HUMAN RESOURCE MANAGEMENT
A Strategic Approach

Harcourt College Publishers

Where Learning Comes to Life

TECHNOLOGY

Technology is changing the learning experience, by increasing the power of your textbook and other learning materials; by allowing you to access more information, more quickly; and by bringing a wider array of choices in your course and content information sources.

Harcourt College Publishers has developed the most comprehensive Web sites, e-books, and electronic learning materials on the market to help you use technology to achieve your goals.

PARTNERS IN LEARNING

Harcourt partners with other companies to make technology work for you and to supply the learning resources you want and need. More importantly, Harcourt and its partners provide avenues to help you reduce your research time of numerous information sources.

Harcourt College Publishers and its partners offer increased opportunities to enhance your learning resources and address your learning style. With quick access to chapter-specific Web sites and e-books . . . from interactive study materials to quizzing, testing, and career advice . . . Harcourt and its partners bring learning to life.

Harcourt's partnership with Digital:Convergence™ brings :CRQ™ technology and the :CueCat™ reader to you and allows Harcourt to provide you with a complete and dynamic list of resources designed to help you achieve your learning goals. You can download the free :CRQ software from www.crq.com. Visit any of the 7,100 RadioShack stores nationwide to obtain a free :CueCat reader. Just swipe the cue with the :CueCat reader to view a list of Harcourt's partners and Harcourt's print and electronic learning solutions.

http://www.harcourtcollege.com/partners

FOURTH EDITION

HUMAN RESOURCE MANAGEMENT
A Strategic Approach

William P. Anthony
Florida State University

K. Michele Kacmar
Florida State University

Pamela L. Perrewé
Florida State University

Harcourt College Publishers
Fort Worth   Philadelphia   San Diego   New York   Orlando   Austin   San Antonio
Toronto   Montreal   London   Sydney   Tokyo

Publisher Mike Roche
Acquisitions Editor Tracy Morse
Developmental Editor CJ Jasieniecki
Marketing Strategist Beverly Dunn
Project Manager Angela Williams Urquhart

Cover Design Graphic World Publishing Services

ISBN: 0-03-033509-4

Library of Congress Catalog Card Number: 2001090841

Address for Domestic Orders
Harcourt College Publishers, 6277 Sea Harbor Drive, Orlando, FL 32887-6777
800-782-4479

Address for International Orders
International Customer Service
Harcourt, Inc., 6277 Sea Harbor Drive, Orlando, FL 32887-6777
407-345-3800
(fax) 407-345-4060
(e-mail) hbintl@harcourt.com

Address for Editorial Correspondence
Harcourt College Publishers, 301 Commerce Street, Suite 3700, Fort Worth, TX 76102

Web Site Address
www.harcourtcollege.com

Harcourt College Publishers will provide complimentary supplements or supplement packages to those adopters qualified under our adoption policy. Please contact your sales representative to learn how you qualify. If as an adopter or potential user you receive supplements you do not need, please return them to your sales representative or send them to:
Attn: Returns Department, Troy Warehouse, 465 South Lincoln Drive, Troy, MO 63379.

Printed in the United States of America

1 2 3 4 5 6 7 8 9 0   048   9 8 7 6 5 4 3 2 1

Harcourt College Publishers

THE HARCOURT COLLEGE PUBLISHERS SERIES IN MANAGEMENT

Anthony, Kacmar, and Perrewé
Human Resource Management: A Strategic Approach
Fourth Edition

Bereman and Lengnick-Hall
Compensation Decision Making: A Computer-Based Approach
Second Edition

Bergmann, Scarpello, and Hills
Compensation Decision Making
Fourth Edition

Boone and Kurtz
Contemporary Business
Tenth Edition

Bourgeois, Duhaime, and Stimpert
Strategic Management: A Managerial Perspective
Second Edition

Bourgeois, Duhaime, and Stimpert
Strategic Management: A Managerial Perspective
Concise Edition

Carrell, Ebert, and Hatfield
Human Resource Management: Strategies for Managing A Diverse Global Work Force
Sixth Edition

Costin
Strategies for Quality Improvement: TQM Reengineering & ISO 9000
Second Edition

Costin
Managing In The Global Economy: The European Union
Second Edition

Costin
Readings in Total Quality Management
Second Edition

Czinkota
Best Practices in International Business

Czinkota
Readings

Czinkota and Ronkainen
Best Practices in International Business

Czinkota, Ronkainen, and Moffett
International Business
Sixth Edition

Czinkota, Ronkainen, and Moffett
International Business
Update 2000

Daft
The Leadership Experience
Second Edition

Daft
Management
Fifth Edition

Daft and Marcic
Understanding Management
Third Edition

Daft and Noe
Organizational Behavior

DeSimone and Werner
Human Resource Development
Third Edition

Dilworth
Operations Management
Third Edition

Gatewood and Feild
Human Resource Selection
Fifth Edition

Greenhaus, Callanan, and Godshalk
Career Management
Third Edition

Harris
Human Resource Management
Second Edition

Hodgetts
Modern Human Relations At Work
Eighth Edition

Hodgetts and Kuratko
Effective Small Business Management
Seventh Edition

Holley and Jennings
The Labor Relations Process
Seventh Edition

Holt
International Management: Text and Cases
Second Edition

Kuratko and Hodgetts
Entrepreneurship: A Contemporary Approach
Fifth Edition

Kuratko and Welsch
Strategic Entrepreneurial Growth

Lesser
Business Public Policy and Society

Oddou and Derr
Managing Internationally: A Personal Journey

Robbins
Business.today: The New World of Business

Robinson, Franklin, and Wayland
The Regulatory Environment of Human Resource Management

Ryan and Hiduke
Small Business: An Entrepreneur's Plan
Sixth Edition

Sandburg
Discovering Your Business Career
CD ROM

Vecchio
Organizational Behavior: Core Concepts
Fourth Edition

Vietor and Kennedy
Globalization and Development: Cases in National Economic Strategies

Wagner and Hollenbeck
Organizational Behavior
Fourth Edition

Weiss
Business Ethics: A Stakeholder and Issues Management Approach
Third Edition

Zikmund
Business Research Methods
Sixth Edition

To Roz, Cathie, and Sarah
To Chuck
To Jerry, Stephen, Matthew, Erin, Jennifer, Emily, and Ellie

Few of you who read this textbook actually will become human resource managers in organizations, but most of you (at some point in your career) will manage a group of people. Also, some of you will be in a position to influence your organization's human resource policy significantly, even if you are not in your firm's human resource department. Of course, no matter where you are in an organization, you will be affected by its human resource policy simply because you are a member of that organization.

The bulk of this textbook examines the formulation and implementation of human resource policy at the *strategic* level. In other words, we are most concerned with the major aspects of how an organization deals with its people—how it acquires them, uses them, rewards them, and separates them. We are concerned with the interplay of the human resource department and line managers as strategic decisions are made and implemented on human resource acquisition and used in organizations. We are also concerned with how strategic human resource decisions interplay with the overall strategic decisions an organization makes.

The book examines typical functions in human resources such as recruitment, selection, training, rewarding (wage and salary analysis), and so on, but it does so from a strategic perspective. Specifically, it explores how these functions integrate with the overall strategy of the firm in order for the firm to become more effective and efficient—in short, more competitive.

Plan of the Book

The textbook is organized into six parts. Part One examines the concept of organizational strategy and how it relates to an organization's human resources. We begin in Chapter 1 by discussing what we mean by a strategic approach to human resource management. In Chapter 2 we examine how managers formulate a corporate strategy within the human resource management realm. In Chapter 3 we examine the global and external environments of the organization and their impact on corporate and human resource strategy.

Part Two focuses on the ways organizations acquire and place people. Human resource planning and information systems are the subjects of Chapter 4. This chapter develops a technology theme that is applied to the human resource strategy planning.

Legal issues such as equal employment, sexual harassment, and managing a diverse workforce are covered in Chapter 5. Chapter 6 discusses job analysis in light of determining job requirements. Chapter 7 then examines how to obtain employees through strategic recruiting and selection methods.

The focus of Part Three is on strategies for maximizing human resource productivity. Assuming that the employees have been hired and placed, we are now interested in maximizing their productivity. First, Chapter 8 looks at how jobs are designed within organizations. Then Chapter 9 looks at orientation, training, and development methods for optimal productivity. Chapter 10 examines how performance appraisal systems can be used to develop employees and make them more productive.

Providing fair and equitable monetary and other rewards that encourage desired performance is the subject of Chapter 11. Finally, Chapter 12 examines the management of quality and productivity improvement.

In Part Four we examine ways of maintaining human resources in the organization. We begin in Chapter 13 by discussing various benefit programs available today for organizations. Chapter 14 looks at health, safety, and stress in today's organizations. Ethics, employee rights, and employer responsibilities are the subject of Chapter 15. Dealing with troubled employees, a major issue today for many organizations, is a major focus of this chapter. Finally, Chapter 16 examines unions and collective bargaining.

In Part Five, Chapter 17 focuses on strategic separation, restructuring, and the virtual organization. Particular emphasis is placed on layoff and termination strategies.

The book concludes with Part Six, a series of comprehensive cases that explain a variety of strategic human resource issues of actual organizations. The emphasis is on applying the ideas learned throughout the book in examining real-world organizational issues.

Hallmark Features

Real-World Examples!

The textbook relies heavily on actual case examples of human resource strategies and practices of organizations. Not only are these examples used liberally in each chapter, each chapter also begins and ends with an actual case of an organization's strategies.

Updated Cases!

Part of the method of human resource strategic analysis is case problem solving. The last part of the textbook is devoted to a compendium of comprehensive cases showing how specific companies integrate their human resource strategy with their overall corporate strategy. The cases are integral to this textbook and make the study of strategy come alive. Many new cases have been added in this edition, and all remaining cases have been significantly updated.

The cases used throughout and at the end of the book have the most value when you try to analyze the situations and suggest courses of action. By applying the concepts discussed in the textbook to case analyses, you will see their relevance in actual organizational situations.

The cases used throughout this book ask you to identify current and potential problems and issues and to formulate strategies for their resolution. This requires that you take a problem- or issue-solving approach to *apply* material in this text. The cases revolve around real organizations you most likely will recognize. They have real human resource problems and challenges. You will need to be both reactive and proactive in examining these cases. Some companies that are included have readily apparent current human resource problems needing immediate solutions. We included other companies because their cases demonstrate good examples of typical human resource policy: They may have few obvious human resource problems at the moment, but problems could be developing on the horizon.

The cases at the end of each chapter are relatively short and are followed by a few questions to guide you in analyzing the cases, using the material covered in the chapter. In reviewing these cases you will see very few "hard" right or wrong answers to the questions. Be concerned with examining both the overall strategies and the human resource strategies involved in each case. Try to determine how well each type of strategy is working and whether the human resource strategy seems to be meshing well with both overall strategy and other functional strategies. Ask yourself what you could do if you were in a position to change things. The cases at the end of the book are comprehensive and require you to integrate the material covered throughout the text in order to analyze them successfully.

"Focus on HR," "HR Challenge," and "You Be the Judge" Boxes!

The textbook contains several examples in each chapter of primary issues currently confronting human resource strategists. "Focus on HR" boxes provide insight into the ways companies and their human resource departments deal with international concerns, ethical concerns, and management of today's culturally diverse workforce. "HR Challenges" boxes offer insight into the different ways that organizations deal with the challenges presented to them on a day-to-day basis. "You Be the Judge" boxes highlight a dilemma and encourage the student to consider whether or not they would have made the same decision.

Resourceful Summary!

Another special feature of the book is its use of management applications. For example, to highlight how any manager, human resource or otherwise, can have an impact on the practices of the human resource function, the summaries at the end of each chapter are provided in the form of "Management Guidelines." These guidelines summarize the key ideas presented in the chapter, but they are restated in the form of guidelines or admonitions for management action.

Focus on Currency!

The fourth edition has been thoroughly updated and includes updated or entirely new cases at the beginning and end of each chapter and at the end of the book. As the awareness on ethics has grown in the workplace, our textbook has increased its emphasis on ethics and how critical it is to strategic human resource management. Because small businesses greatly outnumber large businesses and thousands of new small businesses are formed each day in this country, numerous small business examples and cases have also been included.

Finally, internationalization and the use of new technology have been thoroughly updated. Company website addresses have been added providing students with access to up-to-date information.

Ancillary Package

INSTRUCTOR'S MANUAL

This valuable tool contains not only the Instructor's Manual but also a printed Test Bank and Transparency Masters. This resource has chapter-by-chapter instructional tools, case notes, three varieties of questioning (true/false, multiple choice, and essay), and transparencies created from exhibits featured in the text.

COMPUTERIZED TEST BANK

Available in Windows, MAC, and DOS compatible formats, the computerized version of the printed test bank enables instructors to preview, edit, and add test questions. The tests and answer keys also can be printed in "scrambled" formats.

POWERPOINT/CD-ROM PRESENTATION SOFTWARE

This media active presentation tool will bring lectures and classroom discussions to life. The software is extremely professor-friendly and organized by chapter. This program enables instructors to custom design their own media classroom presentations using overhead transparencies including exhibits from the text.

VIDEO COLLECTION

The video series consists of segments of video that focus on ideas and themes presented in the text.

The Dryden Press will provide complimentary supplements or supplement packages to those adopters qualified under our adoption policy. Please contact your sales representative to learn how you may qualify. If as an adopter or potential user you receive supplements you do not need, please return them to your sales representative or send them to:

Attn: Returns Department
Troy Warehouse
465 South Lincoln Drive
Troy, MO 63379

Acknowledgments

We would like to thank all those individuals who were involved in the first, second, and third editions of this book and the following individuals who assisted in the fourth edition: Ben Alvarez, Ginny Bratton, Ann Marie Breyer, Rhett Brymer, Dejan Bucevski, the late Gordona Cupurdija, Loyd Hawkins, Melanie Keys, Matt Lee, Cathie Anthony Mathe (a *special thanks* for all of her work with the cases and three of the chapters), and Rebecca McNeil.

We are especially grateful to the professors who reviewed the manuscript throughout its various stages for the first, second, third, and fourth editions:

Matthew M. Amano
Oregon State University

Brendan D. Bannister
Northeastern University

Nathan Bennett
Louisiana State University

Linda Bleicken
Georgia Southern University

David E. Bowen
Arizona State University West

Anthony F. Campagna
Ohio State University

Gerald E. Calvasina
University of North Carolina,
Charlotte

Stephen J. Carroll
University of Maryland, College Park

Jeffrey G. Covin
Georgia Institute of Technology

Joseph H. Culver
University of Texas, Austin

Karen J. Cummings
Michigan State University

Dan R. Dalton
Indiana University

Jack Davis
St. Mary's University

Joseph Di Angelo Jr.
Widener University

Thomas G. Gutteridge
Southern Illinois University,
Carbondale

Stephen R. Hiatt
Catawba College

Ken Jennings
University of North Florida

Thomas H. Jerdee
University of North Carolina, Chapel
Hill

Vicki S. Kaman
Colorado State University

Matthew C. Lane
Portland State University

Elaine LeMay
Colorado State University

Robert C. Liden
University of Illinois, Chicago

Stanley B. Malos
San Jose State University

Marc C. Marchese
King's College

Marjorie L. McInerney
Marshall University

Edward Miller
Kean College of New Jersey

Michael T. Quinn
California State University, Long Beach

Shelton Rhodes
Bowie State University

Marcus Hart Sandver
Ohio State University

Sid Siegel
Drexel University

Scott A. Snell
Pennsylvania State University

David Tansik
University of Arizona

Mark A. Wesolowski
Miami University

Donna Wiley
California State University, Hayward

Arthur Yeung
San Francisco State University

Our thanks go to our acquisitions editor, Tracy Morse; developmental editor, CJ Jasieniecki; senior project manager, Angela Urquhart; marketing manager, Kimberly L. Lewis; permissions editor, Linda Blundell; and others who helped in the process. Even though we have been aided greatly by this help, any errors of commission or omission rest with us.

WPA
KMK
PLP
Tallahassee, Florida

William P. Anthony (PhD) (SPHR) is professor of management, Carl DeSantis Professor of Business Administration, and director of the DeSantis Center for Executive Management Education in the College of Business at Florida State University. He received his MBA and PhD degrees from Ohio State University and his bachelor's degree from Ohio University. Dr. Anthony has published more than 80 articles and 14 books. He has been published in a variety of management journals including *Long Range Planning, Human Relations, Academy of Management Executive, Journal of Applied Psychology, Organizational Dynamics,* and *Personnel Journal* among others. He serves as a reviewer for *Human Resource Management Review,* and *The Journal of Managerial Issues.* His book, *Participative Management,* was reprinted 10 times and translated into six different languages. Dr. Anthony consults with a wide variety of business and governmental organizations throughout the United States. His previous clients include Motorola, State Farm Insurance, Intervynals Corporation, The U.S. Department of Defense, The Florida Lottery, Rayonier, Resortquest, Olin Corporation, and Goodwill Industries. He also serves as an expert witness in employment matters. Dr. Anthony has served as chairman of the management department and as assistant dean in the College of Business at Florida State University.

K. Michele (Micki) Kacmar (PhD) is the J. Frank Dame Professor of Business Administration and serves as the director of the Center for Human Resource Management at Florida State University. She received her bachelor's degrees in computer science and communication and a master's degree in communication from Illinois State University. Her PhD degree is in human resource management from Texas A&M University. Prior to joining the faculty at Florida State University she served on the faculty at Rensselaer Polytechnic University. Dr. Kacmar teaches courses in human resource management at the undergraduate level and research design and methodology at the PhD level. Dr. Kacmar's general research interests are in the areas of impression management and organizational politics. She has published more than 50 articles in journals such as *Journal of Applied Psychology, Journal of Organizational Behavior, Journal of Vocational Behavior, Human Relations,* and *Organizational Behavior and Human Decision Processes.* She is currently the editor of the *Journal of Management* and serves as a member of the Editorial Review Board for the *Journal of Applied Psychology.*

Pamela L. Perrewé (PhD) is the Jim Moran Professor of Management and serves as the associate dean for graduate programs in the College of Business at Florida State University. She received her bachelor's degree in psychology from Purdue University and her master's and PhD degrees in management from the University of Nebraska. Dr. Perrewé primarily teaches courses in organizational behavior and human resource management and has taught at the undergraduate, master's, and PhD levels. Dr. Perrewé has focused her research interests in the areas of job stress, coping, organizational politics, and personality. Dr. Perrewé has published more than 50 articles in journals such as *Journal of Applied Psychology, Journal of Management, Journal of Organizational Behavior, Journal of Occupational Health Psychology, Journal of Vocational Behavior, Human Relations, Academy of Management Executive, Human Resource Management Review,* and *Journal of Applied Social Psychology.* She serves as a member of the Editorial Review Board for Human Resource Management Review and Journal of Management. Dr. Perrewé is the co-editor for a new book series titled *Occupational Stress and Well Being.*

CONTENTS

Chapter 3

Chapter 4

Chapter 10

PART FIVE

Strategies Separation
635

Chapter 17

Strategic Restructuring and the Virtual Organization   637

PART

I

The Strategic Approach

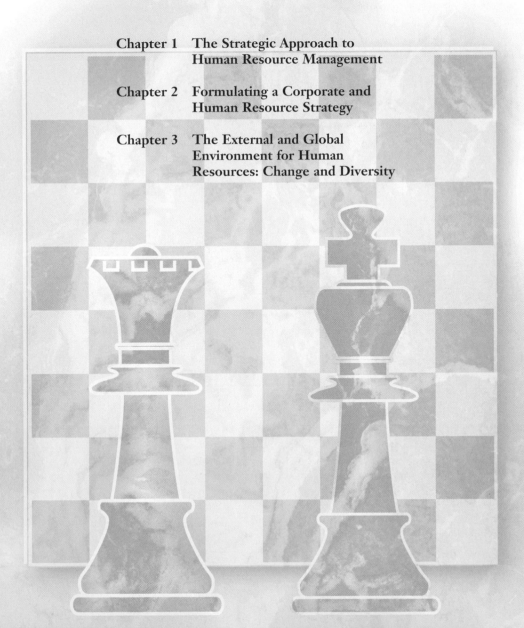

Chapter 1 The Strategic Approach to Human Resource Management

Chapter 2 Formulating a Corporate and Human Resource Strategy

Chapter 3 The External and Global Environment for Human Resources: Change and Diversity

1

The Strategic Approach to Human Resource Management

Chapter Objectives

As a result of studying this chapter, you should be able to

1. Define the concept of strategy and explain the basics of the strategy formulation process.

2. Distinguish the strategic approach to human resources from the traditional functional approach.

3. Explain the relationship of decision making to the strategy formulation process.

4. Understand the decision-making process in organizations and the reasons that human resources management should be an integral part of the process.

5. Explain the environment-organization link and the strategic approach.

6. Explain the relationship of human resource strategy with overall organizational strategy and functional strategy.

7. Understand the history and evolution of the field of human resources.

The environment within which an organization operates is dynamic. External and internal forces are constantly changing the rules of the game, and the organization must amend or adopt new strategies to remain competitive. A change in strategy will determine the direction of each function within the organization, including the human resource management (HRM) function. This chapter examines the definition of strategy and explores the history and practice of HRM. The major goals are to lay the foundation for the way strategy and HRM interrelate and to demonstrate that, in today's complex business environment, a strategic approach to HRM is a necessity.

GM Shrinks and Rebounds

On April 22, 1988, General Motors (GM) Corporation announced a strategic retreat that significantly shrank the largest industrial company in the world for the first time in its 80-year history. GM placed itself on a corporate crash diet in an effort to shed both factories and workers in order to stop its falling net income. It made a similar announcement on December 18, 1991, when it reported plans to close 21 of its plants and eliminate 74,000 jobs in four years, 9000 of which would be white-collar positions. By December 1996, two assembly plants and twelve component plants had been closed, more than 80,000 union workers had been laid off, and the downsizing was having positive results.[1]

GM once claimed almost 50 percent of the U.S. auto market. By 1999 that share had fallen to 29 percent (see Exhibit 1.1A), largely because of the increased sales of imports, Fords, and Chryslers. To match its sales, GM reduced its car production capacity. Unlike in the past, when plant closings and employee layoffs were a regular part of the business cycle, these changes were not temporary. Rather, they represented a major downsizing that resulted in a considerable restructuring of the firm.

The downsizing or retrenchment began in 1988 and continued through the 1990s. Analysts estimated that GM needed to cut at least another 60,000 jobs to bring its cost structure into line with its competitors.[2] During this period, nearly every Japanese automaker opened a new full-scale plant in the United States. While GM eventually hopes to regain some of its market share, the move indicates that the company anticipates an overcapacity in the North American car market, at least in the foreseeable future.

In December 1992, GM was in the midst of this continuing corporate trauma of historic proportions. It had 44 percent of the U.S. car-making capacity, but sales had dropped to 32 percent of the market.[3] To bring the two figures into line, the company planned to close 23 additional plants, cutting at least 74,000 jobs (50,000 hourly and 24,000 salaried workers). It had to carry out a formidable internal restructuring while fending off increasing competition at home, a downturn in foreign car markets, and pressure from the United Auto Workers (UAW).

GM's plants were badly underutilized, running at close to 65 percent of capacity in 1993. Part of the solution lay in condensing the operations by 1994 from three plants running short schedules to two plants running full schedules and eventually eliminating $150 million a year in labor costs plus the cost of one of the plant's operations and equipment.[5]

Although GM's former chairman, Roger Smith, had previously maintained that the automaker's market-share drop was temporary, GM's strategic retreat suggested

EXHIBIT 1.1A GM's SHARE OF THE U.S. CAR MARKET

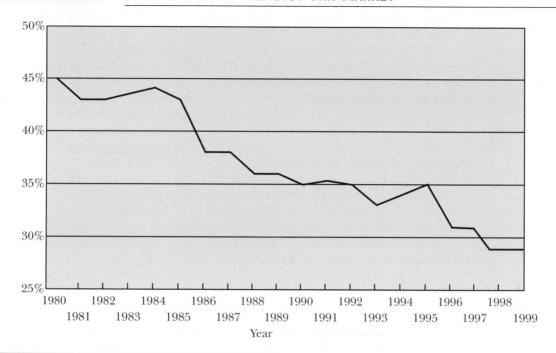

EXHIBIT 1.1B GM's TOTAL PROFITS AND LOSSES (IN BILLIONS $)

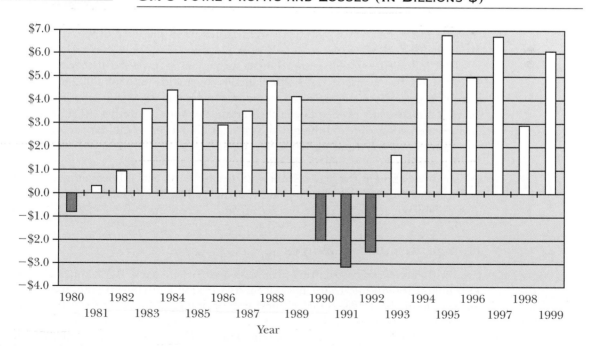

that it shared the belief Ford Motor Company held in 1981 when it went through a similar retrenchment to adjust to a lower market share.

The company set a goal for 1995 to operate at close to 100 percent of its capacity with all plants running two shifts a day, five days a week. GM had not been at the 100 percent level since the spring of 1984. In the 1985 to 1988 period the company varied its strategy from producing all the cars it could to running several plants below capacity for periods of time. In between, the company offered deep discounting with low financing and cash-back offers to clear its oversupply of cars. In addition, GM missed its third quarter 1992 production quota by 95,000 vehicles because of widespread problems in its factories. Working with a mandate from senior management, GM simplified the structure of the company's North American operations, slashed the corporate staff, pared product offerings, and began a sell-off of the company's parts operations. GM announced the spin-off of Delphi Automotive Systems, and its 198,000 employees, in April 1999. These actions have paid off; GM made a profit for each of the years 1996 through 1999 as shown in Exhibit 1.1B, even though its North American market share has dropped to 28.9 percent.

Many have blamed Roger Smith for the lack of vision that resulted in the lagging GM market share and inconsistent production strategy. They believe that GM should have taken steps to downsize years earlier when it became apparent that imports would maintain a strong, permanent share of the market instead of continually denying their existence. Some even argue that the proposed cuts are not enough to make GM fully cost competitive in the global industry.

The possibility of closing plants is a very sensitive subject for employees and the UAW, especially because the labor agreement of fall 1987 was sold to its members based on increased job security. The head of the UAW GM department believed the strategy to close plants was a "loser." In contrast, Joseph Phillipi of Lehman Brothers believed that "despite all its rhetoric, the UAW leadership recognizes what it will take to make GM competitive."[6] While the UAW leadership may have recognized what is needed, on the local level sentiments were expressed in the form of strikes at various plants. In 1996 alone, strikes cost GM over $1 billion.[6]

GM followed a similar entrenchment strategy in Europe during the mid-1980s. This resulted in a profit of $1.88 billion in 1987 over a loss of $568 million in 1986 in European operations. It appears that the retrenchment in North America has produced a similar badly needed financial reversal.[7] For the six months ended June 2000, GM posted profits of $3.6 billion with two record quarters of diluted per-share earnings, continuing the trend started in late 1993.[8]

By gearing its capacity to the low end of the business cycle, GM is following a similar retrenchment strategy instituted earlier by Ford. Since Ford permanently reduced capacity in 1981, it has run plants overtime, added third shifts, or increased production efficiencies to meet increased demand.

Human Resource Changes

Even with its revised cost-cutting plan, GM (jointly with the UAW) contributed over $1.0 billion to educate, train, and retrain its working and laid-off employees during the decade of the 1990s. This is a new way of doing business for GM. In the past, managers competed fiercely with one another, concentrating on their individual departments while ignoring the difficulties blue-collar workers and other departments might be having. But this is all changing. With the realization that personnel, not

<u>technology, is its most important commodity with regard to the bottom line, the company is working hard to replace its old image with one of teamwork and unity.</u> GM is striving for a winning team spirit in hope that this will lead to better productivity, an improved competitive position in the marketplace, and eventually higher profits, more jobs, and job security.

Saturn

One of GM's brightest hopes for recapturing its market share is its Saturn division. GM's Saturn facility in Spring Hill, Tennessee, has a specific competitive goal: to build better cars than the Japanese. Saturn, costing more than $5 billion to bring on line, is taking aim at imports and attempts to sell more than 80 percent of its cars to customers who had intended to buy an import. Because fewer than 5 percent of the car-buying market knew what Saturn was all about, Saturn officials say that generating awareness was the first objective in its early advertising; they did this by focusing on the people behind the car. Most of Saturn's 9000 employees, 20 percent of which is composed of women, were recruited and screened from UAW locals in 38 states and have given up future options to ever work at another GM division. The workers have a shop-floor average salary of $44,000, with 20 percent of that dependent on company profits, productivity, and car quality. In addition, each worker is eligible for a bonus for beating targeted production goals. In 1996, profit sharing and bonus checks contributed an additional $10,000 to individual employee income—the highest incentives paid by any automaker in the United States.[9]

Saturn is breaking ground in four areas.

1. As a partnership between management and the UAW.
2. Through its franchise agreements with dealers, giving them rights to establish multiple outlets over larger-than-average territories.
3. As an integrated manufacturing complex.
4. Through its emphasis on teamwork, both internally with Saturn's employees and externally with Saturn's suppliers.

Saturn's managerial innovations are also having favorable spillover effects in the parent company. GM is beginning to place Saturn personnel in charge of the small car platform within GM.[10]

Saturn sales opened weak across the country with fewer than 100,000 cars sold in 1991. But in the 1992 model year, it sold 170,495 cars, a 236 percent increase over 1991, for a 2.1 percent share of the U.S. car market.[11] Despite production restraints, Saturn sold 286,003 cars in the 1994 model year that ended September 30, 1994. In 1995 Saturn sold 285,674 cars, bringing its client base to more than 1 million owners.[12] Saturn produced 278,636 cars in 1996 and hoped to bring production to 290,000 a year by the end of 1997, but the company finished the year slightly short of the goal with about 278,574 cars.[13]

Increasing competition from Japanese imports has taken its toll on Saturn. While Honda Motor Co. and Toyota have been experiencing record sales in the United States, Saturn and other U.S. small car manufacturing divisions are struggling to maintain market share. Saturn management failed to take the option on developing the scaled-down minivan design that Chrysler released in 2000 as the PT Cruiser. Saturn has also had problems in 2000 with new designs and safety. The Saturn L–series sedan received only one of the four expected top crash-test ratings from the U.S. government in 1999.

Developing Accountability in the Worker

Changes of this magnitude require a skilled, flexible workforce. GM hopes to help employees acquire the new skills, knowledge, and abilities needed for product improvement through education, training, and retraining programs. Approximately 10 percent of former laid-off workers (5000) have been retrained and placed in new jobs with other companies. Almost all currently employed workers went through some type of program at their local GM plant. GM is making this possible by allowing employees to attend classes on a regular basis during company time. However, as illustrated in this case, sobering times in GM's recent past call for employees to account for how they contribute to company performance. Top managers at GM and other organizations now view humans as a strategic resource and, like it or not, are compelled to insist on their active contribution to future success.

Worker accountability programs appeared to succeed by mid-1995 in propelling GM's quality ratings ahead of both Ford Motor Company and Chrysler Corporation.[14]

Conclusion

GM had to make some tough strategic choices that were harmful in some respects to certain segments of the organization. GM's chosen strategy of retrenchment has proved largely successful, and once again the corporate giant is charting excellent performance. This case suggests, however, that a strategic decision affects the multiple functions of the corporation, even at the lowest levels. The functional area of human resources was most dramatically impacted because GM had to increase the number of workers transferred to other plants, slow the rate of hiring, reduce overtime pay, increase the numbers of terminations and layoffs, improve training and retraining efforts, and insist on accountability and contribution to measurable performance standards. Though these changes seemed harsh and dire at the time, the case indicates that retrenchment has bolstered GM's chances for long-term future success.

More information on GM can be found on the Internet at **www.gm.com**. For more information about Saturn, visit the Saturn Web site at **www.saturnbp.com**.

Strategic Choices

When managers, such as those at GM, are faced with deciding on which corporate strategy they should embark, they must make several decisions. The following is only a partial list of some of the strategic choices managers face.

1. Routinely managers must evaluate where they are. They must decide if they should remain with the strategy they have selected and implemented or if they need a new strategy.
2. To make this decision, managers must know exactly what has and has not changed since the current strategic approach was implemented. For example, has the economy changed dramatically in any way that may influence whether or not the selected strategy will continue to be effective?
3. If any changes are suggested, it is important that managers understand the ripple effects these changes may have on other functions. For example, if a growth strategy is selected, will the human resources unit be able to provide the qualified personnel needed to develop this strategy?

4. Finally, managers should try to evaluate the current approach and what any changes to this approach might have on what their competitors do. For example, if GM offers a low financing rate, is Chrysler or Ford in a position to offer an even lower rate, thereby making GM's offer unattractive?

The Strategic Approach

Chances are that you have encountered, or soon will encounter, the strategic approach in your course of studies. It is used in marketing, finance, and information systems courses and serves as the heart of the capstone course in most business programs: the policy or strategic management course. Not until recently, however, has it been widely used as an approach to human resource/personnel management.

Even though you may not become a human resource manager in a firm, you will very likely manage human resources if the position you take gives you some authority over other employees. Even if this does not happen, you will be affected by the human resource decisions made in your firm. You will also have the occasion to ask the human resource unit for advice on hiring, pay increases, discipline, discharge, and other personnel-related issues.

Strategy Defined

A strategy is a way of doing something. It is a game plan for action. It usually includes the formulation of a goal and a set of action plans for accomplishment. It implies consideration of the competitive forces at work in managing an organization and the impact of the outside environment on organization actions.

Although managers have probably managed strategically for many years, the strategic approach is relatively new to management literature. The concept of strategy has its roots in military literature, particularly that developed by the Chinese strategist Sun Tzu.[15] However, Alfred Chandler's work, *Strategy and Structure*, as well as the development of management by objectives (MBO), sets the stage for the present-day popularity of the strategic focus in business and management books.[16]

MBO has been popular in business writings since the mid-1950s when it first was used by Peter Drucker in his classic, *The Practice of Management.*[17] MBO essentially involves three steps: setting a mission or purpose, setting goals or objectives, and determining action plans to achieve the goals or objectives.

The strategic focus accepts these three basic ideas of MBO but goes beyond them by giving explicit recognition to both the outside and competitive environments. The actions and reactions of competition are the heart of the modern approach to strategy. Two popular works of Michael Porter, *Competitive Strategy* and *Competitive Advantage*, no doubt have enhanced this competitive focus.[18] These two books examine how strategy can be used to obtain competitive advantage and have been read widely and referred to by people in both academic institutions and businesses.

For our purpose, we define **strategy** as *the formulation of organizational missions, goals, and objectives, as well as action plans for achievement, that explicitly recognize the competition and the impact of outside environmental forces.*

Before we can clearly see how strategy formulation impacts the human resource function of an organization, we must first understand what human resources in an organization is. The following section provides a brief overview of the duties that are involved in human resources management, a historical look at the field of human resources, and an explanation of the popular functional approach to HRM.

strategy The formulation of organizational missions, goals, and objectives, as well as action plans for achievement, that explicitly recognize the competition and the impact of outside environmental forces.

An Overview of Human Resource Management[19]

Why Human Resources are Important

Investments in human resources pay off for an organization through improved productivity. For example, Jeffery Pfeffer, in his book *The Human Equation*, wrote that success comes from successfully implementing strategy and that the ability to implement strategy comes from the organization's people.[20] Organizations are obsessed with reducing their pay rates when returns from managing people in ways that build high commitment, involvement, and organizational competence are typically on the order of 30 to 50 percent.[21] High commitment management leads to higher productivity, smarter productivity, and increasing responsibility at lower organizational levels. Pfeffer cites Apple Computer as his example of how inattention to human resources can lead to organizational decline. Apple Computer faced challenges from increased competition in the mid-1980s. Apple responded by laying off many of the company's most talented people and irreparably harmed its ability to compete in an industry driven by human innovation. Therefore our approach in this book rests on the fundamental value HRM has to enhance a firm's bottom line. Investments in people pay off for the firm.

The Tasks of Human Resource Management

What sort of activities are included under the province of HRM? As you will see, this book approaches HRM as a fairly broad strategic duty performed by all managers rather than as a more narrowly defined, purely "staff" role played by professional human resource managers. In simple terms, however, we can think of HRM as a variety of tasks associated with acquiring, training, developing, motivating, organizing, and maintaining the human employees of the firm. Given our understanding of strategy, we might add that these tasks should be performed in a way that helps the company deal effectively with any environmental forces and competition and ensures the company's long-term achievement of its goals and objectives.

Human resource managers and academics have debated for some time the point at which HRM ends and other functional management begins. The American Society for Training and Development (ASTD) determined the activities that professionals typically considered to be human resource roles.[22] Among those roles listed were personnel selection and staffing, human resource planning, organization and job design, career development, organization development, training and development, research and information, labor relations, employee assistance and support, and compensation and benefits administration. Much of this book is dedicated to the discussion of these duties and how each should be performed within a strategic framework. In today's complex business environment, strategy formulation and implementation may be the most important duties performed by managers. Later in this chapter we discuss how this important function is performed, but first let's review how the human resource function developed into the multifaceted set of tasks defined by the ASTD's survey.

The Development of Human Resource Management

The Craft System People who worked during the 1600s and 1700s were guided by a craft system. Under this system the production of goods and services was generated by small groups of workers in relatively small workplaces, usually in a home. The work was customized and supervised by a master craftsman. Each master craftsman had several apprentices and journeymen who actually performed the work. When the craftsman retired, the most senior journeyman normally replaced him or her. There was no confusion about career paths and no disputes over wages. This system held for more than 200 years.

As demand for products increased, the craft system could not keep up. Craftsmen had to hire more and more journeymen and apprentices, and the small workplace became more like a small factory. At the same time, machines were being introduced that could be used to help produce high-quality products much faster than experienced craftsmen. These changes helped usher in the Industrial Revolution.

Scientific Management   In the early 1900s, many changes occurred in the workplace. Machines and factory methods that increased production were introduced. However, with this increased production came several problems. Because the machines required several people to operate them, the number of workers increased dramatically. This forced managers to develop rules, regulations, and procedures to control the workers. Some of the regulations required an increase in job specialization, which led to repetitive and monotonous jobs. Specialization also allowed managers the ability to replace quickly and economically any worker who demanded too much or caused a problem. One of the most significant developments that arose during this time was a process called *scientific management*.

The premise of scientific management is that there is one best way to do a job. This one best way is the cheapest, fastest, and most efficient way to perform the task. The process may not be the safest or the most humane, but it does allow the company to make the most profit. Frederick Taylor, the father of scientific management, spent his career collecting data and analyzing the specific motions required to perform various jobs. He then broke the job into specific tasks and refined the motions needed to complete them until the tasks could be refined no more. He then selected, trained, and closely monitored workers who performed the tasks. Those workers who were successful (that is, those who followed the orders of management exactly and by doing so significantly increased their production) earned a great deal of money. Those who were not successful were terminated.

Although scientific management did prove to be an effective management tool that increased the productivity of workers, it was criticized for treating the worker as a tool and not as a person. To compensate for this tendency to depersonalize the work environment, welfare secretaries were hired. People in these positions oversaw programs for the welfare of the employees, such as the installation of libraries and recreational facilities, financial assistance programs, and medical and health programs. The welfare programs were the forerunners of modern-day benefit packages, and the welfare secretary position was the forerunner of the current human resource manager.

Human Relations   The next significant step in the development of human resources occurred in the late 1920s and early 1930s: the Hawthorne studies. Elton Mayo and Fritz Roethlisberger were asked by Western Electric to determine what could be done to increase the productivity of workers at the Hawthorne Works plant in Chicago. While the researchers were specifically examining the effect that lighting had on productivity, their results really had nothing to do with lighting. What they concluded was that the human interaction and attention paid to the workers by the researchers caused their productivity to increase. This finding was the first one to indicate that the social factors in a work environment could have a significant effect on the productivity of workers.

Fueled by the findings of the Hawthorne studies, further research on social factors and how individuals respond to them was undertaken. Results from these studies indicated that the needs of employees must be understood and acted on by management for a worker to be satisfied and productive. Communication between the worker and his or her superior was stressed, as was the need for a more participative workplace atmosphere. More often than not, however, these tactics did little to increase a worker's productivity. The idea that a happy worker is a productive worker failed to be proven, and many of the concepts were modified or abandoned. It is interesting to note that the focus of the human relations era is now the backbone of more recent employee involvement programs that have been found to increase the productivity of workers and increase the profits of companies that adopt them.

Behavioral Science   Expanding on the human relations school of thought of including academic findings from various other disciplines such as psychology, political science, sociology, and biology, the behavioral science era was born. Behavioral science focuses more on the total organization and less on the individual. It examines how the workplace affects the individual worker and how the individual worker affects the workplace. Many believe that the modern fields of organizational behavior (OB), the study of employee behavior in the organization; organizational development (OD), the process of changing employee and organizational attitudes and beliefs; and HRM grew out of the behavioral science era.

The Human Resource Function   As noted, in the early years companies set up welfare secretaries whose jobs were to keep track of employees' welfare. Through the years the welfare secretary's job encompassed more and more duties. As laws were passed that restricted the rights of employers and employees, the welfare secretaries were required to stay informed and determine what impact those laws would have on the organization. The employees in these positions also were required to keep files about employees, maintain payroll systems, and counsel employees. As more and more tasks were delegated to the welfare secretaries, offshoots began to form. One group of welfare secretaries took responsibility for payroll duties, setting wages, and determining raises. A second group focused on hiring and training workers, and yet another concentrated on working with the union to negotiate an acceptable contract. Each of these offshoots eventually became a function of the human resources unit.

So the human resources functional unit has evolved and is now responsible for a large, complex array of duties related not only to the company and the employees, but also to the government and other entities from the external environment. What do these units look like today? What do companies want from their human resource professionals? Exhibit 1.2 gives us some insight into the answers to these questions. This recent ad in *The Wall Street Journal* demonstrates the enormous importance of the human resources function to a company's fortunes. The ad was placed by a Florida company looking for a vice-president of human resources.

EXHIBIT 1.2	THE REQUIREMENTS FOR HR PROFESSIONALS TODAY

Vice-President Human Resources

Florida-based services business of *Fortune* 500 company is seeking experienced, business-oriented HR professional to lead the growth and development of the organization as a key member of the management team.

Responsibilities include managing all aspects of Human Resources function for a large, multilocation operation.

We require a Bachelor's degree in Business (MBA or MA preferred), along with 10–15 years of progressively responsible experience in compensation, labor relations, recruitment/staffing, employee benefits, and organization development. Experience should include working in a TQM and teaming environment. Strong communication and leadership skills a must.

Please send your resume with salary history.

SOURCE: Adapted from an advertisement in *The Wall Street Journal*.

The requirements cited by the company pointed to the central importance of the position. First, the chief personnel officer of this company, and of most larger companies, is given the title of vice-president. The leader of the human resources function is a key member of senior management and probably plays a large part in setting corporate strategy and making major decisions. Additional evidence of the position's lofty status and responsibility relates to the requirement of 10 to 15 years of "progressively responsible experience." The list of responsibilities includes all of the human resources functions, thus making the job a highly diversified, comprehensive management position. In fact, the recruiters seemed to be looking for someone with many of the same qualities and characteristics of today's chief executive officer (CEO). The ad requests someone with extensive experience in working in team settings, strong communication abilities, and highly developed leadership skills. (Also see Exhibit 1.3 for the compensation levels of various human resource positions.) The welfare secretary of old would certainly be surprised at the evolution of this position!

The Strategic Approach to Human Resource Management

The strategic approach to HRM applies the concept of strategy to managing a firm's human resources. This approach has six key elements as shown in Exhibit 1.4. Let's look at each of these.

Recognition of the Impact of the Outside Environment

The outside environment presents a set of opportunities and threats to the organization in the form of laws, economic conditions, social and demographic changes, domestic and international political forces, technology, and so on. Strategic human resource strategy explicitly recognizes the threats and opportunities in each area and attempts to capitalize on the opportunities while minimizing or deflecting the effect

---

EXHIBIT 1.3   COMPENSATION OF HUMAN RESOURCE PROFESSIONALS

The salaries of human resource (HR) professionals increased significantly during the latter half of the 1990s. Median salaries in a few key areas now exceed $200,000. For example, top HR executives who also have industrial relations (union) responsibilities had a median cash compensation level of $201,500 in 2000. This was up by 5.4 percent over 1999. The median pay for HR professionals does not include incentives such as bonuses and stock options, which increase the total compensation package. Approximately 85 percent of senior HR professionals at the vice-president and director levels received incentive pay, which can add as much as 50 percent to the base pay salary.

As shown in Chart 1, highest-paying HR jobs were those that involved industrial relations, labor relations, and international responsibilities. Lower-paying jobs were found in those with primary responsibility in training, quality, or employee relations, yet the cash compensation mean for these jobs was still about $125,000 per year.

Highest pay levels for HR professionals by industry were in the manufacturing and utility sectors, whereas the lowest pay was found in the government, nonprofit, education, retail, and wholesale sectors. Pay also went up with company size. Larger companies paid their HR professionals more than smaller ones did. Firms with less than $500 million in annual revenue paid a median salary of about $109,000, whereas those with $2.5 to $5.0 billion in revenue paid $118,000.

All in all, salaries for human resource professionals are higher than they have ever been. The increases averaged about 5.0 percent per year from 1997 to 2000, exceeding the average of 4.2 percent per year for all salaries in the United States. This reflects the fact that organizations are considering the chief HR professional more and more a key member of the organization's strategic management team.

HIGHEST-PAYING HR JOBS
(MEDIAN TOTAL CASH COMPENSATION)

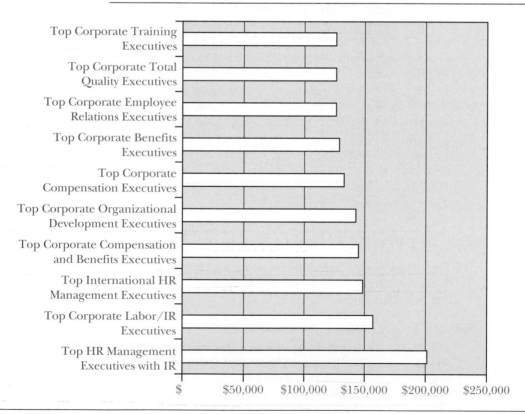

SOURCE: Patricia Schaefer, "HR Pay Keeps Rising," *HR Magazine*, October 2000, pp. 78–83.

EXHIBIT 1.4	CHARACTERISTICS OF A STRATEGIC APPROACH TO HUMAN RESOURCE MANAGEMENT

Human Resource Strategy

- Explicitly recognizes the impact of the outside environment.
- Explicitly recognizes the impact of competition and the dynamics of the labor market.
- Has a long-range focus (three to five years).
- Focuses on the issue of choice and decision making.
- Considers all personnel, not just hourly or operational employees.
- Is integrated with overall corporate strategy and functional strategies.

of threats. For example, GM's strategic decision to open its Saturn plant in Spring Hill, Tennessee, was made only after serious consideration of the potential threat posed by the lack of experienced, qualified technical workers in the area. Top managers, working in close cooperation with human resources experts, had to determine that the company's internal ability to recruit, train, and transfer valuable employees would be strong enough to offset this potential external threat. Decision makers in this situation were also faced with the question of labor availability in the years to come. In other words, success could be achieved only if managers developed ways to deal with the external environment.

Recognition of the Impact of Competition and the Dynamics of the Labor Market

Employers compete for employees just as they do for customers. The forces of competition in attracting, rewarding, and using employees have a major effect on corporate human resource strategy. Forces play out in both local, regional, and national labor markets. The joint GM-Toyota venture, New United Motors Manufacturing, Inc. (NUMMI), through its construction of a plant in Fremont, California, had a major effect on and was very much affected by the local labor market. Labor market dynamics of wage rates, unemployment rates, working conditions, benefit levels, minimum wage legislation, and competitor reputation all have an impact on and are affected by strategic human resource decisions.

Long-Range Focus

A strategic focus tends to set the long-range direction of a company's human resource style and basic approach. Strategy can be changed, but it is not always easy. It depends on the inertia, flexibility, and management philosophy of the firm. The intent, however, is to develop a consistent strategy to guide the firm into its future. Sometimes the word *vision* is used to capture this idea.

Choice and Decision-Making Focus

Strategy implies choosing among alternatives. It implies making major decisions about human resources—decisions that commit the organization's resources toward a particular direction. For example, when Ford established its management–labor worker participation program in the mid-1980s, it did so because of a major decision to increase employee involvement. Of course, the fact that Nissan, Toyota, and other Japanese automakers had successfully used such programs for years probably served as part of the impetus to follow suit. Ford's strategy of employee involvement, based on its "Quality Is Job 1" campaign, was adopted because of a perceived need to resolve issues or prevent new ones from forming—specifically, to improve product quality.

In other words, strategy has a problem-solving or problem-preventing focus. Strategy concentrates on the question "What should the organization do and why?" This action orientation requires that decisions be made and carried out.

Consideration of All Personnel

A strategic approach to human resources is concerned with *all* of the firm's employees, not just its hourly or operational personnel. Traditionally, HRM has focused on hourly employees, including most clerical exempt employees. However, as the province of HRM has broadened, the focus today, at least from a strategic perspective, is on all employees—from top-level management to unskilled operative workers. Consequently, we are just as much concerned with executive pay and benefit plans as we are with hourly wages. We are just as interested in top management's wage and benefit packages as we are with those of hourly union members in the plant. We want to examine management development and training, as well as hourly skill-training programs.

Integration with Corporate Strategy

The particular human resource strategy adopted by a firm should be integrated with the firm's corporate strategy. In other words, corporate strategy should drive human resource strategy. Tom Kelley, former chairman of the American Society of Personnel Administrators' Board of Directors (now the Society of Human Resource Management), remarked that human resource managers "are involved in the strategic planning of global issues, rather than the day-to-day personnel transactions of the previous personnel administrators . . . [and] along with that strategic planning process, it is imperative that the Human Resource Professional establish goals and objectives that support the corporate goals."[23]

If corporate strategy is to grow and dominate a market, such as Apple Computer's strategy in the early 1980s or Intel's and Microsoft's in the 1990s, then human resource strategy should focus on the rapid acquisition and placement of employees. If retrenchment is the strategy, as was shown in the GM case at the beginning of this chapter, then no or low hiring plus layoff and termination of employees is the strategy. Exhibit 1.5 summarizes some key overall strategies and the associated human resource applications that demonstrate this concept.

The key idea behind overall strategic management is to coordinate all of the company's resources, including human resources, in such a way that everything a company does contributes to carrying out its strategy. If all the resources are integrated within an overall, appropriate strategy, additional value to the company is generated by the effective combination of integrated forces. There is no counter productivity, and everything works together in the firm's chosen direction. Excellent coordination and combination of functions often result in a very special phenomenon known as **synergy,** the extra benefit or value realized when resources have been combined and coordinated effectively. This concept, often referred to as **economies of scope,** makes the combined whole of the company (or companies) more valuable than the sum of its parts. It is a true benefit of good strategic management of resources.

synergy The extra benefit or value realized when resources have been combined and coordinated effectively.

economies of scope The concept of synergy that makes the combined whole of the company (or companies) more valuable than the sum of its parts.

EXHIBIT 1.5	EXAMPLES OF ORGANIZATIONAL STRATEGIES AND ASSOCIATED HUMAN RESOURCE STRATEGIES	

Corporate Strategy	Example	Human Resource Strategies
Retrenchment (cost reduction)	GM	Layoffs, Wage Reduction, Productivity Increases, Job Redesign, Renegotiated Labor Agreements
Growth	Intel	Aggressive Recruiting and Hiring, Rapidly Rising Wages, Job Creation, Expanding Training and Development
Renewal	Chrysler	Managed Turnover, Selective Layoff, Organizational Development, Transfer/Replacement, Productivity Increases, Employee Involvement
Niche Focus	Kentucky Fried Chicken	Specialized Job Creation, Elimination of Other Jobs, Specialized Training and Development
Acquisition	GE	Selective Layoffs, Transfers/Placement/Job Combinations, Orientation and Training, Managing Cultural Transitions

Differences from Typical Functional Approach to Personnel

The strategic management approach to human resources and the typical functional approach differ in many ways. As Leonard Schlesinger states, HRM needs to get out of the "people business" and into the business of people.[24] In other words, human resource managers and other human resource professionals need to be full players on the management team.

Exhibit 1.6 enumerates the major differences between the strategic human resource approach and the traditional personnel management approach along six dimensions: planning and strategy formulation, authority, scope, decision making, integration, and coordination. Basically, *the strategic human resource approach is involved in strategic planning and decision making and coordinates all human resource functions for all employees.* The approach vests more authority in the chief human resource officer in the organization. It also views the human resource function as an *integral part* of all corporate functions: marketing, production, finance, legal, and so on. The strategic human resource approach accepts the vice-president of human resources as an integral part of the management team. Exhibit 1.7 shows a typical organization chart that includes human resources in the top level of management and, by doing so, provides the human resource vice-president with the same authority as the other functional vice-presidents. Remember also our job announcement for a human resources vice-president in Exhibit 1.2. This person is an integral part of the overall strategy of the firm.

For the vice-president of human resources to have any significant impact on the corporation, however, he or she must be able to do several things. First, he or she must know when to delegate responsibility and when to remain involved. If a project warrants the top person's input, then the vice-president should remain involved. If the project does not warrant it, the project should be delegated to a knowledgeable subordinate who is instructed to keep the vice-president informed. Second, the

EXHIBIT 1.6 **DIFFERENCE BETWEEN STRATEGIC HUMAN RESOURCE APPROACH AND TRADITIONAL PERSONNEL APPROACH**

Dimensions	Strategic Human Resource Approach	Traditional Personnel Management Approach
Planning and Strategy Formulation	Participates in formulating overall organizational strategic plan and aligning human resource functions with company strategy	Is involved in operational planning only
Authority	Has high status and authority for top personnel officer (e.g., vice-president for Human Resources)	Has medium status and authority (e.g., personnel director)
Scope	Is concerned with all managers and employees	Is concerned primarily with hourly, operational, and clerical employees
Decision Making	Is involved in making strategic decisions	Makes operational decisions only
Integration	Is fully integrated with other organizational functions: marketing, finance, legal, production	Has moderate to small integration with other organizational functions
Coordination	Coordinates all human resource activities (e.g., training, recruitment, staffing, Equal Employment Opportunity)	Does not coordinate all human resource functions

EXHIBIT 1.7 **DEPARTMENTAL STRUCTURE FOR HUMAN RESOURCES**

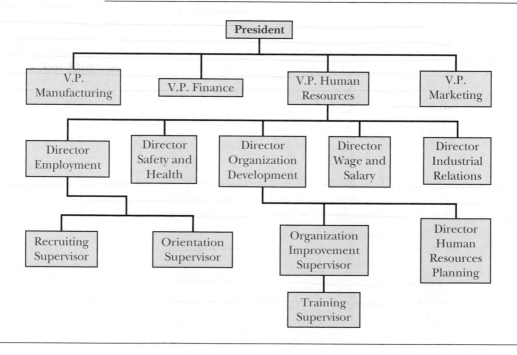

Careers in HR

Careers in HR today provide students with much greater variation and opportunity than in prior years. The breadth and scope of HR positions are as diverse as any other discipline in business. Students can choose a career that combines their key academic interests and personal goals. In many cases, organizations require that HR professionals are proficient in various areas of organizational operations prior to moving to HR. Professionals typically have experience in marketing, management, production, or some other core discipline before entering into HR.

For the student with an interest and background in computer science, information systems, or database management, a career as Human Resource Information Systems Analyst is an option. This position is responsible for analysis of information systems requirements and the development of solutions for the HR department. Requirements for a position of this nature include an understanding of HR theory and practices, a bachelor's degree, and knowledge of HR management software such as Peoplesoft. An individual may find that his or her position in HR is closely tied to the information systems aspect of business by nature of the reporting structure in the firm. Such is the case with a recently advertised position of Assistant Vice-President of HR who reported directly to the Information Technology Vice-President of an investment banking firm.

Consulting is another growth sector for HR specialists. Companies like Booz-Allen and KPMG look for individuals to fill a wide variety of HR positions to complement their management and information systems consulting. Recent positions in this arena include: Instructional Systems Designers/Courseware Developers, Recruiters/Staffing Specialists, and Human Resources Information Systems (HRIS) Analysts/Managers. Instructional Systems Designers assist in the development of instructional systems, courseware, paper and classroom video, and Web-based training. Strong communication skills are a must for such a position. Recruiters and staffing specialists design and implement strategic staffing plans to support business units, and they require strong interview and selection skills. HRIS analyst positions usually require knowledge of HR support software such as Peoplesoft (mentioned earlier), InPower, SAP, ORACLE, and other database management applications.

Individuals who have a desire to maintain connections with the collegiate environment, yet work in industry, may find the position of College Recruiter interesting. This position requires that professionals be able to analyze and develop recruiting needs and strategies of the company as well as cultivate key contacts with universities and relevant departments to develop pools of qualified candidates. A successful college recruiter will typically coordinate on-campus interviewing, develop college internship/externship programs, and conduct extensive interviews. A recent College Recruiter position with W. L. Gore & Associates, named one of "The 100 Best Companies to Work for in America," required a four-year degree, a background in HR (recruiting experience preferred), and a proven track record of handling confidential information.

For more information regarding these and many other unique HR career opportunities, visit the Society for Human Resource Management Web page at **www.shrm.org**. This site showcases a wide variety of careers in HR and recent position postings. Position information can be researched by geographic location, job title, or date of posting. This site can be a valuable resource when choosing the career path in HR that matches your special skills, interests, and future job aspirations.

For more information about careers, check out **www.kccareers.com**.

vice-president must have the respect of his or her peers because it is through these people that things will get done. Keeping the relationships well oiled will help to make the wheels turn when necessary. To make sensible policy decisions, a vice-president must have a good idea of how employees at all levels in the organization think. If a policy decision will be unpopular with the majority of the workers, it will not be a good policy. However, there is no way to know the popularity of a policy without knowing how others think and feel. Finally, a vice-president must have a good rapport with the CEO. To build this needed rapport, the vice-president should become immersed in the business, understand the financial ramifications of the human resource policies, and try to be objective when dealing with the CEO. By practicing these fundamentals, the vice-president of human resources can have a significant impact on the organization.[25]

All Managers are Human Resource Managers

The strategic human resource management approach views all managers as human resource managers. Human resource management issues are not simply the provinces of the human resources unit. Rather, all managers must take responsibility for efficient and effective use of their subordinates. By the same token, human resource managers, because they are in a *staff* position, must view their role as essentially supportive of *operating (line)* managers. That is, they should see their role as advising, helping, and providing expert guidance to line managers on human resource issues. In essence, human resource professionals should view the people they advise as customers and themselves as service representatives.[26]

As environmental changes confront organizations with increasingly more complex people issues, they can, in turn, affect the bottom line—profits or survival of the organization. Keeping abreast of these issues requires a broader understanding of human resource management and an increased time commitment away from the particular business function for the line manager. The human resource department, therefore, is a watchful eye that frees up the line managers across the organization by helping with the people-related business issues and working with the line managers to respond to the issues.[27] Although this relationship can lead to staff-line conflict, such conflict is not necessarily all bad if it results in full discussion of key human resource issues and better role clarification of the parties involved.

A feeling of interdependence among line and staff managers should be generated over time. Human resource managers expect line managers to become very knowledgeable about human resource issues. Line managers believe that it is equally important for human resource managers to become knowledgeable about the interworkings of the business. This seems fairly obvious, but many human resource managers are not adequately familiar with the company's products, markets, and finances. It is difficult for an unfamiliar human resource staff manager to work closely with a line manager in a situation in which expert knowledge of the company is necessary. The human resources staff and other departments should cultivate mutual trust as quickly as possible. The support of other areas is critical, and line departments must be willing to give new ideas and new perspectives a try. The success of the human resources department and its services is also highly dependent on the support and endorsement of all top management, and this too should be sought and cultivated as quickly as possible.

Environment-Organization Link and the Strategic Approach

As we have indicated, the strategic approach explicitly recognizes the impact of the outside environment on both the firm and the formulation of human resource strategy. Chapters 2 and 3 discuss the outside environment and its impact in more depth. However, at this point, we are interested in the impact on strategy formulation from a broad conceptual view.

The outside environment presents a set of *opportunities* and *threats* to the firm. In formulating strategy the firm seeks to take advantage of the opportunities while minimizing or deflecting the threats. What might be a threat to one firm can be an opportunity to another. The oil shocks of the 1970s and 1980s threatened oil-fired electrical utilities but provided great opportunities for coal producers and shippers.

Environmental Scanning

scanning The gathering of information about environmental issues on a regular basis and the interpretation of them in light of the organization's business.

The firm learns of its environment through a **scanning** process. This refers to the gathering of information about environmental issues on a regular basis and interpreting them in light of the organization's business. Scanning is the first step to strategic planning and strategy formulation. A scan and a forecast are developed and serve as the basis for the plan.

Competitive and market analyses are also important to strategy formulation. When the steel industry finally decided to restructure during the severe recession of the 1980s, it chose this strategy largely because of the severe competition from Japanese and German steel makers. Japan and Germany had rebuilt their steel-making facilities (largely with U.S. dollars) after World War II. This technology was more efficient than that in place in the United States. Consequently, during the early 1980s, U.S. steel plants were closed in Pennsylvania, West Virginia, and other industrial areas. Many people lost good-paying jobs and have been unable to find work paying a comparable wage. People who traveled the Monongahela and Eastern Ohio River valleys would see rusted hulks of former steel plants sitting idle and vacant fields where other plants once stood. Much steel-making capacity has been lost to foreign producers.

sustainable competitive advantage A differential advantage a particular organization can achieve over its competition.

A firm tries to achieve a **sustainable competitive advantage** by analyzing competition.[28] This advantage is a long-term distinctive competence that sets one company apart from the competition. It answers the question "Why would someone buy our service or product over someone else's?" This advantage can be based on any number of factors: price, cost, service, quality, image, reliability, convenience, safety, or any combination of the above. For example, Mercedes-Benz has a sustainable competitive advantage in reliability and image over many other automobiles.

Besides competition, the market also brings an industry structure. The industry structure involves a number of factors: growth rates, concentration ratio (the number of firms that have a large percentage of the market), substitute products or services in related industries, technology, change, and so on.

critical success factors The keys to success in a particular industry.

A key aspect in industry analysis is determining **critical success factors,** or keys to success. These are what it takes to be successful in that industry. For example, to be successful in fast foods, a firm must have convenient locations, quick service, a consistent standard of product quality, store cleanliness, mass advertising, high volume, and low margins. Firms such as McDonald's, Wendy's, KFC, Burger King, Hardees, and other fast-food chains are successful because they have largely acquired these characteristics.

Success factors for other industries are different. For example, for department stores, success factors are magnet mall locations, wide variety or choice of merchandise, good service, good- to high-quality merchandise, and a liberal customer return

---

FOCUS ON HR

KFC Finds Success Faster than Others—in China

After 18 months of tough negotiations, Kentucky Fried Chicken (KFC) opened its first restaurant in Beijing, China, in 1988. KFC has dubbed its venture an instant success. By 2000 there were 380 KFC establishments in the People's Republic of China, and KFC is currently the largest fast food retailer in China. KFC currently employs 25,000 people in the city of Shanghai alone, and nearly 150,000 Chinese nationals work for the company throughout China. Individual KFC establishments in China average 10,000-12,000 transactions per week, compared with U.S. store averages of 2000 transactions per week. Research findings of both Burger King and McDonald's indicate that the vital ingredients for fast-food success—high-quality supplies, a disciplined labor force, and receptive consumers—may not be readily available in China.

Daniel Ng, managing director of McDonald's Restaurants in Hong Kong, said that he has been talking with Chinese authorities about the possibility of entering the East Asia fast-food market for the past ten years. He concedes that, while being the first to break into a new marketplace is good, he would rather be sure that it is done right, even if it means being last.

Officials at Burger King held a similar attitude. Their preliminary research study conducted two years prior to the KFC opening indicated that a full-blown feasibility study was ill advised at that point. The main problems they foresaw were the difficulty of procuring supplies and the uncertainty that there would be enough interested customers to ensure a strong return on their investment.

Since 1988, however, Pizza Hut, McDonald's, and Burger King have all opened in China and are enjoying moderate success.

More information on KFC can be found by visiting its Web site at **www.kfc.com**.

SOURCES: Adapted from Brian Caplan, "Kentucky Hatches Its Chickens in Beijing," *Asian Business*, February 1988, p. 17; Susan Oh, "KFC Takes a Big Bite out of Fast Food Market," *South China Morning Post*, March 24, 1994, p. 4; and Carol Casper, *Restaurant Business*, November 1, 1996, p. 5; and **www.kfc.com**.

---

policy, among others. The point is that a firm must know the critical success factors of its industry and formulate a strategy that allows it to meet these factors.

The human resource strategy is based on overall corporate strategy and needs to be consistent with it. A department store emphasizing friendly, competent service to customers must hire, train, and reward employees so that such services are efficiently and effectively provided.

Finally, technology has a major impact on strategy formulation and on human resource strategy in particular. The technology available in the environment, plus that actually adopted by an organization, has a profound effect on job design decisions, which in turn affect many other human resource decisions such as pay, training, work assignment, and leadership. Think of the technology employed by an automobile manufacturer on the assembly line. The configuration of machines, movement, and technical expertise caused by the kind of technology employed creates a set of constraints within which human resource decisions must be made. To change these constraints, the technology must be changed. For example, robotics technology is replacing people who use hand tools in a repetitive manner, such as in welding the frame of a car.

HR CHALLENGES

The Best Companies to Work for

In a 2000 *Fortune* survey of 280 companies and 20,000 employees, it appears that the companies that rated as the most desirable to work for are desperately trying to retain their best employees. Some companies are going to great lengths to keep their best employees. Companies are offering nontraditional benefits such as child care, on-site health care, extra paid vacation, and flex time to keep employees happy and committed. Charles Schwab and SAS Institute both offer their employees massages during business hours. Most of the highest-rated companies offer employee stock options.

With unemployment at a 30-year low in 2000, the best companies were realizing the difficulty of keeping their talented employees. Individuals surveyed at the "100 Best Companies" cited various reasons why they remain with a company. Cutting-edge technology, exciting work, promise of promotions from within, and international assignments were all reasons given for their loyalty. Stock options, performance bonuses, and opportunities to share financially in corporate success were common to most of the top ten–rated companies. However, in an environment where such practices are common, social issues were often cited as setting a company apart from the herd. In a survey of "peak performers" in U.S. companies, respondents indicated that a work environment that "promotes fun and closer work relationships with colleagues" would make them most reluctant to leave the company. Manpower, Inc. indicates that 32 percent of the 16,000 companies they surveyed in the year 2000 were going to add people to their ranks in 2000.

What attracts employees to these companies? The "100 Best Companies" possess one or more of three key traits. *Inspiring leadership* is the first common trait. Herb Kelleher of Southwest Airlines and Mary Kay Ash of Mary Kay, Inc. are both good examples of inspiring leaders. One of Kelleher's focuses is to ensure that his employees believe in him and Southwest Airlines. Mary Kay

Ash is very accessible to her employees. Although she has reached the pinnacle of success, she inspires them to achieve the same level of success. *Workplace facilities and amenities* are the second key factor. Some of the "100 Best Companies" provide their employees with van pools for those who do not want to drive to work, on-site child care, and gymnasiums with tennis and racquetball facilities. Company leadership concedes that the amenities cost a lot, but that they also buy a lot in terms of communicating that they care about their employees. The third trait in common is that these companies instill *a sense of purpose* in their employees. Emphasis on the mission of the company and the people that it serves helps to redirect the employees' focus away from the "hollow notion" of shareholder value.

Are the various perks and elaborate facilities paying off for the "100 Best Companies?" The 58 firms in this group that are publicly traded yielded higher returns to shareholders than the S&P 500 (37 percent versus 25 percent, respectively). According to the *Fortune* magazine survey, the following companies were ranked the top ten companies for which to work in the United States in 2001.

1. Container Store
2. SAS Institute
3. Cisco Systems
4. Southwest Airlines
5. Charles Schwab
6. TDIndustries
7. Fenwick & West
8. Synovus Financial Corp.
9. Edward Jones
10. Plante & Moran

For more information about *Fortune*, visit its Web site at **www.fortune.com**.

SOURCE: Robert Levering and Milton Moskowitz, *Introduction to the Best Companies*, available at **www.fortune.com/fortune/bestcompanies/intro.html**.

Integrating Human Resource Strategy with Corporate and Functional Strategies

GM's corporate strategy of retrenchment and revitalization that we examined at the beginning of this chapter will drive human resource, marketing, operations (production), finance, and other functional policies. GM appears to be resigning itself to a 28.9 percent market share, at least in the foreseeable future, because it has permanently closed 11 plants instead of using temporary layoffs, the traditional way of dealing with sale falloffs in the auto industry. Thus GM's overall corporate retrenchment strategy will have profound effects on its functional strategies, including its human resource strategy. GM has specifically recognized these links in the way it established and operates its Saturn Division. Exhibit 1.8 shows how GM's Saturn project has been used to link corporate strategies to business strategies and finally to human resource strategies.

Corporate Strategy Drives Functional Strategies

As Exhibit 1.9 exemplifies, corporate strategy should drive functional strategy. In other words, a firm determines its overall strategy and then sets functional strategy to carry it out. For example, GM's retrenchment strategy has caused downsizing in human resource management, consolidation in production and operations, cutbacks or at least very moderate growth in marketing (including advertising expenditures), restructuring and consolidation in finance, restructuring of engineering, and so on. GM's major functions will be affected in a substantial way by the retrenchment strategy.

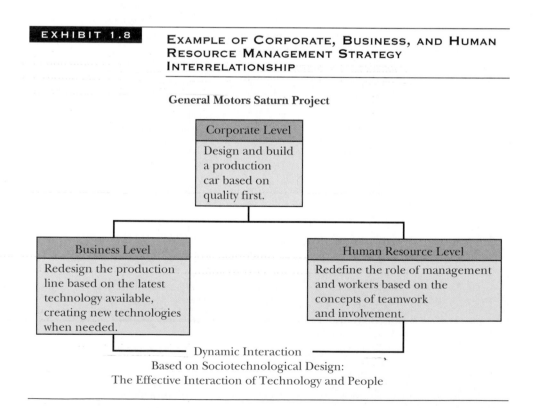

| **EXHIBIT 1.8** | EXAMPLE OF CORPORATE, BUSINESS, AND HUMAN RESOURCE MANAGEMENT STRATEGY INTERRELATIONSHIP |

General Motors Saturn Project

Corporate Level
Design and build a production car based on quality first.

Business Level
Redesign the production line based on the latest technology available, creating new technologies when needed.

Human Resource Level
Redefine the role of management and workers based on the concepts of teamwork and involvement.

Dynamic Interaction
Based on Sociotechnological Design:
The Effective Interaction of Technology and People

HR Not a Priority at Dot-Coms

One survey of more than 200 executives at online companies throughout the United States indicates that ". . . most Internet companies are ignoring fundamental HR and compliance issues even though they are growing rapidly."

- 51 percent do not have a staff member devoted to HR
- 41 percent do not rely on anyone other than themselves for advice on HR matters
- 28 percent rely on friends, neighbors, accountants, brokers, and lawyers for primary advice, rather than HR professionals

Furthermore, even though 76 percent of online companies plan to increase their staffs, 71 percent do not plan to hire an HR person. The study concludes that this lack of focus on HR in dot-com companies results in the fact that ". . . they are leaving themselves wide-open to major liability."

Since the study was conducted, there has been a major shakeout in the on-line industry that began in late 2000. Because of this, it is even more imperative that dot-com companies establish effective HR departments to handle the downsizing and restructuring that is occurring. Provision for orderly changes in human resources staffing patterns and protection from layoff and termination lawsuits require an informed and effective HR department.

SOURCE: Bill Leonard, "HR Not a Priority at Dot-Coms," *HR Magazine*, October 2000, p. 27.

EXHIBIT 1.9 CORPORATE STRATEGY DRIVES FUNCTIONAL STRATEGIES

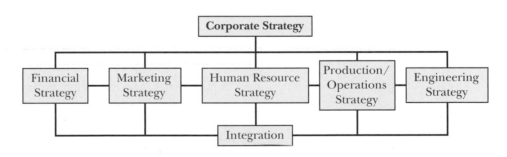

Also, note that in Exhibit 1.9 functional strategy can affect corporate strategy, in that a firm must consider existing functional strategy when setting corporate strategy. For example, the existing human resource strategy and capabilities are major factors to consider in the formulation of corporate strategy.

In addition, various functional strategies must be integrated with one another. It would be inconsistent for GM to adopt a high-growth human resource strategy while scaling back production and operations. Nor would high investment in new plants and equipment be an appropriate financial strategy for retrenchment. Marketing strategy must be focused at an anticipated 30 percent market share instead of the 50 percent to which GM has been accustomed.

The implication for human resource managers is that they must be acutely aware of overall corporate strategy and how human resource strategy dovetails with it. Moreover, they need to be aware of functional strategies and attempt to integrate human resource strategy with them. This awareness argues for participation in the

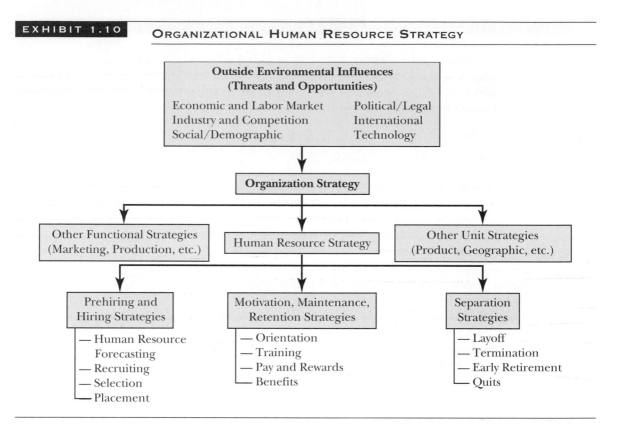

EXHIBIT 1.10 ORGANIZATIONAL HUMAN RESOURCE STRATEGY

Outside Environmental Influences
(Threats and Opportunities)

Economic and Labor Market   Political/Legal
Industry and Competition   International
Social/Demographic   Technology

Organization Strategy

Other Functional Strategies (Marketing, Production, etc.)

Human Resource Strategy

Other Unit Strategies (Product, Geographic, etc.)

Prehiring and Hiring Strategies
— Human Resource Forecasting
— Recruiting
— Selection
— Placement

Motivation, Maintenance, Retention Strategies
— Orientation
— Training
— Pay and Rewards
— Benefits

Separation Strategies
— Layoff
— Termination
— Early Retirement
— Quits

strategy formulation process at both the corporate and functional levels, as discussed previously in this chapter.

A summary model of organizational strategy and its relationship to human resource strategies is presented in Exhibit 1.10. Notice the substrategies that make up overall human resource strategy. Substrategies are developed for prehiring and hiring, motivation, retraining and retention, and separating human resources. Exhibit 1.10 shows the substrategies for each of these areas.

Strategy Formulation, Decision Making, and Problem Solving

The strategy formulation process is not a neat and clean process. It advances in fits and starts and is subject to much revision and ad hoc interpretation. It approximates the "garbage can theory" of decision making in that there is much post hoc attribution or explanation of why certain actions were carried out.[29] Sometimes action drives strategy rather than the reverse. Decision makers then justify a particular course of action by looking for a strategy that supports it.

Thus strategic formulation is a *dynamic* process.[30] It is evolutionary and subject to change as outside environmental conditions, competition, or internal conditions change. This flexibility in strategy formulation and implementation is essential to the process. Because strategy formulation deals with the future (for example, what we will do in the future, how, and why), and because no one can predict the future with certainty, the process must be kept flexible. The firm must be able to respond to changes as they occur—*in spite of* the plans.

The ability of a large corporation such as Ford Motor Company to completely change and refocus strategy in the early 1980s to the "Quality Is Job 1" campaign shows how Ford was able to meet new threats in both domestic (Chrysler) and foreign competition as well as weather the unexpected fuel price shocks of the late 1970s and early 1980s.

logical incrementalism Measured change or reaction to a particular event.

This ability to redirect strategy formulation is sometimes called **logical incrementalism**.[31] This concept refers to the additional measured change or reaction to a particular event. Actions appear to be taken in a step-by-step fashion without the appearance of an overall plan. For example, a particular environmental pressure (such as a new unexpected law) or a competitive threat (such as an unanticipated price cut) could cause a firm to take a calculated course of action that was not originally planned as part of the strategy. A series of these actions might make it appear that the strategy is simply one of **reaction** rather than **proaction;** that is, the company is reacting to the latest threat. In other words, "the squeaky wheel gets the grease."

reaction An approach to strategy formulation or decision making wherein an organization reacts to threats "after the fact."

Although the reactive label might be appropriate if every course of action a firm undertook was in response to a threat, it certainly would not be appropriate if the firm followed a well-formulated strategy but was able to modify it as conditions changed. In this case the firm would be proactive—establishing plans and strategy ahead of time—but flexible. Yet the line between flexibility in strategy and a reactive mode sometimes can be a thin one.

proaction An approach to strategy formulation or decision making wherein strategies are formed in anticipation of problems.

Another way to view this phenomenon is to make a distinction between **intended strategy** and **realized strategy.** The intended strategy is the strategy formulated during the planning period. The realized strategy is the strategy the organization actually follows. Often the realized strategy is different from the intended strategy because unanticipated forces affect the intended strategy or, because of implementation problems, the strategy is modified.

A Reliance on Decisions

intended strategy The strategy formulated during the planning period.

Each of the various components of the strategy process is really nothing more than a series of decisions. In the traditional model of strategic management, once an understanding of the environment has been developed, the company's strategy makers must formulate, implement, and evaluate/control the strategic thrust of the company. These actions call for different but interrelated decisions. For example, after McDonald's decided to add breakfast to its operation and had formulated its breakfast strategy, a whole series of implementation decisions had to be made, including what to serve, how to prepare the food, and how to handle the need for new employees. After implementation, McDonald's management had to make adjustments to the menu and to operations as part of its evaluation and control of the strategy.

realized strategy The "actual" strategy the organization follows.

As a matter of fact, the essence of strategy is decision making. Many questions must be answered, such as the following:

- What should the company do and why?
- How does the company respond to the competition?
- What new products and markets should the company be developing?
- How much does the company want or need to grow?

When dealing with the human resources strategy, more specific questions must be asked, such as the following:

- What must the company's workforce look like in the future?
- Does the company's training program really fit its needs?
- What sort of pay and incentive plan should be developed?
- Should more employees be hired or laid off?

Most managers are flooded with questions such as these and often wonder about the best way to solve the problems and answer the questions.

For more information on McDonald's, visit its Web site at **www.mcdonalds.com**.

Integrating Human Resources in Strategic Decisions

People in organizations make decisions. Even in automatic decisions, such as an automatic cutoff in a launch sequence for a space rocket, someone programmed a computer to shut down the firing sequence if certain data were present or not present. Automatic or programmed decisions are ultimately people driven, even though in some cases tracing back the sequence to the place where human involvement occurred can be complex.

In this section, we examine the human resource impact of decisions from four perspectives. First, we look at the issue of the substitutability of capital for labor. Second, we look at the impact of strategic decisions on human resources in general within the organization. Third, we examine the political forces at work in human resources. Finally, we examine the role of the human resources unit in strategic decision making.

Capital versus Labor

From a strategic and economic perspective, the underlying decision an organization must make regarding its human resources is its capital:labor ratio. Each organization must decide to what extent it will substitute capital for labor and vice versa. In other words, an organization must determine to what extent it will fill its jobs by substituting machines for people.

Since the Industrial Revolution, organizations have substituted capital for labor by using machine power to replace human power. Generally, this has led to higher levels of productivity and lower per unit costs of production. The backhoe replaced the ditch digger; the automatic glass-blowing machine replaced hand blowers; the high-speed printing press replaced the hand press, and so on. Mass production—changeable parts and specialized machines performing the same function over and over again to produce huge quantities—has allowed for tremendous increases in productivity.

Today, the same capital and labor decision is being made in factories, offices, and mines around the country, but it involves substituting smart machines—computers—for other machines and labor. Personal computers replace electric typewriters and calculators in offices; automated management and control systems replace people-controlled machines in paper and steel plants; robots replace welders on automobile assembly lines; automated answering devices replace receptionists who answer telephones and guide people to the right extension; automatic teller machines replace tellers at banks; optical scanners read prices off grocery items, replacing clerks who ring up the price—the list goes on and on.

Organizations invest in these smart machines because, in general, they do the job more cheaply and efficiently than people do. But these changes do not come without both monetary and human costs. Some people who are laid off may never get a job again. Those who do find work may find much lower-paying jobs. Other people enter retraining programs to learn new skills to operate the smart machines. Still others must move and relocate to cities in parts of the country offering suitable employment. Finally, others may become alienated and drop out of society as a form of rebellion against technology.

This technological change brings dislocations, which are the costs of substituting capital for labor. Society as a whole, rather than individual firms, largely bears these costs, so firms often do not consider them when making a technological decision to automate a job or process. In fact, some firms often have no choice. In order to remain competitive from a cost basis in worldwide markets, they *must* automate. We saw this during the 1980s in the steel, rubber, auto, and other major industries, and we will likely continue to see it as other industries—including financial services, insurance, and even housing—become globalized.

The extensive job design consequences of substituting capital for labor by incorporating more technology into jobs are fully explored in later chapters.

Strategic Decision Impact on People in the Organization

In our discussion above, it is obvious that automation of jobs has a significant impact on human resources. However, many important or strategic decisions are often considered nonhuman resource decisions. In other words, restructuring a loan package from lenders is usually considered only a financial decision. A decision to develop a new product is usually looked at from research and development, marketing, engineering, design, and production perspectives. A decision to change a company name or logo is usually a public relations decision.

Yet all of these decisions have a human resource dimension. First, people make the decision. People who make strategic decisions in an organization constitute what is called the **dominant coalition.** The dominant coalition almost always includes top management, but it also often includes people with technical expertise in an area under consideration. More and more frequently, top-level human resource managers are included in the dominant coalition. For example, a computer and information systems specialist in the organization may have a significant role to play in making a decision to purchase a new information management system. The same is true of a design engineer in new product development.

So the composition of the dominant coalition may change, depending on the strategic decision under consideration. The extent to which people further down in the organization have input to membership in the dominant coalition is a major factor in determining the extent of **participation** in the decision process. In general, many organizations have tried to involve their managers and employees more in the decision process and thereby increase their input. However, this involvement is usually in routine or operating decisions rather than strategic decisions. The theory behind employee involvement is that by giving lower-level managers and employees more of a role to play in decisions, they will have a greater commitment to the decision output.

Japanese auto companies exemplify this policy through their **quality circles,** which are groups of employees who meet to recommend ways to improve production and quality. The Motorola Participative Management Program and Florida Power and Light's (FPL's) Quality Improvement Program (which won Japan's prestigious Deming Award in 1989) are patterned after the Japanese participative model.

Involving people throughout the organization in decisions provides an opportunity to consider the human resource impact of the decision. People who eventually have to

dominant coalition Group of individuals in the organization who make strategic decisions.

participation The level of involvement in the decision-making process among managers and employees.

quality circles Groups of employees who meet to recommend ways to improve production and quality.

EXHIBIT 1.11	EXAMPLES OF STRATEGIC DECISIONS THAT HAVE MAJOR AND MINOR IMPACTS ON HUMAN RESOURCES

Examples of Strategic Decisions that Tend to Have a Direct Human Resource Impact

Plant Location	Job Design/Redesign
Plant Closing	Production Technology
Wage Cutting	Supervisory Style
Restructuring	Organization Culture Changes
Collective Bargaining	Market Expansion/Retrenchment
Automation	Mergers/Acquisitions

Examples of Strategic Decisions that Tend to Have an Indirect Human Resource Impact

Loan/Portfolio Restructuring	Public Relations Campaign
Stock Offerings	Changes in Accounting Methods
Logo/Name Change	
Product Feature Change	

carry out the strategic decision made by the dominant coalition may be in the best position to provide input and advice on what must be done to make the decision work.

For example, a plant-closing decision that would involve transfer, retraining, and severance rights for employees certainly would involve the union, if one were present. If no union were present, employees still might be involved through transition committees. Steel companies have used transition committees, even to the extent of allowing the employees to buy the plant, as was done with Wierton Steel in West Virginia.

So obtaining input throughout the organization by using participative management and involvement techniques is a popular way to expose the human resource implications of strategic decisions. Of course, this is best done with decisions that very much affect human resources compared with those that do not. For instance, despite FPL's success in quality attainment, its employees complained that the system was too bureaucratic, so the company has pared down and refocused some of the original structures.[32] Exhibit 1.11 lists samples of decisions that tend to have a direct impact on human resources and those that have little or no direct effect.

For more information about Motorola, visit its Web site at **www.motorola.com**. More information on FPL and the power industry can be found by visiting the Web site at **www.fpl.com**.

Political Influences in Human Resource Management

The strategic perspective of human resource management looks at the long-term implications of human resource decisions and integrates the human resource strategy with the organization's overall strategy. In keeping with the discussion on the dominant coalition, the members in the organization influence the human resource information system. They influence not only who will be hired and promoted but also the criteria used in hiring and job evaluation decisions. Not all behavior is political, but it becomes political when it attempts to manage or control the meanings, norms, and behavior of employees in an organization.

Political influence, like any other behavior in organizations, does not operate in a vacuum. People answer for their actions. This accountability to others can have a substantial impact on their behavior, including political influence behavior. Politics is not "bad" per se; it is a fact of life in most organizations.

Managers may hire employees based on political influence. Although, at the time, they may say that the person hired "fit" better in the organization, the definition of "fit" may be a political one based on whom the managers think they can influence or control. If they hire enough employees who fit their mold, then they can create a powerful political base in the organization. This may not be the best situation for the organization, and the consequences of such behavior will soon become apparent.

Role of the Human Resource Unit in Strategic Decisions

When a strategic decision has a major impact on human resources, such as those decisions listed at the top of Exhibit 1.11, the human resource unit should play a major role in the decision. Human resource professionals are in the best position to advise and otherwise influence the decision process. To become true business partners, human resource managers must focus their attention on issues that are of concern to the company's chief executive.

Traditionally, the human resource unit has *not* been part of the dominant coalition. Largely this is because of the staff or advisory role that human resources plays. However, even though the role of human resources is still largely advisory, the *level* of human resource units has been elevated, as explained in Chapter 2. Today, companies have vice-presidents of human resources both at the corporate and divisional level. This enhances their membership in the dominant coalition. Yet because human resources is essentially staff oriented, the models of influence on decisions tend to fall along the continuum of staff involvement in decision making. Exhibit 1.12 summarizes this continuum, and we discuss it in the following section.

Levels of Staff Involvement in Decisions

The organization's human resource unit can have anywhere from a minimal to a maximum role to play in strategic decisions. At the far left of the continuum shown in Exhibit 1.12, the human resource unit simply provides raw data and information to the dominant coalition. For example, if a company were considering closing a plant, the human resource unit would simply provide the decision makers with information on the number of people affected, severance costs, early retirement costs, and so on, with no analysis.

In the next position to the right, the human resource unit would analyze the data. Graphs and trends might be developed. Interpretive paragraphs would be written and implications would be spelled out regarding the plant closing.

In the middle position the staff role of human resources is carried a step further. Here, specific recommendations as to what the company should do with respect to the human resource issues raised in the closing would be developed but would be unranked. In other words, human resources would simply lay out the options with the associated costs and benefits of each option, but the decision makers would choose the option. In the plant-closing example, human resources might detail the costs and benefits of retraining, transfer, outplacement, early retirement, layoff, and severance programs.

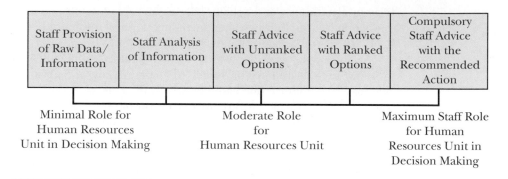

EXHIBIT 1.12 CONTINUUM OF STAFF INVOLVEMENT FOR HUMAN RESOURCES UNIT IN STRATEGIC DECISIONS AFFECTING HUMAN RESOURCES

Staff Provision of Raw Data/ Information	Staff Analysis of Information	Staff Advice with Unranked Options	Staff Advice with Ranked Options	Compulsory Staff Advice with the Recommended Action

Minimal Role for Human Resources Unit in Decision Making

Moderate Role for Human Resources Unit

Maximum Staff Role for Human Resources Unit in Decision Making

In the fourth position to the right, human resources ranks the options as to what they would recommend and why. Finally, in the fifth option, human resources provides the rank order and makes an admonition—no decision could be made without first hearing and considering the options recommended by human resources. The principle of compulsory staff advice forces line decision makers at least to consider staff advice before making the decision, even if they decide not to take it. This gives human resources its strongest staff authority in influencing strategic decisions.

Of course, remember that we are discussing strategic decisions that have a major human resource impact. In those decisions that are strictly human resource decisions—such as how to best administer a pay plan or how to set up a human resource division—human resources exercises line authority over those employed in the unit. The vice-president of human resources (or whatever the head human resource person is called) has line authority to manage the unit.

Possible Line Authority in Strategic Decisions

Taking the previous example a step further, suppose the human resource unit was given not just a staff role to play in making a plant-closing decision, but a line role. In other words, the human resource unit would share in the line authority for the plant-closing decision. The human resource vice-president's "vote" would carry as much weight as the manufacturing vice-president's vote. Here, the authority of the human resource unit is no longer staff but line. This is rare in strategic decision making but does happen occasionally. However, with increasing authority and responsibility being given to the human resource unit, direct line authority over strategic decisions will likely become more common. In fact, a recent study showed that 76 percent of human resource managers surveyed believed that they played a strategic role in making bottom line decisions for the firm. Fifty-three percent of the line managers in these same firms agreed with this assessment. In both government and health services sectors, this percentage was even higher with about 85 percent of human resource managers believing they had the authority to make decisions that contributed to the bottom line.[33]

Strategy, Globalization, and Technology

Three major themes are highlighted throughout the book. These themes are the strategic approach, globalization, and technology. Each of these themes has had a significant impact on human resource management during the past decade. Consequently, we emphasize them throughout the book. Let's examine each of these briefly.

Strategy   As we have indicated in this chapter, we take a strategic focus in human resource management. This focus is explained further in Chapter 2. One of the most significant developments in human resource management has been to accord it the same level of influence held by other functions such as finance, marketing, and operations. This enhanced influence places human resource management strategies at least on par with other functional strategies in organizations.

Globalization   A second major theme throughout the book is the global nature of human resource decisions. Decisions on outsourcing production to a foreign subsidiary to maintaining wages and labor productivity in order to compete in global markets are common ones today for many organizations. Human resource managers can no longer be concerned only with their domestic market and domestic employees. Even small firms are greatly affected by worldwide events. (See the Right Management Consultants case at the end of this chapter.)

As we see in Chapter 3 and throughout the book, international events and global competitive factors have direct effects on a firm's human resource strategies.

Technology   Finally, the third theme we emphasize throughout the book is the technology revolution affecting human resource management. This profound effect is felt by organizations in a variety of ways. For example, organizations are responsible for developing sophisticated training methods to keep employees current with new technology, as well as finding ways to use technology to manage employee databases, human resource planning in production, and payroll and benefits management. Changes in technology have had a major influence on the performance of all human resource functions, from hiring and selection through separation and termination. These changes are noted in each chapter. We also provide Internet addresses throughout each chapter that you can access to obtain more information on the subject being discussed.

Management Guidelines

Based on the material covered in this chapter, we can provide the following management guidelines:

1. Corporate strategy should be determined first, and then human resource strategy should be developed. The human resource strategy that is developed should be consistent with the corporate strategy.
2. Human resource strategy should be consistent with other functional strategies, such as finance, marketing, and engineering.
3. The strategy formulation process should remain flexible and readily adaptable to change.
4. Human resource managers, particularly those at the top of the organization, should be involved in the strategy formulation process.

5. Human resource strategy should consider all human resources in the organization, not just hourly or operative employees.
6. The outside environment and competition should be considered explicitly in formulating both overall organization and human resource strategy.
7. The better and more accurately that managers make sense of the organization's internal and external environment, the better their decisions will be.
8. Human resources should project both intended and unintended consequences of decisions because they might affect human resources.
9. Competition and labor market dynamics have an impact on the success of strategic human resource decisions; human resource managers should develop a realistic match between corporate strategies and the economics of the labor market.

Questions for Review

1. What is meant by the term *strategy?*

2. What is meant by a *strategic approach to human resources?*

3. How does the strategic approach to human resources differ from the functional approach?

4. What role does the outside environment and competition have in formulating organizational strategy?

5. Why should human resource strategy be consistent with both organizational strategy and functional strategy?

6. What roles do problem solving and decision making play in strategy formulation?

7. How has the field of human resources changed over the past 100 years? Why?

8. What is the role of the human resource unit in making strategic decisions?

9. Should human resources exercise more line authority in strategic decision making? Why or why not?

10. How might the labor market constrain the types of strategic decisions rendered by an organization?

CASE

Right Management Consultants Succeeds by Managing Change*

Right Management Consultants has become an international leader in human resources and management consulting by assisting companies and their employees to manage the one constant in business today—change.

At the same time, effectively dealing with change is driving the company's own success. Right has launched fast-track growth by broadening its scope from outplacement services to consulting on the full range of restructuring issues.

*This case was prepared by Tom Shea of Right Management Consultants.

Entrepreneurial Beginnings

Four experienced outplacement and career management consultants—entrepreneurs Frank P. Louchheim, Larry A. Evans, Robert A. Fish, and C. Boardman Thompson—founded Right Management Consultants in 1980 in Philadelphia. In 1982 they expanded the company dramatically to serve a major client with locations throughout the United States. To meet that need, Right opened additional offices and entered into an affiliate agreement with several qualified existing firms, creating a national network of 12 Right offices.

That expansion introduced Right to new markets and opened the door for continuing growth. By 1986, Right had 36 offices in North America with total revenues of $18 million. To expand further in both North America and Western Europe, the company completed an initial public offering in 1986.

Today, Right Management Consultants is the largest publicly traded organization in the industry with more than 150 offices in North America, Europe, Australia, the Far East, and Latin America. There are 8 offices in the Florida division alone and 200 offices worldwide.

Right Management Consultants has served more than 80 percent of the *Fortune* 500 and thousands of other companies and has helped more than 1 million individuals make successful career transitions. In 1991 and 1996, *Business Week* named Right one of "The Top 100 Small Businesses in the United States." *Forbes* magazine in November 1993, 1994, 1995, and 1996 named Right to its annual tally of "The Best Small Companies in the World."

"Several factors account for Right Management Consultants' rapid growth," said Thomas H. Shea, managing principal of the Florida/Caribbean Division. "We emphasize professional training and development for consulting staff, and we've streamlined administrative processes to ensure responsive service. Equally important, Right Management Consultants tailors its services precisely to each client's specific situation and needs."

Expanding Service Focus

Beginning with the first wave of downsizing and restructuring in the mid-1980s, Right began expanding its focus to become business' "partner in managing change." Today, Right confers with companies on restructuring and organizational change issues and with their employees at every level in managing career transitions.

Programs initiated by Right include the customized Key Executive Service for departing CEOs and other senior-level managers. A lead consultant, directing a team of internal/external consultants, works with the key executive in determining the right path, such as an entrepreneurial venture, reemployment, or retirement. The team also assists in developing strategy and positioning and provides a "resource bridge" to reach the goal as quickly as possible. Support services may include those such as personal financial consulting, contract and legal advice, communications/image consulting, and research database assistance.

Another program Right has developed is Spouse Employment Assistance. In the past, corporations provided job search assistance for the spouse of a transferee or new recruit on an informal, as-needed basis. Today, with more than half of America's married couples committed to two careers, a more focused approach is necessary. In addition, the "trailing spouse" is no longer typically a female clerical worker; a male or female executive is just as likely.

Right's program thoroughly prepares spouses for the job search with career goal development, an individualized action plan, and job development assistance, such as tapping local networks that can lead to interviews and opportunities. Right uses its JobBank[SM] and Right Match™ technology to support the effort. JobBank, for example, is a private database listing middle management through key executive positions available nationwide in specific markets.

Managing the Human Side of Change

These specific programs and support services are elements of Right Management Consultants' mission to help corporations manage the human resource issues resulting from reengineering, acquisitions, mergers, and relocations. Services are provided in three basic areas: restructuring planning and implementation, transition management, and recommitment.

In counseling a company facing a major restructuring, for example, Right works closely with the in-house human resources department to develop a customized program. Services include assistance in planning the corporation realignment and career transition support for outplaced key executives and employees at all levels. Right also offers an organizational renewal program for remaining workers taking on new responsibilities and a recommitment program to energize the company after the transition.

Along with helping companies manage change, Right counsels its employees. For example, Individual and Group Career Transition Support prepares employees for reemployment with services such as career decision consulting, assessment of potential, development of self-marketing materials, and effectiveness coaching.

Right's track record underlines the effectiveness of its change management programs. The company's market share has increased in every year of operation and stands at about 15 percent. For 1999, revenues increased 8 percent to a record $181 million, the sixth consecutive year of higher revenues.[34]

For more information on Right Management Consultants, visit its Web site at **www.right.com**.

Questions for Discussion

1. What are the challenges faced by this company when the downsizing effort no longer is a popular human resource strategy?

2. What conflicts do you see between a company of this type and a firm's human resources department?

3. What do you recommend Right do at this time to prepare for the future?

Additional Readings

Ansoff, H. *The New Corporate Strategy*. New York: John Wiley & Sons, 1988.

Anthony, William P. *Practical Strategic Planning: A Guide and Manual for Line Managers*. Westport, CT: Quorum Books, 1985.

Bracker, J. "The Historical Development of the Strategic Management Concept." *Academy of Management Review* 5(1991), pp. 219–224.

Devanna, Mary Anne, Charles Fombrun, Noel Tichy, and E. Kirby Warren. "Strategic Planning and Human Resource Management," *Human Resource Management* 21, Spring 1982, p. 11.

Fossum, John A., and Donald F. Parker. "Building State-of-the-Art Human Resource Strategies." *Human Resource Management* 22, Spring/Summer 1983, p. 97.

Fredrickson, J. *Perspectives on Strategic Management*. New York: Harper & Row, 1990.

Gwynne, S. C. "The Right Stuff." *Time*, October 29, 1990, pp. 74–84.

Hax, Arnoldo C. "A New Competitive Weapon: The Human Resource Strategy." *Training and Development Journal* 39, no. 5 (May 1985), pp. 76–82.

Kelley, Tom, 1989 Chairman of the American Society of Personnel Administrators' Board of Directors (now the Society of Human Resource Management), in an interview by John T. Adams III. "Strategic Partnerships in HRM." *Personnel Administrator*, January 1989, pp. 76–82.

Kotha, S. and B. Vadlamani. Assessing Generic Strategies. *Strategic Management Journal* 16, January 1995, pp. 75–83.

Crivitz, Dennis. *The Human Resources Revolution*. San Francisco, CA: Jossey-Bass, 1988.

Linkow, Peter. "Human Resource Development at the Roots of Corporate Strategy." *Training and Development Journal* 39, no. 5 (May 1985), pp. 85–87.

Mahoney, Thomas A., and John R. Deckop. "Evolution of Concept and Practice in Personnel Administration/Human Resource Management." *Journal of Management* 12, no. 2 (Summer 1986), pp. 223–241.

Miller, Edwin, L., Schan Beechler, Bhal Bhatt, and Roghi Nath. "The Relationship between the Global Strategic Planning Process and the Human Resource Management Function." *Human Resource Planning* 9, no. 1 (1986), pp. 9–23.

Mintzberg, H. "The Strategy Concept I and II." *California Management Review* 30, no. 1 (1987), pp. 11–32.

Ohmae, Kenichi. *The Mind of the Strategist*. New York: Penguin Books, 1983.

Peters, Thomas J., and Robert H. Waterman. *In Search of Excellence: Lessons from America's Best-Run Companies*. New York: Harper and Row, 1982.

Pfeffer, Jeffery. *Competitive Advantage through People: Unleashing the Power of the Work Force*. Boston: Harvard Business School Press, 1996.

Pfeffer, Jeffery. *The Human Equation: Building Profits by Putting People First*. Boston: Harvard Business School Press, 1998.

Porter, Michael E. *Competitive Strategy: Techniques for Analyzing Industries and Competitors*. New York: The Free Press, 1980.

Prahalad, C. K., and G. Hamel. "The Core Competence of the Corporation." *Harvard Business Review*, May–June 1990, pp. 79–91.

Quinn, James Brian, Henry Mintzberg, and Robert M. James. *The Strategy Process*. Englewood Cliffs, NJ: Prentice-Hall, 1988.

Schmid, Hillel. "Managing the Environment: Strategies for Executives in Human Services Organizations." *Human Systems Management* 6 (1986), pp. 307–315.

Stahl, M. J. *Strategic Executive Decision*. New York: Quorum, 1989.

Stahl, Michael J., and David W. Grigsby. *Strategic Management: Total Quality & Global Competition*. Cambridge: Blackwell, 1997.

Thompson, Arthur A., Jr., and A. J. Strickland III. *Strategic Management: Concepts and Cases*. 7th ed. Plano, TX: Business Publications, Inc., 1997.

Ulrich, David. *Human Resource Champions: The Next Agenda for Adding Value and Delivering Results*. Boston: Harvard Business School Press, 1996.

Walker, James W., and Gregory Moorehead. "CEOs: What They Want from HRM." *Personnel Administration*, December 1987, pp. 50–59.

Woodruff, David. "Audi Finally Gets Some Traction." *Business Week*, October 15, 1990, pp. 78–79.

Notes

1. Andrew Osterland, "Why General Motors Will Finally Get Serious about Downsizing," *Financial World*, December 16, 1996, p. 39.
2. Ibid., p. 39.

[3]"General Motors Finds Its Best Salesman Yet," *Economist*, December 12, 1992, pp. 79–80.

[4]"Union Dues," *Financial World*, December 16, 1996, p. 41.

[5]Kathleen Kerwin, "Can Jack Smith Fix GM?" *Business Week*, November 1, 1993, pp. 126–131.

[6]"Union Dues," *Financial World*, December 16, 1996, p. 41.

[7]Alex Taylor III, "GM: Some Gain, Much Pain," *Fortune*, May 29, 1995, p. 80.

[8]General Motors Corporation, *2000 Annual Report*.

[9]"Saturn Workers to Get $10,000 Bonus; Others at GM Get $300; at Ford $1,800; at Chrysler $7,900," *The Buffalo News*, January 30, 1997, City Edition, p. 8B.

[10]Mitchell Fleischer, "Going in the Right Direction: Strategy of Automobile Companies," *ASAP: Automotive Production* 108, no. 9, September 1996, p. 14.

[11]Raymond Serafin, "The Saturn Story," *Advertising Age*, November 16, 1992, pp. 1, 13, 16.

[12]Michael Darling, "GM's Saturn: Colossal Blunder?" *Journal of Commerce*, October 6, 1995, p. 8A.

[13]"Saturn Shares Profits: 9,000 Workers Get $10,000 Each," *Sacramento Bee*, January 31, 1997, p. D2.

[14]Neal Templin, "GM Overtakes Ford as No. 1 in Quality Among Domestic Car Firms, Study Says," *The Wall Street Journal*, May 25, 1995, p. A4.

[15]See Lionel Giles, ed. and trans., *Sun Tzu on the Art of War* (London: Luzae, 1910).

[16]Alfred O. Chandler, Jr., *Strategy and Structure* (Cambridge, MA: MIT Press, 1962).

[17]Peter Drucker, *The Practice of Management* (New York: Harper & Row, 1955).

[18]Michael Porter, *Competitive Strategy* (New York: The Free Press, 1980); and Michael Porter, *Competitive Advantage* (New York: The Free Press, 1985).

[19]This section is based on the following sources: W. F. Cascio, *Managing Human Resources* (New York: McGraw Hill, 1992); M. R. Carrell, F. E. Kuzmits, and N. F. Elbert, *Personnel/Human Resource Management* (New York: Macmillan, 1992); W. B. Werther and K. Davis, *Human Resources and Personnel Management* (New York: McGraw-Hill, 1989); and A. W. Sherman and G. W. Bohlander, *Managing Human Resources* (Cincinnati: South-Western, 1992).

[20]Jeffery Pfeffer, *The Human Equation*, (Boston: Harvard Business School Press, 1998), p. 1.

[21]Ibid., p. 10.

[22]American Society for Training and Development, *Models for Excellence* (Alexandria, VA: ASTD, 1989).

[23]Tom Kelley, 1989 Chairman of the American Society of Personnel Administrators' Board of Directors (now the Society of Human Resource Management) in an interview by John T. Adams III, "Strategic Partnerships in HRM," *Personnel Administrator*, January 1989, pp. 76–82.

[24]Leonard A. Schlesinger, "The Normative Underpinnings of Human Resource Strategy," *Human Resource Management* 22, Spring/Summer 1983, pp. 83–96.

[25]Robert Berra, "What It Takes to Succeed at the Top," *HRMagazine*, October 1991, pp. 34–37.

[26]Peter Rosik, "Building a Customer-Oriented Department," *HRMagazine*, October 1991, pp. 64–66.

[27]Randall S. Schuler, "Repositioning the Human Resource Function: Transformation or Demise?" *The Executive* 4, no. 3, August 1990, pp. 49–60.

[28]Porter, *Competitive Advantage*. This concept is very similar to the concept of differential advantage used in marketing or economic or comparative advantage used in economics.

[29]Michael D. Cohen, James C. March, and Johan P. Olsen, "A Garbage Can Model of Organizational Choice," *Administrative Science Quarterly* 17, no. 1, March 1972, pp. 1–25.

[30]K. Michele Actor and Gerald R. Ferris, "Politics at Work: Sharpening the Focus of Political Behavior in Organizations," *Business Horizons*, July-August 1993, pp. 70–74.

[31]James Brian Quinn, *Strategies for Change: Logical Incrementalism* (Homewood, IL: Richard D. Irwin, 1980).

[32]Stephen Kindel, "What Backlash?" *Financial World*, September 28, 1993, p. 46.

[33]"Human Resources Management Ideas and Trends," *CCH*, no. 433, June 3, 1998, p. 84.

[34]**www.right.com/investor**, accessed October 10, 2000.

2

Formulating a Corporate and Human Resource Strategy

Chapter Objectives

As a result of studying this chapter, you should be able to

1. Describe the strategy formulation process.

2. List and define at least ten generic strategies.

3. Differentiate between business level and corporate strategies.

4. Explain the role of the human resources department in strategy formulation.

5. Understand the importance of functional strategies, especially human resource strategy.

6. Understand how human resource strategy contributes to overall strategy success.

7. Understand the importance of the human resource audit.

8. Explain the contingency approach or situational approach to strategy formulation.

When a company makes decisions about such issues as the market in which it will compete, how it can ensure continued growth over the next several years, and ways in which it can better utilize its human resources, it is formulating corporate strategy. To formulate strategies, managers try to find a way for their organizations to best fit into the environment in which they function. To do this, they must understand the current environment and predict any changes that may occur in that environment, all the while being sure that they understand their customers' needs and desires. Obviously, formulating corporate strategy is a difficult and time-consuming process. This chapter explains how managers go about this process. It also considers the various human resource strategies and how this important functional strategy contributes to a company's overall success.

CASE

Southwest Airlines Flying High with Kelleher[1]

For a little while, it looked as if the major players in the U.S. airline industry had finally struck a crippling blow to the one competitor that had made them all "green with envy." In one announcement after another in the spring and summer of 1994, several travel agencies unveiled their plans to stop using the services of Southwest Airlines. These moves represented a threat to Southwest, with the worst possibility being that many customers of travel agencies nationwide would have limited access to its flights. The reason for the action cited by most of the travel agencies was the fact that Southwest refused to pay their pricey booking fees. Officials at Southwest defended their refusal to pay for several reasons. First, paying such premiums would affect Southwest's overall strategy of offering value prices and quality service. Southwest also refused to pay because its competition owned most of the travel agencies. Southwest was determined not to back down, vowing to beat the competition by doing what no one else seemed to be doing: providing efficient and pleasing service at a very reasonable price. This new threat changed the game a bit, but it certainly did not change Southwest's underlying strategy of efficiency, good service, and low price that had proved very successful.

In response to this action by travel agencies, Southwest chairman Herb Kelleher took an action that exemplifies company strategy. The savvy, bright, and witty head of the nation's highest-rated and most admired airline published a personal letter to customers in numerous publications, including *The Wall Street Journal*. The letter basically stated that Southwest had never bowed to the pressure of competition and that this latest ploy by the competition would be treated no differently. Southwest would work hard, as always, to make things "right" for the customer. Kelleher reported to customers that Southwest was working to make ticket purchase as easy as possible. He noted that negotiations were continuing with the major travel agencies, but in the meantime Southwest was developing a number of ways that customers could purchase tickets, such as by calling a toll-free number. As a result, Southwest was credited for pioneering the idea of "ticketless travel."[2] He was enthusiastic and reassuring. Considering the prevailing reputation of the company and of Kelleher, it appeared that Southwest would not be hampered by this competitive move.

Since then, Southwest has been a pioneer in e-commerce, becoming the first major airline to have its own Web site and offer Internet booking as another way customers can plan their trips on Southwest. By January 2000, more than 25 percent of its monthly passenger revenues came through the Internet site, putting the airline on track to exceed $1 billion in e-commerce revenues for the year. Based on published accounts, in terms of revenues, **www.southwest.com** ranks as one of the largest e-commerce sites and is considered the largest among airlines. Deutsche Banc recently reported that of the ten major U.S. airlines, 20 percent of Southwest's total bookings were made online; Alaska Air came next with 14 percent; and America West was third with 12 percent.[3]

Innovation and Wit in a Serious Business

Why was Kelleher so confident that customers would take his letter seriously? To put it simply, customers seem to enjoy dealing with Southwest. They have described traveling with Southwest as a refreshing adventure, mainly because of its employees and their commitment to the customer and to the company. Southwest is a nontraditional airline. It outperforms the competition consistently by doing a number of things considered radical and innovative when first introduced but that the industry quickly imitates.

Southwest is a domestic airline specializing in linking large- and medium-sized cities throughout the Southwest, South, and Midwest. Originally specializing in short-haul routes (average flight of less than 375 miles), the airline added a few long-haul routes (average flight of greater than 700 miles) in June 1997, accounting for ten percent of total capacity.[4] Southwest offers services that are very good but not fancy. For instance, because Southwest offers mainly short-haul flights, it does not serve an in-flight meal but provides "peanuts-only service," resulting in savings for the customer. It also does not provide seat assignments, which cuts costs. Its low fares attract many customers, like business people who choose to fly rather than drive. Its fares are shockingly low (averaging less than $100 one way), resulting in flights that are almost always full.

With service to 56 airports in 2000, Southwest keeps fares low by its very efficient operations.[5] Its fleet of 295 planes arrive at their destinations just minutes before boarding and are back in the air very quickly—15 to 20 minutes versus the industry average of 60 minutes. Southwest gets high mileage out of each plane every day. Each plane makes ten flights per day, more than twice the industry average. Southwest saves more money than other airlines by making more flights with fewer planes and fewer employees. Southwest planes, all 737s (another cost-cutting ploy) with an average age of just 8.4 years, fly to less-crowded "second airports" such as Love Field in Dallas and Midway Airport in Chicago. Luggage is routed correctly and is waiting for customers at the baggage claim on arrival. In 1999, Southwest was the fifth largest airline in the United States in terms of passengers carried (52 million).[6]

People Make the Difference

An especially notable difference between Southwest and other airlines relates to human resources. Most analysts say that the people at Southwest make the difference. A personality test ranks potential employees, and only 4 percent of the 90,000 people a year who apply for jobs are accepted. Once hired, employees go through rigorous people-skills courses at the University for People, Southwest's training center in Dallas.[7]

Its flight attendants and pilots are very pleasant, even witty. Kelleher is an imaginative, engaging, and witty person. He is a free spirit who enjoys talking to employees about how to solve company problems. One airline analyst remarked that "Herb," as he is known by even the lowest-level employees, is the kind of manager who will stay out late with a mechanic in a bar to find out what the company's problems are. He jokes with colleagues and employees. He encourages a light attitude about work and about helping customers in every way possible. Employees identify closely with him and work extra hard to keep Southwest ahead of the competition in pleasing customers. Obviously, labor relations are excellent because of Herb's hands-on approach.

Gary Kelly, VP and CFO, attributes the company's success to its strong "we care about you" culture that bolsters profit sharing and job security. Its employees own collectively about 13 percent of the company. According to top management, the company "hires for attitude and trains for skills." "Family" is an often-used word at Southwest. Southwest drives this feeling home with its culture committee. Headed by the highest-ranking woman in the airline industry, Executive Vice-President, Customers and Corporate Secretary Colleen Barrett, the committee has more than 100 members from all job levels at Southwest. Employees are impressed by the personal birthday greetings from "Herb and Colleen" and the company's efforts to celebrate all major life events. Christmas parties in July, paper airplane contests, chili cook-offs, and other special events are used to motivate employees and communicate Southwest values. Efforts to promote the Southwest culture have resulted in loyal staff, which is self-perpetuating in that the reputation outside the company helps attract new employees who want to be a part of the Southwest team. The question is, "Can Southwest grow at its current pace without hurting its special culture?" With 29,000 employees in 2000, Southwest's Gary Kelly believes that it is the culture that will enable growth and bring fresh faces and enthusiasm.[8]

A Strategic Human Resource Matter

The strategy of offering highly efficient and superb service would be difficult to pull off without an excellent human resource strategy. Kelleher attracts witty, professional individuals and demands a great deal of them. Employees say that working for Herb is great fun. Flight attendants, for example, go out of their way to amuse and entertain passengers by adding humor to such otherwise mundane activities as the safety lecture and the beverage service. One flight attendant asked passengers to "pass the plastic cups to the center aisle so they could be washed out and used for the next flight." Another flight attendant told passengers, "Those of you who wish to smoke are invited out to our lounge on the wing, where the feature film will be *Gone with the Wind*." Southwest is committed to winning passengers away from its competitors. Attendants invite customers on arrival at a destination, which almost always occurs on time, to "choose Southwest next time." Most passengers do.

The bond between employees and the company is close. Employees know that the company's success depends on their performance. Everyone focuses on efficiency and is committed to improvement. In return for this commitment, the employee gets good pay and a great job. One analyst reports that at most airlines, managers say that people are the most important resource, but only at Southwest is that fact proven day after day. Employees are the key to Southwest's superior efficiency and customer satisfaction. Southwest is a unique company because of an almost unbelievable employee commitment to success. What's interesting is that employees are more than happy to perform so well for the company.

Southwest recognizes the importance of employees and is spending time and money to ensure quality recruitment, training, compensation, motivation, and labor relations. The dividends are paying off. Southwest has lower turnover, higher employee satisfaction and commitment, and a higher ratio of passengers per employee, and it operates more aircraft per employee than any other airline. In 2000 the airline celebrated 27 consecutive years of profitability, a U.S. record. Its safety record has prompted placement on the "most safe" U.S. airline list.[9]

As Kelleher put it in his published letter, "Southwest has survived many challenges during its history."[1] Under Kelleher's leadership, Southwest will likely suffer little from this threat by travel agencies. Southwest has always succeeded, and, with such a well-run company, one must believe that many of Southwest's thousands of customers would forgo the convenience related to making reservations in order to get such a great value.

This case describes a company that has been very successful by providing a high-quality, valuable service to customers. It is evident, however, that a company cannot just go out and provide such services without the key resources and the means to manage them. This case shows that a company's human resource strategy and practices contribute largely to its overall success. Efficiency, professionalism, humor, and quality service characterize most Southwest employees, and company leaders attribute success to the overall pride they exhibit. Southwest's human resource strategy reflects the efforts of managers to maintain this "mix." Southwest's continued success certainly depends on it.

For more information on Southwest Airlines, visit its Web site at **www.southwest.com**.

Strategic Choices

When formulating a corporate strategy, managers must consider several strategic choices. To make the appropriate choice, the following should be addressed:

1. Choosing the strategy that the company should adopt to maintain or improve its position in the marketplace.
2. Ensuring continued sales growth and maintenance of its workforce to avoid retrenchment and layoff.
3. Adapting to its ever-changing environment.
4. Collecting the information it needs to understand and influence its environment.
5. Determining whether to change operating environments. If so, to which one? Why?

As shown in Exhibit 2.1, there are three primary factors that influence strategy formulation: competitor actions, environmental opportunities and threats, and an organization's internal strengths and weaknesses. Strategies are adopted to beat the competition. Competitive actions are anticipated and appropriate strategies adopted. The environment presents threats and opportunities. Strategies are adopted that allow an organization to take advantage of windows of opportunity and to protect itself from outside threats. This is discussed further in the next chapter. Finally, a firm's internal strengths and weaknesses help to drive strategy because a firm wants to take advantage of its strengths and also overcome or correct its weaknesses.

EXHIBIT 2.1   KEY FACTORS IN STRATEGY FORMULATION

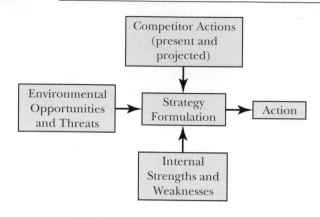

Future Orientation

Strategy formulation is an attempt to anchor the organization to some position in the future. This future orientation is a key concept to strategy formulation. Decisions are made today to formulate strategy that will place the organization at a particular position at a particular point in the future. Every organization attempts to create a desirable future for itself.

For example, in the Southwest Airlines case, Kelleher has a very clear vision of the future of Southwest Airlines. He articulates and shares this vision with employees, building and maintaining a culture that supports employees and attempts to make work fun.

Strategy is goal oriented, and goals exist for the future. In strategy formulation, organizations learn from the past—they learn from their mistakes—but they cannot change the past. "We should have done this" or "We should have done that" has relevance only so far as it specifies what the company should do now.

Philosophical and Ethical Dimensions

Strategy is heavily laden with the personal philosophies and codes of ethics of key decision makers in an organization. Of course, this is clearly seen in family-run organizations, even large ones such as Ford Motor Company in the 1920s. Henry Ford *was* Ford Motor, and his philosophy and ethical values dominated the company.

Yet, even in large organizations in which the power is diffused, the philosophy and ethical values of decision makers shape the strategy. For years, General Motors (GM) has been known as a company that widely distributes decision authority for strategy formulation among members of its executive committee. The personal values and ethics of individuals on this committee come into play in decisions involving product safety, design, fuel economy, dealer relations, customer warranties, labor costs, and so on. For example, in the initial discussion about the installation of passive restraint systems in autos (air bags), some believed that such installation was sound from a moral standpoint, even though the official position of GM was not to install them on all makes and models automatically. This position contrasted with that of Chrysler, which ran a personal pledge from Lee Iacocca in *The Wall Street Journal* advertisements to install such systems in every car and truck Chrysler makes.

EXHIBIT 2.2 EXAMPLE STAKEHOLDER GROUPS OF AN ORGANIZATION

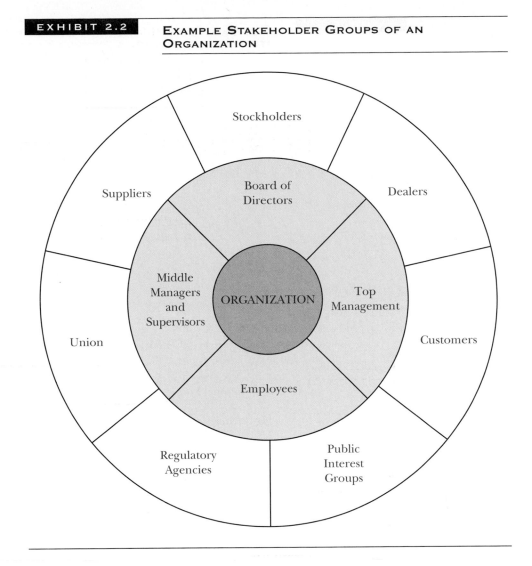

Such a competitive action may have caused GM to change its position on the issue. It certainly won Chrysler wide approval and boosted sales.

Stakeholder Analysis

stakeholders
Constituent groups that have a stake in the organization's operations.

Another major influence on the formulation of strategy comes from **stakeholders**. Stakeholders are groups of people who have a major interest in or claim on the operations or output of the organization.[10] They are also referred to as **constituent groups**. Although the specific stakeholder groups for a particular organization are unique to that organization, Exhibit 2.2 shows examples of stakeholder groups in an organization, and Exhibit 2.3 shows some of the stakeholder groups for a human resource unit.

Notice that some of an organization's stakeholders are actual members of the organization: employees, managers, and boards of directors (except for outside board members unless they are also stockholders). However, notice the range of outside groups—unions, suppliers, dealers, and government regulatory agencies—that can

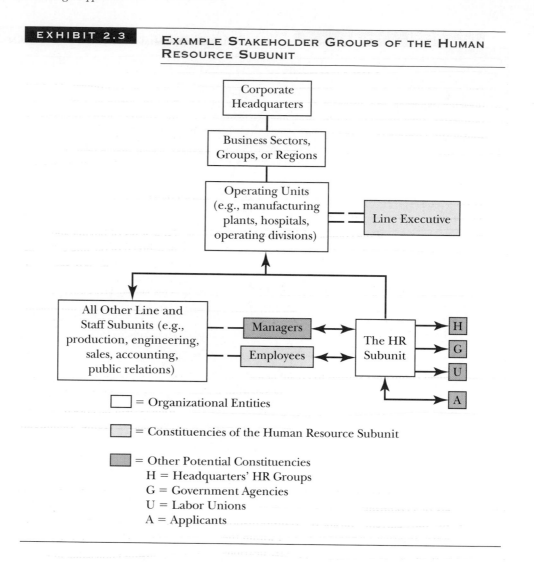

EXHIBIT 2.3 EXAMPLE STAKEHOLDER GROUPS OF THE HUMAN RESOURCE SUBUNIT

☐ = Organizational Entities

▨ = Constituencies of the Human Resource Subunit

▨ = Other Potential Constituencies
H = Headquarters' HR Groups
G = Government Agencies
U = Labor Unions
A = Applicants

affect the formulation of an organization's strategy. Each of these groups lays claims to part of the organization's output. Employees want more wages and job security, stockholders want more dividends and higher stock prices, and customers want quality products and services at the lowest possible price.

Obviously, an organization cannot possibly satisfy all of these groups completely. Therefore it bargains, negotiates, and compromises. No group receives maximum returns on its claims from the organization; rather the organization tries at least minimally to satisfy each group.

Of course, the claims of some groups sometimes become stronger than others. The Teamsters Union pushes strongly for wage increases. Ford's dealers argue for better financing terms. A public interest group from a small Midwestern community storms a corporation's headquarters to protest the local plant's relocation to Mexico. A corporate raider tries to buy enough stock to take control of a company. In each of these situations, the organization must decide what its basic position will be and how this position will affect the organization now and in the future.

HR CHALLENGES

The E-Business Revolution and Cybertrends

While executives of major corporations no longer question whether the Internet will impact their businesses, they may not realize how much it will transform customers, careers, and relationships. Coming is a world linked by increasingly fast, cheap communication in which speed is key, and virtually every business and individual is affected. According to Chuck Martin, author of *Net Future: The Seven Cybertrends That Will Drive Your Business, Create New Wealth, and Define Your Future*, there are five waves of evolution of the commercial Internet:

1. At the Brochureware stage, companies simply transferred what they were doing in their traditional business onto the Internet. A typical example involved putting annual reports and corporate brochures on a company Web site exactly as they appeared in print.
2. The New Content arena took off in 1995, when companies started to create new products and services for the Internet environment. For example, companies began to solicit e-mail responses to various offers.
3. During the third wave, Internet technology infiltrated the organization company wide, creating the intranet. By 1998, many companies started to see the power of the Internet's open technology in connecting all the workers of a company.
4. In the current Business Transformation wave, Internet technology is used within the organization to connect suppliers, distributors, customers, and business partners. These closer connections will enable more streamlined operations both inside and outside of the company.
5. The true e-business wave involves tapping the entire value chain—from product conception and creation, all the way through manufacturing and production, distribution, and ultimately consumption—so that an organization is armed with real-time knowledge from customers. This will allow companies to create and modify products "on the fly" to suit those customers' needs.

Over the course of this five-wave evolutionary process, seven major trends have emerged. These seven "cybertrends"—all driven by technology—will come into increasingly sharp focus as businesses move to the fifth wave.

1. The Cybereconomy Goes Main Street—New ways of buying and selling will create a new breed of on-line consumers who will expect faster delivery, easier transactions, and more factual information.
2. The Wired Workforce Takes Over—The intranet will put more information in employees' hands and create virtual work communities, altering the dynamics of the workplace for both individuals and companies.
3. The Open-Book Corporation Emerges—Boundaries between the corporation and the outside world, including suppliers and customers, will be erased.
4. Products Become Commodities—New interactive dynamics will dramatically change how value is established for products.
5. The Customer Becomes Data—New technologies for analyzing and predicting customer behavior in real time will require companies to organize differently.
6. Experience Communities Arise—People will harness instant global communications, aggregating knowledge in real time.
7. Learning Moves to Real Time, All-the-Time—The new means of networking will create a new generation of empowered and independent learners and require both self-motivation and information sharing to succeed.

SOURCE: Excerpt from Chuck Martin, *Net Future: The Seven Cybertrends That Will Drive Your Business, Create New Wealth, and Define Your Future* (New York, McGraw-Hill, 1999).

Societal Forces

A powerful influence on policy formulation comes from the *societal forces* at work in the environment in which the organization exists. Social forces are the broad trends in the economy, politics, and culture of a society. These ebb and flow with time. These general forces can be sociocultural, political and legal, economic, or technological in nature. For example, in the political area, the liberalism of the Kennedy and Johnson administrations gave way to the conservatism of the Reagan and Bush administrations as the political mood of the country shifted.

Sometimes these shifts are dramatic, as occurred with both the civil rights movement in the United States and the cultural revolution in the People's Republic of China in the 1960s and the Khomeini revolution in Iran in the late 1970s. Other times, the social forces are less dramatic but just as powerful, such as the increasing participation of women in career-oriented jobs that began in the 1960s in the United States. Today, many business and political discussions and decisions are dominated by the fact that the population of the United States, especially in Sunbelt states such as Florida, is aging rapidly. Many new companies and innovative services will capitalize on this change in U.S. society.

The point is that underlying societal forces heavily affect strategy formulation in individual organizations. Of course, this occurs in the strategy formulation process of many organizations. For example, when performing an environmental scan, strategists attempt both to discern and forecast these trends and to position their organization to capitalize on them. This is why John Naisbitt's books *Megatrends* and *Megatrends 2000* were such top sellers for so long during the 1980s and 1990s. Now, with the further development of technology and the Internet, even "cybertrends" have been identified. Many decision makers are hungry for information that expands on and predicts trends.[11] Of course, not everyone agrees with these trends, and some have been severely criticized.[12]

Two Key Strategies for Human Resource Management

Two gross generic categories of strategy seem to have had the greatest impact on human resource management in recent years. Following a review of the literature, Cynthia Fisher classified strategies into two categories:[13]

1. Growth–prospector–high-tech entrepreneurial strategies.
2. Mature–defender–cost-efficiency strategies.

Firms in the growth mode require creative, innovative, and risk-taking behavior from employees. Mature-defender firms need just the opposite kind of behavior—repetitive, predictable, and carefully specified.

Human resource management strategies under each mode are substantially different in terms of function. Human resource management units in growth firms typically recruit at all levels from the external labor market in order to obtain enough employees at all skill levels to meet growth needs. They tend to assess people based on the results they achieve rather than the process they employ or their personal traits. They also tend to look to the long term for success and usually do not pursue innovative efforts that fail. Performance incentives serve as the basis for compensation; when bonuses, profit sharing, and stock options are common, base salaries are modest.[14]

Mature–defender–cost-efficiency competitors follow opposite personnel actions.[15] They tend to recruit primarily at the entry level and promote from within. They emphasize doing things the right way in assessing performance and focus on quantifiable short-term results. Compensation is based on hierarchical wage structures determined by job evaluation. Length of service, loyalty, and other traits are rewarded rather than performance. Financial incentives may be present but tend to be available only to a few select employee groups. Oftentimes, retrenchment and restructuring strategies resulting in layoffs and reductions in force (RIF) occur.

Examples of the Two Key Strategies for HRM

Growth–Prospector–High-tech Entrepreneurial Strategy

Amazon.com was born in a Chevy car, traveling west on Interstate 90. It was 1994 and Jeff Bezos was working on Wall Street, watching Web usage grow by 2300 percent each year. He knew that the Internet would soon be everywhere, so he jumped in his car, drove to Seattle, and launched Earth's Biggest Bookstore. Its first headquarters were in Jeff's garage; its first customers were his friends; and books were the first, best product to sell on the Internet. The main idea was to create a "discovery machine"—a place where people could find and buy any book they wanted and get great customer service, too.

Amazon.com opened its virtual doors in July 1995 with a mission to use the Internet to transform book buying into the fastest, easiest, and most enjoyable shopping experience possible. Today, Amazon.com is the place to find and discover practically anything you want to buy online. The company boasts that 20 million people in more than 160 countries have made it the leading online shopping site. Now Amazon.com offers an extensive array of product categories besides books, including electronics, kitchen products, music, videos, DVDs, camera and photo items, toys, software, computer and video games, tools and hardware, and lawn and patio items.

Recently, Amazon.com announced net sales for the third quarter of 2000 were $638 million, an increase of 79 percent over net sales of $356 million for the third quarter of 1999. For the first time, the Electronics store has grown to become the second-largest U.S. store, behind Books and ahead of Music. In 2001, sales are expected to reach $4 billion.

Amazon.com is working to be the "most customer-centric company on Earth." To reach that goal, it needs exceptionally talented, bright, and driven people, but there is no Amazon.com "type." There are Amazon.com employees who have three master's degrees and some who speak five languages. The company even has a professional figure skater, two race car drivers, a Rhodes scholar, a set of twins, and a husband and wife and their dog. Amazon.com is committed to ingenuity and problem solving, so its employees are considered smart, intense, and dynamic. These innovators typically wear jeans to work and have meetings in the hallway. For working hard with long hours, all employees have stock options that give them an equity stake in the company.

SOURCE: www.amazon.com.

Mature–Defender–Cost-Efficiency Strategy

More often than not, firms that have adopted this strategy have been around for some time. A good example is DaimlerChrysler. The company's struggling Chrysler group recently unveiled a plan to cut material costs by $6 billion, or 15 percent, during 2001-2003. The move, described as the first element of a comprehensive restructuring plan aimed at lowering overall spending, came nearly three weeks after the German automaker installed new management at Chrysler. The U.S. division spends about $40 billion annually with about 900 direct suppliers.

The plan calls for suppliers to cut the prices they charge for materials and all general services by five percent, or $2 billion, effective January 1, 2001. Those cost cuts cover the periods from 2001 to 2003. The second phase of the initiative calls for Chrysler engineers and procurement managers, along with suppliers, to identify an additional 10 percent cost improvement over the two-year period, saving another $4 billion.

Chrysler officials are trying to cut costs to get the once-profitable unit back on track. Chrysler has gone from being the most profitable carmaker to one of the worst, losing more than $1 billion in the second half of 2000.

About 78 percent of Chrysler's total costs come from material costs, said Tom Sidlik, Chrysler's worldwide purchasing chief. "To get quick cost reductions, materials is the way to go," he said. "This is a major cornerstone of the turnaround," said Wolfgang Bernhard, Chrysler's new chief operating officer. "We need results fast. We cannot wait forever."

SOURCE: **www.cnnfn.cnn.com/2000.**

Cost-cutting Competitive Strategy

As we previously stated, the mature–defender–cost-efficiency strategy was common during the 1980s when many organizations attempted to become more competitive by cutting costs. This strategy had a significant effect on human resources in individual organizations that adopted it in at least three major ways: their wages or rate of increase slowed significantly; a significant number of employees were cut or their rate of promotion slowed, especially for higher-paid and staff employees; and production was shifted to lower-wage labor markets, such as the southern United States or developing countries. Sometimes these actions were taken at the initiative of the company; sometimes they occurred as a result of a takeover or merger. Regardless, when an organization adopts a competitive strategy that emphasizes cost cutting, the decision has a profound impact on human resource strategies in all phases of human resource activity: hiring, placement, promotion, pay, layoff, outplacement, retraining, retirement, and so on. The effects and implications of this cost-cutting strategy on human resources are so significant that they will be explored throughout this book. The last chapter is also devoted to this topic.

The popularity of cost-cutting strategies reflects the attempt of corporations to reach a more competitive level on a global basis. Competition with imports produced by foreign manufacturers in lower-wage countries required U.S. corporations to find ways to cut costs to remain competitive. Human resource costs, of course, were not the only ones attacked. Inventory cost and availability were scrutinized as a result of the just-in-time approach to inventory. Just-in-time inventory reflects efforts to shift the carrying costs of inventories to suppliers. Relocation and new plant construction costs could be cut without jeopardizing a firm's competitiveness. This concern with cost cutting will likely pervade human resource and other strategies throughout this decade as global competition becomes even more intense. This will likely occur even as many firms grow and add new employees; they will still be concerned with efficiency.

Role of Human Resources in Strategy Formulation

Up to this point, we have argued that overall corporate strategy should drive functional, including human resource, strategies. That is, a company should first decide what, as a whole, it needs to do to achieve a strategic competitive advantage and then formulate specific strategies for each functional area—marketing, finance, operations/productions, human resources—to carry it out. We have stated that in formulating overall strategy, the company should consider various aspects of each functional strategy. It needs to assess how well it is performing in each functional area.

Thus, in reality, the formulation of corporate strategy is really interactive with the formulation of functional strategy. In other words, by considering its capabilities in each functional area, the company is actually using its existing functional strategy and capabilities to help shape its future corporate strategy.

This interactive effect is an important notion, particularly with respect to human resource strategy. Lengnick-Hall and Lengnick-Hall argue in "Strategic Human Resource Management" that "reciprocal interdependence between a firm's business strategy and its human resources strategy underlies the proposed approach to the strategic management of human resources."[16] Their conceptual diagram, shown in Exhibit 2.4, depicts this interdependence. Notice that the formation of corporate competitive advantage not only influences but also is influenced by human resource

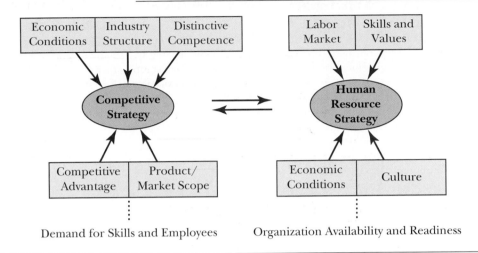

EXHIBIT 2.4   RECIPROCAL INTERDEPENDENCE OF CORPORATE STRATEGY AND HUMAN RESOURCE STRATEGY

SOURCE: Reprinted by permission from Cynthia A. Lengnick-Hall and Mark L. Lengnick-Hall, "Strategic Human Resources Management: A Review of the Literature and a Proposed Typology," *Academy of Management Review* 13, no. 3 (July 1988), p. 467.

strategy. Certainly, economic conditions, industry structure, the labor market, and other factors depicted in the exhibit must be considered in light of the interactive effect of competitive strategy and human resource strategy.

Human resource strategy is now considered to be closely allied or linked to overall corporate strategy; the two go hand-in-hand. Robert Sibson notes in his book 16 critical human resource areas that should reflect any strategic plan. He devotes an entire chapter to each area, including organizational restructuring, educational level of the workforce, and management of cultural diversity.[17] This link is seen in practice as well as in theory. *HRMagazine* reported the findings of a human resources survey indicating that human resource professionals are extremely concerned with strategic, long-term issues that reflect the concerns of top strategic managers. Among the issues dominating the agendas of human resource professionals are improving overall quality, controlling costs associated with employees, and improving overall productivity of workers.[18] At the very least, we must recognize that human resources integrally affects the overall strategy of a company, and, therefore, overall strategy must incorporate human resources considerations.

The importance of human resources to overall strategy is reflected in Super-Lube's success. From Super-Lube's very beginning, a major ingredient in forming its overall corporate strategy was a human resource strategy that stressed competent and courteous employees. This, plus a limited geographic focus, enabled Super-Lube to achieve success in the highly competitive quick-lube market.

Other examples of the link between human resources and overall strategies exist. Ford's "Quality Is Job 1" strategy would have had little chance of success had the company not explicitly considered both present and future human resource capability and strategy when formulating its quality strategy. 3M's strategy of innovation depends

Super-Lube's Sustainable Competitive Advantage

Super-Lube 10 Minute Oil Change is a Tallahassee, Florida–based corporation involved in the quick oil change business. This market offers drive-in, drive-out convenience for oil changes and lubrication. Over 100 separate firms operate in this market; Jiffy-Lube is the largest.

Quick-Lube Industry

The quick-lube industry began in the late 1970s in the upper Midwest. Its primary offering is convenience, because the customer does not have to leave the car for a long period of time for servicing. The primary services provided are oil changes and lubrications, although some companies also provide free tire fills, tune-ups, and brake checks.

The quick-lube industry has grown rapidly because of the demise of full-service gas stations and the rise of self-service brought on by the oil crisis. The social trend toward greater convenience also has been a major reason for the success of the industry. As analysts predicted, the quick-lube oil change business grew rapidly during the past decade. It is estimated that about two thirds of the quick-lube market is now handled by quick-lube type stations and one third by garages, service stations, auto dealers, and "do-it-yourselfers."

Super-Lube

The strategy of Super-Lube can be explained as follows: to be absolutely the best fast oil change facility in the market area served *and* to gain a position of clear market dominance therein. Strategic priorities follow:

1. Complete customer satisfaction through friendly, competent, and courteous service.
2. Highest consistent standards of performance.
3. High level of employee job satisfaction and opportunity for advancement.
4. Comparatively high return to stockholders.

Since its founding in 1983, the company has emphasized fast, competent, courteous service as its key trademark. It prides itself on clean, attractive stations that will make both male and female customers feel comfortable.

Human resources have always played a key role in overall corporate strategy. Bright, helpful, courteous people are hired at substantially above minimum wage. Employees are thoroughly trained in the Super-Lube way from both technical and customer relations standpoints. Within six months, employees are placed on a merit bonus system that supplements their pay.

Currently, there are 16 locations in the Tallahassee, Florida, area, including locations in Quincy, Crawfordville, and Perry. All stations and land are company owned; none are franchised. Total sales for 2000 are estimated at $7 million with net operating revenue at about $0.5 million.

Company founder and president John Lewis attributes the bulk of the company's success to the outstanding employees it has been able to attract and hold. The company has a very good reputation in the entire industry with respect to employee competence and courtesy.

Super-Lube illustrates how a firm was able to use its human resources to help it achieve a strategic competitive advantage in the marketplace. The overall corporate strategy of dominance in a limited market area was achieved by being the first in this market and then using well-trained, polite employees to obtain and keep customer loyalty.

SOURCES: Adapted from Special Stockholders Meeting Report, Super-Lube 10 Minute Oil Change (Tallahassee, FL, 1994-1996), p. 1; Gerald Ensly, "Super-Lube Posted Gross Sales of $18 Million in 1994 from its 600,000 Customers," *Tallahassee Democrat*, August 1995; and **www.superlube.com**.

heavily on programs for innovation instituted with employees. Without innovative employees, the program would not work. The same is true of Florida Power and Light's (FP&L's) Quality Improvement Program. The heart of this program rests with employee Quality Improvement Groups. FP&L spent much money and effort in forming, guiding, and training these groups during the 1980s and 1990s.

A New Role for Human Resources

We see that human resources plays an expanded role under the strategic human resource approach. No longer is human resource strategy simply personnel management strategy with operative employees driven by overall corporate strategy. In short, no longer is personnel management simply left out of the strategic competitive arena. As Michael Porter argues in *Competitive Advantage*, human resource management can help a firm achieve a competitive advantage.[19] By involving human resource considerations when overall strategy is formulated, human resources can help achieve a strategic advantage. This is true for Super-Lube, as well as other firms that have fully integrated human resource considerations in strategy formulation.

In fact, managers are increasingly recognizing human resource management as one of the key considerations for ensuring overall success of the company's strategy. For example, many new training programs for human resource managers are taking a strategic perspective. One sales brochure informed managers that they must somehow use the human resource function as the company's source of competitive advantage. The same program talks of making sure that human resources provides the key competencies necessary for the company's chosen strategy. David Calfee, a management consultant, notes that the critical skills, capabilities, and efforts required of human resources should be reflected in a company's mission statement, the primary statement of its strategic goals. He notes that all employees should "live" the mission statement as they perform even their most mundane duties.[20] Human resource management is generally seen as a way to connect a company's upper-level strategic decisions to the lower-level, day-to-day tasks of all employees. An article in *The Wall Street Journal* reports a computer program that allows managers to set overall company goals. The program then helps each manager formulate goals for his or her department and each employee in an effort to help the company achieve its overall strategy. The program also helps managers to evaluate each employee's performance in meeting the set goal.[21]

One of the most dramatic documentations of the impact of human resources on overall strategy and success was provided by former U.S. Department of Energy Secretary Hazel O'Leary in an address to several hundred HR professionals.[22] O'Leary told the professionals that, for the first time, the large government agency she heads was looking at how jobs were being done and how job performance led to agency success. She reported that her agency was ensuring that all jobs are woven together to meet the goals of the agency. She noted that past efforts of energy secretaries were concerned with allocating and spending budgeted funds rather than the current approach of determining how each job in the agency and the person in that position contribute to the agency's quality. O'Leary concluded that incorporating human resource elements (specifically diversity, quality, and leadership) can lead to the overall success of an organization.

Is there any proof that human resource management and strategy can help a company achieve its overall strategy? An award-winning study by Mark Huselid discovered that a well-formulated human resource strategy and extensive management of human resources led to improved company performance in a number of ways. First, Huselid learned that extensive human resource management improves the quality and performance of employees. Improved quality and performance increase overall company success and achievement of company strategies. Huselid's most important findings were that proper human resource planning and management lead to improved employee performance and improved company performance.[23]

Unfortunately, however, in the 1980s and early 1990s, many companies that focused on human resource strategy issues when forming corporate strategy looked at the issue simply from a cost-cutting perspective. We saw this strategy manifested in the policies of Ford, GM, and Kodak—in short, almost all major older U.S. firms have tried to reduce labor costs to become more competitive.

Because of this cost-cutting strategy, many employees have lost jobs, taken early retirement, or suffered wage cuts. While such actions are often necessary, organizations do not always provide needed transition assistance. Employee assistance, such as severance pay, outplacement (that is, helping a person find a new job), and retraining, could cushion the effect of cost-cutting strategies on labor.

Line versus Staff Conflict

staff-line conflict
Disagreements and jealousy between operating managers/units and staff/support managers and units.

Human resource managers have long suffered from the **staff-line conflict** that tends to arise in many organizations. We review six aspects of this issue and see how this conflict affects the strategic role for human resources.

First, it is important to remember that all managers are human resource managers. That is, all managers have subordinates on whom they rely to carry out work.

Second, the functions of hiring, training, placing, paying, and otherwise dealing with the workforce must be performed by somebody in the organization. If a human resource unit does not exist, then line managers must perform all of these actions themselves. For example, when Southwest Airlines was first formed, line managers made all personnel decisions. As the company grew, a human resource department was added and personnel decisions became its responsibility.

Third, human resource units are set up as specialized departments to help line managers in their role as human resource managers. In other words, human resource units help line managers carry out the human resource functions of hiring, paying, and so on. As Southwest Airlines grew, many of these personnel functions were transferred from line managers to the human resource staff.

Fourth, in some organizations, human resource units are given wide latitude to do some of the hiring, benefit determination, training, and so on. In these organizations, the human resource unit may be criticized for "taking on too much" or "taking too much authority away from line managers."

Fifth, in many organizations, human resource units serve as police units. They enforce the myriad of laws in human resources that a company must abide by: wage and hour, social security, discrimination, benefits, and safety and health policies, for example. These units also are often given the job of enforcing company human resource policy. This results in the human resource unit telling line managers what they can and cannot do according to the law or corporate policy. At Southwest, Kelleher's introduction of a policy manual involved more than just writing the policy; it also required a means to enforce it. This responsibility falls on both the line and staff managers. This division of responsibility can sometimes cause line-staff conflict because goals and objectives can differ among departments.

Finally, because human resource units do not have primary authority to produce or market a product or service but line managers do, line managers often view human resource people as "out of touch" with the real world. Line managers must meet production, sales quotas, and deadlines. They see themselves "on the firing line," or "in the trenches." To them, human resources has none of these deadlines and pressures. Instead, they often see human resource specialists as people who throw roadblocks or hindrances in their way or as people who have the luxury of sitting back in their offices dreaming up new rules and regulations to thwart efficient operations.

This raises the issue of the *credibility* of the human resource unit. Unfortunately, in some organizations, employees in human resource units are often viewed as people

---

EXHIBIT 2.5   SOME WAYS TO ENHANCE THE HUMAN
RESOURCE UNIT'S CREDIBILITY AND
REDUCE STAFF-LINE CONFLICT

---

1. Hire only competent, well-trained, and experienced people for the human resource unit.
2. Clearly spell out human resource responsibilities in relation to line-management responsibilities.
3. Have human resource staff members view their roles as supportive to line-staff members.
4. Have human resource and staff-line members work together in forming personnel policies.
5. Ensure that human resource staff members have firsthand contact and experience with line operations.
6. Ensure that managers remember the important role that human resource plays in reducing burdensome tasks.

---

who could not cut it in a line position. While this problem is not as serious as it once was because the human resource function has become more professionalized, it can be a problem in some organizations and must be addressed.

All of these factors cause staff-line conflict and credibility issues. This conflict and credibility gap can be so serious as to prevent human resources from playing an important role in strategy formulation. Therefore conflict must be reduced and credibility enhanced if the human resources function is to be fully involved in strategy formulation. What can be done? Let us examine some courses of action.[24]

Enhancing Credibility and Reducing Staff-Line Conflict

Exhibit 2.5 notes a number of actions that a company can take to reduce line-staff conflict and enhance the credibility of the human resource unit. First, it should ensure that people who staff the human resource unit are competent, well trained, and experienced in the various human resource functions.

Second, the human resource unit's role should be spelled out clearly in corporate policy vis-à-vis line manager roles. Who has responsibility of what and when needs to be determined, put in writing, and shared among line managers and the human resource unit. Both line managers and human resource professionals should play a role in determining this responsibility.

Third, human resource people should view their role as supporting line staff. The human resource unit exists to help line managers do a better job as human resource managers. Even though the human resource unit must enforce human resource laws and policies, it essentially exists to help line managers and keep them out of trouble.

Fourth, the human resource unit and line managers should work together in formulating human resource policies, programs, and actions. For example, at Clay Electric Cooperative in Florida, even though the human resource unit was given the primary responsibility to come up with a new performance appraisal system, it did so by working with line managers every step of the way. At each step the work of the human resource unit was "bounced off" the line managers in group sessions, and their suggestions were incorporated into modified versions of the system.

Fifth, the human resource unit should practice "managing by wandering around," as Peters and Austin call it in *A Passion for Excellence*.[25] In other words, human resource people should get out of their offices to where the work is done—the factory, office, mine, or field. Human resource isolation from line work can be a serious cause of poor credibility and staff-line conflict. In fact, because of this, many companies, including Procter & Gamble, IBM, and GE, do not place people in human resource positions until they have had line experience and training.

Sixth, line managers need to understand the important and significant role that the human resource unit plays in today's environment. It takes many burdensome chores away from line managers, which actually makes their jobs much easier. Line managers sometimes forget this fact.

Line-staff conflict seldom can be eliminated completely. The points noted here should serve to enhance the human resource unit's credibility and reduce line-staff conflict, thereby opening the door for greater participation of human resource professionals in the strategy formulation process.

Let us turn our attention now to the human resource audit, a program that is helpful in ensuring that the operations of the human resource function meet the needs of the company. The human resource audit is an excellent means to ensure that this function is viewed in terms beyond just costs and benefits. The human resource audit is very important in creating an appropriate linkage between human resources strategy and overall corporate strategy.

Human Resource Audit

Human resource units have been concerned with their effectiveness and efficiency for some time. For example, a survey of human resource departments by the Bureau of National Affairs (BNA) shows that human resource staff ratios to 100 employees have increased slightly from 0.9 to 1.0 from 1996 to 2000, as shown in Exhibit 2.6. However, total human resource expenditures continued to increase approximately 5.5 percent per year from 1996 to 2000 while human resource expenditures per employee remained at about $797 from 1996 to 2000, although they did increase to $994 in 1997.[26]

One way human resource staffs assess their effectiveness and efficiency is through human resource research and human resource audits. Human resource research is one of the primary means by which the human resource department assists the organization in meeting the ever-increasing demand for high productivity in today's competitive marketplace. Human resource research involves evaluating the department's effectiveness in serving the organization's human resource needs. It helps the organization to analyze its human resource practices and policies and determine whether changes and improvements are necessary.[27] One of the key tools for conducting such research is the **human resource audit**. Its main function is to help decision makers understand what is happening with various activities, such as recruitment, hiring, separation, and training.

human resource audit Study of the human resource unit to determine its effectiveness and efficiency.

Why Do an Audit?

A human resource audit often is conducted when management perceives that certain programs or activities are not meeting the goals set for them or that they have other problems.[28] Another reason for the audit is to determine what programs or positions to eliminate when a firm decides to downsize. Programs or activities identified as the least effective are targeted for elimination. For the audit to be effective, the firm must determine what it seeks to achieve by performing it.[29] This will help determine who is to perform the audit and the methods to be used in conducting it.

EXHIBIT 2.6 — **HUMAN RESOURCES DEPARTMENT STAFFING AND EXPENDITURES, 1996–2000**

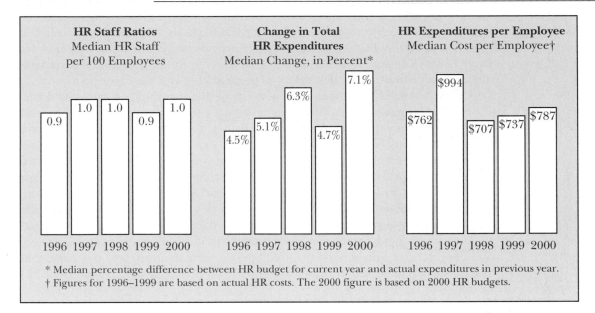

HR Staff Ratios
Median HR Staff per 100 Employees

1996	1997	1998	1999	2000
0.9	1.0	1.0	0.9	1.0

Change in Total HR Expenditures
Median Change, in Percent*

1996	1997	1998	1999	2000
4.5%	5.1%	6.3%	4.7%	7.1%

HR Expenditures per Employee
Median Cost per Employee†

1996	1997	1998	1999	2000
$762	$994	$707	$737	$787

* Median percentage difference between HR budget for current year and actual expenditures in previous year.
† Figures for 1996–1999 are based on actual HR costs. The 2000 figure is based on 2000 HR budgets.

SOURCE: Bureau of National Affairs, *Bulletin to Management*, June 29, 2000, p. S–5.

HR CHALLENGES

Exactly How Do Businesses Evaluate Their HR Departments?

A study by researchers at the University of Iowa indicated that approximately one third of the businesses in their survey seldom or never conduct evaluations of their human resource departments. Another one third said that they conduct human resource reviews at least annually, and the final one third fell somewhere in the middle.

The two most frequently cited reasons for not evaluating the human resource function were difficulty in conducting a scientific evaluation and difficulty in quantifying human resource's return on investment.

However, this did not seem to stop the one third of the respondents who frequently evaluate their human resource departments. When asked what type of evaluation is performed, they indicated a more judgmental and qualitative process is used rather than a quantitative or scientific one. Further, when asked who performs the evaluation, the majority of the respondents indicated that the human resource function evaluates itself.

The results of this study indicate that human resource departments are clearly not being evaluated properly. Further, the true value of the human resource function to the organization is not being made clear. Even in organizations in which evaluations are performed, the informally gathered information by the people in the department will not hold much weight. Before human resource departments can be judged on their merit, procedures must exist for determining how well they perform.

SOURCE: Adapted from Margaret Cashman and James McElroy, "Evaluating the HR Function," *HRMagazine*, January 1991, pp. 70–73.

Performing the Audit

The choice of who will conduct the audit must be made carefully. In-house staff, who are most familiar with the organization, may be selected, but their knowledge may perpetuate past errors and misconceptions. A third-party human resource consultant may be employed. The advantage of having an outsider perform the audit must be weighed against the possibility that the consultant may miss some subtleties of the organization's system or may bring a preconceived set of solutions to the project. An organization's lawyers are able to advise on the legality of programs but lack the expertise to evaluate their effectiveness. The firm must decide which of these options best meets its needs.

The human resource audit involves collecting data. A number of methods, such as employee observation, surveys, questionnaires, and computer data reviews, are used in the process. These techniques are used to gather information and compare it with some expected or predicted outcome. For example, the audits can compare rates or ratios, such as turnover, attendance, or training and development, against past firm or industry levels of performance. Surveys can measure morale and job satisfaction or wages and salaries. All of these factors serve as broad measures of the success of underlying personnel and organizational functions. For example, poor attendance and tardiness rates may indicate poor morale, an overly permissive sick-pay policy, lack of line supervisor discipline, or even a poorly laid-out plant that prevents employees from returning from breaks on time. Exhibit 2.7 provides addi-

EXHIBIT 2.7	HUMAN RESOURCE AUDIT MEASUREMENTS AND THEIR ORGANIZATION'S UNDERLYING INDICATORS
Rate	**Personnel Functions to Examine**
Turnover Rate • Quit rate • Termination rate • Layoff rate • Retention rate • Retirement rate • Length of service rate	Salary and benefits package Supervisory practices Job design Retirement plan
Job Attendance Rate • Absence rate • Tardiness rate	Exit interviews Discipline Convenience of lunchroom and rest room Sick-pay policy
Overtime Rate	Employee planning and scheduling Shortage of staff Selection and training process
Position Vacancy Rate	Recruitment and selection process Salary and benefit package Company image in community
Error/Scrap Rate	Recruitment selection and placement Training and development Job satisfaction
Training and Development Rate	Recruitment and selection Training and development
Grievance Rate	Supervisory practices Job dissatisfaction

tional examples. The technique used depends on the information sought. Surveys are an excellent way to measure effects on large groups; interviews and observations can be used for a more comprehensive analysis of smaller groups. Information obtained may be compared against information from outside sources or internal research.

However the information is gathered, the main purpose of the human resource audit is to evaluate the effectiveness of the organization's human resource function, and the information should reflect this. It should show both the department's strengths and weaknesses and provide management with a clear picture of the department's role in the organization. The audit also should allow management to evaluate the human resource department's broad role in helping the organization meet its strategic goals and objectives.

Results of the Audit

The information gathered during the audit may indicate that a specific program or activity is in fact meeting its goals, in which case no further action is necessary. Or the audit may produce unanticipated results. For example, an audit to examine employee turnover for the past year might indicate that turnover was within reasonable limits. An unexpected result of the audit could be the indication that the firm's reward and compensation plan has contributed to decreased turnover. Sometimes, as a result of the audit, the human resource department can experience re-engineering, which is a restructuring and streamlining of the department in an attempt to make it more efficient.

Contingency for Situational Approach to Strategy

Our discussion of formulating corporate strategy concludes with a review of the situational nature of strategy formulation. Basically, this idea states that what might be good for one firm may not be good for another. The formulation of a proper strategy for a particular firm is firm specific. Thus the strategy is contingent on specific aspects of the firm. The proper strategy is determined by its unique internal characteristics and its specific environmental opportunities and threats. This is true of firms in the same industry—what is right for Ford may not be right for GM and vice versa.

However, the situational or contingency approach does not mean that firms should ignore what other firms are doing. In fact, in the case of their competitors, firms need to consider explicitly the strategies of the competition in formulating their own strategy. A firm can examine its competitors, see what they are doing, and make judgments as to whether its situation is similar enough to allow it to use a comparable or modified version of a competitor's strategy.

Sometimes strategies roll like waves across the business landscape. In these cases a particular strategy catches on with many firms. As pointed out in several places in this book, merger and acquisition and cost cutting were very popular strategies in the 1980s and 1990s. In the area of human resources, two popular strategies have been cutting labor cost and involving human resources. Even though it is tempting to jump uncritically on the bandwagon with wholesale adoption of a popular strategy, each firm should carefully examine the strategy and its own situation to determine if the strategy is, in fact, right for it.

Management Guidelines

We can summarize the key points of this chapter with the following guidelines:

1. Strategy formulation is not a neat and clean process. It moves in "fits and starts" with much backtracking and revision. It is evolutionary in nature more often than it is revolutionary.
2. Strategy and the process of formulating it must be flexible and adaptable.
3. Strategy formulation is an attempt to anchor the organization to some position in the future.
4. The market, especially competition, plays a very important role in the formation of strategy and the firm's sustainable competitive advantage.
5. Stakeholders are a major influence on the formation of strategy.
6. Even though corporate strategy should drive functional strategy, human resource units play an interactive role with respect to overall corporate strategy formulation.
7. Human resources is becoming a key consideration in overall strategy formulation.
8. For human resources to maximize its role in strategy formulation, it must reduce the line-staff conflict and credibility gap that may exist between it and line managers.
9. The human resource audit can be seen as key in collecting important human resources information and ensuring that the human resource function is meeting the needs of the overall strategy.
10. All strategy is situational. The proper strategy for a particular firm depends on the unique situation it faces. What works for one firm may not work for another.

Questions for Review

1. Describe the strategy formulation process and the role strategic planning plays in the process.

2. Why should strategy be flexible and adaptive in nature?

3. In what ways has cost-cutting competitive strategy affected human resources in individual organizations?

4. Explain the purpose of a human resources audit. When is it appropriate to conduct one?

5. What are the components of a human resources audit?

6. We have stated that corporate strategy should drive functional and human resource strategy. We also have stated that the formation of corporate and human resource strategy is interactive in nature. Do you see an apparent contradiction in these two statements? Explain your answer.

7. What are the line-staff conflict and credibility gap that often exist between the human resource unit and line managers? What causes this conflict?

8. How can line-staff conflict and the credibility gap between line managers and the human resource unit be reduced? Why must it be reduced?

9. What do we mean when we say that strategy formation is situational or contingent in nature? Why is this important to understand?

10. What role does a firm's posture on innovation play in strategy formulation?

CASE

AGENCY.COM*

AGENCY.COM is a leading e-business builder in global markets. The company provides strategy, branding, and technology services that help its clients build and grow their interactive business across multiple digital channels—the Web, wireless, and interactive television. Founded in January 1995 by Chan Suh and Kyle Shannon in the living room of Shannon's home, AGENCY.COM has grown to 14 offices worldwide and approximately 1600 employees. AGENCY.COM's client list has grown from one account, Sports Illustrated, to include global business leaders such as Coca-Cola, British Airways, Compaq, and Reuters.

AGENCY.COM is in the business of working with clients to build their businesses through the interactive tools of the Internet, iTelevision (iTV), and mobile wireless technologies such as personal digital assistance and wireless enabled mobile phones. AGENCY.COM has had success in positioning itself in this market; however, the potential exhibited by this industry is attracting new market entrants and has caused the market to become fiercely competitive. This market includes firms that specialize in the online, mobile, and iTV markets, such as marchFIRST, Scient, Viant, Sapient, Xpedior, and iXL, to the likes of larger technology firms that offer broader services, such as Accenture (formerly Andersen Consulting), Arthur Andersen Business Consulting, EDS, and IBM Global. These larger consulting firms are relatively new to this market and are looking to cash in on the revenue potential prevalent in this market, causing this industry sector to become even more crowded.

Toward the end of 2000, many of AGENCY.COM's competitors, such as marchFIRST, Viant, and iXL, announced layoffs as a result of decreased demand in the market for their services. The industry as a whole is down, causing many firms to miss Wall Street analysts' projections and thereby causing industry players' stock prices to plummet. Market watchers are predicting a shakeout in the industry that will cause many cash-strapped firms to close their doors and leave fewer firms standing. Another factor that will contribute to this industry shakeout is the strategy that the larger players—for example, Accenture and IBM—will pursue in wielding their deep pockets to either purchase or merge with weakened industry firms.

AGENCY.COM has managed to maintain its success and meet Wall Street analysts' expectations. Revenues for the third quarter 2000 were up 90 percent from a year earlier, with positive cash EPS of $.07 up 40 percent over second quarter 2000. This success can be attributed to many factors, such as being one of the first market entrants and its decision to steer away from dot-com start-up clients and focus on larger blue-chip clients. One of the most important keys to AGENCY.COM's success has been its ability to attract and keep its talented employees. As a professional services firm, AGENCY.COM possesses an integral asset in its employees. An emphasis of local and corporate management is to create a working environment that favors employees, promotes creativity, and supports project work while maintaining a fun experience. This office "culture" is a fine balance of employees from all different backgrounds, whether from the technology, creative, strategy, client services, or project management competencies. This culture has been cultivated and grown by every office and helps to create synergy and communication in project teams.

As the impending industry shakeout looms in the near future, AGENCY.COM appears to be positioned as one of the industry players expected to be left standing. Corporate management must contemplate how the consolidation of the industry will affect AGENCY.COM. Should it investigate purchasing one or more of its competitors? Should it entertain purchase or merger offers from larger traditional consulting competitors? Management, however, anticipates that the introduction of a new or different culture will disrupt the current culture that AGENCY.COM has built from the beginning. How will these vital employees react? What overall strategy and human resource strategy would you follow under these conditions? Do you think AGENCY.COM has a viable future?

---

*Case written by Craig Mathe.
SOURCES: **www.agency.com**; **www.news.cnet.com**; and **www.internetworld.com**.

Additional Readings

Allio, R. J. *The Practical Strategist.* New York: Harper & Row, 1988.

Baird, L.; I. Meshoulam; and G. DeGive. "Meshing Human Resources Planning with Strategic Business Planning: A Model Approach." *Personnel* 60, no. 5 (1983), pp. 14–25.

Buller, P. F., and N. K. Napier. "Strategy and Human Resource Management Integration in Fast Growth versus Other Mid-sized Firms." Paper presented at the 1990 Academy of Management Meeting. San Francisco, 1990.

Carroll, G. R., and D. Vogel. *Organizational Approaches to Strategy.* New York: Harper & Row, 1988.

Child, J. "Organization Structure, Environment, and Performance: The Role of Strategic Choice." *Sociology* 6 (1972), pp. 2–22.

Dimick, D. E., and V. V. Murray. "Correlates of Substantive Policy Decisions in Organizations: The Case of Human Resource Management." *Academy of Management Journal* 21 (1978), pp. 611–623.

Dyer, L. "Bringing Human Resources into the Strategy Formulation Process." *Human Resource Management* 22, no. 3 (1983), pp. 257–271.

Dyer, L. "Strategic Human Resources Management and Planning." In *Research in Personnel and Human Resources Management.* Eds. K. M. Rowland and G. R. Ferris. Greenwich, CT: JAI Press, 1985, pp. 1–30.

Ettorre, B., and D. J. McNerney. "Human Resources: Managing Human Capital for the Future." *Management Review* 84, no. 6 (June 1995), pp. 56–61.

Finkelstein, S., and D. Hambrick. "Top-Management Team Tenure and Organizational Outcomes: The Moderating Role of Managerial Discretion." *Administrative Science Quarterly* 35 (1990), pp. 484–503.

Fitz-Enz, J. "The ROI of Human Capital: Measuring the Economic Value of Employee Performance." *Amacom, 2000.*

Foltz, R. "Senior Management Views the Human Resource Function." *Personnel Administrator* 27, no. 9 (September 1984), pp. 37–50.

Gilbert, D. R., Jr.; E. Hartman; J. J. Muriel; and R. E. Freeman. *A Logic for Strategy.* New York: Harper & Row, 1988.

Gratton, L. *Living Strategy: Putting People at the Heart of Corporate Strategy.* Englewood Cliffs, NJ: Prentice Hall, 2000.

Green, P. C. *Building Robust Competencies: Linking Human Resource Systems to Organizational Strategies.* San Francisco: Jossey-Bass, 1999.

Grundy, T. "Human Resource Management—A Strategic Approach." *Long Range Planning* 30, no. 4 (August 1997), pp. 507–517.

Guth, W., and I. MacMillan. "Strategy Implementation versus Middle Management Self-Interest." *Strategic Management Journal* 7 (1986), pp. 313–327.

Hasek, G. "The Best of the Best." *Industry Week* 24, no. 15 (August 18, 1997), pp. 18–64.

Herman, R. E. *Keeping Good People: Strategies for Solving the #1 Problem Facing Business Today.* Winchester, VA: Oakhill Pr., 1999.

Hrebiniak, L. G., and W. F. Joyce. *Implementing Strategy.* New York: Macmillan, 1984.

Hussey, D. E. "Human Resources: A Strategic Audit." *International Review of Strategic Management* 6 (1995), pp. 157–195.

Lawrence, P. *Executive Summary—The History of Resource Management in America.* Human Resource Management Future Conference, Harvard Business School, May 9–11, 1984.

Leontiades, M. "Choosing the Right Manager to Fit the Strategy." *Journal of Business Strategy* 2, no. 2 (1982), pp. 58–69.

Lieberman, M.; L. Lau; and M. Williams. "Firm-Level Productivity and Management Influence: A Comparison of U.S. and Japanese Automobile Producers." *Management Science* 36 (1990), pp. 1193–1215.

Lindblom, C. "The Science of Muddling Through." *Public Administration Review* 19 (1959), pp. 79–88.

MacMillan, I. C., and P. E. Jones. *Strategy Formulation: Power and Politics,* 2nd ed. St. Paul, MN: West, 1986.

MacMillan, I. C., and R. S. Schuler. "Gaining a Competitive Edge through Human Resources." *Personnel* 62, no. 4 (1985), pp. 24–29.

McEvoy, G. M., and J. R. Cragun. "Using Outdoor Training to Develop and Accomplish Organizational Vision." *Human Resource Planning* 20, no. 3 (1997), pp. 20–28.

Miles, R.; C. C. Snow; A. D. Meyer; and H. J. Coleman, Jr. "Organization Strategy, Structure, and Process." *Academy of Management Review* 3 (1978), pp. 546–662.

Miller, P. "Strategy and the Ethical Management of Human Resources." *Human Resource Management Journal* 6, no. 1 (1996), pp. 5–18.

Mintzberg, H. "Strategy Formation: Schools of Thought." In *Perspectives on Strategic Management.* Ed. J. Fredrickson. New York: Harper & Row, 1990, pp. 105–235.

Pitts, R. A., and C. C. Snow. *Strategies for Competitive Success.* New York: Wiley, 1986.

Porter, M. E. *Competitive Strategy.* New York: Free Press, 1980.

Porter, M. E. *Competitive Advantage.* New York: Free Press, 1985.

Pruter, R. "Outsourcing Can Significantly Alter the Role of Employee Benefits Departments." *Employee Benefit Plan Review* 52, no. 5 (November 1997), pp. 30–32.

Rumelt, R. P. *Strategy, Structure and Economic Performance in Large American Industrial Corporations.* Boston: Harvard Graduate School of Business Administration, 1974.

Schuler, R. S., and I. C. MacMillan. "Gaining Competitive Advantage through Human Resource Management Practices." *Human Resource Management* 23, no. 3 (1984), pp. 241–256.

Schuler, R. S., and S. E. Jackson. "Linking Competitive Strategies with Human Resource Management Practices." *Academy of Management Executive* 1 (1987), pp. 207–219.

Smart, Bradford D. *Topgrading: How Leading Companies Win by Hiring.* Englewood Cliffs, NJ: Prentice Hall, 1999.

Smith, E. C. "Strategic Business Planning and Human Resources: Part I." *Personnel Journal* 61, no. 8 (1982a), pp. 606–610.

Smith, E. C. "Strategic Business Planning and Human Resources: Part II." *Personnel Journal* 61, no. 9 (1982b), pp. 680–682.

Stumpf, S. A., and N. M. Hanrahan. "Designing Organizational Career Management Practices to Fit the Strategic Management Objectives." In *Readings in Personnel and Human Resource Management.* Eds. R. S. Schuler and S. A. Youngblood, 2nd ed. St. Paul: West, 1984, pp. 326–348.

Sweet, J. "How Manpower Development Can Support Your Strategic Plan." *Journal of Business Strategy* 3, no. 1 (1982), pp. 77–81.

Szilagyi, A., and D. Schweiger. "Matching Managers to Strategies: A Review and Suggested Framework." *Academy of Management Review* 9 (1984), pp. 626–637.

Tichy, N. M.; C. J. Fombrun; and M. A. Devanna. "Strategic Human Resource Management." *Sloan Management Review* 23, no. 2 (1982), pp. 47–61.

Ulrich, D. *Human Resource Champions: The Next Agenda for Adding Value and Delivering Results.* Cambridge, MA: Harvard Business School Pr., 1997.

Notes

[1]Kenneth Labich, "Is Herb Kelleher America's Best CEO?" *Fortune*, May 2, 1994, pp. 44–52; "A Letter to Those Who Appreciate Southwest Airline's Low Fares," Southwest Airlines advertisement, *The Wall Street Journal*, May 4, 1994, p. B12; and Bridget O'Brian, "Giant Reservation System to Dump Southwest," *The Wall Street Journal*, April 22, 1994, p. B1.

[2]Karen Walker, "Proceed with Care, Southwest Airlines Reaches Strategic Development Crossroads," *Airline Business*, 6, no. 13 (June 1997), p. 70.

[3]"Southwest Airlines on Pace to Exceed $1 Billion in Internet Revenue for 2000," Southwest Press Release, Feb. 28, 2000.

[4]"Southwest Airlines Plans Long-Haul Non-stop Service," *Aviation Week and Space Technology*, February 3, 1997, Vol. 146, no. 5, p. 46.

[5]"We Weren't Just Airborne Yesterday, Southwest Airlines—A Brief History," Available at **www.southwest.com** (accessed February 11, 2001).

[6]Ibid.

[7]Ibid.

[8]Katrina Brooker, "Can Anyone Replace Herb?" *Fortune*, April 17, 2000, p. 192.

[9]Ibid.

[10]R. E. Freeman, *Strategic Management: A Stakeholder Approach* (Boston: Pitman, 1984).

[11]John Naisbitt, *Megatrends: Ten New Directions for Transforming Our Lives* (New York: Warner, 1982); and John Naisbett and Patricia Aburdene, *Megatrends 2000: Ten New Directions for the 1990s* (New York: Morrow, 1990).

[12]Emily Yoffe, "Naisbitt's Clip Joint: The Selling of Content Analysis and Megatrends," *Harpers*, September 1983, p. 161.

[13]Cynthia D. Fisher, "Current and Recurrent Challenges in HRM," *Journal of Management* 15, no. 2 (June 1989), pp. 157–180.

[14]Ibid., p. 158.

[15]Ibid., p. 159.

[16]Cynthia A. Lengnick-Hall and Mark L. Lengnick-Hall, "Strategic Human Resources Management: A Review of the Literature and a Proposed Typology," *Academy of Management Review* 13, no. 3 (July 1988), pp. 466–467.

[17]Robert E. Sibson, *Strategic Planning for Human Resource Management* (New York: AMACOM Books, 1992).

[18]Ceel Pasternak, "Benefits," *HRMagazine*, August 1992, p. 27.

[19]Michael Porter, *Competitive Advantage* (New York: Free Press, 1985).

[20]David L. Calfee, "Get Your Mission Statement Working," *Management Review*, January 1993, pp. 54–57.

[21]Walter S. Mossberg, "Personnel Technology: PC Program Lets Machines Help Bosses Manage People," *The Wall Street Journal*, December 24, 1992, p. 7.

[22]Bill Leonard, "U.S. Energy Secretary O'Leary Uses an HR Approach," *HRNews*, October 1993, p. A9.

[23]Mark A. Huselid, "Documenting HR's Effect on Company Performance," *HRMagazine*, January 1994, pp. 79–84.

[24]See also James A. McCambridge and Vicki S. Kaman, "Programs That Strengthen Relations," *HRMagazine*, May 1992, pp. 75–78.

[25]Tom Peters and Nancy Austin, *A Passion for Excellence* (New York: Random House, 1985), p. 11.

[26]Bureau of National Affairs, *Bulletin to Management*, June 29, 2000, p. S-5.

[27]Robert L. Mathis and John H. Jackson, *Personnel/Human Resource Management*, 5th ed. (St. Paul, MN: West, 1988), p. 599.

[28]Johnathan A. Seagal and Mary A. Quinn, "How to Audit Your HR Programs," *Personnel Administrator*, May 1989, pp. 67–70.

[29]Ibid., p. 67.

3

The External and Global Environment for Human Resources: Change and Diversity

Chapter Objectives

As a result of studying this chapter, you should be able to

1. Describe the components of an organization's external and global environments.

2. Explain how an organization knows or learns of these environments and their components.

3. Describe how these environments affect the firm directly and indirectly.

4. Describe the various basic positions an organization can establish with respect to its environment.

5. Understand that the environment must now be considered global, incorporating influential elements from around the world.

The environment within which an organization operates has a profound impact on the organization's success. In today's changing global community, the firm faces many new challenges. The company's ability to adopt or amend strategies to compensate for or take advantage of such changes will dictate its success and even survival. In this chapter, we separate the external environment into areas that influence the company's strategy and operations and that could be potentially major concerns for human resource management. We pay special attention to the emerging global community in which modern firms operate and the implications of this environment to the company and its human resource management efforts.

CASE

Ma Bell Has Learned the Competition Game[1]

"AT&T is no sunset company!" former Chairman Robert E. Allen boasted to shareholders of the communication giant at the company's annual meeting in Atlanta in April 1994. Allen remarked that the worldwide information industry should be worth $1 trillion by 2000 and that he fully anticipates that American Telephone & Telegraph Company (AT&T) will lead the way toward that impressive mark. In fact, analysts predicted that AT&T was on the verge of good performance, but the battle "back" would be difficult.

Since that meeting, AT&T has gone through massive restructuring and leadership adjustments. In 1996, it divided into three companies. In late 1997, C. Michael Armstrong from Hughes Electronics was selected as CEO to replace Bob Allen. AT&T has come a long way to be competitive in an environment of globalization and deregulation.

In late 1983, a federal antitrust suit forced AT&T to divest itself of three fourths of its $150 billion in assets. The trend toward competition, which had been developing in trucking, airline, and other industries since the late 1970s, hit the communications industry, and AT&T in particular, full force. New rules to the ball game were being written. The breakup led to greater flexibility in the regulation of AT&T proper. No longer would monopoly, power, and government regulation provide a safe harbor for AT&T. The environment was being radically restructured. In other words, times were changing.

In fact, most business experts agree that never before has a company been "shaken up" by an external environmental force as severely as AT&T was. The company was forced to change its basic way of doing business. In other words, AT&T's internal operations had been totally reshaped by a force from the external environment.

Meeting this drastic change in the environment has been a major challenge for AT&T. As a regulated utility, costs, not efficiency, drove its profits. Higher costs just expanded the base in which its regulated rate of return was calculated. This automatically boosted earnings. Competition changed all this. First, AT&T had to spin off its regional phone companies—the so-called baby bells—which now operate independently. In fact, AT&T now competes with the regional companies in short long-distance services. The company also lost its monopoly in the long-distance market as satellite technology opened this market to a host of competitive long-distance companies, such as MCI WorldCom and U.S. Sprint, among others. In addition, resellers who buy long-distance time on AT&T lines at wholesale prices and then resell it to customers (10-10 dial-arounds) have emerged. No longer could AT&T count on an assured income stream from long-distance and regional telephone services. It had to compete aggressively in the marketplace.

Competitive Strategy

AT&T's first task was to remove some of the "excess baggage" associated with giant noncompetitive organizations. Costs were cut by eliminating 27,000 jobs plus another 48,000 through layoffs and retirements. This amounted to approximately 20 percent of the company's workforce. As of 2000, AT&T employed 160,000 people. Some work was shifted overseas. For example, residential phones are now made in Singapore. The number of models in AT&T's phone line was cut, and domestic plants were automated. Sales personnel at its retail telephone stores were put on a commission basis. In short, during the restructuring of the early 1980s, the company adopted many of the same cost-cutting tactics used by nonregulated companies.

AT&T desperately wants to remain a leader and "bellwether" in the communications industry. It continues to emphasize its core business while divesting units to improve this focus. AT&T has been forced, however, to rebuild its organization and reorient its human resources to instill a sense of creativity and competitiveness. AT&T has had to change its overall personality or culture. This is certainly a hard thing to do, but the competitive environment, dictated by the government regulators, forced the AT&T staff to change its style. For example, never before had the employees been exposed to the pressure of creating new products and services. Never before had employees been expected to beat competitors in the race for radically new ideas and solutions to human problems. AT&T had always been able to sell itself because it was the "only game in town." The regulatory action meant that AT&T's viability as a firm now rested on the abilities of its employees to adapt.

Employees did develop new products, especially computers suited to AT&T's particular needs. After all, the company believed that its Private Branch Exchange (PBX) and switching systems were, in fact, computers. Company leaders believed that the marriage of telephones and computers was the key union for success in the communications and "information management" industry of tomorrow. In the meantime, AT&T noted the potential importance of cellular technology in the communications industry of the future. In 1994, AT&T received government approval for an $11.5 billion merger with McCaw Cellular, Inc. This made AT&T a leader in the cellular industry.

AT&T also adopted an aggressive marketing campaign. No longer would AT&T wait for customers to discover it. It began to share its vision for the future of communications and illustrate to customers that AT&T was committed to innovation and leadership. In past television commercials, a spokesman told viewers about a day in the future when drivers' licenses will be renewed at ATMs, groceries will be checked a full cart at a time, and faxes will be sent from virtually anywhere. The spokesman vows to the audience that AT&T, an old familiar friend, will lead the way in developing these technologies.

AT&T responded forcefully to MCI and Sprint advertising that was designed to "win away" loyal AT&T customers. AT&T developed creative television, radio, and newspaper ads suggesting that savings associated with switching to the "upstarts" were not substantial. In addition, the advertisements emphasized the superior service and product quality offered by AT&T. The company also developed valuable package plans and discount programs, such as the TRUE campaign, which posed a major threat to the relatively smaller competitors. Also, AT&T strengthened its position in overseas long distance and entered the financial services industry. The company even offers leasing services and a credit card that can also be used as a calling card.

AT&T has continued its metamorphosis. After numerous acquisitions in the 1980s and early 1990s, new focus was required by the latter part of the 1990s. This new focus was on a core business and consolidation. In 1996, AT&T spun off Lucent Technologies and the NCR computer unit. In a separate transaction, the company sold its AT&T Capital Corporation in October 1996. The largest business unit remaining consisted of the core long-distance operation, the wireless service, and 25 percent of Bell Laboratories. This unit retained the name of AT&T. The leadership has also been changing since the 1994 annual shareholders' meeting. In October 1996, John Walter replaced Robert E. Allen as CEO. This leadership ended abruptly in July 1997 when Walter quit and Allen once again was CEO. Late in 1997, C. Michael Armstrong became the most recent CEO of AT&T.

Under Armstrong's leadership, AT&T has actively expanded into cyber communications. During 1998 and 1999, AT&T made several acquisitions, including TCG, the largest alternate supplier of local telecommunications service, and TCI, the second largest cable company in the nation, to form AT&T Broadband & Internet Services and Vanguard Cellular. Since the initiation of Armstrong's cable strategy, AT&T has invested heavily toward the acquisition of and improvement of much of the nation's cable systems. It remains to be seen if this strategy will prove successful. However, at present Armstrong is saddled with some difficult decisions. Thanks to a recent ruling by the Federal Communications Commission, AT&T must sell some of its cable assets, which could potentially reduce its reach in this industry. The company recently announced plans to spin off Liberty Media, part of its TCI acquisition, to alleviate these pressures. At the same time, AT&T is faced with a sizable debt, $62 billion, and falling stock prices. A four-way split may be in the future for the company starting in 2001 and finishing in 2002. While the company has been aggressive in its response to new technological trends, AT&T remains a powerful international company, yet waits to bear the fruits of its latest expansion efforts.

In recent years, AT&T has created many new sales and marketing positions. The employees used to staff these posts were not hired from outside the firm but were transferred from other departments. This was only a small part of AT&T's innovative restructuring plan. While seeking to increase productivity, the company retrained many of its employees to work in sales and marketing positions. The downside of this large retraining project was that because many of these jobs required voluntary transfers on the part of the employees, those who did not take the newly created posts were reassigned or terminated. Even though the firm did not force resignations, it did try to reduce nonrevenue-producing staff positions and streamline overhead costs.

However frugal AT&T has become, it is continuing its generous pension, insurance, and health care plans, along with other benefits. It provides a noncontributory defined pension benefit plan covering substantially all management and nonmanagement employees. Nonmanagement employee benefits are based on a nonpay-related plan, and the benefits for management employees are based on a career-average pay plan. In 1998, AT&T also extended full pension offerings to any employee whose age and time working for the company totaled 65 years, when previously employees needed 30 to 35 years with the company to qualify for this benefit.

Like its current employees, AT&T's retirees are being cared for. The company's provided benefit plan includes health care and life insurance. The company pays the annual insurance premiums, which amounts to about $600 for each of its approximately 140,000 retired employees.

Morale

Though it is apparent that AT&T's aggressive new strategy depends heavily on human resources, all of this change has had an adverse effect on many employees who had grown up in the traditional AT&T culture. Under regulation, attributes such as loyalty, commitment, and longevity were rewarded in a sort of "cradle to grave" management philosophy. The company took care of its employees as long as they went along with the status quo. Innovation, challenge, and new ideas were not rewarded.

Therefore, the changes were particularly difficult for long-time employees brought up in the old system. Many could not adjust and took early retirement, quit, or transferred to the baby bells. Others were fired. Some managed to stay on the job by biding their time until early retirement.

Fortunately, AT&T has been considered one of the most innovative companies in labor relations. Early in the restructuring period, top company managers met with leaders of the company's two unions every few months for so-called common interest forums. Financial figures and improvements in products and services were discussed. In 1985, this meeting process almost collapsed. However, by 1987 it had been revived. Throughout the 1990s, progress was made in improving the layoff process through crisis counseling, retraining, transfer, and attractive buyout packages.

Conclusion

The AT&T case demonstrates the dramatic effect a change in a firm's external environment can have on its overall and human resource strategies. Deregulation changed the rules dramatically, virtually overnight. Employees and managers hired and schooled in one set of rules had to learn an entirely new set. Whereas loyalty and stability were once the primary employee attributes rewarded, innovation and change became the new desirable attributes. Reward systems had to change, socialization and training processes were modified, and performance appraisals now emphasized newly determined employee actions. The uncertainty caused by these changes hurt morale and further affected the company's deteriorating relationship with the unions. Yet, as the case indicates, AT&T is making a sound comeback. It continues to strive toward its goal of being the single resource for consumer communication needs. Today, AT&T focuses on wireless phone service, Internet access, video entertainment, cable systems, and international phone services.

Strategic Choices

An organization makes strategic decisions in dealing with its environment. These decisions serve to link the organization with its environment and to establish the basic direction of the organization, as shown in Exhibit 3.1. A firm can establish several basic strategic postures with the environment. Four postures, which follow the Miles and Snow topology,[2] are outlined as follows:

defenders Organizations that focus on a narrow line of products and strongly defend their position in the market.

1. An organization can adopt a defender strategy. **Defenders** focus on a narrow line of products and strongly defend their position in the market against anyone—competitors, government, and so on. Traditional cigarette companies prior to diversification, such as Liggett and Myers, used this strategy.

prospectors
Organizations that are always looking for new market opportunities and aggressively seek to develop both new products and new markets.

analyzers Organizations that have one product in a stable market and one in a changing market.

reactors Organizations that see major changes in their environments but have difficulty adapting quickly enough to meet the changes.

2. A firm can become a prospector. **Prospectors** always are looking for new market opportunities and aggressively seek to develop both new products and new markets. IBM fits this strategy well, as does the new AT&T.

3. A firm can adopt an analyzer posture. **Analyzers** have a split personality: they have one product in a stable market and one in a changing market. In the stable market, they operate routinely; in the rapidly changing market, they closely watch their competitors and then adapt as best they can. The Schering-Plough Corporation uses this strategy. Known for producing mostly "me-too" drugs (copies of drugs already on the market), the company has one stable product, the antibiotic Garamycin, that has been the mainstay of its prescription drug line. As the company watched its competitors advance in the biotech field, it embarked on a crash program to develop the drug Interferon.

4. Finally, a firm can become a reactor. **Reactors** see major changes in their environment but have difficulty changing quickly enough to meet these changes. Bethlehem Steel and other major steel companies have this strategy primarily because of fixed capital investment, size, and a high wage structure. Changing fast enough to meet foreign competition in steel is a continuing challenge for domestic steel companies.

Adopting any of these strategic profiles will affect human resources. Defenders want aggressively trained specialists in the industry in order to produce and market their narrow line of products. Prospectors want aggressive entrepreneurial types of people who are willing to take risks to develop new products and markets. Analyzers value both stability and innovation in employees, depending on the unit in which the employees work. Finally, reactors want employees who are less resistant to change and able to help the organization move along its chosen path.

Now that we have examined the basic strategic choices an organization makes in dealing with the environment, we can examine the environmental components that affect overall strategy and human resource strategy formulation.

Components of the External Environment

societal environment Outside environmental forces that could affect a company eventually or indirectly.

task environment Outside forces that directly affect a company.

As Exhibit 3.2 illustrates, the external environment is multifaceted and complex. It has many factors, or elements, that can have a major impact on the long-term success of a company. We can generally divide these elements into two broad environmental types: the **societal environment** and the **task environment**.

EXHIBIT 3.1   STRATEGIC DECISIONS LINK THE ORGANIZATION WITH THE ENVIRONMENT

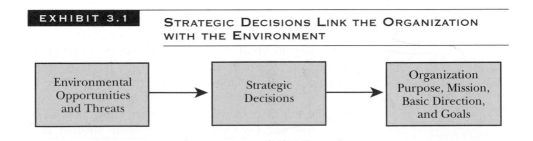

Environmental Opportunities and Threats → Strategic Decisions → Organization Purpose, Mission, Basic Direction, and Goals

EXHIBIT 3.2   EXTERNAL ENVIRONMENT: SOCIETAL AND TASK
ENVIRONMENT FORCES

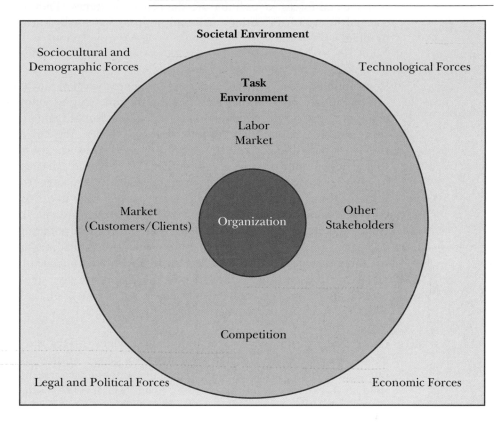

The societal environment involves the varying trends and general forces that do not relate directly to the company but could have an impact eventually or indirectly on the company.[3] Within the societal environment, we typically refer to four general forces: economic forces, technological forces, legal and political forces, and sociocultural and demographic forces. These forces indirectly affect the success of a particular company through their impact on the task environment over time.

The task environment includes those elements that directly influence the operations and strategy of the company. These elements are also affected by the operations of the company.[4] We will consider the task environment elements that follow: *the labor market, competition, the market (customers and clients)*, and *other stakeholders*, such as the government and special interest groups. The task environment elements are in direct contact with the company and are influenced by elements from the societal environment. For example, it became a societal goal and a trend in the 1960s to ensure equal employment opportunity for all Americans. The government soon passed laws prohibiting discrimination of any kind. The labor market was affected by these regulations. In turn, almost every U.S. business has been affected by the laws mandating equality and nondiscrimination in employment practices.

Let's turn our attention now toward a better description and understanding of the societal forces and then to the more directly influential task environment forces. The first societal forces we examine are the economic forces. Then we look at additional societal forces of technology, law and politics, and finally sociocultural and demographic.

Societal Forces

Economic Forces   The economy sets the general level of business. Economic forces can be thought of as mechanisms that "set the tone" or determine the attitudes of all who participate in the conduct of business. These forces regulate the exchange of resources such as money, labor, and information. Often, the implications of economic trends are hard to determine. For example, one might suspect a high level of inflation to deflate the value of a given wage dollar. This deflation can cause a variety of human reactions. For example, employees might demand higher wages to absorb the decrease in purchasing power. Others might seek to work longer hours or find additional employment. Inflation might make many products unaffordable. Labor itself may become unaffordable. All of these implications could affect potentially the success of the company. While the government gathers many statistical measures of the economy, the three that we are most interested in are the gross domestic product, inflation, and real disposable income. Although other measures are also important (for example, leading indicators, lagging indicators, and so on), we focus on these three because they provide good basic descriptions of overall economic activity.

Gross Domestic Product   Gross domestic product (GDP) is a total measure of all goods and services produced in a country for a period of time, usually one quarter or one year. It gives a broad measure of overall economic performance. Exhibit 3.3 shows the U.S. GDP for 1986 through 2000. Even though GDP has had its ups and downs during periods of prosperity and recession, it has grown from $4000 billion to $9800 billion over the 1986 to 2000 period.

Inflation   Inflation measures the increase in the price of products and services. Various indicators measure inflation—for example, the GDP deflator, the producer price index, and the wholesale price index—but the most popular measure of inflation is the consumer price index (CPI). Exhibit 3.4 shows the CPI for the 1987-2000 period. The changes have fluctuated between 1.5 percent to 6.3 percent during this period.

Real Disposable Income   This is a measure of after-tax income adjusted for inflation. It is a broad measure of the amount of money that the citizens of a society have in order to purchase goods and services. Exhibit 3.5 shows how real disposable income increased from 1986 to 1999. Per capita disposable income in current dollars increased from about $13,289 per year in 1986 to $23,244 in 1999.

Exhibit 3.6 shows the difference between the earnings of men and women. Notice that the disparity between men's and women's earnings is no longer steadily closing. Women's weekly earnings were about 76 percent of men's in 1999 versus 58 percent in 1979. However, women's earnings were about 88 percent of men's in 1996. In recent years, both men's and women's earnings have been increasing. One reason for this has been the low unemployment rate.

Technological Forces   Technological forces are the next societal forces we examine. These forces have a major influence on the formulation of overall and human resource

EXHIBIT 3.3 **GDP GROWTH IN THE UNITED STATES**

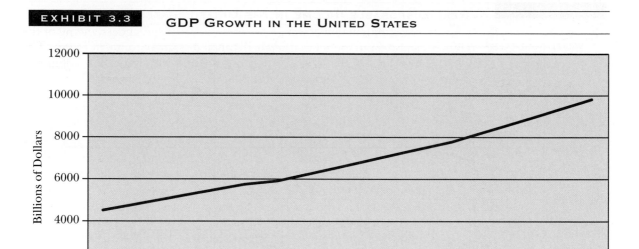

Year

* Year 2000 figure is average of first 2 quarters.

SOURCE: "National Income and Product Accounts," Bureau of Economic Analysis, August 2000.

EXHIBIT 3.4 **CPI 12-MONTH CHANGES, 1987–2000**

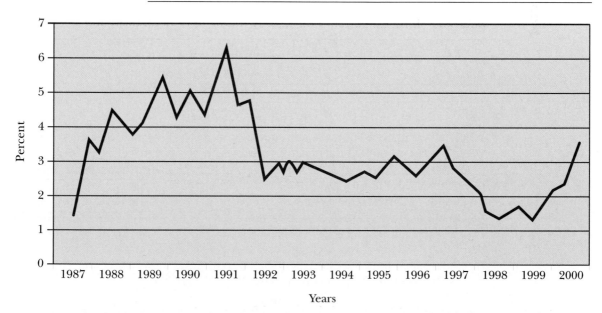

Years

SOURCE: U.S. Department of Labor, Bureau of Labor Statistics, October 2000.

REAL DISPOSABLE INCOME IN THE UNITED STATES

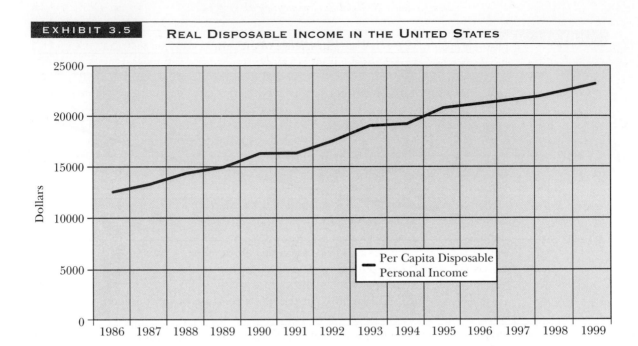

SOURCE: "Survey of Current Business," Bureau of Economic Analysis, April 2000.

MEN EARN MORE; WOMEN EARN LESS

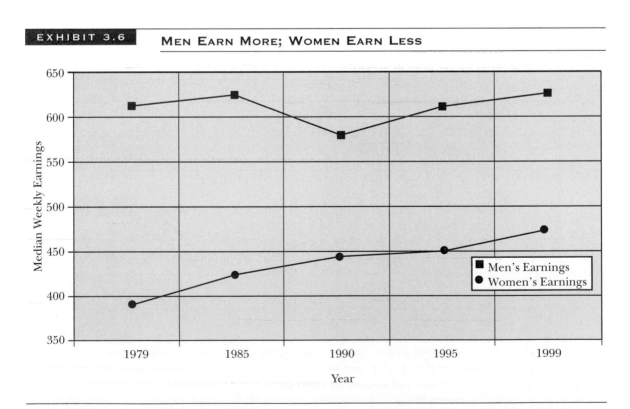

SOURCE: "Highlights of Women's Earnings in 1999," U.S. Department of Labor Statistics, Bureau of Labor Statistics, Report 943, May 2000.

strategy. Technology is the art and science of the production and distribution of goods and services.[5] Technological advances can be reflected in the product itself or in the processes used to design, manufacture, and distribute the product or service. Technology also has a substantial impact on the design of jobs in an organization—a critical human resource issue. It also has a major impact on the demand for products and services produced by companies. Finally, improved technology has led to improved productivity, which has led to wage increases throughout the economy.

The most significant technological advance over the last 25 years affecting employment has been the revolution in information handling brought on by the computer, including the personal computer. The computer has allowed much quicker access to and processing of information and has upgraded job requirements for most clerical and staff assistant jobs. In the book *In the Age of the Smart Machine*, Shoshana Zuboff argues that the effects of the computer have yet to be felt because work itself will change completely as information becomes more readily available right at the workstation.[6] Computers have also spawned robotics—the use of computer-controlled machines—in such diverse areas as welding in auto assembly and forming in steel production. For example, at the Chicago Heights Ford stamping plant, robotic welders and other automated computer-controlled processes reduced the labor force by more than half (from over 1400 people to about 600 employees) over the 1981-98 period. Robotics has led to the development of **artificial intelligence**—the use of computers to simulate the knowledge and thinking patterns of experts. In addition, technology has spread to the service industry, giving rise to automated hotels. While this trend has spread in Europe, it is unlikely that it will threaten human employees in the United States because human labor proves to be much more affordable than automated hotel service.[7]

Other significant technological advances include superconductivity, genetic engineering, fiber optics, and microelectronics. **Superconductivity** refers to transmitting electricity at almost zero resistance. This will revolutionize electrical transmission from power lines to electrical circuitry in computers. **Genetic engineering** refers to artificially changing the DNA molecule in genes to change biological characteristics. **Fiber optics** allows the transmission of data, voices, pictures, or other types of information along a light beam (laser). Finally, microelectronics will result in even smaller computers, new artificial organs, and many other developments in electronics for which space is a limitation.

Technology is changing rapidly, and monitoring and predicting this change is a strategic challenge for all organizations. The development of new products that are not obsolete before they hit the market requires systematic attention to this sector of the external environment. Today, U.S. companies find themselves competing with the advanced minds of scientists and innovators both nationwide and abroad. While rapidly changing technology has many positive effects, it also makes current employee skills obsolete. Training and development become even more critical to ensure that employees have the desired skills to be productive.

Legal and Political Forces The legal and political forces affect each of the elements in the task environment. In fact, probably no other sector of the external environment has had a greater affect on human resource management than the changes in the legal environment over the past 60 years. Legislation has been passed covering virtually every aspect of the employment relationship from hiring to firing. We will discuss major laws and significant court cases as we review key issues in human resource management in the following chapters, particularly in Chapter 5.

artificial intelligence The use of computers to simulate the knowledge and thinking patterns of experts.

superconductivity Transmission of electricity at almost zero resistance.

genetic engineering Artificially changing the DNA molecule in genes to alter biological characteristics.

fiber optics The transmission of data, voice, pictures, or other types of information along a light beam (laser).

The legal environment provides a complex web of rules that very much constrains and specifies what can be done legally in human resource management. These laws developed because of abuses in the labor market: misuse of child labor, sexual harassment, lack of protection against injury, layoff for old age and disability, and systematic discrimination of groups, which resulted in extreme poverty. We sometimes forget the abuses that spawned the plethora of laws related to employment and human resources.

Because of the complexity of the law and the frequency of changing interpretations resulting from court cases and administrative rule making, wise managers rely on legal advice from an attorney when questions arise. In this text, we cover the basics with which most managers should be familiar, but our intent is not to train managers to be attorneys in employment law.

The political aspect of this sector refers to the political processes and mood of the nation, which has ebbed and flowed from conservative to liberal throughout its history. In recent history, the relatively liberal presidential years of Kennedy/Johnson in the 1960s were followed by the conservative years of Nixon, Ford, and Reagan in the 1970s and 1980s. Even the Carter and Clinton administrations are viewed as having been somewhat conservative.

Under the more conservative political climate, especially under Reagan in the 1980s, the enforcement of antitrust laws were not as stringent as they had been previously. Hence, the 1980s saw many takeovers and mergers—a favorite corporate strategy of that decade. Deregulation in the early 1990s, especially in the banking system, encouraged new strategies. The strategy of corporate spin-offs, which proliferated in the early 1990s, was already being replaced by another round of mergers and acquisitions at the end of the decade. Political trends are closely related to sociocultural and demographic trends in that politics is largely shaped by the character and mood of the people of a society. This is the next sector we will examine.

Sociocultural and Demographic Forces   This sector of the environment refers to social and demographic characteristics that make up a society. It includes the society's cultural values, norms, and institutions as well as its physical characteristics of age, sex, and geographic breakdowns. Lifestyle issues are also part of this sector. These forces relate to the ways people think and react, relate to one another, and live their lives. Obviously, these sociocultural and demographic characteristics affect business in general and particular businesses through elements in the task environment, such as customers and the labor force. For example, the increased number of working mothers in U.S. society has increased the concern about and demand for quality day-care facilities for young children. Yet other values in today's society have remained constant over the past 30 years, such as the average workweek. Statistics show that the average U.S. workweek has remained relatively constant at 39.5 hours a week as compared with the averages in 1989 and 1967.[8]

In general, the U.S. population is becoming older and more urban. The most significant population trend of this century has been the baby boom generation born after World War II. As this group ages, the median age of the population will age and lifestyles will change. In 1970, the median age was 28.0. By 1997 it was 35, and it is projected to be 37.3 by 2030. In fact, recent reports project over 20 percent of the U.S. population will be over age 65 by the year 2050. Projections are equally high for this age group in the European Union (28 percent) and Japan (31 percent).[9]

Total U.S. population is expected to increase to 295,009,000 by 2008 from 276,059,000 in 2000.[10] Overall population growth and regional migration have an overall impact on strategy formulation. Labor force composition is driven by population characteristics: age and geographic distribution, growth, and so on. These factors very much affect corporate and human resource strategy.

For example, many companies have moved operations and headquarters to the Sunbelt. A growing labor force, low interest in unions, space, lower taxes, better climate, and lower wage rates have been factors in this movement. The movement feeds on itself. As companies move, so do people. Many families left sections in the upper Midwest and Northeast to find jobs in California, Texas, Florida, Arizona, North Carolina, and other Sunbelt states. However, this trend may be changing with resurging employment opportunities in the Midwestern United States.[11]

The aging population extends worldwide. In 1990, 18 percent of the population in the OECD (Organization for Economic Development), which includes most industrialized nations, was over the age of 60. By the year 2030 that number is projected to be 30 percent. In Latin America and Asia, the percent of population over 60 is expected to double to 14 percent by 2030.[12]

Task Environment Forces

Labor Market The nature of the labor market, including its members' abilities, attitudes, knowledge level, preferred work, and special needs and demands, is determined by all of the elements of the societal environment. Currently, we are seeing special demographic and economic changes that are especially important in shaping the nature of the workforce today and in the next few years. We pay special attention to these changes in this section.

The labor market is a very important factor in determining human resource strategy. The labor market is the configuration of individuals working or available for employment in a particular geographic region—whether a nation, region, state, or local area. Four key measures of the labor market will be examined: unemployment rate, education levels, occupation levels, and the age and gender mix.

Unemployment Rate The unemployment rate measures the number or percentage of people looking for work but unable to find it. It does not measure people not working but *not* looking for work (stay-at-home parents, retirees, and students, for example). These people are simply considered as being "out of the labor force."[13]

Exhibit 3.7A shows the U.S. unemployment rate, whereas Exhibit 3.7B illustrates a comparison of international unemployment rates. Note also in Exhibit 3.7C that the rate for African-Americans has been more than twice that of white people. Exhibit 3.7D shows that the rate for teenagers has been three times as high as the general rule. Of course, during periods of low unemployment, it is often difficult to attract and retain employees.[14]

Education Levels The education level of the U.S. labor force is shown in Exhibit 3.8. Workers with college degrees earn about twice that of those with a high school education.

Occupational Levels The U.S. labor force now includes more white-collar and professional jobs and fewer blue-collar and laborer jobs than in the past (Exhibit 3.9). Notice also the increase in employment in the service industries shown in Exhibit 3.10. With respect to specific occupations, the largest single job percentage climb throughout the first decade of the new millennium is expected to be for computer

EXHIBIT 3.7A   UNITED STATES UNEMPLOYMENT RATES, 1987–2000

Year

* Year 2000 figure is average of first 10 months

SOURCE: U.S. Department of Labor, Bureau of Labor Statistics, November 2000.

EXHIBIT 3.7B   INTERNATIONAL UNEMPLOYMENT RATES, 1987–1999

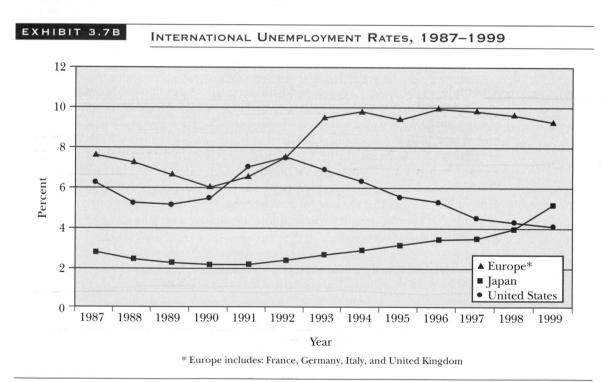

Year

* Europe includes: France, Germany, Italy, and United Kingdom

SOURCE: **www.bls.gov/pub/special.requests/ForeignLabor/flsjec.txt**.

EXHIBIT 3.7C   UNEMPLOYMENT COMPARISON BY RACE

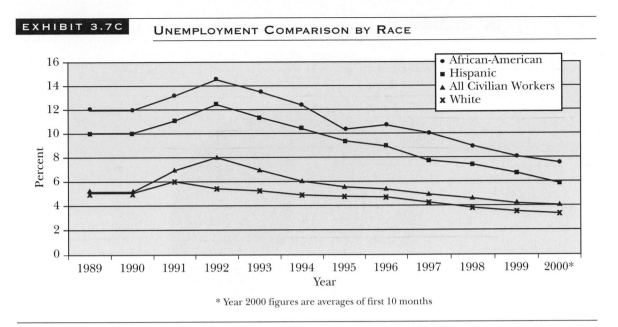

* Year 2000 figures are averages of first 10 months

SOURCE: U.S. Department of Labor, Bureau of Labor Statistics, November 2000.

EXHIBIT 3.7D   UNEMPLOYMENT COMPARISON BY AGE

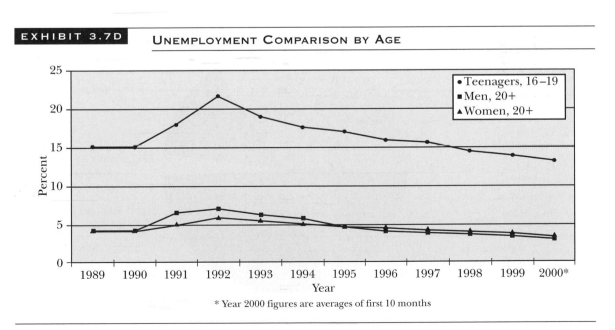

* Year 2000 figures are averages of first 10 months

SOURCE: U.S. Department of Labor, Bureau of Labor Statistics, November 2000.

EDUCATION LEVELS OF THE U.S. LABOR FORCE, 2000*

*AVERAGE OF FIRST 3 QUARTERS IN 2000

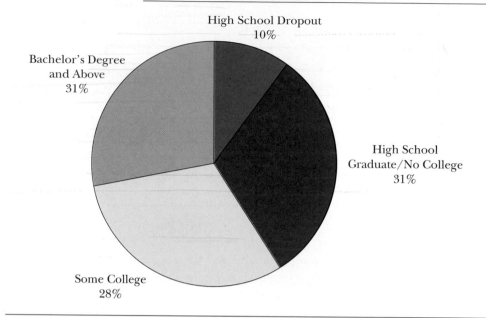

SOURCE: www.bls.gov/pub/special.requests/lf/cpseed3.txt.

EMPLOYMENT BY OCCUPATIONAL GROUP

PERCENTAGE DISTRIBUTION OF EMPLOYED BY MAJOR OCCUPATIONAL CATEGORY, 1998

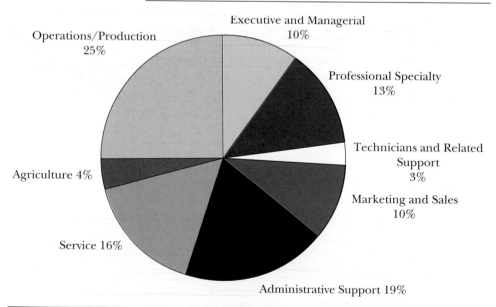

SOURCE: www.slats.bls.gov/news.release/ecopro.t02.htm.

EXHIBIT 3.9B

EMPLOYMENT BY OCCUPATIONAL GROUP
PERCENTAGE DISTRIBUTION OF EMPLOYED BY MAJOR OCCUPATIONAL CATEGORY, PROJECTED 2008

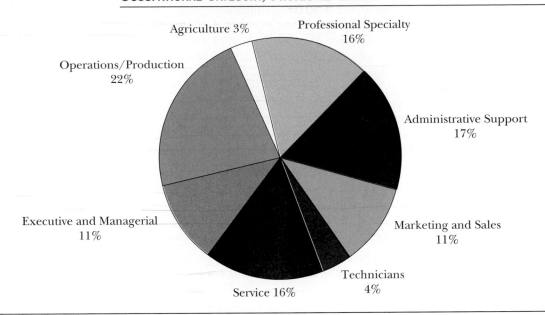

Agriculture 3%

Professional Specialty 16%

Operations/Production 22%

Administrative Support 17%

Executive and Managerial 11%

Marketing and Sales 11%

Technicians 4%

Service 16%

SOURCE: www.slats.bls.gov/news.release/ecopro.t02.htm.

EXHIBIT 3.10

EMPLOYEES IN THREE MAJOR SECTORS, 1950–2000
SERVICE-PRODUCING EMPLOYMENT SURGES IN THE U.S. LABOR FORCE

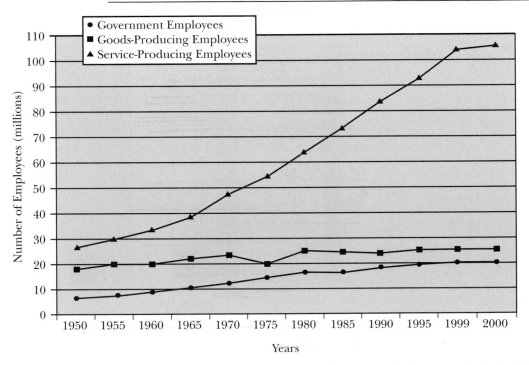

SOURCE: U.S. Department of Labor, Bureau of Labor Statistics, November 2000.

systems analysts. With respect to an occupational field, computer-related professions will grow the most, followed by healthcare.[15]

Age, Race, and Gender Mix   As Exhibits 3.11A and B show, more female employees and older employees are part of the labor force than in the past. Exhibits 3.11A, B, and C also show how the composition of the labor force is projected to change beyond the year 2000. As illustrated in Exhibit 3.11D, the Hispanic population of the United States will increase dramatically in the future.[16]

Labor Force 2001: What Does it Look Like?

The baby boomer generation—those people born between 1946 and 1964—produced millions of new participants in the workforce. This large and comparatively homogenous group of workers made business employment decisions less complex. Now the baby boomers are reaching middle age, and businesses must adapt to the changes in the work force to remain competitive in the new millennium. Winston Wood notes some interesting changes in the job market as a result:

> The economy continues to shift toward high technology, but a coming wave of baby-boomer retirements also will boost demand for more traditional

EXHIBIT 3.11A	SEX AND RACE OF THE LABOR FORCE PROJECTED TO 2008

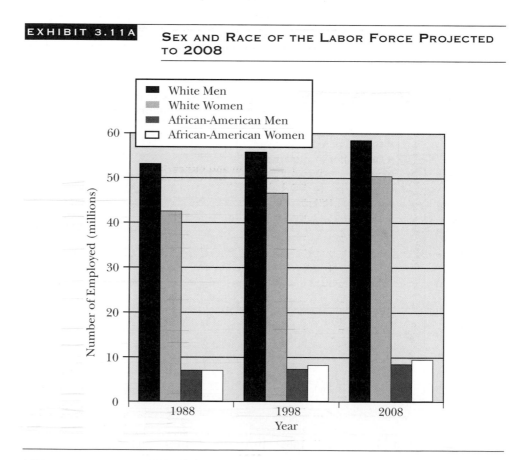

SOURCE: **www.stats.bls.gov/empl/1986.htm**.

EXHIBIT 3.11B   AGE OF THE LABOR FORCE PROJECTED TO 2015

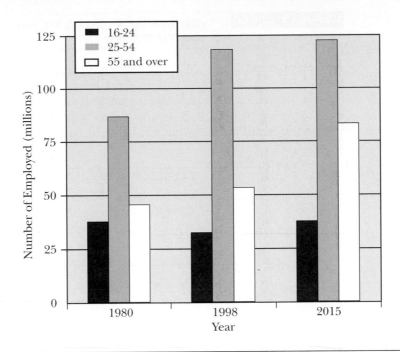

SOURCE: Howard N. Fullerton, Jr., "Labor force participation: 75 years of change, 1950–98 and 1998–2025," *Monthly Labor Review*, December 1999, p. 3–12.

EXHIBIT 3.11C   RACE OF THE LABOR FORCE PROJECTED TO 2015

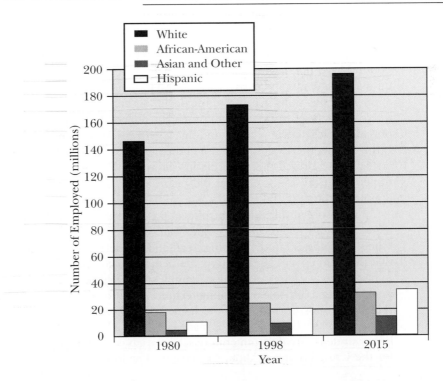

SOURCE: Howard N. Fullerton, Jr., "Labor force participation: 75 years of change, 1950–98 and 1998–2025," *Monthly Labor Review*, December 1999, p. 3–12.

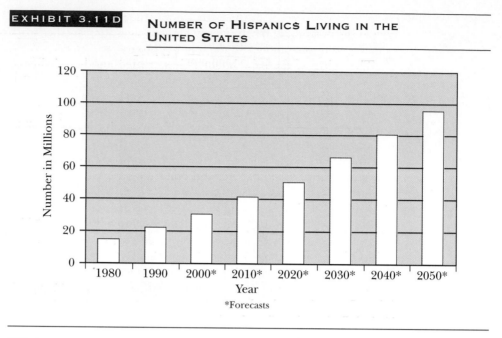

EXHIBIT 3.11D   NUMBER OF HISPANICS LIVING IN THE UNITED STATES

SOURCE: Carla Joinson, "Strength in Numbers?" *HRMagazine*, November, 2000, p. 43–49; U.S. Bureau of the Census.

skills. The Bureau of Labor Statistics predicts employers will replace about 25 percent more retirees between 2003 and 2008 than they did between 1993 and 1998. Demand will be greatest for secretaries, drivers of heavy trucks, elementary-school teachers, and industrial engineers.[17]

One of the greatest challenges that businesses face is the fact that the baby boomers are not having children of their own or are postponing having children until their late 30s and early 40s. As a result, many businesses will have trouble filling entry-level positions because of the declining number of new workers. However, demographers have an eye on California. It seems that California is a proven bellwether of national legislative change, and this may translate into population changes as well. If this is true, there could be a rise in the number of births. Currently, one of every six births in the United States occurs in California. While the state still faces a shortage of people in the 15- to 24-year-old range, it appears that this population will almost double by the year 2040.[18]

This problem of filling entry-level positions is made worse because jobs are demanding more technical skills. The time when a worker could survive with a high school diploma is rapidly coming to an end. More and more businesses are requiring that their employees have writing, mathematical, computer, and other advanced skills to be able to work in today's more complex business environment.[19] Businesses are already having a difficult time filling technical positions (such as computer technicians), skilled/craft positions (such as mechanics and carpenters), and even basic unskilled labor positions.[20] This problem is made even worse by the fact that an increasing number of students are dropping out of school each year. The high school graduation rate for the United States is about 68 percent. The lowest level is found in the Southeast where only 65 percent of the high school students receive degrees.[21] Businesses are now in the position of having to pay higher wages for a smaller work pool and having to invest additional money in job training programs.

The aging of the baby boomers has created another challenge. The workforce that was once predominantly white, male, and middle class is reflecting more diversity. The 1960s and 1970s saw the entry of more women into the workplace. Many today are waiting until they reach their 30s and 40s before they have their first child.[22] Consequently, businesses must cope with maternity leaves, flexible work schedules, and single mothers.

The 1980s began the great wave of minority entries into the workforce. The Americans with Disabilities Act and other factors have urged and inspired physically and mentally challenged individuals to participate more in the workforce. This trend, which is expected to last well into the 21st century, also presents challenges for businesses. As explained in Chapter 5, firms must provide a "reasonable accommodation" for individuals who are physically and mentally challenged. This could mean restructuring jobs in some cases so that these individuals can perform them. From 1998 to 2008, the labor force for women is expected to grow by 15 percent as compared to 10 percent for men. During this same period, all minority labor forces (African-American, Asian, Hispanic, and other) are projected to grow faster than that of whites.[23] *Nation's Business* describes the challenge this way:

> Little by little, senior executives and management experts across America are recognizing that these vast demographic shifts demand a new way of running things—an approach often called **"managing diversity."** This means recognizing that diversity is already a fact of life, learning to understand "culturally different" workers, and creating an environment in which they will flourish.[24]

managing diversity Learning to understand cultural and other differences among workers and creating an environment in which they will be productive.

We address this issue in Chapter 5 and in other sections of the text as appropriate. The increasing number of foreigners settling in the United States is a factor in the impact of cultural diversity on the workplace. In October 1991, a law went into effect that raised the number of legal immigrants entering the United States annually to 700,000. Not only do these new Americans make the workplace more culturally diverse, but they also tend to lower the education level.

All of these changing demographic patterns affect the way firms operate. Old methods and traditions are rapidly becoming obsolete. Business managers must be aware of and adapt to these trends if they wish to succeed in the coming years.

Managers must also consider the very real possibility that the company's products or services could be produced overseas. The trend toward globalization has compelled many managers to learn to deal with distinctly different cultures, norms, practices, and attitudes. The human resources directors of large multinational companies must become well versed in the differing customs and beliefs among various cultures, including such factors as motivation, leadership, interpersonal and interfirm competition, creativity and innovation, daily habits and hygiene, and commitment to the organization. Globalization and diversity should continue to be the key challenge that managers face at the beginning of the 21st century.

Competition

The strategies and practices of competitors have a major direct impact on strategy formulation. If a company discovers that its competitor pays higher wages for similar jobs, the company must decide to match or exceed those wage rates if it expects to attract and retain a productive workforce.

Other strategies of competitors can set the overall level of business for a particular firm. For example, even though Apple Computer has experienced tremendous growth since its founding, it faced major competition when IBM entered the personal computer market in the mid 1980s. IBM is a formidable competitor and initially had an adverse effect on Apple. Apple hired John Scully from PepsiCo as its CEO to design a new corporate and marketing strategy and has rebounded nicely. During the late 1980s and early 1990s, Apple prospered while IBM suffered declines and cutbacks. By the middle 1990s, Compaq, Dell, and other competitors added to the growing personal computer market, and Apple suffered major cutbacks once again.

Competitive factors have always been a major force in strategy formulation, but they took on renewed importance during the early 1980s when the United States experienced its worst recession since the depression of the 1930s. Michael Porter's book *Competitive Strategy* set the tone for the new competitiveness.[25] He presents a model for analyzing the competitive environment, which is shown in Exhibit 3.12. Note that this model considers all relevant aspects of competition from specific competitive actions to substitute products. Essentially, Porter's model indicates that four major factors determine the competitive arena for an industry. These are (1) the potential new entrants into the marketplace, (2) the firm's customers, (3) the actions of various suppliers, and (4) the availability of substitutes for the firm's products. Each of these forces interacts with the others in a dynamic fashion to establish a certain level and type of competition.

For example, the competitive arena of the auto industry is much different than that of the restaurant industry because each of the four major forces at work are so different. Compared with the restaurant industry, the auto industry has few substitute products, few potential new entrants, a rather limited set of suppliers, and customers who make infrequent purchases.

In Chapter 2, we saw how overall corporate strategy formulation affects human resource strategy. We can summarize the competitive arena by noting two major trends. First, competition has become global in many markets, especially consumer electronics and computers, steel, and automobiles. No longer can U.S. firms ignore the strong competition that comes from other countries, especially Germany, Japan, Taiwan, and Korea. Second, U.S. firms experienced a major acquisition binge during the 1980s and 1990s, as we have indicated previously. This series of acquisitions and mergers involved both foreign firms and domestic firms and has served to consolidate the power of many into the hands of a few in many domestic industry sectors. The strategy of acquisition and takeover has been a consistent one during the 1980s and 1990s and has caused firms to design both offensive and defensive competitive takeover strategies. In particular, the *hostile* takeover has been troublesome for many firms. We will examine this in the last chapter of the text.

Market (Customer/Clients)

Another major sector of the task environment that affects strategy formulation is the market. There is no question that the market and industry characteristics drive much of the corporate strategy. This environmental sector is closely related to competition because competitive forces interplay within specific markets. But the sector goes beyond competition. For example, the market itself presents a set of challenges for a

EXHIBIT 3.12 PORTER'S FORCES OF COMPETITION MODEL

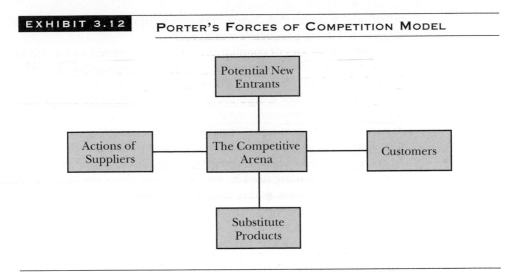

SOURCE: Adapted from Michael E. Porter, "How Competitive Forces Shape Strategy," *Harvard Business Review* 57, no. 2 (March–April 1979), p. 141.

firm, and the firm must know the answers to these questions, among others, concerning the market:

1. Who exactly is the customer?
2. Do we have several distinct customer groups?
3. How shall we define our market(s)?
4. Of what industry and market characteristics must we be aware?
5. How are our market and customers changing?
6. What does it take to be successful in our market(s)?
7. What wage and employment patterns exist in our market(s)?

Developing precise, accurate answers to these questions is critical for successful strategy formulation.

Global Business Environment

Now, let's turn our attention to the global business environment. This environment has had a major impact on human resources, especially during the 1980s and 1990s.

The global business environment has changed dramatically since the end of World War II in 1945. The United States became the world's economic superpower as a result of the war, which destroyed the economies of Great Britain, France, Italy, Germany, and Japan. These nations had to rely on U.S. aid to rebuild. However, these nations began to reassert their industrial might and challenged the U.S. economic supremacy during the 1970s. Traditional U.S. products, such as electronics, steel, automobiles, and heavy machinery, faced stiff foreign competition. The 1980s produced more competition with the rise of newly industrialized countries, such as South Korea, Singapore, and Taiwan.[26] Recent moves by China to improve its industrialization status pose a particularly interesting threat (or opportunity) because of the immense size of the Chinese population and economy.

Some of the most sweeping changes have occurred and continue to occur in the new commonwealth of independent states (the former Soviet Union). Maps became out-of-date overnight as yet another republic announced its freedom. As these new republics acquired their independence, they began to realize that they were not able to become economically stable on their own. Foreign investment and joint ventures have begun. AT&T sold a digital switching system directly to the Armenian government, bypassing Moscow for the first time. Chevron, Amoco, and Mobil Oil have reached an agreement in cooperating with Russia to gain access to the huge Tenghiz oil field. Some firms are waiting until Russia and the republics establish an effective credit and banking infrastructure at the republic level so that the ruble can regain some value. Joint U.S.-Russian efforts have been implemented recently to encourage investment in the Russian market.[27]

The formation of the European Union in the late 1990s and the introduction of their common currency, the Euro, in 1999 have significantly affected the global market. In 1997, the union accounted for over 30 percent of the world's output versus the United States' 27 percent.[28] With the advent of the union, internal trade barriers between countries are being eliminated. This event is a response to the loss of competitive position to other world economic powers. The union, designed to be like the United States, will have many challenges as it attempts to reduce the social welfare programs that the European populations have come to expect. The union faces further challenges in attempting to strengthen and stabilize the Euro.

The changes that occurred over the past few years have resulted in an increasingly complex global business environment and vastly expanded markets. Not only are foreign firms building plants and doing business in the United States, but U.S. firms are operating overseas as well. General Motors, Ford, Xerox, and Texaco all have international subsidiaries big enough to be included in the list of the 500 largest corporations outside the United States.[29] *Fortune* magazine now provides a ranking of the top 500 global firms in addition to its *Fortune* 500 list. Clearly, organizations now compete in a global economy.[30]

Japan has even surpassed the United States in terms of market value of its largest firms. As shown in Exhibit 3.13, the 15 largest industrial firms in the world in terms of market value in 1999 included 7 Japanese firms, 5 U.S. firms, and 3 European firms.[31] The U.S. is no longer the only market in the world.

There has been some debate in recent years as to how U.S. workers currently compare with foreign workers in such measures as productivity and costs. Critics of U.S. workers have found that foreign workers are less costly and more productive.[32] Pessimists have called Americans lazy, unskilled, expensive, and even greedy. Many companies have moved their manufacturing operations to countries where manual, low-wage labor is extremely cheap. On the other hand, compensation (for example, wages and benefits) in the United States has been lower than that in many other industrialized countries. Nonetheless, as shown in Exhibit 3.14, a 2000 report notes that from 1997 to 1999, U.S. compensation costs increased while most countries' compensation costs decreased. This shift in labor costs indicates an increasingly competitive global labor market.[33]

These figures do not, however, tell the whole story. Other data provide a more favorable image of the average U.S. worker. First, when Americans are compared with

EXHIBIT 3.13

1999	1998	Company	Country	Revenue in Millions of Dollars	% Change	Profit	% Change	Assets
1	1	General Motors	U.S.	$176,558.00	9.4	$ 6,002.00	103	$273,921.00
2	4	Wal-Mart	U.S.	$166,809.00	19.8	$ 5,377.00	21.4	$ 70,245.00
3	8	Exxon Mobil	U.S.	$163,881.00	62.8	$ 7,910.00	24.2	$144,521.00
4	3	Ford Motor	U.S.	$162,558.00	12.6	$ 7,237.00	−67.2	$276,229.00
5	2	DaimlerChrysler	Germany	$159,986.00	3.5	$ 6,129.10	8.4	$ 36,142.90
6	5	Mitsui	Japan	$118,555.00	8.4	$ 320.50	37.5	$ 62,360.00
7	7	Mitsubishi	Japan	$117,766.00	9.9	$ 233.70	−4.2	$ 78,949.20
8	10	Toyota Motor	Japan	$115,671.00	16	$ 3,653.40	31.1	$160,572.00
9	9	General Electric	U.S.	$111,630.00	11.1	$10,717.00	15.3	$405,200.00
10	6	Itochu	Japan	$109,069.00	0.3	$ (792.80)	n/a	$ 59,153.90
11	11	Royal Dutch/ Shell Group	Britain/Neth	$105,366.00	12.5	$ 8,584.00	2352.6	$113,883.00
12	13	Sumitomo	Japan	$ 95,701.60	7.5	$ 314.90	n/a	$ 47,819.80
13	18	Nippon Telegraph and Telephone	Japan	$ 93,591.70	22.9	$ (609.00)	2112.9	$179,512.00
14	12	Marubeni	Japan	$ 91,807.40	−1.9	$ 18.50	n/a	$ 54,446.90
15	15	AXA	France	$ 87,645.70	11.3	$ 2,155.80	26.6	$508,647.00

SOURCE: **www.fortune.com/fortune/global500/**.

EXHIBIT 3.14   HOURLY COMPENSATION FOR PRODUCTION WORKERS IN MANUFACTURING, IN U.S. DOLLARS

Country	1997	1999
Germany	26.84	26.18
Japan	19.54	20.89
France	17.99	17.98
U.S.	18.27	19.20
Korea	7.86	6.71
Taiwan	5.90	5.62
Italy	17.57	16.60
Mexico	1.84	2.12

SOURCE: U.S. Department of Labor, Bureau of Labor Statistics, September 2000.

Japanese and European workers (Exhibit 3.15), U.S. workers do not seem quite so expensive. In fact, when one considers that U.S. productivity is among the highest in the world, higher costs for workers may not seem so problematic. Actually, U.S. production rates overall have been on the rise since the mid 1990s. According to a report issued in fall 2000,[34] this increase in productivity has not been matched in most foreign

EXHIBIT 3.15

HOURLY COMPENSATION RATES
JAPAN IS NO. 1 (IN LABOR COSTS IN 1999)

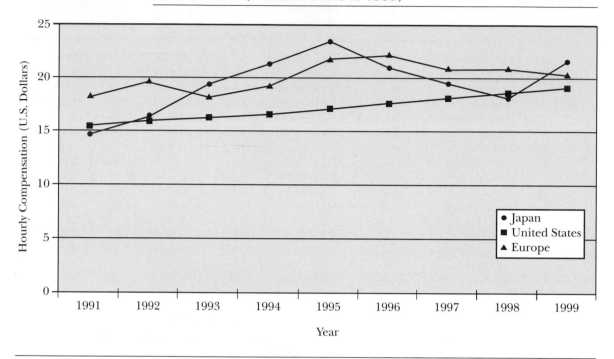

SOURCE: U.S. Department of Labor, Bureau of Labor Statistics, September 2000.

industrial nations. Furthermore, U.S. labor costs have decreased even though levels of productivity would seem to justify increases in compensation.[35] Some feel these changes are due to technological advancement that has spread more quickly throughout the United States than in other foreign nations. Others assert that the increase in U.S. productivity reflects the booming state of the economy.[36] It is most likely a combination of these factors that has contributed to these increases. However, as technology spreads through foreign industrial countries and economic growth in the United States wanes, it is likely that productivity growth will slow in the United States while it increases in other nations.

The 1990s proved the importance of the international sector, which has been more significant in the 1990s and will continue to be as the world economy develops further. This expansion of the international sector presents new *opportunities* for firms, but it also presents new *threats*. As a result, each firm must consider many issues when deciding whether to operate in the global business environment.

Causes of Increased Global Business

Why do firms choose to operate overseas? As our preceding discussion noted, one of the most common reasons is the desire to *reduce costs*. By locating plants abroad, firms can be closer to their supply of raw materials. This step eliminates the need for expensive transportation, insurance, and administration costs. The availability of inexpensive labor abroad also reduces costs. Labor costs in the United States are affected by more than minimum wage, overtime laws, and labor contracts. Taxes, such as social security, unemployment, and worker's compensation, and employee perquisites add to labor costs. In contrast, many nations do not have or enforce wage laws, and labor unions and perquisites are often small or nonexistent. As a result, firms can significantly reduce their labor costs by establishing plants overseas. Finally, costs can be reduced by building semifinished goods abroad. By producing most of an item abroad, especially labor-intensive products, firms can drive costs below domestic costs. To prosper, global firms must invest wherever opportunity is the greatest, whether that means the United States, Mexico, South Korea, or Japan.[37]

Firms will choose to locate abroad because of *less government regulation* in other countries. Two of the most common factors are pollution controls and safety requirements placed on firms. Plant emission controls, OSHA safety requirements, waste disposal, and many other pollution and safety laws increase the costs of doing business in the United States. These requirements may not exist or are waived in other countries, especially in those that are trying to attract new business.

Locating abroad can enable firms to be closer to their product markets. This cuts transportation costs and helps firms to learn the unique characteristics of each market. Such was the case for BMW, which located a new plant in South Carolina, and Mercedes-Benz, which located in Alabama. Locating near the expansive U.S. market was an important factor in BMW's decision to make the move. Other elements BMW considered included the perceived quality of the U.S. workforce and tax and other incentives. Tax and utility benefits offered to the German automaker, along with the strength of the German currency, make the South Carolina plant approximately 20 percent less expensive than the company's Bavarian plants.[38] (See the case at the end of the chapter for more on German companies locating in the Carolinas.)

The international sector can provide access to growth opportunities that are not available at home. Several U.S. banks and stockbrokerages operate subsidiaries in Tokyo to be near the world's largest securities market, which is nearly three times larger than the New York Stock Exchange. So far the results have been mixed. U.S. competitors started off on shaky ground in the mid 1990s. However, after the Asian market plunged in 1996 and 1997, companies such as Citibank made significant gains in the Japanese market, where local customers were driven to bring their business to a stable Western bank. Today, several U.S. banking and brokerage firms, such as Merrill Lynch and Charles Schwab, maintain a strong presence in Japan and are seeking to expand into retail securities. Many anticipate resistance from the Japanese market as this expanse into retail securities develops; however, the huge earning potential of this market continues to attract foreign corporate investment.[39] As John Wadsworth of Morgan Stanley's Tokyo office said in the late 1980s, "The opportunities here are huge."[40] Such opportunities continue to characterize the Japanese market of the new millennium.

Firms also locate facilities abroad to take advantage of labor force quantity and quality. It is not difficult to find areas where the people want to work and where the local government wants foreign firms there to put its people to work. While the labor quantity may be abundant, there can also be problems with quality. Some nations, such as South Korea and Singapore, have an educated and skilled workforce. In other nations some workers, such as farmers migrating to the cities, often lack the basic skills needed for jobs in factories.[41]

Many firms will locate facilities overseas to *avoid or reduce trade and tariff barrier problems.* Japanese automobile manufacturers have been abiding by a self-imposed export quota to the United States since the mid 1980s to avoid potential tariff problems with the U.S. government. This quota does not apply to Japanese cars built in the United States, however. As a result, more and more Toyotas, Hondas, Mazdas, and Nissans are being built in Georgetown, Kentucky; Marysville, Ohio; Flat Rock, Michigan; and Smyrna, Tennessee.[42] These Japanese automobile manufacturers have risen to the top of the American market in productivity and account for a significant portion of sales in the U.S. market. The well-known Harbour Report consistently ranks Japanese manufacturers at the top of the North American auto industry in efficiency and productivity.[43]

In fact, a number of countries have made great efforts recently to establish agreements that limit such tariffs and trade barriers. For example, most of Western Europe is currently considered a free economic trade area, or economic community, with very few tariffs and other restrictions applying to trade across these borders. The unification of currency establishing the Euro has further integrated the European community. In 1993, an interesting debate in the U.S. Congress preceded ratification of the North American Free Trade Agreement (NAFTA), which eliminated many of the problematic trade restrictions hindering trade among the three major North American countries (United States, Canada, and Mexico). Many of the issues discussed previously, such as wage differentials across countries (for example, United States and Mexico) and disparate requirements by the various governments concerning environmental protection, were at the center of the debate on this agreement.

A more far-reaching agreement, known as the General Agreement on Tariffs and Trade (GATT), was approved in 1995. This agreement paved the road to eliminate even more of the hindrances to free trade worldwide.

Improved transportation and communication systems, at least with developed countries, have helped increase the number of firms doing business abroad. Markets that were physically inaccessible 20 or 30 years ago are now open as technologies such as satellites, computers, fax machines, container shipping, and air freight are available. Inducements provided by countries to encourage companies to relocate or start an operation overseas have also led to increased international business. Nations are willing to provide these inducements, often in the form of tax breaks or cheap loans for new plants, to obtain the jobs and foreign exchange created by new business activity.[44]

Important Global Business Arenas

Pacific Rim   In their book *Megatrends 2000,* John Naisbitt and Patricia Aburdene devote an entire chapter to "The Rise of the Pacific Rim." Leveraging both massive labor pools and technology-driven economies, the countries of the Pacific Rim are experiencing the fastest period of economic expansion in history. In the early 1990s, they grew at a rate five times the growth rate during the industrial revolution.[45] No one anticipated the sudden halt in growth, however, when during the late 1990s the Asian economy virtually collapsed. This dramatic downward trend in markets began in Thailand and spread quickly throughout the rest of Asia on the coattails of bad investments coming to light and a panicked investment community. After struggling to recover from this setback, the Pacific Rim is now seeking to reestablish its position in the global market.[46]

The "diamond in the rough," however, might be the world giant, China. A recent U.S. Commerce Department study noted that China's total annual imports are expected to grow by slightly less than $500 billion by 2010. There is little doubt that the absolutely huge population and newly expressed desire to open relations with the world will lead China into a very active role in world trade. China is currently await-ing the final approval for its membership in the World Trade Organization (WTO).[47] Although China's economy was shaken by the Asian recession of the late 1990s, the Chinese government reported strong economic growth rates during the third quarter of 2000, with export rates increasing by 33.1 percent.[48] In 1997, Hong Kong was transferred from British to Chinese rule. This action has created new opportunities for the world, as well as for China.

The vast majority of the Pacific Rim's human resources are unskilled and semi-skilled workers. These workers are being trained and used in factory settings at a frac-tion of the cost the rest of the world would demand. This has stimulated foreign investment in Asian economies, which has produced a huge need for skilled workers. Countries such as Malaysia and Singapore are responding to this demand by improv-ing educational offerings through schools and new training programs.[49]

In spite of recent economic difficulty, the Pacific Rim continues to be an emerg-ing area for new investment and development. The validity of some analysts' percep-tion of the Pacific Rim as being the world's next economic empire, however, is debatable when compared with the potential for the European community.

Europe   In the 1990s, Europe fell behind the world in business operations. Euro-pean cultures had created large social welfare states that served them well after World War II but have not been efficient on a global basis during the highly competitive decade of the 1990s. In 1992, the process of deregulation in Europe began. The Eu-ropean Union (EU) was formed to meet these challenges. To meet competition, steps towards the competitive model found in the United States are being implemented. As the Euro matures, it is certain to have a continued impact in world markets. Members participating in the common currency are considered part of the European Economic and Monetary Union (EMU). At this time the EMU has 15 participants. All partici-pants are expected to attain certain economic criteria within their countries for ac-ceptance into the EMU.[50]

The removal of most of Europe's internal trade barriers is a great step forward for the economies of European countries, aligning them to effectively compete with Japan and the United States. When all of the trade mechanisms are in place, organizations will be better able to react to changes in consumer needs and desires, resulting in more competition and more choices for the consumer. The prospects for the European Union are bright, however many transitions must be undergone before the benefits of a single European market can be realized. Denmark, for example, is currently strug-gling to balance participation in the European Union with its concern for sovereignty.[51] In the future, steps must be taken toward establishing a balance in order to satisfy the concerns of member governments while preserving the stability of the Union.

In anticipation of the European Union's success, investors initially flocked to the region to get an edge on the future. Thus far, however, the European Union has struggled to attract and maintain this investment. This may be attributed to the re-cent decline of the Euro, as well as some lingering economic rigidity predating the formation of the union.[52] Yet the European Union and the Euro are both young. Un-like the Pacific Rim, the European Community's industrial base is more established, as is its consumer base. This means that *both industrial* and *consumer* industries have more choices for profit in the European Union than currently exist in the Pacific Rim.

The *continued* transition of the European Union into a unified economy means that firms will be forced to compete in an open market without internal barriers. With the unification of the EMU come several implications for human resource management. Organizations will begin to rely more heavily on recruiting people with specific skills, such as a knowledge of the politics, tax, and labor laws of newly targeted countries, and the bilingual or trilingual professionals needed to anchor the ventures.

Mexico   Boasting low labor costs and a large population, Mexico is fertile ground for investment. Mexico is trying to emerge from financial and economic difficulties that began in the early 1990s. In December 1994, Mexico experienced currency devaluation and extreme financial market stress. Inflation and interest rates increased drastically. The United States loaned Mexico money to stabilize this potentially disrupting event in North America. Although Mexico had come a long way in improving its infrastructure and encouraging foreign investment, this was a step back for a developing country.

NAFTA, which took effect on January 1, 1994, increased trade among the United States, Mexico, and Canada by reducing and eventually eliminating existing barriers of trade between countries. Intended to add jobs, improve environmental conditions, and reduce the presence of *maquiladoras*, this trade agreement was initially questioned. *Maquiladoras* are U.S.-owned assembly plants that are host to nearly half a million Mexican workers along the U.S. and Mexican border. However, as Mexico regained economic strength in the late 1990s, foreign investment surged. NAFTA's regulations encouraging foreign companies to establish facilities in Mexico deserve partial credit for this new economic growth.[53]

Although some estimates indicate losses of 600,000 jobs in the United States because of NAFTA, the U.S. Department of Labor has a more conservative measure of 210,000 lost jobs during the 1994-99 period.[54] The number of individuals who actually applied for the "trade adjustment assistance program" could explain the discrepancy. This provision was designed to retrain displaced workers for new jobs. Those who put in for this assistance are considered the lost jobs by the Labor Department; not all unemployed workers pursue this program, and therefore, not all unemployed are counted.

The debate over NAFTA has caused enough concern to delay the most recent extension of free trade to other South American countries, especially Chile. In 1997, President Clinton lost a bid to secure "fast track authority." This action would allow a trade pact to go to Congress for a vote without being subject to amendment. Proponents believe that the growing competition in Latin America from Europe and Asia requires new steps by the United States to further strengthen trade relationships.

Ways Global Business Operations Differ from Domestic Business Operations

Global business operations differ from domestic operations in several ways. Culture is often a key issue in these differences. Each nation has its own custom-value orientations, and problems can easily develop in the global environment. Selecting a manager for an overseas assignment has become increasingly difficult. High failure rates from poorly matched past assignments have increased costs. Thus selecting an expatriate is an important human resource function in today's global businesses.[55] Some managers view an international assignment as a career risk. Overseas employees may miss out on business trends and opportunities at home, not to mention undergo the challenges and strains of living in a distant culture especially when there is a language barrier. However, other managers are returning to the United States after successful tenures overseas to find that they have gained desired skills in the business community. Today,

Mexico's Flourishing Border Industry

Since the implementation of the North American Free Trade Agreement (NAFTA) in 1994, *maquiladoras*, U.S.-owned plants that assemble imported products for export, have multiplied along the U.S.-Mexico border and developed into a major driving force behind Mexico's economic expansion. *Maquiladoras* accounted for $63.9 billion in exports in 1999, a 20 percent increase from 1998, and they comprise one half of Mexico's total sales overseas. Approximately 1.3 million people are employed in these plants, and three of every ten jobs created during President Ernesto Zedillo's six-year term are attributed to *maquiladoras*.

The administration of Vincente Fox plans to transform this border industry. Ernesto Ruffo, Mexico's recently appointed border czar, is looking for ways to, "...make northern industry less labor intensive and more capital oriented." Most *maquiladoras* are assembly-line in nature, which is what the administration of President-elect Fox would like to change.

Ruffo seeks to develop training and education in order to make *maquiladoras* more receptive to manufacturing and claims, "In my region, I saw that better education and training played a very important role in making the jump to manufacturing." A shift in focus to manufacturing in the north will promote the nation's entire economy by permitting labor intensive assembly-line plants to shift to the less economically developed areas of Mexico.

SOURCE: Adapted from Tim Duffy, "Mexico's Border Czar Sees Evolution of *Maquiladoras*," *Dow Jones Newswires*, November 29, 2000.

corporations seek out employees with global experience. The key is to carefully choose your international assignment. A manager must consider the long-term goals of the project, how the company communicates with its overseas staff, and how valuable such staff members are to the company.[56] The global business arena is rapidly changing. Less than 20 years ago, it was hard to comprehend the many differences between two cultures such as Japan and America. The humorous problems Michael Keaton's character faced as an American union leader working in a Japanese-managed automobile factory in the movie *Gung Ho* highlight the real differences that often exist between two cultures. The Japanese custom of strong worker loyalties to their companies contrasts sharply with the sometimes volatile labor-management relationship exemplified by the "Big Three" U.S. automobile manufacturers and the United Auto Workers Union.[57] However, things are changing. The younger Japanese generation—those age 20 to 39 years—seem to want different things than their parents do. They are no longer willing to put their employers' needs and desires ahead of their own. They want two-day weekends and diversions, which were denied to their parents. Some Japanese firms have realized that their employees are different than they used to be and that companies must change to meet the needs of the younger generation. These cultural changes have surfaced in the consumer market as well, where Japanese young adults value individuality and advertisers shape their messages to appeal to this value.[58]

The political environment also differs from nation to nation, and this creates both opportunities and risks for international business. We mentioned earlier the huge potential of the Chinese economy. The 1997 repatriation of Hong Kong added even more influence in world trade. Many U.S. firms started doing business in China as part of the government's drive to build its economy. U.S. products manufactured in

The Underground Economy . . .

Across the great cities of Western Europe, police raids are uncovering illegal factories each week where they find immigrants who work in terrible conditions, including children as young as 11 years old who work as much as 20 hours a day. Many Europeans are simply not aware of the atrocities that thousands of immigrant workers undergo in underground sweatshops each day. In fact, it's hard to contemplate these workplace abuses when Western European laws aggressively protect the rights of their workers with high wages, excellent benefits, and many employer restrictions. However, refugees who seek relief from the poverty they experience in their home countries are not aware of and do not enjoy the benefit from the protection of such laws. Actually, the high standard of wages for European workers may in part fuel the demand for the low labor costs of immigrant workers. In exchange for their escape from destitution, immigrants are forced to become part of an underground work force controlled by mobsters that some are equating to "21st century slavery."

One Chinese immigrant turned to the police for help when his 25-year-old wife, while trying to escape her abusive work environment, was kidnapped. The police traced threatening phone calls made to the husband in order to locate his missing wife, and five days later they freed the raped and beaten woman from the captivity of the Chinese criminals. Sadly, the plight of refugees and their exploitation in sweatshops and factories is not new in the global business arena. Pino Arlachhi, executive director of the U.N. Office for Drug Control & Crime Prevention in Vienna, observes, "It's the fastest-growing criminal market in the world." The United States has been battling this problem for years. Former President Bill Clinton signed a law that raises penalties for criminals who traffic women and children. There are not as many similar sanctions in Europe. Some speculate that European policy makers are hesitant to penalize those who fuel this underground economy because it strengthens the overall economy of Europe and increases its competitiveness.

The economic growth in Prato, a suburb of Florence, has been fueled by illegal immigrant labor. According to Giuseppe Gregori, the General Secretary for the Italian labor union in Prato, "We have the world's leading knitwear industry, with sales of $1.2 billion. It is thanks to the Chinese that this sector has been revitalized." However, Gregori acknowledges that Prato's economic growth depends on a labor force that disregards Italian labor and tax laws. While there are 1100 Chinese factories and shops that are officially registered in the city, officials believe that the actual total is much larger, with a substantial portion (40 percent) of their production underground. There are 8000 legal Chinese workers in Prato, but officials suspect that nearly 4000 illegal Chinese immigrants as well as their children toil in appalling work conditions.

In order to crack down on the trafficking of illegal immigrants, Europe must coordinate police across borders. Criminals who are prosecuted often slip away by fleeing to a neighboring country. If police officers are coordinated across borders, such escapes can be prevented. Better communication among police in the nations of Europe can also alert nations to various criminal gangs that operate such businesses between countries. It is doubtful that the underground economy and transport of illegal immigrants will fade without aggressive policing action across the European Union. Until then, officials reveal that the increased earnings from abused immigrant labor may fuel a new kind of criminal organization. The illegal commerce of trafficking and slave labor has "already cast a dark shadow over 21st century Europe."

SOURCE: Adapted from Gail Edmondson, Kate Carlisle, Karen Nickel Anhalt, and Heidi Dawley, "Workers in Bondage," *Business Week*, November 27, 2000, pp. 147-160.

China include trucks, chemicals, processed foods, appliances, and apparel. But concerns about Chinese human rights practices as well as tensions with Taiwan have caused many to oppose China's entry into the WTO.[59] In the late 1990s, China's lack of respect for U.S. copyrights and patents led to heated debates and nearly an all-out trade war. However, just before the U.S. deadline, an agreement was reached. China promised to outlaw theft of software and agreed to protect patents of agricultural chemicals and pharmaceuticals. In return, Washington decided to lighten its view of trading with China. While problems with piracy persist in China today, the relationship between the United States and China has progressed nonetheless. The U.S. government has come out in support of China's formal entrance into the WTO, which is expected to occur sometime in 2001.[60]

Businesses must also face other political risks. The Iranian revolution of Ayatollah Khomeini not only caused the overthrow of the Shah of Iran but also resulted in the nationalization of U.S. business assets. Khomeini made the United States a scapegoat for many of Iran's problems, and his solutions included the nationalization of assets, the taking of U.S. hostages, and the economic isolation of Iran from the Western world. Only recently have these long-standing economic barriers between the U.S. and Iran started to weaken.[61]

Issues such as bribery also take on international significance. In the United States, bribing a public official is illegal. In many nations, however, bribery is an expected part of doing business with the government. The problem becomes worse when cultural clashes occur. It is still a violation of U.S. law for a U.S. firm to commit bribery, even if the recipient of the bribe is the member of a foreign government. How does a firm compete abroad if it isn't allowed to play by the rules of the host nation?

The global legal environment also differs from the domestic environment. Many firms operate with a mix of expatriate managers and local employees. Laws about responsibility for corporate actions are often more severe in other countries than in the United States. If we also consider the impact of technology in the global business arena, the legal ramifications become even more complicated. Take for example the recent case in which the director of "CompuServe Germany" was held accountable for illegal Internet material that was actually posted by the company's customers. Under German law, the company director was severely fined and given a two-year suspended sentence for circulating obscene material through the Internet. What is protected as "free speech" in the United States is a punishable offense in Germany. Until an international standard has been established, global Internet service providers and all multinational corporations that use the Internet must be conscious of these legal issues and the potential risk and liability to their overseas managerial staff.[62]

The infrastructure of each nation also varies considerably. The state of roads, telephone, water, sewage, and other systems may range from modern to nonexistent. All these systems affect a firm's ability to operate in the global environment. If an operation such as a steel plant requires massive amounts of power, the region must be able to supply power to the plant or it must have adequate roads for transporting fuel to it. If the local government is unwilling or unable to provide these services, the firm must measure the worth of building the necessary systems itself.

Business practices also differ in the global environment. What's acceptable in France may not be acceptable in Honduras. These differences may be as small as the standard hours of business or as large as what makes a contract. In many nations a handshake may be as binding as a legal contract in the eyes of a local businessperson. At best, failure to realize these differences causes hard feelings. At worst, it may wind up costing a firm a lot of money.

Firms also face a variety of financial and currency problems that must not be ignored. Exchange rate problems occur when one type of currency is exchanged for another at a time when the exchange rate is unfavorable. A profit in one currency can be a loss in another at the time of exchange. During the recession late in 1997, many Far East Asian economies experienced severe threats to their currencies. South Korea, the

11th largest world economy, was damaged to the point that it required assistance from the International Monetary Fund (IMF). Inflation in foreign countries is more volatile than in the United States and can present a real problem. In addition, firms can be robbed by piracy schemes and other infringements via the relatively prevalent black market. Some nations are unreasonable in their requirements of the foreign company. They may expect large tax payments or further investment. Accounting laws may differ from country to country, resulting in confusion. Finally, certain moral issues such as playing on friendships or favoring relatives over others can cloud the business decisions of managers.

Whatever differences exist, if the firm is organized and managed correctly, it will be able to face any global problem. The following six principles can be used to make a firm's strategy come alive and prosper in a global economy:

1. Build a fluid, dynamic organization so that it is relatively easy to respond to changes and opportunities as they arise. This means that both people and structure must be adaptable.
2. Create mechanisms to respond to revolutionary change instead of routine change.
3. Keep specialization to a minimum and stress interchangeability.
4. Draft the best players, regardless of their expertise. If you hire the best players, they can learn whatever you need and will be instrumental in helping to achieve principle 3 above.
5. Develop from within, but stimulate from without. Because you are hiring the best players, there is no reason to fill positions from outside. However, it is also suggested that new ideas be infused into the organization by hiring consultants or temporary workers.
6. Encourage everyone to take full responsibility for everything. Encourage managers to develop their workers' talents. Encourage workers to make decisions and follow through.[63]

Knowing the Environment

For most organizations, the environment is an ambiguous mass of information. Of course, not everything in the external environment is of equal importance for the organization. Information in some sectors deserves closer monitoring than information in other sectors. How does an organization decide this issue? To answer, we examine the concept of the *enacted environment*.

Enacted Environment

Karl Weick explains that an organization does not and cannot conceivably know everything there is to know in the external environment.[64] Rather, the organization *creates* its own environment out of the external environment. This is called *enactment*. Enactment means that the organization creates a relevant environment for itself by aggressively scoping, narrowing, and scanning the external environment. In effect, the organization creates the environment to which it reacts; it does not react to the entire environment. The difference between creating the environment and reacting to it is a fine but important difference. In effect, the top managers in the organization state, "This is our environment, given what we are trying to accomplish. We will be concerned with these aspects and will ignore, at least temporarily, other aspects of the

FOCUS ON HR

Japanese Inefficiency

According to the Japan Productivity Center for Socio-Economic Development, Japan's workforce is diligent yet highly inefficient. Japan's productivity is the lowest amongst the big seven industrialized nations and rated 20th of the 29 richest countries. This is attributed to the fact that Japanese companies use more workers, compared with other countries, to produce an equal amount of goods. In Japanese department stores, three workers are involved in ringing up a customer's purchase. On construction sites, extra workers are employed to prevent passersby from tripping on equipment. In banks, workers are used to direct customers to tellers and to help them fill out basic forms. This extra service is beneficial to customer service but is superfluous and degrades an employer's bottom line.

The stigma associated with this practice belongs to Japanese cultural business thinking. The idea of employing workers for life and the social drive to keep Japan's 5 percent unemployment rate steady makes it difficult for companies to lay off these superfluous workers.

The negative impact of this cultural practice is growing. As the Japanese economy continues through a decade-long economic slowdown, employers are beginning to cut fixed costs by laying off personnel. Employers are choosing alternative ways to appease social pressure by hiring part-timers or employees on loan who can be let go easier.

SOURCE: Chikako Mogi, "Japan's Diligent Workforce Is Woefully Inefficient," *Tallahassee Democrat*, December 20, 2000, p. 7E.

environment." Organizations then give meaning to the environment based on what they determine to be important for their proper functioning.

An enacted environment implies a *proactive* approach in dealing with the environment. The organization takes an active and aggressive role in actually defining its environment. On the other hand, a *reactive* approach implies that the organization is not aggressive, but merely reacts to its environment. It does not define its environment but instead allows important factors in the environment to define it. The organization reacts to the crisis of the moment.

Unfortunately, an organization may define its environment so narrowly through the enactment process that it neglects to consider important forces that may affect it. For example, very few organizations monitored the Oil Producing Exporting Countries (OPEC) in the early 1970s and were caught completely off guard by its oil embargo and rapid energy price rise in 1973 and 1974. From that point, of course, OPEC actions have been monitored.

GM and other domestic auto manufacturers initially believed overseas competition from Nissan, Toyota, Mitsubishi, Mazda, and other Japanese auto manufacturers would not be a formidable force on a long-term basis and only casually monitored these competitors' actions. They were more concerned with monitoring each others' actions. On the other hand, Japanese automakers were intent on studying U.S. automakers. To get a closer look, many Japanese automakers entered into joint ventures with domestic U.S. automakers. Eventually, the U.S. automakers realized that they were teaching the Japanese in a few short years what it took themselves decades to learn.[65]

Of course, the 1970s and 1980s clearly established the competitive staying power and force of these Japanese auto manufacturers. Many other automobile manufacturers have been trying to imitate their production techniques in the hope of imitating their success. Adam Opel AG built a new car plant in Eisenach, Germany. The goal was to have people think they had entered a Toyota plant, not an Opel plant. The concepts and processes that were implemented were foreign to the workforce; however, this has paved the road for the most successful car plant in Germany. By 1995, the Opel plant was rated the most efficient automobile maker in all of Europe, averaging 59.3 cars per worker each year (compared with other German averages of 23.6 cars per worker per year). This project reflects the increasing globalization and improvement of the auto industry. A Canadian president of the firm is achieving positive results by working for a German subsidiary of a U.S. automaker (GM) that implements Japanese systems.[66]

Environmental Scanning

environmental scanning The process of examining the external environment to determine trends and projections of factors that will affect the organization.

As discussed in Chapter 1, **environmental scanning** is the process of examining the external environment to determine trends and projections of factors that will affect the organization.[67] It is closely related to the strategic planning process and serves as the basis for the forecast on which the plan is built. Assumptions about the future are derived from the plan.

The scan focuses primarily as the organization's enacted environment. The task environment is scanned the most; elements outside the task environment are not ignored, but they receive less attention. Scanning is done to prevent information overload for decision makers. Scanning should focus on providing relevant information for planning and decision making.

The primary environmental areas that should be scanned for human resource management planning and decision making are the labor market, legal environment, and technological environment. This does not mean that other elements, such as the international environment, should be ignored; it does mean that the three sectors identified tend to have a major impact on human resource decisions. Of course, if a firm has overseas operations, these three environmental sectors for each country need to be examined.

Exhibit 3.16 summarizes these concepts of domain, domain consensus, and enactment. Notice that the enactment and scanning process result in a narrowing or focusing of the external environment.

The Role of Human Resources in Environmental Scanning

Human resources is in the best position of any unit in the organization to scan the environment for human resource and labor market issues. As Exhibit 3.16 shows, human resources can help the organization obtain environmental information and feed it to key decision makers. In fact, human resources may play a major role in making the decision, as explained above. Human resources also has the responsibility of obtaining internal organizational information for consideration by strategic decision makers.

boundary spanning The process of scanning the environment in an effort to link the organization to its environment.

Notice that the human resource unit plays a **boundary-spanning** role in that it helps to link the organization to its environment by scanning the environment. We will expand on this linking role when we discuss recruiting and selection as well as termination, retirement, and layoff—other linking processes—in subsequent chapters.

Environmental Summary

We can see that the environment presents a multitude of important but ambiguous information to a firm. Yet for effective strategy formulation, a firm must monitor the relevant portions of each environmental sector: the economy, labor market, technology, social and demographics market, competitors, and legal/political sectors.

EXHIBIT 3.16 **ORGANIZATIONS ENACT AND LIMIT THE ENVIRONMENT**

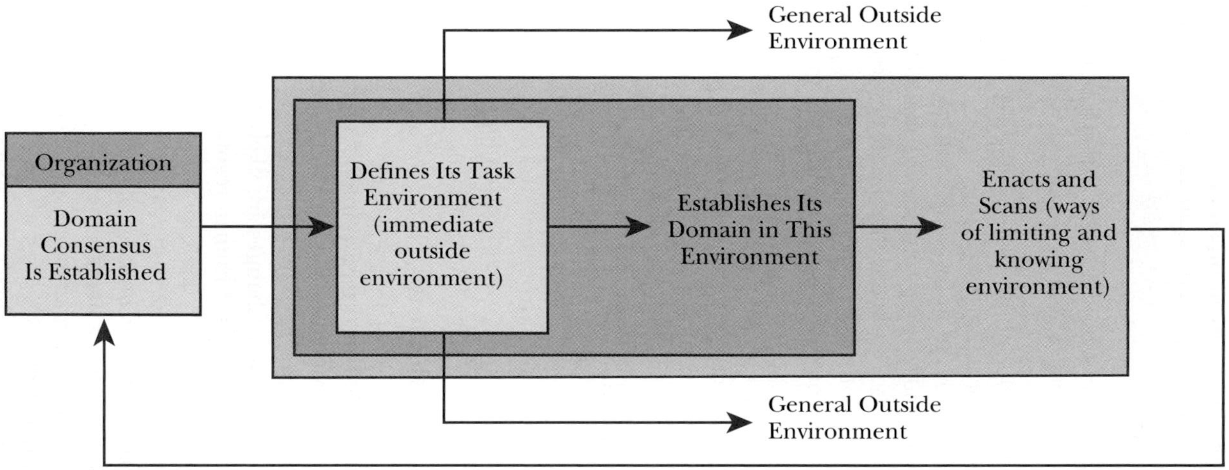

General Outside
Environment

Enacts and
Scans (ways
of limiting and
knowing
environment)

Establishes Its
Domain in This
Environment

Defines Its Task
Environment
(immediate
outside
environment)

General Outside
Environment

Organization

Domain
Consensus
Is Established

Organizations do this through a process of enactment that involves scoping and scanning tactics to reduce the relevant parts of the environment to manageable proportions. In doing this, the organization attempts to establish the set of environmental threats and opportunities presented to it by the environment.

In the next chapter, we see how the organization uses these environmental threats to formulate basic organization and resultant human resource strategies.

Management Guidelines

The information presented in this chapter can be used to generate several guidelines relevant to managers. These guidelines are as follows:

1. The external and global environments are very important to an organization and must be monitored.
2. Organizations monitor and "scan" the environment through a process of enactment and scoping to make the available information manageable.
3. Societal forces influence task environment elements, which influence the firm's operations and strategy.
4. Organizations use this environmental information to formulate overall and basic human resource strategies.
5. Organizations have several choices in designing a basic posture with regard to the environment, from prospector to reactor.
6. The basic strategy an organization chooses has a profound effect on the resultant human resource strategy.
7. Anticipating environmental trends requires a proactive management approach in strategy formulation.
8. Major issues that must be dealt with include the following: companies operate in a global environment; today's work force is diverse and constantly changing; and the rate of technological change is rapid.

Questions for Review

1. Why should an organization be interested in its external environment?
2. What are the basic forces of the societal environment? What are the key elements of the task environment?
3. What profound changes are likely to occur in the labor-market sector, and how will this affect human resource management issues?
4. How is the global environment changing?
5. Why does globalization make management difficult? What changes are occurring in the technological environment, and what are the implications for human resource management?
6. How does an organization scope or limit its external environment for monitoring purposes?
7. What are the basic choices of an organization as to the position it takes with respect to its external environment?
8. What are the environmental changes faced by AT&T as described in the case at the beginning of this chapter, and how have these changes affected basic AT&T strategy?
9. How have these changes affected the human resource strategy of AT&T?

10. Can a large company such as AT&T ever really completely know its environment? Would it be easier for a smaller company, such as a locally owned restaurant in your community, to know its environment? Discuss your answers.
11. Has AT&T performed well in dealing with these changes?
12. Many have written that the external environment changes very rapidly, often in unpredictable ways. Do you agree? Why or why not? Assuming that the environment does change in unpredictable ways, what relevance does this have for both (1) attempting to take a proactive approach and (2) strategy formulation?
13. Why is it important to consider both direct and indirect (eventual) environmental influences?

CASE

For Germans, "Nothin' (Much) Could be Finer"[68]

German companies are becoming increasingly aware that southern U.S. states, especially the Carolinas, have a great deal to offer international enterprises. In recent years, many German companies have expanded their operations in the United States and searched for an appropriate location. A large number have chosen the Carolinas.

So what is the result when the cool, calculating, sophisticated Germans come to the warmth of the U.S. South? It is far from a marriage made in heaven; the two cultures have needed time to get used to each other. Corey Lutynski had her doubts about the German alliances when her boss at Baker Corp., a German-owned forklift maker, threw his stapler into her office to have it filled. A German manager at Baker was alarmed one morning when a large portion of the workforce failed to show up. He later learned that, of course, it was the first day of hunting season.

At first, the U.S. workers were offended when the Germans, attempting to conserve heat, kept their office doors closed. Workers cite the importance of warm, personal relationships at work as opposed to the seemingly aloof style implied by a closed door and the lack of friendly conversation.

A real point of contention has been the disparity in pay and benefits. German workers are some of the highest-paid individuals in the world. In addition, they receive benefits, such as vacations of six or more weeks, that U.S. workers find excessive. One secretary complained that the German bosses were never in their offices, making it difficult for the U.S. workers.

Despite the Growing Pains, Benefits Abound

More than 200 German companies have $4 billion worth of industrial sites in the two-state area known as the Carolinas. What has attracted such companies? One key factor seems to be the reception offered by the Carolina trade representatives. The states, especially South Carolina, are more than willing to offer incentives to cover such things as tax expenses, land development costs, and infrastructure improvements.

The Germans are thrilled about the high-quality state technical and vocational school systems. In general, they are happy about the qualifications of the available workers. The Germans proclaim that costs are low: wages are cheap, especially while the German currency is strong against the U.S. dollar. One German plant, BMW, professes that it considers preserving the image of prestige and precision very important, but it also wants to control costs and appeal to a large segment of the U.S. automobile market. To BMW, South Carolina was the logical choice, and the company plans to increase its investment in the area as a result.

The Germans also claim that the easy-going, likable Southerners are malleable. They tolerate many management practices that many other Americans would find obnoxious, and most Southerners want no part of a union. The Germans call the Carolinians friendly and loyal. The Carolinians appreciate the high-tech training, high wages, and good working conditions.

The Carolinians also are reaping some nice rewards. The Germans are helping in the state's transition from a primarily agrarian economy to a more high-tech industrial-based economy. A huge amount of money is flowing into and throughout the state. The tax base has expanded, and the money can be used to improve such things as highways and schools.

Human Resource Issues

The German expansion into the Carolinas involves many elements related to global business management in general and human resource management in particular. When cultures collide like this, there is a need for accommodation. Both parties in this case have been asked to accept some negatives in order to enjoy the positives that have been delineated. German managers dealing with the Carolinian workers face new challenges, not unlike U.S. managers sent overseas. To deal with the issues important to management and to the workforce, the Germans and the Americans have been forced to forge an understanding of each other's goals and ways of thinking.

A second key element relates to the global business environment that compelled the large German companies to locate in the Carolinas. They considered numerous issues dealing with shipping costs, U.S. market potential, currency fluctuations, and the competitive nature of the local labor market relative to that in other countries prior to making their decision to locate in South Carolina. To the Germans, the key human resource factors of skill, wages, training, and availability were an integral part of their global decision process.

Questions for Discussion

1. What were the strategic issues related to the workforce that the Germans likely considered before deciding to locate in the Carolinas? Why are these issues important?

2. Why do you suspect that German and U.S. workers have different beliefs, attitudes, and behaviors about work? What were the root causes of the minor differences noted in the case?

3. Do you foresee any potential management problems in the future? If so, what are they, what caused them, and how can they be solved (or avoided)?

Additional Readings

Allen, R. E. "Committed to Competition: AT&T, Local Service and the Communication Revolution." The Chief Executive Club of Boston: The Carroll School of Management at Boston College, June 10, 1997.

Badaracco, J. *The Knowledge Link.* Cambridge, MA: Harvard Business School Press, 1991.

Baker, S. "Now Mexico Looks Like a Fiesta for Investors." *Business Week*, August 28, 1989, pp. 42–43.

Beatty, J. "Nasty NAFTA." *Atlantic Unbound.* **www.theatlantic.com** (accessed February 26, 2001), July 1997.

Boyett, J., and H. Conn. *Workplace 2000: The Revolution Reshaping American Business.* New York: Penguin, 1991.

Bradshaw, T. F.; D. F. Burton, Jr.; R. N. Cooper; and R. D. Hormats. *America's New Competitors.* New York: Harper & Row, 1989.

Brauchli, M. W. "Trading in Tokyo." *The Wall Street Journal*, August 16, 1989, pp. A1–6, A8–1.

Carson, C. S. "GNP: An Overview of Source Data and Estimating Methods." *Survey of Current Business* 67 (1987), pp. 103–126.

Carter, S.; J. Rossanto; F. J. Comes; and J. Templeman. "Why the Ayatollah Is Whipping Up a New Wave of Fanaticism." *Business Week*, March 6, 1989, p. 47.

Coates, J.; J. Jarratt; and J. Mahaffie. *Future Work.* San Francisco: Jossey-Bass, 1990.

Daft, R. L.; J. Sormunen; and D. Parks. "Chief Executive Scanning, Environmental Characteristics, and Company Performance: An Empirical Study." *Strategic Management Journal*, March/April 1988, pp. 123–140.

de Cordoba, J. "Wanted in Caracas." *The Wall Street Journal*, August 24, 1989, pp. A1–1, A6–1.

Dess, G. G., and D. W. Beard, "Dimensions of Organizational Task Environments." *Administrative Science Quarterly* 29 (1984), pp. 52–73.

Dowling, P., and R. Schuler. *International Dimensions of Human Resource Management.* Boston: PWS Kent, 1990.

Dreyfuss, J. "Reinventing IBM." *Fortune*, August 21, 1989, p. 38.

Duff, C. "Surging Economy Bypasses Black Men." *The Wall Street Journal*, June 3, 1997, p. A2.

Dunham, R. S., and M. McNamee. "Why Is This Man Smiling?" *Business Week*, June 23, 1997, pp. 34–37.

Dwyer, P.; L. Jereski; Z. Schiller; and D. Lee. "The Raging Battle over 'Intellectual Property.'" *Business Week*, May 22, 1989, p.88.

Egelhoff, W. G. *Organizing the Multinational Enterprise.* New York: Harper & Row, 1989.

Elstrom, P. "Get Busy, Mr. Armstrong." *Business Week*, November 3, 1997, pp. 40–42.

Fahey, L., and W. R. King. "Environmental Scanning for Corporate Planning." *Business Horizons*, August 1977, p. 63.

Fernandez, J. *Managing a Diverse Workforce.* New York: Lexington Books, 1991.

Fischer, A. "What Labor Shortage?" *Fortune*, June 23, 1997, pp.154–156.

Frumkin, N. *Tracking America's Economy.* Armonk, NY: M. E. Sharpe, 1988.

Fuller, G. *The Democracy Trap: Perils of the Post-Cold War World.* Novato, CA: Dutton, 1991.

Fullerton, H. N., Jr. "Labor Force Projections: 1986-2000." *Monthly Labor Review* 110 (1987), pp. 19–29.

Fyock, C. *America's Work Force Is Coming of Age.* New York: Lexington Books, 1990.

Galuszka, P. "The $20 Billion Breakthrough in Kazakhstan." Zhiwriter. **www.nd.edu:81/~astrouni/zhiwriter,** May 13, 1996.

Goldenberg, S. *Hands across the Ocean: Managing Joint Ventures with a Spotlight on China and Japan.* Novato, CA: Dutton, 1988.

Henkoff, R. "Are You (More Than) Ready for a Pay Raise?" *Fortune*, December 8, 1997, pp. 233–234.

Holloway, T. M., and R. W. Peach. "Demographics for the 1990s." *Mortgage Banking*, March 1988, pp. 60–72.

Jamieson, D., and J. O'Mara. *Managing Workforce 2000.* San Francisco: Jossey-Bass, 1991.

Kelly, R. M. *The Gendered Economy.* Newbury Park, CA: Sage, 1991.

Koberg, C. S. "Resource Scarcity, Environmental Uncertainty, and Adaptive Organizational Behavior." *Academy of Management Journal* 30, no. 4 (December 1987), pp. 798–812.

Koretz, G. "The Amazing U.S. Labor Pool." *Business Week*, May 26, 1997, p. 30.

Knouse, S.; P. Rosenfeld; and A. Culbertson. *Hispanics and Work*. Newbury Park, CA: Sage, 1992.

Kraar, L. "Japan's Gung-Ho U.S. Car Plants." *Fortune*, January 30, 1989, pp. 98–108.

Kraar, L. "Korea, Tomorrow's Powerhouse." *Fortune*, August 15, 1988, pp. 75–81.

Licht, W. "How the Workplace Has Changed in 75 Years." *Monthly Labor Review*, February 1988, pp. 19–25.

Main, J. "Business Schools Get a Global Vision." *Fortune*, July 17, 1989, pp. 78–86.

Mendenhall, M., and G. Oddou. *Readings and Cases in International Human Resource Management*. Boston: PWS Kent, 1990.

Mercer, D. *Managing the External Environment*. Newbury Park, CA: Sage, 1992.

Micco, L. "Wage, Education Gaps Narrow for Women: Study." *HRNews*, February 1997, p. 9.

Micco, L. "NAFTA Study Shows Minimal Effect on Employment." *HRNews*, February 1996, p. B7.

Minehan, M. "Aging of the World Population." *Workplace Visions*, September/October 1997, p. 4.

"The Fastest Growing U.S. Ethnic Groups." *HRMagazine*, May 1997, p.160.

Mitchener, B. "Daimler's Alabama M-Class Experiment Has Ripples Spreading Back to Stuttgart." *The Wall Street Journal*, October 17, 1997, p. A18.

Naisbitt, J., and P. Aburdene. *Megatrends 2000: Ten New Directions for the 1990s*. New York: Morrow, 1990.

Ohmae, K. *Triad Power: The Coming Shape of Global Competition*. New York: Free Press, 1985.

Porter, M. *The Competitive Advantage of Nations*. New York: Free Press, 1990.

Potter, E. E. *The American Workplace*. Employment Policy Foundation, 1997.

Prescott, J. E. "Environments as Moderators of the Relationship between Strategy and Performance." *Academy of Management Journal* 29, no. 2 (June 1986), p. 329.

Punnett, B. J., and D. Ricks. *International Business*. Boston: PWS-Kent, 1992.

Schlesinger, J. M. "Working Smarter. Despite Pay Increases, Gains in Productivity, Profits Curb Inflation." *The Wall Street Journal*, May 21, 1997, pp. A1–1, A8–1.

Sekaran, U., and F. Leong. *Womanpower*. Newbury Park, CA: Sage, 1991.

Singleton, L. A. *Global Impact*. New York: Harper & Row, 1989.

Solomon, C. M. "The Corporate Response to Work-Force Diversity." *Personnel Journal*, August 1989.

Solomon, C. "International Business Machines." Standard and Poors Stock Reports, September 1997.

Steers, R. M.; Y. K. Shin; and G. Ungson. *The Chaebol*. New York: Harper & Row, 1989.

Steinmetz, G. "German Absenteeism Hits 20-Year Low." *The Wall Street Journal*, October 21, 1997, p. A17.

Tatsuno, S. M. *Created in Japan*. New York: Harper & Row, 1989.

Thiederman, S. *Bridging Cultural Barriers for Corporate Success*. New York: Lexington Books, 1990.

Notes

[1]Nelson D. Schwartz, "In or Out," *Fortune*, October 13, 1997, pp. 198-202; AT&T Corporate Company Briefing Book, **www.wsj.com** (accessed February 26, 2001), June 30, 1997; "AT&T Directors to Tap Armstrong for Top Posts," *The Wall Street Journal*, October 17, 1997, p. A1; Peter Elstrom, "Get Busy, Mr. Armstrong," *Business Week*, November 3, 1997, pp. 40–42; Robert E. Allen, "Committed to Competition," *Address to Chief Executives Club of Boston*, June 10, 1997; "A Brief Corporate History of AT&T—A Strategic Restructuring for the 21st Century Moving Ahead," **www.att.com** (accessed February 26, 2001), October 17, 1997; "Prepare for Launch: The Global Implication of AT&T Restructuring," **www.att.com** (accessed February 26, 2001), October 3, 1995; John Keller, Geoff Lewis, Todd Mason, Russell Mitchell, and Thane Peterson, "AT&T—The Making of a Comeback," *Business Week*, January 18, 1988, pp. 56–62; Jeffrey A. Tannenbaum, "AT&T to Cut Hiring, Change Jobs of Workers," *The Wall Street Journal*, July 22, 1989,

p. 3; "AT&T to Transfer up to 1500 of Staff to Sales Organization," *The Wall Street Journal*, July 25, 1989, p. 9; Bernard Wysocki, Jr., "Cross-Border Alliances Become Favorite Way to Crack New Markets," *The Wall Street Journal*, March 26, 1990, p. A11; John J. Keller, "AT&T Earnings Rose Strongly in First Quarter," *The Wall Street Journal*, April 21, 1994, p. A4; Carol Kennedy, "The Transformation of AT&T," *Long Range Planning*, June 1989, pp. 10–17; Ronald Smothers, "At AT&T, Taking News of Cutbacks in Stride," *The New York Times*, January 27, 1998, p. D4; Bruce Meyerson, "Speculation Mounts over AT&T's Ability to Pull Off Its Cable Strategy," *The Associated Press*, September 1, 2000; "The Bear at Bay," *The Economist*, September 23, 2000; AT&T Profile: AT&T History, **www.att.com** (accessed February 26, 2001), September 26, 2000; Geraldine Fabrikant, "AT&T Plans Spinoff to Cut Cable Holdings," *The New York Times*, November 16, 2000, p. C1; Geraldine Fabrikant, "AT&T Faces Hard Choices over Its Debt," *The New York Times*, November 20, 2000, p. C1; Allan Sloan, "Malone, Armstrong Want to Carve Up Firm in Preparation for Future Thanksgiving," *The Washington Post*, November 21, 2000, p. E3.

[2]Raymond E. Miles and Charles C. Snow, *Organization Strategy, Structure, and Process* (New York: McGraw-Hill, 1978), pp. 29–30.

[3]These definitions are based on the discussion by Thomas Wheelen and David Hunger, *Strategic Management and Business Policy*, 4th ed. (Reading, PA: Addison-Wesley, 1992), pp. 92–98.

[4]Ibid.

[5]B. J. Hodge and William P. Anthony, *Organization Theory*, 3rd ed. (Boston: Allyn and Bacon, 1988), p. 428.

[6]Shoshana Zuboff, *In the Age of the Smart Machine: The Future of Work and Power* (New York: Basic, 1988).

[7]Ian McGugan, "By Firing All the Humans, France Finally Masters Good Service," *Canadian Business*, August 1997, p. 79.

[8]Bill Leonard, "Average U.S. Workweek Hasn't Changed Much in Past 32 Years," *HRMagazine*, November 2000, p. 36.

[9]Geoff Winestock, "Social Security Reform Rocks the World," *The Wall Street Journal*, October 30, 2000, p. A24.

[10]Howard N. Fullerton, Jr., "Labor Force Projections to 2008: Steady Growth and Changing Composition," *Monthly Labor Review*, November 1999, pp. 19–32.

[11]Robert Rose and Alex Kotolowitz, "Midwest's Revenge: Once the 'Rust-Belt,' Heartland Fares Better than Coastal States," *The Wall Street Journal*, July 30, 1991, p. A11; William H. Frey, "The New Urban Demographics," *The Brookings Review*, Summer 2000, pp. 20–23.

[12]"Aging of the World Population," *Workplace Visions, HRMagazine*, September/October 1997, p. 4; Steve Sternberg, "Earth Welcomes 6 Billionth Baby with Trepidation—All Will Feel Ripple Effect as World Population Booms," *USA Today*, October 11, 1999, p. 5D.

[13]There is some evidence that the unemployment rate actually undercounts unemployment because of the discouraged worker hypothesis. Some people who actually want to work may have given up looking. These people are not counted as unemployed.

[14]It should be noted that during the Great Depression of the 1930s, the unemployment rate reached 25 percent on several occasions.

[15]"Occupational Employment," *Occupational Outlook Quarterly*, Winter 1999–2000, pp. 8–24.

[16]Carla Joinson, "Strength in Numbers," *HRMagazine*, November 2000, pp. 43–49.

[17]Winston Wood, "Work Week," *The Wall Street Journal*, December 12, 2000, p. A1.

[18]"California," *HRMagazine*, April 1991, p. 41; State of California, Department of Finance, *County Projections with Age, Sex, Race/Ethnic Detail*, Sacramento, California, December 1998.

[19]"Investing in GEMS: Global Employees, Mobile and Skilled," *HRMagazine*, January 1991, p. 37; Gene Koretz, "America's Jobs are Changing—But Less Than You Might Think," *Business Week*, January 24, 2000, p. 32.

[20]Martha I. Finney, "The ASPA Labor Shortage Survey," *Personnel Administrator*, February 1989, pp. 36–42; Alison Stein Wellner, "No One Left to Hire," *Business Week*, September 11, 2000, p. F42.

[21]Martha Brannigan, "Work Force Skills Lag in the Southeast, Despite Reforms," *The Wall Street Journal*, February 18, 1992, p. A1; *Digest of Education Statistics*, U.S. Department of Education, National Center for Educational Statistics, **nces.ed.gov/pubsearch** (accessed February 26, 2001), 1997.

[22]David Wessel, "Census Bureau Study Finds Shift in Fertility Patterns," *The Wall Street Journal*, June 26, 1989, p. B1; Amara Bachu and Martin O'Connell, "Fertility of American Women," Current Population Reports, U.S. Census Bureau, June 1998, p. 1–13.

[23]"Labor Force," *Occupational Outlook Quarterly*, Winter 1999–2000, pp. 33–38.

[24]Sharon Nelton, "Meet Your New Work Force," *Nation's Business*, July 1988, pp. 14–15.

[25]Michael Porter, *Competitive Strategy: Techniques for Analyzing Industries and Competitors* (New York: Free Press, 1980).

[26]Ford S. Worthy, "The Perils of Getting Tough on Korea," *Fortune*, June 5, 1989, pp. 263–268.

[27]Peter Galuszka, "The $20 Billion Breakthrough in Kazakhstan," *Zhiwriter*, **www.nd.edu.81/~astrouni/zhiwriter/spool/96050304.htm** (accessed May 13, 1996); "World Bank Launches Online Service for Investors in Russia; Initiative Unprecedented in Scope, Transparency," *Business Wire*, October 6, 2000.

[28]"Why Non-Europeans Should Care about EMU," *The Economist*, March 29, 1997, p. 86.

[29]"The Fortune Global 500," **www.fortune.com/fortune/global500** (accessed February 26, 2001).

[30]Ibid.

[31]Ibid.

[32]Dana Milbank, "U.S. Productivity Gains Cut Costs, Close Gap with Low-Wage Overseas Firms," *The Wall Street Journal*, December 23, 1992, p. A1; Mehrene Larudee and Tim Koechin, "Wages, Productivity, and Foreign Direct Investment Flows," *Journal of Economic Issues* 33, no. 2 (June 1999).

[33]Michael M. Phillips, "U.S. Firms May Lose Labor-Cost Advantage," *The Wall Street Journal*, January 26, 1998, p. A1; David Friedman, "The Jackpot Economy," *The Los Angeles Times*, May 9, 1999.

[34]Christopher Gust and Jamie Marquez, "Productivity Developments Abroad," *Federal Reserve Bulletin* 86, no. 10 (October 2000).

[35]Stuart Silverstein and Leslie Earnest, "U.S. Productivity Rises, Indicating Continued Boom," *The Los Angeles Times*, August 9, 2000.

[36]Louis Uchitelle, "U.S. Productivity Rose at 5% rate in 2nd Half of '99," *The New York Times*, February 9, 2000.

[37]Emily Thornton, Thomas Martin, and Cindy Kano, "What Now for the U.S. and Japan?" *Fortune*, February 10, 1992, pp. 80–95; John McClenahen, "A World of (Top-Line) Difference," *Industry Week* 247, no. 15 (August 17, 1998).

[38]Robert Keatley, "Luxury Auto Makers Consider Mexico: Its Low Cost Labor vs. Image Perception," *The Wall Street Journal*, November 27, 1992, p. A6; Laurie Joan Aron, "Global Rationalization Drives Auto Site Selection," *Site Selection* 44, no. 1 (January 1999).

[39]Steven Butler, "Japan's Down, Citibank's Up," *U.S. News & World Report* 125, no. 9 (September 7, 1998); Charles Smith, "Can the Upstarts Topple the Giants?" *Institutional Investor* 33, no. 9 (September 1999); Steven Butler, "Japan, Say Hello to Charles Schwab-san," *U.S. News & World Report* 127, no. 17 (November 1, 1999).

[40]Marcus W. Brauchli, "Trading in Tokyo," *The Wall Street Journal*, August 16, 1989, pp. A1, 6.

[41]Louis Kraar, "Korea, Tomorrow's Powerhouse," *Fortune*, August 15, 1988, pp. 75–81; Laxmi Nakarmi, Larry Armstrong, and William J. Holstein, "Korea," *Business Week*, September 5, 1988, pp. 44–50; J. Thomas Ratchford, "Exercise the Korea Option," *Research Technology Management* 40 (July/August 1997); Raju Chellam, "Ingredients that Attract R&D," *Business Times*, April 11, 2000.

[42]Thomas O'Boyle, "New Neighbor: To Georgetown, KY, Toyota Plant Seems a Blessing and a Curse," *The Wall Street Journal*, November 26, 1991, p. A11.

[43]Jim Henry, "Japanese, Europeans Increase U.S. Share," *Automotive News*, January 12, 1998; Brian Milligan, "Manufacturing Costs: American Auto Makers Close Gap," *Purchasing* 127, no. 2 (August 12, 1999); Drew Winter, "2000 Harbour Report," *Ward's Auto World* 36, no. 7 (July 2000).

[44]Ford Worthy, "Getting In on the Ground Floor," *Fortune*, 1990 Special Edition, pp. 63–67; Chris Kraul, "Brazil Debates High Cost of Car Plant in Poor State," *The Los Angeles Times*, December 5, 1999; Edwin van der Bruggen, "Say Goodbye to Tax Holidays in Southeast Asia," *Asian Wall Street Journal*, November 27, 2000.

[45]John Naisbitt and Patricia Aburdene, *Megatrends 2000: Ten New Directions for the 1990s* (New York: Morrow, 1990).

[46]"The Perils of Global Capital," *The Economist*, April 11, 1998; Paul Krugman, "Recovery? Don't Bet on It," *Time*, June 21, 1999; Wayne Arnold, "Southeast Asia Losing Ground in New Economy, Report Says," *The New York Times*, September 7, 2000.

[47]Jonathan Peterson, "Senate Poised to Pass China Trade Measure; Commerce: Approval Would Ease the Country's Entry into the WTO…," *Los Angeles Times*, September 19, 2000.

[48]Craig Smith, "China Says Its Economy Grew at 8.2% Rate in 3rd Quarter," *The New York Times*, October 17, 2000.

[49]Maureen Minehan, "Skills Shortage in Asia," *HRMagazine* 41, March 1996; "The Tiger and the Tech," *The Economist*, February 5, 2000.

[50]European Union and World Trade, Europe, **eu.int/en/comm/dg10/infcom/euromove/w-trade/en/trade.htm** (accessed September 4, 1997).

[51]Paul De Grauwe, "Risks of a Roofless Euroland; The Challenges of Further Fiscal and Political Integration Still Lie Ahead," *Time*, January 11, 1999; Roger Cohen, "Identity Crisis for Denmark: Are We Danes or Europeans?" *The New York Times*, September 10, 2000.

[52]"There Once Was an Ugly Duckling," *The Economist*, November 11, 2000.

[53]Linda Micco, "NAFTA Study Shows Minimal Effect on Employment," *HRNews*, February 1996, p. b7.

[54]Jack Beatty, "Nasty NAFTA," *Atlantic Unbound*, **www.theatlantic.com** (accessed February 26, 2001), July 2, 1997; Ben Wildavsky, "Not Happy After NAFTA," *U.S. News & World Report* 126, no. 1 (January 11, 1999).

[55]Allan Halcrow, "Expats: The Squandered Resource," *Workforce* 78, no. 4 (April 1999), p. 42; Valerie Frazee, "Selecting Global Assignees," *Workforce* 3, no. 4 (July 1998), p. 28.

[56]Melinda Ligos, "The Foreign Assignment: An Incubator, or Exile?" *The New York Times*, October 22, 2000.

[57]Louis Kraar, "Japan's Gung-Ho U.S. Car Plants," *Fortune*, January 30, 1989, pp. 98–108; Joseph White, Gregory Patterson, and Paul Ingrassia, "American Auto Makers Need Overhaul to Match the Japanese," *The Wall Street Journal*, January 10, 1992, pp. A1, A4.

[58]Emily Thornton, "50 Fateful Years from Enemy to Friend to __?" *Fortune*, December 16, 1991, pp. 126–134; Paula Lyon Andruss, "Japanese Market Expanding Ad Reach," *Marketing News* 34, no. 22 (October 23, 2000).

[59]Jay Branegan and Adam Zagorin, "In Washington, a Marriage of Convenience for China," *Time* 144, no. 21 (May 22, 2000), pp. 52–53; Ted Plafker, "Beijing Softens Rhetoric on Taiwan; China Plays Down Its Threats of Military Attack," *The Washington Post*, May 23, 2000, p. A23.

[60]Pete Engardio and Laurence Zuckerman, "Yankee Traders Breathe a Sigh of Relief," *Business Week*, February 3, 1992, pp. 39–42; Ching-Ching Ni, "AT&T in Venture to Provide Internet Services in Shanghai," *The Los Angeles Times*, December 6, 2000, p. C1; Craig Smith, "A Tale of Piracy: How the Chinese Stole the Grinch," *The New York Times*, December 12, 2000, p. A3.

[61]Susan Carter, John Rossanto, Frank J. Comes, and John Templeman, "Why the Ayatollah Is Whipping Up a New Wave of Fanaticism," *Business Week*, March 6, 1989, p. 47; Stanley Reed, "When the Dust Settles, Iran May Be Facing West," *Business Week*, June 19, 1989, p. 50; Josh Martin, "When Countries Come in from the Cold," *Management Review* 88, no. 2 (February 1999), pp. 23–28; David Stout, "U.S. to Drop Longtime Ban on Luxuries from Iran," *The New York Times*, March 15, 2000, p. A8.

[62]Mark Konkel, "Internet Indecency, International Censorship, and Service Providers' Liability," *New York Law School Journal of International and Comparative Law* 19, no. 3 (2000), pp. 453–478.

[63]John Dupuy, "Learning to Manage World-Class Strategy," *Management Review*, October 1991, pp. 40–44.

[64]Karl Weick, *The Social Psychology of Organizing* (Reading, MA: Addison-Wesley, 1969).

[65]Brian Dumaine, "The Best Management Books of 1991," *Fortune*, January 27, 1992, pp. 113–114.

[66]Timothy Aeppel, "Opel Designs Car Plant on Japanese Lines," *The Wall Street Journal*, January 21, 1992, p. A16; Nathaniel Nash, "Luxuries They Can't Afford," *The New York Times*, September 13, 1995, p. D1; Adolf Haasen, "Opel Eisenach GMBH—Creating a High Productivity Workplace," *Organizational Dynamics* 24, Spring 1996, pp. 80–85.

[67]Liam Fahey and William R. King, "Environmental Scanning for Corporate Planning," *Business Horizons*, August 1977, p. 63.

[68]Robert Keatley, "Luxury Auto Makers Consider Mexico: Its Low Cost Labor vs. Image Perception," *The Wall Street Journal*, November 27, 1992, p. A6; Michael J. McCarthy, "Why German Firms Choose the Carolinas to Build U.S. Plants," *The Wall Street Journal*, May 4, 1993, p. A1; Tim Venable, "South Carolina: Where the World Comes to do Business," *Site Selection* 44, no. 1 (January 1999), p. 1147–1148; "BMW to Invest 300 Mln USD in South Carolina Plant over the Next Years," *AFX European Focus*, June 27, 2000.

II

Strategies for Human Resource Acquisition and Placement

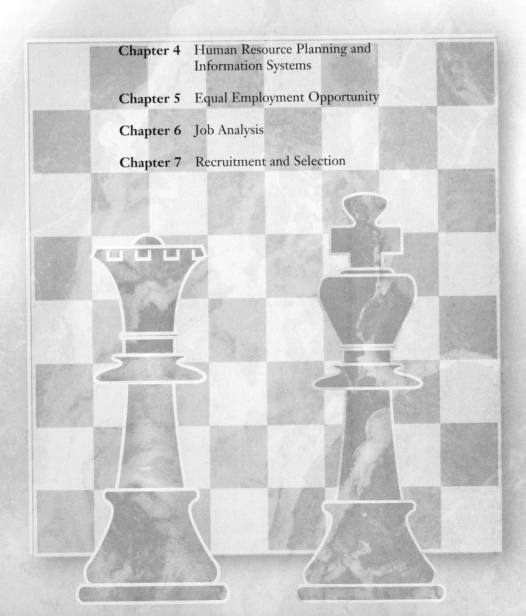

II

Strategies for Human Resource Acquisition

4

Human Resource Planning and Information Systems

Chapter Objectives

As a result of studying this chapter, you should be able to

1. Identify and explain the steps in constructing a human resource plan.

2. Explain the relationship of strategic human resource planning to the staffing function.

3. Discuss human resource costing in organizations.

4. Describe human resource information systems.

5. Explain the critical link between strategic management and human resource information systems.

6. Identify and discuss the factors surrounding the use of human resource information systems.

Technological advancements over the past several years have not bypassed the human resource management functions. In fact, even large companies like the Bellagio Hotel and Casino in Las Vegas have gone "paperless." That is, all of the human resource functions from application to termination forms are done via computers. By using the latest technology, the Bellagio saves money and time and can be more responsive when asked for data about the workforce. Having all of the data about the workforce online and at the fingertips of management allows the Bellagio to better forecast its human resource needs and thus better plan for the future. In this chapter we examine the growing importance of technology in human resources and how this technology can be used by human resource managers to more effectively perform human resource planning.

CASE

How a Computer Keeps Mrs. Fields from Losing Her Cookies[1]

Computers have made the workplace more efficient. Even in the "low-tech" cookie business, operations can be programmed to smooth the production flow as well as schedule personnel. Mrs. Fields Cookies (**www.mrsfields.com**) is a good example of how to use technology in human resource management.

The real Mrs. Fields is Debra Fields, who started the company with her husband Randy, a former systems programmer for IBM. Together they have built a corporation that includes their original company and others, such as La Petite Boulangerie and Retail Operations Intelligence (ROI) Systems. The ROI division sells its expertise to other companies.

From its beginning in 1977, the couple's enterprise has grown substantially. Success in their own business and competition from other businesses led them into other markets and other industries.

The company's strategy was typical of the trends of the 1980s. Increased competition from other cookie companies and from substitutes, such as specialty confectionery companies, caused problems. In 1988, problems from the "combination stores" concept hurt business. Analysts said that the company had made strategic mistakes. The Fields hoped to recoup through diversification and globalization. By 1990, the company was selected by NutraSweet's Desserve Foods Division for a joint marketing effort, the first time NutraSweet had made such a move with another company.

How a Cookie Company Can Use Computers

Paul Quinn heads up ROI, Mrs. Fields' management information systems. He directs the efforts of Mrs. Fields' diversified divisions and markets the systems to over 600 other locations.

One of the features of the ROI system is that it has several components, called *modules*, that handle most of the day-to-day operations in human resource management. Among the modules already up and running are the daily production planner and components that focus on interviewing, setting personnel schedules, and skill testing. One benefit of a computerized human resource information system is that it standardizes routine tasks, such as interviewing prospective employees. A further benefit is that it can customize the standard employment questionnaire based on the individual responses that the applicant has given.

For example, suppose Jane Dough is looking for a part-time job at Mrs. Fields Cookies to help pay expenses while she is in school. She would be instructed to sit at a computer terminal and answer the series of questions that appears on the screen. The questions take about 15 minutes to answer. Some are true/false; others are multiple choice. So far, this could be done with a printed form. However, the computer is programmed to ask additional questions based on Jane's answers. If she says she is interested in temporary work, the computer asks how long she would plan to stay with the company. The follow-up question is similar to one that a store manager might ask in conducting an interview. But not all store managers are able to keep current with legislation affecting employment recruiting practices. The computerized system is updated to make certain that only legal language is used in the interviewing process. The computer package also is programmed to catch discrepancies, such as overlapping dates in previous employment.

After Jane has finished answering the questions, the computer tabulates a score from her responses based on minimum qualifications the company has set. This score provides information to help the manager decide whether or not to hire Jane. However, although the computer program is a part of the human resource information system, it is not there to replace the human resource decision-making system. The computers free up time for the HR managers and allow them to make these important decisions.

Suppose Jane is hired, and after working for a couple of months in the baking operations, she wants to work at the front counter because that position pays more. She must pass the skills test before being considered for the change. The skill training module works like the interviewing module. It asks questions about tasks and gives correct responses and a final score so that Jane can get instant feedback on her skill level. A "help text" explains why an answer was right or wrong, and the test then becomes a tutor. If Jane doesn't pass, she can retake the test immediately or get further training before trying again. Jane isn't the only one who benefits from this system. The human resource staff at the company's headquarters feed her responses into a database. If several sources show the same problem, then the program is checked for wording errors. If there is no problem, then the human resource staff looks at the training techniques, materials, or workforce skill levels for problems. Again, this system is designed to provide information to the people who are responsible for the company's human resources.

More Uses for Computers

In addition to hiring and training, the human resource information system (HRIS) is used by Mrs. Fields Cookies to schedule personnel for production. Information is fed into the computer on a number of employees such as their preferred or available hours, and anticipated traffic in the store. Even breaks are programmed so that each outlet operates at peak efficiency. The system then schedules personnel on an hourly basis. If Jane calls in sick, the labor scheduler module quickly formulates an alternative schedule and alerts the manager.

Although Mrs. Fields is a leader in HRIS management, it is not alone. More than 2000 HRISs were in operation at the beginning of the 1990s, with more systems coming online, according to Dianne and Peter Kirrane, consultants who specialize in expert systems. Older systems using paper forms can make timely information virtually impossible. Today, companies like Arthur Andersen specialize in designing systems to provide the human resource manager with vital information in seconds. These systems also lower overhead by keeping nonessential personnel hires to a minimum.

Despite intense competition, Mrs. Fields tries to keep her cookie business healthy. Part of her strategy is the HRIS used by the company to speed the flow of information from the source to where it is needed throughout the corporation. She was even able to create a sense of company loyalty by giving each store employee a connection to her through voice mail and e-mail.

Strategic Choices

As the introductory case notes, HRISs can play a significant role in all aspects of the human resource function if a company so desires. Whether to use a HRIS and to what extent are just two of the many strategic choices a firm must make. Others include whether to purchase or develop the HRIS programs. Once the data are available online, the issue of privacy arises. Exactly how a company will deal with this issue is another important strategic decision. It is also important to determine whether to keep the HRIS in the HR department or to allow all of the employees to participate in designing and maintaining it. Finally, a company must grapple with the expansion of technology. For example, companies must determine exactly what information and technology to make available to their employees. Should the company support the use of the Internet, e-mail, and access to the World Wide Web, or does providing these services adversely affect performance? Each of these choices will be discussed later in the chapter. However, before we do so, let's first look at the HR planning function.

There are many strategic choices to consider with respect to human resource planning. These key choices can be categorized along several key dimensions.[2] These dimensions reflect the degree to which an organization engages in planning per se. Each dimension represents a choice a firm makes when committing to any type of planning activity. First, the organization can choose to be *proactive* or *reactive* in human resource planning. That is, it can decide to carefully anticipate needs and systematically plan to fill them far in advance, or it can simply react to needs as they arise. Of course, careful planning to better fill human resource needs helps to ensure that the organization obtains the right number of employees with the proper skills and abilities at the time they are needed.

The second decision the organization makes determines its *breadth*. Essentially, the organization can choose a narrow focus by planning in only one or two human resource areas, such as recruitment or selection, or it can choose a broad focus by planning in all human resource areas, including training, rewarding, and so on. This continuum is depicted in Exhibit 4.1.

The third choice involves the *formality* of the plan. The organization can choose to have a rather *informal* plan that is mostly in the heads of its managers and human resource staff, or it can have a *formalized* plan that is clearly spelled out in writing and backed up by supporting documentation and data. Including a computerized HRIS in an organization is one way to help formalize the process.

The fourth choice involves the *degree of tie* the human resource plan has with the strategic plan. The plan can be *loosely tied*, if at all, to the firm's strategic plan, or it can be *fully integrated* with the strategic plan. As we have indicated, integration of the strategic plan and strategic human resource management can best occur by fully integrating the two through strategic human resource planning.

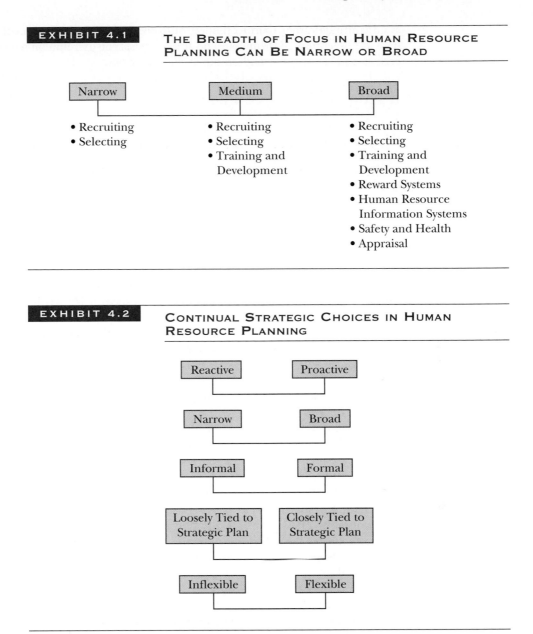

EXHIBIT 4.1 THE BREADTH OF FOCUS IN HUMAN RESOURCE PLANNING CAN BE NARROW OR BROAD

Narrow	Medium	Broad

Narrow
- Recruiting
- Selecting

Medium
- Recruiting
- Selecting
- Training and Development

Broad
- Recruiting
- Selecting
- Training and Development
- Reward Systems
- Human Resource Information Systems
- Safety and Health
- Appraisal

EXHIBIT 4.2 CONTINUAL STRATEGIC CHOICES IN HUMAN RESOURCE PLANNING

| Reactive | Proactive |

| Narrow | Broad |

| Informal | Formal |

| Loosely Tied to Strategic Plan | Closely Tied to Strategic Plan |

| Inflexible | Flexible |

Finally, the fifth choice in the human resource plan involves *flexibility*—the ability of the plan to anticipate and deal with contingencies. As we have indicated, organizations do not like high levels of uncertainty. They reduce this uncertainty by planning, which includes forecasting and predicting possible future conditions and events. Human resource planning can contain many contingencies, which reflect differing scenarios and thereby ensure that the plan is flexible and adaptable, or it can be fairly set and geared to one scenario, thereby requiring much time and effort to obtain change—assuming it can be changed at all.

Exhibit 4.2 summarizes these five major choices faced by organizations in strategic human resource planning. Organizations often tend to be to the left or to the right on all continua rather than to the left on some and to the right on others, although there are exceptions. A firm could be at one end of the extreme on some plan characteristics and at the other end on other characteristics.

The Nature of Human Resource Planning

Human resource planning is the key link between a firm's strategic plan and its overall human resource management function, as shown in Exhibit 4.3. The strategic human resource plan is a projection of how the firm plans to acquire and use its human resources. It affects and is affected by the firm's overall strategic plan, and it serves as the basis for overall human resource management.

Now we begin to look at how organizations fill the jobs. How do they decide how many people they need? How do they determine the skill/ability mix of these people? What should be the mix of hiring from the outside versus promoting from within? How are vacancies estimated? Would the company benefit from a computerized HRIS?

human resource planning The process of making decisions regarding the acquisition and utilization of human resources.

Human resource planning is the process of making decisions regarding the acquisition and utilization of human resources. As such, it is part of the strategic decision-making process. The human resource plan focuses on an analysis of the organization's objectives and the plan for acquiring resources to meet those objectives. The organization's objectives and the resource acquisition process are analyzed in terms of the role that human resources plays in achieving organizational goals.

Human resource planning is the sum total of the plan formulated for the recruiting, screening, compensation, training, job structure, promotion, and work rules of an organization's human resources. It is a process designed to translate the corporate plans and objectives into future quantitative and qualitative employment requirements, together with plans to fulfill those requirements over both the shorter and longer terms, through human resource utilization, employee development, employment and recruiting, and use of information systems.[3]

This definition emphasizes structuring plans to carry out what are considered to be the traditional personnel management functions of hiring, training, compensation, and promotion. Thus, even though the primary focus of human resource planning is on obtaining people to fill jobs, human resource planning is a pervasive function in that it involves planning for the operation of other areas of human resource management as well.

Economic Forces

Human resource planning is influenced by national employment and economic policy planning. National economic policy planning sets the stage for national policy in training and education and the level of economic activity through monetary and fiscal policy. Congress and various federal agencies, (such as the Department of Labor)—particularly the Employment and Training Administration and certain agencies within the Department of Health and Human Services and the Department of Education—play a major role. Laws are passed to encourage certain types of training or the hiring of certain groups. For example, the Jobs Training Partnership Act encourages private sector hiring of disadvantaged groups.

Economic and human resource policy at the national level changes as the priorities of a particular Congress or administration change. For example, under Presidents Kennedy and Johnson, a great deal of effort and funds were spent to develop plans to

EXHIBIT 4.3

STRATEGIC HUMAN RESOURCE PLANNING
SERVES AS THE KEY LINK BETWEEN THE
OVERALL STRATEGIC PLAN AND HUMAN
RESOURCE MANAGEMENT

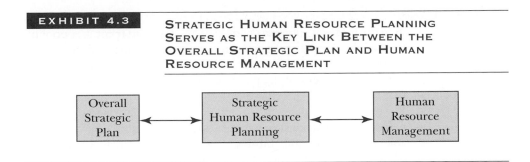

deal with specific employment problems. Most of the programs in this period were directed at improving the employment relationship of minorities and disadvantaged groups, in keeping with the philosophy of the New Frontier of the Kennedy administration and the Great Society of the Johnson administration.

However, during the Nixon and Ford administrations, human resource priorities changed. The emphasis on programs for the disadvantaged and minorities was reduced. Instead, these administrations increased the emphasis on improving the employment situation of veterans and on improving the already existing federal offices, such as the federal-state divisions of employment, to help all levels of employment. The Nixon administration also decentralized the national human resource planning effort by establishing regional offices throughout the nation through the revenue sharing program, and by asking each state to handle its employment planning function.

The Carter administration continued this decentralized approach to human resource planning but sought to increase the scope and funding of programs for the disadvantaged and minorities. The Reagan and Bush administrations reduced the emphasis on the federal government's role in human resource planning and provided incentives for private industry to take over more of the planning and training function. Reagan also instituted the "block grants" concept for the states. Under this plan, money is allocated to state and local governments as a block or whole, not by program or funding category. This allows the states to allocate funds to priority programs with a minimum of federal red tape.[4]

National economic and human resource policy plays a major underlying role in a firm's human resource planning. For example, when federal programs were established to improve the employment opportunities for the unskilled, disadvantaged, and unemployed, all individual organizations were asked to commit extra efforts for recruiting, training, and employing these individuals.

Often federal programs stimulate an organization to increase human resource planning efforts. Federal laws and court interpretations of those laws dealing with equal employment opportunity and affirmative action often make it necessary for many organizations to review their human resource planning process. As noted previously, the thrust of affirmative action planning involves the development of an organizational plan to recruit, train, and employ more minorities and women than the organization presently employs. As organizations review the number of employees presently employed in various positions and develop plans to replace these employees to ensure that minorities are being recruited, they usually end up making a comprehensive review of their total human resource planning system.

The Labor Market

labor market
The pool of qualified applicants from which a company can hire.

To a great extent, organizations view the **labor market** as a pool of skills and abilities that will be tapped as the need arises. For most job requirements, employees with appropriate skills and abilities are readily available. From time to time, organizations experience shortages of people with certain skills or find that the wage level is so high that they cannot "afford" to hire the type of people needed to fill the available jobs. For example, for many years employers faced a shortage of people with computer expertise. The relationship between the organization's job requirements and the available pool of skills and abilities is typically viewed by managers as a sequential process whereby the organization first establishes the best job structure in terms of job content and task assignments, determines each job's worth in the production process (job evaluation), and then proceeds to hire and develop human resources that match these requirements. Often things do not work so smoothly for a firm because the labor market is not perfect and is constantly changing. Shortages and surpluses of skill areas develop, and workers are laid off permanently as plants close. Autoworkers must move from Detroit to Ohio, Tennessee, Kentucky, and California if they want to continue working in the auto industry.

Economists typically indicate four main determinants of the labor supply:

1. The size, age, sex, and educational composition of the population.
2. The demand for goods and services in the economy.
3. The nature of production technology.
4. The labor force participation rates (people working or looking for work) of major subgroups (for example, women).

Skill Changes and Personnel Shortages

Changes in the labor market have led to skill shortages as well as areas of oversupply. When the human resource educational/skill mix differs significantly from the skills required by employers, personnel shortages develop. Employers have jobs open but cannot find people with the skills needed. Many people who want jobs are not hired because they do not have the skills demanded. This mismatch between job skill requirements and the skills of the labor force plagued the U.S. economy during the 1970s and 1980s and can have serious negative impact on the economy of a society. For example, employment rates in traditional industries, such as steel, automobiles, and rubber, have declined as demand and technology in these areas change; yet severe personnel shortages are occurring in such high-tech areas as computers, information processing, and genetic engineering. In many cases, rust-belt jobs in traditional industries in the Midwest have moved to Sunbelt jobs in information systems and services.

This human resource dislocation in part drives inflation, because employers bid up the wage rate for the few qualified workers in the high-demand fields. The wage rates of computer-trained auto mechanics, for example, soared in the late 1980s. At the same time, relative wage rates tumbled in the old-line industries. The federal government has reacted to this situation by encouraging employers to improve the computer-related skills of employees by developing training programs. These programs are embodied in the Jobs Training Partnership Act, a joint federal–private business action that provides the skills necessary for many entry-level jobs in high-tech industries and various federally funded vocational and technical education programs at two-year technical schools.

Because the types of skills needed by employers now are much more sophisticated than they were in the 1970s and 1980s, this most likely will increase the educational attainment level of workers. For example, various new engineering, computer, and medical technical jobs require much higher skills than before. Even today's automotive mechanics will be more highly skilled than their counterparts in the 1980s because of the more sophisticated design of automobile computers, engines, and related systems and because of the tremendous variety in automotive models within a given manufacturer's line.

Thus any human resource plan must assess the human resource educational/skill level of the labor market from which it draws, predict future changes in this mix, assess the effect of federal human resource programs, and then plan recruiting, training, and job design systems that take maximum advantage of the forecasted educational/ skill mix. Human resource management units perform a boundary spanning or scanning role when assessing labor market characteristics. Recognizing that the labor market and federal legislation and activities related to it have a major impact on any company's individual human resource plan, we look now at a model or procedure for constructing a human resource plan.

Model for Human Resource Planning

Exhibit 4.4 shows an overall model or procedure for constructing a human resource plan. We will examine each step in the model.

Determine Growth/Retrenchment Objectives

Notice the impact that outside factors in the environment, as well as market opportunities and the personal values of strategic managers, have in formulating an organization's growth objectives. Growth/retrenchment objectives drive the human resource plan. If an organization decides to scale back, retrench, or restructure, people will be let go. We saw this often in the 1980s. Eastern Airlines, Ford, General Motors, Beatrice, and AT&T, among others, went through major retrenchments. Even very successful companies, such as IBM, experienced periods of retrenchment in the late 1980s.

If a company grows rapidly with little retrenchment, such as Apple or American Express did in the 1980s, employment expands. Growth objectives are a key part of an organization's overall strategic plan. Almost all strategic plans deal with the size the company wishes to be in the future. For example, under Jack Welch, General Electric decided that it wanted to be either number one or number two in every industry it enters; if it is not, it will either not enter that industry or will exit if already in it.[5] This is a key factor of GE's strategic plan. *Managed growth* is a popular phrase because companies can grow too fast; two excellent examples are People Express and Air Florida. Both companies grew faster than their internal operations could handle, and both died. There are costs to growth.

Growth/retrenchment objectives may be expressed in terms of sales, market share, asset size, return on investment, development of new products and services or selling off of product lines, and development of new markets or abandonment of markets.

Human resource departments need to align the strategic human resource plan with the firm's growth/retrenchment strategy. A growth-oriented strategy needs to be supported by a human resource strategy of aggressive recruiting, hiring, and training. Many high-tech companies, such as Apple, NeXT, and Microsoft, were ill-prepared for their rapid growth and either could not find qualified personnel or had to pay

EXHIBIT 4.4   A MODEL FOR CONSTRUCTING A HUMAN RESOURCE PLAN

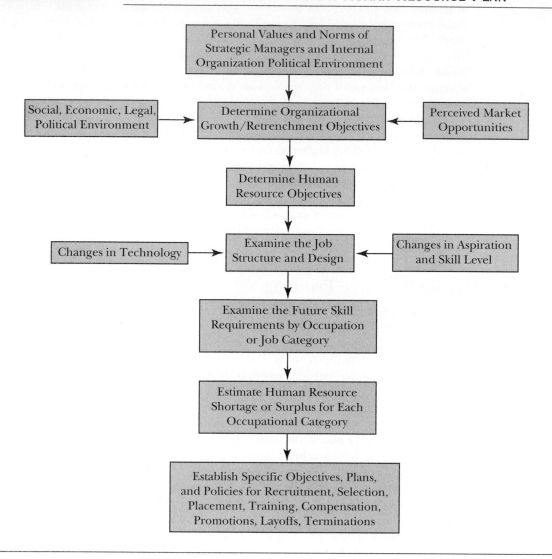

premium prices to fulfill their needs. Because it is not always clear how fast a company might grow, the top executive team needs to be prepared with a set of contingency plans that allow a reasonable range of options.

In contrast to fast-growing firms are those facing retrenchment and declining markets. Here, human resource planning must deal with hard and unpleasant issues. The firm may want to act in a guarded way to avoid alerting suppliers, customers, and employees of an impending cutback. It is important, though, that the strategic plan address these issues to minimize damage and to make the best of a difficult situation. During the mid-1980s, companies in the farm equipment business, such as John Deere and Company, faced massive layoffs. Deere was more successful than most in maintaining its public image and critical human resources through proactive planning and in executing the cutbacks in a humane and thoughtful way. By 1988-1989 the company had returned to high levels of profitability with a trimmed but efficient workforce.[6]

Divestitures and mergers provide a challenge for the human resource department. Merging two or more firms may involve cutbacks or at least reassignment. Conflicting corporate cultures need to be meshed, and this needs to be part of the strategic plan. Divestiture involves issues such as staff reconfiguration, reassignments, and layoffs. Union contracts and other labor agreements may need to be considered. Careful negotiations and agreements with the acquiring company need to be planned for and executed.

planning horizon The time frame estimated to accomplish organizational objectives.

The objectives that companies set are usually expressed in terms of a time frame or **planning horizon**: the length of time over which the objectives and the plan for accomplishing them will occur.

The planning horizon for growth in many organizations seldom exceeds 15 years and is often expressed in terms of short-, intermediate-, and long-range periods. General Electric is widely known for preparing long-range forecasts for products needed in the future. Auto companies, such as Ford, General Motors, and Chrysler, also emphasize long-range objectives. As a rule of thumb, *short range* is defined as a horizon of 1 year or less, *intermediate range* as 2 to 4 years, and *long range* as 5 to 15 years. Often the long-range objectives are quite general, and the intermediate- and short-range objectives are much more specific. This specificity is especially true of short-range or **operational objectives**.

operational objectives Day-to-day short-term objectives.

Human resource professionals often play a role in helping to form growth/retrenchment objectives if the firm has adopted a strategic human resource approach. They can provide advice on how internal staffing needs will likely change as well as the likely availability of people with necessary skills.

Determine Human Resource Objectives

Once the organization's objectives are specified, communicated, and understood by all affected, the human resource unit should *specify its objectives with regard to human resource utilization in the organization*. In developing these objectives, specific policies need to be formulated to address the following questions:

1. Shall we attempt to fill positions from within or by hiring individuals from the labor market?
2. Can we meet our commitments to affirmative action and equal employment opportunity?
3. How do our training and development objectives interface with our human resource planning objectives?
4. What union constraints do we face in human resource planning, and what policies should we develop to effectively handle these constraints?
5. What is our policy toward providing everyone in the organization with a meaningful, challenging job (job enrichment)? Will we continue to have some boring, routine jobs, or should we eliminate them?
6. Can some positions and jobs be eliminated so that we can become more competitive?[7]
7. To what extent can we automate production and operations, and what shall we do about those displaced?
8. How do we ensure that we have a continuously adaptive and flexible workforce?

EXHIBIT 4.5 EXAMPLE OF HUMAN RESOURCE OBJECTIVES

---

1. To develop and implement a pay-for-performance system by January 1, 1995 (large bank).

2. To achieve the staffing plans for the 1997–1999 period (information services company).

3. To reduce employment levels in current manufacturing operations by 10 percent per year from 1993–1995 (plastics manufacturer).

4. To implement a career development plan for all employees by July 1, 1999 (state agency).

5. To ensure that all supervisors receive 60 hours of classroom training prior to appointment of supervision by July 1, 1995 (utility).

6. To establish a computerized human resource skills inventory of all employees by April 1, 1998 (credit union).

7. To reduce employee turnover 33 percent by January 1, 1994 (convenience store chain).

8. To develop and implement an aggressive program to hire older employees by September 1, 1996 (fast-food chain).

9. To achieve a 60/40 inside/outside mix for promotion during the next three years (large restaurant chain).

These are not easy questions to answer, but they go to the heart of human resource planning. Imagine a large company such as Federal Express or IBM facing these questions. With far-flung growing domestic and international operations, development of an overall human resource plan that systematically answers these questions is essential for managed growth.

Exhibit 4.5 shows some actual human resource objectives for organizations. Notice the variety of specific human resource areas addressed: promotion, staffing, training and development, career development, employment levels, pay, and so on. A large firm with a well-developed human resource plan, such as Campbell's or American Express, has a large number of human resource objectives spelled out at the corporate level, and each division has a list of its own subobjectives. These continue down to the unit level as shown in Exhibit 4.6. Taking the objectives to this level is what makes them operational. If the objectives are never taken to the unit level of specificity, they will never be achieved. Translating the objective to the unit level ("the trenches") is required for implementation.

Notice also that human resource objectives should be integrated with other functional area objectives. For example, training and development objectives should be geared toward and integrated with production, sales, and skill needs. Staffing needs should be coordinated with forecasted growth in sales, and so on. This kind of integration is becoming easier to achieve with the use of computer software and hardware. Having human resources play the role of full partner in the strategic planning process helps to ensure better integration among functional areas.

Examine Job Design and Structure

An important step in strategic human resource management is the design of jobs. It is also an important step in human resource planning. Companies should not take the particular configuration of jobs that exist at a specific point in time as unchangeable; in fact, during the 1980s many changes in job design and structure occurred. Think

EXHIBIT 4.6 INTEGRATION OF HUMAN RESOURCE OBJECTIVES

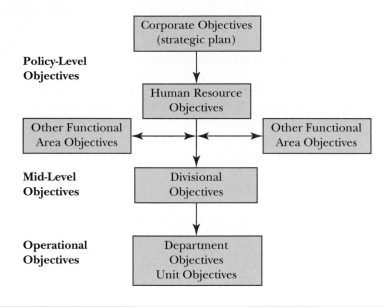

of how much the robotic welding process used in auto assembly differs from the hand welding of earlier times.

Computer-assisted design/computer-assisted manufacturing (CAD/CAM) already has had a major effect on employment in some industries. For example, CAD can greatly increase the work output of designers, such as design engineers in the auto industry, leading to a reduced work force with a very high increase in productivity for the remaining designers. Estimates show that CAD/CAM can improve productivity in an operation by 300 percent.[8]

Therefore examining jobs in light of new technological change will likely result in a reconfiguration of jobs in the organization. This will greatly affect staffing, training, hiring, and other aspects of the overall human resource plan.

A second major factor to be examined in this step involves the aspirations and skill levels of employees. This issue deals with the motivation levels, work ethic, expectations, and job skills employees bring to a job. For years, the trend has been that employees want jobs that are challenging, that require responsibility, and that provide opportunities for advancement and involvement—jobs that require higher skills. Company efforts at involvement and participation through various programs such as **quality circles and quality improvement programs** or **participative management programs** rest on the fundamental belief that employees want an enriched job experience that involves their minds as well as their hands. Motorola, Florida Power and Light, Ford, and Nissan are all companies that have invested heavily in programs of this nature, as we have pointed out elsewhere in this book. The changing nature of employee aspirations, expectations, and skills will cause companies to redefine and restructure jobs to some extent to reflect these changes.

quality circles and quality improvement programs Groups of employees that meet to recommend ways to improve production and quality.

participative management programs A decision-making process that involves managers as well as employees.

The final issue to discuss in terms of technology and human resource planning is the shortages of trained personnel for engineering, computer, and other high-tech–related occupations. Tremendous growth in employment openings in these occupations is forecasted. There also is a projected shortage of people to fill these occupations. From an employer's perspective, this means that it will be increasingly more difficult for organizations to attract and keep people with engineering, computer, and high-tech skills.

Another disturbing phenomenon related to this issue is the "eating your own seed corn" dilemma. Personnel shortages in engineering and computer occupations have caused many firms to hire university faculty members from engineering and computer information programs at salaries greatly in excess of the university salary. This, of course, leads to further shortages in the production of college-educated engineers and computer information specialists for the future. Companies desperate for high-tech employees are going even further up the food chain by recruiting current college students. Companies are offering lucrative salaries in an effort to entice students to quit school and join the company. This is equivalent to college athletes going pro prior to graduation.[9]

Estimate Future Skill Requirements by Occupation or Job Category

Once the new job structure and design are determined, the next step is to examine the skills required in each job category. Forecasting future skill needs and preparing to fill those needs today is a critical feature of the strategic approach to human resource planning. As noted above, job structure changes based on technology or other reasons cause skill changes. Computers in cars require different skills for mechanics. Robot welders in auto assembly changed the skill mix in auto factories. Word processors and personal computers changed the skill requirements for secretaries. For example, one convenience store chain restructured district manager jobs by changing information analysis and reporting requirements and requiring that computers with modems be used.

Occupational skills change over time. Therefore it is important at this stage that an organization have a complete, current listing of all occupational categories in the organization with explanatory job descriptions that specify the duties, skills, and qualifications required for each job. Such a **skills bank** should be computerized and easily accessed for promotion and training purposes. Estimations of how these skills will change need to be built into the human resource plan.

skills bank A list of job descriptions specifying the duties, skills, and qualifications for each job.

For example, during the late 1980s, a large wholesaler in the auto industry in the southeastern United States made a decision that each manager and clerical employee should have a personal computer on his or her desk. This necessitated a massive training program to ensure that all clerical and managerial employees were computer literate so that the PCs would actually be used. The training need was forecast well before the computers were ordered so that a training program could be established and funded, ready to be implemented once the computers were ordered. Key people were sent to off-site training programs so that they could learn to use computers and then train other employees once the computers arrived.

Estimate Human Resource Shortage or Surplus for Each Occupational Category

This takes us to the fifth step in the human resource planning model. The human resource shortage or surplus should be estimated for each occupational and job category. Decisions should be made about what to do to deal with estimated surpluses or shortages in view of the organization's human resource utilization objectives. Exhibit

EXHIBIT 4.7	A PROCEDURE FOR ESTIMATING HUMAN RESOURCE SHORTAGE OR SURPLUS FOR A JOB OR OCCUPATIONAL CATEGORY

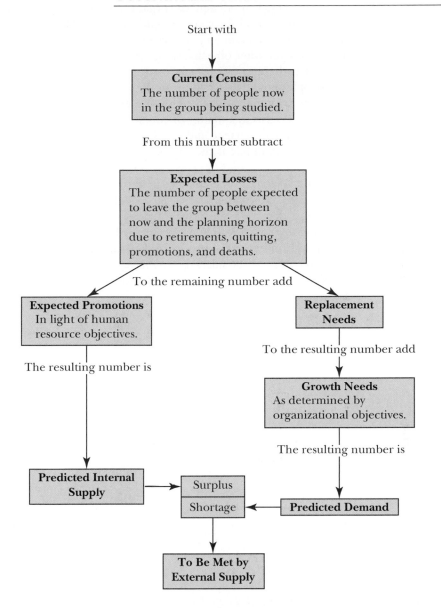

4.7 presents a procedure that is useful in estimating a given surplus or shortage for a particular occupation or job category. Note that this procedure ties in consideration of human resource objectives in filling jobs from within via internal promotions and organizational growth objectives.

If a surplus is predicted for an occupational category, the human resource plan needs to consider whether these individuals will be discharged, temporarily laid off, retrained and transferred, provided with a cash bonus for quitting, given severance pay, or given early retirement. These decisions are probably determined by the organization's overall human resource objectives for training and development.

If a shortage is predicted, the organization must hire from the outside labor market if it expects to fill the resulting job vacancies. This decision may cause the organization to review its human resource objectives with regard to hiring from the outside market vis-à-vis other objectives. For example, if the organization finds that it has to pay a higher than expected wage to attract new people, it may decide to make do with fewer people and either schedule more overtime or subcontract out some of the work. In fact, many organizations do this at least on a temporary basis. Most construction contractors do this as a matter of course, as do most state departments of transportation for road maintenance and construction. Subcontracting and the use of overtime are especially desirable if the shortage is reviewed as temporary (six months or less).

Transition Matrix   The changes or movements of human resources within an organization are called the *flows* of employees. One method of mathematically determining and depicting the flows of people in an organization is through use of a "transition matrix."[10] A simple example will help explain how this works. Assume that an organization had 100 Clerk 1s and 50 Clerk 2s in 1999. As of 2001, only 80 percent of the original 100 Clerk 1s may have remained in that position, and only 60 percent of the original 50 Clerk 2s may still be employed by the organization as Clerk 2s. The transition matrix shows this flow:

	2001	
1999	**Clerk 1**	**Clerk 2**
Clerk 1	80%	
Clerk 2		60%

Suppose that the following conditions actually existed as of 2001: Ten of the Clerk 1s were promoted to Clerk 2, 10 of the Clerk 1s left the organization, 15 of the Clerk 2s left the organization, and 5 were demoted to Clerk 1.

This flow analysis would appear as follows:

	2001			
1999	**Clerk 1**	**Clerk 2**	**Left Organization**	**Total**
Clerk 1	80% stayed	10% promoted	10%	100%
Clerk 2	10% demoted	60% stayed	30%	100%

This information could be integrated into the human resource plan to chart a trend. These percentages are then used as indicators of the probability of transition in each category to project future supply movement. The staffing level in each category at the beginning of a planning period is multiplied by the transition probabilities within each category. Then the columns are summed to yield the future labor supply within job categories.

The analysis is somewhat complex and appears to be used mostly by large firms. Weyerhaeuser, Eaton, and Corning have reported using it with mixed results.[11] Clearly more research and refinement are needed. However, we are likely to see more widespread use as computer software is refined to make transition analysis easier to use.

Computer simulation   Computer simulation of future staffing needs and levels is becoming more common as software to support the simulations becomes available. Disney World uses a computer model to predict its employment levels by job category. This model is especially useful when seasonal factors affect employment.

Because forecasting contains an inherent amount of uncertainty, this technique and others are limited in their usefulness and application by the reliability and validity of the input data. The identification of key variables believed to affect future trends is very important. But selection of these key variables is not enough to ensure success. They must be measured accurately. The data must also be received in a timely fashion because old data are not as useful as new data. Organizations generally rely on past educational and job experience to predict future performance.

However, establishing valid criteria for this type of forecasting is difficult to do—much more difficult than using historical data or future requirements as a means of setting overall organizational objectives.[12] For example, if an organization wished to determine how many workers would be needed in a specific department in five years, a computer model (a representation of reality) might be used. Critical variables would have to be selected. These might include anticipated technological changes, outside labor force changes, required skills, absenteeism and turnover rates, past growth rates within the department, and so on. The model would then give the organization an estimated number of workers.

The firm could obtain not only a single estimate but also, through manipulation or modification of the variables, estimates under varying situations and conditions. For example, Disney develops and runs various alternative future scenarios. How many employees would be needed if the quit rate doubled in certain jobs? How many would be needed if visitor growth rate to the park fell by 25 percent? Forecasting varying scenarios and using the model to manipulate various data under each scenario make computer simulation an extremely useful tool in human resource planning.

Linear Programming   Another technique used to plan and forecast changes in employment by job level is linear programming. Linear programming, a method used to determine the optimal way of allocating scarce resources among competing demands, has been used by Lilian and Rao to describe the movements of people through the organization.[13] It is a quantitative method of analysis used for maximizing an objective function, expressed in the form of a mathematical equation (for example, MAX $z5\$10x1\$30y$), subject to some particular set of constraints, also expressed in mathematical notation (for example, $4x16y,12$; $8x14y,16$). There are several ways to solve linear programming problems, ranging from a graphic method for less complicated problems to computer use for more detailed or complex problems.

Delphi Techniques   Another technique used in planning and forecasting, and recently used in human resource planning, is the Delphi technique.[14] In the Delphi technique, a panel of experts arrives at a consensus of opinion about growth and scenarios. These experts come from numerous related fields, and they complete a detailed questionnaire concerning the issue to be addressed. They also supply their own personal opinions on the issue. Later these experts receive a summary of the responses. If their opinion differs from the summary, they are asked to reconsider their original viewpoint. If they still hold the same opinion thereafter, they are asked to explain their stance. This process is repeated, usually three or four times, until a consensus prediction is reached. One important aspect of the Delphi technique lies in its anonymity. This helps to avoid "groupthink" and to reduce conflict among the panel members.

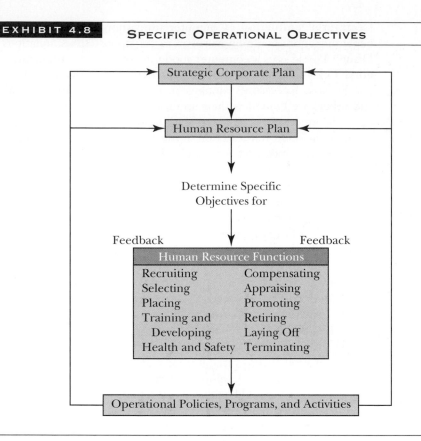

EXHIBIT 4.8 SPECIFIC OPERATIONAL OBJECTIVES

Strategic Corporate Plan

Human Resource Plan

Determine Specific
Objectives for

Feedback   Feedback

Human Resource Functions

Recruiting	Compensating
Selecting	Appraising
Placing	Promoting
Training and	Retiring
Developing	Laying Off
Health and Safety	Terminating

Operational Policies, Programs, and Activities

Delphi processes can be used to derive overall trends in changing job demands. For example, the Florida Association of Independent Insurance Agents used the process to speculate on changing job demands and characteristics in the offices of independent insurance agents. The Delphi technique developed scenarios of highly automated insurance offices using computers and word processors to handle record keeping, billing, and claims payments. These scenarios were "played out" to forecast changing needs in terms of skills and numbers of office employees, including the agent.

Summary of Forecasting Surpluses/Shortages and Changing Skill Needs All of these techniques must be clearly integrated with the needs of line managers, who help supply the necessary data and help make decisions. Plans must be monitored and evaluated to ensure that they are meeting objectives. If necessary, plans must be redesigned as input data or forecasts change. Human resource planning is a dynamic process rather than a static event. In this regard the human resource plan responds to changes in the organization's goals and its environment as well as internal desires for work levels and line manager desires.

Establish Specific Objectives for Human Resource Functions

The final step in human resource planning is to establish specific objectives for each human resource function, from recruiting to terminating.

The overall human resource plan should drive the specific operational objectives established for each human resource function, as shown in Exhibit 4.8. These determine specific operational policies, programs, and activities developed to meet objectives. Both specific functional objectives and operating programs are integrated with the overall human resource plan by means of a feedback loop. If realistic objectives and program activities cannot be set or met under the human resource plan, the plan should be modified. As Exhibit 4.8 indicates, the entire resource plan is integrated with the organization's overall strategic plan. The next section examines human resource costing as it relates to human resource planning.

Human Resource Costing

Making human resource planning decisions because "it's the right thing to do" or because it will "make employees happy" is increasingly a less acceptable reason to justify policy. Today, organizations want to know how human resource policy affects the bottom line. Some of the more common costing measures include HRMex, or the human resource department's expenses as a percent of company operating expense. Human resource managers are increasingly being asked to justify decisions and programs on a cost-benefit basis. They are being held accountable in a financial sense for policy and procedure. They are being asked time and time again, "Are our programs and policies worth it? Are our decisions producing the desired results?"

No doubt cost-competitive factors and restructuring efforts have exacerbated this demand for accountability. But so has the traditional human resource defense of its programs, which has emphasized less tangible benefits such as good morale and job satisfaction. Line managers today want to know how these benefits contribute to the bottom line.

Human Resource Accounting

When asked to name their most important resource, many managers respond with "our people." When asked to put a value on its human resources, most managers say they cannot or that their people are invaluable. Yet valuing human resources has been a subject of inquiry since the late 1960s. The R. G. Barry Corporation of Columbus, Ohio, made the first major attempt to put a value on their human resources.[15] This model uses historical costs (actual expenses for recruiting, training, development, and so on) to determine the firm's investments in its employees and thus the asset value for the employee. This is a traditional way for accountants to value any resource, such as a building.[16] The asset value of the human resource staff can also be computed by calculating the human resource expenditure per employee. This calculation includes the cost of all human resource activities and staff divided by the number of employees covered by human resource services. In 1988 the average per capita expenditure per employee was $629. This value rose to $654 in 1989 and to $730 in 1990.[17]

Some companies are moving further with human resource accounting by attempting to measure and manage their most valuable asset—intellectual capital, or employee knowledge. According to several progressive companies, promoting, managing, and measuring intellectual capital is a critical step in human resource planning.[18] Scandia AFS, a Scandinavia-based insurance firm, recently included in its annual report a description of the important nonfinancial measures that contribute to the company's success. These nonfinancial measures included processes for development and renewal within the organization as well as corporate culture characteristics, such as the proportion of women in the company and how many supervisors were from countries other than Sweden. According to Leif Edvinsson, director of intellectual capital at AFS, the issue is not to measure only financial capital but to have a more balanced measurement system that will ultimately create financial capital. The knowledge of individual workers (human capital) and its relationship to the knowledge of the organization (structural capital) is what is meant by *intellectual capital.* The process of extracting knowledge from employees is, in essence, creating structural capital.

Asset value, replacement costs, present value of future earnings, and value to the organization have also been used to place a value on a firm's human resources. However, a major limitation to all of these approaches is their focus on inputs and outputs. In other words, they do not relate a firm's investment in people with the output the people produce.[19]

Newer approaches attempt to put a dollar value on the behavioral outcomes produced by working in an organization. Costs are determined for such behaviors as absenteeism, turnover, and poor job performance. This method measures the economic consequences of employee behavior, not the value of the individual.

Costing Employee Behaviors

The costing approach may be more useful today when compared with the human resource accounting approach.[20] Financial quantification of a set of common behavior and performance outcomes uses standard cost-accounting procedures applied to employee behavior. To do this, cost elements associated with each behavior must be identified and their separate and independent dollar values computed.[21]

For example, look at costing labor turnover. High turnover can be a very expensive proposition for any organization. To compute turnover costs, dollar figures must be attached to separation costs, replacement costs (including recruiting and hiring), and training and orientation costs. In addition, there is an opportunity cost of having the job unfilled for a period of time or filled with a less-than-fully-trained person. The opportunity cost is the forgone productivity because the job was not filled or because it was filled with a new, less-well-trained employee.

Fast-Food Example   A firm may put up with high turnover if it believes that the costs of curing the problem are higher than turnover costs themselves. Look at a typical fast-food operation such as McDonald's, for example. Suppose that a McDonald's franchise experiences a 100 percent annual average turnover rate, about the national average for fast-food stores. In calculating the costs of this turnover, the costs of people leaving (separation), hiring, training, and forgone productivity would be compared with the costs of reducing the turnover. Assume for a moment that the costs of reducing turnover to, say, 25 percent result in the following:

1. Increasing wages by $1 per hour.
2. Implementing career tracks and promotion routes for all employees.
3. Increasing the benefits package.
4. Allowing employees a more flexible work schedule.

Also assume that when calculating these costs, the franchise determines that they far outweigh the turnover costs. In this case the franchise may put up with 100 percent turnover as the less costly alternative.

incremental approach   A step-by-step approach used by a company to diminish costs incurred because of turnover.

Of course, during the estimation of the costs of the four steps listed above, errors may be made because costs are estimated or projected, *not* actual. Also, it may be possible to reduce turnover by doing only step 1 or steps 1 and 2. In other words, an **incremental approach** could be used to see if a step affects the turnover rate. This would be less costly than attempting all four steps at once.

In order for the HR department to be a full strategic partner, evidence of supporting the bottom line is essential. However, many HR professionals are reluctant to develop costing procedures in their organizations. Some feel that measuring individuals as if they were widgets is distasteful. Others got into HR to avoid having to deal with numbers. It also may be that HR professionals fear the unknown and wonder what would happen if they find their programs to be ineffective. However, having basic bottom line facts may be the best way to combat threats to outsource HR.

The best advice that can be given to HR professionals venturing into the costing arena is to start small. Start by getting a handle on efficiency. Figure out how things are going in your organization, and then benchmark your status against prior performance and competitors. You also can calculate return on investment (ROI) by assigning a monetary value to an HR program and then dividing this number by the cost of the program. It also may be useful to develop HR metrics that are unique to your company. Costing HR is the next great challenge facing HR professionals.[22]

Utility Theory

utility theory
An area of decision making that provides a framework for selecting the decision alternative that provides maximum payment.

Through trial-and-error experience, a firm may develop fairly accurate costs of various behaviors. It may be possible to provide a reasonably accurate estimate of resultant benefits. Yet because choices are involved, the decision should be to select the option that provides the maximum payment or *utility*. The study of this area of decision making is called **utility theory**.[23] Utility theory provides a framework for making decisions that requires decision makers to state goals clearly, specify outcomes of the decision options, and attach differing values or utilities to each outcome. Probabilities for the outcome of each decision also can be specified. This information is used to construct a payoff table or matrix.

Returning to the McDonald's franchise turnover example, we can see how utility theory might work. The objective is to cut turnover. Four possible steps were identified. If we assign a dollar value to the effect of each alternative—the amount it will save in turnover—plus the probability that it will occur, we then have the following payoff matrix:

Effect	Payout		Probability		(Costs saved)
Payoff, Option 1 (Raise wages)	$5000	×	.60	=	$3000
Payoff, Option 2 (Career tracks)	3000	×	.20	=	600
Payoff, Option 3 (Benefits package)	2000	×	.10	–	200
Payoff, Option 4 (Flexible hours)	1500	×	.10	=	150

Clearly, in this example, we will get our highest probable payout by raising wages (Option 1). The effect of this option is that we will reduce turnover costs by $3000 ($5000 estimated cost reduction × .60 probability of occurrence).

The final step is to compare the cost of this option to the cost of the other options in order to compute a cost/benefit ratio for each. This can be computed as follows:

Option	Annual Cost	Annual Payout (Benefit)	Cost/Benefit Ratio
1	$10,000	$3000	.30
2	5000	600	.12
3	4000	200	.05
4	3000	150	.05

With these hypothetical figures, Option 1 would be chosen: it costs the most ($10,000) but has the highest payout relative to cost, giving it the highest cost/benefit ratio of .30.

Of course, this example is hypothetical. Actual figures of a problem of this type would differ because of individual firm circumstances. Furthermore, probabilities, even though based on experience and judgment, are still somewhat subjective. Nevertheless, this affords a much more rigorous analysis of decision options than typical seat-of-the-pants decision making that so often characterizes human resource decisions.

From a strategic standpoint, human resource costing and utility analysis offer much opportunity for the human resource professional. Far more sophisticated models using predictors, criterion cutoffs, and sophisticated mathematical notation are available in the literature. These models, coupled with computer manipulation and software packages, make it possible for even the most minimally skilled novice to incorporate quantitative cost analysis in human resource decisions. The emphasis on controlling human resource costs will likely spur more reliance on these quantitative techniques in the future; however, they are unlikely to completely replace the qualitative decision making discussed at the beginning of the chapter. Judgment will always play a role in human resource decision making.

As we have seen, there are many opportunities in which computers can be used in the planning process. Let's expand on this idea as we now turn our focus to technology and HRISs.

Human Resource Information Systems

The basis for good human resource decisions is good human resource information, which should be provided to both human resource and line managers to facilitate decision making. This concept is known as a decision-support system (DSS). A DSS places information for decision making literally at the fingertips of decision makers. Using personal computers or terminals, human resource and line managers can call up information as needed for making recruiting, promoting, paying, or developing decisions.

system A set of activities that take inputs and transform them into outputs.

A HRIS is made up of numerous elements. Each element must function properly if the **system** is going to benefit the organization. Basically, a system is a set of activities that takes *inputs* (an application for employment in the finance department, for example), *transforms* them into useful items (a hiring approval from the human resource department), and then *outputs* the new items to where they can be used (sends the approval to the finance department). Most systems also have some form of *control* mechanism (the finance department sends back a completed new employee report) that enables supervisors to manage the operation of the system.[24]

Systems may be found on a departmental level, a plant level, or even an organization level. In short, a system is any activity that involves inputs, transformations, outputs, and feedbacks, and one system may be a subsystem—or a part—of another system. The HRIS is usually a part of the organization's larger management information system (MIS), which would include accounting, production, and marketing functions, to name just a few. The special function of HRIS is to gather, collect, and help analyze the data necessary for the human resource department to do its jobs properly. The opening case on Mrs. Fields Cookies is an example of how the HRIS works.

Inputs

The inputs of a HRIS resemble that of a manually based system. Employee information, company policies and procedures, and other personnel-related information must be entered into the system in order to be used. This information is usually entered from documents (such as an application form or an insurance report) into a computer terminal or personal computer connected to a mainframe computer. Information can be typed in, digitally read (or scanned) from documents, loaded into the system from other computers, or retrieved from other machines connected to the computer (for example, a time clock linked to the computer).

A computerized HRIS is superior to a manual system in many respects. Because much of the information is automatically entered into the system, errors are less likely to occur. Also, the HRIS's ability to connect to other computers exposes it to data that would otherwise be too difficult or costly to obtain. For example, the U.S. government and several private organizations maintain databases—or lists of information on certain topics—that can be accessed by computers. If the human resource manager of a New York–based firm realized that its Georgia plant would be needing a new entry-level chemical engineer within six months, he or she could connect into a database that would report the number of persons graduating from college with a bachelor's degree in chemical engineering in the Southeast during the past year and their average starting salaries. Another advantage of an automated HRIS is backlog reduction. A well-designed HRIS will allow for more efficient input operation than a manual system could provide.

Transformations

The transformation portion of the system is most closely associated with the actual computer. It also usually includes the software, or the written instructions that tell the computer what to do, how to do it, and when to do it. Computers and software for HRISs range from simple and inexpensive to complex and expensive. Many small firms can meet their needs by establishing a functional HRIS with a personal computer and standard database and spreadsheet programs. Large multinational firms may need to use a mainframe computer running sophisticated, custom-designed software programs to meet their needs. One of the most sophisticated software packages on the market today is SAP's R/3.

SAP is a German-based software giant run by cochairmen Hasso Plattner and Henning Kagermann. In 2000, SAP was the fourth largest software producer. Additional information about the company can be found on its Web site at **www.sap.com**. SAP's most important product is R/3, a series of tightly interwoven programs that provide organizations a powerful network that can furnish any type of information required to make decisions at the touch of a button. Currently, nearly half of the world's 500 largest companies are using R/3 to run their operations.[25]

Installing R/3 is not the same as installing an over-the-counter software package. According to Michael Hammer, president of Hammer & Company, it is more like an "organizational revolution." Because R/3 is a complex set of programs, it can take several years and millions of dollars to completely implement. However, R/3 appears to be worth the trouble. Corporate managers have described SAP's R/3 system as a light bulb illuminating the darkness of planning and decision making in organizations. Monsanto's vice-president, Bob Barrett, gives R/3 high marks. He attributes Monsanto's ability to slash its production planning time in half—from six months to three months—and its increased bargaining position with suppliers to SAP's R/3. In money terms, R/3 saves Monsanto over $200 million a year.[26]

Not all companies have had the same positive experience as Monsanto. Westinghouse Electric purchased and began installing all of the R/3 modules in 1994. They projected costs of $65 million and payback in two-and-a-half years. However, support from top management was not strong, allowing some of the divisions to resist implementing the required changes. The conversion and payback slowed to a crawl.

Outputs

The next element of the HRIS is the actual use of the newly processed material. The information technology used in the output stage varies. It may involve material produced by printers, terminal screens, or any number of other devices. A well-designed HRIS will begin to show its worth during this stage. It should be noted that a decision support system does not make the decision for the manager but provides high-quality information necessary to make a good decision. For information to be of high quality, it must meet the following five criteria. First, it must be *accurate*. The information must correctly reflect what it reports. A 100-percent accuracy rate is not always needed; for example, less accuracy is needed when measuring employee age trends than in reporting EEO compliance. Information also should be *significant and relevant*. The information provided must be usable, and information must be available in a timely manner. Information should be *comprehensive* and provide a complete picture of the problem and possibly offer alternative solutions. It is important for the information to *be readable and have visual impact*. Information must be easily understandable; it should not be in lists or tables when it can be in graphs and charts. Finally, it must be *consistent in format*. The same information should not come in several different forms when one standard is possible.[27]

These elements, if present, will help to ensure the usefulness of a firm's HRIS. But the question remains: For what do firms typically use their HRIS? The next section on feedback will examine this issue.

Feedback

Feedback represents the managerial control element of a system. The feedback element helps to ensure that the outputs are the ones that the system seeks to achieve. Most HRISs report information on numerous human resource activities. The brief—and not comprehensive—list shown in Exhibit 4.9 gives some of the more common HRIS functions and what is typically included within each function. Some firms' HRISs will have all this information and more. Other firms will only need part of this list to meet their needs. Now that we know what a HRIS is and what it does, we will examine how it can be used as a tool for corporate strategy.

Tying a HRIS to Corporate Strategy

When used properly, a HRIS can be a valuable tool for strategic planning and implementation. HRIS information should help decision makers better understand how human resource management can be a valuable competitive tool. It can be used to monitor morale, efficiency, and labor costs. It can be used to plan for the future human resource needs of the firm or to anticipate changes in the competitive environment. Its use is limited only by the extent to which the organization uses it to make strategic human resource decisions. Many firms are beginning to realize the value of

EXHIBIT 4.9	COMMON HRIS FUNCTIONS

Wages and salaries: Company pay structure, planned raises, and wage histories.

Benefits: Company benefit packages, data on benefits used/accumulated.

EEO compliance: Information on minority hiring, recruitment, and advancement.

Labor relations: Labor contract data, grievance information, and worker seniority lists.

Training and development: Information on various training programs, employees who have received training, and planned training and development activities.

Health and safety: Information on company accidents and the individuals involved, costs of accidents, and other data required by government and insurance reports.

Management succession/career planning: Information on skills, specialties, accomplishments, and possible promotions.

HR planning: Projections of future needs.

Staffing: Job assignments and possible employee specialties.

HR data management: Basic employee information such as wages, social security numbers, and job titles.

Monitoring and reporting HR policy: A DSS component helps organizations compare actual HR performance to desired HR performance.

General organizational data: Organization structure, management levels, and special functions information.

Demographics: Information about worker availability, education, ages.

External databases: Information on other companies or economic trends.

SOURCE: Adapted from Jenkins, M.L., and G. Lloyd, "How Corporate Philosophy and Strategy Shape the Use of HR Information Systems," *Personnel*, May 1985, p. 29; and Walker, A.J., "New Technologies in Human Resource Planning," *Human Resource Planning*, November 4, 1986, pp. 149–151.

using human resources to gain a strategic advantage—or a unique skill or competence that other firms do not have.

It often falls on human resource managers to help top management recognize the need for and value of a HRIS. Because the costs for acquiring and implementing such a system can be substantial, showing the benefits to the firm, including how the system can help strategically align the organization with its goals, is an important step in winning top management support. To do this, the human resource manager needs to think in business terms to determine exactly how a HRIS can help achieve business objectives. First, the manager must identify ways a HRIS system can support the organizational business goals and how using a HRIS can help achieve these goals. Then the manager can develop a HRIS tailored to meet these goals and introduce a deployment strategy for the HRIS. By adopting a value-added perspective such as this, it is possible to link the HRIS directly to the organization's key business strategies.[28]

Types of HRISs

As mentioned earlier, a HRIS can be as small as a single personal computer or as large as one or more mainframe computers connected to each other. Depending on the firm's structure and philosophy of management concerning centralization of resources and decisions, a HRIS can be configured in one of several different ways. The most typical types of HRIS configurations are concentrated, distributed, and independent, or a hybrid combination of these three.[29]

A *concentrated* HRIS places all control and accountability in one centralized location. This placement gives management the greatest degree of control over the system and reduces costs, but it limits the flexibility of persons who need to use or access the system's information.

A *distributed* HRIS features both a central facility and multiple other sites connected to the facility and/or each other. This feature still allows for a great deal of management control over the operation and design of the system while providing some flexibility for its users.

Next, an *independent* system features multiple systems that may or may not be connected to each other. This system provides the greatest amount of flexibility to individual users who can design systems to fit their specific needs. Management control is often minimal, and this can result in increased costs because of different users "reinventing the wheel" or the creation of a new system function that may already exist somewhere else in the organization.

A final HRIS design configuration is the *hybrid* approach. Many firms have found it useful to have certain elements of their HRIS centralized while allowing other functions to be left to the discretion of individual users. In certain circumstances, hybrid systems can be designed to provide the right mix of centralization control and decentralization autonomy within an organization, but they tend to be very expensive because many different functions must be supported.

intranets An internal Web site that can link employees to company-wide information sources.

Implementing any of these types of HRISs has become much easier with the introduction of company **intranets**. In essence, an intranet is an internal Web site that contains "hot buttons" or links to an unlimited number of company-wide information sources.[30] In a survey of more than 300 employers, 57 percent reported that they planned to use intranets for human resource purposes within the next year. Another 84 percent said their benefits enrollments would be online in the near future.[31] It just makes sense that human resource departments were, and continue to be, one of the first departments to develop and use intranets. For example, instead of giving every new employee a company handbook, which is frequently not read and then misplaced, the human resource department can place it on the intranet and allow everyone to access it whenever needed. Further, updates to the online handbook no longer include printing and distributing an addendum. Instead, with a few keystrokes everyone has access to the updates at virtually no cost to the company.[32] Another excellent use of the intranet is form distribution. Insurance and benefits forms can be placed on the intranet and printed off by employees on an as-needed basis, eliminating the need for employees to stop by the human resource department to pick up the forms.

Lately, however, firms have expanded their intranets to include functions other than human resources. For example, let's say a group in marketing needs to have a meeting to discuss the new products about to be unveiled to the public. A conference room needs to be scheduled, so a member of the team fires up the intranet and clicks on the conference room sign-up button. The system asks the user how many people will attend and how long the meeting will be. Based on the information provided, it presents a list of the available conference rooms at this time. The user clicks on the one he or she wants to reserve and provides the requested information (e.g., name under which the reservation should be made, contact telephone number). Once the information has been entered, a new screen pops up. This screen, managed by the catering department, asks whether refreshments are needed for the meeting. After the requested information has been entered, a new screen pops up. This screen, monitored by the audio visual department, asks if any equipment will be needed for the meeting. The options from which to select run from teleconferencing equipment to a flipboard and markers. The meeting, now fully planned, took only minutes. No employee left his or her desk. No other employee's work was interrupted.[33]

Companies have found that intranets have boosted productivity, enhanced morale, and allowed creative employees the opportunity to brainstorm ideas that will help the firm be even more productive in the future. Given all of these benefits, one would think that an intranet would cost a great deal of money to implement. Not true. For as little as a $200 investment in software, a company can have an intranet up and running in less than a week. Even less time is required if the company already has a computer network in place.[34]

Once an organization has decided on the capabilities and configuration of its HRIS, it needs to ensure that its users actually know how to use, and do use, the system. This is the subject of the next section.

Making a HRIS Work

Ensuring that a HRIS works for an organization involves two key issues: training users and tying strategies and decisions.

Just as it is the role of a human resource department to provide training to members of an organization in certain areas, the department also must make sure that its employees and other users are properly trained to use the HRIS. Training often includes introducing users to new terms and familiarizing them with the capabilities of the system. Commercial system developers often provide training to organizations. If the system is developed in-house, then the training function may fall to the department that created the system. However, teaching employees how to use the system is not the only training component needed. It is also critical to teach employees to locate answers to their human resource questions using the system. This requires them to adopt a new mindset of self-service rather than turning to human resources for answers.[35]

The second step in making a HRIS work is tying strategies and decisions. Even if users know how to use the system, it will not serve the organization if they cannot perceive any benefits from its use. As a result, a firm should make sure that the system serves necessary functions and provides information that will aid decision makers in achieving organization goals and strategies. If management believes that the HRIS is not being used effectively, a HRIS audit can be conducted. This entails examining company-specific reasons for having a HRIS and for gathering the data included, as well as the reasons for the procedures used to access the data, the reports it provides, and many other functional characteristics. Misuse, underuse, and potential use all are uncovered.[36]

Privacy and the HRIS

The final issue we will discuss concerning HRISs relates to the privacy of the information it contains. A prime reason for an organization to install a HRIS is to make it easier to find information. This ease of accessing information also has a downside: It is easier for unauthorized individuals to obtain private information (both company and personnel information) or for system users to accidentally disclose private information. Some laws exist that provide penalties for illegally obtaining certain kinds of

Computer Security

As more and more information is made available to employees via the company's intranet, security and privacy become key issues. To encourage employee use of electronic systems and to build their confidence in the system's ability to secure information, it is imperative that a robust security system is in place. Spring Technologies in Falls Church, Virginia, has developed a security system that is virtually impossible to break. Prior to being allowed to access information, an employee's iris is scanned. Because this high-tech thumbprint is unique to each individual, the computer knows exactly who is signing on and can limit access to only the information authorized to this individual. The company's system is currently being used in the airline industry, in prisons to recognize inmates, to secure bank vaults, and to govern access to computer control rooms, but the potential for its use in other industries is unlimited. The system takes a picture of each employee's iris and stores it away for future use. Prior to signing on to a computer the employee's eye is scanned and matched to the stored iris image. Stewart Mann, the company's founder, has big plans for the technology. He envisions a day when iris scans will replace passports, drivers' licenses, and social security cards. Obviously this will eliminate misuse of all of these items, because only the individual belonging to the iris will pass the scan test.

Another innovation in computer security was announced by Polaroid. Its technology uses a fingerprint to determine if the user is authorized to access the computer. Eleven companies have attached fingerprint readers to their keyboards. Like the iris scan, the fingerprint scanner matches the typist's fingerprints to fingerprints stored in a file. Only information authorized to that user is accessible.

SOURCE: Adapted from "How Will New Technology Change the HR Profession?" *Workplace Visions*, SHRM, 2000; and Beth Stanley and Darrell Pope, "Self-Service Lessons," *HRMagazine*, May 2000, pp. 155-164.

employee information, but this does not always stop it from happening. An employee whose employer has accidentally divulged her performance appraisal history (when only her salary history was supposed to be released) to a bank loan division will not be any less upset if it was an accident. Organizations should make every attempt to provide safeguards against revealing private information—whether illegally or accidentally obtained. Protections such as system passwords, restricted access to confidential information on a need-to-know basis, and the physical locking up of files at the end of each day are just the first steps in protecting the organization's reputation, its competitive position, and its legal liability.[37] Other issues that need to be considered include carefully defining and limiting user authorization, verifying that a user is actually the person authorized to use the system, encoding the data if it is transmitted and when it is stored, and using audit trails that provide a clear picture of who accessed what and when. By incorporating some or all of these ideas, the HRIS should be secure.[38]

Summary of Human Resource Information Systems

In summary, a HRIS serves a number of functions within an organization. It can help reduce errors, increase efficiency, and reduce costs for an organization. As a decision support system, it can provide valuable information to decision makers and alert them to potential future problems or opportunities. The HRIS can be used as a strategic tool to help firms better plan and prepare for the future and reduce costs. The HRIS configuration also will reflect the organization's attitude about how human resource decisions are made, whether the HRIS is distributed, centralized, or independent. Of course, for a

HRIS to be effective, users must be properly trained to use it, and it must be used by those whom it is intended to serve. Finally, a computer-based HRIS raises concerns about the privacy of information that it contains. Proper care must be taken to restrict access to the system to those individuals who have a legitimate need for its information.

Other Advances in Technology

Internet A communication tool that can be used to send information to others electronically.

World Wide Web A user-friendly means of accessing information on the Internet.

Two additional topics must be discussed before this chapter ends. The first is the **Internet**, and the second is the multimedia component of the Internet, the **World Wide Web (WWW)**. The Internet is a communication tool that can be used to send and receive information. To access the Internet, you use a computer that can connect to the Internet either via a modem or a direct connection through an existing network. Once on the Internet, you can send messages, often referred to as e-mail, to anyone in the world who has an electronic address. You can send documents, leave or answer messages, and join in a discussion on any number of topics. While the use of e-mail in the business world has increased tremendously just recently, it has not replaced the telephone. In fact, results from a poll of 150 managers who work in the nation's largest 1000 companies indicate that 62 percent will return a phone call before returning an e-mail. So, if you want a more immediate response, the phone may still be your best bet.[39]

Over the past decade the WWW has become an increasingly used method to locate information on virtually any topic. In essence, the WWW is a user-friendly way of locating data on the Internet. With the introduction of hypertext markup language (html), the language used to design Web pages, and easy-to-use browsers, such as Netscape and Mosaic, the WWW has become an online encyclopedia. Individuals and companies create an Internet site called a "home page" using html. Then individuals use browsers to search for information in which they are interested. Exhibit 4.10 provides a list of the WWW sites that can be useful to human resource managers. We will provide additional Web addresses throughout the book to help you locate additional information about important topics.

As mentioned earlier, one of the many strategic choices a company must make concerning the use of technology is how expansive the use of it should be. In 1997, the Society for Human Resource Management (SHRM) conducted a survey of 757 HR professionals to determine how companies are dealing with these strategic choices.[40] For example, companies first must decide whether or not to support and encourage the use of e-mail as a form of communication. According to the survey results, 86 percent of the firms responding support the use of e-mail in their organizations. The next strategic choice is whether or not the e-mail service will be internal only, external only, or both. A very small percentage (5 percent) indicated that e-mail was used only externally. An additional 24 percent allowed in-house e-mail use only. However, the majority (69 percent) provided both internal and external e-mail service to their employees.

One of the main reasons to introduce e-mail into an organization is to increase productivity. If the respondents to SHRM's survey are representative of all companies who use e-mail, it appears that e-mail has achieved this goal. Nearly one third of the respondents (31 percent) felt that e-mail has greatly increased productivity. An additional 49 percent felt that e-mail has increased productivity somewhat. Only 2 percent felt that the introduction of e-mail service decreased productivity.

In order to ensure an increase in performance through e-mail, many companies have restricted the use of e-mail to business purposes only. A total of 73 percent of the

---

EXHIBIT 4.10   WORLD WIDE WEB ADDRESSES FOR HUMAN
                    RESOURCES MANAGERS

Affirmative Action Register	aar-eeo.com
AFL-CIO	www.aflcio.org
Bureau of Labor Statistics	stats.bls.gov
Career Opportunities	monster.com
Employment Standards Administration	www.dol.gov/dol/esa
Employment and Training Administration Statutes	doleta.gov/regs/statutes
Federal Government Statistics	www.fedstats.gov
FMLA	www.dol.gov/dol/esa/fmla.htm
Human Resource Software	www.notjustsurveys.com
International Human Resources	www.euen.co.uk
Job Search Skills	www.winway.com
National Labor Relations Board	www.nlrb.gov
Office of Federal Contract Compliance (OFCCP)	www.dol.gov/dol/esa/public/ofcp_org.htm
Office of Worker's Compensation	www.dol.gov/esa/public/owcp_org.htm
OSHA	www.osha.gov/dol/
OSHA Fact Sheet	www.osha-s/c.gov/oshdoc/toc_fact.html
Pension and Welfare Benefits Administration	www.dol.gov/dol/pwba
PBWA Statutes	www.dol.gov/dol/pwba/public/res/main.htm
PBWA Pamphlets	www.dol.gov/dol/pwba/public/pubs/main.htm
PBWA Minimum Wage	www.dol.gov/dol/esa/public/minwage/main.htm
Retirement Planning	www.isrplan.org
Search Facilities	www.altavista.com or www.lycos.com or www.excite.com or yahoo.com or webcrawler.com or search.opentext.com
Society for Human Resource Management (SHRM)	www.shrm.org
SHRM Student Services	www.shrm.org/students/
Training	www.thinq.com
Wage and Hour Division	dol.gov/dol/esa/public/whd_org.htm

---

companies surveyed indicated that the use of e-mail is restricted to business purposes only. About 10 percent of those who forbid the use of e-mail for personal reasons monitor the e-mail messages sent to ensure adherence to the policy. The surveillance can include tracking where e-mails were sent and randomly reading messages to ensure the content is business-related.

The SHRM survey asked respondents similar questions about the WWW. While nearly 80 percent of the respondents indicated that employees have access to the WWW at work, only 10 percent make this benefit available to all employees. The majority of the firms surveyed (56 percent) indicated that WWW access was restricted to only a few of their employees. Over 60 percent of the companies responding allowed their employees to use the WWW for nonbusiness purposes. However, when this use could occur was often limited. A total of 24 percent allowed their employees unlimited access during breaks and after hours, whereas 5 percent allowed access only on breaks and another 5 percent allowed access only after hours. Few respondents, only 6 percent, felt access to the WWW greatly increased productivity as compared with the use of the Internet. Also, just as many respondents (6 percent) felt that access to the WWW had decreased productivity. These respondents may be right—65 percent of all Internet orders at **www.gamedealer.com** are placed between 9 AM and 5 PM.[41]

Management Guidelines

So we see that the use of technology and human resource planning is an important and fundamental aspect of strategic human resource management. Using technology effectively and human resource planning help to establish a *proactive* approach to human resource management and to integrate human resources with corporate-level strategic planning. Furthermore, these techniques help to ensure that specific objectives, programs, policies, and activities of each human resource function are fully integrated. The following management guidelines should be observed with respect to technology implementation and human resource planning.

1. The human resource plan should be integrated fully with the overall organizational strategic plan, especially the firm's growth objectives.
2. Outside influences of economic conditions, technology, the labor market, and so on should be given adequate consideration when developing the human resource plan.
3. Changes in job design should be recognized explicitly in the plan; the plan should not assume that the structure of jobs in the future will be the same as that of today.
4. The plan should explicitly realize that staffing levels should be based on increasing productivity in order for the firm to remain cost competitive. Just because a job becomes vacant does not mean that it should be filled automatically. Perhaps it should be eliminated or combined with another job.
5. Future shortages or surpluses by job or skill category should be estimated by using computer techniques and quantitative models, as appropriate, to better manage the process.
6. The specific operational objectives of each functional area in personnel should be integrated with the overall human resource plan.
7. Specific personnel programs, policies, and activities should be integrated with the specific functional objectives.
8. HRISs should be used as a decision support system and should alert managers to problems and opportunities.
9. The human resource plan should involve significant line management input at all points in the process.

10. The human resource plan should be kept flexible and adaptable so it can change as conditions change.
11. From a strategic perspective, human resource costing should offer opportunities for the human resource professional.
12. E-mail and intranets can be used to make a company more productive.

Questions for Review

1. What is a strategic human resource plan? Why is it important?

2. What impact do outside forces have on the strategic human resource plan (for example, labor market, technology, economic conditions, and so on)?

3. Why should the human resource plan be integrated with the overall organizational strategic plan? How can this integration be achieved?

4. Outline an overall model or procedure for developing a strategic human resource plan.

5. What are some quantitative techniques for estimating a surplus or shortage in a job category or occupation? Define each technique you list.

6. Why is it important to use the computer and quantitative techniques in human resource planning?

7. How can specific human resource functional objectives be linked with the human resource plan? Why is this linkage important?

8. Why should specific human resource programs, policies, and activities be linked with human resource objectives?

9. Why should a human resource plan be kept flexible?

10. Why should line managers be involved in helping to formulate a human resource plan?

11. What is human resource costing? How is human resource costing a strategic activity?

12. What is the primary purpose of a human resource information system? Discuss the typical HRIS functions and configurations.

13. What is an intranet? How can it be used to make a company more productive?

14. What are some of the key strategic choices companies face when deciding to implement e-mail, an intranet, or access to the World Wide Web?

CASE

Polaroid: Hard Landing[42]

The day after Thanksgiving in 1948, a new camera went on sale at a Boston department store. Worried that it wouldn't sell well, officials of the small company that made it cut the price from $95 to $89.75 at the last minute. They thought the 56 cameras they had produced might be gone by Christmas. The cameras sold out that day.

After struggling more than a decade, Polaroid Corporation, run by a young scientist named Edwin H. Land, had a big winner. Its instant camera developed photos, on the spot, in 60 seconds. It was a technological marvel, and it captivated America.

As Polaroid's laboratories made one breakthrough after another in the 1950s and 1960s, the company grew rapidly. By the early 1970s, its stock was one of the highest highfliers, selling at more than 100 times annual earnings. Polaroid was more than just another success story; it was an icon to American ingenuity. Land exhorted his employees, "Do not undertake a program unless the goal is manifestly important and achievement is nearly impossible."

A Bright Beginning

Polaroid was Land's life mission. By all accounts a genius, he quit Harvard University in 1932, one semester before graduating, to start a research lab. The name of the company, Polaroid, comes from the company's first product, the "polaroid filter," so named because its cellul*oid* filter *polar*ized light. Land developed his polarizing process, a feat that had long eluded scientists, by aligning microscopic crystals in a specific pattern on the celluloid, thus sharply reducing glare when light passed through it.

This discovery was put to use in the making of sunglasses and car headlights, and the revenues from these modest applications provided Land and his new company with money to support other research. Some critics believed that the company, in its early days, resembled a research project run by a group of graduate students.

During World War II, Polaroid survived on military work. It was also during this time that inspiration visited itself on Polaroid and Edwin Land. While he was taking photos in 1943, Land's three-year-old daughter asked why she couldn't see the pictures right away. Land must have realized at that moment that the future looked very bright, indeed.

Perfect Timing

The instant camera took several years to develop and, ironically, didn't use Land's polarizing invention, but rather technologies from Polaroid's labs. But it was the right product at the right time. Americans were just becoming addicted to instant gratification. The baby boom had begun, and proud parents wanted to photograph their growing families. So what if instant cameras and film cost more? Postwar America was increasingly affluent.

Under Land, a savvy showman, Polaroid embraced live television to sell cameras. Entertainers such as Steve Allen took photos in front of the audience. "The essence of TV is dramatization. We had viewers holding their breath. Would it work? Every now and then, it didn't, but that was OK," said Joseph Daly, an executive at DDB Needham Worldwide ad agency, which had the Polaroid account for 30 years. "Never was a product more suited for TV."

It was a period of intense excitement. Many Polaroid employees worked six days a week and loved every minute. "It wouldn't be unusual to work around the clock a few days in a row. Nobody got too tired because it was exciting. We'd sleep on a lab table or office desk or on the floor," recalls Richard Young, a former executive who joined the company in the early 1950s as assistant research director. Polaroid hands held Land in awe, and for good reason. Land's 533 patents are second only to Thomas Edison's 1093.

Polaroid sold its one millionth camera in 1956 and went public the next year. In 1960, sales hit $99.4 million; in 1970, they hit $444 million.

Crowning Achievement

In 1972 came Land's crowning achievement: the pocket-sized SX-70 camera. He was featured on the covers of *Life* magazine ("A genius and his magic camera") and *Time* ("Here comes those great new cameras"). His Polaroid stock was valued at more than $700 million.

The SX-70 scored a great sales success, but Polaroid's stock plummeted because the huge expense of developing the camera held down profit growth. Adding to the pressure, Kodak ended Polaroid's monopoly by entering the instant-camera market in 1976. Polaroid promptly sued, charging patent infringement, but the case would not be decided in its favor until 1985.

Then came Land's greatest flop: Polavision instant movies, which were introduced in 1977. The camera cost too much at $700, didn't have sound, and took only $2\frac{1}{2}$ minutes of film at a time. Land had the right idea but the wrong technology. The Japanese had something better: video recorders, whose hours-long tapes could be reused and played back on a TV set.

Even worse, another Japanese product—klutz-proof 35-mm cameras—took America by storm in the late 1970s and early 1980s. One-hour photo shops made instant cameras moot. From a high of $9.4 million in 1978, Polaroid's instant-camera sales plunged to $3.5 million in 1985. Also during those years, the company profits fared just as badly, skidding from a record $118.4 million on sales of $1.38 billion to $36.9 million on sales of $1.30 billion.

The Downhill Slide

In the late 1970s, things started to go wrong for Polaroid. The market matured while Polaroid stagnated. Its visionary founder lost his vision, and in 1982 Land retired from the company. Newer, better gadgets captured the public's fancy. In 1988 the company became a takeover target. Shamrock Holdings, Inc., a television and radio concern owned by the Roy E. Disney family, tried to buy Polaroid for $2.28 billion.

Polaroid's history is, in some ways, the latest twist in the decline of American industry. But unlike the auto and steel producers, Polaroid isn't an old-line manufacturer. It is one of the earliest postwar high-tech pioneers, a nonunion company lauded for enlightened employee relations. However, its heady growth has given way to hard times for similar reasons. In becoming big, the company became lethargic. The Japanese have emerged as industry innovators, indirectly in Polaroid's case, with 35-mm cameras and video cameras. Instead of adding jobs, Polaroid is cutting them.

Missing Creative Spark

Worse yet, the company has lost its creative spark. "Polaroid hasn't had a breakthrough product for years," says Peter Wensberg, a former Polaroid executive. Despite lavish spending on research, efforts to diversify have been half-hearted, at best.

"The problem for so many big companies is that they don't have an encore," says Thomas V. DiBacco, a professor of business history at American University. "No company can stay very long in a staid position. A lot of firms several decades old—what do they do after they achieve success? It's one of the biggest dilemmas, trying to find the next stage."

Some other companies have had trouble finding the next stage. The sales of Avon Products, Inc., have languished in recent times. Its door-to-door sales strategy has faltered because more and more women work outside the home. Nike, Inc., stubbed its toe when smaller competitors managed to sell athletic shoes as fashion items.

Ignoring the Outside World

Polaroid's management was too inbred to notice that the world was changing, critics say. "Here's a company that had a field to itself for a long, long time. Many executives spent their entire careers on internal problems and technology. Some didn't consider it important to take a close look at the outside world," said Murray Swindell, a former marketing executive and one of Polaroid's many officials who departed in frustration in the early 1980s.

"Polaroid has been very myopic," comments Alex Henderson, an analyst at Prudential Securities Research. He says Polaroid's executives have failed to commercialize the good technology in its laboratories. "They limited their definition of what markets they're in. . . its the 'not invented here' syndrome," he adds. He suggests that Polaroid's imaging technology might be valuable in developing products for the computer publishing and medical-diagnostics markets, but only if the company enters joint ventures with companies offering expertise in those areas. "There's a lot of value in the Polaroid name," Swindell said. "There are any number of products we could have marketed . . . but we couldn't get Land's attention. He preferred to stick to instant photography."

The focus on basic research and development, and not on the exploitation of technology and markets, may be due, in great part, to the philosophy of Polaroid's founder, director of research, and chairman of the board, Edwin Land. Annual meetings contained little by way of sales figures and profit estimates. They were more like a show and tell for Land. He would use the meetings as an opportunity to showcase some of the more interesting developments of the various research teams. Many of these inventions and prospective products never reached production. And Polaroid is still characterized by many as a company that holds too tight a grip on its patents.

After Land's departure, market research was conducted that revealed that the company had been wrong in its assumptions about who was buying their products. Polaroid had thought 80 percent of their consumer cameras were being used for birthday parties and the like. Research showed, however, that 50 percent of these cameras were being used for business purposes such as real estate. Most of the marketing efforts and product designs were being targeted toward the wrong market. This was a major oversight.

Diversification (Growth) or Retrenchment

The company now finds itself in a strategic bind with no easy way out. Some analysts and former executives think that the company should try to diversify, whereas others think that it should stick close to its instant photography line.

Diversification may help bolster losses suffered because of weak sales in Polaroid's principal photography business. Instant photography may have lost its magic, despite the introduction in 1986 of an improved, third-generation camera (Polaroid Spectra). Instant camera sales have slumped while sales of 35-mm cameras have increased dramatically. The 35-mms "have automatic everything: auto focus, auto load, auto rewind, auto zoom," said Jack Crunkleton, the general manager of Camera Shop, Inc., an eastern chain. "Affluent people still count on 35-mm for better quality pictures. It will be hard for Polaroid to get back to the growth days."

Only recently has Polaroid entered the conventional film market, and this represents a major break from the notion that instant photography was the only photography worth pursuing. Polaroid itself argues that instant photography isn't just a quaint gimmick of the past, and it is working on a next-generation system that combines electronics with the use of heat to develop film. The technology could be used to make photographic prints of images stored electronically and initially viewed on computer monitors or TV screens. "Instant imaging will become the dominant form (of photography), surpassing conventional film. . .We do not want to be just 'that other form of imaging'; we want to be No. 1," a spokesperson said. But that won't be easy. "Japanese expertise in the imaging area will really put a lot of pressure on a company like Polaroid," said Young, the former executive.

However, it should be noted that there are still some current uses for instant photography, and Polaroid is capitalizing on them. Polaroid has established itself as the worldwide leader within driver's license bureaus. Polaroid produces more than 300 million driver licenses and other identification documents around the world each year. Its driver licensing, digital imaging, and biometrics system offerings to governments have captured more than 70 percent of the driver licensing market in North America.

Employment Cuts

In 1988, Polaroid went through a major downsizing, eliminating 8500 jobs. In the first quarter of 1995, Polaroid again announced that it would cut its workforce, this time by 5 percent, or 600 workers. Interestingly, in the midst of downsizing, Polaroid was rated one of the best 100 companies for which to work. This may be due in great part to the progressive human resource practices of the company, which include a basic skills training program called Technology Readiness (TR), skill-based pay systems for workers, an aggressive human resource staff training program, and the giving to each employee some ownership of the corporation. Only time will tell whether these adjustments can bring back some of the old magic to a company that, at times, must have seemed like a magical place in which to work.

Restructuring

After thwarting a takeover attempt, Polaroid finally decided that things needed to change in a hurry. They came up with four principal components to incorporate changes to operating structure:

1. Program reductions in certain products.
2. Research and development in manufacturing areas.
3. Strategic refocusing of company's digital imaging business for the medical diagnostic and graphic arts markets.
4. Reduce corporate overhead expenses.

These changes led to losses in earnings per share as well as losses to net earnings in 1995 and 1996. The company attributed those losses to several factors: during this time period (1995-1996) Polaroid incurred one-time costs because of restructuring (this includes increases in marketing expenses and worldwide promotions); they also bought Helios, which turned out to be an unprofitable medical diagnostic and imaging equipment division of the company. They eventually sold Helios to try to reduce some of those losses.

In 1997 Polaroid made an equity investment in a digital imaging venture capital fund that reflected its new emphasis on partnerships and strategic alliances. Gary DiCamillo, Polaroid's chairman and CEO explained that he "is confident that Polaroid's digital strategy will help deliver on customer needs, beginning with our new camera and digital printers," which were made available in 2000. Under their new digital strategy, Polaroid plans to leverage their core imaging technology in the digital marketplace, stake out a position in the mobile, digital, and wireless markets, and capitalize on Polaroid's customer relationships via the Internet. To accomplish this, Polaroid selected theglobe.com for an alliance to promote Polaroid's I-Zone Instant Pocket Camera. While this was Polaroid's first online advertising campaign, it will probably not be their last.

Polaroid has recommitted itself to providing innovative ideas and technologies, which, so far, have led them to increases in worldwide sales and decreases in losses. It looks as if Polaroid is on the right track to recovery.

Questions for Discussion

1. What has been Polaroid's overall growth strategy? How has this affected its human resource planning and strategy?
2. Whose fault is it when employment falls as it has at Polaroid? What responsibility, if any, do operative employees have?
3. Why would employees work virtually around the clock as they did in the early days of Polaroid?
4. How does Polaroid's human resource plan in the 1950s, 1960s, and 1970s compare with its plan for the 1980s and 1990s? How do cutbacks and retrenchment change a human resource plan? Could these cuts have been avoided? If so, how?
5. What other companies do you know of that failed to mature to other growth stages with new products after the initial product played out? What causes this to happen?
6. What benefits are there to Polaroid giving employees some ownership of the corporation?

Additional Readings

Branch, P., and E. Mansfield. "Firm's Forecasts of Engineering Employment." *Management Science* 28 (February 1982), pp. 156–160.

Burack, E. H. "Corporate Business and Human Resource Planning Practices: Strategic Issues and Concerns." *Organization Dynamics* 15 (Summer 1986), pp. 73–87.

Burack, E. H. *Creative Human Resource Planning and Applications.* Englewood Cliffs, NJ: Prentice-Hall, 1988.

Burack, E. H. *Planning for Human Resources.* Lake Forest, IL: Brace-Park Press, 1989.

Burack, E. H., and N. J. Mathys. *Human Resource Planning.* 2nd ed. Lake Forest, IL: Brace-Park Press, 1987.

Butensky, C. F., and O. Harari. "Models vs. Reality. An Analysis of Twelve Human Resource Planning Systems." *Human Resource Planning* 6, no. 1 (1983), pp. 11–25.

Cascio, W., ed. *Human Resource Planning, Employment and Placement.* Washington D.C.: The Bureau of National Affairs, 1989.

Cascio, W. *Costing Human Resources: The Financial Impact of Behavior in Organizations.* Cincinnati: South-Western College Publishing, 2000.

Chamine, S. "Making Your Intranet an Effective HR Tool." *HR Focus* (December 1998), pp. 11–12.

Courtney, R. S. "A Human Resource Plan That Helps Management and Employees Prepare for the Future." *Personnel* 63, no. 5 (May 1986), pp. 32–40.

Dill, W. R., D. P. Gavar, and W. C. Weber. "Models and Modeling for Manpower Planning." *Management Science* 13 (1966), pp. B142–B167.

Gatewood, R. D., and B. W. Rockmore. "Combining Organizational Manpower and Career Development Needs: An Operational Human Resource Planning Model." *Human Resource Planning* 9, no. 3 (1986), pp. 81–96.

Gehrman, D. B. "Objective Based Human Resource Planning." *Personnel Journal* 60 (December 1981), pp. 942–946.

Greer, Charles R., and Daniel Armstrong. "Human Resource Forecasting and Planning: A State of the Art Investigation." *Human Resource Planning* 3, no. 2 (April 1980), pp. 67-78.

Henderson, J. C., et al. "Integrated Approach for Manpower Planning in the Service Sector." *Omega* 10, no. 1 (1982), pp. 61–73.

Hill, A. W. "Strategic Human Resource Planning: How to Succeed." *Management Review* 75 (November 1986), pp. 79–80.

Hollmann, R. W. "Strategic Planning." *Personnel Administrator*, March 1989, pp. 97–100.

Hopkins, D. S. P. "Models for Affirmative Action Planning and Evaluation." *Management Science* 26 (October 1980), pp. 994–1006.

Kanter, Rosabeth M. "Frontiers for Strategic Human Resource Planning and Management." *Human Resource Management* 22 (Spring/Summer 1983), pp. 9–21.

Kerr, Clark, and Paul D. Staudohan, eds. *Economics of Labor in Industrial Society.* San Francisco: Jossey-Bass, 1986.

Klein, E. "Determinants of Manpower Utilization and Availability." *International Labour Review* 122 (March-April 1983), pp. 183–195.

Manzini, A. O., and J. D. Gridley. "Human Resource Planning for Mergers and Acquisitions: Preparing for the 'People Issues' That Can Prevent Merger Synergies." *Human Resource Planning* 9, no. 2 (1986), pp. 51–57.

McAvoy R., and D. M. Hubsch. "Manpower Planning and Corporate Objectives: Two Points of View." *Management Review* 70 (August 1981), pp. 55–59.

Miller, E. L., S. Beechler, B. Bhatt, and R. Nath. "The Relationship Between the Global Strategic Planning Process and the Human Resource Management Function." *Human Resource Planning* 9, no. 2 (1986), pp. 9–29.

Mirengoff, W. *CETA, Accomplishments, Problems, Solutions: A Report by the Bureau of Social Science Research, Inc.* Kalamazoo, MI: W. E. Upjohn Institute for Employment Research, 1982.

Morlock, J. "Impact and Implications of Changing Federal Manpower Policy on the Administration and Implementation of Social Manpower Programs." *Labor Law Journal* 32 (August 1981), pp. 514–518.

Morrison, M. H. "The Aging of the U.S. Population: Human Resource Implications." *Monthly Labor Review* 106 (May 1983), pp. 13–19.

Mould, Jeffrey, and Michael Harper. "Companies Turn to Outsourcing for HR Software Needs." *Workforce*, April 1999, pp.10–12.

Muczyk, J. P. "Comprehensive Manpower Planning." *Managerial Planning* 30 (November/December 1981), pp. 36–41.

Niehaus, Richard. *Computer-Assisted Human Resources Planning.* New York: Wiley, 1979.

Niehaus, R. J., ed. *Strategic Human Resource Applications.* The Philadelphia Conference proceedings. 1987.

Nkomo, S. M. "Human Resource Planning and Organizational Performance: An Exploratory Analysis." *Strategic Management Journal* 8 (1987), pp. 387–392.

Nkomo, S. M. "The Theory and Practice of HR Planning: The Gap Still Remains." *Personnel Administrator* 31 (August 1986), pp. 71–84.

Rothwell, W. J., and H.C. Kazanas. *Strategic Human Resources Planning and Management.* Englewood Cliffs, NJ: Prentice-Hall, 1989.

Rush, I. C. "Strategic Planning for Human Resources." *Business Quarterly* 46 (Summer 1981), pp. 40–43.

Russ, C. F., Jr. "Manpower Planning Systems." *Personnel Journal* 61 (January 1982), pp. 40–45.

Scarborough, N., and T. W. Zimmerer. "Human Resources Forecasting: Why and Where to Begin." *Personnel Administration* 27 (May 1982), pp. 55–61.

Smith, W. J., and F. A. Zeller. "Impact of Federal Manpower Policy and Programs on the Employment and Earnings Experiences of Special Problem Groups of the Unemployed: A Critical Historical Overview." *Labor Law Journal* 32 (August 1981), pp. 518–528.

Strauss, J. S., and E. H. Burack. "The Human Resource Planning Professional: A Challenge in Change." *Human Resource Planning* 6, no. 1 (1983), pp. 1–9.

Subramaniam, S. "Engineering Manpower Planning in an Airline." *Long Range Planning*, August 1977, pp. 56–60.

Sylvia, Robert A. "TOSS: An Aerospace System That's GO for Manpower Planning." *Personnel* 54 (January-February 1977), pp. 56–64.

Thomsen, D. J. "Keeping Track of Managers in a Large Corporation." *Personnel* 53 (November 1976), pp. 23–30.

Ulrich, David. "Human Resources Planning as a Competitive Edge." *Human Resource Planning* 9, no. 2 (1986), pp. 41–50.

Valliant, Richard, and George Milkovich. "Comparison of SemiMarkov and Markov Models in a Personnel Forecasting Application." *Decision Sciences*, April 1977, pp. 465–477.

Witschger, J. "Five Easy Steps to Choosing the Right HR Software Package." *Workforce* (December 1988), pp. 10–12.

Zanakis, S. H., and M. W. Maret. "Markovian Goal Programming Approach to Aggregate Manpower Planning." *Journal of the Operational Research Society* 32 (January 1981), pp. 55–63.

Notes

[1]Greg Matusky, "Rebirth! Businesses Find New Life as Franchises," *Success*, 40 (September, 1993), pp. 64–71; Buck Brown, "How the Cookie Crumbled at Mrs. Fields: Company Seeks to Revive Itself by Diversifying," *The Wall Street Journal*, January 26, 1989, p. B1; "Mrs. Fields Inc.," *The Wall Street Journal*, February 15, 1989, p. B10; Dianne E. Kirrane and Peter R. Kirrane, "Managing by Expert Systems," *HRMagazine*, March 1990, pp. 37–39; and Richard Koenig, "NutraSweet Allies with Mrs. Fields for Diet Food Line," *The Wall Street Journal*, September 19, 1990, p. B6.

[2]Charles Barwick, "Eight Ways to Assess Succession Plans," *HRMagazine*, May 1993, pp. 109–114.

[3]Elmer H. Burach, "Corporate Business and Human Resources Planning Practices: Strategic Issues and Concerns," *Organization Dynamics* 15 (Summer 1986), pp. 73–87.

[4]Richard P. Nathan, "Clearing Up the Confusion over Block Grants," *The Wall Street Journal*, November 3, 1981, p. 3.

[5]Russell Mitchell and Judith Dobrzynski, "Jack Welch: How Good a Manager?" *Business Week*, December 14, 1987, pp. 92–103.

[6]Kevin Kelly, "The New Soul of John Deere," *Business Week*, January 31, 1994, pp. 64–66.

[7]Thomas M. Hunt and George Stalk, "Working Better and Faster with Fewer People," *The Wall Street Journal*, May 15, 1987, p. 14.

[8]Robert J. Koyma, "Low Cost CAD/CAM Units: Major Growth Area?" *Management Information Systems Weekly*, June 3, 1981, p. 4.

[9]Robert J. Grossman. "Robbing the Cradle?" *HRMagazine*, September 2000, pp. 40–45.

[10]K. M. Rowland and M. G. Sovereign, "Markov Chain Analysis of Internal Manpower Supply," *Industrial Relations* 9 (1969), pp. 88–89.

[11]P. F. Buller and W. R. Maki, "A Case History of a Manpower Planning Model," *Human Resource Planning* 4 (1981), pp. 129–138; and J. A. Hooper and R. F. Catalanello, "R. F. Markov Analysis Applied to Forecasting Technical Personnel," *Human Resource Planning* 4 (1981), pp. 41–45.

[12]William P. Anthony, "Get to Know Your Employee—The Human Resource Information System," *Personnel Journal*, April 1977, pp. 179–183, 202.

[13]Gorg L. Lilian and Ambar G. Rao, "A Model for Manpower Management," *Management Science* 21, no. 12 (1975), pp. 1447–1457.

[14]Andre L. Nelberq, Andrew H. Van de Ven, and David H. Gustafson, *Group Techniques for Program Planning: A Guide to Nominal Group and Delphi Processes* (Glenview, IL: Scott-Foresman, 1975).

[15]R. C. Woodruff, Jr., "Human Resource Accounting," *Canadian Chartered Accountant* 97 (1970), pp. 156–161.

[16]R. L. Brummet, E. Flamhol, and W. Pyle, "Human Resource Accounting—A Challenge for Accountants," *Accounting Review* 43 (1968), pp. 217–224.

[17]"The Personnel/Human Resources Department: 1989-1990," *SHRM-BNA Survey #54*, June 28, 1990, p. 10 (Washington, D.C.: Bureau of National Affairs).

[18]Linda Thornburg, "Accounting for Knowledge," *HRMagazine*, October 1994, pp. 50–56; Stephanie Losee, "Your Company's Most Valuable Asset: Intellectual Capital," *Fortune*, October 3, 1994, pp. 68–74.

[19]Wayne F. Cascio, *Costing Human Resources: The Financial Impact of Behavior in Organizations*, 2nd ed. (Boston: PWS-Kent, 1987), p. 5.

[20]Ibid, p. 6.

[21]Wayne F. Cascio, *Costing Human Resources: The Financial Impact of Behavior in Organizations*, 4th ed. (Cincinnati: South-Western College Publishing, 2000).

[22]Ibid, pp. 147–170.

[23]Robert J. Grossman, "Measuring Up," *HRMagazine*, January 2000, pp. 29–35.

[24]Sandra E. O'Connell, "Planning and Setting Up a New HRIS: Part 1," *HRMagazine*, February 1994, pp. 36–40; Robert W. Zmud, *Information Systems in Organizations* (Glenview, IL: Scott-Foresman, 1983), pp. 65–67.

[25]Gail Edmondson, Stephen Baker, and Amy Cortese, "Silicon Valley on the Rhine," *Business Week*, November 3, 1997, pp. 162–166.

[26]Ibid, p. 164.

[27]Kirk J. Anderson, "Putting the 'I' in HRIS," *Personnel*, September 1988, pp. 12–24.

[28]William A. Minneman, "Strategic Justification for an HRIS That Adds Value," *HRMagazine*, December 1996, pp. 35–38.

[29]Robert D. Marceluk, "Accountability and Control of Human Resource Information," *Personnel Administrator*, July 1985, pp. 24–26.

[30]Mike Frost, "Build It Yourself," *HRMagazine*, September 1996, p. 30.

[31]Bill Leonard, "HR Departments Take Advantage of Intranets," *HRMagazine*, April 1997, p. 10.

[32]Martha I. Finney, "Harness the Power," *HRMagazine*, January 1997, pp. 66–74.

[33]Ibid, p. 68.

[34]Ibid, p. 69.

[35]Beth Stanley and Darrell Pope, "Self-Service Lessons," *HRMagazine*, May 2000, pp. 155–164.

[36]Joe Pasqualetto, "New Competencies Define the HRIS Manager's Future Role," *Personnel Journal*, January 1993, pp. 91–99; Joanne Wisniewski, "The Needs-Based HRIS Audit," *HRMagazine*, September 1991, pp. 61–64.

[37]Helen LaVan, Nicholas J. Mathys, and Wayne Hochwarter, "Insecurity in Numbers," *Computers in Personnel*, Spring 1989, pp. 51–53.

[38]Lynn Adams, "Securing Your HRIS in a Microcomputer Environment," *HRMagazine*, February 1992, pp. 56–61.

[39]Elaine McShulskis, "To E-mail or not to E-mail," *HRMagazine*, January 1997, p. 18.

[40]Society for Human Resource Management, "1997 SHRM E-mail and WWW Survey," October 1997.

[41]"How Will New Technologies Change the Human Resource Management Profession?" Workplace Visions, SHRM, No. 3, 2000.

[42]Richard L. Bunning, "Models for Skill-Based Pay Plans," *HRMagazine*, February 1992, pp. 62–64; Nanette Byrnes, *Financial World*, September 28, 1993, pp. 38–39; Barbara Carton, "Polaroid to Cut Work Force by up to 5%, Take Charge; Operating Loss Is Likely," *The Wall Street Journal*, February 6, 1995, p. 7A; Company Press Release, "Retransmission: Infocorp Announces Strategic Alliance with Polaroid Identification Systems" June 5, 2000;

Company Press Release, "Polaroid Launches Major Online Advertising Initiative on theglobe.com's Happy Puppy Site," June 5, 2000; Marilyn W. Daudelin, "HR Development at Polaroid," *Personnel Journal*, February 1991, pp. 56–63; Mary Ann Castronovo Fusco, "Employment Relations Programs," *Employment Relations Today*, Spring 1989, pp. 89-92; Ronald Grover, "Maybe I'll Raid You And Maybe I Won't," *Business Week*, September 5, 1988, p. 25; K. H. Hammonds, "Why Polaroid Must Remake Itself Instantly," *Business Week*, September 19, 1988, pp. 66-72; Lawrence Ingrossio, "How Polaroid Went from Highest Flier to Take-over Target," *The Wall Street Journal*, August 12, 1988, pp. 1, 16; Lawrence Ingrossio, "Kodak's Motion Denied by Judge in Polaroid Case," *The Wall Street Journal*, August 12, 1988, p. 16; Michael Ozanian, *Financial World*, June 6, 1995, pp. 42–45.

5

Equal Employment Opportunity

Chapter Objectives

As a result of studying this chapter, you should be able to

1. Discuss the strategic choices available to firms regarding equal employment opportunities.

2. Understand the meaning of Title VII of the Civil Rights Act and the procedures the Equal Employment Opportunity Commission (EEOC) follows in investigating claims and trying cases filed under Title VII, and how cases are tried and investigated by the EEOC.

3. Describe the regulations that prohibit employment discrimination because of sex, race, national origin, religion, handicaps and health-related issues (including AIDS), or status as a Vietnam veteran.

4. Discuss equal employment opportunity (EEO) case law.

5. Describe the components for strengthening or establishing affirmative action programs.

6. Discuss the Equal Pay Act of 1963 and some of the controversies surrounding comparable worth.

7. Understand the issues regarding managing a diverse workforce and the importance of having a diverse workforce.

8. Discuss strategic EEO guidelines for managers.

This chapter examines the role of equal employment opportunities and management of a diverse workforce. Specific laws prohibiting employment discrimination based on sex, race, national origin, age, religion, disabilities and health-related issues (including AIDS), and status as a Vietnam veteran are covered. Affirmative action programs, the issue of "equal pay for equal work," and the Equal Pay Act are covered, as is the controversial topic of comparable worth. Finally, the issue of managing a diverse workforce is addressed.

CASE

Home Improvement Giant Settles Gender Discrimination Suits[1]

Home Depot, the largest home-improvement chain in the United States, agreed to pay $104 million to settle gender discrimination suits. The September 1997 settlement came three days prior to the trial date of a class-action suit in California. Under the agreement, $65 million was slated to settle the California class-action suit, and $17 million was scheduled to upgrade employment programs countrywide and to settle three other gender-based discrimination cases in Louisiana, New Jersey, and Florida. The remaining $22.5 million was slated for plaintiff attorney's fees in the four cases. The action represents one of the largest gender discrimination settlements in U.S. history. Other suits include State Farm for $250 million in 1992, $107 million paid by Lucky Stores Inc. in 1994, and an $81.5 million settlement by Publix Supermarkets in January 1997.

The Problem

The California class-action suit (*Butler, et al.* v. *Home Depot*) was originally filed in December 1994. The lawsuit involved more than 25,000 women who worked in or applied to work in the company's West Coast Division between November 5, 1992, and September 22, 1997. The West Coast Division encompasses 10 states. The suit alleged that Home Depot discriminated based on gender in nearly all aspects of its personnel decision making, including hiring, gender-based segregation of jobs, training, transfer opportunities, promotional opportunities, and compensation. The plaintiffs based their arguments on manager subjectivity regarding hiring and pay criteria and statistical evidence showing a disproportionately high number of women in cashier and operations positions, whereas men primarily occupied the sales, merchandising, managerial, and supervisory positions. The data suggest a high level of segregation by gender. Jacqueline Genero, one of the eight original plaintiffs, said that when the suit was filed she had been named the first employee of the year at the store where she worked but was denied the $500 bonus paid to male recipients. She said that she made $8 an hour, whereas men doing the same work earned $16 more.

Three other gender-based suits that had not yet been certified for class-action treatment had also been filed against Home Depot. A Louisiana case (*Griffin et al.* v. *Home Depot*) alleging gender discrimination in Home Depot's Northeast, Southeast, and Midwest Divisions was filed in January 1995. A New Jersey case (*Tortajada* v. *Home Depot*) alleged discrimination in the company's nine-state Northeast Division. A Florida case alleged discrimination in the 11-state Southern Division. The EEOC had sought court permission to intervene in the suit filed in Louisiana. This activity is conducted only a few times a year and is reserved for situations in which officials believe a public policy issue needs to be addressed.

No Wrongdoing

Despite the settlement, Home Depot denies discrimination. In a statement, the firm maintained that it provides opportunities for all of its associates to develop. "The Home Depot believes that entering into these agreements is in the best interest of our associates, customers, and stockholders as it will allow the company to avoid distractions to our business," said Bernard Marcus, the company's chairman. "We are committed to putting these lawsuits behind us and focusing on what we do best." According to Suzanne Apple, Home Depot's director of community affairs, "We felt confident we could have successfully defended ourselves in court, but settling the California case pretty much took the teeth out of the other three cases."

According to Stephen Bokat, general counsel of the U.S. Chamber of Commerce, "Companies are settling claims, even if they dispute them, because of the risks and expense entailed in fighting a class-action lawsuit." Ann Reesman, general counsel of the Equal Employment Advisory Council, confirms. "It means Home Depot made a business decision," Reesman said. "Win or lose, they'd spend a lot of money. They were in a no-win situation."

"The settlement will enhance Home Depot's ability to compete in the future," said Mike Baller, co-lead counsel for the 11 women who filed the California case. According to Chris Roush of the *Atlanta Constitution*, if a jury had heard the case and found Home Depot responsible for discrimination, the company may have paid as much as $65 billion. However, "The size of the settlement certainly seems to confirm the EEOC's view that there are serious employment problems at Home Depot," said Ellen Vargyas, legal counsel of the EEOC.

Change in Employment Practices

Fast-growing firms often concentrate on growth at the expense of employment practices. Conditions of the settlement require Home Depot to implement new employment practices, and the company has hired executives to oversee this directive. A federal judge will oversee Home Depot's compliance with the settlement for five years. The Atlanta-based retailer must set up a formal system for employees to inform managers when they want to be considered for promotion to sales and management positions. This action involves installing an in-store computer or telephone system on which its 115,000 employees can apply for other jobs in the company. Dubbed the "Job Preference Process," it is designed to steer more women into sales and management jobs. The company will retrain managers in equal employment opportunities and implement a formal internal complaint procedure to resolve concerns. The company will develop job-related qualifications for sales, supervisor, and manager positions to remove subjectivity. In addition, Home Depot is required to publish a pamphlet describing the agreement, to be posted in stores and made available to each worker.

The concept of equal opportunity is an ideal basic to the free enterprise system. The positive growth of any economy results from nurturing and using the ability of all persons to the fullest extent. Merit, not irrelevant factors such as race, sex, or religion, is the most important consideration in our society. Under a meritorious system, the best performers and competitors should be rewarded.

This concept means that all persons have an equal opportunity to demonstrate their merit. Unfortunately, a substantial number of employers have discriminated against certain classes of individuals based on characteristics such as gender or race. As a result, the government passed laws to end discrimination that prevented members of society from having an equal chance at available employment and the training and experience necessary to pursue all employment opportunities.

Strategic Choices

An organization has a number of important strategic choices to make regarding EEOs. These choices are outlined as follows:

1. The organization can choose to be proactive or reactive in its strategy toward EEOs.
2. The organization can choose the breadth of its focus.
3. The organization can decide on the depth of its EEO plan.
4. The organization can choose the degree of the tie between its EEO plan and the overall strategic plan of the firm.
5. The organization can decide on the degree of formality in its approach to EEO.

Strategic Choices for EEO

Proactive or Reactive An organization can decide to plan carefully and anticipate any potential discriminatory practices. This means examining new *and* existing employment policies to ensure equal opportunities. In addition, proactive organizations can develop equal opportunity programs, including affirmative action programs, to ensure that any discriminatory practices are eliminated. Affirmative action programs are discussed later in this chapter. Some organizations, however, are more reactive to EEOs and minimally satisfy only those regulations required by law and demanded by the courts.

Breadth An organization can choose a narrow focus by meeting EEO regulations in hiring and promotion decisions only. However, organizations can choose a broader scope by ensuring equal opportunities in areas such as training, rewarding, and so on. Although organizations are required by law to ensure fair and equal treatment in all areas of employment, many organizations fall short of this requirement.

Depth The organization can choose to have an EEO plan that mostly involves only a few employees (for example, the heads of the human resource department) in its management and enforcement. On the other hand, it can involve all organizational personnel in an effort to promote *commitment* to nondiscriminatory practices throughout the organization.

Tie with Strategy The organization's EEO policies can be tied loosely, if at all, to the firm's overall strategic plan. Conversely, the EEO policies can be fully integrated with the strategic plan of the organization. Integration of the firm's EEO policies and its overall strategic plan can best occur by fully integrating the two through strategic human resource planning.

Formality Finally, the organization can choose to have a rather informal plan that depends on the knowledge of its managers or personnel staff regarding EEO regulations. On the other hand, the organization can have a formalized plan that is clearly defined in written policy and supported by documentation and data.

Employment Discrimination[2]

Discrimination can be defined as the process of responding to a person differently based on that person's individual differences. This is often the goal for human resource managers. These managers make selection decisions by discriminating among the applicants. For example, when six applicants apply for one job, one has to be selected. As long as decisions of this type are based on the abilities of the applicants, discrimination is legal. Discrimination becomes illegal, however, when the differences used to separate individuals are non-job-related characteristics such as gender, race, national origin, or handicap. This chapter discusses *illegal* discrimination acts defined by Title VII of the Civil Rights Act of 1964. Exhibit 5.1 is one firm's stated philosophy and policy regarding employment decisions.

Title VII of the Civil Rights Act

Title VII of the Civil Rights Act of 1964 prohibits discrimination against any individual based on race, color, religion, sex, or national origin in any employment condition (for example, training and hiring). Title VII was amended in 1972 to strengthen its enforcement and to expand its coverage to include government employees, educational institutions, and private employers of more than 15 persons. Title VII was amended again in 1978, making it illegal to discriminate because of pregnancy, childbirth, or related conditions.

Finally, the Civil Rights Act of 1991 was enacted. The need for this new act was precipitated in part by the 1989 Supreme Court rulings on discrimination in the workplace. In 1989 the Supreme Court, in *Wards Cove* v. *Antonio*, set new limits in the area of civil rights by reexamining laws against job discrimination. The significance of the Supreme Court's decisions on civil rights is best understood when compared with earlier decisions on fair employment legislation. In one of the landmark employment cases, *Griggs* v. *Duke Power Company*, the Court ruled in 1971 that companies must be able to prove that their selection procedures do not discriminate unfairly. In essence, the *Griggs* v. *Duke Power Company* case involved promotion and transfer policies requiring employees to have a high school diploma and satisfactory scores on two aptitude tests. One of these tests, the Wonderlic Intelligence Test, failed African-Americans at a higher rate than Caucasians. In addition, fewer African-Americans had high school diplomas than Caucasians. Passing the aptitude test and having a high school diploma were not judged to be job-related requirements. The Court held that when plaintiffs demonstrate that otherwise neutral employment practices disproportionately and adversely affect minorities and women, they have demonstrated that a Title VII violation exists. To avoid this violation, employers had to demonstrate that (1) the plaintiff's statistics were wrong or (2) the practices at issue were dictated by business necessity.

According to civil rights activists, the Court (1) put limits on the abilities of individuals to bring employment discrimination suits (*Wards Cove* v. *Antonio*), (2) allowed challenges to affirmative action programs that had been in effect for years (*Martin* v. *Wilks* and *Lorance* v. *AT&T*), and (3) decided that federal governmental laws do not

---

| EXHIBIT 5.1 | AN INSURANCE COMPANY'S EMPLOYMENT PHILOSOPHY AND POLICY |

---

1. We have an obligation to our policyholders to determine realistically our needs for employees and to select the best-qualified available personnel to handle the insurance business.
2. We shall hire, promote, compensate, and provide terms, conditions, and privileges of employment solely on the basis of the company's personnel requirements and each individual's qualifications.
3. In fulfilling our obligations, we will not practice, tolerate, or condone discrimination because of race, color, religion, sex, national origin, age, or handicap.
4. We shall comply at all times with the letter and the spirit of all national, state, and local laws pertaining to employment.
5. Just as we will not discriminate against prospective employees because of race, color, religion, sex, national origin, age, or handicap, we will not terminate any competent person to make room for another on the basis of any of these reasons.

---

cover racial harassment in the workplace (*Patterson* v. *McLean*). According to civil rights leader Ralph G. Neas, overturning the *Wards Cove* v. *Antonio* decision was the number one legislative priority of the civil rights community during 1990 (see Exhibit 5.2 for more information on these controversial Supreme Court decisions).[3]

The Civil Rights Act of 1991 was, for the most part, in response to the U.S. Supreme Court decisions in 1989. The new civil rights law makes it easier for certain workers to sue their employers over alleged job discrimination. The law creates new, but limited, rights for women and the disabled to collect money damages that already are available to racial minorities. In addition, the act provides for compensatory and punitive damages for victims of intentional discrimination. Jury trials may be requested. Further, the new law applies to on-the-job problems as well as hiring issues.[4] Exhibit 5.3 summarizes the major provisions of the 1991 Civil Rights Act.

compensatory damages Compensation awarded because of trauma incurred in the workplace.

Compensatory and Punitive Damages   **Compensatory damages** include emotional pain and suffering, mental anguish, and a loss of quality of life. Compensatory and punitive damages are in addition to back pay, which is still covered under the Civil Rights Act of 1964. The total compensatory and punitive damage package cannot exceed $50,000 for organizations with 15 to 100 employees; $100,000 for organizations with 101 to 200 employees; $200,000 for organizations with 201 to 500 employees; and $300,000 for organizations with more than 500 employees.

Glass Ceiling Commission An organization focusing on breaking down the barriers to the advancement of minorities and women in the workplace.

Glass Ceiling Commission   Women and minorities remain underrepresented in management decision-making positions. Under the Civil Rights Act of 1991, Congress established the **Glass Ceiling Commission** to help alleviate this problem. Essentially, the Commission considers how prepared women and minorities are for advancement and what opportunities are available. The Commission next determines the business policies in place that affect the promotions as well as makes comparisons with businesses that have actively promoted women and minorities and their success.

EXHIBIT 5.2   SUMMARY OF EEO CASE LAWS THAT PRECEDED THE CIVIL
RIGHTS ACT OF 1991

Patterson v. *McLean* (1978)

The plaintiff, an African-American, filed a racial harassment case against the McLean Credit Union because she had not received a promotion or raise while employed there. Further, she was told "blacks work slower than whites" and thus had grounds for a discrimination suit. The Supreme Court ruled that the section under which she filed (Section 1981 of the 1991 Civil Rights Act) was not appropriate because it dealt only with making and enforcing contracts, and her situation did not fall under this section. This decision narrowed the view of Section 1981 by not covering racial harassment in the workplace.

Wards Cove v. *Antonio* (1989)

Wards Cove involved two salmon-packing companies in the Northwest. Each firm hired only minority workers (Eskimos and Filipinos) for the lower-paid, unskilled packing jobs during the salmon season. Other more skilled jobs (e.g., engineers or mechanics), which were not seasonal, were given only to nonminority workers. Because of the statistical differences between the representation of minorities in the skilled jobs, the plaintiffs sued, claiming discrimination. The Supreme Curt ruled against previous decisions and said that statistical disparity does not establish a prima facie case. The results of this case limited the ability of employees to bring employment discrimination suits by shifting the burden of proof to the employee.

Martin v. *Wilks* (1989)

In this case, the National Association for the Advancement of Colored People (NAACP) sued the city of Birmingham, Alabama, because the city was not hiring minority firefighters. To avoid litigation, the city entered into a consent agreement to hold a certain number of positions open for minority candidates. The Caucasian firefighters objected to the agreement but did not take part in developing it. Later, the Caucasian firefighters challenged the agreement under Title VII and the 14th Amendment. The Supreme Court ruled in favor of the Caucasian firefighters and said that they had not been given adequate opportunity to participate in making the agreement that violated their rights. This decision opened the door for reverse discrimination challenges to affirmative action plans that have been in place for years.

Lorance v. *AT&T* (1989)

AT&T's seniority system was changed from companywide to departmentwide. In other words, a person's seniority did not go with him or her after a transfer but started over. Union men favored the change, but the women opposed it. A few years later when layoffs occurred, the women field a suit claiming the departmentwide seniority system discriminated against them. The Supreme Court ruled that the 300-day filing deadline from the time of the act in question had long passed and it dismissed the case. This decision limited the ability of employees to challenge past changes that may have a future discriminatory impact.

City of Richmond v. *Croson Company* (1989)

The city of Richmond had set aside 30 percent of its contractual work for minority business enterprises since the city was 50 percent African-American, and historically less than 1 percent of the contracts had been awarded to local African-American companies. Croson, an African-American, was denied a city contract even though he was the only bidder. He sued and the lower courts decided in his favor. However, the Supreme Court ruled against him. This decision made preferential treatment (i.e., Affirmative Action plans) for minority groups discriminated against in the past unprotected by law.

| EXHIBIT 5.3 | MAJOR PROVISIONS OF THE 1991 CIVIL RIGHTS ACT |

- *Damages and Jury Trials:* Provides for compensatory and punitive damages for victims of intentional discrimination suing under Title VII, the Age Discrimination Act (ADA), or federal employment sections of the Rehabilitation Act. The combined amount of compensatory and punitive damages depends on the size of the employer, with caps ranging from $50,000 to $300,000. Jury trials may be requested by any party seeking compensatory or punitive damages.
- *"Race Norming" of Employment Tests:* Prohibits adjustments in test scores, use of different cutoff scores, or other amendments to employment-related tests based on race, color, religion, sex, or national origin.
- *Expanded Coverage under Section 1981:* Amends interpretation of language in Supreme Court decision in *Patterson* v. *McLean*, regarding the right "to make and enforce contracts." Prior to this decision, section 1981 was applied to race discrimination in all aspects of the employment contract, that is, hiring, duration of employment, and contract termination. After the *Patterson* decision, Section 1981 applied to hiring only. The Civil Rights Act of 1991 restores the pre-*Patterson* interpretation specifying that the term "make and enforce" contracts includes all benefits, privileges, terms, and conditions of the employment relationship. This is significant since there are no caps on awards for compensatory and punitive damages under Section 1981.
- *Mixed Motive Cases:* Reverses *Price Warehouse* v. *Hopkins*, in which the Supreme Court held that an employer could avoid liability for discrimination by showing that it would have made the same employment decision in the absence of discrimination. Under the new act, this rule is changed by providing that an illegal employment practice has occurred if discrimination was a motivating factor, even though other factors also motivated the employment decision. In such cases, plaintiffs may recover declaratory and injunctive relief, attorneys fees, and costs.
- *Disparate Impact:* Reverses the Supreme Court decision of *Wards Cove* v. *Antonio*, which stated that plaintiffs injured by disparate impact discrimination had to prove that the challenged practices were not significantly related to legitimate business objectives. Under the 1991 act, an employer must demonstrate that a challenged practice is job-related and consistent with "business necessity" after the plaintiff has shown that the employment practice caused a disparate impact. Once the employer has met its burden, the plaintiff must prove that an alternative practice exists having less of a disparate impact and that the employer refused to adopt it. If the employer can prove that its employment practice does not cause disparate impact, it is not required to show the practice is required by business necessity.
- *Extraterritorial Employment:* Defines *employee* in both Title VII and the ADA to include U.S. citizens employed abroad and provides exemptions for otherwise unlawful employment actions if compliance violates laws of the foreign country where the employee works. Additionally, the 1991 act creates a presumption that violations of Title VII by foreign corporations controlled by a U.S. employer are violations by the U.S. employer itself.
- *Glass Ceiling:* The Glass Ceiling Commission was established to study barriers to advancement of minorities and women in the workforce and to recommend means of overcoming those barriers. Also establishes the National Award for diversity and excellence in executive management.

SOURCE: Adapted from L. Z. Lorber, "Legal Report: The Civil Rights Act of 1991," *Society for Human Resource Management*, Spring 1992; and M. Kobata, "The Civil Rights Act of 1991," *Personnel Journal*, March 1992, p. 48.

What is Discrimination?

Discrimination in employment decisions is usually manifested in one of three ways: (1) disparate treatment, (2) adverse impact, and (3) present effects of past discrimination.[5]

disparate treatment The use of different standards for different applicants or employees.

Disparate Treatment A manager who intentionally treats an applicant or employee differently because of race, color, religion, national origin, sex, or age is guilty of **disparate treatment**. One example of disparate treatment is rejecting Asian applicants because of the concern that one or more might be an illegal alien. Another case of

Danish Women Begin to Sing "I've Been Working on the Railroad"

The government-owned Danske Statsbaner (DSB), the Danish state rail system, has implemented an aggressive policy to place women on the management fast track. For example, one woman, Birthe Oestergaard Peterson, went from working the switch signals on the night shift to heading the team that plans Denmark's train schedules. DSB's plans include training programs to give women the skills needed to become engineers. It offers seminars for female workers such as one on "Is Management for Me?" DSB also has instituted a confidence-building job development program for secretaries. To attract women, DSB offers 24-hour daycare. Recruiters and managers have been told to look for qualified women, and male managers were placed in discussion groups with women to help break down the stereotypes each held.

Since it began its program, DSB has increased the proportion of female workers from 11 percent to approximately 20 percent. Even more exciting is the fact that the number of female executives has increased from 1 percent to 10 percent, front-line managers from 2 percent to 12 percent, and female train conductors from virtually zero to 40 percent.

Even with these advances, DSB has a long way to go. "There is still a glass ceiling," reports Tore Haakomsson, the personnel lawyer for DSB. He also noted that there is still pay inequity between men and women at DSB and that the company cannot find enough women to recruit. To overcome this problem, it has initiated its own training programs, such as teaching metalworking skills to women, so they can become locomotive engineers.

Some argue that the firm is going too far. One woman declined a job offer when she found that she was the only female applicant out of 50. She realized that getting a job just because she was a woman was not good for the company or for her. Other women feel differently. One of the first women to break into top management, Anne-Lise Bach Soerensen, has seen both her responsibility and salary double. She is now taking business trips out of the country and actively helping the women in positions below her to rise through the ranks. Recognizing the potential in one of her assistants, Soerensen enrolled her in the management training program.

SOURCE: Dana Milbank, "Danish Women Given Inside Track on the Rail," *The Wall Street Journal*, May 16, 1994, p. A11.

disparate treatment is application of a rule against applicants or employees of a protected group. For example, an organizational rule that allows men to marry but prohibits women from marrying treats women differently from men and violates Title VII. Finally, disparate treatment can arise from sexual, racial, religious, or national-origin harassment. For example, managers violate the law if they make sexual advances or demands as a condition for employment or promotion.

adverse impact
The effect of using one set of standards that results in a disproportionate number of minorities being treated unfairly.

Adverse Impact   Seemingly neutral qualifications for employment or promotions have been found to have an **adverse impact** on some minority groups. That is, selection and promotion tests that screen out minority candidates adversely affect them and are discriminatory. It has been found that some job qualifications thought to be necessary for effective performance in organizations are not actually needed and have an adverse impact on members of minority groups, women, or older workers. For example, requirements of minimum height or weight can have adverse impact on women and some ethnic groups. Some employment tests tend to eliminate certain minority groups disproportionately yet have a questionable relationship to job performance.

| EXHIBIT 5.4 | EXAMPLE OF THE FOUR-FIFTHS RULE |

A company hired 193 of the 344 Caucasian applicants who applied, 40 of the 49 Hispanic applicants, 110 of the 209 African-American applicants, and 62 of the 89 Asians who applied. The selection ratio for each group follows:

- Caucasian applicants: 193/344 = 56%.
- Hispanic applicants: 40/49 = 82%.
- African-American applicants: 110/209 = 53%.
- Asian applicants: 62/89 = 70%.

The most favorably treated group in terms of selection ratio in this example is the Hispanics with a selection ratio of 82 percent.

To avoid discriminating against the Caucasian, African-American, and Asian applicants, each of the other groups must have a selection ratio of at least 80 percent of 82 percent, or 66 percent. Since their selection ratios were less than 66 percent, both Caucasian and African-American applicants were discriminated against by the hiring plan used by this firm, but Asians and Hispanics were not.

The *Uniform Guidelines on Employee Selection Procedures*, developed by the EEOC, the Department of Labor, the Department of Justice, and the U.S. Civil Service Commission, provides guidance on ways to develop selection systems that avoid having an adverse impact and therefore do not violate Title VII. One of the recommendations included in this document is the Four-Fifths rule. In essence, this rule states that the selection rate of any minority group should be at least 80 percent (i.e., four fifths) of the group with the highest selection ratio. A selection ratio is simply the number of applicants selected divided by the number of applicants who applied. Exhibit 5.4 provides an example of how to apply the Four-Fifths rule.

Past Discrimination   The third way employers have been guilty of discrimination is by perpetuating the effects of past discriminatory policies. For example, a policy of hiring persons who are referred by current employees before hiring other applicants may appear to be a nondiscriminatory policy. However, if the workforce is Caucasian because of discrimination in the past, the use of an employee referral policy in hiring may tend to perpetuate the Caucasian workforce, because new recruits might come primarily from the Caucasian community.

Seniority systems have been challenged because of their perpetuation of past discrimination practices. However, if a seniority system was not developed out of an intent to discriminate, it is not unlawful, even though it may result in restrictions of employment opportunities. For example, if women were not hired into an organization until recently, a promotion system based on seniority would have an unequal impact on female employees. The promotion system in this case would be considered nondiscriminatory (if it were developed without the intent of being discriminatory) because it applies equally to all groups.

Types of Discrimination

Sex Discrimination   Title VII of the Civil Rights Act of 1964 prohibits discrimination because of the sex of a person. When the sex of an employee or job applicant is one of the factors on which an employment decision is based, the decision is most likely unlawful. The use of height or weight requirements may be challenged and found to be discriminatory if the requirements eliminate a significantly larger number of women than men. Other types of sex discrimination include refusing employment to a woman based on the assumption that parenthood might cause her to be absent more than a male employee. Sex stereotyping can also result in unlawful sex discrimination. For example, if a male manager evaluates the performance of a female subordinate more critically because she demonstrates stereotypically masculine characteristics (for example, assertiveness), he is guilty of sex discrimination.

Even though sex-based stereotypes should not be considered when hiring workers, they still exist in the workplace and often hinder women's chances for promotion and raises. The most damaging stereotyping is that women have lower career commitment than men do. If a woman is in her child-bearing years, managers ask themselves whether they should invest in her, knowing she might leave. More than likely the answer is no, even if the woman cannot or chooses not to have children. A second damaging stereotype is that women are too emotional to handle management positions. When men blow up, they are considered to have a good reason; when women do it, they are considered to be emotional. Finally, women are either too aggressive or not aggressive enough. Those who are too aggressive are considered shrews; those who are not aggressive enough are not considered management material.[6]

Although overt discrimination may be waning in corporate America, covert, subtle discrimination is on the rise. Deborah Flick, a diversity trainer, equates subtle sexism to water torture—one drip at a time. Even though it is hard to detect, it can be devastating to a woman and her career. Exclusion is one example. Women are left out of decision making, important meetings, and business trips. The results of exclusion are lawsuits, adverse impact on women's careers, and the loss of important contributions by women.[7]

Sexual discrimination lawsuits are still prevalent. One Wall Street firm, Kidder, Peabody & Co., has had more than its share of suits. According to interviews with 15 women who are former Kidder employees, ranging from entry-level associates to managing director, top executives froze them out of top jobs, limited their pay, and verbally harassed them.[8]

A successful sex-discrimination lawsuit has forced a popular Miami Beach restaurant, Joe's Stone Crab, to look harder for waitresses. In the past, only men were hired as servers. Traditional all-male restaurant-hiring policies are illegal under federal discrimination law. Although a single-gender wait staff is a common phenomenon, it is still clearly illegal. The company's reliance on employee referrals contributed to its downfall because the male wait staff told male friends about the available jobs and discouraged women from applying.[9]

Interestingly, homosexuals are not covered under Title VII. The Civil Rights Act does not prohibit organizations from refusing to hire or for firing someone because he or she is a homosexual. Although there are no federal laws, state and local laws do exist in certain areas. Specifically, Connecticut, Hawaii, Massachusetts, New Jersey, and Wisconsin prohibit discrimination based on sexual orientation by private and public employers. Further, California, Minnesota, New Mexico, New York, Ohio, Pennsylvania, Rhode Island, and Washington have an executive order by their respective governors making it unlawful for the government to discriminate on the basis of sexual orientation.

Sexual Harassment   Sexual harassment is also a violation of Title VII of the Civil Rights Act. The highly publicized hearings regarding sexual harassment charges made by law professor Anita Hill against then Supreme Court nominee Clarence Thomas made the issue of sexual harassment more salient.[10] Essentially, sexual harassment means unwelcome verbal or physical conduct from others of a sexual nature. According to the EEOC guidelines, behavior becomes sexual harassment when:

1. Submission to sexual conduct is made either explicitly or implicitly a term or condition of an individual's employment.
2. An individual's submission to or rejection of sexual conduct is used as the basis for employment decisions affecting that individual.
3. Unwelcome conduct unreasonably interferes with an individual's work performance or creates an intimidating, hostile, or offensive work environment.[11]

The first two items illustrate *quid pro quo* (literally, "something for something") harassment; the third illustrates hostile environment sexual harassment. Each will be discussed.

quid pro quo Something for something.

Quid pro quo harassment occurs when unwelcome sexual advances or requests for sexual favors are made explicitly or implicitly as a condition for employment. For example, if a manager tells a job applicant that, in terms of hiring, "It would be beneficial for you to go out on a date with me," this would constitute *quid pro quo* sexual harassment. The rules for establishing a prima facie *quid pro quo* case were established in the *Barnes* v. *Costle* (1977) ruling. The District of Columbia circuit court suggested that two criteria are needed to establish such a case: disparate treatment of women versus men and a tangible employment consequence.[12] The disparate treatment requirement is needed to show that only women are being harassed. If, however, a bisexual manager was harassing both men and women equally, there would be no case. In *Barnes*, the court found that she was harassed because she was a woman and that men in her office were not being, and were not likely to be, harassed, thus indicating disparate treatment.[13]

One well-known example of a *quid pro quo* court case is *Bundy* v. *Jackson*.[14] The plaintiff in the case was Sandra Bundy, who held the position of personnel clerk with the District of Columbia Department of Corrections. Jackson, the defendant, made repeated sexual advances toward her. Jackson began as her peer but was later promoted to the director of the agency. Bundy indicated that two other supervisors, Arthur Burton and James Gainey, also made sexual advances toward her. When she complained to their boss, Lawrence Swain, he asked her to begin a sexual relationship with him. When she was passed over for promotion, she was told the reason was that her work was not adequate. However, because she had never been told that her work was unsatisfactory, she sued on the grounds of discrimination. The U.S. Court of Appeals found that Bundy had been discriminated against because of her sex and extended the definition of discrimination to include sexual harassment.

hostile environment An organizational environment or surrounding that promotes or tolerates sexual harassment.

Hostile environment sexual harassment involves unwelcome conduct that interferes with the employee's job performance or creates an offensive working environment. This type of discrimination was first recognized in the 1986 Supreme Court case of *Meritor Savings Bank* v. *Vinson*.[15] The employer argued that if no tangible losses in terms of compensation or the job itself occurred and that there was no stipulation that sexual conduct was the only way to retain the job, Title VII did not hold. That is, the only type of sexual harassment covered by Title VII is *quid pro quo*. Because *quid pro quo* harassment could not be proved in the *Meritor* case, lower courts found that the bank was not liable. However, the U.S. Supreme Court had a different interpretation. It held that hostile environment sexual harassment, as defined in the EEOC guidelines, was unlawful. It further found that any activities that create an abusive working environment are unlawful sexual harassment.

Every employee has the right to work in an environment free of discriminatory intimidation or insult. Photographs and posters of nude women in the workplace and verbal or written obscenities can be defined as creating a sexually hostile environment. If an employee is subjected to a hostile environment, it can be very costly to an organization. For example, in an October 1997 ruling, Continental Airlines was ordered to pay $875,000 in damages to a female pilot who said she repeatedly complained, to no avail, about pornography strewn about the airplane cockpits.[16]

One must also be aware of hostile work environments that may arise through the proliferation of electronic mail. Nearly two dozen employees, or ten percent of the workforce, at the New York Times Co.'s business office were fired. During a fraud investigation, managers found a number of potentially offensive e-mails, some of which had been sent by or forwarded to other employees in the office. Although one or two explicit e-mail messages typically aren't enough by themselves to prove that a workplace environment is hostile, such e-mails can bolster other damaging evidence. At a subsidiary of Chevron Corp., e-mails containing such jokes as "25 reasons beer is better that women" were used, along with other evidence, in a sexual harassment claim that was settled in 1995 for 2.2 million dollars.[17]

An employer should take all necessary steps to prevent sexual harassment in the workplace. Some guidelines to prevent harassment include developing a written policy prohibiting sexual harassment, informing managers and employees of the policy and of appropriate action to take if they are harassed, promptly investigating any complaints, and taking appropriate action against the offender (Exhibit 5.5). Even if the employer has a policy against sexual harassment, the employer can still be held liable for the actions of managers, employees, and even customers and vendors if the employer *knew* or *should have known* about the occurrence and failed to take appropriate action. In the case of *Lockard* v. *Pizza Hut, et. al.*, an Oklahoma court ordered an Oklahoma Pizza Hut franchisee to pay $200,000 in compensatory damages for allowing a hostile work environment created by two customers who harassed a waitress. *Lockard* involved a manager who disregarded his employee's complaint that she was being sexually harassed. In *Rodriguez-Hernandez* v. *Miranda-Velez*, a female employee sued her employer under Title VII, alleging that she was discharged from her job after complaining to her employer about the sexual advances made by a high-level executive of one of her employer's most important clients. The First Circuit Court upheld the jury's verdict for the plaintiff based on the customer's harassing behavior.[18] The best defense against sexual harassment claims is to have a well-designed grievance procedure and to encourage employees to speak up.[19] Exhibit 5.6 presents a company's policy on sexual harassment. A policy statement should be consistent with the firm's grievance procedure and be specific and objective.[20]

Companies need strong sexual harassment policies for a number of reasons. Business owners who ignore issues of sexual harassment are running big risks as companies of all sizes increasingly face lawsuits. Interestingly, complaints to the EEOC more than doubled—to 15,342 in 1996—since Anita Hill testified in 1991.[21] Sexual harassment can happen anywhere. One study shows that 90 percent of *Fortune* 500 companies have dealt with sexual harassment complaints. More than one third of these companies has been sued at least once, and about one quarter has been sued over and over again. All of this litigation costs the average large corporation $6.7 million a year, or an average of $200,000 for each complaint investigated.[22]

Not all employees are able to take their case to court, however. In the securities industry, the path taken to report a harassment incident is through the firm's internal

| EXHIBIT 5.5 | SAMPLE OF GUIDELINES TO PREVENT SEXUAL HARASSMENT |

1. Develop a written policy prohibiting sexual harassment.
2. Inform managers and employees of the policy.
3. Inform managers and employees of the appropriate action to take if they are harassed.
4. *Promptly* investigate any complaints.
5. Take appropriate action against the offender.

| EXHIBIT 5.6 | EXAMPLE OF A COMPANY POLICY ON SEXUAL HARASSMENT* |

1. Sexual harassment is a violation of the corporation's EEO policy. Abuse of anyone through sexist slurs or other objectionable conduct is offensive behavior.
2. Management must ensure that a credible program exists for handling sexual harassment problems. If complaints are filed, the complaints should receive prompt consideration without fear of negative consequences.
3. When a supervisor is made aware of an allegation of sexual harassment, the following guidelines should be considered:
   a. Obtain information about the allegation through discussion with the complainant. Ask for and document facts about what was said, what was done, when and where it occurred, and what the complainant believes was the inappropriate behavior. In addition, find out if any other individuals observed the incident, or similar incidents, to the complainant's knowledge. This is an *initial* step. In no case will the supervisor handle the complaint process alone.
   b. If the complaint is from an hourly employee, a request for union representation at any point must be handled as described in the labor agreement.
   c. The immediate supervisor or the department head and the personnel department must be notified immediately. When a complaint is raised by, or concerns, an hourly employee, the local labor relations representative is to be advised. When a complaint is raised by or concerns a salaried employee, the personnel director is to be advised.
4. The personnel department will conduct a complete investigation of the complaint for hourly and salaried employees. The investigation is to be handled in a professional and confidential manner.

*Policy example is based on General Motors' Corporate policy on sexual harassment.

grievance procedures. This may seem to be a reasonable solution, but it apparently does not work well. The case of Helen Walters is an example. She filed a complaint against her boss for calling her a "hooker" and a "bitch," brandishing a riding crop in front of her, and leaving condoms on her desk. In any court of law, she could clearly establish a prima facie case of hostile environment. However, she lost her grievance even though her boss readily admitted to all of the acts of which he was accused. The problem lies in the grievance panel members. The three-person panel is appointed and paid by the industry organization such as the New York Stock Exchange. Nearly 90 percent of the panel members are men, roughly half are retired, and their average age is 60. According to Marilyn Stringer, a former Paine Weber sales assistant, asking arbitrators with this type of profile to judge a sexual harassment case is like asking the "brother of the fox who raided the hen house." Unlike Ms. Walters, Ms. Stringer won her grievance, but her award was only $300, a far cry from the average settlement won in court cases.[23]

Although nine of ten sexual harassment cases filed are by women, the number of cases filed by men is on the rise.[24] One of the most celebrated cases of a man suing a woman for sexual harassment is *Gutierrez* v. *Martinez*. In May 1993, a Los Angeles court awarded Sabino Gutierrez $1.017 million in damages in the suit he had brought against Cal-Spa and its chief financial officer, Maria Martinez. Reports indicated that the jury did not believe either party, but they apparently liked Gutierrez more than Martinez. She was described as being a cold, hard, ice princess. As the story goes, Martinez befriended Gutierrez when he first began working at Cal-Spa. At that time he could not speak English and could not read or write. She mentored him, and he rose from being an hourly employee to a production supervisor, overseeing a staff of nearly 70, with a salary of about $45,000 a year. However, when he announced that he was engaged, Gutierrez claims that Martinez demolished his office, threw away his personal things, and demoted him in retaliation. Martinez says that she was the one being harassed. She claims that Gutierrez made a sexual advance toward her the month his first child was born. She also claims that he would not attend a company function because he could not stand to see her with her husband. The truth of what happened may never be known, but people who worked with them and knew both sides say the truth resides somewhere between their stories.[25]

What the court requires as proof of sexual harassment changes continually. The Supreme Court held in *Harris* v. *Forklift Systems* that an individual does not have to have a nervous breakdown to qualify as suffering from the effects of harassment. Instead, an abusive work environment, even if it does not seriously affect the worker's psychological well-being, can detract from his or her ability to perform the job and should be considered hostile.[26] However, for every court ruling that moves the plight of sexual harassment forward, one that moves it backward can be found. For example, in the case of *Burns* v. *McGregor Electric Industries*, the court ruled that even though the sexual advances Ms. Burns faced from her boss were unwelcome and not solicited, they were not offensive to her because of her personal history, her appearance on the stand, her manner of dress, the location of her tattoo, and the fact that she had appeared nude in a magazine.[27]

Pregnancy Discrimination Under the Pregnancy Discrimination Act of 1978, a female employee or job applicant may not be treated differently from a male because of her pregnancy or capacity to become pregnant. Essentially, a woman is protected against being fired, being refused a promotion, or not being hired because she is pregnant or has had an abortion. As long as they can still work, pregnant employees cannot be forced to quit or go on leave. Some states have variations of a parental leave law that enable both parents to take time off from work to care for their newborn child. However, only a few states require the employer to guarantee the same job to the employee on return.

Special problems arise when an organization manufactures or uses products or processes that may be harmful to female reproductivity or the unborn child. Interestingly, a policy that excludes women from the workplace because of reproductive or fetal hazards may violate Title VII, even if it can be justified by scientific evidence.

EEOC filings for alleged pregnancy-related discrimination have been found to be quite lucrative. For example, Lana Ambruster, a former claims adjuster for California Casualty Management Company, was awarded $2.7 million, including $1.5 million in

EXHIBIT 5.7	U.S. SUPREME COURT RULINGS ON SEXUAL HARASSMENT

During the spring and summer of 1998, the U.S. Supreme Court issued three rulings that further defined sexual harassment. First, in *Oncale* v. *Sundowner*, the Court ruled that sexual harassment law applies not only to heterosexuals but also to people who harass coworkers of the same sex. In *Farager* v. *Boca Raton*, the Court ruled that employers are liable for actions of their supervisors in sexual harassment even if the employer did not know of the harassing behavior. Finally, in *Burlington Industries* v. *Ellreth*, the Court allowed a woman to sue her former employer over threats a supervisor allegedly made but never carried out.

These cases emphasize that employers must have sexual harassment policies in place that are tailored to their business and filled with real-life examples. Employers must communicate them to all concerned, including the CEO, through training, posters, and memos. They must provide a means for employees to file a complaint and must provide a means to have a fair and impartial investigation of the complaint by the employer even if it means bringing in an outside investigator to ensure a fair and impartial review. Furthermore, they should assess employees' familiarity with the sexual harassment policy on a regular basis through tests and other means.

SOURCES: Edward Felsenthal, "Rulings Open Way for Sex-Harass Cases," *The Wall Street Journal*, June 29, 1998, p. A3; and Joann S. Lubin and Timothy D. Schellhardt, "High Court's Harassment Rulings Confuse Employers," *The Wall Street Journal*, June 30, 1998, p. B1.

punitive damages. She claimed that her boss threatened to fire her if she came back from her honeymoon pregnant. Two months later, when she told him she was expecting a child, he placed her on written probation. She was fired two months later. California Casualty said that she was fired for performance reasons and had been warned about her poor performance. The firm also mentioned that the allegedly discriminatory remarks by Ms. Ambruster's boss were taken lightly by the other employees.[28] Please see Exhibit 5.7 for additional rulings from the U.S. Supreme Court on sexual harassment that occurred about the same time.

Race Discrimination   Race discrimination means that employment decisions are based on an employee's race or color. Charges of race discrimination remain the most common type of EEO complaint. Under Title VII, employers have a responsibility to maintain a bias-free work environment and correct any discriminatory situations. As with sexual harassment, it is unlawful to engage in racial harassment. Racial harassment includes making racial and ethnic slurs or jokes directed at minority employees or in the presence of minority employees. In addition, it is unlawful to address minority employees by their first name if nonminority employees are addressed by titles such as "Mr." or "Ms." The failure of a nonminority employee to train a minority employee properly is also considered a form of racial harassment.

Almost any factor can be used to determine whether minorities have been treated differently from nonminority employees. For example, performance ratings, average salaries, records of termination, and employee training opportunities are ways in which minority groups can be compared with nonminority groups. Thus it is important for managers to maintain accurate records of all employment decisions.

The restaurant industry has been hard hit with race-bias allegations. Three major chain restaurants—Shoney's, Wendy's, and Denny's—have been targets of race-bias filings with the EEOC. Shoney's trouble started in the small town of Marianna, Florida. Henry and Billie Elliott, comanagers of a Captain D's Seafood restaurant, which is owned by the parent company Shoney's, were fired because they refused to practice immoral, illegal policies. For example, they were instructed by their area manager to "find more attractive white girls" to hire and to cut the hours of the African-American workers to force them to quit, so Caucasians could be hired to replace them. After the Elliotts promoted two African-American employees, the area manager demoted the two African-American employees and fired the Elliotts. When they were fired, the Florida couple sued. The court found for the Elliotts and ordered Shoney's to distribute $105 million in damages and back pay to approximately 10,000 African-American workers who had worked for Shoney's or had been denied employment.[29]

Unlike Shoney's, Denny's was sued by customers who claimed to have been discriminated against. The charges included the fact that African-Americans were required to prepay for their meals as well as pay cover charges in some Denny's restaurants in California. The suit also noted that Denny's promotional offer of providing customers a free birthday meal was not offered to African-American customers. Finally, the suit claims that managers used a racial coding system in which the term *blackout* meant that too many African-American customers were in the restaurant. The lawyer for Denny's explained that the "late-night" policies such as prepayment and cover charges were installed to address "security problems."[30]

Racial discrimination is not confined to the restaurant industry. Brooks Brothers, an apparel retailer, settled a lawsuit alleging discrimination in hiring. Brooks Brothers was accused of using a policy in which nonminority applicants are told that a job is open, but minority applicants are told that it is closed. This discrimination was identified by finding "testers" to apply for advertised openings. Testers are equally qualified individuals who differ only with respect to race or gender. In the case of Brooks Brothers, the nonminority testers were told the job was still open, although the minority testers were informed that the job had been filled. Critics argue that testing is not perfect and should not be used to prove discrimination. Supporters of the system say it is one of the few ways subtle discrimination can be shown.[31]

National Origin Discrimination   Employment discrimination based on national origin affects members of all national groups and groups of persons of common ancestry or heritage. National origin discrimination differs from race or color discrimination because other factors besides skin color or obvious race identification may be the basis for discrimination. For example, an employee's or job applicant's Cajun accent or manner of speaking cannot be part of the employment decision. Similar to race discrimination and harassment, the employer is responsible for the conduct of its employees regarding ethnic slurs and other harassing comments or actions.

The EEOC reported that national origin discrimination claims have increased. This increase has been attributed to the nationwide job insecurity and downsizing as well as the increase in immigration to this country. According to William Ho-Gonzales, who heads the Office of Special Counsel (OSC) for Immigration Related Unfair Employment Practices, many people fear that "foreigners" are coming to take away the few jobs left for Americans. The OSC investigates national origin discrimination charges in businesses with 4 to 14 employees; the EEOC handles those with more than 14.[32]

HR CHALLENGES

Immigration Act Compliance

With the continuing influx of immigrants into the U.S. workforce, the need for proper identification and work authorization forms has become a primary concern to American businesses. Headlines alert the public to the problems of not only hiring illegal aliens but also discriminating against immigrants. In 1986 the Immigration Reform and Control Act was established to clarify the hiring process of immigrants and to curb employment discrimination by providing clear, concrete guidelines for employers to follow in the hiring process.

It is important that employers be aware of the dynamics of the act and remember it when hiring immigrants. Employment decisions should *not* be based on national origin, citizenship status, foreign appearance, name, or accent but on an employee's qualifications. Any decision based on these attributes may be construed as discriminatory, resulting in a host of legal headaches.

According to the act, employers are required to complete an I-9 verification form within three business days of the hire. This necessitates the documentation of not only the employee's identity but of work authorization as well. The following is a list of documents that can establish both identity and work authorization. The employer should be careful not to ask for "more" or "better" proof from one group of individuals than from another because this, too, may be viewed as discriminatory.

The following documents establish identity and work authorization:

1. U.S. Passport
2. Certificate of U.S. citizenship
3. U.S. Citizen ID Card
4. Certificate of Naturalization
5. Alien Registration Card with photograph
6. Unexpired foreign passport with attached employment authorization
7. Temporary Resident Card with attached employment authorization

Finally, employers should *never* knowingly hire illegal aliens. The legal ramifications of this type of employment practice are serious and far outweigh any perceived benefits. By using these guidelines to comply with the Immigration Act's requirements, the employer will ease the hiring process and reduce any threat of discrimination.

SOURCE: Contributed by Donald Levine, Esq., (Chicago, IL: Levine & Ginsburg Ltd., 1998).

Some of the discrimination claims investigated by the EEOC have been based on the way applicants or employees talk. For example, Cambodian-American Planna K. Xieng alleged that the bank he worked for overlooked him for a promotion because of his accent. The bank felt that he did not have good enough English skills to calm irate customers.[33] The court awarded Xieng $389,000 in damages.

Many cases are not making it to the courts, however. Instead, employers have been settling cases without admitting liability. A Filipino nurse from Pomona, California, challenged a hospital's "English-only" policy as being discriminatory against bilingual workers. The hospital paid an undisclosed amount but admitted no guilt to settle the case.[34]

Age Discrimination and Harassment The Age Discrimination in Employment Act (ADEA) of 1967 protects employees 40 years of age and older from discrimination based on their age. In general, an employer cannot force an employee to retire after turning 70. In addition, an employer generally cannot refuse to hire or promote an individual because he or she is 70 or older. Unlike Title VII, ADEA allows victims of age discrimination or harassment to have their case heard before a jury. In the fall of 1990, President George Bush signed into law the Older Workers Benefit Protection Act. This law was enacted to include employee-benefit programs under the coverage of the ADEA.[35]

Employers have a duty under the law to maintain a work environment free from age discrimination and harassment just as they do to provide an environment free of sexual discrimination and harassment. A preference for employees who will remain on the job for a long time might be considered unlawful if it excludes older workers. An employer must demonstrate a bona fide occupational qualification if challenged on eliminating individuals from certain positions because of age.

Subjective hiring or promotion decisions should be examined carefully. For example, qualities such as "energetic" might be viewed as not applying to older workers. In addition, cost-cutting is not a legitimate reason for firing older workers and replacing them with younger and equally qualified employees merely because the older employee earns more money, although this is often done through early retirement programs. For example, an employer may make an exceptionally good offer to a group of older employees to encourage retirement. This is legal as long as it is made to all employees over a specific age in an occupational class and if no one is compelled to retire. Interestingly, age discrimination claims filed with the federal government went down to approximately 15,500 in 1996 from close to 20,000 in 1993.[36] One reason for the decrease in age bias claims may be because age bias suits are becoming harder to prove.[37] Plaintiffs must now show that their employer intentionally discriminated against them. Employees are not allowed to argue that they were discriminated against simply because the layoff affected older workers more than others. Unlike federal laws on race and sex discrimination, which specifically allow plaintiffs to make claims against employers based on the adverse impact on groups, the federal age discrimination statute does not specifically state anything about this.

Successful age-bias claims have resulted in fairly lucrative awards. It appears that members of juries can visualize themselves as old and therefore can relate to the plaintiff. Further, the jury has the ability to provide double back pay if an organization's wrongful conduct is found to be willful.[38] This was the outcome for Walter Biggins, who was fired at the age of 62 just weeks prior to his pension vesting. The jury awarded him $419,000 in damages and then doubled it because the jury believed that Hazen Paper Company had willfully violated the ADEA.[39]

In 1992 the ADEA was extended to cover retired workers. The EEOC filed suit against a plumbers and pipefitters union on behalf of the retired workers who were trying to get work through the local union. The union refused to let retired workers sign up for work unless they forfeited their retirement benefits. The court ruled that the policy discourages retired employees from seeking to return to the workforce and frustrates the ADEA's goal of promoting employment opportunities for older workers.[40]

To avoid the risk of age-based lawsuits, firms can and must take action. To begin, they must analyze their recruitment strategies. They must ensure that brochures and other information distributed to potential employees picture older workers. They must develop messages that attract mature workers. Firms must ensure that their recruitment activities target the mature audience. For example, some firms offer an "unretirement" party and invite individuals interested in rejoining the workforce. Organizations should advertise in sections of the newspaper other than the classifieds. The American Association for Retired Persons (AARP) can help firms locate retired employees who want to work. Hiring older workers is only one step, perhaps the

HR CHALLENGES

Double Damages for Age Discrimination

In *Brown* v. *M&M Mars*, the U.S. Court of Appeals for the 7th Circuit ruled that to receive double back pay damages under the federal Age Discrimination and Employment Act (ADEA), a plaintiff does not need to prove that the employer's conduct was "outrageous," only that the employer knew or demonstrated reckless disregard for the discrimination laws regarding older workers. Brown had been a supervisor and was discharged for not handling a production problem properly.

Rejecting the company's position that the discharge was based on performance, the jury found that age was a determining factor. The 7th Circuit confirmed the jury's finding that the company's articulated reasons for discharging Brown were a cover-up and that there was sufficient circumstantial evidence to support the jury's award of double damages.

SOURCE: *Resource: Legal Report*, Society for Human Resource Management, October 1989, p. 15.

HR CHALLENGES

Sixtysomething

Much of America is mentally trapped in stereotyping people over 60 years old as being worn out, having slow minds, and longing for retirement. Despite the fact that federal laws are against mandatory retirement, our culture seems to push employees toward leaving organizations early. In 1950 about half of all men at the age of 65 were still working; today only 15 percent still work, and the median retirement age has dropped to 61.

A recent survey by the American Association of Retired Persons (AARP) showed that as many as 40 percent of retired people would prefer to return to the workforce.

America is facing an era of labor shortages. With the number of 18- to 44-year-olds expected to drop by 1.6 million over the next decade, the country will need its older workers as never before. Progressive corporations are reversing the recent trend toward younger workers. For example, McDonald's actively recruits older employees, offering them flexible working hours and training them in a "McMasters" program. Sears, Roebuck, and Co. has expanded its part-time staff, with

much reliance on older workers. Finally, Polaroid (among other companies) offers "retirement rehearsals," allowing its employees to try out a short-term leave before retirement; if the change is too dramatic and the employee is unhappy, the job is still there.

Public leaders are needed to help spread the practice of using older workers. Warren Buffett has built an investment empire by paying close attention to both his companies and employees. When asked about leaving a woman in charge of one of his companies after her 94th birthday, he said, "She is clearly gathering speed and may well reach her full potential in another 5 or 10 years. Therefore, I've persuaded the Board to scrap our mandatory-retirement-at-100 policy. . . My God, good managers are so scarce I can't afford the luxury of letting them go just because they've added a year to their age."

SOURCE: Adapted from David R. Gergen, "Sixtysomething," *U.S. News & World Report*, April 16, 1990; and Phaedra Brotherton, "Tapping into an Older Workforce," *Mosaics: SHRM Focuses on Workplace Diversity*, Volume 6, March/April, 2000.

easiest, in avoiding age-based discrimination suits. If older workers do not feel welcome, they will not remain. To create a positive environment for them, sensitivity training programs should be offered to employees to make them aware of the advantages older workers bring to the workplace. It is also important to offer flexible schedules or a variety of hours, especially as older workers ease out of retirement. These

YOU BE THE JUDGE

Using Peyote: Religious Discrimination?

Discriminating against a job applicant because he uses peyote, a mescaline hallucinogen derived from a cactus, as part of his religion was determined a violation of Title VII of the Civil Rights Act. In *Toledo* v. *Nobel-Sysco, Inc.*, the plaintiff applied for a truck-driving job with Nobel, a restaurant supply business. The job required driving on mountain roads and working on weekends. When the plaintiff applied for the job, he was told that he was qualified, provided he had not used drugs during the last two years (a policy specified in Nobel's employment advertisements). The plaintiff informed the company that he had used peyote twice in the past six months as part of his religion with the Native American Church. The Native American Church believes that peyote heals and helps its practitioners communicate with God. When he was rejected, the plaintiff filed a claim alleging religious discrimination. Although peyote is legal for use in religious services, the company was concerned with liability should the driver have an accident. Experts agreed that an individual should not drive a truck for at least 24 hours after using peyote.

During the hearings, Nobel offered the following to the plaintiff: reinstatement with $500 in back pay, a limit of two peyote ceremonies per year, a requirement that he give one week's notice prior to taking part in a ceremony, and permission to take time off after each ceremony. The plaintiff refused all offers.

The Tenth Circuit reversed an earlier trial court's decision and ruled that a settlement made during the course of an administrative proceeding is *not* a reasonable attempt to accommodate. Because Nobel had made no attempt to accommodate the plaintiff until a discrimination charge was filed, the plaintiff had no obligation to cooperate with the employer. The court found that Nobel would not experience undue hardship in accommodating the plaintiff. You be the judge. Do you think the court made the right decision?

SOURCE: Adapted from *HRNews*, Society for Human Resource Management, February 1990, p. A9; and *The Florida Law Weekly, Federal* 4, no. 12 (April 20, 1990), pp. S254–S255.

---

actions may seem to represent a big investment, but the benefits of hiring older workers will far outweigh the costs in just a short time.[41]

Religious Discrimination   Lule Said, a native of Somalia, was a student at Boston University when he began working at Northeast Security Inc. in 1991. As a devout Muslim, Said must pray five times a day. According to Said, Northeast told him not to pray during his 16-hour work shifts. He eventually gave up praying but was still demoted to a part-time position. After filing a complaint, Said was awarded $300,000 in damages in 1996. Northeast appealed, and in a ruling issued August 14, 2000, Said's award was upheld.[42]

Title VII of the Civil Rights Act prohibits employment discrimination on the basis of religion, including all aspects of religious practice and beliefs. Discrimination occurs when an employee is forced to choose between giving up an employment opportunity or a fundamental belief or practice. The most common problem occurs when an employee asks the manager to accommodate a religious need and a scheduling conflict must be resolved (e.g., conflict might arise if management asks a Seventh-Day Adventist to work on Saturdays).

When religious conflicts arise, the employer must make every effort to reasonably accommodate the employee. Reasonable accommodations include the use of voluntary substitutes, flexible work scheduling, transfers to other departments, or changes in job assignments or training methods. Agnostics and atheists are also protected from religious discrimination. For example, an atheist cannot be forced to attend meetings that include prayer. Employers who can demonstrate that they are unable to reasonably accommodate an employee's or job applicant's religious practice or beliefs without undue hardship on the company are not engaging in religious discrimination.

In October 1993 the EEOC defined religious harassment as conduct that "denigrates" or shows "hostility or aversion" toward someone because of his or her religion. This conduct must create an offensive work environment and interfere with performance or employment opportunities. Although most people would view the EEOC's guidelines as fair, they are still challenged. Interestingly, the challenge often comes from religious conservatives. They argue that they may not be able to hold morning prayers, pray before meals, or hold lunchtime Bible studies if someone in the organization finds it "offensive" and sues. The pressure in the debate was strong enough to push more than 100 members of Congress to support a House resolution calling for EEOC to withdraw the guidelines. EEOC would rather explain how the existing law is designed to protect everyone's rights than change its guidelines.[43]

Handicap Discrimination The Rehabilitation Act of 1973 prohibits all federal contractors from discriminating against persons with physical or mental handicaps and requires them to take affirmative action to employ job applicants or employees with such handicaps.[44] Acquired immune deficiency syndrome (AIDS) is now classified as a form of handicap; thus this disease is covered under the Rehabilitation Act. Although most handicaps are readily detectable, some are not. The law covers both types. In addition, the law covers cases in which an employee does not have a handicap but is perceived as having one. Managers should not assume that a particular employee is not capable of performing certain types of jobs. Instead, the manager should allow the employee to decide whether he or she can perform a specific job. Although the Rehabilitation Act applies only to companies with a federal government contract or subcontract, many states have laws that cover all employers.

Handicapped individuals are protected under law if they are handicapped but are qualified and able to perform the job. Employers are required to make *reasonable accommodations* for handicapped employees. Often, accommodation involves no more than common sense and does not need to be expensive to be effective. Wheelchair users need space for their chairs entering and leaving a building as well as in work areas. Local building codes state the amount of space required. Wheelchair ramps, wide doorways, and accessible restrooms are all necessary to accommodate handicapped workers in wheelchairs. Specially designed workstations in which desks or worktables can be raised and lowered mechanically can help the handicapped worker to feel more comfortable and perform effectively.

A variety of devices is available for telephones to amplify hearing and speech for hearing-impaired employees. Individuals with severe hearing loss can use more elaborate telecommunication devices. Individuals with vision impairments can be accommodated in various ways. For example, raising lettering or Braille symbols on signs and elevator buttons can be extremely helpful. Agencies dealing with specific disabilities, such as state commissions for the blind and visually impaired, and state and local rehabilitation facilities are sources of assistance in providing successful accommodations.

The law does not extend to alcohol or drug abusers.[45] However, it is recommended that a company encourage any employee with an alcohol or drug abuse

HR CHALLENGES

Mental Impairments Stimulate Debate

A significant proportion of the complaints under the Americans with Disabilities Act (ADA) that are sent to the Equal Employment Opportunity Commission (EEOC) allege discrimination on the basis of emotional or mental impairment. Although approximately 13 percent of the claims are related to mental impairments, the EEOC did not issue guidance about employers' and employees' rights and responsibilities until 1997. A summary of the EEOC guidance follows:

1. Employers cannot ask applicants if they have a mental disability or have ever been treated for mental illness.
2. Employers should provide reasonable accommodations such as flexible work schedules for those in need.
3. Employers do not have to tolerate inappropriate behavior or workplace violence that might be attributed to mental illness.

Unfortunately, many HR professionals and managers argue that these guidelines create more confusion. For example, the guidance fails to address potential conflicts between the ADA and the Family and Medical Leave Act. Further, the guidance seems to limit an employer's ability to request reasonable fitness levels in examinations and enforce conduct and appearance codes. For the EEOC's guidance, see the SHRM home page at **www.shrm.org**. You can download a copy of the enforcement guidance from EEOC's Web site at **www.eeoc.gov**.

SOURCE: Adapted from Jonathon A. Segal, Esq., "The Surprising Path of the ADA," *HRMagazine*, July 1997, pp. 75-83; and Linda Micco, "Employers Criticize EEOC Guidance on Psychiatric Disabilities," *HRNews*, May 1997, p. 10.

problem to seek professional help (such as through an Employee Assistance Program) prior to any disciplinary measures or discharge. In addition, the law does not extend to employees who currently have contagious diseases or infections and who, because of this disease, would be a direct health or safety threat to others. AIDS cases do not fall under this category because research has shown that AIDS cannot be transmitted through casual contact. Employers should not wait until they are confronted with an AIDS case before developing a comprehensive AIDS policy. Policies and educational programs need to be implemented before a crisis situation occurs. Medical evidence showing that AIDS cannot be contracted through casual contact will not appear genuine to employees if the evidence is presented to them *after* a coworker is known to have AIDS.

Americans with Disabilities Act   The Americans with Disabilities Act (ADA) of 1990 prohibits discrimination against individuals with disabilities. Under the ADA, the term *disability* is defined as it is in Title V of the Rehabilitation Act of 1973; however, the ADA is *not* limited to federal grantees or contractors.[46] The ADA has been described as "revolutionary" because of the scope of protection it provides to individuals with disabilities. The ultimate goal is the integration of persons with disabilities into all segments of society.[47]

The ADA is made up of five sections.[48] Title I (employment) makes it illegal to discriminate against a qualified individual with a disability and imposes an obligation for employers to make reasonable accommodations for the disabled. The ADA covers physical and mental impairments such as visual, speech, and hearing impairments; cerebral palsy; epilepsy; multiple sclerosis; AIDS; cancer; heart disease; mental retardation; and emotional illness.[49] The ADA prohibits most preemployment health questions. Although a user of illegal drugs is not protected under the ADA, a rehabilitated drug user or someone who is participating in a supervised rehabilitation program is protected.

Title II (public service) makes it illegal for state or local governments to discriminate against qualified disabled persons in the provision of public services and includes requirements regarding the accessibility of public transportation for individuals with disabilities. Title III of the ADA (public accommodation) makes it illegal for public accommodations (such as restaurants, retail stores, or places of recreation) to discriminate against individuals with disabilities in the provision of goods, benefits, services, facilities, privileges, advantages, or accommodations. In addition, Title III requires existing public accommodation to be made accessible.

Title IV of the ADA (telecommunications) requires all common carriers in interstate communication to ensure that telecommunications systems are available to individuals with hearing and speech impairments and to provide reasonable technological accommodations. Title V (miscellaneous) is a more general "catch-all" provision that relates ADA to other laws. Among the provisions, retaliation against individuals who exercise their rights under the act is made illegal. For additional and up-to-date information on the Americans with Disabilities Act, see the U.S. Department of Justice's ADA home page at **www.usdoj.gov/crt/ada/adahom1.htm**.[50]

According to the EEOC, an employer is required to use a four-step method to identify reasonable accommodation. First, the employer should determine the purpose of the job and the essential functions required in performing the job. Next, the employer should consult with the individual with the disability and determine his or her physical and mental abilities and his or her precise limitations. Third, in the discussions with the individual with the disability, the employer should try to identify possible accommodations and the effectiveness of each in helping that person perform the essential functions of the job. Finally, the employer should consider the preferences of the individual with the disability and then select the accommodation that best serves the needs of that individual and the employer. The employer is free to choose among effective accommodations and may choose the one that is less expensive or easier to provide.[51]

Reasonable accommodations do not have to be expensive. More than one half of all job accommodations cost employers absolutely nothing, according to the U.S. General Accounting Office, and another 30 percent of accommodations cost less than $500. Although building structural modifications are sometimes necessary, many employers find accommodation solutions by adjusting work schedules (e.g., for those who have night vision impairments), restructuring job processes, or using a team approach. Sometimes process accommodations require the cooperation of other employees so that others in the team are able to do a task the disabled worker cannot perform.[52]

Those cases that have made it to court provide good examples of what employers should not do. For example, in *EEOC* v. *AIC Security Investigation, LTD.*, the EEOC represented a senior executive with terminal brain cancer who was fired by his employers despite the fact that he could still perform his job. The complainant, Charles Wessel, was fired three days after the ADA took effect. According to his employer, Wessel's health problems were interfering with his job performance. However, no record of counseling, reprimands, or other evidence to document his poor performance was ever provided. The company claimed that Wessel was absent 25 percent of the time during 1992 for cancer treatment and that he therefore could not perform his job adequately. The court disagreed, noting that a number of Wessel's tasks could be performed over the phone whether the phone be in his car, home, or office. Where the work is done is immaterial as long as it is done. The jury awarded Wessel $572,000 in back pay and damages. The judge later reduced this amount to $222,000, which is the cap on damages allowed by the 1991 Civil Rights Act. It appears that the company's attitude toward Wessel, who was forced to seek employment during the remaining few months of his life, made an expensive impression on the jury.[53]

The first civil penalty imposed under the ADA was a $20,000 fine. It was levied against a Denver business with more than 100 parking lots and garages that allegedly failed to provide handicapped-accessible spaces. In addition to the $20,000 penalty, the firm was required to provide over 400 handicapped-accessible parking spaces. This decision showed a significant shift in attitude from a warning and announcement approach to an enforcement approach. The Department of Justice, which imposed the penalty, said that businesses should be aware of the ADA and take corrective action regarding potential violations.[54]

Employers have won a major decision in addressing just who is considered disabled. In three cases held in 1999—*Sutton* v. *United Airlines* (130 F.3d 893), *Murphy* v. *United Parcel Service* (141 F.3d 1185) and *Albertson's* v. *Kirkingburg* (143 F.3d 1228)—the U.S. Supreme Court ruled that individuals who have physical impairments but who can function normally with mitigating measures, such as eyeglasses or medication, generally are not disabled under the ADA. Although employers should consider the new decisions as a major victory because they help bring order to the chaos caused by the ADA's lack of clarity, caution should still be practiced. A very real possibility still exists that individuals who successfully use mitigating measures will be considered disabled under the law.[55]

Equal Employment Opportunity Commission

The EEOC enforces compliance with Title VII, the Equal Pay Act, the Pregnancy Discrimination Act, the Age Discrimination Act, the Rehabilitation Act, and the Americans with Disabilities Act. The EEOC has the authority to process, investigate, and conciliate grievances alleging discrimination. *Conciliation* is the process of trying to reach an out-of-court settlement.

Any charge filed against an organization must be made within 180 days of the discriminatory act. When there is a state or local agency with the authority to handle discrimination, the charging party must file the complaint with the agency. An individual dissatisfied with the decision has 30 days after the state or local ruling to file with the federal EEOC. The EEOC then conducts an investigation to determine if reasonable cause exists that discrimination occurred. The charging party is interviewed and counseled on EEOC procedures. If reasonable cause is believed to exist, the EEOC attempts to conciliate the dispute. If reasonable cause is not found, the case is dismissed.

After a charge is filed, the employer is notified within 10 days and a fact-finding conference is held subsequently. The charging party and the employer present evidence to an EEOC specialist (conciliator). The EEOC specialist tries to work out a satisfactory settlement with both sides. If the EEOC is unable to conciliate the charge, it will be considered by EEOC attorneys for a possible lawsuit to be filed in federal district court. However, if the EEOC decides not to file a lawsuit, a "right to sue letter" is issued permitting the charging party to take the case to court. However, this suit must be filed within 300 days of the discriminatory act taking place. The only exception to the 300-day rule is in the case of a change in a seniority system that will eventually lead to intentional discrimination. (Exhibit 5.8 presents the EEOC complaint processing system.)

In discrimination court cases, the burden of proof begins with the plaintiff. The plaintiff must prove to the judge that discriminatory acts took place. If the plaintiff is able to do this, a prima facie case of discrimination has been established. If the plaintiff is unable to do so, the case is dismissed. If a prima facie case is established, the burden of proof switches to the defendant, who must present arguments to rebut the charges and offer a legal reason for its actions. If successful, the burden of proof shifts once again to the plaintiff, who has one final chance to discredit the defendant's case. The type of evidence needed to establish a prima facie case and the defense of the firm differs with the type of discrimination being charged. Exhibit 5.9 outlines the evidence required for each. This information is discussed in the following sections.

Adverse Impact

Court cases relating to adverse impact require that the plaintiff demonstrate statistically that the practices used by a firm affect various groups differently. The Four-Fifths rule is an example of one type of statistic that can be used to establish a prima facie case. This statistical demonstration is often accomplished by comparing the percentage of minorities in the firm to the percentage of minorities represented in the relevant labor market. The relevant labor market refers to all individuals who qualify for the job. Often the relevant labor market is limited in geographic scope. For example, it is highly unlikely that an individual would commute more than 100 miles one way for a job that pays $5 an hour. Hence, the relevant labor market for such a position may be limited to the population in a 100-mile radius of the firm. However, if the position is chief of medicine at the city hospital, then the relevant labor market expands geographically to encompass virtually the whole world, because it is likely that an individual will move a great distance to take this type of job.

Once the plaintiff has established a case, the defendant can use one of three options to rebut the charges: business necessity, bona fide occupational qualification (BFOQ), or validation data. Each of these defenses is a legal exception to discrimination. When a firm claims a business necessity, it is arguing that hiring people other than those it has selected will jeopardize the safety of customers or other employees. The firm must show that if the selection procedures were not used, the risk to customers or current employees greatly increases. It is not enough for the firm to say that not using the procedures in question would result in a substantial cost or loss to the firm. That is, the Court has not defined business necessity in economic terms.

When claiming a BFOQ defense, a company must prove that no person from a protected class could adequately perform the job. This type of defense has been used mainly in gender or religious discrimination cases. For example, the shower room attendant at the YWCA should be a woman; no man qualifies for this position. The preference of the customer is not a BFOQ. That is to say, firms that hire only men because their clients prefer to work with men could not claim a BFOQ defense. However, genuineness or authenticity has been upheld in the courts as a BFOQ. This allows a director to hire a woman to play the female lead in a play or a dance troop to hire only Polynesians for the Tahiti Fire Dance portion of their show. The hiring

EXHIBIT 5.8   EEOC COMPLAINT PROCESSING SYSTEM

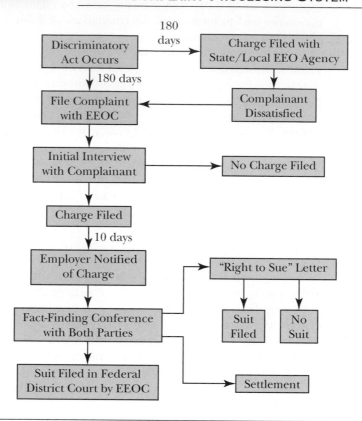

EXHIBIT 5.9   EVIDENCE PRESENTED IN TITLE VII DISCRIMINATION SUITS

Adverse Impact

- **Plaintiff** must demonstrate statistically that the practice in question affects various groups differently.
- **Defendant** can use either business necessity, bona fide occupational qualification, or validation data to rebut the charges.
- **Plaintiff** must show that an alternative practice can be used and that the alternative practice results in less adverse impact.

Disparate Treatment

- **Plaintiff** must demonstrate that (1) he or she belongs to a minority, (2) he or she applied for and was qualified for the job, (3) he or she was rejected for the job, and (4) that the job remained open.
- **Defendant** must show job-based reasons for the action taken.
- **Plaintiff** must prove that the reasons given are a pretense and the true reason for the decision was prejudice.

practices of Hooters, a national restaurant chain notorious for its scantily clad waitresses, were assumed (by Hooters) to be legal under this exception. The argument was that the "Hooter-girl" was an essential component to the marketing goals of the restaurant and that there was nothing illegal about passing over a man for the job because only women can meet the BFOQ for the job. Interestingly, however, Hooters was sued by men who were denied employment by the restaurant chain, and the company agreed to pay $3.75 million to settle the lawsuit. Although there will be men in waiter positions, the agreement also provides that women will still make up the bulk of the serving staff.[56] However, not all firms have been successful using this defense. When Johnson Controls tried to ban women of child-bearing age from working in areas that could lead to birth defects, it used BFOQ. In *UAW* v. *Johnson Controls* (1991), Johnson Controls argued that a BFOQ of being a man was necessary to protect job holders from having children with birth defects. The Supreme Court ruled that BFOQs are limited to policies that directly relate to the worker's ability to do the job.

The final defense a firm can claim is validation evidence. To use this defense, a firm must have performed a validation study in which the results clearly link the requirements for the job to the procedure in question. For example, if the firm is being sued because it uses a selection test that has a higher pass rate for whites than for minorities, the firm must prove that the skills measured by the test are essential to adequate job performance. Hence, any person failing the test would not be able to adequately perform the job and should not be hired.

Disparate Treatment

As in an adverse impact case, the plaintiff claiming disparate treatment must begin by establishing a prima facie case. The requirement for establishing a prima facie case in a disparate treatment case was spelled out in the 1973 *McDonnell-Douglas* v. *Green* case. Hence, the requirement is often referred to as the *McDonnell-Douglas Rule*. Specifically, this rule requires that the plaintiff prove four things: (1) that he or she belongs to a minority, (2) that he or she applied for and was qualified for the job, (3) that he or she was rejected for the job, and (4) that the job remained open. These four steps taken together show that the firm *intentionally* discriminated and thereby establish a prima facie case.

The defendant must deny the allegations. To do this, it must provide clear and specific job-related reasons for its actions. In the case that set the precedent (*McDonnell-Douglas* v. *Green*), Green argued that his layoff was racially motivated. McDonnell-Douglas defended its actions by saying that Green had been rejected from the job because he had participated in a protest and took illegal actions against the company. The court accepted this defense.

If the court accepts the defendant's case, the plaintiff can rebut the reasoning. To do this the plaintiff must show that what the defense offered was simply a "pretext" and that the real reason for the firm's actions was discrimination. This could be done by showing evidence that when the position was eventually filled, nonminority applicants with very similar qualifications were hired over minority applicants. In the *McDonnell-Douglas* case, Green could have rebutted McDonnell-Douglas's claims if he could have shown that the rehire practices McDonnell-Douglas used to fill his vacant position favored nonminority applicants or that McDonnell-Douglas had a general practice of discriminatory practices against minority applicants.

Affirmative Action[57]

Similarities exist between the legal concepts of "discrimination" and "affirmative action"; however, there are important differences. EEO laws are designed to rid the workplace of current and future discriminatory acts. Affirmative action is designed to remedy past discrimination by requiring employers to hire and promote minorities and females based on the number of *qualified* minorities and females in the relevant labor market.

Who is Required to Develop Affirmative Action Programs?

According to the Executive Orders 11246, 11375, and 11478, federal contractors and subcontractors are required to develop, implement, and maintain a written affirmative action program (AAP). Specifically, companies with at least 50 employees and a $50,000 contract or subcontract with the federal government (or with another company doing business with the federal government) are usually compelled to develop, implement, and maintain a written AAP on an annual basis. If a company does not meet these criteria, it is not required to comply. For example, a company with 5000 people and a $5000 contract with the federal government is not required to comply with AAP regulations. However, companies found guilty of discrimination may be required to have an AAP.

Court decisions have made a distinction between *voluntary* and *required* AAP. Many employers have developed an affirmative action program on a volunteer basis. That is, they realize that having a diverse workforce is a wise policy and take steps to locate and hire qualified minority applicants. If an AAP is voluntary, the employer is not required to adhere to the goals of the plan. However, if a plan is required, an employer has been ordered by the court to have an AAP and is obligated to adhere to the goals of the plan.

How Affirmative Action Works

According to Seligman in "How Equal Opportunity Turned into Employment Quotas,"[58] affirmative action operates on four levels. The first level is *pure nondiscrimination* and embodies a willingness to treat all races and both sexes the same in employment decisions. Many critics find the approach insensitive to the deleterious effects of past discrimination because this level of affirmative action may not significantly increase minority and female employment in nonstereotyped positions.

The second level of affirmative action hires and/or promotes employees entirely based on merit. However, this level includes a concerted effort to expand the number of minority and female applicants and employees (such as minority-focused recruiting efforts).

The third and fourth levels of affirmative action programs use *preferential hiring* and *quota systems*, respectively. Preferential hiring means that the company systematically favors minorities and females in hiring and promotion decisions. Use of the quota system includes preferential hiring and advocates a specific number of minorities and females that should be hired and/or promoted in the organization.

Reverse Discrimination

Critics of preferential hiring and the use of quota systems have argued that they can lead to reverse discrimination against white males. *Reverse discrimination* occurs when an equally or more qualified nonminority, usually a Caucasian male, is not hired or promoted in favor of a racial or sexual minority group member. For example, in *City of Richmond* v. *Croson Company* (1989), the Supreme Court addressed the problem of reverse discrimination. The Richmond City Council adopted the Minority Business Utilization Plan, which required prime contractors (to whom the city awards construction contracts) to set aside 30 percent of the dollar amount of the contract for minority business enterprises. The Court held that the minority contractor set-aside requirement denied equal protection because it discriminated on the basis of race. Essentially the Supreme Court recognized that preferential treatment for "protected classes" can have a discriminatory effect against other groups, who may be in the actual majority of the population.[59]

Chrysler was found guilty of reverse discrimination in 1993. Mary Hand Frost, a Caucasian woman from Oklahoma, sought a Dodge dealership in Edmond, Oklahoma, under Chrysler's Marketing Investment Program. Under the terms of this program, Chrysler pays dealers to operate and manage its dealerships with the understanding that the dealer can buy out Chrysler's interests. Candidates for the program can either be graduates of Chrysler's Minority Dealer Development Program or have business experience that qualifies them for the position. According to Ms. Frost's claim, she approached a Chrysler zone representative about the dealership and was informed that she was the most qualified applicant, having spent 14 years selling new and used cars, and was more or less assured of getting the assignment. Chrysler denied her application, and the dealership was run by an interim manager until an African-American candidate was found. The judge noted that "the evidence in the case strongly suggested that Chrysler's affirmative action program was a mere pretext for rejecting the application of the plaintiff, a white female," and granted a summary judgment against Chrysler. The Court decided against Chrysler for three reasons: The firm failed to demonstrate that there was "conspicuous" racial imbalance that it was trying to correct, the firm did not recruit from other racial minorities, and the program should have been temporary.[60]

It is important that employers realize that nothing about affirmative action requires companies to recruit, hire, or promote employees not qualified to do the job under question. Affirmative action means that employers should make every effort to place minorities and females in jobs in which these groups are underutilized. The objective of this government directive is equitable treatment and a fair opportunity for all to compete on an equal footing. Although some view affirmative action as reverse discrimination, this is not the dominant opinion. Public support appears strong for ending reverse discrimination but not for scrapping affirmative action initiatives that level the playing field for women and minorities.[61]

Establishing Affirmative Action Programs

Many employers face penalties for violation of equal employment opportunity and affirmative action regulations. The development of a comprehensive affirmative action program is an important step in avoiding expensive litigation. Elements of an effective program, shown in Exhibit 5.10, include underutilization and availability analyses, the examination of current job specifications and descriptions, the development of goals and timetables, effective recruiting, and the development of a comprehensive inventory of existing employee skills. Each of these is described in the following text.

Underutilization and Availability Analyses An underutilization analysis examines the number of protected group members (e.g., minorities) employed and the types of

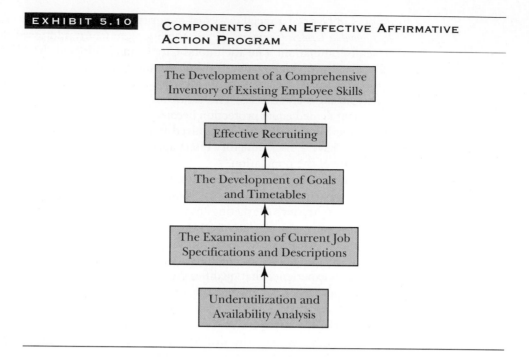

EXHIBIT 5.10 COMPONENTS OF AN EFFECTIVE AFFIRMATIVE ACTION PROGRAM

The Development of a Comprehensive Inventory of Existing Employee Skills

Effective Recruiting

The Development of Goals and Timetables

The Examination of Current Job Specifications and Descriptions

Underutilization and Availability Analysis

jobs they hold in an organization. An availability analysis examines the number of protected group members who are available to work in the relevant labor market. The firm should determine where minorities and women are clustered, excluded, or underutilized based on reasonable expectations from the labor market. An availability analysis can be developed with data from a state labor department or the U.S. Census Bureau. The availability analysis is the basis for determining whether underutilization is occurring within a company.

Examination of Current Job Specifications and Descriptions Employers should examine the current job specifications and descriptions in their company to ensure their accuracy. The firm should establish prescribed qualifications and wage scales based on the actual job to ensure that barriers to minorities and women are not present. Irrelevant qualifications or qualifications that exceed the requirements of the job have been the cause of many lawsuits.

Development of Goals and Timetables Employers should correct underutilization of minorities and women by establishing measurable and realistic hiring and promoting goals. In addition, employers should develop realistic timetables by which these goals are to be actualized. The firm's goals should remedy exclusion and/or underutilization of protected groups in specified jobs.

Effective Recruiting Employers can actively recruit minorities and women to fill positions that have been found to exclude or underutilize minorities and women. Systematic record keeping should describe the flow of minorities and women seeking employment and promotions. Job application forms should not contain information about race or sex.

Inventory of Existing Employee Skills   A comprehensive skills inventory of current employees can help to establish a baseline for training and development programs. Employers can learn the skill level of the firm's employees, which is important for identifying qualified employees to fill higher-level positions. Employers also can use this information to create training and development programs for all employees, including minorities and women. General Motors, for example, has spent millions of dollars to provide a variety of educational programs for minorities and women.

Legal Issues in Compensation

The Equal Pay Act of 1963

The Equal Pay Act (EPA) requires that men and women who work for the same organization be paid the same for work that is equal in skill (such as experience or training), effort (mental or physical effort), responsibility (the degree of accountability), and working conditions (the physical surroundings and hazards).[62] This act was passed as an amendment to an earlier compensation law called the Fair Labor Standards Act of 1938. Essentially, the Fair Labor Standards Act applies to employees engaged in interstate commerce.[63] The EPA also forbids wage discrimination on the basis of sex but extends coverage to employees in executive, administrative, professional, and outside sales force categories, as well as employees in most state and local governments, hospitals, and schools. Pay discrimination against minorities and women is also covered under Title VII. The EPA of 1963 was designed to close the salary gap between men and women. However, the gap still exists because women still make approximately 71 cents to every dollar made by a man. Experts argue that wages will not approach equality in the near future because the EEOC is not doing much to enforce the law. According to the EEOC, people prefer to file under Title VII gender discrimination because the EPA has a two-year time limit.[64]

Some people believe that the wage gap should not be closed because women are less qualified than their male counterparts. However, research appears not to support this claim. Dr. Peter Hammerschmidt, an economist at Eckerd College in St. Petersburg, Florida, analyzed the pay and credentials of 194 corporate managers randomly selected from 800 participants who enrolled in a leadership course at Eckerd. He found that the men he studied earned approximately 18 percent more than women.[65]

Another reason that the pay gap has not narrowed is that discussing one's salary in the workplace is taboo. Hence, underpaid women and overpaid men do not know each other's pay rate. Women find out in subtle ways, however. For example, when Marcia Rafter's counterparts were purchasing boats and homes that she could not afford, she began to wonder why. Even though she was rated number 1 or 2 every quarter, she was told that as a single woman, she did not need as much money as did men who had families. This policy of basing salary on need is not limited to women. Men, especially when their wives work, and particularly if they have no children, also are being told that their need is not as great as some of their coworkers. This policy may be a factor in the decrease in wages for men.[66]

Pay differentials between equal jobs can be justified, however, when they are based on a seniority system, a merit system, a system based on measuring earnings by quality or quantity of production, or any factor other than sex. Under the EPA, employers must correct any pay inequities by raising the pay of lower-paid employees, not by lowering the pay of higher-paid employees. For up-to-date information regarding earnings gaps by sex and gender, visit **www.uaw.org**.

Comparable Worth

Comparable worth means that jobs requiring comparable knowledge, skills, and abilities should be paid similar amounts. Comparable worth and the EPA differ in that the EPA requires equal pay for male and female employees who perform work that is substantially equal. Comparable worth means employers are required to provide equal pay for work of *equal value*. For example, a 1980 court case examined whether nurses (a predominantly female job) should be paid the same as tree trimmers (a predominantly male job).[67]

The issue of comparable worth was developed primarily as an answer to the persistent wage gap between men and women employees. On average, women's earnings are approximately 70 percent of men's earnings. Comparable worth advocates that employees who work on "comparable" jobs (even though the actual job duties may differ) should be paid equally. Rather than comparing jobs based on job duties, proponents of comparable worth advocate comparing jobs based on four factors: (1) knowledge and skill level, (2) effort, (3) responsibility, and (4) working conditions.

The most publicized comparable worth case occurred in the state of Washington. The state was sued by the American Federation of State, County, and Municipal Employees (AFSCME). The union alleged that women who worked for the state of Washington were experiencing pay discrimination. The state's job evaluation plan placed many of the jobs traditionally held by women at a higher level than those held by men, but the wage rates were less than those for jobs traditionally held by men. Although the discrimination charges were upheld in U.S. District Court, the U.S. Supreme Court ultimately ruled against the women, claiming comparable worth. However, following the decision, the state of Washington and the AFSCME reached a settlement in which the state paid $41.4 million on pay equity adjustments from April 1986 through June 1987 to employees such as nurses, library technicians, and clerk typists.[68]

One of the biggest problems facing comparable worth advocates is the cost of replacing the supply-and-demand market with a government-run job evaluation system. Closing the earnings gap between men and women has been estimated as costing well over $300 billion a year.[69] In addition, some have argued that a more effective solution would be to encourage women to enter nontraditional occupations and provide them with equal access to education, training, and employment, rather than raise the price of labor for specific jobs.[70]

Current Strategic Issues in Equal Employment Opportunity

The Glass Ceiling

The term *glass ceiling* refers to the often subtle attitudes and prejudices that create barriers that block women and minorities from climbing the corporate ladder[71] or, in some cases, even moving laterally.[72] Glass ceilings have caught the attention of the Department of Labor. After reviewing a study done by researchers at the University of California, Los Angeles, in conjunction with Korn/Ferry International, the Department of Labor announced plans to begin investigating and removing glass ceilings in large government contractors.

The UCLA/Korn/Ferry study revealed that women and minorities held less than 5 percent of the senior management positions among the *Fortune* 500 companies surveyed.[73] Further, it is estimated that just 2 percent of senior executives at large corporations are women.[74] Given that women and minorities represent over

50 percent of the workforce, these facts are of concern to officials at the Department of Labor.[75]

In a study that tracked the career paths of male and female MBAs, evidence of glass-ceiling effects was discovered. Over the time of the study, females received on average the same number of promotions as men; however, they experienced lower salary increases, fewer managerial promotions, and lower hierarchical levels compared with men of similar background and experience.[76]

Pursuant to the discovery of glass-ceiling effects, investigations were begun to find out why women and minorities cannot penetrate the invisible barriers, other than as a result of overt and covert discrimination. An 18-month study by the Department of Labor revealed that, in many cases, women and minorities were not given critical training early on that would have made promotions possible. In addition, women and minorities were often passed over for the higher visibility projects that would have allowed them to prove themselves. Finally, Caucasian males were found to mentor and help other Caucasian males. Given that very few top management positions are occupied by women and minorities, less mentoring seems to be occurring with the groups who need it the most.[77] Mentoring has been found to be related to organizational advancement.[78] Mentors provide critical thinking, share inside information, lend social support, and serve as a buffer between the organization and the mentored employee. Women who have been mentored have been found to advance more rapidly than those without mentors.[79] However, women are less likely to develop a mentoring relationship than men.[80] Because mentoring appears to be a factor in organizational success, encouraging it may help to crack glass-ceiling barriers.

Managers should be aware of the possible glass ceiling within their organization. The following guidelines can help to encourage women and minority promotions into higher-level positions:

1. *Formal Training.* If promotions depend on critical and specialized skills, it is important that training opportunities are offered to all employees.
2. *Networking.* Encourage women and minorities to communicate and exchange information and ideas about the job (that is, to engage in networking). In addition, managers can bridge various "networks," including Caucasian male networks, by arranging for representatives from different networks to meet and discuss job-related issues. Of course, it is also important to discourage Caucasian males from networking in private clubs in which women and minorities are officially excluded.
3. *Mentoring.* Mentoring refers to an informal relationship between top managers and newer, lower-level employees that helps the newer employees gain status and get promoted. Mentors often achieve these results by explaining the corporate culture, providing strategic advice, suggesting career moves, and supporting these employees for promotion. As mentioned earlier, the Department of Labor found that some Caucasian male managers tend to mentor other Caucasian males. One way to overcome this tendency is to create a more formalized mentoring program and to pair top managers with women and minorities.
4. *Diversity Training.* Top managers may need to have some diversity training in order to understand gender and cultural differences. For example, diversity training programs have shown why women make decisions differently than men.

Breaking the subtle barriers of the glass ceiling will require the efforts of human resource professionals. The human resource professional should not only make sure that discrimination does not exist but also make sure companies make a good faith effort to allow women and minorities to advance. Continuing to maintain glass ceilings will not go unnoticed for long, and the cost of "fixing" their ill effects may be a major cost to organizations in the future. Interestingly, a growing number of women who began their careers in the 1970s are now beginning to break though the cracks of the glass ceiling. On January 1, 1997, Jill Barad became chief executive officer of Mattel, Inc., the first woman to take the reins of a major American company. Other large corporations that have top-level women executives include AT&T, Goldman Sachs & Co., and Kraft Foods. The women who have begun to break through this glass ceiling have some things in common besides their intellect, motivational skills, hard work, and willingness to take risks. These women are almost all in their 40s and were among the first group of women admitted to top business schools such as Harvard. They came up through the ranks of their respective companies, usually through the operations side. Most took over divisions that no one else wanted and turned them around. These women also made some tough personal choices regarding motherhood and working through "female" sicknesses such as breast cancer.[81]

Managing Workplace Diversity

Today's workforce is becoming increasingly diverse, and many believe the playing field for men, women, and minorities has already been leveled. Just ask the majority of voters in California who, with the sweeping passage of Proposition 209, effectively wiped out affirmative action practices throughout the state. Although affirmative action has done much to open doors for women, minorities, and older employees, the retention and advancement of a diverse workforce will require dramatic changes in corporate culture and human resource policies.[82] For example, the concept of treating everyone equally has been replaced by emphasizing individualism. The corporate culture must consider the ethnic, cultural, educational, and gender differences that represent today's workforce. New human resource policies should reflect the unique needs of individuals rather than focusing on only one "mold" for all employees.[83]

The goal of managing a diverse workforce is to create a culture in which each employee has the opportunity to make a full contribution to the organization and to advance on the basis of excellent performance.[84] Although more women and minority workers are being hired, this is not enough to ensure a diverse workforce. Exhibit 5.11 gives examples of company strategies for attracting and promoting women.

Whether minorities remain in the organization and thrive seems to depend on how well they adapt to the culture in which they work.[85] Some cultures are more accepting and hence more successful at managing diversity. Lawrence Otis Graham published the book *The Best Companies for Minorities*, which recognized the 85 best companies among the *Fortune* 1000 for hiring minority members. This book indicates that although the workplace is becoming a more hospitable place for minority workers, there is still room for improvement. Graham's goal was to list the top 100, but he found only 85 worth citing.[86] One of the many statistics listed in the book is a ranking of firms with minorities in management positions. Topping the list is Levi Strauss with 36 percent, followed by Turner Broadcasting with 26 percent. Other firms such as Coors and Corning made the list even though their numbers were not impressive but because they supported minority causes and had strong diversity programs under way.

As Graham's book notes, some firms are managing diversity well, but others are not and are losing minority employees. In one study, researchers found that six factors kept minority employees from remaining with a firm: (1) how frequently they had to

EXHIBIT 5.11   WHERE DIVERSITY GETS TOP BILLING

Strategies of Some Employers Seeking to Attract and Promote More Women

Avon Products The cosmetics maker set minimum quotas for hiring women and linked managers' pay to performance on diversity. Now, managers win awards for promoting women. Overseas, Avon identifies and grooms women for management.

Colgate-Palmolive Mandatory two-day diversity training for all employees includes role-playing and video presentations. High-potential women are cross-trained to gain broader experience in different roles.

Coopers & Lybrand The accounting firm wants women to account for 30% of new partners by 2000. To get there, it has created mentoring programs and sensitivity training and ties part of partners' bonuses to meeting diversity goals.

Dow Chemical Senior management takes responsibility for diversity and wants women to account for at least as many promotions as men. Men participate in company-sponsored women's groups to understand gender issues.

Hoechst Celanese Hiring and promotion of women are expected to mirror the college recruiting pool by 2001. A quarter of managers' bonuses is tied to diversity progress; senior managers oversee the strategy and serve as mentors.

Motorola Using census data, it has set goals for diversity in management that it aims to reach by 2000. Top execs are required to name the woman or minority best suited to succeed them: Those people are targeted for career development.

SOURCE: *Business Week*, February 17, 1997, p. 67.

fight stereotypes, (2) the level of discrimination and harassment in the workplace, (3) how excluded and isolated the minority employees felt, (4) how employee-friendly policies were, (5) whether career development was available, and (6) how closely minority employees' values aligned with those of the organization. One woman noted that the day she arrived at her new job, she saw buyers yelling, cursing, and threatening sales representatives. Among the words uttered were racial and sexist slurs. It took only one day before she was back actively seeking employment.[87] It is difficult to keep minority employees in this situation.

Other firms, and even cities, have found ways to overcome these turnover factors. For example, Talladega, Alabama, has been dubbed the "user-friendly" city for disabled people, and for good reasons.[88] Talladega is custom fitted to citizens with disabilities. Its crosswalks announce the name of the street as well as when it is safe to cross. Bank statements are printed in Braille as are menus at local restaurants, even at McDonald's. Even pizza delivery people can use American Sign Language to communicate with the customer on delivery. One reason for the disabled-accepting culture is the fact that the Alabama Institute for the Deaf and Blind is located here. It did not take long for the community to realize that it could be prosperous if it accepted its large contingent of disabled people. However, the term *disabled* no longer fits the citizens of Talladega because they do so much: hold jobs, raise families, and support the community. Distinctions between disabled and nondisabled have disappeared. Diversity is the norm.

Diversity is not always the norm for a number of large corporations. Texaco's racial law suit has prompted a new look at diversity in organizations. The lawsuit by

Texaco employees received national attention when secret tapes of top executives making disparaging remarks about African-Americans were released. Diversity experts argue that top-level executives must be committed to diversity not only by promoting it but by embracing it. The EEOC found reasonable cause to believe Texaco had violated Title VII of the Civil Rights Act. Workers claim they were denied promotions and advancement opportunities because of their race. After the tapes went public, Texaco offered a $176 million settlement that included giving all of its African-American workers a ten percent raise. This agreement is the largest settlement of a racial discrimination case in U.S. history. For more information about the Texaco controversy, visit the Society for Human Resource Management online at **www.shrm.org\press**.[89]

The idea of managing a diverse workforce is still relatively new to human resource professionals. Many people are still struggling with the concept, its definition, and its usefulness. There is a great deal of resistance to diversity in the workplace, and the growing attention paid to diversity has led to a growing alienation of Caucasian males within many organizations.[90] Caucasian males are feeling the pinch of job insecurity resulting from downsizing. They see themselves as the first to be placed on the chopping block in the name of diversity. According to Thomas Kochman, a professor at the University of Illinois at Chicago, "Race and gender have become factors for white men, much the way they always have been for other groups. White males are like the firstborn in the family, the ones who have had the best love of both parents and never quite forgave the second child for being born. What they are dealing with is a sense of entitlement."[91]

The second child of whom Caucasian males are resentful appears to be more like a set of sextuplets. Specifically, managers named six different groups as having minority status, including women, older workers, disabled workers, workers for whom English is a second language, African-Americans, and gay and lesbian workers.[92] Individuals who belong to more than one of these groups are even more highly sought than those from only one group. Judge Deborah Batts is one individual who can claim to belong to three of these groups. Confirmed as a federal judge in New York in June 1994, Judge Batts has an impressive resume. She graduated from Radcliffe and Harvard, practiced law for six years in private practice, served five years as a federal prosecutor, and taught law at Fordham University for ten years. She is a woman who also is an openly gay African-American. She does not want to be known as the "gay judge," but gay activists believe that her appointment will do a great deal for their cause.[93]

What can employers do to protect themselves from discrimination claims? Gilbert Casellas, the former chairman of the EEOC, argues that in the new millennium, employers need to have procedures in place that follow the law. But they also need to make sure that their people are following those practices and procedures and need to provide as many credible outlets and mechanisms as possible that allow people to file complaints so they don't have to go outside the organization.[94]

Management Guidelines

Title VII suits based on alleged violations of the law prohibiting discrimination in employment and executive orders requiring affirmative action have been litigated for decades. Penalties for EEO violations not only include monetary sanctions against organizations but also public embarrassment and the possible loss of consumer loyalty.

Thus it is imperative that organizations develop and implement a comprehensive plan to ensure equity in employment decisions. Components of an effective affirmative action program were discussed earlier in the chapter. The following strategic guidelines will help to ensure the success of affirmative action programs and EEO policies and help develop and support a diverse workforce:[95]

1. All levels of management, including top management, should be committed to the entire program. If employees perceive a lack of commitment from management, they may become less willing to try to make the program work and be suspect of management's motives for implementing EEO policies or AAPs.

2. Every employee should understand fully the organization's policy on equal employment. Managers and employees need to be aware of both their obligations and their rights.

3. The organization should appoint an EEO officer with the following responsibilities:
   a. The handling of all contracts with and approval of information submitted to government agencies.
   b. The coordination of the organization's EEO programs.
   c. The interpretation of EEO laws, regulations, statutes, and executive orders with the assistance of the organization's legal counsel.
   d. The dissemination of information to all employees regarding the organization's EEO policies and guidelines.

4. Top management, including EEO officers, should ensure that the organization recruits, selects, trains, transfers, promotes, lays off, and compensates employees on the basis of ability and other meritorious qualifications without discrimination because of sex, race, color, religion, age, national origin, or ancestry.

5. Top management should ensure that the organization does not discriminate against any qualified job applicant or employee because of a mental or physical handicap or status as a disabled or Vietnam-era veteran.

6. Managers should act to *remedy any deficiencies* in the firm's EEO programs and AAPs. This includes evaluating the utilization of minorities, females, physically or mentally handicapped individuals, and disabled or Vietnam-era veterans.

7. Managers should consider *establishing results-oriented goals* and timetables to eliminate the underutilization of minorities and females throughout the organization. If quotas or goals are used, this does not mean that the organization should hire unqualified applicants or promote unqualified employees. Quotas and goals should be developed subject to the availability of qualified minority and female applicants.

8. Managers should be careful *not to limit, segregate, or classify employees* in any way that would tend to deprive them of employment opportunities or adversely affect any employee's status because of sex, race, color, religion, age, national origin, or ancestry.

9. Managers should ensure that the organization *does not use sexual or racial stereotyping* in any oral or written description of an applicant or employee. In addition, managers must eliminate any sexism or racism, whether conscious or otherwise, in any evaluation process.

Questions for Review

1. What are the important strategic choices managers should make regarding EEOs?
2. Discuss Title VII of the Civil Rights Act. What does this act prohibit? Be specific.
3. What is a bona fide occupational qualification (BFOQ)? Give an example of a BFOQ.
4. The chapter covered three ways to demonstrate discrimination in employment decisions. What are they?
5. What is the difference between sex discrimination and sexual harassment?
6. What is the difference between race discrimination and national origin discrimination?
7. How has recent EEO case law affected civil rights?
8. What is the difference between EEO laws and affirmative action?
9. What is reverse discrimination? Give an example.
10. What are the components of an effective AAP?
11. What is the difference between the Equal Pay Act and comparable worth?
12. Do you believe implementing comparable worth laws and guidelines would have a positive or negative impact on the workforce? Do you believe comparable worth is realistic?
13. What are ways to manage diversity?

CASE

An Example of Subtle and Not-So-Subtle Discrimination in the Workplace—Whose Responsibility?

The following is an excerpt from an essay written by an employee of a *Fortune* 500 company that was undertaking an initiative to diversify its workforce. All of the incidents reported are actual situations encountered by the author of the essay. This particular essay was written by an African-American, but the same feelings and problems experienced by this individual also are experienced by virtually every individual who falls into a protected class. The following is a cover letter from the area director attached to the employee's essay. The director circulated these items to all managers in his area of the company in an effort to help others understand what minority members face every day.

Dear Senior Managers,

As we advanced our careers, many of us were challenged directly or indirectly by the culture of our organization. The very culture that adds stability and meaning to the organization oftentimes gets in the way of our aspirations and goals. We have either learned to address these barriers or have been supported along the way to cope or to take action. Thus, we have moved ahead in the organization.

For some of our employees, the ability and opportunity to resolve incongruities in behavior and practices is not an easy task. The support systems needed to help address these issues are not available. This becomes a daily struggle—a painful experience that drains their energy and robs them of enthusiasm. For our business, these conditions thwart our ability to put the full talent and skills of all our employees to work for us.

The attached essay was written by one of our black employees who, over the years, has directly experienced the pain of some of our inexpedient practices and behaviors. It is a compelling case study of the impact that our decisions and behavior have on employees who feel or are, in fact, excluded.

The plight of this essay's author is intolerable. We cannot afford to have these types of conditions at this company. Please send your diversity representative your reactions and, most important, your comments and recommendations on the concerns raised.

The essay:

Throughout this essay, I will attempt to illustrate the development of the corporate African-American by discussing personal events encountered during my five years in this company. I intend, through an analysis of my own personal experiences, to show the reader the types of obstacles placed before corporate blacks and the impact these obstacles/events have on their development. Simply, I hope to sensitize the reader to the cumulative effect of the daily racial incidents many corporate African-Americans confront. I caution the reader not to dismiss the following incidents as a comedy of mishandlings unique to me alone, because to do so would mitigate the value of the message. The fact is, similar incidents as those described below infest the lives of most corporate African-Americans.

In June 1988, I began working for this company. I brought along the enthusiasm and dreams that every fresh graduated new entrant into the workforce brings. I could hardly wait to find my desk and dive in. I ached to impress someone, to show all the right people that I was ready to begin my journey to the top. Of course I understood I would have to pay my "dues" along the way, but I was willing (after all that's what I'd been doing in college all these years!).

The first six months were almost perfect. The learning was interesting and stimulating, and a bond of friendship had grown between myself and other new employees starting the same day as I (referred to as my cohorts). We attended training together by day, and hung out together by night. Other employees were supportive also. Especially the black ones. They seemed supportive, but lifeless—at least professionally. By lifeless, I mean they did not seem to expect much from the company. I sensed that the battle to survive preempted the battle to progress, but mine would not falter. So long as I concentrated on my performance, I could not be denied.

For the next few months, work was wonderful. April 1989 was the first performance review session for which my cohorts and I were eligible. The possible ratings included an "E" for excellent, an "H" for above average, and an "S" for satisfactory performance. Anyone below an "S" was on the way out the door. I received an "H." At first I was disappointed because I thought I deserved an "E," but at lunch that day, my cohorts and I discussed the ratings we each received, and I realized that many received "S's" and none received "E's." I still thought I deserved an "E," but I felt a little better.

On May 5, 1989, while sitting in my cubicle, I was approached by a white coworker and asked if I listened to "nigger music." Right out of the blue, this person walked into my space and the first thing out of his mouth was this question. I reported the incident to management, and they investigated. Within a few days, the coworker was demoted, and I was assured that this was a "Single Isolated Incident" (SII).

In October of 1989, a special promotion window was declared to promote any deserving grade 7 employees (which included me and my cohorts) to a grade 8. The morning the promotions were to be announced, my desk phone rang off the hook. Each phone call was from one of my cohorts informing me that their boss first asked them into his office and sat them down to announce the promotion. I must have peeked over the walls of my cubicle 100 times before my boss finally arrived to invite me to his office. As I faced him in his office, I tried to contain my smile, but I am sure I had a pretty stupid looking smirk on my face. However, as my boss began to speak, that stupid smirk was drowned in confusion. My boss informed me that there were just not enough promotions in our area for me to receive one. However, he reassured me that I would be eligible next year.

I could not believe my ears. I knew for a fact that some of those joy-filled phone calls were from individuals who received lower ratings than mine. How in the hell could they get promoted and not me? By the way, not one of the phone calls was from an African-American. I was so upset that I requested a meeting with my boss's boss. We met the next day. After explaining my case, he explained his position. He told me he knew how I felt, but that there were just more promotions available in other areas. He told me it was a "Single Isolated Incident" and not to let it upset me.

I looked forward to April 1990 because that was the next promotion period. I recall my supervisor approaching my work space and inviting me to his office. This was it. The moment I had been waiting for. I entered his office and awaited his words. After extending my new promotion to grade 8, he sat back and waited for my grin and thank you. We were both surprised by my reaction. I was appalled. I was just given a promotion that was six months overdue and I was supposed to jump for joy? I thanked him for the promotion and shook his hand and retreated back to my area to think. Soon, one of my friends called to tell me he had been promoted to a 9. The call was from a white man who had the same performance ratings I did.

April arrived again and I was somewhat unsure about my promotional prognosis. I knew I had an above-average year, but was not sure when to expect a 9. Once again I was called into my boss's office for the news. I was not given a promotion, but my raise was relatively high. Over the next few days I learned that most of my cohorts received their promotions to 9 even though my performance ratings were higher than theirs. I began to think that the old cliche—a black person must do more to get equal—may be right. I decided to get equal.

In January 1992 I enrolled in an evening MBA program. I looked up the corporate ladder and concluded that an MBA would ensure positive treatment. I was pleasantly surprised to find other company employees also enrolled in the program. I began to study and socialize with a group of five or six folks who had served similar time at the company. Although I was the only African-American in the group, this was not surprising to me.

I announced my plans for graduate school to my immediate supervisor first. I am not sure what I expected to be his reply, but I knew it would be positive. He surprised me by saying that I needed to realize that an MBA would not change the way the company looked at me. I would hear this statement many more times from other employees and other managers.

I attended classes two nights a week from 6 PM to 9 PM. It was difficult finding adequate time to study, so in addition to studying at home, I would find an empty conference room at work and study there during lunch. During the week of midterms and finals, I would also keep my books at my desk and sneak a peek whenever possible. I often had to quickly shove my books aside or cover them when my project leader or boss came by. Sometimes I was not quick enough and would be reprimanded for studying on the job. I never thought to question their position because, after all, it was company time. I would simply put my books away and find something else to do.

One afternoon I got together with my study group to prepare for an exam. What I learned from that study session has affected my relationship with the company profoundly. As we began to talk, I heard stories of the grand support each received from their respective supervisors. Each was given unrecorded afternoons and even days off to study and were able to study at their desks when they needed to. They were given company computers to support their schoolwork and other allowances. I believe this incident marked the beginning of the "absenteeism effect." Simply, as a work environment becomes increasingly less supportive and oftentimes blatantly exclusionary, the resulting stress and frustration will attack the physical and mental health of the target. The relief is found in less exposure to the cause. . .the workplace.

One afternoon in January of 1993, I was standing at the fax machine faxing three pages of notes for a classmate from another company. My boss happened into the fax room and noticed I was faxing schoolwork. He called me to his office and informed me that company resources are not be used for school. He asked me if I wanted to go to school or work. I replied that I did not believe the two were mutually exclusive; he disagreed.

Because his stance about my MBA made me wonder if he may do something to make them mutually exclusive, I decided to go to HR for an impartial audience. In January of 1993 I arranged to meet my HR representative. For more than an hour I voiced my concerns with regard to my lack of support with school and various other issues. I was assured that my issues would be handled in a way that would not jeopardize my future.

The result of my actions was a meeting with my boss and his boss. They sat on one side of the table and I sat on the other. Unbelievably, no member of HR attended. They made their disappointment in my going outside the department evident. Although I was able to voice some of my concerns, I spent most of the meeting apologizing for my actions. At the conclusion of the meeting my boss did apologize for his statement and informed me that "it was out of line." However, his apology sounded like a statement for the record, not an apology. He also pledged to support my school efforts. To his credit, he has improved. In fact, I can even use the fax now.

It is my impression that HR identified the potentially discriminating actions of my management and asked that they be discontinued, resulting in an apology and support of my schooling. However, it was not apparent that any attempt was made to address the discriminatory thinking of my management. Clearly, no firm can control the thoughts and feelings of its agents; however, the actions of these agents can certainly be managed. Until there are true consequences for the discriminatory actions of the agents, the more than occasional "mistake and apologize" incident will continue to thrive.

I have come to realize that the impulse to solely address the particular racial act, as opposed to the root of the act, is not limited to HR. In fact, throughout this essay, I am only highlighting a very small fraction of the SIIs that I have personally encountered. I have limited my report to events which would be documented by myself and others. This documentation will most likely be necessary because I expect the reaction to this essay will be one of defensive reflex. Much like the HR reaction above, the impulse will be to first dispute the facts, and those that cannot be disputed, explain.

SIIs are certainly not limited to such personal experiences as described above. In fact, it might be said that many of the most damaging SIIs afflicting the African-American workforce are delivered by single thunderous blows, affecting the entire black community at once. I have heard countless discussions among my white coworkers professing their contempt for having to "pay for the crimes" they themselves did not commit. It became obvious that to many of them, my presence served only as a reminder of what they thought they had to give up. The SIIs that result from this dilemma are difficult to articulate because of their abstract intangible nature. Perhaps this will help you understand:

Have you ever worked with someone who obviously resented your presence but was forced to work with you anyway? Or with someone who considers you a personal threat to his/her security? If you have not, I assure you the contempt and fear is [sic] felt, even through smiles and handshakes. Now consider an environment where the person described above is the norm instead of the exception. Every encounter attacks your self-esteem.

It is not my intention to focus the attention of the reader on the details of my personal SIIs. It is my intention to sensitize the reader to the existence and frequency of racially motivated SIIs and bare [sic] out the effect on its victims. Clearly, most people, regardless of color or gender, can identify the blatant act of racism but few recognize the cumulative effect of many small hidden acts. Even with regard to the small SIIs the reflect [sic] is to view each one individually. This perspective tends to make the victim of the individual SII seem irrational in his/her reaction. For example, consider yourself to be the target of a series of single words, each shouted individually at one hour intervals. At the delivery of the final word, you (the target) come to understand the insulting nature of the entire sentence, and react. To the casual observer who happened to witness only the delivery of the single final word, your reaction will appear irrational. "Why are you getting so upset over a word?" Until the existence of the not-so-blatant daily racial blows suffered by most African-American employees is acknowledged, and the cumulative effect of these daily reminders is understood and respected, the recovery period cannot begin and the true value of diversity will never be realized.

Questions for Discussion

1. What are some of the ways in which the not-so-blatant discrimination felt by this employee affected the success of the organization?

2. How do you feel about the statement that HR deals with the problem, not the cause of the problem? How could HR actually deal with the cause?

3. Can you describe a situation in which you felt not-so-blatantly discriminated against? What was the outcome of the situation?

4. What suggestions do you have for this company for implementing a diversity plan that will be effective?

5. Do you think the employee who wrote this essay was simply overreacting? Why or why not?

Additional Readings

Buhler, Patricia. "Scanning the Environment: Environmental Trends Affecting the Workplace." *Supervision* 58 (March 1997), pp. 24–33.

D'Souza, Dinesh. "Beyond Affirmation Action: The Perils of Managing Diversity." *Chief Executive*, December 1996, pp. 44–46.

Hale, Noreen. *The Older Worker: Effective Strategies for Management and Human Resource Development*. San Francisco: Jossey-Bass, 1990.

Hall, Francine S., and Elizabeth L. Hall. "The ADA: Going Beyond the Law," *Academy of Management Executive* 8, no. 1 (1994), pp. 17–32.

Hodgson, Morgan D. "ADEA Waiver Rules and Enforcement Guidance." *Employment Relations Today* 23 (Winter, 1997), pp. 75–84.

Jackson, Kathy. "Stallkamp Leads Chrysler's Push for Diversity," *Automotive News*, March 3, 1997, p. 3.

Konrad, Alison and Frank Linnehan. "Formalized HRM Structures: Coordinating Equal Employment Opportunity or Concealing Organizational Practices?" *Academy of Management Journal* 38 (1995).

Lebo, Fern. *Mastering the Diversity Challenge: On-the-Job Applications for Measurable Results*. Delray Beach, FL: St. Lucie Press, 1996.

Powell, Gary N. "Male/Female Work Roles—What Kind of Future?" *Personnel* 66, 7 (1989), pp. 47–50.

Powell, Gary N. *Gender and Diversity in the Workplace*. Newbury Park, CA: Sage, 1994.

Rousseau, Rita. "Employing the New America." *Restaurant and Institutions* 107 (March 15, 1997), pp. 40–46.

Stern, Barbara. "Holding Executives Accountable: Linking Diversity Performance to Compensation." *The Diversity Factor*, Fall 1995, pp. 11–15.

Turner, Ronald. *The Past and Future of Affirmative Action: A Guide and Analysis for Human Resource Professionals and Corporate Counsel*. Westport, CT: Quorum Books, 1990.

White, M. B. "Power Lines: Networks and the Diversity Initiative." *The Diversity Factor*, Winter 1996, pp.2–7.

Notes

[1]Vicki Butler, et al., Plaintiffs, v. Home Depot, Inc., Defendant. Theresa Frank, Katherine Toma, and Kathleen York, et al., Plaintiffs, v. Home Depot, Inc., Defendant, No. C-94–4335 SI, C-95–2182 SI, United States District Court for the Northern District of California, August 28, 1997, decided, 1997 U.S. Dist. Lexis 16296, **web.lexis-nexis.com/ universe**; Petition for a Writ of Certiorari to the United States Court of Appeals for the Ninth Circuit, Home Depot U.S.A., Inc., Petitioner, v. Vicki Butler, et al., Respondents, No. 96–943, December 12, 1996, Lexis-Nexis, **web.lexis-nexis.com/universe**; Mark Albright, "Home Depot Settles Sex Bias Claims," *St. Petersburg Times*, September 20, 1997, p. 1E; The Associated Press, "Home Depot to Pay Women $65 Million in Bias Suit," *Chicago Tribune*, September 21, 1997, p. H3; Chris Roush, "Home Depot Required to Set

Up Special Job Application System," *The Atlanta Journal and Constitution*, September 25, 1997, p. 2F.

[2]The discrimination discussion that follows is based on the *Equal Employment Opportunity Manual for Managers and Supervisors*, a publication of the American Society for Personnel Administration and Commerce Clearing House, Inc. (1989).

[3]Tim Smart, "This Civil Rights Bill May Fly—If It Stays Light Enough," *Business Week*, February 5, 1990, p. 35.

[4]P. M. Barrett, "Some Specifics About the New Law," *The Wall Street Journal*, November 4, 1991, p. B1.

[5]D. P. Twomey, *A Concise Guide to Employment Law* (Cincinnati: South-Western, 1986).

[6]Patricia Hamilton, "Running in Place," *D&B Reports*, March/April 1993, pp. 24–26.

[7]Carol Kleinman, "How Women Can Deal with Today's Underground Sexism," *Tallahassee Democrat*, March 30, 1994, p. 18D.

[8]Leah Nathans Spiro, "The Angry Voices at Kidder," *Business Week*, February 1, 1993, pp. 60–63.

[9]Linda Micco, "EEOC: Employers Should Heed Restaurant Bias Case," *HRNews*, August, 1997, p. 7.

[10]For discussions of the hearings, see *Time*, October 21, 1991; and *U.S. News & World Report*, October 21, 1991.

[11]Section 1604.1 of the EEOC Guidelines based on the Civil Rights Act of 1964, Title VII.

[12]Arthur Gutman, *EEO Law and Personnel Practices* (Newbury Park, CA: Sage, 1993).

[13]Junda Woo, "Harassing Both Sexes Equally Isn't Excuse," *The Wall Street Journal*, June 16, 1994, p. B5.

[14]*Bundy* v. *Jackson*, 641 F.2d 934, 24 FEP 1155 (D.C. Cir., 1981).

[15]*Meritor Savings Bank* v. *Vinson*, 477 U.S. 57 (1986).

[16]Associated Press, "Pilot Wins $875,000 in Suit Complaining of Porn in Cockpits, *The Wall Street Journal*, October 17, 1997, p. B2.

[17]Ann Carrns, "Those Bawdy E-mails Were Good for a Laugh—Until the Ax Fell," *The Wall Street Journal*, February 4, 2000, p. 1

[18]Adam Jack Morrell, "Nonemployee Harassment," *Legal Report*, January-February 2000, pp. 1–2.

[19]S. J. Garvin, "Employer Liability for Sexual Harassment," *HRMagazine*, June 1991, pp. 101–108.

[20]M. Lengnick-Hall, "Checking Out Sexual Harassment Claims," *HRMagazine*, March 1992, pp. 77–81.

[21]Karen Donovan, "Avoiding a Time Bomb: Sexual Harassment," *Business Week Enterprise*, October 13, 1997, pp. 20–22.

[22]Anne Fisher, "Sexual Harassment: What to Do," *Fortune*, August 23, 1993, pp. 84–88.

[23]Margaret A. Jacobs, "Riding Crop and Slurs: How Wall Street Dealt with a Sex-Bias Case," *The Wall Street Journal*, June 9, 1994, p. A11.

[24]Sarah Cohen, "More Men Claiming Sexual Harassment," *Tampa Tribune*, January 24, 1994, p. 11.

[25]Elizabeth Kadetsky, "The Million Dollar Man," *Working Woman*, October 1993, p. 461.

[26]Kellyanne Fitzpatrick, "What to Expect from Plaintiff Jones and Defendant Clinton," *The Wall Street Journal*, May 11, 1994, p. A15.

[27]"Women and Work," *Employment Relations Bulletin*, January 1993, p. 2.

[28]Sue Shellenbarger, "As More Pregnant Women Work, Bias Complaints Rise," *The Wall Street Journal*, December 6, 1993, p. B11.

[29]Brett Pulley, "Culture of Racial Bias at Shoney's Underlies Chairman's Departure," *The Wall Street Journal*, December 21, 1992, p. A11; "Shoney's Settles EEO Dispute," *HRNews*, March 1993, p. A3; and Jan Pudlow, "Marianna Couple's Stand Was a Victory for Thousands," *Tallahassee Democrat*, February 7, 1993, p. A11.

[30]Benjamin Holden, "Parent of Denny's Restaurants Signs Bias-Case Decree," *The Wall Street Journal*, March 26, 1993, p. A5.

[31]Ron Suskind, "Brooks Brothers Settles Job-Bias Suit: Inquiry Used Controversial 'Tests,'" *The Wall Street Journal*, April 21, 1993, p. B7; and James P. Scanlan, "Measuring Hiring Discrimination," *Labor Law Journal*, July 1993, pp. 387–394.

[32]Mary Ann Barton, "National Origin Discrimination Claims Rising," *HRNews*, December 1993, p. 5.

[33]Catherine Yang, "In Any Language It's Unfair," *Business Week*, June 21, 1993, pp. 110–111.

[34]Ibid.

[35]D. Israel and G. McConnell, "New Law Protects Older Workers," *HRMagazine*, March 1991, pp. 77–79.

[36]U.S. Equal Employment Opportunity Commission, "Age-Bias Claims Down," *USA Today*, August 27, 1997, p. B1.

[37]Frances A. McMorris, "Age-Bias Suits May Become Harder to Prove," *The Wall Street Journal*, February 20, 1997, pp. B1 and B13.

[38]Milo Geyelin, "Age-Bias Cases Found to Bring Big Jury Awards," *The Wall Street Journal*, December 17, 1993, p. B11.

[39]"Supreme Court Says Years of Service Not a 'Proxy for Age' in Bias Case," *Business & Legal Reports*, 0888-6228/93, p. 3.

[40]"Age-Bias Law Covers Retired Workers," *HRNews*, February 1993, p. A19.

[41]Catherine Fyock, "Finding the Gold in the Graying of America," *HRMagazine*, February 1994, pp. 74–76.

[42]"Muslim Security Guard's Prayer for Relief Granted, Massachusetts Commission Against Discrimination Upholds $300,000 Award," *HR Comply*, 12 September 2000, **www.hrcomply.com/said.html** (accessed March 6, 2001).

[43]Richard Schmitt, "EECO May Pit Church vs. State at Work," *The Wall Street Journal*, June 8, 1994, p. B8.

[44]E. J. Conry, G. R. Ferrera, and K. H. Fox, *The Legal Environment of Business*, 2nd ed. (Boston: Allyn and Bacon, 1990).

[45]Ibid.

[46]P. A. Morrissey, "How Is Disability Defined?" *HRNews*, January 1991, p. 6.

[47]R. Pimentel and M. Litito, "Shining Light on ADA," *HRMagazine*, February 1992, pp. 47–49.

[48]The following section is based on D. Gold and B. Unger, "ADA Prohibits Most Preemployment Health Questions," *HRNews*, March 1992, p. A5; and W. F. Casio and J. W. Walker, *HRM Update* (New York: McGraw-Hill, 1992).

[49]S. R. Meisinger, "The Americans with Disabilities Act: Begin Preparing Now," *HR Legal Report*, Winter 1991, pp. 1–12.

[50]Mike Frost, "Technology Solutions HR Cyberspace: The E-Mailbag," *HRMagazine*, September 1996, p. 34.

[51]Neville Tompkins, "Tools That Help Performance on the Job," *HRMagazine*, April 1993, pp. 84–91.

[52]Barbara Gamble Magill, Esq., "ADA Accommodations Don't Have to Break the Bank," *HRMagazine*, July 1997, pp. 85–88.

[53]Ibid.

[54]Garwood, McKenna, and McKenna, "EEO," p. 1.

[55]Timothy S. Bland, "The Supreme Court Focuses on the ADA," *HRMagazine*, September 1999, pp. 42–43.

[56]"Hooters Agrees to Hire Men," *Tallahassee Democrat*, Associated Press, October 1, 1997, p. 9E; C. Simon, "Restaurant Seeks Waitresses," *The Wall Street Journal*, October 7, 1997.

[57]This discussion was based largely on the *Equal Employment Opportunity Manual*.

[58]D. Seligman, "How Equal Opportunity Turned into Employment Quotas," *Fortune*, March 1973, p. 162.

[59]Conry et al., *The Legal Environment of Business*.

[60]Arlena Sawyers, "Chrysler Found Guilty of Reverse Discrimination," *Automotive News*, June 21, 1993; and Harry N. Tuchman, "Will an Employer That Voluntarily Implements an Affirmative Action Program Be Subjected to Possible Liability Under Title VII of the Civil Rights Act of 1964?" *Employment Relations Today* 21 (Spring 1994), p. 111.

[61]Owen Ullmann, "The GOP Assault on Affirmative Action Is Getting Serious," *Business Week*, November 17, 1997.

[62]U.S. Department of Labor, *Equal Pay for Equal Work Under the Fair Labor Standards Act* (Washington, D.C.: Interpretive Bulletin, August 31, 1971).

[63]U.S. Department of Labor, *Employment Relations under the Fair Labor Standards Act* (Washington, D.C.: Employment Standards Administration, Wage and Hour Division, revised May 1980, reprinted August 1985).

[64]Joan Rigdon, "Three Decades after the Equal Pay Act, Women's Wages Remain Far from Parity," *The Wall Street Journal*, June 9, 1993, p. B11.

[65]Ibid.

[66]Ibid.

[67]*Lemons* v. *City and County of Denver*, 620 F.2d 228, 1980.

[68]*AFSCME* v. *State of Washington*, 770 F.2d 1401, Ninth Circuit, 1985.

[69]"Twenty Questions of Comparable Worth," The Equal Employment Advisory Council, 1984. Reprinted in *Personnel Administrator* 30, April 1985, p. 65.

[70]Julie M. Buchanan, "Comparable Worth: Where Is It Headed?" *Human Resources: Journal of the International Association for Personnel Women* 2 (Summer 1985), p. 12.

[71]S. B. Garland, "Throwing Stones at the 'Glass Ceiling,'" *Business Week*, August 19, 1991, p. 29.

[72]J. Lopez, "Study Says Women Face Glass Walls as Well as Ceiling," *The Wall Street Journal*, March 3, 1993, p. B1.

[73]C. M. Dominguez, "A Crack in the Glass Ceiling," *HRMagazine*, December 1990, pp. 65–66.

[74]J. B. White and C. Hymowitz, "Broken Glass: Watershed Generation of Women Executives Is Rising to the Top," *The Wall Street Journal*, February 10, 1997, pp. A1, A8.

[75]Garland, "Throwing Stones at the 'Glass Ceiling.'"

[76]T. H. Cox and C. V. Harquail, "Career Paths and Career Success in the Early Career Stages of Male and Female MBAs," *Journal of Vocational Behavior* 39, no. 1 (1991), pp. 54–75.

[77]Garland, "Throwing Stones at the 'Glass Ceiling.'"

[78]K. E. Kram, "Phases of the Mentor Relationship," *Academy of Management Journal* 26, no. 4 (1983), pp. 608–625.

[79]B. R. Ragins, "Barriers to Mentoring: The Female Manager's Dilemma," *Human Relations* 42(1), 1989, pp. 1–22.

[80]Ibid.

[81]White and Hymowitz, "Broken Glass: Water-shed Generation."

[82]B. Rosen and K. Lovelace, "Piecing Together the Diversity Puzzle," *HRMagazine*, June 1991, pp. 71–84.

[83]L. Bayots, "Launching Successful Diversity Initiatives," *HRMagazine*, March 1992, pp. 91–97.

[84]B. Rosen and K. Lovelace, "Fitting Square Pegs into Round Holes," *HRMagazine*, January 1994, pp. 86–93.

[85]"Diversity Training Is a Culture Change, Not Just Training," *1993 SHRM/CCH Survey*, May 26, 1993, p. 1.

[86]Leon Wynter, "Corporate America's Best Bets for Minorities," *The Wall Street Journal*, December 22, 1993, p. B1.

[87]Rosen and Lovelace, "Fitting Square Pegs into Round Holes."

[88]Tony Horwitz, "Talladega, Alabama, Is a User-Friendly City for Disabled People," *The Wall Street Journal*, February 14, 1994, p. A1.

[89]L. Micco, "Texaco Racial Suit Prompts New Look at Diversity Plans," *HRNews*, December 1996, pp. 1, 7; E. Smith, "Playing the Corporate Race Card," *Black Enterprise*, January 1997, p.19.

[90]Michele Gordon and Ann Therese Palmer, "White, Male, and Worried," *Business Week*, January 31, 1994, pp. 50–56.

[91]Ibid.

[92]Vanessa J. Weaver, "Diversity: One Size Doesn't Fit All," *Mosaics: SHRM Focuses on Workplace Diversity*, Vol.6, May/June 2000.

[93]Frances McMorris, "Judge Brings New Look to Federal Bench," *The Wall Street Journal*, September 13, 1994, p. B16.

[94]B. Leonard, "Interview: Life at the EEOC," *HRMagazine*, January 1998, pp. 83–90.

[95]These "Management Guidelines" are based largely on the work of Walter Manley, Esq., unpublished manuscript (1989) and on the content of the chapter.

6

Job Analysis

Chapter Objectives

As a result of studying this chapter, you should be able to

1. Discuss the strategic choices regarding job analysis that are available to organizations.

2. Define job analysis.

3. Describe the steps involved in a typical job analysis.

4. Be familiar with various methods of conducting a job analysis.

5. Discuss how job descriptions and job specifications can be developed from the results of a job analysis.

6. Understand the many ways that the results of a job analysis can be used in other functions of human resource management.

Before an individual can be hired to perform a job, the requirements of that job must be identified. Before the level of pay for a job can be established, the qualifications required to perform the job must be determined. Similarly, before the performance of an employee can be evaluated or a decision can be made as to whether or not an employee needs to be trained, what the employee should be doing must be identified. Therefore, before any of these human resource functions can be performed, there must be a thorough understanding of the domain of the job. To do this, human resource professionals use a job analysis, which is a means of collecting information about various aspects of a job. Results from a job analysis serve as the foundation for many of the human resource functions, including selection, compensation, performance evaluation, and training.

CASE

Whirlpool's Use of Job Analysis

When you hear the name Whirlpool, you naturally think of home appliances. Over the past 80-plus years, Whirlpool has developed a national and international reputation for producing quality appliances. Whirlpool claims to be the largest home appliance manufacturer and marketer in the world. The brand names of the products sold include Whirlpool, KitchenAid, Roper, and Estate. Whirlpool also produces the appliances sold by Sears under its store brand, Kenmore.[1] More information about Whirlpool can be found on its home page at **www.whirlpool.com**.

There is a constant need for replacement parts for Whirlpool products. The Whirlpool division that provides these parts is located in the small town of La Porte, Indiana, approximately two hours east of Chicago.

The parts distribution warehouse in La Porte receives orders from retail customers, appliance stores that sell Whirlpool products, and Sears. Each of the orders is entered into a computer file and held until the end of the day. At the end of each day, a computer program develops the orders into processing schedules; the 600-plus employees at the warehouse, working three shifts, are assigned to fill those orders. Whirlpool guarantees its customers, who consist of national distributors, regional parts distribution centers, factory service branches, and international accounts, a 24- to 72-hour turnaround from the time the order is processed.

Manual Parts Distribution System

Until 1994 the locating, picking, packing, and shipping activities at the warehouse were all part of a manual system. Essentially, the orders were printed on six-inch cards called pick tickets. At the beginning of each shift, a worker was assigned a deck of pick tickets to process. Each ticket directed the employee to a certain location in the warehouse and informed him or her how many parts to pick. The employee then stapled the pick ticket to the part and delivered the part to the appropriate packing station. On arrival at the packing station, a packer surveyed the items to be packed, selected a box of suitable size, and packed the parts in any way that he or she felt was appropriate. Finally, these boxes were delivered to the dock and packed in trucks to be shipped to the waiting customer. The trucks were packed in the order in which the boxes arrived at the docks and in a way that most efficiently utilized the space available. Both of these contingencies were determined by the person at the dock as the boxes arrived.

Automated Parts Distribution System

In an effort to become more efficient as well as productive, Whirlpool decided to automate each of these warehouse functions by using a variety of computerized systems linked together via a central computer system. Obviously, this decision would change the way in which every job in the warehouse was performed. Virtually all of the redesigned jobs would require some computer expertise. For example, pickers, under the automated system, would be directed by handheld computers programmed to plot the most efficient pick paths instead of allowing the pickers to determine the order in which the parts were picked. Packers would be required to use a computer terminal set up at their packing station that told them which size box to select, which parts to place in the box, and in what order. Finally, the packed boxes would travel on a computerized conveyor belt and arrive at the appropriate dock in the order in which they were to be packed onto the truck. John Haywood, national director of parts operations, says the system has led to a near-perfect record of parts fulfillment. Since the improvements, on-time deliveries improved to 99.9 percent, up from about 85 percent under the manual system.

Along with these major production changes, in order to be more flexible, Whirlpool also wanted to cross-train as many of the employees as possible on each of the new automated jobs. Whirlpool realized, however, that before any training began, it needed to ensure that its current workforce possessed the knowledge, skills, and abilities (KSAs) required by the new automated jobs. To accomplish this goal, a job analysis was performed.

Job Analysis

The first step in Whirlpool's job analysis was to determine the KSAs required by the current jobs. To do this, the Common-Metric Questionnaire (CMQ) by Psychological Corporation was administered to three employees in each position in the warehouse. Multiple respondents from the same position were used so that the information gathered could be cross-checked. The results from the job analysis were used to ascertain the level and variety of KSAs that warehouse employees used on a daily basis. Results indicated that the physical requirements of the current job (i.e., lifting, pulling, pushing, walking) were much more extensive than the mental requirements (i.e., decision making, mathematical requirements).

Next, because the warehouse had not been automated yet, a substitute location had to be used to collect data about the KSAs required by the redesigned jobs. The parts distribution warehouse for Radio Shack in Dallas, Texas, was used for this purpose. This facility was already using equipment similar to what Whirlpool planned to install. Some differences in the equipment and its functioning existed, but the basic KSAs required were similar enough to be useful. Therefore the CMQ was administered to several employees at the Radio Shack location, and the data gathered were used to determine the KSAs required by the automated jobs. Results from this analysis indicated that the physical requirements did not exceed the mental requirements. Instead, the physical requirements of the redesigned jobs were much less than those under Whirlpool's current manual system, but the mental requirements were often higher. For example, in many of the picking jobs under the automated system, the parts came to the picker instead of the picker going to the part. Hence, the number of physical movements under the automated system decreased. However, it was still necessary to verify that the part that arrived was the appropriate part and that the correct number of parts was available. If either or both of these could not be verified, the picker had to use the computer to correct the problem, thus increasing the mental requirements of the job.

Comparison of Requirements: Previous and Redesigned Jobs

The results of the job analysis at the two locations were then compared to determine whether any KSAs required by the automated system were not currently being used in the manual system. Based on this analysis, a needs assessment test was developed. This test focused on the KSAs found to be required from the Radio Shack analysis and was administered to each Whirlpool warehouse employee. The results from this test indicated that only a handful of employees lacked the KSAs required to perform the automated jobs. Prior to beginning the automation training, Whirlpool offered classes (e.g., a refresher course on numerical problem solving) free of charge to the employees who lacked the specific KSAs required by the job.

Because the human resource manager at the Whirlpool plant realized that even planned changes can cause major problems (e.g., employee resentment) in the future, he made a proactive strategic decision to try to prevent possible problems. A thorough job analysis of the current manual and of proposed automated jobs allowed Whirlpool to pinpoint differences in KSAs. The company then set up pretraining for the employees who lacked the KSAs required by the new job requirements prior to their participation in the actual automation training. This allowed the conversion to the newly automated jobs to proceed smoothly and effectively.

This case presents typical changes that many companies have faced as they have integrated computers into the workforce. Think how different a secretary's job is today compared with what it was just a few years ago, before personal computers sat on every secretary's desk.

The computer has had a revolutionary effect on jobs. Many jobs in factories, offices, and mines have been totally redesigned because of the computer. Paper making, steel manufacturing, rubber and glass manufacturing, and many other processes are all very different than they were even a few years ago because of computers. The activities performed by employees no longer include packing, pulling, lifting, and walking. Instead they consist of sitting at a terminal or computer console and pushing buttons. As more and more computerized changes occur in the workplace, companies must be sure to update the requirements for jobs. Any job that changes because of computers, or for any other reason, should be analyzed. The purpose of this chapter is to describe how this analysis should be performed.

Strategic Choices

Because the results of a job analysis can be applied to many aspects of human resource management, even making the decision to perform a job analysis is a strategic decision in itself. However, several other strategic considerations about job analysis should be mentioned.

1. Managers must decide the extent to which employees can participate in the job analysis process. Involving employees in the job analysis process may be wise for a number of reasons. First, if workers are asked to participate in the

process, they feel more ownership for the results and accept them more easily. Further, employees trust the results more because they know they took part in developing them. However, a disadvantage of employee involvement in the job analysis process is that employees may try to inflate the importance of their job. Therefore, it is important to use more than one job incumbent in the job analysis process so that information gathered about the requirements can be double-checked for accuracy.

2. A second strategic decision about performing a job analysis is to determine how detailed it must be. Should the results of the job analysis be extremely specific, such as how long it should take to perform each task, or should they just highlight the major components of the job? The answer to these questions depends on the use of the job analysis results. If a company wants to determine the salary of an individual performing the job, the major components might be sufficient. However, if the results are to be used to determine the type of training that should be offered to individuals recently hired to fill a position, more specific results are needed.

3. When a job analysis should be conducted is another strategic decision managers must make. It may be useful to conduct a job analysis when a job has changed in any major way (e.g., new equipment or procedures are introduced) or when a job is added. Also, if a department, division, or organization is restructured, the jobs affected by the restructuring should be analyzed.[2] Another indication that it is time to conduct a job analysis is that the turnover rate for a job is higher than the organization's average rate. This may indicate that the job is extremely difficult and that modifications to it may be warranted.

4. Finally, managers must decide whether to use a traditional or future-oriented job analysis. Traditional job analysis methods are used to collect information about how the job is currently being performed. However, if an organization is changing rapidly because of constant growth or technological changes, a more future-oriented approach to job analysis may be desired. To reorient traditional job analysis approaches to have a future perspective, managers need to predict changes that should occur in the industry during a specific time period and determine how jobs will probably need to be performed in the future.[3] It is also critical to ensure that the job analysis approach is compatible and supportive of the company's strategic business directions.[4]

The Components of a Job

A variety of activities are involved in performing any job in an organization. Sometimes the activities of two different jobs are extremely similar and other times they are very different. For example, customer service representatives are required to answer phone calls from customers who have problems or complaints and to direct them to the person or area that can solve the problem. Similarly, receptionists and secretaries often serve this same function. However, receptionists and secretaries also may be required to open mail and screen calls—functions that customer service representatives may not be required to perform.

To truly understand a specific job and to be able to make comparisons among or between jobs, anyone analyzing a job should know that it can be broken into several components and arranged into a hierarchy of the work activities. This hierarchy is depicted in Exhibit 6.1. As the exhibit illustrates, the lowest-level component is an

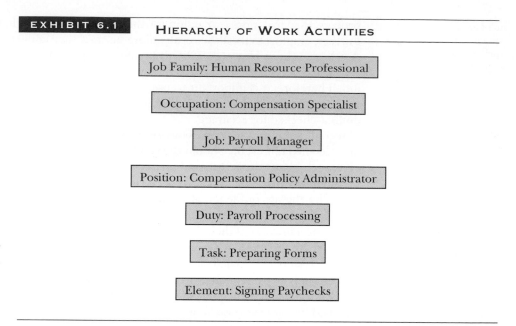

EXHIBIT 6.1   HIERARCHY OF WORK ACTIVITIES

Job Family: Human Resource Professional

Occupation: Compensation Specialist

Job: Payroll Manager

Position: Compensation Policy Administrator

Duty: Payroll Processing

Task: Preparing Forms

Element: Signing Paychecks

element The smallest practical unit into which any work activity can be subdivided.

task An identifiable unit of work activity that is produced through the application of a composite of methods, procedures, and techniques.

duty Several distinct tasks that are performed by an individual to complete a work activity for which he or she is responsible.

position The combination of all the duties required of one person performing a job.

job A group of positions that are similar enough in their job elements, tasks, and duties to be covered by the same job description.

occupation Jobs that are combined across organizations based on the skills, effort, and responsibilities required by the jobs.

element. An **element** can be defined as the smallest practical unit into which any work activity can be subdivided.[5] An example of a job element for a payroll manager is signing the paychecks each pay period. When several elements are combined to produce a predetermined output, an employee has completed a task. A **task** is an identifiable unit of work activity that is produced through the application of a composite of methods, procedures, and techniques.[6] A task for a payroll manager might be preparing the required forms to have the checks cut each pay period.

The next step in the hierarchy of work activities is a **duty**, which can be defined as several distinct tasks that are performed by an individual to complete a work activity for which he or she is responsible. One of the duties of a payroll manager is to process the payroll each pay period. This involves performing all of the elements (e.g., signing the checks) and tasks (e.g., ordering the checks to be printed) required to fulfill this responsibility. The combination of all of the duties required of one person in performing a job is referred to as a **position**. Each person in the organization holds a position. The position of payroll manager could include ensuring the integrity of the data used to compute the amount of pay; verifying the accuracy of the deductions required by the local, state, and federal governments; and physically processing the weekly payroll.

The next level in the hierarchy is a job. A **job** is a group of positions that are similar enough with respect to their job elements, tasks, and duties to be covered by the same job description. More than one person in an organization can hold the same job. For example, several employees in an organization may perform the job of night-shift supervisor. With respect to our payroll example, the job is payroll manager.

An **occupation** is a combination of jobs across organizations based on the skills, effort, and responsibilities required by the jobs. For example, our payroll manager may be called a benefits coordinator in another organization, even though he or she performs the same job elements, tasks, and duties. These two jobs could be grouped

job family A category in which similar occupations are grouped together.

together under the occupation of compensation specialist. Finally, similar occupations can be grouped together into a **job family**.[7] Compensation specialists can be combined with other occupations in the field of human resources (e.g., staffing specialists) and placed into the job family of human resource professional.

Job Analysis

job analysis Collecting data about the jobs performed in an organization.

Simply stated, a **job analysis** involves collecting data about the jobs performed in an organization. However, this definition is probably too simplistic when all of the different types of information that must be collected are considered. For example, the data collected should clearly describe exactly what is required to perform a specific job. This should include the knowledge, skills, and abilities (KSAs) that the incumbent must possess. **Knowledge** is defined as the degree to which a job holder is required to know specific technical material. **Skill** is defined as adequate performance on tasks requiring the use of tools, equipment, and machinery. Finally, **abilities** refer to the physical and mental capacities needed to perform tasks not requiring the use of tools, equipment, or machinery. A frequent addition to the KSAs needed to perform a job is other characteristics. **Other characteristics** include specific requirements needed to perform the job that fall outside the KSA domain. Examples include possessing a particular type of driver's license required by truck drivers or chauffeurs or residency requirements for public employees (e.g., having to live inside the city limits).

knowledge The degree to which a job holder is required to know specific technical material.

skill Adequate performance on tasks requiring the use of tools, equipment, and machinery.

abilities Physical and mental capacities needed to perform tasks not requiring the use of tools, equipment, or machinery

A job analysis also must consider where the job is completed. For example, is the environment dangerous, hot, or isolated? In addition, it is important to determine any machinery or tools that must be used to perform the job. Exhibit 6.2 provides a more complete list of the types of information that should be collected when performing a job analysis. Further information about the job analysis process can be found through the home page for the Society for Human Resource Management (SHRM) at **www.shrm.org.**

Because such a variety of information must be collected when conducting a job analysis, the exact procedures followed will vary from organization to organization and according to the purpose of the analysis. However, there is a series of steps that all job analyses should include. These steps are listed in Exhibit 6.3 and are discussed in the sections that follow.

Step 1—Determine the Purpose for Conducting a Job Analysis

other characteristics Specific requirements needed to perform a job that fall outside the KSA domain (e.g., possessing a certain type of driver's license).

The first decision human resource managers typically make is the purpose for conducting a job analysis. Has the company been experiencing rapid growth or downsizing and, thus, found the need to add to, delete from, or change the current job in any way? Has a merger taken place? Are employee salaries equitable?[8] The purpose for conducting a job analysis should be explicit and tied to the overall strategy of the firm in order to increase the likelihood of a successful job analysis. Making the decision about the purpose of the job analysis will allow managers to also determine the type of information that should be collected. That is, decisions can be made about whether data should be collected on work contexts, work inputs, work outputs, or on all of these components of the job.

Step 2—Identify the Jobs to be Analyzed

The second task managers typically undertake is deciding which jobs need to be analyzed. If a formal job analysis has never been performed, then this task is

EXHIBIT 6.2	TYPES OF INFORMATION TO BE COLLECTED BY A JOB ANALYSIS

Work Activities

- Job-oriented activities (description of the work activities performed, expressed in "job" terms, usually indicating what is accomplished, such as galvanizing, weaving, cleaning, and so on; sometimes such activity descriptions also indicate how, why, and when a worker performs an activity; usually the activities are those involving active human participation, but in certain instances they may characterize machine or system functions).
- Work activities/processes.
- Procedures used.
- Activity records (such as films).
- Personal accountability/responsibility.

Worker-Oriented Activities

- Human behaviors performed in work (such as sensing, decision making, performing physical actions, or communicating).
- Elemental motions (such as those used in time and motion studies).
- Personal job demands (human expenditures involved in work, such as energy expenditure).

Machines, Tools, Equipment, and Work Aids Used

- Computers (hardware and software).
- Safety equipment (goggles and gloves).
- Office tools (phone, fax, and books).

Job-Related Tangibles and Intangibles

- Materials processed.
- Products made.
- Knowledge dealt with or applied (such as law or chemistry).
- Services rendered (such as laundering or repairing).

Work Performance

- Work measurements (i.e., time taken).
- Work standards.
- Error analysis.
- Other aspects.

Job Context

- Physical working conditions.
- Work schedule.
- Organized context.
- Social context.
- Incentives (financial and nonfinancial).

Personal Requirements

- Job-related knowledge and/or skills (such as education, training, or work experience required).
- Personal attributes (such as aptitudes, physical characteristics, personality, interests required).

SOURCE: Adapted from J. McCormick, "Job and Task Analysis," in *Handbook of Industrial and Organizational Psychology* (Chicago: Rand McNally College Publishing Company, 1976), pp. 652–653.

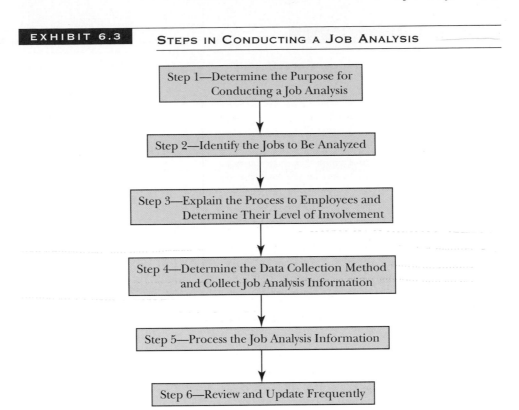

EXHIBIT 6.3   STEPS IN CONDUCTING A JOB ANALYSIS

Step 1—Determine the Purpose for Conducting a Job Analysis

Step 2—Identify the Jobs to Be Analyzed

Step 3—Explain the Process to Employees and Determine Their Level of Involvement

Step 4—Determine the Data Collection Method and Collect Job Analysis Information

Step 5—Process the Job Analysis Information

Step 6—Review and Update Frequently

easy—analyze all of the jobs. If, however, the organization has undergone any changes that have affected only certain jobs, or new jobs have been added, then managers must pinpoint the exact jobs to be analyzed. Also, existing jobs that have a high turnover rate may benefit from a job analysis. The turnover rate may indicate that the job has grown too complex and may need to be modified.

Step 3—Explain the Process to Employees and Determine Their Level of Involvement

The purpose of conducting a job analysis should not be kept from the employees and managers. They should be informed of who will be conducting the analysis, why the job analysis is needed, whom to contact if they have questions or concerns, the schedule or timetable of events, and their role in the job analysis. Too often employees are uncertain about these issues and begin to feel that their jobs are being threatened. To reduce any anxiety employees may be experiencing, communication is of the utmost importance. If anxieties and uncertainties exist among employees, accurate job analysis information will be difficult to obtain. Another means of reducing anxiety and adding validity to the process is to form a committee (elected by the employees) to represent various jobs and to verify that the job analysis information gathered is accurate. These elected committee members also can help answer questions and concerns employees may have.

Step 4—Determine the Data Collection Method and Collect Job Analysis Information

The fourth step consists of actually collecting the job analysis information. Managers must decide which method or combination of methods will be used and how to

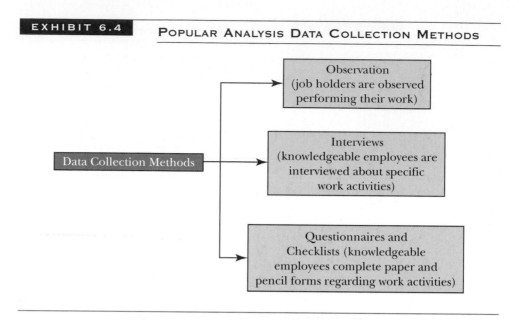

EXHIBIT 6.4   POPULAR ANALYSIS DATA COLLECTION METHODS

collect the information. Once this has been determined, managers must make sure that the information collected is complete. If additional information is required for purposes of clarification, it is best to go back immediately and gather it while the job analysis issues are still salient to employees.

Because the information needed to be collected about a job varies depending on the purposes to be served by the organization, a number of methods can be used to collect job analysis information. Managers should consider using a number of different methods of data collection because it is unlikely that any one method will provide all the necessary information needed for a job analysis. The use of multiple methods to collect job analysis data provides a means of cross-checking the accuracy of the data collected. The information collected from incumbents may not be completely accurate for a variety of reasons. First, incumbents may not recall all of the components of their jobs during an interview because performance of the same job for an extended period of time often causes it to become rote. Employees may try to inflate the importance of their jobs in order to appear more valuable to the organization to ensure job security or to seek a salary increase. Also, people mold the jobs they do to fit themselves. Therefore conflicting responses may be obtained from people performing the same job. Finally, none of these responses may describe the performance of a job exactly the way the company would like it to be performed.

Three of the most popular forms of data collection include (1) observation of tasks and behaviors of the job holders, (2) interviews, and (3) questionnaires and checklists. These are summarized in Exhibit 6.4 and are discussed in the following sections.

observation method A method of job analysis in which job holders are observed performing their work.

Observation   To collect job analysis data via the **observation method**, job holders are observed performing their work. Observation may be continuous or intermittent based on work sampling (observing only a sampling of tasks performed). For many jobs, observation may be of limited usefulness because the job does not consist of physically active tasks. For example, observing a bookkeeper reviewing reports or filling out forms may not lead to very valuable information about the job. Thus observation is most useful when the job is composed of physically active tasks, such as those performed by an assembler on an automobile production line or a receptionist handling phone calls and visitors. However, even with more active jobs, observation does not always reveal vital information, such as the importance or difficulty of the tasks. Given the limitations of using observation as the only data collection method for job analysis, it is helpful to incorporate additional methods for obtaining job analysis information. Observation is most helpful to managers or job analysts as a means to gain a general familiarity with the job.

One specific job analysis method that uses observation is the **critical incident method**. To use this method, incumbents, supervisors, or other "experts" are asked to recall incidents that they witnessed (i.e., observed) that they consider critical to a successful job performance.

This approach focuses on the things a worker does (incidents) that distinguish that person as an effective or ineffective employee. To be considered critical, an incident must occur in a situation in which the intent of the act seems clear to the observer and its consequences leave little doubt about the effects. The data collection process results in a mass of incidents descriptive of effective and ineffective job behaviors in critical situations. In addition, they describe behaviors that reflect outstanding versus poor performance on the job. These incident descriptions are examined and put into job dimension categories that characterize particular facets of job performance. The critical incident approach is frequently used to support the competencies approach to job analysis.[9] The competency approach is broader and more behavioral oriented than traditional job analysis approaches. This approach separates the "can-do" competencies (KSAOs) from the "will-do" competencies, or the behavioral component (motivation and willingness to perform).[10] The competency approach was introduced as a means of supporting the strategic direction the firm adopted.

Interviewing To collect job analysis data via the **interview method**, employees knowledgeable about a particular job (for example, job holders, supervisors, or individuals who have worked on the job before) are interviewed about the specific work activities that the job comprises. Usually a structured interview form is used to record information. Exhibit 6.5 is a sample structured interview form used to collect data.

Interviewing can be a rather time consuming and thus costly method of data collection. For example, if a company has 25 jobs and two people are interviewed for each job for 30 minutes, the time involved in the interview process alone is a minimum of 25 hours, not counting the interviewer's time. Managerial and professional jobs are more complicated and may require between one and two hours of interviewing. There are also costs involved in training interviewers to perform the job analysis interviews, transcribing the interviews, and then evaluating the content. Given the time-consuming nature of interviews, managers and job analysts might prefer to use the interview as a means to answer specific queries generated from observations and questionnaires.

Questionnaires and Checklists If the **questionnaire or checklist data collection method** is used, a list of all of the possible tasks that are performed in a job must be generated. Then, at least one employee knowledgeable about the job completes the questionnaire. It is desirable to have two or even three people complete the questionnaire for purposes of verification. The use of questionnaires and checklists is most efficient when a large number of employees are involved or when a number of widely dispersed employees are to be questioned about their jobs. The questionnaire allows

---

critical incident method One job analysis method that uses observation of "critical" incidents.

interview method Employees knowledgeable about a particular job are interviewed about the specific work activities that the job comprises.

questionnaire or checklist data collection method An inexpensive way to collect information about a job wherein a detailed list of all tasks performed in a job is compiled and given to at least one employee knowledgeable about the job.

EXHIBIT 6.5	JOB ANALYSIS STRUCTURED INTERVIEW FORM

Name _____ Age _____

Date _____ _____ Length of Time with Company

_____

Present Job Title and Grade _____

Dept. _____ Section or Group _____ Supervisor's Name _____

_____

1. Purpose of job: _____

_____

_____

_____

2. Describe major duties of your job: _____

_____

_____

_____

3. Other, less important job duties: _____

_____

_____

_____

4. Machines or equipment used:	*Continually*	*Frequently*	*Occasionally*
_____	_____	_____	_____
_____	_____	_____	_____
_____	_____	_____	_____

for a relatively quick and inexpensive way to collect information about the job. Additional data collection is often necessary if some questions need clarification or some information is missing. Follow-up observations and interviews are not uncommon if a questionnaire or checklist is chosen as the primary means for collecting the job analysis information.

Questionnaires and checklists provide the employee with a simplified method for providing important information. The difficulty arises in constructing a structured questionnaire. It must be extremely detailed and comprehensive so that valuable information is not missed. Obviously, management must decide whether the benefits of

EXHIBIT 6.6	PREFABRICATED JOB ANALYSIS QUESTIONNAIRES AND CHECKLISTS

Job-Element Method (JEM)

Developed by Ernest Primoff; establishes selection standards and validates selection tests for jobs in the federal government.

Ability Requirement Scales (ARS)

Developed by Edwin Fleishman; lists 50 physical and nonphysical abilities that may be necessary for performing a job.

Comprehensive Occupational Data Analysis Program (CODAP)

Includes task checklists for 216 of the 240 Air Force specialties.

Position Analysis Questionnaire (PAQ)

Developed by Ernest J. McCormick and his colleagues; consists of 194 elements that are grouped within 6 major divisions and 28 sections.

Management Position Description Questionnaire (MPDQ)

Developed by Walter W. Tornow and Patrick R. Pinto; includes 208 items that describe a manager's job.

Functional Job Analysis (FJA)

Developed by Sidney Fine; produces information about what a worker does and how a task is performed.

Common-Metric Questionnaire (CMQ)

Developed by Robert J. Harvey; is comprehensive enough to be used with any job found in any organization.

---

a simplified method of data collection outweigh the costs of its construction. Strategically, managers would most likely favor methods of data collection that do not require much work up front if the content of jobs changes frequently. However, another option might be to adopt an existing structured questionnaire. Exhibit 6.6 lists a variety of prefabricated job analysis questionnaires and checklists that can be used to perform a job analysis. Each of these is briefly discussed in the following sections.

job-element method A method of job analysis that yields worker-oriented information.

Job-Element Method   The Civil Service has used the **job-element method** to identify the worker characteristics associated with effective performance. People familiar with the job identify the KSAs and personal traits (job elements) needed to perform the job. As Exhibit 6.7 illustrates, each of these job elements is rated on four scales: barely acceptable (number of barely acceptable workers who have this element), superior (can element distinguish between superior and inferior employees?), trouble likely (probability of trouble occurring if an employee does not have the element), and practical (practicality of expecting to find people with the element). The job-element method helps the human resource manager decide whether the element is a characteristic workers must have before beginning the job or whether it is an element likely to require training.

Ability Requirement Scales   The **Ability Requirement Scales** focus on worker characteristics rather than job characteristics. Unlike the job-element method,

EXHIBIT 6.7	JOB-ELEMENT INSTRUMENTS

Rater's Name and Grade
Job Rated: Title and Grade

Element	Barely Acceptable Workers 2 All Have 1 Some Have 0 Almost None Have	To Pick Out Superior Worker 2 Very Important 1 Valuable 0 Does Not Differentiate	Trouble Likely if Not Considered 2 Much Trouble 1 Some Trouble 0 Safe to Ignore	Practicality Demanding This Element 2 All Openings 1 Some Openings 0 Almost No Openings
Ability to add 2-digit numbers	2	0	2	2
Can cook hamburger	0	1	1	0
Can scrub floors, etc.	1	1	1	2

Ability Requirement Scales A method of job analysis that focuses on worker characteristics rather than on job characteristics.

however, the scales in this technique yield standardized information. Tasks are described, contrasted, and compared in terms of the abilities that a given task requires of the performer. These abilities are relatively enduring traits of the employee performing the task. An assumption is made that each task requires specific abilities for effective performance. Tasks requiring similar abilities are placed in the same category.

Abilities are listed under perceptual-motor, physical performance, and cognitive domains. Behaviorally anchored scales define the abilities to be rated. Specifically, a set of behaviorally anchored scales measures how much each of 37 abilities is needed to perform the job. For example, the verbal comprehension ability has behavioral anchors that range from "understanding a comic book" to "understanding in its entirety a mortgage contract for a new home."

Comprehensive Occupational Data Analysis Program (CODAP) A structured job analysis questionnaire consisting of a list of tasks relevant to some occupational area.

Comprehensive Occupational Data Analysis Program The **Comprehensive Occupational Data Analysis Program (CODAP)** is a structured job analysis questionnaire consisting of a list of tasks relevant to some occupational area. This instrument uses job "experts" (individuals familiar with the content of the jobs) to create a list of tasks and then rate each task according to the relative amount of time spent on it. Because the list of tasks involved in the performance of a job is likely to differ across jobs, task inventories must be developed separately for each occupational area. These ratings are entered into a computer (CODAP is a computer program that summarizes job analysis ratings), analyzed, and converted into job dimensions. The Air Force has used task inventories successfully for years to monitor the changes that occur in jobs as a result of technological or personal changes.

Position Analysis Questionnaire (PAQ) A questionnaire that contains 194 job elements an employee rates by judging the degree to which an element is present.

Position Analysis Questionnaire The **Position Analysis Questionnaire (PAQ)** contains 194 job elements. Employees familiar with a particular job rate it on the 194 descriptors by judging the degree to which an element (or descriptor) is present. These elements are grouped into six general categories.[11] Exhibit 6.8 describes the categories and gives examples of rating scales used to collect information and rate jobs. The PAQ has been researched thoroughly and enables a statistical comparison

| EXHIBIT 6.8 | POSITION ANALYSIS QUESTIONNAIRE (PAQ) |

Organization of the PAQ

The job elements in the PAQ are organized in six divisions as follows (examples of two job elements from each division are included):

1. *Information input.* (Where and how does the worker get the information he or she uses in performing his or her job?)
   Examples: Use of written materials
   Near-visual differentiation
2. Mental processes. (What reasoning, decision-making, planning, and information-processing activities are involved in performing the job?)
   Examples: Level of reasoning in problem solving
   Coding/decoding
3. *Work output.* (What physical activities does the worker perform, and what tools or devices does he or she use?)
   Examples: Using keyboard devices
   Assembling/disassembling
4. *Relationships with other persons.* (What relationships with other people are required in performing the job?)
   Examples: Instruction
   Contact with public, customers
5. *Job context.* (In what physical or social contexts is the work performed?)
   Examples: High temperature
   Interpersonal conflict situations
6. *Other job characteristics.* (What activities, conditions, or characteristics other than those described above are relevant to the job?)

Rating Scales Used with the PAQ

There is a provision for rating each job on each job element. Six types of rating scales are used:

Letter Identification	Type of Rating Scale
U	Extent of Use
I	Importance to the Job
T	Amount of Time
P	Possibility of Occurrence
A	Applicability
S	Special Code (used in the case of a few specific job elements)

A specific rating scale is designated to be used with each job element, in particular the scale considered most appropriate to the content of the element. All but the "A" (Applicability) scale are 6-point scales, and "0" (which is coded as "N") is for "Does not apply," as illustrated below:

Rating	Importance to the Job
N	Does not apply
1	Very minor (importance)
2	Low
3	Average
4	High
5	Extreme

SOURCE: Reprinted by permission from Ernest J. McCormick, *Job Analysis: Methods and Applications*, copyright Pudue Research Foundation.

of the dimensions of jobs in an organization to be made. Responses to the PAQ can be sent to PAQ Services in Logan, Utah, for scoring. This analysis provides an estimate of worker attributes predictive of success in a particular job. In addition, this analysis provides a comparison of a specific job with other job classifications. The use of the PAQ is not as widespread as one might believe because above-average reading skills are necessary to use it.

Management Position Description Questionnaire (MPDQ) Thirteen factors used to describe managerial jobs.

Management Position Description Questionnaire An instrument similar to the PAQ has been developed to describe managerial jobs. The **Management Position Description Questionnaire (MPDQ)** developed the 13 factors shown in Exhibit 6.9 that may be used to describe managerial jobs. These factors resulted from a 208-item questionnaire completed by 434 managers.

functional job analysis (FJA) A method of job analysis in which the functions of a job can be examined in relation to three classifications: data, people, and things.

Functional Job Analysis Functional job analysis (FJA) is an instrument that examines the functions of a job in relation to three classifications: data, people, and things. Within each of these classifications are degrees or levels with corresponding numbers (Exhibit 6.10). The lower the number, the more the job is involved with that particular function.

Common-Metric Questionnaire (CMQ) One of the newest job-analysis packages available, designed to be completed by the job expert and a job analysis administrator.

Common-Metric Questionnaire The **Common-Metric Questionnaire (CMQ)** is one of the newest job analysis packages available for sale. Designed to be useful for any job in any organization, the CMQ is completed by the job expert (i.e., incumbent, supervisor, or job analyst), but some sections must be completed by a job analysis administrator. The CMQ is divided into five sections with between 41 and 80 questions in each section. The respondent reads each question and determines whether it is applicable to his or her job. If it is not, it is simply skipped. If it is applicable, then various other questions pertaining to that one item also must be answered. Because the questionnaire is designed to cover every possible job in an organization, some (many) of the items may be irrelevant to the position being analyzed. However, the respondent must first read each item to determine whether it is relevant. Thus a great deal of time may be required to complete the entire list of questions. Further information about the CMQ can be found on Robert Harvey's Web site at **harvey.psyc.vt.edu**.

Step 5—Process the Job Analysis Information

Once the job analysis information has been collected, it is important to place it into a form that will be useful to managers and human resource departments. One way to do this is to develop a specialized form on which the job analysis results can be printed. Using a form for reporting the results serves several purposes. First, it can be used as a step to verify that all required information has been collected. If during the transfer process a blank on the form cannot be completed, it becomes obvious that more data must be collected. Also, a standardized reporting format makes it easy for a manager to compare several different jobs to a specific criterion of interest. All he or she has to do is focus on the fields on the form that are of concern and compare them across the different jobs analyzed.

Step 6—Review and Update Frequently

The final step is actually an ongoing phenomenon. Given that organizations are dynamic, jobs seldom go unchanged for very long. Managers and personnel specialists need to review job descriptions and specifications frequently. This review should be

| EXHIBIT 6.9 | MANAGEMENT POSITION DESCRIPTION QUESTIONNAIRE (MPDQ) FACTORS |

1. *Product, Marketing, and Financial Strategy Planning:* Indicates long-range thinking and planning. The incumbent's concerns are broad and oriented toward the future. They may include such areas as long-range business potential, organizational objectives, company solvency, business activities the company should engage in, and new idea evaluation.

2. *Coordination of Other Organization Units and Personnel:* The incumbent coordinates the efforts of others over whom he or she exercises no direct control, handles conflicts or disagreements when necessary, and works in an environment where he or she must cut across existing organizational boundaries.

3. *Internal Business Control:* The incumbent exercises business controls, that is, reviews and controls the allocation of human and other resources. Activities and concerns are in the area of assignments of supervisory responsibility, expense control, cost reduction, setting of performance goals, preparation and review of budgets, protection of the company's monies and properties, and employee relations practices.

4. *Products and Services Responsibility:* Activities and concerns of the incumbent in technical areas related to products, services, and their marketability. Specifically included are the planning, scheduling, and monitoring of products and services delivery along with keeping track of their quality and costs. The incumbent is concerned with promises that are difficult to meet, anticipates new or changed demands for the products and services, and closely maintains the progress of specific projects.

5. *Public and Customer Relations:* A general responsibility for the reputation of the company's product and services. The incumbent is concerned with promoting the company's products and services, the goodwill of the company in the community, and general public relations. The position involves firsthand contact with the customer, frequent contact and negotiation with representatives from other organizations, and understanding the needs of customers.

6. *Advanced Consulting:* The incumbent is asked to apply technical expertise to special problems, issues, questions, or policies. The incumbent should have an understanding of advanced principles, theories, and concepts in more than one required field. He or she is often asked to apply highly advanced techniques and methods to address issues and questions, which very few people in the company can do.

7. *Autonomy of Action:* The incumbent has a considerable amount of discretion in the handling of a job, engaging in activities that are not closely supervised or controlled, and making decisions that are often not subject to review. The incumbent may have to handle unique problems, know how to ask key questions even on subject matters with which he or she is not intimately familiar, and engage in free-wheeling or unstructured thinking to deal with problems that are themselves abstract or unstructured.

8. *Approval of Financial Commitments:* The incumbent has the authority to approve large financial commitment and obligate the company. The incumbent may make final and, for the most part, irreversible decisions, negotiate with representatives from other organizations, and make many important decisions on almost a daily basis.

9. *Staff Service:* The incumbent renders various staff services to supervisors. Such activities can include fact gathering, data acquisition and compilation, and record keeping.

10. *Supervision:* The incumbent plans, organizes, and controls the work of others. The activities require face-to-face contact with subordinates on almost a daily basis. The concerns revolve around getting work done efficiently through the effective utilization of people.

11. *Complexity and Stress:* The incumbent has to operate under pressure. This may include activities of handling information under time pressure to meet deadlines, frequently taking risks, and interfering with personal or family life.

12. *Advanced Financial Responsibility:* Activities and responsibilities concerned with preserving assets, making investment decisions, and making other large-scale financial decisions that affect the company's performance.

13. *Broad Personnel Responsibility:* The incumbent has broad responsibility for the management of human resources and the policies affecting them.

SOURCE: Adapted from W. W. Tornow and P. R. Pinto, "The Development of a Managerial Job Taxonomy: A System for Describing, Classifying, and Evaluating Executive Positions," *Journal of Applied Psychology* (1976), pp. 61, 410–418.

EXHIBIT 6.10	FUNCTIONAL JOB ANALYSIS CLASSIFICATIONS	
Data	**People**	**Things**
0 Synthesizing	0 Mentoring	0 Setting Up
1 Coordinating	1 Negotiating	1 Precision Working
2 Analyzing	2 Instructing	2 Operating–Controlling
3 Compiling	3 Supervising	3 Driving–Controlling
4 Computing	4 Diverting	4 Manipulating
5 Copying	5 Persuading	5 Tending
6 Comparing	6 Speaking–Signaling	6 Feeding–Offbearing
	7 Serving	7 Handling
	8 Taking Instructions–Helping	

SOURCE: *United States Department of Labor, Dictionary of Occupational Titles*, 4th ed. (Washington, DC: United States Government Printing Office, 1977) p. xviii.

done with an eye on the corporate strategy. If there have been shifts in the strategic focus of the organization, then changes in the job requirements might be needed to reach the organization's strategic goals. The job analysis process can be time consuming and costly. Thus it is to the organization's advantage to update information on all jobs rather than repeat the entire process in a few years. If no major changes have occurred within the organization, then a complete review of all jobs should be performed every three years.[12] Obviously, more frequent reviews are necessary if organizational changes occur.

Job Analysis Data Output

job description
Description of the duties, responsibilities, working conditions, and activities of a particular job.

The data collected from the job analysis can be used for a variety of purposes. One of the most important is in writing job descriptions and job specifications. **Job descriptions** describe the duties, responsibilities, working conditions, and activities of a particular job. A sample job description is shown in Exhibit 6.11. **Job specifications** describe employee qualifications, such as experience, knowledge, skills, or abilities, that are required to perform the job.

Job Description

job specification
Description of employee qualifications, such as experience, knowledge, skills, or abilities, that are required to perform a particular job.

Job descriptions vary in terms of the level of detail provided. However, several components are present in virtually every job description. For example, the title of the job is always provided. It is important that the title be descriptive of the job so that people reading it immediately understand what the job entails. Some type of summary that describes the work performed in the job and the worker requirements also are extremely important to include in the job description. Other sections frequently found in a job description include a job summary (a paragraph that provides an overall description of the job), a separate section for each KSAO that specifically states what is required by the job, importance ratings for the KSAOs, and the date the job analysis was conducted.

EXHIBIT 6.11	SAMPLE JOB DESCRIPTION

Job Title	Comp Admin	Structure	US Exempt Admin
Job Code	399	Country Code	USA
Job Status	Active	Country	United States
Effective Date	09/01/99	Mgr Status	Non-Manager

Basic Function:

Under general supervision, responsible for performing staff support activities to develop, implement, and administer compensation policies and programs. Conducts special studies and recommendations on subjects such as incentive compensation, bonus plans, sales compensation, stock option programs, etc. Reviews requests for new or revised classifications to determine appropriate salary grade assignment.

Duties and Responsibilities:

Section 1—For Use by Non-U.S. & U.S. (U.S.-ADA Essential)   % Work Time

1. Formulates recommendations regarding development of company salary structure, FLSA exemptions, job revisions, organizational structures, etc. — 10

2. Analyzes competitive salary information to determine company's competitive positions. — 10

3. Counsels management regarding proposed salary adjustments for conformance to established guidelines, policies, and practices. — 15

4. Conducts special compensation and HR studies and analyses. — 20

5. Administers job evaluation process; evaluates level of job responsibilities, activities, duties, and requirements in order to equitably place into established grade structure. — 10

6. Administers stock option grant process. — 10

7. Assures proper HRIS and personnel file records are maintained and provides work direction to the HRIS records coordinator. — 15

Section 2—For Use by U.S. Only (ADA Non-Essential)

1. Completes surveys. — 5

2. Performs related duties as required. — 5

*Note: Percent of Work Time must equal 100%   **100%**

Knowledge and Skills Required:

Education/Training/Work Experience:
Bachelor's Degree or equivalent in Business, Human Resources or related field.
Special Knowledge & Skills:
Mathematical aptitude; good working knowledge of HR/personnel practices and principles, especially in the area of state and federal laws pertaining to compensation; good analysis skills; and ability to communicate effectively orally and in writing. Strong interpersonal skills in dealing with all levels of personnel and management.

Scope of Responsibilities:

(Budget/Dollars and People—Organizational and Functional)

EXHIBIT 6.12   JOB TITLE AND DESCRIPTION FROM DICTIONARY OF
OCCUPATIONAL TITLES

166.117-018 Manager, Personnel (Profess. & Kin.)

Plans and carries out policies relating to all phases of personnel activity. Recruits, interviews, and selects employees to fill vacant positions. Plans and conducts new employee orientation to foster positive attitude toward company goals. Keeps record of insurance coverage, pension plan, and personnel transactions, such as hires, promotions, transfers, and terminations. Investigates accident and prepares reports for insurance carrier. Conducts wage survey within labor market to determine competitive wage rate. Prepares budget of personnel operations. Meets with shop stewards and supervisors to resolve grievances. Writes separation notices for employees separating with cause and conducts exit interviews to determine reasons behind separations. Prepares reports and recommends procedures to reduce absenteeism and turnover. Contracts with outside suppliers to provide employee services, such as canteen, transportation, or relocation service. May keep records of hired employee characteristics for governmental reporting purposes. May negotiate collective bargaining agreement with BUSINESS REPRESENTATION LABOR UNION (profess. & kin.).

SOURCE: United States Department of Labor, *Dictionary of Occupational Titles*, 4th ed. (Washington, DC: United States Government Printing Office, 1977), p. 98.

Dictionary of Occupational Titles (DOT)
A valuable source for locating standardized job descriptions, published by the U.S. Department of Labor and providing information on more than 12,000 occupations.

One valuable source for locating standardized job descriptions is the **Dictionary of Occupational Titles (DOT)**. The U.S. Department of Labor publishes the DOT, which provides information on over 12,000 occupations. The job description for a personnel manager from the DOT is presented in Exhibit 6.12.

The numbers next to the job title (166.117-018) are important for using the information in the DOT. The first three numbers (166) represent the occupational code, title, and industry, respectively. The next three numbers (117) represent the degree to which a typical human resource manager is involved with data, people, and things, respectively. The final three numbers indicate the alphabetical order of job titles within the same occupational grouping that have the same involvement over data, people, and things. The DOT job descriptions are endorsed by the federal government.

Managers can adapt the standardized job descriptions from the DOT to the specific jobs within their firm. The DOT is particularly useful when a large number of jobs needs to be analyzed. Rather than "starting from scratch," managers can use the DOT as a guide. The DOT may also prove invaluable to managers who are not human resource specialists.

The DOT will eventually be replaced by O*NET. O*NET, the Occupational Information Network, is a comprehensive database of worker attributes and job characteristics. The goal of O*NET is to be the nation's primary source of occupational information. O*NET is a user-friendly resource for public and private firms striving to develop their workforce's skills. Like the DOT, a variety of jobs are indexed in O*NET along with the required KSAs for these jobs. For more information about O*NET, visit their Web site at **www.onetcenter.org**.

Job Specification

The personal qualifications an employee must possess in order to perform the duties and responsibilities depicted in the job description are contained in the job specifications. Typically, job specifications detail the knowledge, skills, and abilities relevant to

EXHIBIT 6.13   JOB SPECIFICATION

Department: Executive President's Office   *Job Title:* Executive Secretary
Reports to: President

Required Knowledge, Skills, and Abilities:

1. Knowledge of office routines and procedures.
2. Knowledge of the executive secretarial field.
3. Skill in the operation of computerized office equipment.
4. Skill in typing, filing, answering the telephone, and composing routine letters and reports.
5. Ability to act as a liaison between company officials, board members, customer executives, and state and federal government officials when president is out of town.
6. Ability to plan and prioritize work.

---

a job, including the education, experience, specialized training, personal traits, and manual dexterity required. A sample job specification is provided in Exhibit 6.13. At times, an organization may also include the physical demands the job places on an employee.[13] The physical demands of a job might include the amount of walking, standing, reaching, or lifting that is required of the employee. In addition, the condition of the physical work environment and the hazards employees may encounter may be included among the physical demands of a job.

The job specification is important for a number of reasons. First, certain jobs have qualifications required by law. For example, airline pilots, attorneys, and medical doctors all need to be licensed. Another type of job specification is based on professional tradition. For example, university professors must usually hold a Ph.D. or equivalent degree if they are going to be in a tenure-track position. Whether having a Ph.D. or its equivalent is important for teaching and research is still debatable and has not been empirically verified beyond question. Finally, job specifications might involve establishing certain standards or criteria that are deemed necessary for successful performance. This depends primarily, however, on the judgment of the employer.

For example, secretarial and clerical workers may be required to demonstrate typing speeds in excess of 100 to 120 words per minute. Management positions may be available only to those applicants with at least three to five years of experience in a similar position. It is important to remember, however, that these job specifications must be linked directly to the job description. Specifically, job specifications must be job relevant. It is also important to keep the firm's strategic plan in mind. Including job specifications that will support the successful implementation of this plan is essential.

The Americans with Disabilities Act (ADA) of 1991 has had a significant impact on the development of job descriptions and job specifications. ADA prohibits employers from discriminating against qualified individuals with disabilities. Specifically, a qualified individual with a disability refers to someone who can, with or without "reasonable accommodation," perform the "essential functions" of the job. Reasonable accommodation refers to any accommodation that does not impose an undue hardship on the business. These can include lowering counters, installing ramps and lever door knobs, or providing interpreters. The essential functions of a job are the fundamental job duties required of the position as determined by the employer. The essential job duties traditionally are identified by a job analysis and then are documented in the job description and the job specifications. Job analysis outputs can be used to illustrate the job relatedness of the job requirements and to help establish the

EXHIBIT 6.14	TRADITIONAL USES OF JOB ANALYSIS INFORMATION	
	Programs for Salary Rated	**Programs for Hourly Rated**
Job Evaluation	98%	95%
Recruitment, Selection, and Placement	95	92
Labor and Human Resource Relations	83	79
Utilizing Human Resources	72	67
Training and Development	61	63

SOURCE: Jean L. Jones, Jr. and Thomas A Decoths, "Job Analysis: National Survey Findings," copyright May 1974.

business necessity of these requirements.[14] Both steps are critical to complying with ADA. Thus, in order to comply fully with ADA, a firm must know the job, and job analysis is the best way to do this.

Uses of Job Analysis Data

Once the job analysis has been conducted, the data can be applied to a variety of human resource functions. Exhibit 6.14 describes the traditional ways in which the results from a job analysis can be used; the following sections describe them in more detail.

Job Evaluation

The information gathered during a job analysis can be used as input for the organization's job evaluation system. The job evaluation determines the worth of a particular job to the organization. This information is primarily used to determine the pay for the job. Thus employees should be paid more for working on more difficult jobs. Job analysis information is instrumental in determining which jobs contain more difficult tasks, duties, and responsibilities. This is discussed further in Chapter 11 on compensation systems.

Recruitment, Selection, and Placement

A good job analysis should provide information useful in planning for recruitment, selection, and placement. This information coupled with the firm's strategic plan will allow managers to plan for the staffing of their organizations. Further, selecting an individual for a job requires a thorough understanding of the type of work to be done and the qualifications necessary to perform the work. Selecting individuals to fill positions is effective only if there is a clear and accurate understanding of what the job entails. Job analysis information is also useful for detecting unnecessary job requirements. For example, a manager for a manufacturing plant may be able to hold recruiting and salary costs down if the job analysis reveals that it is not necessary for first-line supervisors to have a college degree. Finally, placing employees into jobs by means of promotions and transfers is made easier if the details of what the job entails are known and the qualifications necessary to do the job are well understood.

Labor and Human Resource Relations

Information generated from the job analysis can help both labor and management understand what should be expected from each job incumbent and how much employees should be compensated for performing a particular job. Obviously, the information generated from the job analysis is most beneficial if it is clearly communicated to both employees and management. This communication can help alleviate perceived inequities among employees. For example, many employees would like to know why their jobs do not pay as well as other jobs. Much of the controversy about comparable worth revolves around this issue. Comparable worth is discussed in more detail in Chapter 5.

Utilizing Human Resources

All managers would like to utilize their employees optimally. However, performance appraisals often reveal that many employees are not adequately performing their jobs. Job analysis information can help both employees and managers pinpoint the root of the problem. By comparing what the employee is supposed to be doing with what the employee is actually doing, supervisors can determine whether the employee is performing adequately and, if not, what areas need improvement. Sharing this information with the employee can be enlightening for both parties. Employees may not have realized what was expected of them and what their work role entailed. Thus job analysis information can help clear up any uncertainties employees might have regarding their work performance and work role.

Training and Development

Job analysis information also can be useful for training and development needs. By clearly depicting what the job entails and what qualifications are necessary to do the job, managers should be able to discover any qualification deficiencies. Most deficiencies are probably best remedied by training or retraining employees. In addition to identifying training needs, job analysis information is helpful in career development. Specifically, managers will be able to tell employees what will be expected if the employee desires a transfer or promotion. This information can help employees prepare for career advancement.

Another development opportunity organizations can offer is to encourage employees to sit for certification exams. SHRM offers two levels of certification, Professional in Human Resources (PHR) and Senior Professional in Human Resources (SPHR). HR professionals also can be certified in compensation. Job analysis plays an important role in the development of certification exams. For example, the National Association of Purchasing Management (NAPM) recently revised its Certified Purchasing Manager (CPM) exam.[15] The revisions were based on a comprehensive job analysis conducted to gather current information from purchasing professionals in the field. The main reason for revamping the exam was to broaden the scope of tasks completed in this profession and to make the focus of the exam more strategic in nature. Neither of these goals could have been accomplished without a thorough job analysis.

Organization Strategy and Job Analysis

All of the job analysis methods discussed in this chapter are viable alternatives for the human resource manager. Unfortunately, many methods are chosen simply because the human resource manager is familiar with them. Only a few researchers have discussed job analysis as an activity that can enhance the strategy of an organization.

Given that job analysis provides managers with clear descriptions and specifications about jobs, it is possible to determine which jobs are the most critical for a particular organizational strategy or objective. For example, if management decides to downsize an organization, the information provided by the job analysis should prove invaluable once a company decides which jobs to retain, change, or eliminate. Similarly, an organization with a growth strategy can use this information to identify the areas that need expansion or development.[16]

Management Guidelines

The following strategic guidelines should be examined when deciding whether to conduct a job analysis:

1. The reasons for conducting a job analysis should be clearly specified (such as establishing wage rates or recruiting) to help ensure that all relevant information is examined.
2. The primary purpose for conducting a job analysis should serve as input for the types of information collected (for example, work activities, machines and tools used, or job context).
3. The purpose for the job analysis, the types of information required, the time and cost constraints, the extent of employee involvement, and the level of detail desired should be specified before choosing one or more of the available methods of data collection.
4. The strategy of an organization can influence which human resource activities will be emphasized. In turn, certain human resource activities (such as selection or performance appraisal) may require different job analysis methods.
5. Managers should follow or include the following steps when conducting a job analysis:
   a. Determine the purpose for the job analysis.
   b. Identify the jobs to be analyzed.
   c. Determine the data collection method.
   d. Explain the process to employees and involve them.
   e. Collect job analysis information.
   f. Process the job analysis information.
   g. Review and update frequently.
6. The job analysis should be designed so that job descriptions and job specifications can be derived easily.
7. Managers should communicate all relevant information to employees concerning the job analysis to prevent unnecessary uncertainty and anxiety.
8. If major organizational changes have taken place, managers should consider conducting a job analysis.
9. If major organizational changes are anticipated, managers should consider conducting a more future-oriented job analysis.

Questions for Review

1. Why should managers conduct a job analysis? What purpose does it serve?
2. What are the advantages and disadvantages of using each of the described data collection methods?
3. What are the steps in the job analysis process?

4. What are the pros and cons of involving employees in the job analysis process?
5. What is a future-oriented job analysis? When would you want to use it?
6. What are job descriptions and job specifications? What is their relationship to the job analysis?
7. How often should a job analysis be conducted?
8. What are the various methods of job analysis?
9. Under what conditions should each of these job analysis methods be used?

CASE

Job Analysis as a Means of Revamping Training for the Gas Industry in the Netherlands[17]

As the environment in which a business operates changes, so must the business. One industry that experienced tremendous changes in recent years is the gas industry in the Netherlands. Specifically, the distribution processes used by the gas industry were changed so drastically by new technologies that the training programs that were in place to teach gas technicians their jobs became obsolete. In an effort to keep pace with the changes, the gas industry commissioned a group of researchers to develop new training programs. To accomplish this goal, job analysis was used.

The job analysis project was designed around four major questions that needed to be answered:

1. What tasks and subtasks must be performed by specific employees in the gas and energy distribution industry?
2. What knowledge, skills, and abilities (KSAs) are required by these tasks and subtasks?
3. What changes will the tasks outlined go through in the near future?
4. Are there any significant differences between the tasks performed by the gas side of the industry as compared with the energy side?

To answer these questions, a model based on a general job analysis approach was developed. At the heart of this model is an activity, the smallest unit of analysis, which is conceived of as an action directed at the realization of a task. A task, the next level in the hierarchy, is a prescribed activity. Coherent sets of tasks define a job. Jobs can be described in job descriptions, and related jobs can be combined into job families. A job profile is a graph that depicts the relative importance of the tasks accomplished by the employees within a job. The KSAs required by a job can be outlined and presented in a KSA profile. One or more KSA profiles can be used to determine the curriculum required in a course. Courses can be combined to form modules. Each module is oriented toward a specific learning goal and is linked directly to the performance of a task. How well the task is performed after training can be evaluated and compared to a prescribed standard. Once again, all of these components are based on and determined by a job analysis.

Several data collection formats were used to perform the job analysis. First, job experts were interviewed. Qualitative data also were collected by studying documents about jobs, tasks, and the KSAs provided by the gas and energy companies involved. Mailed questionnaires also were used to collect more quantitative data. Each firm involved also was asked to nominate a key informant who could be contacted to fill in the data gaps when needed. The data were collected in a three-stage process.

Stage 1

Interviews were held with each of the key informants to collect data about the structure of the organization, human resource management policies and procedures, jobs and tasks, education levels of the employees, career patterns available for the workers, and the training policies of the firm. The results from the interviews were used to develop the first part of the questionnaire sent out in Stage 2, and written job descriptions provided by the informant were content analyzed and edited to form the second part of the questionnaire. Finally, the training documents available were analyzed to develop the third (i.e., learning goals and course content) and fourth (i.e., inventory of available courses) sections of the survey.

Stage 2

Because of the large number of specific tasks and subtasks identified, the second part of the survey had to be tailored to one of three different job families: logistics, support, and administrative staff; gas-technical specialists, inspection, service, and public relations; and managers, assistants to the managers, and supervisors of technical personnel. However, parts 1, 3, and 4 of the survey were identical for each job analyzed.

Stage 3

The final stage was a conference that included the informants, the course instructors, and key members of the training staffs for each of the firms involved. The preliminary results of the interviews and surveys were presented. The conference attendees were encouraged to modify the proposed course content and procedures to better meet their individual needs.

The end results of the job analysis process were two courses designed to allow the workers to be fully competent in their jobs. The courses were based on learning goals that stressed the KSAs needed to perform the jobs in question. Further, the courses incorporated as much of the existing information and training methods as possible to make the transition process easier for the employees.

Questions for Discussion

1. How did the job analysts go about answering the four major questions that prompted this study?

2. What exactly is a KSA profile and how was it used? How could this profile be used in the other human resource functions, such as selection, compensation, or performance appraisal, that use job analysis as a basis?

3. Using a job you are familiar with, define an activity, a task, a job, and a job profile. For what purposes can these items be used?

4. Although a variety of means of collecting the job analysis data was used in this case, which ones discussed in the text were not applied? Describe how they could have been utilized.

5. This case indicates that a variety of firms that normally competed with one another banned together to develop industrywide courses. What is another industry that could benefit from this type of project?

Additional Readings

Ash, R. A., and S. L. Edgell. "A Note on the Readability of the Position Analysis Questionnaire (PAQ)." *Journal of Applied Psychology* 60 (1975), pp. 765–766.

Cain, P. S., and B. F. Green. "Reliabilities of Selected Ratings Available from the Dictionary of Occupational Titles." *Journal of Applied Psychology* 68 (1983), pp. 155–165.

Conley, P. R., and P. R. Sackett. "Effects of Using High- versus Low-Performing Job Incumbents as Sources of Job-Analysis Information." *Journal of Applied Psychology* 72 (1987), pp. 434–437.

Conway, James M. "Analysis and Design of Multitrait-Multirater Performance Appraisal Studies." *Journal of Management* 22 (1996), pp. 139–163.

DiNisi, A. S.; E. T. Cornelius III; and A. G. Blencoe. "Further Investigation of Common Knowledge Effects on Job Analysis Ratings." *Journal of Applied Psychology* 72 (1987), pp. 262–268.

Dowell, B. E., and K. N. Wexley. "Development of a Work Behavior Taxonomy for First-Line Supervisors." *Journal of Applied Psychology* 63 (1978), pp. 563–572.

Friedman, L., and R. J. Harvey. "Can Raters with Reduced Job Descriptive Information Provide Accurate Position Analysis Questionnaire (PAQ) Ratings?" *Personnel Psychology* 39 (1986), pp. 779–789.

Gael, Sidney. *Job Analysis: A Guide to Assessing Work Activities.* San Francisco, CA: Jossey-Bass, 1983.

Harvey, Robert J.; Lee Friedman; Milton D. Hakel; and Edwin T. Cornelius III. "Dimensionality of the Job Element Inventory. A Simplified Worker-Oriented Job Analysis Questionnaire." *Journal of Applied Psychology* 73, no. 4 (1988), pp. 639–646.

Harvey, Robert J., and Susana R. Lozada-Larsen. "Influence of Amount of Job Descriptive Information on Job Analysis Rating Accuracy." *Journal of Applied Psychology* 73, no. 3 (1988), pp. 457–461.

Harvey, Robert J., and Mark A. Wilson. "Yes, Virginia, There is an Objective Reality in Job Analysis." *Journal of Organizational Behavior* 73, no. 3 (2000), pp. 457–461.

Hunt, Allen H., and Timothy L. Hunt. *Human Resource Implications of Robotics.* Kalamazoo, MI: W. E. Upjohn Institute for Employment Research, 1982.

Levine, E. L.; R. A. Ash; and N. Bennett. "Exploratory Comparative Study of Four Job Analysis Methods." *Journal of Applied Psychology* 65 (1980), pp 524–535.

Levine, E. L.; R. A. Ash; H. Hall; and F. Sistrunk. "Evaluation of Job Analysis Methods by Experienced Job Analysts." *Academy of Management Journal* 26, no. 2 (1983), pp. 339–348.

McCormick, E. J.; P. R. Jeanneret; and R. C. Mecham. "A Study of Job Characteristics and Job Dimensions as Based on the Position Analysis Questionnaire (PAQ)." *Journal of Applied Psychology* 56 (1982), pp. 347–368.

McGregor, Douglas. *Human Side of Enterprise.* New York: McGraw-Hill, 1960.

Miller, A. R.; D. J. Treiman; P. S. Cain; and P. A. Roos, eds. *Work, Jobs, and Occupations: A Critical Review of the Dictionary of Occupational Titles.* Washington, D.C.: National Academy Press, 1980.

Mullins, Wayman C., and Wilson W. Kimbrough. "Group Composition as a Determinant of Job Analysis Outcomes." *Journal of Applied Psychology* 73, no. 4 (1988), pp. 657–664.

Tornow, W. W., and P. R. Pinto. "The Development of a Managerial Taxonomy: A System for Describing, Classifying, and Evaluating Executive Positions." *Journal of Applied Psychology* 61 (1976), pp. 410–418.

Notes

[1] Gary Hoover, Alta Campbell, and Patrick Spain, *Hoover's Handbook of American Business* (Austin, TX: The Reference Press, 1992), p. 568.

[2]"HR's Role in the Reengineering Process," *Personnel Journal*, December 1993, p. 48H.

[3]William J. Rothwell and N. C. Kazanas, *Strategic Human Resource Development* (Englewood Cliffs, NJ: Prentice-Hall, 1989), p. 140.

[4]Jeffery S. Schippmann, *Strategic Job Modeling: Working at the Core of Integrated Human Resources* (Mahwah, NJ: Lawrence Erlbaum Associates, 1999), p. 114.

[5]Richard Henderson, *Compensation Management* (Englewood Cliffs, NJ: Prentice-Hall, 2000), p. 106.

[6]H. L. Ammerman, *Performance Content for Job Training* (Columbus, OH: Center for Vocational Education, Ohio State University, 1977), p. 21.

[7]"Managers Make Pay Decisions through Job Families," *Personnel Journal*, June 1993, p. 64D.

[8]Paul Dorf, "Classify Jobs Properly to Avoid Overtime Trap," *HRMagazine*, April 1994, pp. 29–30.

[9]Kenneth H. Pritchard, "Introduction to Work (Job) Analysis," SHRM White Paper. Available to SHRM members at **www.shrm.whitepapers/documents/61407.asp**.

[10]Schippmann, *Strategic Job Modeling: Working at the Core of Integrated Human Resource*, p.26

[11]Ernest J. McCormick, *Job Analysis: Methods and Applications* (New York: AMACOM, 1979), pp. 144–145.

[12]Robert L. Mathis and John H. Jackson, *Personnel/Human Resource Management* (St. Paul: West, 1985), p. 177.

[13]Kristen Shingleton, "Job Audits as Interviews: Define Physical Requirements," *HR Focus* 69, no. 7 (July 1992), p. 11.

[14]Kenneth H. Pritchard, "ADA Compliance…Job Analysis is Key," SHRM White Paper, available to SHRM members at **www.shrm.whitepapers/documents/61242.asp**.

[15]Kathryn Belyea, "NAPM will roll out revised CPM exam in 2001," *BUYLINES* (Cahners Business Information), p. 32.

[16]J. E. Butler, G. R. Ferris, and N. K. Napier, *Strategy and Human Resources Management* (Cincinnati, OH: South-Western, 1991).

[17]J. M. van der Veen and A. M. Versloot, "A Research-Based Model for Job Analysis," *Journal of European Industrial Training* 17 (1993), pp. 15–23.

7

Recruitment, Selection, and Retention

Chapter Objectives

As a result of studying this chapter, you should be able to

1. Discuss the recruiting methods available to organizations.

2. Understand the selection process organizations use to choose future employees.

3. Describe methods used to retain effective employees.

4. Explain strategies for effective recruitment, selection, and retention.

5. Discuss how an organization's strategy can affect its recruitment and selection process.

Recruiting and selecting the right employees have always been a challenge for managers. For example, when the labor market is tight, there are fewer applicants than positions. This means that companies have to be more creative in their recruiting efforts and offer more benefits—monetary as well as nonmonetary.[1] This also means that retention issues grow in importance. As more and more workers are wooed away by competitors, companies must find ways to make employees want to stay.[2] Approximately 83 percent of new entrants into the labor force will be minorities, immigrants, and women.[3] This diversity among workers will call for new strategies and approaches to recruitment, selection, and retention. This chapter examines these and other important issues in the areas of recruiting, selecting, and retaining employees.

CASE

Xerox Manages Worker Diversity[4]

With the rapidly shifting demographic makeup of the workforce, U.S. corporations are facing an ever-increasing diversity of workers. Between 1986 and 2000 there was a 12 percent drop in the number of Caucasian non-Hispanics entering the labor force. This rate continues to decline. The biggest growth was seen in the number of women entering the workforce (51 percent), followed by Hispanics, the fastest-growing minority with a 15 percent growth rate. Blacks accounted for 13 percent of all new entering employees, whereas Asian and other minorities accounted for 6 percent of all new workers during this time period.

Encouraging and Promoting Minorities

The Xerox corporation (**www.xerox.com**) has acknowledged the shifting makeup of its workforce and believes that the proper management of worker diversity will become a necessity in the future. David Kearns, former CEO of Xerox, states that "we have to manage diversity right now and much more so in the future. American business will not be able to survive if we do not have a large diverse workforce because those are the demographics." Kearns goes on to state, "If you fail to include women and minorities, you've restricted yourself from a major part of the labor pool, which economically doesn't make sense. Beyond that, one of the major advantages you get out of having women and minorities in business is that they bring in a whole new set of ideas. Right now, American business needs new ideas and thought if we're going to compete on a worldwide basis."

Xerox has supported its beliefs by encouraging and promoting minorities into fast-track management positions. Although the average percentage of minorities in managerial positions across U.S. firms was 9 percent in 1989 (based on figures from the Equal Employment Opportunity Commission), 26 percent of Xerox managers were minorities by the end of 1996. About 20 percent of Xerox senior executives are women or minorities or both.

Xerox also exceeded the industry average of 12 percent by filling 18 percent of its professional positions with minorities. Xerox was presented with an award by the U.S. Labor Department for its aggressiveness towards recruiting and promoting women and minorities into the ranks of management.

Training is Key to Success

Simply recruiting and hiring a diverse workforce does not guarantee success. The key to Xerox's success comes from the implementation of training programs that foster support and cooperation among minorities. "You can't just hire large numbers of women and minorities and think it'll work," Kearns cautions. "You need a process to identify the right experiences people will need to move ahead. You need to have training programs for your managers that talk about managing diversity. What are the issues of managing minorities and women, because there are things that are different?"

Xerox began to encourage the development and management of diversity during the 1970s when the managers of Xerox's affirmative action program looked at the careers of ten top executives to determine which key position helped them the most in their careers. The result of the study showed that the pivotal position for success was the first-level sales manager. The managers of the affirmative action program also discovered that all 500 first-level sales manager positions were held by Caucasian employees.

Encouraging Affirmative Action

Xerox started to encourage affirmative action by basing 20 percent of a manager's performance review on the manager's success with human resource management, which included affirmative action. The performance program has met with some resistance from Caucasian managers. As Theodore Payne, Xerox's affirmative action manager, states, "There are some . . . who just could not adjust."

To avoid upsetting the informal structures already established, Xerox did not try to dismantle the Caucasian male "old boy" network within Xerox; instead, the company encouraged the growth of networking. The minority caucuses met on their own to develop advancement strategies. A major change sought and won by the caucuses was to allow the posting of "stepping stone" job openings, which was a major breakthrough because a number of major U.S. corporations still refuse to implement this policy.

By selecting the best people from all minority groups, Xerox believes that it is better prepared than most other U.S. firms to compete in an ever-increasing global market. As a top marketing executive at Xerox states, "We'd like to be able to stand up and say that we've done that [beaten international competition] as a multicultural company . . . I think that will serve as a beacon for the rest of American industry."

Strategic Choices

Diversity is only one of many issues currently facing U.S. corporations as they attempt to recruit, select, and retain the best individuals in available jobs. Other issues include locating qualified workers, developing selection procedures that treat all applicants equally, using temporary or part-time workers to help manage costs, and retaining talented employees. Managers have to make a number of choices regarding their recruiting and selection strategies, because all of these issues should be considered when managers develop their recruitment, selection, and retention plans. These strategic choices are outlined as follows:

1. Organizations can choose to "make" or "buy" their employees (that is, hire less-skilled workers or hire skilled workers and professionals).
2. Organizations make strategic decisions regarding the budget allocated for recruiting and selecting employees.
3. An organization can make a strategic choice to explore untapped labor sources.
4. Organizations make strategic decisions regarding the technological sophistication of their recruiting and selection devices.
5. An organization can choose the extent to which internal versus external recruiting methods are used (that is, recruiting within the organization or outside the organization).
6. An organization must decide whether to develop a plan to retain qualified workers.

Make or Buy Decision

Organizations can make a strategic decision to hire less-skilled labor and invest in training and educational programs, or they can recruit and hire skilled labor and professionals. Essentially, this is the "make" (hire less-skilled workers) or "buy" (hire skilled workers and professionals) decision. Managers who recruit only skilled labor and professionals can expect to pay considerably more for these employees.

The advantage to hiring skilled labor and professionals is that they possess the necessary skills to begin working immediately and require little training. However, the amount of money it might take to attract skilled labor and professionals may outweigh the benefits. In addition, many organizations may prefer to conduct their own training programs to ensure some measure of standardization. For example, IBM has an elaborate training program designed to promote not only skill acquisition but also socialization and commitment to the organization.

Budget

As we learned in Chapter 4, HR professionals traditionally have not focused on determining the cost of HR programs, including recruiting. If most firms do not attempt to determine their hiring costs, they are not in a position to control these costs rationally. Organizations can make a strategic decision to control hiring costs only after determining the approximate cost per hire. Information on employee recruitment, selection, orientation, and start-up (such as training) costs is imperative if managers choose to develop and manage cost-effective programs. The costs associated with employee replacement in organizations also should be figured into the cost per hire. Hewitt and Associates estimated that the cost to replace one departed worker is one-and-a-half times the salary of the individual being replaced.[5]

The process of recruiting can be very expensive. Keep in mind that recruiting costs include the direct costs of advertising and promotional materials, referral bonuses, relocation expenses, sign-on bonuses, background checks, and costs to develop and use selection tests. Add to these costs the wages of employees who recruit, process paperwork, interview, provide tours, give tests, train, conduct orientation, and the wages for support staff who hook up phones, computers, and create identification badges, and you begin to see why recruiting is so expensive.[6] Even though these costs seem high, they are only a fraction of what Japanese firms pay to hire a new college graduate.[7] The high price per candidate seems worth it to Japanese firms because once hired, the individual will more than likely stay until he or she retires 30 years later.

Managers also must consider geographical factors when budgeting for recruiting and selection. Some areas may have a severe shortage of workers and an intense competition for qualified applicants that necessitates more extensive recruiting methods, more incentives (such as benefits), and a higher salary to attract qualified workers. However, more and more these conditions appear to be nationwide. Companies are reporting that the labor market continues to tighten. With more than half of the states reporting unemployment rates lower than 5 percent, companies are being forced to get creative with their recruiting techniques. Moira Oliver, director of HR for the Hyatt Orlando, is looking for new recruits as far away as Poland, Hungary, and Ukraine.[8] She also visits U.S. cities with higher unemployment rates than Orlando's 3.3 percent, offering potential employees discounted U-Haul rental rates to lure them to relocate to Florida. Michael Clute, CEO of Marine Service, tells a similar story. His company will pay an applicant $100 cash just to show up for an interview. They have raised salaries over 30 percent, supplemented their benefits package, and offered rooms in a local hotel for out-of-town workers.

In order to attract and retain the best talent in a tight labor market, companies are becoming increasingly clever and generous with the benefits it offers employees. For example, Wilton Connor of Wilton Connor Packing keeps his largely female and minority workforce on the job by hiring two laundresses per shift who wash, dry, and fold employees' family laundry while they work. Connor also employs a handyman who makes repairs at workers' homes, and he offers van service to and from work with stops at day-care facilities in town.[9] These relatively inexpensive perks allow Connor to control his turnover rate.

Another way to interest employees in a job is to offer more free time. Flexible work schedules, including part-time, telecommuting, job sharing, or a compressed workweek, are being offered to individuals who value their time as much as their money.[10] Other "softer" benefits being offered by firms desperate to hire include child- and elder-care services on site or credit for such services.[11] Interestingly, Silicon Valley companies that have traditionally ignored these softer benefits have recently joined the bandwagon. Nearly 160,000 jobs in the Silicon Valley go unfilled every year. Reasons include the high cost of housing in the area, causing long commutes from more affordable locations, and an aging workforce that has begun refocusing their attention on their families.[12]

Sign-on bonuses also appear to be effective recruiting tools for some applicants. For example, companies can offer middle managers a hefty sign-on bonus to recruit and win them over. However, the company also wins, because it does not have to disrupt the pay balance between the new hire and current employees if the extra payment is a one-time lump-sum bonus rather than a higher salary.[13] Sign-on bonuses are also big with recent college graduates.[14] Many firms will offer relocation support (e.g., house-hunting trip, moving vans) or the option of taking the cash equivalent. Recent college graduates are more likely to take the cash than the moving support. Other firms offer a sign-on bonus to recent college graduates in the form of a gift certificate to a clothing store. Developing a work wardrobe can be expensive, and the initial support for this expense is often welcomed.

It can also help to lure and retain employees if development and career advancement opportunities are available. To ensure its employees don't see their job as a dead end, Cisco hires in-house headhunters. These professionals are trained to identify qualified candidates and to bring these people to the attention of managers for promotion and advancement consideration.[15]

All of these benefits are needed if companies want to keep their employees. Because the companies are understaffed, increased demands are being placed on the workforce. These demands have produced record levels of stress and turnover, perpetuating the problem of understaffing.[16] These stressful times have created a less-than-gentle environment for resigning. For example, after giving his two weeks' notice, one employee e-mailed all 2000 employees at the firm complaining about management's unwillingness to do what was needed to keep employees. Others have made their two-week notice contingent on being paid a bonus to stay. The worst action taken by departing employees is to raid their old departments and lure away additional employees.[17]

Untapped Labor Sources

Organizations can make a strategic decision to tap into less-traditional labor pools. Three labor sources receiving the attention of recruiters recently are the handicapped, the homeless, and welfare recipients. Handicapped workers, also called *physically challenged* workers, have not been pursued seriously as potential hires by many organizations. However, the fact that 68 percent of handicapped persons are employable and *want* to work, coupled with the limited number of applicants for entry-level, low-skilled jobs, has made recruiters aware of this valuable employee resource.[18] Although special accommodations are often needed (see Chapter 5 on equal employment opportunity), handicapped workers offer organizations a plethora of knowledge, skills, and abilities (KSAs).

Another labor source that has been left untapped is the homeless. Although still in experimental stages, Days Inns successfully placed numerous homeless people into jobs. Homeless workers are offered a hotel room for a small fee, along with wages. Days Inns hopes to fill more vacant positions and offer homeless individuals a new beginning.[19]

There has been an increased interest in hiring welfare recipients since President Clinton signed the Personal Responsibility and Welfare Reconciliation Act of 1996. This act required 25 percent of the people receiving welfare assistance to be either working or involved in a work-training program by September 30, 1997. The percentage will continue to rise until it reaches 50 percent on September 30, 2002. In essence, this act required one million people to be placed in jobs in one year with an additional million being placed over the following five-year period.[20]

To entice businesses to develop programs to train and hire welfare recipients, the government offered tax credits to businesses. The Work Opportunity Tax Credit can provide up to $2100 per employee hired off the welfare rolls.[21] Aramark, a firm that hires a large percentage of low-wage workers to work in the concession stands in its food courts, hospitals, and convention centers nationwide, viewed the tax credit as a means of saving hundreds of thousands of dollars. However, six months after the tax cuts were introduced, few benefits were seen by Aramark. Of the 900 employees Aramark tagged as eligible for a tax credit, only a quarter actually qualified. The reasons for the discrepancy are two-fold: tough program restrictions and the inability of Aramark's managers to generate the required paperwork in a timely fashion.

A more recent untapped labor market are refugees expelled from their homelands because of civil unrest. For example, Dee Zee Manufacturing in Des Moines, Iowa, has begun hiring Bosnian refugees. Some speak almost fluent English and many have valuable training and skills. Further, these employees are extremely grateful for being given a chance to start over and demonstrate via loyalty to the firm. This reduces turnover rates and lowers costs, resulting in a win-win situation for all.[22]

From Welfare to Workforce

Many Americans erroneously assume that welfare recipients simply do not want to work. We can open any newspaper to the classified advertisement section and locate numerous ads placed by companies searching for workers. It would seem that anyone on welfare wanting a job should simply answer some of those countless ads. If this were the case, however, the American Works Company, located in Hartford, Connecticut, and New York City, would be out of business.

American Works has been extremely successful tapping into a labor force typically ignored by the business world. By exclusively recruiting and training welfare recipients for entry-level positions, American Works gets people off welfare and into the workplace, saves the taxpayers money, and provides hiring employers with a valuable tax credit. If the social benefits of helping welfare recipients find jobs were included, American Works' profits would be even greater.

The crucial element in the American Works' approach to finding jobs for those on welfare who want to work is its focus on assimilating the worker into the system. American Works teaches basic interviewing and job skills, as well as proper English. It also acts as a mediator between the applicant and employer during a four-month trial period while the employee is adjusting to the new job. Roughly 70 percent of the employees trained by American Works are retained by the companies, and almost 90 percent stay in the job past the first year. Overall, companies are pleased with their new employees, stating that compared with other applicants, they are better prepared to accept responsibility and are more motivated and ready to work.

Chrysalis, a Los Angeles–based assistance agency, extends this service to the homeless. By offering full-service help that includes job-search training, interview rehearsals, hygiene items, haircuts, interviewing clothes, and a place to receive mail and phone calls, Chrysalis has helped more than 400 homeless people find jobs. The officials at Chrysalis use statistics to show how effective their services are. For example, it spends $350 per client to help him or her find work. Welfare would pay the same person $343 a month for *not* finding a job. For every 100 people Chrysalis places, they will earn $1,152,000 rather than costing the taxpayers $411,600.

SOURCES: Adapted from "From Welfare to Work Force," *HRMagazine*, July 1991, pp. 36-38; and "Homeless 1 Employment 5 Ex-Homeless," *Management Review*, June 1993, p. 7.

Technological Sophistication

Organizations make strategic decisions regarding the methods used in recruiting and hiring. Often these decisions are influenced by available technology. Computerized resume scanning and tracking systems have made finding the right person for the job much easier. However, finding the right computerized system may be harder than finding a good applicant, because over 55 such systems are available.[23]

Although each computer-based applicant tracking system is unique, these systems share common features. First, clerks scan resumes into the system. These clerks are also responsible for verifying the accuracy of the scanning process and for requesting a computer-generated "thank you letter" to each applicant. When managers need an employee, they provide a recruiter with the requirements of the job and the recruiter searches the database using keywords. If the pool is too small, requirements are relaxed; if it is too large, requirements are tightened (e.g., number of years' experience could be decreased or increased). Use of such systems has many advantages. Companies can reduce their reliance on recruitment agencies by generating their own applicant pools. Assessing resumes by computer is more efficient and faster than manual assessment, so it speeds the hiring process. Finally, unsolicited resumes are no longer viewed as a source of irritation but as a valuable resource.[24]

Computers have given employers and job applicants a wide scope of options in the initial screening stage. For example, some firms have implemented an online application system. When an applicant arrives at the company for an interview or simply walks in to inquire about openings, he or she is asked to complete a computer application. The application program greets the applicant and feeds questions, one by one, to him or her. Once all of the questions have been answered, a copy of the application is printed for the applicant to sign. The benefits of such a system are obvious. First, the form is easy to read and all sections are completed. Next, because the information is already in the computer, it can be used by various other human resource systems, such as resume scanning systems or skills databases. However, because the system does require some degree of computer literacy on the part of the applicant, it may not be appropriate for every position or every applicant.[25]

"Telerecruiting" has become increasingly popular. Telerecruiting allows the screening process to be done by telephone. Large organizations have begun to form telerecruiting departments, which screen job applicants and put their resume information in a computer.[26] This procedure has enabled managers to interview and hire new employees more quickly. Employers who do not have the staff or budget to develop a telerecruiting department can get assistance from outside services.

The latest method of recruiting is via the Internet. With more than 30 million people "surfing the net," posting job openings online can greatly expand the applicant pool.[27] The Internet appears to be suited for recruiting. To facilitate the process several job post sites are available on the World Wide Web (WWW). Headhunter (**www.headhunter.net**) lists more than 6000 jobs from more than 200 different employers. On an average day, 70,000 job searchers access their database. Another job search Web site that enjoys incredible traffic is **www.monster.com**. However, some firms using these sites have been flooded with resumes and inquiries.[28] Companies ill equipped to handle the load may find the Internet is not such a great recruiting tool.

Internal Versus External Recruiting Methods

Internal recruiting methods include posting position openings, distributing memos within the organization, and searching organizational databases for a match between the skills required to perform the job and the skills held by current employees. This method of recruiting looks to internal sources to fill positions and encourages promotions from within. External recruiting methods include advertising position openings in newspapers and magazines and looking to external sources to fill positions. Whether managers choose internal or external methods depends on the degree to which the organization's strategy encourages promotions and transfers from within the organization. Recruiting from within can lead to job satisfaction and motivation if employees see new career opportunities available. In addition, filling positions with existing employees ensures, to a large extent, that these employees are socialized to the organization's culture or "personality." However, problems can arise if the internal promotion system is not viewed as fair.

The best way to avoid negative backlash when hiring or promoting from within is to install fair procedures. People are more willing to accept a loss if they view the loss as fair and square.[29] If steps are taken to ensure a fair internal promotional process, most people will accept their loss and remain a productive and useful organizational citizen.

External recruiting helps to bring new ideas and approaches to the organization. In the university system, faculty positions are almost always filled by using external

EXHIBIT 7.1	INTERNAL VERSUS EXTERNAL RECRUITMENT: ADVANTAGES AND DISADVANTAGES

Internal Recruitment

Advantages	Disadvantages
1. Employees familiar with organization.	1. Political infighting for promotion.
2. Lower recruiting and training costs.	2. Inbreeding.
3. Increase morale and motivation for employees.	3. Morale problem for those not promoted.
4. Probability of success due to better assessment of abilities and skills.	

External Recruitment

Advantages	Disadvantages
1. New ideas and approaches.	1. Lack of "fit" between employee and organization.
2. "Clean slate" regarding company-specific experiences from which to build.	2. Lowered morale and commitment of employees.
3. Level of knowledge and skill not available in current organization.	3. Increased adjustment period.

recruiting methods and sources. In academia, new ideas and approaches are encouraged; thus Ph.D. students rarely become part of the faculty at the school where they receive their degree.

Recruiting Methods

Most job openings are filled with people from within the organization, and entry-level positions are the most likely to be filled by external sources.[30] Methods of internal recruiting include job posting, skills inventories, job bidding, and referrals. Methods of external recruiting include school and college recruiting, advertising, using employment agencies and executive search firms, and the Internet and WWW. The advantages and disadvantages of internal versus external recruitment are depicted in Exhibit 7.1. Each of these methods will be discussed in the following section.

Internal Recruiting

job posting
Publicly posting job openings so that all qualified employees in the organization can apply if they so desire.

Job Posting   Many positions can be filled as a result of posting the job opening on bulletin boards, announcing the opening in the company newsletter, or posting the position announcement on the company's intranet. A **job-posting** procedure enables employees to strive for a better position within the company. Notices of position openings should include all important information about the job (e.g., brief job description, the education or training required, the salary, and whether it is full time or part time).

Bellagio Casino and Resort in Las Vegas, Nevada, requires that all jobs be filled internally if possible. To facilitate this goal, job posting is used. When a manager informs HR of an opening, the job description is posted on the job board where it remains for seven days. Any employee who is interested and qualified for the job completes a job interest card and returns it to HR. HR loads the records of all interested employees into an applicant queue. After seven days the manager with the opening looks at the queue and rejects or accepts the applicants based on qualifications for the job. All accepted applicants must be interviewed and dismissed before the manager can look at outside candidates. This policy has helped keep qualified employees at Bellagio and established their turnover rate as one of the lowest on the Strip.

Although posting jobs can be an efficient method of recruiting, a number of problems have been associated with it. For example, job posting can lead to conflict if an employee perceives he or she is more qualified for the job than his or her peer who is hired. In addition, having employees compete for jobs can put a supervisor in a very stressful situation. A supervisor might have to decide among three very qualified employees, all of whom would do a good job.

skills inventory
A list of each employee and the KSAs each possesses.

Skills Inventory   Another internal recruiting method is the use of **skills inventories**. Essentially, a skills inventory includes a list of employee names, their education, training, present position, work experience, relevant job skills and abilities, and other qualifications. The organization can search through the company skills inventory to identify potential candidates for the position opening.

job bidding
Process by which unionized workers apply for open positions.

Job Bidding   When a union is present, the labor-management agreement usually includes **job-bidding** procedures. These procedures typically specify that all jobs covered by the agreement must be filled by qualified applicants from within the bargaining unit. Those interested in the vacancy "bid" for the job by applying if they are qualified. The position is filled by the individual with the highest seniority from among the qualified applicants. In some cases, applicants take competitive examinations and the position is filled by the highest-scoring applicant. In either case, only those currently employed are permitted to apply. This has the effect, especially among blue-collar and other unionized jobs, of filling only entry-level positions from external sources.

Using a job-bidding system is normally very easy. The negotiated contract specifically outlines how the procedure is to work by designating who is qualified to bid, how often bids can be made, and how the bid is to be processed once submitted. However, a job-bidding system can present difficulties. For example, when one division of Whirlpool completely changed the way its jobs were performed by introducing computers, every single job had to be bid for because all of the old jobs were eliminated. The workers had one week to analyze job descriptions of the new jobs and bid on their top three choices. Once the bids were in, the head supervisor and his assistant analyzed the bids, trying to match the workers to the jobs following the formula outlined in the contract. This process took two days. Once completed, the job assignments were posted for inspection by the employees. Many workers found that they had been assigned a job for which they had not even bid because coworkers with higher seniority had filled all of the jobs they had requested. Hence, these employees immediately submitted new bids for different jobs, causing the process to begin all over again.

Referrals   An excellent source of information is current employees who may know someone who would be qualified and interested in the open position. To entice employees to make employee referrals, some companies offer a referral bonus. An employee who recommends someone who is hired receives a small bonus, usually between $100 and $1000. Obviously, this source of information is very low cost, yet it can yield a number of good prospects because normally only individuals who are happy in their jobs recommend their company to their friends and family. People tend to associate with people like themselves; therefore if the employee fits in well in the organization, chances are his or her referrals will too. Good employees are not going to refer someone who might tarnish their reputation or will cause more work for themselves.[31] Employees whose referrals are hired are often willing to serve as a mentor to ensure their referrals succeed in the company. The use of referrals also makes it easier to implement teams, because many pairs of workers are already working as a team. However, managers should be aware that when the organization does not have a representative number of minorities, referrals have been considered a violation of Title VII of the Civil Rights Act.[32] Some companies have taken employee referrals to a new level. These firms focus their sites on a key player in a rival organization deemed the "Pied Piper." Firms know that if they can snag the Pied Piper, others will naturally follow.[33]

External Recruiting

School and College Recruiting   Recruiting at high schools or vocational schools is often the strategic approach adopted by organizations with position openings at the entry level or in internal training programs. Recruiting at the college level serves as a major source for acquiring managerial, professional, and technical skills.[34] College recruiting can be expensive, so human resource managers should be certain that a college degree is needed for successful performance in the position openings. In general, professionals (such as engineers and human resource managers) are recruited nationally whereas more technical or lower-level jobs are recruited regionally or locally.

One of the most important decisions that human resource managers must make is from which schools and colleges to recruit. Many organizations make a strategic decision to recruit from certain schools or colleges exclusively. The rationale for limiting the number (besides time and money) includes recruiting from only prestigious schools to enhance the reputation of the organization, from schools to which the organization makes financial donations, or from schools from which previous hires have performed effectively. Another reason to focus on only a few schools is to establish a presence on campus and develop a relationship with key players.[35] College recruiting has become fiercely competitive because the supply of students, especially in technical fields, is far less than the demand. Graduating seniors recognize this and have begun interviewing earlier. Many will take a job in early fall with a start date of the following summer after graduation. Firms that have an ongoing relationship with a school will be aware of these changes and be ready to act when necessary.

Some firms have decided not to wait for students to graduate. Instead, they are recruiting juniors. By offering lucrative salaries and benefits, firms hope to persuade students to forego their college degree and take a job early.[36] This places students focusing in their studies in the same league as those focusing on their game. Big bucks for an early out is no longer just for athletes. Besides, if it doesn't work out, the student can always go back to school, complete his or her degree, and be recruited all over again.

Advertising   Advertising job openings in newspapers, magazines, newsletters, and other media sources (such as radio) is a relatively inexpensive recruiting mechanism. *The Wall Street Journal*, for example, has a large section devoted to managerial and professional openings. Advertising is useful for filling open positions quickly.

However, advertising does not usually target a specific audience. For example, Mc-Donald's often includes an abbreviated application blank on every paper placemat. These placemats are given to customers when they pick up their food order. McDonald's views every customer as a potential employee! The cost of screening candidates may preclude the use of media sources for most jobs other than entry level. The effectiveness of media advertising for position openings should be examined periodically. Evaluating the success or failure of recruiting efforts by counting the number of qualified candidates is *not* a recommended method. For example, it is far more expensive and time consuming to screen 100 applicants and find 5 qualified candidates than to screen 15 applicants and find 5 qualified candidates.[37] However, when developing advertisements for open positions, steps can be taken to increase their effectiveness.

Clearly written, specifically defined advertisements will attract qualified applicants, dissuade unqualified ones from applying, and make the recruiting process more efficient. But what exactly should be included in an employment advertisement? Obviously, the answer depends on the job. For example, the ad may require applicants to submit salary history, which can be used to determine whether the salary for the current opening will be attractive to the applicant. This may turn off some applicants, because revealing this information limits their ability to negotiate a good deal.[38] A more useful and practical way to attract only those who will be satisfied with the salary offered is to include in the advertisement an anticipated starting salary range with a disclaimer stating that actual salary will depend on the candidate's experience and credentials.

Interestingly, some award-winning ads do not follow these guidelines. For example, Booz-Allen and Hamilton won a Creative Excellence Award for their "Keeping it Simple" ad campaign. Trying to capitalize on its selection by *Working Mother Magazine* as one of the 100 best companies to work for in America, Booz-Allen and Hamilton ran an ad that had the words "We believe business should always have a human side" under a vertical line up of paper clips and diaper pins. The campaign was highly successful, illustrating that sometimes simple is better.[39]

Public Employment Agencies All states provide employment services to job seekers and employers. An effort has been undertaken in recent years to improve the image and the services provided by the public employment service. Traditionally, employers and job seekers believed that the public employment system was useful only for filling blue-collar, unskilled jobs. In part, this resulted from the association that the public employment system has with the payment of unemployment compensation. Another problem with the service has been its preoccupation with filling placement goals or quotas at the expense of effective screening of candidates for jobs. Individuals without proper qualifications were sometimes sent to particular jobs simply because the service was attempting to meet its referral and placement quotas. However, the service has been used successfully by employers, even though it has been focused on unskilled or low-skilled jobs.

Private Employment Agencies Private employment agencies vary considerably in size and effectiveness as good sources of employees and must be chosen carefully by employers and job seekers alike. For a fee, these agencies conduct the preliminary applicant screening for the organization. Agencies usually charge the job seeker a fee if he or she is hired by an employer through the agency. The employer may agree to pay all, part, or none of this fee. Regardless, the fee is usually based on some multiple of the employee's salary. Unfortunately, some agencies are more concerned with placing employees quickly than in effecting a good match between the employee and the organization. Human resource managers can reduce problems if they supply the employment agency with a detailed description of the position to be filled. Similar to that in a well-written employment advertisement, relevant information about the job should include a job title, job description, education level needed, special training or skills required, and pay ranges.

Executive Search Firms   Some employment agencies focus their efforts on seeking quality management-level employees. An executive search is characterized by aggressive action on the part of consultants and management who actively pursue the optimal candidate. The search seeks to identify those whose careers are on track with their current employers and those who are not actually looking for another job but would be interested in considering another opportunity. Recently, some companies have decided not to limit this type of recruiting activity to executives. Recruiting for any position within the organization can be done by sending out "scouts" to look for good employees who are not necessarily looking for another job.[40]

Whereas most recruiting activities focus on selecting from those who apply, search activities focus on selecting from among candidates who have to be found. Because search activities are often directed at candidates from companies with competitive products or services, the industry backgrounds of those identified are usually closely related to the industry of the organization conducting the search.[41]

Because it is often difficult to locate professional applicants at higher levels in the organization, the recruiting process may have to take a different approach. It is important to make sure that the applicant believes his or her best interests are kept in mind, as well as those of the company. Attention should be paid to the candidate's home life by, for instance, helping the spouse/family become knowledgeable about the company and its location.[42] It is also important for the company to be aware of its own best interests when using an executive search firm. In 1996, the Association of Executive Search Consultants (AESC) modified its ethical standards and practice guidelines. The reason is that AESC does not have the resources to police its members, so it turned the policing over to the firms.[43] One of the major changes involved is the lifting of the two-year block on recruiting from a client organization after a placement has been made.

Another change in the conduct guidelines is that search firms are no longer required to disclose conflicts of interest. Although AESC recommends that firms do disclose them, the wording was changed from "must" to "should." Conflicts of interest (e.g., recruiting for both Coca-Cola and PepsiCo) will restrict the candidates that search firms can present to a client. Hiring firms would obviously want to be aware of the conflicts of interest and may even pass on a firm if the conflict appears too great. However, given that the search firms no longer are required to make these confessions, hiring firms are at a definite disadvantage.

Hiring firms should also be aware that the new AESC guidelines now suggest that candidates' backgrounds be checked thoroughly prior to being presented to a client. However, with the change from "must" to "should," reference checking is frequently the *last* step performed—and usually after the individual being investigated has been placed. Given the potential for lost revenue, negative information is rarely uncovered.

These changes place more of a burden on companies that hire search firms to specify the rules to follow. At a minimum, firms should delineate:

- How long the client organization is off limits to the search firm.
- The parts of the client organization that are off limits.
- Specifications of the search firm's conflicts of interest as well as which firms are off limits for each search.
- The search firm's policy on recruiting candidates it has placed.
- Specifications of when reference checking will be conducted and how thorough the check will be.

Another key change in executive search firms is how they are being paid. When placing a top executive in a small start-up firm, many search firms will ask for company stock in exchange for a lower fee. This helps the small start-up firms strapped for cash utilize the services of an agency they otherwise could not afford. It also encourages consultants to focus on the long-term viability of the company to help ensure a large payoff when the company goes public.[44]

The Internet and the WWW   As previously mentioned, one of the fastest-growing recruitment methods is the Internet and the WWW.[45] According to a report by Internet Business Network, an online consulting firm, more than 1.2 million jobs are currently listed on the Internet and over 1 million resumes have been posted online.[46] One of the most well-known WWW sites for job searchers and recruiters is **www.monster.com**, which offers vast job and resume banks and expansive career resources.[47]

Even though the numbers indicate a heavy usage, a survey by William Olsten Center for Workforce Strategies revealed that only one in five companies responding to the survey said they used the Internet to recruit. Further, of those who did indicate they used the Internet to recruit, just 1 percent of the hires came from this source as compared with 48 percent of the applicants who found their way to the company through traditional print advertisements.

The companies that do use the Internet as a recruiting source appear to be happy with the process and the results. Over two thirds of the companies responding to a recent survey rated the Internet more cost effective than most or all other recruitment methods available.[48] Other advantages of recruiting on the Internet were offered by Internet users responding to a different survey.[49] These included access to more people, broader selection of applicants, ability to target the type of applicants needed, access to applicants with technical backgrounds, convenience, speed, ease of use, and economy.

Several disadvantages also surfaced. For example, not everyone has access to the Internet, so some qualified applicants are not being considered. Also, the increased volume of applicants can be a problem. Some companies without a computerized tracking system are flooded by applications and have insufficient time to review and respond to them. Companies feel they also might be missing out on the "passive job seekers," those individuals who would accept a new job at certain firms but who are not actively searching via the Internet.

There are a few key issues a firm must consider when deciding whether or not to join the trend of recruiting on the Internet:

1. Understand what all potential users want from the recruiting component of the Web page. Consider the needs of external applicants, internal candidates, and the HR department. Some firms have found focus groups useful in identifying components to include on their Web page.

2. Spend some time thinking about how the Web page will be organized. Numerous options are available. For example, the page could be organized by business unit, by job function, or by geographic location, just to name a few.
3. Make sure all of the resources you will need are available. Is there someone on staff who has been assigned to develop and update the Web page? Are there enough staff available to respond to the online requests and to mail requested additional information? Is there a computerized system in place to track the flow of applications?
4. Examine what other companies are doing. By benchmarking with other companies, tried-and-true methods can be incorporated into your online recruiting procedures, saving you time and money by not having to work the kinks out of your own system.

Utilizing Recruiting Sources

Companies frequently use a variety of internal and external recruiting strategies to locate and hire their workers. Although one technique may work well for some organizations, the same technique may prove ineffective for others. Some techniques may mesh well with the organization's competitive strategy, but others do not.

By integrating both internal and external recruiting techniques, a company can develop an overall recruiting plan that is specifically tailored to support its overall strategy and result in the selection of highly qualified applicants. Exhibit 7.2 is an illustrative description of one possible recruitment plan. Plans such as this one are needed for a variety of reasons. First, to ensure productivity, a fully staffed workforce is needed. When employees are asked to do too much for too long, both morale and productivity can sag. Also, more than one applicant must be recruited to fill one position. In fact, it may take hundreds of applicants to fill one position, depending on the position. Exactly how many recruits are needed can be determined from past recruitment efforts. Specifically, a yield ratio can be developed for each position to be filled. A **yield ratio** is the number of candidates who pass a particular recruitment hurdle divided by the number who attempted the hurdle. For example, we would calculate a ratio for each step outlined in Exhibit 7.2 in the recruiting process in which a decision about an applicant was made. One set of possible yield ratios is provided in Exhibit 7.2 in parentheses after each decision point in the diagram. Specifically, 20 internal candidates of 1000 possible (20/1000) were found by the human resource department and passed on to the hiring department. It selected 3 of these 20 to interview and 1 of the 3 (or zero of these 3) to whom to offer a job. On the external side of the diagram, 10 of 250 applicants were passed on to the hiring department, with 4 receiving interviews and 1 or none receiving an offer. This scenario, although fictitious, is not far from reality. The overall point is that a large applicant pool may be required to hire even one person for the job, and hence prior planning must be done. Finally, it is important to keep in mind that this plan should mesh with and support the organization's overall strategic plan. For example, if the organization makes the strategic decision to promote only from within, then a detailed internal recruitment plan should be developed.

yield ratio Percentage of candidates passed on to the next step in the selection process.

Retaining Employees

One of the primary roles of a recruiting effort is to attract a number of qualified applicants; however, retaining those employees selected is also an important issue. Too often a recruiter attempts to "sell" the organization to the candidate and subsequently

EXHIBIT 7.2   POSSIBLE ORGANIZATIONAL RECRUITING PLAN

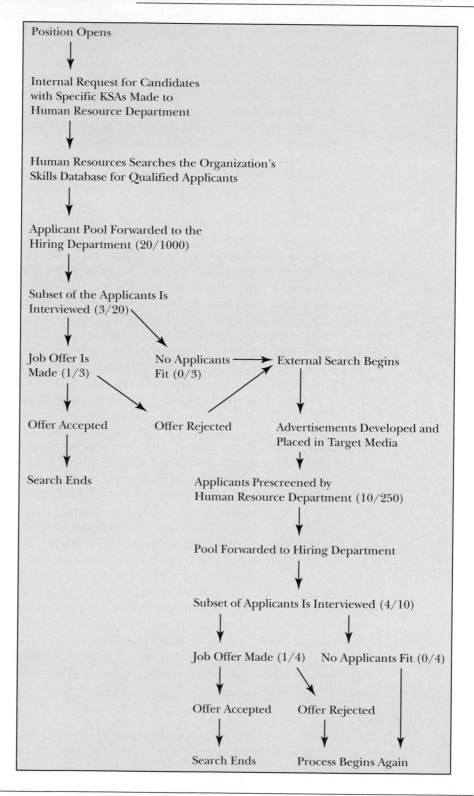

inflates the positive characteristics of the organization while minimizing any negative features. This is often termed the *flypaper* approach, which assumes that if an organization can attract people, these new employees will "stick" with the organization. One survey found that job candidates can be enticed to join a company if offered a large enough salary, but another survey revealed that retaining those same employees requires strong leadership skills among top management.[50]

F. Leigh Branham, author of "Keeping the People Who Keep You in Business," recommends four keys to keep top performers: (1) be a company for which people want to work, (2) select the right person in the first place, (3) manage the joining-up process, and (4) coach to maintain commitment.[51] Let's look at some examples from companies that have successfully used these principles.

Be a Company for Which People Want to Work There are a variety of ways companies can be viewed as one for which people want to work. For example, making one of the lists of the "100 Best Companies To Work For" can make an organization attractive to recruits and employees alike. Another approach that has been successful for Goldman Sachs is to make employees view the organization as a market leader so that those who leave will be forced to take a step down. Top management at Home Depot believes that empowering employees with decision-making authority creates an environment that keeps people. Home Depot recognizes that its salespeople are the ones touching the customer, so it makes them associates rather than workers, indicating how valuable their services are viewed.[52] Even the U.S. Navy has been making the job of a sailor more attractive in an effort to retain junior sailors. Admiral Albert Konetzni, who inherited a personnel crisis when he took over command of the Pacific submarine fleet in 1998, has acquired a reputation for being a sailor's friend. He took $500,000 from his parts budget and hired civilians to do grunt work like painting and maintenance. He also purchased $12,000 of conveyor belts out of his travel budget to ease the loading of the submarines. He then reduced the number of hours worked while in port to 40 hours a week. These efforts paid off, and the Pacific Fleet now boasts a second tour of duty sign-up rate that is twice the rate of the rest of the Navy.[53]

Select the Right Person in the First Place The old computer adage "garbage in, garbage out" also applies in hiring. Desperate organizations that take any warm body pay the price in turnover. Tavern on the Green, a famed eatery in New York City, boasts that over 35 percent of its staff have been employed for over ten years. This is a remarkable feat given the volatility in the hospitality industry. How do they do it? By carefully selecting the best applicants for the job. To determine who the best applicants are, the company requires candidates to pass a prescreening telephone application, have at least four hours of interviews with department heads, undergo personality tests and a drug test, and then participate in 5 hours of orientation and 40 hours of classroom training. Although the process is not quick, it does produce the type of employee the Tavern is looking for.[54] The same philosophy has served Southwest Airlines well. After ten years of analyzing the behavior of Southwest employees, Libby Sartain, Vice President of People, and her staff have calibrated their interview questions to test for specific needs and requirements of each job. They also tap qualities that all Southwest employees need, such as common sense and good judgment. Southwest gets a lot of opportunity to use these questions because they interview over 70,000 people to hire 5000 employees each year. It appears that their methods are working; Southwest reports a 9 percent turnover rate, the lowest in the industry.[55] A similar approach is used by Capital One Financial. In 1998 the company gave 1600 of its employees a five-hour test to determine characteristics of high performers. They used the results to create a performance database against which applicants are judged. In addition, applicants are required to take an intelligence test and a personality test designed to provide Capital One a clear reading of how the candidate will perform on the job.[56]

Manage the Joining-up Process   Trying to make employees feel at home right from the start has paid off for Cisco Systems. Even during a year when Cisco acquired 20 companies, they only lost 7 percent of their employees. Their key to retention is to do everything it can from day one to make new employees feel welcome. For example, when a new employee arrives at work they find everything they need to be productive (e.g., e-mail account, phone line, computer, printer) already set up. Cisco has designed an orientation session that not only provides standard information such as benefits, but also provides useful and unique information like how to navigate the Web site and how to succeed in Cisco's culture. Finally each new employee is assigned a sponsor (who is not his or her boss) to ease the transition even more.[57]

Coaching to Maintain Commitment   One company famous for developing management talent is GE. Once a year current managers at GE are asked to put together a report outlining their accomplishments, strengths, and ideal next moves. The managers discuss the reports with their managers, who recommend a select few to Jack Welsh and Bill Conaty, the head HR official. From the recommendations 360 managers are selected to attend the company's management training programs at its Crotonville campus in upstate New York. The courses, staffed by key managers the students hope to replace, teach employees how to grow and develop. GE is convinced that giving top people the chance to develop within the company will keep them around. The approach used by Enron is to make it easy to move within the company so employees won't have to look outside. Employees are strongly encouraged to manage their careers by moving around in the firm and acquiring new skills. This approach keeps employees happy and provides Enron with a highly skilled workforce.[58]

Alternatives to Recruitment

Another strategic decision businesses can make is *not* to recruit. Instead, they can rely on alternative staffing options. Some of the most common options are outlined in Exhibit 7.3 and discussed below. **Temporary workers** are employees hired on an as-needed basis. The need could be for a specific project (e.g., opening a new restaurant) or for a specific time (e.g., seasonal workers). Temporary workers are generally contracted through a temporary employment agency. However, some firms hire in-house temporary employees for a specific length of time. There are over 7000 U.S. temporary agencies, with the largest, Manpower, employing over 600,000 employees.[59] When contacted, a temporary agency immediately sends the contracting firm fully qualified employees and bills the firm for their wages. The temporary agency is responsible for these employees who are on its payroll. Temporary agencies were used in the past mainly when extra secretarial support was needed, but this has changed. More and more frequently, organizations are turning to temporary agencies to help staff managerial positions, although a search is underway or to provide an employee for a project that has a definite ending date.[60] Long-term temporary assignments are becoming more common. In order to ease the permanent workload of the workforce,

temporary workers Employees hired on an as-needed basis.

EXHIBIT 7.3 COMMON ALTERNATIVE STAFFING OPTIONS

Traditional Temporary Help

In a traditional temporary worker arrangement, a potential employee is recruited, tested, screened, and employed by a temporary staffing agency. The temporary agency assigns qualified individuals to work at a client's site, generally to support or supplement the current workforce. The need could range from covering for an employee who has called in sick to helping meet a deadline on a large project that may take a few months to complete. Temporary employees can be supplied by a variety of agencies, especially if the requirements for the job are highly specialized like engineers or other types of scientists.

Long-Term Temporary Assignments

It is becoming increasingly popular for an organization to staff part of its workforce with temporary workers on an ongoing basis. These individuals are not considered short-term replacements, but more a part of the regular workforce. The number of individuals employed in this way will change with the needs of the business. One advantage of this type of staffing arrangement is that any downsizing is done with the temporary workers, providing the core employees with a feeling of job security.

In-House Temporary Employees

Organizations may hire temporary workers on their own payroll, but will more than likely not pay them benefits. These individuals can be cross-trained to work on a variety of jobs so they can be plugged in where needed. This staffing arrangement provides the organization with maximum flexibility.

Temp-To-Perm Programs

Some temporary hiring firms serve as feeders for their clients. The client company will agree to hire a temporary worker as a permanent worker after a probationary period. Provided the temporary employee performs competently during the probationary period, the client company will move the worker to its payroll.

Part-Time Employees

Workers who work less than 40 hours a week are considered part-time employees. They can be on the organization's payroll or assigned via a temporary agency. Frequently these individuals will receive limited, if any, benefits.

Employee Leasing

A company may transfer some of its employees to a leasing firm or Professional Employer Organization (PEO). The leasing firm then leases back the workers to perform the same jobs they did for the client company. However, the leasing firm is now responsible for cost and work associated with the typical HR functions such as payroll, benefits, and record keeping.

Temp-To-Lease Programs

Sometimes a firm will contract with a temporary staffing agency to provide temporary workers. After the temporary employees satisfactorily complete a probationary employment period, they are transferred to a leasing agency with whom the client company also has contracted. This is like a promotion for the workers as their jobs become "permanent" and they are now eligible for all benefits offered by the PEO.

Independent Contractors

Independent contractors are self-employed individuals who market a specific skill they possess to a variety of companies. A company will hire them for a specific project or contract. Payment is usually based on the time and effort the individual put forth on the project and expenses are frequently reimbursed.

Outsourcing Services

An independent company with expertise in a specific area will contract with a firm to take full responsibility for that specific function in the organization.

SOURCE: Adapted from Thomas C. Greble, "A Leading Role for HR in Alternative Staffing," *HRMagazine*, February 1977, pp 99–103.

companies have begun hiring temporary workers for periods longer than the duration of a project. It is also possible for temporary workers to be offered a permanent position if they perform competently. The most important benefit of temporary employees is decreased cost. All recruitment costs are eliminated, as are the costs of benefits for these employees and outplacement or severance costs. More information on temporary workers can be found on the home page for the National Association of Temporary Staffing Services at **www.natss.com.**

part-time workers Employees who work less than 35 hours a week.

Part-time workers are those who are employed on a continuing basis but work less than full time, normally less than 35 hours a week. Although at one time this was considered a less-than-optimal working arrangement for employees, this view is rapidly changing. Nearly one fifth of the total workforce is now part time, and 85 percent of those are working part time by choice. Because of the increased number of full-time workers opting for a permanent part-time working arrangement, companies have begun offering benefits for part-time workers. In a recent survey by the Conference Board, 97 percent of the companies responding offered benefits to its permanent part-time workers.[61]

leased employees Employees who are hired through a leasing company for a fee.

Organizations can **lease employees** in the same way that they lease cars. Just as an organization would not own a leased car, it would not employ a leased employee. Instead, it would pay the firm that does employ the worker (own the car) a leasing fee. This fee is generally more than the worker would earn in base salary if working for the leasing firm, but the leasing firm is not responsible for paying benefits, which often makes the fee less than would be paid if the employee were hired directly. Under a leasing agreement a firm terminates a group of employees, who are then hired by a leasing agency, which leases them back to the original organization. An organization that leases employees is responsible only for giving them a place to work and work to do, as well as supervising them. Training costs, benefits, health insurance, and all of the other human resource administration costs are the responsibility of the leasing agency, not the organization. This type of arrangement has been the salvation of small businesses. With only a few employees, most small businesses could not qualify for competitively priced health-care plans. However, by pooling several small businesses into one leasing agency, more affordable rates can be negotiated.[62]

Leasing firms, frequently referred to as Professional Employer Organizations (PEOs), are one of the fastest-growing areas for HR. At the end of 1997 approximately 2500 PEOs were managing more than 2 million employees.[63] Because most of the functions performed by PEOs, such as payroll, benefits administration, and maintaining personnel records, are HR activities, some fear PEOs will be the death of HR functions in organizations. There may be some truth in this assertion. Ninety-three percent of the large firms with HR functions have outsourced at least some of their HR activities. However, the rapid growth in PEOs is not from large organizations but from small businesses that have no HR departments. Hence, PEOs may actually increase the demand for HR professionals.

In some instances, companies have combined a temporary hiring arrangement with a leased program. When using a temp-to-lease program, individuals who are hired through a temporary agency and work out well are moved to a PEO firm to become leased workers. Workers who get moved to the PEO become eligible for the better benefits offered by a PEO.

independent contractors Individuals who contract with multiple companies to provide a specific skill or ability.

Independent contractors are individuals who have a specific KSA that organizations need. These individuals offer to apply their talent to a specific problem for a variety of companies. They are paid for the product they produce and sometimes

---

Recruiting Practices That Get the EEOC's Attention

To avoid disparate treatment charges, recruiting firms should keep the following in mind:

- Prior to using any type of selection test, it should be thoroughly tested for job validity. To accomplish this, a firm can hire a consulting firm to conduct a scientific validation study. Validation evidence of this type has held up in various court cases.

- If using an interview, make sure that it is highly structured and that all interviewers ask exactly the same questions. Being able to prove consistency in the interview process will be extremely valuable in court. If a panel of interviewers is used, check the composition of the panel. If only one race, sex, and age group is represented, think about changing the panel. Finally, inter-

viewers should be instructed to write down only job-related items about the candidate. Margin notes can and have been used by a plaintiff to make a prima facie case.

- Be leery of testers. Testers usually work in pairs and apply for the same job. Both applicants will supply virtually identical resumes, with the only significant difference being race, sex, or age. If the applicant from the protected class gets turned down for the job and the majority candidate is hired, the testers may be able to sue for discriminatory practices.

SOURCE: Adapted from Jennifer Click, "Blend Established Practices with New Technologies," *HRMagazine*, November 1997, p. 60; and Theresa Donahue Egler and Jennifer G. Velez, "Your Hiring Practices Could Be Put to the Test," *HRMagazine*, March 1997, pp. 126–130.

---

for expenses incurred while developing the product. Many consultants and writers work in this fashion. Real-estate agents are generally considered to be independent contractors.

outsource To turn over complete responsibility of a specific business function to another firm.

Finally, just as PEOs have begun playing the role of an HR department for some firms, companies may elect to **outsource** one or more of their business functions. Peripheral business functions are the best candidates for outsourcing. Maintaining computer equipment or the fleet of company cars are two possible areas that companies may elect to outsource.

Recruiting and the Legal Environment

Recruiting and hiring employees must be done within the legal environment of the organization. The Focus on HR box about legal issues discusses recruiting practices that get the Equal Employment Opportunity Commission's (EEOC's) attention. To avoid problems in the early stages of the hiring process, preemployment application forms should not ask questions that later could be used in recruitment materials to unfairly discriminate against a candidate. Specifically, job applicants and screening interviews should never include questions referring to the candidate's gender, religion, or race. Employers need to obtain a certain amount of information from the job candidate, but there is a correct and an incorrect way to ask these questions.

Affirmative action principles should also be observed in the recruiting process. For example, it is recommended that minorities be used in the recruiting process and minority leaders contacted for possible employment candidates. Using the phrase "an equal opportunity employer" is important, but this alone is not enough to fulfill the goals of affirmative action. Because affirmative action plans include goals for increasing the number of minorities and women holding certain jobs, the organization's recruiting efforts should be directed toward meeting these goals. Many organizations make an effort to recruit from predominately female and/or black colleges. For example, the Xerox case in this chapter demonstrates how making a strategic decision to recruit, hire, and train minorities can help meet the affirmative action goals of the corporation while achieving a diverse workforce. Affirmative action is discussed in more detail in Chapter 5.

Evaluating Recruiting Methods

Given the importance of recruiting to the organization, the methods used in recruiting should be evaluated periodically. One of the most important reasons to evaluate recruiting methods is to determine the costs versus the benefits of various methods. When recruiting methods do not attract enough applicants, many organizations respond by raising starting salaries. Although some job applicants may be enticed by money, this may not be the most cost-effective method of recruiting. Further, employees within the organization may perceive inequity if new employees are brought in at a similar or even higher salary.

Recruiting costs include factors such as the cost of advertising, the salaries and travel expenses of recruiters, travel expenses of potential job applicants, and recruiting agency fees. These costs must be weighed against factors such as the proportion of acceptances to offers. At a minimum, organizations should compare the length of time applicants from each recruiting source *stay* with the organization with the cost of *hiring* from a particular source. The effectiveness of recruiting methods varies among organizations and even jobs within the same organization.

The Selection Process

selection
Choosing an individual from a pool of recruited applicants.

Selection is the process of choosing individuals who have the necessary qualifications to perform a particular job well. Organizations differ as to the complexity of their selection systems. Some organizations make a strategic decision to fill positions quickly and inexpensively by scanning application forms and hiring individuals based on this information alone. Other organizations, however, make a strategic decision to choose the best person possible by having an elaborate and sometimes costly selection system. These systems may require potential employees to fill out application forms and provide information for a background check, take a number of job-related tests, and perform well through a series of interviews. Most organizations have more than one selection process. Exhibit 7.4 presents an overview of the selection process. Each element in this process will be discussed.

Application Blanks and Resumes

The initial screening of potential employees is usually done by examining resumes and/or having the applicant fill out an application blank. Items that should be requested on an application include general biographical information; an extensive employment history including most recent jobs, employers' names, addresses, dates of employment, positions held, and reason for leaving; personal references; and the applicant's signature showing consent for the employer to investigate all of the information provided. An incomplete application should automatically disqualify a candidate.[64] Much of the information gathered on application blanks is objective so that the human resource manager can verify it. Verification of information on an application is becoming increasingly important to avoid claims of negligent hiring. An employer

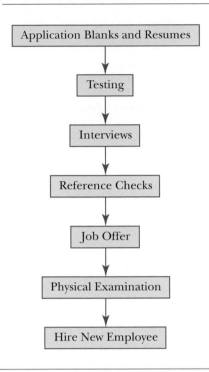

EXHIBIT 7.4	THE SELECTION PROCESS

negligent hiring
A finding that an employer is responsible for using poor selection procedures after an employee inflicts harm on a customer or other third party.

is guilty of **negligent hiring** if he or she failed to perform a thorough background check on an employee whose infliction of harm on a customer or third party could have been predicted by the employing firm. For example, a carpet-cleaning company was found to be guilty of negligent hiring and was ordered to pay $1 million to the parents of two University of Florida students who were strangled by an employee who was in their apartment to clean the carpet. A thorough background check would have revealed that the employee was a bad risk because he had been arrested on drug charges, had violently resisted arrest, and had been fired from two previous jobs.[65] Another important reason for verifying information provided on application blanks and resumes is that job applicants are increasingly lying about the qualifications they have. James E. Challenger, president of Challenger, Gray, and Christmas, Inc., has seen a variety of deceptive practices in his four decades of job search counseling.[66] For example, a "Wizard of Oz" resume is one in which the applicant claims to have performed duties or assumed responsibility for things he or she did not do. Other resume writers will try to enhance their salary bargaining position by indicating their salary "including tips" was higher than it was. Challenger has also seen a great many "Phantom College Degrees." Sometimes applicants slip up when doing this. For example, one applicant boasted that he had played varsity football at the University of Colorado's main campus in Denver. However, the University of Colorado's main campus is in Boulder.[67]

Once the application has been verified, it can be scored numerically to make it more comparable with others. The process of quantifying an application is called

EXHIBIT 7.5	RESUME BLOOPERS

Please disregard the attached resume, it is terribly out of date.

Here are my qualifications for you to overlook.

I am a great team player I am.

Very experienced with out-house computers.

I have lurnt Work Perfect 6.0, computor and spreadsheat programs.

My intensity and focus are at inordinately high levels, and my ability to complete projects on time is unspeakable.

I am an outstanding worker; flexible 24 hours a day, 7 days a week, 365 days a year.

In my last position I set up an entire office including furniture, lighting, computers, filing cabinets, and office procedures. I also have a flair for floral arrangements and catering.

I hold a B.A. in Loberal Arts.

I never take anything for granite.

To Home-Ever it concerns.

I have expertise in dealing with customers' conflicts that arouse.

I seek challenges that test my mind and body, since the two are usually inseparable.

I am good at checking out customers.

Reason for leaving: maturity leave.

Received a plague for Salesperson of the Year.

Wholly responsible for two (2) failed financial institutions.

I will not accept employment in foreign countries, including New York and California.

My compensation should be at least equal to my age.

I am writing to you as I have written to all *Fortune* 100 companies every year for the past three years, to solicit employment.

I have an extensive background in public accounting. I can also stand on my head.

Flunked the CPA exam with high grades.

Overlooked all areas to ensure an overwhelming success.

Completed 11 years of high school.

At the emphatic urging of colleagues, I have consented to apply for your position.

There is acuracy in all phases of my work.

Thank you for your consideration and I hope to hear form you shorty.

SOURCE: Elaine McShulskis, "Resumes as Entertainment," *HRMagazine*, April 1997, p. 22; Robert Half, *Finding, Hiring, and Keeping the Best Employees* (New York: Wiley & Sons, 1993).

weighted application blank (WAB) An application in which numeric "weights" are assigned to important questions in order to create a numeric score.

weighting an application. The use of a **weighted application blank (WAB)** involves placing a value or score for the items on the application that have been found to predict successful job performance. Applicants receive points according to the information they report on the form and can then be ranked based on their total points.

Although weighted application blanks have been found to be predictive of future performance,[68] the time and cost of developing an effective system are often prohibitive.

Cover letters and resumes are often used instead of application blanks. Managers sometimes ask for both a resume and an application blank, because the resume contains only the information the applicant is willing to voluntarily share. Because the cover letter and resume represents the individual, it is imperative that they contain no errors. A recent survey by SHRM found that 76 percent of those surveyed indicated that typos and grammatical errors cause them to remove the applicants from the pool.[69] Exhibit 7.5 provides some examples of bloopers that personnel expert Robert Half has collected over the past 40 years.

Although an applicant may believe that his or her resume is the way to get a foot in the door, this is probably not the case. According to Challenger, the odds that an unsolicited resume will result in employment are very poor because employers have been inundated with resumes from laid-off workers seeking jobs. When a hiring decision must be made, the decision maker normally turns to people he or she knows rather than to a pile of unsolicited resumes.[70]

Reliability and Validity in Testing

Selection testing is a means of obtaining standardized information from potential employees. Standardization means that the test contains the same content for each applicant and is administered and scored the same way for everyone. Using tests as a selection device is useful only when the tests are reliable and valid.

reliability Proof that a selection method consistently produces a similar score.

Reliability   Test **reliability** means that the test is consistent in its measurement. For a test to be consistent in its measurement it must be free from error. The more error in the measurement, the less reliable it will be. However, every measure has some error in it. If a person steps on a digital scale five times in a row, chances are that the weight reported will not be the same in each instance. It may read 155, 157 twice, 156, and 155. Although the reading of the scale changed over these five times, the actual or true weight did not. The variation in the readings was due to error in the measurement of the weight.

This example illustrates that every measurement is composed of two parts: *true score* and *error*. This error can be systematic. *Systematic error* occurs when the measure is incorrect by the same amount each time it is used. For example, if an oven always heats to 340 degrees when it is set for 350 degrees, the 10-degree difference is systematic error. It is always present, and it is always the same. The error in measurement also can be *random*. This type of error is not consistent. The weight example used above is an example of random error. The measure fluctuated up and down but not always by the same amount.

Error can be introduced into a selection test in many ways. For example, the person taking the test may make errors as a result of being worried, anxious, bored, or fatigued and by not working to his or her full potential (i.e., not producing his or her true score). The test itself could introduce error if two tests were developed that were designed to be equivalent but were not because one contained items that were not appropriate or were extremely difficult. Also, the environment in which the measure is being made—a room that is extremely hot or extremely cold—could cause error.

correlation coefficient A numerical index that represents the degree of relationship between two variables.

Before ways to measure reliability can be presented, we must first discuss correlation coefficients, because this statistic is often used to calculate the reliability of a measure. Essentially, a correlation coefficient is a numerical index that represents the degree of relationship between two variables. A **correlation coefficient** indicates the direction as well as the strength of a relationship. Correlations vary from +1.00 to −1.00. A negative correlation means that as one variable increases, the other variable decreases (e.g., as you party more, your grades fall). Conversely, a positive correlation means that both variables move in the same way (as you study more, your grades rise). The strength of the relationship is determined by the magnitude of the correlation. The closer the correlation comes to 1.00 (or −1.00), the stronger the relationship. A zero correlation indicates no relationship between two variables. Exhibit 7.6 illustrates the concept of a correlation coefficient, and Exhibit 7.7 presents a variety of scatterplots and the resulting correlation coefficients.

EXHIBIT 7.6	CORRELATION COEFFICIENT

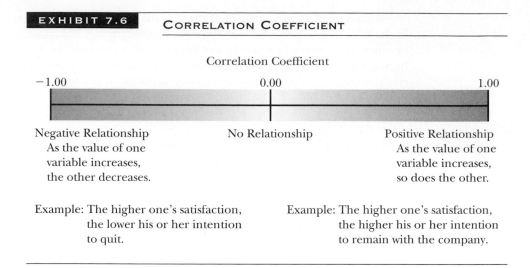

EXHIBIT 7.7	EXAMPLES OF SCATTERPLOTS AND THE RESULTING CORRELATION COEFFICIENT

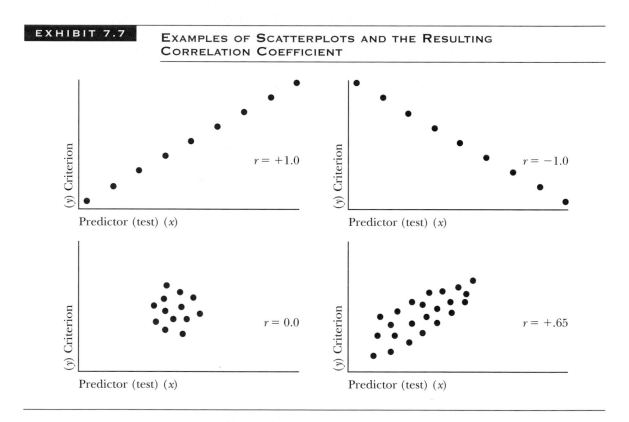

Methods for Estimating Reliability The reliability of a scale or test can be estimated in a variety of ways. Five different types will be discussed here: test-retest, parallel forms, split-half, interrater, and internal consistency. The estimate of reliability for the first four methods is a correlation coefficient. It is suggested that a correlation of .80 or higher indicates good reliability. The final method uses a coefficient alpha, which represents the average correlation of each item on the test with each other item. This value also should be .80 or higher.

Test-Retest Method   As the name implies, this method of estimating reliability requires that a test be given twice. Specifically, a group of people completes the test. This same group of people takes the same test at a later date. The scores on the two tests are correlated to produce the reliability estimate. The resulting coefficient is often referred to as the **coefficient of stability**. The idea behind this method is that if the test or measure is stable (i.e., reliable), the scores on each administration should be similar and hence correlated. It is important that the two administration times be far enough apart that the respondents will not remember their answers on the first test and simply repeat them. However, it is also important to note that if the administrations are too far apart, the individuals may have changed in some way (e.g., completed a class) that will also change their answers.

coefficient of stability   A measure of how reliable a selection test is over time.

Split-Half Method   The split-half method of estimating reliability splits the results from one administration of the test into two equal halves and correlates the results from the two halves. This is often accomplished by correlating the odd items with the even ones. This method is based on the notion that if the questions within the scale are similar enough to one another (i.e., reliable), the correlations between them should be high. It is important that each half be representative of the test's content and format. For example, if the test has two different types of question formats (e.g., multiple choice and true-false), an equal number of each should be included in each half.

Parallel Tests Method   To use the parallel tests method of estimating reliability, two equivalent forms of the same test must be generated. The two tests do not have to be identical, but they should cover the same material and be equal in length and difficulty. These two tests are either given to the same group at the same time or, as with the test-retest method, the same group completes one form at one time and a second form at a different time. In either case, the scores from the two tests are correlated. The resulting correlation is referred to as the **coefficient of equivalence**. In other words, if the correlation is high (greater than .80), the two forms are seen to be equivalent to one another. Obviously, the difficulty in using this method arises in developing two tests that are truly equivalent.

coefficient of equivalence   A measure of how similarly two measures tap the same construct.

Interrater Method   Interrater reliability refers to the agreement between two raters who use the same measure to evaluate a candidate. This type of reliability is often used in interview settings. Essentially, two different interviewers interview the same applicant using the same interview format. After the interview, each interviewer rates the applicant on a scale. The ratings from the two different interviewers are correlated to determine the agreement rate between them. This correlation is the interrater reliability coefficient. Interrater reliability may be low for many reasons. For example, the interviewers may not receive the same response from the applicant to the same question. Further, each interviewer may weigh the information received differently. Finally, the questions asked may differ for a number of reasons. Hence, low interrater reliability coefficients may mean that the interview procedure is faulty or that it was not followed correctly.

Internal Consistency Method   An internal consistency estimate of reliability determines whether each item is measuring the same construct. For example, if items were designed to test the applicant's ability to complete a balance sheet, but some of them asked the applicant about the innerworkings of a particular computer spreadsheet, the internal consistency of the test would not be high. In essence, each item is correlated with each other, and the average of these correlations is reported. A number of statistical procedures can be used to calculate the internal consistency of a measure; the most frequently used is Cronbach's **coefficient alpha**.[71]

coefficient alpha
A measure of the internal consistency of a test.

Validity   Specifically, if a test is valid, it accurately and consistently measures what it purports to measure. A test must be reliable if it is valid, but the reliability of a test does not ensure validity. Thus a test might accurately and consistently measure "something," but if human resource managers do not know what that "something" is, the test is reliable but not valid. For example, if you were given a ruler that was marked incorrectly (one inch actually was two inches long) and asked to measure the width of the cover of this book, you would report four inches. Likewise, anyone else given this ruler would do the same. Thus we would have a reliable measure of the width of the book because everyone reported the same value. However, is this value correct? No. The book is actually 8 inches wide. Hence, the measurement made with this ruler is not valid because it is not measuring the true width of the book.

There are many different ways to assess validity. In the sections that follow, four different types of validity will be discussed: content, face, construct, and criterion related (i.e., concurrent and predictive) validity.

Content Validity   Every test developed seeks to measure some underlying concept. For example, a typing test could measure someone's knowledge of typing rules. Further, there is a pool of questions that, if asked, would help to determine whether a person understands these rules. This pool could include questions concerning how many type lines are on a page or how many blank lines are needed in triple-spaced material. However, the pool would not include items about banking procedures or cooking instructions. This pool of questions is often referred to as the **content domain**. Thus, if every question on the measure is drawn from the content domain for that concept, the test has content validity. The more questions on the test from outside the domain, the lower the content validity.

content domain
All questions possible on a specific topic.

It is also important to note that the concept being measured (e.g., typing knowledge) must be relevant to a particular job. A good job analysis can help the human resource manager determine whether the specific KSA measured by a test is needed for adequate performance of the job. Content validation also must demonstrate that the items, questions, or problems required to be completed by the applicant are representative (from the domain) of the types of situations and problems the applicant would encounter on the job.[72] For example, suppose a typing test focused mainly on centering and headings, but the job required the applicant only to do this sort of typing once a year. Although the test was composed of items from the content domain of typing, it was not composed of situations that were relevant to the job. Hence, the content validity of this test as a selection tool for this job would be low. To determine content validity, a panel of experts who know the specific KSA required to successfully perform the job in question can be used.

face validity
How well the questions appear to tap the construct of interest.

One specific type of content validity is known as **face validity**. Essentially, a measure has face validity if the people required to take it view the items on the test as job related. In other words, on the face of it, the test appears to be tapping the KSAs required by the job. Face validity also is determined by experts, usually test takers. At the end of the test, questions that ask whether the items were appropriate for or related to the job might be included to gather information about the face validity of the measure.

Construct Validity   A *construct* is any characteristic that a human resource manager seeks to measure for selection purposes. For example, creativity, anxiety, motivation, and intelligence are all constructs. A test is said to have construct validity when the scores obtained from it can be interpreted accurately as measuring the construct intended to be measured, that is, whether a scale developed to measure motivation did indeed measure motivation. However, determining just how well a scale measures the identified construct is not easy, especially when the construct is an abstract one such as creativity. Hence, no one study can determine construct validity. Instead, a series of studies must be used. For example, the construct of interest, its components, and the way the job behavior relates to it must be defined. The degree to which the measure developed to evaluate this construct compares with other measures that are reported to measure the same thing must be determined. In addition, two groups that should possess very different levels of the construct under investigation should be identified and the results from the administration of the test to these two groups compared.

Criterion-Related Validity   Human resource managers use criterion-related validity to determine how well a test predicts an outcome. In simple terms, it is a correlation between a predictor (resume, application form, test results, letter of reference, and so on) and a criterion measure (performance appraisal instrument, performance ratings on some dimension, and so on). The higher the correlation, the better the test (predictor) predicts the outcome (criterion). The two ways to perform a criterion-related validity study are concurrent and predictive.

Performing a concurrent validity study is fairly easy. It entails developing a test or measure to use in future selection decisions. This test is then given to a group of employees who are currently employed in the organization. At or about the same time that the test is administered, performance data about these individuals are collected. The performance data and the test results are then correlated. The idea behind this validation technique is that those who score high on the test should also be the ones who have a good performance evaluation rating *if* the test is valid. Therefore a high correlation indicates that the test should be able to select qualified employees in the future.

There are limitations to this type of validity study. First, the employees currently doing the job will have more knowledge about the job than will job applicants. Hence, the question arises as to whether these two groups really are comparable. Also, everyone currently performing the job knows how to do it. Hence, no one should score poorly on the test unless the test is not related to the job. Therefore the scores will be clustered with very little variance. When a distribution of scores contains little variance, restriction of range has occurred. **Restriction of range** occurs when all of the scores are grouped together rather than distributed over the possible range of scores. If these scores are plotted, the scores are all clustered together, similar to the third example in Exhibit 7.7. The correlation for scores such as these will be low because the relationship depicted is not linear. This may lead human resource managers to assume that the test does not measure job-relevant factors when in reality it does.[73]

The goal behind predictive validity is to gather the data about the test from the same population that will take it. In other words, to overcome the problem found in

restriction of range All of the test scores group together rather than distribute themselves over the possible range of scores.

concurrent validity that the test takers (i.e., incumbent workers) have more knowledge than the applicants, actual applicants are used to validate the test in predictive validity. Specifically, a test is developed and is given to persons applying for the job. However, the scores on this test are *not* used to select the applicants; some other means are used. Approximately six months later, the performance measures of the individuals hired are collected. The tests taken when these individuals applied for the job are then correlated with the performance ratings. The higher the correlation, the more predictive the test.

Some problems are associated with predictive validity. For example, if only a few people are hired each year, it may take years to gather enough tests to compare to the performance ratings. Consequently, only the largest companies may be able to utilize this technique. A long period of time must be invested in determining validity, and it is possible that the results may indicate that the tool is a poor predictor.

Types of Selection Tests

A number of selection tests have been developed to aid the human resource manager in hiring employees. The following section covers mental ability tests, work sample tests, trainability tests, personality and interest inventories, and honesty tests as selection devices.

Mental Ability Tests   Pencil-and-paper tests have been developed by psychologists and are used by organizations to measure mental ability and aptitude. Ability and aptitude tests examine a variety of traits, such as general intelligence, understanding of spatial relationships, numerical skills, reasoning, and comprehension. Having been administered to over 2 million people, the Wonderlic Personnel Test is perhaps the most widely used measure of general intelligence. The Wonderlic is a timed test in which applicants are given 12 minutes to complete up to 50 questions. The questions tap a variety of abilities including numerical calculations, analogies, and spatial relations. Because of its wide-scale use (even the National Football League uses it), normative data are available for comparison purposes. Further, the test is rather inexpensive to use, costing as little as $1.50 per applicant.

One firm that has used pencil-and-paper tests to its advantage is BBC Engineering. Pencil-and-paper ability tests were designed to replace the initial interview. Once prepared, trial tests were administered to volunteers who worked at BBC. Concurrent validity results indicated that strong job performance correlated with high test scores. Now the recruitment staff sends applicants a "self-selection guide" full of information about the job, including sample items from the tests. With the implementation of the new system, the quality of the candidates has improved. BBC attributes this to the fact that unqualified workers self-select themselves out of the pool.[74]

Work Samples   Also called performance tests, work sample tests measure the ability to *do* something rather than the ability to *know* something.[75] These tests may measure motor skills or verbal skills. Motor skills include physically manipulating various types of job-related equipment. Verbal skills include problem-solving and language skills. Work sample tests should test the *important* aspects of the job. Because job applicants are actually performing a small portion of the job, it is difficult to "fake" one's ability on these tests.

One of the most effective ways to design work sample tests is by using the results of a job analysis. Because the results of a job analysis indicate which tasks are most critical and which are required for successful completion of the task, it is easy to determine which activities need to be represented on the tests. Provided that the materials are not too costly, requiring work samples that parallel what is actually done on the job can be an excellent way to locate only the most qualified applicants. Some examples of work sample tests include reading a blueprint for errors, correctly identifying the order in which 30 subcontractors work on a project from start to finish, locating construction errors in a building, and developing a daily schedule that matches the skills employees who are to work that day possess with the jobs that need to be accomplished.[76]

One company that has virtually perfected the use of work samples is Toyota. Since Toyota opened its doors in Georgetown, Kentucky, over 200,000 people have applied for the 7500 jobs in the assembly plant. In an effort to weed out all but the very best candidates for the jobs, Toyota developed a selection process that mirrors what employees will be required to do on the job.[77] It also included a hefty component on teamwork, because its work environment requires individuals to work as a team.

Six days a week, 24 people a day are run through the selection process. Starting at 6:30 AM, candidates are placed on a simulated assembly line where they are required to take part in the same activities they would perform if hired. Following the work simulation, applicants spend a few hours inspecting parts, participating in group problem-solving sessions, and completing written exams. In all, candidates spend 12 hours being evaluated on a variety of tasks. Some do not make it through the full 12 hours. Some self-selectors cut out after lunch whereas others ask for a bathroom break, never to return.

Trainability Tests   For jobs in which training is necessary because of (1) the skill level of the job applicants or (2) the changing nature of the job, trainability tests are useful. Essentially, the goal is to determine the trainability of the candidate. In the first step of the process, the trainer demonstrates how to perform a particular task. Then the job applicant is asked to perform the task while the trainer helps to coach him or her through the process several times. Finally, the candidate is expected to perform the task independently. The trainer carefully monitors the performance, recording any errors, to determine the overall trainability of the job applicant.

Both work sample tests and trainability tests have been shown to have high to moderate success predicting job performance.[78] Many managers, as well as job applicants, prefer these types of tests over the cognitive ability or aptitude tests because of their face validity (that is, the tests are *perceived* to be valid measures of future work performance by applicants and managers). Essentially, job applicants are more readily able to understand why they are suited or not suited for a particular job by actually performing the job or a portion of it.

Personality and General Interest Inventories   Personality and general interest inventories are tests that have no "correct" or "incorrect" answers. Interest tests are used to measure an individual's work and career orientations. Personality tests focus on identifying traits or typical behaviors of individuals and are used to measure a variety of traits, including aggression, self-esteem, and Type A behavior.

Over the past decade, there has been an increased interest placed on five personality characteristics referred to as the Big Five. The Big Five include emotional stability (being calm, optimistic), extraversion (being social, talkative), openness to experience (being imaginative, curious), agreeableness (being trusting, sympathetic), and conscientiousness (being dependable, determined). Several measures of the Big Five are available to use. One is the Personal Characteristics Inventory (PCI), which asks applicants to indicate their level of agreement with 150 sentences that describe behaviors (e.g., I enjoy trying new and different things).[79] The measure takes about 30 minutes to complete and only requires a sixth-grade reading level. Other tests designed to measure the Big Five include the NEO Personality Inventory and the Hogan Personality Inventory (HPI).[80]

General interest inventories are used to determine vocational interest. Results from these tests can be used to ensure a strong job-person and organization-person fit. Two of the most widely used inventories are the Meyers-Briggs Type Inventory (MBTI) and the Strong Vocational Inventory Blank (SVIB). Results from the MBTI place applicants in one of 16 categories that have been found to be related to the Big Five. The SVIB places applicants in one of six categories (e.g., realistic, artistic) to which jobs can be matched.

Although personality tests can be costly, they can help human resource managers determine individual characteristics not obtained from a resume, thus increasing the likelihood of finding a good "fit" between the job position and the employee. Most human resource managers and psychologists caution, however, that personality and general tests are not usually predictive of performance on the job and should not be used as selection devices. Nevertheless, some evidence exists in support of the use of personality inventories as a selection device.[81]

A serious criticism of personality and general interest inventories is their tendency to be invasive in that they seek to "uncover revealing data about a person's psyche."[82] Companies that use this type of preemployment test must therefore ensure that the information they seek and the way they use this information are relevant to the job in order to prevent lawsuits by rejected applicants. The legal challenges to written preemployment tests, in particular personality inventories, could result in legislation restricting their use,[83] especially after the well-publicized *Soroka* v. *Dayton Hudson Corporation* case, in which Target stores were sued for using a personality inventory to select security guards for their stores. Target admitted no wrongdoing, but it did settle the case for $2 million—a costly sum for not doing anything wrong.

Honesty Tests   In an attempt to identify employees who do not have a propensity to steal, firms may rely on honesty tests as a selection tool. Until 1988, the best way to assess an applicant's honesty was by performing a polygraph test. A polygraph, or lie detector, measures an individual's respiration, blood pressure, and perspiration while the individual answers a series of questions. Changes from the baseline for any of these indicators may mean the person is lying. However, in 1988, President Reagan approved new legislation that disallowed polygraph testing for preemployment screening of applicants.[84]

The more current way in which honesty is measured is via a pencil-and-paper test. Research has shown that thieves will give themselves away when asked direct questions about their honesty.[85] Specifically, thieves believe that everybody steals. Hence, if they indicate that they do not steal, they believe their test results will be flagged because everyone else will have admitted to stealing. So, they admit to stealing. Further, they suspect that their employers know they are stealing and openly admit to their crimes, even though they may tone down the actual severity of their transgressions. In other words, it is difficult for thieves to fake honesty. For this reason, honesty tests can be good predictors of applicants with the propensity to steal.

Exactly What Are Personality Inventories?

Personality inventories attempt to discern general personality characteristics by asking applicants questions. Although there are numerous types, in general personality inventories are designed to identify applicants' personality traits or expected behavior in order to assess their fitness for employment.

Personality inventories can be administered in several ways. One means is to have applicants read the questions and complete a computer-readable answer sheet by filling in the circles that correspond to their responses with a number 2 pencil. The answer sheets are either sent to the test developer for grading or graded by the employer using a grading system purchased from the test creator. Another alternative is to have the test creator telephone the applicants and read them the questions. Respondents indicate their answers by pressing certain keys on the telephone keypad. A more personalized option is to have the applicant participate in a face-to-face interview with a psychologist who asks the questions.

Because the focus of questions found on personality inventories is on personal beliefs, some of the questions may be intrusive and illegal. For example, questions that refer to religious affiliation or practices may cause disparate treatment in that employers may use answers provided to decide not to hire an individual. Questions that may fall into this category include the following:

- Do you ever argue a point with an older person whom you respect?
- Do you feel marriage is essential to your present or future happiness?
- Do you tend to be radical in your political, religious, or social beliefs?
- Would you like to be a church worker?
- Would you like to be a priest, minister, or rabbi?
- Would you like to read the Bible as a way of having fun?

Another problem that employers may face when using personality inventories as a selection device is invasion of privacy. This is exactly what happened in the Target case. Some items that may invade an applicant's privacy include the following:

- I am fascinated by fire.
- I feel sure there is only one true religion.
- I would like to be a florist.
- My sex life is satisfactory.
- I am very strongly attracted to members of my own sex.
- Evil spirits possess me sometimes.

SOURCE: Adapted from Daniel P. O'Meara, "Personality Tests Raise Questions of Legality and Effectiveness," *HRMagazine*, January 1994, pp. 97–100.

The Interview

Most organizations, regardless of size, use interviewing as a selection method. Interestingly, interviews have been criticized for being unreliable sources of information because of perceptual and judgment errors on the part of the interviewer.[86] For example, interviewers often form a first impression of the job applicant based on information obtained on the application blank or the first two minutes of the interview. Initial impressions are often resistant to change, even though they are made with little objective information. Interviewers may base subsequent questions and judge the candidate's responses on these first impressions in an attempt to confirm their beliefs about the candidate.

halo effect Rating someone high or low on a number of characteristics simply because he or she possesses one characteristic.

Another type of perceptual error is called the **halo effect**. In this case, one characteristic or behavior of the job applicant (positive or negative) overrides all or most other characteristics. For example, if an applicant comes to the interview dressed very professionally, the interviewer might unconsciously evaluate other characteristics (such as dependability or knowledge of the business field) as also being of a professional nature.

contrast effect
Evaluating an applicant as higher or lower based solely on the perceived quality of previous applicants.

Contrast effects also have been found to distort interviewers' judgments about job applicants. Contrast effects occur when the interviewer evaluates a job applicant by comparing this person with previous job applicants. For example, an average applicant might be judged as excellent if prior applicants were of very poor quality. Similarly, this same person might be evaluated lower if he or she follows a high-quality applicant.

Other perceptual errors that can distort an interviewer's evaluation include stereotyping, leniency, strictness, and central tendency errors. These perceptual errors are discussed in detail in Chapter 10 on performance evaluations.

Establishing a system for conducting an interview can improve the reliability and validity of interview assessments.[87] These guidelines should be followed when establishing a system for interviewing:

1. Determine the job requirements through a formal job analysis.
2. Focus on only those KSAs and other characteristics necessary to perform the job well.
3. Develop interview questions based on the information gathered in the job analysis.
4. Conduct the interview in a relaxed setting. Try to put the job applicant at ease by giving general information about the company and asking simple questions.
5. Evaluate each candidate according to his or her relevant job KSAs.

In addition to these guidelines, human resource managers must choose which *type* of interview to conduct. Interviews can be classified into three general categories: structured, semistructured, and unstructured. The following sections describe each of these categories.

Structured   When conducting a structured interview, the interviewer asks questions from a prepared list and does not deviate from this list except for some follow-up questions. During the interview, the interviewer records his or her thoughts and reactions on a standard organizational form. When different interviewers reach the same or very similar conclusions about a given candidate, the interrater reliability is high. Generally, structured interviews result in a high interrater reliability and can be helpful if gathering precisely the same information from each candidate is very important. In addition, structured interviews help to ensure that all necessary information is obtained. Unfortunately, this type of interview is very restrictive; thus important and relevant information about the candidate may never be discussed. This approach can also be frustrating to job candidates who are not allowed to elaborate on or qualify their responses.

behavioral description interview Asking applicants questions about how they performed in the past in order to predict how they will perform in the future.

Two common types of structured interviews are the behavioral description interview and the situational interview. The **behavioral description interview** was developed by Tom Janz based on the notion that the best predictor of future performance is past performance.[88] Behavior-based interviews allow you to gather and evaluate information about what candidates have done in the past to predict how they will act in the future. To develop a behavior-based interview, you should start with a thorough job analysis of the job for which the interview is being developed.[89] Be sure to uncover the specific KSAs required by the job as well as appropriate and important behaviors performed by the job incumbents. Next, you need to develop interview questions that

To Tell the Truth

NEWSFLASH: American employees steal $40 billion worth of goods and services from businesses every year! Such an astounding figure was estimated by the U.S. Chamber of Commerce and works out to $7125 a minute in thefts, which is 10 times the cost of the nation's street crime. It is no wonder that U.S. employers are grasping at any tools that might assist them in policing dishonest employees. The methods employers choose to screen applicants may be dependent on factors outside of their control, however.

What "guns" are available to help employers screen applicants and fight the crimes committed by employees inside organizations? The 1988 Employee Polygraph Protection Act declared preemployment screening by polygraph illegal in most cases (the government can still use polygraph testing). Credit checks have proven to be unreliable predictors of honesty. Although helpful, background and reference checks are proving to be less and less valuable to employers because the applicants' former employers are less willing to provide information beyond verifying when the candidate was employed. One obvious reason that companies are hesitant about providing information about a former employee is the fear of the potential legal ramifications.

One tool employers may use to screen dishonest applicants is the paper-and-pencil assessment instrument known as an *integrity* or *honesty test*. Although honesty tests certainly have their share of critics, the American Psychological Association (APA) released a report stating that the preponderance of the evidence supports the idea that some of the tests can help predict which prospective employees may be undependable or may steal. The question has been raised, however, whether the users of these tests even understand how to interpret what the scores means. The APA report recommends better training for employers who use and interpret the exams and proposes that the tests not be used as a primary or sole means for assessing an applicant's qualifications. Although an earlier report released by the Congressional Office of Technology Assessment raised questions about the reliability of honesty tests, the APA report may serve to reduce those concerns. At any rate, the debate about whether honesty tests should be used as a preemployment screening device is certainly not over.

SOURCES: Adapted from R. Zemke, "Do Honesty Tests Tell the Truth?" *Training*, October 1990, pp.75–81; and G. Fuchsberg, "Prominent Psychologists' Group Gives Qualified Support to Integrity Test," *The Wall Street Journal*, March 7, 1991, p. A6.

---

will elicit the desired behaviors. For example, if the job requires a great deal of coordination among workers, you could ask candidates to describe a time when they were required to coordinate a large project or several people's work output. Once all of the questions have been generated, the specific order in which they will be asked needs to be formalized. You also need to generate standards on which to judge the responses given by the applicants. The best way to do this is to try out the questions on incumbents and then have a group of experts score the responses. Answers that are judged as "good" should easily show the qualities the question was designed to elicit. If a candidate was asked to describe a time when he or she met a difficult goal, a good response would be one that showed the steps taken and how the candidate overcame obstacles to reach the goal. An average response may include the candidate just discussing how the goal was achieved but not offering any indication of how difficult the goal was to achieve. Finally, a poor response would be one in which the candidate was unable to come up with a response or the goal was not difficult. The final step is to train the interviewers. The interviewers will need to be trained on how to ask the questions, how to probe for more details, the specific order to follow, how to take notes, what to include in the notes, the benchmark responses, and how to judge a candidate's response against the benchmarked answers. Because there is a great deal to be learned, interviewer training may take several days. Allowing interviewers to practice on applicants is also a good idea.

By using behavioral description interviews, John T. Phillips, director of Training and Development at S.C. Johnson & Son, Inc., hopes to discover whether the job applicant will "fit" with the company. A job candidate might be told, "Give me a specific example of a time you had to reprimand an employee and tell me what action you took. In addition, what were the results of your reprimand?"[90] Note the specific nature of the question rather than a general one, such as "How would you reprimand an employee?"

However, these interviews are not always kind to the applicant. Applicants are generally not prepared for questions such as "Tell me about a time in the past when you had to get someone to do something for you. How did you go about it?" This could be followed up with questions such as "How did the person react to your actions?" or "How did it turn out?" Because the applicant is not expecting such questions, he or she may have to sit quietly and think about an example that fits the situation. A silence of only 30 seconds feels like five minutes, and the applicant may begin to fill the quiet by talking about an example that does not fit. Hence, in this type of interview, applicants who think well on their feet generally succeed. However, if this is not a characteristic needed in the job, this type of interview may not be the appropriate one.

situational interview A type of interview in which interviewees are asked to describe how they might act in a given situation.

The second type of structured interview is the **situational interview**, which was developed by Gary Latham and his associates.[91] To create this type of interview, job experts develop questions focusing on situations that might arise in the actual job. For example, an applicant for a teller position might be asked to describe how he or she would act if an irate customer came to his or her window. The job experts also develop above-average, average, and below-average responses to which interviewers can refer to judge the quality of an answer. Finally, situational interviews usually are conducted with a panel of interviewers, each of whom independently rates the applicant. These ratings are then averaged to produce an overall rating for the applicant. This type of interview is kinder to the applicant because a past example does not have to be provided. However, this same kindness is a potential problem for this type of interview procedure. Specifically, an applicant may respond in the manner that he or she thinks will get the job, not necessarily in the way he or she would actually act. Hershey Foods uses the behavioral description type of structured interview. Candidates are asked what they would do to resolve a real-life work problem. They are given a work situation and asked how they would respond if actually confronted with this situation.[92] Exhibit 7.8 provides examples of both behavioral and situational interview questions.

Semistructured In a semistructured interview, only the major questions are prepared in advance and are recorded on a standardized form. This type of interview involves some planning on the part of the interviewer but allows for some flexibility regarding exactly what and how questions are asked. Although the interrater reliability of the information is not as high as with the structured interview, the information obtained may be richer and possibly more relevant. In essence, this approach to interviewing allows the interviewer to ask the key questions without imposing unnecessary restrictions on the interviewee. Interviewers go into the interview knowing what they hope to learn from a candidate and then ask questions to elicit this information. One way this is accomplished is by asking the candidate a very broad question and then getting more and more specific with follow-up questions. For example, an inter-

EXHIBIT 7.8	EXAMPLE INTERVIEW QUESTIONS

Behavioral Description Questions

1. Describe a time when you had to get someone to do something for you. Please include what you needed done, why you needed it done, who you asked for help, and how you got them to help you.

    Follow up probes:
    How did they react when you asked?
    How long did it take to convince them?
    Why did you use this approach?
    How did it turn out?

2. Describe a time when you had difficulty achieving a goal or deadline. Please describe the goal or deadline, what obstacles were in your way, and how you tried to overcome the obstacles.

    Follow up probes:
    How did you feel during this time?
    How did you stay motivated?
    What kept you from quitting?
    How did it turn out?

3. Describe a time when you helped someone overcome a problem or complete a task. Please include in your example who the person was, what the task was, and how you helped.

    Follow up probes:
    How did they react when you offered to help?
    How long did it take to help them?
    Why did you offer to help?
    How did it turn out?

Situational Questions

1. It's an hour before you need to leave for work. Your spouse and two teenagers are sick in bed with the flu. What would you do?

    Good Answer: Find someone to check in on them and come to work.
    Fair Answer: Come to work, but leave early to check on them.
    Poor Answer: Call in sick and stay home to take care of them.

2. You are a sales associate in women's wear. A male customer has been in your area for 15 minutes. He looks confused and frustrated. What would you do?

    Good Answer: Approach the man and ask if you can help him.
    Fair Answer: Move near where he is standing and rearrange stock so he can call to you for help if he needs it.
    Poor Answer: Remain behind the register.

3. An employee who reports to you has been coming in late for the past few days. This is highly unusual for this worker and you are curious as to why his or her behavior has suddenly changed. What would you do?

    Good Answer: Greet the employee as he or she arrives at work and take him or her to your office to discuss the problem.
    Fair Answer: Explain to the employee that his or her behavior is unfair to the other employees and ask him or her to arrive on time from now on.
    Poor Answer: Ignore the problem and hope it goes away.

viewer might ask a college applicant to talk about a class he or she recently completed. Based on the information provided by the candidate, many different paths could be taken in follow-up questions. One possibility would be to focus on a group project that was required. Another would be to ask the applicant to summarize the one main point that he or she remembered from the class. Whichever approach is taken, it is selected to provide the most job-relevant information about the applicant as possible.

Once this approach is exhausted, a new general question is posed and the process is repeated.

Unstructured The unstructured interview involves little or no planning on the part of the interviewer. Because of a lack of planning, the interviews tend to vary greatly between interviewees and also between interviewers. In addition, important job-related issues may be left unexplored. Unstructured interviews have low interrater reliability and seldom yield valid or useful information. Thus unstructured interviews are not recommended as a selection device.

Improving the Interview

A company can take a variety of steps to improve the quality of its interviews. For example, it is important that the negative as well as positive aspects of the job are mentioned.[93] The interview is usually thought of as a means of selling the company, but if only positive information is presented, the hopes and expectations of applicants may be unrealistically high. When this occurs, turnover rises and satisfaction plummets. Another improvement involves revamping the interview system to make sure that it can identify the type of people the firm wants to hire.[94] Because the demographic makeup of the workforce is changing so rapidly, the interview procedures organizations use may also need to change. Taking a closer look to ensure that the interview procedures are gender and race neutral is a wise organizational decision.

Drexelbrook Engineering took steps to improve its screening interview.[95] First, the applicant is asked to complete an application form while seated at a table where information about the company is available. Whether or not the applicant looks at the material is noted. Next, the interviewer studies the application to determine whether any information has been omitted and why the applicant left (or wishes to leave) the last (current) place of employment. The interviewer then engages the applicant in verbal interaction to judge his or her verbal expression and appearance. The interviewer is instructed to explore the applicant's needs. If he or she is currently unemployed, when can he or she start? If currently employed, what does he or she do in the present job? Next the interviewer talks about the company and the job to be filled. Finally, the applicant is asked what he or she wants to know. The types of questions asked are noted. The interview ends on a friendly note with a specific promise of when the applicant will hear from the company. Although this may not seem like a great deal of information, it is more than adequate to determine whether to consider the applicant. Because this system collects more than just information about the verbal qualities of the applicant, the hiring decisions made have improved since the system was implemented.

Reference Checking

Most organizations ask an applicant for a list of references that includes previous supervisors or coworkers. Because the employee generates the list of references, these individuals will most likely present a positive image of the applicant. Letters of recommendation are also considered a type of reference. Again, these letters are usually solicited by the applicant, so many employers do not consider these as a good selection device by themselves. Studies have found, however, that if the letter contains specific behavioral examples, the applicant is viewed more favorably.[96]

Another reason that references can be overly positive is that many organizations are afraid to provide accurate appraisals of their former or present employees for fear of lawsuits.[97] Instead, they simply provide dates of employment as references. However, this is not as safe as one might imagine. Following this policy also can open a firm to litigation. For example, negligent hiring can occur because of the acceptance of a weak reference. As previously discussed, an employer can be held liable if an employee causes injury to a third party (customer, coworker, and so on) and it is proven that the employer failed to adequately check the employee's background. Employers have a duty to find out if an employee is unfit. Charges of **negligent referrals** can be lodged by a third party or an employer against another employer for giving a reference that either misstated or omitted facts about the individual. For example, a Florida judge held the ex-employer liable for not giving a negative reference on a former employee.[98] The former employee was fired from Allstate for bringing a gun to work. When Fireman's Fund Insurance called Allstate for a reference, no mention of the illegal and inappropriate behavior was mentioned. Allstate was found liable after the same employee shot and killed three of his coworkers at Fireman's Fund. Further, under the compelled self-publication doctrine, an employer can be held liable for defamation, even if it provides only dates of services, if a former employee is compelled to report to his or her prospective employer the reason for termination. The increase of cases involving these issues indicates that potential employers believe that they have the right to accurate information and that former employers have a duty to report it. Providing anything else is a risky proposition.

> **negligent referrals** Lodging a complaint against a third party or an employer for giving a reference that either misstated or omitted facts about the individual.

A firm can take several steps to use reference checking to its advantage.[99] First, the organization must decide, usually through a thorough job analysis, what key qualities are needed for the job. Reference checkers should ask questions designed to elicit information that will tell whether the applicant possesses these qualities. Some of these qualities might be a person's commitment to project completion (i.e., getting things done) or ability to predict needs before they arise (i.e., to plan). Giving the reference two alternatives helps to identify strengths and weaknesses. For example, asking whether the individual prefers to work with people or with technical equipment elicits specific information. If you are looking for the one they do not mention, you have revealed a weakness. Faxing a form to the reference giver that is signed by the applicant and indicates that he or she waives his or her legal right to action against the reference giver also may help. Finally, using open-ended questions will provide more information than simple yes-no questions.[100]

Physical Examination

Many organizations require a complete physical examination prior to hiring to ensure that the candidate is physically able to perform the job. However, the reason for the exam must be deemed a bona fide occupational qualification. For example, airline pilots are required by law to undergo an extensive physical examination. Physical examinations can also be useful for placement purposes. Individuals with lung or breathing problems may be best placed into jobs void of any smoke, dust, or fumes. In addition, a good physical examination should document any physical problems to avoid the possibility of worker compensation claims being filed against the company for a preexisting condition.

Physical examinations can also include drug and alcohol testing. Employers are reluctant to hire individuals who abuse drugs or alcohol, partially because of the higher absenteeism and turnover rates among these employees. In addition, employees do not work to their full potential and are more susceptible to accidents when they are under the influence of drugs or alcohol. Although many employees find substance abuse—testing programs in violation of their privacy, local, state, and federal regulations have not provided a standard and definitive set of guidelines for testing.

Acquired immune deficiency syndrome (AIDS) testing has become a very controversial topic for businesses.[101] In general, most medical specialists believe that AIDS testing in organizations is unnecessary because the disease cannot be contracted from AIDS patients under normal working conditions. Although AIDS testing is not part of a routine physical examination, some cities, such as San Francisco, have adopted city ordinances prohibiting discrimination on the basis of AIDS. Discrimination issues regarding AIDS were discussed in Chapter 5.

Many large companies choose to employ an in-house physician to perform physical examinations. A company physician has the advantage of knowing the physical demands and hazards for jobs and may be better able to help make knowledgeable decisions about hiring or placement. Obviously, the cost of an in-house physician may be prohibitive of many organizations. Exhibit 7.9 summarizes many of the selection methods discussed here and the frequency with which organizations use them.

Job Offer and Hiring

The final steps in the selection process are making the job offer and hiring the candidate. When employers extend a job offer to a candidate, it usually describes the types of duties and responsibilities the new employee will be expected to perform. The employer usually discusses salary (although this is often established well before the actual hiring occurs), benefits, promotions, vacation time, sick leave, employee assistance programs, and other policies of the organization. Although many of these were probably discussed during recruitment, it is always wise to keep important organizational policies and strategies salient to the employee. Finally, important documents are completed and signed (such as the employment contract and benefit forms), and the new employee begins his or her new job and new role as a member of the organization.

Managerial Selection Devices

assessment centers
Processes in which applicants are asked to perform a variety of job-related tasks and then judged on their performances.

Selection devices for managers can differ from nonmanagerial employee selection. In general, selection devices for managers should assess numerous skills and abilities because of the wide range of skills needed for successful performance. **Assessment centers** (which can last from one day to one week) were developed to tap these numerous managerial skills by collecting work sample information. An assessment center is not a place but a process. In this process, trained professional evaluators, called *assessors*, observe, record, and evaluate how a candidate performs in simulated job situations.[102] Generally, a variety of tasks are required to be completed by the applicants. Some of the most common ones include (1) in-basket techniques, in which the job candidate must decide how to organize numerous letters and memorandums by priority and ask for more information, delegate, or make a decision regarding them, (2) leaderless group discussions, in which the candidate engages in a typical simulated meeting, (3) role-playing, in which the candidate interacts with other "managers" or "subordinates," and (4) speech making. Each potential manager is assessed by several raters to increase the reliability of the hiring or promotion decision. Assessment centers have been found to be a valid means of assessing managerial potential,[103] but they are extremely costly; thus they are usually used for upper-level or top managerial positions.

However, one firm, Mercury Communications in England, has found that assessment centers can be used for front-line staff selection as well. In a two-year period,

EXHIBIT 7.9	SELECTION TECHNIQUES AND THE FREQUENCY OF USE

Technique	Percentage of Firms Reporting Use
Reference checking	96%
Interviews	94
Application forms	87
Ability tests	78
Medical examinations	50
Mental ability	31
Drug tests	26
Personality inventory	17
Weighted application forms	11
Honesty tests	7
Lie detector tests	5

SOURCE: A. M. Ryan and P. Sackett, "A Survey of Individual Assessment Practices by I/O Psychologists," *Personnel Psychology* 40 (1987), pp. 455–488; Bureau of National Affairs, *1988–89 Survey of Fortune 500 Companies*, Washington, D. C.; and I. T. Robertson and P. J. Makin, "Management Selection in Britain: A Survey and Critique," *Journal of Occupational Psychology* 59, pp. 45–57.

Mercury had to select 1000 customer service representatives. When a firm hires such large numbers, turnover can be a problem. Unless the person hired can do the job well, fit well in the organization, and like the job, he or she will quit, usually very quickly. To avoid this problem, Mercury decided to design an assessment center to select telecommunications customer assistants. The perfect applicant would have active listening skills, customer sensitivity, and the ability to cope in a pressurized environment. To locate individuals with these skills, the assessment center requires applicants to participate in simulated exercises with customers, a criteria-based interview, a keyboard skills test, and psychometric tests. From the initial pool of 1600 applicants, 350 were sent through the assessment center. Of these, 127 were hired. The process resulted in about 18 hires per week.[104]

Although the validity of assessment centers tends to be high, some problems recently have been identified with this selection device. For example, some researchers have found that assessment centers can produce hostile or defensive reactions among some candidates.[105] Also, assessment center formats have been found to cause a high level of anxiety in some applicants. Further, the "audience effect" may be detrimental to the performance of some individuals. That is, some participants may not perform as well as they are capable because the assessors constantly watch them.[106] Hence, when assessment centers are used, it is important to keep in mind that these problems could prevent the identification of qualified applicants.

HR CHALLENGES

Selecting Expatriates

As more and more organizations expand internationally, selecting the appropriate expatriate for these new international jobs becomes an important consideration. Recent reports indicate that between 40 and 70 percent of all expatriate placements do not serve their allotted appointments. Reasons for early returns vary, but the most common are the spouse's inability to adjust, the employee's inability to adjust, the employee's lack of personal and/or emotional maturity, and other family problems. There are two ways to combat these problems: develop better procedures to select expatriates and provide training for the expatriate and his or her whole family.

With respect to improving the selection procedures, several suggestions can be made. Research has found that three qualities—self-orientation, other orientation, and perceptual orientation—are needed for an expatriate to succeed in an international placement. *Self-orientation* means that the individual has good mental health, high self-esteem, and self-confidence. *Other orientation* means that the individual can get along well with others, has strong language skills, and understands nonverbal language. Finally, *perceptual orientation*

means that the individual has the ability to understand why foreigners act as they do and can accept these actions. To ensure that the expatriate selected possesses these qualities, the selection procedure should incorporate selection techniques that measure them.

Cross-cultural sensitivity training for the expatriate and his or her entire family has been found to decrease turnover rates. Before they leave the country, family members can be enrolled in culture and language classes. This will help them to better understand what to expect on arrival. Also, cultural counselors should be available on arrival. These counselors provide services that include helping to secure a place to live, registering with the authorities, shopping, or assisting with any other problems that arise during the move. Incorporating one or both of these suggestions should help to increase the expatriate's length of stay.

SOURCES: Bill Leonard, "Guardian Angels Help Overseas Employees," *HRMagazine*, April 1994, pp.59–60; Byron Sebastian, "Integrating Local and Corporate Cultures," *HRMagazine*, September 1996, pp. 114–121; and Marvina Shilling, "Avoid Expatriate Shock," *HRMagazine*, July 1993, pp. 58–63.

Strategies for Effective Recruiting and Selection

The organization's strategy can affect the recruiting and selection process. In general, organizations with different strategies should recruit different types of individuals for employment.[107]

Organizations in a retrenchment mode have shed all but their most stable and productive products and services, narrowing their focus. As a result of their narrow focus, these types of organizations seldom make major changes in their technology, structure, or methods of operation. They devote most of their attention to improving efficiency. Firms in this mode would emphasize "making" employees rather than "buying" highly trained or educated employees. Thus little recruiting is done above the entry level, and selection is based on weeding out undesirable or unqualified applicants. To make sure the employees retained are experts, firms in a retrenchment mode might emphasize training their employees. Thus new hires might be given trainability tests or intelligence or aptitude tests to identify those individuals most likely to learn from training.

Organizations in a growth mode search for product and market opportunities and experiment with responses to emerging environmental trends. Often, these types of organizations create change and uncertainty to which competing organizations must respond. Growth firms emphasize "buying" their employees rather than "making" employees through elaborate training programs. Recruiting methods are sophisticated at all levels of the hierarchy, and efforts are focused on identifying appropriate skills and acquiring qualified individuals. Given the emphasis on "buying" employees, training programs are limited. Thus growth firms might prefer to use work sample tests as a selection device.

The organizational strategy not only affects a firm's recruiting approaches and selection criteria but also affects which attitudes and personality traits are seen as the best match or "fit" between the applicant and the organization.[108] For example, employees with a need for risk taking and a high tolerance for change and ambiguity would be well suited in an organization with a growth strategy. Conversely, an employee with a need for structure and a low tolerance for change and ambiguity might be better suited in an organization with a retrenchment strategy.

Managers must not only be sure that the selection criteria are job related but also should consider whether the criteria are consistent with the strategies and culture of the organization. The relationships between strategy and recruiting and between selection and training are still somewhat speculative. These relationships assume that staffing decisions are (1) consistent with one another and (2) consistent with the strategy of the firm.[109] Thus these relationships should be viewed only as a general guide for managers.

Management Guidelines

Decisions regarding recruitment, selection, and retention are crucial for effective organizational performance. The following management guidelines should be helpful when making these decisions:

1. Managers should consider recruiting minorities, females, handicapped, and older workers as the workforce demographics change.
2. Managers can often improve employee satisfaction, commitment, and retention rates by promoting from within the company when feasible.
3. Career development should usually be part of any training program for new hires.
4. Preemployment forms should be free of questions that could be perceived as discriminating.
5. Affirmative action principles, if observed in the recruiting and selection process, can help to develop a more diverse workforce.
6. Measurement reliability and validity should always be considered in the recruiting and selection process.
7. The specific recruiting and selection methods should be consistent with the strategic thrust of the firm.

Questions for Review

1. What types of strategic choices do managers have when deciding on recruiting and selection efforts?
2. What are some alternatives to recruiting?
3. What is negligent hiring? What are negligent referrals? How can they be avoided?
4. Why should selection measures be reliable and valid? What does this mean?

5. What is a correlation coefficient?
6. How does the strategy of the firm affect the recruiting and selection process?

Hiring the Educated—A New Approach to Staffing the Automobile Factory[110]

Working in a factory is often a tedious, boring, and relentless job. Because of these job characteristics, highly educated workers have not been considered appropriate candidates for such work. Placing educated people in a monotonous job without any possibility for advancement was thought to be a good recipe for turnover. However, this theory is being reconsidered. Both Ford and Chrysler are looking for better-educated employees to staff their automobile lines. The reason? Things are changing.

First, old plants where cars were made by hand by skilled craftsmen are virtually nonexistent. In their place stand high-tech factories. Training the workers who staffed the old plants to run the new ones has been a nightmare. In one specific example, training hours reached one million because of the poor skills of the workers, the vast majority of whom had not even finished high school. By selecting educated employees, a firm's training costs should decline.

Second, team-based management is becoming a necessity. Prior to 1995, Chrysler (**www.chrysler.com**) had 1 salaried worker for every 25 hourly workers. That figure has now dropped to 1 to 48. Because there are not enough supervisors, workers will have to supervise themselves. Educated workers have more potential to do this than workers who have not finished high school.

Third, the nature of the work is changing. When a line worker notices a problem in production, he or she can stop the line, inform the authorities, and help to find a way to fix it. Performing these tasks will require better-educated workers.

Fourth, competition is changing. All of the auto manufacturers have entered the global market, and they need qualified workers to help them succeed. To compete, Ford and Chrysler have begun to use the manufacturing techniques developed by their foreign competitors. However, these competitors select from among the best and brightest graduates from technical schools to employ in their plants. To compete, Ford and Chrysler will have to recruit better-educated employees too.

But what educated worker would want this type of job? Plenty of them. With job opportunities so tight for college graduates, jobs that once were considered beneath them are now viewed as plum. Jeffrey Pancheshan holds an MBA from the University of Windsor; he earned his degree to find a good job. The best job he found was working in a Chrysler car plant in Windsor. He is not alone. Twenty-six percent of the workers hired at the Windsor plant in December 1993 were college graduates. This is quite a change from the situation five short years prior, when 10 percent of the workforce had so much trouble reading and writing English that the union and the company had to institute a remedial education plan for the workers.

Chrysler recently implemented a program to educate and prepare students at the high school level who are potential future employees of the company. One element of the program is a day when the students visit the Chrysler Technology Center and get an in-depth look at the work skills appropriate for the jobs there. Another aspect of the program is courses that are offered at high schools to help ease the transition for those individuals going straight from the classroom to a work environment. And lastly, Chrysler offers top high school students apprenticeships with a number of benefits and incentives, including a job when their training is complete. This gives the student hands-on experience and an idea of what to expect when they get into the working world.

The current flood of highly qualified applicants is a very different situation for auto manufacturers than they previously experienced. Twenty and 30 years ago, Ford had trouble getting enough people to show up for work to keep its lines running. Recently, it had 110,000 applicants for 1300 positions. Although this may sound like an enviable position, designing a selection system to weigh each applicant's qualifications was no easy process.

To accomplish this task, Ford designed a selection system that incorporated a number of tests and procedures. Specifically, each applicant was given a test that lasted three-and-one-half hours. The test included working math problems, including the use of fractions and percentages; reading technical material and answering questions about it; performing a variety of dexterity tests; and demonstrating the ability to work as a team. Applicants who scored in the top half of the group and who had solid work histories were then interviewed by at least two employees who were responsible for selecting the most promising prospects. Then each applicant had to pass a drug test and a physical exam to ensure they had adequate physical ability to perform the job.

What type of employee does a selection system like this choose? About one third attended college, and 4 percent have college degrees. Ninety-seven percent have high school diplomas. Some have completed trade school, and many are military veterans. The average age is higher than the past, nearly 30 years as compared with 17 to 18 years when high school dropouts were hired.

But what about turnover? Can a highly educated person be placed in a dead-end, boring job and be expected to stay? This question will only be answered with time. Both Ford and Chrysler recognize the potential for problems and realize that keeping these employees will be a challenge. But they also acknowledge that it takes a different person to build today's cars than it did to build them for these new workers' parents.

Questions for Discussion

1. What do you think Ford's overall strategic perspective is? How well does its new selection system support this strategy?

2. What steps are included in Ford's selection procedure? According to the chapter, what other techniques could it incorporate?

3. Are there any other factors that are causing the auto companies to alter their selection procedures and look for more educated employees?

4. How do you think this scenario will play out? Will the educated workers leave? Will they stay?

5. What type of work will the high school dropouts and immigrants who used to be selected to work in these car plants now be doing?

6. What benefits will Chrysler get from educating high school students?

Additional Readings

Bies, Robert J., and Debra L. Shapiro. "Voice and Justification: Their Influence on Procedural Fairness Judgements." *Academy of Management* 31 (September 1988), pp. 676–685.

Buck, David N. "Staffing Internal Audit Departments in the Year 2000." *Internal Auditor* 47 (April 1990), pp. 24–30.

Cosentino, Chuck; John Allen; and Richard Wellins. "Choosing the Right People." *HRMagazine* 35 (March 1990), pp. 66–70.

Cowan, Robert A. "Sacred Cows—Roadblock to Professional Staffing?" *Manufacturing Systems* 8 (March 1990), pp. 58–61.

Dossin, Milton N., and Nancie L. Merritt. "Sign-On Bonu$e$ Score for Recruiters." *HRMagazine* 35 (March 1990), pp. 42–43.

Dreyfuss, Joel. "Get Ready for the New Work Force." *Fortune* 121 (April 23, 1990), pp. 165–181.

Elliott, Brian. "Astride the Demographic Time-Bomb." *Accountancy* (United Kingdom) 105 (March 1990), pp. 110, 112.

Greenbury, Linda. "What Do I Want to Do?" *Women in Management Review* (United Kingdom) 3 (1988), pp. 202–206.

Harrison, Sheila S., and Geraldine D. Jones. "Star Search: The Black Enterprise Executive Recruiter Directory." *Black Enterprise* 20 (April 1990), pp. 74–82.

Herman, Roger E. "The Competitive Environment." *Security Management* 34 (April 1990), pp. 107–110.

Hildenbrandt, Herbert W., and Jinuyin Liu. "Chinese Women Managers: A Comparison with Their U.S. and Asian Counterparts." *Human Resource Management* 27 (Fall 1989), pp. 291–314.

Kaman, Vicki S., and Cynthia Bentson. "Roleplay Simulations for Employee Selection: Design and Implementation." *Public Personnel Management* 17 (Spring 1988), pp. 1–8.

Kleinschrod, Walter A. "Temporary Help Complete Your Personnel Picture." *Today's Office* 24 (January 1990), pp. 28–40.

Koch, Jennifer. "Apple Ads Target Intellect." *Personnel Journal* 69 (March 1990), pp. 107–114.

Landes, Jennifer. "GAMC Report: Agent Referrals Produce Agents." *National Underwriter* 94 (March 26, 1990), pp. 3, 22.

Lee, Paula Munier. "The Employee Equation: A New System for Solving Your Business's 'People Problems.'" *Small Business Reports* 15 (April 1990), pp. 61–71.

Licht, Walter. "How the Workplace Has Changed in 75 Years." *Monthly Labor Review* 111 (February 1988), pp. 19–25.

Marx, Jonathon. "Organizational Recruitment as a Two-Stage Process: A Comparative Analysis of Detroit and Yokohama." *Work & Occupations* 15 (August 1988), pp. 276–293.

Matte, Harry. "Cheese Plant Closing Opens New Doors." *Personnel Administrator* 33 (January 1988), pp. 52–56.

McQuaid, Maureen, and Daren Winkler. "Using PMTs in Handicapped Workshops." *MTM Journal of Methods-Time Measurement* 13 (1987), pp. 50–58.

Packer, Arnold. "Skills Shortage Looms: We Can Handle It." *HRMagazine* 35 (April 1990), pp. 38–42.

Rhodes, David W. "Shootout in the Classroom." *Journal of Business Strategy* 11 (March-April 1990), pp. 50–52.

Samorodov, Aleksandr. "Coping with the Employment Effects of Restructuring in Eastern Europe." *International Labour Review* 128 (1989), pp. 357–371.

Schnorbus, Paula. "The Confidence Game." *Marketing & Media Decisions* 23 (May 1988), pp. 133–148.

Smith, Charles. "Cosmic Disturbance: Political Scandal Hits Operations of Japan's Recruit Group." *Far Eastern Economic Review* (Hong Kong) 143 (March 30, 1989), pp. 44–45.

Sonnerfield, Jeffrey A., and Maury A. Peiperl. "Staffing Policy as a Strategic Response: A Typology of Career Systems." *Academy of Management Review* 13 (October 1988), pp. 588–600.

Stanton, Michael. "Cooperative Education: Working Towards Your Future." *Occupational Outlook Quarterly* 32 (Fall 1988), pp. 22–29.

Supposs, Dean A. "What Accident Histories Can Tell You." *Business & Health* 7 (March 1989), pp. 43–44.

Sweeney, Dennis C.; Dean Haller; and Frederick Sale, Jr. "Individually Controlled Career Counseling." *Training & Development Journal* 41 (August 1987), pp. 58–61.

Tobias, Lester L. "Selecting for Excellence: How to Hire the Best." *NonProfit World* 8 (March-April 1990), pp. 23–25.

Zhou, Songnian. "A Trace-Drive Simulation Study of Dynamic Load Balancing." *IEEE Transactions on Software Engineering* 14 (September 1988), pp. 1327–1341.

Notes

[1] Joann S. Lublin and Joseph B. White, "Dilbert's Revenge," *The Wall Street Journal*, September 11, 1997, p. A11.

[2] Donald E. Robinson and Timothy Galpin, "In for a Change," *HRMagazine*, July 1996, pp. 90–93.

[3] E. Blacharczyk, "Recruiters Challenged by Economy, Shortages, Unskilled," *HRNews*, February 1990, p. B1.

[4] Ibid; J. Braham, "No, You Don't Manage Everyone the Same," *Industry Week*, February 6, 1989, p. 29; and L. E. Wynter and J. Solomon, "A New Push to Break the 'Glass Ceiling,'" *The Wall Street Journal*, November 15, 1989, p. B1.

[5] Rochelle Shapre, "Work Week," *The Wall Street Journal*, October 7, 1997, p. A1.

[6] Carla Johnson, "Capturing Turnover Costs," *HRMagazine*, July 2000, pp. 107–119.

[7] "For Your Information," *Personnel Journal*, May 1991, p. 16.

[8] Gail DeGeorge, "Sign of the Times: Help Wanted," *Business Week*, November 10, 1997, pp. 60–61.

[9] "Hiring Line: How to Land Workers in a Tight Market," *The Wall Street Journal*, September 10, 1997, p. S21.

[10] Sue Shellenbarger, "More Corporations Are Using Flexibility to Lure Employees," *The Wall Street Journal*, September 17, 1997, p. B1.

[11] "Despite Downsizing, Shortage Creates Job Wars," *HRMagazine*, September 1996, pp. 19–20.

[12] Pui-Wing Tam, "Silicon Valley Belatedly Boots Up Programs to Ease Employees' Lives," *The Wall Street Journal*, August 29, 2000, p. B1+.

[13] "HRM Update," *HRMagazine*, January 1997, pp. 24–25.

[14] Michelle Neely Martinez, "How Top Recruiters Snag New Grads," *HRMagazine*, August 1997, pp. 61–64.

[15] Patricia Nakache, "Cisco's Recruiting Edge," *Fortune*, September 29, 1997, pp. 275–276.

[16] "Record Number of Companies Say They're Understaffed," *HRMagazine*, April 1997, pp. 26–27.

[17] Julie Foster, "That's It, I'm Outta Here," *Business Week*, October 9, 2000, pp. 96–98.

[18] Blacharczyk, "Recruiters Challenged by Economy, Shortages, Unskilled," p. B4.

[19] Ibid.

[20] Bill Leonard, "Welfare Reform: A New Deal for HR," *HRMagazine*, March 1997, pp. 78–86.

[21] Rochelle Sharpe, "Great Expectations," *The Wall Street Journal*, August 21, 1997, p. A11.

[22] Andrea C. Poe, "Refugees to the Rescue," *HRMagazine*, September 2000, pp. 81–84.

[23] Jim Meade, "Where Did They Go?" *HRMagazine*, September 2000, pp. 81–84.

[24] Larry Stevens, "Resume Scanning Simplifies Tracking," *Personnel Journal*, April 1993, pp. 77–79.

[25] Lyn Murphy, "Streamline the Application Process," *HRMagazine*, July 1993, pp. 35–38.

[26] B. Leonard, "High-Winning Game Plan," *Personnel Administrator*, September 1989, pp. 58–62.

[27] O'Connell, "Technology in the Employment Office," p. 34.

[28] Meade, "Where Did They Go?" p. 81.

[29] Ken Jordan, "Play Fair and Square When Hiring from Within," *HRMagazine*, January 1997, pp. 49–51.

[30] B. Schneider and N. Schmitt, *Staffing Organizations*, 2nd ed. (Glenview, IL: Scott, Foresman, 1986).

[31] Kathryn Tyler, "Employees Can Help Recruit New Talent," *HRMagazine*, September 1996, pp. 57–60.

[32] R. Mathis and J. Jackson, *Personnel/Human Resource Management*, 5th ed. (St. Paul: West, 1988).

[33]Bernard Wysocki Jr., "Yet Another Hazard of the New Economy: The Pied Piper Effect," *The Wall Street Journal*, March 30, 2000, pp. A1+.

[34]A. E. Marshall, "Recruiting Alumni on College Campuses," *Personnel Journal*, April 1982, pp. 264–266.

[35]Andrea C. Poe, "Face Value," *HRMagazine*, May 2000, pp. 60–68.

[36]Robert J. Grossman, "Robbing the Cradle," *HRMagazine*, September 2000, pp. 40–45.

[37]C. Edwards, "Aggressive Recruitment," *Personnel Journal*, January 1986, pp. 40–48.

[38]Nancy Hatch Woodward, "Asking for Salary Histories," *HRMagazine*, February 2000, pp. 108–112.

[39]Michelle Neely Martinez, "Winning Ways to Recruit," *HRMagazine*, June 2000, pp. 57–64.

[40]E. E. Spragins, "Hiring Without," *Inc.*, February 1992, pp. 80–87.

[41]J. B. Spangenberg, "Executive Search: A Misunderstood Resource," *HRNews*, February 1990, p. B6.

[42]"Clever Recruiting," *Executive Edge*, May 1993, p. 3.

[43]William G. Hetzel, "Negotiate Up Front When Using Search Firms," *HRMagazine*, October 1996, pp. 62–66; and "HRM Update," *HRMagazine*, February 1997, pp. 22–26.

[44]Sherry Kuczynski, "Taking Stock," *HRMagazine*, February 2000, pp. 50–54.

[45]Samantha Drake, "HR Departments Are Exploring the Internet," *HRMagazine*, December 1996, pp. 53–56.

[46]Mike Frost, "The Internet's Hire Purpose," *HRMagazine*, May 1997, p. 30.

[47]"Browse Click Career," *Fortune*, May 29, 2000, pp. 223–226.

[48]O'Connell, "Technology in the Employment Office," p. 35.

[49]Alice M. Starcke, "Internet Recruiting Shows Rapid Growth," *HRMagazine*, August 1996, pp. 61–66.

[50]Kevin Salwen, "Money Gets 'Em," *The Wall Street Journal*, April 12, 1994, p. A1.

[51]F. Leigh Branham, *Keeping the People Who Keep You in Business* (New York: AMACOM, 2000).

[52]Nicholas Stein, "Winning the War to Keep Top Talent," *Fortune*, May 29, 2000, pp. 132–138.

[53]Greg Jaffe, "How Adm. Konetzni Intends to Mend Navy's Staff Woes," *The Wall Street Journal*, July 6, 2000, p. A1+.

[54]Deborah S. Roberts, "Two Companies Battle High Turnover—And Win," *Recruiting & Retention*, May 2000, pp. 6–7.

[55]Stein, "Winning the War to Keep Top Talent," pp. 134–136.

[56]Ibid, pp. 133–134.

[57]Ibid, p. 138.

[58]Ibid, p. 134.

[59]Jaclyn Fierman, "The Contingency Work Force," *Fortune*, January 24, 1994, pp. 30–36.

[60]Marcie Schorr Hirsch, "When a Key Person Leaves," *Working Woman*, June 1994, pp. 20–23.

[61]"Permanent Part-Timers," *HRMagazine*, September 1996, p. 20.

[62]Timothy L. O'Brien, "Rise in Employee Leasing Spurs Scams," *The Wall Street Journal*, March 22, 1994, p. B1.

[63]Carolyn Hirschman, "All Aboard," *HRMagazine*, September 1997, pp. 80–85.

[64]"Suggested Hiring Procedures," *Risk Management*, October 1992, p. 58.

[65]"Company Liable in Slayings," *Tallahassee Democrat*, March 13, 1994, p. 4C.

[66]"Job Hunters Resorting to Questionable Ethics," *HRMagazine*, February 1997, p. 27.

[67]"Did I Say Harvard? I Meant Hartford," *Tallahassee Democrat*, February 16, 1994, p. B2.

[68]J. Hunter and R. Hunter, "Validity and Utility of Alternative Predictors of Job Performance," *Psychological Bulletin* 96, 1984, pp. 72–98.

[69]"Cover Letters and Resume Survey," SHRM Research, 1999.

[70]Bob Tippee, "The Resume: A Contrary View," *Oil & Gas Journal*, December 6, 1993, p. 13.

[71]L. J. Cronbach, "Coefficient Alpha and the Internal Structure of Tests," *Psychometrika* 16, 1951, pp. 297–334.

[72]C. H. Lawshe, "Inferences from Personnel Tests and Their Validity," *Journal of Applied Psychology* 70, (1985), pp. 237–238.

[73]R. L. Thorndike, *Personnel Selection: Test and Measurement Techniques* (New York: Wiley, 1949).

[74]Philip Schofield, "Improving the Candidate Job-Match," *Personnel Management*, February 1993, p. 69.

[75]W. Cascio, *Managing Human Resources: Productivity, Quality of Work Life, Profits* (New York: McGraw-Hill, 1989).

[76]David D. Robinson, "Content-Oriented Personnel Selection in a Small Business," *Personnel Psychology*, Spring 1981, pp. 77–87.

[77]Micheline Maynard, "Toyota Devises Grueling Workout for Job Seekers," *The Wall Street Journal*, August 11, 1997, p. 3B.

[78]W. Cascio and N. Phillips, "Performance Testing: A Rose among Thorns?" *Personnel Psychology*, Winter 1979, pp. 751–766.

[79]Michael Mount and Murray Barrick, *Manual for the Personal Characteristics Inventory* (Libertyville, IL: Wonderlic Personnel Test, Inc., December 1995).

[80]P. Costa, Jr., and R. McCrae, *Revised NEO Personality (NEO-PI-R) and NEO Five-Factor (NEO-FFI) Inventory Professional Manual* (Odessa, FL: Psychological Assessment, 1992); and J. Hogan and R. Hogan, "How to Measure Employee Reliability, " *Journal of Applied Psychology*, 1989, pp. 273–279.

[81]D. Day and S. Silverman, "Personality and Job Performance: Evidence of Incremental Validity," *Personnel Psychology*, Spring 1989, pp. 25–36; and R. Helmreich, L. Sawin, and A. Carsrud, "The Honeymoon Effect in Job Performance: Temporal Increases in the Predictive Power of Achievement Motivation," *Journal of Applied Psychology* 71 (1986), pp. 185–188.

[82]K. M. Evans and R. Brown, "Reducing Recruitment Risk through Preemployment Testing," *Personnel* 65, September 1988, pp. 55–64.

[83]R. Zemke, "Do Honesty Tests Tell the Truth?" *Training* 27, October 1990, pp. 75–81.

[84]S. Moss, "Polygraph Protection Act," *Personnel Today* 3, Fall 1988, p. 2.

[85]"Searching for Integrity," *Fortune*, March 8, 1993, p. 140.

[86]R. Arvey, "The Employment Interview: A Summary and Review of Recent Research," *Personnel Psychology*, Summer 1982, pp. 281–322.

[87]B. Felton and S. Lamb, "A Model for Systematic Selection Interviewing," *Personnel* 59, 1982, pp. 40–49.

[88]Tom Janz, Lowell Hellervik, and David Gilmore, *Behavior Description Interviewing* (Boston: Allyn and Bacon, 1986).

[89]Alice M. Starcke, "Tailor Interviews to Predict Performance," *HRMagazine*, July 1996, pp. 49–54.

[90]Solomon, J. "The New Job Interview: Show Thyself," *The Wall Street Journal*, December 4, 1989, p. B1.

[91]Gary P. Latham, Lise A. Saari, Elliott D. Pursell, and Michael A. Campion, "The Situational Interview," *Journal of Applied Psychology*, August 1980, pp. 422–427.

[92]A. Karr, "Creative Interviewing Takes Firmer Hold, and the Job Pinch Worsens," *The Wall Street Journal*, May 8, 1990, p. A1.

[93]T. L. Brink, "A Discouraging Word Improves Your Interviews," *HRMagazine*, December 1992, pp. 49–52.

[94]K. Michele Kacmar, "Look at Who's Talking," *HRMagazine*, February 1993, pp. 56–58.

[95]"A Structure for Job Interviews," *HRMNews*, February 10, 1993, pp. 3–4.

[96]B. Wonder and K. Keleman, "Increasing the Value of Reference Information," *Personnel Administrator*, March 1984, pp. 98–103.

[97]Karen Matthes, "Staying Neutral Doesn't Mean You're Protected," *HRFocus*, April 1993, p. 3.

[98]Anne Field, "Would You Hire This Person Again?" *Business Week*, June 9, 1997, pp. 32–34.

[99]Paul Falcone, "Reference Checking: Revitalizing a Critical Selection Tool," *HRFocus*, December 1992, p. 19.

[100]Carolyn Hirschman, "The Whole Truth," *HRMagazine*, June 2000, pp. 87–92.

[101]P. Myers and D. Myers, "AIDS: Tackling a Tough Problem through Policy," *Personnel Administrator*, April 1987, pp. 95–108.

[102]"Assessment Centers Help Target Employees for Management Selection," *HR Measurements*, January 1993, pp. 1–2.

[103]B. Gaugler, D. Rosenthal, G. Thornton, and C. Bentson, "Metaanalyses of Assessment Center Validity," *Journal of Applied Psychology* 72 (1987), pp. 493–511.

[104]Mike Thatcher, "'Front-line' Staff Selected by Assessment Center," *Personnel Management*, November 1993, p. 83.

[105]P. A. Iles and I. T. Robertson, "The Impact of Personnel Selection Procedures on Candidates," in *Assessment and Selection in Organizations*, ed. P. Herriott, (Chichester: Wiley, 1989).

[106]Clive Fletcher and Claire Kerslake, "Candidate Anxiety Level and Assessment Center Performance," *Journal of Managerial Psychology* 8 (1993), pp. 19–23.

[107]J. Olian and S. Rynes, "Organizational Staffing: Integrating Practice with Strategy," *Industrial Relations*, Spring 1984, pp. 170–183.

[108]G. Milkovich and W. Glueck, *Personnel Human Resource Management: A Diagnostic Approach* (Plano, TX: Business Publications, 1985).

[109]S. Rynes, H. Heneman III, and D. Schwab, "Individual Reactions to Organizational Recruiting: A Review," *Personnel Psychology*, Autumn 1980, pp. 529–542.

[110]Neal Templin, "Dr. Goodwrench: The Auto Factories Are Hiring Better-Educated Workers, Including College Grads," *The Wall Street Journal*, March 11, 1994, p. A11.

III

Strategies for Maximizing Human Resource Productivity

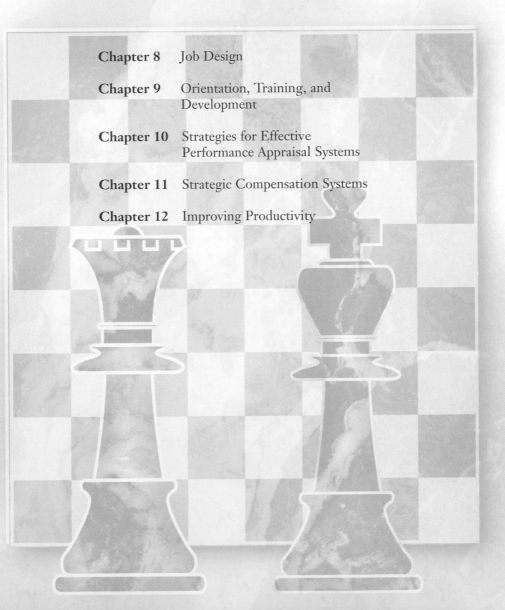

8

Job Design

Chapter Objectives

As a result of studying this chapter, you should be able to

1. Discuss the various environmental, organizational, and behavioral factors that need to be considered in job design.

2. Discuss early approaches to job design.

3. Describe the various individual and group design options.

4. Discuss the sociotechnical model and the characteristics of autonomous work groups.

5. Describe how the job characteristics model can aid managers in job design or redesign.

6. Discuss the relationship between organizational strategy and job design.

7. List and describe the steps involved in the strategic framework for job redesign.

How a job is designed has a tremendous impact on the effectiveness of the organization and the quality of work life for employees. Given the importance of job design, it should be tied directly to the strategies and goals of the organization.

Job design can be thought of as a blueprint of tasks required to accomplish a job successfully. Job design and redesign techniques have become more complex because of the downsizing that has plagued many organizations. Essentially, fewer challenging jobs are available, and employees are sometimes placed in jobs for which they are clearly overqualified.[1]

CASE

Fearful Skies and the Bored X-Ray Operators[2]

As Americans make plans to fly abroad, many still find themselves concerned about terrorism. The airplane explosion over Lockerbie, Scotland, more than a decade ago still concerns many flying overseas. It is difficult to forget how terrorists planted a bomb aboard Pan Am Flight 103 in December 1988, killing 270 people.

The U.S. government has tried to respond to dangerous terrorists' threats. Because bombs can be hidden and disguised in ordinary items such as radios and laptop computers so that X-rays cannot spot them, the Transportation Department considered a total ban on such items. However, the fact remains that there are few defenses against sophisticated terrorists. Worse yet, even those procedures that exist can fail through human error, when airport workers are overloaded and overwhelmed by hoards of impatient passengers and mountains of luggage.

The Lockerbie case is sobering. Two Libyans were suspected in the bombing incident, and the United States negotiated with Libya to have them tried in the United States. The two said to be responsible for this were indicted, and investigators now know the bomb was planted inside a radio-cassette recorder hidden in a suitcase.

X-Ray Limitations

All X-ray machines depend on interpretations by operators, some of whom may be ill trained or poorly motivated. The Transportation Department task force reports that training of U.S. X-ray screeners was described as "perfunctory." The President called for a commission to investigate aviation security measures. The commission recommended numerous changes including new screening technologies, more training, and better coordination of security measures across countries.

To avoid paying high airline wages and flight benefits, U.S. carriers generally hire outside security firms to perform screening. The firms, which often are hired by submitting the lowest bid, pay screeners poorly, sometimes only slightly above the minimum wage. Two contractors interviewed by the task force said fast-food chains were their chief competitors for staff. "The restaurants occasionally paid more . . . and even if pay were the same, had the advantage because they provide meals as well," the task force said.

Perhaps the biggest problem is the nature of the job itself. "Anyone standing in front of a monitor watching suitcase after suitcase go by is bound over time to become tired and inattentive," the task force stated. At peak periods, it added, screeners are confronted with "long lines of anxious passengers, putting the screening crew under extreme pressure" to rush bags through.

In Europe, government employees usually screen passengers, with U.S. carriers often performing a second screening. But the same problems afflict screeners overseas, of course.

Since the Lockerbie disaster, the U.S. Department of Transportation has ordered U.S. carriers to intensify security procedures on all bags checked in Europe and the Middle East. Federal regulation requires that bags be searched or X-rayed, and all must be matched to a passenger on board. But even today, bags checked on carriers at many airports around the world are neither searched nor X-rayed. They are put, unexamined, on airplanes.

Pan Am charged the Federal Aviation Administration with approving security procedures in Frankfurt that the airline found, after the Lockerbie crash, to be in violation of federal regulations. Pan Am did not match each bag checked with a passenger on board; it simply relied on the X-ray screeners to identify bombs in unmatched bags. Terrorists countered by using unwitting bomb carriers.

For example, an Irish woman passed through London Heathrow security—which was equipped with an X-ray machine—with a suitcase that was packed with a bomb prepared by her Arab boyfriend. The timer was concealed in a calculator, and the bomb was in the bottom of the suitcase. Fortunately, El Al security personnel at the gate discovered the bomb just before the woman boarded.

One of the major problems is with the way an X-ray machine operator's job is designed. The work is so repetitive, it is no wonder that the workers become bored, tired, and inattentive. Given the potential disastrous effects of an inattentive X-ray machine operator, airlines might consider evaluating the current job design. Redesigning the work of airline X-ray personnel to be more interesting and motivating could save lives.

Poor job design is not always associated with life or death consequences; however, in an era of shrinking profits and increased global competition, corporations cannot afford to neglect continuous product and process improvement. Job design and redesign strategies can help companies maintain their competitive edge by making the most efficient use of their resources (human, capital, and technological).

Strategic Choices

The decision to initially design or later redesign jobs in an organization should not be made hastily. Managers must consider a number of factors before deciding on a job redesign effort. Any job redesign program should be examined carefully and be consistent with the overall strategy of the organization. Environmental, organizational, and behavioral factors should be considered before designing jobs for the first time or redesigning jobs because of a needed change.

Environmental Factors

Political System   All organizations are affected by the political systems in their environment. Organizations must comply with international, national, state, and local laws, regulations, and ordinances if they want to survive. Managers need to be aware of a plethora of laws because virtually every aspect of their organizational operations is affected by legal considerations. In the United States, numerous laws cover wages, hiring practices, benefits, drug testing, and safety standards. These laws can have a direct or indirect impact on the design of the job. For example, safety regulations may directly affect the design of certain jobs. Consider a factory worker who walks between dangerous machinery or moving belts because this is the most efficient path to obtain needed supplies. The Occupational Safety and Health Act (OSHA) would most likely prohibit such behavior. The organization should redesign this job to avoid employee injuries and a fine from OSHA. If a number of jobs required employees to walk through dangerous areas, the organization might need to consider a total redesign effort.

Organization managers must also consider the political systems in other countries. Organizations in the United States are affected by problems such as grain shortages in the Soviet Union and international terrorism. The opening case to this chapter demonstrates the need for the jobs of airline X-ray operators to be redesigned to better detect terrorist bombs. It is vital that managers consider their political and economic environments in order to design or redesign jobs within the organization.

Social Expectations The acceptability of a job's design is partially due to societal expectations. Culture, the work ethic, and religion all help to shape societal expectations. For example, uneducated immigrants flocked to America in the early days of the automobile industry. They were willing to accept low-paying jobs that were routine, physically difficult, and demanding of long work days. Often these immigrants were willing to accept this type of job because they had left countries where work was unavailable. Today, however, employees are better educated and expect a higher quality of work life from their jobs. Failure to meet these expectations can lead to low motivation, dissatisfaction, low performance, and high absenteeism and turnover.

Organizational Factors

Automation One important decision that managers must make when designing jobs initially or when considering job redesign is whether they want to automate the job and, if so, to what degree. Job redesign through automation has been undertaken by many companies, including companies in the automobile and steel industries, in order to cut labor costs. Reducing labor costs has helped many organizations to achieve or remain competitive in world markets. One strategic choice the firm must make is to decide how much it wants to substitute capital for labor through automation, robotics, and other highly technical innovations. A company can reduce per unit labor costs by increasing automation, thus reducing labor costs. For example, PepsiCo developed a beverage dispenser that fills cups by computer.[3] General Motors introduced robotics on the assembly line, changing many of the jobs while making others obsolete.

In some instances, more interesting and challenging jobs can be opened for employees in the organization by automating the more repetitive and routine jobs. Automation (for example, word processors or laser printers) has given secretaries more time for new and higher-level duties. Firms are training secretaries as managerial assistants and paraprofessionals. Thus secretarial skills are broadening, partially because of automation. At Quanex Corporation in Houston, many secretaries take on marketing or personnel responsibilities.[4] However, automation should not be seen as a panacea for job enrichment. Automation often leads to more routine jobs, a decrease in social interaction, displacement, or even the elimination of jobs.[5] Continual performance of repetitive and routine jobs, although efficient, can lead to employee boredom, fatigue, tardiness, absenteeism, performance decrements, and ultimately lower productivity. This issue will be explored in greater detail later in the chapter.

Technology   Many managers want to have state-of-the-art equipment in their organization. Often keeping up with the latest developments in the technical field can help keep a company on the "cutting edge." For managers who master the newest in office technologies, the payoff can be more power and greater control.[6] Just as often, however, investing in expensive equipment can serve to be a waste of resources. Investing in a new computer system, for example, may not be cost effective. Not only should the cost of the equipment be a concern, but also managers must consider the costs of any additional training needed to teach employees the new system, any loss of productivity because of training or computer downtime during implementation, and how jobs will be affected. For example, some very specific workplace effects attributable to computerization have been identified from the research.[7] The implementation of a computer-aided design system has been found to increase and change communication patterns on the job, increase skill requirements, and increase the formalization of work methods. Interestingly, computer-aided designs have not affected job displacement or wages significantly.

If managers fail to understand and prepare for the revolutionary capabilities of high-technology computer systems, new technology can become as much an expense and inconvenience as a benefit.[8] If the new system changes a number of jobs, additional considerations need to be made. First, are the employees skilled enough to work their newly designed job? Do they want to take on additional (or fewer) responsibilities? Will the time and effort required for training and learning be cost effective? How well can the organization respond to new incentives if jobs are substantially changed?[9] Finally, are the employees committed to the job redesign change and willing to try to make it work? A longitudinal study examined the adjustment of unskilled workers transferring from traditional assembly lines to computer-automated batch production. Results suggest that actual changes to jobs increased employee stress and decreased job satisfaction, organizational commitment, and the perceived quality of work life.[10]

An essential ingredient for a successful job redesign effort is employee training. Ingersoll-Rand, for example, developed a special program designed to help employees cope with plant modernization.[11] Ingersoll-Rand, in Athens, Pennsylvania, is the primary manufacturing location for the company's power tool division. Parts of the plant were over 100 years old. To remain competitive, Ingersoll-Rand needed to modernize its machinery. Employees had been operating conventional machine tools (such as cranks, dials, and buttons); however, as a result of the job redesign effort, employees were expected to operate numerically controlled machinery. They had to perform computer setups, interact with this new technology, and integrate these skills with their regular work teams. Essentially, production methods went from the traditional assembly-line system to cellular manufacturing. Penn State University's Institute for Research in Training and Development conducted a training program on two levels: basic skills (reading, writing, and arithmetic) and floor skills (the daily skills needed to operate the computerized equipment). The results have exceeded expectations. The training program helped Ingersoll-Rand profit from plant modernization because computerization has kept costs down and has enabled the company to offer products priced competitively. Just as important, the employee response to the program was extremely favorable: 99 percent of the eligible employees volunteered to participate. In addition, many of these employees went beyond the training program and continued their education in the classroom. Managers should carefully analyze all aspects of any job redesign program to give it the best chance for success.

Cross-Functional Integration   Cross-functional integration is the act of combining several jobs into one. A number of organizations have begun cross-functional integration in order to cut labor costs and raise productivity. For example, Motorola rewards workers who learn a variety of skills and, as a consequence, has found that its defect rate has dropped by 77 percent.[12] Service firms have been particularly interested in cross-functional integration because of the typical high turnover rates in the service industry. For example, Manor Care, which operates the Sleep Inn hotel chain, designed its hotels with the flair of an industrial engineer. By simplifying jobs and carefully examining the time it takes to complete them, Manor Care is able to combine jobs and keep its staff size down.[13] A typical 100-bed Sleep Inn employs only 12 full-time employees, 13 percent fewer than the average no-frills hotel. To simplify housekeeping, the nightstands are bolted to the walls so that workers do not need to vacuum around the legs. The closet has no doors to open and shut. The shower is round to prevent dirt from collecting in the corners. These labor-saving devices give housekeepers more time to do additional tasks, such as working with room service or even at the front desk.

The hotel's security system helps the owners keep track of the time it takes a housekeeper to clean a room. The employee inserts a card that tells the front-desk computer where the housekeeper is located and when he or she entered the room, finished cleaning it, and exited it. This same computer can bar a guest's access to the room after checkout time and can automatically turn off the heat or air-conditioning. Thus, by simplifying jobs, combining jobs, and utilizing technology, Manor Care has been able to cut its labor force and raise wages while remaining competitive.

Behavioral Factors

Labor Pool Skill Mix   Before attempting a job design or redesign program, managers should decide whether their employees' skills will match or "fit" the new jobs. Sometimes additional training is all that is necessary. However, on occasion, employees will not have the abilities or education to perform the newly designed jobs. This can lead to dissatisfaction, frustration, and poor performance. If the job design or redesign effort simplifies the work too much, employees may become bored, apathetic, unchallenged, and dissatisfied. These individual factors could lead to poor performance and lower productivity even if the job has been designed to be more efficient.

Unfortunately, most companies cannot afford to train workers to perform the duties required by a job redesign. A significant proportion of the individuals looking for work today lack the necessary skills to read computer manuals, program robotic welders, perform statistical quality control, and the like. Many of the new entrants to the job market will not be qualified for jobs of the future.[14]

Companies have responded by making jobs less complex and more routine. You may have noticed that the numbers on the registers of fast-food restaurants have been replaced by symbols corresponding to the requested food item. The price of each item, the total price, and the change from the transaction are automatically computed. Some restaurants even have registers that dispense the correct coin change to the customer via a change chute!

Designing Jobs to Fit the Needs of Employees or Technology   Designing or redesigning jobs can be made to fit the employees, the existing technology, or a combination of both. Managers must decide which direction they believe is most appropriate for their organization. Designing jobs for people involves an important

Jobs Disappear—When *Work* Becomes More Important

On the surface, Koch Industries and Amazon.com don't have much in common. Koch, based in Wichita, Kansas, employs 14,000 people worldwide and is America's second largest privately held company. It has a 60-year history in industries as diverse as chemicals, agriculture, financial services, and oil and gas. Koch employs everyone from farmers in Montana to commodities traders in London.

Amazon.com, based in Seattle, employs 5000 people and is publicly traded. Six years ago, Amazon led the way as a standard bearer of a whole new industry—e-commerce—and employed Internet-savvy business professionals. But despite their outward differences, Koch Industries and Amazon.com are remarkably similar in one respect: They don't hire people for traditional job slots. They hire people to do work.

Walk into the HR departments of these companies, and you won't find a complex system of job classifications, pay grades, promotional charts, and job descriptions. "We don't have any of that normal HR structure," says Paul Wheeler, vice president of HR for Koch Industries. Neither does Amazon.com. "We focus on what needs to be done," explains Scott Pitasky, director of strategic growth—which is Amazon's word for HR. "Here, a person might be in the same 'job,' but three months later doing completely different work."

As disorganized as it may sound, these companies are actually role models for 21st century human resource practices. Why? Because their HR professionals understand that the traditional way of organizing work in which a person is hired, paid, and trained to do a *specific job* is simply too rigid for today's ever-changing marketplace.

To succeed, more companies will have to follow Koch and Amazon's lead and seriously begin to rethink the way they organize and accomplish work. Simply put, jobs as we know them are fast becoming relics of a bygone era. Whereas employers, employees, paychecks, and careers will remain, the rigid lines we draw around work itself will be gone.

SOURCE: Adapted from Shari Caudron, "Jobs Disappear," *Workforce*, January 2000, pp. 30–32.

examination of the wants, needs, and desires of employees. Managers of car and light truck fleets often overlook the needs of their drivers when buying the cars and trucks. Some managers, however, view their drivers as customers, often allowing the drivers a choice of which vehicles to use. Patsy Brownson, of Cox Enterprises, Inc., allowed her entry-level drivers to pick any four-door sedan (under a certain set amount), which she then purchased for company use. She found that the drivers seemed to be happier with their choice, had pride in their vehicles, and took better care of them.[15] Jobs can be designed to increase the meaningfulness of the work for employees' satisfaction and motivation. The job characteristics model, which addresses the issue, will be discussed later in this chapter. Designing jobs to fit the technology is often a primary concern. For example, organizations that have large amounts of money invested in machinery and equipment (such as the General Motors assembly line) must keep these capital investments in mind if job redesign is considered. Another approach of management to design or redesign is to consider the needs of both the technology and people simultaneously. This is called a *sociotechnical system*. Basically, it involves forming autonomous work groups that recognize the importance of integrating the social system with the technical system. This approach will be explored further later in the chapter. Before examining new approaches to job redesign, early job design efforts will be discussed.

Early Job Design Efforts

Scientific Management   Frederick Taylor, the father of "scientific management," focused on the efficiency of operations after the turn of the century. Taylor's scientific management principles and general management philosophy emphasized the following components:

1. Specialization (narrow range of tasks per job).
2. Clear and specific job descriptions.
3. Systematic scheduling of work and rest breaks.
4. Close supervision.

Utilizing the scientific management approach, industrial engineers and job analysts focused on specialization in designing jobs so that they would not exceed the abilities of the workers. As a result, most jobs were mechanistic and reduced to extremely simple and repetitive tasks. These tasks lent themselves to time and motion studies and piece rate reward systems. Although efficient, scientific management overlooked the human element when designing the job. Many workers became bored, tired, and dissatisfied with their repetitive jobs. In effect, the personal goals of the employee (growth and challenge) were sacrificed for the goals of the organization (productivity).

Human Relations   In the early 1930s, managers became aware of the need to emphasize employee morale and cooperation. Treating employees as "human beings" as opposed to machines and acknowledging their needs was the emphasis of the human relations movement. Historically, three critical factors gave impetus to this new approach to management: the Great Depression, the labor movement, and the Hawthorne studies.[16] The Depression was due to a number of factors, including a piling up of business inventories and consumer resistance to rising prices. After the stock market crash, management realized that production was not the only important organizational factor. Marketing, finance, and personnel also needed to be emphasized. Unemployment, a weakening of confidence, and a general discontent made human problems more salient to managers. Human relations became a more significant issue.

The passage of the Wagner Act in 1935 gave employees the right to organize and unionize. The organized labor movement helped make managers aware of the employee concerns. Typical areas of employee concern included fair wages, decent working conditions, and reasonable hours. Although many organizations initially resisted labor interference, organized labor became legal and management (some more willingly than others) began to work with employees to resolve grievances and emphasize employee relations.

The final contributing factor to the human relations movement was a series of studies conducted at the Hawthorne Works of the Western Electric Company outside Chicago. Conducted under the direction of Harvard professor Elton Mayo, the Hawthorne studies demonstrated the importance of group influences in affecting individual behavior and performance. These studies concluded that group norms and standards had a more significant impact on worker output than did money. Together, the Great Depression, the labor movement, and the Hawthorne studies gave impetus to a new organizational emphasis—the human factor. Today, managers are interested in determining how to design jobs to better motivate their employees.

The importance of job design can be seen in the results of a study that surveyed over 56,000 people. Individuals were asked to rate the most important factor in a job.

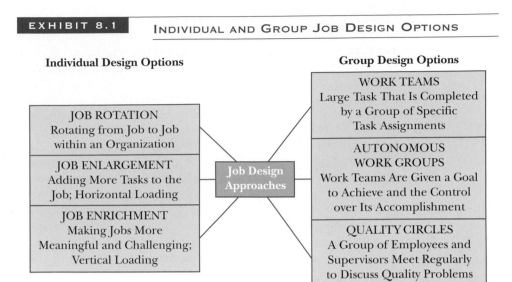

EXHIBIT 8.1 INDIVIDUAL AND GROUP JOB DESIGN OPTIONS

Individual Design Options

Group Design Options

JOB ROTATION
Rotating from Job to Job within an Organization

JOB ENLARGEMENT
Adding More Tasks to the Job; Horizontal Loading

JOB ENRICHMENT
Making Jobs More Meaningful and Challenging; Vertical Loading

Job Design Approaches

WORK TEAMS
Large Task That Is Completed by a Group of Specific Task Assignments

AUTONOMOUS WORK GROUPS
Work Teams Are Given a Goal to Achieve and the Control over Its Accomplishment

QUALITY CIRCLES
A Group of Employees and Supervisors Meet Regularly to Discuss Quality Problems and Solutions

Interesting work was rated as the most important factor in a job over security, pay, advancement opportunities, pleasant coworkers, or a considerate boss. Thus it appears that the job itself can provide a significant source of motivation for employees.[17]

The Sociotechnical Model The work environment includes both technical and social aspects. These two systems are interrelated and influence each other. The sociotechnical model proposes a fit among the needs of individuals, groups, and technological processes for effective organizational goal attainment. This approach gave impetus to autonomous work groups and work teams, which provide employees with control over the design and management of their work. General Foods is one of the widely publicized companies using a sociotechnical approach (see the HR Challenge box, "Autonomous Work Teams"). The sociotechnical approach to job design was started in the 1950s by the Tavistock Institute in London. One of the first studies conducted by this research team examined the effects on productivity of implementing an efficient long-wall method (assembly line) in a coal mine.[18] The intervention experiment failed because management did not consider the problems associated with removing the coal miners from their small autonomous work groups.

Job Redesign Approaches

As shown in Exhibit 8.1, a variety of individual and group job design options is available for managers. Job rotation, job enlargement, and job enrichment are among the approaches concerned with designing or redesigning individual tasks. Approaches for designing or redesigning jobs or groups include forming work teams, autonomous work groups, quality circles, job sculpting, and communities of practice.

job rotation
The systematic movement of workers from one job to another in an attempt to minimize monotony and boredom.

Job Rotation **Job rotation** does not change the actual job content, but it rotates employees from one job to another after a specified period of time. Job rotation often increases the number of employee skills and duties and can add flexibility to the organization. For example, organizations that emphasize specialization and train employees on only one task do not have the flexibility to substitute employees on jobs if someone is absent or abruptly quits. However, training every employee to be a "jack of all trades" is not always advantageous to the organization.

job enlargement
An increase in the number of tasks an employee performs.

Job Enlargement   **Job enlargement** (horizontal job loading) increases the number of tasks an individual performs, thereby increasing the diversity of a job. Adding more tasks to the job increases variety for the worker. Job enlargement's major shortcoming is that many workers do not perceive enlargement as adding variety but as simply giving them more work to do. Thus job enlargement can add variety to highly specialized jobs; however, it does little to add meaning and significance to the job.

job enrichment
An increase in the meaningfulness of the work and the responsibilities of an employee.

Job Enrichment   **Job enrichment** (vertical job loading) increases the depth of a job by expanding it vertically. Managers must add meaningfulness to the job and allow workers more control over their work if the job is to be perceived as enriched. In addition, workers should receive feedback regarding their performance. The following list illustrates how Travelers Insurance enriched the jobs of its keypunch operators:[19]

1. The random assignment of work was changed so that each operator was responsible for specific accounts.
2. The task of keypunching was expanded to include some planning and control functions.
3. The operators were given direct contact with clients. If a problem arose, the client dealt with the operator—not a supervisor.
4. The operators were given the control to plan their schedules, prioritize their work, and correct their own coding errors.
5. Weekly computer printouts of errors were sent to the operator rather than to the supervisor.

Travelers Insurance found the results of its enrichment program to be outstanding. The changes saved Travelers an estimated $90,000 a year. The quantity and quality of performance increased, errors and absenteeism were reduced, and worker attitudes seemed to improve.

Companies that have employees on assembly lines face a difficult job in trying to use job enrichment, given that these jobs tend to be monotonous with seemingly little room for improvement. Some large corporations such as Texas Instruments, Corning Glass Works, and IBM are all using different methods of job enrichment in an attempt to increase the production levels while keeping the turnover rate low. Examples include giving employees a sense of increased autonomy and giving them all titles of managers and operators in order to help even out the status field.

work team   A group of employees who have been assigned a large task to complete.

Work Teams   The goal of a work team is to implement job enlargement at the group level. In a **work team**, a group of workers is given a large task to complete and the team members are responsible for deciding on specific task assignments, solving production problems, creating their own schedules and deadlines, and continually improving work activities. The members of the work team can rotate the tasks among members or assign specific tasks to members. The group has a supervisor who oversees the entire operation.[20] The supervisor must concentrate on coaching and training while keeping the team's focus in line with the goals of the entire organization.[21] Construction builders often use work teams to complete a house, for example.[22]

Research suggests that the success of work teams is primarily due to the leaders' and workers' awareness of time constraints and their roles.[23] Working on a team and leading a team are two very different tasks. Many team leaders want to be viewed as a peer by the members of the team, yet team leaders are often responsible for handling performance reviews. No longer are team leaders solely part of the operation. They walk a fine line between working on the operations of a project and organizing team efforts and planning for the project's success. For example, a fast-growing computer company, FORE, uses the team approach.[24] FORE concentrates on developing a system of computer networking that includes delivering real-time video and voice at a faster rate than most existing systems. When FORE went public in 1994, it employed about 200 people. It had over 1400 employees and revenue increased about 68 percent in 1997. Given the growth and emphasis on teams, many of FORE's young employees who sought work in the operations side of computers have found themselves thrown into the challenging position of team leader. Team leaders are not considered management, so many leaders are able to balance their leadership role with the opportunity to remain in the actual operations.

Implementation of work teams can present problems for the organization. Supervisors and managers often feel that the use of work teams dilutes their power and authority. Further, if the number of team members is too large (over 15), smaller interest groups tend to develop.[25] In order for more teams to be successful, management must consider these problems and monitor the transition process carefully. By keeping the groups small in number and providing clear, explicit roles for the supervisor, the organization can ensure that the opportunity for team success is high.

Autonomous Work Groups   Forming autonomous work groups recognizes the importance of integrating the social system with the technical system. In essence, an **autonomous work group** is responsible for achieving a complex goal and is given a considerable amount of control over work assignments, rest breaks, prioritizing, inspection procedures, and so on. Some autonomous work groups even have the freedom to select their members. Autonomous work groups can be thought of as implementing job enrichment (vertical loading) at the group level.

Monsanto Chemical Company made some dramatic changes at its fibers plant in Greenwood, South Carolina. Monsanto instituted its own version of autonomous work groups. The employees in the work groups divided the work and made key decisions themselves. One of the workers said that he knew 20 years ago that he could direct his own job, but nobody wanted to hear what he had to say. Workers became involved in decision making and quality control. Autonomous work groups enabled Monsanto to use fewer supervisors, which, subsequently, left more money for employee training. Programs like this are not without problems, however. By focusing on quality and productivity, employees can become less safety conscious and injuries may increase. In addition, the reduction in management positions results in few promotions. Nonetheless, the autonomous work group approach will remain because once you give people freedom, you cannot take it back without lowering employee morale.[26]

Managing Autonomous Work Groups   Autonomous work groups need a manager but not one who attempts to plan, organize, or control the group. These activities are the responsibilities of the members of the work group. Managers of autonomous work groups should carefully monitor any organizational changes that might affect the

autonomous work groups
Work groups that have been assigned complex tasks and the authority to decide the best way to get the job done.

Autonomous Work Teams

The General Foods pet food plant in Topeka, Kansas, was designed around the concept of autonomous work groups. Each work group consisted of 7 to 14 members, including a group leader. Every group was responsible for deciding members' work tasks, selecting new members, and developing and training new members. The plant was designed to facilitate informal gatherings for better coordination and social interaction by removing unnecessary status symbols such as plush offices or preferential parking spaces. In addition, the company decentralized with top management. Decentralization was thought to be motivating and necessary if employees were actually going to be working in autonomous work groups.

The Topeka plant began to show some fairly impressive improvements. Fixed overhead was 33 percent lower than comparable plants, quality rejects were reduced 92 percent, employee morale was good, the plant's safety record was excellent, and turnover and absenteeism were low. Although General Foods no longer owned the plant, many of these positive characteristics remained. However, top management attempted to take control of the operations, which has caused numerous problems. Managers are sometimes insecure about letting employees have considerable control over their own work and work-related decisions because they fear a loss of power. Managing autonomous work teams without alienating management is achieved by heavily integrating the team concept throughout the organization and training management.

Research indicates that to receive high performance from autonomous work teams, a number of factors should be considered. For example, employees should agree with team goals, the level of team goals should be high but reachable, employees must be willing to be cross-trained, they should participate in decision making, and they should have a sense of team commitment. To be effective, teams should be self-managed and empowered to organize their work and make decisions.

SOURCE: Adapted from B. Glacel, "Teamwork's Top Ten Lead to Quality," *Journal for Quality and Production*, January/February, 1997, pp.12–16; M. Martinez, "Factory Flexibility for Shift Workers," *HRMagazine*, August, 1994, p. 24; B. Dumaine, "The Trouble with Teams," *Fortune*, September 5, 1994, pp. 86–92; and R. E. Walton, "The Topeka Story: Teaching an Old Dog New Tricks," *The Wharton Magazine*, Spring 1978, pp. 38–46.

work group and should serve as a liaison between the work group and top management. Unfortunately, many managers do not have the training or skills to act in an advisory, consultative, or liaison role. Thus, it is imperative that all managers of autonomous work groups receive the appropriate training required to perform the broader organizational assignment. In addition, these managers need to be given the power to help develop effective work teams that are consistent with the overall goals of the organization.[27]

quality circles
Regular meetings of a group of employees and supervisors to discuss quality problems and solutions.

Quality Circles   The concept of a quality circle primarily focuses on maintaining and enhancing the quality of a product. It is a management-employee group effort designed to find and solve production and coordination problems. Although originally developed in the United States and referred to as quality control circles, the name has been shortened to quality circles (QCs). Japan has used quality circles extensively, and they have become increasingly popular in the United States.[28] Typically, **quality circles** include a group of 7 to 10 employees and supervisors who meet at regular intervals (usually once a week) to discuss quality control problems and solutions. The Lockheed Missile and Space Company was one of the first U.S. organizations to implement and study the effects of an extensive quality circle program. Results of its program are reported to have saved the company six dollars for every one dollar it spent on the process. In addition, defects in manufacturing declined by two-thirds and job satisfaction among quality circle members increased.[29] The potential for improving individual performance and organizational effectiveness has given impetus to the respect and support that quality circles receive from many management and union members.[30]

To achieve the potential benefits from a quality circle, management must be committed to the concept and provide good training to the members. Employees must not be allowed to use the meeting time to explore problems with working conditions, environmental issues, or salary and benefit systems. Instead, the focus must be on work-process problems and concerns.[31] In fact, many of the problems found in trying to implement Japan's popular quality circles in the United States are due to misconceptions about their true intent and purpose.[32] However, if the proper focus is attained, quality circles can produce tremendous benefits for almost any U.S. company.

Quality circles have been critical to the performance of engineers at Honda R&D North America, Inc. In many companies, quality circles have been limited to the factory floor. At Honda, however, quality circles are used throughout the organization. One of the problems at Honda R&D was that 80 percent of engineers' time was being spent on computer terminals that had response times that were too slow. Rather than simply complain about the system, the senior design engineer established a quality circle consisting of herself, two body design engineers, two interior design engineers, two people from information systems, and one person from the technical training area. They worked to find the root causes of the slow-down problems and switched their system to a more workstation-based system requiring new computer equipment. Although an investment in equipment was necessary, the engineers' productivity increases more than made up for the initial capital outlay.[33]

Job Sculpting   Many talented professionals leave their organizations because senior managers don't understand the psychology of work satisfaction; they assume that people who excel at their work are necessarily happy in their jobs. But the fact is, strong skills don't always reflect or lead to job satisfaction. People will only stay if the job matches their *deeply embedded life interests*.

Job sculpting is the art of matching people to jobs that allow their deeply embedded life interests to be expressed. It is the art of forging a customized career path in order to increase the chance of retaining talented people. Research has found that there are eight deeply embedded life interests for people. Deeply embedded life interests do not determine what people are good at—they drive what *kinds* of activities make them happy. At work, that happiness often translates into commitment. It keeps employees engaged, and it keeps them from quitting.

Job sculpting begins when managers identify each employee's deeply embedded life interests (Exhibit 8.2). If managers promise to job sculpt, how do they deliver? Each change in assignment provides an opportunity to do some sculpting. However, this can be hit or miss. Job sculpting can be most effective when it is incorporated into the performance review. In making job-sculpting part of the performance review, it becomes systematized; in becoming systematized, the chances of falling through the cracks are minimized. Once managers and employees have discussed deeply embedded life interests, it is time to customize the next work assignment accordingly.

| EXHIBIT 8.2 | THE EIGHT DEEPLY EMBEDDED LIFE INTERESTS |

Application of Technology—People with the life interest application of technology are intrigued by the inner workings of things. They are curious about finding better ways to use technology to solve problems.

Quantitative Analysis—People who see mathematical work as fun when others consider it drudgery.

Theory Development and Conceptual Thinking—People with this deeply embedded life interest are drawn to theory – the why of strategy interests them more than the how.

Creative Production—These people always enjoy the beginning of projects the most, when there are many unknowns and they can make something out of nothing.

Counseling and Mentoring—For these people, nothing is more enjoyable than teaching: This usually translates into coaching and mentoring. People with a high interest in counseling and mentoring are often drawn to organizations such as museums, schools and hospitals that provide products or services that they perceive to hold a high social value.

Managing People and Relationships—People with this deeply embedded life interest enjoy dealing with people on a day-to-day basis. They derive a lot of satisfaction from workplace relationships, but focus much more on outcomes than do people in the counseling and mentoring category.

Enterprise Control—Whether or not they like managing people, these people find satisfaction in making the decisions that determine the direction taken by a work team, a business unit, a company division, or an entire organization.

Influence through Language and Ideas—People who love expressing ideas for the sheer enjoyment that comes from storytelling, negotiating, or persuading. These people feel most fulfilled when they are writing or speaking. People in this category sometimes feel drawn to careers in public relations or advertising.

SOURCE: Adapted from T. Butler and J. Waldroop, "Job Sculpting, the Art of Retaining Your Best People," *Harvard Business Review*, September-October 1999, pp 144–152.

| EXHIBIT 8.3 | A SNAPSHOT COMPARISON |

Communities of practice, formal work groups, teams, and informal networks are useful in complementary ways. Below is a summary of their characteristics.

	What's the Purpose?	Who Belongs?	What Holds it Together?	How Long Does it Last?
Community of practice	To develop members' capabilities; to build and exchange knowledge	Members, who select themselves	Passion, commitment, and identification with the group's expertise	As long as there is interest in maintaining the group
Formal work group	To deliver a product or service	Everyone who reports to the group's manager	Job requirement and common goals	Until the next reorganization
Project team	To accomplish a specific task	Employees assigned by senior management	The project's milestones and goals	Until the project has been completed
Informal network	To collect and pass on business information	Friends and business acquaintances	Mutual needs	As long as people have a reason to stay in contact

SOURCE: Adapted from E. Wenger and W. Snyder, "Communities of Practice: The Organizational Frontier," *Harvard Business Review*, January–February 2000, pp. 139–145.

Communities of Practice   A new organizational form is emerging that promises to complement existing structures and radically galvanize knowledge sharing, learning, and change. It is commonly called the community of practice (see Exhibit 8.3).

What are communities of practice? In brief, they're groups of people informally bound together by sharing expertise and passion for a joint enterprise—engineers engaged in deep-water drilling, for example, consultants who specialize in strategic marketing, or frontline managers in charge of check processing at a large commercial bank. Some communities of practice meet regularly; others are connected primarily by e-mail networks. They may or may not have an explicit agenda on a given week, and even if they do, they may not follow it too closely.

Communities of practice can drive strategy, generate new lines of business, solve problems, promote the spread of best business practices, develop people's professional skills, and help companies recruit and retain talent.

Communities of practice are emerging in companies that thrive on knowledge. The first step for managers is to understand what they are and how they work. The second step is to realize that they are a fountainhead of knowledge development and therefore the key to the challenge of the knowledge economy. The third step is to appreciate the paradox that these informal structures require specific managerial efforts to develop them and to integrate them into the organization so that their full power can be leveraged.

Communities of practice are the new frontier. They may seem unfamiliar now, but in five to ten years they may be as common in discussions about organizations as business units and teams are today—if managers learn how to make them a central part of their company's success.

Strategic Guidelines for Job Design

One of the most comprehensive frameworks for job design is the job characteristics model. It proposes specific characteristics of jobs that can lead to important psychological states. In turn, these psychological states lead to a number of positive personal and work outcomes.[34]

The Job Characteristics Model   As shown in Exhibit 8.4, the job characteristics model recognizes that certain aspects of the job are inherently motivating for most people and that individuals may perceive and respond to the same stimuli differently. Thus, its designers, Hackman and Oldham, proposed that the relationship between core job characteristics and the psychological states is moderated by an individual's growth need strength. Similarly, the relationship between the psychological states and the personal and work outcome is moderated by growth need strength. *Growth need strength* is the need to learn, grow, and be challenged. This means that employees who perceive their jobs as being high on the core job characteristics and who have a high growth need strength are more likely to experience the psychological state. If employees perceive the psychological states from their work and they have high growth need strength, they are more likely to experience the personal and work outcomes. In essence, this model works best for employees with a need to learn, grow, and be challenged (high growth need strength).

The five core job characteristics are defined in the following terms:

1. *Task identity.* Seeing a whole piece of work. Employees can complete a task from beginning to end with an identifiable outcome.

EXHIBIT 8.4 HACKMAN-OLDHAM'S JOB CHARACTERISTICS MODEL

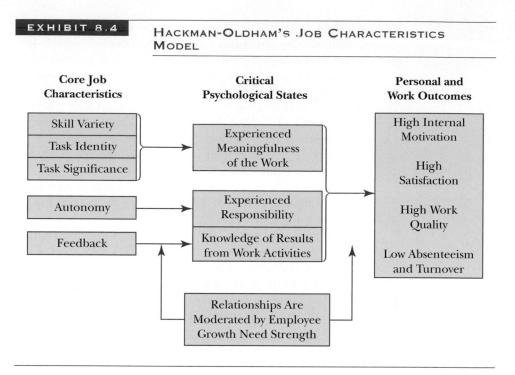

SOURCE: Adapted from J. R. Hackman and G. R. Oldham, "Motivation through the Design of Work: Test of a Theory," *Organizational Behavior and Human Performance* 16 (1976), pp. 250–279.

2. *Task significance.* Importance of the job. The characteristic is determined by the impact the employee's work has on others within or outside the organization.
3. *Skill variety.* The degree to which employees are able to do a number of different tasks using many different skills, abilities, and talents determines the skill variety.
4. *Autonomy.* The degree to which employees have control over their work. This refers to the amount of discretion and independence employees have regarding such things as scheduling, prioritizing, and determining procedures for task completion.
5. *Feedback.* The degree to which the job offers information to employees regarding performance and work outcomes.

The three psychological states are defined in the following terms:

1. *Experienced meaningfulness.* The degree to which employees perceive the work as being meaningful, valuable, and worthwhile.
2. *Responsibility.* The degree to which employees feel accountable and responsible for the outcomes of their work.
3. *Knowledge of results.* The degree to which employees know and understand how well they are performing on the job.

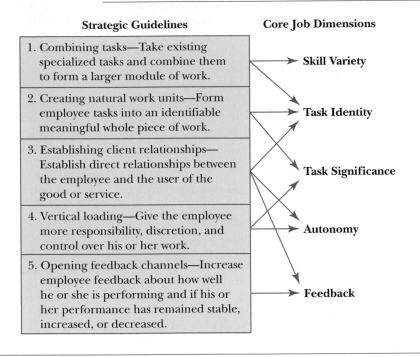

| EXHIBIT 8.5 | STRATEGIC GUIDELINES OFFERED BY THE JOB CHARACTERISTICS MODEL |

Strategic Guidelines　　　　　　　**Core Job Dimensions**

1. Combining tasks—Take existing specialized tasks and combine them to form a larger module of work.

2. Creating natural work units—Form employee tasks into an identifiable meaningful whole piece of work.

3. Establishing client relationships—Establish direct relationships between the employee and the user of the good or service.

4. Vertical loading—Give the employee more responsibility, discretion, and control over his or her work.

5. Opening feedback channels—Increase employee feedback about how well he or she is performing and if his or her performance has remained stable, increased, or decreased.

- Skill Variety
- Task Identity
- Task Significance
- Autonomy
- Feedback

SOURCE: Adapted from J. R. Hackman, G. R. Oldham, R. Janson, and K. A. Purdy, "A New Strategy for Job Enrichment," *California Management Review* (Summer 1975), pp. 57–71.

Although the five job characteristics are widely accepted, evidence suggests that an expanded set of job characteristics among other modifications may be more predictive of employee attitudes and behaviors.[35] Further, the characteristics of the job should match the abilities and needs of job holders.[36]

Job Diagnostic Survey　Hackman and Oldham developed a questionnaire for testing the job characteristics model, called the Job Diagnostic Survey.[37] The survey contains measures of the core job characteristics, critical psychological states, personal and work outcomes, and growth need strength. Research results indicate that the job diagnostic survey can discriminate among different jobs.

Strategies for Managers　The job characteristics model offers managers strategic guidelines for increasing core job dimensions in the workplace. As depicted in Exhibit 8.5, each strategic guideline affects one or more job characteristics.

An application of the job characteristics model offers some evidence that use of this model can improve both employee satisfaction and performance.[38] Sales jobs in a large department store were redesigned in the following manner:

1. *Skill variety.* Salespeople were asked to try to think of and use different selling approaches, new merchandising displays, and new record-keeping methods.

2. *Task identity.* Salespeople were asked to keep a personal record of daily sales in dollars, keep a daily record of the number of sales/customers, and determine a display area that would be theirs and keep it orderly and finished looking.

3. *Task significance.* Salespeople were reoriented to the store objectives, reminded of the importance of their display areas to selling, and told that, to the customers, the salespeople are "the store."

4. *Autonomy.* Salespeople were encouraged to develop and use their own unique sales approaches, select their own breaks, and make suggestions for improvement in any phase of policy or operations.

5. *Feedback.* Salespeople were encouraged to keep personal records of their performance, observe and help each other with selling techniques, and invite supervisor and customer reactions to merchandise, service, and so forth.

The salespeoples' effective performance behaviors (conversing with customers, handling returns, and showing merchandise, for example) increased, while ineffective performance behaviors (such as socializing with coworkers or leaving their work stations without legitimate reason) decreased. Satisfaction also increased for this group of salespeople. Another group of salespeople who did not receive the intervention (the control group) showed no change in performance. This is an example of how job redesign can be used as a strategic intervention for both employee and organizational benefits.

Organizational Strategy and its Relationship with Job Design

An organization's job design should be consistent with its overall strategy. Beginning in the early 1970s, Raymond Miles and Charles Snow examined the competitive strategies of several hundred companies in more than a dozen different industries.[39] Over time, they realized that all of the competitive approaches revolved around a few fundamental business strategies. Miles and Snow found that successful firms displayed a consistent strategy supported by complementary organizational structures, designs, and management processes. Those firms in which the strategy was poorly aligned with the structure, design, or process of the organization performed less well than the other three types.[40]

One way to view the strategic initiatives of organizations is to examine whether organizations have adopted a growth or retrenchment strategy. Under growth strategies, organizations are concerned with their competitive markets as well as hiring and retaining top employees. Under these conditions the design of the job should offer autonomy for job occupants. Employees need to have the autonomy to make decisions quickly, and their autonomy should match their responsibility. Further, flexibility is an important goal for organizations with a growth strategy.

Building flexibility into an organization is not often an easy and inexpensive task. For example, Ford Motor Company started a flexible manufacturing plant to build innovative modular engines for the 1990s.[41] Ford took a billion-dollar gamble on its modular engine concept. U.S. automobile manufacturers typically design individual factories to build a single engine type. The factories produced the same basic engine for decades. This seemed to work fine when the U.S. automotive industry could count on steady sales and stable markets. However, changing government fuel-economy regulations, intense competition from the Japanese, and changes in consumer tastes have forced many automobile manufacturers to reevaluate their mechanistic factories. Ford's new plant has flexible manufacturing equipment, and the modular design allows for the production of more than a dozen engine sizes and configurations on one line. In addition, this new plant design allows inexpensive, rapid shifts to smaller, lighter engines.

Under retrenchment strategies, managers are more concerned with cost cutting and achieving economies of scale. The concern is with organizational survival. Hence, the decision making may become more centralized and the design of an individual's job less autonomous. Flexibility is also important for organizations with a retrenchment strategy. The type of flexibility sought is often with regard to employee skills. Downsizing the organization without sacrificing the critical skill mix is crucial to organizational survival. One way to keep the critical skill mix is through job rotation. Job rotation involves lateral moves such that employees know how to do a number of different jobs within the organization.[42] This type of flexibility can help organizations undergoing retrenchment to survive.

Work Flexibility: A Current Strategic Issue in Job Design

The 1980s was called the *decade of career obsessions*.[43] However, in the 1990s and into the new millennium, men and women are trying to create a better balance between work and family. Back in 1989, Felice Schwartz wrote a controversial article in the *Harvard Business Review* on women managers and their conflict between career and family. She suggested that businesses needed to adapt to this conflict by introducing flextime, job sharing, and other personnel policies that would add flexibility to work schedules.[44]

flextime   A work schedule that gives workers some control over when they begin and end their work day.

The controversy stems from Schwartz's conclusion and recommendation that corporate officials treat women in managerial positions according to whether they are on a *career track* or a *career/family* track, also called the *mommy track*. Critics have been concerned that this could provide companies with a rationale for discrimination against women who have or plan to have children. In other words, the fear is that career tracks would be equated with "fast" tracks, and mommy tracks would be equated with "slow" or "dead-end" tracks.[45] Regardless of problems associated with career tracking, organizations are pressed by employees and society in general to offer more flexible work schedule options for *both* men and women. Another issue involves employees' need to take leaves from their jobs to take care of family responsibilities. Women may need maternity leaves, men may wish to care for young children, and more and more Americans are experiencing the demands of caring for elderly relatives. In response to this issue, LinguiSystems has initiated parental leave, which gives employees (father or mother) time off with pay to be with the newborn. The first two weeks are at full pay, the following four weeks are at $150 a week, and the remaining six weeks are unpaid. Insurance benefits are not interrupted during the leave period.[46]

job sharing   A work schedule where two part-time employees share one full-time job.

compressed work schedules   Work schedules that allow for a 40-hour workweek in fewer than the traditional five days.

The most popular option for introducing flexibility into the job is **flextime**, which gives full-time employees some latitude as to when to begin and end their work days. "Flextime is the number-one driver of employee retention," contends Kathie Lingle, National Director of Work/Life at KPMG LLP. Money, she adds, isn't necessarily the key to holding good employees. "Time is now as scarce as money," says Lingle, "and employees are much more likely to stay with an employer who gives them a say in setting their work schedule."[47]

telecommuting   A work method that allows workers to complete their work at home or at another location and communicate with their place of business through electronic media.

Job sharing occurs when an employee shares his or her job with another employee. Advantages and disadvantages to job sharing can be seen in Exhibit 8.6. **Compressed work schedules**, in which employees put in their 40 hours in less than a full five-day workweek (for example, working ten hours for four days), and working at

EXHIBIT 8.6	ADVANTAGES AND DISADVANTAGES OF JOB SHARING FOR EMPLOYERS AND EMPLOYEES

For Employers

Advantages	Disadvantages
The organization can retain experienced and valued staff.	Administration costs for training, accommodation and other employment expenses could be higher.
This provides flexible opportunities for employees, increasing satisfaction and impacting positively on their productivity.	Communication may be a problem in jobs where continuity is essential.
If one job sharer is ill or on leave, there is continuity as at least part of the job gets done.	If one job sharer leaves, the employer has to find another job sharer.
Potential exists for job-share partners to cover each other's absences or help out during peak periods.	Job sharers will not both be able to attend the same meetings or appointments.

For Employees

Advantages	Disadvantages
This can be a flexible work option for those who wish to work part-time without necessarily sacrificing their career.	Working fewer hours reduces income.
Management positions, requiring a full-time presence, can be available to those wishing to work part-time.	Employers may be reluctant to allow certain jobs, higher-level or management jobs, to be shared.
Job sharing is attractive to those with family responsibilities.	Participating in job-share arrangements may affect promotional prospects.
This provides a way for individuals to earn an income and pursue other interests, studies, or leisure activities.	Communication may be a problem if job sharers do not overlap and may require new procedures to ensure sufficient communication.

SOURCE: Adapted from *Family Friendly Work Practices*, 1997, Department of Productivity and Labour Relations, pp. 1–10; **www.wa.gov.au/gov/doplar/w%26f/ffwp/fam4.html**.

home are also popular options that emphasize the importance of flexibility in the workplace.

Telecommuting is a popular trend in which employees can work from their home or another location of their choice and communicate through the use of computers, express mail, facsimiles, and improved telephone networks. For example, even in the early 1990s, Charles Lazarus, the chief executive of Toys 'R' Us, had a computerized office in his vacation house on Long Island.[48] His system tied into his company's sophisticated computer system, allowing him to track the sales of all of the company's 20,000 products in any part of the world.

Although women (especially baby boomers in their late 30s and 40s) seem to be leading the push for more flexibility in their work schedules, men are also interested in flexible scheduling. In fact, a survey by Robert Half International, an executive recruiting firm, determined that more than half of the 500 men polled said they would be willing to cut their salaries as much as 25 percent to have more family or personal time, and about 45 percent said they would likely decline a promotion if it meant spending less time with their families.[49]

More and more companies are experimenting with flexible work schedules and finding, for the most part, that workers like the changes and are more productive.[50] However, some worry that telecommuters and other flexible workers will become invisible to the companies they serve and fall off the fast track to success.[51] Some home workers lament the loss of personal space and personal freedoms in their home offices.[52] Some are afraid to go to the bathroom for fear of missing an important phone call! The virtual corporation, a futuristic conglomerate of just-in-time employees, throwaway executives, and temporary workers, is more fact than fiction.[53] This drive for corporate flexibility runs into the belief that competitive advantage relies on a dedicated, motivated workforce. Ultimately, job redesign provides promise for a compromise between the needs of flexibility and the necessity of worker involvement.

Whether managers choose to redesign (or design) a small portion of the organization, a new plant, or the entire firm, a well-integrated job design plan is crucial. The following section discusses the steps involved in implementation.

Strategic Framework for Implementation

Recognizing the need for job redesign is one of nine steps in an integrative strategic implementation framework designed by Ricky Griffin.[54] The nine steps are summarized in Exhibit 8.7.

Recognition of the Need for Change   The first step in strategic job redesign is the recognition that a change is needed. A number of factors in the workplace typically serve as indicators that a change is needed. Employee complaints about their job and a subsequent decline in motivation and performance are often the first signs that the design of the job needs improvement. If managers want to retain and attract good employees, a well-designed, motivating job is imperative.

Another factor that could lead to strategic job redesign is the technology available to an organization. New computer advancements for more efficient production processes often necessitate new work methods. If companies want to stay competitive, they may make a strategic decision to acquire state-of-the-art equipment. New equipment or methods often create the need to redesign some jobs.

Selection of the Intervention   After determining that a change is needed, managers must decide on the appropriate intervention. Job redesign is only one of the many options available to the human resource manager. For example, the recognition of a drop in employee motivation and performance could be the result of numerous factors—poor communication, leadership, or training—and not necessarily a poor job design. If, however, employees complain of boring, unchallenging work, job redesign may be the most logical intervention. This step requires managerial experience, intuition, and tacit knowledge to choose the appropriate intervention strategy.

Diagnosis of the Work System and Context   An in-depth diagnosis of the work system and its context is important after management decides to implement a job redesign program. Human resource managers need to ensure that any job redesign effort is consistent with the existing work system. In *Task Design*, Ricky Griffin described six areas to be examined when diagnosing the work system and context:[55]

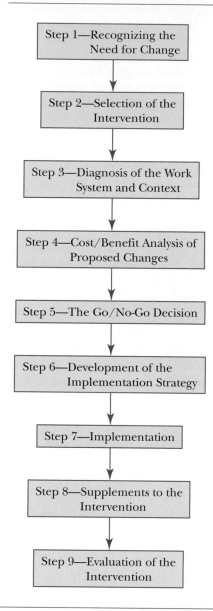

| EXHIBIT 8.7 | A STRATEGIC FRAMEWORK FOR IMPLEMENTING JOB REDESIGN IN ORGANIZATIONS |

SOURCE: Adapted from R. W. Griffin, *Task Design: An Integrative Approach* (Glenview, IL: Scott, Foresman 1982), p. 208.

1. *Diagnosis of existing jobs.* For example, evaluate using methods such as job analyses and the job diagnostic survey.
2. *Diagnosis of the existing workforce.* For example, compare the current performance, motivation, and satisfaction of employees with the desired level of performance, motivation, and satisfaction.

3. *Diagnosis of technology.* For example, technology may be a constraint because expensive equipment and heavy machinery are necessary.
4. *Diagnosis of organization design.* Categorize the organization as being either mechanistic or organic. Determine the organization culture. Is it accepting of change?
5. *Diagnosis of leader behavior.* The cooperation of the supervisor is crucial in order to reinforce a job redesign effort.
6. *Diagnosis of group and social processes.* The degree of group cohesiveness is crucial if the job redesign effort includes the development of autonomous work groups.

Cost/Benefit Analysis of Proposed Changes The possible costs of a job redesign intervention must be balanced against potential benefits. Cost to an organization might include new machinery, downtime during the transition, and possible wage increases because of increased employee responsibility and task performance. Benefits from the job redesign effort include an increase in worker motivation, satisfaction, commitment to the organization, and performance and a decrease in absenteeism, turnover, tardiness, errors, and grievances. The goals of a job redesign intervention should be realistic, and the benefits should outweigh any costs incurred.

The Go/No-Go Decision After conducting a cost/benefit analysis, managers should make a decision to "go with" a job redesign intervention or consider other alternatives. It is important for managers to consider both short-term and long-term consequences and determine how this meshes with the overall strategy of the organization. Even after a systematic cost/benefit analysis, managers often believe that they do not have all of the information to make the correct decision. Managers must rely on both quantitative information as well as their expertise and intuition.

Development of the Implementation Strategy Strategy considerations for implementation include (1) who will plan the job redesign intervention, (2) what actual job changes will have to be made, (3) who will be affected by these changes, and (4) when the intervention will take place. These strategic issues should be systematically developed prior to initiating any changes. Some researchers advocate a participative approach using employees, supervisors, and consultants to plan the job redesign intervention.[56] Others, however, advocate participation in some situations and a top-down approach in others.[57] The decision for participation will depend on the degree to which employees have important information, see the need to accept the change, and desire to add their input to the plan.

Decisions also have to be made regarding the jobs to be changed, who would be affected by the change, and whether the intervention will be individual based or group based. For example, group-based interventions (such as autonomous work groups) should be used only if there is an obvious benefit over individual-based interventions, because of their added complexity.[58] Finally, the planning group must determine the time frame for implementation. Considerations include how long it will take to purchase new equipment, install it, and train the employees to use it.

Implementation The actual intervention seldom occurs without unforeseen problems. The best protection against implementation difficulties is to carefully diagnose the work situation, develop a specific strategy, and follow a detailed plan based on the previous steps.

Supplements to the Intervention   Supplemental changes are often necessary, particularly regarding contextual factors in the organization. For example, changes in the structure of the organization, workflow patterns, or reward system may be necessary because of the job redesign intervention. For example, if autonomous work groups are formed, the organization cannot continue to pay workers based on individual achievement. Group performance as opposed to individual performance becomes the basis for evaluation. Thus the organizational reward system should reinforce the job redesign intervention.

Evaluation of the Intervention   The final step determines whether the job redesign intervention was effective. If managers want to see the impact of a change, then employee perceptions, performance, and other work-related outcomes need to be measured prior to actual intervention. After the intervention, they should be measured again and compared with the outcomes prior to the intervention. Unfortunately, this step is often not included as part of an organizational job redesign effort, possibly because of additional time and cost constraints. Managers should thoroughly examine the effects of any intervention and evaluate the cost and benefits incurred. This information is invaluable as input for future strategic decisions in the workplace.

Management Guidelines

Deciding how to design a job or implement a job redesign program is an important decision for managers. The management guidelines that follow should be considered before making these types of decisions:

1. Human resource managers need to carefully monitor the interaction between employees and jobs in their organizations to ensure that a productive relationship is achieved and maintained.
2. Job design or redesign should be undertaken only after careful consideration is given to environmental, organizational, cost, and behavioral factors.
3. After job redesign, managers need to update job descriptions, specifications, and performance evaluation criteria.
4. The reward system in the organization should reflect the new roles and responsibilities caused by job design or redesign.
5. The employees' growth need strength and their desire for job redesign should be given at least as much consideration as the costs and technical aspects of efficiency before developing and implementing a job design or redesign program.

Managers should use a strategic framework for job redesign as a guide throughout the entire job design or redesign program to ensure a systematic and consistent approach.

Questions for Review

1. What are the strategic choices managers should make before considering redesigning jobs?

2. What were some of the problems associated with scientific management?
3. What are the various individual and group job design options?
4. What is the job characteristics model? Explain how growth need strength affects the model.
5. How can a manager increase the core job dimensions for his or her employees? What strategies are available?
6. What is the strategic framework for implementing job redesign? Discuss it and explain the importance of intervention evaluation.
7. Should a job redesign be undertaken if it will improve efficiency even if the employees do not want it? Explain your answer.
8. What are the fundamental premises of the sociotechnical model? What are some advantages to using autonomous work groups?
9. Can employees be trained to work in autonomous work groups if they are unwilling or incapable of doing so? Explain your answer.
10. In what ways could the X-ray jobs discussed in this chapter's opening case be redesigned? How could this be accomplished?

CASE

Toyota's Production System: Life in the Fast Lane?[59]

Toyota's Production System (TPS) is legendary. In fact, some automotive executives and engineers believe that it is the benchmark in manufacturing and product development. This is why many visit Toyota's manufacturing complex in Georgetown, Kentucky, each month. The visitors, who work for competing automakers, are given intensive, comprehensive plant tours at no charge.

The TPS does not apply just to manufacturing, however. TPS techniques apply to almost every aspect of the business, including product development, supplier relations, and distribution, and permeate to the soul of Toyota. Perhaps this is the reason why others have not been successful in copying the production system. Hence, TPS has evolved into a competitive advantage for Toyota, the world's third largest automaker as measured in unit sales. The company is recognized as the world's most proficient automaker and sets the standard in efficiency, productivity, and quality largely due to TPS.

Despite its international success, global expansion has been somewhat difficult for Toyota because of competition and flaws related to TPS. For instance, the company has not developed a single facility that is as efficient as the ones it has in Japan. According to Wharton School professor John Paul MacDuffie, who has been studying the international automobile industry for more than ten years, "This is a difficult system to take globally." Indeed, many factors influence the success of TPS. Inside a plant, its success depends on highly experienced managers working with a motivated, well-trained workforce. Outside the plant, TPS requires a network of dedicated, capable suppliers that can operate in sync with Toyota.

TPS in concept is simple: Maximize flow, eliminate waste, and respect people. But its implementation and coordination are rather complicated. For example, John Shook, an American who worked for Toyota in Japan in 1983 and now directs the Japan Technology Management Program at the University of Michigan, says, "TPS takes an incredible amount of detailed planning, discipline, hard work, and painstaking attention to detail." The company designs the work to flow from process to process without peaks or valleys and expects its products to arrive in just the right quantity for the customer. The result is a smooth-running plant with little or no waste. Every movement has a purpose, and there is little slack.

In the past, there was no stockpile of parts on the production line. Therefore suppliers and workers were under considerable pressure to perform their jobs as scheduled and even to work overtime if they fell behind. Recently, Toyota has been trying to make jobs easier for its employees in lieu of the persistent labor shortage in Japan. The company has replaced the long, noisy production line with segments or mini-assembly lines, each with a quiet conveyor designed by Toyota engineers. On each line, teams of 15 to 20 workers install integrated systems and are allowed to stockpile small buffers of unfinished parts at the end of each segment in case of an interruption.

Toyota has sought to make work both less strenuous and less tedious. Mini-assembly lines allow greater flexibility for moving the chassis up and down according to the work involved, practically eliminating the need to stoop, bend, or crane the neck. The machines, which are powerful and precise, are designed to work together with men and women who are dexterous, flexible, and intelligent. Workers are also responsible for machine maintenance, which has further diversified work, cut costs, and improved standards.

Takahiro Fujimoto, a Harvard Business School graduate who teaches at Tokyo University and has studied the company, says, "Toyota's real strength resides in its ability to learn. Its employees are problem-conscious and customer-oriented, and this preparedness is the source of the company's dynamic capability. The company's practices are constantly changing, even though its basic principles are unchanged." This capacity to adapt is a fundamental ingredient in Toyota's success.

Innovations have included job rotation, cross-training, and assembly-line improvements. For example, workers at Toyota's Kyushu plant rotate jobs on two- and four-hour shifts throughout the day. Toyota has gradually introduced the practice at older assembly plants. Job rotation has not only eliminated stress injuries and reduced fatigue, but it has also boosted productivity.

Some team leaders discovered that workers could easily move from one job to another, provided that they had the necessary skills. So Toyota has placed dummy cars on some factory floors where workers practice different assembly tasks. Plant manager Kiyotoshi Kato credits the job redesign approaches for giving line workers a better understanding of the production process and increasing worker flexibility.

Applying the principles of TPS requires leadership, teamwork, and communication among workers. Some areas, such as product development, require not only creativity and freedom to produce innovative designs, but also discipline and control regarding scheduling, resources, and quality. In addition, the supportive organizational culture encourages employees to learn from their mistakes and from the successes and failures of each other.

Even though Toyota's system is a huge success, the company is constantly making adjustments to it. In the early 1990s, it introduced automation into its factories but then backed away when the machinery proved too costly and inflexible. So instead of replacing workers, Toyota designed machines to make them more productive. More recently, Toyota reorganized its engineers into three groups—front-wheel-drive cars, rear-wheel-drive cars, and trucks—to make it easier for different projects within the groups to share common components among themselves. This new grouping effectively took power away from Toyota's chief engineers, who were blamed for contributing to the cost and complexity of new models by competing among themselves. In addition, this arrangement fosters creativity by reducing the tendency of chief engineers to mimic what is already available in the marketplace.

Despite Toyota's success with TPS in Kentucky and elsewhere, it remains a very difficult system to establish outside Japan. The smooth integration of manufacturing, engineering, and parts supply requires common purpose, static-free communication, and experienced management, all of which are found in greater quantities in Japan, where everyone comes from a common culture and speaks the same language. Some observers say that none of its operations work as well as the ones in Japan. The system is large, unique, and hard to duplicate—even for Toyota.

One of the big problems is the lack of well-trained local managers. For instance, Toyota's Japanese plant managers typically have 20 years of experience in TPS, whereas local managers often start with little or none. The company must develop managers regardless of their origins to support its global ambitions.

Nearly all of Toyota's future growth will have to come from overseas, and the company is clearly headed in that direction. So, as Toyota evolves from a multinational company into one that is truly global, TPS will have to continue to change too.[60]

Questions for Discussion

1. What is the relationship between Toyota's organizational strategy and TPS?

2. What organizational and behavioral factors need to be considered in order to effectively duplicate or imitate TPS?

3. How does Toyota use the team approach?

4. How has TPS affected workers' jobs and responsibilities and the quality of cars produced?

5. Do you think the human relationships required for TPS are unique to Japan? Why or why not?

6. How would you suggest Toyota train local managers for TPS?

Additional Readings

Adenburg, D. "Spirituality at Work." *The Washington Post* 120 (April 15, 1997), p. D5.

Butler, T., and J. Waldroop. "Job Sculpting, the Art of Retaining Your Best People." *Harvard Business Review*, September–October 1999, pp 144–152.

D'Andrea-O'Brien, C. and A. F. Buono. "Building Effective Learning Teams: Lessons from the Field." *SAM Advanced Management Journal* 61, no. 3 (Summer, 1996), p. 4.

Glacel, B. P. "Teamwork's Top Ten Lead to Quality." The Journal for Quality and Participation, 20, no. 1 (January–February 1997), p. 12.

Horowitz, A. S. "Rotate!" *Computerworld* 30, no. 45 (November 4, 1996), p. 90.

Howard, J. L. "The Effects of Organizational Restructure on Employee Satisfaction." *Group and Organizational Management* 21, no. 3 (September 1996), p. 278.

Maynard, R. "A Client-Centered Firm's Lesson in Team Work." *Nation's Business* 85, no. 3 (March 1997), p. 32.

Robinson, M. "Desktop Video Servers for Workgroups." *Advanced Imaging* 12, no. 3 (March 1997), p. 32.

Shaiken, H., S. Lopez, and I. Mankita. "Two Routes to Team Production: Saturn and Chrysler." *Industrial Relations* 36, no. 1 (January 1997), p. 17–45.

Stites-Doe, S. "The New Story about Job Rotation." *Academy of Management Executive* 10, no. 1 (February 1996), p. 86.

Van Auken, P. "Do You Dare to Be a Team?" *Supervision* 58, no. 1 (January 1997), p. 8.

Wenger, E., and W. Snyder. "Communities of Practice: The Organizational Frontier," *Harvard Business Review*, January–February 2000, pp 139–145.

Zachary, G. P. "The New Search for Meaning in 'Meaningless' Work." *The Wall Street Journal*, January 9, 1997, p. B1.

Notes

[1] R. D. Middlemist and M. A. Hitt, *Organizational Behavior: Managerial Strategies for Performance* (St. Paul, MN: West, 1988), p. 171.

[2] William M. Carley, "Fearful Skies: Airline Security Offers Only Weak Protection against Bombs on Jets," *The Wall Street Journal*, May 10, 1989, pp. 1, 12; "Pan Am Employees Allege FAA Approved Use of Family Security Measures in Europe," *Aviation Week & Space Technology*, April 9, 1990, p. 63; "On the Trail of Terror," *U.S. News and World Report*, November 13, 1989, pp. 44–46; Andrew Blum, "Court Chides Insurers in Pan Am Bomb Case," *The National Law Journal*, November 28, 1994, p. A7; and "Commission Offers Recommendations to Improve Airline, Airport Security," *Aviation Week & Space Technology*, May 21, 1990, p. 125.

[3] A. Murray, "Jobs Don't Guarantee a Sound Economy," *The Wall Street Journal*, October 24, 1988, p. 1.

[4] A. Karr, "Secretaries Seek More Authority, with Some Success," *The Wall Street Journal*, August 22, 1989, p. 1.

[5] O. Shenkar, "Robotics: A Challenge for Occupational Psychology," *Journal of Occupational Psychology*, March 1988, pp. 103–112.

[6] J. Dreyfuss, "Catching the Computer Wave," *Fortune*, September 1988, pp. 78–82.

[7] A. Majchrzak, T. Chang, W. Barfield, R. Eberts, and G. Salvendy, *Human Aspects of Computer-Aided Design* (Philadelphia: Taylor & Francis, 1987), pp. 160–196.

[8] R. Hayes and R. Jaikumar, "Manufacturing's Crisis: New Technologies, Obsolete Organizations," *Harvard Business Review*, September–October, 1988, pp. 77–85.

[9] P. Collins, J. Hage, and F. Hull, "Organizational and Technological Predictors of Change in Automaticity," *Academy of Management Journal*, September 1988, pp. 512–543.

[10] A. Majchrzak and J. Cotton, "A Longitudinal Study of Adjustment to Technological Change: From Mass to Computer-Automated Batch Production," *Journal of Occupational Psychology*, March 1988, pp. 43–66.

[11] J. Sheedy, "Retooling Your Workers along with Your Machines," *The Wall Street Journal*, July 31, 1989, p. A10.

[12] N. Alster, "What Flexible Workers Can Do," *Fortune*, February 13, 1989, pp. 49–52.

[13] D. Wessel, "Working Smart: With Labor Scarce, Service Firms Strive to Raise Productivity," *The Wall Street Journal*, June 1, 1989, pp. A1, A12.

[14] J. C. Szabo, "Finding the Right Workers," *Nation's Business*, February 1991, p. 19.

[15] J. Candler, "Treating Drivers like Customers," *Nation's Business*, December 1993, pp. 56–58.

[16] Fred Luthans, *Organizational Behavior*, 6th ed. (New York: McGraw-Hill, 1992), pp. 23–25.

[17] Clifford E. Jergensen, "Job Preferences (What Makes a Job Good or Bad?)," *Journal of Applied Psychology*, June 1978, pp. 267–276.

[18] E. Trist and K. Banforth, "Social and Psychological Consequences of the Long-Wall Method of Coal-Getting," *Human Relations*, February 1951, pp. 3–38.

[19] J. Richard Hackman, Greg R. Oldham, R. Janson, and K. Purdy, "A New Strategy for Job Enrichment," *California Management Review*, Summer 1975, pp. 57–71.

[20] B. Dutton, "A Case for Work Teams," *Manufacturing Systems* 9, no. 7 (July 1991), p. 58.

[21] Ibid.

[22]Ibid.

[23]C. J. Gersick, "Time and Transition in Work Teams: Toward a New Model of Group Development," *Academy of Management Journal*, March 1988, pp. 9–41.

[24]M. Murray, "Who's the Boss?" *The Wall Street Journal*, May 14, 1997, pp. A1, A14.

[25]G. S. Odiorne, "The New Breed of Supervisor: Leaders in Self-Managed Work Teams," *Supervision* 52, no. 8 (1989), pp. 14–17.

[26]J. Ellis, "Monsanto Is Teaching Old Workers New Tricks," *Business Week*, August 21, 1989, p. 67.

[27]J. R. Hackman and G. R. Oldham, *Work Redesign* (Reading, MA: Addison-Wesley, 1980); C. Manz and H. Sims, "Leading Workers to Lead Themselves: The External Leadership of Self-Managing Work Teams," *Administrative Science Quarterly*, March 1987, pp. 106–129.

[28]P. C. Thompson, *Quality Circles: How to Make Them Work in America* (New York: AMACOM, 1982).

[29]R. L. Cole, "Made in Japan—Quality Control Circles," *Across the Board* 16 (1979), pp. 72–78.

[30]T. Tang, P. Tollison, and H. Whiteside, "The Effect of Quality Circle Initiation on Motivation to Attend Quality Circle Meetings and on Task Performance," *Personnel Psychology*, Winter 1987, pp. 799–814; and A. Whatley and W. Hoffman, "Quality Circles Earn Union Respect," *Personnel Journal*, December 1987, pp. 89–93.

[31]P. F. Koons, "Getting Comfortable with TQM," *Bureaucrat* 20, no. 2 (Summer 1991), pp. 35–38.

[32]S. Watanabe, "The Japanese Quality Control Circle: Why It Works," *International Labor Review* 130, no. 1 (1991), pp. 57–80.

[33]G. Vasilash, "A New Spin on Quality Circles," *Automotive Production* 108, no. 10 (October 1996), pp. 56–59.

[34]J. Richard Hackman and Greg R. Oldham, "Motivation through the Design of Work: Test of a Theory," *Organizational Behavior and Human Performance* 16 (1976), pp. 250–279.

[35]S. J. Zaccaro and E. F. Stone, "Incremental Validity of an Empirically Based Measure of Job Characteristics," *Journal of Applied Psychology*, May 1988, pp. 245–252; Y. Fried and G. Ferris, "The Validity of the Job Characteristics Model: A Review and Meta-Analysis," *Personnel Psychology*, Summer 1987, pp. 287–322.

[36]C. T. Kulik, G. R. Oldham, and J. R. Hackman, "Work Design as an Approach to Person-Environment Fit," *Journal of Vocational Behavior*, December 1988, pp. 278–296.

[37]J. Richard Hackman and Greg R. Oldham, "Development of the Job Diagnostic Survey," *Journal of Applied Psychology* 60 (1976), pp. 159–170.

[38]Fred Luthans, Barbara Kemmerer, Robert Paul, and Lew Taylor, "The Impact of a Job Redesign Intervention on Salespersons' Observed Performance Behaviors," *Group and Organization Studies*, March 1987, pp. 55–72.

[39]R. Miles, C. Snow, A. Meyer, and H. Coleman, Jr., "Organizational Strategy, Structure, and Process," *Academy of Management Review*, July 1978, pp. 546–562.

[40]Ibid.; and R. Miles and C. Snow, "Designing Strategic Human Resources Systems," *Organizational Dynamics* 13 (Summer 1984), pp. 36–52.

[41]D. Woodruff, "A Dozen Motor Factors—Under One Roof," *Business Week*, November 20, 1989, pp. 92–93.

[42]S. Stites-Doe, "The New Story about Job Rotation," *Academy of Management Executive* 10, no. 1 (1996), pp. 86–87.

[43]C. Trost and C. Hymowitz, "Careers Start Giving In to Family Needs," *The Wall Street Journal*, June 18, 1990, pp. B1, B5.

[44]C. Trost, "How One Bank Is Handling a 'Two Track' Career Plan," *The Wall Street Journal*, March 3, 1989, pp. B1, B8.

[45]"Women and Work," *Employment Relations Bulletin* 7, no. 8 (April 1989).

[46]S. Nelton, "A Flexible Style of Management," *Nations' Business*, December 1993.

[47]R. McGarvey, "Time on Their Side," *Entrepreneur*, July 1999, pp. 79–81.

[48]L. Castro, "Managers Declare Independence to Run Businesses from Their Personal Utopias," *The Wall Street Journal*, September 3, 1991, pp. B1, B4.

[49]Ibid.

[50]S. Shellenbarger, "More Companies Experiment with Workers' Schedules," *The Wall Street Journal*, January 13, 1994, pp. B1, B6.

[51]S. Shellenbarger, "I'm Still Here! Home Workers Worry They're Invisible," *The Wall Street Journal*, December 16, 1993, pp. B1, B4.

[52]B. Fryer, "Home Work," *Working Woman*, April 1997, pp. 59–60.

[53]J. Fierman, "The Contingency Workforce," *Fortune*, January 24, 1994, pp. 30–36.

[54]Ricky W. Griffin, *Task Design: An Integrative Approach* (Glenview, IL: The Scott Foresman Series in Management and Organizations, 1982), pp. 207–227.

[55]Griffin, *Task Design*.

[56]Raymond J. Aldag and Arthur P. Brief, *Task Design and Employee Motivation* (Glenview, IL: Scott, Foresman, 1979).

[57]Hackman and Oldham, *Work Redesign*.

[58]Ibid.

[59]Ken Zino, "We've Got to Make It," *Parade Magazine*, September 4, 1988, pp. 22–25; J. Mitchell, "GM to Discontinue the Buick Reatta, Citing Slow Sales," *The Wall Street Journal*, March 5, 1991, pp. A4, A5; and "Reatta Plant to Produce Electric Cars," *Washington Post*, March 5, 1991, p. P8.

[60]Adapted from A. Taylor III, "How Toyota Defies Gravity," *Fortune*, December 8, 1997; pp. 100–108; S. Butler, "Life in the Fast Lane," *U.S. News and World Report* 121, no. 25 (December 23, 1996), pp. 47–48.

9

Orientation, Training, and Development

Chapter Objectives

As a result of studying this chapter, you should be able to

1. Describe the elements of an effective orientation program.

2. Explain the role training and development play in improving performance.

3. List and describe training and development methods.

4. Understand how to evaluate a training program.

It is imperative that organizations integrate their employees into the organization so that they can become effective, productive members soon after joining the firm. Several effective ways to do this is through orientation, training, and development. Orientation teaches new employees about the organization's history and values and outlines expectations for employee performance. Training helps individuals hone the skills they will need to effectively perform their jobs. Development is broader than training and is tied more closely to the skills and aptitudes of the employee. To explore these topics, we examine the important elements of orientation, training, and development programs.

CASE

Orientation at Bellagio Resort

Bellagio is one of the largest resorts on the world famous "Strip" in Las Vegas, Nevada. Hiring at Bellagio is constant, because to run efficiently, over 9000 employees are needed. Recruiting is fairly easy for many positions, as Bellagio is known as one of the best places on the Strip to work. However, some positions are so unique (e.g., underwater welders, seamstresses who must be able to swim 100 yards, and gourmet chefs) that extra effort is required to locate potential employees with the skills required. Once an employee has been hired, regardless of the position or skills, he or she must attend an orientation session before he or she is allowed to work. Orientation is offered twice a week. It starts at 7:30AM and continues until mid-afternoon. As you can imagine, a great deal of information is provided during that time.

Orientation begins when a new hire arrives at the Employment Center by 7:15AM. He or she signs in and takes a seat in the waiting room. A few minutes later, after a computer has been loaded with the new hire's information, the employee is escorted to the computer. A brief description of the process he or she will follow is offered, and the employee is asked to answer whatever questions the computer asks. Screen by screen the new employee types in the information required by law and other information needed to complete the new hire's personnel folder. The computer work takes between 15 and 30 minutes, depending on the new hire's typing and English skills. For employees who prefer, the computer session can be switched to Spanish with the click of a function key.

Once the computer work is finished, the new hire begins "processing." During processing a member of the employment department explains key organizational rules, answers any questions about the computer work, verifies that the computer work is complete and accurate, gives the new employee a handbook for which he or she must sign to indicate that it was received by the employee, orders a name badge, and makes a photo identification card for the employee. When processing is complete, the new hire returns to the waiting room until 8:30AM when the group is given a tour of the facilities and is then escorted to the training room for the next portion of the orientation.

During the next segment of the orientation program, the new hires participate in an information session. The training department, with the help of employees who have volunteered to participate in the orientation program, runs this session. This means that a cocktail waitress, a front desk clerk, or a member of the gardening staff could help facilitate the session. The volunteer presenters are trained in how and what information to present prior to their participation in the session. The session is interactive and involves several presentation forms. Oral quizzes are conducted throughout the session with those providing correct answers receiving a small prize. Because the session runs through the lunch hour, lunch is catered. Free food is included in the session as a way of introducing the new hires to one of the many benefits provided by Bellagio: free food in the employee cafeteria.

At the close of the classroom session supervisors arrive at the training room to collect their new hires. The supervisor conducts a tour of the area in which the new employee will work and reviews major work rules such as hours to be worked, the best way to navigate the back of the house to get from the employee entrance to the work area, and any unique rules the area may have. The supervisor also introduces the new hire to the other employees with whom he or she will be working. The supervisor reviews the work that the employee will be performing and answers any questions he or she may have.

The final stop in the orientation process is wardrobe. The new hires are fitted for their uniforms and told to return to wardrobe 15 minutes prior to their first shift to pick up their customized uniform. They also are informed of another benefit offered by Bellagio: free dry cleaning of the uniform. All the employee has to do is drop off a dirty uniform at the end of their shift and return the next day to retrieve it, cleaned, pressed, and ready to wear. The locker room procedure also is explained. Specifically, when an employee arrives at work in street clothes, he or she goes directly to the locker room. On arrival the employee tells the seamstress in the locker room his or her identification number. The seamstress types in the number on a computer and the rack of uniforms spins until the employee's uniform is in front. The employee is given the clean uniform and a garment bag with a lock and key. The employee takes everything into one of the dressing rooms, changes into his or her uniform, and places all of his or her personal belongings in the garment bag, and locks it. The employee delivers the locked bag to the seamstress and walks away with the only key to the bag, ensuring that his or her valuables are safely secured until the employee retrieves the bag at the end of the shift.

Bellagio's orientation program serves a variety of purposes. First, all of the required paperwork is completed during this time, ensuring that new employees are paid on time and that Bellagio is conforming to all of the employment laws. Second, it provides new hires with a great deal of information about Bellagio and provides the company the opportunity to reinforce its expectation of providing guests exceptional service. The orientation process involves many different current employees as well, illustrating Bellagio's commitment to cross-training and teamwork. Finally, it makes the new employees feel welcome and reassures them that accepting the offer from Bellagio was the right decision.

Strategic Choices

An organization must make four basic choices with regard to developing employees:

1. Does the firm want employees who are content following established rules of the organization, or does it want employees who challenge rules that are ineffective and search for more productive ways to perform their jobs?
2. Should the organization develop its human resources ("grow its own"), or should it focus on hiring employees who are already developed ("buy its own")?

3. Should the organization find ways to improve the performance of marginal workers, or should it simply replace them?
4. How well does the organization's development strategy match the organization's overall strategy? If the match is not good, decisions about what and how to change must be made.

Each of these choices is analyzed in the following sections.

Continuous Improvement

All organizations want their employees to follow rules to some extent to prevent an organizational anarchy. Organizations need rules, procedures, and policies to function as an organization. Structural hierarchy and job descriptions spell out job duties, responsibilities, authority, and reporting relationships.

So the issue is not whether to hire employees who accept and conform to the rules. Rather, the issue is how much agreement to have. Following rules and procedures reduces variation and uncertainty. Uncertainty reduces risk because it enhances predictability. But predictability comes at a price—when there is "too much" acceptance, innovation and creativity are stifled. When innovation and creativity among organizational members are stifled, the organization finds it difficult to come up with new ideas, approaches, products, and creative solutions to problems.

So, the issue becomes how to achieve the stability that is needed to function as an organization and, at the same time, to encourage employees to develop their creativity. Companies such as Nissan and Toyota have solved this problem through the quality circle concept to encourage creativity among employee groups. As noted in Chapter 8, employees meet periodically to discuss ways to improve both production and quality. 3M uses a form of "intrapreneurship" that encourages employees to actually form minicompanies within it to develop and market new products and ideas.[1] This is how the highly successful Post-it notes and Thinsulate were developed for 3M.

Yet not all firms want creativity from their employees. Even a highly successful company such as Walt Disney World has a very specific dress code. The dress code for Walt Disney World cast members (this is what employees at Disney are called) is laid out clearly in the *Handbook for Cast Members*. A quick look through this handbook illustrates how detailed the guidelines are. For example, two pages are devoted to exactly what constitutes an acceptable and unacceptable sideburn. To the untrained eye, there is virtually no difference between the pictures that illustrate this section. However, cast members are trained to be able to recognize a difference.

Developing People Versus Hiring Developed People

The second key decision regarding training and development involves the extent to which the firm will train and develop employees versus hiring already well-trained and developed persons. For example, Procter & Gamble exerts a great deal of time and effort in the comprehensive training of new employees, whereas Parker Foods, a much smaller organization based in Colorado, tries to hire people with extensive experience. The same is true of IBM compared with a smaller computer company such as Standard.

Size is often a major factor in this decision. Larger companies often can afford to spend extensive amounts on training and developing new employees; most of the

FOCUS ON HR

In Search of Talent

Every organization needs good people. Where can they be found? One answer is to look within the organization. Many highly qualified employees are under the noses of their bosses but are never recognized. The following are some techniques that managers have used to locate hidden talent:

1. Argue with an employee. If he or she immediately changes his or her opinion to match yours, look elsewhere for the talent you need.
2. Watch how people clock in and out. Those who walk with purpose in both directions have more on the ball than those who straggle in and run out.
3. Watch whom a manager goes to for help in solving a problem. That employee has the most potential and talent, or he or she wouldn't be asked for an opinion.
4. Determine who comes up with the solutions, not who finds problems. Those who solve the problems and then come to you to explain what they did have talent. Those who simply come in and say there is a problem lack foresight.
5. Try not to pick a clone. Just because someone looks and acts like you doesn't make that person the most talented. Look for differences so that your strengths will be different from his or hers.

Once the talent in the ranks has been recognized, do everything in your power to groom these people. Finding a replacement for high-potential, high performers is far more difficult than locating talent in the organization.

SOURCE: Robert McGarvey, "Talent Scout," *USAir Magazine*, April 1993, pp. 68-73.

---

firms that offer training are large *Fortune* 500 companies that can afford to do so. Both IBM and Procter & Gamble have served as training grounds for hosts of smaller firms in their respective industries. Statistically, however, this accounts for a very small percentage of companies providing training for U.S. workers. Only five tenths of 1 percent of all the companies in the United States deliver 90 percent of the workplace training.[2] Some critics believe that not nearly enough money is being spent on training the U.S. workforce. Most agree that organizations should be spending at least 5 percent of their funds on training; however, the figure is closer to 2 percent.[3] Further, some firms spend nothing on training whereas others concentrate the training they do provide on managers, technical employees, and professionals.[4] When training is provided, it often does not focus on what employers list as the number one deficiency of the U.S. workforce: written communication.[5]

Frequently, a company will hire untrained and inexperienced people for two major reasons. First, they can get them for a fairly low wage rate and, second, they can train the employees in their preferred way of carrying out the job. Many companies hire new college graduates for these reasons while shunning more experienced and expensive employees. Another factor that influences this decision is the firm's policy to promote from within versus hiring from the outside.

Firms such as GM and Polaroid have a strong promote-from-within policy and, therefore, tend to hire inexperienced people at entry-level positions in order to provide promotion opportunities. Apple Computer, on the other hand, hires experienced people for higher-level jobs primarily because of the very rapid growth the firm experienced in the 1980s. In fact, Apple hired many people from IBM, a firm known for its thorough training and orientation program. This presents a dilemma for many firms that provide thorough training: they may end up training employees who leave and eventually work for competitors. Some firms known for their sophisticated training programs, such as Electronics Data Systems (EDS), have tried to prevent this from happening by requiring new employees to sign a form indicating that they will repay EDS for their training if they take a job with a competitor during a specified number of years after completing the EDS training program.

So the organization must decide how much time, effort, and money it wishes to invest in a training and development program relative to its position on hiring well-trained and experienced employees. Of course, even those firms that hire well-trained and experienced employees will have at least a minimal training and development program to show employees "how we do it here."

Improving Versus Replacing Poor Performers

A third key strategic choice in the development of employees involves how much the firm will invest in an employee to improve subpar performance. Several key issues must be considered: the probability of improving the performance, the cost of improving it, legal considerations, replacement costs, and top management philosophy.

When employees do not perform their jobs to the standards expected in some companies, they are terminated. In other companies, they are coached, counseled, and trained in hopes of improving their performance. With the emphasis on drug and substance abuse rehabilitation and the legal protections prohibiting discriminatory actions (including termination) based on age, sex, race, religion, or disability, companies often seek ways to improve employees' performance instead of terminating them. Employee Assistance Programs (EAPs) have been developed to help the substance abuser or troubled employee. In addition, many employers fear that termination for poor performance could result in litigation charges of discrimination. Because of this, employers who at one time might have immediately terminated an employee (for drunkenness, for example) now may continue the person's employment but require that the employee enter an EAP.

Thus today an employer must decide whether additional training can salvage marginal performance or whether a swift termination policy is more desirable.

Strategy and Training and Development

An organization's strategy and the importance it places on training and development are closely related. For the corporate strategy to be implemented, a well-trained, competent workforce is needed to complete the goals and initiatives put forth in the strategic plan. On the other hand, training and development of employees can facilitate or limit the very strategies that are even considered.

If an organization wishes to grow by entering new markets, fully trained employees who can help achieve this goal are necessary. If the organization does not place a high priority on training and development, this initiative may fail as the unprepared employees struggle to achieve the growth expected. However, if an organization values training and development and works closely with new employees to ensure they are fully trained to perform their jobs, virtually any strategic approach is possible.

Managers need to understand the dynamics of the strategy/development connection. It is important not only in the successful formulation and implementation of strategy but in filtering what type of strategy is even possible in the first place. Strategic decisions often lead to new objectives that require specific skills to implement.

FOCUS ON HR

Disney's Orientation Program

One of the most successful orientation programs for U.S. firms is the one developed by the Disney organization. Everyone—all employees hired at all levels—attends Disney University and must pass Traditions I before going for specialized training. Traditions I is an all-day experience in which the Disney philosophy, tradition, and culture are presented.

At Disney, employees are called "cast members," and whenever they work with the public, they are "on stage." Customers are called "guests." Employees are told about all functions and how they relate to the "show." They are reminded of how important their role is in making the show a success. Even ticket takers receive four eight-hour days of instruction in order to learn locations of restrooms, when the parade starts, show schedules, and so on. In other words, they are required to know more than the ticket-taking job; they are also expected to know other information to make the guest's stay as enjoyable as possible.

Disney emphasizes the "Disney Way" in orientation, training, and follow-up employee evaluations. Because of this emphasis, the company is sometimes criticized for "brainwashing" its employees. The firm requires conformity to the Disney Way, and employees are given little opportunity to express creativity and innovation.

Yet when one examines the success of Disney theme parks, the wide use of part-time and student help, and the critical nature of their jobs in terms of customer contact, a rigid, highly formalized orientation and training program is probably the best. And of course, it's difficult to argue with success.

SOURCE: Adapted from Thomas J. Peters and Robert H. Waterman, Jr., *In Search of Excellence* (New York: Harper & Row, 1982), p. 168.

Sometimes it may be necessary to train and develop employees before it is possible to undertake a certain strategy.

Orientation

orientation Familiarizing new employees with the rules, policies, and procedures of the organization.

Before a new hire can become a productive part of the organization, he or she must become familiar with "how things are done" in the organization. Probably nothing does more to bring a new employee up to speed than an orientation program. **Orientation** is the process of welcoming new employees, bringing them into the organization, and familiarizing them with its operations and culture. Orientation occurs two ways: formally and informally. The formal orientation is conducted by the organization. Informal orientation occurs through daily interactions with fellow employees.

Formal Orientation Programs

formal orientation An orientation program sponsored and developed by an organization.

A **formal orientation** program is sponsored and developed by the organization. Its primary purpose is to welcome new employees and acquaint them with the rules, policies, and procedures of the organization. It should be held as soon as possible after a new hire begins the job, usually the first day of work, so that the new employee does not have time to pick up any "bad habits." Some proactive companies even start the orientation process prior to the first day of work by contacting employees who have been hired but whose start date is in the future. Information about the company, benefits offered, or new initiatives can be shared with future employees. Keeping in touch will help to build a bond between the new hire and the firm even before he or she begins the job.

EXHIBIT 9.1	TIPS FOR BUILDING A STRONG ORIENTATION PROGRAM

The very first step in welcoming new employees into the organization is the orientation program. However, an ever-increasing number of firms are sending a stale, stagnant message to their employees. To fix this problem, organizations need to focus on updating and revamping their orientation programs. Some suggestions for making needed changes follow:

1. Keep the paperwork portion of the orientation light the first day. Information overload can be a real turnoff for employees. Try to separate the required paperwork into two piles: those forms that must be completed the first day and those that can wait a week or two.
2. Start the orientation with an informal meeting with the new recruit's immediate supervisor. The meeting should be brief, no more than 20 minutes, and it should start on time. This meeting will serve two purposes. First, the employee will see that his or her immediate supervisor is a person with whom he or she can come to with problems and concerns. Second, it shows that the firm and the supervisor stress punctuality.
3. Alternate heavy information such as benefits and insurance forms with short taped or live accounts of the organization by the CEO or other important and not-so-important organizational members. This helps to reassure the new employees that the organization is made up of people, not just forms and rules.
4. Provide the new employees with a glossary of terms unique to the organization. This can be done in a variety of ways. For example, two long-time employees can act out a scene in which the organization's jargon is used and then allow the new employees to guess what the terms stand for. Afterward, the same scene can be acted out by two new employees who have mastered the corporate lingo. Having employees learn the organization language up front is an easy way to help them begin to think like an organization member. This exercise also cuts down on the feeling of being an outsider once the employee begins working.
5. Find a buddy for each new employee. Matching employees with new recruits does not have to focus on the job to be performed. Sometimes it may be useful to match people on a personality basis rather than on a job basis. This allows new employees to build links with employees outside their immediate department, further reinforcing the organization's culture of working together as an organization.

In "Where the Training Dollars Go," Chris Lee reports that 76 percent of firms with 50 or more employees have a formal orientation program.[6] Several companies have excellent ones—IBM, Frito-Lay, and Dana Corporation among them. Many of these firms follow the suggestions outlined in Exhibit 9.1 that highlight the way to develop a strong orientation program.

Some firms have overall orientation programs designed for any and all employees; others develop specific orientation programs for one job classification or one unit. Exhibit 9.2 shows the elements of the Quaker Oats orientation program for college graduates in sales. Notice that the Quaker philosophy is an important part of the program. Also note that some sales techniques (presentation skills and promotional materials) also are covered. All new sales hires are put through this three- to six-month orientation before receiving additional sales training.

Common Components of an Orientation

Welcoming   Orientations frequently begin with an official welcoming of the employee. In small organizations, this should be done by the CEO. In larger organizations,

EXHIBIT 9.2 ELEMENTS OF QUAKER OATS' ORIENTATION OF
COLLEGE GRADUATES AS SALES TRAINEES

Field Training with District Manager
Quaker's Company Philosophy
Presentation Skills
Organization Structure
Use of Sales Promotion Materials, Trade Allowances, and Consumer Events
Administrative Details

- Payroll
- Health insurance
- Leave and vacation policy

- Pension benefits
- Employee benefits
- Forms

SOURCE: Reprinted by permission from *Quaker Sales Careers: Leadership Through Innovation,* copyright Quaker Oats Company. All Rights Reserved.

someone from human resources and/or the immediate supervisor should welcome the employee and make him or her feel comfortable and accepted.

Meeting the Boss and Fellow Employees   The employee should be introduced to those with whom he or she will work by either the supervisor or someone from human resources. In some cases, a peer employee or buddy might introduce the new employee to his or her coworkers. These introductions are very important and should not be taken lightly.

Completing Paperwork   All essential paperwork should be completed during orientation so that the employee is paid accurately and on time. Various tax and insurance forms as well as time cards, citizenship-resident documentation, and other items need to be completed properly in a timely fashion. There is nothing more aggravating for a new employee than to miss the first paycheck or to be paid improperly because the correct forms were not completed accurately. Someone in the company should be given the responsibility to be the expert on new hires. This person should ensure that all needed forms for new hires are completed promptly and accurately.

Reviewing the Employee Handbook   One critical step in the orientation program is a review of the employee handbook. Exhibit 9.3 is the table of contents of a typical one. As this table of contents indicates, this handbook contains a vast amount of information. It would be impossible to discuss it all, but at least a brief mention of each section should be made. Sections that need to be covered carefully might include employee benefits and retirement programs as well as company policies, rules, regulations, and expectations. Some attention also might need to be paid to grievance procedures and disciplinary procedures.

employment-at-will An employment situation in which either the employee or employer can terminate the working relationship for any reason at any time.

Specific language about the term of employment also should be stated in the handbook, and new employees should be made aware of this passage. Terminology in the handbook should be chosen carefully to avoid **employment-at-will** litigation. In essence, under employment-at-will, the employer or the employee can terminate their relationship for good cause, no cause, or even bad cause without warning because their relationship is based on an implied contract, not a written one.[7] Employees who believe that they have been dismissed unfairly can file a wrongful discharge lawsuit in the hope of getting their job back, and the odds of winning are on their side.

EXHIBIT 9.3   TABLE OF CONTENTS FROM EMPLOYEE MANUAL

In approximately 70 percent of these cases, the court has ruled in favor of the employee, costing the employer court costs of up to $250,000, as well as damages that average around $500,000.[8]

Wrongful discharge suits have generally been heard for four different reasons. First, the employee can argue that the employer violated public policy by firing him or her. This line of defense includes dismissing an employee for refusing to perform some illegal, unethical, or unsafe procedure. A second defense is that the employer did not deal with the employee fairly and in good faith. If an employee was fired just before his or her retirement benefits were to begin, the organization could be found not to have acted in good faith. The employer also can be charged with tortuous acts toward an employee; an example of this is an employee seeking a job outside the company whose job search was sabotaged by the company, which then dismissed the employee. The company could be held at fault. Finally, if an employer breeches an implied contract, an employee can sue for wrongful discharge. Cases of this type relate to verbal statements made during an interview that allude to or imply a long-term commitment on the part of the employer and/or statements in the employee handbook that suggest that after a probationary period, employees move to "permanent" status. In just such a case in Michigan, the court ruled in favor of the employee and against Blue Cross and Blue Shield.[9]

Introducing Job Duties and Performing Initial Training   Of course, the job duties were discussed during the hiring interview. However, they should be reviewed as part of the orientation process. The job description, goals (objectives), and employee performance evaluation form and process all should be reviewed. The employee needs to know the following:

- What he or she is to do (job description).
- What is to be accomplished (job goals or objectives).
- How he or she will be evaluated (performance evaluation).

Failure to clearly point out and discuss these items at the time of hiring will likely cause many problems later. The employee also needs to be given initial training about how the job is done at the particular company with specific follow-up training conducted later.

Conducting a Follow-Up Session   Finally, after a period of one to three months, a follow-up session should be held with the employee by either the supervisor or someone in human resources. This may occur at the end of the employee's probationary period. A follow-up session is a good idea to give both the employee and the employer time to assess whether a good choice has been made. A careful review of the employee's performance at the end of the probationary period and a review of the company policies and rules will help ensure that the employee is fitting in properly.

We now examine how the informal orientation process operates in the organization.

Informal Orientation

informal orientation An orientation that an employee receives from other employees.

Informal orientation occurs when new hires receive information about the organization and how to perform their jobs from current employees. Organizations hope that the information passed to new hires from current employees matches the information given during the formal orientation program. The stronger the belief of the employees in the organization's culture, the closer the two types of information will be.

Many companies go to great lengths to ensure a match between information provided formally and informally. For example, Dana Corporation, under the leadership of former Chairman Rene McPherson, emphasized a one-page statement of philosophy, which was communicated to new and existing employees over and over again. This helped to reinforce corporate philosophy with existing employees as well as new ones. This philosophy covers four key points:[10]

1. Face-to-face communication of all performance figures with all employees is critical.
2. Training and the opportunity for development should be provided to all employees.
3. Job security should be provided for all people.
4. Incentive programs based on ideas, suggestions, and hard work should be established as a reward.

A short, simple, straightforward statement, such as the one above, consistently emphasized and communicated, can do much to ensure that the formal orientation strategy is reinforced on the job. This is particularly so if the CEO exemplifies the organization's mission. CEOs carry great symbolic power when they exemplify a strategy they desire the firm to implement.

Reinforcing Behavior

In addition to the exemplary role played by the CEO in reinforcing a desired strategy, the organization should have systems that reinforce behavior that helps achieve this strategy. For example, if participation and employee involvement are keystones in implementing a desired organizational strategy, then employees and managers who engage in participative behavior should be rewarded for it. These rewards could be in the form of salary increases or incentive pay, promotions, praise, and symbols (such as plaques or certificates). Negative sanctions could be used for those who do not participate in desired activities, such as the absence of rewards as well as managerial and peer censure in the form of verbal and written comments. At the extreme, it might even involve termination.

Let's now turn our attention to the training and development strategies and programs that organizations use to enhance and improve the performance of their employees.

Training, Development, and Performance Improvement

The goal of training and development programs of all organizations should be to maintain or improve the performance of individuals. In so doing, employees will have the required skills to implement the firm's strategy and ensure the success of the organization.

Many organizations spend much time, effort, and money on training and developing their employees, including managers. In some organizations, such as Federal Express, this system is very sophisticated and quite formalized. Federal Express uses a database of 25 interactive videodiscs to train its 35,000 employees. Before a courier ever delivers a package, he or she receives three weeks of training; a customer service agent receives five weeks of training before answering a call.[11] In other organizations, training and development are very informal and unstructured. Whether the system is highly structured, a major responsibility of any organization is to *invest* in the education and development of its employees by formulating and implementing a human resource development strategy that includes programs, objectives, and procedures for development programs, on- and off-the-job training, and other learning experiences.

Training and Development

training Providing an employee with skills that can be used immediately on the job.

development Providing an employee with knowledge that may be used today or in the future.

Training refers to providing instruction to develop skills that can be used immediately on the job. It has a narrow focus and should provide skills that will benefit the organization rather quickly. **Development**, on the other hand, has a broader scope. It involves developing knowledge that may be used today or sometime in the future. It may not be focused on either the present or future job but more on meeting the organization's general long-term needs. The payoff is less direct and can be measured only in the long term.[12] One Web site that provides additional information on training and development is **www.astd.org**. This site is the home page for the American Society of Training and Development, and it offers extensive excerpts from its monthly magazine, *Training and Development.*[13]

If an organization taught its managers to use *Lotus 1-2-3* to manage their budgets, that would constitute training. If these same managers took courses in general systems theory and management information systems to help the company develop into a more efficient, effective organization over the long term, the effort would more properly be labeled as a development activity. Both are obviously important and need emphasis.

management development Training and development programs for supervisors and managers.

The terms *training* and *development* refer to the total structure of on-the-job and off-the-job programs used by organizations in developing employee skills and knowledge necessary for proficient job performance and career advancement. **Management development** refers to the training and development programs for supervisors and managers and often excludes programs for professionals (such as engineers, salespeople, and accountants), skilled operative employees (such as draftsmen, tool and die makers, and bookkeepers), and semiskilled and unskilled operatives (such as assembly line workers, packers, and material handlers), unless these individuals are being prepared for supervision or management.

Any meaningful training and development system must be integrated closely with other human resource strategies in the organization if it is to operate most effectively. Organizations that have effectively integrated training and development with other human resource strategies in performance appraisal, promotion, or pay advances recognize the importance of the training function. This integration also helps to ensure that development strategies help support other related personnel strategies.

Training Responsibilities

Top management, human resources, the immediate supervisor, and the employee share the major responsibilities for training and development. Each is described in the following text.

Top Management   The commitment of the CEO and top management is critical for effective training to take place throughout the organization. Managers tend to manage as they are managed. Any developmental program that doesn't have the attention, understanding, and commitment from top management will be limited severely in terms of the basic changes it can produce.

Career Paths Help Keep Training and Development on Track

As the abundance of baby boomers continues to clog corporate ladders, organizations are making changes. Many firms have implemented dual-career tracks to allow more individuals to climb up the corporate ladder. Generally, one ladder is the management track, and the other is a professional track. By installing two tracks, organizations hope to change the idea that moving into management is the only way to "make it to the top."

To develop these dual-career paths, one firm, British Petroleum Exploration (BPX), assigned teams to develop two truly comparable tracks in terms of responsibility, rewards, and influence for management and for individual contributors. Current paths were scrapped and the teams began developing things as they should be done, not as they were currently being done. The result was a dual-career track that employees could jump between and progress up as BPX's needs, abilities, and interests changed. Many other firms, such as ITT, IBM, and NCR, have similar programs.

The benefits of these types of programs are evident. However, there are potential costs as well. For example, even though the ladders are designed to let employees move from one to the other, at some point this becomes impossible. This is especially true for managers who have been away from the technical aspects of the job so long that their skills are obsolete. Also, the organization's compensation costs can increase as employees begin to climb their chosen ladders. Further, organizational costs for implementing and monitoring the system can also be quite high.

However these new career paths are enacted, the human resource unit will have the major responsibility for them. Making sure that all of the human resource professionals understand the process can make the transition period and subsequent operations of the dual tracks much easier.

SOURCE: Adapted from Robert Goddard, "Lateral Moves Enhance Careers," *HRMagazine*, December 1990, pp. 69–74; James McElwain, "Succession Plans Designed to Manage Change," *HRMagazine*, February 1991, pp. 67–71; and Milan Moravec and Robert Tucker, "Transforming Organizations for Good," *HRMagazine*, October 1991, pp.74–76.

YOU BE THE JUDGE

The main goal behind developing managers is to ready them for their next position, or to make them promotable. When a person is ready for promotion, a change in job level with a commensurate increase in responsibility and pay is normally determined by his or her immediate supervisor. However, a recent study found that the qualities supervisors look for when determining if one of their subordinates is ready for a promotion differ based on the gender of the candidate. For example, when asked why a male candidate was deemed ready for a promotion, decision makers noted in 75 percent of the cases that they had a high level of comfort with the candidate. Comfort with the candidate was only mentioned by 23 percent of the decision makers when discussing a female applicant. One supervisor explained "comfort level" by indicating that he knew the candidate well and that they had an effective relationship. He knew how the employee would act and react in situations and that he could count on him to be stable and consistent over time.

A second characteristic that differed across genders when it came to promotions was familiarity with the job. This is when the supervisor promotes individuals only into positions with which they are already familiar. Continuity was found to be an important factor in promotions for women but not for men. More than 35 percent of the decision makers mentioned familiarity with the job when discussing a promotion for a woman, but only 6 percent mentioned the quality when deciding to promote a male candidate. One supervisor interviewed explained that although a woman he supervised was well prepared for a higher-level job, he did not promote her until a position became available in the plant where she currently worked. He felt it would be easier for her to handle the new responsibilities if the people with whom she would be working already knew her. When the candidate was asked by the researchers how she felt about the decision, she said she felt restricted. She said she would have preferred an earlier promotion at a different facility rather than waiting for a job in her current location. What do you think about the decision this manager made?

SOURCE: Adapted from Michelle Martinez, "Prepared for the Future," *HRMagazine*, April 1997, p. 85.

FOCUS ON HR

Becoming the First Woman Training Manager for a Dutch Firm

Paulette Pellani is a training manager with Philips Electronic Corporation of North America. Pellani recently did what no woman has done before. She took a position as a training manager in Holland. In an effort to internationalize its staff, Philips Gloeilampenfabrieken, the home office of the giant Dutch electronics enterprise, asked Pellani to be the first woman to hold a training manager slot. How could she refuse this once-in-a-lifetime opportunity?

She describes her two-year stint as an investment and a learning experience. She knew that the skills she would gather while living abroad would make her martketable to other firms if her position disappeared while she was overseas. To keep her face familiar, she visited her old office every time she was in town on business.

Pellani admitted that she did have to wrestle with a gender gap problem. For example, she provided a lot of directions for lost guests and made more than a dozen copies for people before she realized that she shouldn't. She decided that she would make sure that people understood her position from the beginning. When introduced to someone, she would simply mention that her job was the same as the man who introduced her. Because she was the first and only woman to hold this position, she was not easily forgotten. However, when she learned that her replacement was a Dutch woman, she knew that her services had been appreciated. Now back in the states for more than a year, she is ready to go again.

SOURCE: Adapted from Cynthia Barnum, "U.S. Training Manager Becomes Expatriate," *HRMagazine*, April 1994, pp. 82–84.

Top management has the responsibility to provide the general policies and procedures required to implement the training program. They need to provide administrative control to ensure that managers and employees comply with the program and give it a conscientious commitment.

Setting the proper culture for encouraging training and development rests with top management. If top management does not do this, establishing the proper climate in the organization will be very difficult.

The Human Resource Department The human resource department in the organization performs essentially a staff support function. It *assists* line management in training and development by providing expertise and resources and sponsoring training conferences and programs.

The Immediate Supervisor Each employee's immediate supervisor and those higher on the organizational hierarchy have the direct responsibility to ensure that training and development occur. The supervisor should encourage employees to develop themselves and should provide time for this to occur. The immediate supervisor, indeed the whole organization, must provide the atmosphere, resources, and encouragement for self-development.

The Employee Even though human resource professionals and line managers must facilitate and manage the training and development process, the primary responsibility lies with the individual. The employee has the responsibility for demonstrating interest in personal career development relative to the goals of the organization. Finally, each employee should encourage other employees to take advantage of development opportunities.

10

Strategies for Effective Performance Appraisal Systems

Chapter Objectives

As a result of studying this chapter, you should be able to

1. Discuss some of the major strategic choices regarding the performance appraisals that are available to organizations.

2. Discuss the process of the performance appraisal.

3. Examine the various methods of performance appraisal, including those based on a standard human resources comparison system and results-oriented performance appraisals.

4. Identify a number of perceptual errors that can affect the objectivity and validity of the performance appraisal.

5. Discuss the relationship between the strategy of the organization and the performance appraisal process.

6. Examine the requirements for an effective performance appraisal system.

Performance appraisals are useful tools not only for evaluating the work of employees but also for developing and motivating employees.[1] Unfortunately, performance appraisals also can be a tremendous source of anxiety and frustration for both the manager and the employee. This is often due to the uncertainties and ambiguities that surround many performance appraisal systems. In general, performance appraisals can be thought of as a means to verify that individuals are meeting performance standards that have been set. Performance appraisals also are a way to help individuals manage their performance. The terms *performance appraisal* and *performance evaluation* are used interchangeably throughout this chapter. The purpose of this chapter is to examine the role of performance appraisals in human resource management and the relationship between performance appraisals and the strategy of the organization.

CASE

Performance Management at St. Luke's Hospital[2]

One goal of any useful performance appraisal system is to differentiate between high and low performers. This sounds simple, but it is not so easy to implement. Rating scales that tend to lump all employees together in the middle, supervisors who have a difficult time rating a worker poorly, and cultures that reward longevity instead of performance interfere with the goal of differentiation in performance appraisals. One firm that is striving to overcome these problems is St. Luke's Hospital in Fargo, North Dakota. St. Luke's dramatically redesigned its performance appraisal process in an effort to identify and reward high-quality performers.

St. Luke's instituted its new performance appraisal system, the Performance Review and Development System (PRDS). Even the title focuses attention on the goals of the system: to make people aware of their performance and to provide guidance to improve that performance. In designing this system, St. Luke's took a strategic approach. That is, it developed the new performance appraisal system to dovetail with its overall strategic plan. Specifically, the hospital was in the midst of redesigning itself so that all service groups in the organization would epitomize St. Luke's corporate commitment to excellence, customer service, and support for one another.

The Strategic Plan

St. Luke's strategic efforts were multifaceted. First of all, it changed titles of all employees to *associate*. Hence, there were no longer titles such as physician, nurse, and staff; instead, everyone was an associate. Next, St. Luke's empowered its associates at the customer level. This provided them with the opportunity to serve a customer to the best of their ability and prevented them from hiding behind the phrase, "I can't; it's not allowed." In addition, the hospital integrated the organization's needs with those of its associates to foster individual growth and development. Next, decision making was decentralized so that those who were affected by a decision were included in making it. Finally, the PRDS was developed to include corporate commitments such as quality, customer service, and individual growth in the performance appraisal process and as a means of recognizing and rewarding individuals and teams for high-quality performance.

The actual development of the PRDS was undertaken by a multidisciplinary task force of 16 individuals including hospital managers and a college professor.

They began by clarifying the goals of the task force, reviewing current performance appraisal systems, and envisioning the ideal system of performance review and management.

The Previous Appraisal System

The one feature of the previous appraisal system that all members of the task force objected to was the fact that there were two different appraisal forms: one for management and one for nonmanagement. The management format accentuated objectives and contained consistent standards for all management. However, the forms were not individualized to each manager's job description. The system did not mention team objectives, and neither differential weights nor special categories were included to individualize the form. The overall view of the task force and the associates was that the previous management appraisal system was rather subjective.

The appraisal form for nonmanagement positions focused on job-related accountabilities, included specific measures of performance, and incorporated differential weighting schemes. However, it did not include objectives for individuals or teams, nor did it encourage personal growth and development. Training opportunities were not available for nonmanagement associates, although they were for management personnel.

The implementation of the system also had some problems. First, it required each individual to have a performance review yearly, but individuals in some areas had not received a formal appraisal in several years. Because there had been no means to track compliance with the yearly appraisal requirement, it was often ignored. Second, even though there were five rating levels available for use, only three, the highest ones, were ever used. This resulted in inflated ratings and the inability to distinguish between top and average performers.

Based on their analysis of the former system, the task force decided to develop only one performance appraisal system that would be used for all positions in the hospital. Several items were identified as being important to include in the new system, including tying behavioral criteria to corporate commitments and training individuals who would perform the appraisals. A variety of raters also was to be used, including self, peer, customer, and supervisory raters. The rating scale had to be redesigned, an appeals process added, and a monitoring system developed to ensure that the appraisals were completed yearly. Finally, the task force decided to use computers as much as possible in the new evaluation procedures. To achieve these goals, the PRDS system includes three major components: ongoing responsibilities and objectives, shared values, and self-development.

Ongoing Responsibilities and Objectives

Based on each individual associate's job responsibilities as outlined in the job description, jointly developed ongoing responsibilities were identified by the associate and the appraiser. In addition to the ongoing responsibilities that are always part of the associate's job, both parties agreed to specific objectives that have deadlines and ending dates. Both ongoing responsibilities and the temporary objectives are then assigned a weight totaling 100 percent. The weights can differ with each new appraisal period so that strategic changes needed by the organization can be factored into the appraisal system to keep the objectives of the organization and the individual associates in agreement. This portion of the rating system is worth 60 percent of the total percentage available.

Shared Values

The shared values component of the appraisal system focuses on *how* the job is done, not what is expected. This segment of the PRDS was designed specifically to reflect the firm's corporate commitments to excellence, customers, and support for one another. It is assessed by using 14 items such as, "Does this associate meet customer needs in an effective and timely manner?" This evaluates the degree of commitment the individual has in the areas of excellence, customer service, and support for other associates. Responses to the 14 items are solicited from managers, peers, subordinates, and customers to obtain the most accurate assessment possible. The importance of this component of the appraisal process is emphasized by assigning it 40 percent of the total evaluation.

Self-Development

This component of the evaluation is not numerically scored as the other two are. However, it is an important part of the total performance appraisal process. Because of the high expectations for each of the associates with respect to quality service, constant self-development is essential. This segment also fits nicely with St. Luke's strategic thrust for continuous quality improvement.

Implementation

All appraisers received training in how to use the PRDS before it was implemented. Since its initiation, several positive outcomes have occurred. First, because the process is interactive, the appraisers no longer are expected to know when each individual is to be appraised. Instead, the associate can and does initiate the appraisal on his or her anniversary date. This means that an individual can no longer go years without receiving feedback about his or her performance. The shared values component (i.e., *how* the job is done) underscored the importance of the organization's commitment to excellence, customer service, and support for one another. Associates have expressed a more positive attitude toward the appraisal system as well as the feedback they receive. No longer do they feel as though they are simply being evaluated on their performance but that the focus is on their work toward achieving personal and organizational goals. Finally, using a variety of raters such as customers, peers, and the employees has resulted in ratings that associates see as fairer and more informative.

It appears that St. Luke's has developed a successful performance appraisal system that will allow individuals to work toward improving themselves as they advance the hospital's goals. Appraisal systems of the type described in this case are deemed fairer and more accurate by all those involved than the more traditional systems. Organizations can enjoy substantial benefits from appraisals, including the knowledge that the most deserving performers will be identified accurately and rewarded appropriately. Such employee knowledge contributes directly to productivity. Further, well-designed appraisal systems can alleviate some of the negative attitudes both managers and employees frequently hold. How this can be done successfully is the focus of this chapter.

Strategic Choices

Managers have a number of strategic choices to make regarding the performance appraisal system. Some of the most important choices are outlined in the following section.

1. Managers should decide on the *objectives* and *purpose for the performance appraisal*. Will the evaluations be for correcting problems, for determining rewards, or for other purposes? Will the evaluations be individual or group based?
2. Managers can choose between *formal and informal procedures* for the performance appraisal. Should the reviews be structured and occur at a specific point in time (formal), or should the manager and the subordinate discuss problems and ways to correct them as they occur (informal)?
3. Performance appraisal formats can emphasize more *objectivity versus subjectivity*. Should managers use their own judgments when evaluating subordinates, or should more concrete factors such as number of units produced and absenteeism be used to evaluate an employee?
4. Managers must decide on the *frequency* of the performance appraisals. Most often, yearly appraisals are performed. However, with new job procedures in which feedback about performance is given monthly, daily, and even hourly, perhaps less frequent formal reviews could be performed. On the other hand, if the job provides no specific feedback about performance, yearly intervals may be too long between appraisals.
5. Managers must decide *who conducts* the performance appraisal. Immediate supervisors are the frequent choice, but, as you will see in this chapter, they are by no means the only choice.

Performance Appraisal Objectives

One human resource objective for using performance appraisal systems is to determine who should be promoted, demoted, transferred, or terminated. However, these are not the only human resource functions that are related to performance appraisals. For example, an organization may use the results from a performance appraisal to determine who needs formal training and development opportunities. Further, such opportunities may be used as a reward for individuals whose appraisals were positive. A variety of developmental opportunities that can be used as a reward are presented in Exhibit 10.1.

Performance appraisals also can be used to motivate and improve performance. By showing an individual where his or her strengths lie and pointing out areas that still need improvement, an evaluator can help focus an employee's attention on a course that will produce the most positive benefits. In addition, reinforcing behaviors that have produced strong positive results should motivate the individual to continue to perform in this manner.

| EXHIBIT 10.1 | AVAILABLE DEVELOPMENTAL OPPORTUNITIES THAT CAN BE USED FOR EFFECTIVE PERFORMANCE |

On-the-Job
    One-on-One Supervisor Training
    Job Rotation
    Role-Plays
    Computer-Assisted Instruction
    Programmed Instruction
    Organization-Sponsored Training
    In-Basket Exercises
    Special Projects/Assignments
    Reference Material Review
    Mentoring
Off-the-Job
    College Courses
    Professional Seminars
    Networking
    Professional Certificate Programs
    Field Trips
    Correspondence Courses
    Research/Writing Assignments
    Benchmarking
    Executive Development Programs

SOURCE: Robert Lucas, "Performance Coaching: Now and for the Future," *HRMagazine*, January 1994, p. 13.

A well-designed performance appraisal system also can encourage individuals to work together as a team. If this is an organization's goal, it must face several challenges in designing and implementing such a system. Obviously, the traditional, individual-focused performance appraisal systems are no longer appropriate. In fact, applying an individual results-based appraisal system to individuals who perform highly interdependent tasks may discourage team efforts. Instead, peer pressure may be enough to motivate team members to perform.[3] Rather than using the supervisor in the evaluation process, self-managed group members can evaluate each other. Because self-managed teams require a unique approach to performance appraisals, the process may need to be redesigned.

Formal Versus Informal Performance Appraisals

Formal performance appraisals usually occur at specified time periods once or twice a year. Formal appraisals are most often required by the organization to evaluate employee performance. Informal performance appraisals can occur whenever the supervisor feels communication is needed. For example, if the employee has been meeting or exceeding standards consistently, an informal performance appraisal may be in order simply to recognize this fact. Discussions can take place in a variety of places in the organization, ranging from the manager's office to the cafeteria. Of course, it is always wise to discuss employee performance in private.

Many organizations encourage a combination of both formal and informal appraisals. The formal appraisal is most often used as the primary evaluation. However, the informal appraisal is very helpful for more frequent performance feedback. Informal appraisals should *not* take the place of a formal performance evaluation.

Objective Versus Subjective Performance Appraisals

Organizations must choose the degree to which performance appraisals are to be objective (evaluating performance against specific standards) versus subjective (evaluating how "well" an employee performs in general). Although at first glance it may seem that objective measures are the best strategic choice for an organization, subjective measures can be helpful when identifying desirable characteristics that are difficult to quantify. For example, objectively measuring communication skills or management potential is an extremely difficult task. The formal performance appraisal should contain both objective and subjective measures of performance.

Standards for performance appraisals should be based on job requirements. Job requirements should include documented performance standards based on a thorough job analysis. From a strategic view, it is often best for an organization to encourage objectivity in the formal appraisal process (that is, the employee should be rated on behavior rather than attitudes). Not only can this help to alleviate some of the ambiguities for employees and managers (such as determining what an *attitude* really is), but from a legal standpoint, objective measures are easier to defend. Unfortunately, the more objective performance appraisals, such as the behaviorally anchored rating scale discussed later, are often extremely time consuming and expensive to develop. Thus the organization must weigh the costs and benefits of developing such a format.

Frequency of Performance Appraisals

Traditionally, most organizations recommend that performance appraisals be conducted every 6 to 12 months for employees. Interestingly, many employees report that their performance is evaluated much less frequently.[4] Infrequent performance appraisals are most often due to the manager's negative view of the process. It can be stressful for both the employee *and* the manager, especially when employee performance has been below expectations. Thus, the manager may want to avoid this situation.[5] In addition, the manager may view the performance appraisal process as extra work and, thus, burdensome. Regardless of the reasons, managers should be encouraged (possibly through training) to view the process as an opportunity to communicate with their employees and as a means to improve performance and to develop employees.

Research has shown that many employees believe performance feedback should be given more frequently than once or twice a year.[6] In fact, more than 80 percent of the employees asked rank feedback about their performance as one of their top five priorities, whereas only 45 percent feel they receive adequate feedback.[7] Interestingly, the employees desire informal rather than formal evaluations. The former can reduce the anxiety connected with formal assessment by minimizing "surprises"

Computerizing Performance Feedback

Giving feedback is never easy. Individuals do not want either to give or to receive negative feedback. Therefore constructive criticism may come across as an attempt to undermine one's self-esteem instead of the way it was intended. One way to overcome this problem is to use a computer to provide feedback. Because computers are viewed as analytic and not personal, the feedback may be more readily accepted.

One such system is Acumen's *WorkStyles*. It asks a person to rate himself or herself on 176 questions on a scale ranging from "extremely so" to "not at all." After the input procedure, which usually takes between 15 and 30 minutes, the software analyzes the individual's work style on 12 different assessment scales that encompass three orientations: satisfaction, people, or task. The individualized feedback provides a complete picture of how individuals perceive themselves. Also, individuals can use the system any time to better understand how they are doing. The system also can be used to plot one's improvements and to make one more self-aware. One of its best features is that negative feedback is presented in a positive way and therefore is more likely to be accepted.

Another computerized feedback system is called *TEAMS 360 Degree Feedback*. The software is designed to help evaluators collect performance evaluation data from multiple sources such as supervisors, colleagues, direct reports, and customers to provide an all-inclusive view of an individual's behavior. The program also can be used to plot the performance of a group, department, division, or company. Because a variety of raters are used, a "trimmed mean" approach is calculated. In essence, the highest and lowest scores are deleted to provide a more accurate rating of the individual. Another advantage of this system is that the review can be tied directly to the job description of the person being evaluated, thus customizing the review process. With the current emphasis on team environments, the use of multiple raters may become commonplace in the workplace in just a few years. Software such as this package should make changes in the evaluation process easier for organizations.

SOURCE: Adapted from Walter C. Borman, "360-Degree Ratings: An Analysis of Assumptions and a Research Agenda for Evaluating Their Validity," *Human Resource Management Review* 7, no. 3 (1997), pp. 299–316; Charlene O'Brien, "Assessment Tool Makes Giving Feedback Easier," *HRMagazine*, May 1994, pp. 99–103; and Debra J. Cohen, "TEAMS 360 Degree Feedback Offers Varied Ways to Create Feedback Surveys," *HRMagazine*, November 1993, pp. 32–38.

concerning behavior identified long before the session but not mentioned. Thus one strategy that an organization might use is to encourage frequent informal appraisal sessions between managers and employees while limiting the formal and more labor-intensive sessions to one or two every year. Under this approach, the employee meets with the supervisor at the beginning of the year to establish goals and objectives for the upcoming year. The two meet regularly throughout the year to ensure the employee is on track. Supervisors should also meet regularly and communicate with employees to discuss new priorities, status of existing projects and other matters.[8] The formal review at the end of the year should be much less stressful for both parties, given the continuous feedback that has occurred during the year.

How Am I REALLY Doing?

Lou Hoffman, the owner of a Silicon Valley public relations firm, Hoffman Agency, does not have a boss. And, like most small-business owners, he does not have a board of directors. So, as one might suspect, Hoffman did not receive annual evaluations. Just because he was the boss, he figured that did not mean he was above the need for reviews. In fact, he felt that this element was missing in his professional life. Hoffman turned to his employees for help—he gave the job of evaluation to them.

In the spring of 1995, Hoffman hired a consultant, Allison Hopkins, president of Core Elements Inc., a Saratoga, California, human resources consulting firm that advises small to midsize businesses. Her assignment was to conduct confidential employee interviews and to provide Hoffman with a report card that he promised to share with his workers. Basically, she asked questions about both Hoffman and his nine-year-old agency. Hopkins led discussions on a range of subjects including hot issues such as firing nonperformers, availability of financial information, and Hoffman's priorities.

Despite Hoffman's first review—a very unpleasant experience as he recalls because his staff criticized his internal communication skills—he advocates such evaluations. He believes they help to identify early warning signs of problems. The reviews are meant to check his leadership style and make sure that there is no trouble brewing among his employees. The 41-employee company posted $3.6 million in revenue last year, a sum that Hoffman believes he could not have reached without the critiques.

Even though employees were suspicious at first, many now feel empowered by the interviews. Some view Hopkins as a kind of buffer zone, encouraging more open, honest input. But experts are divided on the value of the process. For instance, William Cockrum, an adjunct professor at the John E. Anderson Graduate School of Management at the University of California at Los Angeles, believes subordinates rarely have the experience to evaluate a superior properly. Also, David Bradford, a senior lecturer at Stanford University's Graduate School of Business, suggests that such reviews might discourage workers from confronting their boss when problems arise. On the other hand, James Schrager, a senior lecturer in business policy at the University of Chicago's Graduate School of Business, is more positive. He says small-business owners often become isolated and blind to the need for change. Seeking employees' opinions provides valuable information and boosts morale. What do you think?

Source: S. Beck, "How'm I Doin'? No, Really." *Business Week Enterprise*, September 1, 1997, pp. 10–11.

Who Conducts the Performance Appraisal?

Employee evaluations can be performed by a number of individuals or groups. In matrix-type organizations, for example, employees most often have two immediate supervisors and receive ratings from both of them. Having more than one rater can increase the reliability of the performance evaluation. A number of potential sources of performance ratings are discussed in the following sections.

Supervisors

The most common evaluator is the employee's immediate supervisor. It has been estimated that more than 90 percent of all performance appraisals are completed *only* by the immediate supervisor.[9] To be able to evaluate the employee effectively, the supervisor should have frequent contact with the employee and be able to obtain the specific information regarding his or her performance. Although it might be assumed that this degree of contact occurs regularly, many supervisors do not actually have much opportunity to observe their employees' behavior. For example, an employee who heads up a branch firm in a different city or even state from the "home office" may have little direct contact with his or her supervisor. Although the supervisor may be able to gather relevant information about this employee, the supervisor may benefit from obtaining information from some of the additional sources described in the following section.

Coworkers

In certain situations coworkers may evaluate their peers' performance. Although coworkers may be somewhat uncomfortable and resistant to evaluating their peers, at least one study has shown that peer evaluations are more stable over time and may be the *most* accurate evaluations of employee performance.[10] An organization may choose to encourage peer evaluations, particularly if the contact between supervisor and employee is limited. Also, if self-managed work teams are used, peer rating is an important component in the performance appraisal system.

Employees

Occasionally, employees are given the opportunity to assess their own performance. Although many are reluctant to engage in self-ratings, this information can be extremely valuable to the supervisor. Large discrepancies between the supervisor's and employee's evaluation should be reason for concern. Discrepancies often occur due to a lack of communication and performance feedback from the supervisor. For example, if employees hear nothing from their supervisor for months, they might erroneously conclude that they are performing well (or poorly). When a comparison of evaluations indicates a discrepancy, this information can be used to convince the manager to increase the amount of feedback to the employee in the future.

Research has found that employees who are given the opportunity to evaluate themselves have a tendency to inflate their ratings.[11] One study reported that mean self-ratings for a group of workers were at least one standard deviation higher than those of the supervisors. Further, the range of ratings given by the employees for their performance was much smaller than those provided by their supervisors.[12] Interestingly, however, women tend to rate themselves lower than do their supervisors.[13]

Finally, self-evaluations have been found to be extremely helpful when used for employee development purposes.[14] Self-evaluations can encourage discussions about the employee's strengths and weaknesses from both the employee's and supervisor's points of view. In addition, some companies are now encouraging employees to fill out "discussion forms" (see the following HR Challenges "Employee Discussion Form") so that the supervisor is better able to help the employees in career development. If an organization's strategy is to hire inexperienced workers at a low salary ("make" versus "buy") and to promote from within, self-evaluations and discussion forms are an excellent way to motivate and develop employees.

Subordinates

Subordinates are valuable sources of information when examining the performance of supervisory employees.[15] It is important to encourage subordinates to be candid if the information is to be at all useful. Candor, of course, is most likely to occur when subordinates are guaranteed anonymity and have no fear of reprisal.[16] Information from subordinates is helpful not only for determining how well a manager leads, communicates, plans, delegates, and organizes but also for identifying general problem areas

Employee Discussion Form

To encourage subordinates to talk about their self-evaluations, organizations have used discussion forms much like the example shown here.

Handy-Dandy Stores

Please complete prior to the performance appraisal interview.

Name:
Supervisor's Suggested Decision Date:
Discussion Date:
Present Job Title:

Please circle any of the following comments, questions, or ideas you want to talk about during your performance appraisal. For those areas you circle, I would like you to write down any specific thoughts you want to discuss.

1. My Job
   A. Responsibilities I'm unclear about:
   B. Things I'd like to do more of:
   C. Things I'd like to do less of:
2. Our Organization
   A. Things I'd like to know more about:
   B. Barriers that keep me from doing a better job:
3. Me
   A. Training and development I'd like to have:
   B. My future in this organization:
   C. Other areas I'm concerned about:

within a department. The use of subordinate input for managerial evaluations can be valuable if the information is gathered in an atmosphere of trust and candor.

Computers

Computer-aided management involves the use of computers to monitor, supervise, and evaluate employee performance electronically. It has been estimated that as many as 30 million visual display terminal users are evaluated and monitored by electronic methods.[17] Monitoring employees by computer is open to serious invasions of privacy issues. Some lawmakers are already attempting to introduce legislation that would limit the use of computer monitoring in organizations.[18] Despite the concerns, computerized appraisals could be a valuable aid to human resource managers. "Lately, HR departments have been treated as not central, which goes against the concept that their role is to improve the organization," said Forrester Research analyst Bobby Cameron. "So they look at ways to improve the performance of the human asset. Self-service is the answer."[19] Computer monitoring must include benefits for both the employees and the employers if it is to be effective. Exhibit 10.2 outlines benefits of using computer monitoring of performance.

Computers have an additional use in the appraisal process. DuPont and the University of Minnesota built and tested a multiple-rater appraisal system. The artificial intelligence component can evaluate ratings and determine whether they are reliable. Also, the system can pinpoint problems, such as a particular question that is being misinterpreted or a specific evaluator who is out of line when compared with all other raters. The problems can be relayed back to the evaluator or the group that developed the system for corrections. By using computers in this manner, the evaluation process can become more valid and reliable over time.[20]

Customers

In service organizations the customer is in a perfect position to provide performance feedback. For example, guests checking out of a hotel are frequently asked to complete

EXHIBIT 10.2	RESULTS OF USING COMPUTER MONITORING OF PERFORMANCE

1. ***Response-Outcome Dependency.*** Computer monitoring indicates to the worker which responses are correct. In turn, this can lead to an increase in the performance of desired behaviors. It also makes undesired behaviors stand out.
2. ***Effective Feedback Vehicle.*** Summary reports from the computer can provide immediate feedback to employees so that they can choose to modify their behavior.
3. ***Constructive Expectations.*** Electronic performance monitoring sets specific standards accompanied by expectations that are incorporated into the daily work routines. Workers have a clear idea of what is expected of them.
4. ***Reduced Unpredictability.*** Computer monitoring allows the employee to track his or her performance throughout the year. Thus, the yearly performance evaluation should be less of a surprise.
5. ***Direct Accountability.*** Performance monitoring by computer is a direct measurement of work, making it difficult for an employee to cover up errors or to blame others. Thus, those employees who are good performers would be the most likely to accept electronic monitoring.
6. ***Better Training Programs.*** Gathering summary information regarding the types of mistakes most commonly made could lead to training programs that precisely target the problems.
7. ***Objective Documentation.*** Electronic monitoring can identify good performers objectively because the computer generates a quantitative appraisal.
8. ***Increased Flexibility.*** Flexibility can occur because "fast" workers will have more control over scheduling of required work. "Slower" workers can be allowed some additional time to complete the tasks if the computer information shows that the worker output is adequate.

SOURCE: Adapted from D. Shair, "CompStar Adds Efficiency and Flexibility to Performance Reviews," *HRMagazine*, October 1997, pp. 37–40; and N. F. Angel, "Evaluating Employees by Computer," *Personnel Administrator*, November 1989, pp. 67–72.

a response card about their stay and indicate whether any staff member enhanced the visit. Hampton Inn asks guests to "catch an employee in the act" of making their stay more enjoyable. Any employee who is singled out by a satisfied customer for a job well done earns a Hampton Inn sticker, which the employee can display prominently on his or her name tag. This type of constant evaluation works as a reinforcing mechanism for Hampton Inn's motto: "100 percent satisfaction guaranteed."

The Job

Finally, employees at all levels in the organization can receive feedback from the job they perform. For example, when a secretary mistakenly presses the wrong button on his or her word processor, a beep sounds. This negative feedback is a reminder that the last behavior was inappropriate. Similarly, workers who are linked by an interdependent work situation—that is, one person cannot perform his or her job without input from someone else—are constantly aware of their level of performance as they realize that others are waiting for them to supply the needed part or information. To use this type of performance feedback successfully, organizations must carefully design the jobs their workers perform.

Which and How Many Evaluators Should Be Used?

The organization's choice of type and number of evaluators to use is not easy. The strategy of the firm, the culture within the firm, and the purpose of the evaluation must be taken into consideration. For example, if the culture and strategy of an organization emphasize efficiency and one-on-one supervisor-subordinate relationships, the most effective way to evaluate performance might be to have only the input from the immediate supervisor and/or from computer monitoring. On the other hand, if the organization emphasizes development, training, and promotions from within, performance information might be solicited from a variety of sources including supervisors, coworkers, and the employee. Collecting information from a number of different sources can increase the reliability of the performance appraisal and is attracting ever-increasing attention.

360-degree feedback The process by which an individual's performance is assessed through confidential feedback from managers, peers, customers, and the individual himself.

The review process known as **360-degree feedback,** in which an individual receives performance feedback from subordinates, peers, supervisors, and even internal and external customers, is the hottest new approach to performance appraisals. Those who have used this multi-rater feedback process tend to be very positive about the value added. For example, approximately 75 percent of the users judge 360-degree feedback to be successful. Further, approximately 92 percent of managers who have experienced the process find it to be helpful.[21] Multi-rater feedback can focus on performance issues often neglected in the typical supervisor/subordinate appraisal. There is a realization that the traditional approach to performance appraisals is not adequate with the new emphasis on teamwork, empowerment, and total quality management.[22] Instead, a more flexible system that incorporates feedback from the people with whom the employee most closely works is more appropriate.[23] However, as with most new techniques, it does present some problems. For example, with so many reviewers involved, conflicting and unclear messages about performance could result. When there are conflicting evaluations, how can the more accurate ones be determined and when should this be done? Another problem involves the type of format to use to poll different constituencies. Because each party is concerned with different aspects of an individual's performance, one generic form may not be suitable. Also, if multiple forms are used, how can the ratings be compared and combined? Although the 360-degree feedback method presents some problems, the interest generated by this type of appraisal appears to indicate that the advantages outweigh the problems.

An interesting development in the 360-degree feedback appraisal system has been the integration of the feedback process with the intranet. Many companies are learning that the intranet and Internet are great vehicles for gathering 360-degree feedback. This method offers a faster, more convenient alternative to the traditional pencil-and-paper method. Appraisers also tend to perceive this method as more secure and confidential. An ancillary benefit to using a Web-based system allows the HR administrator more flexibility in tracking reviews.[24]

Performance Appraisal Process

Developing and conducting performance appraisals should not be done in isolation. The performance appraisal is closely related to a number of human resource management activities that should be considered. Exhibit 10.3 illustrates some of these relationships that are described in the following section.

Job Analysis

The performance appraisal should be based on a thorough job analysis. The results of the job analysis can be used to produce a job description, which describes the work to be performed, and job specifications, which outline the requirements necessary to

| EXHIBIT 10.3 | WHERE THE PERFORMANCE APPRAISAL PROCESS FITS WITH RESPECT TO OTHER HR FUNCTIONS |

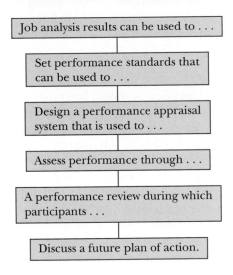

Job analysis results can be used to . . .

Set performance standards that can be used to . . .

Design a performance appraisal system that is used to . . .

Assess performance through . . .

A performance review during which participants . . .

Discuss a future plan of action.

accomplish the job. A discussion of job analysis is presented in Chapter 6. Only when the duties, responsibilities, working conditions, and activities of a job are clearly defined can performance be evaluated.

Performance Standards

Performance standards should be derived from the job analysis information. Based on this information, the levels of performance deemed to be acceptable versus those that are unacceptable are developed. In essence, this determines a standard against which to compare employee performance. A good performance standard describes what an employee should have produced or accomplished upon completing a specific activity. It focuses on the results or the degree of accomplishment achieved by the worker. The standard should answer questions such as what, how much, and by when. For example, a performance standard for a sales representative might be to obtain $2000 worth of new business by the end of the quarter. This standard informs the sales representative what (new business), how much ($2000), and by when (end of the quarter).

Performance standards should meet several important requirements. First, the standards should be written so that anyone who reads them will recognize the difference between acceptable and unacceptable behavior. In the preceding example, any quarter in which the sales representative did not sign $2000 worth of new business would be considered unacceptable. Second, the standard should challenge the employee while being realistic. Setting an extremely high standard to motivate employees to perform at their maximum level may backfire. Instead of motivating an individual to work hard to achieve the goal, it might cause employees to give up and not try at all because they believe that achieving the high expectation is impossible. Defining the methods by which the activity is to be accomplished may also be useful. For example, a sales representative who steals customers from other representatives achieves the goal but at the expense of other sales representatives. Therefore the standard must state clearly what qualifies as an appropriate behavior (obtaining new business). Finally, it is important that a timeframe be specified and that the goal be observable and measurable. Simply asking a sales representative to increase customer satisfaction is not enough. Exactly how and when this should be accomplished (e.g., reduce the number of complaint letters received in one quarter by 50 percent) must be stated.

The Performance Appraisal System

deficient Job dimensions that fail to measure all the important aspects of performance.

contamination Evaluation error that occurs when extraneous factors not central to overall successful performance are included in the evaluation of one's job performance.

distortion Evaluation error that occurs when components of a job are not emphasized in relation to their importance to the job.

relevant A job dimension that measures only aspects of performance that are truly important in determining job effectiveness.

In general, employees should be evaluated on a number of specific dimensions of job performance. Each of the specific dimensions of job performance used to evaluate an individual's performance should be developed so that it is not deficient, contaminated, distorted, or irrelevant. Job dimensions that fail to measure all of the important aspects of performance would be viewed as **deficient**. When extraneous factors that are not central to overall successful performance are included in the evaluation of one's job performance, **contamination** has occurred. Job dimensions that suffer from **distortion** do not emphasize each component in relation to its importance to the job. Finally, a job dimension that measures only aspects of performance that are truly important in determining job effectiveness would be considered **relevant**. An example that includes each of these elements may be useful in understanding the distinction of each of these concepts. To effectively perform the job of airline reservation agent, a person must be able to effectively use the computerized reservation system, make changes to tickets, reserve tickets, and assign seats. These four components are all relevant to the job. If we rank them from most important to least important and weigh them accordingly, we will have a job dimension that is free from distortion. If we add the dimension of getting along with the other booking agents, we introduce contamination because this component is not absolutely critical to performing the job well. Finally, if we do not include the ability to make seat assignments, the job dimension is deficient because it does not measure all of the important aspects of this job.

Using a single global or overall measure can present difficulties. Global measures are more prone to distortion on the part of the evaluator. The Supreme Court ruling in 1975 regarding *Albemarle Paper Company* v. *Moody* was based on the fact that no specific job dimensions of performance were assessed.[25] Raters were asked to evaluate employees by comparing them to one another based on a single, global rating. The Court found significant racial differences on the criterion (the overall rating), with no objective information to back it.

Assessing Performance

The actual performance assessment is the determination of the employee's strengths *and* weaknesses. One purpose of a performance appraisal is to improve the employee's performance. As a result, performance weaknesses must be determined. However, it is also important to reinforce existing behavior that is deemed to be strong.

If multiple evaluators are used, assessing performance also includes compiling all evaluations into summary form. If evaluators' assessments are in agreement, high interrater reliability exists and summarizing the ratings is not problematic. However, if there is a substantial amount of disagreement about the employee's performance, interrater reliability is low. The supervisor must use this information as more of a heuristic device or guide for the final evaluation.

Performance Review

The performance review is the actual discussion that transpires between the rater and the ratee regarding the ratee's performance. Research suggests that the performance review should be approximately 60 minutes long and be a mutual discussion.[26] However, employee responses to an employment survey indicated that most performance reviews are relatively short.[27] In fact, most employees reported that their last performance review session lasted less than 15 minutes!

Because the performance review involves two people, the appraiser and the appraisee, the review should entail an exchange of information between these two parties. This information exchange can take many forms. Three of the most common include closed reporting, open reporting, and coaching. Each of these is discussed in the following section.

Types of Performance Review

closed reporting A method of performance review in which the appraisee has very little input into the discussion.

open reporting A method of performance review in which, after the reporting is complete, the appraiser listens to the reactions of the appraisee.

coaching A method of performance review in which the appraisee evaluates his or her own performance while the appraiser serves as a coach, not a critic.

Types of Performance Review   The three types of performance reviews can be viewed as three points on a continuum that measures the degree of involvement of the appraisee. At one extreme of the continuum is the **closed reporting** method. When it is used, the appraisee has very little input into the discussion. Instead, the appraiser reports how the appraisee performed during the time period considered and then attempts to persuade the appraisee to accept this evaluation. In the middle of the continuum is the **open reporting** approach. This method begins as with closed reporting, with the appraiser identifying the strengths and weaknesses of performance, but then the appraiser listens to the reactions of the appraisee. Finally, a **coaching** approach anchors the other end of the continuum. In this type of performance review, the employee evaluates his or her own performance while the appraiser serves as a coach, not a critic.

If employed under the appropriate circumstances, each of these methods can prove useful. For example, the closed reporting method could be used in situations in which the performance appraisal is simply an activity that must be done each year but is not used as a basis for human resource decisions. Likewise, the open reporting method is appropriate when extenuating circumstances may have affected the individual's performance on the job, and the appraisee needs to make the appraiser aware of these issues. Finally, the coaching method can be used when the individual being appraised holds a job that has very few clear-cut standards on which to base an assessment. One job that might not have clear standards is that of a research scientist. A person in this position could spend several years working on a product before it is actually marketable. During those years working on the project, the scientist is in the best position to know the type of goals he or she can reach and how to describe them.

Problems Related to Performance Reviews   Closed reporting, open reporting, and coaching have both strengths and weaknesses. First, both the closed and open reporting approaches can make the person being evaluated defensive. It is human nature to want to defend oneself when weaknesses are identified. Therefore, as soon as they are mentioned, the person being evaluated may "tune out" what is being said and prepare to defend himself or herself.[28] This leads to a second problem, which is trying to accomplish too much in one session. For example, if a pay increase is an outcome of the appraisal process, as soon as it is mentioned, it tends to remain the topic of discussion, and any suggestions for future improvement are ignored. Further, if the feedback given to the appraisee is even partially negative, he or she may not be receptive

---

EXHIBIT 10.4   TIPS FOR A SUCCESSFUL PERFORMANCE REVIEW

- Give the employee fair notice about when the review is to take place.
- Ask the employee to think about and evaluate his or her own performance prior to the review session.
- Prepare for the review by examining information available about the employee's performance. Seek additional information if needed.
- Begin the session on a positive tone to set the employee at ease and make him or her receptive to the performance review process.
- Explain the format of the performance review session.
- Make the employee aware of the uses of the performance appraisal results (e.g., training and development, salary decisions, promotion decisions).
- If needed, set a second meeting to discuss nonperformance-related issues such as the salary increase, future goals, or developmental suggestions.
- Encourage the employee to participate, especially when his or her appraisal differs from yours.
- Review the standards to which the employee will be compared to remind him or her that the process is not completely subjective.
- Make sure to praise the employee for his or her accomplishments during the evaluation period. Recognize his or her achievements, and indicate where the employee has excelled.
- Highlight, but do not dwell on, areas in which performance did not meet the standards.
- Discuss ways to improve performance in the areas in which the employee was weak or to solve problems that have caused the employee to be less effective than desired.
- Make sure that the employee fully understands the appraisal.
- End the discussion on a positive note.

SOURCE: Adapted from Dick Grote, "Getting the Most out of the Review Process," *HR Focus* 74, no. 1 (January 1997), p. 15; Kathryn Tyler, "Careful Criticism Brings Better Performance," *HRMagazine*, April 1997, pp. 57–62; and James G. Goodale, "Seven Ways to Improve Performance Appraisals," *HRMagazine*, May 1993, pp. 77–80.

to suggestions for addressing the problems in the future.[29] Instead, he or she may have a closed mind (sometimes indicated by a defensive posture, such as crossed arms). In these situations, the constructive criticism offered is viewed only as criticism. To avoid this, eliminating the discussion of salary and focusing only on ways to improve performance should help to concentrate on the appraisee's performance.

Another element that can cause an ineffective review is an unprepared appraiser. Nothing upsets an appraisee more than having an appraiser who does not know what he or she has accomplished during the evaluation period. To perform an effective performance review, an appraiser must take the time to carefully review and evaluate the performance during the time period in question. Only after he or she is familiar with the performance is the appraiser ready to discuss the evaluation.

Improvement of Performance Review   The problems outlined previously can be improved in a variety of ways. Exhibit 10.4 lists several of these. The one thing that is important to keep in mind is that both the appraiser and the appraisee will be nervous. Giving and receiving performance feedback is often looked at as a negative experience. By following the suggestions listed in Exhibit 10.4, the performance review session can be more helpful and positive for all involved.

As organizations move toward a more employee-oriented strategy, the supervisor-subordinate formal appraisal may not be effective. Instead, a performance review discussion based on the employee's evaluation of his or her own work for a specified period of time may be more useful. When this format is followed, the manager becomes a counselor instead of an evaluator. This type of review session appears to be more useful and enjoyable for both the evaluator and the employee.[30]

Setting a Plan of Action   By this point in the review, the employee should have an accurate idea of his or her performance evaluation. The employee should know his or her strengths and weaknesses. Recapping key points and asking the employee to summarize the major issues discussed is usually a good way for the supervisor to ensure joint understanding before the performance review ends.

At this point the supervisor and employee should focus on the future. Job performance objectives should be discussed to establish a plan of action. The employee as well as the supervisor should have input in this process. This is often an appropriate time to explore the employee's career interest and developmental needs. The employee should be aware of the supervisor's expectations in regard to the plan.

Finally, the supervisor reviews the job performance and plan of action developed, and then sets objectives, based at least in part on the plan identified, for the next rating period. This will provide the employee with direction and guidance about what is expected. The employee needs to understand areas *where* improvement is needed and *how* to strengthen job performance (such as additional training). In closing the discussion, the supervisor may wish to reassure the employee that he or she is interested in the employee's success and should indicate a willingness to talk further at a later date.

Given the importance of the performance evaluation, it is surprising that most supervisors do not receive any training in this area.[31] Comprehensive training programs can help ensure the success of any performance appraisal system and of a system already in place. New evaluators should be trained, and current evaluators' skills can be fine-tuned.

Types of Performance Appraisal Methods

A number of different performance appraisal methods or formats are available. Some methods focus more on employee behavior (for example, planning or organizing); others are more results oriented and emphasize the *results* of employee behavior (such as the extent to which an employee reaches goals and objectives). Within the behavioral methods, employees can be evaluated based on an organizational or departmental standard, or they can be evaluated relative to others.

Behavioral Performance Appraisal Methods

Checklists   In its simplest form, the checklist is a list of descriptive statements and/or adjectives describing job-related behavior. If the evaluator perceives the employee as possessing a particular trait, the item is checked. If the evaluator does not perceive the employee as possessing this trait, the item is left blank. Each item listed reflects either a positive or negative quality that an employee could possess. One point is added for every positive item checked, and one point is subtracted for every negative quality checked. Qualities left blank are excluded from the calculations. An example of a checklist is provided in Exhibit 10.5.

EXHIBIT 10.5   EXAMPLE OF A CHECKLIST APPRAISAL FORM

Instructions: Read each item below and determine whether the individual you are rating exhibits this quality. If the answer is "yes," place a check in the blank in front of the statement. If the answer is "no," leave the blank empty.

_____ Asks for assistance when encountering problems.

_____ Recognizes others' contributions to his or her production.

_____ Maintains good relations with other workers.

_____ Takes initiative when faced with a new situation.

_____ Requires an excessive amount of instructions when confronted with a new situation.

_____ Can see more than one alternative to a situation.

_____ Continually meets deadlines.

EXHIBIT 10.6   EXAMPLE OF A WEIGHTED CHECKLIST

Instructions: Below is a list of qualities upon which you are to rate each employee. If you believe that the employee possesses the quality listed, place a check in the blank in front of the item; otherwise, leave the blank empty.

	Value*
_____ Is asked for advice by others.	3.0
_____ Follows directions well.	2.0
_____ Does not work well in group settings.	−1.0
_____ Works well without direct supervision.	2.5
_____ Continually misses deadlines.	−2.0
_____ Applies quick fixes to recurring problems.	−1.0
_____ Treats others fairly.	1.0

*These values would not be included on the actual rating form.

---

weighted checklist A checklist used for performance evaluation that places weighted values on each response; the weighted responses are then summed to provide an overall rating.

Weighted Checklists   The checklist described previously evenly weights each item. When this type of weighting scheme is not appropriate, a **weighted checklist** can be used. This method uses essentially the same format as the one described previously. However, after the list has been completed, a weighted value is applied to the responses. The evaluator does not know how the items are weighted. The points assigned to the weighted responses are then totaled to provide an overall rating. An example of a weighted checklist is provided in Exhibit 10.6.

Graphic Rating Scale   One of the most widely used performance evaluation formats is the graphic rating scale. There are many reasons for its widespread use. First, graphic rating scales are easy to use. Evaluators can rate a large number of individuals in a short amount of time. Also, these scales are easy to understand and explain to the ratees. Finally, they are simple to develop and change when needed. The ratings

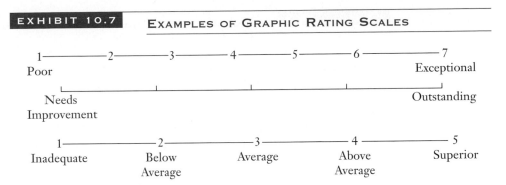

EXHIBIT 10.7   EXAMPLES OF GRAPHIC RATING SCALES

1 = Clearly inadequate performance. Consistently performed below expectations and did not meet a majority of the objectives.

2 = Performance did not meet objectives in several key areas. Results were generally achieved in an unacceptable manner.

3 = Performance met all objectives. Results were achieved in an effective fashion. Represents good, solid performance.

4 = Performance met all objectives and exceeded objectives in several key areas. Results were achieved in a manner that surpassed the generally accepted norms for the position.

5 = Truly exceptional performance. Performance exceeded all objectives. Results were achieved utilizing superior techniques.

are made using a scale that is divided into several levels, usually 1 to 5, with adjectives such as "unsatisfactory" and "outstanding" anchored at the two extremes of the scale (i.e., 1 = unsatisfactory and 5 = outstanding). The evaluator reads the quality to be rated and then determines at what level, if at all, the individual demonstrates it. A graphic rating scale can be used to rate an employee's overall performance, but usually it rates a number of characteristics such as quality of work and knowledge of the job, and then the values on each of the individual characteristics are summed to create an overall rating. An example of a graphic rating scale is provided in Exhibit 10.7. Similar to weighted checklists, certain items on a graphic rating scale can be weighted differentially.[32]

Mixed-Standard Scale   One variation of the graphic rating scale is the mixed-standard scale. Instead of rating a behavior, such as attendance, the evaluator is given three conceptually compatible statements describing that behavior at high, medium, and low levels. These statements are mixed with sets of three statements that describe various other qualities to be rated. The evaluator is asked to rate each individual on each item by indicating whether he or she exhibits "better than" (indicated by a +), "as good as" (indicated by a 0), or "worse than" (indicated by a −) performance on the behavior described in each statement. A special scoring key is used to translate the ratings into a numerical score. The key is based on the ratings within a behavioral category. That is, all three ratings for a category are examined and matched to a pattern in the scoring key. A score is then assigned for that pattern. For example, if an individual was rated "better than" (i.e., +) on each of the three statements designed to determine the behavioral dimension attendance, that individual would earn a 7 for that category. If he or she was rated "worse than" (i.e., −) on all three behaviors, the value

| EXHIBIT 10.8 | EXAMPLE OF A MIXED-STANDARD ASSESSMENT FORMAT |

Instructions: Read each statement provided. Using the scale below, rate the individual on each statement. Place your response in the blank in front of each item.

Scale

+	This employee's performance is **better than** the behavior described in this statement.
0	This employee's performance is **as good as** the behavior described in this statement.
−	This employee's performance is **worse than** the behavior described in this statement.

_____ *1.* Always at work unless a critical emergency has arisen.

_____ *2.* Always volunteers for difficult assignments.

_____ *3.* Misses work less than twice a month.

_____ *4.* Mistakes are present in virtually all work completed by this individual.

_____ *5.* Requests only assignments he or she has performed in the past.

_____ *6.* While rare, corrections sometimes must be made to work submitted by this individual.

_____ *7.* Will take on challenging assignments if requested to do so.

_____ *8.* Has more than two absences a week.

_____ *9.* Assignments are always accurate.

Note

Statements 1 (high), 3 (moderate), and 8 (low) represent the three levels of absenteeism.

Statements 2 (high), 7 (moderate), and 5 (low) represent the three levels of drive.

Statements 9 (high), 6 (moderate), and 4 (low) represent the three levels of ability.

Scoring Key

Determine the pattern of responses within a behavioral dimension and match that pattern to the matrix below. The score for each pattern is provided at the end of the line.

	Statements		
High	**Moderate**	**Low**	**Score**
+	+	+	7
0	+	+	6
−	+	+	5
−	0	+	4
−	−	+	3
−	−	0	2
−	−	−	1

assigned would be a 1. Finally, it is important to note that all of the possible patterns are not represented in the scoring key. For instance, the pattern of 0 0 0 is not listed because the ratings given to the moderate and low behaviors have to be higher (or equal to if it is a 1) than the rating assigned to the high behavior. That is, if an individual is "as good as" (i.e., 0) on a high behavior, he or she will naturally be "better than" (i.e., +) a moderate example of this same behavior. Exhibit 10.8 provides an

EXHIBIT 10.9	FORCED-CHOICE RATING SCALE EXAMPLE

Please check the statement that *best* describes the employee:

Statement	Discriminability index	Favorableness index
___ 1. Shows patience with slow learners.	1.72	2.82
___ 2. Lectures with confidence.	.51	2.75
		Unknown to Evaluator

Note that the statements are similar in their social desirability but differ in their ability to determine high from low performers (that is, discriminability).

example of a mixed-standard appraisal form, including the scoring key. The mixed-standard scale gives a wider range of scores than the simple graphic rating scale.

Forced-Choice Scale   The forced-choice scale was designed to increase objectivity and decrease subjectivity in ratings by camouflaging the "best" responses.[33] With many appraisal formats, raters are able to easily locate the positive and negative items and therefore can inflate the score they provided by rating the positive items high and the negative items low. Forced-choice ratings scales make padding ratings more difficult because raters are required to select an item from a pair of items that most closely reflects the individual being rated. Although *both* items are equally positive, only one is important for the job in question. Because the raters cannot tell by reading the items which one is more important, they cannot intentionally inflate their ratings. Exhibit 10.9 illustrates an example of a forced-choice scale for a teacher. The statement with the highest ability to discriminate is worth one point. The other item is worth zero points. Thus the subject would receive one point if the rater chose item 1 and zero points if the rater chose item 2. One problem with this procedure is the difficulty in developing items that are not related to performance but that appear to be.[34]

critical incident
An example of a highly effective or highly ineffective performance.

Critical Incident Method   A **critical incident** is a written description of a highly effective or highly ineffective performance. To use the critical incident method to appraise an individual's performance, the evaluator keeps a journal of critical incidents for each individual being evaluated. It is important that the evaluator record the incident as soon as it happens; relying on one's memory at a later date often proves ineffectual. Examples of a highly favorable and a highly unfavorable critical incident recorded for a sales clerk at a large department store chain might read as follows:

> A customer approached a sales clerk and asked for a specific line of clothing. The clerk showed the customer to that section of the store. She then offered to help the customer locate a specific item within the line. After realizing that the store did not have the particular color, style, and size the customer wanted, the clerk called the other stores in the area until she located the item and placed it on hold for the customer.
>
> Near the end of an evening, a customer approached the cash register where a sales clerk was positioned and requested that the clerk ring up her purchases. The clerk asked the customer to go to a different counter because he had already counted his money drawer and did not want to have to do so again.

Critical incidents should contain (1) the circumstances that preceded the incident, (2) the setting in which the incident occurred, (3) precisely what the employee did that was effective or ineffective, (4) the consequences of the incident, and (5) the extent to which the consequences were within the employee's control. At the end of the evaluation period, these reports are used to appraise the employee's performance. Although recording employee behavior can help the evaluator remember the range of behavior that occurred during the evaluation period, it is very time consuming and difficult to quantify.

Behaviorally Anchored Rating Scale (BARS)   BARS is a sophisticated method of evaluating employee performance based on employee *behavior* rather than attitudes or assumptions about motivation or potential. BARS is a numerical scale that is anchored by specific narrative examples of behaviors that range from very negative to very positive descriptions of performance.[35]

BARS is a difficult and time-consuming scale to develop. Each job must be analyzed and a list of critical incidents developed by experts in the job. Once the critical incidents are developed, they are matched to a set of performance dimensions that are then scaled from effective to ineffective performance. Exhibit 10.10 illustrates one aspect of a BARS for a manager. The BARS technique offers a high degree of interrater reliability and objectivity because of its emphasis on behavior. Unfortunately, because of the complexity and expense of setting up the scale, managers should carefully consider the administrative investment before adopting BARS as their performance appraisal technique.

The performance appraisal methods just discussed base the employee's evaluation on some type of standard. The standard may be set at the department or the organization level. The next three performance appraisal methods evaluate the employee's performance relative to that of others in the employee's department. These are called *personnel comparison systems*.

Personnel Comparison Systems

Ranking   The ranking method is used to evaluate an employee on his or her overall performance. To use this method, the evaluator places the employees in a specified group (e.g., all subordinates reporting to a supervisor) in order from the "best" performer to the "worst" performer. In essence, the evaluator simply looks down the list of employees to be rated and selects the individual he or she believes had the best overall performance for the evaluation period. This name is written at the top of a sheet of paper and crossed off the list of names. This process is repeated until all the names have been crossed off the list. Another ranking approach is called **alternative ranking**. Under this method, the rater selects the best overall performer, writes the name on a new sheet of paper, and then crosses the name off the list of ratees. Next, the appraiser selects the overall worst performer, crosses off that name, and transfers it to the new list. He or she then selects the best performer from those left on the list. This alternating process continues until all employees have been ranked.

One advantage to the ranking method is that it does not allow the evaluator to rate everyone high. Unfortunately, rank ordering produces ordinal data; thus the *amount* of difference between employees is unknown. For example, it is impossible to determine if the employee with the second highest ranking is close to the highest performer or if a large gap exists between them.

alternative ranking   A ranking approach in which the rater selects the best overall performer, writes the name on a sheet of paper, and crosses the name off the list of ratees. Next, the rater selects the overall worst performer, transfers the name to the bottom of the sheet, and crosses off that name. From the remaining names, the

EXHIBIT 10.10   BEHAVIORALLY ANCHORED RATING SCALE EXAMPLE

Position: _____

Job Dimension: _____

Plans work and organizes time carefully in order to maximize resources and meet commitments.

9

8   Even though this associate has a report due on another project, he or she would be well prepared for the assigned discussion on your project.

7   This associate would keep a calendar or schedule on which deadlines and activities are carefully noted, and which would be consulted before making new commitments.

6   As program chief, this associate would manage arrangements for enlisting resources for a special project reasonably well, but would probably omit one or two details that would have to be handled by improvisation.

Plans and organizes time and effort primarily for large segments of a task. Usually meets commitments, but may overlook what are considered secondary details.

5   This associate would meet a deadline in handing in a report, but the report might be below usual standard if other deadlines occur on the same day the report is due.

4   This associate's evaluations are likely not to reflect abilities because of overcommitments in other activities.

3   This associate would plan more by enthusiasm than by timetable and frequently have to work late the night before an assignment is due, although it would be completed on time.

Appears to do little planning. May perform effectively, despite what seems to be a disorganized approach, although deadlines may be missed.

2   This associate would often be late for meetings, although others in similar circumstances do not seem to find it difficult to be on time.

1   This associate never makes a deadline, even with sufficient notice.

Forced Distribution   This method requires the evaluator to place a certain percentage of employees into each of several categories based on overall performance. For example, 10 percent of the employees must be placed in the "unsatisfactory" category, 15 percent must be placed in the "fair" category, 50 percent must be placed in the "satisfactory or average" category, 15 percent in the "good" category, and 10 percent in the "outstanding" category. Similar to the ranking method, forced distribution forces the evaluator to discriminate between the employees; however, the absolute difference between them is not known. Exhibit 10.11 provides an example of a possible distribution schedule.

rater chooses alternately the best and worst performers until all employees have been ranked.

Paired Comparisons   When the paired comparisons method is used, the evaluator compares all possible pairs of subordinates on their overall ability to do the job.

EXHIBIT 10.11	EXAMPLE OF A FORCED DISTRIBUTION PERFORMANCE APPRAISAL METHOD

Performance	Percentage distribution
Highest Level Employees who exhibit this level of performance *continually* produce more than is required, before it is due, and the work is of exceptional quality.	No more than 7%
Above-Average Level Employees who exhibit this level of performance often produce more than is required, sometimes beat their deadlines, and frequently produce work of above-average quality.	No more than 17%
Average Level Employees who exhibit this level of performance produce the work required, meet their deadlines, and produce acceptable work.	No more than 45%
Below-Average Level Employees who exhibit this level of performance sometimes fail to produce the work required, often miss their deadlines, and frequently produce work that is unacceptable.	No more than 21%
Lowest Level Employees who exhibit this level of performance *continually* fail to produce assigned work, miss deadlines, and produce work that is unacceptable.	No more than 10%

From each possible pair of employees, the evaluator selects the employee with the higher overall ability to do the job. The number of comparisons required by the evaluator is based on a simple formula: number of pairs = $[N (N - 1)]/2$ where N is the number of people who will be rated. Thus 10 subordinates require 45 comparisons $[10 (10 - 1)]/2$.

Due to the subjectivity of evaluating "overall performance," some managers use a number of different job-related dimensions when comparing. If the rater compares all employees on more than one dimension (D), the number of pairs = $D([N \{N - 1\}]/2)$. Thus, 10 employees compared on only five different job dimensions would result in 225 comparisons $(5\{[10 (10 - 1)]/2\})$. Obviously, this method can become very cumbersome if there are many employees to evaluate or if the evaluation uses a variety of job dimensions.

Problems with Personnel Comparison Systems   At first glance, comparison systems appear easy to implement and use, intuitively appealing, and simple to explain to others. However, these types of appraisal systems have some negative aspects. First, comparison systems are highly subjective. Many rating systems ask the evaluator to make a global judgment about an individual's performance. This is a difficult, if not impossible, task. Further, because individuals are compared with one another, this squelches team spirit and encourages competition. This may be effective for some positions such as sales, but those companies that wish to use a team-based management approach would find it counterproductive to implement an appraisal system based on comparisons.

The ranking and paired comparison methods become difficult to manage when a large number of employees must be evaluated. These systems also become unwieldy when a variety of dimensions are evaluated instead of overall performance. One of the major disadvantages of the forced distribution method is that the performance of the employees to be evaluated may not fit the imposed distribution. Think about this from an exam perspective. Let's say you earned a 97, the *second highest* grade, on the first exam in this class. Let's suppose further that your instructor decided to use the distribution system described in Exhibit 10.11, making the highest level of performance the *A*s and the lowest level of performance the *F*s. Finally, let's say that there are 25 students in your class. Applying the distribution outlined in Exhibit 10.11 to your exam grade would place you in the *B* range, or the above-average level of performance. Because there are 25 students in the class, no more than one person can be in the top level (i.e., no more than 7 percent). Obviously, you would disagree with this grade assignment. The point is that the performance distribution may not reflect the distribution that is forced on it.

Results-Oriented Performance Appraisal Methods

The following two performance appraisal formats are results oriented. Thus the evaluator is rating the outcomes of the employee's behavior rather than the actual behavior.

Management by Objectives (MBO) A frequently used performance appraisal method is management by objectives (MBO). MBO has been around for more than 30 years and is usually credited to Peter Drucker. Drucker was trying to design a systematic approach to setting objectives and performing appraisals by using results that would lead to improved organizational productivity. Research findings indicate that MBO does indeed increase productivity. In 68 of 70 studies, productivity gains were reported by organizations that have implemented MBO programs. However, this research also indicated that the degree of productivity increase was directly linked to whether or not top management fully supported the MBO process. In organizations in which top management did support MBO, the average productivity gain was 56 percent. However, in organizations where there was no, or limited, top-level management support for the program, productivity gains averaged only 6 percent.[36]

Although there are a number of variations, MBO generally consists of the following steps: setting organizational objectives, setting individual objectives, and appraising according to results.

Because MBO takes a top-down approach, top management must decide the overall objectives of the organization and the departments. Objectives should always be stated so that they can be measured or quantified. Also, the objectives should include target dates for completion and action plans that discuss the process of achieving these objectives.

After the overall objectives have been set, individual objectives for employees at each level of the organization (e.g., upper-level management, then middle-level management, then lower-level management, and finally employees with no supervisory responsibilities) are set. Employee objectives and the specified period of time for the accomplishment of these objectives are determined jointly by the supervisor and the employee. See Exhibit 10.12 for an illustration of an MBO performance worksheet. The objectives set should be specific, measurable, challenging, and accepted by both parties.

EXHIBIT 10.12	HANDY-DANDY STORES' PERFORMANCE OBJECTIVES WORKSHEET

Directions: This sheet is to be completed at the *beginning* of the appraisal period.

Employee Name: Sam Swanson   Length of Time in Position: 4 years

Employee Number: 189   Date Prepared: 9/1/99, revised 4/1/01

Job Title: District Manager   Department/Region: Lakeland, Florida

Strategic planning goals	Results expected	Time frame (by when)
1. Reduce turnover 33%	Reduce turnover 33% in all stores	9/1/98
2. Improve store appearance	Paint outside of all stores	4/98
3. Improve store mgr. part.	Send store mgrs. to mgt. dev.	8/1/98
4. Improve communications	Send all mgrs. to comm. training	8/1/98
5. Increase sales	Increase sales by 10% per store	9/1/98
6. Reduce shrink	Reduce shrink losses by 45%	9/1/98

Maintenance/routine goals	Results expected	Time frame (by when)
1. Monitor costs	Reduce costs by at least 8%	9/1/98
2. Reduce stockouts	Reduce stockout level by 20%	9/1/98
3.		
4.		

Personal development goals	Results expected	Time frame (by when)
1. Improve communications	Attend communications workshop	9/1/98
2. Improve computer skills	Attend community college course on computers	9/1/98
3. Improve planning ability	Develop written plan for stores; attend planning workshop	9/1/98

Employee Signature   Supervisor Signature

These objectives play an important role in the feedback process and the final evaluation. Specifically, employees should be given periodic feedback on their progress toward their stated goals and objectives. In addition, the final performance appraisal should be based on how well the employee met the objectives set forth. Obviously, situations arise that might require the initial objectives to be modified throughout the year, such as a change in the competition or the economy. Changes in objectives can be made during periodic reviews or feedback sessions. The use of MBO or a variation of MBO as a performance appraisal technique is popular, partly because of the high level of employee involvement.

Work Planning   Work planning is similar to MBO except that its primary focus is the periodic feedback and review. Less emphasis is given to setting each objective in terms of being measurable. Thus work planning allows the supervisor latitude for "judgment calls" regarding whether or not the employee met the objective.

Tips for Developing a Legally Defensible Performance Appraisal

Based on outcomes of various court cases that centered on the performance appraisal, the following list suggests ways to create a legally defensible performance appraisal system. While reading this list, keep in mind that there is no such thing as a completely safe performance appraisal system.

1. Begin with a job analysis that determines the necessary characteristics for successful job performance.
2. From the job analysis results, determine performance standards.
3. These standards must be communicated and accepted by the employees who will be judged by them.
4. Using the standard as a guideline, develop a rating scheme. The scheme should measure clearly defined individual components of job performance rather than global or undefined measures. The standards and rating scheme should be distributed to all raters.
5. The type of scale selected is not significant from a legal perspective. The courts have not indicated any problems with using simple graphic rating scales or trait ratings. However, when these types of methods are used, it is helpful to avoid abstract trait names such as "loyalty" and to anchor the scales with brief, logically consistent tags.
6. Train the raters to use the scale correctly. Focus on how to apply the standards when making decisions. It is important that the raters uniformly apply the standards because in many cases in which the organization lost the court case, the plaintiffs showed the standards were not uniformly applied.
7. Include a mechanism for appealing the rating. The appeal should be directed to upper-level management.
8. Document all appraisals. These are very useful in court cases.
9. Provide a way for poor performers to receive corrective guidance. When the organization has made an attempt to help poor performers, the court ruled more favorably toward the organization.

SOURCE: Adapted from William Lissy, "Performance Appraisals Can Be a Weapon for Employees," *Supervision* 58, no. 3 (March 1997), pp. 17–19; Gerald Barrett and Mary Kernan, "Performance Appraisal and Terminations: A Review of Court Decisions Since *Brito* v. *Zia* with Implications for Personnel Practices," *Personnel Psychology* 40 (1987), pp. 489–502; and David Rosen, "Appraisals Can Make or Break Your Court Case," *Personnel Journal*, November 1992, pp. 113–118.

Selecting a Performance Appraisal Method

In general, there is no one *best* performance appraisal method.[37] However, depending on the situation, certain methods might be better than others. For example, if *objective* performance data are available, then MBO is a good strategy to use. If, however, employees are going to be compared for determining pay increases, promotions, and so on, then some common denominator must be determined to make comparisons among many employees. This usually implies a numerical rating of performance, such as ranking or rating methods rather than MBO or work-planning methods in which employee objectives can vary. Thus the *purpose* of the performance appraisal is an important consideration when choosing a performance appraisal method.

An increasingly important factor in selecting a performance appraisal method is whether or not the technique is legally defensible. Although there is no way to *guarantee* a completely "safe" performance appraisal, managers need to be aware of the outcomes of court cases that made judgments about the performance appraisal process. In general, the important cases suggest, among other things, that the courts do not reject subjective reviews such as those made by the employee's immediate supervisor. Further, the use of objective measures, such as production figures, does not ensure favorable decisions for the organization. In each case, it is up to the court to determine if subjective or objective measures are appropriate for the job in question. It also has been found that techniques used to develop and refine the performance appraisal process, such as training raters and validating the process, do not guarantee winning court cases. These practices are useful to ensure a quality performance appraisal process and are used to help ensure that the standards are being applied evenly to all employees.[38]

Another consideration to make when choosing an appraisal method is how well it will control the types of rater errors that most likely will be encountered. To better explain this factor, the following section defines and describes typical rater errors or biases that can occur in the performance appraisal process.

Perceptual Errors in Evaluation

Performance evaluations can be biased due to a variety of perceptual errors made by raters. Regardless of the performance criteria or the scientific nature of the appraisal method, perceptual error can occur. Typical errors include the halo effect, stereotypes, attributions, recency effects, leniency, strictness, and central tendency. Each of these is examined in the following sections.

Halo Effect

The halo effect occurs when the rater allows one trait or characteristic (either positive or negative) of the employee to override a realistic appraisal of other traits or characteristics. For example, if an employee is always on time to work, a supervisor might allow this positive characteristic to influence his or her evaluation of this employee's performance on other dimensions. Thus this employee might be judged as a good performer—not because of actual performance, but because of the halo effect. The halo effect has been examined extensively in the performance appraisal literature.[39] Some approaches used to control halo effects include using performance appraisal simulations prior to evaluations, and having raters listen to short lectures on the halo effect before rating employees.[40]

Of the different types of performance appraisal methods described in the previous section, several would be more susceptible to halo error than others. For example, any of the scales that request the evaluator to judge the individual on more than one factor, such as checklists and the graphic rating scale, could be subject to halo effect error. The best method to use to avoid or reduce halo effect error might be the critical incident approach, provided that the evaluator collected negative as well as positive incidents. Also, adding a weight, which is unknown by the evaluator, to the factors evaluated may help to alleviate this error. Finally, as with most of these errors, raters can be trained to recognize this bias and to work to overcome it.

Stereotyping

Stereotyping occurs when the rater places an employee into a class or category based on one or a few traits or characteristics. For example, an older worker may be stereotyped as being slower, more difficult to train, and unwilling to learn new approaches. Obviously, this perceptual error could negatively affect the overall performance evaluation. Of course, the older worker being evaluated may not fit this stereotype at all and may be quick to pick up new concepts and anxious to participate in new training programs. Some research has indicated that the composition of the group from which the stereotyped employee comes may influence whether or not the stereotype influences the rating. For example, women received lower ratings when the proportion of women in the group of employees was small; however, the stereotype did not lower ratings for African Americans who came from a group that had more Caucasians than African Americans. These results suggest that some stereotypes may be stronger than others.[41] Similar to reducing the halo effect, stereotyping may be controlled by offering specialized training to raters and making the problem associated with stereotyping salient. Further, avoiding scales that are not tied to performance standards can help to reduce stereotyping errors.

Attributions

Another perceptual error that can affect the validity of the performance appraisal involves the attributions the rater makes about employee behavior. Making an attribution means to assign causation for another's behavior.[42] For example, if a supervisor attributes an employee's good performance to external causes, such as luck, holding an easy job, or receiving help from coworkers, then the performance evaluation will not be as positive as if the supervisor had attributed good performance to internal causes, such as effort or ability. Similarly, if the supervisor attributes poor performance to external causes rather than internal causes, the performance evaluation will not be as negative. Frequently, attribution errors can be avoided by using BARS, because this method requires the evaluator to rate the behavior but not judge it.

Recency Effects

Recency errors occur when performance is evaluated based on performance information that occurred most recently. Essentially, supervisors rate the employee's most recent behavior. Recency errors are most likely to occur when there is a long period of time between performance evaluations (such as a year). Because recent employee behavior is the most salient to a supervisor, using a method that requires the rater to keep a log of employee performance throughout the year, such as the critical incidents approach, and forcing the rater to review the log before making a rating can help to alleviate this problem.

Leniency/Strictness Errors

Leniency and strictness errors occur when the rater tends to use one of the extremes of a rating scale. When leniency errors occur, most employees receive very favorable ratings, even though it is not warranted by their performance. Leniency errors can occur for a number of reasons. For example, a supervisor may be uncomfortable confronting particularly aggressive employees with less than favorable evaluations. To avoid conflict, the supervisor might choose to rate everyone high. It is also possible that the supervisor's own performance evaluation is based partially on the performance of his or her work group. Rating everyone favorably gives the impression that the entire work group is very effective.

Strictness errors, which are basically the opposite of leniency errors, occur when the rater erroneously evaluates most employees unfavorably. In this case, supervisors may simply want to appear "tough," or they may have unrealistic expectations of performance. Regardless, most employees are assigned ratings at the lower end of the performance scale.

Both of these errors can be eliminated by using any of the personnel comparison systems discussed previously. For example, the forced distribution method requires that the rater place a certain percentage of the people being evaluated in various categories, from outstanding to below average. By forcing the rater to use all of the categories, both leniency and strictness errors will disappear.

Central Tendency Errors

Central tendency errors occur when the rater avoids the extremes of the performance scale and evaluates most employees somewhere near the middle of the scale. This error results in most employees being rated as "average." Leniency, strictness, and central tendency errors limit the ability of the performance appraisal to discriminate between the performances of workers. Thus employees are grouped together at the low, mid-point, or high end of the scale; it is virtually impossible to differentiate performance levels among the employees. As with the leniency and strictness errors described previously, using a human resources comparison performance appraisal method can help to alleviate this problem.

Strategy and the Performance Appraisal Process

The performance appraisal system can be used to promote a variety of management goals and objectives. In addition to systematically encouraging high levels of performance, the system is useful in identifying employees with potential, rewarding performance equitably, and determining employees' needs for development. These are all activities that should support the organization's strategic orientation. Although these activities are clearly instrumental in achieving corporate plans and long-term growth, typical appraisal systems in most organizations have been focused on short-run goals.[43]

Organizational Strategy

Strengthening the linkage between the performance appraisal system and the organization's long-term strategic plans can improve organizational effectiveness. By designing a performance appraisal system that matches the organization's strategy, individuals should naturally perform in such a way to support the organization's mission. A clear linkage between the two also can help to build a culture that will further reinforce the organization's strategy. In addition, if the system is designed to help employees manage rather than critique their performances, there is a better chance for both the organization's and individual's goals to be met.[44] The following discussion examines the organizational strategy as it relates to performance appraisal systems.[45]

When an organization is operating under a retrenchment strategy, primary attention is devoted to improving the efficiency of existing operations. Successful organizations in retrenchment use performance appraisals as a means of identifying training needs and of skill building. On the other hand, when an organization is under a growth strategy, searching for new product lines or market opportunities is common. The emphasis is often on the identification and acquisition of human resources outside the organization. The focus is on identifying staffing needs as opposed to training needs.

Identifying Successful Versus Unsuccessful Appraisal Systems

Performance appraisal systems can fail for a variety of reasons. Exhibit 10.13 illustrates some of the reasons that trouble may occur.[46] The following discussion focuses on diagnosing the problems of an unsuccessful performance appraisal system.

EXHIBIT 10.13	COMMON PROBLEMS WITH UNSUCCESSFUL PERFORMANCE APPRAISAL SYSTEMS

1. A poorly defined appraisal system
2. A poorly communicated appraisal system
3. An inappropriate appraisal system
4. A poorly supported appraisal system
5. An unmonitored appraisal system

SOURCE: Adapted from C. Lee, "Smoothing Out Appraisal Systems," *HRMagazine*, March 1990, pp. 72–76.

YOU BE THE JUDGE

"Communicating" Performance Appraisal Information

A manager circulated an employee's performance appraisal that contained false information about the employee to other managers within an organization. When the employee was subsequently fired, he filed a defamation lawsuit, charging that the performance information was "published" because it was seen in writing by other managers. For defamation of character to legally occur, "injurious falsehoods" about an individual must be "published" and communicated to another.

The Indiana Supreme Court pointed out that several states view the circulation of documents within the workplace as simply communication and that this does not satisfy the requirement that defamatory material be published. However, other states have taken the opposing viewpoint, arguing that injury to one's reputation within a corporate environment can be just as devastating as that caused by defamation published outside the organization. The court ruled that refusing to characterize an internal document as a "publication" was unacceptable and that this would deprive employees of their right to seek legal counsel for damage to their reputation. Should performance appraisals be considered "published" when circulated within an organization? You be the judge.

Source: Adapted from William E. Lissy, "Performance Appraisals Can Be a Weapon for Employees," *Supervision* 58, no. 3 (March 1997), pp. 17–18.

Poorly Defined Systems A poorly defined system means that something is wrong with the design. For example, the system might lack written documentation to use as a guide. Often poorly defined systems emerge out of "tradition." Another possibility is that the system is not well defined. The performance appraisal system must be tied directly to clearly stated organizational objectives and strategies. Managers should not have to guess the objectives of the organization, the purpose of the performance appraisal, and how these issues tie together.

Poorly Communicated Systems Even a sophisticated appraisal system is doomed to fail if it is not communicated properly to everyone involved. The evaluators and the employees should have similar expectations about the purpose and the importance of the appraisal system. For example, the employee should know whether the performance appraisal system will consist of periodic reviews of performance aimed at changing work behavior or if it is to be an annual evaluation to determine salary and promotion opportunities.

Inappropriate Systems   Some of the most common characteristics of inappropriate systems include measurement of inappropriate types of performance (those that are not job related), asking the wrong people to do the evaluating, conducting the performance appraisal discussions too infrequently, and using a rating system that is not suited to the performance being measured. Any of these problems could lead to an ineffective performance appraisal system.

Poorly Supported Systems   The performance appraisal system can fail if it is supported only by top management. Even a good appraisal design can fail if the people using it are not committed to its success. Similarly, if the performance appraisal system is accepted and supported by employees, but not by top management, management may not choose to use the information gained from the appraisal. Essentially, a successful performance appraisal system should be accepted and supported by all who use it.

Unmonitored Systems   If problems with the performance appraisal system go unmonitored, they can become serious over time. For example, suppose that raters are consistently making leniency errors so that everyone receives high ratings. If this problem goes undetected, the performance appraisal becomes meaningless. Thus a performance appraisal system, even a good one, can fail if problems are not monitored regularly.

Criteria for a Successful Performance Appraisal System

Successful performance appraisal systems have a number of common characteristics. The following discussion focuses on the criteria for a successful performance appraisal system, which are listed in Exhibit 10.14.

Clear Objectives   A good performance appraisal should be built around unambiguous objectives. These objectives should cover all levels and areas of the organization and reflect the needs of each. The appraisal system should be clear in its purpose. Participants should know whether it is being used to determine raises and promotions or to determine development needs. It is important to clearly delineate who should participate in the system. That is, will employees at all levels be involved or will some areas or layers in the organization be excluded? Finally, participants must be aware of what type of information will be collected, how often, and who will have access to this information.

Management and Employee Endorsement   To be effective, the appraisal system should be supported by the entire workforce. This includes management support for possible expenses such as additional training, employee meetings, appraisal forms and other materials, and staff time. In addition, employees can benefit from involvement in the performance appraisal. For example, many companies encourage employees to do a self-appraisal as a means for discussion. The information solicited by self-appraisals should be consistent with both the organization's objectives and individual goals.

Flexibility   An organization must design its system with enough flexibility to adapt to any changes that might occur. For example, the appraisal system should be flexible enough to accommodate different management philosophies, employee subcultures,

EXHIBIT 10.14	CRITERIA FOR A SUCCESSFUL PERFORMANCE APPRAISAL SYSTEM

1. Construction reflects clear objectives
2. Endorsement by management and employees
3. Flexibility to adapt
4. Predictable timing of appraisal
5. Performance dialogue
6. Appropriate appraisal form
7. Periodic system checks

SOURCE: Adapted from R. S. Dreyer, "Why Employee Evaluations Fail," *Supervision* 58, no. 7 (July 1997), pp. 19–21; and C. Lee, "Smoothing Out Appraisal Systems," *HRMagazine*, March 1990, pp. 72–76.

and geographic locations. Sometimes it is necessary to establish different sets of procedures for very different employee groups or locations.

Predictability The timing of the performance appraisal(s) and any other feedback sessions should be predictable. For example, some organizations have an annual performance appraisal close to the hiring anniversary date of the employee. This enables the employee to prepare for the evaluation. Some organizations have two separate performance appraisals each year—one for salary considerations and one to assess employee development needs. Regardless of the number of evaluations, the employee should always have advance knowledge of what to expect in the performance review and when to expect it.

Performance Dialogue Performance discussions between the rater and the employee are perhaps the most critical component of a successful performance appraisal system. Performance reviews should not emphasize a "tell-and-sell" approach, in which the rater tells employees how good or bad their performance has been and attempts to convince them to accept this rating. Using a tell-and-sell approach can alienate employees and destroy the possibility of open communication in the future.

Instead, the performance review should emphasize a dialogue between the evaluator and the employee. During the discussion the employee should be given the opportunity to see all written appraisals of his or her performance, discuss them with the evaluator, and respond to them both verbally and in writing. Some organizations encourage employees to fill out a self-appraisal form to facilitate these dialogues.

Appraisal Form The importance of an appropriate appraisal form should not be overlooked. Many organizations simply adopt some "standard" form that may or may not be tailored to their goals and objectives. Failure to tailor the appraisal form to the objectives of the organization can lead to ratings based on irrelevant or unimportant issues. It is important that the form contain questions that directly relate to the employee's job in terms the employee can understand.

Periodic System Checks Systematically evaluating the validity of the performance appraisal system should be a key feature. As previously mentioned, an unmonitored system can create havoc within an organization if problems go undetected. At a minimum, the performance appraisal system is consistent with the strategic objectives of the organization. Validity checks should occur more often if problems have been detected with the system.

Management Guidelines

This chapter has examined a number of issues regarding the process and requirements of an effective performance appraisal system. Various methods of performance appraisals have been presented, as well as a number of perceptual and system errors that can hinder the success of an appraisal system. The following management guidelines on performance appraisals are offered as an aid to managerial decision making:

1. Performance appraisals should be based on a thorough job analysis that is current regarding both job descriptions and job specifications.
2. Performance standards should be developed from the job analysis as input into the performance appraisal.
3. Performance appraisals should evaluate a number of specific behaviors as opposed to evaluating "overall job performance" using one or a few global measures.
4. The performance review discussion should be a two-way communication between the evaluator and the employee.
5. The performance appraisal should be used not only as a means of evaluating performance but also as a means of motivating and developing the employee.
6. The *purpose* of the performance appraisal and the *objectives* of the organization must be considered carefully before deciding on a performance appraisal method.
7. Training programs should be implemented to (a) help raters avoid common perceptual errors in evaluations and (b) help raters with their performance review/feedback skills.
8. The link between the performance appraisal system and the organization's long-term strategic plans should be clearly defined.
9. In general, a successful performance appraisal system should be built around clear objectives, have the support of both management and employees, be flexible enough to adapt to organizational changes, and foster open discussions between supervisors and employees.
10. The validity of the performance appraisal system should be examined at regular intervals.

Questions for Review

1. What are some of the major strategic choices that organizations should make prior to implementing a performance appraisal system?
2. Why is a job analysis important to the performance appraisal system design?
3. What are the differences between the behavioral methods and the personnel comparison methods of performance appraisal?
4. What is the purpose of a performance appraisal?

5. What is the relationship between the performance appraisal system and the strategy of the organization?
6. How does the halo effect differ from stereotyping?
7. What are some ways an evaluator can avoid recency effects?
8. How can evaluators avoid leniency, strictness, and central tendency errors in ratings?
9. What are some characteristics of an unsuccessful versus a successful performance appraisal system?

CASE

Xerox Revamps Performance Appraisal System[47]

Xerox Corporation was faced with a problem—its performance appraisal system was not working. Rather than motivating the employees, its system was leaving them discouraged and disgruntled. Xerox recognized this problem and developed a new system to eliminate it.

The Old System

The original system used by Xerox encompassed seven main principles:

1. The appraisal occurred once a year.
2. It required employees to document their accomplishments.
3. The manager would assess these accomplishments in writing and assign numerical ratings.
4. The appraisal included a summary written appraisal and a rating from 1 (unsatisfactory) to 5 (exceptional).
5. The ratings were on a forced distribution, controlled at the 3 level or below.
6. Merit increases were tied to the summary rating level.
7. Merit increase information and performance appraisals occurred in one session.

This system resulted in inequitable ratings and was cited by employees as a major source of dissatisfaction. In fact, the Reprographic Business Group (RBG), Xerox's main copier division, reported that 95 percent of its employees received either a 3 or 4 on their appraisal. Merit raises for people in these two groups only varied by 1 to 2 percent. Essentially, across-the-board raises were being given to all employees, regardless of performance.

The New System

Rather than attempting to fix the old appraisal system, Xerox formed a task force to create a new system from scratch. The task force was made up of senior human resources executives; however, members of the task force also consulted with councils of employees and a council of middle managers. Together they created a new system, which differed from the old one in many key respects:

1. The absence of a numerical rating system.
2. The presence of a half-year feedback session.
3. The provision for development planning.
4. Prohibition in the appraisal guidelines of the use of subjective assessments of performance.

The new system has three stages, as opposed to the one-step process of the old system. These stages are spread out over the course of the year.

The first stage occurs at the beginning of the year when the manager meets with each employee. Together, they work out a written agreement on the employee's goals, objectives, plans, and tasks for the year. Standards of satisfactory performance are explicitly spelled out in measurable, attainable, and specific terms.

The second stage is a mid-year, mandatory feedback and discussion session between the manager and the employee. Progress toward objectives and performance strengths and weaknesses are discussed, as well as possible means for improving performance in the latter half of the year. Both the manager and the employee sign an "objectives sheet" indicating that the meeting took place.

The third stage in the appraisal process is the formal performance review, which takes place at year's end. Both the manager and the employee prepare a written document, stating how well the employee met the preset performance targets. They then meet and discuss the performance of the employee, resolving any discrepancies between the perceptions of the manager and the employee. This meeting emphasizes feedback and improvement. Efforts are made to stress the positive aspects of the employee's performance as well as the negative. This stage also includes a developmental planning session in which training, education, or development experiences that can help the employee are discussed.

The merit increase discussion takes place in a separate meeting from the performance appraisal, usually a month or two later. The discussion usually centers on the specific reasons for the merit raise amount, such as performance, relationship with peers, and position in salary range. This allows the employee to better see the reasons behind the salary increase amount, as opposed to the summary rank, which tells the employee very little.

A follow-up survey was conducted the year after the implementation of the new appraisal system. Results were as follows:

Eighty-one percent better understood work group objectives.
Eighty-four percent considered the new appraisal fair.
Seventy-two percent said they understood how their merit raise was determined.
Seventy percent met their personal and work objectives.
Seventy-seven percent considered the system a step in the right direction.

In conclusion, it can be clearly seen that the new system is a vast improvement over the previous one. Despite the fact that some of the philosophies, such as the use of self-appraisals, run counter to conventional management practices, the results speak for themselves.

Questions for Discussion

1. What type of performance appraisal is central to the new system at Xerox? Which, if any, of the criteria for a successful appraisal system does this new system have?

2. Given the emphasis on employee development, what implications does this have for hiring and promotions?

3. How do you think management feels about the new performance appraisal system? Why?

4. Are there any potential negative aspects of the new performance appraisal system?

Additional Readings

Borman, W. C., and G. L. Hallam. "Observation Accuracy for Assessors of Work-Sample Performance: Consistency Across Task and Individual-Differences Correlates." *Journal of Applied Psychology* 76 (1991), pp. 11–18.

Borman, W. C., Leonard A. White, E. D. Pulakos, and S. H. Oppler. "Models of Supervisory Job Performance Ratings." *Journal of Applied Psychology* 76 (1991), pp. 863–872.

Giles, W. F., and K. W. Mossholder. "Employee Reactions to Contextual and Session Components of Performance Appraisal." *Journal of Applied Psychology* 75 (1990), pp. 371–377.

Glen, R. M. "Performance Appraisal: An Unnerving yet Useful Process." *Public Personnel Management* 19 (1990), pp. 1–10.

Greenhaus, J. H., S. Parasuraman, and W. M. Wormley. "Effects of Race on Organizational Experiences, Job Performance Evaluations, and Career Outcomes." *Academy of Management Journal* 33 (1990), pp. 64–86.

Hanges, P. J., E. P. Braverman, and J. R. Rentsch. "Changes in Raters' Perceptions of Subordinates: A Catastrophe Model." *Journal of Applied Psychology* 76 (1991), pp. 878–888.

Jourden, F. J., and C. Heath. "The Evaluation Gap in Performance Perceptions: Illusory Perceptions of Groups and Individuals." *Journal of Applied Psychology* 81, no. 4 (1996), pp. 369–379.

Kamouri, A. L., and W. K. Balzer. "The Effects of Performance Sampling Methods on Frequency Estimation, Probability Estimation, and Evaluation of Performance Information." *Organizational Behavior and Human Decision Processes* 45 (1990), pp. 285–316.

Kane, J. S. and K. A. Freeman. "A Theory of Equitable Performance Standards." *Journal of Management* 23, no. 1 (1997), pp. 37–58.

Klimoski, R., and L. Inks. "Accountability Forces in Performance Appraisal." *Organizational Behavior and Human Decision Processes* 45 (1990), pp. 194–208.

Larson, J. R., and C. Callahan. "Performance Monitoring: How It Affects Work Productivity." *Journal of Applied Psychology* 74 (1990), pp. 530–538.

Londao, M., and A. J. Wohlers. "Agreement Between Subordinate and Self-Ratings in Upward Feedback." *Personnel Psychology* 43 (1991), pp. 375–390.

Ludeman, Kate. "Customized Skills Assessments." *HRMagazine*, July 1991, pp. 67–85.

Maurer, T. J., and R. A. Alexander. "Contrast Effects in Behavioral Measurement: An Investigation of Alternative Process Explanations." *Journal of Applied Psychology* 76 (1991), pp. 3–10.

McEvoy, G. M. "Public Sector Managers' Reactions to Appraisals by Subordinates." *Public Personnel Management* 19 (1990), pp. 201–212.

Meyer, Herbert. "A Solution to the Performance Appraisal Feedback Enigma." *Academy of Management Executive* 5 (1991), pp. 68–76.

Mount, M. K., M. R. Sytsma, J. F. Hazucha, and K. E. Holt, "Rater-Ratee Race Effects in Developmental Performance Ratings of Managers." *Personnel Psychology* 50, no. 1 (Spring 1997), pp. 51–70.

Nathan, B. R., A. Mohrman, and J. Milliman. "Interpersonal Relations as a Context for the Effects of Appraisal Interviews on Performance and Satisfaction." *Academy of Management Journal* 34 (1991), pp. 352–369.

Nathan, B. R., and N. Tippins. "The Consequences of Halo 'Error' in Performance Ratings: A Field Study of the Moderating Effect of Halo on Test Validation Results." *Journal of Applied Psychology* 75 (1990), pp. 290–296.

Sackett, P. R., and C. L. Z. DuBois. "Rater-Ratee Effects on Performance Evaluation: Challenging Meta-Analytic Conclusions." *Journal of Applied Psychology* 76 (1991), pp. 873–877.

Solomon, R. J. "Developing Job Specific Appraisal Factors in Large Organizations." *Public Personnel Management* 19 (1990), pp. 11–24.

Waldman, D. A., and B. J. Avolio. "Race Effects in Performance Evaluations: Controlling for Ability, Education, and Experience." *Journal of Applied Psychology* 76 (1991), pp. 897–901.

Williams, K. J., T. P. Cafferty, and A. S. DeNisi. "The Effect of Performance Appraisal Salience on Recall and Ratings." *Organizational Behavior and Human Decision Processes* 46 (1990), pp. 217–239.

Zigon, J. "Team Performance Measurement: A Process for Creating Team Performance Standards." *Compensation and Benefits Review* 29, no. 1 (January–February 1997), pp. 38–48.

Notes

[1] D. Waldman and R. Kenett, "Improve Performance by Appraisals," *HRMagazine*, July 1990, pp. 60–69.

[2] L. Fleury, R. Hanson, and J. McCaul, "Review System Supports Customer Focus," *HRMagazine*, January 1994, pp. 66–69.

[3] "Labor Letter," *The Wall Street Journal*, September 7, 1993, p. A1.

[4] J. Laumeyer and T. Beebe, "Employees and Their Appraisal," *Personnel Administrator*, December 1988, pp. 76–80.

[5] Robert McGarvey, "But I'm Doing a Great Job," *USAir Magazine*, May 1993, pp. 62–69.

[6] H. J. Bernardin, "A Performance Appraisal System," in R. A. Berk, ed., *Performance Assessment*, (Baltimore: Johns Hopkins University Press, 1987), pp. 277–304; Christopher Rhoads, " A Year-Round Schedule Said to Take Sting out of Performance Reviews," *American Banker* 162, no. 28 (1997), p. 6.

[7] Kate Ludeman, "Customized Skills Assessments," *HRMagazine*, July 1991, pp. 67–85.

[8] "Employers Must Revisit Purpose, Timing of Evaluations" *Miami Daily Business Review*, October 4, 1999.

[9] D. L. DeVries, A. M. Morrison, S. L. Shullman, and M. L. Gerlach, *Performance Appraisal on the Line* (New York: Wiley, 1981).

[10] K. Wexley and R. Klimoski, "Performance Appraisal: An Update," in K. Rowland and G. Ferris, eds., *Research in Personnel and Human Resources Management*, (Greenwich, CT: JAI Press, 1984), Vol. 2, pp. 35–80.

[11] See M. M. Harris and J. Schaubroeck, "A Meta-Analysis of Self-Supervisor, Self-Peer, and Peer-Supervisor Ratings," *Personnel Psychology* 41 (1988), pp. 43–62; and G. C. Thornton, "Psychometric Properties of Self-Appraisals of Job Performance," *Personnel Psychology* 33 (1980), pp. 263–271.

[12] C. C. Hoffman, B. R. Nathan, and L. M. Holden, "A Comparison of Validation Criteria: Objective versus Subjective Performance Measures and Self versus Supervisor Ratings," *Personnel Psychology* 44 (1991), pp. 601–619.

[13] "Gender Gap," *The Wall Street Journal*, July 21, 1992, p. A1.

[14] D. Campbell and C. Lee, "Self-Appraisal in Performance Evaluation: Development versus Education," *Academy of Management Review* 13 (1988), pp. 302–314.

[15] Albert Karr, "Rating the Boss," *The Wall Street Journal*, July 11, 1991, p. A1; Kate Ludeman, "Upward Feedback Helps Managers Talk the Talk," *HRMagazine*, May 1993, pp. 85–93; and Harry Gaines, "How Do You Rate?" *Sky*, September 1993, pp. 20–34.

[16] J. Segal, "Ignorance Is No Defense," *HRMagazine*, April 1990, pp. 93–94.

[17] N. Angel, "Evaluating Employees by Computer," *Personnel Administrator*, November 1989, pp. 67–72.

[18] "Is Your Friendly Computer Rating You on the Job?" *U.S. News and World Report*, February 18, 1987, p. 66.

[19] Linda Castellitto, "Collaboration Tools Help the Bottom Line," *Intranet World News*, June 15, 1998, p. 1.

[20] Mark Edwards, "Accurate Performance Measurement Tools," *HRMagazine*, June 1991, pp. 95–98.

[20] Bodil Jones, "How'm I Doin'?" *Management Review* 86, no. 5 (May 1997), p. 9.

[20]Robert C. Jones, Steve Quisenberry, and Gary W. Sawyer, "Business Strategy Drives Three-Pronged Assessment System," *HRMagazine*, December 1993, pp. 68–72.

[20]Matthew Budman and Berkeley Rice, "The Rating Game," *Across the Board*, February 1994, pp. 35–38.

[20]Huet-Cox, G. Douglas, "Get the Most from 360-degree Feedback: Put it on the Internet," *HRMagazine*, 44, no. 5 (May 1999), p. 92.

[25.]*Albemarle Paper Company* v. *Moody*, 422 U.S. 405, 1975.

[26]D. L. Kirkpatrick, "Performance Appraisals, Your Questions Answered," *Training and Development Journal*, 1986, pp. 68–71.

[27]Laumeyer and Beebe, "Employees and Their Appraisal."

[28]Richard Ringer, David Balkin, and Wayne Boss, "Managing Employee Emotion," *HRMagazine*, May 1993, pp. 140–144.

[29]Leon E. Wynter, "Black Managers Reject White Bosses' Criticism," *The Wall Street Journal*, February 2, 1994, p. B1.

[30]Herbert Meyer, "A Solution to the Performance Appraisal Feedback Enigma," *Academy of Management Executives* 5, 1991, pp. 68–76.

[31]Laumeyer and Beebe, "Employees and Their Appraisal."

[32]F. J. Landy and J. L. Farr, "Performance Rating," *Psychological Bulletin*, April 1980, pp. 72–107.

[33]F. Blanz and E. E. Ghiselli, "The Mixed Standard Scale: A New Rating System," *Personnel Psychology* 25 (1972), pp. 185–199.

[34]D. A. Bownas and H. J. Bernardin, "Suppressing Illusory Halo with Forced-Choice Items," *Journal of Applied Psychology* 76 (1991), pp. 592–594.

[35]D. Gold and B. Unger, "Evaluating Employees Through Rating Scales," *HRNews*, July 1990, p. 5.

[36]R. Rodgers and J. E. Hunter, "Impact of Management by Objectives on Organizational Productivity," *Journal of Applied Psychology* 76 (1991), pp. 322–326.

[37]J. Maiorca, "How to Construct Behaviorally Anchored Rating Scales (BARS) for Employee Evaluations," *Supervision* 58, no. 8 (August 1997), pp. 15–19; H. J. Bernardin and R. W. Beatty, *Performance Appraisal: Assessing Human Behavior at Work* (Boston: PWS Kent, 1984).

[38]G. V. Barrett and M. C. Kernan, "Performance Appraisal and Terminations: A Review of Court Decisions Since *Brito* v. *Zia* with Implications for Personnel Practices," *Personnel Psychology* 40 (1987), pp. 489–503.

[39]K. R. Murphy and W. K. Balzer, "Systematic Distortions in Memory-Based Behavior Ratings and Performance Evaluations: Consequences for Rating Accuracy," *Journal of Applied Psychology* 70 (1986), pp. 39–44.

[40]See, for example, R. Smither, *The Psychology of Work and Human Performance* (New York: Harper & Row, 1988), p. 164.

[41]P. R. Sackett, C. L. Z. DuBois, and A. W. Noe, "Tokenism in Performance Evaluation: The Effects of Work Group Representation on Male-Female and White-Black Differences in Performance Ratings," *Journal of Applied Psychology* 76 (1991), pp. 263–267.

[42]See, for example, J. H. Harvey and G. Weary, "Current Issues in Attribution Theory and Research," in M. R. Rosenzweig and L. W. Porter, eds., *Annual Review of Psychology* 35 (1984), pp. 427–459; and M. J. Martinko and W. L. Gardner, "The Leader/Member Attribution Process," *Academy of Management Review* 12 (1987), pp. 235–249.

[43]Fombrun and Laud, "Strategic Issues in Performance Appraisal: Theory and Practice," in K. Rowland and G. Ferris, eds., *Current Issues in Personnel Management*, 3rd ed., (Boston: Allyn & Bacon, 1986).

[44]Clive Fletcher, "Appraisal: An Idea Whose Time Has Gone," *Personnel Management*, September 1993, pp. 34–37.

[45]R. Miles and C. Snow, "Designing Strategic Human Resources Systems," *Organizational Dynamics*, 1983, pp. 36–52.

[46]The following discussion is based on C. Lee, "Smoothing Out Appraisal Systems," *HRMagazine*, March 1990, pp. 72–76.

[47]Woodruff Imberman, "Pay for Performance Boosts Quality Output," *IIE Solutions* 28, no. 10 (October 1996), pp. 34–37; Norman R. Deets and D. Tyler, "How Xerox Improved Its Performance Appraisals," *Personnel Journal*, April 1986, p. 50.

11

Strategic Compensation Systems

Chapter Objectives

As a result of studying this chapter, you should be able to

1. Describe the various influences on the design and implementation of compensation systems.

2. Discuss the lead, match, and lag pay level policies available to organizations.

3. Explain the concept of pay for performance and the advantages and disadvantages associated with it.

4. Summarize the major issues in communicating salary information.

5. Understand the relationship between motivation and compensation.

6. Differentiate among salary, incentives, commissions, profit-sharing plans, and gain-sharing plans for groups and individuals.

7. Be familiar with a variety of nonfinancial rewards that may be useful when designing compensation systems.

Designing and implementing an effective compensation program is a critical human resource activity. It may be difficult to say exactly how much a compensation system can influence an organization, but the creative use of compensation plans can work to maximize human resource productivity and contribute significantly to the achievement of human resource and organizational objectives. A pay system can reinforce an overall corporate objective of increased profitability, focus on both individual and team effort, and emphasize both short-term and long-term strategies. How best to pay people continues to challenge human resource managers.[1]

CASE

The Eleven-Million-Dollar Men[2]

Several years ago, Phillips–Van Heusen (PVH) participated in a costly battle against an unfriendly takeover. It won but realized that major restructuring, especially in its financial area, was required to remain competitive. One change that was instituted was an incentive compensation program for senior management. The goal of this plan was to use financial incentives to motivate individual performance and to reinforce a team-oriented culture that focused management's attention on achieving strategic goals. One of these strategic goals was to gain a measure of control over its destiny by eliminating the cyclical swings of its notoriously fickle business.

In essence the plan allows that each of the senior executives, regardless of the size of their operations, earn $1 million if earnings per share (EPS) grow 35 percent during a four-year period. The first $500,000 is earned in increments when EPS goals are met each year. The second $500,000 is the bonus for making the combined target in the fourth year. Even if they miss their target one year, they can make it up by the last year and still earn the full $1 million.

As retailers moved to limit the number of brands on their shelves or to push store brands, PVH found its merchandise being squeezed off the shelves of department stores and decided to fight back. In response, PVH expanded its wholesale business and created its own retail division, setting up a chain of specialty stores and factory outlets to sell its own products. The potential for competition between PVH's own wholesale and retail divisions had to be minimized. Thus a major objective of the incentive plan was to foster camaraderie and cooperation between those units.

The plan worked. Soon after its introduction, the senior executives, already close friends, jelled as a team. They began to meet more frequently, talk more openly about operations, and work harder to make each division more profitable. Cooperative efforts multiplied. Salespeople in the sweater and shirt divisions teamed up to sell color-coordinated combinations, boosting sales for both divisions. All groups contributed recommendations for a new chain to upscale mall stores targeted at shoppers who have "outgrown The Gap."

Plan participants easily met their goals for the first year this plan was in operation. The second year, however, was tough on them. Even though the participants outlined and followed a detailed plan, the year was fraught with unpredictable events that rendered the plan unsuccessful. For example, civil unrest in some countries hurt the production of sweaters, and severe weather conditions closed three suppliers in Puerto Rico for two weeks. Last, the Campeau retail empire's financial problems delayed payments for PVH merchandise. Soft sales in the retail division sealed the company's fate, and it failed to reach that year's target.

Mike Culang, sweater division chief, spoke for all when he said, "It will be terribly difficult, but with our mind-set the way it is, if there is a way to make it, we will make it." Also, Phillips is truly satisfied with the results of his plan: "The plan reinforced the religion and put everybody in his own confessional. Now each of these guys is terribly supportive of every other division of this company. You don't find that very often in corporate America."

Regretfully, the bonus portion of the executive compensation package had to be eliminated because of competitive pressures in the mid-1990s. However, even as it was eliminated, the compensation committee noted how important the bonus was to the culture and the competitiveness of PVH and vowed to reinstate it. True to their word, as of 1997, the executive bonuses were back.

Strategic Choices

The design of an organization's compensation system may have a critical impact on its ability to achieve its strategic goals. For this reason the reward system's philosophy and objectives must reinforce and reflect the organization's culture, external environment, and business strategy.[3] Among other things, reward systems can influence (1) who is attracted to and who remains with an organization,[4] (2) an employee's motivation level,[5] and (3) the organization's operating costs.[6] Managers must face several strategic choices with respect to the organization's reward system.

1. Management must decide the *importance of external equity* in the organization's compensation system. This decision is manifested in the type of pay policy implemented by the firm. The firm must make the strategic choice about how much to pay employees with respect to the competition. Is the firm going to pay the highest wages in the market to ensure attracting the most qualified applicants, or is the firm going to match the market salary or even pay less? This strategic choice is one of the most important choices an organization must make. It frequently forms the basis on which the rest of the compensation system is built.

2. An additional strategic choice a firm faces is *how closely the compensation plan will be linked to the organization's overall strategic plan*. It is important that the compensation plan reward behavior that will lead to the accomplishment of the organization's overall goals. Rewarding managers for meeting short-term goals at the expense of long-term goals may indicate a reward system that is inconsistent with the organization's overall strategy.

3. With respect to raises, a firm must choose between *merit pay raises* (paying for performance) or *across-the-board raises*. Firms that elect to pay for performance face the challenge of setting standards of performance against which the employees can be compared. Firms that decide to provide equal raises across the board face the challenge of keeping highly productive workers motivated and committed to the organization.

4. Firms also must choose the *level of pay secrecy* the organization will enforce. Many firms have decided that how much an individual is paid is between the firm and that individual. Employees who violate this agreement may be terminated. Other firms have more open views on pay secrecy and publicly post the salaries of their employees.

5. An organization must also determine its stance on *internal equity* when designing compensation systems. Firms that strive to ensure that the pay structure among different jobs is based on the relative worth of these jobs to the organization have selected a strong internal equity stance. Other firms that determine pay based on the person in the job, not the job itself, may have internal inequity with respect to compensation.

6. Finally, managers must decide how to *mix intrinsic rewards* (rewards that come from performing the job) and *extrinsic rewards* (rewards that come from a person outside the job) when developing a compensation system. When monetary rewards are not available or applicable, firms must locate other means by which to reward employees. Managers can make the strategic choice to design jobs so that intrinsic rewards are available to workers.

External Environmental Variables

When developing and designing a compensation system, organizations must take into consideration the external environment in which they do business. Many external environmental factors affect an organization, but only a few have a direct effect on an organization's reward system. Three of these—the nature of the competition, the nature of the labor market, and governmental regulations—are discussed in the following sections.

Nature of the Competition

The level of competition a firm faces in the product market is an important consideration when a compensation system is designed. When an organization has many product competitors, cost control assumes greater significance. Price pressures generally are downward, and increased costs from salary increases cannot be passed on to customers without risking loss of market share. In this situation, noneconomic rewards (such as promotions, job enrichment, and training and development programs) may assume greater importance in the pay scheme. Few competitors, on the other hand, increase flexibility in the design of the compensation system because wage increases are absorbed into the cost of the product or service.

An example of an industry with few competitors is flight simulation training. Simulflite and FlightSafety International are the only two organizations (outside of individual airline companies) that provide pilots with such training. Because their services have a high level of demand and have no practical product substitutes, they are able to pass on any increase in costs to their customers.

Nature of the Labor Market

A discussion of the impact of the nature of the labor market on designing reward systems focuses on two issues: labor supply and demand, and the wage levels that competitors are paying to their employees. When demand for labor is greater than the supply, competition for the scarce resource of labor increases, bidding up the cost of labor. Applicants can afford to "shop around" for a company that pays a higher salary when labor is in demand. When the supply of labor is greater than the demand, the competition among job applicants for a limited number of positions permits companies to pay lower salaries. This type of labor market exists in the cruise line industry. The majority of the 55,000 cruise line employees are from Third World countries. Even though the hours are long (between 16 and 18 hours a day) and the wages are low (roughly $1.55 an hour), the jobs are in great demand. Applicants flood the cruise line hiring agencies around the world. This is because cruise wages compare very favorably with salaries available in the workers' native lands. In addition, cruise ship jobs offer some added benefits not available in the workers' homeland: the opportunity to earn tips and room and board. Cruise ship workers are monitored closely. After two infractions such as tardiness, dirty quarters, or mingling with customers, the worker can be fired and the coveted position can be offered to someone else.[7]

This is not the only way that wages paid by competitors in the labor market can influence a company's wages. Some industries or individual organizations pay higher salaries than others as a policy. Certainly, high-tech and research and development industries must attract highly qualified employees. One way to do this is to pay more than other employers in the area. The strategic choice of paying above the market rate is discussed in more detail later in the chapter.

Government Regulations

Specific employment legislation affecting compensation decisions is addressed in Chapter 4, and it is included here again because of its significant organizational impact. Federal legislation affects almost every aspect of the compensation plan. It places a lower limit on wages that can be paid, affects raise and incentive decisions, proscribes wage discrimination, and requires that certain benefits be paid for all employees.

Recent changes in tax legislation have further complicated benefit decisions for many companies and made it very difficult to determine the employment tax status of an organization's workers. For federal employment tax purposes, one set of rules applies to employees, and a completely different set applies to independent contractors. Although the costs of misclassifying workers can be very high, it is extremely difficult to categorize workers with accuracy. For example, an employee may be classified as a statutory employee—an employee whom the Internal Revenue Code specifically classifies as an employee for FICA and FUTA purposes, but as an independent contractor for income tax withholding purposes. This crossover of status makes it important for an organization to categorize the employee for each specific tax purpose rather than in one set category.[8]

A second governmental regulation is minimum wage. The history of the minimum wage is presented in Exhibit 11.1. When the minimum wage rate is increased, small businesses, which have to increase pay rates to comply with the new wage law, have to cut back on staff to stay in business. The owner of a small motel in Wisconsin noted that the last increase in the minimum wage cost her motel about $5000 a year. Raising room rates to cover this cost will only decrease occupancy rates and thus reduce income even further. Also, if the hotel really had an extra $5000 to spend, it would much rather invest in new carpeting for the rooms than spend it on labor costs.[9]

The change in the minimum wage law, agreed to by Congress in late 1989, raised the minimum wage from $3.35 to $3.80 in April 1990. A second increase from $3.80 to $4.25 took effect April 1991. Minimum wage jumped again from $4.25 to $4.75 in October of 1996 and then again in September of 1997 to its current level of $5.15.[10] The law has a loophole that allows employers to pay a lower "training wage" to new employees for up to six months while they are learning the job.[11] Originally, the minimum wage law was designed to hold the minimum wages paid to unskilled or part-time workers at one-half of the average U.S. hourly wage. However, it has not always reached its goal.

In an effort to pay people enough to support a family in decent living conditions, some areas have passed living wage laws. Under a living wage law, companies that

EXHIBIT 11.1	THE HISTORY OF MINIMUM WAGE		
Date	**Minimum Wage**	**Date**	**Minimum Wage**
October 24, 1938	$0.25	January 1, 1975	$2.10
October 24, 1939	0.30	January 1, 1976	2.30
October 24, 1945	0.40	January 1, 1978	2.65
January 25, 1950	0.75	January 1, 1979	2.90
March 1, 1956	1.00	January 1, 1980	3.10
September 3, 1961	1.15	January 1, 1981	3.35
September 3, 1963	1.25	April 1, 1990	3.80
February 1, 1967	1.40	April 1, 1991	4.25
February 1, 1968	1.60	October 1, 1996	4.75
May 1, 1974	2.00	September 1, 1997	5.15

contract with cities and counties must pay their employees at a rate higher than minimum wage. Living wage rates vary by area, and some locations even have a dual track—a higher rate for firms that do not pay benefits and a lower rate for those that do. The highest living wage rate is in Kankakee County, Illinois, with a rate of $11.42 an hour regardless of whether benefits are paid, and the lowest rate is $6.22 paid in Buffalo, New York, by firms that offer benefits. Proponents of living wage laws believe that the extra pay makes a significant difference in the people it touches. Those against the initiative argue that living wage laws cut into profits, reduce jobs and hours, and encourage automation or relocation of businesses forced to pay a higher wage.[12]

Internal Environmental Variables

Internal as well as external environmental variables are important to organizations when developing compensation systems. Four of the most salient internal variables—corporate strategy, management philosophy, the type of job, and productivity—are examined in the sections that follow.

Corporate Strategy

The overall corporate strategy provides the direction for the organization. Because its focus is primarily long term, the pay system should be designed to support this focus. One way to accomplish this goal is to tie the compensation system to the developmental stage of the company. Different combinations of pay are designed to fit with the strategic conditions faced by the firm. As shown in Exhibit 11.2, six organizational stages are possible, ranging from start-up through maturity, decline, and renewal. Each of these cycles requires a different combination of base pay, incentives, and benefits.

For example, a mature organization would have several product lines and strong earnings. The focus of its human resource department would be on cost cutting, consistency of program application, and efficiency. The most effective pay mix would offer a competitive base pay, incentives, and benefits. It is possible that a

EXHIBIT 11.2   STRATEGIC PAY AND THE ORGANIZATION LIFE CYCLE

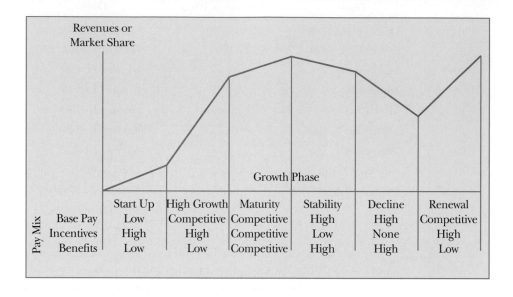

Pay Mix		Start Up	High Growth	Maturity	Stability	Decline	Renewal
	Base Pay	Low	Competitive	Competitive	High	High	Competitive
	Incentives	High	High	Competitive	Low	None	High
	Benefits	Low	Low	Competitive	High	High	Low

SOURCE: George Milkovich and Jerry Newman, *Compensation*, 2nd ed. (Homewood, IL: BPI/Irwin, 1987), p. 16. Reprinted with permission.

single organization could have more than one compensation strategy and system. Within an organization the various subdivisions or units may be in different stages in their life cycle. This would require separate compensation plans for different divisions.

Management Philosophy

One component of management philosophy is the value it places on its human resources. This value is reflected in the relationship between management and line employees. Take, for example, this statement of company mission for Herman Miller, Inc., a manufacturer of office furniture. Central to the company's mission is that it attempts to share values, ideals, and goals and to have respect for each person. To implement this mission, Miller installed a plan in 1950 that pays every employee a quarterly bonus based on attainment of production goals, employee cost-saving suggestions, customer satisfaction, and the company's return on assets. As you can see, an organization's culture is reflected in its pay system.

The Type of Job

Jobs differ in many ways. These differences include the variety of tasks performed; the amount of physical or mental effort; the pleasantness of the working conditions; the degree of autonomy (control over how, when, and what to do); the responsibility for labor, materials, and equipment; and the amount of interaction with others.

Contrast the job of a coal miner with that of a computer analyst. A coal miner's job is mainly physical, involves a limited number of tasks under working conditions that most of us would find unpleasant (working underground, in dangerous conditions, with the potential for health problems in the long run) with little or no control over how, when, or what to do on the job. A computer analyst, on the other hand, mainly uses mental skills, may have a wide variety of tasks (debugging programs, developing and writing computer programs, and systems planning), and works in a climate-controlled, generally pleasant environment with some freedom in program development and perhaps control over job priorities. It's possible that both of these jobs could exist within a large organization. How can a company develop a system that equitably compensates both types of employees? Their job tasks vary considerably; yet, each is a valuable employee to the organization.

Where the employee performs his or her job may also change the value and compensation associated with the position. For example, in the early 1990s U.S. managers who accepted positions overseas often made more money than their stateside counterparts.[13] A manager who made $100,000 in the United States earned three times that when transferred to London. That same manager would have made close to $1 million if transferred to Stockholm or Tokyo.

Today, however, most multinational companies compensate their expatriates according to a fairly rigid formula often called the balance sheet approach. Often, that includes paying them their stateside salary, plus allowances for foreign taxes and the higher cost of overseas housing and basic goods and services. Although most companies will tack on a premium of 10 to 15 percent to a person's salary, these premiums are carefully crafted so that employees do not see their standard of living increase or decrease substantially.[14]

Another key component in determining the value and compensation of a job is whether the job is performed by an individual or by a team. The use of teams in organizations has increased dramatically during the past decade. One recent survey found that 73 percent of all U.S. organizations used some form of teams to accomplish their goals.[15] Management is extremely excited about teams because they have been shown to increase productivity by 25 percent.[16] The increase in productivity often leads to an increase in wages for workers. However, just exactly how to pay individuals for team production is not always clear.

Take for example the Frito Lay plant in Kirkwood, New York.[17] John Powenski joined Frito Lay in 1994. When he arrived at Frito Lay he brought a strong positive feeling about teams and began changing the structure of the Frito Lay plant to incorporate teams. He started at the top. He implemented a Leadership Team composed of managers from all of the areas. The Leadership Team acted as a champion for the team approach, which was very well received. Teams trained together, planned together, and provided evaluative performance feedback to one another. In essence, the culture changed. However, when Powenski tried to implement a compensation system based on team performance, the transition hit a brick wall. The change was too great and too fast. Due to the backlash, Powenski was forced to roll back the new compensation system and reinstate the old one. However, he says this is temporary and will try it again in the future.

In the meanwhile, it might be possible for Powenski to institute a goalsharing program. Under a goalsharing program, groups or teams are rewarded monetarily for meeting specific goals that are not necessarily tied to the bottom line. The reward is in addition to employees' normal salary and is often a percentage of their total compensation for the year. In order for a goalsharing plan to work, several key components should be included:

1. Select only a few goals—three to five—so that people will remain focused on the goals.
2. Allow employees to help set the goals.
3. Carefully define the team so that units within the firm are not competing with one another.
4. Make the achievement of goals measurable in ways that employees can see and understand.
5. Weight some goals more heavily to align with and emphasize the strategic initiatives of the organization.
6. Reevaluate the goals at least annually.

Goalsharing programs are not quick fixes. It may take a few years for a plan to fully suceed.[18]

Productivity

pay level The average wage rate paid for a specific group of jobs.

Productivity, as you have learned, is simply the ratio of outputs (product or service provided by the company) to inputs (for example, costs in terms of labor, capital, energy, materials, and machinery). Any increase in labor costs decreases productivity unless output increases or other costs decrease. How to minimize the impact of these salary increases on productivity requires careful consideration.

pay level policy Whether the firm has decided to pay the same, more, or less to its workers than do its competitors.

Now that we've examined some of the major external and internal environmental variables that influence compensation decisions, let's turn our attention to a number of strategic options that must be considered. These options include the organization's pay level policy, the mix of extrinsic and intrinsic rewards, pay-for-performance systems, and pay secrecy versus openness.

Strategic Compensation Options

In the development of a pay system, several policy decisions must be made. Three of the most critical are pay level policy, pay structure policy, and types of rewards offered.

Pay Level Policy

external equity The degree to which an organization's wages are competitive with those of its competitors.

An organization's **pay level** is simply the average wage rate paid for a specific group of jobs.[19] Pay level is important because it influences both the organization's ability to attract and retain competent employees and its competitive position in the product market. **Pay level policy** refers to how an organization's pay level compares with its competitors' pay levels. The concept of **external equity**, the degree to which an organization's wages are competitive with those of its competitors, is reflected in a firm's pay level policy.

External equity occurs when an employer pays wage rates that correspond to those prevailing in the external labor markets. Factors that are potentially important to consider when defining the labor market include geography or location of the organization, the education or technical background required, the industry type, licensing or certification requirements, and the experience required by the job.

wage and salary survey A report of the current wage or salary earned by incumbents holding jobs in a variety of organizations.

Wage and salary surveys are designed to help the compensation analyst make informed decisions about wage rates that will maintain external equity. A wage and salary survey reports the current wage or salary earned by incumbents holding jobs in a variety of organizations. An organization can choose to conduct its own survey or use data collected by others. Creating an in-house survey will result in up-to-date comparisons; however, these surveys can be costly. When designing a wage and salary survey, managers must be concerned about (1) selecting which jobs should be examined, (2) defining relevant labor markets, (3) selecting firms to be surveyed, (4) determining information to be asked, and (5) determining data collection techniques.

Outside wage and salary surveys use data collected by others to determine external equity. Surveys are available from a variety of sources including the Bureau of Labor Statistics, trade groups, and professional compensation analysts (such as the Hay Group). Salary information also is available on the World Wide Web. For example, the Bay Area Library in Oakland, California, has compiled a list of hundreds of salary surveys and provides links to them from their Web page (**jobsmart.org/ tools/salary**).[20] (You can also try the home page for the Society for Human Resource Management [SHRM] at **www.shrm.org**. Specifically look for their "HR Links" button and then click on "compensation." Inside the compensation area will be a subsection that concerns salary surveys.) Although less expensive than creating an in-house survey, using information collected by others may not be as relevant or timely.

Basically, three pay level policy options may be chosen: lead, lag, or match.[21] Employers with a lead policy pay higher wages than the average wage paid in the labor market. Employers who choose a lag policy pay lower than average wages, whereas employers with a match policy "match" the market wage rate.

Why does an organization choose one pay level policy over another? The basic answer to this question is that the organization chooses the pay level that (1) maximizes its ability to attract and keep qualified employees, (2) is within its ability to pay, and (3) allows it to remain competitive in its product market.

Many organizations use a "match" policy. This enables them to recruit and retain a competent (but not superior) workforce, to pay their employees a wage that is perceived as fair, and to keep their labor costs in line with those of their competitors. Organizations who desire to attract the "cream of the crop" and therefore obtain higher product quality, lower turnover, less pay dissatisfaction, and therefore fewer unionization attempts or labor disputes, select a lead policy. Firms that can offer employees some benefit (such as the ability to perform a job that is consistent with employees' beliefs and values) other than a high salary or that always face an overabundance of qualified labor can choose a lag policy.

Some firms also may use one form of pay policy at one point but may be forced to switch to another at some future point. For example, in the early 1980s, the utility company Public Service Company of New Mexico faced economic prosperity, a positive regulatory environment, high growth, and an increase in available workers. During this time, Public Service prided itself on paying employees better than the going rate. In other words, it followed a lead pay policy. This policy served the company well until the end of the 1980s. At this time a general downturn in the overall economy occurred. Further, deregulation and diversification entered the picture. Public Service was forced to cut 20 percent of its workforce to remain competitive and now pays its remaining employees well below market rates.[2]

pay ranges The range of wages allowed by a specific wage classification and the amount of overlap between the ranges.

Pay Structure Policy

A company must also make a decision about **pay ranges**, the range of wages allowed by a specific wage classification and the amount of overlap between the ranges. The

EXHIBIT 11.3	TYPOLOGY OF JOB EVALUATION METHODS	
	Whole Job	**Specific Job Factors**
Job vs. Job	**Ranking Method**	**Factor Comparison Method**
	Identify the job with the most "worth" to the company. Identify the next job with the most worth. Continue this until all jobs are in a hierarchical order.	Select compensable factors and describe the jobs in terms of these factors. Rank the jobs on each factor. Weight each factor in terms of its relative importance to the organization. Calculate the total points for each job.
Job vs. Standard	**Classification Method**	**Point Method**
	Decide how many grade levels the job value structure is to be broken into (usually varies from 5 to 15) and write generic descriptions at each level. Compare the job descriptions with the description of the grade levels. Assign each job to the grade level it most closely matches.	Select compensable factors and develop levels (with points attached) for each factor. Analyze the job in terms of the compensable factors and determine which point level best fits the job. Assign points for each factor for the total points for each job.

government puts an absolute minimum on any pay range, but, in practice, an organization must decide on the maximum and minimum pay for any job or set of jobs in the pay structure. This maximum and minimum are based on the worth of the job that is determined through a job evaluation.

internal equity Setting wage rates that conform to the job's internal worth to the employer.

   Internal equity is the objective of setting wage rates that conform to the job's internal worth to the employer. A **job evaluation** is a formal process by which management assigns wage rates to jobs according to some preestablished formula. Most job evaluation techniques employ compensable factors in assessing job worth. A compensable factor provides a basis for defining the internal worth of a job. The most commonly used compensable factors are (1) skills required by the job, (2) responsibility for people and/or equipment, (3) effort required, and (4) working conditions. Four general types of job evaluations can be seen in Exhibit 11.3. Job evaluation techniques can be differentiated on the basis of (1) whether the job being evaluated is *compared with other jobs* directly or *against some standard* and (2) whether the comparison is based on the *job as a whole* or on *specific factors* in the job.

job evaluation A formal process by which management assigns wage rates to jobs according to some preestablished formula.

   A large spread between the minimum and maximum salary allowed in a pay range is termed a *wide pay range*. The wider the pay range, the longer the employee can stay in the same job and still receive pay increases. Wide pay ranges are common in organizations that have only a few pay grades. A **pay grade** is a group of jobs that have the same classification with respect to pay. Wide pay ranges are needed so that employees have room for movement in the pay range for a number of years before reaching a maximum. An organization with many pay grades, however, generally has narrower pay ranges, and the maximum paid for any job can be reached more quickly. Companies using this type of pay structure encourage their employees to receive pay raises through promotion and movement through pay grades instead of promotion and movement within the pay grade. Exhibit 11.4 pictorially summarizes the pay structure components described previously.

pay grade A group of jobs that have the same classification with respect to pay.

EXHIBIT 11.4   EXAMPLE ORGANIZATIONAL PAY STRUCTURE

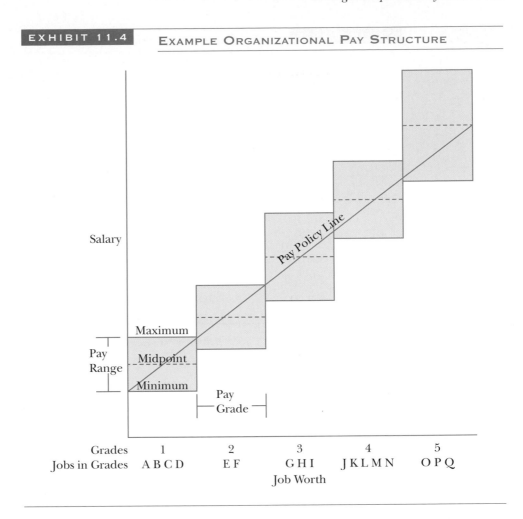

Grades	1	2	3	4	5
Jobs in Grades	A B C D	E F	G H I	J K L M N	O P Q

Job Worth

broadbanding
The collapsing of job clusters or grades of positions into a few wide bands, which creates a flatter organizational structure.

    Broadbanding is a concept that refers to the collapsing of job clusters or grades of positions into a few wide bands, creating a flatter organizational structure. An example of the pay grades before and after broadbanding was implemented is shown in Exhibit 11.5. Broadbanding is intended to focus management and employee attention on important matters in the delivery of pay and career development. One goal of broadbanding is to enhance the manager's ability to compensate people for what they contribute to the organization beyond what is called for in their job descriptions. Further, broadbanding can direct employee attention to career growth. A flat structure of pay opportunities makes it salient that only significant increases in job responsibility merit moving to a higher pay band.[23]

    Most organizations that have implemented broadbanding have done so in the past few years. Managers at General Electric (GE) have used broadbanding extensively and have reported great success. Philip Morris, after investigating this pay practice, decided against implementing it. GE and Philip Morris have different organization strategies and cultures, and those of Philip Morris did not meet the necessary requirements for successful broadbanding.[24] Examples of cases in which broadbanding is most likely to be successful include:

| EXHIBIT 11.5 | AN EXAMPLE OF BROADBANDING |

Old Grades			New Bands		
Grade	Minimum	Maximum	Band	Minimum	Maximum
1	$14,900	$19,500	1	$15,000	
2	$16,200	$21,300			$26,300
3	$17,600	$23,200	2	$18,000	
4	$19,100	$25,300			$31,500
5	$20,700	$27,600	3	$22,500	
6	$22,500	$30,100			
7	$24,700	$33,200			$39,400
8	$26,900	$36,200	4	$27,000	
9	$29,200	$39,500			
10	$31,700	$43,000			
11	$34,500	$46,900			$52,000
12	$37,500	$51,200	5	$35,500	
13	$40,800	$55,800			$67,400
14	$44,400	$60,800	6	$46,100	
15	$48,300	$66,300			
16	$52,500	$74,600			$87,700
17	$58,100	$82,800	7	$60,000	
18	$64,400	$92,000			
19	$71,400	$102,100			$114,000
20	$80,500	$115,400	8	$81,000	
21	$90,900	$130,400			
22	$102,600	$147,300			$153,800
23	$115,800	$166,500	9	$109,300	
24	$130,700	$188,100			$207,700
25	$147,200	$219,300	10	$147,600	$280,400
26	$169,100	$252,200	11	$199,200	$387,500
27	$256,700	$383,600	12	$278,900	$529,900

1. The organization experiences a significant precipitous event.
2. The organization is ready for a change in its compensation system.
3. Top management is committed to broadbanding.
4. The organization has a decentralized compensation administration.
5. The managers are empowered.

One form of pay grades that has fallen from favor is the two-tier pay system. This system allows existing workers to maintain their wage level while new employees are paid at a lower wage rate. Only a decade ago, two-tier wage scales were an extremely useful tool for dealing with escalating labor costs. However, today those that remain are a thorn in the side of both management and labor. New employees, who worked side by side with the longer-tenured workers, performed the same jobs, received less pay, and thus began to complain. As the size of the workforce receiving the higher wages began to shrink because of retirement and attrition and the number of the lower-paid employees began to increase, the inequities between the two groups became too great. Only a few of the newly negotiated contracts now hold two-tier wage level clauses.[25] Interestingly, the opposite problem—**wage compression**—is even more prevalent. This most often occurs when, because of inflation, new hires are brought in at about the same salary or higher salaries than the current employees are paid. Organizations argue that to attract qualified employees, they must be willing to pay a premium. Unfortunately, organizations do not always adjust the salary levels of the current employees, which can lead to perceptions of inequity and dissatisfaction among employees.

wage compression Pay situation arising when new hires are brought in at about the same salary as or a higher salary than the current employees.

Extrinsic Versus Intrinsic Rewards

So far our discussion has centered on the financial reward system for the organization. However, financial remuneration is not the only alternative the company has for compensating its employees. Economic downturns in the 1980s and early 1990s have led to increased cost consciousness for many companies. Companies have found it difficult to increase salaries, provide cash bonuses, or otherwise provide tangible rewards to their employees. In the absence of cash, some firms are looking for alternative ways to motivate employees.

Some nonmonetary motivators for which managers have reached during lean times include intellectual challenges, a sense of purpose, more flexibility and responsibility, greater freedom and recognition, and increased input in decision making. To instill a sense of purpose, managers have doubled the praise bestowed on their staff to let their employees know how much their work is appreciated. Other managers have tried to assign extremely challenging projects to employees to increase their mental stimulation. Assigning employees challenging projects can keep them from becoming bored and increase their intrinsic motivation for the job. Offering an employee a change in job title, which includes more prestige, also can be an effective nonmonetary reward. Finally, companies have found that flexibility is important in lean times. Sharper Image relaxed its dress code at headquarters for employees who did not meet the public. Employees are now allowed to wear sweaters and slacks and can even wear jeans on Fridays.[26]

What kinds of benefits do individuals get from the nonmonetary rewards? Some examples are a sense of pride and feeling of accomplishment when a job is done well, pleasure received from doing a task that is interesting and challenging, participation and involvement in decision making, and an opportunity for personal and professional growth. The important point is that the design of the job itself, how it is performed, and what one wears while performing it can be used to reward the individual. These types of rewards can have a powerful effect on motivation.

A Strategic Approach to Compensation

An organization's compensation system should be consistent with the overall strategy of the organization. Successful firms display a consistent strategy supported by complementary organizational structures, designs, and management processes. Two major strategic initiatives that occur in businesses today are growth or retrenchment. Firms following these two strategies would view the compensation process very differently. Firms in a growth mode would focus on employee performance and especially on external performance. This would force firms to pay attention to external competitiveness and equity. Total compensation packages would be oriented toward incentives and would be driven by recruitment needs. Firms following a retrenchment strategy would be mainly concerned with overall costs and would seek ways to reduce the firm's overall compensation costs. Hence, nonmonetary rewards would be used instead of monetary rewards. Further, the firm's focus would be more internal (i.e., survival) than external competitiveness.

Pay for Performance

It used to be that hourly workers were paid by the hour, salaried workers were paid by the year, and only upper management received bonuses. Many companies now, however, have decided that this method does not work well enough and are experimenting with a variety of pay concepts to improve employee performance.

If a major goal of compensation is to motivate employees to work at their best level, then pay for performance is an intuitively appealing idea. After all, employees who are more productive are more valuable to the organization and should be rewarded for their superior performance.

The move toward paying employees for their contributions, not simply for their time spent at work, has been driven by the need for U.S. firms to be more productive—to do more with less. The "less" normally extends into pay with pay-for-performance plans, which usually start with reduced base wages and salaries but reward employees with handsome bonuses for hitting targets or meeting goals.[27]

The types of firms that have found ways to incorporate a pay-for-performance reward system vary greatly. For example, in the early 1990s, American Airlines ground personnel, who were represented by the Transport Workers Union, ratified a contract that tied pay hikes to performance. Under this contract, baggage handlers could earn pay increases by getting luggage to passengers more quickly. This type of contract incentive provided a benefit to all involved, including travelers, the airline, and the baggage handlers.[28] Pay-for-performance systems also have been introduced on Wall Street. Shearson Lehman, for example, introduced a plan called BONUS. Each letter in BONUS stands for a specific way in which a stock can perform: buy, outperform, neutral, underperform, and sell. Analysts are expected to rate stocks in terms of these outcomes, and, through the use of computers at the end of the year, their predictions are checked against what the stocks actually did. Analysts' bonuses are related to how well they predicted during the year.[29]

The two pay-for-performance systems described previously have one clear advantage over many other pay-for-performance systems: it is easy to measure performance. With respect to the baggage handlers, there is a specific time at which the plane's cargo doors can be opened. This time can be registered and compared with the time when the luggage from that flight begins to reach the luggage carousel. Similarly, Shearson can compare the actual data about the stocks and ratings made by the analysts and develop a result that can't be questioned.

Quantifying and defining performance standards is often a stumbling block in the development of pay-for-performance systems. For such systems to work effectively, distinctions among employees' work must be made. However, because most managers are unwilling to make these distinctions and because few companies force them to do so, most pay raises simply move in a lockstep fashion. Further, frequently it is a struggle to determine what workplace behavior is fair and meaningful to measure and reward. The measures frequently are global measures of safety and quality that, although they may be easier to quantify, may not be the workplace behavior that will actually increase productivity.[30]

The difficulty involved in determining and quantifying performance standards is not the only barrier to implementing a pay-for-performance system. Other problems rest in the traditional mind-set of employers with respect to what employee compensation should include. For example, many firms believe that they have an obligation to keep employee pay even with inflation. This is normally accomplished by cost-of-living raises, which are equal across the board. After employees are provided with cost-of-living raises, frequently little money is left to reward outstanding performers. Similarly, if firms strive to maintain external equity and tie their pay scales to what the competition is paying, the majority of money earmarked for raises may end up being spread across the board instead of directed to the most productive workers. Finally, companies can inhibit their ability to use a pay-for-performance system by striving to keep all workers at the midpoint of the salary range and by allowing managers to provide inflated performance appraisals, which increase expectations of large and deserved raises.[31]

How the pay-for-performance system is developed and implemented, who decides performance-based raises, and who benefits from pay-for-performance systems also affect the success of the programs. Pay-for-performance systems that were implemented via a "slam dunk" approach (someone from the top ordered someone below to implement a pay-for-performance system—pronto) frequently fail. The parameters of successful pay-for-performance systems must be negotiated and agreed to by all involved. In addition, in some environments, pay-for-performance systems are not appropriate, and introducing a system in these environments will result in failure.[32]

Once implemented, the way the program is managed also can result in problems. For example, in many firms, the immediate supervisor determines the merit increases subordinates will be paid, which allows them an extremely broad level of discretion and a good degree of control over the workers.[33] Although middle-level managers may have the ability to determine the merit increases for their subordinates, they are all but forgotten in pay-for-performance reward systems. According to compensation consultants, barely 1 percent of the salary paid to middle-level executives earning from $20,000 to $50,000 is paid through a pay-for-performance system.[34] Further, middle-level managers are frequently evaluated to satisfy budgetary needs, not to reward performance. If merit raises are provided, they are far too small and not as much, proportionally, as they should be with respect to lower-performing colleagues.[35]

Pay-for-performance reward systems have been implemented in an unlikely location—Japan. Once noted for paying for amount of time in a particular pay grade and rewarding seniority, Japan has begun to take steps to link employee pay with performance. Much of the change can be traced to the changing demographics in the Japanese workforce. As the age of the workforce increases, more and more employees expect to be promoted, because promotion after a certain time in grade was common in the past. However, with the top-heavy situation being experienced by Japanese firms, these traditions must change. The change has frequently been a push for pay and promotion for performance. Nissan is a good example of a Japanese company looking to change. It told workers that promotions would be based on ability rather than tenure. Ryobi, a die cast maker, took pay-for-performance one step further and now bases middle managers' salaries on performance. This is quite a switch from the tenure-based salary structure that had been in place since the company began. Ryobi hopes that the change in compensation will increase managers' activity and spur initiative.[36]

Ryobi's desire to increase managers' activity and initiative is but one of the positive outcomes that can stem from a well-designed pay-for-performance reward system. Other potential benefits include a movement toward focusing on the results rather than on the methods and focusing on the group or the whole instead of the individual.[37] Pay-for-performance systems also can be used to get employees to learn to think like shareholders. This is the main goal of the pay-for-performance system at General Dynamics. Top management at General Dynamics believes that if management can get employees to think and act like shareholders, this partnering of interest will result in financial rewards for both. In addition, these rewards will be tied to the long-term success of the organization.[38]

Executive Pay and Pay for Performance

Many elements of the total compensation package are offered to top executives. Frequently, an executive's base salary is the lowest form of compensation received. Instead of a high base salary, executives receive a combination of perks leading to a total compensation package that is well above the average pay of the workers or shareholders of the firm. The perks that are included in a compensation package differ with respect to the industry, the board of directors, and the firm. Further, perks change over time.

Some of the items that have been added to the list of executive compensation perks in the past few years have created some controversy. One such item is a pension, often called *golden parachutes*, which guarantees to protect executives from hostile takeovers and bankruptcies. Shareholders and employees argue that it is not fair that they risk losing their investments and jobs when the firm is taken over or files for bankruptcy although top executives stand to lose nothing. Companies defend the action, saying that it protects executives from losing the benefits that they have earned. Further, companies that normally offer such a plan are in some trouble in the first place. It is difficult to retain qualified top executives in troubled firms without some type of guarantee.[39]

The coverage of executive parachutes has been extended from a loss of job resulting from often uncontrollable external evils, such as hostile takeovers and bankruptcies, to much more controllable and personal reasons for loss of a job, such as poor performance, personality conflicts, or illegal activities.[40] Take the case of J.P. Bolduc, president and CEO of W.R. Grace & Co., who was forced from his position after allegations of sexual harassment. His severance package was $43 million. The story was similar for Michael Carpenter who resigned as CEO of the Kidder Peabody Group during an insider trading scandal. His parachute provided him with a $10 million severance package. One of the largest settlements, and one that created a great deal of backlash for the company, was the $90 million payment made to Michael Ovitz after he was terminated by Disney for poor performance. Shareholders sued and withheld votes to reelect board members and to confirm the lucrative new contract for chairman and CEO, Michael Eisner.[41]

A second issue that concerns many stakeholders is the increased use of stock options in executive compensation plans. A stock option gives the holder the right to buy a certain number of shares at a set price some time in the future. Because the benefits of stock options depend on the stock price, this option does not necessarily guarantee

YOU BE THE JUDGE

What Were They Thinking?

According to *Business Week*, the highest paid CEO in 1999 was Charles B. Wang, CEO of Computer Associates (CA). The reason for his first place ranking was a generous stock option granted to him by CA's Executive Compensation Committee. Specifically, he received 12.2 million shares of stock valued at $655 million in a stock grant plan. But the plan covered more than just Wang. More than 6 million shares went to Sanjay Kumar, president and COO, and 2 million shares went to Russell M. Artzt, an executive vice-president, making the total stock plan worth more than $1 billion. What did these men do to earn such a deal? They raised CA's stock price from $20.00 to $53.33 in three years. To cover the cost of the stock plan, CA had to charge $675 million against earnings. Naturally the announcement quickly sank the stock price, dropping it to the low 20s. However, by the middle of 2000, it had risen back to the mid 50s. How did the stockholders react? With anger and lawsuits. In November of 1998, Judge Myron T. Steele, a Delaware Chancery Court Judge, decided two shareholder's lawsuits in favor of the shareholders. The three executives were ordered to return 9.5 million of the 20.3 million shares awarded to them. CA appealed. In March of 2000, CA announced a settlement in the two cases. The three men agreed to give back 4.5 of the 9.5 million shares ordered returned by the judge. So what do you think? Is any CEO worth $655 million?

SOURCE: Adapted from Anthony Bianco, "The Package That Launched a Dozen Lawsuits," *Business Week*, April 17, 2000, p. 108.

a large payoff. For example, in 1999 the top five executives at Borders Group Inc. took stock options in lieu of a salary, banking on the soaring stock price to make them rich. Even though Borders' posted record sales and profit that year, the executives' stock options were under water (i.e., the stock was selling at less than the option price), and one executive had to borrow money to pay his living expenses. The next year four of the five elected to take their salary in cash.[42]

The dipping stock prices that plagued 1999 changed the composition of executive pay. Even though exercised stock options made up more than 80 percent of the average long-term compensation plan for CEOs in 1999, for the first time in three years the average salary and bonus increased. In 1998 this figure was $2.1 million. In 1999 the figure rose to $2.3 million. A total of 78 percent of the CEOs received a pay raise in 1999, up from 71 percent in 1998.[43]

Gains in executive compensation during the past few years have angered many stakeholders.[44] The tough economic times have made employees, who have been asked to tighten their belts and do more with less by top executives in their firms, ask the executives, "What about you?" For example, when the top management of United Press International (UPI) asked workers for a 90-day, 35-percent wage reduction, union officials said yes, but only if managers took an equal cut and no bonuses were awarded to executives.[45]

Many people agree that CEO compensation systems may need to be revamped but do not agree on how this revamping should be accomplished.[46] Some groups are suggesting reviving the fixed-ratio theory of executive pay.[47] This theory is based on the idea that the highest-paid executives in the firm should make no more than X times the amount earned by the average worker in the firm (that is, a ratio of X to 1). Agreement with respect to what X should be is not clear. For example, Socrates, the Greek philosopher, suggested 5 to 1 as a solid ratio. However, more recently, Peter

Drucker, the renowned management consultant, suggested a 20-to-1 ratio. However, in 1999 the average CEO earned 475 times what the average blue-collar worker earned.[48]

The fixed-ratio theory also may need to be extended to compare salaries at the top. A study that examined the turnover of the top five executives of 460 companies during a five-year period found that large pay gaps between the CEO and the remaining four executives doubled turnover rates. Biomet had the lowest pay gap and also had the lowest turnover—none. Louisiana-Pacific had the largest gap and had 13 changes in the top five executives during the five-year period studied. These results indicate that extremely high CEO pay has a variety of negative consequences.[49]

An alternative compensation plan designed to make CEOs more accountable for their pay is an economic value added (EVA) plan. Essentially an EVA plan evaluates corporate performance by comparing what a firm earns with its cost of capital. If the firm earns less than its costs, shareholder value decreases, indicating a poor-performing CEO. A Stern Stewart survey showed that firms that use an EVA plan gained more than 8 percentage points more per year than competitors that did not use such a plan. However, other studies indicated no difference in performance between EVA and non-EVA firms.[50]

Another option is to compare the CEO's salary to shareholder return and/or return on equity. When *Business Week* applied these formulas to CEO pay in 2000, A. Jerrold Perenchio, CEO of Univision, and David S. Wetherall, CEO of CMGI, took the top two slots, indicating they earned their pay. Occupying the bottom two slots were Stephen M. Case, CEO of America Online, who grossed more than $303.3 million during a three-year period, and Michael D. Eisner, CEO of Disney, who was paid a whopping $639.9 million during a three-year period. According to *Business Week*, neither of these gentleman earned his keep.[51]

Pay for Performance at Individual and Group Levels

Although often considered as a method of payment for CEOs, the concept of pay-for-performance is being implemented at all levels in the organization in a variety of ways. The methods can be divided into three major types: individual, group, and a combination of the two. For individuals, pay-for-performance can take the form of merit pay, incentives, and bonuses. At the group level, profit sharing, gain sharing, and stock ownership are the most prevalent.[52] Each of these options is discussed in the sections that follow. This discussion begins by examining base pay and then introduces the various types of pay-for-performance plans most commonly used today.[53]

base pay The basic cash received for the work performed, adjusted for the individual's skill, education, experience, or some other attribute.

Base Pay However a system is designed, most compensation programs use some form of **base pay**, which is the basic cash received for the work performed, adjusted for the individual's skill, education, experience, or some other attribute. The base pay may be either hourly (paid by the hour) or salaried (paid weekly, biweekly, monthly, or yearly). Base pay can be supplemented by incentives, lump-sum bonus payments, or some other form of extra compensation such as overtime pay.

Individuals who are paid an hourly wage rather than a weekly salary are generally classified as "nonexempts." By law, nonexempt workers are to receive time and a half for each hour over 40 they work per week. However, some firms are using technology as a means of cutting down on overtime pay. Instead of having individuals remain on the job after 40 hours, they are sent home with a pager. If needed, the workers are paged and are required to return to work within a predetermined window.

The legal question that must be answered is whether time spent on-call, but not actually responding to a call, is time that must be compensated. The Department of Labor's interpretation of the Fair Labor Standards Act is not very helpful on this issue. They suggest that such time may need to be compensated. This lack of clarity has led to a surge of federal cases on overtime liability. In general, courts require on-call employees to be compensated for their time if they cannot use that time effectively for their own purposes.[54]

Incorrectly categorizing nonexempt employees as exempt can be a costly mistake as can not completely following the wage and hour provisions of the Fair Labor Standards Act (FLSA). If a firm is found guilty of violating the FLSA, the Department of Labor can audit two years of payroll records. This is raised to three years if the company acted "willfully." The penalties for repeated and willful transgressions can be up to $1000 per incident and unpaid wages. How easy is it to violate the FSLA? Employees who regularly work through lunch or skip breaks in order to complete assigned work constitute a transgression of the law.[55]

Merit Pay   Perhaps the most familiar form of pay-for-performance plan is merit pay, which rewards work behaviors that have already occurred. Frequently, merit raises are based on the level of the individual's performance in the past year relative to some standard of performance. Merit pay can be given either as an increase to the base salary or as a lump-sum payment.

A primary issue in merit pay-for-performance systems is whether pay truly is based on performance. Many researchers believe that the majority of merit pay systems simply do not work. Merit pay does not increase productivity because the difference in merit pay between the outstanding and poor performers is so small that the pay increase ends up being no incentive at all. For example, one survey of 459 companies found that top performers received, on average, a 7.7 percent increase whereas average performers received an average increase of 4.7 percent. Although these figures appear to be significantly different, the difference in pay after taxes is approximately $20 a week for a $40,000-per-annum employee. In these terms the monetary increase is barely enough to cover lunch out for the week and can hardly be a motivating factor for high-quality workers.[56]

Another issue in merit pay-for-performance plans is whether employees perceive the relationship between pay and performance, if it does exist. Because it is often so unclear how a person got a higher or lower raise than another, it takes an enormous leap of faith for an employee to determine that pay and performance are really related. To address these problems, companies are getting rid of subjective appraisals and are setting up bonus plans based on specific performance goals. These plans include a strong, positive correlation with performance. If performance increases, so does pay. If, on the other hand, performance goes down, so does pay.[57]

When an organization is considering whether a performance-based pay system would work for it, the potential benefits and costs must be weighed carefully. Four major considerations are listed here.

1. If an organization employs *mostly* professionals, implementing a merit program is risky. Professional employees often have a marketable skill for which employers are always willing to pay. Thus, if the new merit compensation system does not meet their expectations of what their compensation should be, they will be likely and able to leave the organization.

2. Employees who like what they are doing and who are enjoying a good deal of intrinsic motivation from their jobs may not like the extra pressure of external rewards placed on their job when a merit system is implemented. In this case it is better to let the employees enjoy their jobs without adding performance pressures.

3. If cooperation, teamwork, and work groups are valued above competition, individual initiative, and superstars, then a merit pay plan is not advisable. Merit plans tend to make individuals work to better themselves, perhaps even at the expense of others in the workplace.

4. For any merit pay system to be effective, management must enforce it. If managers are unable or refuse to take on the tough roles required by a merit pay system, such as providing accurate performance appraisals, the system will not work.[58]

Incentives   Like merit plans, incentive plans tie pay to some standard of performance. This standard can be defined as cost-saving goals, quality standards, or production levels, among others. However, incentives differ from merit pay in that they are future oriented; they are used to induce desired behavior. Their time orientation may be short term, long term, or a combination. They also may be tied to individual and/or group performance.

straight piece-work plan   A type of individual incentive plan that pays a constant amount for each unit that is produced.

standard hour plan   A type of individual incentive plan that ties pay to a standard amount of time it takes to perform a service or complete a task.

Most individual incentive plans are of two types: (1) the **straight piecework plan**, which pays a constant amount for each unit that is produced, and (2) the **standard hour plan**, which ties pay to a standard amount of time it takes to perform a service or complete a task. Under a straight piecework plan, an assembly line worker may receive 25 cents for each fishing tie that is completed. An example of the standard hour plan might be found at an appliance repair shop. Standard rates are determined for doing certain repairs, based on the average length of time it usually takes to do the job. If the standard time for a motor repair job is two hours, the repair person is paid for two hours. If the job is finished in less than two hours, the repair person is still paid the full amount. On the other hand, if the job takes longer than two hours, the repair person still earns the same amount.

Many companies have combined the basic incentive plan with a form of year-end bonus. Lincoln Electric in Cleveland is a shining example of a successful piecework plan instituted in 1934. Lincoln pays each factory worker for each acceptable piece that is produced. In addition, each employee receives a year-end bonus based on a yearly merit rating of the employee's dependability and ideas as well as quality and amount of output. For employees, the payoff has been bonuses averaging almost 98 percent of yearly wages. For Lincoln, the payoff has been operating for 54 years without a losing quarter and 40 years without a layoff.

Group plans are similar to individual plans in that pay is tied to performance, but a major goal is to increase cooperative efforts and to coordinate activities. Essentially, incentives are based on an increase in profits or a decrease in costs, relative to a "base year." The size of the group may range from work teams to the entire organization, with unitwide and organizationwide plans growing in popularity.

The use of both individual and group incentive plans by all sizes of firms continues to increase. In 1993 it was estimated that more than half of all companies offered some form of incentive to workers below the top executive level. One reason for the increase in use of incentives is that they actually seem to work. For example, introducing an incentive plan to workers has helped Domino's Pizza to witness an increase in sales, Ford Motor Company to improve morale and quality of work, Avis to reduce customer complaints by 35 percent in one year, and Warner Lambert Company to witness an increase in the performance of its managers.[59]

There probably are as many incentive plans existing as there are firms using them. However, there is some agreement on the types of plans that work best. Two of three companies that implemented incentive plans indicated that productivity increased when the plan offered to pay incentives to workers in discrete units for meeting specific targets.[60] One small company, headed by Hugh Aaron, that made color concentrates for the plastics industry capitalized on this formula and was able to increase productivity during even the leanest times.

After witnessing a flat profit line month after month after a period of intense growth, Aaron decided that something had to be done. To increase sales he added to the salesforce, increased advertising, and purchased more equipment to enable him to produce more product. Profit continued to remain flat. His strategy did allow him to win some new clients, but he lost an equal number. He decided it was time to take a new approach, and he began focusing on the production line.

An incentive plan was introduced to reward plant workers when each production line produced more than the historical average of items per hour. Because the production line was run by a group of workers, teamwork improved and "slackers" received so much social pressure that most quit. When members of a team quit, the remaining team members requested that those positions not be filled. Because the bonus was split with the entire production line, fewer workers meant bigger rewards for the remaining workers. The new incentive system allowed production that used to take more than 100 employees to be performed with fewer than 40 employees, and production increased more than 50 percent.

The incentive plan clearly produced a win-win situation. For every dollar in bonus the employees earned, the company earned two. Management met with the workers to express its appreciation for the level of performance it was receiving and was informed that even more could be produced, but only if management would make one promise. The promise was that if the workers did increase productivity even further, the historical average production figures on which the incentive program was based would not be changed. Management quickly agreed, in writing, and production levels increased to a point at which the profits and productivity were higher than either side ever dreamed.[61]

Not all incentive programs result in a happy ending. Nearly one third of the respondents to a survey of more than 600 companies using incentive programs stated that their programs were ineffective or needed improvements. One reason that some of the programs did not work is that they were introduced primarily because the competition was doing the same thing. When the goals and conditions surrounding the plan are not clearly thought out and linked to overall firm performance goals, any incentive program is doomed to failure.[62]

skill-based pay
A form of incentive-based pay wherein employees are paid for the skills they possess, not just the skills performed.

A form of incentive-based pay that has received a great deal of attention in the past few years is **skill-based pay**. Under a skill-based pay plan, employees are paid for the skills they possess, not just the skills performed. Among the advantages of this type of pay system is reduced competition among workers for higher supervisory ratings. Because an individual's pay is determined by his or her ability, not the supervisor's rating, competition between workers is reduced. Similarly, supervisor costs decrease because as the workers' skills increase, they take on the responsibility for functions previously performed by supervisors. Finally, employees begin to have a greater understanding of how each position fits into the overall production process.

Although the advantages of a skill-based pay plan seem impressive, some disadvantages are associated with it. First, the training costs are high. Frequently, the skills needed by workers are job or company specific, and for the employees to gain these skills, in-house training must occur. The costs of setting up the programs and reduced production during the times employees are attending the training classes make a skill-based pay plan a costly proposal. An additional cost involved in this type of incentive program is the increase in the overall hourly wage costs. As employees complete the training programs, the overall hourly wage costs will increase. Although highly trained employees allow the firm more flexibility, the wage costs must still be considered. Finally, even though employees consider a skill-based pay plan as fair, compensation problems can still occur. Disagreements about the difficulty of the training, the time required, and the frequency with which the skills are required to be used may arise. Ways with which to deal with these problems must be developed.[63]

The increase in mergers, acquisitions, takeovers, and shutdowns in the past several years has produced a new type of incentive: stay bonuses. **Stay bonuses** include a variety of cash bonuses and other inducements offered by firms to keep valued workers on the payroll during corporate reorganizations or closedowns. Frequently offered only to employees at higher levels in the organization, stay bonuses have begun to trickle down to even the lowest levels of the workforce. For example, an office equipment company paid sales commissions even when there were no sales in order to maintain "business as usual" while it prepared to close. Often the most likely lower-level employees to benefit from stay bonuses are workers who have skills that are difficult to replace. These skills may be job or company specific, or simply a skill that is currently in demand in the marketplace. Other employees who may be involved in stay bonuses are experienced workers. For example, when Marico Acquisition Corporation acquired Rouge Steel Company, experienced workers were offered bonuses of up to $13,000 over three years if they would remain with the firm.[64]

stay bonuses A variety of cash bonuses and other inducements that firms offer to keep valued workers on the payroll during corporate reorganizations or closedowns.

Gain-Sharing Plans Although gain-sharing plans have been around for more than 50 years, their recent increase in popularity has made them the fastest-growing type of incentive. Gain-sharing plans involve a participative management approach. The pay for gains results from a reduction of costs, whether or not the organization is profitable at year end. Gain-sharing plans mold employees' perceptions about what they need to do to improve the organization's results overall and along the way.[65]

One widely used cost-saving plan that was developed in 1937 is the Scanlon plan. The Scanlon plan focuses on decreasing labor costs without decreasing output. The two major components of the plan are (1) the development of a productivity norm and (2) the use of a dual-committee system to encourage companywide participation in decision making. In the development of a productivity norm, a base year is chosen that is neither a boom nor a bust year. The base year also must be fairly recent so that it represents current factors in the organizational environment. Worker committees are responsible for evaluating suggestions from employees about how to cut costs or improve productivity. Money is added to a bonus pool created each time that output exceeds the productivity norm. Each month a portion of the fund is distributed to the employees and a portion is reserved in case of a poor month. Anything remaining in the pool is paid out at the end of the year.[66]

Improshare

Programs based on Improshare stress quality and quantity goals derived from engineering standards. The bonus formula used in these types of plans is based on productivity standards that emphasize quality and quantity in relation to total labor hours expended. Improshare plans need not include an employee involvement component, but such an element has been used successfully in conjunction with quality circles and other types of work team situations.

Carrier, a subsidiary of United Technologies, introduced Improshare to its employees in 1988. In its first year, productivity increased 24 percent over its base year (1986), and rejects decreased dramatically. Savings in labor costs are split 50-50 between the company and its employees, with each employee receiving the same percentage bonus. In 1988, 2500 employees shared $3 million in bonus pay. Carrier claims that its success is due to employee involvement. Plant productivity is posted daily on the bulletin board; quarterly meetings to discuss the budget, business conditions, and the economy are held with all employees in groups of 70 to 80; and employees are encouraged to talk to plant managers about their ideas.

SOURCE: Adapted from E. Ost, "Gain Sharing's Potential," *Personnel Administrator,* July 1989, pp. 92–96.

The Rucker plan, a second gain-sharing program, is also based on employee involvement but does not make as extensive use of employee committees as does the Scanlon plan. Instead, a suggestion box may be introduced in place of employee committees. The Rucker plan also has a bonus formula that is based on value added. Because it is less radical than the Scanlon plan, the Rucker plan is frequently used by firms attempting to change their traditional management style by slowly adding employee involvement.[67] Unlike the typical Scanlon plan, the Rucker value-added formula allows workers to benefit from savings in production-related materials and supplies. Many of these plans also have a reserve pool set aside for low productivity months. If the money in the reserve pool is not used during the year, it is paid out as an additional bonus to employees at the end of the year.[68] A more recent innovation in gain sharing is Improshare, developed in the 1970s by Mitchell Fein. The nearby HR Challenge "Improshare" box more fully describes this innovation.

Successful gain-sharing plans can produce a number of important results for organizations, as noted in the Improshare example. However, when deciding whether to implement a gain-sharing plan to achieve some of these benefits, several factors must be considered. First, it is important to clearly define the eligible employees of a group or unit to be included. Who is selected to be included and excluded may very well determine the success of the plan. Second, a great deal of time should be spent specifying the measures and formula calculations that will be used to determine the rewards. The measures and calculations must be easy enough to implement and explain to those involved, but they must also be accurate and reward only the behavior that helps produce the wanted results. Finally, the proportion of total gains to be allocated to eligible employees and the frequency with which these gains will be paid must be defined clearly. The program should be designed to reward the behavior desired as soon after it occurs as possible.[69]

Profit-Sharing Plans   Profit sharing ties employees' bonus pay to the success of the company by focusing on profits. Profit-sharing plans generally reward employees only when a certain profit level is reached. These profits typically are distributed in cash, deferred until a future time (retirement, severance, or disability), or paid in a combination of the two methods.

Profit sharing has several advantages. Generally, the incentive formula is simple and easy to communicate. Pay is variable because the plan pays only when the firm is profitable. Last, it promotes interest in the overall financial health of the company for both management and line employees.

Many companies have found success with profit-sharing plans. Hewlett-Packard believes profit sharing is a powerful tool for improving productivity.[70] Until recently, H-P used deferred profit sharing only for upper-management levels. Now it pays cash bonuses to middle management and white-collar staff each year that specific profit goals are met.

Another believer in profit sharing is Aluminum Company of America (Alcoa). After suffering from several years of downsizing and reorganization, Alcoa decided to use profit sharing as a way to share its hard-earned success with the employees who helped reach its goals. The plan begins once Alcoa's U.S. aluminum operating profits exceed 6 percent of the company's U.S. assets. Salaried employees received cash bonuses averaging 7 percent of each worker's salary. Alcoa believes that profit sharing, combined with a merit raise system that replaced automatic yearly raises, gives it more flexibility in its compensation system.

As you will see in the ending case of this chapter, National Semiconductor has successfully blended the best of profit sharing and gain sharing. However, profit sharing does have its disadvantages. When payments are made annually, long-term goals may be ignored and short-term goals emphasized. Further, many times profits are beyond the control of company employees. As a result, employees who have made sacrifices or worked harder may feel cheated when their efforts do not pay off.

Profit sharing is not always a success. Profits are influenced by a variety of variables, and many employees fail to see how their performance is tied to organizational performance. When payout is deferred for many years, the connection between performance and reward is further blurred.[71] However, some programs may succeed because they change the culture of the firm, leading employees to develop a broader view of the organization and its goals and inspiring greater commitment to those goals.[72]

For incentives to work, companies need a clear idea of their strategy and goals. Next, they must focus on jobs that can be measured and require peak performance levels. Companies also must allow individual business units to tailor their plans to their specific situations and provide conditions under which the program can be modified or even eliminated. Finally, incentives need to be separated from base pay so that employees can more readily see the link between rewards and performance. These recommendations do not ensure success, but they certainly increase its likelihood.

Commissions   Commission plans are typically developed for sales employees. They may be either straight commission plans, which pay the employee a percentage of sales that are made, or a combination of salary and commission (and/or bonus). The percentages vary by industry, product, and nature of the sales job. For example, real estate commissions paid to the selling agency average around three percent, with up to two percent going directly to high-performing agents. Plans also vary in the determination of how sales are calculated. Using the point-of-sale figures may encourage a very different set of sales behaviors than using the point of delivery.

Companies are working harder to make their commission plans more effective. Behlen Manufacturing in Columbus, Nebraska, ties its commissions partly to company profits. One fourth of the commission on selling a preengineered building depends on the company's profit on the deal. A different plan is used by an Indianapolis product distributor, Seal Products, Inc. Seal pays up to four times as much when the sale is harder to make than when the customer walks in the front door and the salesperson only has to show the product for the sale to happen. Seal believes its new plan helped boost sales by 25 percent in 1990.[73]

Major department stores have begun switching employees from salary to commission in an effort to boost sales. The concept of an all-commission sales force in department stores is not new. Nordstrom's, a Northwest service-oriented department store chain, has been using this type of compensation system successfully for quite some time. As lagging sales continue to force stores to close and squeeze profit margins, retailers are looking to imitate Nordstrom's success.

The change in compensation plans has not been as smooth as some would have liked. For one thing, simply placing a salesperson on a commission-based compensation system does not create a customer-oriented salesperson. Customer service is a part of the culture and must be instilled and communicated throughout the organization. Similarly, some employees who had been working for the firm on a salary basis for many years had to be terminated because they were unable to effectively function on a commission-only basis. New salespeople also were turning over as quickly as old. One firm saw its turnover rate jump from 4 percent before the introduction of commission-based pay to more than 18 percent after the introduction.

Some employees were thankful for the change in pay policies. These were the people who have been able to increase their pay under the new system. For example, a clerk at Bloomingdale's in New York City was paid $7 an hour and 0.5 percent commission on sales of up to $500,000 under the old compensation system. The total compensation package for this employee would be $16,220 per year based on a 40-hour work week for 49 weeks of the year ($13,720 for hours worked + $2500 in commission). Under the new plan, an employee who sells $500,000 worth of merchandise would earn $25,000 a year (5 percent of $500,000).[74]

The use of commissions offers both advantages and disadvantages. Certainly commissions reward performance, are easy to communicate and administer, and allow fluctuation in pay. On the other hand, a straight commission plan may create a high variability in pay from one period to the next and may generate lower organizational commitment. Further, the emphasis on volume of sales may cause employees to pay less attention to nonselling duties. Lastly, using commissions assumes that money is the primary motivator of employee behavior.[75]

For these reasons, the majority of organizations use a combination plan. A survey by the American Compensation Association found that more than 70 percent of sales compensation plans were of the salary plus commission or bonus type.[76] Aside from offering greater income security, it also motivates employees to perform even those duties that do not have an immediate sales-connected payoff. These advantages seem to outweigh the potential disadvantages of increased complexity and consequently higher administration costs.

Stock Ownership Plans   Stock ownership generally is a form of long-term incentive that traditionally has been available only for middle- to top-level management. In theory, managers who are partially paid with company stock have a higher interest in the long-term profitability of the company. Frequently, employees are required to remain with the firm for a specified time to qualify for ownership. Both the number of firms that require this and the length of employment required have risen in recent years.[77] In general, the success of stock ownership depends on the situation and how it is used. In small organizations, stock ownership decreases the need for other forms of incentive plans; in larger organizations, stock ownership is more successful when used in conjunction with other pay-for-performance systems.[78] Three major forms of stock ownership plans are stock options, stock purchase, and employee stock ownership plans (ESOP). They are discussed in the following sections.

Stock Options   Two types of stock options are the classic stock option and the restricted stock option. A classic stock option gives the employee the right to buy the company's stock during a certain period of time (usually 10 years) for a set price. That price usually is the market value of the share on the day the option was offered. If the price rises above that level, the employee can exercise the option to buy the stock and immediately resell it for a "risk-free" gain. Offering stock options to managers is intended to ensure their personal interest in the future of the firm. Firms hope, but do not always require, that managers hold their stock as long as they are with the company. Some companies have no record-keeping procedure to check to see whether managers sell or keep their stock. In a restricted stock option, the employee is given the shares with the restriction that they may not be resold for a specified period of time, generally five years. During that five years, the employee receives all dividends and voting rights. Even if stock prices fall, the sale of the stock still brings a certain sum of money to the employee.[79]

The use of stock options has dramatically increased during the past few years. Leading the way in this expansion are high-tech firms such as Microsoft. Greg Maffei, chief financial officer at Microsoft, dubbed the use of stock options as the "virtuous cycle."[80] As Maffei explains, Microsoft has enjoyed an extremely strong growth in their stock price—an average of 60 percent per year since 1986. In addition, Microsoft believes in rewarding employees with stock options and has done so very generously—on average, 2500 per employee. Microsoft's generous stock option plan helps in other ways too. Because people recognize the potential windfall that can be made through stock options, they are willing to take a pay cut to work for Microsoft. Being able to pay below-market wages for highly qualified and committed employees lowers Microsoft's salary expenses. But the stock option plan gets even better. When employees "cash in" their options, Microsoft can deduct the amount employees receive on their options as an expense on their taxes. In 1996 Microsoft was able to reduce its tax liability by $352 million through the use of stock options.[81]

The wave of technology and dot-com firms capitalizing on their ability to pay lower wages by offering stock options on their soaring stocks may have crested. With technology stocks tanking in the stock market, employees are beginning to prefer cash to options. Some firms are heeding the requests. For example, Priceline.com introduced a new compensation plan that was implemented in the fourth quarter of 2000. The plan included large cash bonuses aimed at retaining key workers. Other firms have hung in with options, but many have been forced to reassign a new price as many of the original options were under water (selling at less than the original option price).[82]

The dot-coms are not the only businesses jumping on the stock options bandwagon. Andersen Consulting introduced "eUnits" in 2000, which represent a stake in the $200 million venture capital invested in e-commerce companies. When and if the firms go public, Andersen employees can cash in their eUnits.[83] All the ruckus about stock options may be worth it. One study that examined shareholder return during a five-year period reported that companies that provide more stock-based incentives in their compensation plan delivered higher shareholder returns.[84]

Stock Purchases   In the same way that stock options can tie executives to the company's fate, workers allowed to purchase stock have a greater interest in the company's success and frequently demonstrate higher morale. Organizations frequently allow employees to purchase stock shares either at regular market value or at a reduced value. Often the offer is for a limited time, commonly 30 days, or ongoing, in which the money needed to purchase the stock is withheld from the worker's paycheck. For small organizations with participative management style, performance frequently improves and productivity increases. For large organizations, the effect is less pronounced unless all employees are allowed to participate in the plan.[85]

Employee Stock Ownership Plans (ESOPs)   ESOPs work differently from stock purchase plans. Currently, about one fourth, or about 10 million, of all corporate employees have enrolled in an ESOP. This type of stock ownership plan, pioneered in the 1950s, allows employees to borrow against corporate assets to purchase stock. In some cases, however, employees accept wage concessions in return for stock. When companies do well, ESOP participants can amass significant nest eggs. PepsiCo implemented a program to encourage employees to take initiative in improving individual and organizational performance.[86] A key to the program was an ESOP that allows long-term employees to accumulate large gains based on annual salary, salary growth, and share price.

In recent years, ESOPs have provided two additional benefits to firms. The first is that they provide tax advantages to companies that give shares of stocks to their employees. Fifty percent of the interest on loans granted companies for use in ESOPs is tax exempt. A second benefit is that ESOPs can be used as a defense against hostile takeovers.

The benefits that ESOPs provide also shed light on factors that must be considered before such plans are devised. Workforce retirement needs, changes in the economy, and market position of the organization are key to the successful development and implementation of an ESOP. In Wall Street terms, individuals involved in ESOPs are holding extremely undiversified portfolios. If the portfolio remains unprofitable, the holders will have nothing left with which to diversify.[87]

Development of Well-Rounded Compensation Systems

Many firms are attempting to develop a well-rounded compensation system. To do this, they are using a variety of compensation options. Exhibit 11.6 is an example of an overall compensation package that includes a variety of options. This package is offered to managers of Toys "R" Us. Another example, which describes an overall compensation package that has gone through some revisions lately, follows.

General Motors (GM) set up a new compensation system designed to push its salaried employees to work harder—and to help push those who don't out the door. The move, affecting 112,000 low-level managers, clerical workers, and other white-collar staffers, is part of a trend to tie compensation more closely to performance to make pay more variable from year to year. Two years earlier, GM had stopped giving annual cost-of-living raises. Temporarily suspended salary increases have been

---

EXHIBIT 11.6   STORE MANAGEMENT BENEFITS AT TOYS "R" US

Benefits package effective as of February 1994. This policy may change over time.

Stock Options	Management personnel receive stock options which are normally exercisable in four years and nine months after the date they are granted at the original option price. Options are issued each year, usually in November, at the then current price. The number of options granted is dependent on your position at the time of grant. (At this time, a manager's stock option is 100 shares).
Incentive Programs	In addition to regular compensation, a performance-oriented incentive award may be achieved annually. The following table summarizes the current award levels by classification.

Position	Incentive Range
Manager	0–15% of base salary
Assistant Director	0–22.5% of base salary
Store Director	0–30% of base salary

Unlike some other companies, the Toys "R" Us incentive bonus is designed to be paid. Our annual budgets actually provide for funding of all incentive awards at the target amount levels shown.

Profit-Sharing and Savings Plan	An employee shall be eligible to participate in the profit-sharing and savings plan as of the first day of the month in which he or she completes one year of service. The company contributes a portion of its profits to the profit-sharing plan. This contribution is usually equal to 8% of participants' compensation for the calendar year. With 5 years or more of service you become 100% vested. You can contribute anywhere from 1% to 10% of your pre-tax income to the plan. The Company will make a matching contribution of up to one-half of the first 6% that you contribute. For example, if you contribute 6%, the Company will add another 3% for a total of 9%.
Stock Purchase Plan	Eligibility: Age 18 years or older and completion of 90 days of continuous service. The employee Stock Purchase Plan enables you to invest in company stock through automatic payroll deductions. The company will add 10% to your contribution and pay all commissions on purchases made through payroll deductions.

SOURCE: Copyright © 1994 Toys "R" Us, Inc.

---

reinstated, but with a new philosophy: "A merit increase is something you have to earn," says Roy Roberts, vice-president for personnel. "To treat people fairly, you have to treat people differently." GM's new strategy involves base-pay merit raises, lump-sum payments, and profit sharing. The top 5000 managers also have seen changes. Their 70-year-old bonus plan was scrapped, decreasing annual pay for many executives by 50 percent. Instead of cash and stock right away, these managers receive restricted stock grants that will take years to mature. All of this is to get people to work harder and encourage better cooperation.[88]

Pay Secrecy Versus Openness

Organizations differ as to the amount and type of information about pay that they readily communicate to their employees. To be sure, an organization that purports to use a pay-for-performance system increases employee trust and confidence in the system when it communicates to its employees how that system works, what level of raises will be received for different levels of performance, and pay increase schedules. Other information such as pay maximums and minimums for various job classes or even specific individual salaries also may be communicated.

Next, Inc., hangs a list of all employees' salaries in its company offices in Redwood City and Fremont, California. Phillip E. Wilson, vice-president of human resources, maintains that "anything less than openness doesn't establish the same level of trust."[89] Calfed, Inc., a bank in California, is more in the middle between pay secrecy and openness policies. Vanessa Jorgenson, a branch manager, believes that she is better able to handle pay problems and has a better chance of keeping people she has trained because of the bank's open pay policy. Calfed's performance guide, which she discusses with employees, includes data about how to compute a merit raise and salary brackets for every job.

However, the majority of companies prefer a policy of pay secrecy because they believe it gives them more freedom to make pay decisions and keeps employee pay dissatisfaction low. Communicating information about a pay system that is not performance related also can reduce employee motivation. The results from a salary survey of 388 human resource professionals further documents the level of pay secrecy in the workplace. Whereas 81 percent of the respondents reported that some information about pay ranges in the organization is made available to employees, 48 percent allowed employees to see only their own pay ranges and did not reveal pay structures for other positions; approximately 20 percent indicated that no pay-scale information was provided to employees.[90]

Many employees also believe that pay secrecy is the best policy. For some, pay may be tied to the employee's ego. Others may simply be embarrassed about their pay or not want to know about others' pay for fear that it would just make them angry. At Electronic Data Systems, new hires are required to sign a form that acknowledges certain companywide policies. One of these policies states that employees are permitted to reveal their salaries but that they can be fired if such a disclosure leads to "disruptions."

All of the discussion so far assumes that money is a source of motivation to employees. In the following section, the relationship between motivation and compensation is discussed.

Motivation Theory

The general topic of motivation was discussed in an earlier chapter. In this section, the relationship of equity theory, expectancy theory, and reinforcement theory to compensation is more fully explained.

Equity Theory

equity theory
The belief that employees examine the relationship between their outcomes from the job and their inputs to the job. This ratio is then compared to the ratios of relevant others.

A major goal of all compensation systems is fairness or perceived equity. Employees often determine their own individual perception of compensation equity by using the formula espoused in **equity theory**.[91] Equity theory proposes that employees examine the relationship between their outcomes from the job (such as pay, job satisfaction, recognition, and promotion) and their inputs (such as education, experience, skill, and effort). This ratio is then compared with the ratios of others (for example, other employees or the employees at a previous job). If the ratios are perceived as inequitable, dissatisfaction may result.

Dissatisfaction probably does not occur if positive inequity (the person feels overrewarded) is the result of the comparison. Research has shown that workers have been found to be happy when they believe they are paid more than they are worth. Further, this happiness also occurs when workers believe that their colleagues are over-rewarded.[92]

When negative inequity (the person is underrewarded) occurs, employees are generally dissatisfied. This dissatisfaction motivates the employee to reduce that inequity by increasing outcomes or decreasing inputs (either cognitively or physically) or changing the comparison in other ways so that the ratios are more equitable. Employees who want to increase their outcomes could ask for a raise or promotion, seek greater recognition, or even change the perception of the level of satisfaction received from the job. Alternatively, the employee may choose to decrease inputs by using such mechanisms as cognitively downgrading the skill level or amount of experience or by not working as hard.

Research on equity theory has shown that individuals who believe they are paid too little relative to what others earn or what they think they *should* earn may become dissatisfied. This dissatisfaction may cause them to seek new employment, to become less productive, or to be absent more often. Thus an individual's perception of equity is an important consideration in both the design and administration of the reward system.

In regard to wages, women often experience inequity in the workplace. From just after World War II until the 1980s, working women earned about 60 cents to every dollar their male counterparts earned. This gap narrowed in the 1990s to 74 cents on the dollar.[93] Frequently, the inequality is rationalized by the types of jobs women hold, such as nurse, school teacher, and domestic help. However, even when women move into more male-dominated jobs, their salaries do not always improve. For example, although more women are managers, they are not earning top salaries. Nationwide, 40 percent earn less than $500 a week, or $26,000 a year. Further, less than 10 percent of female managers earn gross annual wages of $52,000 to $78,000—a salary that one might assume a middle- to upper-level manager might make in the United States.[94] Although women have made gains in narrowing the gender pay gap during the last decade, pay inequity still exists.

Expectancy Theory

In *Work and Motivation*, Victor Vroom's expectancy theory suggests that employee behavior is a function of the outcomes that are received for the work and the value of those outcomes to the individual.[95] Essentially, the theory has three key concepts: (1) performance-outcome expectancy, (2) value (or attractiveness), and (3) effort-performance expectancy.

The performance-outcome expectancy simply means that an individual believes that every behavior is connected to an outcome, and different levels of that behavior may be connected to different levels of that outcome. The attractiveness of that outcome differs from one individual to the next. For some, the outcome may be a highly valued reward; for another, the same outcome may be perceived as a punishment. For example, the individual who is afraid of the water or is terrified to get in front of a group will not be motivated to work hard enough to "win" an ocean cruise or receive recognition as "Employee of the Month" at an organizationwide meeting. These outcomes are not attractive to that employee.

Last, individuals evaluate the effort-performance expectancy relationship. In essence, the employee asks whether or not he or she is capable of performing successfully at certain levels and then translates those perceptions into probabilities of success. He or she then chooses those behaviors that have the highest likelihood of success for obtaining valued outcomes.

When designing compensation systems using expectancy theory, employers must follow several guidelines.

1. Make a clear connection between performance and outcome.
2. Develop flexible reward systems that provide a variety of potentially attractive outcomes.
3. Determine what rewards are valued by employees.
4. Make sure that employees have the appropriate training and ability to perform the job successfully.

Reinforcement Theory

Reinforcement theories explain an individual's behavior as a response to a stimulus in the environment. Edward Thorndike's law of effect is the basis for many contemporary models of reinforcement and explains how a person's own actions in a situation interact with the environment to influence future reactions in that environment.[96] In essence, this law maintains that behavior that is positively reinforced (rewarded) tends to be repeated in that situation; behavior that is punished tends not to be repeated in similar situations. Rewards are positive reinforcers that strengthen the relationship between the situation and the behavior. They can be as subtle as a pat on the back or a smile or as obvious as a bonus or company car.

The important point, again, is that rewards that are connected to a behavior encourage that behavior to be repeated. As in expectancy theory, the manager must make sure that rewards are applied in a timely fashion so that employees (1) make the connection between behavior and outcome and (2) repeat the desired behavior in the future. Whether the behavior is short term or long term in focus and whether quality or quantity issues are relevant, management should understand the relationship between outcomes, their value to employees, and the impact that they have on employee behavior.

Management Guidelines

1. Designing a reward system that reinforces the organization's business strategy can make the organization more competitive, increase its effectiveness, and help management focus on both short-term and long-term goals.
2. The goals of the compensation system can include
   a. Attraction and retention of employees.
   b. Cost efficiency.
   c. Legal compliance.
   d. Equitable salaries for all employees.
   e. Motivation of employee performance.
3. An organization's external environment interacts with its internal environment to influence the choice of compensation systems.
4. Effective reward systems include both intrinsic rewards (those that result from the job itself) and extrinsic rewards (those that are provided by others in the organization) to increase employee motivation.
5. Pay-for-performance plans are becoming increasingly popular because of their ability to tie pay to individual employee or group performance.
6. Three critical factors involved in pay-for-performance plans include the ability to

    a. Tie pay to performance.

    b. Accurately measure performance.

    c. Provide appropriate incentives.

7. Individual incentive plans tend to encourage competition among workers; group plans are more likely to encourage cooperative efforts and teamwork.

8. Three motivation theories (equity, expectancy, and reinforcement theory) provide important insights into the role that rewards play in influencing employee behavior.

9. Internal and external equity, or perceived fairness, both in the design and implementation of the compensation system, increases employee acceptance of the system and lowers pay dissatisfaction.

10. All rewards are not relevant to all employees. Managers must identify what employees value and then try to match rewards with employees.

Questions for Review

1. What are the important external and internal environmental variables affecting compensation plans? Which are most important? Why?

2. In what way does the competition in the labor market affect the wages a company has to pay?

3. What is one important objective for a compensation system? Why?

4. Define the term *pay-level policy* and discuss the three types of policies. Under what conditions might a company select each strategy?

5. Do you agree or disagree with the following statement? Defend your answer: "Money is the most important tool that a manager has for motivating employees."

6. How does expectancy theory relate to employee compensation?

7. Why have pay-for-performance plans increased in popularity recently? What are some problems associated with them?

8. What is the difference between gain sharing and profit sharing?

9. Why would a manager choose to use an individual incentive plan rather than a group plan?

10. If you were to design a pay system for sales employees at a large men's clothing store, how would you set it up and why?

CASE

National Semiconductor's Hybrid Incentive Plan[97]

Moving to a team environment has many advantages. However, as National Semiconductor found, it also has some drawbacks. For example, if individuals are asked to work in teams, solve problems in teams, and think like a team player, why are they rewarded as individual contributors? The goal of a team environment is virtually undermined by the system set up to reward a team member's individual behavior.

To overcome this problem, National Semiconductor set out to redesign its incentive plan. Its goal was to develop a plan that rewarded performance that helped to reach operational goals. In other words, it aligned its strategic business plan with its incentive plan.

The first step in redesigning its incentive plan was to establish a companywide task force. The task force included 20 members from all levels in the organization as well as all pay grades (i.e., exempt, nonexempt, and managerial). The task force was charged with designing an incentive plan that would be perceived as fair companywide while being flexible enough to meet the unique needs of each business unit.

Task force subcommittees were formed. Each subcommittee had a specific area to research, including benchmarking, communication, fit and integration, assessment of readiness for incentives, and incentive plan design.

Benchmarking

The benchmarking subcommittee contacted 11 different companies to determine why their incentive plans were or were not working. From this research, they learned that many companies were struggling to make their plans work. Common problems included goals that were too complex to understand; goals that were in conflict among departments or areas; lack of input by the employees in the development of the incentive plan; lack of communication about the plan; incentives that were actually part of an individual's salary, not above and beyond it; and lack of support from top management.

To avoid making these same mistakes, the task force developed six guiding principles for the development of the incentive plan. These included (1) linking incentive plan goals with strategic business plans, (2) ensuring alignment between a business unit's goals and management's goals, (3) having goals that employees are easily able to understand, (4) making sure that the plan included monetarily quantifiable goals, (5) guaranteeing that the level of payout opportunity be appropriate for the degree of goal difficulty, and (6) involving employees in the design, goal-setting, implementation, and evaluation of the plan.

Communication

To avoid the problems other companies experienced when implementing an incentive system, the task force decided to communicate, up-front, that its goal was to develop corporate guidelines for incentive pay plans. It was determined that frequent communication would help to manage expectations of the employees and keep them informed as well. Monthly updates were provided via newsletters and videos.

Fit and Integration

It soon became apparent that the current performance appraisal process did not fit well with the team environment or the goal of the new incentive system. After gathering information from employees and managers through focus groups, one major change was implemented. Specifically, feedback on an individual's performance from peers and internal customers was integrated into the assessment system to better reflect the focus of the new team environment.

Assessment of Readiness

Within each business unit, a committee for readiness was appointed. This committee determined whether the business unit it represented was ready to implement the incentive program. These committees asked questions such as "Are management and supervisors supportive of the incentive pay plan changes?" and "Is there already an established team environment?" The outcomes from the answers they received have included the identification of valuable areas for the organizational improvements and action plans to implement those improvements.

Design of the System

The subcommittee assigned to design the incentive plan had the largest task. To accomplish it, members began by evaluating the two most frequently used team incentive plans: profit sharing and gain sharing. Recognizing that each had positive and negative elements, they decided that a combined plan would be the best. They proposed a plan that had the financial focus of profit-sharing plans and the operational focus of gain-sharing plans. Specifically, their incentive formula provided an increased amount of sharing with employees as the business unit performed better on both its profits and a few identified operational goals. Further, increased sharing was awarded for reaching more difficult goals.

Setting Goals

As the benchmarking group found, conflicting goals among groups, including other business units and management, can undermine the effectiveness of a team incentive system. Hence, to avoid this, goals were tied to the unit's preapproved annual business plan with gains defined as performance above the baseline goal set by the business plan. The task force came up with three levels of goal difficulty: baseline goals, challenging goals, and stretch goals. Baseline goals were defined as the easiest goals to achieve. That is, there was an 80 percent chance that the goal would be achieved. Challenging goals, which received a higher reward when met, were deemed to be achievable 50 percent of the time. Hence, these goals were challenging and achievable. The highest goal level was called a *stretch goal,* which was expected to be reached only 20 percent of the time. Significant breakthroughs would be needed to accomplish this goal level. The three-tiered goal levels system was applied to both the financial goals and operational goals.

Employee Involvement

To gain wider acceptance of the goals set, individual business units selected a design team that was charged with collecting the data needed to determine the financial and operational goals for the business unit. This type of employee involvement is crucial for the acceptance of the plan.

How Much Is Enough?

Once the goals were set, employees needed to know how much they could expect to receive if they reached each level of goal. A range of 3 to 10 percent of one's base salary seemed to be what other companies were paying, based on data collected. However, payment plans of this type were still based on individual salary levels and did not conform to the goals of the new system. Instead, National Semiconductor decided to base the pay on the business unit's total payroll. Specifically, 2 to 5 percent could be expected for reaching challenging goals; 4 to 10 percent could be expected for reaching stretch goals. The payment guidelines were set up to ensure that the payments received would be financially self-funded, would be perceived as fair given the level of goal achievement required, and would be large enough to be motivating.

Disbursing the Funds

The final issue that the task force grappled with was how the money should be paid. Payouts are commonly made in two ways: as a percentage of salary or as an equal-dollar amount. After a lengthy debate, it was agreed that the equal-dollar amount, although favoring the lower-paid individuals in the unit, was more in line with the overall team goal of the incentive system and was selected as the disbursement method.

This Is Only a Test

Instead of immediately implementing the new incentive system, several pilot tests were performed. These test cases had positive results, and several gain-sharing opportunities resulted. As long as the business strategies remain aligned with the performance goals, the plan has an excellent chance to succeed.

Questions for Discussion

1. The task force itself may have had competing goals. Where might this have happened?

2. How motivating do you think the stretch goals are? Why?

3. Discuss the payout percentages implemented. Do you see these figures as motivational? Why?

4. Describe some of the pros and cons for percentage-based and equal-dollar disbursement systems? Which method do you think should have been used? Why?

5. Do you think the incentive plan will increase or decrease competition between units? What type of impact would this change in competition have on the achievement of the company's overall goals?

Additional Readings

Aaron, Hugh. "Making Incentives Pay During a Recession." *The Wall Street Journal*, October 29, 1990, p. A14.

Balkin, David, and Luis Gomez-Mejia. "Matching Compensation and Organizational Strategies." *Strategic Management Journal* 11 (1990), pp. 153–169.

Belcher, David W., and Thomas J. Atchison. *Compensation Administration*. Englewood Cliffs, NJ: Prentice-Hall, 1987.

Bergmann, Thomas, Harvey Gunderson, D. Weil, and B. Baliga. "Rewards Tied to Long-Term Success." *HRMagazine*, May 1990, pp. 67–72.

Bunning, Richard. "Skill-Based Pay." *Personnel Administrator*, June 1989, pp. 65–70.

Commerce Clearing House. *Executive Compensation*. Chicago, IL: Commerce Clearing House, Inc., 1989.

Drazin, Robert, and Ellen R. Auster. "Wage Differences Between Men and Women: Performance Appraisal Ratings vs. Salary Allocation as Locus of Bias." *Human Resource Management* 26 (1987), pp. 157–168.

Ellig, B. "Pay Policies While Downsizing the Organization: A Systematic Approach." *Personnel* 60 (1983), pp. 26–35.

England, John. "Developing a Total Compensation Policy Statement." *Personnel*, May 1988, pp. 71–73.

Finkelstein, Sidney, and Donald Hambrick. "Chief Executive Compensation: A Synthesis and Reconciliation." *Strategic Management Journal* 9 (1988), pp. 543–558.

Foulkes, Fred. *Executive Compensation: A Strategic Guide for the 1990s.* Boston: Harvard Business School Press, 1990.

Gomez-Mejia, Luis. *Compensation and Benefits.* Washington, DC: BNA Books, 1989.

Gomez-Mejia, Luis, David Balkin, and George Milkovich. "Rethinking Rewards for Technical Employees." *Organizational Dynamics* 18 (1990), pp. 62–75.

Graham-Moore, Brian, and Timothy Ross. *Gainsharing Plans for Improving Performance.* Washington, DC: BNA Books, 1990.

Hufnagel, Ellen. "Developing Strategic Compensation Plans." *Human Resource Management* 26 (1987), pp. 93–108.

Kerr, Steven. "On the Folly of Rewarding A, While Hoping for B." *Academy of Management Journal* 18, December 1975, pp. 769–783.

Kerr, Steven, and John Slocum. "Managing Corporate Culture Through Reward Systems." *Academy of Management Executive* 1 (1987), pp. 99–108.

Kotlikoff, Laurence, and David Wise. *The Wage Carrot and the Pension Stick.* Kalamazoo, MI: W.E. Upjohn Institute, 1989.

Lawler, Edward. *Strategic Pay.* San Francisco: Jossey-Bass, 1990.

Leader, Laurie. *Wages and Hours: Law and Practice.* Albany, NY: Matthew Bender, 1990.

McCaffrey, Robert. *Employee Benefit Programs: A Total Compensation Perspective.* Boston: Kent Publishing, 1988.

Martin, James, and Thomas Heetderks. *Two-Tier Compensation Structures.* Kalamazoo, MI: W.E. Upjohn Institute, 1990.

Michael, Robert, Heidi Hartmann, and Brigid O'Farrell. *Pay Equity: Empirical Inquiries.* Washington DC: National Academic Press, 1989.

Ost, Edward. "Gain Sharing's Potential." *Personnel Administrator*, July 1989, pp. 92–96.

Patton, Thomas. *Fair Pay.* San Francisco: Jossey-Bass, 1988.

Rock, Milton, and Lance Berger. *The Compensation Handbook.* New York: McGraw-Hill, 1991.

Roth, William. *Work and Rewards: Redefining Our Work-Life Reality.* Westport, CT: Greenwood Press, 1989.

Schneier, G. "Implementing Performance Management and Recognition and Rewards (PMRR) Systems at the Strategic Level: A Line Management Driven Effort." *Human Resource Planning* 12 (1989), pp. 205–220.

Tomasko, R. "Focusing Company Reward Systems to Help Achieve Business Objectives." *Management Review* 71 (1982), pp. 8–18.

VonGlinow, Mary Ann. "Reward Strategies for Attracting, Evaluating, and Retraining Professionals." *Human Resource Management* 24 (1985), pp. 191–206.

Wallace, Marc, and Charles Fay. *Compensation Theory and Practice.* Boston: Kent Publishing, 1988.

Notes

[1] Jaclyn Fierman, "The Perilous New World of Fair Pay," *Fortune*, June 13, 1994, pp. 57–64.

[2] Christopher Knowlton, "11 Men's Million-Dollar Motivator," *Fortune*, April 1990, pp. 65–67.

[3] L. L. Cummings, "Compensation, Culture, and Motivation: A Systems Perspective," *Organizational Dynamics*, Winter 1984, pp. 33–34.

[4] W. H. Mobley, *Employee Turnover: Causes, Consequences, and Control* (Reading, MA: Addison-Wesley, 1982).

[5] Edward Lawler, *Pay and Organizational Development* (Reading, MA: Addison-Wesley, 1981).

[6] Edward Lawler, "The Strategic Design of Reward Systems," in C. J. Fombrun, N. Tichy, and M. Devanna, eds., *Strategic Human Resource Management* (New York: Wiley, 1984), pp. 127–147.

[7]Joshua Harris Prager, "For Cruise Workers, Life Is No 'Love Boat,'" *The Wall Street Journal*, July 3, 1997, pp. B1–B8.

[8]Joel Walters, "Employment Tax Issues," *HRMagazine*, April 1990, pp. 72–76.

[9]Jeffrey Tannenbaum and Udayan Gupta, "Timing of New Basic Wage Hurts Firms," *The Wall Street Journal*, April 9, 1991, p. B1.

[10]Robert W. Thompson, "Democrats Hail Study Citing Wage Hike Benefits," *HRNews*, September 1997, p. 6.

[11]Albert Karr, "Compromise on Minimum Wage Reached," *The Wall Street Journal*, November 1, 1989, p. A3.

[12]Carolyn Hirschman, "Paying Up," *HRMagazine*, July 2000, pp. 35–41.

[13]C. Conte, "U.S. Hard Hats and Managers Rank High in International Pay Comparisons," *The Wall Street Journal*, March 3, 1992, p. A1; and D. Lohse, "For Foreign Postings, the Accent Is on Frugality," *The Wall Street Journal*, June 23, 1995, p. C1.

[14]Stephanie Overman, "In Sync," *HRMagazine*, March 2000, pp. 86–92.

[15]C. James Novak, "Proceed with Caution When Paying Teams," *HRMagazine*, April 1997, pp. 73–78.

[16]Elaine McShulskis, "Teamwork Can Lead to Higher Wages," *HRMagazine*, July 1996, p. 16.

[17]Novak, "Proceed With Caution When Paying Teams," p. 74.

[18]Charlotte Garvey, "Goalsharing Scores," *HRMagazine*, April 2000, pp. 99–106.

[19]The group may include (1) all jobs in the company, (2) all jobs in a specific department(s), or (3) whatever combination of jobs that the company wishes to analyze.

[20]Mike Frost, "Technology Solutions," *HRMagazine*, April 1997, p. 34.

[21]Much of this discussion relies on D. Belcher and T. Atchison, *Compensation Administration*, 2nd ed. (Englewood Cliffs, NJ: Prentice-Hall, 1987); and G. Milkovich and J. Newman, *Compensation* (Homewood, IL: BP1/Irwin, 1990).

[22]Amanda Bennett, "When Money Is Tight, Bosses Scramble for Other Ways to Motivate the Troops," *The Wall Street Journal*, October 31, 1990, p. B1.

[23]Kenan S. Abosch, Dan Gilbert, and Susan M. Dempsey, "Broadbanding: Approaches of Two Organizations," *ACA Journal: Perspectives in Compensation and Benefits*, Spring 1994, pp. 46–53.

[24]Ibid.

[25]Arthur Berkeley, "Companies Drop Tiered Pay Systems," *HRMagazine*, August 1990, p. 69.

[26]Bennett, "When Money Is Tight."

[27]John Greenwald, "Workers: Risks and Rewards," *Time*, April 15, 1991, pp. 42–43; Shawn Tully, "Your Paycheck Gets Exciting," *Fortune*, November 1, 1993, pp. 83–98.

[28]Harris Collingwood, "Pay for Performance at American Airlines," *Business Week*, June 19, 1989, p. 41.

[29]William Power, "Wall Street Firms Link Analysts' Pay to Performance," *The Wall Street Journal*, September 19, 1989, p. B1.

[30]Amanda Bennett, "Paying Workers to Meet Goals Spreads, but Gauging Performance Proves Tough," *The Wall Street Journal*, September 10, 1991, pp. B11.

[31]Selwyn Feinstein, "Pay for Performance Means Redefining What's Right," *The Wall Street Journal*, February 20, 1991, p. A1.

[32]Jerry McAdams, "Performance-Based Reward Systems: Toward a Common-Fate Environment," *Personnel Journal*, June 1988, pp. 103–113.

[33]Selwyn Feinstein, "Pay for Performance Hangs Mostly on Boss's Subjective View," *The Wall Street Journal*, October 24, 1989, p. A1.

[34]Albert Karr, "Middle Managers Are Ignored in Accelerating Switch to Pay for Performance," *The Wall Street Journal*, January 9, 1990, p. A1.

[35]Selwyn Feinstein, "In Federal Government, Pay for Performance Doesn't Seem Very Effective," *The Wall Street Journal*, December 12, 1989, p. A1.

[36]Yumiko Ono and Marcus Brauchli, "Japan Cuts the Middle-Management Fat," *The Wall Street Journal*, August 8, 1989, p. B1.

[37]Stephenie Overman, "Compensation Responds to New Marketplace," *HRNews*, June 1990, p. 7.

[38]William Anders, "Hefty Bonuses for Hefty Gains," *The Wall Street Journal*, May 20, 1991, p. A18.

[39]Ron Suskind, "More Executives Get Pension Guarantees to Protect Against Takeovers, Failures," *The Wall Street Journal*, July 5, 1991, pp. B11; and Julia Flynn, "Continental Divide over Executive Pay," *Business Week*, July 3, 1995, pp. 40–41.

[40]Jim Bernstein, "Platinum Parachutes," *Working Woman*, May 1997, p. 20.

[41]Bruce Ovwall and Joann S. Liblin, "Plutocracy," *The Wall Street Journal*, February 24, 1997, pp. A1–A8; and Bruce Orwall, "Disney Holders Decry Payouts at Meeting," *The Wall Street Journal*, February 26, 1997, p. A3.

[42]Jennifer Reingold, "Executive Pay," *Business Week*, April 17, 2000, pp. 100–112.

[43]Ibid.

[44]Kevin Salwen, "Shareholder Proposals on Pay Must Be Aired, SEC to Tell 10 Firms," *The Wall Street Journal*, February 13, 1992, p. A1.

[45]Carol Hymowitz, "More Employees, Shareholders Demand That Sacrifices in Pay Begin at the Top," *The Wall Street Journal*, November 8, 1990, p. B11.

[46]Ira T. Kay, Gary M. Lawson, and Diane Lerner, "Executive Pay Under Attack," *HRMagazine*, June 1994, pp. 93–97.

[47]Jacqueline Mitchell, "Herman Miller Links Worker-CEO Pay," *The Wall Street Journal*, May 7, 1992, p. B1.

[48]Reingold, p. 110.

[49]Rich Jurgens, "Look Out Below," *Wall Street Journal*, April 6, 2000, p R3.

[50]Robert McGough, "EVA Pay Plans Aren't a Big Hit in the New Study," *The Wall Street Journal*, May 3, 2000, p. C1+.

[51]Michael Arndt, "Who Earned Their Keep and Who Didn't," *Business Week*, April 17, 2000, p. 103.

[52]See Edward Lawler, "Pay for Performance: A Strategic Analysis," in Luis R. Gomez-Mejia, ed., *Compensation and Benefits* (Washington, DC: Bureau of National Affairs Books, 1989), for a thorough discussion of the strategic implications of individual and group pay-for-performance plans.

[53]This section borrows from Milkovich and Newman, *Compensation*, and Gomez-Mejia, *Compensation and Benefits*.

[54]Christopher S. Miller, Steven J. Whitehead, and Elizabeth Clark-Morrison, "On-call Policies Help Avoid Overtime Pay," *HRMagazine*, July 1996, pp. 57–64.

[55]Paul Falcone, "Exempt vs. Nonexempt," *HRMagazine*, June 2000, pp. 207–214.

[56]Ira Kay, "Do Your Workers Really Merit a Raise?" *The Wall Street Journal*, March 26, 1990, p. A8.

[57]Ibid.

[58]Barry Wisdom, "Before Implementing a Merit System . . . ," *Personnel Administrator*, October 1989, pp. 46–50; and Bill Leonard, "New Ways to Pay Employees," *HRMagazine*, February 1994, pp. 61–62.

[59]Selwyn Feinstein, "Worker Incentives Proliferate," *The Wall Street Journal*, December 12, 1989, p. A1; and Shawn Tully, "Your Paycheck Gets Exciting," *Fortune*, November 1, 1993, pp. 83–98.

[60]Selwyn Feinstein, "Labor Letter," *The Wall Street Journal*, December 5, 1989, p. A1.

[61]Hugh Aaron, "Making Incentives Pay during a Recession," *The Wall Street Journal*, October 29, 1990, p. A4.

[62]Selwyn Feinstein, "Incentive Plans Keep Spreading Beyond Executive Suites. But Do They Work?" *The Wall Street Journal*, November 6, 1990, p. A1.

[63]Richard Bunning, "Skill-Based Pay," *Personnel Administrator*, June 1989, pp. 65–69.

[64]Selwyn Feinstein, "Labor Letter," *The Wall Street Journal*, March 12, 1991, p. A1.

[65]Judy Huret, "Paying for Team Results," *HRMagazine*, May 1991, pp. 39–41.

[66]Gary Florkowski, "Analyzing Group Incentive Plans," *HRMagazine*, January 1990, pp. 36–39.

[67]Edward Ost, "Gain Sharing's Potential," *Personnel Administrator*, July 1989, pp. 92–96.

[68]Florkowski, "Analyzing Group Incentive Plans," p. 37.

[69]John Dantico and Sandra Sipari, "Gainsharing: Consider a Plan for All Reasons," *HRNews*, February 1991, p. 12.

[70]Michael Shroeder, "Watching the Bottom Line Instead of the Clock," *Business Week*, November 7, 1988, p. 64.

[71]Pinhaus Schwinger, *Wage Incentive Systems* (New York: Halsted, 1975).

[72]R. Bullock and E. Lawler, "Gainsharing: A Few Questions and Fewer Answers," *Human Resource Management* 23, 1984, pp. 23–40.

[73]Roger Ricklets, "Whither the Payoff on Sales Commissions," *The Wall Street Journal*, March 6, 1990, p. B1.

[74]"Now Salespeople Really Must Sell for Their Supper," *Business Week*, July 31, 1989, p. 50.

[75]Several excellent articles and books provide details for designing sales compensation plans. For example, see Bruce Ellig, "Sales Compensation: A Systematic Approach," *Compensation Review*, 1982, pp. 21–45; and J. Barry and P. Henry, *Effective Sales Incentive Compensation* (New York: McGraw-Hill, 1981).

[76]Gomez-Mejia, *Compensation and Benefits*.

[77]Selwyn Feinstein, "Stay or No Pay," *The Wall Street Journal*, February 27, 1990, p. A1.

[78]Gomez-Mejia, *Compensation and Benefits*.

[79]Graef Crystal, "Incentive Pay That Doesn't Work," *Fortune*, August 28, 1989, pp. 101–104.

[80]Justin Fox, "Free Money," *Fortune*, July 7, 1997, pp. 52–62.

[81]Laura Jereski, "Found Money," *The Wall Street Journal*, May 13, 1997, pp. A1–A10.

[82]Susan Pulliam, "New Dot-Com Mantra: 'Just Pay Me in Cash, Please'," *The Wall Street Journal*, November 28, 2000, p. C1+.

[83]Susan J. Wells, "Stock Incentives vs. Wage Pressures: What Gives?" *HRNews*, September 2000, p. 9.

[84]Carlos Tejada, "Work Week," *Wall Street Journal*, November 21, 2000, p. A1.

[85]John McMillan, Ken Allen, and Robert Salwen, "Private Companies Offer Long-Term Incentives," *HRMagazine*, June 1991, pp. 63–66; and John McMilliam and Chris Young, "Sweetening the Compensation Package," *HRMagazine*, October 1990, pp. 36–39.

[86]Dawn Anfuso, "PepsiCo Shares Power and Stock with Workers," *Personnel Journal*, January 1995, p. 79.

[87]James White, "As ESOPs Become Victims of '90s Bankruptcies, Workers Are Watching Their Nest Eggs Vanish," *The Wall Street Journal*, January 25, 1991, p. C1.

[88]Jacob Schlesinger, "GM's New Compensation Plan Reflects General Trend Tying Pay to Performance," *The Wall Street Journal*, January 3, 1989, p. B1.

[89]Julie Solomon, "Hush Money," *The Wall Street Journal*, April 25, 1990, pp. R22–R24.

[90]"Most New Hires Start at the Low End," *HRNews*, April 1991, p. 2.

[91]For two classic articles regarding equity theory, see J. Stacey Adams, "Toward an Understanding of Inequity," *Journal of Abnormal and Social Psychology* 67, 1963, pp. 422–436; and George Homans, *Social Behavior: Its Elementary Forms* (New York: Harcourt Brace Jovanovich, 1961).

[92]Selwyn Feinstein, "Pay Satisfaction Runs High, Especially at Companies That Street Teamwork," *The Wall Street Journal*, October 9, 1990, p. A1.

[93]"The Shrinking Gender Wage Gap," *HRMagazine*, April 1997, p. 29.

[94]M. Mahar, "More Women are Calling the Shots, but They're Still Making Less than the Guys," *Working Woman*, June 1994, p. 18.

[95]Victor Vroom, *Work and Motivation* (New York: Wiley, 1964).

[96]Edward L. Thorndike, *Animal Intelligence* (New York: Macmillan, 1911), p. 244.

[97]Darlene O'Neill, "Blending the Best of Profit Sharing and Gainsharing," *HRMagazine*, March 1994, pp. 66–70.

12

Improving Productivity

Chapter Objectives

As a result of studying this chapter, you should be able to

1. Understand the concept of productivity.

2. Recognize ways to increase productivity through organizational restructuring.

3. Understand how to increase productivity through individuals.

4. Recognize ways to increase productivity through leadership.

5. Define *involvement* and explain the benefits of having an involved staff.

6. Be familiar with techniques available to help increase employee involvement.

A main goal of any organization is to be productive. Some organizations successfully reach this goal, whereas others fail. Although each successful organization follows a different formula, some common productivity principles are found in all successful organizations, such as training and development, companywide communication, and trust in employees. These and other productivity principles are examined in this chapter.

CASE

Motivating Motorola[1]

In recent years, U.S. managers have taken a closer look at the effectiveness of Japanese management and have questioned why workers in the United States seem to lack motivation and why U.S. productivity has declined. What is it about Japanese management style that motivates Japanese workers and increases productivity? In short, corporate America continues to struggle with how to motivate workers.

Motorola—A Leader

Motorola, one of the world's leading high-tech companies, set out to resolve the motivation problem with its workers. Rather than merely mimic Japanese management style, Motorola adopted a strategic approach that adds a U.S. twist to the Japanese style. Although Motorola has embraced such Japanese tactics as driving relentlessly for market share, sharply upgrading quality, and constantly honing manufacturing processes to pare costs, it has exploited "Yankee know-how" in areas where Japanese companies have been notoriously weak, such as marketing and software development. "U.S.-style" Japanese management has put Motorola in the driver's seat in telecommunications. Worldwide, Motorola is recognized as a leader in productivity.

Strategic Approach

Robert W. Galvin, the son of the founder of Motorola, engaged in a top-to-bottom overhaul of Motorola's market share both at home and abroad. Motorola has committed itself to a more participative management style and prepares its workers to participate *effectively* by emphasizing education and training for all employees. The company has also emphasized research and development, high quality and low cost, and interdepartmental collaboration.

Education and Training

To instill the workforce with the new corporate goals, Motorola launched a massive education drive for all employees, both workers and managers. The company spends more than $100 million a year on educating its employees by offering courses in global competitiveness and risk taking, for example. The courses also teach workers practical skills in statistical process control and ways of reducing product cycle times. Training programs help workers to develop new skills and problem-solving techniques. Motorola offers executive programs to discuss real-world topics and problems that do not necessarily have clear-cut answers. Such programs enable managers to deal more effectively with a changing environment. Finally, Motorola has instituted a leadership development program for new vice-presidents. These new executives are able to learn and practice essential leadership and innovation skills through intensive seminars.

By investing in training and development, Motorola is helping its employees to gain confidence in their ability to participate effectively in the decision-making process. Like Motorola, other leading corporations have incorporated case studies into their training and development programs that utilize their own real-life strategic and business issues. Thus participants in the programs are gaining more practical and applicable experience from which to draw on in the future.

Collaboration

In an effort to create unified team spirit, Motorola is tearing down the traditional walls that isolate various departments, such as design, manufacturing, and marketing. Motorola is attempting to establish a new tradition of collaboration among disciplines. Representatives from each discipline are now encouraged to get involved in new projects from the start. New-product venture teams composed of five or six employees from different departments are formed to discuss and develop new product ideas, and interdepartmental functional teams rally to ensure that new ideas are successfully developed.

As can be seen in the Motorola case, the company has chosen to break away from the traditional "American way" of doing business. The change in Motorola's attitude toward spending money on programs whose benefits are not immediate is a nontraditional strategic approach. Money spent on training and education is viewed as more of an investment than a cost. Motorola has realized that an investment in its workforce ensures the company a greater sense of enthusiasm and commitment among its employees. This point of view is distinct from other business strategies; it notes the way that employment policies and practices create resources and competencies that achieve competitive advantages. Human resource professionals are a key ingredient in developing firm-specific, valuable resources that affect long-term profits earned by the firm.[2] However, there are other possible strategic choices businesses can make. Some of these choices are outlined in the next section.

Strategic Choices for Productivity

Choosing to include employee involvement in the management of the organization as a means of increasing productivity is a strategic decision in itself. Included in this decision, however, are several other considerations:

1. Top management must decide how much faith it has in its employees. Should managers simply ask for input about how to improve the organization, or should they instill in their employees the power necessary to implement these changes? The level of involvement that employees are allowed in an organization is a strategic choice that upper-level management must make, and it ultimately will be based on how much trust management has in its employees.

2. To enable a staff to be productive, the organization must provide the tools needed to perform effectively. These tools can take on a variety of forms, such as education, equipment, or information. Whatever form they take, providing

of these tools is expensive. Managers must make a strategic choice concerning how much the firm is willing to invest in equipping the employees.

3. Another strategic choice that managers must make is whether or not the organization's culture is supportive of an involved work environment. Because it is difficult to change or adapt an organization's culture, top management must be behind a decision of this nature. Opening up lines of communication and sharing responsibility and power with subordinates may be difficult for some managers to do. However, if the managers see their bosses openly communicating and sharing responsibilities, they may be more open to trying these techniques with their subordinates, too.

What is Productivity?

In simple terms, productivity can be defined as output per hour.[3] But this is far too simple. Productivity comes in various forms. For example, some define productivity as the change in unit labor costs, or how much each item costs to produce. Others suggest that productivity is the value of production over paid hours. This ratio determines profitability as well as productivity. Whichever way productivity is defined, it is used to determine whether the firm has been successful.

Defining productivity in service organizations is not easy. Although output per hour could be measured by the number of customers serviced, other factors come into play. Two of the recurring factors are quality and service.[4] In practice, the goal of most service organizations is to provide the fastest, most efficient, and friendliest service possible to any and all customers. In terms of productivity, this may mean that minimizing errors or eliminating reworking is stressed. Or it may mean that smiling and offering to go the extra mile for a customer is stressed. In any case, the idea is to make the service industry more productive by having better serviced customers.

Measuring Productivity

The techniques for measuring productivity are as varied as the industries in which the measurements are taking place. Traditional techniques were developed to measure assembly-line productivity. These measures are based on tracking output in units or dollars per inputs, usually in the form of human hours spent working on the relevant tasks. These figures are still used in many production-oriented firms today.[5] But what do these figures actually mean? Researchers at MIT suggest that each worker can be viewed in terms of his or her "value added." In the car plants in Japan, it is difficult to find any worker who cannot be defined as adding value. However, in the European plants, these researchers found that many people add no value, but instead correct mistakes that never should have been made in the first place.[6]

In the service and professional areas, traditional productivity measures have fallen. It is difficult, if not impossible, to measure some types of activities with respect to output per input. When the traditional measures are used in nonproduction areas, great productivity numbers may not result in good outcomes. One example of this was found at Motorola. Recruiters for Motorola were assigned the goal of spending less per hire each year as a measure of productivity. Each year productivity rose. Things should have been good, but they were not. The quality of the new hires began to decrease. Obviously, if you spend only a few dollars to select employees, the new hires selected may not be qualified or effective workers. By cutting costs in this way, the thoroughness of the screening process will deteriorate. To solve this problem, Motorola changed its policy. It now measures recruitment productivity by how well its recruits do at Motorola after being hired. For example, recruiters are measured on items such as how well qualified the person was for the job and whether the salary was determined correctly by whether the new hire leaves soon after employment for a higher paying job. Under the new productivity measures, price per recruit has risen, but so has the quality of the recruits.[7]

Other industries also have developed unique ways to measure productivity in nonproduction areas. In the hotel business, it is almost impossible to stay overnight in a hotel or motel and not see some type of customer response card asking for a rating of it at some point in a stay. Many of the large chains ask guests upon checkout whether they completed a response card. Other chains leave them in rooms, and many are personalized with the name of the person who cleaned the room that day. In addition to customer input, Quality Inns tracks the number of minutes it takes to clean a room, how many meals are served in an hour, and how frequently a booking agent can turn a call into a reservation.[8]

Whatever method is used, it is important that the results are used to do what they are intended to do—improve productivity. After realizing that other productivity measures, besides the recruitment area, were causing problems down the line, Motorola revamped its entire productivity measurement scheme. Motorola now defines productivity in terms of the opportunity to make mistakes. Most mistakes made are not made because of poor quality of employees but because of the way people are told to do their job. Over the years, procedures and policies have become antiquated, complicated, and redundant. Managers at Motorola strive to locate poor procedures and replace them with more efficient ones. This new perspective has saved Motorola both time and money.[9]

Ways to Increase Productivity

Increasing organizational productivity can be initiated from the organizational level, the individual level, and the group level. The following sections examine how to increase organizational productivity through restructuring, individual approaches, and leadership. Employee involvement and total quality management are discussed later but also relate to increasing productivity.

Organizational Restructuring

Many firms have tried to become more productive through organizational restructuring.[10] Organizational restructuring can take on a variety of forms: downsizing, mergers and acquisitions, joint ventures, and globalization. We will look at each of these in turn.

Downsizing   Companies that faced a decrease in sales, market share, or profits in the 1980s and early 1990s began to realize that their human resources were expensive and underutilized. To be more competitive, companies made a strategic decision to gradually lower their payroll numbers. The first step was to use attrition. By not replacing employees who retired or quit, substantial gains were made with respect to overall costs. Employees who were asked to take on the work done by others at first were disgruntled but accepted the change after realizing that it was helping them keep their jobs.

However, as the economy began to degrade, older workers began to postpone retirement indefinitely once mandatory retirement was abolished. Some realized that the pension they would receive would not be enough to support them in the manner in which they were accustomed with the current economy; others decided they were not ready to face the golf course on a daily basis. Similarly, voluntary turnover decreased as well. The poor job market, fueled by the weak economy, made any job better than the unemployment line. Attrition was no longer a suitable tool for **downsizing** the workforce.

downsizing
Reducing the size of the workforce.

The next step was budget cutting. In this stage, managers were given mandates to decrease their budgets anywhere from 5 to 50 percent. The easiest way to do this was to reduce the size of the workforce. Often automation could be introduced to make a job that once took as many as a dozen people to complete manageable by only one or two. The other ten employees were dismissed. Another technique was to reduce the number of people all performing the same job by doubling the work load for half of them and dismissing the other half. Creative ways to cut staff were the focus of most managers during this time. The person with the ax became a very unfriendly sight, even after the cuts were completed. Morale dipped extremely low, even for the survivors. It was difficult for the manager who rearranged the workforce to lead it again after the dust settled.

Some companies fought to keep the morale of the firm up during even the worst times. Firms that communicated the changes early and provided the employees who were to be released with the opportunity to retrain or develop new skills before termination increased the morale for both the leavers and stayers. In addition, the survivors who were asked to take on more responsibility and work were asked what they needed to make their jobs easier. Training, equipment, and more control were provided as a means of keeping the remaining workers satisfied.[11] However, the quality of the product or service often takes a beating because of downsizing.

Downsizing and budget cutting are only reactions to the problem. They cannot even be considered strategies.[12] These techniques may have helped to save several large companies, such as Caterpillar and Ford Motor Company, but they do not provide a lasting solution to the problem. Human resource professionals should be aware that the negative effects of downsizing are felt not only by those who leave but also by those who stay. Significant adjustments must be made by workers, especially older workers, who may have believed that they would be employed for life. Some firms have found that acquiring or merging with another company may be a more long-term strategic approach to increase productivity.

mergers and acquisitions
The union of two or more corporate interests or organizations.

Mergers and Acquisitions **Mergers and acquisitions** are the union of two or more corporations. Although the financial value of these deals is easily calculated, the human value is unclear. Often in mergers and acquisitions, the human resource division is completely left out of the picture. Likewise, the people who are being acquired are frequently given scant attention. In a survey, only 37 percent of the acquirers indicated that they audited the management and personnel prior to buying the firm. Further, the majority of these audits were to examine human resource policies that may limit the buyers' freedom to act, not to examine the personnel themselves.[13]

As mergers and acquisitions become increasingly common, it is important for human resource managers to become involved in the acquisition or merger process early on. To do this successfully, we suggest the following:

1. Get to know the members of the acquisition/merger team. If they speak a different language, either literally or figuratively, learn it. They will be more open to your human resource concerns if you are more aware of theirs.

2. Bring something with you. Show them that you have training programs that could be beneficial to both sides of the merger. Explain how you can help to merge the two cultures. Show them that you are willing to help in any way.
3. Be realistic about what information they will provide you and how much interest they will have in your offers.
4. Be timely. Show them that you are willing to work under their time frame.
5. Maintain a balanced viewpoint. Try not to get bogged down in trivial issues but continue to focus on the bigger picture.[14]

Other issues that human resource managers should be aware of during a merger or acquisition include the fact that personnel uncertainty will be extremely high. The only way to manage this is through accurate and frequent communication about the process. As employees try to manage the uncertainty in their lives, they will flip-flop continually between supporting the change and hating it. Realizing that this behavior is common can help to avoid confusion for human resource managers. Employees will go through culture shock as the two cultures collide, and they will tend to pull out their support and patience if they anticipate more changes to the culture than they can handle. Communication, again, is one way to avoid this problem.[15] Finally, it is important to note that not all mergers and acquisitions will be positive events. Research has shown that about 50 percent of the acquisitions examined were clear failures.[16] Many of these ventures failed because the acquirers did not realize the effectiveness of the current management and structure of the acquired firm, and they altered it on arrival. Inevitably, the acquired staff was demoted or misplaced and eventually turned over. Ironically, the reason the acquirers wanted the acquired firm in the first place—the management team—may have vanished.[17]

joint venture
Method of implementing a growth strategy in which two or more companies join forces for a common purpose.

Joint Ventures **Joint ventures** are another way in which organizations can become more productive. By using the strongest skills of each partner in the joint venture, the outcomes can be better than they would have been with each side working alone. Whenever two parties join forces, they both have a stake in the claim, and what is good for one side may not necessarily be good for the other. GM faced that dilemma when Toyota asked if it could build Toyota trucks in the United States. There were large and certain payoffs for Toyota if GM said yes. If Toyota could build trucks in the United States, it could avoid the 25 percent tariff placed on imported trucks. The payoffs for GM were not so clear. Certainly, the profits at the plant would increase, which would be good for GM. However, GM still competed with Toyota in the marketplace, and allowing Toyota to have an even less expensive truck available to the U.S. consumers was not good business for GM. Thus joint ventures should have clear payoffs for both parties.[18]

Globalization The term *globalization* raises many questions in the minds of U.S. business people. What exactly is globalization? Does it mean that a certain percent of sales, say 25 percent, must take place overseas? Does it mean that top management must have experience in a variety of countries? Or is it more of a global perspective, in which top officials scan the entire world before making decisions?[19] Globalization is all of this and more.

Globalization requires having global standards for quality, pricing, service, and design.[20] For instance, if a firm manufactures products for the European market, or if it sells machinery, electronics, food products, pharmaceuticals, or other goods in

Mercedes in Alabama

Rural Vance, Alabama, with a population of about 400, is about the last place you would expect to find a Mercedes factory. But the German automaker began production on a new M-class sport-utility vehicle, priced around $35,000, at the Vance plant last year.

Mercedes had some solid reasons for setting up a plant in the United States. For example, labor costs in Germany are about 50 percent higher than in a small Southern town in the United States. The Vance plant also gives the company an insider's view to the American market and functions as a test for future foreign manufacturing ventures.

Andreas Renschler, CEO of the Alabama factory, set out to create a new corporate culture that was separate from headquarters. Starting in 1993, he deliberately pieced together the management's top tier: a balanced team, consisting of four Germans and four Americans. Renschler hoped that these executives would provide guidance on how a foreign automaker might best go about setting up a factory in the United States.

Regarding workers, Mercedes learned that it did not matter all that much that the workforce in Alabama was so different from that in Stuttgart. The key was to find individuals who could be trained. Ultimately, the automaker looks for people who can get along with others and follow directions. In addition, the company ensures that all factory-floor jobs are done in accordance with standard methods and procedures (SMPs). The SMPs are designed by German engineers and posted at workstations for easy reference by American employees. In fact, the American line workers need permission to make the slightest change in their methods. For the average American, this management style takes some getting used to. Despite the cultural differences between Germans and Americans, the Vance factory has proved to be a success. The design of the plant has proved especially efficient. The automaker has clearly gained valuable experience in how to set up and operate a plant in a foreign country.

SOURCE: Adapted from J. Martin, "Mercedes: Made in Alabama," *Fortune*, July 7, 1997, pp. 150–158.

Europe, it will soon need to address the ISO 9000 quality program, which is a blueprint for international standards of manufacturing excellence.[21] Ford's Escort was one of the first U.S. products to be built on a global scale. But globalization takes more than just setting and adhering to standards; it also requires global leadership.

Globalization is definitely a strategic business decision, one that can and will be made by more and more companies as entry into other areas of the world becomes increasingly easier. What does it mean to the human resource department if an organization decides to go global? The ramifications seem endless. For one thing, training will be affected. Not only will it be important to train American employees who plan to go overseas in the language of the country in which they will be placed, but also it will be just as important to inform them of the culture of the country. Being literate in both word and deed will make the transition easier and more positive. What are the training needs of overseas employees coming to the United States to work? The organizational culture and jargon must be taught to the new employees in a way that they will understand but that is not demeaning. Further, socialization programs must be in place to ensure a smooth transition for these new employees.

Aside from training issues, human resource professionals will face many other problems. What performance appraisals, reward programs, and compensation are needed? Many of these functions have been so Americanized that they will not be effective with foreign workers. In Japan, telling one worker that she or he is doing better than the rest and rewarding that worker for doing so is not appropriate. Japanese workers want to fit in and be like the rest. They do not want to be recognized. Recognizing one worker in a group may cause work group problems, resulting in the need for conflict resolution techniques. Would it be wise to use the American models such as confronting one another and working out the problem? Probably not. This is not appropriate behavior in many foreign cultures. What about wages? Do you pay these new workers what their counterparts in the country from which they came would make, or do you pay them American wages? What if they are transferred back? Do they go back to their home country's pay base? The list of problems goes on and on. Suffice it to say that globalization will have a significant impact on the human resource function of any organization that selects a globalization strategy.

Individual Approach

Two major components influence whether or not an employee is productive: ability and attitude. Ability is simply whether or not the person is able to perform the job. It is influenced by whether the person has the training, education, skills, and tools and works in an environment necessary to perform the job. Attitude, on the other hand, refers to whether the person *wants* to perform the job. Attitude is influenced by the employee's level of motivation as well as satisfaction with and commitment to the job to be performed. Organizations have a great deal of control over both of these areas. Organizations that provide well-developed training and development programs, educational reimbursement plans, and state-of-the-art equipment can expect employees with extremely high ability. Likewise, organizations with strong personnel policies with respect to compensation, rewards, promotions, and career development usually have employees with positive attitudes toward their job and the company. The following sections examine more closely the options organizations have with respect to increasing employees' abilities and positive attitudes.

Ability   To have employees who are able to perform their jobs effectively, organizations must hire people with the knowledge, skills, and abilities needed to perform the job or must provide training that will develop these qualities. They must also be sure to provide a work environment that is conducive to performing well. This means that the tools and equipment that employees must have to succeed are provided. Furthermore, the organization's environment or culture also must be designed to promote high-quality performance. To achieve these goals, many organizations use a variety of techniques. Let's look first at training, development, and education of the workforce.

The type of training and development required by lower- and higher-level employees differs. At the lower level, employees generally are provided with specific training designed to make them immediately more productive on the job. Higher-level employees receive this type of training, but they also receive more developmental types of training. Developmental training is designed to help employees now, as well as in the future, by readying them for assignments with more and more responsibility. However, it has become more and more obvious that firms that have a large number of lower-level employees, such as the hospitality and fast-food industries, may need to begin developing them as well as training them.

In the past, employees in the fast-food and hospitality industries were treated in the same manner that equipment was treated. They were replaceable. The jobs were designed to be "idiot-proof" so that they could be performed by any person who walked in off the street. However, because of the demographic changes in the marketplace, the increasing costs of turnover, and the ever-increasing demand for quality service, this is no longer feasible. Organizations are quickly realizing that the management techniques used in the higher levels may be applicable at the lower levels as well.[22]

Workers are increasingly taking responsibility to ensure they are well trained. Unfortunately, there is a common perception that their initiative is not recognized by their supervisors. Interestingly, according to a survey by Towers Perrin, a management consulting firm, 94 percent of the respondents consider it their responsibility to remain current in their job skills. A positive finding from this survey was that approximately 75 percent said they were satisfied with their jobs, which is up from 58 percent in 1995.[23]

Attitude   Employee attitudes have a crucial effect on any firm's bottom line. An employee's attitude determines whether a defective part is placed into a product, whether the customer continues to patronize the firm, and whether the firm is productive. Employees who are burned out, turned off, cynical, demoralized, or any combination of these fail to buy into the spirit of the firm. And their bad attitudes are infectious.

Research has found that when cynical employees distrust their bosses, it is reflected in their work. Cynical employees are less productive, less efficient, and less willing to accept change. The problem lies not only with the worker, however. Cynical bosses who treat employees without dignity are also to blame.

Companies that have realized the impact that employee cynicism and other negative attitudes have on the bottom line have taken steps to combat it. Nancy Austin, a management consultant, argues for several ways to combat poor attitudes. First, let employees know they matter and that they are important. Second, keep vital information flowing freely. This gives the employee a sense of control about how things are going. Third, give employees a stake or ownership in the company (e.g., company stock). Finally, lighten it up. Humor is an excellent way to combat poor attitudes.[24]

Kodak established a humor task force that was charged with building a humor room at corporate headquarters when it was decided that the company needed to lighten up. It seems to be working. When Kodak's downsizing announcement coincided with the release of the movie *Honey, I Shrunk the Kids*, ingenious Kodak employees circulated a spoof memo entitled "Honey, I Shrunk the Company." Humor can also be big business. Consulting firms that specialize in humor have been doing a brisk business by teaching firms to give up the old notion that humor is dependent on putting someone else down. Instead, the focus is on teaching the firm to laugh at itself.[25] Exhibit 12.1 outlines some helpful hints for how one can go about having fun at work.

What does this all mean? Why should human resource professionals be concerned with employee attitudes? One clue can be taken from a survey of Baldrige award winners.[26] They suggest that effective human resource policies can significantly influence the attitudes of workers toward their companies. These positive attitudes often translate to less absenteeism and turnover, greater satisfaction and commitment, and, ultimately, more productivity in the workplace for companies that successfully motivate their employees. The previous examples show some of the ways human resource managers are contributing to increased productivity and, in some ways, not only reinforce business strategy but also create new strategies to gain competitive advantage.[27]

As previously mentioned, no one technique improves employees' attitudes across the board. Instead, a combination of motivational tools should be used. Also, it is

---

EXHIBIT 12.1   HOW TO START HAVING FUN AT WORK

---

1. Get to know your people. Then you'll understand what will be fun for them.

2. Acknowledge people's help. Write someone a personal letter of thanks for exceptional work performance. Then go by and shake his or her hand.

3. Think of someone you really respect but who may not know it. Tell the person.

4. Make a joke about yourself. Tell someone one of the most embarrassing things that ever happened to you.

5. Pull a practical joke on someone who can take it.

6. Send someone a gift when he or she has done something exceptional for you or your organization.

7. Pick one or two people to "grow." Make them your special projects and help them in any way you can. (You do not need to tell them you are doing this.)

8. Create a social committee to organize events. Get actively involved in this committee.

9. Tell everyone coming to your next meeting to bring their best joke or work-related story with them to tell everyone at the meeting. (If you want, you could judge the best one and give the person a prize.)

10. Try this for a prize: When someone does a particularly great job of something, do his or her job for a day.

11. Throw a party for the people you work with, or throw a party for your customers and clients.

12. Get everyone involved in skits they make up about their strengths and their weaknesses at work.

13. Ask a customer, coworker, or supervisor to help you learn something new.

14. Make a list of three things you will do tomorrow to make your work more fun. Do them.

15. Start a new contest at work that is tied to people's performance. You could even create a contest just for yourself. If you are successful at meeting your goal, do something special for yourself.

SOURCE: D. Abramis, "Fun at Work," *Personnel Administrator*, November 1989, p. 63; N. Austin, "When Companies Get the Blues," *Working Woman*, October, 1996, pp. 21–23.

important to remember that the tools must be consistent with the corporation's culture for them to be effective. Exhibit 12.2 outlines a list of suggestions for human resource managers who are trying to find out what it takes to motivate employees to be productive.

Leadership and Productivity

An area's productivity, or lack thereof, can frequently be traced to the leaders provided to that area. In a study of 12 major companies, workers believed that they and the people with whom they worked were committed to providing a quality product. The problem in doing this, they reported, arose at the management level, specifically top management. Two thirds of the workers surveyed indicated that quality of the work completed was not an important measure of performance in their organization. This belief was frequently supported by top managers who verbally stressed the importance of quality workmanship but offered incentives based only on the number of units produced.[28]

One of the first people to even discuss the idea of enhancing quality productivity through leadership was the statistician Dr. W. Edwards Deming. Although he was

EXHIBIT 12.2	MOTIVATION TIPS FOR HUMAN RESOURCE MANAGERS

1. Select the best. Motivation comes from within an individual. Therefore, if you hire only the people who have the potential to be motivated, half of the battle is won.

2. Use the Pygmalion effect. If you truly believe in your employees, they will believe in themselves. Take the time to psychologically invest in your employees.

3. Track success. Provide challenging goals with which employees agree and compare their performance regularly to these goals. Make sure to do this in a manner that is not critical or demeaning.

4. Recognize contributions. Provide public recognition for employees who have performed well. Be sure to be consistent about when the rewards are provided. For example, select an employee of the week and announce his or her name at a weekly meeting.

5. Provide incentives and rewards. Remember that the psychological reward of the incentive is often greater than the monetary reward. Also, incentives can be a useful motivator in the short term.

6. Empower employees. Make employees responsible for the company's product or service. Listen to what they have to say and use their ideas.

7. Enhance career development. Use training and development as a tool to ready employees for the next step in their career paths. Invest in your employees just as you would invest in new equipment.

SOURCE: Adapted from K. Dawson and S. Dawson, "How to Motivate Your Employees," *HRMagazine*, April 1990, pp. 78–80; B. Azar, "Corporations Seek Help Fitting Goals Together," *APA Monitor*, July, 1997, pp. 14–15.

virtually given saint status in Japan, Deming's philosophy, which helped to rebuild Japan after World War II, was virtually ignored in the United States. He died in December 1993 at the age of 93, but his ideas will continue to have an impact on U.S. firms as they strive to become more productive in the twenty-first century.[29] A tireless teacher, Deming was concerned with whether management's interest in quality was deep enough to ensure lasting improvement. Deming's management philosophy is stated in the form of 14 principles. These principles are listed in Exhibit 12.3. As you read them, notice how closely they reflect the ideas currently being accepted and used in U.S. firms.

One of Deming's suggestions was to change the management style that has been used in U.S. business for decades. This is a very difficult task. For managers to support quality production, they must abandon many of the techniques they have used for years in favor of more open and sharing techniques. Delegating the power, prestige, and control that took managers years to build is a bitter pill to swallow, even if it is for the good of the company. However, some managers have been able to mold their leadership styles successfully to promote the new quality-minded workplace. Let's examine a few of these cases.

Success Stories   Xerox Corporation, which won the prestigious Malcolm Baldrige National Quality Award that is explained in Exhibit 12.4, has found a way to remold the corporate culture to one that supports and emphasizes quality. The focus at Xerox is on the individual. If each person who works for Xerox becomes a quality advocate and is extremely knowledgeable about the techniques used to perform his or

| EXHIBIT 12.3 | DEMING'S 14 PRINCIPLES FOR MANAGERS |

1. Create constancy of purpose toward improvement of product and service with the aim to become competitive, to stay in business, and to provide jobs.

2. Adopt a new philosophy. We are in a new economic age created by Japan. We can no longer live with commonly accepted styles of U.S. management, nor with commonly accepted levels of delays, mistakes, or defective products.

3. Cease dependence on inspection to achieve quality. Eliminate the need for inspection on a mass basis by building quality into the product in the first place.

4. End the practice of awarding business on the basis of the price tag. Instead, minimize the total cost.

5. Improve constantly and forever the system of production and service to improve quality and productivity and thus constantly decrease costs.

6. Institute training on the job.

7. Institute supervision. The aim of supervision should be to help people, machines, and gadgets do a better job. Supervision of management is in need of overhaul, as well as supervision of production workers.

8. Drive out fear so that everyone may work effectively for the company.

9. Break down the barriers between departments. People in research, design, sales, and production must work as a team to foresee problems of production.

10. Eliminate slogans, exhortations, and targets for the workforce that ask for zero defects and new levels of productivity. Such exhortations create only adversarial relationships. The bulk of the causes of low productivity belong to the system and thus lie beyond the power of the workforce.

11. Eliminate work standards that prescribe numerical quotas for the day. Substitute aids and helpful supervision.

12. Remove the barriers that rob the hourly worker of his or her right to pride of workmanship. The responsibility of supervisors must be changed from sheer numbers to quality. Remove the barriers that rob people in management and engineering of their right to pride of workmanship. This means abolish the annual rating, or merit rating, and management by objective.

13. Institute a vigorous program of education and retraining.

14. Put everyone in the company to work to accomplish the transformation.

SOURCE: Adapted from *Out of the Crisis* by W. Edwards Deming by permission of MIT and The W. Edwards Deming Institute. Published by MIT, Center for Advanced Educational Services, Cambridge, MA 02139. Copyright 1986 by The W. Edwards Deming Institute.

her job, the result is a quality product. To achieve this goal, Xerox developed a "Leadership through Quality" program that focuses on skills training, customer satisfaction, strong union support, and community involvement. By making each employee responsible for the company's success, providing the skills and tools necessary to perform the job, and reinforcing the goals, Xerox has reached its goal of creating a total quality organization.[30]

Another successfully managed company is McDonald's. The founder, Ray Kroc, purchased the franchise rights from Dick and Mac McDonald, who ran a small fast-food take-out kitchen in San Bernardino, California. He realized that the formula they used—quick, good food at reasonable prices—was worth his investment, and he knew that the brothers had no intention of expanding. Kroc, who died in 1981 at age

Exactly Who Is W. Edwards Deming?

William Edwards Deming was born on October 14, 1900. After growing up in Iowa and Wyoming, he obtained his first degree in electrical engineering in 1921 from the University of Wyoming. He continued his education at the University of Colorado, earning a master's degree in mathematics and physics, and he received his Ph.D. from Yale in mathematical physics in 1928. He began working for the U.S. Department of Agriculture, where considerable attention was being placed on statistical experimental design. Deming enjoyed this work and wanted to continue it. To do this, he moved to London to study under the "father of statistics," Sir Ronald Fisher.

During summer jobs while in school, Deming had learned of the work of Walter Shewhart. Shewhart focused on the statistical control of processes and charting these controls. He believed that there were two variables in the output process: controlled and uncontrolled. While Shewhart focused his attention on improving production processes, Deming realized that these ideas were applicable to all aspects of business. He proved his assumption was correct by applying the concepts to the administrative processes used to prepare the 1940 census, on which he worked.

After this success, he began to teach people involved with the war effort about his 14 principles of quality management. Although they listened and implemented some, they never internalized his ideas. After the war, businesses were not interested in becoming more efficient because the United States was the only country producing anything. There was virtually no competition.

General Douglas MacArthur asked Deming to join him on two trips to Japan to help advise the Japanese in how to reconstruct their country. The contacts he made while on these trips made Deming famous in Japan. He gave the same speech to Japanese managers that he had given to U.S. managers, but the Japanese listened and implemented his 14 principles. His teachings helped Japan become what it is today.

Deming was "introduced" to the United States in a 1980 documentary called "If Japan Can, Why Can't We?" produced by Clare Crawford-Mason. She interviewed Deming and marveled at the fact that he was living only minutes from the White House, yet *no one* would listen to his remedy for the stagnation in U.S. business. However, after her story aired, Americans began to listen. Deming traveled throughout the United States, giving his seminars to U.S. managers, and some even began to implement his ideas. Two of the most well-known converts are Nashua and Ford. Both of these companies have benefited greatly from Deming's advice.

SOURCE: Adapted from Henry Neave, *The Deming Dimension* (Knoxville: SPC Press, 1990).

84, has been described as short tempered, politically conservative, tireless, perpetually optimistic, and a fanatic for cleanliness. He motivated workers through maxims that continue to adorn bulletin boards in today's McDonald's. Some of the all-time favorites include "Free enterprise will work if you will" and "If you've got time to lean, you've got time to clean."[31]

Sam Walton, or Mr. Sam as he was known by his employees, was another interesting success case. Beginning in 1962, Walton developed his single store into a 1300-store retail chain known as Wal-Mart. Walton followed a savvy, innovative, and carefully mapped strategy to build his chain, which was masked by the cheerleading front that was Walton's style. He avoided putting stores in cities, instead focusing on the heartland of America. His employees are called *associates* and work more like teammates than employees. Each store is in healthy competition with other Wal-Mart stores for recognition as the "best of the area." The rewards are shared by the entire store and doing so builds a more teamlike environment.

| EXHIBIT 12.4 | THE MALCOLM BALDRIGE NATIONAL QUALITY AWARD |

This award was established in 1987 to promote quality awareness, to recognize the quality achievement of U.S. companies, and to publicize successful quality programs and strategies. The criteria are expressed fairly broadly so that they may be applied to both manufacturing and service firms. The seven categories that are viewed as important to quality are listed with the maximum number of points that evaluators may award, depending on their assessment of a company's programs and performance.

1998 Examination Items and Point Values

1998 Examination Categories/Items	Point Values	
1.0 Leadership		**110**
1.1 Leadership System	80	
1.2 Company Responsibility and Citizenship	30	
2.0 Strategic Planning		**80**
2.1 Strategy Development Process	40	
2.2 Company Strategy	40	
3.0 Customer and Market Focus		**80**
3.1 Customer and Market Knowledge	40	
3.2 Customer Satisfaction and Relationship Enhancement	40	
4.0 Information and Analysis		**80**
4.1 Selection and Use of Information and Data	25	
4.2 Selection and Use of Comparative Information and Data	15	
4.3 Analysis and Review of Company Performance	40	
5.0 Human Resource Focus		**100**
5.1 Work Systems	40	
5.2 Employee Education, Training, and Development	30	
5.3 Employee Well-Being and Satisfaction	30	
6.0 Process Management		**100**
6.1 Management of Product and Service Processes	60	
6.2 Management of Support Processes	20	
6.3 Management of Supplier and Partnering Processes	20	
7.0 Business Results		**450**
7.1 Customer Satisfaction Results	125	
7.2 Financial and Market Results	125	
7.3 Human Resource Results	50	
7.4 Supplier and Partner Results	25	
7.5 Company-Specific Results	125	
Total Points		**1,000**

| EXHIBIT 12.5 | WARREN BENNIS'S SEVEN CHARACTERISTICS OF A LEADER |

- **Business literacy:** Does he or she know the business? Does he or she know the real feel of it?
- **People skills:** Does he or she have the capacity to motivate, to bring out the best in people?
- **Conceptual skills:** Does he or she have the capacity to think systematically, creatively, and inventively?
- **Track record:** Has he or she done it before and done it well?
- **Taste:** Does he or she have the ability to pick the right people—not clones of himself or herself but people who can make up for his or her deficiencies?
- **Judgment:** Does he or she have the ability to make quick decisions with imperfect data?
- **Character:** The core competency of leadership is character, but character and judgment are the qualities that we know least about when trying to teach them to others.

SOURCE: Adapted from M. Loeb, "Where Leaders Come From," *Fortune*, September 19, 1994, pp. 241–242.

One of the most successful and beloved corporate leaders was Roberto C. Goizueta, the late CEO for Coca-Cola. His devotion to the company and to its products made him wealthy and also enriched his shareholders. Goizueta's intensity and desire to increase shareholder wealth became Coca-Cola's dominant management theme through the 90s. His basic strategy was if a business didn't add value, get rid of it. Another notable achievement was Goizueta's ability and vision to build a management team that could absorb the loss of his death in 1997. He had the foresight to have top management executives running the operations for years prior to his death.[32]

What Does it Take to Be a Good Leader? To be a good leader, one must have good followers. All of us may not be managers in our lives, but each of us fulfills the role of follower. It seems no matter how high a person climbs up the corporate ladder, he or she always has a boss. A boss can make a job easier by hiring good followers. But what exactly is a good follower? Good followers manage themselves well. They are committed to the organization, its purpose, its mission, and to others. They focus their efforts for maximum impact. Finally, they are courageous, honest, and credible.[33]

According to Warren Bennis, one of the foremost authorities on the subject of leadership, good leaders must have certain qualities. The most indispensable quality is a guiding vision and a clear idea of what he or she wants to accomplish; a good leader needs a strongly defined sense of purpose.[34] Bennis differentiates between leaders and managers. He says that leaders are people who do the right things; managers are people who do things right. The major difference is that leaders think about dreams, missions, visions, strategic intent, and purpose. Managers, however, think more about control mechanisms. Leaders ask the what and why questions, not just the how questions. Exhibit 12.5 illustrates the seven characteristics that define a leader, according to Bennis. Headhunters Thomas Neff and James Citrin, who have done extensive research on corporate leadership, found America's top business leaders all share the six principles outlined in Exhibit 12.6.[35]

Workplace Diversity Once a person has a qualified staff of effective followers, he or she needs to be a leader who can motivate and challenge each and every one of his

EXHIBIT 12.6	**WINNING STRATEGIES OF CORPORATE STARS**

1. Live with integrity, lead by example. "Integrity builds the trust in senior management that is . . . critical for high-performing organizations."

2. Develop a winning strategy of "Big Idea." "A successful leader must go to the company's roots and build on the things the organization truly does best."

3. Build a great management team. Great leaders hire managers "whose skills and experiences complement their own, but whose passion, attitudes, and values are one and the same."

4. Inspire employees to greatness. "Communicate continuously. Listen carefully, genuinely tolerate failure as a learning experience."

5. Create a flexible, responsive organization. "The best leaders have redesigned their organizations to make sure decisions can be made fast."

6. Use reinforcing management systems. "Compensation . . . must be consistent with and reinforce the value and strategy of the organization."

SOURCE: Adapted from "In Search of Leadership," *Business Week*, November 15, 1999, pp. 172–176.

or her workers. Companies are concerned about keeping these employees committed to their work and keeping them productive. Providing on-site child-care facilities, flexible work schedules, parental leave, and tuition reimbursements for children of employees are just some of the ways in which companies are trying to retain their workers.[36] Further, because of the cultural and generational diversity in the workplace, one management style will not be effective with all workers. For example, four distinct generations of workers exist in the current workforce: the swing generation (born 1910–1929), the silent generation (born 1930–1945), the baby-boom generation (born 1946–1964), and the baby-bust generation (born 1965–1976). Each of these generations has a different opinion of work and values different things.

The swing generation was involved in the rebuilding of the United States after World War II. Many of the workers in this generation have retired, but the ones who remain in the workforce often long for the "good old days" and may not be willing to accept change as quickly as the other generations. The silent generation has quietly gathered real estate, boats, and IRAs for their upcoming retirement. Members of this generation still hold the majority of the power positions in business, and they view the world with a lack of true interest and no desire to make it better for those who come after. The baby-boom generation believes in the rights of the individual worker, that no one should be dismissed without cause, and that each employee should be rewarded on a merit basis, regardless of race, creed, color, or age. The baby boomers are beginning to take on more roles of responsibility as the silent generation begins to retire. Finally, the baby-bust generation has no real sense of oneness. This generation believes that there is a true difference between the have's and the have-not's with respect to economic status and skills. For these workers, managers must be aware of the potential variation in the quality of the workers from this generation.[37] This may explain, in part, the profusion of leadership training courses available to firms seeking to upgrade their managers' leadership skills. Offerings range from a $29 book to a $65,000 speech. Teaching leadership in its many forms has become an industry in itself.[38]

If top management can develop the goals for the organization and then find a way to incorporate the needs and rights of each generation into these goals, everyone will be a winner. Let's take a closer look at the blending of leadership and culture.

Leadership and Culture   What makes one company able to attract and retain quality leadership? One answer to this question is the overall organizational environment, or **culture.** Organizations that have better-than-average management also have been found to have the following qualities:

culture The overall organizational environment.

1. Strong human resource policies for compensation, promotion, development, and training.
2. Clear communication of job possibilities in the firm.
3. High-quality career planning.
4. An overall quality work environment.[39]

An organization's choice and use of culture are strategic decisions. Various types of cultures are available for organizations to use; however, the leadership style of the firm must mesh with its chosen culture. Researchers have argued that an organization's cultural values influence its human resource strategies, including selection and placement policies, promotion and development procedures, and reward systems.[40] Human resource managers must be aware of the strong links between the strategies of managers with regard to organizational culture and the resulting impact on psychological climates that foster varying levels of commitment to increases in productivity. For example, Sun Hydraulics prides itself on a unique management culture that encourages employees to be innovative and creative by leaving them alone. CEO Clyde Nixon's philosophy is to stay out of people's way so they can get the job done. Sun Hydraulics' employees do not have titles or even job descriptions. Workers cooperate with each other and have the autonomy to switch roles in the production process at will. Everyone knows what everyone else is doing, so if some do not pull their share, it's noticed.[41]

When an organization's culture is not in sync with the management or with the rapidly changing times, that organization may decide to change its image and develop a new corporate culture. To be successful at changing a corporate culture, other companies that make this strategic decision should be aware of several things. First, corporate culture can never be imposed. A company cannot force employees to change their values simply because it is in the best interests of the organization. However, it can change someone's behavior. By changing an employee's behavior, the company can hope that his or her attitudes will change in the process. Management must be aware of this subtlety and attempt to help guide the change.

Another concern a corporation must keep in mind when developing or changing its culture is that certain cultures work best in specific environments. To determine what culture is right for a company, the goals, mission, and direction of the organization must be taken into consideration. The culture should be developed to support the organization's goal. By focusing on what the organization wants to accomplish, how to do this and what environment is needed become apparent. A culture that supports the organization's goals and environment can then be developed. Employee involvement is critical to the success of a changing corporate culture and overall productivity. The following sections examine employee involvement in detail.

Employee Involvement

employee involvement Strategy that allows workers more responsibility and accountability.

Employee involvement (EI) can be induced by a series of strategies that firms can adopt to allow workers more responsibility and accountability for preparing a product or offering a service. The term itself can refer to a wide range of practices, from simply soliciting employees' work-improvement ideas in small group meetings with

Union Enforced Quality

United Auto Workers in the Saturn plant in Spring Hill, Tennessee, donned black and orange arm bands and participated in a work slow down. Although it may look like yet another labor problem, it really isn't. It is a management problem. What were the employees after? They wanted management to stop increasing output because the speedup was causing quality to decrease. The union leader explained that the workers were not going to sacrifice quality to increase productivity because the workers knew, and management temporarily forgot, that their future depended on making a high-quality product. Management conceded that the union was absolutely right. The workers' concern for quality reinforced the urgency of getting the quality problems fixed, and fixed fast.

The reason that management bumped up the total cars produced from 700 to 900 cars a day is simple: Consumers consider Saturns to be good cars and want to buy them. Saturn generates extraordinary customer satisfaction, as indicated by numerous customer testimonials and a Customer Satisfaction Index in which Saturn ranked third, just behind luxury cars Lexus and Infiniti. A four-day event for Saturn owners brought 38,000 people to a small town to partake in plant tours and other festivities. Saturn owners recommend their cars to more people than owners of any other make. As the workers realized, just turning up the speed is not the answer. The Saturn plant is so well tuned that problems in production will lead to a complete shutdown in the assembly area in just six minutes. The faster the lines go, the greater chance of a problem. The greater a chance of a problem, the fewer the cars that are actually produced. The management team at Saturn is fortunate to have their workers so concerned about quality.

SOURCE: David Woodruff, "At Saturn, What Workers Want Is—Fewer Defects," *Business Week*, December 2, 1991, pp. 117–118; and R. Serafin, "Saturn Bounces Back with Its Basic Appeal," *Advertising Age*, January 30, 1995, p. 4.

A Plant Manager Keeps Reinventing His Production Line

At Dana Corp.'s plant in Stockton, California, there is always room for improvement. That underlies the culture created by Mark Schmink, the founding plant manager. Since 1995 the plant has been making truck chassis for a single customer: Toyota Motor Corp. This automaker increasingly expects a price cut from Dana. Therefore, according to Mr. Schmink, 48, "Every dollar has to come out of the process."

Because the operation at Stockton is committed to constant productivity gains, the plant manager searches endlessly for finding better ways to do things. For instance, Mr. Schmink improved an already efficient assembly process by creating a culture of inventiveness. One way he accomplished this was by insisting that every employee learn every job in the plant and that no one receive a permanent assignment. These guidelines maintained fresh perspectives by allowing employees to learn how each job fit into the entire operation.

Mr. Schmink also believed that a diverse workforce promotes a diversity of ideas. In fact, 19 different nationalities are represented by the plant staff, which totals less than 300 workers. Even though individuals and worker-teams questioned most of the plant's operations, Mr. Schmink demanded that each employee submit two ideas in writing each month. Astonishingly, 81 percent of the suggestions proved worthwhile to implement. Furthermore, Mr. Schmink celebrated every reached goal as if it were an occasion. He also provided continuous feedback to his workers by displaying minute-by-minute productivity figures on electronic signs.

Mr. Schmink's management philosophies, coupled with his management style, have created a culture that fosters ongoing productivity improvement at the plant. Even though the 21-year Dana veteran resigned this past year, the culture he created still lives on.

SOURCE: Adapted from T. Petzinger Jr., "A Plant Manager Keeps Reinventing His Production Line," *The Wall Street Journal*, September 19, 1997, p. B1.

front-line workers to forming self-managed work teams of workers who are given total control over their jobs and working environment. Also included in the concept of EI is the idea that unions or other worker-represented groups should have the power to participate in the plant- and company-level decision-making process.[42]

EI is based on two principles that managers have been familiar with for many years. The first is that people tend to support what they helped to create. For example, someone who is actively involved in developing new policy for handling the return procedures for a product is more likely to help ensure that it is carried out correctly, to make sure that it really does work, and to sell it to their friends and coworkers. The second principle underlying EI is the idea that people who know most about the inner functioning of an operation are those who actually perform the work. Asking for information and participation of the people actually performing the job can provide insights not available from managers or consultants.[43]

Benefits of Employee Involvement

As more and more firms have begun to implement EI techniques, the benefits of doing so have begun to surface. The following is a list of just some of the possible positive repercussions of using EI in an organization.

1. EI provides subordinates a greater understanding of decisions because they are more likely to be involved in making those decisions.
2. Similarly, employees who have a say in the decision are more committed to implementing it.
3. Involving employees in the decision-making and planning practices of the organization provides a greater understanding of the organization's objectives and improves their commitment to achieving these objectives. In addition, employee commitment and loyalty have been associated with higher productivity.[44]
4. EI provides greater fulfillment of psychological needs, and therefore it provides greater employee satisfaction.
5. EI can capitalize on the increased social pressure other members will place on fellow workers to comply with the decisions the group made as a whole.
6. EI provides a greater team and organizational identity, which is shown through greater cooperation and coordination among members at all levels.
7. When conflict does arise under EI situations, the people involved are better able to constructively deal with it.
8. EI produces better decisions.[45]

Communication and Involvement

One of the key components of successful implementation of EI is open and truthful communication among and between employees at all levels in the organization. Various techniques can be used to open the lines of communication in an organization; some are more appropriate for service firms, and others are more useful in manufacturing situations. Further, the usefulness of some techniques depends on the level in the organization from which the employees are drawn.

Advancements in technology have presented managers with a variety of communication tools from which to choose. Techniques such as voice mail and videoconferencing revolutionized the business of communicating in the workplace in the 1990s.[46]

Less technical ways to communicate with employees exist as well. One frequently used method for getting a pulse on the workplace is simply by asking. Employees can be polled in several ways. Many firms use attitude surveys, which request employee opinions on topics such as benefits and compensation and the cafeteria menu. Another way to gather employee input is to interview them. Firms can either hire consultants to perform the interviews or use employees who have been trained in interviewing techniques to collect the information. Although this is more formal, it has been found to be one way to generate a great deal of information in a limited amount of time.[47]

When managers are asked by their supervisors to communicate with lower-level employees, the response is generally, "But I *already* do that." The problem is that managers who think they may be talking with and listening to their employees in reality are not. Managers who fall into this category are often referred to as "deaf, dumb, and blind." It's not that deaf managers cannot hear; they don't take the time to listen. It's not that dumb managers cannot speak; they have been taught to read from scripts and teleprompters and not to talk to employees. It's not that blind managers cannot see; they limit their reading to electronic mail and spreadsheets.

Many of these problems are due to the environment in which the managers work. For example, if a manager's schedule is planned for him or her and booked three weeks in advance, he or she literally doesn't have the time to talk with employees, unless it is scheduled on the calendar.[48] However, some managers have personalities that make them poor communicators.

Employees report that the message they receive from their managers is, "I want to hear what you have to say, but give it to me and let's get on with things." This rushed or hurried approach does not make employees feel that what they have to say is important. It makes them feel that they are simply being listened to because their supervisors were *told* to listen to them. The only way communication is effective is if the employees feel that the managers care about what they have to say and if managers care about the employees as people, not just as employees.[49]

Techniques for Employee Involvement

Because communication is at the heart of all employee involvement efforts, managers can employ various ways to talk with and listen to their employees. Several different EI techniques, which are popular in the U.S. workplace, are described in the following sections.

employee empowerment Strategy of pushing the decision-making level down to the lowest level of qualified employees.

Empowerment   Whether the concept of **employee empowerment** is real or rhetoric has been a hot topic for debate. People on one side of the argument suggest that many employers are simply talking about empowering their employees and doing very little to make it happen. Other people are actually taking steps to empower their employees. These steps generally include pushing decision making down to the lowest level in the organization to the most qualified people who can make the decision. Organizations that employ empowering techniques also try to applaud both the successful and unsuccessful risk-taking behavior of employees. These firms take the attitude that each failure is a learning experience and more is learned by failing then by not doing anything at all. Managers in empowered organizations urge employees to find their own ways to boost productivity.[50] These managers ask employees to question silly rules and find better ways to do things, and then they allow the employee to use the resulting new procedures.[51]

Essentially, empowerment means that management vests decision-making or approval authority in employees instead of keeping it for themselves. Empowerment has become important for several reasons. First, globalization and competition have increased, requiring more and more innovation, which requires more freedom for the innovators. Second, the increased competition has forced U.S. businesses to be more productive than ever before.[52]

Lockheed Martin takes a team approach to empowerment. To encourage employee involvement the company has switched to integrated process teams. The integrated team approach encourages anyone who has needed information about a project to speak up and take control of that aspect of the project. This way, employees are involved in the project from the beginning.[53]

Suggestion Boxes   The suggestion box was the forerunner of quality circles, as discussed in an earlier chapter. The reasoning underlying each of these concepts is the same: employees who do the work should have good ideas of how to do it better. Unlike quality circles, which involve only a few people, suggestion boxes encourage all employees to participate. Frequently, the suggestor's identity is kept anonymous until the suggestion is implemented and then an award is presented. This helps people feel more secure about participating.

Sometimes the suggestion box format can be turned into a formal program. For example, Consolidated Edison Company of New York implemented a Front-Line Feedback program. The program requested that employees who work directly with the customer suggest ways in which service could be improved. Employees whose ideas were accepted earned $50, and they and their suggestions were written about in the company newsletter. Many of the recipients felt that the money was nice, but the recognition was better.[54]

The outcome of this program highlights one of the most beneficial reasons for implementing a suggestion box. The public recognition employees receive for submitting winning ideas boosts their self-esteem. Employees have an increased sense of their true abilities when their ideas are deemed good enough to be implemented by a firm. Every time a fellow worker uses the new method, the employee can say, "That's *my* idea."[55]

Ownership   One piece of information a stock buyer can use when deciding which company to invest in is the degree of ownership that top management has in the firm. If top managers are paid a salary that does not depend on the success of the company, then the investor should pass on the stock. If, however, the management's salary is tied to the productivity of the firm—that is, a large portion of the salary is in the form of stocks—then the investor should buy it. The investor wants someone who is running the firm to have the same interests the investor does—profitability. Managers who have a strong ownership in the organization will think in terms of profitability.[56]

The concept also can be pushed further down into the firm. Workers who have an ownership in the firm also want the firm to be more productive. Armed with this philosophy, many firms are considering employee ownership. Exhibit 12.7 provides an example of this concept in action. The belief is that employees who have more say in the direction of their workplace become more productive and more competitive globally.[56]

At Dana Corporation, each business unit or plant runs its own suggestion box program. The philosophy is that the employees are responsible for keeping their

EXHIBIT 12.7	INVOLVEMENT THROUGH OWNERSHIP

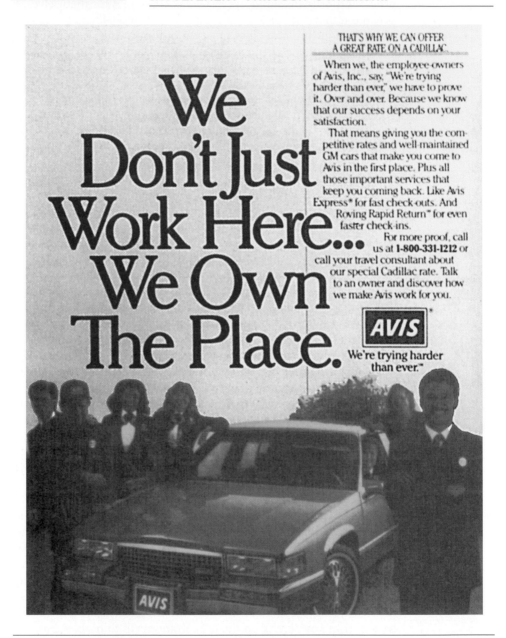

total quality management (TQM) An integrated management system designed to achieve an extremely high level of customer satisfaction.

plants competitive. In 1997, Dana Corporation used approximately 70 percent of all suggestions by giving the workers the opportunity to put their ideas into effect.[58]

Total Quality Management One concept that seems to incorporate all or many of the topics discussed in these past few sections is **total quality management (TQM).** TQM is an entirely new way of doing things. It asks employees to challenge old rules and find new and better ways to get things done. This can be accomplished in a group, individually, at the bottom of the organization, or at the top. The key is that everyone is involved.

TQM is a strategic, integrated management system for achieving customer satisfaction that involves all managers and employees and uses quantitative methods to continuously improve an organization's processes. TQM is designed to achieve customer satisfaction, make continuous improvements, and give responsibility to everyone. To achieve this goal the organization must develop performance standards and valid ways to measure these standards. It must strive to focus on the customer, on communication, and on employee involvement. Top management must support and direct the TQM effort by showing a commitment to training and by rewarding and recognizing quality work.

The process of implementing TQM in an organization can be viewed in three phases. To begin, the firm must have an awareness of the need to change. This vision must be supported by the knowledge that workers need to be trained and educated and that the tools they use to do their jobs may need to change. Once the organization recognizes these things, it then becomes committed to implementing TQM, which is the second phase. During this stage, the firm must develop support structures that include steering committees and TQM boards. These groups are responsible for determining the standards and capabilities of the firm. They also must be sure that the resources needed are provided and that the training required is available. Finally,

---

HR CHALLENGES

An Efficiency Drive: Fast Food Lanes Are Getting Faster

"HimayItakeyourorderplease?" says the drive-through greeter at Wendy's Old Fashioned Hamburgers. This greeting takes only one second—a triumphant two seconds faster than is suggested in Wendy's guidelines—and the speed of it was clocked by a high-tech timer installed in January. In just three months, the timer—which measures nearly every aspect of drive-through performance—helped knock eight seconds off the average takeout delivery time at this restaurant. But manager Ryan Tomney wants more. "Every second" he says, "is business lost."

Wendy's, the nation's third-largest hamburger chain, leads the competition in drive-through productivity. Cars spend an average of 150.3 seconds in their drive-thru. This is 16.7 seconds faster than McDonalds, their closest competition.

Yet far from gloating, Wendy's is scrambling to improve it's drive-through speed, and for good reason. Not long ago, drive-through was a hole punched through the wall to supplement dining room sales. But today, almost 65 percent of fast food revenue is coming through that hole.

The drive-through is the new battlefront for increasing revenues. It is "critical because it's over half of our business" says McDonald's CEO Jack Greenberg. For every six seconds saved at the drive-through, sales increase by 1 percent.

How are these fierce competitors increasing drive-through productivity? Through the implementation of technology, product development and employee retraining. Burger King's drive-through improvement plans will facilitate "beating the car to the window with food" and see-through bags that will allow customers to check their order more quickly. Arby's is working on a high viscosity version of it's special sauce that is less likely to spill. And McDonald's is testing salad containers that fit in the cup holder of its customers' cars.

The fight is on, and the customer may turn out to be the ultimate beneficiary of the drive-through wars!

SOURCE: Adapted from J. Ordonez "An Efficiency Drive: Fast Food Lanes Are Getting Even Faster," *The Wall Street Journal*, May 18, 2000.

performance improvement teams are established. At this point, the organization is ready to implement TQM. The performance teams begin to analyze the processes in the workplace with an eye toward improving them. During this analysis, seven basic quality tools can be used. They include:

1. Process flow analysis—provides a step-by-step chart of the steps involved in the process under investigation.
2. Cause-effect diagram—examines the root cause of painful symptoms.
3. Run chart—illustrates the trends and results over a specified period of time for a particular situation.
4. Control chart—indicates the variation from normal in the situation over time.
5. Scattergram—indicates whether or not a linear relationship exists between variables.
6. Histogram—depicts the distribution from the mean and how close to normal it is.
7. Pareto chart—prioritizes categories from most to least important.[59]

TQM groups initiate changes and are recognized for their accomplishments. Once in place, TQM continues to provide the organization with a way to constantly push itself to be more and more productive. Proponents of TQM argue that many firms' TQM efforts do not succeed because of a lack of support from top management or because of the mistaken view that results should be immediate.[60] Only time will tell whether TQM will continue to be a successful tool for continuous process improvement or a management fad relegated to the deep recesses of old college textbooks.

Management Guidelines

The productivity and involvement of employees should be major priorities for managers. However, no one set of steps can be followed to make all employees productive and involved. Nor are all companies more productive by simply involving their employees. With these two warnings in mind, let's review some suggestions for managers who want to build a more productive and involved workforce.

1. Almost all of the concepts discussed in this chapter rest on one principle: management must trust its employees. For example, to provide employees with the knowledge necessary for them to set their own goals, they must understand what output is expected overall. For employees to know if the new technique they are suggesting is feasible, they have to know how much the old method costs. For employees to make the sound business decisions that they were empowered to make, they must have the necessary information. If management is not willing to trust its employees, it cannot have an involved organization. An unwillingness to trust employees may imply that quality employees were not selected in the first place and the company's hiring policies need to be reworked. However, if a company hires only competent, qualified employees, then trusting them with organizational information should not be a problem.
2. Productivity can also be stifled by inappropriate or out-of-date equipment. Managers must remain knowledgeable about current machines and techniques available in the field to help employees do their jobs. Investing in

equipment to help increase productivity is one good way for firms that cannot use involvement techniques to increase productivity.

3. Before any steps can be made toward encouraging employees to become involved in the organization, a serious study of the overall corporate culture must be made. Will the current corporate culture allow management to initiate involvement programs? Which techniques, if any, are appropriate for the organization? Implementation of a new policy that runs counter to the culture will not be effective.

4. Start small. Once management decides to use involvement techniques, it should select one small project to begin with and see how it goes. Making too many changes all at once, even if they are all good ideas, may be too much for employees to handle.

5. Do not overlook the advantages of training employees. By providing training to employees, a manager can build a smarter, more loyal workforce. The payoff from training is frequently increased productivity and lower turnover.

6. Remember that employee attitudes can be shaped. Monetary rewards coupled with strong promotional and career path planning can increase morale, productivity, and commitment to the organization's goals.

Questions for Review

1. What is productivity? Discuss three ways in which productivity can be affected.
2. How can training and development help to increase productivity?
3. How can managers influence employee attitudes? Why would they want to?
4. What is employee involvement? What are some of the benefits of involving employees in the organization?
5. How can communication be used to help involve employees in their jobs?
6. In what ways are two of the techniques for increasing employee involvement similar? Different?
7. How would you go about increasing involvement in a plant that assembled toys? In a plant that plucked and cut chickens? In a law firm? In a mail-order catalog organization?

CASE

Bruegger's Bagel Bakery[61]

It's the fourth quarter, your team is down by seven points, and the ball is at midfield with less than one minute left to play in the game. What strategy do you put into action to move your team down the field? Do you tighten up and get conservative, or do you loosen up and call the unexpected play? Further, do you, as the coach, call the play, or do you let the quarterback call it? Mike Dressell, Nordahl Brue, and Jim Briggs (who has since left the business), founders of Bruegger's Bagel Bakery, would probably opt for the latter. When the trio first considered the idea of opening a bagel bakery, they knew they had to develop a decentralized approach; that is, they knew they wanted to let the individual managers call the plays. Because each of them was busy in another occupation (Dressell had a construction company, Brue was an attorney, and Briggs was an accountant), they didn't have the time or knowledge to get involved in operating decisions.

Passing the Ball, Not the Buck

Basically, Dressell, Brue, and Briggs adopted the attitude that if you wanted something done right, you didn't necessarily have to do it yourself. Rather than getting involved directly in operating decisions, the founders made a strategic decision to hire local managers to run their bagel shops. Local managers were offered a partnership that gave them a 20 percent ownership of the individual shops they supervised. The managers were empowered with the responsibility and authority to make decisions that affected their "cluster" of units. Offering the managers financial incentives beyond their salaries, the owners wanted the managers to have a higher stake in the survival of their shops and therefore more incentive to make things work.

Initially, the playing field was left wide open for local managers in terms of developing their own techniques for managing their shops, watching costs, and creating their own menu items. The principal partners took a sideline approach to overseeing each manager's game plan but would occasionally visit some of the units. Overall, they liked what they saw, as was evident in Brue's comment that "managers took lots of initiative." Bruegger's created an environment that encouraged ingenuity and innovativeness. Each cluster manager was in the driver's seat, and all of the managers knew who buttered their bagels, so to speak—it was none other than themselves! Various clusters of stores offered different styles of bagels (some lighter, some darker) and different lines of beverages. Some had paper goods with the company logo; others didn't. Some offered creative bagel delights, such as pizza bagels; others offered more traditional bagels. Again, the decisions were made by the individual managers of each cluster of stores, thereby adding an element of uniqueness to each.

Smell of Victory

Since the principal partners first considered the idea of Bruegger's Bagel Bakery in 1983, the company has grown rapidly. The first market was in Albany, New York, and in less than three years, they added other markets, including Cedar Rapids, Iowa; Minneapolis, Minnesota; Boston, Massachusetts; and Raleigh-Durham, North Carolina. Obviously, Dressell and Brue's strategic business plan has worked well. Despite their success, however, the principal partners have not closed their eyes to the possibility that change is needed.

A Slight Shift in the Game Plan

As the company continued to grow, Bruegger reached a point at which the decision to set some companywide standards became evident. Although the partners wanted to continue giving managers the freedom to make decisions affecting their individual clusters, they believed there was a need to coordinate the activities of the various stores. Stephen Finn, President of Bruegger's Corp., believed the best way to manage growth effectively is to develop a strong corporate culture.

Bruegger's strategic philosophy had always been in line with the idea of empowerment. The partners wanted their managers to have "bragging rights" for the success of their individual stores. After all, Bruegger's success reflected the individual management techniques and decision making. Although the principal partners did not want to interfere with the managers' decisions to offer particular products, they did persuade the managers to rely on market research to ascertain the viability of keeping certain items on the menu.

Conclusion

Bruegger's Bagel Bakery has demonstrated that setting standards can be done without "robbing" managers of the motivation to run their shops the way they choose. By empowering people with responsibility and authority and by giving them a stake in their business, Bruegger's has the benefit of many minds working on the same problems and working to ensure the survival of the company.

Questions for Discussion

1. The strategic philosophy behind Bruegger's Bagel Bakery is based on at least one of the strategic choices mentioned at the beginning of the chapter. How has Bruegger's been able to implement this strategic choice to develop a successful organization?

2. Various concepts discussed in this chapter have been implemented at Bruegger's. What are two? Discuss how they have been utilized effectively by Bruegger's.

3. Of what strategic choices described in this chapter has Bruegger's failed to take advantage? What suggestions do you have for implementing these strategies?

4. If you were asked to measure Bruegger's productivity levels, how would you do it?

Additional Readings

Allnoch, Allen. "IE Knits Productivity with Ergonomics Tool." *IIE Solutions* 42, no. 1 (January 1997), pp. 16–17.

Baldwin, Timothy T., Camden Danielson, and William Wiggenhorn. "The Evolution of Learning Strategies in Organizations: From Employee Development to Business Redefinition." *Academy of Management Executive* 9, no. 4 (November 1997), pp. 47–58.

Beckhard, Richard, and Wendy Pritchard. *Changing the Essence: The Art of Leading Fundamental Change in Organizations.* San Francisco: Jossey-Bass, 1992.

Bell, Robert R., and John M. Burnham. *Managing Productivity and Change.* Cincinnati: South-Western, 1991.

Bolman, Lee, and Terrence Deal. *Reframing Organizations.* San Francisco: Jossey-Bass, 1991.

Boyett, Joseph H., and Harry P. Conn. *Workplace 2000: The Revolution Reshaping American Business.* New York: Dutton, 1991.

Brown, Stephen, Evert Gummesson, Bo Edvardsson, and Bengtove Gustavsson. *Service Quality.* New York: Lexington Books, 1990.

Carnevale, Anthony Patrick. *America and the New Economy.* San Francisco: Jossey-Bass, 1991.

Casson, Mark. *Enterprise and Competitiveness.* New York: Oxford Press, 1990.

Deming, W. Edwards. *Out of Crisis.* Cambridge, MA: Cambridge University Press, 1986.

Denton, D. Keith. *Horizontal Management: Beyond Total Customer Satisfaction.* New York: Lexington Books, 1991.

Ernst and Young Quality Improvement Consulting Group. *Total Quality: An Executive Guide for the 1990s.* Homewood, IL.: Dow Jones-Irwin, 1990.

Gardner, William L. and Bruce J. Avolio. "The Charismatic Relationship: A Dramaturgical Perspective." *Academy of Management Review* 23, no. 1 (January 1998), pp. 32–58.

Graham-Moore, Brian, and Timothy L. Ross. *Gainsharing for Improving Performance.* Washington, DC: BNA Books, 1990.

Gordon, Judith R. and Karen Whelan. "Successful Professional Women in Midlife: How Organizations Can More Effectively Understand and Respond to the Challenges." *Academy of Management Executive* 12, no. 1 (February 1998), pp. 8–27.

Juran, J. M. *Juran on Quality by Design.* New York: Free Press, 1992.

Ketchum, Lyman, and Eric Trist. *All Teams Are Not Created Equal.* Newbury Park, CA: Sage, 1992.

Kinlaw, Dennis. *Developing Superior Work Teams.* New York: Lexington Books, 1990.

Koestenbaum, Peter. *Leadership: The Inner Side of Greatness.* San Francisco: Jossey-Bass, 1991.

Kotter, John P., and James Heskett. *The Corporate Culture Connection.* New York: Free Press, 1992.

Lewis, Jordan D. *Partnerships for Profit.* New York: Free Press, 1990.

Maidani, Ebrahaim. "Comparative Study of Herzberg's Two-Factor Theory of Job Satisfaction Among Public and Private Sectors." *Public Personnel Management* 20 (1991), pp. 441–448.

McIntosh, Stephen. "Buying Time by Delegating." *HRMagazine*, October 1991, p. 47.

Miller, Danny. *The Icarus Paradox: How Exceptional Companies Bring About Their Own Downfall.* Scarborough, Ontario: Harper Collins Canada, 1990.

Morgan, Gareth. *Images of Organizations.* Newbury Park, CA: Sage, 1990.

Orsburn, Jack, Linda Moran, Ed Musselwhite, and John Zenger. *Self-Directed Work Teams: The New American Challenge.* Homewood, IL: BusinessOne Irwin, 1990.

Quinn, Robert. *Beyond Rational Management.* San Francisco: Jossey-Bass, 1991.

Robson, George. *Continuous Process Improvement: Simplifying Work Systems.* New York: Free Press, 1991.

Rummler, Geary A., and Alan P. Brache. *Improving Performance.* San Francisco: Jossey-Bass, 1990.

Ryan, Kathleen D., and Daniel K. Oestreich. *Driving Fear out of the Workplace: How to Overcome Barriers to Quality, Productivity, and Innovation.* San Francisco: Jossey-Bass, 1991.

Sandy, William. *Forging the Productivity Partnership.* New York: McGraw-Hill, 1990.

Schein, Edgar. *Organizational Culture and Leadership.* San Francisco: Jossey-Bass, 1991.

Shapero, Albert. *Managing Precessional People.* New York: Free Press, 1989.

Thibodeaux, Mary, and Dale Yeatts. "Leadership: The Perceptions of Leaders by Followers in Self-Managed Work Teams." Paper presented at the 1991 International Conference on Self-Managed Work Teams. Dallas, 1991.

Thornburg, Linda. "The Push to Improve." *HRMagazine*, December 1990, pp. 36–39.

Tjosvold, Dean, and Mary Tjosvold. *Leading the Team Organization.* New York: Lexington Books, 1992.

Wellins, Richard, William Byham, and Jeanne Wilson. *Empowered Teams.* San Francisco: Jossey-Bass, 1991.

Womack, James, Daniel Jones, and Daniel Noos. *The Machine That Changed the World.* Boston: MIT, 1990.

Yeatts, Dale. "Self-Managed Work Teams: Innovation in Progress." *Business and Economic Quarterly*, Fall/Winter, 1990/1991, pp. 2–6.

Yasuda, Yuzo. *40 Years, 20 Million Ideas: The Toyota Suggestion System.* Cambridge, MA: Productivity Press, 1991.

Zeithaml, Valarie A. *Delivering Quality Service.* New York: Free Press, 1990.

Notes

[1]E. B. Baatz, "Motorola's Secret Weapon," *Electronic Business*, April 1993, pp. 51–54; A. K. Gupta and A. Singhal, "Managing Human Resources for Innovation and Creativity,"

Research-Technology Management, May–June 1993, pp. 41–48; D. Eller, "Motorola Trains VPs to Become Growth Leaders," *HRMagazine* 40, no. 6 (June 1995), pp. 82–87.

[2]P. Cappelli and H. Singh, "Integrating Strategic Human Resources and Strategic Management," in D. Lewin, O. S. Mitchell, and P. D. Sheres, eds., *Research Frontiers in Industrial Relations and Human Resources* (Madison, WI: IPRA, 1992); and B. E. Becker and M. A. Huselid, "High Performance Work Systems and Firm Performance: A Synthesis of Research and Managerial Implications," in G. R. Ferris, ed., *Research in Personnel and Human Resources Management*, vol. 16 (Stamford, CT: JAI, 1998) 53-102.

[3]G. Koretz, "The Surge in Factory Productivity Looks Like History Now," *Business Week*, October 8, 1990, p. 24.

[4]R. Henkoff, "Make Your Office More Productive," *Fortune*, February 25, 1991, p. 72.

[5]A. Taylor, "New Lessons from Japan's Carmakers," *Fortune*, October 22, 1990, p. 166.

[6]Vic Heylen, "Europeans Keep Progress off Assembly Line," *The Wall Street Journal*, June 3, 1991, p. A10.

[7]Henkoff, "Make Your Office More Productive," p. 76.

[8]A. Karr, "A Special News Report on People and Their Jobs in Offices, Fields, and Factories," *The Wall Street Journal*, April 10, 1990, p. A1.

[9]Henkoff, "Make Your Office More Productive," p. 76.

[10]Robert Tomasko, "Restructuring: Getting It Right," *Management Review*, April 1992, pp. 10–15.

[11]B. Reilly, "The New Deal: What Companies and Employees Owe One Another," *Fortune*, June 13, 1994, pp. 44–52.

[12]McCormick and Powell, "Management for the 1990s."

[13]J. Hunt, "Hidden Extras: How People Get Overlooked in Takeovers," *Personnel Management*, July 1987, pp. 24–28.

[14]Baytos, "The Human Side of Acquisitions and Divestitures," p. 170.

[15]R. Ford and P. Perrew, "After the Layoff: Closing the Barn Door Before All the Horses Are Gone," *Business Horizons*, July–August 1993, pp. 1–7.

[16]D. T. Bastien, "Common Patterns of Behavior and Communication in Corporate Mergers and Acquisitions," *Human Resource Management* 26, no. 1 (Spring 1987), p. 28.

[17]P. O. Gaddis, "Taken Over, Turned Out," *Harvard Business Review*, July–August 1987, p. 9.

[18]P. Ingrassia and J. White, "GM Mulls Tough Call in Toyota Venture," *The Wall Street Journal*, June 10, 1988, p. A2.

[19]G. Anders, "Going Global: Vision vs. Reality," *The Wall Street Journal*, September 22, 1989, pp. R20–21.

[20]J. Main, "The Winning Organization," *Fortune*, September 26, 1988, pp. 50–60.

[21]T. P. Pare, "Rebuilding a Lost Reputation," *Fortune*, May 30, 1994, p. 176; and L. S. Richman, "Reengineering under Fire," *Fortune*, April 18, 1994, p. 186.

[22]J. Solomon, "Managers Focus on Low-Wage Workers," *The Wall Street Journal*, May 9, 1989, p. B1.

[23]R. W. Thompson, "Employees Seek 'Shared Destiny,' Study Finds," *HRNews*, November 1997, p. 4.

[24]N. K. Austin, "When Companies Get the Blues," *Working Woman*, October 1998, pp. 21–23.

[25]D. Milbank, "In These Gloomy Times, Some Companies Provide Employees with Comic Relief," *The Wall Street Journal*, February 19, 1991, pp. B1.

[26]M. A. Barton, "Baldrige Winners Stress HR Practices," *HRNews*, November 1993, p. 7.

[27]Cappelli and Singh, "Integrating Strategic Human Resources and Strategic Management."

[28]S. Feinstein, "Blame Bosses If Quality Is Poor," *The Wall Street Journal*, July 10, 1990, p. A1; and Jerry Bowles, "Is American Management Really Committed to Quality?" *Management Review*, April 1992, pp. 42–46.

[29]J. A. Byrne, "Remembering Deming, the Godfather of Quality," *Business Week*, January 10, 1994, p. 44.

[30]S. Overman, "Leader Helps Improve Competitiveness," *HRMagazine*, May 1990, pp. 58–60.

[31]E. Carlson, "McDonald's Kroc Bloomed Late, but Brilliantly," *The Wall Street Journal*, May 23, 1989, p. B2.

[32]S. Perman, "The Man Who Knew the Formula," *Time*, October 27, 1997, pp. 101–103.

[33]R. E. Kelley, "In Praise of Followers," *Harvard Business Review*, November–December 1988, pp. 142–147.

[34]Adapted from "In Search of Leadership," *Business Week*, November 15, 1999, pp.172–176.

[35]M. Loeb, "Where Leaders Come From," *Fortune*, September 19, 1994, pp. 241–242.

[36]R. Naylor, Jr., "The Best Companies for Working Mothers," *Tallahassee Democrat*, September 14, 1994.

[37]"Managing Generational Diversity," *HRMagazine*, April 1991, pp. 91–92.

[38]J. Huey, "The Leadership Industry," *Fortune*, February 21, 1994, pp. 54–56; and B. O'Reilly, "How Execs Learn Now," *Fortune*, April 5, 1993, pp. 52–58.

[39]J. P. Kotter, "How Leaders Grow Leaders," *Across the Board* 25, no. 3 (March 1988), pp. 38–42; and O'Reilly, "How Execs Learn Now."

[40]J. E. Sheridan, "Organizational Culture and Employee Retention," *Academy of Management Journal* 35, no. 5 (1992), pp. 1036–1056.

[41]A. Henderson, "Corporate Freeform," *Florida Trend*, August 1997, pp. 52–56.

[42]J. Hoerr, "The Strange Bedfellows Backing Workplace Reform," *Business Week*, April 30, 1990, p. 57.

[43]S. Bicos, "Employee Participation Without Pain," *HRMagazine*, April 1990, p. 89.

[44]R. Jacob, "Why Some Customers Are More Equal Than Others," *Fortune*, September 19, 1994, pp. 215–224.

[45]N. Margulies and S. Black, "Perspectives on the Implementation of Participative Approaches," *Human Resources Management* 26, no. 3 (Fall 1987), p. 386.

[46]S. Antilla, "What's on TV? Our 10 A.M. Meeting," *Working Woman*, February 1992, pp. 42–43.

[47]B. Shimko, "All Managers Are HR Managers," *HRMagazine*, January 1990, p. 67.

[48]M. Falvey, "Deaf, Dumb, and Blind at the Helm," *The Wall Street Journal*, April 10, 1989, p. A14.

[49]P. Farish, "HR Update," *Personnel Administrator*, May 1989, p.19.

[50]A. Karr, "Empowering Workers: Is It Real or Overplayed?" *The Wall Street Journal*, June 18, 1991, p. A1; and A. Markels, "Team Approach: A Power Producer Is Intent on Giving Power to Its People," *The Wall Street Journal*, July 3, 1995, p. A1.

[51]T. Peters, "Another Bright Idea Squashed by Congress," *The Wall Street Journal*, November 22, 1989, p. A12.

[52]Jeffrey Gandz, "The Employee Empowerment Era," *Business Quarterly*, Autumn 1990, pp. 74–79; and Peter Fleming, "Empowerment Strengthens the Rock," *Management Review*, December 1991, pp. 34–37.

[53]T. L. Wolff, "Power to the People," *Workforce Diversity*, Fall 1997, pp. 24–28.

[54]"The Power of Suggestions at ConEd," *Personnel Journal*, January 1988, p. 11.

[55]R. Meehan, "Programs That Foster Creativity and Innovation," *Personnel*, February 1986, p. 32; and B. Miller, "Not All It's Cracked Up to Be?" *Across the Board*, November 1991, pp. 24–28.

[56]K. Fisher, "Ownership Counts," *Forbes*, November 14, 1988, p. 362.

[57]M. J. McCarthy, "Administration Looks Favorably on Idea of Employee Ownership," *The Wall Street Journal*, December 23, 1993, p. A6.

[58]R. Teitelbaum, "How to Harness Gray Matter," *Fortune*, June 9, 1997, p. 168.

[59]Carla C. Cater, "Seven Basic Quality Tools," *HRMagazine*, January 1992, pp. 81–83.

[60]G. Guchsberg, "'Total Quality' Is Termed Only Partial Success," *The Wall Street Journal*, October 1, 1992, p. B1.

[61]Adapted from B. G. Posner, "Raising the Stakes," *Inc.*, March 1990, pp. 100–103; and telephone conversation with company official at home office in Albany, New York, October 3, 1994; R. L. Allen, "Bruegger's Bagel Bakery; Hot Concepts!" *Nation's Restaurant News* 29, no. 21 (May 22, 1995), pp. 88–90.

IV

Strategies for Maintaining Human Resources

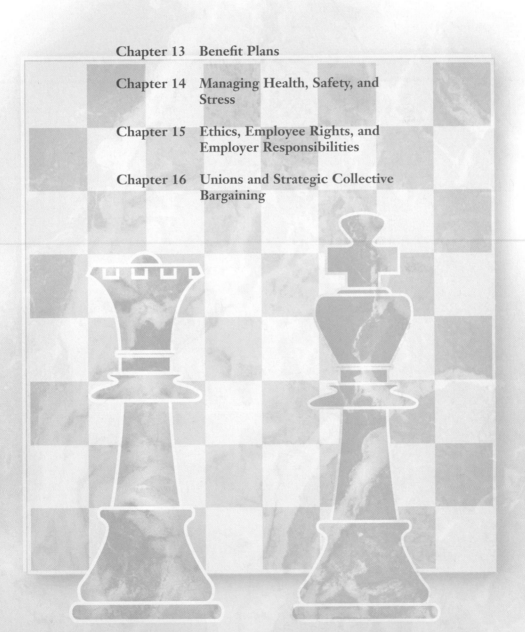

13

Benefit Plans

Chapter Objectives

As a result of studying this chapter, you should be able to

1. Explain the strategic choices available to a firm in the area of benefits.

2. List and define various forms of benefits.

3. Distinguish between traditional benefit plans and "cafeteria" or choice plans.

4. Be aware of possible trends in the future of benefits.

Increasing costs and the passage of new legislature have caused major changes in benefit plans during the past years. (For a monthly compendium of major benefits trends see **www.hr2000.com/mercer/main.htm**.) With all of these changes comes confusion. Many employees have difficulty understanding a firm's benefit program, let alone comparing it with those of other firms.[1] In the past, employers provided a fixed set of benefits to all employees, but this practice is changing. In the midst of today's competition, employers are becoming partners with their employees. By communicating with employees to learn more and, in some cases, to discover their needs, employers are offering flexible plans to accommodate a wide array of needs.

CASE

Manor Care[2]

Manor Care, Inc., is a company in the lodging and health-care industries, headquartered in Silver Spring, Maryland. In an effort to be the employer of choice, the company is offering a new employee benefits package, Benefits of Choice. The highlights of the new plan include the following:

- A cash accumulation retirement plan that, at retirement, provides lower-paid employees a higher percentage of their salary than it gives more highly paid employees.
- A medical program that provides greater flexibility by accommodating small families.
- A decrease in coinsurance family rates of about 50 percent for long-term employees.
- A decrease in employee contributions to the group insurance plan.
- An increase in the employer match to the 401(k) savings plan, which rewards length of service.

The first challenge the company faced in revising its benefits plan was to create a pension plan in which its frontline employees could afford to participate.

Communicating the Benefits

Realizing that effective communication is critical to the success of any new program, Manor Care conducted extensive educational activities during a three-week open enrollment period. Forty-nine Manor Care human resource professionals were trained for two days on the intricacies of the new plan. Then, during the three-week open enrollment period, the human resource professionals made presentations to groups of five to ten employees in sessions given around the clock every hour to accommodate all three shifts. Sessions began with a 10-minute video, followed by a 30- to 45-minute period that consisted of overhead slides illustrating the mechanics and meaning of the plan to each employee. At the end of the presentation, employees were given take-home packets to help them gain a better understanding of the new benefits package. In addition, the company implemented a national toll-free number for employees who needed more counseling.

The company now communicates the benefits on an ongoing basis. A human resource person in each of Manor Care's centers who has been trained on presenting the benefits plan is responsible for orientation of all new employees. The company has also hired a full-time benefit communications person whose responsibility is to maintain a constant flow of plan communication through bulletins as well as in-service programs such as brief refresher seminars.

Giving Employees a Choice

Manor Care's goal with the training was not to guide the employee's decisions but to provide the information needed for them to make the best choice, depending on each individual's circumstances. This information was helpful to employees in clarifying the more flexible benefit approach of the new design. As an additional aid, the terminology was explained to help employees understand it. For example, *flex dollar credits* were referred to as *cash out options*. It should be noted that there was no two-tiered communication effort to address upper-level management.

Getting Immediate Results

The communication effort had an amazing effect. Almost at the same time the plan was introduced and communicated, "voluntary turnover across the corporation dropped almost 15 percent in all classifications. The turnover of front-line service employees decreased almost 20 percent," according to the president of human resources for Manor Care, Inc.

Providing Cost-Effective Education

Manor Care also noted that the educational effort proved to be quite cost effective. The 20 percent decrease in turnover of nursing assistants (2000 fewer recruits each year) experienced by Manor Care has resulted in a savings of $2000 to $2500 per employee. The savings more than paid for the investment (which consisted of costs of the video, staffing the hotline, training instructors, sending presenters to locations, and printed literature) of $5.00 to $7.50 per employee.

In short, Manor Care is very pleased with the success of its new effort. The plan has helped to retain employees and recruit new ones. It has also played a role in the company's increase in quality of customer service.

Strategic Choices

Human resource managers are faced with a multitude of benefits choices available. How does one decide which to offer? Frequently, the decisions boil down to three fundamental strategic choices managers must make. Each of these is outlined here.

1. How much of the money that is used to cover employee benefits should be paid by the employer, and how much of it should be covered by the employee? When this decision is being made, concepts such as corporate culture, corporate strategy, employee rights, and employer responsibilities must be kept in mind. If the firm wants to boast that it offers a comprehensive benefits package, it must not require that the employee pay the majority of the costs. Likewise, if the firm is following a cost containment strategy, it will not want to pick up the total cost of the benefit package. However, when firms require

employees to help foot the bill for benefits, employees may opt out of the coverage. One recent study found that six million Americans declined the insurance offered by their employers because the payments required were too high.[3]

2. Second, managers must decide how comprehensive their plans should be. Some firms pride themselves on covering any possible need the employee might have. Other firms may decide that only health insurance is important and offer only that to their employees. It may be difficult for some to believe that an employee would select to work for a firm that offers only health insurance, but many workers do. As we have seen in past chapters, not everyone is motivated by money or, in this case, benefits.

3. Finally, managers must make a fundamental choice about how flexible the benefits program will be. The changes occurring in today's workforce make some of the traditional benefit packages obsolete. For example, if both husband and wife work, it may be to their benefit to have one spouse cover dental and the other cover major medical because the plans are more comprehensive or less expensive. What they really do not need is for both of them to be covered under both plans. To allow these types of variations in benefit plans, flexibility is a must.

Let's look at each of these choices in more detail.

Who Pays for the Benefits?

In the past, the employer has been responsible for paying most of the cost of a benefit program. This included premiums and deductibles for insurance as well as premium contributions. This began during World War II when employers were prevented from giving wage increases. Instead, they substituted benefit programs that were not under wage-price controls. However, the trend is being reversed, especially in health insurance.[4] The U.S. health-care system is the world's most expensive. From 1971 to 1991 the cost of medical care rose nearly 70 percent faster than inflation.[5] In the mid 90s health-care costs stabilized, but by the late 90s started to increase again. The increase for 1999 was 3.7 percent, but this more than doubled to 7.6 percent in 2000.[6] But health-care costs are just one of the components of the total benefits package. The Bureau of Labor Statistics estimated that in March 1996, fringe benefits accounted for 28.1 percent of total compensation costs for private employers. This was down from 28.4 percent in March of 1995 and 28.9 percent in March of 1994. The cost climb continues—benefit costs were 5 percent higher in 2000 than they were in 1999.[7] An average employee's hourly compensation is $17.49, with wages and salaries comprising $12.58 of this and benefits costing $4.91 per hour.[8] With the pressure to keep labor costs under control, employers will be forced to make a strategic decision regarding benefits: How much will we ask the employee to pay?

How Comprehensive a List of Benefits Shall Be Offered?

compulsory benefits A range of benefits that all employers must offer, as mandated by law.

A second strategic choice faced by employers involves the breadth and depth of coverage. All employers must offer a certain range of benefits. These are called **compulsory benefits**, such as workers' compensation and unemployment insurance, which are mandated by law.

Beyond these compulsory benefits, employers have a wide choice of benefit packages. Most major employers offer a comprehensive list of benefits, and this list will

| EXHIBIT 13.1 | THE CHANGING BENEFIT MIX OF THE 1990s |

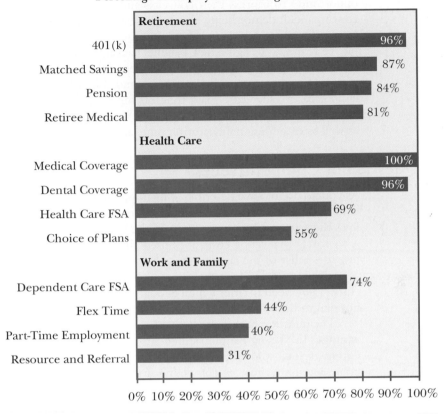

Percentage of Employers Providing Benefit

Retirement
- 401(k) — 96%
- Matched Savings — 87%
- Pension — 84%
- Retiree Medical — 81%

Health Care
- Medical Coverage — 100%
- Dental Coverage — 96%
- Health Care FSA — 69%
- Choice of Plans — 55%

Work and Family
- Dependent Care FSA — 74%
- Flex Time — 44%
- Part-Time Employment — 40%
- Resource and Referral — 31%

0% 10% 20% 30% 40% 50% 60% 70% 80% 90% 100%

likely continue to grow. Exhibit 13.1 shows the results of a research study of 1034 major U.S. companies. Ninety-two percent of the *Fortune* 100 companies, 56 percent of the *Fortune* 500 industrials, and 43 percent of the *Fortune* 500 service companies participated in the survey. Note that the surveyed companies offer a broad mix of benefits. All of the companies offer medical coverage, but only 31 percent offer any type of resource and referral services.[9] As employees become more family oriented, the benefit mix will likely change. For example, as employers seek to expand the workweek, employees may expect additional family benefits, such as child care, to compensate for the lost time at home. If other companies begin to offer these benefits, will most employers in the geographic area begin to offer them? The extent of benefit offerings is a strategic question for each employer.

How Flexible Shall the Benefit Offerings Be?

The third strategic choice involves the flexibility of benefit offerings. The employer needs to decide whether a standard list of benefits shall be offered to all employees or whether employees will be allowed to pick and choose among benefit offerings in a cafeteria-style plan.

In an effort to improve the current benefits package, Pitney Bowes, Quaker Oats, Nike, Salomon Brothers, and many others have solicited employee involvement. The starting points are usually surveys and focus groups in which employees are given an opportunity to express their concerns and fears about various issues. Some common concerns include not being able to purchase a home, to send children to college, and to care for elderly parents. After gathering the information, companies then ask employee teams to design a new benefits package offering more choices without raising costs. As a result, companies have broadened the benefits mix and increased employee morale. Employer-provided matching funds for college tuition, offering subsidies for child care or elder care, paid time off for family leave, group discounts on auto or home insurance, discounted mortgages, legal services, and financial planning advice, as well as extending paid vacation time, are among the newest benefits offerings.[10]

The Question of Competitiveness

As you no doubt have determined by now, one key underlying strategy that prevails in benefit offerings is *competitiveness*. Employers want to offer a benefit package that allows them to compete successfully in the labor market for employees but not one that is so costly that labor costs are raised above those of the competition. Exhibit 13.2 provides a list of the reasons given by employers for offering employee benefits. Essentially, employers face the same dilemma with benefit costs as they do with wage costs: They need to offer a high enough wage to attract and hold good employees but not one so high that labor costs exceed those of competitors.

competitive advantage A combination of the ends (goals) for which the firm is striving and the means (policies) by which it is seeking to reach those ends that gives it an advantage over its competitors.

The question becomes whether benefits can be used to achieve a **competitive advantage**. In "Using Employee Benefits," H. W. Hennessey argues that they cannot.[11] Citing various studies showing that employees know little of their own benefit program, let alone those of competing firms, he argues that benefits cannot be used to achieve a competitive differential in hiring. Furthermore, the complexity of current benefit offerings with varying coverages and costs makes it difficult for all but the most diligent employees to understand the package.

differential advantage An edge on competitors achieved by distinguishing or creating a product or service that is unique within the industry.

The implication is that if a firm wishes to achieve a **differential advantage** in its benefit offering, it must know what is being offered by competitive employers in the labor market and then design a program that is better. Next it must very clearly communicate this difference to all job applicants and present employees. Unless these two steps are taken, the benefit program will not be a way to gain a competitive advantage.

Some employers do not wish to gain a competitive advantage with their benefit program; rather, they want to remain competitive. That is, they want to offer a package of benefits that compares with, even though it does not surpass, that of their competition. However, a firm may throw in a unique benefit or two as a means of setting themselves apart from the competition.[12] Of course, even with this approach, clear communication of benefits to job applicants and present employees is essential.

One company that has done a great job communicating the benefits message is AlliedSignal in Morristown, New Jersey. To spread the word about benefits the HR department developed a communication plan. First, they divided all of the benefits offered into four categories: health and well being, financial well being, life-planning tools and resources, and learning. This made it easier for employees to focus on the benefits of interest to them without having to wade through those that were not of interest. Next, they developed a consistent layout and look to all benefits materials so employees would easily recognize the information as benefits related. Finally,

EXHIBIT 13.2	REASONS GIVEN BY EMPLOYERS FOR OFFERING EMPLOYEE BENEFITS

Company Size in Number of Employees

Reason	1–10	10–49	50–99	100–499	500+
Attract good employees					
Salaried	10%	38%	44%	57%	53%
Hourly	33%	48%	27%	46%	47%
Reduce turnover					
Salaried	30%	19%	32%	19%	11%
Hourly	33%	22%	42%	18%	18%
Motivate employees					
Salaried	10%	22%	4%	10%	32%
Hourly	11%	19%	8%	21%	12%
Tax-free benefits					
Salaried	40%	22%	12%	8%	6%
Hourly	22%	4%	0%	0%	0%
Keep out the union					
Salaried	0%	0%	4%	2%	0%
Hourly	0%	4%	12%	9%	18%
Meet union requirements					
Salaried	0%	0%	0%	0%	0%
Hourly	0%	4%	8%	5%	0%
Other					
Salaried	10%	0%	4%	4%	0%
Hourly	0%	0%	4%	2%	6%

SOURCE: Adapted from N. Sutton-Bell, "Are Employers Meeting Their Benefits Objectives?" *Benefits Quarterly* 2, no. 3 (1986), pp. 14–20.

employees received a personal benefits planner. The planner included a form employees could complete to determine how much Allied spent on their benefits and information on all of the other benefits offered. The planner continued the same benefits color scheme and had tabs for easy referencing. The plan resulted in an increase in employee understanding, which translated into bottom line savings.[13]

Composition of Benefit Plans

Most companies today, especially larger ones, offer a wide variety of benefits. Some of the benefits are compulsory (required by law); others, while not required by law, have been offered for so many years that firms are virtually obligated to continue to offer them. In this section, we explore the various types of benefits offered. We classify benefits into seven major categories as follows:

- Required or mandatory security
- Voluntary security
- Retirement-related security
- Time-off–related security
- Health insurance
- Financial services
- Social and recreational services

Specific examples in each category are shown in Exhibit 13.3.

Required Security

Federal and state governments require that employers provide a certain minimum level of protection or a security floor for each employee. There are three primary areas of compulsory security: workers' compensation, unemployment compensation, and Social Security benefits.

workers' compensation Payments for injuries received while on the job.

Workers' Compensation **Workers' compensation** protects the employee from costs resulting from injury on the job. These costs are paid entirely by the employer. Thus industrial accidents are viewed as a cost of doing business, and, like any other cost, the company is responsible for keeping the costs as low as possible by furnishing a safe workplace and safe work procedures.[14]

Workers' compensation started with the Federal Employee's Compensation Act of 1908 and the state laws of California, Washington, Wisconsin, and New Jersey passed in 1911. All states now have workers' compensation laws.

contributory negligence Doctrine whereby an employee is unable to collect on a lawsuit if the employee is at all liable.

Prior to the passage of workers' compensation laws, if an employee was injured on the job, he or she had to prove negligence on the part of the employer. This was very difficult. Under the doctrine of **contributory negligence**, even if the employee was only 1 percent negligent and the employer 99 percent negligent, the employee could not collect in the suit. Because most employers had no health insurance plans for employees at the time, the net effect was that employees injured on the job had to pay for their medical care entirely on their own. Of course, most workers simply did not have funds to do so.

Workers' compensation originally covered only physical injury. However, today it has been expanded to cover emotional consequences resulting from physical injury. In some cases, job stress and strain are covered if they lead to emotional illness. Furthermore, even an accident at a company-sponsored party may be covered if employees are expected to attend.

Employers pay premiums into a state or private insurance fund. Premiums are based on the company's experience with accident and job-related illness rates: the higher the accident rate, the higher the premium. Thus employers have an incentive to provide a safe workplace and instruction in safe work habits. However, insurers often refuse to set premium prices for small companies to their level of injury. The result is that some small firms that have had no accidents are placed in a pool with all other firms in their industry and end up paying a much higher premium than is warranted.[15]

Employees collect workers' compensation either in the form of cash paid directly to the employee or in the form of reimbursement for medical expenses, pain, and suffering. When work is missed, the employee is paid for lost work time. Although the amount varies from state to state, payment for lost work time resulting from illness or injury averages about two thirds of the employee's regular earnings.

EXHIBIT 13.3   A TYPOLOGY OF BENEFITS

Category	Example benefit programs					
Mandatory Security	Workers' compensation	Unemployment compensation	Social Security			
Voluntary Security	Severance pay	Supplemental unemployment benefits	Golden parachutes			
Retirement-Related Security	Pension funds	Vesting	Retirement anuity	Individual retirement accounts	401(k) plans	
Time-Off-Related Security	Vacation pay	Holiday pay	Sick leave	Disability leave	Paid and unpaid leaves of absence	Military reserve time
Health and Other Insurance	Medical	Dental	Disability	Life	Legal insurance	Wellness and fitness programs / Employee Assistance Programs (EAPs)
Financial Services	Profit sharing	Stock plans	Moving assistance	Tuition reimbursement	Legal services	Financial counseling / ESOPs
Social and Recreational Services	Paid club membership	Professional and trade association dues and meeting costs	Child/elder care	Flex-time	Service awards (such as watches, jewelry)	Company-sponsored social events (e.g., the Christmas party)

SOURCE: Adapted from Robert L. Mathis and John H. Jackson, *Human Resource Management* (West Publishing Company, 1997) p. 442.

Importance of Benefits Keeps Growing

In the past, benefits were not very important, but today their importance is increasing. In a Gallup poll of 1000 Americans, 75 percent consider health insurance, pensions, vacations, and other benefits to be very important in deciding whether or not to take a job. In contrast, only 70 percent in 1991 and 57 percent in 1990 thought these benefits were very important. These benefits are likely to become even more important in the future.

The majority of the people surveyed said that they would not accept a job that did not provide health insurance. Individuals with health insurance stated that they would need to earn an average of $4570 more to give up health benefits. In an effort to attract and maintain competent employees, employers will need to offer a competitive benefits package. In many cases, the benefits package greatly influences the decision to accept or decline an employment offer.

SOURCE: Albert R. Karr, "Benefits Keep Growing, at Least in Importance to Workers," *The Wall Street Journal*, November 17, 1992, p. A1.

All but three states (Texas, New Jersey, and South Carolina) have compulsory workers' compensation plans with which every employer must comply. Under the elective laws in the three exception states, employers have the option of accepting or rejecting the act. If the employer rejects it, the employee must sue to initiate compensation.

To control rising costs of workers' compensation, several hospitals in Massachusetts have formed a self-insurance group and are paying a total of $2.5 million into a workers' compensation fund. The administrators of the fund have promised that a nurse will contact the injured employee within a day of when a claim is filed. This early involvement is intended to decrease the number of days missed from work, which will reduce hospital costs.[16]

Workers' compensation costs for companies rose between 1985 and 1993. In 1993, employers paid $60.8 billion, double the amount paid in 1985. However, some change in the trend appeared in the mid 1990s. Workers' compensation costs for 1995 were down from 1993 to $57.1 billion, equivalent to a 6.3 percent decline. The U.S. Bureau of Labor Statistics reported an additional 5 percent decline in the number of injuries and illnesses reported by private employers in 1996.[17]

The downward trend ended in the late 1990s. Several factors led to the change. First, insurance companies that held their rates stable during the late 1990s to remain competitive began to raise them in 2000. Additionally, fluctuations in the market and lower interest rates further fueled the increases. Third, increased wages raised workers' compensation costs because the rate companies pay to cover workers' compensation is indexed off wages paid. Fourth, the types of injuries covered increased. For example, mental health claims are just one of the many new injuries covered. Finally, medical costs that also remained stable in the mid 1990s began to rise in 2000.[18]

Criticism of Workers' Compensation   Because benefits and plans vary so much from state to state, organized labor and others have lobbied for more federal control and regulation. Of course, employers and business groups have strongly resisted this because they believe their costs will increase. States also prefer to have their own plans, because those with low benefit levels use that fact as a strong inducement when attracting new industry.

Today, employers are paying $40 billion a year to compensate and care for injured workers, with medical bills accounting for 40 percent and compensation for the other 60 percent. Insurers and companies that self-insure pay $20 billion a year for medical care for injured workers.[19] These rising costs have some managers worried about how they will pay the premiums. For example, Jean Stinson, a railroad contractor in Florida, lost a great deal of business when her company's workers' compensation liability jumped 187 percent in one year. To cover the $250,000 in costs, she raised her bids. However, her customers decided to put all but the necessary projects on hold. She faced a similar problem at the beginning of 1992 when Florida's rates again were increased by 25 percent.[20]

As some employers find ways to pay workers' compensation premiums, others are devising methods to avoid paying them. Stafcor, an employee leasing agency in California, has found a loophole in the law. The company administers its own workers' compensation program by combining it with its health insurance plan. Stafcor asserts that its "24-hour program," which covers employees on and off the job, is perfectly legal under the Employee Retirement Income Security Act of 1974 (ERISA). This loophole in this federal law allows Stafcor to save as much as 40 percent of the average $4 to $5 per $100 of payroll that California companies now pay to cover their workers in the state's program.[21] To deal with higher costs, top management must become involved. The following are several steps recommended to help managers keep workers' compensation benefits in line:

1. Collect facts about the history of the firm's workers' compensation. Compare these figures to profits, sales, and salaries to see if they are out of proportion.
2. Be sure to understand the current programs in safety and health. Are there areas that can be improved?
3. Invite outside vendors, especially insurance carriers, who often have innovative plans and can propose alternative plans that will help curb rising costs.
4. Become more involved in the workers' compensation reforms in the states in which the company does business. Its voice may help to change the process.
5. Communicate information about workers' compensation benefits to employees—it can keep them from taking an adversarial stance.
6. Show concern in an emergency. The use of in-house clinics that can provide immediate attention to injuries can reduce the need for outside care.
7. Penalize careless managers. Charge claims to the operating unit in which the injury occurs.
8. Get employees back to work fast. The longer the employee stays away from work, the more attitudes toward him or her and work change. The employee may never come back.
9. Find out what's causing injuries. Many injuries can result from common problems that are easily fixed.[22]

unemployment compensation
Payment to employees for time missed because of layoff or termination.

Unemployment Compensation **Unemployment compensation** pays employees for work time missed because of layoff or termination. This is a state-administered plan, but it was established as part of the Social Security Act of 1935. The law was passed during the height of the depression to provide income for the millions of people out of work, thus helping to revive the economy. Employers fund this program by paying up to 3.5 percent of an initial amount (often $7000 of an employee's salary).

Most employees are eligible for benefits unless they are fired for misconduct. They collect 50 percent to 80 percent of pay, depending on the state, for up to 26 weeks as long as they actively seek employment. During periods of high unemployment, Congress extends the period for collecting benefits up to another 26 weeks. Unemployment compensation has been criticized for encouraging fraud and laziness. Yet it has provided a floor of income for people who leave their jobs usually through no fault of their own. The law requires people receiving unemployment compensation to actively seek work, thus officially encouraging them to go to work as soon as they can.

Some have suggested that the federal law should be changed to eliminate abuse, provide stronger requirements for work-search behavior, and provide more funding for the plan, especially during recessions. Standardization among the states also has been advocated.

Social Security   Virtually everyone who works today is covered by Social Security. Social Security benefits are provided when an employee retires at age 65. It also covers old age, disability, and survivors' insurance. Even such programs as Medicare and Medicaid fall under Social Security. In fact, several welfare programs, such as Aid to Families with Dependent Children (AFDC), the program that distributes food stamps, fall under the Social Security Act of 1935. However, our concerns are with those provisions of the program that deal with employment-related issues.

The Social Security program was established by the Social Security Act of 1935. This law was passed during the depression as part of President Franklin D. Roosevelt's New Deal program. The rationale was that government needed to provide a mandatory social insurance program to provide a minimum income for those who retire or are disabled on the job and for their survivors. Although initially limited in coverage, virtually everyone who works today (even farmers, who are not included in most programs) is covered by the law.

Social Security Funding   Social Security is funded jointly by the employee and employer through a tax on a set amount of wages. Both the tax and the minimum wage covered have consistently increased throughout the years, as is shown in Exhibit 13.4, but benefits also have increased greatly and are now indexed to inflation.

The Social Security fund is not a strict insurance fund as found in a private insurance company. Rather, the contributions of current employees pay the benefits of current retirees and other eligible recipients. In fact, there is some concern that once the baby boomers begin to retire in the first decade of the next century, there will not be enough people working to cover the massive benefit payments needed to fund such a large number of retirees.

Social Security also provides disability payments to an individual who is disabled on the job for as long as the person lives. These payments are rather modest, however. They also are made to survivors (immediate family) under certain conditions if a person covered by Social Security dies while working or retired.

Finally, Medicaid benefits are funded under the Social Security Act, and pay health-care benefits for the elderly who are covered under the Social Security Act.

To better fund the program, some changes were made in 1983 in an act passed to amend the basic law. Social Security begins to pay some benefits at age 62, but the normal retirement age is 65. By 2002, the retirement age will increase by two-month increments to age 67 for all employees born in 1960 or later. The age for coverage for widows and widowers will also increase from 60 to 65. Finally, the act was changed so that people with higher incomes pay a tax on their Social Security income.

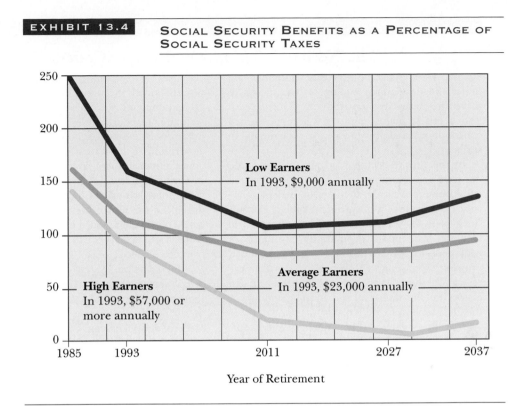

EXHIBIT 13.4   SOCIAL SECURITY BENEFITS AS A PERCENTAGE OF SOCIAL SECURITY TAXES

Year of Retirement

The Future Challenges of Social Security   Beginning in 1993 for high wage earners, and in 2002 for average wage earners, some Americans will be getting less in benefits than the accumulated value of what they and their employers paid in taxes. However, lower-income workers will still benefit from the program. As can be seen in Exhibit 13.4, Social Security is almost guaranteed to be a bad deal for high- and average-income workers.

A recent survey conducted by the Employment Benefit Research Institute showed that 65 percent of working Americans expect to pay more into Social Security than the amount that they will actually receive. If this persists, it will become more difficult to gain support for Social Security from average- and high-income individuals.

In addition, meeting the needs of the huge population of aging baby boomers will threaten to bankrupt the Social Security system. Even though Social Security taxes on employees and employers rise annually, there is some doubt that all of the aging baby boomers will be cared for properly under Social Security, especially as life expectancy continues to increase.

Voluntary Security

severance pay
Money given to an employee at termination.

Two of the major security benefit programs used by employers are voluntary: severance pay and supplemental unemployment benefits (SUB). **Severance pay** is pay given to the employee at termination. Its purpose is to provide funds to tide the employee over until he or she finds another job. The amount varies from several weeks of pay for hourly workers to several years worth of salary for executives.[23]

The Need to Fill Empty Retirement Coffers

Many pension plans, both private and public, are underfunded because employers have failed to make the necessary contributions. During economic crises, many employers have postponed contributions, and now problems are beginning to surface.

In the private sector, many contributions do not have enough money to pay benefits to vested employees. In addition, the Pension Benefit Guaranty Corporation, a government agency that insures plans in a manner similar to the Federal Deposit Insurance Corporation's insurance of bank deposits, has a $2.8 billion deficit—and it is growing. According to Robert Reich, former Secretary of Labor, "At the present time the problem is not dire, but the trend is disturbing and now is the ideal time to fix it."

It is almost certain that employees and taxpayers will be affected in some way by this problem. What can be done to adequately deal with it before a major crisis emerges?

"Although relatively few people are aware of the problem, state and local pension plans across the country are more than $125 billion short of the money they will need to meet their pension promises." For example, Dale Barry of Maine always dreamed of retiring from his state job at age 60 and enjoying the fruits of his labor. However, well after reaching age 60, Mr. Barry and 21,000 other public employees in Maine are still working as a result of the state's $2.6 billion pension account underfunding. When federal civilian and military employees are included, the gap between the amount saved and the amount required is an astonishing $1.24 trillion. As with the problems facing persons employed in the private sector, employees and taxpayers will have to assist in dealing with the problem.

Americans often are told not to rely solely on Social Security because it may not be available for their retirement. Should Americans also not rely on the pensions their employers promised? These are very serious issues. What can be done to ensure that our pensions will be available when we reach retirement age?

SOURCE: Richard D. Hylton, "Don't Panic about Pensions—Yet," *Fortune*, April 18, 1994, p. 1211; and Leslie Scism, "Public Pensions Are So Underfunded That Trouble Is Likely," *The Wall Street Journal*, April 6, 1994, p. C1.

---

golden parachute Amount paid to executives in the case of a hostile takeover.

Golden parachutes, a form of severance pay, are paid to executives as a form of compensation if they are terminated during a hostile takeover. Executives who fear hostile takeovers often are able to obtain a golden parachute clause in their contract, which states that they will be paid a large amount—often several years worth of salary—if they are terminated. Because hostile takeovers usually result in termination of many executives in the acquired company, this protects those executives and is a deterrent to hostile takeovers, because such a large amount of cash is needed to fund the golden parachutes.

supplemental unemployment benefits (SUB) Amount given in excess of unemployment compensation received from the state.

The second form of voluntary security is **supplemental unemployment benefits (SUB).** These are payments made by the employer to an employee who is temporarily laid off. They are made in addition to unemployment compensation received from the state. These payments were pioneered by the auto industry (during economic recessions, model changeovers, and so on). In the auto industry, employees receive up to 95 percent of their normal wage through SUB and unemployment compensation.

Retirement

More than 90 percent of full-time workers at companies with more than 100 employees are covered by retirement plans, according to the Employee Benefits Research Institute. Yet only 43 percent of firms with fewer than 100 employees have pension

Two Bad Options

Imagine that you have worked for your company for more than 15 years. You have reached the point at which you have become vested in the retirement program, and you are looking forward to the pension you will receive when you retire. Now imagine that your employer outsourced your jobs and gave you two choices: you can work for the new company who won the outsourcing contract for less benefits, including your pension, or you can be laid off. This is exactly what happened to the employees of the Santa Fe Terminal Services Company who transferred cargo between railcars and tracks at a rail yard. As you might imagine, they sued, charging that contracting out their jobs was a way for the Sante Fe Railway to avoid providing benefits that were promised to them under their collective bargaining agreement.

The appeals court ruled that the workers had the right to sue over the loss of pension benefits but not the other benefits guaranteed under the contract. Pensions were specifically noted as relevant in the lawsuit because once an employee is vested in a pension plan, he or she has a legally enforceable right to collect this benefit. The case was remanded all the way to the Supreme Court. Can you guess what their decision was?

The Supreme Court was unanimous in their decision in favor of the workers. From the employee's perspective, if the court had ruled otherwise, there would be potential for employers to discriminate against those who had high medical bills or retirement benefits. The Supreme Court's ruling clarified federal benefits protection and indicated that companies cannot discharge workers just to cut their health and benefits costs. Good news for the workers; bad news for companies.

coverage.[24] About 45 percent of all civilian workers work in firms of 100 or fewer employees, so a large percentage of employees are not covered by pensions. In fact, Congress is considering several bills to encourage more widespread use of pensions by employers; the incentives include portability, tax credits, and reduced paperwork.

Pension plans are considered rewards for long service and are not incentives to work more efficiently or effectively unless the premium is tied to a stock option plan, as Sears' is. Pension plans are used primarily to retain a loyal workforce.

Employment Retirement Income Security Act (ERISA) of 1974   This law was passed to correct many abuses in pension coverage and to set rules and regulations. It is the major law regulating pensions. It is complex, detailed, and, at least for small firms, costly to follow. Hence, many small firms have terminated their pension coverage to avoid the voluminous paperwork; yet the law has provided increased security to ensure that employees actually receive their pensions when they retire.

The Internal Revenue Service (IRS) has also developed guidelines to try to control discrimination in pensions. Specifically, rules were established so that higher-paid employees would not benefit more than lower-paid employees.[25] Higher-paid employees in 1990 were defined by the IRS as any employee paid more than $85,485 a year or $56,990 if he or she was in the top 20 percent of a company's earners.[26]

unfunded plan
Plan that pays pensions out of current earnings generated by the company.

funded plan
Plan that pays benefits out of money set aside and invested specifically for paying pension benefits.

Funding of Pensions   Funds for paying pension benefits are acquired in two basic ways. An **unfunded plan** pays pensions out of current income generated by the organization. A **funded plan** pays benefits out of money set aside and invested specifically to pay pension benefits; this is the more popular method because a specific fund is set aside to pay benefits. Current income of the firm, which can vary widely from year to year depending on economic conditions and other factors, is generally viewed as too variable and risky a way to fund pensions.

insured pensions Funds administered through an insurance company that guarantees payment of benefits.

Insurance for Pensions   **Insured pensions** are administered through an insurance company that guarantees payment of the benefits. **Uninsured pensions** are administered by the employer and are considered to be less stable and sound than insured pensions. However, some insured pensions are not too safe. For example, Pacific Lumber's retirement payments to its workers were delayed and threatened to be cut completely when the state took over First Executive Corporation's largest insurance units in California and New York. These insurance units, which were responsible for Pacific Lumber's pension plan, invested heavily in junk bonds, and when the bottom fell out of that market, the insurance units had to be taken over. Workers like Bill Hunsaker, who worked for Pacific Lumber for 47 years, were devastated. Hunsaker's medical bills for his wife and himself stacked up, and promises from the company did little to ease his pain.[27]

uninsured pensions Plans administered by the employer; considered to be less stable and sound than insured pensions.

noncontributory pension Plan in which all pension funds are paid by the employer.

Contributions   A **noncontributory pension** is one in which the employer pays all of the funds for the pensions. In a **contributory pension**, both the employee and the employer fund the pension.

contributory pension Plan that is funded by the employer as well as the employee.

Pension Benefits   Retirement plans come in two main types: defined contribution and defined benefit plans. Exhibit 13.5 illustrates the number of employees involved in both and the assets associated with each. A **defined contribution plan** is one in which the contribution rate paid by the employee is *fixed* and retirement benefits *vary*. Profit sharing, employee stock ownership plans (ESOPs), and thrift plans are defined contribution plans. In a **defined benefit plan**, the benefits paid to employees are *set* as are the methods used to determine them. This allows the use of statistics to determine the employer contribution. Because a defined benefit plan provides a greater assurance of benefits and predictability of benefits available at retirement, older employees generally prefer this type of plan.[28]

defined contribution plan Plan in which the contribution rate paid by the employee is fixed and retirement benefits vary.

defined benefit plan Plan in which the benefits paid to the employees and the method to determine the benefits are set.

Defined benefit plans have become more costly to administer because of tax and accounting rules. Consequently, more firms have adopted defined contribution plans, in which salary and service determine annual payments to an employee's account. Defined contribution plans are popular with firms for other reasons. For example, this type of plan makes it fairly easy for companies to modify their retirement plans, usually lowering employee benefits. Let's explore some of the ways companies can cut their pension plans.

First, we need a numeric example to serve as a baseline. Three numbers are frequently used to calculate a pension payment: years of service, average salary during the past three years, and a multiplier that is set by the firm. For our hypothetical example, let's say that Fred has worked for us for 20 years, his average salary during the past three years is $40,000, and our company uses a multiplier of 1.5 percent. If we do the math (20 × 40,000 × .015), we learn that Fred is entitled to $12,000 a year at age 65. Given the downturn in our profits and a dip in the stock market, we decided that we cannot afford to pay Fred $12,000 a year, so we cut the multiplier from 1.5 to 1.0. Fred now gets $8000 a year. Another option is to redefine what the average salary is based on. Let's say Fred received a 10 percent bonus every year. We could deduct that amount from his average salary, reducing his payout to $10,800 while using the

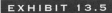

EXHIBIT 13.5   RETIREMENT PLANS BY TYPES

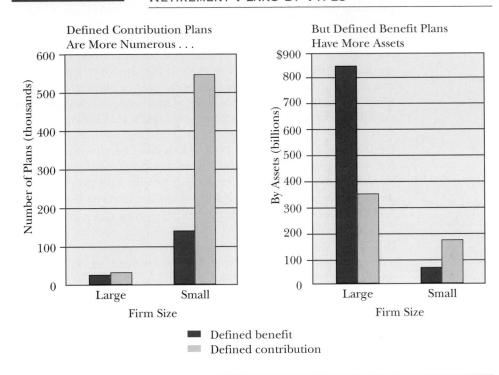

original multiplier. Still a little too high? Another change we can make is to average Fred's salary over ten years instead of three. This should lower his payment because he earned a lower salary a decade ago, and averaging it in will drop the overall average used in calculating the payout. Other options include capping the number of years of service that can be used in the equation and freezing the plan on a certain date so that any additional years of service or salary increases cannot be included in the calculations. Pension calculation changes to reduce payouts such as those noted previously have been made by a host of companies, including IBM, Ameritech, Duke Energy, Dow Chemical, KMart, and Lucent Technologies.[29]

portable pension plan Plan that allows employees to move their benefits from one employer to another without incurring a loss.

Portability   In a **portable pension plan**, employees can move their pension benefits from one employer to another without losing benefits. Portability has become an increasingly important aspect of pensions because the average worker changes jobs every two to three years before age 30 and four to seven years thereafter. To deal with these demographic changes, in 1978, the Internal Revenue Service addressed the demand for portable pensions by creating 401(k) plans and reducing the number of years needed for vesting. In 1991, the Department of Labor proposed the Pension Opportunities for Workers Expanded Retirement (POWER) to simplify and increase the flexibility of pension systems. As the baby-boom generation continues to age, there will be even more demand for portability and security for retirement.[30] If an employee is not in a portable pension, then a lump-sum benefit must be taken at termination, provided the employee is vested.

vesting The right to receive benefits from a retirement plan.

Vesting Rights   **Vesting** is the right to receive benefits from a retirement plan. A person becomes vested after working and contributing for a period of time. Five- and ten-year vesting periods are common. If the employee leaves prior to the vesting requirement, the only funds the employee receives on employment termination are the funds the employee has contributed. Once vested, however, pension rights are retained and both employee and employer funds are received.

Retirement Equity Act of 1984   This law liberalized pension regulations that affect women, guaranteed access to benefits, lowered the vesting age, and prohibited employers from discriminating against people who take leaves of absence (such as pregnancy leave). Other provisions of the act lowered the age at which workers can receive pension credits and the age at which they can enroll.

Individual Retirement Accounts (IRAs)   A popular retirement fund is the individual retirement account. Although IRAs are funded entirely by the employee, they are popular because the salary money contributed, up to $2000 per year, is not subject to taxes under certain total income limitations. Also, the interest earned on the amount set aside is not taxed regardless of total income.

Money can be set aside until age $70\frac{1}{2}$ and can be withdrawn without penalty beginning at age $59\frac{1}{2}$. Funds drawn prior to that date are subject to income tax plus a 10 percent penalty. The major advantages of an IRA are that the employee can decide how to invest the extra retirement income, and a tax shelter is created because income tax is deferred until retirement when total income is presumably lower and, hence, taxed at a lower rate. Alternatively, employees can invest in a Roth IRA. Under this plan taxes are paid up front, making the money taken out at retirement tax free.

401(k) Plans   Named for the section of the IRS code that set them up, 401(k) plans work much like an IRA in that they serve as a tax shelter for a portion of income until retirement. The difference is that the employer deducts the salary, and the money can be invested in only a limited set of employer-approved funds. Also, a larger amount can be set aside in these plans—$7000 per year or up to $9000 for educators. These plans are popular with higher-paid managers and executives, as shown in Exhibit 13.6. In fact, the gap between highly paid workers (those earning more than $66,000 a year) and lower-paid workers participating in 401(k) plans has risen every year. In 1995 the gap was only 14 percent (77 percent versus 63 percent). In 1996 the gap grew to 26 percent, and in 1997 90 percent of highly paid workers participated in 401(k) plans compared to 64 percent of lower-paid workers, resulting in a gap of 34 percent.[31] In an effort to lure lower-paid employees to enroll in 401(k) plans, employers offer classes to educate employees about the benefits.[32] Some firms have installed automatic enrollment facilities in which employees are automatically enrolled in the company's 401(k) plans at the default levels unless they sign a form opting out of the program.[33] These measures were taken for several reasons. First, lower-paid, often younger workers are frequently unwilling to sign up for retirement benefits, even though they should. By making it easier to sign up and harder not to, employers are encouraging employees to begin retirement planning at an earlier age. In addition, the

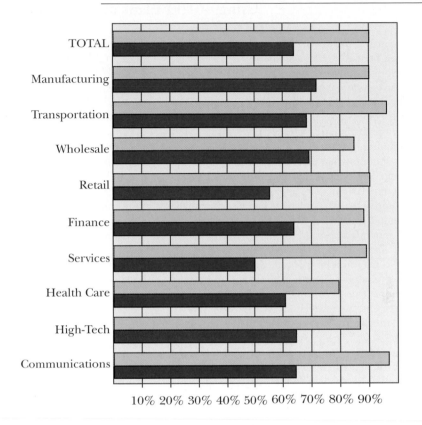

| EXHIBIT 13.6 | AVERAGE PARTICIPATION RATE FOR EMPLOYEES OFFERED 401(K) PLANS |

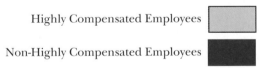

Highly Compensated Employees

Non-Highly Compensated Employees

level of contribution allowed by higher-paid employees is dependent on the level of contribution made by lower-paid employees. There are complex reporting formulas imposed by the federal government that are used to determine if lower-paid employees are being discriminated against with respect to enrollment in 401(k) plans. However, effective in 1999, companies can exempt themselves from the nondiscrimination testing if they make an across-the-board 401(k) contribution of 3 percent to all eligible employees.[34]

One way to entice more employees to participate in 401(k) plans is to make them more attractive. For example, younger employees may be turned off by having to put money away that they will not be able to touch for more than 30 years. Including a loan option in the 401(k) plan may be all that is needed to win these folks over.[35] Another complaint professional employees have is that they could earn more money if they took the cash and invested it in the stock market. To overcome this objection,

---

Using 401(k) Plans at Coors

During 1990, Coors Brewing Company increased 401(k) participation by 16.5 percent and hiked pension benefits by an average of 7.1 percent for all employees. Employees have become involved in their retirement plans. More than one third of Coors employees have requested a computer program to project their retirement benefits. What sparked this dramatic increase? Coors says it's simply communication.

Coors implemented a campaign called the Tax Effective Retirement Account (TERA). This plan was designed to increase employee participation in the company's 401(k) plan. When Coors realized that employees failed to see their retirement income should come from three sources—pensions, Social Security, and personal savings—they decided to do something about it. The TERA promotion focused on helping employees understand the importance of making steady contributions to a retirement savings account to maintain a style of living after retirement to which they have grown accustomed.

One key to the program's success was the TERA turtle, which served as the mascot for the program. The turtle, inspired by the Aesop's fable of the tortoise and the hare, represented that the way to win the retirement race is with steady, dependable savings. All employees who enrolled in the 401(k) plan received a turtle lapel pin, and all nonparticipants who requested a personalized computer projection received a pin too. If the nonparticipants joined, they also received a turtle

coffee mug as did those who increased their deferral percentage. To maintain interest in the program, Coors sponsored a weekly drawing for $100. However, the name pulled as the winner could collect only if the person was wearing a turtle pin.

All of these efforts paid off for Coors. In just 10 months, participation in TERA jumped from 73 percent to 84 percent of the workforce. More than 2200 employees increased their deferral percentage and more than 1200 employees signed up for first-time participation. Coors believes that its efforts will help to ensure that its employees will be able to retire in style.

Coors is a success story. However, the majority of companies have yet to attain its level of success. The latest evidence from a Gallup survey of defined contribution plans revealed that while 401(k) participants are more familiar with investment terminology than are others surveyed, they lack overall investment knowledge.

Companies are faced with the challenge of educating their employees. IDS helps its employees by issuing GAP statements, which are designed to identify retirement income needs and to demonstrate how to attain the goals. As a human resource manager, what improvements would you make to ensure better understanding of pension plans?

SOURCES: Adapted from Shari Caudron, "Boosting Retirement Benefits," *HRMagazine*, December 1991, pp. 76–79; and Richard F. Stolz, "State-of-the-Art in 401(k)," *Advertisement*, 1993.

---

some firms have modified their 401(k) plans to include a "self-directed" option. Under this plan employees can use their tax-qualified retirement savings to trade stocks, bonds, and mutual funds.[36] While administering 401(k) plans that include these options are more difficult, they do encourage more employees to participate.

Keogh Plans   Keogh plans, or self-employment plans (SEPs), are retirement plans that self-employed individuals can use for retirement. These act much like an IRA in that a $2000 limit is observed, and the individual directs the plan. Of course, the income and interest are sheltered from taxation until withdrawn.

Early Retirement   Most companies offer early retirement whereby a person can retire at a lower age with fewer benefits. This is attractive, especially if a person can supplement company retirement with 401(k), IRA, or Keogh retirement plans. Many companies will "encourage" early retirement when attempting to reduce the number of employees by offering an extra one-time bonus for them to take early retirement. However, they cannot force people to retire against their will. Because of a 1986 amendment to the Age Discrimination in Employment Act, most employees can no longer be forced to retire.[37]

Forcing older workers out the door has not been a problem. Actually, in some cases, the reverse has occurred. For example, a petroleum firm that offered early retirement to its workers was forced to temporarily shut down a refinery because nearly every worker at the power plant that supplied the power for the refinery took early retirement. West Virginia's early retirement plan is costing the state $11 million more than it saved. DuPont was forced to hire back as consultants some of the employees it lost through an early retirement offer because almost twice as many people accepted the offer as the company had anticipated.[38]

As a way to avoid a mass exodus of older workers, firms have begun offering a phased retirement option. Under this plan, employees remain with the company and work part time. In return the company provides the employee with a one-time lump payment of their pension. This program creates a win-win situation. Employees get their retirement up front and can invest the funds any way they choose—often earning more than they would have leaving it in the pension plan. They also get to ease into retirement rather than stop working cold turkey. The company benefits too. First, it retains a great deal of corporate knowledge by keeping older workers on the payroll, but it reduces their costs because they are working only part time. Further, the firm's pension liabilities for its older employees are greatly reduced, making the bottom line stronger.[39]

Statistics indicate that the number of employees who opt for early retirement offers may continue to increase. For example, in 1955, 65 percent of the men over age 55 were working, but this figure had dropped to only 46 percent by 1980. For the men in the age group of 65 to 69, 57 percent were employed in 1955 as compared with only 29 percent by 1980. The figures are not so dramatic for women, but there has been an increase in their retirement percentages as well.[40] One thing that may make potential retirees think twice about early retirement is a lower standard of living after retirement. For a retiree who earned $40,000 in 1988 to maintain that standard of living, the retiree would need an income of about 68 percent of that amount plus Social Security benefits. By 1992 the amount had risen to 77 percent of that amount. Two of the major culprits for the increase are higher medical costs and lower savings.[41]

For years, employers have promised employees health-care coverage after retiring. However, a new accounting rule requiring companies to show a liability for retirees' health benefits on their financial statements is putting pressure on management to trim costs to improve the bottom line. An easy solution to this is to increase the amount of the premiums paid by retirees. However, some companies have even eliminated the coverage completely.[42]

Procter & Gamble took a different approach. Since the early 1990s it has had an investment trust fund designated to fund retirees' health benefits. The rise in the stock market coupled with lower-than-expected health-care costs yielded an unexpected boost to Procter & Gamble's bottom line. In addition, the fund is now "overfunded" so Proctor and Gamble will not have to cut benefits for retirees.[43]

Time-Off–Related Benefits

Most companies offer time-off–related benefits in the form of holiday pay, vacation pay, and leaves of absence.

Holiday Pay   Most employers provide pay for all established holidays such as New Year's Day, Memorial Day, Fourth of July, Thanksgiving, and Christmas. Other firms also provide holiday pay for Christmas Eve, the day after Thanksgiving, and the employee's birthday. Federal employees also receive pay for President's Day, Veteran's Day, Martin Luther King's birthday, and Columbus Day. The average number of holidays given is ten per year, and many employers offer floating holidays, such as the employee's birthday.[44] Unionized companies negotiate holidays as part of the labor agreement.

Vacations   Most employers offer paid vacations that range from one to six weeks per year, depending on length of time (seniority) with the company. In one poll, employees rated paid vacations and holidays as the third most important benefit behind medical insurance and pensions.[45]

sabbatical
Extended leave of absence granted to employees for renewal purposes.

Leaves of Absence   Leaves are given for military service, jury duty, elections, disability, funerals (bereavement), sickness, and maternity/paternity. Longer leaves called **sabbaticals** are also given for renewal or special service. Nearly half of the Fortune 100 Best Companies to Work For in America provide employees sabbaticals.[46] Sabbaticals are becoming more and more popular with high-technology firms, as shown in Exhibit 13.7. For example, Intel employees are eligible for eight weeks off with full pay and benefits after every seven years of full-time employment. Intel says sabbaticals accomplish two things: they allow employees time to revitalize themselves and they reward employees for longevity in a positive way. Because private-sector employees can use their sabbaticals for any purpose, as long as the purpose does not conflict with the interests of the employer, many workers elect to take extended vacations and return to work de-stressed and more productive.[47] Brooks Fisher did just that. After working 100+ hours a week, which included constant travel, he asked for some extended time off. Intuit, Inc., his employer, readily agreed. Fisher spent the time reacquainting himself with this family and studied jazz piano.[48]

maternity leave
Leave of absence associated with child bearing, usually six weeks or more.

The 1978 Pregnancy Discrimination Act requires that **maternity leave** be treated in the same manner as any other medical disability or condition that involves a leave. If an employer has certain guarantees for employees on leave as to rights to certain jobs and pay on return, these also must be made available to women on maternity leave. Companies are finding that with the increase in the number of women in the workforce, an up-to-date maternity leave policy is extremely important. Firms that do not have such a policy may find themselves losing valuable employees.[49]

As a response to employees' need for leaves for fathers of newborn or young children and for other reasons, such as to care for ill or elderly family members, President Clinton signed into law the Family and Medical Leave Act on February 5, 1993, which became effective on August 5, 1993. In the case of a collective bargaining agreement, the act does not apply until the expiration of any existing agreement or one year after enactment, whichever is earlier. All employees who work at least 12 months for employers with 50 or more employees within a 75-mile area of a given workplace are covered. The major elements of the act include 12 weeks of leave during any 12-month period for one or more of the following: birth of a child; placement of a child for

EXHIBIT 13.7	SABBATICAL OFFERINGS FROM HIGH TECHNOLOGY FIRMS

Firms That Offer Sabbaticals

Firms	Sabbatical	Eligibility
Adobe Systems	3 weeks paid	5 years
Advanced Micro Devices	2 months paid	7 years (for exempt classes)
Apple Computer	6 weeks paid	5 years
Autodesk	6 weeks paid	4 years
Centigram Computer	4 weeks paid	4 years
Intel	8 weeks paid	7 years
Microsoft	8 weeks in paid leave or cash	7 years (upper-level key employees)
Silicon Graphics	6 weeks paid	4 years
Storage Dimensions	2 weeks paid	4 years
Sybase	6 weeks paid	5 years
Tandem Computers	6 weeks paid	4 years
3Com	4 weeks paid or 2 weeks off at double pay	4 years

SOURCE: Judith Harkham Semans, "Taking Off from the Hi-Tech Grind," *HRMagazine*, September 1997, p. 128.

adoption or foster care; caring for a spouse, child, or parent with a serious health condition; or the serious health condition of the employee. The 12-week leave can be taken in a variety of ways. For example, the employee could take days as needed or use the leave to reduce the workweek or day.[50]

The Family and Medical Leave Act requires that fathers be offered the same child-care leave as mothers. These so-called gender-blind leaves are also mandated by 14 states.[51] However, not many fathers are taking them. Although more dads may be changing diapers and helping with child rearing, few can afford to take leave from work, for both financial and career reasons. Normally, after childbirth, the mother cannot work, so the father's paycheck becomes more important. Even with the guarantee that they will return to the same job, men fear taking the leave. Some critics say that the men have watched women who have been "guaranteed" the same position after returning from maternity leave who end up in a less than equal role, and they do not want to face the same outcome.[52]

In an effort to combat potential problems, Cigna implemented a program called "The Expectant Manager." The plan was aimed at managers and explained their role in accommodating pregnant employees, complying with federal laws, dealing positively with pregnancy issues, and minimizing costs of pregnancy complications.[53] In addition, Cigna unveiled their "Healthy Baby Program." This program encourages early and regular prenatal care. The goal is to cut medical costs by producing healthy, full-term babies. It appears to be working. Over the past five years the program has saved Cigna $2.4 million.[54]

disability leaves
Leaves offered to
individuals who
are hurt or be-
come ill on the
job.

Disability leaves are offered by employers to employees who are hurt or become ill on the job. These leaves are above and beyond those provided under Social Security and Workers' Compensation. While an insurance program of some sort usually funds them, they involve absence from the job and are discussed in this section. In a Gallup poll, 53 to 59 percent of the respondents said that becoming disabled would probably mean the loss of their savings, standard of living, or jobs.[55] Employers as well as employees must develop innovative solutions to this problem.

Some organizations are actively seeking ways to minimize disability costs by trying to find ways to keep the employee on the payroll. For example, when an assistant professor at the University of Pittsburgh became disabled with chronic fatigue syndrome, she, her rehabilitation specialist, and her university developed a way in which she could continue her teaching. She videotaped her lectures and held telephone office hours. This unique arrangement not only saved the university $63,000 in disability benefits, but it also kept the position filled with an employee who loves her job.[56]

Another way to cut costs associated with disabilities is to implement a managed disability care program. Managed disability programs focus on making sure disabled workers receive the care and rehabilitation they require to help them return to work as quickly as possible. Implementation of such a program requires a medical case manager. This manager should be a nurse with disability expertise. This expertise should include knowledge of relevant laws (e.g., Americans with Disabilities Act) and the knowledge of when to involve Social Security specialists or rehabilitation experts.[57] An additional emerging trend designed to cut disability costs is to limit disability insurance benefits to employees with "self-diagnosed" illnesses such as chronic fatigue syndrome, back pain, and stress. UNUM Life Insurance Company, the largest group disability carrier in the United States, is championing the movement. They have suggested a two-year limit on self-reported illnesses that cannot be confirmed with medical tests. A total of 39 states have approved the plan.[58]

There also has been some reaction to disability coverage with the passing of the Health Insurance Portability and Accountability Act of 1996 (HIPAA). One provision of this act is that both employees and employers can deduct the cost of long-term care (LTC) insurance from their annual income taxes. This new law has stirred interest in employers. Insurers say they have received more inquires than normal from firms since the passage of HIPAA. The current LTC market is composed virtually of only individual policies. Of the $2.5 billion of total LTC premiums, $2.1 billion came from individual policyholders. However, this is expected to change.[59]

Health and Insurance-Related Benefits

Employers offer various types of insurance coverage, including medical, disability, dental, life, legal, and auto insurance.[60] Health and insurance benefits are a major expense for most firms. Maintaining adequate coverage while keeping costs within bounds is a challenge for organizations.

Health Benefits   In the late 1980s and early 1990s, health-care costs rose by double digits.[61] In an effort to get the spiraling costs under control, organizations undertook major cost-containment programs. Some of the more popular cost-cutting programs are shown in Exhibit 13.8 and are explored in more detail in the following sections.

Cost-Containment Methods
Health Maintenance Organizations (HMOs)   With HMOs, health care is prepaid. Prevention is emphasized. Employers contract with an HMO, which has doctors on

WAYS THAT EMPLOYERS TRY TO CUT HEALTH-CARE COSTS

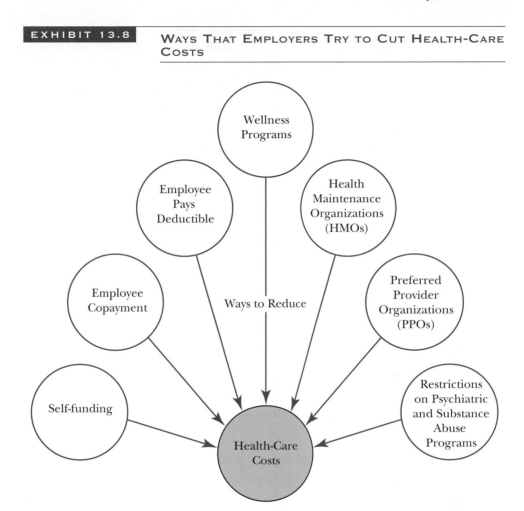

its staff. (Hospitalization is usually not covered.) For a fixed fee per enrolled employee, employees can visit the physician as often as necessary for a very small per unit charge. Thus preventive medicine can be practiced, in an attempt to prevent sickness and illness from escalating. Employees are required to work through their primary physician who refers them to other care or hospitalization. This practice also helps to keep costs down because the primary physician can do screening. In 1993, 19 percent of employees with health benefits were enrolled in HMOs. In 1997 this figure had jumped to 30 percent.[62] HMOs save money by negotiating lower fees with doctors, hospitals, and other suppliers, by scrutinizing medical decisions, and by discouraging wasteful or unnecessary procedures.[63] Sometimes the incentives the doctors receive for not ordering tests can actually harm the patient. Cindy Herdich went to her primary physician twice complaining about severe stomach pain. The first time she was told she had a urinary infection and was given antibiotics. On the second visit her doctor believed she had an ovarian cyst. To confirm her diagnosis her doctor scheduled an ultrasound. The first available appointment was eight days later. That test revealed a burst appendix that had abscessed. After immediate surgery Ms. Herdich survived but sued the HMO for valuing saving money over saving a life.[64]

Preferred Provider Organizations (PPOs)   Another form of contract health service is the PPO. This is a group usually organized by a hospital or a group of physicians. It operates much like an HMO, but a larger group of physicians is usually involved and a "looser" organization is provided in that the physicians are still independently operating under the umbrella of an HMO. A PPO allows employees more choice than does an HMO. Costs can still be kept low through prenegotiated fees, rapid claims payment, cost controls, and claims review procedures. In 1997, 35 percent of all employees covered by health benefits were enrolled in a PPO, up from 27 percent in 1993.[65]

Employee Copayment   Another cost-cutting initiative is to require employees to pay a part of their annual monthly premium. For example, the State of Florida government pays about three-fourths of individual health-care premiums and one-half of family coverage premiums for its employees. The employee picks up the rest.

Employee Payment of Deductible   The deductible system requires that the employee pay an initial fee for each office or hospital procedure. In some cases the employee pays 20 percent of each visit for an 80:20 cost-sharing ratio. This is called a copayment. In other cases the employee must pay a certain amount per year before insurance coverage pays. For example, HealthTrust's new health-care plan has a current deductible of $200, but for individuals participating in high-risk activities, it imposes a $1000 deductible.[66]

In effect, requiring employees to pay a deductible helps to reduce costs and claims for minor illnesses. Of course, it *discourages* employees from obtaining preventive treatment and early diagnosis of illness because the deductible must first be established.

Self-Funded Insurance   Self-funded plans are funded by the employer, not an insurance company.[67] In this instance, the employer sets aside a certain amount of money to pay claims during the year (for example, $1 million). In addition, a contract often is written with a health insurance company such as Blue Cross/Blue Shield or Aetna to cover claims over the amount set aside and to administer the claims payment process.

Self-funded insurance can cut costs in several ways. First, the employer earns interest on the money set aside for claims, provided it is invested. Second, by paying such a huge deductible (for example, $1 million), the actual policy with the insurance carrier can be very low. Third, the agent (the carrier) is eliminated on the bulk of the claims.

Self-insurance has become very popular as a cost-cutting strategy. For it to work, an employer should have at least 100 or more employees over which to spread the costs.

Wellness/Fitness Programs   Many companies are becoming more aggressive in preventive actions to cut health-care costs. For example, IBM has fitness rooms and jogging tracks in many of its facilities. More and more companies and communities have no-smoking policies in the workplace and encourage employees through contests and awards to give up smoking. Some employ health and fitness experts to advise executives and managers. Others, such as Xerox, sponsor employee teams to run in major races like the Boston Marathon. Although done primarily for social reasons, many firms sponsor employee athletic teams and tournaments in bowling, softball, golf, and basketball. Others sponsor weight-loss programs whereas others demand it.[68] The law firm of Klarquist, Sparkman, Campbell, Leigh, and Whinston produced a chart that indicates the healthy weight of individuals, much like an insurance chart. Employees out of their weight range are required to pay their own health insurance, although those within the range receive free coverage. Rita DelRey, a legal secretary for the firm, finds the program troubling. After losing 33 pounds she was still 12 pounds over the weight allotted for her height and age and is required to pay $56 a month for health insurance until she drops the remaining 12 pounds. She says she looks and feels great and does not want to lose any more weight. However, her bosses disagree.

Some firms are even paying employees to get healthy. Bank of Delaware employees receive $6 a month if they agree to wear a seat belt and promise to attend several health seminars. If they agree to take a fitness evaluation and adhere to the prescribed exercise plan, they can earn $9 a month. If they participate in both, they earn $12 a month.[69] U-Haul is taking the reverse approach by fining employees who do not have a healthy lifestyle. Any employee who is overweight, underweight, or who smokes is required to pay up to $10 a paycheck.[70] These companies are not alone. International Paper Corporation, which was hit with seven claims that topped $200,000 in 1989, moved to limit exposure caused by life-style excesses. The company now charges extra insurance or increases the deductibles for workers who smoke, are overweight, do not wear seat belts, or who drive while intoxicated.[71]

Providing More Information   Companies are providing information and encouraging employees to shop for medical care as they would for any other service. NCR Corporation has provided a schedule showing what the company will pay for 11,000 procedures. This gives employees a starting point to negotiate with their present doctors or to find a new one. Employees who choose not to use the company's managed care networks could end up paying a larger percentage of some doctors' bills.[72]

Other companies, such as International Paper, have a more comprehensive plan. For example, an employee in Greenville, South Carolina, facing gallbladder surgery can use the company's files to learn that International Paper will pay a maximum of $1219 to the surgeon, $257 per day for a semiprivate room, and $178 a day for nursing care. In addition, the files inform the employee that 19 surgeons in the area perform the procedure with fees ranging from $958 to $1900. The files also indicate where doctors went to school, completed their residencies, whether they are board certified, at which hospitals they work, and whether they will discuss fees.[73]

Restrictions on Psychiatric and Substance Abuse Programs   Initially, employers attempted to restrict psychiatric and substance abuse programs. However, the trend among large companies that recognize the importance of their employees' mental health is to provide a flexible set of benefits with few, if any, restrictions. Employers are beginning to see that restricting mental health coverage costs more in the long run.[74] Scientific literature shows a strong interrelationship between mental health and medical services. For example, it is more cost effective to treat alcoholics in clinics that help them stop drinking than it is to treat them for gastric disorders.[75]

Other Techniques   To reduce the cost of prescription drugs, companies are looking at new ways to deal with pharmacies. Some options include joining discount mail-order drug plans,[76] requiring that prescriptions be filled using generic drugs when they are available, and negotiating with local pharmacies to lower prices on drugs. Some firms are even toying with the idea of an in-company pharmacy. The employer would gain control over prescription costs, but the overall price tag may not make it worthwhile.[77] Another in-company trend is employers providing medical care for workers at job locations or in company-run clinics to lower health-care costs and reduce employee downtime resulting from visits to doctors' offices.[78]

School unions in California have developed trusts to manage health-care costs and to reduce the friction between unions and management. The trust is a board of about 16 members who meet regularly to find ways to cut costs through wellness programs and negotiating new contracts with doctors and pharmacies.[79] Some firms have limited costs by tailoring the insurance programs to their specific needs and by not paying for services not used by their employees.[80] Others have reduced their costs by focusing on the "at-risk" portion of their workforce: those who have terminal diseases such as cancer, heart and respiratory diseases, and childbirth and mental health needs.[81]

Even cities and states are getting into the action. When Clevelanders found out that they could load their sick employees on a plane and fly them 750 miles to the Mayo Clinic for treatment and still pay less than they would have if their employees checked into the nearby Cleveland hospitals, they knew it was time to do something. They enlisted the help of hospital administrators to obtain costs for hospital procedures and used a computer program to determine what facilities offered the most effective and efficient services. Employees were then directed to the "winning" facility.[82] Approaches like this are being used by other areas as well in an attempt to set up a market approach to health care in which only the most efficient and effective survive.[83]

One alternative to the market approach being used by several cities is a "pay-or-play" proposal.[84] Basically, this approach requires employers to provide medical coverage to all employees (play) or contribute to a government-financed health plan through a new tax (pay).[85] Some firms, such as Chrysler, have announced that they would drop their corporate insurance and pay into the public pool instead if the tax costs were less than the nearly 17 percent of the payroll that now goes to health insurance.[86]

Finally, some firms that have cut their portion of the payment for employees' insurance costs have established "flexible spending accounts" (FSAs) to ease the burden on employees. An FSA is an account funded by an employee's pretaxed income that can be used to pay for specified health-care bills, such as deductibles, day care, or medical bills. There are several benefits to this type of account. For example, the money is not taxed. Also, it reduces the employee's taxable income. However, if the employee does not spend the money by the end of the year, it is lost.[87]

Evaluation of Cost-Cutting Measures As Exhibit 13.9 shows, corporate cost-cutting efforts were effective. In 1994 health-care costs dropped. In 1997 health-care costs increased only slightly. However, by 1998 the downward trend was over. Further, survey after survey indicates that the rise in health insurance costs will set new records each year through 2003.[88] Reasons for the increase abound. For example, the migration of the American workforce to managed care plans during the last few years has saved corporations a great deal of money. However, there are not enough employees left to move to managed care to sustain the drop in health-care costs.[89] In addition, employers cut health-care costs by covering fewer employees.[90] Attempts to cut retiree health-care costs have been met by aggressive resistance by retirees.[91] Yet the

EXHIBIT 13.9   ANNUAL CHANGE IN AVERAGE TOTAL HEALTH
BENEFIT COSTS

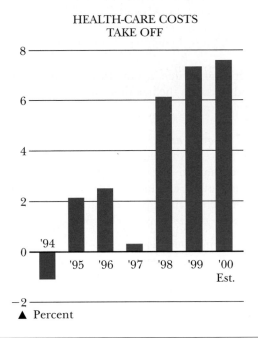

HEALTH-CARE COSTS
TAKE OFF

▲ Percent

courts have ruled that retiree medical coverage is no longer a "sacred cow" and that employers have the right to change or terminate health benefits for retirees.[92] And change they will. Sixty-two percent of the firms surveyed indicated that they will raise or will definitely consider raising insurance premium contributions for retirees,[93] and 1 in 20 says they will cancel the plan altogether.[94] The Government Accounting Office estimates that annual health-plan costs for retirees will climb to $22 billion in 2008 from about $9 billion in 1988.[95] However, once again, there are too few retirees left who can be cut in the future to sustain the downward cost trend.

Unable to reel in health-care costs by using any of the techniques used in the mid 1990s, firms had to find new approaches. One new strategy was to provide employees with a set amount of money to pay for health benefits. Employees used this amount to purchase a health-care insurance plan. The plans from which employees pick cover a wide range of options, from no-frills HMOs to traditional fee-for-service plans. This approach has been dubbed the "defined contribution" health benefit system, borrowing the term from pension benefits. This approach allows employees to control their health benefits. If the plan they selected doesn't work for them, they are free to move to another. This will also keep costs down, because the amount of money a firm pays for health care is fixed.[96] Daimler Chrysler decided it could save money if it got more involved in the delivery of health care. So it arranged a 5-day workshop at a local hospital to help the staff streamline its emergency room operations. The goal was to uncover inefficient, redundant, and costly practices. Its efforts worked, providing Daimler Chrysler employees with better health care at a lower price.[97] Merrill Lynch found it could save money by focusing on quality of care and early detection. It began by forming a company called Active Health Management Inc. This company examined the treatment of Merrill's high cost employees—those whose medical expenses exceeded $50,000 in one year. They found misdiagnoses and poor follow-up. A medical consultant for Merrill contacted the doctors and made a few suggestions whereas Active Health followed up later. By focusing on early detection and proper first diagnoses, Merrill Lynch has decreased its health-care costs.[98]

Additional Issues in Health Insurance   Several additional issues are having a profound effect on the health insurance and medical industries and will, consequently, affect employers.

COBRA Law that requires employers to provide extended health care coverage to employees who leave an organization.

Legal Requirements   In addition to the previously mentioned reasons for rising health-care costs, requirements mandated by the **Consolidated Omnibus Budget Reconciliation Act (COBRA)** passed in 1986 also have increased health-care costs.[99] Under the law, employers with 20 or more employees (except the federal government and churches) must provide extended health-care coverage to the following groups, *even when not employed* by the company:

1. Employees who quit.
2. Employees who are terminated, but not for "gross misconduct."
3. Widowed or divorced spouses and dependent children of former or current employees.
4. Retirees and their spouses whose health-care coverage ends.

Employees receive coverage for six months after leaving the company and must pay the group rate themselves. Its various requirements on notification, coverage period, and so on have caused COBRA to be a somewhat burdensome and costly law requiring more paperwork for most employers.

One way to limit the paperwork is to use computer software designed for COBRA reporting. Two such applications are COBRA Administration Manager for Windows by William Steinberg Consultants and COBRA Administration Manager by COBRA Solutions. Both programs provide a "to do" list of all of the steps required to satisfy COBRA requirements. Cost for the software ranges from $200-$300 per user.[100]

A second, more recent, law that also affects health insurance costs is HIPAA. The major impact on costs for organizations arises from HIPAA-reporting requirements. All employees who leave an employer are allowed to "port" or transfer their coverage of existing illnesses to their new employer's insurance plan without being treated as preexisting conditions. An employee earns credit for every month, up to 12, that he or she is covered by his or her former employer's insurance plan. These months can then be transferred to the new employer. If an employee has 12 months or more of credit, he or she is covered immediately by the new employer. Every employee who leaves an organization must be issued a health-care certificate that outlines the creditable coverage. In addition, employers must notify all employees and their dependents who left their insurance plan between October 1996 and May 31, 1997, of their creditable coverage. Fines of up to $100 a day per person can be levied against employers who fail to locate former employees and their dependents.[101]

An Aging Population   The U.S. Census Bureau indicates that the United States will become a gerontocracy as the baby boomers age and the birth rate remains low. By the year 2010, 33.8 percent of the nation will be over age 50.[102] Older people consume vast amounts of health care, which will likely increase as medical advances keep older people alive for longer periods of time. How will the nation adequately fund the care of its elderly in the twenty-first century?

In his book *The Retirement Myth*, Craig S. Karpel states that the baby-boom generation has virtually no hope of retiring in comfort. He reports that 59 percent of the elderly today depend on the government for more than half their income. He predicts that more Americans will be working past retirement age to offset the impact of lower government subsidies.[103]

AIDS   Acquired immune deficiency syndrome (AIDS) is a deadly disease for which, at the time of this writing, there is no cure. At the beginning of 1989, 87,188 people were diagnosed with AIDS, producing 49,976 deaths.[104] Once thought to be a disease of male homosexuals, now male heterosexuals, women, and children have it. Costs of finding a cure and treating the disease are likely to place a heavy burden on our medical system. Employers should be aware that placing an exclusion or ceiling for AIDS on insurance benefits may be illegal. As the number of legal remedies available to AIDS patients rises, the risk of employer liability climbs.[105]

Drug Testing   The use of illegal drugs in society has caused many employers to adopt a drug-testing policy. This policy might involve testing at the time of the employee's hire or unannounced tests while employed. There are legal guidelines and prohibitions to follow to have valid tests (chain of custody, invasion of privacy issues, and so on). Drug use on the job and its prevention are critical health issues with which many employers will continue to be concerned.

Expansion of Coverage   Many firms are beginning to offer coverage for dental, chiropractic, and optometric work in addition to mental health coverage. With the passage of the Mental Health Parity Act of 1996, firms may need to reevaluate their mental health benefits to ensure they align with the act. Although the act does not require firms to offer mental health coverage, it does impose some restrictions on employers who already offer this benefit. For example, if the medical benefits offered an employee have no annual or lifetime limits, then limits cannot be imposed on the mental health insurance coverage either. If there are medical insurance limitations, only these limitations can be applied to the mental health insurance.[106] In addition, states are requiring employers to add coverage for such medical services as care by lay midwives, ambulance transport, and breast reconstruction.[107]

Nonmedical Insurance Benefits   Besides health-related insurance, employers also provide other forms of insurance. For example, many employers provide life insurance policies based on a group rate. According to a recent survey by the International Society of Certified Employee Benefits Specialists, life insurance is offered by more employers than any other product.[108] A typical level is 150 percent of an employee's annual salary, but executives often receive much more than this as part of an executive compensation package. *Long-term disability coverage* is also provided by many employers, which provides a continuation of income in the event of a long-term injury or illness.

Legal insurance is provided by some firms, often in the form of prepaid or negotiated fees between the employer and a group of attorneys. The employee often shares in the premium for this insurance and/or in the fee payment at the time of the service.

Some firms also offer group rates for automobile, home, or personal property insurance at rates that are often lower than individual rates. Firms are willing to offer these types of insurance coverages to their employees because the paperwork and administrative costs are very limited and the goodwill the programs generate is significant.[109]

Financial, Social, and Recreational Benefits

perks Noncash compensation in the form of special benefits or privileges.

Many companies offer a variety of financial benefits to managers and employees. These benefits include **perks** (perquisites), which are special types of additional or added noncash compensation in the form of benefits or special privileges. Care must be exercised when defining these additional benefits. Employees often perceive programs that benefit only executives as aristocratic, and benefits given only to highly compensated employees can be found to be discriminatory as well as subject to employer and employee taxation. Employers are encouraged to seek employee input in defining benefit package components.[110] Let's examine these additional benefits.

Nonfinancial Benefits The use of a company car, company expense accounts, club memberships, help in buying and selling a home, and the use of company-owned resort condominiums are examples of perks available to managers, executives, and some employees. Also, financial planning and counseling, including tax preparation advice, are often offered to managers and executives. During times of low unemployment, companies must get creative with the benefits offered. Some of the more unique options included massage therapy, concierge services, dry cleaning, nap time, and pet health insurance.[111]

Additionally, most medium and large companies offer *credit unions* to employees for lending and saving services. Some firms offer purchase discounts to employees in the form of buying clubs or employee discounts on company merchandise.

employee investment plans Employees set aside money to invest in company-sponsored programs.

Thrift/Stock Benefits Employee **thrift**, **saving**, or **stock purchase investment plans** are also popular. For example, in a stock option plan, an employee is often guaranteed the right to buy shares of company stock at a discount or at a certain price. Alternatively, the company may purchase the stock for the employee. (This is taxable compensation unless it is in the form of a defined stock plan; then the tax is not levied until the stock is actually taken by the employee.)

employee stock ownership plan (ESOP) Profit-sharing plan in which employees are offered the opportunity to buy stock in the organization.

ESOP When stock is provided as a part of a profit-sharing plan, an **employee stock ownership plan (ESOP)** is developed. (ESOPs are also discussed in Chapter 12.) ESOPs receive favorable income tax treatment and have become very popular. They give employees a sense of ownership in the company and allow them to share in the company's success and profits.[112]

ESOPs also have been used in leveraged buyouts (LBOs) of firms by employees.[113] From 1980 to 1987, the number of employee buyouts of firms rose from 500 to 1500, a 300 percent increase. However, in 1989 and 1990, things began to slow down. In 1989, 830 new ESOP plans were established and in 1990, only 480 ESOPs were formed. Since then, the rate of growth has steadily declined to about 400 per year. The main reason suggested for the slowdown was that tighter credit restrictions limited borrowing.[114]

In the early 1980s, workers used ESOPs to buy relatively small companies or to become buyers of last resort for large troubled companies. However, by the late 1980s and 1990s, because of favorable tax treatment and as a tactic to thwart hostile takeovers, healthy companies, such as Avis, were purchased by employees through LBOs financed through ESOPs.

As the economy began to worsen in the late 1980s and early 1990s, some ESOPs lost favor with employees. Falling stock prices and rising corporate bankruptcies are rendering some ESOPs null and void. At Thomson McKinnon, where brokers and other employees owned as much as 77 percent of the firm's shares, ESOP employees saw their plan devalued from $140 million to nothing. In 1989, employees received a letter indicating that it was possible that their ESOP would have no value whatsoever.[115]

By 1995, many of the 12,000 ESOPs in the United States denied employees the right to vote on typical "shareholder" issues and often withheld key financial information. For example, morale at Avis in 1995 was very low as a result of declining profits and a 50 percent drop in share value since 1993.[116]

Educational Benefits   Many firms offer a tuition reimbursement plan for employees who attend a school, college, or university. Usually the firm requires that the employee take a course related to work, although this is often broadly defined, and that a passing grade is earned in the course.

Child-Care Benefits   Working women with small children have become very common in our society. To support these women, firms have begun to open on-site day care programs. Approximately 8000 workplaces had on-site day care centers in 2000, up from only 204 in 1982.[117] Exhibit 13.10 shows how each region of the country ranks in respect to corporate-sponsored child care. For more specific information on nonprofit child care available in communities across the United States, see the following Web sites and click on publications: **www.familiesandwork.org**, **www.nww.org**, and **www.dol.gov/dol/wb**.

Costs of day care and the inconvenience of taking and picking up children are stumbling blocks for many working parents. Home care either from relatives or neighbors is often unavailable or simply too expensive. The quality of care is also an issue. All of these factors are increasing the pressure on employers to provide affordable, quality, and convenient child care for employees who desire it as part of the insurance package. Some firms are responding to this need.[118]

St. Joseph's Hospital in Marshfield, Wisconsin, is a 524-bed hospital in a town of 20,000. The hospital employs 2200 employees, many of whom require child care. Because demand was so great, the hospital opened an on-site day-care center in 1981. In 1989 it expanded its facilities so that it could take care of twice as many children—130. It also extended the hours to midnight and allowed up to 50 children during the evening. Because the center has a waiting list, the hospital can no longer use it as a recruiting tool. However, it can use the benefits offered by the hospital, which are much better than other local facilities, as a recruiting tool for day-care workers.[119]

Some critics argue that child care is being used as a tool to discriminate against employees. For example, Merck & Company opened a day-care facility years ago in Rahway, New Jersey, after one of its top female scientists threatened to resign. However, the monthly cost of using the facility was $680. Professionals can easily afford this service, but secretaries cannot. The company is anxious not to appear to favor one type of employee over another, and it should be.[120] Not only are nonprofessional workers disgruntled, but so are childless workers. Some 40 percent of the childless workers surveyed felt they were subsidizing health-care benefits for employees with

EXHIBIT 13.10   PERCENTAGE OF COMPANIES OFFERING CHILD-CARE PROGRAMS BY REGION

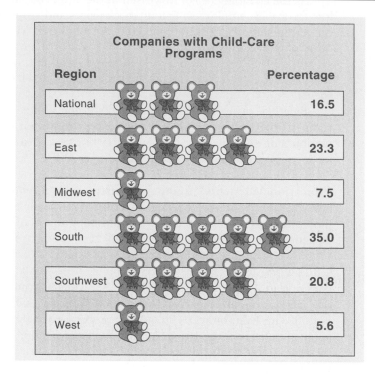

Companies with Child-Care Programs

Region	Percentage
National	16.5
East	23.3
Midwest	7.5
South	35.0
Southwest	20.8
West	5.6

children. Further, childless employees often are required to take up the slack when employees need time off for child-care reasons, further fueling the bad feelings.[121] Companies need to keep in mind that 60 percent of the workforce does not have a child under 18 in the household. Thus day care benefits actually benefit a minority of the workforce.[122]

Child care may be one area in which the Japanese can learn something from Americans. Tokyo parents flocked to the first corporate child-care center, which opened as a result of a joint venture between Bright Horizons Children's Center in Cambridge, Massachusetts, and Temporary Center Corporation, Tokyo's largest temporary placement agency. On the day the center opened, all 44 slots were taken and there was a waiting list. Every person who visited the center during its developmental phase enrolled his or her child. With demand so high, two additional facilities have been planned.[123]

Elder Care   A study of benefit directors indicated that 77 percent of them believed that elder care—care of the elderly—will be a major growth benefit in the future.[124] The number of elderly citizens increased greatly in the 1990s, and with the baby boomers aging, increasing demands will be placed on employers to provide benefit plans to assist with the care of aged parents and aged employees.

One study uses the "dependency ratio" to explain this issue.[125] This ratio compares the number of current workers to the number of dependents. Dependents are defined as those below age 18 and above age 64. Between 1950 and 1982, the ratio of youthful dependents fell from 51.0 per 100 workers to 44.1 and is expected to drop to 36.2 by the year 2008. At the other end, the elderly dependency ratio climbed from 13.3 to 18.8 in the same period and is expected to soar to 41.9 by the year 2008. Thus, the number of retirees is expected to continue to grow at a much faster pace relative to the number of current workers.

With more and more retirees living longer, a greater number of employees will be supporting their retired parents in addition to their own children. Hence, strong demand will be placed on employers to help with this burden. One study estimated that 44 percent of the nation's workforce needed elder-care services.[126] Elder care givers liken the work to raising a baby, except that you watch the baby grow and you watch the parent die. The costs required to care for an older person are huge—so huge, in fact, that care givers who miss 8 hours or more a week from work will lose more than $650,000 in wages and reduced retirement benefits over their lifetime.[127] Fannie May in DC developed an in-house elder care referral system. A licensed social worker is available to meet one-on-one with employees facing elder care issues. The social worker helps employees assess the situation and offers suggestions about available services and options. Employees say they have saved several days of work by using this benefit rather than investigating the options themselves.[128]

Cafeteria Plans   Because of the variety of options in the benefit area, many employers have shifted to or are considering "cafeteria plans." As noted earlier, cafeteria plans allow employees to pick and choose from a variety of benefit options much as a person chooses food at a cafeteria. This allows a person to tailor a benefit program that meets his or her needs. Employees generally purchase benefits with flex credits allocated through their employers or through a salary reduction agreement.[129]

For example, a young, single-parent mother may place greater value on child care, health care, and similar benefits than a 55-year-old male who may be more interested in retirement benefits, long-term health care, and life insurance. Some employees may want to buy extra vacation days; others would like to trade in the ones they have for cash.[130] Cafeteria plans allow for such switches.

Half of the companies with such programs say they have been able to demonstrate cost savings as a result. Frequently, the cost savings come in the form of higher employee contributions.[131] Accurate prediction of employee selections also can help control costs.[132]

Nine of ten flexible benefit plans surveyed offered major medical and hospital coverage. More than half the plans included life insurance, long-term disability, and dependent care. Flexible plans were most popular in the western part of the country, in medium-sized and large companies, and in the education/government/nonprofit sector. One survey indicated that 90 percent of the 1000 employees surveyed preferred a job that offered flexible benefits over one that did not.[133]

Family Friendly Benefits   Organizations have come to recognize that employees distracted by personal concerns will not be as productive as employees with clear minds. In an effort to ease employees' minds, a wide array of family friendly benefits are being offered.[134] For example, offering employees flexible scheduling, where employees are allowed to start and/or end work at a time that is convenient to their lives, has grown to more than 70 percent.[135] Other family friendly benefits include compressed workweeks, job sharing, telecommuting, dependent care flexible spending

---

FOCUS ON HR

Just Who Should Be Covered?

As the traditional American lifestyle continues to change, some employees are asking that some not-so-traditional dependents be included on their insurance. For example, some employees want their retired parents to be included on their policies. Older workers are sometimes dropped from their own employer's insurance policies after they retire, and it is much too costly to purchase insurance for older citizens, especially if they are in poor health. On the other end of the spectrum, some children get married, have children, and then, for various reasons, move back home. Some employees are requesting insurance help for the children of their dependent children. Also, unmarried live-in domestic partners and their children are frequently asked to be included on the insurance policies employees hold. Sometimes allowing this to happen stirs up quite a controversy.

In September 1991, Lotus Development Company became the nation's first well-known company to offer health insurance to partners of its gay and lesbian employees. To qualify, gay and lesbian couples must sign an affidavit stating that they are each other's "sole spousal equivalent and intend to remain so indefinitely." They must also state that they live together and that they are responsible for each other's welfare. The announcement was expected to raise protests from within and from outside the organization, but not the kind of ruckus that ensued, especially from within. Lotus employees sent so many internal mail messages using the company's electronic mail system that it crashed. Some employees showed up for meetings scheduled by the human resource department to discuss the issues while others simply discussed it in the halls and elevators and at lunch.

Why all of the commotion? Some employees believe that if other companies don't follow Lotus' lead, the company will become a magnet for gay employees. Others argue that the provision is unfair because single heterosexual employees are being discriminated against. All of the arguments can be traced back to strong opposition to a homosexual lifestyle in the business community. Following Lotus' lead, more than 70 major companies (including Silicon Graphics, MCA, Microsoft, Viacom, Oracle Systems, Apple, and Time Warner's HBO) offer domestic partner benefits, with most coverage being limited to gay employees.

But organizations must face the fact that the definition of family has changed. Currently, only 25 percent of the households would fall under the 1950s Ozzie and Harriet model in which the husband works and the wife stays home to raise their two children. Some firms, such as Digital Equipment, are rewriting their statement on the definition of family and are requiring each employee to define for himself or herself what his or her "family" includes.

SOURCES: Adapted from William Buckley, "Lotus Creates Controversy by Extending Benefits to Partners of Gay Employees," *The Wall Street Journal,* October 25, 1991, p. B11; Ceel Pasternak, "Health-Care Coverage for Nontraditional Dependents," *HRMagazine,* November 1990, p. 21; and David Jefferson, "Gay Employees Win Benefits for Partners at More Corporations," *The Wall Street Journal,* March 18, 1994, p. A11.

---

accounts, child or elder-care referral services, emergency/sick child care, on-site child/elder care, and subsidized child/elder care.[136] Companies being more sensitive to employees' needs outside of the job allow employees to be more productive at work.

Future Benefit Changes

Although no one can accurately predict the future state of benefits with a high degree of certainty, one analysis suggests the following trends:[137]

1. *More Paid Leave.* Leave will be provided for long-term "refresher" sabbaticals and for social service pursuits.

2. *Education and Training.* Rapidly changing job skill requirements and a shortage of new entrants into the labor force will compel employers to regularly offer education and training programs, leaves, and reimbursement for a wide variety of training to employees.

3. *Career Planning.* Many employers will offer formal career counseling programs to help employees plan careers that adjust to their changing lives.

4. *Housing.* Moving assistance and mortgage aid will become even more common.

5. *Late Retirement.* As baby boomers age and shortages of workers and skills increase, companies will be bending over backwards to help their older employees. TRW's Pat Choate calls these "platinum handcuffs" consisting of company-paid vacation trips, shorter hours, and bonus plans that reward employees for staying on past a certain age or period of service.

6. *Domestic Partner Benefits.* In August 2000 the Big-Three automakers joined 93 other companies in offering health benefits to same-sex partners. Some feel the move will set a precedent.[138] Objections to offering benefits to these significant others are sure to arise, ensuring more attention being placed on this issue in the future.[139]

7. *Vacations.* Employees will be able to "buy" extra vacation time if they deserve it by trading it for other available benefits such as sick leave or even a portion of hospital care.

8. *Computers.* Firms will expand the use of intranets and the World Wide Web to help support the benefits offered to their employees and to help control costs.[140]

Corporate Effort to Measure Benefit Cost-Effectiveness

Ideally, to determine the cost effectiveness of a benefits program, controlled experiments comparing the advantages and costs of one type of benefit with the advantages and costs of an alternative benefit need to be conducted. AT&T is conducting a study with its insurers comparing the medical claim data of 1600 participants in a wellness program with a control group of 1800 nonparticipants.[141] They expect that wellness program participants will have a lower use of hospitals and doctors, thereby saving medical costs overall.

Some companies attempt to measure problems that would occur if benefits were *not* provided. These costs usually include such negative consequences as turnover, absenteeism, and tardiness. For example, Corning Glass Works decided to measure out-of-pocket expenses associated with turnover, such as interview costs and hiring bonuses. Costs were estimated at $16 million to $18 million annually. This led to a look at the causes of turnover and the adoption of new policies in flexible work hours and career development in order to cut turnover.[142]

Some companies are even attempting to measure more complicated linkages among benefits and other factors. One company that has attempted to quantify productivity figures and flexible scheduling is Merck & Company. It interviewed and surveyed a large number of managers and developed a list of 30 cost variables attached to turnover. After developing several methods of cost determination, Merck determined that, depending on the job, turnover costs it 1.5 to 2.5 times the annual salary paid for the job.[143] As a result of this study, the company is attempting to enhance the benefit programs that it believes reduce turnover.

In a study of day care at Union Bank in California, using before and after day-care cost data on absenteeism, turnover, and maternity leave time for both a control group and an experimental group, Union concluded that the day-care center saves the bank $138,000 to $232,000 a year.

Measurement Issues   Quantifying the benefits of any one program is more difficult than estimating its costs. It is also difficult to estimate the costs of failing to implement programs that would reduce absenteeism, turnover, and lost productivity. Yet employers will devote more time and attention to doing this as benefit options proliferate and as their costs increase.

Human resource managers in all areas are being asked to demonstrate how their programs and actions contribute to the bottom line. Nowhere is this more evident than in the management of benefits. With adequate cost and effectiveness data for various benefit options, human resource managers are in a better position to make strategic decisions about which benefit programs an organization should have.

Management Guidelines

Several key guidelines in the benefits area need to be recognized from a strategic viewpoint:

1. Benefits should be strategically managed, not just "administered."
2. Benefit costs and options are increasing dramatically. Many choices are available, and many ways to reduce costs have been found. Human resource managers need to be aware of the possibilities to provide the best advice to their organizations.
3. The cost-effectiveness of benefits and benefit contributions to the bottom line is and will continue to be emphasized.
4. Benefits can best be used to gain competitive advantage by maintaining or increasing benefit levels while decreasing benefit costs.
5. A changing heterogeneous workforce will require a flexible or cafeteria-style program.
6. Management of benefits must comply with a host of federal and state regulations and requirements.
7. Because present and prospective employees are often unaware of the value of benefits provided them, benefit packages should be clearly and succinctly communicated to employees on a regular basis.
8. Health-care and insurance costs as well as retirement costs for the elderly will likely increase dramatically as baby boomers age and life spans are increased, thereby placing pressure on employee benefit plans.

Questions for Review

1. Why is it that so many potential and present employees are unfamiliar with the benefit plan offered by an organization?
2. What strategic choices does an employer face in managing a benefit program? What factors affect the decision on each choice?
3. Why are health-care costs rising so much? What have organizations done to reduce them?
4. Who should pay the cost of health care: the employee, the employer, or the government? Explain your answer.

5. What are cafeteria-style benefits? Why are they so popular?
6. How should benefit plans tie into an overall human resource strategy?
7. How will the structure of benefits likely change as our population ages?
8. Assume that you were asked to determine the value or worth of a wellness-fitness program for a company. How would you go about this?
9. Although managers believe that benefits aid in attracting, motivating, and retaining employees, studies show little support for this belief. Why do you think that benefits may not be helping to attract, motivate, and retain employees?

CASE

Medical Reform in the Twin Cities[144]

Managed competition is radically changing health care in Minneapolis-St. Paul, Minnesota. The current experiences of residents may indicate how the nature of health care may change in the future.

After using virtually every cost-containment device known, 24 major employers in Minneapolis-St. Paul, including Dayton Hudson Corp., Honeywell, Inc., Ceridan Corp., and the State of Minnesota, formed the Business Health Care Action Group in response to rising health-care costs and the current number of uninsured residents. The goal of the group is to use purchasing power to change the way medicine is practiced. Under managed competition, large purchasing groups similar to business coalitions buy care from competing health plans that, in theory at least, thrive only by delivering a high-quality, low-cost product. The program is designed to reduce health-care costs for employers as well as risk. To achieve this goal, the Twin Cities' firms put their employee health group up for bids and selected a single organization that, among other things, is committed to documenting and improving doctors' performance while encouraging preventive medicine.

Finding a supplier was not an easy task. The coalition invited more than 150 doctors and health plan administrators to conferences to explain its requirements. In response, about 20 health-care organizations bid for the contract, but only two came close to meeting the coalition's requirements. One was Minnesota Blue Cross and Blue Shield, which argued that it was successfully using six years' worth of accumulated data on physician and hospital performance to encourage cost-effective care. The coalition viewed Blue Cross and Blue Shield as a third party that wanted to set the rules and rejected its bid. Group Care, Inc., a consortium formed from the marriage of two local HMOs—Group Health, Inc., and Med Centers, Inc.—that joined with the Mayo Clinic in nearby Rochester, Minnesota, was selected. Park Nicollet Medical Center, a 360-doctor group in Minneapolis, is the main physician group in the consortium. Group Care, Inc., was selected because most of its doctors are salaried and thus not compensated according to the number of procedures performed. In addition, Group Care, Park Nicollet, and Mayo have already developed practice guidelines for more than 50 medical conditions. For example, Park Nicollet has new technology that allows a woman with a questionable mammogram to learn whether she has a malignancy without having surgery. A new computer-guided machine enables a radiologist instead of a surgeon to perform the biopsy, eliminating the wait for surgery, the surgeon's fee, and hospital costs related to the surgery.

In an effort to develop guidelines for dozens of other medical conditions, the consortium founded a $7 million research institute. One of the first items on the agenda is to create a policy that nearly eliminates all X-rays and physical therapy for back pain patients in the first six weeks of treatment. Through intensive research, doctors have found that 90 percent of all back pain cases resolve themselves in six weeks with proper exercise, heat and ice treatment, and the use of aspirin. The new institute is dealing with many issues that will contribute to changes in health-care provision in Minnesota and other areas.

Demands from the Business Health Care Action Group have pushed the Minnesota health-care community to a frenzy of mergers and acquisitions as it strives to reorganize its jumble of independent doctors and hospitals into streamlined networks that compete on the basis of quality, service, and price. In short, practically every hospital and thousands of doctors in the Twin Cities are competing for patients on the basis of cost as well as quality.

As with most changes, there is some opposition. Opponents of the new system (primarily some doctors) argue that the Twin Cities area is on the "bleeding edge" of medical reform. At any rate, a number of the highly trained specialists have reason to be concerned, for many of them will be replaced by primary-care doctors. To reduce costs the coalition of employers aims to cut back on the care delivered by expensive cardiologists, orthopedists, and other specialists.

In addition, the fee structure is changing. Instead of the usual itemized hospital bills and separate doctors' fees, health services are offered for a bundled amount. Also, if employees want to, they can use doctors outside of the coalition for a 30 percent copayment.

Employees also face changes. They are expected to attend seminars on how to be better patients. Doctors complain that some patients undermine cost-effective medical practice by demanding costly and unnecessary procedures. For example, a patient may demand unnecessary imaging tests for routine complaints because they assume that insurance picks up most of the tab. This new integrated health system is beneficial to the employers because they don't have to chose a health care provider for their employees anymore. The employees get to choose for themselves and family members need not choose the same system. Now, however, employees need to be informed consumers and become much more sophisticated in order to be able to make decisions on their health care which were at one time made for them.

To encourage participation in the new plan, companies are using videos that explain the plan and attest to the quality of care and lower out-of-pocket costs. In February 1993, two months after its inception, 35,000 employees and dependents had joined the plan, with projections of 250,000 employees and their dependents joining.

The coalition is expecting the market to reform via consumer choice. Three steps to this conversion are to (1) organize the system so that health systems are accountable and provide standard information on quality and patient satisfaction, (2) give that information to the consumers, (3) let the consumers make the choice. Whether the changes in the Twin Cities will improve quality and contain costs is unknown at this time. The short-term goal of the coalition is to reduce the cost growth to the overall inflation rate. The goals of the coalition are being criticized by some and adopted by others. Two other employer coalitions are launching similar efforts, and a law was passed in 1992 to provide care for the uninsured by requiring that organized networks of doctors and hospitals provide them care.

The recent changes in the Twin Cities may in fact spread throughout the United States and become the basis of a new medical system. The impact of health-care changes is uncertain, but we can be sure that the Twin Cities are well on their way to dealing with the inefficiencies in the current system.

Questions for Discussion

1. What is the goal of a business coalition such as the Business Health Care Action Group in Minnesota? How does such a plan work?

2. What is required to make such a plan successful?

3. Would a plan like the Twin Cities' plan work in your geographic region? Why or why not? Cite reasons.

4. What benefits does the plan have for the employers who use it? For the employees?

Additional Readings

Brockhart, James, and Robert Reilly. "Employee Stock Ownership Plans after the 1989 Tax Law: Valuation Issues." *Compensation and Benefits Review*, 1990.

Callan, Mary, and David Yeager. *Containing the Health Care Cost Spiral.* New York: McGraw-Hill, 1990.

Cave, Douglas, and Larry Tucker. "10 Facts about Point-of-Service Plans." *HRMagazine.* September 1991, pp. 41–46.

Crawford, Lou Ellen. *Dependent Care and the Employee Benefits Package.* Westport, CT: Quorum Books, 1990.

Denenberg, Tia S., and R. V. Denenberg. *Alcohol and Drugs: Issues in the Workplace.* Washington, D.C.: BNA Books, 1983.

Flexible Benefits: Will They Work for You? Chicago: Commerce Clearing House, 1991.

Haar, Jerry, and Sharon Kossack. "Employee Benefit Packages: How Understandable Are They?" *Journal of Business Communication*, 1990, pp. 185–200.

Harrington, Harry, and Nancy Richardson. "Retiree Wellness Plans Cut Health Costs." *Personnel Journal* 69 (1990), pp. 60–62.

Hay/Huggins Benefits Comparison. Philadelphia: The Hay Group, 1987.

Hayes, Cheryl, John Palmer, and Martha Zaslow. *Who Cares for America's Children.* Washington, D.C.: National Academic Press, 1990.

Iseri, Betty, and Robert Cangemi. "Flexible Benefits: A Growing Option." *Personnel*, 1990, pp. 30–32.

Koenig, R. "Comparison Shopping: Companies Seek New Data on Health-Care Costs to Gain Leverage in Bargaining for Services." *The Wall Street Journal*, April 22, 1988, pp. 19R–20R.

Konrad, W., and G. DeGeorge. "U.S. Companies Go for the Gray." *Business Week*, April 3, 1989, p. 66.

Lee, Alice, and Fred Lee. *A Field Guide to Retirement: 14 Lifestyle Opportunities and Options for Successful Retirement.* New York: Doubleday, 1991.

Lock, E., K. Shaw, L. Saari, and G. Latham. "Goal Setting and Task Performance 1969-1980." *Psychological Bulletin* 90 (1981), pp. 125–152.

McGregor, Eugene. *Strategic Management of Human Knowledge, Skills, and Abilities: Workforce Decision Making in the Post-Industrial Era.* San Francisco: Jossey-Bass, 1991.

Masterson, Joe. "Benefit Plans That Cut Costs and Increase Satisfaction." *Management Review*, April 1990.

Meadows, Anne. *Caring for America's Children.* Washington, D.C.: National Academy Press, 1991.

Mitchell, O. "Fringe Benefits and Labor Mobility." *The Journal of Human Resources* 17, no. 2 (1982), pp. 286–298.

——. "Fringe Benefits and the Cost of Changing Jobs." *Industrial and Labor Relations Review* 37, no.1 (1983), pp. 70–78.

Mowday, R., L. Porter, and R. Steers. *Employee Organization Linkages: The Psychology of Commitment, Absenteeism, and Turnover.* New York: Academic Press, 1982.

1987 Employee Benefits. Washington, DC: Chamber of Commerce of the United States, 1987.

Niedzieielski, J. "Intranets Aid Benefit Choices," *National Underwriter Property and Casualty Risk & Benefits Management* 102, no. 5 (1998), pp. 16–17.

Phillips, Mary Ellen, Carol Brown, and Norma Nielson. "An Expanding Employee Benefit: Personal Financial Planning with Expert Systems." *Management Accounting,* September 1990, pp. 29–33.

Pillsbury, Dennis. "Nipping Workers' Comp in the Bud." *Risk and Insurance,* October 1991.

Porter, M. *Competitive Advantage: Creating and Sustaining Superior Performance.* New York: Free Press, 1985.

——. *Competitive Strategy: Techniques for Analyzing Industries and Competitors.* New York: Free Press, 1980.

Roberts, Karen, and Sandra Gleason. "What Employees Want from Workers' Comp." *HRMagazine,* December 1991, pp. 49–54.

Rosenbloom, Jerry S., and G. Victor Hollman. *Employee Benefit Planning,* 2nd ed. Englewood Cliffs, N.J.: Prentice-Hall, 1986.

Schiller, B., and R. Weiss. "Pension and Wages: A Test for Equalizing Differences." *The Review of Economics and Statistics* 62, no. 4 (1980), pp. 529–538.

Shanklin, Catherine. "Unemployment Insurance: Survive the System." *Personnel Journal,* March 1990.

Smith, Doyle. *Kin Care and the American Corporation: Solving the Work/Family Dilemma.* Homewood, IL: Business One Irwin, 1991.

Spirig, John. "Human Resources Information Systems Can Help Employers Plan and Implement Flexible Benefits Programs." *Employment Relations Today* 16 (1989), pp. 9–17.

Stepina, L., H. Hennessey, and B. Weschler, eds. *Florida's Compensation System: A Comprehensive Study of Career Service Pay and Benefits.* Final Report, Contract #1986–068, 1987. (Available from State of Florida, Department of Administration, Carlton Bldg., Tallahassee, FL.)

Sutton, N. "Are Employers Meeting Their Benefit Objectives?" *Benefits Quarterly* 2, no. 3 (1986), pp. 14–20.

——. "Do Employee Benefits Reduce Labor Turnover?" *Benefits Quarterly* 1, no. 2 (1986), pp. 16–22.

Taulbee, Pamela. "What's Ahead for Retiree Health?" *Business & Health,* December 1990, pp. 25–36.

Wilson, M., G. Northcraft, and M. Neale. "The Perceived Value of Fringe Benefits." *Personnel Psychology* 38, no. 2 (1985), pp. 309–320.

Notes

[1]M. Wilson, G. Northcraft, and M. Neale, "The Perceived Value of Fringe Benefits," *Personnel Psychology,* 38, no. 2 (1985), pp. 309–320.

[2]Dawn Gunsch, "Benefits Program Helps Retain Frontline Workers," *Personnel Journal* 72, no. 2 (1993), pp. 88–92; Beth Rogers, "Clarifying the Choices," *HRMagazine,* March 1993, pp. 40–43.

[3]Laurie McGenley, "More Workers Drop Health Insurance From Employers," *The Wall Street Journal,* November 10, 1997, p. B16.

[4]Glen Ruffenach, "Health Insurance Premiums to Soar in '89: Workers Likely to Take on More of Costs," *The Wall Street Journal,* October 25, 1988, p. B1.

[5]Craig J. Cantoni, "Manager's Journal," *The Wall Street Journal,* August 18, 1997, p. A14.

[6]Yochi J. Dreazen, "Rise in Benefits Costs Take on Urgency," *Wall Street Journal,* June 2, 2000, p. A2+.

[7]Ibid.

[8]Bill Leonard, "Ratio of Benefits to Total Pay Continues to Decrease," *HRMagazine,* December 1996, p. 8.

[9]Rick Wartzman and Hillary Stout, "Clinton Health Plan Would Use Regulation to Spur Competition," *The Wall Street Journal,* September 13, 1993, p. A7.

[10]Sue Shellenbarger, "Firms Try to Match People with Benefits," *The Wall Street Journal*, December 17, 1993, p. B1.

[11]H. W. Hennessey, Jr., "Using Employee Benefits to Gain Competitive Advantage," *Benefits Quarterly*, Winter 1989, pp. 51–57.

[12]Nancy Hatch Woodward, "Beyond Basic Benefits," *HRMagazine*, September 1997, pp. 53–56.

[13]Howard C. Smith, "Get Your Message Across With Graphics," *HRMagazine*, January 2000, pp. 84–88.

[14]James Swanke, "Ways to Tame Workers' Comp Premiums," *HRMagazine*, February 1992, pp. 39–41.

[15]Barbara Marsh, "Rising Workers' Compensation Costs Worry Small Firms," *The Wall Street Journal*, December 31, 1991, p. B2.

[16]Ron Winslow, "Hospitals Team Up to Trim Workers' Comp," *The Wall Street Journal*, December 8, 1989, p. B1.

[17]Robert W. Thompson, "Employers' Worker Comp Costs Decline in 1995," *HRNews*, February 1998, p. 3.

[18]William Atkinson, "Is Workers' Comp Working?" *HRMagazine*, July 2000, pp. 50–61.

[19]Greg Steinmetz, "States Take on the Job of Holding Down Medical Costs of Workers' Compensation," *The Wall Street Journal*, March 3, 1993, p. B1.

[20]Marsh, "Rising Workers' Compensation Costs Worry Small Firms," p. B2.

[21]Ronald Grover, "How Workers' Comp Could Get Mangled," *Business Week*, December 14, 1992, p. 44.

[22]Michael Pritula, "Workers' Comp: Tranquilizing a Benefit Gone Mad," *The Wall Street Journal*, January 13, 1992, p. A14; and Mark D. Fefer, "What to Do about Workers' Comp," *Fortune*, June 29, 1992, pp. 80–82.

[23]Bill Leonard, "Severance Packages for Mid-level Executives Rise Steeply," *HRMagazine*, October 1996, p. 8.

[24]"Labor Letter," *The Wall Street Journal*, September 13, 1988, p. A1.

[25]Linda Thornburg, "The Pension Headache," *HRMagazine*, January 1992, pp. 39–46; Wallace Campbell, Jr., "Plans That Upgrade Pensions," *HRMagazine*, November 1991, pp. 71–73; and Selwyn Feinstein, "IRS Regulations on Pension Plans Promise Headaches for Major Employers," *The Wall Street Journal*, May 22, 1990, p. A1.

[26]Selwyn Feinstein, "Rules Change for Pensions: Who Gets What," *The Wall Street Journal*, July 3, 1990, p. B11.

[27]Pauline Yoshihashi, "Junking of Pensions Angers Mill Workers," *The Wall Street Journal*, April 18, 1991, p. A5.

[28]Allen Steinberg, "Best Bets for Retirement," *HRMagazine*, January 1992, pp. 47–50.

[29]Ellen E. Schultz, "Pension Cuts 101," *The Wall Street Journal*, July 27, 2000, p. A1.

[30]Ellen Schultz, "Changing Jobs Means Having to Find a New Home for Cash in Retirement Plan," *The Wall Street Journal*, March 9, 1992, p. C11; and "Pension Portability," *HRMagazine*, February 1992, pp. 99–100.

[31]Ellen E. Schultz, "Rich-Poor Gap in 401(k) Plans Widen," *The Wall Street Journal*, August 21, 1997, p. C11.

[32]Elaine McShulskis, "Investments 101," *HRMagazine*, September 1996, p. 26.

[33]Roger Thompson, "The Positive Side of Negative Elections," *HRMagazine*, November 1997, pp. 112–117.

[34]Ibid., p. 113.

[35]Alison Stein Wellner, "Borrowing from the Future," *HRMagazine*, July 2000, pp. 99–104.

[36]Ellen Hoffman, "Self-Directed Accounts: 401(k)s With a View," *HRMagazine*, March 2000, pp. 115–124.

[37]Richard Hill and Patricia Dwyer, "Grooming Workers for Early Retirement," *HRMagazine*, September 1990, pp. 59–63.

[38]Joann Lubin, "Bosses Alter Early-Retirement Windows to Be Less Coercive—and Less Generous," *The Wall Street Journal*, February 8, 1991, p. B11.

[39]Ellen E. Schultz, "'Phased Retirement' Option for Workers Is Mainly a Boon for Their Employers," *The Wall Street Journal*, July 27, 2000, p. A6.

[40]Catherine Fyock, "Crafting Secure Retirements," *HRMagazine*, July 1990, pp. 30–33.

[41]Christopher Conte, "Falling Behind," *The Wall Street Journal*, March 3, 1992, p. A1.

[42]Ellen E. Schultz, "This Won't Hurt," *The Wall Street Journal*, October 25, 2000, p. A1.

[43]Ellen E. Schultz and Robert McGough, "Using a Trust Fund to Help Pay Retiree Benefits in the Future Can Help the Bottom Line Now," *The Wall Street Journal*, October 25, 2000, p. C1+.

[44]*Paid Holidays and/or Vacation Policies*, Personnel Policies Forum no. 130 (Washington, DC: Bureau of National Affairs, November 1980), p. 1.

[45]Jolie Solomon, "The Future Look of Employee Benefits," *The Wall Street Journal*, September 7, 1988, p. 29.

[46]"Give Me a Break," *The Wall Street Journal*, May 5, 1992, p. W1+.

[47]Judith Hackham Semas, "Taking Off from the Hi-Tech Grind," *HRMagazine*, September 1997, pp. 122–129.

[48]"Give me a Break," p. W4.

[49]Gene DeLoux, "Is Your Maternity Policy Ready for the '90s?" *HRMagazine*, November 1990, pp. 57–59.

[50]Linda Thornburg, "Family Leave Law Effective August 5," *HR News*, March 1993, p. A1.

[51]Albert Karr, "The Daddy Track," *The Wall Street Journal*, April 30, 1991, p. A1.

[52]Suzanne Alexander, "Fears for Career Curb Paternity Leave," *The Wall Street Journal*, August 24, 1990, p. B11; and Albert Karr, "Maternity Leave," *The Wall Street Journal*, April 28, 1992, p. A1.

[53]Elaine McShulskis, "Managing Pregnant Employees," *HRMagazine*, July 1997, p. 29.

[54]Elaine McShulskis, "Healthy Babies Help Reduce Costs," *HRMagazine*, September 1997, p. 28.

[55]Albert R. Karr, "People Worry about Being Disabled and Needing Long-Term Care," *The Wall Street Journal*, November 24, 1992, p. A1.

[56]Jim Mishizen, "In the Eye of the Health-Care Storm," *HRMagazine*, September 1991, pp. 47–50.

[57]Drew King, "A Comprehensive Approach to Disability Management," *HRMagazine*, October 1996, pp. 97–102.

[58]"Limits to Disability Insurance," *HRMagazine*, October 1996, p. 24.

[59]Carolyn Hirschman, "Will Employers Take the Lead in Long-Term Care?" *HRMagazine*, March 1997, pp. 59–66.

[60]"Most Employers Offer Disability Leaves," *American Society for Personnel Administration/Resources*, December 1988, p. 4.

[61]Mike McNamee, Gail DeGeorge, and Ron Stodghill II, "Health Care Inflation: It's Back!" *Business Week*, March 17, 1997, pp. 28–30.

[62]Ron Winslow, "Health-Care Inflation Kept in Check Last Year," *The Wall Street Journal*, January 20, 1998, p. B11.

[63]Eckholm, *The President's Health Security Plan*, pp. 13–14.

[64]Thomas Fields-Meyer, Vicki Bane, Brian Karen, and Lorna Grisby, "A Patient's Anger," *People*, March 13, 2000, pp. 99–100.

[65]Winslow, "Health-Care Inflation Kept in Check Last Year," p. B1.

[66]Bill Leonard, "Health-Care Provider Heals Itself," *HRMagazine*, July 1993, p. 51.

[67]Karen Munson and David Israel: "Self-Insurance Checkup," *HRMagazine*, February 1992, pp. 83–87.

[68]Ceel Pasternak, "Incentives for Wellness," *HRMagazine*, August 1991, p. 19; and Greg Jaffe, "Corporate Carrots, Sticks Cut Health Care Bills," *The Wall Street Journal*, February 3, 1998, p. B11.

[69]Hilary Stout, "Paying Workers for Good Health," *The Wall Street Journal*, November 26, 1991, p. B11.

[70]Aaron Bernstein, "Health Care Costs: Trying to Cool the Fever," *Business Week*, May 21, 1990, pp. 46–47.

[71]Selwyn Feinstein, "Companies Target Catastrophic Illnesses in Bid to Curb Soaring Health Cost," *The Wall Street Journal*, July 30, 1990, p. A1.

[72]Glenn Ruffenach, "Firms Use Financial Incentives to Make Employees Set Lower Health-Care Fees," *The Wall Street Journal*, February 9, 1993, p. B1.

[73]Ibid., p. B6.

[74]Carol Hymowitz and Gabriella Stern, "Cutting Psychotherapy May Trim Productivity," *The Wall Street Journal*, August 10, 1994, pp. B1, B8.

[75]Merritt C. Kimball, "The Trend to Give What's Appropriate," *HRMagazine*, January 1994, pp. 49–50.

[76]Ceel Pasternak, "Dealing in Drugs," *HRMagazine*, March 1992, p. 26.

[77]Ceel Pasternak, "In-Company Pharmacy?" *HRMagazine*, September 1991, p. 23.

[78]Albert Karr, "Make Workplace Calls?" *The Wall Street Journal*, May 7, 1991, p. A1.

[79]Glen Ruffenach, "California School Unions Use Trusts to Cut Costs," *The Wall Street Journal*, March 3, 1992, p. B1.

[80]John Sturges, "Examining Your Insurance Carrier," *HRMagazine*, February 1992, pp. 43–46; and William Wymer, George Faulkner, and Joseph Parente, "Achieving Benefit Program Objectives," *HRMagazine*, March 1992, pp. 55–62.

[81]Stephenie Overman and Linda Thornburg, "Beating the Odds," *HRMagazine*, March 1992, pp. 42–47.

[82]John Morley, "The Cleveland Health-Care Experiment," *The Wall Street Journal*, February 10, 1992, p. A16; and Walt Bogdanich, "Clevelanders Bet Top Health Care Will Be Cheaper," *The Wall Street Journal*, February 2, 1992, p. B11.

[83]Ron Winslow, "How Local Business Got Together to Cut Memphis Health Costs," *The Wall Street Journal*, February 4, 1992, p. A11; Alain Enthoven, "How Employers Boost Health Costs," *The Wall Street Journal*, January 24, 1992, p. A14; and David Wessel and Walt Bogdanich, " Laws of Economics Often Don't Apply in Health-Care Field," *The Wall Street Journal*, January 22, 1992, p. A11.

[84]Edmund Faltermayer, "Let's Really Cure the Health System," *Fortune*, March 23, 1992, p. 46–58.

[85]Stuart Butler, "'Pay or Play' Health-Care Is Bound to Be a Loser," *The Wall Street Journal*, January 3, 1992, p. A6; Hilary Stout, "Health Care Choices: A Bigger Federal Role or a Market Approach?" *The Wall Street Journal*, January 15, 1992, p. A11; Linda Thornburg, "U.S. Health Care Called a System in Crisis" *HRNews*, January 1992, p. A14; Christine Keen, "National Health-Care Reform: Politics vs. Policy," *HRNews*, February 1992, p. A5; and Linda Thornburg, "Medical Community Proposes National Health-Care Reforms," *HRNews*, February 1992, p. A11.

[86]"Pay or Play," *The Wall Street Journal*, January 21, 1992, p. A1.

[87]Jill Fraser, "Flexible Spending," *Inc.*, October 1990, pp. 164–167; and Georgette Jason, "Medical Reimbursement Accounts Are a Good Deal for Many Workers," *The Wall Street Journal*, July 26, 1991, p. C1.

[88]Susan J. Wells, "Avoiding the Health Care Squeeze," *HRMagazine*, April 2000, pp. 46–54.

[89]Ron Winslow, "Health-Care Costs May be Heading Up Again," *Wall Street Journal*, January 21, 1997, p. B11.

[90]David Wessel, "Firms Cut Health Costs, Cover Fewer Workers," *The Wall Street Journal*, November 11, 1996, P. A1.

[91]Richard Schmidt, "Retirees Fight Cuts in Health Benefits," *The Wall Street Journal*, December 8, 1988, p. B1.

[92]Gary Laugharn, "Caught in the FASB Crossfire," *HRMagazine*, July 1990, pp. 38–42.

[93]Ceel Pasternak, "HRM Update," *HRMagazine*, August 1991, p. 19.

[94]Timothy Schellhardt, "Retirees Benefit Cuts Won't End Soon," *The Wall Street Journal*, September 19, 1990, p. B1.

[95]Albert Karr, "Labor Letter," *The Wall Street Journal*, February 7, 1989, p. A1.

[96]Ron Winslow and Carol Gentry, "Health-Benefit Trend: Give Worker's Money, Let Them Buy a Plan," *The Wall Street Journal*, February 8, 2000. P. A1.

[97]Wells, p. 47.

[98]Carol Gentry, "Doctor Yes," *The Wall Street Journal*, May 23, 2000, p. A1+.

[99]Gary Kushner and Gina Williams, "COBRA: Answers to the Most-Asked Questions," *Legal Report* (Alexandria, VA: Society for Human Resource Management), 1990.

[100]Roderick W. Munn, "Specialty Software to Tame the COBRA," *HRMagazine*, August 1997, pp. 45–50.

[101]Mark Howard, "HIPAA: What's That?" *Florida Trend*, August 1997, pp. 62–64.

[102]Walecia Konrad and Gail DeGeorge, "U.S. Companies Go for the Gray," *Business Week*, April 3, 1989, p. 66.

[103]James H. Smalhout, "The Not-So-Golden Years," *The Wall Street Journal*, June 29, 1995, p. A14.

[104]Marilyn Chase, "Science Edges Closer to Designing Drugs to Defeat AIDS Virus," *The Wall Street Journal*, March 3, 1989, p. A1.

[105]David Israel and Debra Scott, "AIDS-Related Insurance Ceilings Are Risky," *HRMagazine*, November 1990, pp. 85–86.

[106]Ronald E. Bachman, "Time for Another Look," *HRMagazine*, March 1997, pp. 93–96.

[107]David Stipp, "Laws on Health Benefits Raise Firms' Ire," *The Wall Street Journal*, December 28, 1988, p. B1.

[108]"Voluntary Benefits Popular," *HRMagazine*, March 1997, p. 30.

[109]Joanne M. Cole, " Personal Insurance: A No-Cost Option Employees Favor," *HRMagazine*, November 1997, pp. 65–70.

[110]Bill Leonard, "Perks Give Way to Life-Cycle Benefit Plans," *HRMagazine*, March 1995, pp. 45–46.

[111]Robin A. Friedman, "Perking up the Workplace," *Florida Trend*, November 2000, p. 46.

[112]Dominic Bencivenga, "Employee-Owners Help Boost the Bottom Line," *HRMagazine*, February 1997, pp. 79–83.

[113]James P. Miller, "Some Workers Set Up LBOs of Their Own and Benefit Greatly," *The Wall Street Journal*, December 12, 1988, pp. A1, A6.

[114]"Employee Stock Ownership Plans Spread More Slowly in 1990," *The Wall Street Journal*, March 12, 1991, p. A1.

[115]James White, "As ESOPs Become Victims of '90s Bankruptcies, Workers Are Watching Their Nest Eggs Vanish," *The Wall Street Journal*, January 25, 1991, pp. C1.

[116]James S. Hirsch, "Avis Employees Find Stock Ownership Is Mixed Blessing," *The Wall Street Journal*, May 2, 1995, pp. B1, B4.

[117]Bill Leonard, "Employers Explore On-Site Day Care Options," *HRMagazine*, May 2000, p. 29.

[118]Stephenie Overman, "3M Arranges Summer Child Care," *HRMagazine*, March 1991, pp. 46–47.

[119]Linda Thornburg, "On-Site Child Care Works for Health-Care Industry," *HRMagazine*, August 1990, pp. 39–40.

[120]Janet Guyon, "Inequality in Granting Child-Care Benefits Makes Workers Seethe," *The Wall Street Journal*, October 23, 1991, p. A11.

[121]"Do Childless Employees Feel Cheated?" *HRMagazine*, July 1997, p. 26.

[122]Andrea C. Poe, "The Baby Blues," *HRMagazine*, July 2000, pp. 79–84.

[123]Sue Shellenbarger, "U.S.-Style Child-Care Wins Fans in Japan," *The Wall Street Journal*, February 12, 1992, p. B1.

[124]Solomon, "The Future Look of Employee Benefits," p. 29.

[125]*America in Transition: Benefits for the Future* (Baltimore: Employee Benefits Research Institution, 1988).

[126]"Blue Cross and Blue Shield of New Jersey Announces Pilot Program for Child and Elder Care Services," *PR News Wire* via DowVision, March 28, 1995.

[127]Russell V. Gerbman, "Elder Care Takes America by Storm," *HRMagazine*, May 2000, pp. 51–58.

[128]Susan J. Wells, "The Elder Care Gap," *HRMagazine*, May 2000, pp. 39–46.

[129]Richard Gisonny, "Benefits and Taxes," *HRMagazine*, February 1991, pp. 37–42.

[130]Albert Karr, "Vacations for Sale," *The Wall Street Journal*, September 17, 1991, p. A1.

[131]Glenn Ruffenach, "Odds and Ends," *The Wall Street Journal*, March 27, 1991, p. B1.

[132]Melissa Barringer, George Milkovich, and Olivia Mitchell, "Predicting Employee Health Insurance Selections in a Flexible Benefits Environment," *On Center* 1, 1992, p. 7.

[133]Albert Karr, "Favoring Options," *The Wall Street Journal*, April 30, 1991, p. A1.

[134]Alice M. Starcke, "Equitable Plans Help Balance Work and Life," *HRMagazine*, May 1997, pp. 53–58.

[135]"Work and Family Benefits are Increasingly Popular," *HRMagazine*, July 1997, p. 26.

[136]*1997 SHRM Benefits Survey*, prepared by the SHRM Issues Management Program, Alexandria, VA.

[137]Solomon, "The Future Look of Employee Benefits," p. 29.

[138]Norihiko Shirouzu, "Gay Couples to Get Benefits at Auto Makers," *Wall Street Journal*, June 9, 2000, p. A3+.

[139]Starcke, "Equitable Plans Help Balance Work and Life," pp. 55–56.

[140]Bill Leonard, "Benefit, Point and Click," *HRMagazine*, July 2000, pp. 43–48.

[141]Jolie Solomon, "Companies Try Measuring Cost Savings from New Types of Corporate Benefits," *The Wall Street Journal*, December 29, 1988, p. B1.

[142]Ibid.

[143]Ibid.

[144]Ron Winslow, "Employers' Attack on Health Bills Spurs Change in Minnesota," *The Wall Street Journal*, February 26, 1993, p. A1.

14

Managing Health, Safety, and Stress

Chapter Objectives

As a result of studying this chapter, you should be able to

1. Outline the strategic choices available to managers with respect to the management of employee safety, health, and stress.

2. Discuss the Occupational Safety and Health Administration (OSHA) and explain its purpose, scope, and procedures.

3. Examine some of the current health and safety problems facing employees, such as repetitive motion problems and AIDS, of which managers need to be aware.

4. Present information regarding fetal protection available in the workplace.

5. Identify types and consequences of workplace stress and present ways to reduce it.

6. Discuss possible organizational strategies available to help improve and maintain the health and safety of workers.

Employee health and safety represent an area undergoing continual change. Materials that were not considered hazardous in the past have been found to be extremely dangerous as the long-term effects of exposure became known. New ailments caused by acts performed or equipment used on the job are coming to the public's attention more and more.[1] Pressure on employees from both home and work can cause emotional and physical problems, increased health-care costs, and decreased productivity at work.[2] Because of the flux in this area, it is imperative that organizations remain informed and aware of the changes taking place.

CASE

Smart Management in the Danger Zone: Health and Safety at Georgia-Pacific[3]

Before 1991, the 241 plants and mills operated by Georgia-Pacific, the Atlanta-based forest products giant with $13 billion in annual revenues and more than 47,000 employees, had a terrible safety record. Working in dangerous places, such as paper mills, saw mills, and plywood factories, where employees faced deafening noise, razor-sharp blades, long chutes of lumber, and giant vats of boiling water and chemicals, was just part of the job at Georgia-Pacific. In fact, there were nine serious injuries per 100 employees each year, and 26 workers lost their lives on the job between 1986 and 1990. In 1991, however, all of that started to change when A. D. "Pete" Correll took over as president and chief operating officer of Georgia-Pacific.

During the 1990s, Georgia-Pacific has recorded one of the best safety records in the industry. Eighty percent of its plants operated last year without any injuries at all, and best of all, no workers died anywhere. Now safety comes first. So how did Georgia-Pacific make this dramatic safety turnaround? Simply stated, the company has changed the way people think about their work and how they do it. As a result, workers' attitudes and behaviors have changed. According to Barry Geisel, who runs the company's plywood factory in Madison, Georgia, "The biggest challenge has been trying to change everybody's old habits and assumptions."

Georgia-Pacific improved safety by altering its "stubborn" corporate culture through ten ideas:

1. *Realize that you can change how people work.* In the past, most employees assumed that they had no control over whether accidents happened or not. This attitude has changed.
2. *Whatever you do, do not call it a program.* Many employees do not take programs seriously. If you want results, make it clear that the new order of things is not a passing phase but a pervasive and permanent commitment.
3. *Be sure you understand why you have a problem in the first place.* Most workers do not generally do things without a reason. If you want to solve the problem, find out what the reason was and then fix that. For instance, one reason why workers took dangerous risks was to keep the line moving. Now any employee can shut down any production line rather than take a chance on an injury.
4. *Be consistent.* Steve Church, a senior manager at headquarters in Atlanta, said, "What would be the point in saying something is your number 1 priority if you're not going to treat it that way?" At Georgia-Pacific division meetings, the first thing on the agenda is always safety. Following through on what you say is very important.

5. *Reinforce your message every way you can.* Georgia-Pacific thoroughly and obsessively conveys its "safety first" message through training sessions, meetings, posters, stickers, buttons, T-shirts, and jackets. It lets people have fun with it. According to Mike Skinner, Georgia-Pacific's director of workers' compensation, "There's no good reason why, just because something is important, it also has to be boring."

6. *Reward good behavior.* Georgia-Pacific's supervisors and managers are evaluated and compensated based on how they do in four areas, and safety is one of them. In fact, it carries the same weight as production.

7. *Take advantage of people's natural urge to compete.* For the past few years Alan Ulman, Georgia-Pacific's director of internal communications, has been researching what motivates employees to change their work habits. Through his annual (anonymous) employee surveys, he has learned that workers want to do their jobs more safely to avoid letting down their team, which is competing against similar teams companywide to see who can claim the fewest accidents.

8. *Do not let a "right-sizing" distract anybody from the task at hand.* Last year Georgia-Pacific needed to cut overhead, so it did away with about 2500 salaried jobs, including many line supervisory positions. By that time, employees had bought into the new ways of doing things, and safety performance in the plants continued to improve—even without a boss on hand to remind them.

9. *Share success stories throughout the company.* Most of the success stories tend to describe near misses and discuss ways of avoiding coming that close to an accident. Near-miss reports are shared on the company's SafeTV network, index cards, faxes, and bulletin boards.

10. *Never let up.* According to Correll, Georgia-Pacific's safety goal is zero accidents. Thus the company cannot ever stop emphasizing and reinforcing safety, because if it does, its safety record could start to slip.

Strategic Choices

The decisions managers make regarding the health and safety of their workers become increasingly more important as time passes because of ever-increasing penalties, some aimed directly at the top management,[4] for willfully endangering the lives of employees. Many of the decisions made are based on strategic choices available to the organization. Some of these strategic choices follow:

1. Managers must determine the *level of protection* the organization will provide employees. Some firms, for financial or liability reasons, prefer a minimum level of protection; others prefer a maximum level.

2. Managers can decide whether *safety regulations will be formal or informal.* Formal regulations are written and carefully monitored whereas informal regulations are enforced through peer pressure or good training.

3. Managers also can be *proactive or reactive in terms of developing procedures or plans* with respect to employee safety and health. Proactive managers seek to improve the safety and health of their employees prior to a need to do so; reactive managers fix safety and health problems after they occur.

4. Managers can decide to use the *safety and health of workers as a marketing tool* for the organization. This type of strategy involves advertising that Company

X is a great place to work because of how much it cares about the worker. "Safety before production" could be this company's motto. Other firms take the opposite strategy and stress output more than safety.[5]

Keep in mind as you read this chapter that managing health, safety, and stress in the workplace involves making strategic choices in the form of trade-offs. A company may desire a high level of protection but may not always have the resources to achieve its goals with regard to safety. Strategic choices concern fundamental questions about the level of risk a company can afford and the degree of liability it intends to accept. Managers must strike a balance between what is desired and what can be provided. A knowledge of the legal aspects of occupational health and safety can help human resource managers as they work with company managers to formulate strategic plans. The foundation for all safety and health programs in U.S. businesses is the Occupational Safety and Health Act of 1970, discussed in the next section.

Occupational Safety and Health Administration[6]

Occupational Safety and Health Act of 1970

Because of the overwhelming number of workers killed on the job (more than 14,000 in 1970) and the emotional and economic impact these problems caused, Congress passed the Occupational Safety and Health Act of 1970. This act was designed to offer, as far as possible, every working man and woman a safe and healthy work environment.

To include as many employers and employees as possible, Congress passed the Occupational Safety and Health Act under the Commerce Clause of the United States Constitution. By defining the act under this clause, all employers and employees of businesses affecting interstate commerce are included. The few exceptions to this act include federal and state government employees, the self-employed, and domestic servants.

The Birth of the Occupational Safety and Health Administration

Occupational Safety and Health Administration (OSHA)
A federal administrative agency that has the authority to set health and safety standards, conduct inspections, and enforce penalties for violations and/or noncompliance with its regulations.

The **Occupational Safety and Health Administration (OSHA)** was created as the primary administrative agency for the Occupational Safety and Health Act of 1970. OSHA is within the Department of Labor and has the authority to set safety and health standards, conduct inspections to ensure compliance with them, and seek enforcement actions for noncompliance. This authority is supervised by the Secretary of Labor.

The act also created two other agencies: the National Institute of Occupational Safety and Health (NIOSH) and the Occupational Safety and Health Review Commission (OSHRC). NIOSH is a research center for occupational safety and health. As such, it studies various health and safety problems occurring in the workplace and provides technical advice and standard recommendations based on its findings. OSHRC is the enforcement arm. OSHA may recommend a penalty for a discovered violation to OSHRC, but only OSHRC may actually impose the penalty.

How OSHA Works

The Organizational Health and Safety Act provides the Secretary of Labor with the authority to establish three different types of health and safety standards: interim, permanent, and temporary emergency standards. Interim standards were those established from the date of the act for two years that usually generated from preexisting national consensus standards. Permanent standards are either newly created or revised from interim standards. They often stem from suggestions taken from interested parties (such as unions, employers, or NIOSH) or from an appointed advisory committee. Permanent standards must be published in the Federal Register to provide the public time to respond. If publishing the standard results in a requested public hearing, OSHA must schedule and publicize one. OSHA has 60 days after the close of public comment in which to publish the standard, its effective date, and reasons for its adoption. If the Secretary of Labor believes that workers are in grave danger from a newly found hazard, he or she has the authority to bypass the permanent standard formalities and establish temporary emergency standards. Once the temporary standard is published, it becomes effective immediately but for only six months. At the time of publishing, the Secretary must also begin the normal procedure for establishing a permanent standard after the temporary emergency status has expired.

Employer Responsibility

The Occupational Safety and Health Act charges employers with three major responsibilities: to furnish and maintain a healthful work environment, to keep records of occupational injuries and illnesses, and to comply with OSHA standards. With respect to the first responsibility, the act specifically states that employers must provide a workplace that is free from recognized hazards that are likely to cause death or other serious physical harm. The McDonald's case (see the HR Challenges box) illustrates how a recognized hazard can be a costly mistake. To prove a violation of this general requirement, the Secretary of Labor must show that the employer failed to produce a hazard-free environment; that a hazard existed that was recognized by either the employer or the industry; that a hazard exists that did or may cause death or serious harm; and that there was a means by which the employer could have eliminated or reduced the hazard. If all four elements are not proven, the Secretary's case has not been met.

The act also requires that organizations with eight or more employees keep records of any occupational injury or illness if it results in death, loss of consciousness, transfer to another job, medical treatment other than first aid, or one or more lost work days. Occupational injury is defined as any injury that results from a work-related accident; occupational illness is any condition resulting from exposure to environmental factors at the workplace. The information must be recorded on specific OSHA forms. The organization is required to post this information once a year so that employees are aware of the records, and the organization must present these records if requested to do so by an OSHA compliance officer.

Inspections

To enforce its standards, OSHA conducts workplace inspections in all establishments covered by the act. Obviously, this is a monumental job. With its current budget, OSHA can visit only a small percentage of the millions of workplaces every year. To concentrate its efforts on the areas most in need of inspections, OSHA has established a four-tier priority system. It gives top priority to cases in which death or serious injury have occurred, followed by cases of valid employee complaints, high-hazard industries, and, finally, general random inspections.

An inspection is unannounced, except for conditions of imminent danger when advance notice is given to allow the employer the opportunity to correct the situation

A Matter of Degree

When members of a New Mexico jury learned they had been summoned to determine whether a woman who ordered hot coffee at a McDonald's drive-through should be compensated for the burns she received when it spilled as she was putting cream and sugar in it as she held it between her legs while driving, they were incredulous. It seemed that McDonald's had an open-and-shut case. According to opinion polls and radio talk show callers, the public felt the same way when the jury awarded the woman nearly $3 million, finding that McDonald's had served "defective" coffee. The defect? The coffee was too hot and customers should have been warned about the possibility of serious burns. In a seven-day trial, the jury learned (and saw photographs) of the 81-year-old plaintiff's extensive burn-related injuries. It was not sympathy alone, however, that apparently motivated the jury. The jury felt that $160,000 ($200,000 reduced by 20 percent to reflect the degree of fault attributable to the plaintiff for causing her own injuries) was sufficient to compensate her. An additional $2,700,000 was awarded as punitive damages to punish the defendant for intentional, reckless, wanton, or malicious conduct.

It was found that McDonald's coffee (at about 180 degrees) was 20 to 40 degrees hotter than that of most of its competitors in the Albuquerque area. Indeed, McDonald's marketing research showed that its customers preferred its coffee precisely because it was so steaming hot. The company's operations and training manual mandated that coffee be brewed at 195 to 205 degrees and held at 180 to 190 degrees for optimum aroma and taste. So how could a jury find the coffee to be "defective"? In the first place, McDonald's own witnesses acknowledged that the company was aware of previous instances in which customers had been burned seriously by its coffee. However, the company decided against either turning the temperature down or warning customers and took the position that hot coffee burns were statistically insignificant, given that the company sells billions of cups of coffee each year. Moreover, the company failed to consult burn experts. Had such experts been consulted, McDonald's would likely have learned, as the jury heard from the plaintiff's expert witness, that coffee held at 160 degrees would take about 20 seconds to cause third-degree burns; at 180 degrees, it would take 12 to 15 seconds, and at 190 degrees, less than 3 seconds. To the jurors the company seemed callous and uncaring, and so it punished the corporation by awarding the plaintiff a sum equal to about two days of its companywide coffee sales (about $1.35 million a day). Although the amount was later reduced, this was still very costly for McDonald's.

The lesson for employers? Recognize that some situations and activities in the workplace may be as safe as possible and yet still present risk of harm to employees. In such "unavoidably unsafe" circumstances, a failure to warn of possible dangers may be sufficient to result in liability. Even misuse or carelessness by an employee may result in liability if a sympathetic judge or jury believes that the employer should have foreseen the misuse and warned employees specifically about it.

SOURCE: A. Gerlin, "A Matter of Degree: How a Jury Decided That a Coffee Spill Is Worth $2.9 Million," *The Wall Street Journal*, September 1, 1994, p. A1.

as quickly as possible. The inspector must present proper identification and a warrant to conduct the inspection. A warrant is not needed if the employer consents to the inspection, if the site is open to public view, or if there is an emergency situation in which imminent danger to employees would not allow the time needed to obtain a warrant.

The compliance officer may be escorted on a tour by a representative of the employer or the employees. On this tour, the inspector may question workers and employers in private, take samples, make readings, observe, take photographs, and inspect records. At the end of the inspection tour, the compliance officer holds a closing conference with the employer to review the findings and report any possible

EXHIBIT 14.1	VIOLATIONS OF THE OCCUPATIONAL SAFETY AND HEALTH ACT	
Willful	Conscious, intentional, or deliberate decision or a careless disregard for the OSHA standards or indifference to employee safety	Criminal: Up to $10,000 fine or up to six months in prison Civil: Up to $10,000 fine
Repeated violations	Prior violation of the same standard	Up to $10,000 fine
Serious	Substantial likelihood that death or serious physical harm could result	Up to $1,000 fine
Nonserious	Causes an unsafe work environment but probably would not cause death or serious physical harm	Up to $1,000 fine, but only if 10 or more nonserious violations are cited
De minimus	Violation has no immediate relationship to job safety	Notice issued

violations found. The inspector then reports to the area director, who has six months to decide whether or not to issue a citation and impose a penalty.

Violations, Citations, and Penalties

The Occupational Safety and Health Act delineates the types of violations possible. Exhibit 14.1 provides an overview of these as well as the penalties associated with each violation. The area director, after reviewing the compliance officer's report, sends a certified letter outlining the citations and the proposed penalties. Normally, 30 days are provided as the abatement period during which time the employer must correct the violation or OSHA imposes the penalty. The act allows civil sanctions for each day in which the violation has not been corrected after the abatement period.

Willful violations are the only type that include a prison sentence as well as a fine. OSHA can cause top officials to rue the day they were less than diligent in enforcing OSHA regulations. In one case, Howard Elliott, president of Elliott Plumbing & Heating, was sentenced to six months in jail, of which 45 days must be served, for willfully failing to comply with OSHA trenching standards. Failing to abide by the standards resulted in the death of two of Elliott's company's workers. Elliott was placed on probation for three years and was also fined $21,452 in a lump-sum payment, or $544 per month for three years, to cover restitution for funeral expenses and lost earnings.[7] In a more severe case, Phillips Petroleum Company was fined $5.7 million for willful safety violations in connection with a chemical plant explosion near Houston that resulted in 23 deaths and more than 130 injuries.[8]

Managing an OSHA Inspection

Workplace inspections by OSHA are conducted for one of three reasons: (1) in response to an accident, injury, or fatality; (2) in response to an employee complaint alleging an OSHA violation; or (3) as part of OSHA's regularly scheduled inspections. Although a company cannot prevent an OSHA inspection, employers should always know how to manage an inspection. Employers should expect the following:[9]

1. *Opening Conference.* The employer should hold an opening conference for his or her management team and OSHA representatives. During this initial conference, the employer can explain company policy and procedures regarding OSHA inspections. Employers should explain that any document requests must be in writing and that any documents containing confidential information (e.g., trade secrets) must be kept confidential by OSHA. During this opening conference the employer should also set up a procedure with OSHA to determine the schedule of employee interviews.

2. *The Walkaround.* During the actual physical inspection of the workplace, the OSHA inspector should be accompanied by a member of the management team. OSHA inspectors should not be allowed to wander off alone into work areas.

3. *Employee Interviews.* Although OSHA may interview employees at the workplace, the employer is entitled not to have business disrupted; however, employees should not be discouraged from talking with OSHA inspectors.

4. *Closing Conference.* The employer should insist on a closing conference to correct any misunderstandings or errors. This is also an opportunity to inquire about any citations that are likely to occur.

5. *Postclosing Conference.* The employer may want to bring additional information to the attention of the OSHA inspector. This is also the time to consider a precitation settlement if violations have been found.

6. *Postcitation.* If a citation is issued, the employer may ask for an informal meeting with the OSHA inspector to present any last-minute information. After receiving a citation, an employer's notice of contest must be filed within 15 working days.

"Right to Know" Legislation

"right to know" legislation State laws that guarantee employees the right to know whether there are harmful substances in the workplace.

Many states have passed **"right to know" legislation** that guarantees individual workers the right to know of hazardous substances in the workplace, requires employers to inform employees' physicians of the chemical composition of workplace substances, and notifies local officials and residents when local employees are working with hazardous substances. The laws vary from state to state, but it is not uncommon for them to require training programs for employees who work with hazardous materials to inform them about the properties of the materials, safe handling procedures, and emergency treatments for overexposure. Also, many states have enacted legislation that requires labels for containers of toxic substances.

Safety and Health Problems for Employees

cumulative trauma disorders (CTD) Medical problems caused by repetitive motions using the same muscles.

Although the sweatshop work environment has all but disappeared, employers are still concerned about employee productivity.[10] One way in which increased productivity can be achieved is through automation. Sometimes, however, the introduction of new technology can be responsible for adding safety and health problems.[11] One example is the **cumulative trauma disorder (CTD)** caused by repeated motions of the same muscles hundreds or thousands of times each day. These work-related injuries are also known by other terms, such as *repetitive stress injuries, carpal tunnel syndrome,* and *musculoskeletal disorders (MSD).* According to OSHA, work-related injuries afflict as many as 1.8 million workers a year.[12]

Work-Related Injuries

Computers and CTD   The personal computer has changed the American office. Its introduction into the workplace has enabled typists to move 40 percent faster than when using a typewriter because no manual margin adjustments or paper changes are required with computers.[14] However, this change in the variety of hand motions required to type has caused an increase in the reported cases of CTD in all jobs associated with keyboarding. "According to Labor Department statistics, repeated-trauma cases peaked at 332,100 in 1994, up from 23,000 in 1980."[15] The objective is to curb the rise of CTDs, such as the well-known carpal tunnel syndrome. CTDs, which commonly affect a worker's wrists and hands, are the fastest-growing type of workers' compensation claim.[16]

OshKosh B'Gosh, the Wisconsin-based manufacturer, found that most of its workers' CTD problems arose from small, awkward motions that required force and were highly repetitive. Neither the chairs nor the worktables on the shop floor were adjustable, so workers had to lean over and reach, which put great stress on the hands. After an extensive study the safety team at OshKosh was authorized to buy a new chair for each person on the production line, 7000 in all, at $100 each. Among other changes, OshKosh rotates workers through different jobs within the plants so that different parts of their bodies can get a rest.[17] Safety precautions, such as those at OshKosh, can prevent injuries due to cumulative trauma disorders.

Ergonomic Programs

ergonomics
The study of job designs that match the best human-machine fit.

Other corrective measures management can take include introducing an appropriate ergonomics program (**ergonomics** is the study of job designs that maximize the human-machine interface) that focuses on fitting the job to the worker, not the worker to the job. Ergonomics programs also train workers to be aware of the possible symptoms of CTDs and MSDs and ways to curtail these injuries.[18] A properly positioned terminal and keyboard punctuated with frequent breaks can go a long way to reduce or eliminate CTD.[19] Nancy Larson, a corporate agronomist at 3M in St. Paul, Minnesota, explained that effective ergonomic programs tend to evolve in four basic levels. Most companies start programs by trying to fix an MSD problem reported by a specific employee. At the next level, companies become more proactive and try to think of how the solution to the specific MSD problem might be applied to other jobs. At this level, companies are doing some training and researching ergonomics as they design and purchase new equipment. At level three, businesses start understanding how ergonomics helps them increase their profitability. When ergonomics is at the fourth level, it has become a valued part of the business culture.[20] Larson gave a specific example of how an implemented ergonomics program increased profitability. When a worker on a packaging line complained of some discomfort, the site's ergonomics team decided to investigate. The workers were packing cartons with a product that included two different size pails, gloves and a stir stick. The ergonomics team eliminated the need for the pails and stir stick and decided to use a separated sealed pouch. According to Larson, "By getting rid of the pails we decreased the need for warehouse space and cut costs because the plastic pouches were cheaper. We reduced reaching motions. The new product was easier for the customer to use, and we're saving $250,000 annually."[21] In fact, Larry Hettinger, director of human factors and ergonomics at Arthur D. Little in Cambridge, Massachusetts, noted that 95 percent of more than 50 ergonomics audits that Arthur Little has conducted in recent years have resulted in positive Return on Investment (ROI). In other words, the costs of solving problems relating to MSDs are usually outweighed by increases in profitability.[22] Interestingly, OSHA may soon be citing employers for ergonomic violations. OSHA has for years vowed to create employer guidelines for ergonomically designed workstations. An oversight commission has given OSHA the official "go ahead" to cite employers for safety hazards involving lifting and repetitive motions.[23]

Chemicals in the Workplace

Some health problems, such as CTD, are considered threats to workers whereas others, such as chemical poisoning and lung disease, have long plagued workers. Chemical poisoning is an old problem, but several chemical health risks, such as indoor air pollution and passive smoking, have gained attention. Another reason that chemicals in the workplace have received increased attention is OSHA's issuing of new standards for hazardous materials in May 1988 under the title Hazard Communication Standard. This standard, which once applied only to manufacturers, requires every workplace in the country to identify hazardous substances on the premises, list them, and train employees in their use.[24] To comply, employers must observe the following procedures:

1. Identify and list hazardous chemicals in the workplace.
2. Obtain and retain a material safety data sheet (MSDS) for each chemical and make these sheets available to employees.
3. Create and maintain a written chemical communication program.
4. Identify workers who should be trained and provide training that includes instructions in each substance's dangers and safe handling techniques, how to read the Material Safety Data Sheet (MSDS) and warning labels, and what to do in case of an emergency.[25]

Because of the complexities of the regulations and the severity of the penalties for noncompliance, OSHA designed and distributed a "Hazard Compliance Kit."[26] It contains loose-leaf materials designed to provide employers with simple instructions regarding compliance with OSHA's hazard communication standard.

Indoor Air Pollution   The 1976 American Legion convention in Philadelphia will be remembered for many years to come. At this convention, 29 people died from Legionnaire's disease contracted from a bacteria in the hotel's cooling tower that spread through the ventilation system.[27] This was one of the first and most highly publicized cases of "sick building syndrome."

Sick building syndrome is an outgrowth of the energy crisis of the 1970s. Buildings were designed with sealed windows and heavy insulation, resulting in inadequate fresh air and poor ventilation systems. The buildup of chemicals from photocopying machines, cleaning liquids, and solvents has caused workers to complain of headaches, dizziness, and bleeding.[28] Four women with such symptoms, who were fired because they refused to work in the building, sued their employer, its parent company, the building's designer, and the contractor.

Only a handful of lawsuits have been filed on the grounds of indoor air pollution, but the Environmental Protection Agency (EPA) estimates that the economic costs of indoor air pollution totals tens of billions of dollars in such forms as lost productivity, medical care, lost earnings, and sick days. William J. Fisk and Arthur H. Rosenfeld, researchers from the Lawrence Berkeley National Laboratory in Berkeley, California, estimate that companies could save up to $58 billion annually by preventing sick building illnesses. The researchers believe that creating offices with better indoor air would save an additional $200 billion in worker performance improvements. Further-more, they found that the financial benefits of improving office environments are as much as 8 to 17 times larger than the costs of making those improvements.[20] With the increase in both litigation and indirect costs, architects are redesigning buildings so that fresh air is available, and engineers are improving air circulation systems for of-fice buildings.[30]

Smoking in the Workplace

The 1990s will likely be referred to as the decade of the smoke-free workplace. The movement toward eliminating smoking in the workplace has been fueled by reports that virtually all companies are working to eliminate workplace smoking. Reasons given for these actions include concern for employee health, worker complaints, the EPA's classification of environmental tobacco smoke (ETS) as a human carcinogen, and the increase in state and local laws.[31]

Although not cited, employers may want to see their employees quit smoking for a variety of other reasons. Smokers are 50 percent more likely to be hospitalized than are nonsmoking employees. Smokers lose 80 million work days a year because of their habit, and their absenteeism rate is 50 percent higher than that of their nonsmoking counterparts. Smokers have twice as many job-related accidents as nonsmokers, in part due to loss of attention, hand occupation, eye irritation, and coughing.[32] Smok-ers also have been found to have more car accidents.[33]

Smokers are not the only victims of the deleterious effects of smoking. The EPA concluded that "secondhand" smoke has a "serious and substantial public health im-pact" on nonsmokers.[34] Environmental tobacco smoke comes from two sources: main-stream smoke, which is inhaled directly by the smoker, and sidestream or secondhand smoke, which is emitted by the lighted end of the cigarette. Secondhand smoke, which is unfiltered, has higher concentrations of carbon monoxide, ammonia, and other harmful chemicals than does mainstream smoke and can be inhaled more deeply into the lungs because of its smaller particle size.[35] A number of companies have made a strategic decision to promote a smoke-free workplace. Merck & Co., a pharmaceuti-cal corporation based in Rahway, New Jersey, has taken somewhat extreme measures; it has severely restricted smoking in all of its 24 sites in the United States. Further, it also has banned smoking at Merck-sponsored off-site events. To help its employees kick the habit, Merck does the following:

1. Reimburses employees and their dependents for successful completion of ap-proved smoking-cessation programs.
2. Encourages smokers to quit through a year-long communications program.
3. Helps fund a smoking clinic at a local hospital.
4. Donates money to the American Cancer Society and the American Lung As-sociation to support public education and no-smoking programs.
5. Produces an antismoking commercial that airs repeatedly on 14 commercial radio stations serving communities surrounding Merck sites nationwide.[36]

Strategies for effective management of smoke-free environments include (1) com-municating with employees concerning smoking policies (both smokers and non-smokers should be consulted); (2) clearly defining a policy and sticking to it;[37] (3) treating the issue with dignity and seriousness; (4) offering incentives and/or help for smokers to quit smoking; (5) working with the union; and, most important, (6) ensuring that top management is seriously committed to the health of all employees.[38]

Asbestos in the Workplace[39]

Asbestos is a fiber that was used extensively in insulation for more than a century until it was linked to cancer. Workers who were exposed to asbestos contracted a form of cancer called *asbestosis*, which slowly suffocates its victims. The first lawsuit filed by a worker exposed to asbestos was in the 1950s. The lawsuits continued for the next 40 years, with plaintiffs winning big beginning in the 1980s when juries learned that companies knew the risks associated with asbestos but did nothing to protect the workers. Some of the judgments were so high that companies were forced to file Chapter 11 bankruptcy to protect themselves.

As the rewards and the number of suits continued to grow, the asbestos manufacturers' insurance companies grew tired of paying and began to reread the contracts for loopholes. Many filed suit against the asbestos manufacturers, and these cases also ended up in court.

Asbestos suits were becoming so common that lawyers specialized in such cases. It is estimated that more than 1100 law firms around the country were involved in defending asbestos manufacturers, insurance firms, or victims.

The solution to the escalation of lawsuits came in the form of the Asbestos Claims Facility, a one-stop settlement shop for asbestos claims. The designers saw it as a faster, less costly, and more orderly way to resolve claims. Fifty companies, who included the largest asbestos manufacturers and insurance companies, joined the facility. These companies provided funding for the facility to use in settling claims quickly and without the use of the courts.

Soon after its inception, the flood of claims turned into a deluge. New claims poured in at a rate of 1300 a month, more than triple the rate from a few years before. With more than 60,000 claims pending, the Asbestos Claims Facility folded. Seven of the biggest participants withdrew their financial support, which accounted for more than 60 percent of the funding available. Companies and plaintiffs alike were forced to return to the overcrowded courts to reach a settlement.

Accidents and Death on the Job

Research has found that when a father holds a hazardous job, the son is more likely to follow in his footsteps.[40] Sons appear to believe that they can control the dangers associated with the job. Another contributing factor is the rate of pay: the higher it is, the higher the chance of the son choosing a hazardous career. However, education level and race have been found to decrease the rate of occupational following. Research has found that the higher the level of education attained by the son, the less likely he is to perform his father's job. Also, white males are more likely to pursue their fathers' careers than are black males.

Both the type of job one holds and the type of person holding the job influence the accident rate. Research has found that left-handed men are one third more likely to have accidents on the job than right-handers because of the bias of right-handed equipment.[41] Furthermore, although it was always assumed that blacks, who tend to work in more dangerous occupations, had a higher accident rate than whites, recent reports contradict this assumption. A study by the National Center for Health Statistics reported that whites have slightly higher rates of work-related accidents than blacks, especially in the growing service sector.[42]

An ever-increasing cause of accidents and death on the job is violence in the workplace. A review of litigated cases shows various types of workplace violence. A youth who was struck by an usher carrying a flashlight sued the theater operator for damages. A fast-food restaurant employee sued her employer for fraud and bad faith after being injured in a robbery. She charged that the employer promised police protection and other security measures but reneged on his promises. A woman, who was raped and sexually abused by an individual employed by a corporation to prepare bids for construction jobs, sued the employer for negligent retention of the employee and vicarious liability for the employee's violent actions.[43] One of the leading causes of death for women in the workplace is murder.[44] Women often work in retail establishments where the number of homicides is high because of easy entrance by strangers.[45] OSHA has drafted guidelines for night retailers aimed at reducing the risk of violence. Among some of the structural changes suggested are "bullet-proof" glass and video surveillance systems.[46] A draft of OSHA's guidelines for workplace violence is available on the Internet at **www.shrm.org/hrnews**.

The causes of workplace violence are varied; in most cases, employers can be held responsible because they are obligated by law to provide a safe working environment for their employees and a safe place for nonemployees to conduct business.[47] To protect themselves, employers should make a strategic decision to implement policies and practices designed to limit the risk of employing unfit, dangerous, or incompetent employees. In addition, because there is a higher level of awareness and concern about workplace violence, human resource professionals should become familiar with security selection and program design.[48] Prevention and preparation are the keys to minimizing the threat of workplace violence, so human resource professionals should take steps to familiarize themselves with the various options and strategies available to their companies. The HR Challenges box on workplace safety emphasizes the need to include the concept of teamwork into the safety improvement process.

Acquired Immune Deficiency Syndrome (AIDS) Issues in the Workplace

AIDS has become a serious health threat to Americans. AIDS also has caused significant confusion and disruption in the workforce. Individuals who have AIDS are protected by federal, state, and local legislation. This protection is guaranteed under the ADA of 1990 because AIDS is considered a disability.[49] This protection generally comes in the form of protection against discrimination and is based on the fact that the virus cannot be spread by casual contact.[50]

The Center for Disease Control and Prevention (CDC) has long concluded that the kind of nonsexual, person-to-person contact that generally occurs among workers and clients or consumers in the workplace does not pose a risk for transmission of HIV, the virus that causes AIDS.[51] However, even with these reassurances, some employees fear working with coworkers who are infected with AIDS. The fear may stem from the fact that employees know little about AIDS, and what they do know is extremely frightening.

When employees realize that they are working with an infected coworker, they sometimes issue an ultimatum: "Either that person goes or we go, and if we go, we'll go public." To some employers, this can be an extremely effective scare tactic. Few employers want to be faced with the empty tables, beds, or desks that may appear after the public learns that a chef, chambermaid, or engineer has AIDS.[52] What choice does the employer have? Discharging an employee with AIDS violates the law. If

Workplace Safety: Lessons from Japanese Management

Forty years ago Japan had an industrial injury and illness rate five times that of the United States. By 1990, the United States had an injury and illness rate almost six times that of Japan. Today, Japanese employees and managers are working together to promote safety and health. Slogans such as "anzen nakushite seisan nashi"—without safety there can be no production—are spoken frequently by Japanese employees and managers.

The Japanese behavioral approach to promoting workplace safety may be useful for managers in the United States. Specific examples of Japanese strategies for promoting workplace safety and health include the following:

- *Continuous Improvement.* Employees and managers are trained to think constantly about changes to the production process that can improve safety and health conditions.
- *Morning Exercise and Safety Check.* Stretching exercises are followed by a safety check involving two employees who check each other for any safety or health problem (e.g., jewelry that might get caught in machinery).

- *Articulation of Hazards and Contingencies.* Employees learn to identify the hazards involved in their workstation, and they develop a contingency plan should the hazard they study occur.
- *Hazard Prediction Cards.* To help employees remember the wide range of possible hazards, cards listing generic hazards are given to workers to carry.

Successful work safety and health programs in Japan and the United States have incorporated employee empowerment and the teamwork concept into the safety processes. In Japan there is a high degree of cooperation among labor, management, and government. Given that one of the best ways to improve safety and health in an organization is to examine the "best practices" of other successful organizations, managers in the United States may want to examine some of the "best practices" in Japan.

SOURCE: Adapted from W. Neal, "Workplace Health, Safety: A Continuing Process," *HRNews*, September 1994, p. 18; and R. Wokutch, "New Lessons from Japanese Management," *HRMagazine*, September 1994, pp. 72–78.

---

other employees leave and make the situation public, the business could suffer irreparable damage.

The only choice available to employers is to prevent employees from acting irrationally by educating them about AIDS. Several guidelines must be followed if the educational program is to be effective:

1. One goal of the program is to be certain that employees understand how AIDS is contracted. If they understand that the activities required to contract AIDS are not practiced in their workplace, the irrational behavior should disappear.
2. Because the message presented includes sexual references, the presentation should be informed and professional so that the workers do not feel that management is infringing on their personal lives. To achieve this goal, it may be necessary to hire an external expert to present the educational program.
3. Finally, it is imperative that *all* employees attend the sessions.[53]

If these guidelines are followed, employers may not be faced with ultimatums.

Enterprising organizations are taking innovative and proactive approaches to the AIDS crisis in the workplace. First and foremost is the establishment of a responsible AIDS policy that outlines equal treatment for employees, legal responsibilities, education, and confidentiality concerns.[54] The potential for devastation with such a disease is obvious, but those firms that prepare in advance will be able to minimize the

---

EXHIBIT 14.2 TIPS FOR IMPLEMENTING A SAFETY PROGRAM THAT WORKS

---

1. Avoid asking workers to "do as I say, not as I do." Managers and supervisors must serve as role models for the safety program. If workers see their supervisors performing jobs in an unsafe manner, they feel they have every right to do so too. It is the manger's responsibility to perform the job exactly as outlined by the safety program.
2. Avoid having a "participatory facade." Asking for employee suggestions for improving workplace safety will be effective only if the suggestions are implemented in a timely fashion. If the ideas provided by workers are ignored or implementation is postponed, when they are eventually implemented, the workers will not be motivated to support them.
3. Avoid the problem of workers believing that "if I'm not in on it, I'm not up on it," by allowing workers at all levels to participate in the development of the safety program. If workers or managers feel that the program is being pushed down their throats without concern for their feelings, they will not be motivated to abide by the rules.
4. Workers will want to know "what's in it for me." While the company is sure to benefit from increased safety through reduced medical and insurance costs, workers may not see a personal advantage to abiding by the new safety plan. Including an incentive for workers often reverses this trend and increases compliance. However, be sure that the incentive is awarded frequently and as soon as possible after good compliant behavior occurs in order to tie the reward to the behavior you want to see repeated.

SOURCE: Adapted from R. A. Reber, J. A. Walling, and D. L. Dubon, "Safety Programs that Work," *Personnel Administrator*, September 1989, pp. 66–69; C. M. Ford, "Building Safety into Operating Procedures," *Occupational Hazards* 59, no. 2 (February 1997), pp. 39–43.

---

impact. There have been some advancements that offer hope to those afflicted with the AIDS virus. In 1996 the federal government approved protease inhibitors, a drug that has been somewhat successful in combating the deadly AIDS virus. In 1997 government officials announced the first drop in AIDS deaths nationwide since the discovery of the virus. New AIDS drugs have given impetus to individuals returning to work who are afflicted with the disease because they find themselves with a good expectation of longevity. Human resource professionals must attend to this new development.[55]

Safety Programs that Work

For a safety program to be effective, it must be followed. All too often a program is implemented and ignored. There are various reasons that some programs work and others do not. Exhibit 14.2 provides tips for implementing safety programs that work. One of the most important items in this list is that workers must be aware that the program is to their advantage, not just for the company's benefit. This has been referred to as the "What's in it for me?" problem.

Workplace Stress

What Is Stress?

Stress has been defined as the interaction between the individual and the environment characterized by physiological and psychological changes that cause a deviation from normal performance.[56] This deviation from normal may have a positive or negative

---

EXHIBIT 14.3 CATEGORIZATIONS OF OCCUPATIONS

Active Jobs. These jobs have a heavy pressure to perform but provide leeway in problem solving. Hours may be long but are partly at the worker's discretion. There are chances to advance and to learn new skills. Initiative is a big part of the job. Examples: farmers, doctors, engineers, executives, and other professionals.

Low-Strain Jobs. These are the self-paced occupations. There are low demands form others and a high degree of decision freedom. What is done, in what order, and often at what pace are determined by the employee. Examples: tenured professors, carpenters, repairmen, or artists.

Passive Jobs. These jobs require a low degree of skills and mental-processing ability and have little leeway for learning or for making decisions. This type of job offers almost no latitude for innovation. Some jobs may actually cause workers' sills to decline. Examples: janitors, billing clerks, or data-entry operators.

High-Strain Jobs. These jobs have a heavy pressure to perform, but provide no leeway in decision making. Hours and procedures are rigid and the threat of layoffs is present. The jobs provide no opportunities to learn new skills. It is extremely difficult to take an unscheduled break or to take time off for personal reasons. Examples: assembly-line workers, telephone operators, or waiters/waitresses.

SOURCE: Adapted from R. Karasek and T. Theorell, *Healthy Work* (New York: Basic Books, 1991); R. Winslow, "Lack of Control Over Job Is Seen as Heart Risk," *The Wall Street Journal*, July 25, 1997, pp. B1, B3.

---

outcome. A moderate amount of stress can help to stimulate employees to work longer, harder, and better. However, an extremely low level of stress can leave employees unstimulated, resulting in low productivity. An extremely high level of stress can lead to poor performance from the diversion of increased energy from production and from dealing with the stress itself.

Stress has both an internal and an external factor. Internal factors are primarily a person's attitudes and expectations. Difficulty living up to these values may cause self-induced stress. External factors can be divided into two categories: physical and psychological. Physical stressors can include poor ventilation or lighting or physically demanding tasks. Examples of psychological stressors include demands of the job or demands from home.[57]

An increase in a person's stress level can result in several physical changes. These changes, often referred to as a *stress response*, include increased blood pressure, heart rate, and respiration; an increased output of mental activity and gastric juices; and changes in the blood flow patterns. These changes can result in employee responses such as fatigue or anxiety.[58]

Causes of Stress

It is difficult to categorize stressors as high level or low level or to even list them because a situation that creates a high level of stress for one person may not cause any stress for another. Further, a person who views a situation as stressful one day may not view it as stressful on another day. However, it is safe to say that every aspect of a person's life is a potential source of stress. Specifically, stress can come from pressures at work or at home, or because of personality traits.

Work Pressures   The type of job a person holds has a significant impact on the degree of stress he or she faces at work. Some occupations have a great deal of stress

EXHIBIT 14.4	HOW HEALTHFUL IS YOUR JOB?

Place the number that best agrees with your feelings about each of the following statements with respect to your job in the blank before each statement. Total scores below 14 indicate a job that encourages good health. Total scores over 30 indicate a stress-inducing job.

Strongly Agree		Neither Agree Nor Disagree		Strongly Disagree
1	2	3	4	5

_____ My job requires me to make maximum use of my skills and offers me a chance to increase them.

_____ I am free from worker-as-child disciplines. I control the machines on which I work, I can participate in long-term planning, and I have flexible work hours.

_____ The demands placed on me are mixed. The changes made are challenging but predictable. I have some input with respect to the magnitude of changes made.

_____ Collaboration on my job is encouraged.

_____ My workplace believes in the democratic process. I have an avenue to air and settle grievances.

_____ I know what it is I produce and why it is necessary. Customers provide me feedback so that I know how well I am performing.

_____ My job allows me time and energy for activities other than work.

SOURCE: Adapted from K. Karasek and T. Theorell, *Healthy Work* (New York: Basic Books, 1991).

associated with them; others are less stressful. Exhibit 14.3 is a four-part categorization of occupations based on the tasks associated with the job. Surprisingly, the high-strain jobs listed are the jobs in which the highest levels of stress and stress-related diseases are reported. It appears that the bossed, not the bosses, are the ones who suffer the most from the effects of stress. These individuals have little control but high accountability. Employees who hold active jobs report the lowest levels of stress-related diseases; the passive and low-strain employees fall in between. To determine how healthful your job is, take the quiz in Exhibit 14.4.

Another way in which the workplace can cause an employee stress is by living and working with the constant fear of being replaced. Frequently this means consolidating jobs and laying off employees. Even IBM, which was famous for its policy of lifetime employment, found itself in a position in which it had to lay off workers. Other types of consolidation that have continued since the late 1980s are mergers and acquisitions. These types of activities also led to a reduction in the workforce as the newly merged company found itself with two identical accounting or human resource departments. Yet another worker fear is automation. Workers and managers alike know that one machine can do the jobs of many workers and never requires a coffee break. As corporations restructure, managers are finding that they must do more with less.[59]

The stress from the fear of being replaced or from actually being replaced can cause severe reactions. In one Citibank unit in which 2000 jobs were eliminated, two employees killed themselves and the number of traffic accidents experienced by employees increased significantly.[60] After Westinghouse Electric announced a restructuring and downsizing plan, employees were surveyed. Researchers found a higher than average prevalence of depression among white-collar workers induced by the stress of the impending changes.[61] Approximately 38 percent of employers who cut jobs from 1990 to 1995 saw an increase in psychiatric and substance-abuse claims, compared with 29 percent of firms that didn't cut jobs.[62]

Home Stressors   Americans have seen dramatic changes in the family structure in the last 15 years. Single-parent families, which include fathers raising children, and dual-career couples are commonplace. These changes have made the conflict between parent as parent and parent as paid employee an extremely deep source of stress and anxiety in the American family today.[63]

Mothers frequently report stress induced by the guilt of not being a good parent when work pressures are high and not being a good employee when home pressures take priority. Of 3000 working mothers surveyed, 16 percent reported that they felt intense guilt about spending too little time with their children and spouses or not spending enough time on themselves. These mothers reported little support at home and few work rewards.[64]

Fathers, too, have begun to wrestle with the pressures from both career and family. One survey of more than 1600 employees at a large public utility company indicated that almost as many men as women (36 percent versus 37 percent) reported feeling "a lot of stress" in balancing their work and family lives.[65] A separate survey of more than 1200 employees at a Minneapolis company found that more than 70 percent of the fathers under the age of 35 had serious concerns about problems they were having managing work and family conflicts with their spouses. More than 60 percent of the male respondents reported that family concerns were affecting their work goals and plans. Many indicated that they were not seeking promotions or transfers because they needed to spend more time with their families.[66]

Research suggests that women may be better able to handle the stress of both family and career. Researchers had 166 couples in Detroit keep diaries of when they felt extreme pressure from both work and home or when they had arguments. The results indicate that men, not women, reported more incidents. Evidence also showed that men were more likely to have work problems spill over into family time and vice versa than women. Researchers suggested that differences in upbringing and role expectations have made women better able to handle family/work stress.[67] Interestingly, good work experiences can buffer people from stress at home and vice versa.[68]

Personality   Individuals who have what has been referred to as *Type A personalities* (hard-driving workaholics) have long been thought to be prime candidates for heart problems.[69] The reason behind this is that Type As have a strong bodily reaction to stressful situations. Their heart rate and blood pressure rise, causing increased blood flow to their muscles. This change in their systems, when repeated throughout their lives, can place severe strain on their hearts and eventually cause damage. Evidence suggests, however, that not all Type As are prone to coronary heart disease. By looking at the various components of Type A behavior, it has been found that only the anger and hostility components of Type A behavior are associated with heart disease.[70] This means that the chronically angry and hostile person is the one who is most at risk.

Other personality characteristics can lead to increased stress as well. Researchers have found that certain personal characteristics draw certain individuals to specific jobs. These jobs, in turn, tend to cause stress in the people they attract. For example,

EXHIBIT 14.5	STRESS INDICATORS CHECKLIST

These symptoms can indicate stress, especially when appearing in groups and when they represent major changes in behavior. People may exhibit symptoms and suffer from stress even if they are not aware of feeling pressured.

BEHAVIORAL
Heavy smoking, increased use of alcohol, drug use, high-risk behavior, violence, overeating, hyperactivity, sleep disturbances, nightmares.

ATTITUDINAL
Boredom, cynicism, distrust, despair, feelings of helplessness, self-righteousness, feeling trapped, self-doubt.

EMOTIONAL
Anxiety, feelings of being overwhelmed, fear, paranoia, perceived lack of control, guilt, depression, anger, panic, feelings of tension, pressure.

SOCIAL
Withdrawal from friends, marital/relationship problems, restricted social contacts, critical toward self, conflict with spouse, overdependence on others.

PHYSICAL
Headaches, abdominal pain, indigestion, nausea, fatigue, frequent colds, weight loss or gain, heart palpitations, vision problems.

MENTAL
Difficulty concentrating, inability to make decisions, short attention span, intrusive images, self-blaming, frequent daydreams, avoidance of certain thoughts.

SOURCE: Adapted from J. Kelly, "Get a Grip on Stress," *HRMagazine* 42, no. 2 (February 1997), pp. 51–55.

clergy, who often have a distorted view of "selflessness," tend to have extremely high levels of stress that may eventually lead to burnout because they ignore their own needs and give too much of themselves to others.[71]

Consequences and Expenses of Job Stress

Stress can cause physical and emotional problems for people who suffer from excess stress. The most frequent disorders range from chronic fatigue to depression brought on by insomnia, anxiety, migraine headaches, emotional upsets, stomach ulcers, allergies, skin disorders, lumbago and rheumatic attacks, high blood pressure, tobacco and alcohol abuse, overeating, family abuse, cynicism, distrust, and even colds. In severe cases the end results can even be death from heart attacks, accidents, or suicide.[72] Exhibit 14.5 describes typical symptoms from experienced stress.

All of the medical complications associated with stress are an ever-increasing burden on the medical costs for companies. Some experts have estimated the overall cost for many large corporations at more than $200 million a year for employee medical benefits. This figure rises to more than $150 billion a year when the costs to the overall economy caused by repercussions of stress, such as reduced production due to ill, absent, or unmotivated employees, are factored in.[73]

Balancing Work and Family

Balancing work and family is clearly not an easy task for working couples. As the parents of baby boomers age, many working adults find themselves caring for not only their children, but also their parents. In response to a concern about work and family conflict, organizations have begun to adopt a number of family-friendly work policies. Work schedule flexibility and dependent care benefits represent the most prevalent work-family pro-grams. Work programs that include flexible work-ing schedules for their employees have shown an increase in productivity, job satisfaction and a de-crease in employee absenteeism.

SOURCE: B. B. Baltes, J.W. Briggs, J.A. Wright, and G.A. Neu-man, "Flexible and Compressed Workweek Schedules: A Meta-Analysis of Their Effects on Work-Related Criteria," *Journal of Applied Psychology*, 1999, 84, pp. 496–513.

Stress Reduction Techniques

In an effort to reduce their costs, companies have begun implementing stress reduc-tion or control programs for their employees. These programs represent proactive strategies toward stress management and come in a variety of forms, depending on the needs of the employees. Commonly found programs include discussion groups, stress education classes, relaxation techniques, time management programs, physical fitness programs, weight-loss clinics, drug and alcohol rehabilitation clinics, family counsel-ing, hobbies, sports, and goal-setting classes.[74] Given that in 1998 career stress was the number one health problem for working adults, identifying methods to reduce expe-rienced stress is critical.[75]

Stress in one's life is virtually unavoidable. For those who are not lucky enough to have a stress reduction program available to them, or for those who are between pro-grams, here are a few techniques:

1. List items that cause stress. Isolate the ones you can fix and concentrate your time and effort on them. Avoid the ones that you can do nothing about.
2. We all need to take pride in our accomplishments and receive praise from oth-ers. If your job does not provide for these needs, find an activity that does.
3. Experiment with different forms of relaxation, such as exercise, sports, or med-itation, until you find one that relieves your anxiety.
4. Remember that a sense of control and a reason to live lead to a healthy and productive life.[76]

Strategies for Improving Health and Safety

Besides providing some flexibility, managers have the extremely important role of providing a safe and healthy environment for their employees. The opportunities available for doing this have become more and more varied over time. Two of the most important strategic choices regarding health programs currently are fitness, drug testing, and rehabilitation plans.

Fitness Programs

The number of health and fitness programs sponsored by corporations has increased. Perhaps one reason for these increases is the fact that health promotion has proved to be a cost-effective organizational strategy. Each dollar invested in workplace health education can yield $1.42 over two years in lower absentee costs. Some companies have reported absences from illness dropping by as much as 15 percent.[77] Other studies have found that the difference in the productivity of participants and nonparticipants in organization-sponsored health programs was valued at more than $1 million.[78]

The key to building an effective organization fitness program is to follow some basic rules. First, employees must see something in it for themselves or their family. If employees see it as just another cost-cutting ploy, they will not be responsive to it. To make it appeal to employees, a firm should offer incentives and rewards. Second, it must appeal to all employees and therefore should be varied and fun. The firm should ask employees what they want.[79] Finally, do not have a workplace environment that contradicts the firm's goals. Some examples of fitness programs include banning smoking in the workplace, providing nutritional meal alternatives in the cafeteria, and sponsoring fun runs rather than bake sales.[80]

Companies that have followed these guidelines have reported great success. One of the most impressive was introduced by Mesa Limited Partnership, a holding company in Amarillo, Texas, headed by T. Boone Pickens. The first phase of the program is a computerized health-risk appraisal. All participants are eligible to receive up to $240 annually for participating. They must complete a written test and submit to a glucose, cholesterol, and blood pressure screening. Results from these tests are used in phase 2: goal setting for weight loss or weight control, strength improvement, and general health maintenance. To get employees to participate in phase 2, monetary incentives are provided to participating employees.[81]

Drug Testing and Rehabilitation

One area of employee safety and health that continues to evolve is drug testing. Substance abusers have been shown to file five times as many workers' compensation claims as nonabusers. However, drug testing remains a controversial issue in the workplace.[82] In 1988 President Reagan issued Executive Order 12564 establishing a drug-free workplace in the federal government. This order established a drug testing program for federal workers. Also in 1988, Congress passed the Drug Free Workplace Act to abolish drug use among employees within any organization that works directly with the federal government.[83]

The Drug Free Workplace Act states that employers must notify their employees of drug-free workplace requirements, outline actions that will be taken against those who violate the requirements, and establish awareness programs that include supervisory staff training in identifying drug abuse.[84] However, as organizations implement these requirements, they must not violate the rights guaranteed their employees under the Fourth Amendment, specifically, the right to be free of illegal search and seizures.

One would expect employees to hold a negative view concerning drug testing in the workplace, but at least one survey has found the opposite to be true. An attitude survey of the Anchorage Telephone Utility indicated that employees actually held a more favorable view than expected. Employees indicated that although they felt drug testing was an invasion of their privacy, they did not feel that it was unreasonable. However, they also indicated that all levels in the organization should be required to participate if a drug testing program is enforced.[85]

Motorola, Inc. has implemented a random and universal drug testing program with the ultimate goal of improving customer service and productivity.[86] Implementation of the program was not easy. Motorola incurred extensive first-year costs of nearly $1.5 million, and the program was met with some employee resistance.[87] However, Motorola saw a decrease in positive drug tests among employees to a low of about 1 percent. Other benefits derived from a successful drug testing program include increased productivity and lower absenteeism. Other companies have reported similar successes. For example, Burlington Northern reduced the rate of employees testing positive for drug use to only 0.5 percent of the total workforce and has substantially lowered insurance claims costs since the implementation of its drug testing program.[88]

The legal aspects of drug testing in the workplace are complicated, especially with regard to the provisions of the ADA, which provides protection from discrimination for recovering substance abusers. Before a company engages in any type of drug testing, it must make sure that the testing complies with state and federal laws and guidelines.

One positive outcome of the drug testing issue is the continued development of employee assistance programs (EAPs) to help employees who are found to be using drugs. One of the requirements of the Drug Free Workplace Act is that employees who are convicted of drug usage must be required to satisfactorily complete a rehabilitation program. Many organizations pay for or offer these programs to their employees because firms are finding that EAPs may be more helpful in curbing drug abuse than is drug testing.[89]

Company-sponsored EAPs are designed to help employees whose personal problems have an adverse impact on their job performance. These programs may be administered in-house or through outside organizations. EAPs can be designed to help employees with a variety of personal problems, ranging from alcohol and drug abuse to marital problems, financial concerns, depression, and stress.[90] Whether or not a program is deemed successful depends on the definition of *success*. Overall, drug rehabilitation success has not been high. Some firms believe that they are very successful if they can keep 20 to 30 percent of their members off drugs.

The Cost of Insurance for Small and Large Businesses

Health-care insurance has become a nightmare for thousands of small businesses because of soaring premiums. Although the percentage increase may seem small, the actual number of employees who lost their insurance coverage may be as high as one million.[91]

Although Congress continues to debate the appropriate makeup of health-care legislation, small businesses can take several steps to reduce their insurance costs. First, companies can become involved in insurance pools designed specifically for small businesses. Some states are creating insurance pools for small companies. This will provide lower premiums for participating firms because the monetary foundation is larger and the risk of an expensive claim is reduced. Some large insurance companies are also providing small-group risk pools designed to cover small business insurance needs. However, to qualify, four low-risk employees must be enrolled for every one high-risk employee.[92]

Another alternative is called *partnering;* it involves direct contracting with health-care providers. The major building blocks of partnering include making long-term exclusive contracts between employers and health-care providers; promoting a healthy workplace through maintenance and wellness programs; sharing risks and rewards among the providers, employers, and employees; and communicating among all participants. This alternative is available to small businesses that band together to form coalitions.[93]

The most extreme alternative being considered by some employers is turning health-benefits decisions and responsibilities over to the employees entirely. Employers would provide each employee with a set amount of money for health benefits. The employee could then choose a health-insurance plan, and the company would successfully cap health-benefits costs. Xerox Corp. has already implemented a similar plan with an added bonus. When employees spend less than their allotment, they can choose to contribute what is left to some other benefit such as disability or dental insurance. Not only do employees have more choices regarding health benefits, but putting consumers in control has promoted more market efficiency. When consumers become dissatisfied, they just switch plans. In the long run, this could suppress soaring health-care insurance premiums.[94]

Human resource professionals need to become more involved in the employee health-care process. A more detailed knowledge of the benefits and costs of various alternatives provides more strategic choices concerning the long-term health and well-being of employees.

Management Guidelines

The following guidelines represent many of the important elements that organizations need to include as part of an effective health and safety program. Management must give employee safety and well-being serious consideration and ensure that these issues never be neglected or ignored. An effective health and safety program can help ensure that the strategic plan, goals, and objectives of the company are realized.

1. Employee health and safety programs should be a major priority for management because they save lives, increase productivity, and reduce costs. These health and safety programs should stress employee involvement, continued monitoring, and an overall wellness component.
2. Jobs that employees currently perform should be examined in an effort to locate the ones that may present a potential health or safety problem for employees. Steps should be taken to eliminate these problems.
3. It is important to be aware of the health risks that production may cause workers. All sources of workplace chemicals or of other health concerns should be recorded and all employees made aware of these records.
4. Safe-handling procedures for harmful substances should be developed and employees should be trained in these procedures.
5. Employee assistance programs should be developed to help employees deal with emotional, physical, or other problems caused by their employment.
6. Jobs should be analyzed for potential sources of stress and redesigned to eliminate these pressures.
7. Employers should strive to meet and surpass the health and safety guidelines imposed by OSHA. Frequent and continual updating of procedures may be necessary to remain in compliance.
8. A firm that decides to offer a fitness or wellness program to employees should be sure that it is something they will want to use and should make it easy for them to participate. Offering incentives to participate may also be useful.
9. AIDS informational campaigns in an organization should focus on reducing the workers' fear about AIDS through education.

10. As court decisions continue to change and redefine the rules in the workplace, it is imperative that human resource managers be up-to-date with respect to the rules and regulations governing their industry. Providing educational incentives for these managers will help them achieve this goal.

Questions for Review

1. When and why was the Occupational Safety and Health Act passed? Describe some of the provisions of this act.
2. What are two of the current safety and health problems facing U.S. businesses today?
3. If asked to design an employee health and safety program that would help to eliminate accidents in the workplace, what would your plan include?
4. What is the relationship between job stress and productivity?
5. How can employers reduce job stress?
6. What are some techniques that employers can use to ensure that employees participate in fitness or wellness programs?
7. Why is it important for organizations to provide informational programs about AIDS?
8. Fetal protection policies have almost always been directed at female workers. Why is this? Why is it not important to protect potential fathers from chemicals that may harm their potential children?
9. What are some of the tips managers should be aware of when developing safety programs that work?
10. If an organization makes a strategic decision to stress employee health and well-being, what are some of the potential advantages of adopting this strategy?

CASE

Safety in the Workplace—Whose Responsibility?[95]

"On this site, 146 workers lost their lives in the Triangle Shirtwaist Co. fire on March 26, 1911. Out of their martyrdom came new concepts of social responsibility and labor legislation that have helped make American working conditions the finest in the world."

This quotation appears on a plaque commemorating the 146 people who died in the fires at Triangle Shirtwaist Company. The majority of those who died were low-paid young women who were trapped inside the building. Management at Triangle routinely kept doors locked to prevent employees from stealing. Although Triangle had four major fires in the nine years prior to the 1911 blaze, they failed to prepare their workers for just such a crisis (for example, no fire drills were conducted).

The Triangle fire was a landmark incident that led to legislation requiring companies to install sprinkler systems, have wider exits, unlock doors, and conduct regular fire drills. This incident, along with other workplace accidents, focused attention on the need for employers to provide a safe and healthful work environment for their workers and eventually led to the creation of OSHA.

However, an accident called into question the effectiveness of health and safety regulations in the workplace. Despite efforts to improve working conditions, has significant improvement been made in the last 90 years?

Fire at Imperial Food Products Plant

September 3, 1991, started out as a typical workday for workers at the Imperial Foods Products plant in Hamlet, North Carolina. Workers arrived to work on Tuesday morning and began preparing for the day. No one had any reason to suspect that this day would be any different from any other. At 8:30 AM, however, an event took place that would change the lives of each and every worker at Imperial; a fryer at Imperial's chicken-processing plant caught fire, leaving 25 workers dead, more than 40 injured, and countless grieving. Although workers were heard banging on doors screaming "Let me out!" witnesses outside were unable to open the locked doors. Just as at Triangle, management at the Imperial plant also routinely kept doors locked to prevent employees from stealing. In addition to locked doors, one of the exits was blocked by a delivery truck, and workers had to wait for it to be moved.

Safety in the Workplace

With the exception of those who work under extremely hazardous conditions, most of us rarely think about safety in the workplace. We assume that the company will provide a safe environment and that officials at OSHA will ensure that the company is not in violation of safety regulations. Unfortunate and tragic accidents at the workplace, however, remind us that this idealistic situation is not always in accord with the realistic situation.

In 1970, OSHA began requiring employers to keep exit doors clear so they can serve as escape hatches. Why, then, was Imperial placing its employees at risk by keeping exits locked on a continual basis in an environment in which fires have posed a threat in the past? Similar to Triangle, Imperial had had three fires in the previous 11 years, and it also did nothing to prepare workers for such a crisis, such as conducting fire drills. Federal laws allow states to set up their own regulatory agencies, and although OSHA is responsible for monitoring these state programs, they rarely enforce safety regulations in the states that currently have their own programs.

State Programs

North Carolina is among the states responsible for performing their own inspections and fining those in violation. Imperial Foods, however, had never been inspected in its 11 years of operation, which is not surprising considering that North Carolina's state legislature had cut the safety budget by 40 percent.

Although not every state program is so lax in enforcement, many have been less than rigorous in their effort to protect workers on the job. The business community often pushes for state-run programs in an effort to "keep the monkey off their backs" and to reduce costly fines that may be imposed on them by the federal government. North Carolina, for example, fined Perdue Farms, another poultry-processing plant, $39,000 for exposing workers to repetitive motion injuries in two plants; in contrast, Cargill, Inc., was fined $1 million by OSHA for similar violations at plants in Georgia and Missouri. This is an indication of why companies may prefer to be out from under OSHA's thumb and why they may prefer to keep the control at the state level.

What Now?

The incident in North Carolina has prompted renewed interest in health and safety in the workplace. Under the Clinton administration, OSHA's enforcement policy has never been more clear. OSHA intends to use high-cost, high-profile litigation against employers to "encourage" compliance with the law. Although state-run OSHA programs were intended to be as strict or more strict than the federally run OSHA programs, this had not been the case during the 1980s and 1990s. All state-run OSHA programs are under the federal government, and the cost of not following federal guidelines at this time is extremely high.

OSHA fines and the number of penalties assessed are likely to increase, and any employer violating OSHA standards could be criminally prosecuted. Although any new legislation will not make restitution for those who lost their lives in the fires at both Triangle and Imperial, it may serve to prevent similar accidents from occurring in the future.

On Monday, March 9, 1992, three management officials of the Imperial Foods plant were indicted on charges of involuntary manslaughter. Families of those killed in the fire filed criminal charges against the managers who allowed the safety violations to occur. Imperial Foods Products' owner Emmett Roe was sentenced to 19 years and 11 months in jail. Roe plea bargained so that his son and the plant's operations manager did not serve any jail time. This raises the costs of willfully violating safety standards to a new level.

Questions for Discussion

1. How true is the opening quotation in this case today, given all of the workplace hazards discussed in this chapter? What can be done at any and all levels to make this quotation true?

2. Would a state inspection of the Imperial Foods plant have prevented this accident? Why or why not? What could have been done to prevent it?

3. The case mentions fines imposed by OSHA and the state for exposing workers to CTD. Do you think the differences in the size of the fines caused the companies to react differently to them? Why or why not?

4. How appropriate do you think it is for states to have control of the safety of the workplace? Devise a state plan that would allow for effective policing of workplace safety. Why hasn't your plan been implemented?

Additional Readings

Erickson, P. *Practical Guide to Occupational Health and Safety.* San Diego, CA: Academic Press, 1996.

Fassel, D. *Working Ourselves to Death: The High Cost of Workaholism and the Rewards of Recovery.* San Francisco: Harper, 1990.

Hargreaves, W., M. Shumway, T. Hu. *Cost-Outcome Methods for Mental Health.* San Diego, CA: Academic Press, 1997.

Heenan, M. "Are Safety Audits Confidential?" *Pit and Quarry* 89, no. 7 (January 1997), pp. 14–15.

Kaplan, H. *Psychosocial Stress.* San Diego, CA, Academic Press, 1996.

LaBar, G. "Awards and Incentives in Action." *Occupational Hazards* 59, no. 1 (January 1997), pp. 91–93.

MacLachalan, J. "Firm Promotes Safety First Throughout the Workplace." *The Business Journal* no. 2 (February 24, 1997), pp. 39–43.

Moller, A. P., M. Milinski, and P. Slater. *Stress and Behavior.* San Diego, CA: Academic Press, 1998.

Pritchard, R. E., and G. C. Potter. *Fitness Inc: A Guide to Corporate Health and Wellness Programs.* Homewood, IL: Dow Jones-Irwin Books, 1990.

Smith, C. C. *Recovery at Work: A Clean and Sober Career Guide.* San Francisco: Harper Collins Publishers, 1990.

Notes

[1] Stanley Kalin, "The Ubiquitous Nip Point: The Booby Trap of Industry," *Experts-at-Law*, September–October 1990, pp. 39–42; and Phil Kuntz, "What a Pain: Proposed OSHA Rules for Workplace Injuries Make Companies Ache," *The Wall Street Journal*, September 18, 2000, p. 1.

[2] S. A. Joure et al., "Stress: The Pressure Cooker of Work," *Personnel Administrator*, March 1989, pp. 92–95.

[3] A. Fisher, "Danger Zone," *Fortune*, September 8, 1997, pp. 165–167.

[4] "Contractor Sentenced under OSHA after Two Die," *American Society for Personnel Administration/Resource*, February 1989, p. 15; see also B. D. Platt, "Negligent Retention and Hiring in Florida: Safety of Customers versus Security of Employers," *Florida State University Law Review*, 1993, pp. 697–716.

[5] C. Ansberry, "Nucor Steel's Sheen Is Marred by Deaths of Workers at Plants," *The Wall Street Journal*, May 10, 1991, p. A11.

[6] The following discussion is based on D. P. Twomey, *A Concise Guide to Employment Law EEO & OSHA* (Cincinnati: South-Western, 1986), pp. 109–134.

[7] "Contractor Sentenced under OSHA after Two Die," p. 20.

[8] A. R. Karr, D. D. Medina, and C. Solomon, "OSHA Seeks to Fine Phillips Petroleum $5.7 Million for 'Willful' Safety Breaches," *The Wall Street Journal*, April 20, 1990, p. A4.

[9] W. Goldsmith, "Preparing for and Managing an OSHA Inspection," *Society for Human Resource Management/HRNews/Legal Report*, Summer 1994, pp. 1–4.

[10] S. Cohen, "Pain with the Paycheck," *Tallahassee Democrat*, November 12, 1989, p. D11.

[11] E. Scalia, "OSHA to Business: Slow Down, You Work Too Fast," *The Wall Street Journal*, January 13, 1994, p. A18.

[12] Phil Kuntz, "What a Pain: Proposed OSHA Rules for Workplace Injuries Make Companies Ache," *The Wall Street Journal*, September 18, 2000, pp. 1, A14.

[13] Ibid.

[14] A. Gabor, "On-the-Job Straining," *U.S. News & World Report*, May 21, 1990, pp. 51–53.

[15] Phil Kuntz, "What a Pain: Proposed OSHA Rules for Workplace Injuries Make Companies Ache," *The Wall Street Journal*, September 18, 2000, p. 1.

[16] M. Lotito and F. Alvarez, "Integrate Claims Management with ADA Compliance Strategy," *HRMagazine*, August 1993, pp. 86–92.

[17] M. Fefer, "Taking Control of Your Workers' Comp Costs," *Fortune*, October 3, 1994, pp. 131–136.

[18] R. F. Bettendorf, "Curing the New Ills of Technology," *HRMagazine*, March 1990, p. 35; and Robert J. Grossman, "Make Ergonomics," *HRMagazine*, April 2000.

[19] C. Conte, "Fighting Technostress," *The Wall Street Journal*, May 4, 1993, p. A1.

[20] Robert J. Grossman, "Make Ergonomics," *HRMagazine*, April 2000, p. 39.

[21] Ibid.

[22] Ibid, p. 40.

[23] L. Micco, "OSHA May Cite Employers for Ergonomics Violations," *HRNews*, June 1997, p. 4.

[24] S. L. Jacob, "Small Business Slowly Wakes to OSHA Hazard Rule," *The Wall Street Journal*, November 22, 1988, p. B2.

[25] Ibid.

[26] "OSHA Issues Hazard Compliance Kit," *American Society for Personnel Administration/Resource/Legal Report*, February 1989, p. 20.

[27]A. D. Marcus, "In Some Workplaces, Ill Winds Blow," *The Wall Street Journal*, October 9, 1989, p. B1.

[28]Ibid.

[29]Michelle Conlin, "Is Your Office Killing You?" *Business Week*, June 5, 2000, p. 118.

[30]Ibid.

[31]R. M. Yandrick, "Smoking in the Workplace: More Employers Prohibit Smoking," *HRMagazine*, July 1994, pp. 68–71.

[32]C. Pasternak, "High-Cost Habit," *HRMagazine*, October 1990, p. 23.

[33]"Smoking Employees Post Cost Risks," *Communications*, September–October 1990, p. 1.

[34]S. Overman, "New EPA Study," *HRMagazine*, February 1993, p. 73.

[35]J. S. Harris, "Clearing the Air," *HRMagazine*, February 1993, pp. 72–79.

[36]C. Pasternak, "Totally Smoke-Free," *HRMagazine*, February 1990, p. 21.

[37]Lin Grensing-Pophal, "Smokin' in the Workplace," *HR Magazine*, May 1999, p. 64.

[38]Yandrick, "Smoking in the Workplace: More Employers Prohibit Smoking," pp. 68–71; and Harris, "Clearing the Air," pp. 72–79.

[39]The following discussion is based on C. F. Mitchell and P. M. Barrett, "Trial and Error: Novel Effort to Settle Asbestos Claims Fails as Lawsuits Multiply," *The Wall Street Journal*, June 7, 1988, p. A1.

[40]D. Feinstein, "Labor Letter," *The Wall Street Journal*, September 26, 1989, p. A1.

[41]G. Feinstein, "Labor Letter," *The Wall Street Journal*, August 8, 1989, p. A1.

[42]A. L. Otten, "People Patterns," *The Wall Street Journal*, April 6, 1989, p. B1.

[43]R. P. Hunter, "Workplace Violence: A Growing Trend," *Legal Report for the Society for Human Resource Management*, Summer 1990, p. 1.

[44]D. Harbrecht, "Talk about Murder Inc.," *Business Week*, July 11, 1994, p. 8.

[45]L. Thornburg, "When Violence Hits Business," *HRMagazine*, July 1993, pp. 40–45.

[46]L. Micco, "Debate Flares over OSHA's Night Retail Guidelines," *HRNews*, January 1997, p. 3.

[47]J. A. Segal, "When Charles Manson Comes to the Workplace," *HRMagazine*, June 1994, pp. 33–40.

[48]S. Overman, "Be Prepared Should Be Your Motto," *HRMagazine*, July 1993, pp. 46–49.

[49]J. A. Segal, "HIV: How High the Risk?" *HRMagazine*, February 1993, pp. 93–100.

[50]T. J. Dilauro, "Relieving the Fear of Contagion," *Personnel Administrator*, February 1989, p. 52.

[51]W. F. McHugh, "AIDS in the Workplace: Policy, Practice, and Procedure," *AIDS in the Workplace: Florida and Federal Legal Guidelines 1989*, December 1988, p. 39.

[52]J. A. Segal, "AIDS Education Is a Necessary High-Risk Activity," *HRMagazine*, February 1991, p. 82; and V. Alliton, "Financial Realities of AIDS in the Workplace," *HRMagazine*, February 1992, pp. 78–81.

[53]Ibid.

[54]R. Knotts and J. L. Johnson, "AIDS in the Workplace: The Pandemic Firms Want to Ignore," *Business Horizons*, July–August 1993, pp. 5–9.

[55]SHRM, "New AIDS Drugs Spawn, 'Return to Work' Issues," *Workplace Visions*, May/June 1997, pp. 5–6.

[56]J. D. Brodzinski, R. F. Scherer, and K. A. Goyer, "Workplace Stress," *Personnel Administrator*, July 1989, pp. 76–80.

[57]Ibid.

[58]Ibid.

[59]L. Smith, "Burned-Out Bosses," *Fortune*, July 25, 1994, pp. 44–52.

[60]T. F. O'Boyle, "Fear and Stress in the Office Take Toll," *The Wall Street Journal*, November 6, 1990, p. B1.

[61]R. Winslow, "Workplace Turmoil Is Reflected in Depression among Employees," *The Wall Street Journal*, December 13, 1989, p. B1.

[62]N. A. Jeffery, "Disability Claims Mirror Rising Job Cuts," *The Wall Street Journal*, November 21, 1996, p. A2.

[63]"Workplace Stress," *HRMagazine*, August 1991, pp. 75–76.

[64]A. R. Karr, "Guilty or Innocent?" *The Wall Street Journal*, May 14, 1991, p. A1.

[65]C. Trost, "Men, Too, Wrestle with Career-Family Stress," *The Wall Street Journal*, November 1, 1988, p. B1.

[66]Ibid.

[67]A. L. Otter, "How Work, Home Stress Affects Working Couples," *The Wall Street Journal*, February 22, 1991, p. B1.

[68]B. Azar, "Quelling Today's Conflict between Home and Work," *APA Monitor* 28, no. 7 (July 1997), pp. 1, 16.

[69]S. A. Joure et al., "Stress: The Pressure Cooker of Work," *Personnel Administrator*, March 1989, p. 92.

[70]R. Williams, *"The Trusting Heart: Great News about Type A Behavior* (New York: New York Times Books, 1989).

[71]R. Sandroff, "Is Your Job Driving You Crazy?" *Psychology Today*, July–August 1989, pp. 41–45.

[72]A. Bennett, "Is Your Job Making You Sick?" *The Wall Street Journal Reports*, April 22, 1988, p. 1; "Coming to Terms with Stress," *ILO Information*, February 1991, p. 1; M. Snider, "Stress May Be Something to Sneeze About," *USA Today*, August 29, 1991, p. 1A; and R. Winslow, "Study Uncovers New Evidence Linking Strain on the Job and High Blood Pressure," *The Wall Street Journal*, April 11, 1990, p. B4.

[73]S. Cartwright and C. L. Cooper, *Managing Workplace Stress* (Thousand Oaks, CA: Sage, 1997).

[74]G. Smith, "Meditation, the New Balm for Corporate Stress," *Business Week*, May 10, 1993, pp. 86–87.

[75]B. Condor, "Reducing Stress Can Improve Health," *Tallahassee Democrat*, March 4, 1998, p. 15E.

[76]D. Robinson, "Stressbusters," *Parade Magazine*, July 22, 1990, p. 12.

[77]S. Feinstein, "Health Promotion Brings Dollar-and-Cents Return, a Study Shows," *The Wall Street Journal*, September 18, 1990, p. A1.

[78]P. N. Keaton and M. J. Semb, "Shaping Up the Bottom Line," *HRMagazine*, September 1990, pp. 81–86.

[79]Michelle Nelly Martinez, "Using Data to Create Wellness Programs that Work," *HR Magazine*, November 1999.

[80]C. Garzona, "How to Get Employees behind Your Programs," *Personnel Administrator*, October 1989, pp. 60–62.

[81]Keaton and Semb, "Shaping Up the Bottom Line," p. 81.

[82]"Drug Testing in the Workplace," *Occutrax*, July–August 1993, p. 1.

[83]S. Mazaroff and J. P. Ayres, "Controlling Drug Abuse in the Workplace: The Legal Groundrules," *Human Resources Management Legal Report*, Spring 1989, p. 1.

[84]J. Deming, "Drug-Free Workplace Is Good Business," *HRMagazine*, April 1990, pp. 61–62.

[85]D. McGlothin and T. Stimson, "Employees Hold Favorable View of Drug Testing," *Society for Human Resource Management/HRNews*, August 1991, p. 14.

[86]H. G. DeYoung, "Motorola's Preemptive Strike against Drug Abuse," *Electronic Business* 48, no. 5 (March 1993), pp. 72–74.

[87]Ibid.

[88]B. Oliver, "Fight Drugs with Knowledge," *Training & Development*, May 1994, pp. 105–109.

[89]A. Karr, "Labor Letter," *The Wall Street Journal*, August 21, 1990, p. A1.

[90]D. Gold and B. Unger, "Better Pregnancy Benefit Not Discriminating," *Society for Human Resource Management/HRNews*, January 1990, p. 7; and Charlene Marmer Solomon, "Behavioral Health: The Forgotten Benefit," *Workforce*, February 2000.

[91]A. Bernstein, "Small Companies Are in Big Pain over Health Care," *Business Week*, November 26, 1990, pp. 187–190.

[92]Ibid.

[93]C. F. Hendricks and G. L. McManis, "Partnering for Employee Health Care," *Personnel Administrator*, November 1989, pp. 32–37.

[94]Ron Winslow, "Health-Benefits Trend: Give Workers Money, Let Them Buy a Plan," *The Wall Street Journal*, February 8, 2000, p. 1.

[95]Bill Bishop, "Those Who Died in the Plant Fire Are Waiting for Justice," *Tallahassee Democrat*, September 15, 1991, p. 3B; S. B. Garland, "What a Way to Watch Out for Workers," *Business Week*, September 23, 1991, p. 42; "Three Indicted in Plant Fire," *Tallahassee Democrat*, March 10, 1992, p. 3A; J. E. Roughton, "The OSHA Man Cometh," *Security Management* 39, no. 2 (February 1995), pp. 41–46; and "Price of Neglect," *Time*, September 28, 1992, p. 24.

15

Ethics, Employee Rights, and Employer Responsibilities

Chapter Objectives

As a result of studying this chapter, you should be able to

1. Describe the strategic choices managers face with respect to ethical considerations, employee rights, and employer responsibilities.

2. Be familiar with the laws pertaining to employee rights.

3. Understand the ethical and legal responsibilities of employers to both their employees and the community at large.

4. Discuss the way to manage a problem employee.

5. Delineate the characteristics of a good disciplinary climate.

Ethical behavior, employee rights, and employer responsibilities are dynamic segments of the human resource management field. Important related issues are constantly developing, and new issues emerge with startling frequency. Organizations that do not pay attention to the latest developments in the ethics-rights-responsibility field are likely to face large lawsuits and many forms of hostile actions from both employees and the government. We examine these and a number of other related issues in this chapter, including discrimination, employment at will, privacy, and due process, to name only a few.

CASE

I Believe in the Second Coming of Christ and Other Test Questions[1]

How would you feel if you were asked the following true/false questions as part of a job application test?

- I am very strongly attracted to members of my own sex.
- I believe in the second coming of Christ.
- I have no difficulty starting or holding my urine.

These questions are part of an ongoing battle over employee rights and the employer's need to know. They are just some of the more than 700 questions that are part of a test routinely used by many organizations in the hiring process. The test helps evaluate an individual's personality characteristics, including honesty, motivation, and ambition.

The controversy over personality testing is part of a larger battle emerging over an employer's right to test current and potential employees. Testing can take many forms, including personality tests, polygraph tests, drug tests, and even genetic tests. On a broader scale, the issue includes the employer's ability to obtain and use other kinds of supposedly confidential employee information such as medical records and credit histories. At stake is the very question of an employee's privacy and an employer's need to know about its employees.

Polygraph Tests

Polygraph machines were once one of the most commonly used devices for determining employee honesty and truthfulness regarding specific events. In general, polygraph tests measure changes in a subject's physiological reactions (through a series of electrodes) as the subject answers a set of questions. Certain kinds of changes indicate that the subject was experiencing stress and possibly lying. Despite its widespread use, it was generally believed to be unreliable in determining whether the subject was telling the truth or a lie. Subjects' individual physiological characteristics and testing conducted by improperly trained examiners all complicated the test's reliability. In addition, many organizations tended to place too much emphasis in the test results without taking into account other circumstances or evidence. All of these factors proved to be insurmountable. Congress and President Reagan outlawed the use of polygraph tests by organizations by passing and signing, respectively, the Employee Polygraph Protection Act of 1988.

Personality Tests

Organizations have long used personality tests, and these are being more widely used since polygraphs have been outlawed. Popular tests include the Minnesota Multiphasic Personality Inventory (MMPI), the California Personality Inventory (CPI), and the Inwald Personality Inventory (IPI). In addition to some of the issues related above, personality tests can be used to determine whether a person is introverted, extroverted, self-driven, or other-directed and has a host of other personality traits.

Many components of these tests are widely accepted. For example, it is generally agreed that an organization has the right to know whether an applicant for a sales position is introverted or extroverted. The problems arising with these tests stem from some of their predictive components and their probing into what many contend are private areas that are not job related.

Many of these tests were designed for specific purposes but are administered in a wide variety of situations. Like the problems with polygraph testing, the tests often are administered by untrained professionals. A long line of court cases and government legislation is likely to occur before the hows, whens, and whys of personality testing are resolved.

Changes in employment laws complicate possible resolutions even further. In 1992 the Americans with Disabilities Act (ADA) became law with the aim of protecting disabled individuals from unfair employment practices. In particular, the ADA strictly set forth provisions regarding the use of medical examinations in the hiring process in that a medical examination can be given after a job offer has been extended to an individual but not as an employment screening device. Questions arose among employers about whether or not personality tests were considered a medical examination and therefore covered under the ADA provisions. To clarify the ADA, the Equal Employment Opportunity Commission (EEOC) published some guidelines stating that personality tests were not considered part of the ADA's definition of medical examinations and therefore could be used at any time during the employment process.

Financial Data and Medical History or Testing

The increasing use of personal credit and medical histories in the hiring process is also a hotly debated subject. This issue includes the right of organizations to demand that potential employees undergo various medical tests, such as the acquired immune deficiency syndrome (AIDS) test, as a condition of employment. Although this information is supposedly confidential, technology has given organizations the ability to gather much of this information. Some concerns that arise given this new technology are test accuracy and the need for employers to know whether an employee has AIDS. The blood test for HIV AIDS is not perfect and shows the existence of the virus, but not whether the AIDS condition is present.[2] Most states have some provision regarding AIDS testing as part of the employment process, either prohibiting testing altogether or allowing tests only when an individual consents to a test.

Two large issues are emerging here. The first is strictly a question of access. Does your future boss have the right to know that your mother had leukemia or that your aunt has a history of chronic depression? Does he or she have the right to demand that you undergo genetic testing? Or how about knowing that you missed a Visa payment in March 2001?

In general, it is important to remember that if a question is illegal in an interview, then surreptitiously obtaining the information is not permitted. However, under some circumstances, an employer would be negligent in missing certain elements of a background check. When it comes to inquiries regarding more complicated issues than simple legal background checks, we enter a new and perhaps dangerous area. For example, genetic traits can also be assessed in some medical testing procedures, and the Congressional Office of Technology Assessment recently indicated that issues of fairness and reliability must be dealt with in genetic testing. If tests are not used and analyzed properly, misleading conclusions can be drawn about a person's susceptibility to certain diseases or environmental exposure. A 1998 court ruling regarding genetic testing of employees at Lawrence Berkeley Lab in California says that genetic tests violate workers' privacy.[3] The privacy of the individual and the extent to which employers and society need to know medical and financial histories are still critical issues in the employment process.

Organizations assert that this information is vital for several reasons. First, they argue that the skyrocketing cost of medical coverage makes it necessary for them to know an employee's complete medical history before that person is hired. In many instances organizations are requiring applicants to undergo certain kinds of medical exams, such as AIDS tests. This can help them plan their medical expenses, employee absenteeism, and turnover, among other things. In addition, the trend for insurance companies not to cover illnesses or diseases for individuals who have "preexisting conditions" is increasing. Many argue against these practices, which they assert to be essentially clever methods by organizations to practice discrimination against perceived undesirables.

Second, organizations argue that this information, especially financial information, can help determine employee reliability. They argue that employees who cannot manage their own finances are viewed as being unlikely to be able to manage a department's budget. Organizations have also used the negligent hiring doctrine as a basis for obtaining employee medical and financial data.

Drug Tests

Perhaps some of the most talked about and controversial tests today are drug tests. More than 80 percent of large corporations engage in some type of employee drug screening.[4] The most common of these tests are urinalysis and hair sampling. (See the "You Be the Judge" box regarding genetic testing.) Drug testing is a particularly sensitive issue for several reasons. First, many people believe that drug tests, especially urinalysis, are particularly intrusive of their privacy. Second, organizations that do not screen for drug users are most open to lawsuits concerning the negligent hiring doctrine. A third emerging issue is that of the conflict between the individual's right to privacy and the public's right to safety. The public policy issues are by no means settled and will be debated for some time.

The first issue concerns public safety. The right to perform drug tests on employees who are directly responsible for public safety, such as military personnel, police officers, airline pilots, and bus drivers, is being supported increasingly by both court precedent and public legislation. Another issue relates to the increasing frequency of employees winning court cases against organizations that conduct poorly planned and poorly implemented drug-testing programs. This includes nonrandom

YOU BE THE JUDGE

Do Genetic Tests Violate Workers' Privacy?

Genetic testing of employees is a controversial issue. The state and federal entities that run the Lawrence Berkeley Laboratory have had to defend charges of employment discrimination and violations of employees' constitutional right to privacy. At issue in the case were tests performed on blood and urine samples given by black, Latino, and female lab employees. The seven plaintiffs who were employed at the lab in clerical or administrative positions provided these samples as part of their required preplacement physicals. The plaintiffs later learned that, without their knowledge or consent, the samples were tested for syphilis, pregnancy, and the sickle cell anemia trait.

On February 3, 1998, the Ninth U.S. Circuit Court of Appeals ruled, "If unauthorized, the testing constituted a significant invasion of a right that is of great importance. . . ." An individual's health or genetic makeup is a personal subject that is likely to implicate privacy interests. The plaintiffs maintained that they were never told what tests would be conducted on their blood and urine samples and that they never consented to the tests for the sickle cell trait, syphilis, or pregnancy. Should Lawrence Berkeley seek consent from employees before running tests not usually performed in an occupational health exam? *You be the judge.*

SOURCE: Adapted from Jennifer Click, "Court Says Genetic Tests Violated Workers' Privacy," *HRNews*, March 1998, p. 6.

---

testing or testing without justifiable cause, improper administration of tests, or other forms of discriminatory actions. Like the other testing issues, the future of drug testing employees is uncertain. Although it is safe to say that drug testing is still part of organization life, it is unwise to predict exactly what form drug testing will be allowed to take in the future.

These issues relating to employee testing represent only one portion of the ethical behavior, employee rights, and employer responsibility segment of human resource management. Many of these issues are emotion packed, and virtually everyone has an opinion or strong feeling about them. Although managers have laws, precedents, and corporate policies to guide their behavior, sometimes these may not be enough. The decisions that managers make concerning these issues are difficult and often extremely important to the organization.

Strategic Choices

Many factors influence the choices managers make about how they will carry out their responsibilities in recognizing and respecting employee rights. The organization must establish policies to guide managers to consider the appropriate factors when they must make choices. In doing so, organizations should consider the following:

1. How can it ensure that its managers are treating employees with the respect they deserve?
2. What type of ethical standards should the organization set for its managers? How should these standards be disseminated to the managers?
3. Is there ever a time when a manager has the right to violate an employee's right to privacy?

EXHIBIT 15.1	STATEMENT OF A HOSPITAL'S CORE VALUES

1. We will treat each employee with respect.
2. We will observe the Golden Rule when dealing with all employees regardless of rank or job title.
3. We will make every effort to communicate with each employee and will listen to each.
4. We will respect the individual rights of each employee as a human being.
5. We will make every effort to involve each employee fully in his or her work.

---

4. How does an organization keep all of its managers up-to-date with respect to the legal ramifications of their treatment of employees?

Strategic Factors

The main factors that directly influence managers' decisions about how they will treat employees include (1) management philosophy, (2) the tightness of the labor market, (3) the law, (4) union and employee power, and (5) organizational culture as it relates to discipline and control.

Management Philosophy

The main question relating to management philosophy is the extent to which top management and other managers throughout the organization believe in protecting employee rights. If top managers strongly believe in protecting employee rights, they will more likely ensure that company policy and actions respect these rights. They will more likely treat their subordinates with respect and expect them to do likewise. Furthermore, they will develop and communicate a set of core values that manifest these beliefs.

If, on the other hand, top management holds little regard for the rights of individual employees, very little, if anything, will be communicated about protecting these rights. Employees will more likely be treated as common factors of production without explicit consideration or respect for individual human dignity. In her study of General Motors, Maryann Keller shows how this basic orientation among top management permeated the organization and was a major cause for the decline of GM's competitiveness in the labor market.[5] By creating a stifling bureaucracy that provided little respect or allowance for individual differences, managers were not encouraged to recognize individual rights explicitly. Keller quotes an employee's letter that points out management's failure to recognize him as a human being. She indicates that mutual respect for the rights of each party, management and workers, is the way for GM to pull out of its tailspin.

Sometimes an organization formulates a set of core values that act as a basic guide for the treatment of employees. For example, Exhibit 15.1 is a set of core values for a large hospital in the southeastern United States. These core values appear in the employee manual and the firm's strategic plan and are posted in the lobby of the hospital. In addition, they have been printed on wallet-sized cards that all managers and employees were encouraged to carry with them. It is certainly possible for an organization to develop such statements of core values for public relations purposes, but the fact that this statement was developed by the CEO and other members of the top management team and was circulated so widely gave the statement real meaning.

Tightness of the Labor Market

The second variable that affects the extent to which a firm respects the rights of employees is the tightness of the labor market. If labor is plentiful and readily available at prevailing or below prevailing wage rates, firms are less likely to respect individual rights than if labor markets are tight, everything else being equal. This occurs because management knows that disgruntled and unhappy employees who quit or are fired can be replaced easily when there is an abundant supply of labor.

The United States experienced this most dramatically during both the great immigration waves of the early twentieth century and the Great Depression of the 1930s. During these periods, employee rights were frequently abused because of the abundance of labor relative to the demand. Child labor, long hours, unsafe and unhealthy working conditions, low wages, and arbitrary and discriminatory treatment were all too common during these periods. In fact, because of these abuses, industrial unions were formed and legislation was passed in an attempt to protect the rights of employees. These two factors are discussed following.

Legislation

To the extent that legislation exists and that it is vigorously enforced, employee rights will be protected. If laws and court cases clearly define employee rights and if agencies exist specifically to uphold these laws, employers will more likely respect employee rights by observing the law and fearing sanctions. Initially, much of the law protecting employee rights was passed at the state level. For example, early in this century, Wisconsin had laws regulating child labor and working conditions for women. Such laws varied greatly among states that had them, but many states had no legislation. It was not until federal legislation was passed that comprehensive coverage and enforcement practices occurred.

Unions and Employee Power

The greater the power of employees to protect their rights, especially through collective action (unions), the more likely employers will respect employee rights, all other things being equal. If employers know that employees can take concerted action to enforce rights, the power of employees is heightened. To a large extent, respect for rights depends on a power relationship: those who have power tend to get their way. Their rights are protected because they have the power to enforce their protection.

Unions have played a very strong role in defining and protecting employee rights. By uniting, employees have greatly increased their power in relation to employers. Unions have acted as advocates for employees both in collective bargaining with employers and in lobbying Congress for legislation to protect employee rights.

Culture

The final variable we consider is culture. Both the external culture and the organization's internal culture are key variables in terms of how the employer defines employee rights. For example, historically communist countries, such as the former Soviet Union, guaranteed employees jobs, resulting in a very low reported unemployment rate. Western countries traditionally have not actually made this guarantee, although

EXHIBIT 15.2	CORPORATE VALUES OF APPLE AND HEWLETT-PACKARD CONCERNING THEIR EMPLOYEES

Apple's Statement of Values

Individual Performance—We expect individual commitment and performance above the standard for our industry. Only thus will we make profits that permit us to seek our other corporate objectives. Each employee can and must make a difference in the final analysis. *Individuals* determine the character and strength of Apple.

Individual Reward—We recognize each person's contribution to Apple's success, and we share the financial rewards that flow from high performance. We recognize also that rewards must be psychological as well as financial and strive for an atmosphere where each individual can share the adventure and excitement of working at Apple.

Hewlett-Packard's Statement of Values

Our People—To help HP people share in the company's success, which they make possible; to provide employment security based on their performance; to ensure them a safe and pleasant work environment; to recognize their individual achievements; and to help them gain a sense of satisfaction and accomplishment from their work.

SOURCE: Apple Computer and Hewlett-Packard.

most have a national economic policy of full employment to be achieved through monetary and fiscal policy (government spending, taxation, and central bank actions). Former communist countries experimenting with free enterprise will likely allow some unemployment to exist in the future.

Internal culture—organizational culture—also determines employee rights. A culture that places great value on employees and the worth of the individual will likely define and protect more employee rights than a culture that does not value employees as individuals. Exhibit 15.2 presents the corporate values of Apple Computer and Hewlett-Packard in relation to their employees. Apple and Hewlett-Packard have reputations as two of the most innovative and highest performing firms in the computer industry. Yet, as Exhibit 15.2 shows, their approaches to their employees are completely different. Hewlett-Packard is known as a company that historically fosters and nurtures its employees. Its pay scale is average for the computer industry, but it is committed to a no-layoff policy.[6] Apple, in contrast, is often viewed as a high-stress organization with high levels of employee turnover. In turn, Apple places a great emphasis on financially rewarding high performance. Apple does not even have a formal retirement policy, because, as one Apple executive states, "We don't expect people to last that long." Another Apple executive asserts, "Someone who worries about a retirement plan isn't an Apple type of person."[7] It is obvious that these two organizations take different attitudes toward employee rights. Much of this difference is a result of their corporate cultures.

The key factors that affect the strategic choices employers have in defining employee rights and management responsibilities are as follows: management philosophy, the tightness of the labor market, the law, union and employee power, and the outside as well as the organizational culture. These variables are interrelated and work together. Therefore it is important to try to understand their cumulative effect to understand how rights and responsibilities are viewed in individual organizations.

Ethics

The focus of this chapter is on the discussion of employee rights and employer responsibilities. However, as important as these topics are to practicing human resource managers, many of the problems facing organizations today arise from the decisions managers make concerning what may or may not be ethical behavior. This "gray area" between what is legal and what is patently illegal is the domain of ethical dispute. For instance, is it ethical to take home pens and pencils from the office? Is it okay to make a short, personal long-distance call on the company phone, use the company mail for a few personal items, or take the company car on a trip to the mall? Is it unethical to "pad" an expense account? Should an employee follow company orders that conflict with the teachings of his or her church? Should a family member be hired even if there was a more qualified person available? Should an employee withhold information from a local reporter who is investigating whether or not the company is dumping hazardous waste into a local river?

These are examples of ethical dilemmas that individuals face; there are no absolute right or wrong answers. Some situations are minor and more familiar, and some are more serious, but all concern areas in which explicit guidance (in the form of written policy or regulation) may be lacking. There are no agreed-on ethical standards that guide all behavior in organizations because ethical behavior depends on what society considers the norm for such behavior and on who is judging the behavior. No doubt, some may find that certain behaviors are more suspect than others; others may find that all of the behaviors cited are unethical. And because ethics is such an individual quality, individual interpretations of what is and is not ethical serve to keep the gray area in constant ebb and flow.

Consider the source of an individual's ethical code. Ethics and values are intimately related. Values are learned early in life from parents and family, peers, teachers, and significant others and are either reinforced or altered by subsequent experience. Values consist of those enduring beliefs that specify that a certain mode of conduct or end-state of existence is personally or socially desirable. Values tend to be learned in an all-or-nothing fashion (i.e., it is *always* right to tell the truth), but they are subject to modification (i.e., "fudging" the numbers on a tax return isn't really lying because everyone does it to a degree). The wide variation in child-rearing practices and upbringing contributes in part to the wide variation in how people behave and how they evaluate the behavior of others.

Ethics follow from values and concern an individual's beliefs about what is right or wrong, good or bad. There is always a degree of subjective judgment involved. As such, questions about ethics concern matters well beyond mere compliance with organizational policy and state and federal laws.

Ethics and Strategic Choices

An organization that wants to be perceived as ethical cannot simply hope that its members will act ethically; it must take action to ensure that individuals know what appropriate behavior entails.[8] In recent years courses on business ethics have been added to the curriculum of many major universities. In-house ethics training classes at large corporations have been developed. Orientation programs often include sections on the ethical stance of the organization. Some organizations have even set up formal ethics offices complete with an ethics officer who is responsible for creating and maintaining the company's ethics program. The HR Challenges box "Ethics—Is

Ethics—Is It Just Another Fad?

What is behind the rush to install ethics programs in U.S. universities and industries? In the aftermath of the 1980s, have revelations about ethical improprieties such as insider trading scams and the savings and loan fiasco spurred businesses to action? Some believe that ethics training is no more than window dressing construed to give the appearance that businesses have changed their tune. Take, for example, the case of the second largest U.S. defense contractor, General Dynamics, which set up one of the first corporate ethics offices. This occurred after news leaked that Congress was investigating them on charges that they billed for unauthorized services (including charges for expensive dinners and the services of a dog kennel).

One prominent business school lauded its new ethics program in an alumni newsletter. The newsletter described the program on one page, which included new elective courses on ethics and a student code of ethics; on another page it described in the main feature story a course in Creativity in Business taught by Michael Milken. Milken was the junk bond trader who bilked many people, including many elderly individuals and those on a fixed income, out of millions of dollars. He was later convicted and served a few years in a federal minimum-security prison.

Perhaps the drive to install ethics programs is something less than internally motivated. In November 1991 strict federal sentencing guidelines concerning unlawful business practices took effect. In addition, new guidelines were developed to help organizations set up internal mechanisms, including the establishment of ethics offices, for preventing, detecting, and reporting criminal conduct in the workplace. Perhaps the establishment of ethics programs is in response to an increased threat of government sanctions or poor publicity.

Supporters of ethics training argue that teaching ethics allows individuals to experience decision-making opportunities that involve ethical questions, thereby exposing individuals to the consequences associated with their actions. Supporters suggest that values can be learned, and that exposure to ethical dilemmas heightens awareness of appropriate value systems, thereby helping to improve decision-making skills in today's complex business environment. What do you think?

SOURCE: Adapted from N. K. Austin, "The New Corporate Watchdogs," *Working Woman*, January 1994, pp. 19–20; and S. P. Robbins, *Organizational Behavior*, Englewood Cliffs, NJ: Prentice-Hall, 1993, p. 566.

It Just Another Fad?" describes ethics programs and asks the question of whether the emphasis on ethics in universities and businesses is more smoke than substance. In essence, the discussion questions whether the investment in ethics training (a strategic choice) is worth it.

Ethics and the Human Resource Manager

This discussion of ethics is applicable to the day-to-day activities of human resource managers. The high costs of unethical behavior are increasingly being felt by individuals and organizations alike. For instance, the Bureau of Justice Statistics reported that employment discrimination lawsuits in the private sector more than tripled in the 1990s. According to the Society for Human Resource Management (SHRM) and the law firm of Jackson Lewis, 53 percent of organizations that responded to a 1999 survey had been named as defendants in at least one employment-related lawsuit in the past 5 years. Another SHRM/Jackson Lewis survey (1997) reported that 23 percent of organizations polled had an individual named as a defendant in an employment-related lawsuit, of which 16 percent were HR directors or HR managers.[9] The following is a list of reasons that ethics have become such a hot topic in the business literature.

1. There appears to be a widespread breakdown in ethical conduct among senior managers. As the double standard is employed to allow top management to take advantage of the system and is gradually revealed to the American public (beginning with the savings and loan scandal and Wall Street problems), people are growing concerned and are asking for changes.
2. Time and productivity can be stolen more easily than goods and services. Workers who are treated as professionals may take advantage of the freedoms they enjoy. Experts estimate that payroll could be cut by 20 percent without any change in productivity.
3. The family, where the ethical values were conveyed, has all but disappeared. The "family meal," during which family members discuss their problems and learn the "correct" way to solve them, no longer exists.
4. Organizational loyalty is declining sharply as employees adopt a "what's in it for me" attitude. This attitude shift often has been a reaction to selfish acts of management, such as leveraged buyouts and golden parachutes, witnessed by workers.[10]

What can organizations do to ensure that ethical standards are upheld? We suggest a combination approach based on an appropriate management philosophy that is transmitted and reinforced within the culture of the organization. This approach includes at a minimum a set of written ethical guidelines that specify standards for appropriate conduct backed by top management support and visible demonstrations that ethical behaviors are encouraged and rewarded. These guidelines can help to make ethical actions a cornerstone of corporate culture and provide businesses with a source of increased competitive advantage. Such was the case at Johnson & Johnson, the makers of Tylenol, when someone poisoned several bottles of the product. Knowing that Johnson & Johnson viewed ethical treatment of customers as a priority, workers in drug and grocery stores did not hesitate to check with headquarters before removing millions of bottles of Tylenol from store shelves.[11] The threat to customers, in the minds of Johnson & Johnson, far outweighed the costs of destroying great quantities of Tylenol, even though only a few tainted bottles had been found. In the long run this disaster contributed to the implementation of tamper-proof packages on medicine and food products, and Johnson & Johnson now enjoys an even more prominent position as a trusted supplier of quality pharmaceuticals because of the way it handled the situation.

Defining what constitutes ethical business practices is not easy and becomes increasingly difficult as organizations internationalize. See the HR Challenges box regarding ethics in a global market. As top organizational managers search for a universal code of ethics, they become increasingly aware of the role of cultural differences. For example, if a company practices gender equality regarding status and pay, what is the role of the company if a woman from the company, working in a foreign country, is treated by the locals as a second-class citizen, following that country's norms, values, and beliefs? Does the company have an obligation to her? Similarly, if a company has a rule prohibiting the acceptance of gifts, but the country in which you are doing business views *not* accepting a gift as an insult, what should your company do?

Conducting Business "Ethically" in a Global Market

Most managers with global experience believe that there should be a set of shared global ethical values. Rushworth Kidder, from the Institute for Global Ethics, conducted a values survey and found the following common values: love, truth, freedom, fairness, community, tolerance, responsibility, and reverence for life. The problem is that even if there is an underlying agreement on values, these values may be prioritized differently in different cultures.

A general rule of business is that a company doing business in other countries should comply with all of the laws of those countries. A corporation must be responsible to what the society is demanding. Further, a company can use what is called "ethical displacement," which means that ethical dilemmas are displaced upward to a higher level. For example, a company policy might solve a dilemma for a manager who is offered a gift. The manager might explain that it is not his or her decision but that company policy prohibits accepting gifts.

Initiating an ethics program in today's multicultural environment is a complex task for any manager, but the following guidelines may help:

- Make ethics an important and salient issue by developing a clear code of conduct for employees that is value based and addresses cross-cultural issues.
- Provide employees with opportunities to learn and understand ethical dilemmas as well as alternatives for resolving these dilemmas. Study the best practices of other multicultural firms.
- Continually review and update the company's ethics policy and communicate this policy to employees frequently.

SOURCE: Adapted from S. Richter and C. Barnum, "When Values Clash," *HRMagazine*, September 1994, pp. 42–45; B. Rogers, "Serious about Its Code of Ethics," *HRMagazine*, September 1994, pp. 46–48; and D. Bottorff, "How Ethics Can Improve Business Success," *Quality Progress*, February 1997, pp. 57-60.

The Law and Employee Rights

Because many rights have been codified either in legislation or case law, we now examine one key aspect of employee rights—the law. We do not intend to cover each and every aspect of the law; much of this has been done in other chapters. Our intent here is to highlight those aspects of the law that deal with rights and responsibilities. We review three key areas of the law: discrimination, employment at will, and rights. The basic legislation and case law in each area is summarized.

Discrimination

antidiscrimination laws Employment laws that say all employment decisions should be based on job-relevant factors such as skill, knowledge, and ability.

Employees have the right to employment free from discrimination based on race, color, creed, religious belief, country of national origin, age, sex, or physical or mental handicap. This protection covers all aspects of employment—from hiring to placement, training, promotion, pay, discipline, or termination. The primary laws prohibiting discrimination are Title VII of the 1964 Civil Rights Act and the 1990 ADA, as amended and as interpreted by case law. Employees are also protected against sexual harassment because this has been defined as a type of sexual discrimination.

The **antidiscrimination laws** are quite complex, but basically they require that employment decisions should be made strictly on factors relevant to the job. This means that the decisions should be based on skill, job knowledge, and abilities—factors that relate to a person's ability to do the job. Even such factors as experience and educational level could be ruled as discriminatory if these factors are not relevant

EXHIBIT 15.3 EMPLOYMENT-AT-WILL CLAUSE EXAMPLES

Strong Form

I understand that if I am employed by _____ Company, my employment and compensation can be terminated with or without cause and with or without notice at any time, at the option of either the company or myself. I also understand that neither this application for employment nor any present or future employee handbook or personnel policy manual is an employment agreement, either expressed or implied, and that no employee or manager of _____ Company, except the vice-president of human resources, has any authority to enter into any agreement for employment for any specified period of time or to make any agreement contrary to the foregoing.

Moderately Strong Form

In the event of employment, I understand that my employment is not for any definite period or succession of periods and is considered an "at-will" arrangement. This means that I am free to terminate my employment at any time for any reason, as is the company, so long as there is no violation of applicable federal or state law.

Soft Form

I understand that no representative of the company is authorized to state or imply that a contract for permanent employment shall exist between the company and me.

SOURCE: Adapted from R. Hilgert, "Employers Protected by At-Will Statements," *HRMagazine*, March 1991, pp. 57–60; J.J. Moran, *Employment Law* (Upper Saddle River, NJ: Prentice-Hall, 1997).

to a particular job. In fact, they could serve as institutional forms of covert (hidden) discrimination if white people consistently have higher levels of education than minority groups and if this educational level is irrelevant to the job. From an employment standpoint the skills and knowledge that education and experience represent are the desired qualities. In other words, just because a person has a certain formal education level or years of experience does not necessarily mean that the person has the required skill or knowledge to do the job. Employers use education and experience to represent skill and knowledge because it is a screening device easy to use and because so few sophisticated tests exist to test job knowledge and skill (and those few are relatively expensive to administer); it is much easier to require a certain education level and use this prerequisite to screen out the mass of applicants.

Discrimination can be overt or covert. The law has essentially eliminated overt discrimination, but covert discrimination is more difficult to identify and therefore eliminate. The major controversial aspects of discrimination, particularly affirmative action, which was adopted as national policy even before the passage of Title VII as a way to eliminate discrimination, was discussed previously.

employment at will A policy under which employers are free to discharge their employees for any reason unless the discharge is limited by contract or state or federal statute.

Employment at Will

The policy of **employment at will** exists in many states. It means that an employer or an employee is free to break the employment relationship "at will" unless there is a written or implied employment contract. Examples of employment-at-will statements are provided in Exhibit 15.3. The rationale behind this concept is the belief that an employee ought to be free to quit to seek employment elsewhere and that an employer ought to be able to terminate an employee to hire another one.

Five primary factors temper the employment-at-will concept: (1) an employment contract, (2) civil service protection, (3) antidiscrimination laws, (4) unions, and (5) discharges contrary to the public interest.[12]

Employment Contract   In an individual employment contract, a clause specifying reasons for terminations is usually spelled out. This protects the employee from termination for other reasons. The following is an example of such a clause:

This agreement shall, at the employer's sole option and without further notice, be terminated on the occurrence of any one or more of the following events:

1. The conviction of the employee of a felony.
2. The conviction of the employee of a misdemeanor involving moral turpitude.
3. Gross negligence by the employee in the performance of his or her duties.
4. The willful and intentional commission of any act or failure to act, which the employee knew or should have known would result in substantial and material harm to the employer's business or goodwill.

These are vague terms and would need to be specifically defined by a court or arbitrator if contested by the employee. Yet if this were in an employment contract, these would be the only reasons that an employee could be terminated.

In the absence of a written contract, courts often infer a contract of employment. For example, if in the employee handbook a statement is made that a new employee moves from probationary to permanent status after a period of time, such as 90 days, courts have held that the word *permanent* implies a contractual relationship. For this reason, employers should use the word *regular* instead of *permanent* in employee manuals, other publications, and policy statements unless they wish to imply permanent status.

An implied contract can also be inferred from oral statements made by superiors in the organization.[13] For example, organizations should be careful about saying things like the following at the time of hire: "We plan to keep you here for your entire career" or "We view our relationship as a long-term, permanent one." Statements similar to these have been ruled in cases as an implied contract of lifetime employment in the supreme courts of New Jersey, New Mexico, and Michigan.[14]

The costs an organization incurs to protect itself from wrongful termination lawsuits are being passed on to employees in the form of fewer jobs. To offset the costs involved, some firms are simply hiring fewer people. However, it appears that the actual court costs are minimal—the actions organizations take to prevent litigation are costly. Many firms are spending more per employee to avoid litigation than they are spending for litigation itself.[15]

To minimize a firm's chances of being sued over an implied contract, it should take the following steps:

1. Establish a written at-will statement and place it on all applications. Make potential employees sign the form.
2. Stipulate the standards of conduct for employees and the kinds of conduct that will lead to termination.
3. Indicate that even though the firm uses progressive discipline, it is by no means a guarantee of employment and the progression can be suspended at any time.
4. Reserve the right to dismiss the employee without following disciplinary procedures.

YOU BE THE JUDGE

Relocation Can Lead to an Implied Contract

Getting employees to transfer to a new location seems to be getting more and more difficult. Issues such as dual careers, children having to change schools, especially high school, and extreme differences in the cost of living or quality of life sometimes make it hard to sell an employee on a transfer.

All too frequently, when managers are trying to convince an employee to make a move, the use of seemingly harmless words to persuade the employee can be interpreted legally as an implied contract. For example, mentioning that the move will "be worth the employee's effort over the long haul" or that this move is "simply one more step in the employee's career ladder" may be considered by a court as an implied contract.

A case decided on this issue illustrates this problem. After 25 years of service as an accountant at Dresser Industries, Thomas Krause had worked his way up to the highest accounting position in southern Louisiana. During a general cutback, he was demoted and told that he would have to move to Oklahoma City to keep his job. After being assured by his supervisor that if he moved his job would be safe because future job cuts would be determined by seniority, he decided to move to Oklahoma City. When he arrived there, he found that the only other accountant was the 27-year-old son of a senior vice-president. Soon the ax fell and he was fired. When the VP's son found a new position at Dresser but Krause didn't, he sued for both age discrimination (he was 52 at the time of the firing) and for wrongful discharge under the implied contract theory. He won on both accounts—$168,000 for the age discrimination claim and an additional $166,000 for the wrongful discharge suit. Do you believe this is fair? You be the judge.

As this one example shows, relocation is a gray area. Managers must be made aware that what they say may be used against them later if the transferred employee is terminated. Honesty may very well be the best policy.

SOURCE: Adapted from Jack Raisner, "Relocate without Making False Moves," *HRMagazine*, February 1991, pp. 46–50; T. Brady, "The Legal Horrors of Truth-in-Hiring Lawsuits," *Management Review* 85, no. 10 (October 1996), pp. 53–56.

5. Do not establish a probationary period for new hires. They may expect that if they pass the probationary period, they are guaranteed employment.[16]

Civil Service Protection Employees working for government agencies are protected from discharge without justifiable cause through civil service rules and regulations. These specify dischargeable offenses as well as the procedure to be used.

Discrimination Law People cannot legally be dismissed from a job if it occurs because of their race, creed, color, religious belief, country of national origin, sex, age, or physical or mental handicap except as provided by the law.

Unions The fourth factor that modifies the employment-at-will doctrine is the presence of a union. Unions, through the collective bargaining process, negotiate and enforce a collective bargaining agreement called a *contract*, which specifies causes and procedures for discharge. See the You Be the Judge box regarding relocation and "implied" contracts. These items, as well as other aspects of unions and collective bargaining, are discussed in the next chapter.

Discharges Contrary to the Public Interest The final factor that modifies the employment-at-will doctrine concerns discharges for reasons that involve the public interest. For instance, if an employee is fired for going against his supervisor's orders to dump battery acid down the drain and into the local sewer (an act clearly against the public interest), that employee may sue for wrongful termination. Every employee has the right to disobey orders that violate laws and to feel free to speak when violations occur (commonly referred to as *whistleblowing*). However, not all free speech in the workplace is protected. An employee is not protected if he or she violates the confidentiality of business information or makes unfounded accusations about management.[17] The law does not protect those who "cry wolf."

Types of Rights

Any list of employee rights is likely to be incomplete. No one source lists employee rights just as no one source lists the rights we have as citizens of our country. However, both legislation and case law, as well as certain key documents such as the Constitution, provide a framework to use in listing employee rights. For our purposes, we will look at the following seven rights:[18]

1. Privacy.
2. Fair treatment.
3. Safe and healthful workplace, including freedom from a hostile environment regarding sexual harassment.
4. Collective bargaining.
5. Communication and involvement in the organization.
6. Notice of plant closings and of disciplinary action.
7. Due process.

Privacy

The right to privacy is grounded in the U.S. Constitution. The Fourth Amendment prevents unreasonable search and seizure. Most state constitutions provide for some form of protection similar to that of the Fourth Amendment. Ten states even have specific privacy guarantees in their constitutions. Beyond this, the law is complex and unclear. Most of the privacy concept has evolved as the result of the decision of hundreds of past court cases. The right to privacy is an ever-changing and evolving concept. Basically, however, the right to privacy means that employees are free to work without undue interference from their employer and that employee records are protected from examination unless a legitimate interest exists. Monitoring employee behavior without invading an employee's right to privacy can raise some sensitive issues.[19] For example, does an employer have the right to search an employee's desk? How can drug tests be conducted without violating the right to privacy? How can employers monitor the conversations held by telephone operators without violating privacy rights? In a specific case the U.S. Department of Transportation is considering requiring long-haul truck drivers to use electronic recorders monitoring their time on the road. Although the motive is to ensure that the drivers are taking enough time off for rest, some drivers see the recorders as an invasion of their privacy.[20] There are even software programs that were designed to monitor and record every keystroke an employee makes, regardless of whether the data are ever saved in a file or transmitted over a network.[21] See the HR Challenges box regarding how far an employer's arm can reach.

As the new millennium begins, it is clear that voice mail, e-mail, the Internet, and PCs have revolutionized the workplace. However, there is a more troublesome side to

How Far Can the Employer's Arm Reach?

As a manager, do you have the right to know whether an employee has been accused of a crime while in your employ? Is it legal to terminate an employee because of his or her violation of the law, even if the employee is extremely productive and has never missed a day's work? Does the severity of the crime matter? What if the employee was convicted of child molestation or drunk driving or armed robbery? Managers who must answer these tough questions are being guided by an every-increasing body of laws.

In general, the case law suggests that misconduct outside the workplace in some cases may not be a lawful justification for employee discipline. As a defense, an employee could argue that what he or she does outside of work is none of the company's business as long as the employee is still productive. This defense is being taken more and more seriously as privacy issues become a significant area for judicial examination.

The employer's best defense is to link the crime to some aspect of the job. For example, Pepsi-Cola was able to terminate a vending-machine serviceman who was convicted of child molestation because he worked unsupervised in areas where children frequented. Employers could argue that the employee's presence in the workplace is disruptive. In one case workers were so repulsed by an employee who was accused of sexual misconduct that the peer pressure they exerted on him made him quit. However, the firm would have chosen to terminate him if he did not quit on his own on the grounds that the employee's misconduct had a disruptive impact on the workplace.

These issues are very controversial. Some states, such as Hawaii, have laws that specifically preclude employers from basing disciplinary actions on the fact that the employee has been arrested for a crime; other states do not have such laws. Further, businesses also enjoy special protection in this area by some laws. Regardless of the laws protecting either side, the employer is frequently placed in a difficult situation that must be handled with extreme care.

SOURCE: Adapted from L. Lewis, "Big Brother Is Watching," *Progressive Grocer* 76, no. 2 (February 1997), pp. 22–28; and S. Bergsman, "Employee Conduct Outside the Workplace," *HRMagazine*, March 1991, pp. 62–64.

---

these technological advances. Today's electronic systems also provide us with the means to view others' e-mail messages, listen to voice-mail messages or telephone conversations, and view what is currently on someone's computer screen from another room.[21] Employers argue that monitoring and surveillance are critical to ensure a safe and secure workplace. Workers, on the other hand, feel their rights to privacy are being ignored. Employee monitoring has become one of the most controversial issues in human resource management today. According to corporate lawyer Eric Joss, it is "the hottest employment law topic of the 1990s."[22] These issues will be explored more fully in the case at the end of the chapter.

Fair Treatment

fair treatment
Employee freedom from arbitrary and capricious behavior on the part of the employer.

The second right we examine is the right to **fair treatment** by employers. By *fair treatment*, we mean freedom from arbitrary and capricious behavior on the part of the employer. It means that individual employees will not be singled out for discipline when others also deserve it, and that overt favoritism on the part of the employer will be minimized. It also means that in the absence of mitigating circumstances, precedence will be followed by the employer. Fair treatment has been cited as the most serious ethical problem with which human resource managers must deal.[23]

Safe and Healthful Workplace, Including Freedom From Sexual Harassment

The Occupational Safety and Health Act of 1970, as amended, gives employees the right to a safe and healthful workplace. The law set up the Occupational Safety and Health Administration (OSHA) to enforce the law and to conduct inspections, levy fines, and, in severe cases, shut down operations. Finally, the law gives employees the right to complain to OSHA about safety violations without fear of retribution from employers.

The concept of fair treatment was applied to Microsoft Corp. in 1997 when the software giant lost its appeal of a workers' benefits case. A federal appeals court ruled that Microsoft knowingly and wrongly excluded certain employees from lucrative benefits by improperly classifying them as temporary or contract workers. These so-called contract workers had worked at the company for years and did the same work under the same management team as other full-time workers.[24]

Hostile Environment   In the landmark case of *Vinson v. Meritor Savings Bank, FSB*, the U.S. Supreme Court ruled that Vinson had been subjected to sexual harassment on the job by her employer, Meritor Savings Bank, because the employer had created a **hostile environment** with regard to sexual harassment. A series of activities took place involving off-color jokes, fondling, and even sexual intercourse. The plaintiff, Vinson, did not complain until she was terminated for excessive sick leave, even though the company had a complaint procedure in place. She claimed that she was afraid to complain for fear of losing her job. The court ruled in her favor and stated that the employer had created a hostile environment that prevented Vinson from voicing her complaint.[25] The EEOC guidelines define a hostile environment as one in which sexual harassment interferes with the employee's work behavior or creates an offensive work environment.[26] Since passage of the Civil Rights Act of 1991, which allows victims of sexual harassment to sue for punitive and compensatory damages, companies are taking a harder look at their work environments to ensure that they are not sexually offensive.[27]

> **hostile environment**   An organizational environment or surrounding that promotes or tolerates sexual harassment.

Collective Bargaining

Employees have the right to form or to join unions to bargain collectively with their employers with regard to wages, hours, and other terms and conditions of employment. This right is protected by federal law. By bargaining collectively, employees increase their power relative to their employer. This increased power enables them to secure those aspects desired in an employment relationship, such as higher wages and improved hours, working conditions, and terms and conditions of employment.

Communication and Involvement in the Organization

Employees have the right to be informed about all aspects of their jobs and their employment. They also have the right to be fully involved in their employing organization. In some countries this right is commonly adhered to by employers who communicate with and involve their employees through quality circles, suggestion programs, and consensus decision making. However, U.S. employers have not always believed in this right, although more employers such as Ford, GM, 3M, Motorola, and Florida Power Corp. have embraced this right.

No doubt, some would argue that although this communication and involvement might be good management practice, it does not constitute an employee right.

However, we take the position that for an employee to properly do his or her job, he or she must be kept informed about what is expected of him or her.[28] Furthermore, as an employee, an individual is entitled to full membership privileges in the employing organization. This includes participation in the benefit programs offered and access to information on organizational operations, at least in so far as they relate to the individual's job duties and responsibilities. Some argue that this right also includes the right to knowledge of organizational missions, goals, and objectives.[29] Finally, an employee has the right to know how he or she will be evaluated, including the criteria and the process used. This right is part and parcel of the right to be communicated with on aspects related to job duties and expectations.

Notice of Plant Closings and of Disciplinary Action

WARN Worker Adjustment and Retraining Notification Act of 1988, a federal act that requires advance notification to employees of plant closings.

Federal law requires that employers provide notice to employees of planned plant or facilities closings. The Worker Adjustment and Retraining Notification Act of 1988 (WARN) was passed by Congress after nearly 15 years of legislative battling. **WARN** basically requires that all firms employing more than 100 full-time workers give at least 60 days' advance notice of any plans to close plants or lay off workers. Firms are required to notify their employees under the law if a plant closing results in the loss of more than 50 jobs at one location. Notice is required in mass layoff situations if the firm lays off more than 500 people for more than 6 months or if it lays off 50 workers that constitute more than 33 percent of its workforce. Firms that employ fewer than 100 people are exempt from the law.

In addition, it is a well-established practice in arbitration hearings that an employer must give notice to employees on new rules or regulations or when it intends to enforce a previously existing but unenforced rule or regulation. Employees cannot be expected to adhere to rules and regulations that have not been made public or otherwise communicated to them. Even an existing rule or regulation that the organization has not been enforcing is unenforceable unless the organization first puts employees on notice stating that the rule will be enforced from this day forward.

For example, a no-smoking rule existed in a warehouse of a large consumer products manufacturer. This rule had been communicated to employees; in fact, no-smoking signs were clearly posted on walls in the warehouse. The rule was clearly stated in the employee handbook. The penalty for violating the rule was also clearly stated—an immediate 3-day suspension without pay on the first offense and termination on the second offense.

due process Employees' right to tell their side of the story and to have all facts considered in an impartial manner when charged with a rule violation.

However, this rule was enforced neither by the supervisors in the warehouse nor by the warehouse superintendent. When the old superintendent retired and a new one was appointed, he decided to enforce the rule. The morning of his first day on the job, he suspended an employee caught smoking. The employee filed a grievance through the union, which went to third-party arbitration. The arbitrator ruled that the suspension was improper because past practice showed that the rule existed on paper only because the company had not enforced it. He ruled that the employer should have first put all employees on notice that the rule would be enforced, even though it had not been in the past. This ruling is well established in arbitration cases—the arbitrator looks to past practice prior to making the ruling.

Due Process

The final right we examine here is the right to due process. **Due process** refers to the right to a fair hearing or adjudication that considers all facts in an impartial manner

HR CHALLENGES

Resolving Disputes with Your Company

Nearly six in ten human resource professionals responding to a recent Society for Human Resource Management (SHRM) survey said their organizations had been sued over employment issues within the past 5 years. As the number of employment lawsuits skyrockets, many companies are instituting alternative dispute resolution (ADR) programs. The benefits to these programs are well known: faster and cheaper than litigation, settle disputes in a more confidential manner, and often result in more creative, tailored solutions. Although ADR programs vary, many incorporate an open-door policy in which workers having problems with a supervisor can talk to other managers up the ladder.

One of the first choices employers must make is whether to use arbitration, mediation, or some combination of the two. With mediation, a third party works with all individuals to devise a solution. On the other hand, with arbitration, an arbitrator, typically an attorney or retired judge, imposes a final solution that is usually binding and not subject to appeal. According to a recent survey by Cornell University, Price Waterhouse, and the Foundation for Prevention & Early Resolution of Conflict, out of 600 major U.S. corporations, 88 percent used mediation in the past 3 years, 79 percent used arbitration, and 41 percent used a combination of mediation and arbitration.

ADR programs can benefit employers and employees alike, but only if the programs are well designed and specially tailored to an organization's specific needs. The most important step in designing an ADR program is assessing the history of employment conflicts. For instance, what kinds of disputes have arisen and how often? Why did those disputes occur? How are disputes currently handled, how long does the process take, and what does it cost? What changes have been recommended and why? In addition, ADR program designers should consider the culture of the organization and employees' feelings about using an informal complaint mechanism. Employee surveys, interviews, and focus groups can be useful ways to acquire this information, which will help define the goals of an internal ADR program.

SOURCE: Adapted from Jennifer Click, "SHRM Survey Finds Many Employers Being Sued." *HRNews* 7 (July 1997); Todd Gutner, "When It's Time to Do Battle with Your Company," *Business Week* 130 (February 10, 1997); Carol Wittenberg, Susan Mackenzie, Margaret Shaw, and David Ross, "And Justice for All," *HRMagazine* 131, no. 6 (September 1997).

when a person is charged with a rule violation. In most cases this means the right to file a grievance and have it heard. In a unionized organization, this right is protected by the labor agreement and the grievance process is usually spelled out in the contract. Even in a nonunion organization, a grievance process is often spelled out. A typical grievance starts with the immediate supervisor and ends with arbitration, which is a binding ruling by an outside neutral third party. This process allows both the employee and the employer to state their cases—to have "their day in court," so to speak.

Of course, if arbitration is not present in a grievance process, an employee can sue an employer for damages. This due process procedure is usually more time consuming and costly than a grievance and arbitration. See the HR Challenges box on the new alternative dispute resolution (ADR) programs.

Employer Responsibilities

To this point, we have discussed the rights of employees. Employers have responsibilities with respect to these rights. This responsibility is not the reverse side of the same coin, although employee rights do suggest corresponding employer responsibilities. However, employers have responsibilities to the community at large as well as to employees. Some concepts concerning the social responsibilities of business are discussed here.

For example, actions of employers often have impact beyond the immediate boundary of the organization. This was the key issue in the U.S. government's loan guarantee to Chrysler a number of years ago. It was reasoned that it would be better for the federal government to guarantee the loans to Chrysler in hope of saving the company than to let the company go bankrupt and thereby throw thousands of people out of work. The potential costs in unemployment insurance, food stamps, and other welfare programs were thought to far exceed the costs of guaranteeing the loan. In retrospect, the decision appears to have been the correct one because the company recovered nicely and even paid off the loans ahead of schedule.

Therefore firms have responsibilities not only to their employees and stockholders but also to other groups and to the community at large. Making charitable donations, supporting the United Way, backing arts groups, supporting colleges and universities, and working to reduce or eliminate drugs and crime are but some activities firms can participate in to improve the quality of life in the communities where they operate. Although firms may have selfish motives for doing these things—they want good schools and safe streets for their employees—the community as a whole benefits.

Responsibilities to Stakeholders

stakeholder
Any organizational constituency or group that has a vested interest in what an organization does or does not do.

One way to view these responsibilities of companies is from the perspective of a **stakeholder.** This approach holds that organizations serve multiple constituencies, and each group has a set of expectations or a vested interest in what the organization does. Consequently, the organization has a responsibility to each of these groups. Exhibit 15.4 lists some of the stakeholder groups for a large corporation. Notice that the corporation has a responsibility to try to fulfill the expectations of each of the stakeholder groups. For example, owners want a return on their investment so the organization strives to earn a profit. Employees want good wages, security, and fair treatment. Customers want a product or service at desired quality, quantity, place, time, and price. Government agencies want taxes and want the organization to obey appropriate laws.

In fulfilling these obligations to these various groups, organizations often face conflicting expectations. For example, employees make a claim to profit in the form of higher wages or other incentive pay, such as profit sharing. They compete with owners who want a share of profit in the form of dividends. The organization must balance these competing interests. Requests for financial support for college and university programs come from many institutions of higher learning; the corporation must decide which ones it will support and which ones it will not. This requires the organization to practice the art of compromise and to properly assess the power of each stakeholder and the consequences of not fulfilling the expectations of each.

In the next section we briefly discuss employer responsibilities as they pertain primarily to employees. However, it is important to recognize that these responsibilities are tempered by other responsibilities to other stakeholder groups.

Responsibility to Know the Law

"Ignorance of the law is no excuse" is an old saying that is especially pertinent to employee rights. The law is so complex and changes so rapidly that it is vital that both human resource managers and other managers try to stay abreast of the law as best

EXHIBIT 15.4	EXAMPLES OF ORGANIZATION STAKEHOLDERS

Internal Stakeholders	External Stakeholders
Employees	Suppliers
Management	Distributors
Board of directors	Board of directors
(internally chosen)	(externally chosen)
Owner (sole proprietorship)	Customers
	Government agencies
	Public interest groups
	Stakeholders

they can as well as seek legal assistance on a regular basis. Actively staying current on legal matters is an important responsibility of human resource managers today. Communicating legal requirements to line managers is a very important part of every human resource manager's job. Human resource managers must read extensively, attend workshops on legal matters, and communicate frequently with counsel to keep line managers properly educated and informed as to what they legally can and cannot do.

Responsibility to Communicate with Employees

Human resource managers should communicate effectively with employees and should ensure that line managers also communicate effectively with employees. This responsibility is related to the employee right to notice described previously. The right to notice cannot be fulfilled if the employer does not adequately communicate with employees.

Today, companies use many forms of communication. In addition to the standard ways of face-to-face communication through one-on-one encounters and meetings, letters, memoranda, postings, telephoning, and reports, organizations now use the fax machine, videos, and electronic communication (e-mail). For example, IBM, among other organizations, regularly uses videos in the communication process, not only from central headquarters but also within regions. A multimedia approach seems to be more effective in reaching employees than using just one communication medium, and adding visual images enhances the communication process.

Responsibility to Treat Employees with Human Dignity

A third employer responsibility is to treat employees with human dignity. People are not just another factor of production as is a machine, desk, or factory. They deserve respect and consideration. This is sometimes difficult to achieve, as we saw during the massive restructuring effort in the 1980s when thousands abruptly lost their jobs. Yet ethical values and our system of morals based on the Judeo-Christian ethic as well as our political system give people certain rights to be treated with dignity and respect. The movie *Roger and Me* demonstrated the conflict that can result when a large corporation (GM) takes action to close a plant that the citizens of the town wish to keep open. In situations such as this, individual rights and dignity are sometimes lost in the process, and the question becomes who can exercise the most power to assert their rights as they interpret them. Certainly, GM has the right to close a plant, but those involved have the right to be treated with human dignity.

Responsibility to Bargain Collectively

The law requires that employers bargain collectively with employees if a union has been certified as the bargaining agent. The employer has no choice about whether to bargain in good faith or not. However, the employer does have a choice in trying to keep a union from forming. An employer can legally take action to keep a union from forming, although strict guidelines about what can and cannot be done must be followed.

Responsibility to Provide Due Process

As noted previously in this chapter, the right to a fair treatment and a fair hearing on the part of the employee requires that the employer accept the responsibility to provide due process. When a union is present, due process is usually obtained through the grievance process. Governmental organizations usually provide some type of civil service hearing procedure. Nonunionized employers often have impartial panels of employees and managers to hear an employee complaint or grievance. Many Japanese companies do this. For example, Toyota uses a series of committees made up of elected worker representatives and appointed managers to hear disciplinary cases involving workers.

In the next section we look at a particularly difficult situation that is all too common in organizations today: the problem employee. Employee rights and employer responsibilities come to a head in situations that involve a problem employee. Because this is so difficult a situation and involves rights and legal responsibilities, we devote the remainder of the chapter to the issues involved.

Managing the Problem Employee

Suppose you find yourself in this position: One of your employees comes to work acting very strangely. He seems to be in a fog and unable to concentrate, but you do not smell alcohol on his breath. Furthermore, you have noticed this employee acting in this manner several times over the past 6 weeks. You have talked with him twice in the past about this "spacey" behavior only to be told that everything was all right and that the employee was simply tired and under a lot of stress because of an impending divorce. Yet you suspect drug use and are concerned that the employee's judgment and coordination are severely impaired. What do you do? If you order a drug test, will you violate the employee's right to privacy? If you take no action, will you be held liable for any accident or injury caused by the employee?

This example shows just how difficult it is to handle problem employee situations.[30] The employer must find a way to deal effectively with the problem employee situation while protecting the employee's rights. In this example the employer would be much better off if the firm had a policy on drug testing that was approved by legal counsel and circulated to all employees prior to the incident. The employer would also be better able to handle this situation if the company had an employee assistance program (EAP). Without a drug policy and an EAP, the employer can still take effective action. That action is the subject of the remainder of this chapter.

The Problem Employee

All employees have problems from time to time. They are usually transitory and clear up with little if any help from the employer. However, if this is not true, the person may be a problem employee, characterized by the following factors:

- Has a major problem.
- Has a chronic problem that recurs.
- Has a problem that requires high costs to resolve.
- Has a problem that will result in high costs if not resolved.

From a strategic standpoint, the organization must decide how much action it can afford to take in resolving the problem: that is, how much can it afford to spend to salvage an employee? The answer to this question is usually not easy to determine and depends on a number of factors:

- The law.
- The importance of the employee to the organization.
- The ease with which the organization can replace the employee.
- The returns that will come to the organization by saving the employee.
- The organization's human resource philosophy.

Of course, these factors are not always easy to determine, especially the costs and potential benefits involved in the process.

Taking Action versus Not Taking Action

At first, managers typically ignore problem employees for several reasons. They hope the problem is not serious. They believe the problem will go away on its own. They are unsure about what to do. They have other things on their minds that divert their attention from the problem employee situation. Of course, in many cases, the problem does clear up with little, if any, managerial action. This reinforces the inactivity on the manager's part. But if it does not resolve itself, the manager is in a difficult situation because he or she has let the problem go on for some length of time.

From a strategic standpoint, this becomes dangerous because the costs associated with clearing up the problem at this point can become quite high. In addition, if the organization is tolerant of a problem employee's behavior, other employees will notice this, providing a precedent. Should tolerance for this type of behavior become established in the organization's culture, it will be very difficult and costly to correct.

Consequently, it is recommended that managers take immediate action when a problem employee is initially encountered. Waiting can exacerbate the situation and make it very difficult and expensive to rectify later. Of course, managers need good policy guidance from human resource professionals to help take action that is both effective and legal.

Cost Issues

The costs involved in resolving a problem employee situation are difficult to predict. At the onset, managers do not know how much it will cost them to resolve the situation. It is difficult to predict just what will work, what will be covered by insurance, and what the costs of lost production are because of the problem employee's behavior. Furthermore, opportunity costs are associated with trying to correct problem

Model Employment Termination Act (META)

The current state of wrongful discharge litigation is still in a state of uncertainty. Some complainants become rich with awards for damages; others with similar complaints receive nothing. Neither the employers nor the employees benefit from such actions. To correct this problem, the Model Employment Termination Act (META) was introduced.

One reason for the random outcomes in the courts for wrongful discharge cases is the ever-increasing common-law exception being developed on a case-by-case basis as states decide wrongful discharge cases brought on by termination in employment-at-will situations. The main provision of META supports arbitration instead of court litigation for discharges. The arbitrator will be severely limited in the amount of damages that can be awarded, usually to back pay and up to 4 years of future pay.

META also provides a universal definition of just and unjust dismissals that could be used by all states. Just discharges would be those based on performance problems, economic problems, company relocations, and the like.

META favors the employers for several reasons. First, the threat of large settlements are gone; only back and front pay can be offered. Second, because just cause is clearly defined, there is no fear of a poor interpretation of the situation. Finally, an arbitrator, not the court system, decides the case. This is less costly and frequently quicker.

The employee also receives some benefits. First, all employees must be made aware of the process when terminated. In the past many suffered in silence because they did not know they had any other options. Also, because the termination policy is standardized across states, employees have a clearer idea of why and how the termination process works.

SOURCE: Jeremy Fox and Hugh Hindman, "State to Address Model Termination Law," *HRNews*, January 1992, p. 1; Society for Human Resource Management, "Supreme Court Voids Gag Order of Former Employee," *HRNews*, February 1998, p. 8.

employee behavior: The manager could be doing something with his or her time and effort other than trying to deal with the problem employee.

Because of these costs, many managers become frustrated and simply attempt to terminate the employee. Termination is sometimes an effective solution, but it is considered the "capital punishment" in the employment relationship and generally should not be the first action taken. In addition, such termination may cause many liabilities such as wrongful discharge; discharge that could be interpreted to violate a union contract or civil service protection in government; or discharge that might be judged to be discriminatory based on race, sex, age, creed, and so on. For these reasons, termination should be carefully thought out and substantiated with documentation that will stand up in a hearing or court of law. See the HR Challenges box regarding the Model Employment Termination Act (META).

A final note on the termination of problem employees concerns the provisions of the ADA of 1990, which protects recovering alcohol and drug abusers because these illnesses are considered treatable. If termination is carried out without first trying to rehabilitate the employee, a court or hearing officer may order reinstatement based on the fact that the employee was dismissed on the basis of a handicap—a reasonable accommodation was not first attempted (perhaps a rehabilitation program). Options other than termination are discussed following.

The Counseling Process

Managers should counsel problem employees to the extent that they can and should readily refer them to professional counseling as necessary. This is one reason that having an EAP program is so beneficial in dealing with problem employees.[31] We are not suggesting that managers attempt a full-blown counseling program with the employee, but that management constructively confront the employee about the problem and attempt to find out more information about what is going on and how the behavior can be changed.

These are a few counseling guidelines appropriate for managers to follow:

- Talk with the employee to specifically define the problem in terms of the behavior that needs to be changed.
- Focus on behavior that the employee can change and that is within his or her control.
- Enlist the employee's assistance in determining specific suggestions for changing the behavior in order to create a sense of ownership on the part of the employee for the solution to the problem.
- Jointly establish a means of monitoring and follow-up with the employee to verify compliance.
- Emphasize the consequences of not fulfilling the "behavior contract"— specifically deal with the question of what will happen to the employee. Schedule follow-up meetings with a timetable.
- Offer encouragement and indicate that you support the employee and that you want him or her to do better.

Avoid getting involved in personal off-the-job problems with the employee, and certainly avoid telling the employee specific steps he or she should take in his or her personal life.[32] For example, do not ever tell an employee that he or she should divorce his or her spouse. If the problem rests here, suggest marriage counseling.

Types of Problem Employees

Managers can encounter a variety of problem employees. We do not list every type here, nor do we go into extensive detail as to how to handle each type. Rather, our purpose is to identify each type and to point out some strategic considerations that must be kept in mind from a rights and responsibilities standpoint.

Alcohol/Drug Abuser Alcohol and drug abuse is still common in organizations. The primary consideration here is to give the employee the opportunity to rehabilitate without risking injury to self or others and without doing damage to the organization's operations. As indicated earlier in the chapter, it is essential for the organization to have a policy on drug and alcohol use and drug testing and to thoroughly communicate and enforce it. Exhibit 15.5 presents some guidelines that organizations may follow when adopting a drug/alcohol policy. It is also important to have or have access to an EAP.

Approaching alcohol and drug abuse as a treatable medical problem is legally safe and usually protects employee rights better by giving the employee the opportunity to correct behavior prior to disciplinary action or termination.

EXHIBIT 15.5   GENERAL ALCOHOL/DRUG POLICY DEVELOPMENT GUIDELINES

- Address the problem of alcohol and drug abuse squarely.
- Conduct proper investigations of suspected violations.
- Follow appropriate disciplinary guidelines.
- Train supervisors and educate employees.
- Develop a policy on rehabilitation or employee assistance.
- Be sensitive to employees' privacy rights.
- Take reasonable steps to protect employees and others from harm caused by substance abusers.
- Know the applicable statutes and regulations.
- Practice good employee relations.

In addition:

- Define the problem in workplace terms while avoiding legal, moral, and medical definitions.
- Safeguard privacy, due process, and confidentiality.
- Avoid conflict with applicable federal, state, and local statutes and regulations.
- Apply substance-abuse policies equitably throughout the organization.

SOURCE: Adapted from S. J. Smits and L. Pace, "Workplace Substance Abuse: Establish Policies," *Personnel Journal*, May 1989, p. 88; and J. E. Bahls, "Drugs in the Workplace," *HRMagazine*, February 1998, pp. 81–87.

Marginal/Low Performer   This employee is one who is just meeting minimum standards of job accomplishment. From a strategic standpoint, it is better for the organization to create a culture of involvement and leadership to inform the employee of the situation and to provide guidance to improve it. A reward system that provides financial and nonfinancial incentives for top performance can work to prevent or alleviate problems of this type.

Tardy/Absent Employee   A person can be absent or tardy for many reasons, but if a person is gone, regardless of the reason, his or her work is not getting done or must be done by others. To avoid being placed in the position of ruling on the appropriateness of the reason for absence or tardiness, many organizations offer these options:

- Flexible working hours (flextime).
- Accumulation of leave time that can be taken for either vacation or illness.
- Bonuses at the end of the year or at retirement for unused sick leave.
- Wellness programs that encourage employees to develop good health and fitness habits, thereby reducing illness.
- Day care for employees with small children.
- The organization should have a clearly stated policy concerning absences; violations may result in loss of the job.

Whatever policy the organization adopts, it should be communicated effectively to all employees and enforced consistently. With the advent of newer work arrangements, such as telecommuting (working at home via computer link to office), the tardiness and absence problem that sometimes plagues organizations may subside as an issue.

Saboteur/Thief   Our system believes that an individual is innocent until proven guilty. Yet continuing the employment of a person suspected of a criminal act against the organization can be disastrous. How can the organization protect itself from criminal actions while protecting the rights of a suspected employee?

One common action taken by employers is to suspend suspected employees with or without pay until a hearing can be held to determine whether the evidence indicates guilt. Assuming a speedy and fair hearing is held, the organization can either reinstate the employee or take other disciplinary action up to and including termination and prosecution through the courts.[33]

Caustic/Sarcastic/Negative Attitude   An employee characterized in this way can be the rotten apple that spoils the barrel in that the poor attitude can become contagious. This situation must be dealt with by focusing on the behavior that results from the negative attitude. For example, if this attitude causes the employee to lose his or her temper when working with customers or other employees, it is appropriate for management to point out that such behavior will not be tolerated in the future. If the attitude results in spreading vicious lies, gossip, or character assassinations, the employee must be confronted with such remarks and told to stop making such statements.

Changing an attitude is very difficult because it is not directly observable and is open to much debate. For example, just what exactly is a "bad attitude?" Unlike a negative attitude, a negative behavior is observable and verifiable.

The final section of this chapter addresses the issue of discipline and relates it to the protection of employee rights and the handling of problem employees. Creating the proper disciplinary climate is important for preventing and resolving disciplinary issues while protecting the rights of employees.

Building a Good Disciplinary Climate

From a strategic standpoint, management has a responsibility to create the proper disciplinary climate rather than just allow any climate to evolve. This means that management and human resource managers must have in mind a set of desirable criteria. A good disciplinary climate includes the following:

- Self-discipline over externally imposed discipline.
- Positive and future orientation.
- Prevention and correction.
- Progressive nature.
- Proper communication.
- Fair and impartial administration.
- The right of appeal.

We briefly look at each of these characteristics.

Self-Discipline over Externally Imposed Discipline

The best discipline is the kind that employees impose on themselves. They do the right thing because they know it is expected and they want to do it. Such discipline is difficult to reach in many organizations. Instead, many external control measures are imposed to ensure that people do the right thing. Some level of external control is always necessary, but the emphasis should be shifted to creating a culture that fosters and rewards self-control and self-discipline. For example, Thomas J. Peters and Robert H. Waterman, in their book *In Search of Excellence*, report on the astounding success of IBM. They attribute this success to IBM's focus on its people:

> Treat people as adults. Treat them as partners; treat them with dignity; treat them with respect. . . .Thomas J. Watson, Jr. [former CEO of IBM], puts it well: "IBM's philosophy is largely contained in three simple beliefs. I want to begin with what I think is the most important: *our respect for the individual.* This is a simple concept, but in IBM it occupies a major portion of management time. We devote more effort to it than anything else."[34]

Peters and Waterman report on dozens of companies that succeed by enabling their employees to control themselves. The advantage of self-control is that the bureaucratic red tape and cumbersome reporting and check-up procedures are greatly reduced. Instead, managers *manage by exception.* People are assumed to be doing the right thing unless they demonstrate otherwise. Managers need only monitor in a general sense and become involved only when performance does not meet standards and is not quickly self-corrected. This approach reflects Theory Y assumptions about people as described earlier in the book. People want to work and want to do a good job, and the manager's role is to create conditions that allow this to happen.

Positive and Future Orientation

Discipline should focus on positive actions expected in the future rather than on negative ones experienced in the past. This means that the climate should focus on explaining what behaviors are expected and how employees can achieve these behaviors rather than on punishing behaviors of the past.

Prevention and Correction

A good disciplinary climate prevents as well as corrects undesirable behavior. Of course, from a strategic standpoint, it is better to prevent undesirable behavior from occurring in the first place than it is to correct it after the fact. In other words, there must be incentives to do the right thing and anticipated negative sanctions for doing the wrong thing. These negative sanctions can serve as a deterrent provided they are:

- Known ahead of time.
- Administered in a timely fashion.
- Equally applied to everyone (the "hot stove" rule: the consequence is immediately applied to everyone who touches the hot stove).

Corrective actions should focus on just that: correcting the behavior. This means that managers and human resource managers must clearly spell out in very specific terms what the employee must do and must instruct the employee on how to do it. Incentives for compliance as well as negative sanctions for noncompliance should also be indicated clearly.

Progressive Nature

Progressive discipline means that the severity of the sanction increases with the severity and repeated nature of the offense. Some actions might warrant immediate dismissal, such as theft; others trigger a series of steps. Exhibit 15.6 shows part of the progressive discipline schedule used by a restaurant chain for a series of relatively

EXHIBIT 15.6	AN EXAMPLE OF PROGRESSIVE DISCIPLINE

Disciplinary problem: failure to report to shift on time

First offense: Oral warning

Second offense: Written warning

Third offense: Loss of one shift's pay

Fourth offense: Three days off without pay

Fifth offense: Dismissal

---

minor offenses that range from showing up late for one's shift to failing to clean up one's workstation at the end of the shift. Notice that the disciplinary action proceeds from a relatively light sanction of oral warning to a serious one of termination. Of course, this schedule is clearly spelled out to the employees ahead of time so they know what to expect.

Proper Communication As indicated, proper communication with employees is essential for good discipline. Employees must be absolutely clear as to expectations. They must also know what is required to achieve these expectations and what happens to them if they do not. Further, they need to be put on notice properly if a previously unenforced rule is now going to be enforced.

To ensure good communication, a variety of methods should be used to clearly communicate expectations and desired behavior: face-to-face meetings, written handouts, bulletin board postings, and videos. Sunshine Junior Stores, Inc., a convenience store chain in the southeastern United States, makes extensive use of videos in new-employee orientation where expectations, policies, procedures, and rules are clearly covered. The advantage of a video is that the desired and undesired behavior can be demonstrated very clearly.

Fair and Impartial Administration

Finally, the disciplinary process should be fairly and impartially administered. This means that individual rights should be protected and that favoritism should largely be absent from the process. People are treated alike regardless of their relationship to key people, wealth, or other factors. In practice, of course, this is difficult to achieve. But the system must be perceived as fair if it is to be respected and voluntarily followed. In a union situation the concepts of fairness and equity are often spelled out in the labor agreement. Because the employees have had some say on discipline through their union in collective bargaining negotiations, a union system might have higher perceptions of equity than in a nonunion situation.

The Right of Appeal

Perceptions of fairness and equity also involve the right of appeal. A dissatisfied employee should have the right to appeal a disciplinary decision to a person or board. As we see in the next chapter, this right is clearly spelled out in union agreements. In nonunion situations the right might involve simply appealing the decision to the next higher level of supervision.

These rights and responsibilities are further discussed in Chapter 16, which deals with unions. Unions present a special strategic challenge to organizations because they provide employees with an organized way to make their wishes known and to seek redress for grievances. The next chapter explores these differences and challenges for organizations.

Management Guidelines

The following management guidelines are based on the issues addressed in this chapter.

1. Five basic factors influence management's approach to its responsibilities and employee rights: management philosophy, the tightness of the labor market, the law, union and employee power, and organizational culture. Managers must consider the balance these factors create when developing their approach to rights and responsibilities.
2. The law has a large influence on employee rights. Legislation on discrimination, employment at will, and privacy all play major roles in management's creation of employee rights policies.
3. Employee rights policies must include seven basic areas. These areas are privacy, fair treatment, workplace health and safety, organization communication and employee involvement, notice of plant closings and disciplinary action, and due process. Management failure to adequately deal with any of these areas is likely to result in severe organizational problems.
4. Management must seek to reduce the conflict between its responsibilities to its internal and external stakeholders without unduly harming any one group, such as employees. This can usually be accomplished by making ethically correct decisions.
5. Management responsibilities include knowing the law, providing open communication, treating all employees with dignity, bargaining collectively, and providing due process.
6. Management must treat problem employees according to its own rules and methods.
7. Employee discipline is essential to organizational success. In general, the best policies are those that emphasize employee self-discipline. Good discipline policies are positive and future oriented, emphasize prevention and correction, are progressive and properly communicated, and are fairly and impartially administered. Poor policies are likely to produce organizational turmoil and severely hamper company performance.

Questions for Review

1. What arguments can an employer use to justify having a drug or AIDS testing policy? Why might an applicant or employee be concerned about such a test?
2. What are three examples of how the culture of a society can influence employer treatment of their employees?

3. Many firms that thought they were operating under an employment-at-will doctrine later ended up in court defending themselves. What are two precautions that managers can take to ensure that their organization does not get sued for a wrongful discharge?
4. This chapter lists and describes seven basic employee rights. What are two? Explain them.
5. What is the stakeholder concept with respect to employer responsibilities? What are some of the problems with this approach?
6. What are organizational ethics? How are ethical standards instilled in people? What, if anything, can an organization do to raise or alter the ethical standards of its employees?
7. What can be done to help a problem employee?
8. What are four different types of problem employees? Compare and contrast how a manager should deal with each type.
9. How should one go about developing a good disciplinary climate?
10. At your yearly performance evaluation interview, you are informed by your boss that she has been spying on you periodically throughout the year to gather accurate information to be used in your appraisal. You receive high marks and a large raise. How do you feel about the fact that your boss has been spying on you? What if you receive a poor evaluation and no raise? Would it change your opinion about the boss's spying?

CASE

The Clash Between Employee Rights and Employer Monitoring[35]

Imagine that you are at work and need to use the phone. How would you feel if you knew that your employer might be listening in on your conversation? Is your employer justified in listening to you in an effort to save expenses and monitor your job performance? Or is this an invasion of your right to privacy? The technology exists today for employers to electronically monitor employees' phone calls, watch what they type at their computer terminals, read their electronic mail, and watch them talk to their coworkers.

The advent of the modern electronics age has made the privacy issue one of the decade's hottest topics in employee rights. Consider the following situations:

General Electric uses fisheye lenses mounted in wall and ceiling pinholes to watch employees suspected of crimes.
DuPont uses long-distance cameras to watch employees on its loading docks.
Delta Airlines monitors booking agent productivity through its computer system.
Management Recruiters, Inc., monitors computer-based employee schedules to see who interviews the most candidates.
Holy Cross Hospital in Silver Spring, Maryland, mounted a surveillance camera in the women nurses' locker room to investigate missing narcotics.
Safeway Stores uses electronic systems in its trucks to monitor employee driving habits.

Until recently, police departments in Connecticut, Rhode Island, West Virginia, and Utah routinely tapped all incoming and outgoing phone calls to the barracks—including privileged defendant-attorney conversations.

Which of these actions are fair and which represent an invasion of employee privacy? Almost all forms of electronic monitoring have been challenged in court (see for example, *James* v. *Newspaper Agency Corporation* for phone monitoring or *McIntyre* v. *United States* for bugging), but federal, state, and local legislation and court decisions still do not make clear what is acceptable and what is not.

Most challenges to electronic monitoring are based on the "reasonable expectation of privacy" doctrine. This doctrine generally holds that there are situations in which a person can reasonably expect to be free of any form of monitoring or surveillance. Any invasion of this reasonable expectation of privacy should not be allowed. Unfortunately, what constitutes a reasonable expectation of privacy is not clear. In "Protecting Private Employees," Terry Dworkin suggests that in areas in which employees have high expectations of privacy, such as private offices, changing areas, and bathrooms, the use of electronic monitoring equipment could lead to successful employee suits against the employer unless the employer can show a great need for the surveillance. However, she adds that there are even exceptions to this rule. A recent federal court case, *Postal Workers Union* v. *United States Postal Service*, held that "relative lack of scrutiny" in these areas did not necessarily create a reasonable expectation of privacy.

Furthermore, violations of privacy rights generally are a combination of civil and criminal offenses. Often, victims must sue in civil court to obtain damages and must prove that the employer's monitoring was done without sufficient cause to do so. In criminal cases, courts have generally held that people give up a great deal of privacy expectations when they become employees of an organization. Even when privacy rights are generally established, organizations can often monitor their employees by informing workers that monitoring is a general policy or by making workers sign privacy waivers as a condition of employment.

Another problem is that it is believed that the use of monitoring techniques generally harms employee morale, strains labor-management relations, and often produces increased stress in employees under surveillance. Managers are strongly cautioned to consider these side effects when developing a monitoring policy. All of these problems associated with employee monitoring make it one of the most controversial human resource issues.

Questions for Discussion

1. What ways besides electronic monitoring are available to managers to determine how productive employees are?

2. One aspect of the human resource function is to hire employees who the organization can trust. If managers feel compelled to spy on employees to reduce employee theft, is human resource failing at its job?

3. Telephone operators who are aware that their manager may be listening or watching them have reported high incidents of headaches, back pain, fatigue, shoulder soreness, anxiety, and sore wrists. Obviously, these problems could

reduce an employee's effectiveness. Do you think that these managers are hurting productivity by monitoring their employees?

4. Several software packages on the market can be used by managers to spy on their employees by tapping into the employees' computers and viewing what is on their screens. Often these programs can be run without the knowledge of the employee. Should it be illegal for software companies to market this type of product? Why or why not?

Additional Readings

Barrar, Peter, and Cary Cooper. *Managing Organizations in 1992.* New York: Routledge, 1992.

Barrett, Paul. "High Court Upholds Workers' Comp Law in Setback to Employer-Rights Advocates." *The Wall Street Journal,* March 10, 1992, p. A3.

Bellingham, Richard, and Barry Cohen. *Ethical Leadership: A Competitive Edge.* Amherst, MA: HRD Press, 1991.

Bible, Jon. "When Employers Look for Things Other Than Drugs: The Legality of AIDS, Genetic, Intelligence, and Honesty Testing in the Workplace." *Labor Law Journal,* April 1990, pp. 195–213.

Brady, Teresa. "The Legal Horrors of Truth-in-Hiring Lawsuits," *Management Review* 85, no. 10 (October 1996), pp. 53–56.

Carrell, Michael, and Christina Heavrin. "Before You Drug Test." *HRMagazine,* June 1990, pp. 64–68.

Center for Employment Relations and Law, College of Law, Florida State University. "Wrongful Discharge." *Employment Relations Bulletin,* January 1990.

Daniels, Robert. "Storm Is Brewing between Employers, Employees over the Right to Privacy." *The Wall Street Journal,* August 10, 1990, p. B6A.

Dworkin, Terry. "Protecting Private Employees from Enhanced Monitoring: Legislative Approaches." *American Business Law Journal* 28 (1990), pp. 59–85.

Etziono, Amitai. *The Responsive Society.* San Francisco: Jossey-Bass, 1991.

Goff, J. Larry. "Corporate Responsibilities to the Addicted Employee: A Look at Practical, Legal, and Ethical Issues." *Labor Law Journal,* April 1990, pp. 214–221.

Greengard, Samuel. "Privacy: Entitlement or Illusion," *Personnel Journal* 75, no. 5 (May 1996), pp. 74–83.

Hawkins, Robert. "Diversity and Municipal Openness." *Public Management,* January 1992, pp. 33–35.

Hayes, Arthur. "Layoffs Take Careful Planning to Avoid Losing the Suits That Are Apt to Follow." *The Wall Street Journal,* November 2, 1990, p. B1.

Henshaw, Georgeanne, and Kenwood Youmans. "Employee Privacy in the Workplace and an Employer's Right to Conduct Workplace Searches and Surveillance." *Society for Human Resource Management Legal Report,* Spring 1990, pp. 1–5.

Israel, David, Pamela Sweeny, and Michael Mitchell. "Workplace Surveillance Risky Business for Employers." *HRNews/Society for Human Resource Management,* January 1990, p. 15.

Kelly, Kevin, and Michael O'Neal. "This Turnaround Will Be Tougher Than Al Cheechi Thought." *Business Week,* December 24, 1990, pp. 28–30.

Lowman, Rodney L. *The Ethical Practice of Psychology in Organizations.* Washington DC American Psychological Association and Bowling Green, OH: Society for Industrial and Organizational Psychology, 1998.

Miceli, Marcia, and Janet Near. *Blowing the Whistle.* New York: Free Press, 1992.

Oliver, Bill. "Do You Drug Test Your Employees?" *HRMagazine,* October 1990, p. 57.

Rosen, Benson, and Catherine Schwoerer. "Balanced Protection Policies." *HRMagazine,* February 1990, pp. 59–64.

Rothfeder, Jeffrey, Michelle Galen, and Lisa Driscoll. "Is Your Boss Spying on You?" *Business Week,* January 15, 1990, pp. 74–75.

Salaman, Graeme. *Human Resource Strategies.* Newbury Park, CA: Sage, 1992.

Segal, Jonathan. "Follow the Yellow Brick Road." *HRMagazine*, February 1990, pp. 83–86.

Segal, Jonathan. "Test Suspected Users Only." *HRMagazine*, November 1990, p. 79.

Sheppard, Blair, Roy Lewicki, and John Minton. *Organizational Justice.* New York: Free Press, 1992.

Willard, Richard. "Drug Test All Employees Randomly." *HRMagazine*, November 1990, p. 78.

Zachary, G. Pascal. "Bruised Apple." *The Wall Street Journal*, February 15, 1990, p. A1.

Notes

[1]Michael Carrell and Christina Heavrin, "Before You Drug Test," *HRMagazine*, June 1990, pp. 64–68; David Gold and Beth Unger, "Weigh Legalities in Formulating AIDS Policy," *HRNews*, August 1991, p. 5; M. K. St. Clair and D. W. Arnold, "Preemployment Screening: No More Test Stress," *Security Management*, February 1995, p. 73; R. E. Smith, "Corporations That Fail the Fair Hiring Test," *Business and Society Review* 88 (Winter 1994), pp. 29–33; and G. D. Webster, "Hiring Dos and Don'ts," *Association Management*, November 1992, pp. 100–102.

[2]Jon Bible, "When Employers Look for Things Other Than Drugs: The Legality of AIDS, Genetic, Intelligence, and Honesty Testing in the Workplace," *Labor Law Journal*, April 1990, pp. 195–213.

[3]J. Click, "Court Says Genetic Tests Violate Worker's Privacy," *HRNews*, March 1998, pp. 6–7.

[4]A. Fisher, "Big Brother Wants a Closer Look at Your Hair," *Fortune*, June 23, 1997, p. 163.

[5]Maryann Keller, *Rude Awakening: The Rise, Fall, and Struggle for Recovery of General Motors* (New York: William Morrow, 1989).

[6]Thomas Peters and Robert Waterman, *In Search of Excellence: Lessons from America's Best-Run Companies* (New York: Warner Books, 1982), pp. 244–245.

[7]G. Pascal Zachary, "Bruised Apple," *The Wall Street Journal*, February 15, 1990, p. A1.

[8]S. Carlson and P. L. Perrewé, "Institutionalization of Organizational Ethics through Transformational Leadership," *Journal of Business Ethics* 13 (1994), pp. 1–10.

[9]Alan Weiss, "Seven Reasons to Examine Workplace Ethics," *HRMagazine*, March 1991, pp. 69–74.

[10]Ibid.

[11]"Unfuzzing Ethics for Managers," *Fortune*, November 23, 1987, pp. 229–234.

[12]Forty states have enacted some form of legislation that modifies the employment-at-will concept. For more information on employment-at-will legislation, see Michael Goldblatt, "Preserving the Right to Fire," *Small Business Report*, December 1986, p. 87; and Darrel Brown and George Gray, "A Positive Alternative to Employment at Will," *Advanced Management Journal*, Summer 1988, pp. 13–16. In 1987 Montana became the first state to pass a wrongful discharge law, which essentially allows workers to challenge the employment-at-will doctrine in court under several conditions. For more information on the Montana law, see Jonathan Tompkins, "Legislating the Employment Relationship: Montana's Wrongful-Discharge Law," *Employee Relations Law Journal*, Winter 1988/1989, pp. 387–398.

[13]"Distribution of Employee Manual Does Not Give Rise to Contract," *Employment Law Report*, November 1991, p. 1; and Ellen J. Pollock, "Ruling Frowns on Employers' False Promises," *The Wall Street Journal*, October 7, 1992, p. B11.

[14]See, for example, Amy Dockser Marcus, "Courts Uphold Oral Pledges of Lifetime Employment," *The Wall Street Journal*, December 12, 1989, p. B1.

[15]Milo Greyelin and Jonathan Moses, "Rulings on Wrongful Firing Curb Hiring," *The Wall Street Journal*, April 9, 1992, p. B3.

[16]Debbie Keary, "Minimize the Risk of Wrongful Discharge, Urges Brown," *HRNews*, June 1990, p. 7.

[17]D. Farber, "Free Speech Is Not a Crime, But It Can Still Get You Fired," *Newsday*, February 12, 1990.

[18]We recognize that this list is somewhat arbitrary and that other authors might have a different list. However, our list generally conforms to accepted listings. See James Hunt, *The Law of the Workplace: Rights of Employers and Employees* (Edison, NJ: BNA, 1988).

[19]Jonathan Segal, "A Need Not to Know," *HRMagazine*, October 1991, pp. 85–90; J. Rothfeder, "Computers May Be Personal, but Are They Private?" *Beyond Computing*, January/February 1994, pp. 50–53; and Ellen E. Schultz, "Employee Beware: The Boss May Be Listening," *The Wall Street Journal*, July 29, 1994, p. C11.

[20]Anna Wilde Matthews, "For Truckers, Electronic Monitors Rev Up Fears of Privacy Invasion," *The Wall Street Journal*, February 25, 2000, p. B1.

[21]Rothfeder, Galen, and Driscoll, "Is Your Boss Spying on You?" p. 74.

[22]Ibid.

[23]"Most Serious Ethical Problems Involve Differences in the Way People Are Treated Based on Favoritism or Relationship to Top Management," *1991 SHRM/CCH Survey*, June 1991, p. 3.

[24]C. McCoy and D. Bank, "Microsoft Loses Appeal in Worker-Benefits Case," *The Wall Street Journal*, Friday, July 25, 1997, pp. A1, A3.

[25]See Kenneth L. Sovereign, *Personnel Law*, 2nd ed. (Englewood Cliffs, NJ: Prentice-Hall, 1989), pp. 87–93.

[26]29 CFR 16.011 (A).

[27]Troy Segal, "Getting Serious about Sexual Harassment," *Business Week*, November 9, 1992, pp. 78–82.

[28]Paul Staudohar, "New Plant Closing Law Aids Workers in Transition," *Personnel Journal*, January 1989, pp. 87–90.

[29]David W. Ewing, "Corporate Due Process Lowers Legal Costs," *The Wall Street Journal*, October 23, 1989, p. A14.

[30]Cecily A. Waterman and Teresa A. Maginn, "Investigating Suspect Employees," *HRMagazine*, January 1993, pp. 85–87.

[31]Ellen E. Schultz, "Be Careful What You Tell Your Firm's Counselors; It May Be Used against You," *The Wall Street Journal*, May 26, 1994, p. C11.

[32]"Employees' Rights, after Hours," *Manager's Legal Bulletin*, 1994, Alexander Hamilton Institute Incorporated.

[33]Michael Allen, "Security Experts Advise Firms to Avoid Panic, Excess Zeal in Probing Data Leaks," *The Wall Street Journal*, September 20, 1991, p. B11.

[34]Peters and Waterman, *In Search of Excellence* (New York: Warner Books, 1982), p. 238.

[35]Israel, Sweeny, and Mitchell, "Workplace Surveillance Risky Business for Employers," p. 15; Daniels, "Storm Is Brewing between Employers, Employees," p. B6; Rothfeder, Galen, and Driscoll, "Is Your Boss Spying on You?" pp. 74–75; Henshaw and Youmans, "Employee Privacy in the Workplace," pp. 1–5; Gene Bylinsky, "How Companies Spy on Employees," *Fortune*, November 4, 1991, pp. 130–140; and L. Harper, "Concern about Privacy," *The Wall Street Journal*, May 17, 1994, p. A1; P. Barlas, "Ex-Watkins Employees File under Unique Privacy Suit," *The Business Journal* 14, no. 4 (May 13, 1996), pp. 1–3.

16

Unions and Strategic Collective Bargaining

Chapter Objectives

As a result of studying this chapter, you should be able to

1. Identify strategic issues that affect labor unions today.

2. Describe the current state of union growth and decline.

3. Discuss the role and objectives of unions in society today.

4. Explain the laws that regulate relations between unions and management.

5. Identify strategic variables and choices regarding the collective bargaining process.

6. Distinguish between adversarial and cooperative problem-solving union roles.

7. Debate the pros, cons, and legalities of "union-busting" tactics and union avoidance techniques.

8. Outline the formal bargaining process, including preparation, negotiations, settlement, and mediation and arbitration.

One of the most significant issues facing managers in the 21st century is the changing role that unions are playing in the economy. Important economic shifts have affected not only companies and unions, but also the very essence of their relationship. Worldwide markets, changing demographics, and attitude changes make it necessary for managers, particularly human resource managers, to understand the strategic role of unions.

This chapter looks at international competition, attitudes towards unions, and legislative solutions that have dramatically affected the role of unions and management. The impact of these and other important concerns on the collective bargaining process is also discussed.

CASE

Caterpillar Moving Forward Into the Future or Turning the Clock Back?[1]

"Quality People Working Together"

—Banner in late 1980s that union member Bob Thorpien convinced the company to erect.

"Cat Treats Workers Like Dogs"

—Sign displayed by Mr. Thorpien in June 1994. When he was suspended by the company for his actions, the United Auto Workers (UAW) staged the ninth wildcat strike since the fall of 1993.

The name *Big Blue* is synonymous with IBM, and *Bright Yellow* represents the Big Cat to tens of thousands of farmers, construction workers, and owners. Caterpillar Company, maker of Big Cats, is based in the heart of middle America in Peoria, Illinois. Over the last half of the century, Caterpillar has become the largest worldwide producer of construction and earth-moving equipment and of large powerplants (engines) that are used in farm equipment, trucks, and construction equipment. Like the auto industry, the construction and earth-moving equipment industry grew dramatically after World War II. Times were good and profits high, which led to the growth and strengthening of the major labor union, the UAW. During the 1960s and early to mid 1970s, negotiations between the company and the union were difficult, but the ultimate settlements were generous, and profits remained high. Between 1955 and 1982, ten strikes occurred during ten contracts.

During these prosperous years, efficiency often was of little concern; the shop floor was described by one union member as being like a "playground." Workers came in drunk or stoned on drugs, and union stewards spent a great deal of time trying to keep them from being fired. Given the overall economic prosperity, however, such inefficiencies were tolerated and the large wage and benefit packages could be passed along to the customer in the form of higher prices.

The Best of Times Become the Worst of Times

In the late 1970s the economic bubble burst. A grain embargo against the Soviets, issued by then President Carter, led to a precipitous decline in farm incomes and land prices. Interest rates climbed to dizzying heights, in some cases in excess of 20 percent. Caterpillar, which had enjoyed market domination in a number of countries most affected by the economic crisis, had planned massive expansion of its facilities. When the market for construction equipment dried up, Caterpillar had to stop construction of two new plants in Burlington, Iowa, and Morton, Illinois, after the structural steel had been erected. Both were ultimately torn down.

Rather than needing new capacity, Caterpillar could not keep existing capacity busy. Costs were spiraling out of control and demand was down. Workers were laid off and, in many cases, permanently furloughed. The number of UAW employed by Caterpillar in 1979 declined from approximately 23,000 in the Peoria area alone to fewer than 12,000 in 1984, and has declined since. The situation was grim for both the union and the company. No longer were layoffs limited to the blue-collar workforce; managerial ranks were being reduced as well. In 1982 the UAW conducted a 205-day strike that led many to believe that the old adversarial relationship had to be changed.

New Ideas and New Approaches: Will They Play in Peoria?

Once both the company and union realized that the 1980s were a repeat of the temporary layoff–hire-back cycle of the past, there was a very strong incentive to work together. New management concepts such as quality circles, just-in-time inventory, and total quality management were becoming popular in the mid 1980s. Companies such as Deere, General Motors, and other UAW shops were experimenting with new cooperative arrangements. This was difficult often for both management and union. Their long-term adversarial relationship was more comfortable and the rules more certain and predictable than these new arrangements. Managers frequently believed that they did not want to give control to the "workers." Union officials who sought too much cooperation were accused of "selling out." Nevertheless, over time many of the deeply held suspicions were put aside to save as many jobs as possible.

In the spring of 1986, Caterpillar managers and UAW representatives met in Michigan to try to develop a more cooperative spirit. The meetings went so well that one union official remarked, "I'm getting worried; I'm agreeing too much with you guys." An outflow of this session was the employee satisfaction process (ESP). In Aurora, Illinois, plant workers helped plan everything, including the purchase of machinery and reorganization of the assembly line. Rich Clausel, one of the workers, summed up the new positive attitude of many of the union members: "For the first time, I felt when I went to work, I made a difference." Even doubtful employees like Bob Thorpien were won over. He suggested that training classes be held to help new workers in his area; he ended up teaching the classes himself.

Clausel took the challenge seriously. At home he read about employee involvement programs and freely shared his knowledge and ideas with other workers. He moved from his line job to become one of the facilitators. New alliances and friendships formed between old rivals, and problems were approached creatively. The UAW workers enjoyed an increased sense of value. Furthermore, Caterpillar's costs decreased and productivity increased. It saved almost $5 million from 241 team-generated ideas in the Aurora plant. Downtime and product defects declined. Clausel and a company official even went so far as to conduct workshops for hourly, salaried, and managerial employees, demonstrating that bad attitudes hurt product quality. Was this the beginning of a new era of good feelings that many had wanted for years?

Chairman Fites Arrives: A Knight on a White Horse or a Black Cat?

Meanwhile, the Peoria headquarters applauded such efforts, but the company continued to suffer through the recession of the early 1990s. Economic performance was lackluster. In an effort to reverse the decline, Caterpillar named Donald Fites chairman in 1992. He wanted to embark on a radically different strategy. He reorganized the company into profit centers and engaged in an effort to hold down costs as he attempted to make the company competitive in the world market. To him, holding down costs meant taking on the UAW. The auto industry, farm equipment industry, and construction industry had a tradition of **pattern bargaining**, whereby a settlement between one company and a union is used as a model for the other companies in the industry. For example, the UAW might target Ford in a given contract cycle for negotiation. Whatever agreement the UAW is able to get with Ford would be accepted later by GM and Chrysler. In 1991 Deere & Company was the targeted company in the construction/farm equipment business. Deere agreed to a very lucrative package of wages and benefits. In addition, it agreed to other concessions and provided increased job security. Caterpillar determined that a similar package based on the pattern bargaining concept would involve an approximate 26 percent increase in costs. Fites refused to go along with the pattern bargaining and offered a package worth 17 percent. He argued that Deere served a different market and did not face the same worldwide competitive battles as faced by Caterpillar.

The UAW was outraged and launched a strike on November 4, 1991. On November 5, the UAW suspended the ESP. Clausel was caught between the company and his union. He initially crossed the picket line to jeering union members. After 2 days, he joined the strikers, but the damage had been done. The ESP was dead and Clausel was censured from ever running for a union office. Fites took an extremely tough line. Bolstered by the antiunion sentiment of the 1980s and growth of management power, he threatened to hire permanent replacement workers. The union ended the strike, and Fites imposed a mandated agreement. Many saw this as a major embarrassment for the union and the end of a promising new era in labor-management relations. Production was slowed, grievances increased significantly, and new ESP buttons were issued by the union that read Employees Stop Participating.

From a bottom-line standpoint, the company may have come out ahead. The mandated contract, as compared with the UAW demands, saved about $80 million over 3 years as opposed to the estimated $50 million savings from the employee involvement plans. Many wondered, however, whether the long-term damage to morale and productivity could ever be undone.

Company Perspective: The Proof is in the Profits

By 1994 Caterpillar's sales and profits had risen dramatically, recovering from the recession-plagued years 1991 and 1992 (Exhibit 16.1). The 1994 earnings were $955 million on sales of $14 billion worldwide, finishing Caterpillar's fifth consecutive quarter of record profits in March 1995. Financial records were also set for 1997—record profits of $1.66 billion on sales of $18.92 billion. Caterpillar set an internal sales record of $20.97 billion in 1998. However, in recent years Caterpillar's profits have been waning due to the sluggish domestic economy and shaky overseas markets. Company officials report that this downward trend in profits is expected to persist as a result of the continued slowing of the economy as well as increased spending. Caterpillar maintains that the imposed settlement of 1992 was necessary and that labor

pattern bargaining A type of contract bargaining in which one settlement is used as a model for other settlements in a given industry.

EXHIBIT 16.1   CATERPILLAR BY THE NUMBERS

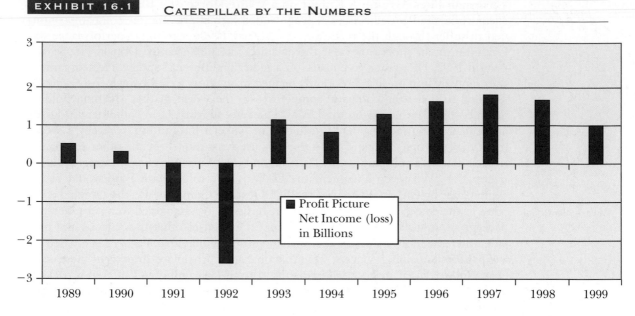

	1993	**1994**	**1995**	**1996**	**1997**	**1998**	**1999**
Sales (billions)	$11.62	14.33	16.07	16.52	18.92	20.97	19.70
Net income (loss) millions	$ 0.652	0.955	1.136	1.361	1.665	1.513	0.946
Earnings (loss) per share	$ 1.61	2.35	2.86	3.54	4.44	4.17	2.66

MAJOR PRODUCTS: Earth-moving, construction, and materials-handling equipment; diesel engines; and financial services to customers.

MAJOR COMPETITORS: Deer & Co.; the Case Corp, unit of Tenneco Inc.: Komatsu Ltd. and Hitachi Ltd. of Japan; and Fiat Spa of Italy.

SOURCE: Robert L. Rose, "Labor Strife Threatens Caterpillar's Booming Business," *The Wall Street Journal*, June 10, 1994, p. B4; Caterpillar Annual Reports 1994–1999, www.cat.com.

relations are really pretty good. It blames much of the current discord on "peer pressure." Even with threatened strikes and work slowdowns, productivity has increased. Management clearly believes that it won the battle and the war. The lean, efficient organization is poised to take advantage of the growing market for its products worldwide.

Union Perspective: Time Does Not Heal All Wounds
The UAW sees the situation very differently. The discord in the plants is growing, and a series of wildcat strikes has occurred since 1993. Grassroots rebellion may be building as exemplified by Thorpien's sign, "Cat Treats Workers Like Dogs." During the 1991-1992 labor dispute, the company had severe financial problems and the union believed that it had very few options. With increasing demand and increasing profits, as well as a backlog on several of the products, the UAW perceived that the balance of power might be shifting. The humiliating defeat in 1992 weighed heavily not only on union officials but also on the **rank-and-file** members. Most of the walkouts were not

rank and file
Regular union members, not union leaders.

led from the top down but by line workers, who complained about harassment and gratuitous suspensions. More than 80 complaints were filed with the Nation Labor Relations Board. In December 1996 the NLRB issued two significant new decisions upholding workers' union rights at Caterpillar. The NLRB ruled that Caterpillar unlawfully discharged Robert Boze. The chairman of Local 974's Unit VII at Caterpillar's plant in Mossville, Illinois, was fired in December 1993, in retaliation for participating in protected union activities. The NLRB also issued findings that Caterpillar violated Section 8(a)(1) of the National Labor Relations Act when it unlawfully placed a gag order on Boze on his return to the plant and affirmed a determination by Judge Rose that Caterpillar supervisor Charles Haddad unlawfully told a union steward to stay away from Boze because he was a troublemaker. Between 1992 and August 1997, the NLRB issued complaints against Caterpillar on nearly 400 unfair labor practice allegations.

The Future: Cat and Mouse or Will the Union Come Roaring Back?
The outlook for Caterpillar and the UAW still remains unclear. Despite the company's financial success and recognition for its employment programs, Caterpillar continues to be the focus of the NLRB and OSHA. In 1996 and 1997 NLRB ordered Caterpillar to cease and desist from harassment of workers and to post notices informing workers of their rights and promising to abide by the law. In August 1997 OSHA imposed tougher penalties against Caterpillar for failure to guard machinery properly against possible harm to workers. At the beginning of 1998, UAW Vice President Richard Shoemaker stated that constructive discussions had taken place between representatives of the UAW and Caterpillar. In March 1998 the company and union settled and signed a new contract which is in force until 2004. Subsequently, Glen Barton succeeded Donald Fites as the new CEO of Caterpillar.

The economic conditions both in this country and worldwide affect demand and profits for the company. Ironically, the better the outlook for Caterpillar, the more likely the UAW is to press its claims. With the continued profit declines forecasted for the company, the tension between Caterpillar and the UAW may dwindle. The Clinton administration, which enjoyed strong support from organized labor, had initiated federal legislation via executive order to prohibit the permanent replacement of striking union members in companies performing government contract or subcontract work. This order, discussed later in this chapter, was very controversial, and if it remains federal law, the strategy employed by Caterpillar in the 1991–1992 strike would be rendered useless.

Caterpillar's experience should cause concern in company managers and union officials alike. It raises several significant questions that must be dealt with in this century, including the following:

1. Can managers and union members work in cooperative team efforts without violating collective bargaining agreements? What do management and labor have to gain or lose by these arrangements?
2. Are cooperative efforts such as those discussed at Caterpillar merely a short-term departure from the long-term animosity between labor and management, or are they the beginning of a new era?
3. When a new corporate strategy such as that installed by Donald Fites is deemed necessary, what role, if any, should unions have in determining the creation and implementation of that strategy? What are the perils of inclusion and exclusion?

4. To what degree do outside environmental issues such as economic and political conditions affect the relationship between management and labor?
5. Did the election of the Clinton administration represent a significant shift in the balance of power between labor and management, reversing the decline of union power during the 1980s and 1990s? How will that balance change under the new Bush administration?

Strategic Choices

Managers have a number of strategic choices to make regarding the role of unions in the organization. Some of the most important choices follow:

1. Managers who work for unionized organizations must decide what type of union-management relationship they want. Once determined, they must take appropriate steps to make this type of relationship a reality. Many additional strategic choices will arise as these steps are determined and taken.
2. Managers who work for organizations without a union must decide how important it is to keep the union out of the company. If it is determined important to remain nonunion, management must determine the necessary steps to keep unions out.
3. Management must also choose the type of bargaining tactics to use during contract negotiations with unions.
4. Managers who wish to decertify an existing union must be aware of laws concerning this.

The Historical Development of Unions

To fully understand today's trends in the labor movement, managers should appreciate the historical basis and development of unions over the last 150 years. Much of the current policy debate and the future direction of the labor movement is rooted in the unique U.S. experience with unions that has developed within the context of democratic institutions.

The Early Labor Movement

union hiring hall
Office that maintains a list of qualified union members available for work.

industrial unions
Unions whose members work in "industrial" professions such as manufacturing or mining.

Early attempts at organization go back to around the time of the American Revolution. The earliest movements involved mostly craft organizations and were local in nature.[2] These unions had a common bond of common skill. They sought to protect their chosen occupation through entrance requirements, apprenticeship training, and a form of certification using the journeyman and master designations. This practice assured employers that they could depend on the quality of work provided by a union member. These same concepts of controlled entrance, apprenticeship training, and quality assurance serve as the basis of craft unions even today. In fact, craft unions often operate a **union hiring hall** that maintains a list of qualified individuals for work. This actually helps employers with the recruiting, screening, hiring, and training functions. The American Federation of Labor (AFL) eventually grew as the group or federation of allied craft unions.

History of Industrial Unions

Prior to the 1930s, organizing industrial (factory, mining, and so on) workers met with little success. In the 1930s, however, **industrial unions** began to grow in both numbers and power. Some would argue that the powerful emergence of the unions in the 1930s was a result of excesses and the unchecked power of large emerging corporate entities.[3]

The AFL was against industrial unions because it viewed the workers as unskilled. The unwillingness of the AFL to pursue industrial unionism eventually resulted in the formation of the Congress of Industrial Organization (CIO), which served as the federation for the developing industrial unions. During the 1950s the AFL and the CIO merged, and now most, but not all, unions are members of the AFL-CIO union federation in the United States (the most notable nonmembers include the West Coast Longshoremen and, until 1987, the Teamsters).

Because members of industrial unions typically are not highly skilled, industrial unions do not perform the same screening, training, and placement functions performed by craft unions. Unions' strength lies in numbers; they seek to get as many employees into the union as possible.

Legal Framework

collective bargaining The contract negotiation and enforcement process between union and management representatives.

As unions began to grow, many bloody, violent battles erupted between unions and management. The courts and the federal government played a role in trying to stem this violence and to provide a web of rules to govern unionization and **collective bargaining**, the process of contract negotiation and enforcement between union and management representatives about issues such as wages, hours, and working conditions. Each of these rules is described and summarized in Exhibit 16.2.

Changes for Unions in the 21st Century

In the early 1990s approximately 16 to 17 million workers in the United States belonged to a union of some type. Membership in the public and education sectors increased in the early 1990s but decreased in the late 1990s. Public sector employee membership peaked at 40 percent but decreased to 37 percent by 2000.

Although the *number* of union workers remains moderately stable, the increase in membership does not reflect the increase in the overall labor market. Since 1983 union membership has fallen 9 percent to about 16.2 million. This represents only about 13.5 percent of the labor force, which is the lowest percentage since the Great Depression (Exhibit 16.3).[4] In 1983 to 2000, union membership in the private industries declined from 17 percent to 9 percent. The percentage had been as high as 40 percent in the mid 1950s.[5] A major reason for this decline is global competition, which has drawn millions of low-skill U.S. jobs to Asia and other third-world countries. For example, 500,000 U.S. jobs in the apparel and textile industries were lost in the 1980s. Of course, many of these jobs were nonunion, but the downward pressure on wages has weakened the power of existing unions and discourages the formation of new locals. The fear that the North American Free Trade Agreement (NAFTA) would encourage even more relocation of jobs to Mexico was the reason that organized labor, in general, opposed it. In November 1997 the UAW and the anti–fast-track coalition succeeded in blocking the passage of trade legislation that would have eased expansion of NAFTA to other Latin countries. The union feared that passage of such legislation would put the quality of jobs, food supplies, air, and water at risk to the American public (see the Legislative Review later in this chapter).[6]

There is some evidence, however, that the steep decline in union membership experienced during the 1980s may be leveling off. There was no decline in union membership between 1998 and 1999. The National Education Association (NEA) is now recognized as one of the largest and most powerful unions in the country. Among

---

EXHIBIT 16.2	MAJOR LEGISLATION AND LEGAL CASES AFFECTING UNIONS

GENERAL COURT INJUNCTION
A court order is used to control the actions of another party. These were used by employers to stop strikes, boycotts, picketing, and organizing activity but are rarely used today.

SHERMAN ACT (1914)
Originally passed to break up monopolies and trusts, it was used against unions because they were viewed as monopolies in restraint of trade.

CLAYTON ACT (1914)
Sought to exclude unions from provisions of the Sherman Act.

DUPLEX CASE (1921)
Supreme Court affirmed earlier right to prosecute unions under antitrust legislation.

RAILWAY-LABOR ACT (1926)
First favorable legislation for unions. Gave railway workers the right to organize and bargain collectively.

NORRIS-LAGUARDIA ACT (1932)
Made it much more difficult for employers to obtain a court injunction and eliminated yellow-dog contracts under which an employee had to sign a pledge never to join a union to gain employment.

WAGNER ACT (1935)
Guaranteed the right of employees to form, join, assist, and bargain collectively. Formulated procedures for establishing a union and limited employers' actions. Created the National Labor Relations Board (NLRB).

JONES AND LAUGHLIN STEEL CASE (1937)
Supreme Court upheld the Wagner Act as a valid regulation of interstate commerce.

TAFT-HARTLEY ACT (1947)
Prohibited unions from refusing to bargain in good faith, using secondary boycotts, and featherbedding (paying for time not worked), among other things. Set the stage for "right to work" laws.

LANDRUM-GRIFFIN ACT (1959)
Regulated the internal working of unions and set standards for union treatment of members.

---

potential union organizing targets during the remainder of the 21st century are the following:

- Service sector employees.
- Professional associations (such as the NEA).
- Sunbelt state workers.
- Small businesses.

No one expects labor unions to regain the power they had in the 1940s and 1950s, but the destruction of unions would be considered detrimental to the economy.

According to the 1994 *Economic Report of the President*, the decline of union power results in a drop in pay for millions of people and could threaten the American social fabric.[7] Indeed, the pay increases for union members actually lagged behind those of their nonunion counterparts during the 1980s.

EXHIBIT 16.3 UNION MEMBERSHIP AS A PERCENTAGE OF LABOR FORCE

Labor's Diminished Role in the Workplace
A Smaller Share of Workers . . .

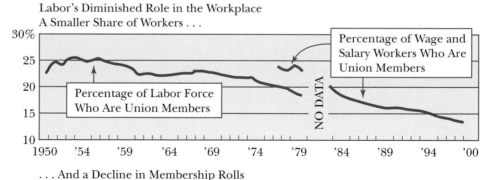

. . . And a Decline in Membership Rolls

SOURCE: Glenn Burkins, "Union membership fell further in 1997," *The Wall Street Journal*, March 18, 1998, Labor Department, **www.bls.gov**.

Of increasing concern for U.S. workers is the erosion of benefit packages such as health care and pension benefits. In 1980, 63 percent of workers in companies with more than 1000 employees had employer-provided health care. By 1991 that percentage had dropped to 56 percent, and by 1999 it stood at 51 percent.

Interestingly, a survey from Roper Starch Worldwide, Inc., reported that employee job satisfaction was at its lowest in 21 years. Could this be signaling an opportunity for unions to strengthen membership and bargaining power?[8] Some managers argue that unions have been their own worst enemy and caused their own decline in the 1980s. To remain competitive on a worldwide basis, these managers contend that unions must become more realistic and cooperative.[9] New attitudes are beginning to emerge in some quarters. In these cases both unions and companies are exhibiting a willingness to try new cooperative arrangements. In a landmark report in February 1994, the AFL-CIO encouraged its members to become partners with management to increase productivity. Efforts such as those between Xerox and Amalgamated Clothing & Textile Workers and LTV and unionized steel workers are becoming more common. The Caterpillar case at the beginning of this chapter, however, demonstrates how fragile these agreements can be, given the background of the traditional adversarial role between labor and management. This was critical in 1995 as the Bureau of Labor and Statistics estimated that 42 percent of the nation's union contracts expired, the largest percentage in 11 years.

Immigrants Add to Union Strength

During union negotiations for hotel workers in Minneapolis, contract negotiators had to explain proposals in eight languages to Local 17. Unions across the country have opened their doors to new immigrants (people traditionally considered the enemy). This is a result of the declining union membership and the strong U.S. economy.

Members of Local 17 come from Somalia, Ethiopia, Tog, Vietnam, Tibet, and Bosnia. Andrew Haeg of National Public Radio reported, "Unions from around the country watched this strike (Minneapolis) and noted that immigrants make perfect union members. Many have escaped poverty, torture, and war, all to find a better life, and they're not afraid to keep fighting for it." Their determination led to a 26 percent wage boost over 5 years for the lowest paid workers.[10]

Labor's Diminished Role in the Workplace

The future of unions is uncertain. The success of unions in the next 10 to 15 years clearly will be based on how well they match their objectives and strategies with the opportunities and threats in the environment. Unions must establish a strategic fit, as must other organizations. This means that unions must reevaluate their role in society given the major changes in the workplace over the last 20 years. A 1994 AFL-CIO report recognized that change was needed.[11] Let's look at some of these present and potential roles of unions and discuss how they are changing or might change.

Advantages of Unionization

Members' Perspective

Union membership provides a number of advantages to workers. Unions negotiate wages and benefits for their members and seek to provide them job security, social affiliation, training and development, and the opportunity to exert political influence. These are the most important roles of unions.

However, Reynolds states that union leaders are no longer billing themselves merely as the guardians of organized labor but also as employee rights advocates. They seek cooperation instead of confrontation and participation in both decision making and profits.[12] As unions seek to diversify their membership, issues such as health benefits for part-time employees, child care, flexible hours, and pension security continue to be of importance; but many workers who enjoy such benefits are now seeking increased influence in decision making at their workplaces.[13]

Wages and Benefits   Unions act as a collective bargaining agent for the rank and file within a company. In the late 1990s the success of these negotiations was somewhat limited. Union leaders contend, however, that in an age of givebacks and concessions, they have prevented deeper erosion and unfair singling out of workers for cuts. Increasingly, unions have turned their attention to issues such as job security in exchange for lower raises or, perhaps, actual reduced wage rates.

Health care benefits have become an area of contention between labor and management. With an aging workforce at one end and young families or single-parent families at the other end, basic health care is a high priority. The premiums have risen far more sharply than the general inflation rate, as we saw in Chapter 14. Many workers expect the employer to pay a full 100 percent of a health care premium, but, as previously discussed, employers are seeking to share the costs, reduce benefits, and raise deductibles.[14] From 1979 to 1988, the share of workers aged 25 to 64 with employer-paid health care actually decreased from 63 percent to 56 percent. Some of this was due to deunionization, and some due to a shift to small companies. Smaller companies are particularly hard pressed to provide benefits. Failed attempts to reform the nation's health care system in 1994 focused on this particular issue.[15]

In 1996 the Big Three automakers decided to attack the high costs of health care by treating providers like suppliers. They began expecting top quality at the lowest cost and telling health care providers exactly how to reduce costs. For example, the auto makers went to Wayne State University's Karmanos Cancer Institute in Detroit. The experts redesigned the institute's operations, breaking up traditional departments and grouping people who treat the same patients. They also helped the institute create a single computerized record for each patient. As the largest U.S. private employer, GM is also the largest private purchaser of health care. Its health benefits cover so many Americans that there are only three major ZIP codes where GM doesn't have a person covered. GM's new type of managed care showed an improvement in productivity at the institute of 30 to 50 percent. The UAW generally approves of the company's moves to scrutinize health care providers. Doing so relieves workers of blame for the cost. "The demand for health care is not driven by the patient; it's driven by the doctor."[16]

Job Security   Provision of job security continues to be an important issue for union members. In the era of the "go-go" 1960s, when jobs were plentiful and employment was steady, the job security issue was often one of providing protection against what the union considered unfair retribution and arbitrariness on the part of management or protection against cyclical layoffs, such as those that occurred in the steel and auto industries. Work rules and rigid job classifications also were developed to keep a certain number of jobs intact. When a company had considerable financial resources and slack, having extra positions was not a problem. Unions, such as the UAW, negotiated contracts with pay clauses to cover layoffs (supplemental unemployment benefits) and other clauses, such as the "30 and out provision" whereby a worker could retire after 30 years of service, regardless of age, with a very attractive financial package. Today, in the age of cutbacks, buyouts, and global competition, unions have difficulty maintaining these clauses.

Because of the economic turbulence since the 1970s, long-term employment is no longer assumed. When the slack disappeared, layoffs and givebacks became pervasive. Akio Morita, former chairman of Sony, espouses the Japanese philosophy of lifetime employment. He severely criticized the layoff practice of U.S. businesses: "American management treats workers as just a tool to make money. When the economy is booming, they hire more workers, and when the recession comes, they lay off the workers. But recession is not caused by the workers."[17] However, because of the severe recession in Japan in the mid 1990s, some Japanese firms laid off workers. Some large U.S. companies have no-layoff policies, but several of them have discontinued this policy under increasing financial pressures; these companies include Bank of America, Eastman Kodak, Morgan Guarantee, R.J. Reynolds Tobacco, and IBM.

Union leadership has increasingly turned to the issue of guaranteed job security in exchange for reduced wages, **two-tiered wage systems** (new workers are paid a lower wage scale than existing employees), easing of work rules, and so forth. Companies such as Maxwell House are making the distinction between job security and employment security. Employees with at least 5 years of seniority may be guaranteed

two-tiered wage system   A wage system in which newer employees are paid less than more experienced employees for performing the same job.

YOU BE THE JUDGE

Fast Track and the Union

On September 16, 1997, former President Clinton unveiled a long-awaited proposal to obtain special powers to negotiate trade deals. Fast Track, the common name for the Reciprocal Trade Agreement Authorities Act of 1997, would allow the president to negotiate trade agreements that cause changes in tariffs and other domestic laws without amendments by Congress. They could only vote up or down on the agreements.

The Florida Fruit & Vegetable Association (FFVA), along with the UAW and the anti-fast-track coalition, were against this legislation for several reasons, including the following:

- Lack of adequate safeguards and trade remedies for perishable and seasonal commodities.
- Potential of expanding NAFTA.
- Risk of job loss for Americans.
- Decrease in quality of goods received.

On November 10, 1997, the Clinton administration conceded defeat when a majority in the House could not be obtained. Clinton did continue attempts to gain fast-track authority for the White House in subsequent Congressional session but did not succeed. Under President George W. Bush's new administration, experts anticipate another push for this negotiating authority from the White House.

SOURCES: Douglas Harbrecht, "Free Trade: Fast Talk, Slow Action," *Business Week* Online News Flash, April 30, 1997, p. 1, available at **www.businessweek.com/bwdaily/dnflash/april/nf70430c.htm** (accessed March 21, 2001); Donna Smith, "Clinton Unveils Fast Track Trade Legislation," *Yahoo News*, September 16, 1997, pp. 1–2, available at **www7.yahoo.com/text/headlines/970916/politics/stories/trade_4.html** (accessed March 21, 2001); "Fast Track," January 30, 1998, pp. 1–2, available at **www.ffva.com/fastrack.htm**; "Fast Track Win Boosts Labor," *UAW: Washington Report*, November 21, 1997, 37, no. 17, available at **uaw.org/uawreleases/washington_report/3717/wr371701.html**; William Miller, "The cloud over Clinton—will it affect business?," *Industry Week*, March 2, 1998, pp. 10–11; James Cox, "Foreign trade: Expect eventual push for fast-track authority," *USA Today*, December 14, 2000, p. 3B.

no layoffs (except in the event of extreme economic conditions), but they are not necessarily guaranteed their present job duties.

A relatively new approach to the job security issue has been for unions to become more actively involved in mergers and buyouts through union-sponsored employee stock ownership plans, as discussed in Chapter 14. Some labor leaders believe workers can bring a different investment perspective to the company. Public stockholders want the highest rate of return, but union member-owners may be more interested in good wages or job-saving capital investment programs.

Union ownership poses interesting questions. What will happen if the union is forced to impose wage cuts on its members? The employee buyout of United Airlines in July 1994 tested whether this type of reconfiguration can work. The UAL purchase represented the nation's second largest employee-owned company ever. One factor complicating this buyout was the fact that multiple unions are involved. (See the United HR Challenges box.) Just how this will affect the human resource function is a serious, unresolved question at this time.

social affiliation
Community and social support and services offered by a union to its members.

Social Affiliation Unions offer important **social affiliation** for their members to provide a sense of community and to help avoid alienation caused by the work routine. Unions may sponsor social events and involve members in the community. During hard economic times, the union can help ease the problems associated with shutdowns and reduction in income by providing a sense of social and psychological support.

Training and Development   Many unions are instrumental in the training of their membership. As we discussed earlier, this is particularly true of craft unions. They often provide apprenticeship programs to develop highly skilled workers. As plant closedowns continue, industrial unions will need to be more involved with the company in helping their members to be retrained for new jobs requiring new skills. When International Harvester was preparing to shut down permanently its Rock Island, Illinois, plant, the union and management negotiated significant funds for retraining and basic job search programs in cooperation with state and local officials.

Political Influence   Unions often support political issues or causes. A great deal of legislation protecting workers (union and nonunion as well) has been passed as a result of direct lobbying or union support.

mandated bene-fits Benefits required by the federal government to be given to workers.

In recent years labor has advocated more **mandated benefits**, such as guaranteed medical insurance, higher minimum wages, and time off for family emergencies as provided for by the Family and Medical Leave Bill passed in 1993. It is certainly more efficient to seek these on a national scale than to resort to local union, state legislature, or even industry-wide efforts. With organized labor's shrinking percentage of the workforce, these national efforts allow labor to build coalitions with other political and social advocacy groups that may share some or all of its views on certain issues. These coalitions may be one way to maintain past union political clout.

Involvement in politics can be a double-edged sword, however. One of the difficulties with political action is that union members may hold a wide diversity of views. When union leaders take an official position or support a certain candidate, they risk the estrangement of rank-and-file members.

Management's Perspective

As noted previously, management seeks to protect the company's interests. Issues of importance to management are discussed in the following section. As a general rule, management has resisted unionization and has viewed it as a severe limitation of management's power and discretion. Management resistance can be classified into two types of strategies: **union suppression** and **union substitution**. Union suppression includes a variety of active legal (or perhaps illegal) opposition tactics during an organizing campaign. Union substitution entails progressive and proactive human resource policies designed to reduce the desire for a union. Such tactics may include high wages, complaint resolution systems, and participation plans such as profit sharing. Sloane and Whitney have defined the following five different management philosophies toward labor:

union suppression Management tactics, legal or illegal, to keep a union out of a company.

union substitution Management's creation of positive work conditions so that employees will not want to unionize.

1. Conflict involves open hostility and direct action opposing the objectives of labor. It was widespread before World War II and led to bitter strikes, union militancy, and sometimes even physical violence. Today open conflict is rare because of laws protecting the rights of both employers and employees.
2. An armed truce philosophy consists of a letter-of-the-law approach. The company believes that the interests of the union and the interests of the company are far apart. The company will stay inside the law but will be very rigid in bargaining and will insist on strict adherence by the union of even the smallest details of the contract.
3. A power bargaining approach recognizes the reality of a union but focuses on maximizing the power and posture of the company at the bargaining table.

EXHIBIT 16.4　　ADVANTAGES OF UNIONIZATION

UNION MEMBERS' PERSPECTIVE

Negotiation of wages and benefits

Job security protection

Social affiliation

Training and development opportunities

Social/political influence

COMPANY MANAGEMENT PERSPECTIVE

Reduced number of negotiations

Specification of work rules, disagreements, and grievances

Efficient communication and enforcement of predictable standards

---

4. The accommodation philosophy recognizes the rights of union members. The company adjusts to the reality of the union and tries to minimize conflict and disputes. There still is, however, a clear distinction between management and union roles.

5. A cooperative approach means accepting the union as an active partner in the decision-making process.[18]

high commitment policy A company's policy to develop highly motivated and well-trained employees.

Strauss states that a **high commitment policy** is a viable alternative to the traditional practices of the past. According to Strauss, high commitment policies are designed to develop broadly trained, highly motivated employees who are prepared to exercise high orders of discretion. The organization commits itself to provide job security and a career, not just a job. Specific high commitment policies may include the following:

1. Broad job classifications, team-oriented decision making, quality of work life programs.

2. Lifetime employment or efforts at least to moderate dislocation during economic downturns.

3. Training in both skills and attitudes along with orientation programs that stress corporate values.

4. New compensation plans, including profit sharing and pay for knowledge.[19]

A variety of attitudes exists today in the employer-union area. Many companies and unions are experimenting with a more cooperative role or the high commitment policy.[20] On the other hand, labor disputes such as the one at Caterpillar seem to be moving in the opposite direction. Regardless of the philosophy of the company, unions can play several key roles that can actually be helpful. These include reducing the number of individual negotiations, specification of work rules, procedures for disagreements and grievances, and easier communications. Each of these is discussed following and is listed in Exhibit 16.4.

Reduced Number of Negotiations　　Once a contract is negotiated with the union, managers need not worry about being approached by individual workers for raises or special benefit considerations. The manager merely needs to refer to the contract. From a planning perspective, this provides greater accuracy in forecasting costs. Multiple-year contracts can greatly reduce the time that must be spent on the compensation issue. Of course, the preparation for the negotiations and the actual sessions put a heavy load on managers, particularly human resource managers, once every contract cycle.

If a dispute over wage and benefit issues arises, the company deals with the representative of the union, not with the individual worker. Although union representatives may be more skillful in negotiations than are individual workers, the negotiation process with them is more predictable, and procedures are usually outlined in the contract.

Specification of Work Rules and Procedures for Disagreement and Grievances

A union contract can clearly define work rules and guidelines for settling disagreements and grievances. If an individual worker disagrees with an action taken by his or her supervisor, but the supervisor is acting within the rules agreed to by the union, the problem is not between the supervisor and the employee but is an issue that the union steward must work out with the worker. This may reduce the information-processing load on the supervisors and the human resource department. Lyles contends that, for financial reasons, companies may prefer keeping a union intact. He uses the example of a company not giving an employee a wage increase. If the employee is represented by a union, the dispute goes through a grievance process. If the company cannot resolve the issue and has to go to arbitration, it may spend $2500. On the other hand, without a union, the dispute may end up in court and the same complaint may cost the company $250,000.[21]

Efficient Communication and Enforcement of Predictable Standards

Communication can be facilitated by a union contract. In many cases the company communicates with the union and the union in turn with its members. Because the contract often spells out in some detail the various procedures, work rules, and ways of handling disputes, the total number of channels may be reduced as compared with the situation for a union-free environment. This may eventually benefit management as well. If participative management is introduced into a plant, the communication channels that already exist can be used to help smooth the environment.[22] A 1993 National Labor Relations Board ruling prohibits communication with teams regarding work rules and working conditions if they are seen as going around union agreements. Managers in union companies need to be clear about the NLRB ruling when working with teams.[23]

Unions can be the source of highly qualified, well-trained, and disciplined workers, which can help to maintain productivity and high standards. This is especially true for craft unions, such as carpenters, electricians, steamfitters, millwrights, tool and die makers, and the like. They may have long apprentice programs, certification examinations, and high levels of craft pride. Building contractors often hire from union halls rather than maintain their own employee rolls. One advantage to the employer is the ability to hire only for the duration of the project. The company, although being assured of adequately trained employees, does not have to permanently employ workers in slack demand phases.

Unionization holds advantages for both members and management. Management can reap certain benefits from a carefully and skillfully managed union relationship.

HR CHALLENGES

United Airlines: United We Fly; Divided We Crash

In recent years the skies have been stormy and turbulent for the airline that touts the motto "Fly the Friendly Skies of United." The nation's largest air carrier, with 101,500 employees and 614 aircraft, has been plagued with chronic financial losses and increasing competition. United's shareholders and employees alike had been unhappy with the results and perceived sacrifices over the 1984-1995 period. The company has tried to hold down costs but has had little success in competing with the low-cost, higher productivity airlines. Starting in 1987, several attempts were made to engineer an employee buyout. In fact, between 1987 and 1994 five separate buyout plans were advanced. During 1993 the situation became more serious, and United's management proposed either a buyout/concessions deal or the real threat of asset sales and massive employee layoffs. With so many stakeholders pressing their individual interests, including management, stockholders, several unions—including machinists, pilots, and flight attendants—and even nonunion employees, a historic agreement was reached in July 1994.

The precedent-setting $4.8 billion buyout involved workers' investment of 55 percent in the company in exchange for wage cuts and other concessions designed to make United a sleeker airline. The stockholders voted acceptance by an overwhelming 70 percent majority. Support by union members was certainly not unanimous. The pilots' union, which was leading the buyout, faced significant objections from many members of the machinists' union, who believed that double-digit wage cuts were a steep price to pay. Nevertheless, enough members went along to seal the deal. Under the agreement, the unions were given three seats on the board of directors and therefore had input into the selection of the new CEO Gerald Greenwald, the former Chrysler executive who helped to engineer the automaker's turnaround.

In the years since the creation of the ESOP that made United employees its majority owners, the results have been amazing. For 1999, net earnings were $10.06 per share and earnings were $1.23 billion, both almost doubling the 1995 numbers. U.S. pension plans have been at fully funded levels since 1996. There were also dramatic improvements in service, with United establishing an industry benchmark by increasing the amount of space available to passengers in domestic flights. In an attempt to create a culture of cooperation and trust, United began a program called Vision 2000. This program is a commitment to competitive compensation and universal profit-sharing that will allow all employees as well as shareholders to benefit from superior financial performance resulting from improved customer service. United's success was tested, however, when the ESOP expired in April 2000. During contract talks, pilots refused to work overtime, voluntarily causing the cancellation of more than 20,000 flights from April to August. United reached a new agreement with the Air Line Pilots Association on October 26, which is retroactive to April 12 and expires in September 2004. The airline suffered additional cancellations, however, during November because of maintenance-related problems. A federal judge issued an order on November 17 instructing United mechanics to cease what the airline claimed was a planned work slowdown. Since then the airline has operated at normal levels and is working to negotiate a new contract with the machinists' union. United officials reveal that this new contract will make United mechanics, like its pilots, the best paid in the business.

Although United reported losses of $64 million in October 2000 as a result of the tumult it suffered over the summer, the outlook holds promise for the future. In May 2000 James Goodwin, who succeeded Greenwald as CEO in July 1999, announced plans for a $4.3 billion acquisition of US Airways, the nation's sixth largest airline. With this takeover, United anticipates yearly revenue increases from $18 billion to more than $25 billion.

SOURCE: Frank J. Dooley, "Why Airlines Crash," *The Wall Street Journal*, March 30, 1994, p. A16; Susan Chandler, "A United United Is Still a Way Off," *Business Week*, May 23, 1994, p. 32; UAL Corporation 1996 Annual Report; David Field "UAL 'nice guy' in tough spot CEO Goodwin loses union support more than US Airways merger," *USA Today*, July 16, 2000, p. 1B; Laurence Zuckerman, "Summer Delays Take Toll on UAL," *The New York Times*, October 20, 2000, p. C16; Frank Swoboda, "Airlines Discuss Service Problems," *The Washington Post*, November 16, 2000, p. E11; Laurence Zuckerman, "United Gets Order Against Its Mechanic," *The New York Times*, November 18, 2000, p. C1; "United Cancels Fewer Flights," *The Washington Post*, November 24, 2000, p. E02; "United-ALPHA 2000 – Summary," available at **www.ual.com** (accessed January, 2001).

Using Teams Could Be Hazardous to Your Company's Health

Using employee teams to solve problems can be a tricky and difficult issue in light of a controversial 1992 NLRB ruling against Electromation, Inc. of Elkhart, Indiana. Suppose that several employees approach a company's human resource manager, asking that smoking be banned in the plant. Other employees object to this outright ban and prefer that the current policy of designated smoking areas be maintained. The manager decides that the best way to resolve this conflict is to form an employee committee. This sounds like a good idea, but it may violate the law, according to the NLRB ruling.

In the case of Electromation, the Teamsters Union objected to committees that had been formed to deal with issues such as absenteeism, smoking policies, communication networks, attendance bonuses, and pay progression for premium positions. The Teamsters contended that such committees violated a prohibition against company unions. The NLRB agreed. Compounding the problem, the NLRB confused the difference between what constitutes a company union and a team. The NLRB ruling bans employer domination of the team or any attempt to interfere with ongoing company and labor relationships. A team is defined very broadly as any group of two or more employees who discuss workplace problems with management members in an attempt to resolve them.

U.S. Representative Steve Gunderson (R-Wisconsin) argued that the effect of this ruling may be very chilling to even the most successful employee involvement teams. He contends that "the effect is that management refinements concerns—including health and safety concerns—may be illegal if they result from dialogue between management and an employee group. . . . How can any committee talk about any issue in the workplace without crossing the fine line into conditions of work?"

In 1996 Congress approved a bill developed to protect such employee involvement programs, called the Team Act. However, the bill was 14 Senate votes short of the number necessary to override a presidential veto, and President Clinton vetoed the bill. Labor unions, a large constituency of former President Clinton, perceive such programs as a threat in that they wrongly assume the role of unions in representing employee interests.

Despite the obvious intentions of the Electromation ruling, employers seem to be experimenting more with nonunion groups. Management attorneys claim that although their clients do not openly disobey Electromation, they do not rigorously adhere to the policy restrictions set forth in the ruling. Nearly a decade after the Electromation ruling, nonunion employee teams continue to exist in a "zone of fuzzy compliance."

SOURCE: Adapted from Steve Gunderson, "NLRB Muddies Regulator Waters," *The Wall Street Journal*, February 1, 1993, p. A10; Del Jones, "CEOs: Legalize worker teams," *USA Today*, June 24, 1996, p. 1A; Jonathan Marshall, "Work Teams Under Attack," *The San Francisco Chronicle*, July 5, 1996, p. E1; Chris Black, "Labor gets edge in Senate," *The Boston Globe*, July 11, 1996, p. 51; Michael LeRoy, "Are employers constrained in the use of employee participation groups by section 8(a)(2) of the National Labor Relations Act?," *Journal of Labor Research*, Winter 1999, pp. 53–71.

Of course, management also pays a price for these benefits. In the late 1980s Trowbridge identified several approaches that unions and companies were exploring. More than a decade later, companies and unions continue to employ these approaches, which include the following:

1. Gainsharing, that is, paying workers exceeding base productivity levels.
2. Employee participation in decision making, also known as jointness programs.
3. Employment security and productivity agreements.
4. Corporate acceptance of the union in a partnership role.[24]

The point here is that, once a company has been unionized, managers need to make the best of the situation and exploit potential new areas of productive relationships.

The Role of Labor Unions in Society Today

As the Caterpillar case indicates, the role, power, and relative influence of unions changed dramatically in the 1980s and 1990s. Human resource managers need to be aware of these changes. Several strategic variables must be considered to understand the labor situation in this century. Let us consider them one at a time.

Strategic Variables

Competition When high-quality, price-competitive foreign products started making inroads in the 1970s and 1980s, many previously insulated U.S. corporations had to compete with the manufacturing facilities of countries such as Japan, China, Poland, and Mexico that had significantly lower wage rates. Often higher-quality products could be sold at a significantly lower rate than products made in the United States.

Fluctuating currency exchange rates, along with what many economists and politicians considered unfair trade barriers for U.S. products, made the strong export industry decline. During the 1980s, for example, the United States went from the status of being the largest creditor nation to that of being the largest debtor nation. This foreign competition limits the ability of U.S. companies to pass along higher labor costs in the form of increased prices.

Foreign competition is increasing. The growth of sophistication among third-world nations such as Korea, Malaysia, and the People's Republic of China promises to keep pressure on U.S. companies. The growing power of Europe, particularly of Germany, offers competition to many U.S. core industries. Political and economic changes in Eastern Europe and the dissolution of the Soviet Union promise additional sources of competition as well as opportunity. To summarize, the industrial corporations that have been the stronghold of labor unions must now truly compete in a worldwide market.

Domestic competition by nonunion workers can radically affect a labor union's ability to negotiate. Consider, for example, the long and bitter dispute between Local P-9 of the United Food and Commercial Workers and the George A. Hormel Company in Minnesota. For years, the company and union prospered together and there was relative labor peace. Then Iowa Beef Processors (IBP) became more aggressive. IBP set out to be a low-cost, price-leading firm by holding labor costs to a minimum. Riding the antiunion sentiment of the late 1970s and early 1980s, IBP was successful in setting up nonunion shops. In the process it created significant price competition for established union firms such as Oscar Meyer, Wilson Foods, and Hormel. To remain competitive, Hormel sought major concessions from its unionized workforce. The result was a long and bitter strike. An interesting feature of this labor dispute was that the national union was opposed to it and ordered the strike ended, but the P-9 defied the national union and continued the walkout.[25] This **nonunion competition** has become a major concern for large national unions. In many cases the choice is between a crippling strike seeking wage and benefit concessions and forcing the company into bankruptcy.

nonunion competition Competition from a company that does not employ a unionized workforce.

Antiunion Sentiment Clearly, the 1980s saw a dramatic shift in the sentiment toward unions. According to a Gallup poll, labor's approval rating dropped from 76 percent in 1957 to about 66 percent in this new millennium having increased some 10 percent since 1981.[26] A number of factors contributed to that change, including

International Labor Markets Are a Two-Way Street

The Exit Route

Organized labor fought hard against the passage of the North American Free Trade Agreement (NAFTA). Labor has argued that such agreements result either in loss of U.S. jobs to offshore facilities, including Mexico, or in suppressing U.S. wage rates under threat of reallocation. This indeed may be true in certain low-wage factories that employ unskilled workers. Monroe Manufacturing Company of Monroe, Louisiana, provides a case in point. Monroe, which produces a variety of baby products, pays many of its workers the $5.15 minimum wage. President Edward Hankin bluntly tells his workers: "You know what the job paid when you applied for it . . . if I can't compete in America with American jobs, I'll take your jobs overseas where we can be competitive." The workers face a dilemma. Many of them find that the wage is not enough to support a family, but the company has argued that it can take the jobs out of the country, paying hourly rates of 70 cents in Mexico and 8 cents in China.

Ironically, the low wage rate and low skill levels make this labor force difficult to organize. Union organizers can argue that the employees are not receiving a fair rate, but the company can counter that it will move work out of the country if it has to pay higher rates. Workers do not consider these to be idle threats because more than 1.2 million manufacturing jobs were moved to other countries during the 1980s.

The Entry Route

On the other hand, European car manufacturers indicate that worldwide competition can actually benefit U.S. skilled workers. In an attempt to expand its North American sales and given the relatively high expense of producing automobiles in Europe, Mercedes-Benz has built a new plant in Alabama. BMW likewise opened a South Carolina facility in 1995. A partnership of government, private sector, and labor leaders worked very closely with these companies to convince them to locate

in these southern states. These plants join an already long list of foreign auto plants in the United States, including Honda's in Marysville, Ohio, Toyota's in Georgetown, Kentucky, and Mazda's in Flat Rock, Michigan.

Those who wish to promote and preserve free and open markets worldwide give the following reasons for supporting international trade:

- Free trade benefits American businesses and consumers by ensuring that markets are open to U.S. exports and that American consumers have a greater and more affordable selection of products at home.
- Free trade ensures America's competitive edge in the global economy.
- Free trade is good for the U.S. economy. It encourages the creation of trade-related jobs, which pay more than non-trade related jobs.

In the years following the passage of NAFTA, the consensus is that the feared effects of this agreement have not materialized. In fact, by 1997 the Labor Department reported that although 128,303 U.S. workers had lost their jobs as a result of the agreement, 2.2 million jobs had been created each year of NAFTA's existence. As the United States proceeds into the 21st century, it continues to strive toward trade liberalization. Although existing worker anxieties must be addressed, the elimination of remaining trade barriers, estimated to generate more than $600 billion in purchasing power for consumers globally, promises substantial benefits to those in the United States and the rest of the world.

SOURCE: Ron Suskind, "Tough Vote: Threat of Cheap Labor Abroad Complicates Decisions to Unionize," *The Wall Street Journal*, July 28, 1992, pp. A1, A8; AIADA Homepage, "AIADA Position on International Trade," January 30, 1988, p 1, available at **www.aiada.org/gr/issues/trade/pptrade.htm**; Paul Magnusson, Elisabeth Malkin, Bill Vlasic, "Nafta: Where's That 'Giant Sucking Sound'?" *Business Week*, July 7, 1997, p. 45; Joe McKinney, "NAFTA: Four years down the road," *Baylor Business Review*, Spring 1999, pp. 22–23; Robert Litan, "Trade policy: What next?" *The Brookings Review*, Fall 2000, pp. 41–43.

EXHIBIT 16.5   FACTORS LEADING TO ANTIUNION SENTIMENT

Well-publicized union corruption cases
Personal inconvenience of public from strike or slowdown
Perception of inflationary wages caused by unions
"Me" generation unwilling to join communal group
Strikes by professionals, such as teachers, viewed as "unprofessional"
View that unions have narrow, parochial interests and are antithetical to the common good
Political rhetoric of Reagan administration during the 1980s

well-publicized union corruption cases—such as that of Jackie Presser, the Teamsters president—which still contribute to the perception of corruption even today; [27] the disruption of the public conveniences via airline, train, or bus strikes, such as the public transit workers' strike in Los Angeles in the summer of 1994; a public perception that high union wage settlements led to inflationary cycles; and a generation more dedicated to personal goals than to group action. Also, strikes by public employees, such as teachers, produced very mixed reactions. Many Americans believed that the unions epitomized parochial greed rather than the public good.

President Reagan's firing of the air traffic controllers in 1981 may have served as the watershed that demonstrated the change in the public's attitude toward labor. Even though such **illegal strikes** by public employees happened on occasion, it was unthinkable that the employees would actually be fired. Although there may have been some protests over these firings, there certainly was not a mass public outcry. In fact, the action was perceived by many as a bold, courageous step by the president. Exhibit 16.5 illustrates several factors that may lead to antiunion sentiment.

illegal strike A strike by a union that is prohibited by law or statute from conducting a work stoppage.

As mentioned earlier in this chapter, there is some evidence that the antiunion sentiment may have moderated some during the 1990s. Some of the tactics used by management during the 1980s such as firing pro-union employees with impunity have moderated antiunion sentiments. Successful examples of cooperative efforts to improve productivity at companies such as Deere, Xerox, and General Electric have led many managers and the general public to have a more positive perception of unions. According to the Bureau of Labor Statistics, contract settlements for 1996 were continuing to decrease.

It seems that the decrease in union membership has bottomed out for the time being. The AFL-CIO reported an increase of 100,000 union members in 1998 and an additional increase of approximately 200,000 members in 1999. These levels dropped off somewhat in 2000, however. This changing trend in union membership is attributed to increased union recruitment efforts as well as improved public perceptions of organized labor. In the late 1990s negative attitudes toward unions in the United States decreased from 31 to 23 percent although positive perceptions among the U.S. public increased from 33 to 39 percent.[28]

It is critical for human resource managers to be aware of public sentiment in this area as well as their particular organizational climate because such trends ultimately affect most organizations. In what may be more favorable to unions, the Clinton administration agreed to rehire the fired air traffic controllers the Reagan administration had fired in 1981. This appears to have been a symbolic gesture because most former air traffic controllers had secured other jobs or had permanently retired.

Dispersion of Labor   Much of the successful labor-organizing activity earlier in the century was based in the Northeast or Midwest, where there were large concentrations of industrial installations. For example, the auto industry was concentrated in states like Michigan and Ohio, the farm implement industry in Iowa and Illinois, steel making in Pennsylvania, and apparel in the Northeast. Because the factories were large and geographically concentrated, it was easier to organize and to control the labor supply in these areas.

Several important changes have occurred during the last 20 to 30 years. More factories and facilities are moving into smaller, rural communities, often in the Sunbelt states. One reason for the shift is the **right-to-work legislation** (workers need not join a union if one is present) that is more common in the Sunbelt region. In addition, many new specialized companies are small. Medoff maintains that unions cannot survive unless they learn to represent workers in small units. He estimates that about one half of all nonunion workers are employed in companies that hire fewer than 100 workers.[29] Former head of organizing at the AFL-CIO, Richard Bensinger, adds that increased recruitment of union members requires a "massive cultural change."[30] Large corporations may prefer to set up a more decentralized system with smaller plants. Service organizations, because of their need to be near the customer, also result in small units. The change in economy away from the **smokestack industries** toward a service and information-based economy may have profound effects on the ability of labor organizers who try to use traditional approaches to implement collective bargaining agreements.

Economic Conditions and Employment   From 1982 to 1991 and then again from 1992 to 2000, the U.S. economy experienced the longest sustained economic expansions in history. (A brief recession occurred in 1991 to 1992.) Overall job growth was occurring, despite the decline of employment in industries such as steel and autos. The United States experienced phenomenally low unemployment rates, less than 4 percent on average, in 2000. During relatively prosperous times, when jobs are plentiful and wages are rising, unions have difficulty attracting new members. It is hard to organize new unions around the issues of unemployment and poor wage and working conditions. In *Megatrends 2000*, Naisbitt and Aburdeen forecasted an ever-increasing shortage of skilled labor in the 1990s and into the present century.[31] From 1989 to 1999, employment in manufacturing decreased by 4.4 percent and this downward trend is expected to continue through 2008.[32] Many of the remaining manufacturing jobs will be affected seriously by computer-integrated manufacturing, robotics, and just-in-time inventory systems (JIT).

An interesting and new phenomenon occurring during the economic recovery of 1992-1998 has potentially negative consequences for union membership. Even though the economy was growing at a rapid rate in excess of 4 percent for several of these years, companies such as IBM, AT&T, and Kodak were making large cutbacks.[33] Part-time employment, which usually increases during a recession, did so during the recovery. Companies were filling positions not only with part-timers but also temporary workers, both of whom are less costly, especially because they typically are not paid benefits and present few problems when their employment is terminated. (These issues are explored in more depth in the next chapter.)

In this situation unemployed or underemployed workers might again turn to labor unions for help in difficult times. Human resource managers need to study the trends in their business to be able to predict the likely effect of such economic changes on the company's labor relations environment.

---

right-to-work legislation   State laws that give workers the right to refuse to join a union and yet be able to work in a unionized shop.

smokestack industries   Traditional, heavy industries such as steel, coal, and chemical making, as well as auto making.

FOCUS ON HR

Unionizing Healthcare Professionals

Historically, society in general has perceived healthcare professionals as choosing that vocation because they are altruistic and primarily motivated by compassion and caring. As in many professions, union organization in the health industry has been slow. In the last 20 years, however, profound changes have occurred. Dramatic technological breakthroughs, shirting demographics, increased government regulation and participation, an increase in for-profit facilities, and rapidly increasing costs have led healthcare workers to become more aggressive in seeking job security and in becoming a voice in healthcare reform.

In the fall of 1999, the American Medical Association formed their own labor organization, Physicians for Responsible Negotiations. Since then, doctors around the country have started to acquire bargaining agents to handle negotiations with their HMOs. Although money, benefits, and working conditions are important issues, the doctors really want to recapture from insurers the power to practice medicine as they see fit.

Another issue attracting new members to unions of healthcare professionals concerns the ratio of staff to patients. Healthcare workers contend that fewer staff caring for more patients will reduce the quality of service. As society wrestles with issues of healthcare rights, universal coverage, cost control, and access to services, it must also deal with the fact that these issues impact the relationship between healthcare managers, their employees, and their patients. Whether a growing union presence in the healthcare industry is helpful or harmful to the nation's healthcare goals is unclear. If driven to save money, a manager may inadvertently thwart many of his or her goals if the result is the installation of a union that, perhaps, neither the manager nor staff really wanted in the beginning.

SOURCE: Robert Tomsho, "Mounting Sense of Job Malaise Prompts More Health-Care Workers to Join Unions," *The Wall Street Journal*, June 9, 1994, pp. B1, B8; David Whitford, "Now the Doctors Want a Union," *Fortune*, December 8, 1997, p. 32; Tedd Mitchell, "Why doctors are thinking about unionizing," *USA Weekend*, July 16, 2000, p. 04.

Law As explained in Chapter 15, more and more employee rights have been codified into the law through court decisions and the legislative process. This trend has the potential to forge revolutionary changes in the workplace and the way companies manage people.[34] Broad legislation has been written to protect employees in the areas of privacy, severance pay, plant shutdowns, and discrimination based on age, sex, and race. Health and safety issues have been addressed at both the state and federal levels. It is clear that many times large labor groups such as the AFL-CIO led these actions. Unions recently lobbied for the Family Leave Bill (which was signed into law in 1993), the prohibition of striker replacement through legislation introduced in Congress in 1994, and health care reform (neither of the bills passed).

The lobbying and passing of legislation may be a mixed blessing for the unions, however. Support of issues provided the unions a platform on which to attract new members. However, once legislation has been passed or defeated and court cases have been completed, the public may no longer be aware of the efforts unions make on behalf of their members.[35]

Legal solutions usually apply to a much broader segment of the labor force than do those gained in collective bargaining; therefore the differential advantage of belonging to a union may narrow. Given the costs associated with belonging to a union, such as dues, limitation of individual action, and the requirement to participate in strikes, membership may be unattractive to potential members. Freedman argues that labor failed to recognize several potential issues that later became legislative priorities. She argues that unions might have moved directly toward a strong equal-opportunity agenda at the end of World War II, but they did not. Instead, unions fought to preserve

FOCUS ON HR

Union Attempt to Organize Amazon.com Employees

During early 2001 the Washington Alliance of Technology Workers, or WashTech, led a drive to organize about 400 Amazon customer service agents in Seattle, Washington. Amazon.com was in the midst of layoffs affecting about 1300 employees. These employees were being given the option of signing separation agreements that contained "nondisparaging" clauses in exchange for an enhanced separation compensation package. These clauses prohibit employees from making any derogatory comment in any format about the company. The WashTech union believed that the Seattle Amazon employees were especially targeted for these agreements because the office was slated to be closed during 2001, and the greatest union activity was occurring there. The union saw this as an attempt by the company to prohibit former employees from saying bad things about the company during the union organizing drive. Laid-off employees still received a severance package, but it was not nearly as generous as the one received by those that signed the nondisparaging clause.

Unions have had little success in organizing employees of dot-com companies. Few other unions have attempted to organize Internet company employees. In early 2001 the Northern California Media Workers Guild tried to organize customer-support workers at San Francisco-based eTown.com, a consumer electronics information site owned by Collaborative Media. At the time of this writing it had not been successful.

SOURCE: Nick Wingfield, "Amazon's Layoffs Include Agreement Linking Benefits to Speech Curbs," *The Wall Street Journal*, February 1, 2001, p. B1.

privilege, seniority, and preference of the past. As Freedman points out, the unions have been lukewarm toward legislation to correct past discriminatory practices, and in many cases have led the fight against such reforms.[36] Often the public has suspected that unions are basically special-interest groups representing a privileged elite.[37]

The trend toward legally based employee rights protection is likely to increase despite the decline of unions. Nonunionized members can bring potential pressure to bear that may, over time, result in significantly more benefits than organized labor can produce. The human resource manager must carefully monitor the legislative and court actions at the national, state, and local levels.

Enlightened Management   It is often argued that the management of many companies has taken a more progressive view toward the human resources of the organization. Unions have long maintained that they would have little reason to exist if it were not for poor and self-serving management. Whether for humane reasons or economic self-interest, many companies have begun to understand working in harmony with their unions makes sense. After 6 years of trying to organize workers at the Nissan plant in Smyrna, Tennessee, the UAW acknowledged defeat. The results of the 1989 election were convincing: 1622 workers voted against the union; 711 were in favor of it. Bucky Kahl, the director of human resources at the plant, stated, "We pride ourselves in being a company that functions in a participatory way. The vote was a statement of support for the strongly participatory management."[38] Less than a decade later, the UAW tried once again to unionize the Nissan plant in Smyrna. Their efforts failed by such a large margin that the UAW did not even call for a vote.[39] Management can take an openly hard line or a more subtle approach in avoiding unionization. In *The Transformation of American Industrial Relations*, Kochan, Katz, and McKersie argued that during the late 1950s and early 1960s, managers in nonunion plants started introducing innovative, new systems of human resource management into

| EXHIBIT 16.6 | STRATEGIC VARIABLES AFFECTING UNIONS |

COMPETITION
Foreign and domestic competition poses a threat to the unions' power base.

ANTIUNION SENTIMENT
The 1980s reflected growing suspicion and disfavor toward unions, but that may be changing.

DISPERSION OF LABOR
Many companies are relocating or building new plants in the South and rural areas, or in foreign countries, to escape the stronghold area of unions, particularly unions in the northeastern and midwestern United States.

ECONOMIC CONDITIONS AND EMPLOYMENT
Strong growth in jobs and nonunion wages have dampened the incentive to join organized labor. Use of more part-time and temporary workers has also reduced union bargaining power.

LAW
Many basic employee rights are now legislated or decreed by court decisions, thereby removing many issues from bargaining and negotiation.

ENLIGHTENED MANAGEMENT
Management tends to be better trained and more effective in dealing with human relation issues without being forced to by contracts.

CHANGING DEMOGRAPHICS/JOB SECTOR CHANGES
More older workers, part-time employees, women, and minorities are entering the workforce. Unions have been the stronghold of white male workers for the past 50 years or so. More jobs are being created in the service and information sectors, while there has been a relative decrease in the manufacturing sector.

their shops.[40] A number of union companies, such as Motorola, General Motors, Ford, Honeywell, Mead, Xerox, and GTE among others, have publicly committed to changes in the way they manage their employees.[41] An important question for both unions and management in this century is whether unions have a reason to exist in their present form and with their present objectives if management improves.

"graying" of the workforce The increase in the average age of workers because of the "baby boom" of the 1940s and 1950s and the "birth dearth" of the 1960s.

Changing Demographics   The changing demographics of the U.S. labor force can have a significant effect on the union movement. The **"graying" of the workforce** can potentially pit one segment against the other. For instance, older workers may be much more interested in pension and retirement benefits; younger workers may desire current high wages.

The entry into the workforce of more minorities and women may make union growth unlikely. The demographic shifts will be dramatic. Today's workforce is approximately 88 percent white non-Hispanics. Many of the current core workers are middle-aged and will be retiring from the workforce in the next few years. By 2025 the percentage of white non-Hispanics in the workforce is expected to drop to about 8 percent. From 1998 to 2015, the average increase of minorities in the workforce is at least 2 times greater than that of white non-Hispanics.[41] Unions that protect the seniority system will find it difficult to support the demands of the new type of worker. These workers will be concerned with different economic, cultural, and sociological issues. Exhibit 16.6 summarizes the critical variables discussed in the previous sections.

EXHIBIT 16.7	EXAMPLES OF THE ECONOMIC AND POLITICAL OBJECTIVES OF UNIONS

Economic Issues—Bread and Butter

Category	Example
Wages	United Auto Workers bargaining with Ford for a 6 percent annual increase for three years
Benefits	Teamsters asking for full family health coverage to be paid by employer
Seniority	Steelworkers negotiating with USX to give priority to longer tenured employees in awarding overtime hours
Working Conditions	Airline Pilots Association working out an agreement with United Airlines on maximum number of nights away from home
Security	UAW agreeing to two-tiered wage structure in return for nonlayoff clauses

Political issues

Category	Example
Political Endorsements	AFL-CIO endorsement of Bill Clinton in the 1992 and 1996 presidential elections
Political Action Committees (PACs)	Contribution of campaign funds to local, state, and national candidates
Endorsement or Opposition to Government Policies	During the Vietnam War era, certain unions supported, while others opposed, the war
Endorsement of Certain Political Stances	The American Federation of Teachers encouraged defense cuts and more money for education

Strategic Choices Facing Unions

Several strategic choices are open to unions as they fight for their survival and position in society. Each of these is discussed following and summarized in Exhibit 16.7.

Bread-and-Butter Issues versus Political Objectives

bread-and-butter issues
Bargaining objectives based on economic rather than social or political concerns.

Unions differ, of course, as to their particular objectives and goals, but the goals of unions in the United States can be separated into two broad classes. **Bread-and-butter issues** include economic concerns of members, such as wage rates, life and health insurance, paid vacations, and job security. Historically, unions have emphasized these issues. When Samuel Gompers was asked what unions wanted, he boldly declared, "More!" The late Jimmy Hoffa said the success of the unions depended on their ability to deliver "the highest buck."[42]

The second goal of unions involves political issues. Unions have supported or opposed the country's foreign policy objectives or allocation of government spending programs, such as increasing spending for education, over the years. The political influence of U.S. unions is usually indirect.

Union Membership Declines Despite Its Privileges

In 1986 the AFL-CIO created the Union Privilege program. The program was designed to help union members away from the job. John Ross, the communications director for the program, said he wanted the membership to turn to the union for any need.

The goal is to attract people who are not part of any collective bargaining unit as associate union members. Offering associated program benefits would tie them to the union and the union movement.

Several benefits are currently offered by the program:

- A credit card with no annual fee and a low interest rate.
- A union credit card to assist in establishing or reestablishing credit.
- Mortgages with rates at or below the national average and low down payments and closing costs with special deals for first-time homebuyers.
- College loans and job skills training loans for members and families.
- Emergency automobile service for members and families.
- Life insurance plans that Union Privilege says are up to 25 percent lower than comparable plans.
- Prescription discounts for union members and their families. The mail service prescription plan allows members to save up to 30 percent on most brand name medications and more on generic drugs.
- Savings on dental (30 percent savings) and vision care (50 percent savings).

- Legal services including a free 30-minute consultation and a 30-percent discount on services.
- College scholarship awards ranging from $500 to $4000 for members and families.
- Several other programs and services, including discounts on flowers, tax preparation, car rentals, and hearing care.

Despite the campaign to revitalize America's unions, recruiting has risen only modestly and has been unable to keep pace with the growth of the overall workforce. Although the image of organized labor has improved in recent years, it seems that organized labor has lost its appeal to some workers for several reasons. First, workers feel that the union no longer has "bargaining clout." Due to international competition and deregulation, the ability of the union to raise an employee's salary has decreased significantly. Also, the need for the union has decreased because of legislation protecting employees against wrongful termination and discrimination. Finally, with the most rapid job growth occurring in industries where unions have little presence and employment levels decreasing in the primary industries of labor unions, union membership continues to wane.

SOURCE: Adapted from Stephanie Overman, "The Union Pitch Has Changed," *HRMagazine*, December 1991, pp. 44–46; Stuart Silverstein, "Labor's 1997 Organizing Record: CAT yields to UAW Walkout," *LA Times*, November 8, 1997, p. 1; Steven Greenhouse, "Unions Hit Lowest Point in 6 Decades," *The New York Times*, January 21, 2001, p. 20; "The Union Plus Benefits—At a Glance," available at **www.unionprivilege.org/benefits/index.htm** (accessed January 2001).

Generally, U.S. unions have done best with the economic issues, and although in the past decade the economic paradigm seems to have faded from the forefront, with the new global economy in place, unions may be looking toward the establishment of coordinated bargaining practices across national borders in the future.[43] As noted previously, when unions have become involved in political issues, they frequently have stirred up hostility not only among the general population but also among their members. For example, even though the AFL-CIO endorsed Jimmy Carter in 1980 and Walter Mondale in 1984, the rank and file voted for Ronald Reagan in both elections. Since 1964 only three union-endorsed presidential candidates have won election: Johnson, Carter (first term), and Clinton.

A Change in Role?

adversarial relationship A management-union relationship in which each side is in competition with or seeks different objectives from the other.

Over the past century or so, the union-employer relationship has basically been an **adversarial relationship** with each side having different objectives or interests. Unions have defined their role as challenging management rather than cooperating with it. Unions believed this was the best way to advocate their members' interests, a philosophy consistent with the U.S. pluralistic political and economic system. However, many union members and company managers are now questioning whether the relationship is necessarily adversarial or if a closer cooperation might be needed in this era of global competition.

Cooperative efforts between companies and unions are increasing, including those by Xerox and the Amalgamated Clothing and Textile Workers Union, as well as National Steel Corporation and United Steel Workers of America. Frequently, the driving force behind these efforts is the threat to close a local plant or facility or a major cutback of the labor force.

jointness program Cooperative efforts by both unions and management.

Unions have responded to, talked about, and actually implemented workplace innovations, such as **jointness programs** (where workers and management pursue joint decision-making strategies) in a variety of ways. Many unions have offered their wholehearted cooperation and collaboration with the innovations. They follow this path because they believe that the adversarial relationship is hurting their members and that a change may help everyone involved. Finally, the unions can use the innovations to assert their own interests. For example, the innovations may improve the quality of work life for their members, and bargaining units will be sure to include the improvement in the next negotiated contract.[44]

From a strategic human resource management perspective, these cooperative experiments are important. If they are to yield beneficial results, the human resource professionals and line managers must rethink their positions just as the labor movement is doing. It may be as difficult for the managers of the company to reorient their stance toward cooperation as it is for the union leadership to put aside a long history of confrontation. Substantial training efforts can facilitate these changes. Cohen-Rosenthal and Burton indicate that any joint union-management training effort needs to include the following:

- An explanation of what the program is and how it will work.
- The basic principles, processes, and procedures of the program.
- Skills training in the specific areas necessary to meet the goals and objectives of the program.
- A component on commitment and motivation.[45]

Domain Considerations

Exhibit 16.8 is an illustrative presentation of several environmental factors that affect the union's strategic choices. Earlier we mentioned the changes in the economy that have affected the traditional strength of the unions: for example, the decline of smokestack industries, the increase of service sector jobs, the movement of jobs to the Sunbelt, a more global economy with worldwide competition, and the increase of jobs in small companies.

Several additional factors also need to be considered. High-technology jobs are often filled by well-trained, often college-educated individuals. This presents a new type of worker who has to be communicated with differently. Professionals such as accountants, nurses, doctors, and market researchers may consider themselves more

EXHIBIT 16.8 FACTORS AFFECTING STRATEGIC CHOICES OF UNIONS

closely aligned with management than with the unions. Yet the growth of professional positions has been significant, and unions must consider such groups for inclusion as the number of unskilled or semiskilled jobs declines in other sectors. Exhibit 16.9 dramatically demonstrates the decline in the traditional industrial unions and the increased membership in the government, service, and professional unions. Notice the steep decline of membership in the auto, electrical, machinists, and steelworkers unions. In contrast, membership in public, service, and education unions has increased.

The entry of more women into the labor force has expanded the issues that unions must support. For example, although women now hold more than 53 million jobs, representing 45 percent of the labor force, they earn only about 64 cents for each dollar earned by men. Unions must therefore support equality in wages between genders. Another concern of many women, as well as some men, is the need for child care support.

Today women comprise 40 percent of union membership compared with 18 percent in 1960. Unions seek to increase female membership because union growth is the fastest in industries that are dominated by women, such as textiles, hotel and hospitality services, and healthcare.[46] Although seeking to attract women to membership, unions also need to look at inequalities in their own houses. The appointment of Linda Chavez-Thompson as the first executive vice president of the AFL-CIO represents the union's effort to respond to these changing demographics of the labor force.[47]

One of the most significant trends in the labor movement in the last 40 years or so has been the growth in public-sector unionization. Employees at the federal, state, and local levels have participated in this phenomenon. John F. Kennedy's 1960 campaign promise and his 1962 Executive Order 10988 were regarded by the postal workers and federal workers as their **magna carta**, or their statement of rights and

magna carta A statement of rights and privileges.

EXHIBIT 16.9	UNION MEMBERSHIP DISTRIBUTION

In 1996, as wage and salary employment continued to rise, the number who were members of unions totaled 16.3 million, little changed from the prior year. Nearly three-fifths of union members (9.4 million) were in private industry, where they constituted 10.2 percent of wage and salary employment. There were 6.9 million union members in government (federal, state, and local), where they accounted for 37.7 percent of wage and salary employment. The following chart shows the distribution of membership based on industry and occupation.

Occupation	Employed	Union Percentage
Managerial and professional specialty	30,942	13.6
Executive, administrative, and managerial	14,263	5.5
Professional specialty	16,679	20.4
Technical, sales, and administrative support	34.187	9.5
Technicians and related support	3,828	10.7
Sales occupations	12,658	4.3
Administrative support, including clerical	17,701	12.9
Service occupations	15,897	13.2
Protective service	2,154	39.5
Service, except protective service	13,743	9.1
Precision production, craft, and repair	11,615	22.8
Operators, fabricators, and laborers	17,428	23.0
Machine operators, assemblers, and inspectors	7,584	23.1
Transportation and material moving occupations	4,862	25.6
Handlers, equipment cleaners, helpers, and laborers	4,981	20.2
Farming, forestry, and fishing	1,892	4.9

Industry		
Agricultural wage and salary workers	1,710	1.9
Private nonagricultural wage and salary workers	92,059	10.2
Mining	538	14.1
Construction	5,387	18.5
Manufacturing	19,653	17.2
Durable goods	11,642	18.5
Nondurable goods	8,011	15.4
Transportation and public utilities	6,623	26.5
Transportation	4,006	27.0
Communications and public utilities	2,617	25.9
Wholesale and retail trade	23,638	5.6
Wholesale trade	4,357	6.2
Retail trade	19,280	5.5
Finance, insurance, and real estate	6,863	2.4
Services	29,357	5.7
Government workers	18,210	37.6
Federal	3,284	31.7
State	5,132	30.5
Local	9,795	43.4

SOURCE: Bureau of Labor Statistics, "Development in Labor-Management Relations: Union Members Summary," **stats.bls.gov/news. release/union2.nws.htm**, January 29, 1988, pp. 1–2.

Unions Go "Digital"

Unions have long been considered part of the "Old Economy." The "New Economy" of digital, wireless, and high technology was believed separate and apart from unions and striking workers. Recently, mergers in the telecommunications industry gave union representatives a chance to challenge these beliefs. The merger of Bell Atlantic, GTE, and Vodafone created Verizon—and a host of labor problems. The Communications Workers of America (CWA) and the International Brotherhood of Electrical Workers (IBEW) made up 53 percent of the workers at Verizon, and they wanted the opportunity to sign up the nonunion employees brought into the company as a result of the merger. An 18-day strike in August of 2000 secured a future for these in unions in the newly formed Verizon.

CWA and IBEW strikers won the right to negotiate union contracts from Verizon when 55 percent of employees signed union cards. The union also limited the ability of Verizon to transfer work to nonunion divisions. The new contract also included limits to overtime, a 12-percent pay increase, a one-time grant of 100 stock options, and a 14-percent increase in pensions. Most importantly, Verizon had to make concessions in the unionization of the fast-growing wireless business. This was a major issue in the strike and a major departure in union philosophy. Union negotiators in previous years had been willing to protect current union workers at the cost of the unions' future.

However, the strike did reveal some internal problems for the workers. Workers in some regions signed a contract and returned to work while others were still striking. The CWA and the IBEW acknowledged that negotiating contracts for workers from different areas of the country was difficult. This will be one of the main difficulties when 129,000 union contracts with SBC Communications expire in April of 2001.

SOURCE: Deborah Solomon and Yochi Dreazen, "Verizon, Striking Factions Continue Talks." *The Wall Street Journal*, August 23, 2000, pp. A3, A10; Yochi Dreazen, "Minefield of Pacts Underlay Verizon Talks," *The Wall Street Journal*, August 25, 2000, pp. A2, A6; Robert Kuttner, "Verizon's Crash Course," *Business Week*, September 11, 2000, p. 28.

privileges.[48] This order provided postal workers with the ability to bargain collectively in all aspects of their job except wages. However, later legislation (Postal Reorganization Act of 1970) granted them the right to bargain for wages as well. The continued growth in public-sector employment and the relatively high percentage of union membership are changing the balance of the private and public influence in the overall labor movement.

The union movement must make strategic choices as this century begins regarding where it will position itself. Should it double its effort at organizing what is left of the basic manufacturing industries? Should it change its approach and organize more white-collar workers? Should it change its outlook toward women and minorities and move more of them into union leadership positions?

These are more than minor considerations; they determine whether the labor movement will remain a viable force in society. In 1985 the AFL-CIO issued a landmark report on "The Changing Situation of Workers and Their Unions." It recognized these questions and the shifting environment and suggested more cooperative and productive relationships with management. This was confirmed by the AFL-CIO in 1994. The only areas in which union percentage participation increased in 1999 were the nontraditional areas of the service occupations and state employees.

Consolidation

A final strategic choice facing unions is the extent to which they should consolidate. Should unions merge with one another to increase power and reduce costs? This

EXHIBIT 16.10 KEY VARIABLES IN THE COLLECTIVE
BARGAINING PROCESS

tactic of merger and consolidation has been popular with businesses for many years. Unions are now considering and taking such action. There have been 39 union mergers in the 1990s. Yochi Dreazen pointed out in the September 1, 2000 issue of *The Wall Street Journal* that small unions gain power from mergers, and large unions gain new dues payers without membership drives. For example, in July 1995 the UAW, United Steel Workers of America, and International Association of Machinists signed an agreement to merge into one union. Their agreement called for the gradual integration of such key union departments as organizing and lobbying. The combined union is estimated to have nearly 2 million members. This consolidation was intended not only to reduce overhead but also interunion rivalry in competing for organization of the same workers. Between 1990 and 1999, there have been more than 39 union mergers.[49]

Strategic Variables Facing Management

Managers many times must work with a union. The union may be a long-standing fixture that was organized in response to problems and abuses of past decades, or it may have recently been organized at the particular company in response to current management or economic conditions. Regardless of how and why the company became unionized, the managers must consider several key strategic variables in the collective bargaining process. Five of these variables are discussed in the following sections and are presented in Exhibit 16.10.

Harmony

Probably the biggest change that occurred during the 1980s from a strategic standpoint is the reduction in the confrontational approach between union and management and an increase in the more collaborative approach. Most managers recognize the value of harmony in creating a work climate that can lead to high productivity. Harmony involves working together on common goals without conflict or discord. At the same time, experienced managers would also agree that harmony may be a necessary but not sufficient condition for productivity. For example, harmony almost always could be achieved in the short run by simply agreeing to every union demand. However, in most cases, short-term harmony would result in financial bankruptcy and business failure.

Discord between a company's management and its union can have a direct negative impact on customers. For example, the strike by the Teamsters Union against United Parcel Service (UPS) over the weight of packages to be handled by UPS delivery personnel could have been devastating on businesses relying on UPS for short delivery schedules. Fortunately, the strike was settled quickly.

Managers must examine their history with the union and keep in touch with the current attitudes of supervisors and union members to increase the commitment to harmony whenever possible. With the fast-changing environment, managers and union officials may find that past bitter disputes color the present attitudes, which may be highly detrimental to the current interest of both sides.

Management generally recognizes the importance of harmony to the work climate. However, as noted previously, the potential return to an adversarial relationship is a trend that very well could continue and that managers in general, and human resource managers in particular, should monitor.[50]

Power

Unions exist to advance their members with respect to wages, benefits, and working conditions. Unions are seen to have power when they are able to deliver these for their members; when they are not able to do so, they are perceived as losing their power. Members may consider the union to have lost power if it has accomplished its agenda, leaving little, if anything, to negotiate with management. At the other extreme, members may become concerned that the union has lost power when it must make concessions or accept givebacks during negotiations as a way to save jobs.

When enlightened management commits to work with unions to solve disputes, the rank and file may question whether union leaders have become too cozy with managers, which was a situation discussed in the Caterpillar case. In such instances union officials may find it necessary to provoke a dispute to reassert their power or at least create the perception of a power play. It has even been suggested that managers sometimes let the union win these relative **nonissues** to avoid more serious problems. Exhibit 16.11 lists conditions that can lead to the perception of union power loss.

nonissue An objective that is insignificant and that may be given up for a symbolic purpose.

Power is also an issue for management. Managers may feel compelled to demonstrate that they are in charge. Many traditional managers view cooperation as unwisely giving away management rights and responsibilities. The board of directors should ensure that management exercises power only to achieve the company's objectives, not to fulfill the ego needs of the managers.

power tactics Negotiating tactics based on a side's perception of its power rather than on a willingness to bargain based on rightness or fairness.

The use of **power tactics** in negotiations has a long-standing historical precedent. Use of such tactics in bargaining may be an attempt to intimidate the union into making concessions that management might not otherwise be able to obtain. For example, management might suggest that plant closings or cutbacks might be necessary if the union will not concede to its demands. Likewise, a union might threaten to strike at an inopportune time over long-standing disagreements. For example, the union might make strike threats at a time it knows the company is in a high-demand situation and is making substantial profits. A strike at such a time could cause the company to lose business (and profits) to its competitors.

The relative balance of power has shifted in the last few years to favor management. Unions have accused management of deliberately resorting to power and

| EXHIBIT 16.11 | CONDITIONS THAT CAN LEAD TO THE PERCEPTION OF UNION POWER LOSS |

More enlightened management committed to working out issues rather than disputing them.
Recent cooperative efforts by union officials that contrast sharply with their past aggressive confrontational approach.
Necessary givebacks demanded by the company.
Reduction in overall number of employees and union membership.
Reduction in union campaigns, strike benefits, and so on caused by decreasing union budgets.
Fewer union-supported candidates being elected to political office.

| EXHIBIT 16.12 | CORPORATE STRATEGY AND COLLECTIVE BARGAINING IMPACT |

Strategy	Collective Bargaining Impact
Low-cost producer	Tough negotiations over wages
High-quality/ high-price goods	More flexibility in work rules to utilize skilled workers
Lower costs by cutting expenses	Seek wage concessions; reduce benefits
Downsizing—reducing overcapacity and inefficient plants	Layoff clauses, earlier retirements, seniority revisions, improved productivity
Merger and acquisitions	Common contract provisions; change in pension language

union busting
Management's removing a union or rendering a union ineffective.

making totally unreasonable demands that will force strikes, allowing the company to hire permanent replacement workers, which the unions call disguised **union busting**. Labor lobbyists continue to work on a striker replacement bill. Thompson argues that the simple, underlying motivation of the Striker Replacement legislation is power-union power.[51] He goes on to say that often the only defense a company has is to let the union strike rather than yield to unreasonable demands. If union workers had no risk of permanent replacement, the number of strikes would increase significantly.

Early in 1995, President Clinton supported the shift back to labor's power by initiating Executive Order 12954 to prohibit companies doing more than $100,000 worth of business with the federal government from hiring replacement workers during a strike. Companies found in violation of the order could lose contracts or become ineligible for future contracts. This order was, however, invalidated by the courts the following year.[52] Even though the Executive Order affected many companies, no national legislation has been passed.

grand strategy
A company's long-term plan and direction.

Clearly, power bargaining by either management or unions can have unintended and destructive consequences.

The Relationship of Corporate Strategy to the Collective Bargaining Process

A company's **grand strategy**, or long-term plan, must be considered in determining its position in the collective bargaining process. Exhibit 16.12 lists several corporate

FOCUS ON HR

Leadership Has a Price

In the summer of 1993, Northwest Airlines, the nation's fourth largest airline, was on the verge of bankruptcy. To avoid this dismal scenario, employees agreed to take an $886 million cut in wages. Top managers took an approximate 20 percent pay cut. Employees, including managers, received 34.2 percent ownership in the airline. CEO John J. Dasburg's agreement included a base salary of $463,906 plus an incentive-based bonus of $450,705. Finally, Dasburg was paid a special $750,000. In an unusual move, Dasburg agreed to give it back.

Commenting on the move, he said, "It's more important to this airline to accomplish its goal than it is for me to have another $750,000. Leadership sometimes has a price, and sometimes it includes my pocketbook."

Management has generally maintained that executive compensation is solely an issue among the company, the board of directors, and its management team.

Employees could make no legal claim on this issue, but CEO Dasburg's action may have been determined by both pragmatic and ethical considerations.

SOURCE: Adapted from "Northwest Air Chief Agrees to Give Back $750,000 Bonus under Union Pressure," *The Wall Street Journal*, March 28, 1994.

---

strategies and their impact on collective bargaining. For example, a company pursuing a low-cost price strategy may have to take a very tough stance in negotiating any significant increases in wages and benefit costs that would negate its competitive advantage. The company may be more agreeable to quality-of-work-life issues or to sharing decision making so long as costs are not forced up as a result. Another company may choose to pursue a product differentiation strategy that relies on a special, highly trained labor force. If the company can easily pass along these costs, it may yield on wages but seek concessions that require a reduction in the number of labor classifications, which would allow more flexibility in scheduling skilled craftspeople for a variety of tasks.

culture A company's or union's accepted way of doing things.

Companies that have been involved in mergers and acquisitions present special strategic problems for managers. One salient problem is bringing together two differing **cultures**.[53] When unions are involved, the problems may be intensified. Entirely different unions, with different goals and expectations, may be inherited, or different locals of the same international union may be involved. USAir's merger with Piedmont, generally hailed as a model of success, caused significant headaches in combining existing contracts with various unions. Fraze, referring to the merger, argued, "The thorniest problem for company officials has been the merger of existing contracts among the various employee unions."[54] Particularly difficult was the issue of pilot seniority, which determined who would sit in which seat and the resulting salary. The pay difference between the pilot and copilot is significant. This issue is currently slowing the proposed merger of United Airlines with US Airways.[55]

In this book we have argued that human resource planning and strategy must be tied together. This proactive stance provides an organization with the proper mix of personnel for its present as well as future needs. A significant change in strategic direction may very well require different human skills than companies currently possess. In the collective bargaining process, constraints and opportunities need to be examined carefully in terms of current and future strategic thrusts and whether the contract allows enough flexibility for training, relocating, promoting, hiring, or laying off personnel as needed.

Management Position Toward Unions

Managers have historically held different views toward unions. Some have been opposed to them at any cost and have even engaged in intimidation to avoid the entry by a union or to get rid of an existing one. Although this extreme position is usually rare today, management's philosophy toward unions in the 1980s reflected an increasing hostility, or at least a high level of opposition, toward unions. Some managers may believe that the next century provides an opportunity to correct the negative view they have held toward organized labor.

National Labor Relations Board (NLRB) The federal agency that concerns itself with labor issues.

Regardless of the shift, the collective bargaining process often indicates the company's level of power vis-à-vis organized labor. In the late 1980s and early 1990s, union leaders sometimes accused management of deliberately provoking labor problems by negotiating in bad faith. Clear guidelines have been set by the **National Labor Relations Board (NLRB)** regarding good faith negotiations, but labor would argue that the NLRB has not enforced these provisions as closely as it may once have.

Union Removal or Decertification versus Union Busting

During the 1980s and early 1990s, attempts were made to remove unions from companies. From the perspective of the unions, this union-busting activity has been perceived as a sinister attempt to take away the rights that workers have gained through hard-fought battles with companies for more than a century. Many times managers have argued that unions have become excessively powerful, are out of touch with the needs of their members, and are unwilling to recognize that U.S. companies are engaged in worldwide competition. These managers see the removal of the union or the reduction of its power as beneficial to everyone concerned, except perhaps union leadership.

decertification The removal of a union as the official legal representative of a company's workforce.

A union can be removed through the formal process of **decertification**. Until the Taft-Hartley Law of 1947, it was generally assumed that once a union was certified, it was forever.[56] Decertification is more or less the reversal of the certification process. It must be initiated by the union members. The petition must be signed by at least 30 percent of the bargaining unit members. The timing of the filing is important. The petition must be signed by at least 30 percent of the bargaining unit members and must be filed within 60 to 90 days. If all procedures are followed, the NLRB schedules an election.[57] A majority of votes to decertify is required. Unions have been decertified by their members over the past several years.[58] Management cannot initiate decertification, but it can legally support the decertification after the petition is filed by using the following strategies:

1. Meeting with union members to discuss the merits of becoming a union-free shop.
2. Providing legal assistance in preparing for decertification.
3. Changing the corporate culture and atmosphere so that workers feel they no longer need a union as an intermediary.

An alternative to a formal decertification election process has been used in recent years. Employees can oust the union by collecting 50 percent or more of the bargaining unit's employees' signatures and then demanding that the management stop any further bargaining with the union's representatives.[59]

If a company desires to remove a union, it must remember the following:

1. To be very careful in following the rules laid down by the NLRB to prevent the decertification election from being voided. At the same time, it cannot be timid in voicing its position within the legal guidelines.

2. To be prepared to change its corporate environment to the extent that employees no longer need a union.
3. To prepare the human resource function to change its emphasis after a union is removed from that of grievance handling and contract negotiation to creating an atmosphere in which productive cooperative arrangement can be facilitated.

Avoiding Unionization

Moving to Another Region of the Country

In an expanding market, a company may leave its union facilities intact and seek to open new facilities in a union-free environment. However, the closing of labor union–dominated facilities in the North and opening of new plants elsewhere without a union has been more typical. This strategy has been especially offensive to unions and is seen as one of the many antiunion and union-busting strategies that labor considers unfair and even immoral. It is illegal to close or move a plant solely to avoid a union, but a firm can often make a case that the move is based on cost savings brought about by lower taxes, a newer plant, or lower wages. As a result of this type of action, unions are seeking to bring more security issues to the bargaining table. Communities that stand to lose a major tax base are supporting unions on these issues.

During the 1970s and 1980s, a number of communities, states, and localities provided a variety of subsidies in forms of training dollars, wage subsidies, and tax abatements to lure new business into a community, provide funds for an expansion, or at least avoid major shutdowns. In return for those incentives, cities have often joined union lawsuits when companies decide to move to a more attractive location.[60] Although companies may argue persuasively that economic conditions do not allow them to compete effectively using high-priced labor, and in some cases outdated equipment, the argument often falls on unsympathetic ears. Community leaders counter that companies lose a measure of freedom if they accept public money. Dan Boroff, city manager of Clarksbury, West Virginia, states that companies "have the freedom to come and go" but they should not "accept taxpayer dollars to subsidize these moves."[61] The implication is that the strategic flexibility of a company may be greatly impaired by these agreements.

Often local and state legal action is taken to prohibit or restrict plant closing. In addition, action can be taken at the federal level under the 1988 Worker Adjustment and Retraining Notification Act, which took effect February 4, 1989. It requires companies that hire more than 100 workers to notify their employees at least 60 days in advance of a plant closing.[62] This allows workers and communities to better prepare for the impending closure. This legislation was heavily supported and lobbied for by organized labor in an attempt to slow its eroding power base.

Moving to Foreign Countries

offshore Outside the United States, as in Mexico, Canada, or overseas countries.

Another manifestation of the attempt to escape unionization involves going **offshore,** that is, transferring jobs from the United States to countries that are predominantly nonunion. These are often third-world or developing countries that desire and welcome industrial jobs. Although the workers may be paid anywhere from one half to less than one tenth of what their U.S. counterparts would receive, in many countries this wage puts the worker in a much higher economic class than most other workers in the same country. When the wages are low enough and productivity rates are similar to those in the United States, increased shipping costs and other costs associated with doing business in a foreign land are not considered serious limitations to competitiveness.

In other situations, however, companies choosing to move jobs to foreign countries to reduce labor costs experience problems that at least partially offset the advantages of doing so. Many critics, particularly organized labor, are quick to point out these problems, including the following:

1. Lower productivity per worker because of inadequate education, training, and incentives.
2. Lower quality of goods because workers are less skilled.
3. High costs of doing business in a foreign country.
4. The perception of a lack of loyalty to the United States, causing backlash by the U.S. public.
5. Lack of infrastructure-good schools, roads, medical facilities, shipping and storage facilities, and so on.

Some analysts maintain that these criticisms are basically the self-serving propaganda of unions and believe that U.S. companies cannot compete in world markets unless they produce for markets in a variety of countries. Locations can range from technologically advanced countries to third-world countries, depending on a variety of factors such as labor costs and proximity to markets.

These issues will not be resolved soon but will directly affect the collective bargaining process. Whether a given company is selling in global markets today or not will not insulate the company or its unions from opportunities to avoid unionization by moving to foreign countries. Very likely, more and more domestic and foreign competitors in almost all industries will consider using a mixed U.S. and foreign labor force as a competitive strategic weapon. Union officials and company management need to be concerned because this type of international workforce will likely become more important as a bargaining issue.

The fight over the passage of NAFTA illustrated the strong differences of opinion over the issue of jobs and competitiveness. For the most part, organized labor fought the bill and was supported by a majority of the Democratic members of Congress. They feared that the passage of NAFTA would continue to erode union strength and cost U.S. jobs. Nevertheless, a coalition of business groups, Republicans in Congress, and President Clinton prevailed in passing the agreement. They argued that a few jobs might be lost in the short term, but in the long term, NAFTA would open new markets and result in a net creation of jobs in the United States. At the time of this writing job loss caused by NAFTA continues to be very small. Only time will tell whether it is a good piece of legislation from labor's perspective.

Outsourcing

outsourcing
Buying parts or services externally rather than producing them internally.

A relatively recent trend that has become a major point of contention in contract bargaining is the issue of outsourcing. **Outsourcing** occurs when a company subcontracts work to other companies that had previously been done in-house. Consider, for example, a machined component for a large truck transmission that costs $150 for materials and uses 6 hours of labor at a labor rate of $33 per hour (including benefits); the total cost of the part is $348. The company may seek a small job shop that has a nonunion workforce and an average wage rate of $21 per hour. If the outsourcing

---

EXHIBIT 16.13	SOME WORKER CONCERNS THAT MANAGEMENT MUST ADDRESS TO MAINTAIN GOOD INDUSTRIAL RELATIONS

Economic-Related Issues
- Wages and benefits
- Secure pension and retirement benefits
- Assignment of hours and overtime
- Layoff provisions and protection
- Profit sharing
- Promotions
- Subcontracting limitations

Quality of Work Life Issues
- Clean, safe work environment
- Recreational facilities
- Day-care subsidies and/or on-site day care
- Work team involvement, such as quality teams
- Grievance procedures
- Recognition for work accomplishment
- Training and development programs that can lead to advancements
- Internal hiring policies when possible

---

subcontractor takes a $32 per piece margin, the total cost comes to $314. The company may decide to reduce its union labor force and buy externally.

The company can accrue other benefits by specifying that it will pay for only "perfect" parts, thereby eliminating scrap. If demand falls, the company can eliminate its contract and not be saddled with long-term unemployment compensation liabilities. Of course, outsourcing has some liabilities as well, but it has led unions to accuse companies of using it as just one more union-busting tactic. It is likely that outsourcing will become a more important collective bargaining issue. Unions often try to negotiate a say in which parts or services can be subcontracted.

Managers and union leaders do need to recognize, however, that outsourcing can work to the benefit of both parties in certain situations. It provides more flexibility for the company in adjusting to varying demands and can provide a more stable core of unionized workers. When a downturn occurs, these external contracts can be eliminated before well-trained, experienced union members are laid off.

Making a Union Unnecessary

union-free shop
A company that has no union representation of workers.

Many companies have never had a union or have had one that has been decertified. If a company wants to remain a **union-free shop**, it must take care to develop and maintain policies that will balance the needs of the company to make a fair profit with the legitimate needs of the workers. Managers must remember that economic issues are not the only issues that concern workers. Exhibit 16.13 lists a variety of issues that should be addressed.

It is not uncommon for companies to clearly state their commitment to remain union free and try to persuade employees that the company has their best interests at

Negotiation Rules to Follow to Reach an Agreement

Robert J. Harding, a veteran labor negotiator, offers seven rules to follow in negotiations to enhance the chances of reaching agreement.

1. Use the preliminary meetings to set the ground rules for future sessions. For example, the negotiators might agree that negotiations will take place during normal business hours, not in all-night marathon sessions.
2. Document carefully all meetings. Include who was there, what was said, what the intent was behind contract language, and what proposals and counterproposals were made. At the end of each day's session, the note taker can dictate the outline of the sessions and have typewritten documents prepared for review. Missing information or disagreement can be filled in. This documentation will help not only in the negotiation process but also in interpreting the contract once it is signed.
3. If the company CEO is well regarded by the employees, consider using him or her in certain negotiating sessions, particularly the early ones. This helps the CEO understand the position of the union.
4. Within the bounds of what is legal, establish a comprehensive file on the in-plant union negotiating committee. This can be a basis for

better participation and drawing out the union members who are perhaps the most qualified to speak on a given issue. For instance, if a worker has been with the company 20 years and a management representative believes that the current proposal might not benefit her, the representative might pose a question such as, "Janet, are you aware that the current proposal will give workers with 20 years' seniority only about half the benefits as those who have been with the company from 5 to 10 years?"

5. Accept union negotiators as equal peers. Never underestimate their abilities. A condescending attitude can hurt the process and may result in winning an ego battle but losing the contract war. Many of the union people are street smart and savvy when it comes to negotiations.
6. Sustain strong communication links with managers and first-line supervisors after the contract is settled. They are the ones who actually administer the contract on a day-to-day basis.
7. If an impasse is reached, consider federal mediation. This demonstrates good faith and a commitment to avoid a bitter labor dispute.

SOURCE: Adapted from Robert J. Harding, "Seven Tips for Successful Collective Bargaining," pp. 220–221.

heart. A formal policy statement is frequently made to indicate that the success of the company is based on the skill and efforts of its employees and that in the opinion of the management, unionization would interfere with the respect that the company has for its employees. The statement might go on to say that a union-free environment is in the best interest of the employees, the customers, and the company itself.[63] Such a statement may be included in an employee handbook and emphasized during new employee orientation sessions.

The company should be very careful in its policy considerations to consider all effects a given policy will have on the union-free environment. In some situations a company may have paid a substantial price to maintain its nonunion status. For example, a company fearing a union may be very generous in granting wage increases in an attempt to discourage union organizers. But the company may find that the cost increases cannot be fully supported by the market price of its product, thereby decreasing the company's bottom line. Having made such sacrifices to remain union free, the company must not risk its union-free status over some minor disagreement with the workforce. These issues cannot be left to chance but need to be a part of a

EXHIBIT 16.14   THE COLLECTIVE BARGAINING PROCESS

Preparing for negotiations

Settlement (negotiations, mediation, arbitration, last-resort options)

Ratifying settlement

Implementing settlement

Contract administration

comprehensive human resource management strategy that is linked with corporate and business unit strategies.

Violence and Sabotage as a Result of Negotiation Breakdowns

Sabotage and violence are not common today, but they still happen. Managers need to develop contingency plans to deal with outbreaks of violence should they occur. But first and foremost, careful planning should prevent this from happening. Today, most union officials and company managers realize that bargaining disagreements should be discussed only at the bargaining table. Discussing these issues with people other than the bargaining teams can cause very real danger to lives and property.

In summary, company management should seek an ironclad commitment from its union leaders to avoid, prevent, and denounce the use and advocacy of violence and sabotage. In especially bitter disputes management should have a plan to protect the lives and property of those involved.

The Collective Bargaining Process

The collective bargaining process consists of seven stages: (1) preparing for negotiations, (2) reaching a settlement through contract negotiation, (3) reaching a settlement through mediation and arbitration, (4) reaching a settlement through last-resort options, (5) ratifying the settlement, (6) implementing the settlement, and (7) administering the contract. These phases are illustrated in Exhibit 16.14.

Mandatory, Permissive, and Prohibited Negotiating Issues

It is important in designing a strategic negotiating approach that management and the negotiating team understand the types of issues that can be negotiated as well as those prohibited. The 1947 Taft-Hartley law defines three types of negotiating issues:

mandatory issue
An issue that is required by law to be bargained on.

1. **Mandatory issues** must be negotiated by law. They include such items as wages, hours, benefits, and other terms and conditions of employment. These have the most direct impact on workers' day-to-day functioning. Refusal to bargain on these issues can result in charges of unfair labor practices and an NLRB investigation. These issues are mandatory for both sides, not only the employer.

| EXHIBIT 16.15 | EXAMPLES OF MANDATORY, PERMISSIVE, AND PROHIBITED BARGAINING ISSUES |

MANDATORY ISSUES

Wages

Benefits, including insurance, vacation, holidays

Overtime rules and compensation

Subcontracting work

Posting procedures of job openings

Layoff plan

Shift differentials

Safety

Promotions

Stock purchase plans

Seniority

Management rights clause

Retirement age

PERMISSIVE ISSUES

Pricing policy of firm

Pensions and benefit level and rights of retired personnel

Supervisory compensation

Supervisory discipline

PROHIBITED ISSUES

Featherbedding

Hot-cargo agreements

Discrimination against protected classes

Closed-shop agreements

Union or agency shop clauses in right-to-work states

Secondary boycott agreements

permissive issue An issue that can be bargained on but that is not required by law to be bargained on.

prohibited or illegal issue An issue that cannot be bargained on by law, even if both sides wanted to bargain on it.

2. **Permissive issues** may be discussed only if both parties agree to do so. Permissive issues often include items that are of mutual interest, including a company's pricing policy, the pensions and benefits of retired workers, or safety rules. Neither the union nor the employer can refuse to sign a contract based on failure to reach agreement on a permissive issue.

3. **Prohibited or illegal issues** are strictly forbidden by law. They cannot be subject to negotiation even if both parties want to negotiate them. Included are closed-shop agreements, discrimination against protected classes of individuals, featherbedding, and hot-cargo agreements.

Additional examples of the three types of issues are listed in Exhibit 16.15.

In most contracts a special section called a managerial prerogative clause reserves certain rights for management that are not specifically enumerated in the contract. It might read like this:

> It is herewith recognized that all management functions shall be retained by the company. These functions include, but are not limited to, the full, complete, and exclusive control of direction of the workforce, scheduling of production, operation of the plant, acquisition of materials, production of products, location of such production, and the methods of sale and distribution of its products; the right to change or establish job classifications and descriptions; the right to introduce new or improved procedures; the right to abolish any job or department; the right to make and enforce reasonable shop rules; and the right to hire, fire, suspend, train, discipline, discharge, advance, transfer, lay off, and recall employees. These rights shall all be the function of management unless expressly stated otherwise within this agreement.[64]

Basically, managerial prerogative clauses allow management a great deal of discretion in the day-to-day and strategic management of the company. Traditionally, unions have taken the attitude that management can make decisions, which the union will challenge if it perceives them to be unfair. Management has sought maximum flexibility and has been reluctant to give up any more control than is absolutely necessary. These past attitudes, however, may be changing on both sides. For a variety of reasons, more cooperative-collaborative relationships may be in the offing.

In exchange for concessions the union may ask for a larger role in decision making. With increased foreign competition, the union and management may decide to work jointly on increasing productivity. Decisions to develop a collaborative environment will have a definite and profound effect on the collective bargaining process in two ways. First, the issues negotiated may change from economic issues to those related to quality of work, decision control, and jointly determined investment decisions. Second, such collaboration can take both management and unions into uncharted waters. Roles may not be as clear as before. Human resource managers must think through the implications of these changes before they get to the bargaining table. Many benefits are to be gained from cooperative efforts, but there is a price to be paid in terms of control on the part of management and increased responsibility and accountability on the part of the unions.

Preparing for the Negotiating Process

Each side should be prepared for negotiating by understanding its own strategic position, analyzing its strengths and weaknesses as well as those of the other side, and selecting the team for negotiating. Preparations should include a high level of planning and research.

Understanding the Strategic Position   Each side in the negotiating process should understand its overall mission. The company must understand its corporate mission and how the negotiated issues will affect it. The union must identify its objectives. Each side may identify certain "non-negotiable" issues on which it will not bargain.

Analyzing Strengths and Weaknesses   Labor negotiators for both company and the union should be as informed as possible of the strengths and weaknesses of both their own side and of the opposing side. Each is likely, therefore, to investigate the other's position; information concerning the company's finances, inventory levels, sales forecast, and market share is important. Information about the union, such as the level of its strike funds, should also be considered. These data must be accurate so that each side can evaluate its position and that of the other side. Sometimes the best way to identify current issues is by obtaining a clear understanding of the history between the company and the union and of the past negotiation behavior of each side.

Both the company and the union use the information obtained to create realistic negotiation scenarios. For example, a company with strong sales and low inventory could see this as a vulnerable position. To prevent this from hampering its negotiations, the company might choose the defensive and expensive strategy of increasing production for several months prior to negotiations. A union that has a large amount of strike funds is likely to come to the bargaining table with a different position than one with low funds. Such strengths and weaknesses should be evaluated carefully in planning negotiation objectives and tactics.

The human resource factor is an important element that each side should consider. For example, if a firm has workers who are so highly skilled that it could not operate in the event of a work stoppage, the union might use this fact to its advantage. If operations are automated to the extent that a certain level of service can be maintained, as has happened during recent labor disputes in the telephone industry, management might use this to its advantage.

Selecting the Negotiation Team   Each side must exercise great care in choosing its negotiators. Such factors as age and educational level should be considered. Union negotiators are usually less well educated and younger than management representatives, but union representative are often more "street smart."

Within the limits of propriety, it is highly recommended that each side analyze the personalities of members of the negotiating teams and try to predict how the different people will behave in the negotiating session. The following questions may help in this preparation:

1.   Who is the most influential person on both sides?
2.   What sort of emotional tactics are team members likely to employ?
3.   Can some negotiators be "read" more easily than others?
4.   Based on past negotiations, what are the tactics that each side should be prepared for, and how can one react to these tactics to gain an advantage?

Reaching a Settlement Through Contract Negotiation

Contract negotiations are the actual bargaining between the two parties to reach agreement as to a contract. It is one specific aspect of the entire collective bargaining process, which is an ongoing procedure because both sides work under the terms of the existing contract. Collective bargaining sets the tone for contract negotiations. For example, if the union and the firm have experienced constant disagreements and grievances during the current 3-year contract, this confrontation atmosphere is almost sure to affect negotiations for the next contract.

The result of successful negotiations is a written contract, signed by each party, that will govern the employment relationship for the period covered by the contract. Both parties must be willing to compromise on issues until a reasonable accommodation is reached. Negotiation between the union and management is the give-and-take process between them to reach a mutually acceptable agreement.

Tactics Used in Negotiations   Each party tries to maximize its position relative to that of the other party. In doing so, it may use a variety of tactics. Each party may use one or more different tactics while negotiating. For example, **bluffing and posturing** involves appearing to be interested in obtaining a concession that can later be traded away for a different concession. **Window dressing** refers to making a list of extraneous, unimportant demands that can be easily traded away if obtained. **Timing** is another tactical device that saves important issues until late in the negotiation process. **Misrepresentation** refers to the use of false data or facts to use as bargaining leverage. It borders on lying, perhaps, and involves using fabricated data, withholding data, or actually stating a position that the party does not believe. Careful preparations by the negotiators should ameliorate the vulnerability of each side to these tactics.

Importance of Power in Negotiations   The success of negotiations depends on the relative power of each party to get the other side to do something it would normally not do or to refrain from doing something it would normally do. The 1992 contract imposed by Caterpillar's Fites was the result of a pure power play; union members grudgingly gave in to his demands because they felt powerless to do anything about it.

One party to have power over another in the bargaining relationship, it must have something the other wants. A car sale provides a good example of this. It is much easier to sell a car at the price wanted if the other person really wants it. In the employment relationship, the union wants higher pay, better hours, and job security. The employer has these things. It needs a stable, skilled workforce that it can employ in a flexible manner to produce a sufficient quantity of quality goods at competitive prices and a reasonable level of profitability. The union controls the labor factor of production, and the employer provides the materials and equipment to produce the goods. The two parties then negotiate with each other over what each one can give up relative to what the other wants. Thus negotiating involves making a trade-off. Exhibit 16.16 is a simplified negotiating model. In the model in Exhibit 16.17, the two parties bargain not only with each other but also among themselves to please their constituencies, who do not always agree on what their positions as a group should be. Plant management and the company's board of directors are among the constituencies. Those of the union include local membership and the national union office.

Reaching a Settlement Through Mediation and Arbitration

In some cases the negotiation process breaks down and a settlement cannot be reached through normal channels. Rather than resort to a strike on the part of the union and a lockout or hiring of replacement workers by the company, the two parties may seek the outside intervention of a third party. **Mediation** involves having a neutral third party try to break a bargaining impasse. Mediators may be called on to get the parties to start negotiating again, clarify points that have been misunderstood, suggest alternative compromises that have not occurred to the bargaining parties, and improve trust and communication. Mediators have no power to enforce a settlement, but they may bring a fresh viewpoint into the process that can reopen the negotiations.

The Federal Mediation and Conciliation Service (FMCS) was created as an independent agency by the 1947 Taft-Hartley Act. Labor, management, or both can seek the assistance of FMCS, or they can seek some other third party to mediate the negotiating process. Because these mediators have no power to force a settlement, they must have a reputation of being impartial, fair, well informed, and patient.

bluffing and posturing
Feigning interest in winning a concession when that concession will actually be traded away later in the interests of a true issue.

window dressing
A group of unimportant demands that can be traded away easily if needed.

timing   Saving arbitration of important issues until late in the negotiation process.

misrepresentation   Using false data or inaccuracies in advocating a position.

mediation   Employing a neutral third party to try to break a bargaining impasse.

EXHIBIT 16.16 A SIMPLIFIED MODEL OF THE NEGOTIATING PROCESS

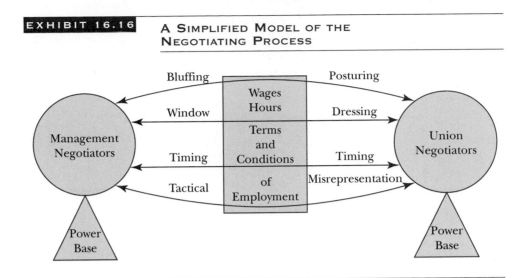

arbitration Employing a neutral third party to break a bargaining impasse via a recommendation that binds both sides to agreement.

contract rights arbitration Settlement of an impasse regarding the actual administration of a contract.

interest arbitration Settlement of an impasse regarding the content of a contract.

Arbitration, on the other hand, involves a neutral third party listening to both sides, evaluating the evidence, and making a binding recommendation. Arbitration is of two basic types: contract rights arbitration and interest arbitration. **Contract rights arbitration** consists of settling impasses in the actual administration of the contract and is usually the outcome of a grievance procedure that cannot be settled by the parties. **Interest arbitration** involves the terms of the contract itself. Whereas interest arbitration is used in the public sector, where strikes are illegal, it is rarely used in the private sector.[65] Normally, neither of the bargaining parties is willing to give up control of such basic issues as wages, benefits, working conditions, and so forth. They generally would rather rely on the negotiation process and the threat of economic pressure. In *The Labor Relations Process*, Holley and Jennings point out that relying on interest arbitration has some additional drawbacks: delays and extra costs may occur; the arbitration may put a damper on the working environment; arbitrators may be inconsistent from case to case; arbitrators may end up splitting the difference, causing the parties to take extreme positions; and reliance on the arbitration process may lead to overreliance on arbitration rather than working out differences through negotiations.[66]

Contract rights arbitrators generally come from two sources: either the FMCS or the American Arbitration Association (AAA). The AAA is a nonprofit organization that acts as a clearinghouse for qualified arbitrators. To be considered, potential arbitrators must be able to present their credentials and must be recommended by a representative of labor, management, and a neutral third party. A fairly large number of arbitrators and mediators tend to be members of the legal profession and may specialize in labor law.

Sometimes the parties cannot conclude a workable agreement. They may have not sought mediation, or the mediation efforts were not successful. With binding arbitration, both parties must agree to accept the outcome. If either party or both parties refuse to agree to arbitration, then a labor stoppage is almost assured.

The FMCS requires unions to file a 30-day notice of all contract expirations. It estimates that about 2 to 3 percent of these expirations involve a strike. Gramm, however, asserts that this may be misleading because of the number of small companies in

EXHIBIT 16.17 AN EXTENDED MODEL OF THE NEGOTIATING PROCESS

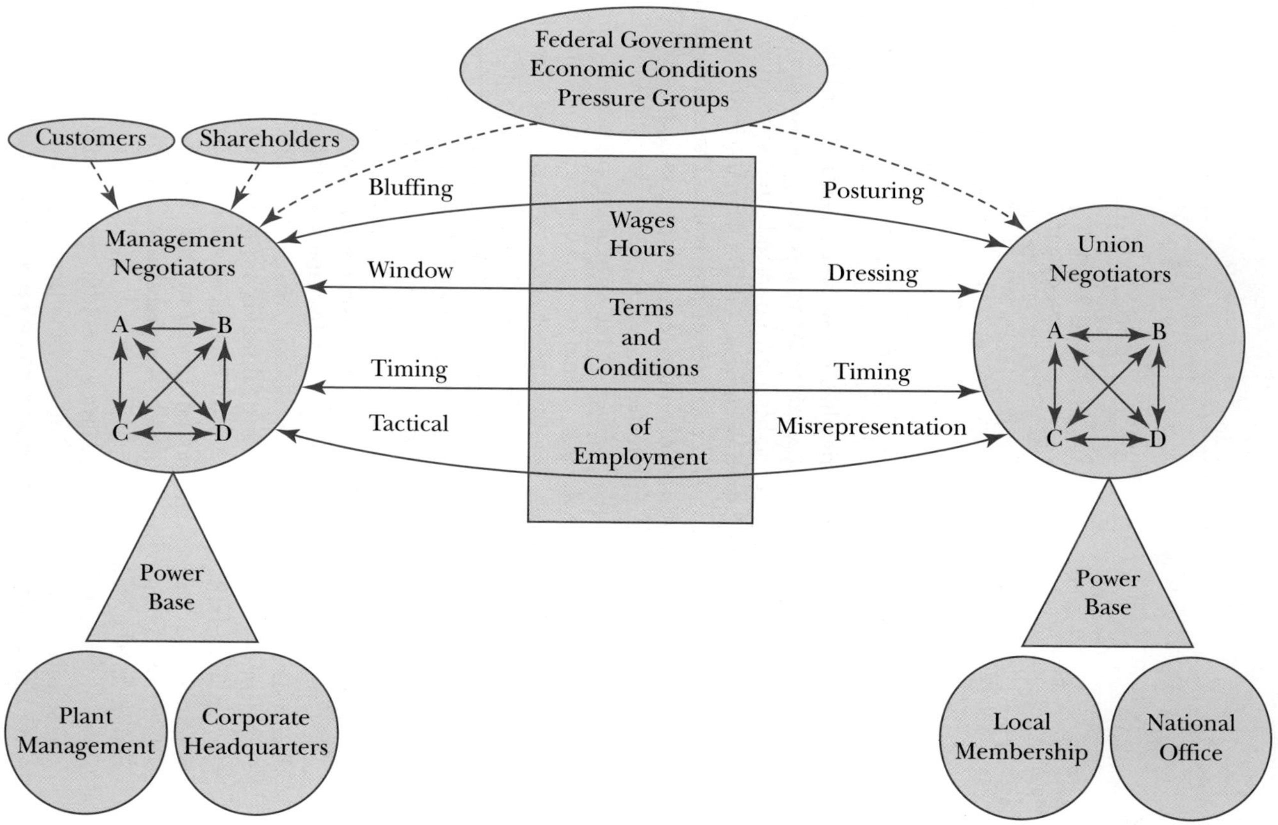

EXHIBIT 16.18	WHAT A STRIKE COULD COST UNION MEMBERS*					
Weeks of strike	Hours lost	Wages lost	Union benefits	Net loss	Hours to make up	Weeks to make up
1	40	$ 680	$ 300	$ 380	894.1	22.4
2	80	1360	600	760	1,788.3	44.7
3	120	2040	900	1140	2,682.4	67.1
4	160	2720	1200	1520	3,576.6	89.4
5	200	3400	1500	1900	4,470.7	111.8
10	400	6800	3000	3800	8,941.5	223.5
15	600	10200	4500	5700	13,412.2	335.3
20	800	13600	6000	7600	17,883.0	447.1

*Example assumes a company offer of $17.00 per hour (3 percent over previous rate) versus a union demand of $17.82 per hour (8 percent).

Table illustrates the point at which the union members will make up their losses due to the strike, assuming the company finally meets the union's 8 percent demand.

the FMCS sample. Her research indicates that between 1971 and 1980, companies with more than 1000 employees had a strike rate of 13.8 percent for a total of 2644 work stoppages. This rate decreased substantially throughout the 1990s.[67]

Reaching a Settlement—Last Resort Options for the Union

strike A refusal by labor to work.

Strike A union frequently takes a strike authorization vote to give its negotiating team a bargaining lever. A **strike** is a refusal by labor to work. It is not casually used. The union measures carefully the cost-benefit factor in considering a strike. Timing is crucial. For instance, if the demand for the company's product is high and in a growth phase, the company may not want to bear the opportunity cost of lost sales or alienated customers. On the other hand, if demand is slack and inventory is high, labor's threat of a strike may ring hollow. As noted previously, companies sometimes work overtime to build up inventories in anticipation of tough bargaining and a potential strike; this is common in both the steel and auto industries, among others.

A strike may force the company to give in on key union demands, but it is a high-risk strategy for the union. A 1989 Supreme Court ruling determined that if a company hires **replacement workers** during a labor walkout, it does not have to fire those workers once the strike is over (*TWA* v. *Independent Federation of Flight Attendants*). This can effectively eliminate or greatly reduce the size of the union. Even if replacement workers are not hired, it can take a significant amount of time to make up for losses incurred in a strike situation.

replacement workers Workers hired either temporarily or permanently to perform the jobs of striking employees.

For example, imagine the workers of a canning factory striking over a dispute of a 3-percent, company-offered raise versus an 8-percent, union-demanded raise. If the average worker would make $17.00 under the company's offer, Exhibit 16.18 demonstrates how long it would take to make up the lost wages under different strike lengths, assuming that the company finally gives in. Of course, there is the risk that the company may (1) hire replacement workers, (2) agree only to the previous 3-percent raise, or (3) lower the raise to 1 percent or even ask for a decrease. This example presumes that the worker receives a $300-per-week strike benefit package from the union fund and unemployment. Some union members might receive more; some might receive less. Even with a relatively short strike, union members may take up to two thirds of a year to make up for the losses. In the case of a prolonged 20-week strike, it could take several years to make up for the losses. The company correspondingly has to weigh the long-term cost of increasing pay and benefits against the potential of lost revenue and profits.

Both the company and the union have to evaluate carefully not only the possibility of lost profits and wages but also intangibles such as reputation, competitiveness, discord, and various other social and psychological factors. Human resource managers and union leaders have come to realize that other avenues are generally more attractive to settle even wide differences. Yet unions sometimes strike on a small wage difference as a matter of principle, although this is not as common today as it was during the 1960s and 1970s. In fact, work stoppages fell to a near-record low in 1999. There were only 17 major work stoppages affecting 73,000 workers in 1999. This averages to workers being idle 1 of every 10,000 available work days.[68]

boycott An agreement by union members not to buy or use a targeted company's goods or services.

Boycott   A **boycott** can be defined as an agreement of union members not to buy or use the goods or services of a company targeted for a strike. Secondary boycotts, in which the union openly encourages suppliers and customers not to sell to or purchase from the targeted company, were made illegal by the Taft-Hartley Act. Boycotts are difficult to use effectively because in most cases the share of a company's sales made to union members and their families is a small proportion of the total sales volume.

A local business that operates in a strong pro-union community may be the most vulnerable. An example would be a grocery store that has a union contract with its checkout clerks. In the event of a labor dispute, the workers' families and friends may stop shopping at that store. Although that may not be enough of an economic lever, other union members from unrelated industries as well as other community members may join in the boycott in sympathy. According to the law, the union that is in dispute with the chain could not openly solicit a secondary boycott. However, it may happen through word of mouth and media attention to the issue. Even these quasi-secondary boycotts rarely meet the objectives of the unions. The boycott against California lettuce, led by labor leader Cesar Chavez during the 1980s, was eventually dropped without forcing the growers to concede to Chavez's demands.

Reaching a Settlement—Last Resort Options for the Company

lockout A management prohibition of union members entering the company facility.

The Lockout   A management tactic somewhat akin to a strike is a **lockout**. Management may prohibit union members from entering the facility and instead run the company with management employees and temporary replacement workers. As industries become more automated and less reliant on highly skilled employees, lockouts are more feasible. The communications business is becoming much more automated. As noted earlier, telephone companies, for instance, increasingly depend on computer hardware and software that minimizes the need for human intervention. Think about what happens when you make a long-distance call with a credit card. By using a touch-tone phone, you can complete the call without any direct human intervention. Such technology made it possible for NYNEX managers during a labor dispute in 1989 to continue all the company's basic services with management employees.

Other industries that are becoming increasingly automated are banking, continuous-process operations such as oil refining and chemical manufacturing, and even retailing with an increased emphasis on self-service and phone-based orders.

Replacement Workers   The lockout tactic often utilizes temporary workers to get the union back to the negotiating table and move toward a settlement that will allow the resumption of normal operations. In recent years replacement workers have been hired not just to temporarily fill the gap but also to permanently replace the striking union members. The 1981 firing of the air traffic controllers (PATCO union members) by the Reagan administration and subsequent hiring of replacement controllers actually paved the way for a more widespread use of this tactic. As mentioned earlier, a controversial 1989 Supreme Court decision confirmed an employers' right to keep the replacement workers after a strike is over. From the union's perspective, this is a powerful counter to a strike, and it can result in the effective end of a union's influence in a company, as demonstrated by the UAW's return to work at Caterpillar when its CEO threatened to hire replacement workers. Union leaders have accused management of deliberately provoking strikes to allow management the opportunity to hire replacement workers who will decertify the union.

As mentioned previously, former President Clinton signed an Executive Order in 1995 prohibiting the hiring of replacement workers in firms with government contracts. National labor leaders have been pressing Congress to pass a restrictive law to prohibit the hiring of permanent replacement workers in all firms. National labor policy has tended to recognize two parallel but competing rights. Unions have been given the clear right to strike, but businesses have been given an equal right to stay open.[69] Continuing into this century, these competing rights will certainly be at the center of attention in legislative and court decisions.[70]

Ratifying a Settlement

In large organizations the final settlement is the result of a complex procedure over an extended period of time. Settlements in smaller companies are frequently more straightforward.

ratification process   A vote of the rank-and-file union members on whether to accept or reject a negotiated contract.

In large organizations, the immediate union bargaining team typically submits the settlement to a representative council. If the council approves the agreement, the rank and file vote on it. This is called the **ratification process**. If the rank and file do not accept the settlement, their negotiators go back to the table. In recent years approximately 10 percent of the negotiated contracts were not ratified on the first vote. This should not happen if union leadership is in close contact with the desires and needs of its membership.

Implementing a Settlement

Assuming that ratification does take place, the following steps should be taken to implement it:

1. The contract provisions should be submitted to lawyers on both sides to determine that the agreed-on provisions are transferred into appropriate language that is both understandable and enforceable.
2. Appropriate news releases and a joint union-company news conference may be appropriate. Whatever the outcome of negotiations, it is better for the parties involved to explain the facts rather than let them be disseminated by rumor or

innuendo. The union may focus on the shutdown of a production line at a plant, but to the company, the fact that it is giving workers the chance to be retrained, retired, or relocated is just as important.

3. Internal publications from the union and company should communicate the most important aspects of the agreement.

4. If the settlement involves major changes in work rules, compensation packages, or benefit allowances, human resource managers should prepare and offer appropriate training and development programs for both managers and workers. For example, if a new quality improvement program and related compensation rules are included in a new contract, management cannot assume that everyone will understand them; specific technical training may be needed. If the company-union relationship is poor, it may be important for the first-line supervisory staff to attend sessions on appropriate human relations topics.

5. Both the union leadership and company management need to state their commitment clearly to make the agreement work, recognizing that whether the process was smooth or rough, all the parties must now work together to abide by the settlement.

Administering the Contract

Once the contract is ratified, its day-to-day implementation is critical. If a contract is well written and clearly specifies the responsibilities of both sides, administering the contract becomes relatively easy. The tone of the negotiations can affect the contract administration process. If the contract is settled without a strike or lockout, the agreement is less likely to lead to grievances. If the negotiations were tough and resulted in a prolonged walkout, the day-to-day administration may develop into a version of the cold war.

The administration of a settlement that is less than satisfactory to one or both sides can be difficult. One or each party may try to obtain concessions not obtained by the negotiations by what is called grievance bargaining as the contract is implemented and interpreted. Suppose, for example, that the contract stipulates that a worker be paid for at least 4 hours when he or she is called in by a department head for unscheduled work, perhaps on the weekend. Suppose also that a supervisor calls in the worker for unscheduled duties that take 2 hours to perform. The company might justify paying the worker for only 2 hours, not 4 as the contract requires, because a supervisor, not a department head, called in the worker.

The union obviously would support the employee, stating that it does not matter who called in the employee; the fact is that the employee came in and worked 2 hours and should be paid for 4. Such a case would likely go to arbitration, especially if the company is trying to find a means to do away with this call-in provision and has not been able to eliminate it in actual contract negotiations. The company is attempting to win something through arbitration that it could not win at the bargaining table.

letter of the law
The strict, inflexible interpretation of a contract.

It is not uncommon for companies to try to circumvent strict **letter-of-the-law** interpretation of the contract. Managers will argue that during a 3-year contract, economic and competitive conditions can change so radically that they need some flexibility. Depending on the union's strengths and goals, it may agree to this flexibility. It is very possible that both parties may benefit from some flexibility. If this is so, it should be built into the contract during the negotiation process rather than relying on the grievance and arbitration process, which can be extremely costly and disruptive.

It should be obvious that the negotiation process cannot be taken lightly, nor can the consequences of the signed contract be ignored. From a strategic viewpoint, long-term implementation should always be kept in mind during the negotiation process. Frequently, the management team involved in the bargaining process is not involved in the day-to-day administration as are the first-line supervisors. Therefore the management team should carefully review the feasibility of the provisions, anticipate potential areas of conflict, and try to preempt as many of these situations as possible. Management should establish an effective channel of communication between these supervisors to ensure that ongoing problem areas are properly dealt with in any subsequent negotiations.

Grievances   Even when a satisfactory agreement is negotiated, inevitable disagreements occur regarding contract language. Management has the primary responsibility of administering the contract. The union watches carefully to be sure that the contract language is observed. In most contracts a specific procedure is spelled out about how complaints and concerns over contract administration will be handled. Grievances have several causes.

The grievance process usually involves submission of a complaint to the first-line supervisor. It can be settled at that level, or it can be submitted to as many as three or four more levels. If it cannot be settled in this way, it may go to arbitration.

Misunderstanding or Misinterpretation   A contract may vary from a few pages to more than 50 pages, but because not every eventuality can be anticipated, the language is written in general terms. The worker and supervisor might interpret the language differently. For a variety of legal reasons, the contract may be full of legal terms. The average supervisor or worker may interpret these provisions in his or her own particular way. Long-term employees may think they understand the agreement and not bother to read the actual contract, assuming that the new contract is just about the same as the old one. This can lead to a contract violation due to neglect.

Premeditated Contract Violation   Occasionally, one side or the other will intentionally commit a **premeditated contract violation** to draw attention to an issue that could not be resolved in the negotiations process. For instance, a union might be unhappy about a work rule that allows a supervisor to change a worker's assignment to a different machining operation more than three times in a shift. The union worker may complain and deliberately slow down after being transferred the third time to test management's intent to enforce the contract. Management may choose to ignore the worker's behavior and in the future assign a worker to a maximum of two machines, leading to a de facto drop of the provision. Or the management may discipline the worker, the worker subsequently may file a grievance, and the union may force the grievance to binding arbitration, where it hopes to get a change in the contract provision.

Management, likewise, sometimes forces an issue for economic reasons. Changes in economic conditions might make a work rule too restrictive to allow the company to remain competitive; thus the management may disregard the rule. The union may ignore the violation if it serves union interest to do so, or it may immediately file a grievance. The outcome of these willful violations is often a function of the relative power of the management and the union, which could change dramatically during the

premeditated contract violation   A deliberate attempt to violate the terms of a labor agreement by either a union or management.

course of a contract. Some provisions in contracts that run from 2 to 5 years are usually open to negotiation every year.

Smoke Screen Violations   It is possible that a grievance may be filed for a less-than-obvious reason. If the union leadership seems to be losing control, or if the members are starting to wonder whether the union officials are too cozy in their relationship with the company, the union may provoke a grievance to prove to the membership that it is in control and serving the needs of the members after all.

Management as well may provoke a problem in an attempt to embarrass the union or test its power. If the management of the company is working to move to a union-free environment, a series of violations may serve as a means to divide the union into factions.

Such **smoke screen violations** can be very risky and dangerous because the other party may misinterpret the intent and take retaliatory action. It is recommended that disagreements be dealt with whether during the contract negotiations or through a formal grievance process rather than by covert political moves.

smoke screen violation   An obvious contract violation that disguises an underlying problem or disagreement.

Management Guidelines

Some of the managerial implications from this chapter include the following:

1. It is important for managers to understand that the nature of union activity has changed dramatically in the last 20 years because of a variety of circumstances encompassing economic shifts within the United States and global economy, demographic changes, and political and social attitudes. As a percentage of the workforce, union representation has declined significantly. Managers of facilities both with and without unions need to be aware of these changes.

2. Unions must determine the degree to which they should concentrate on "bread-and-butter" issues, working conditions, job security, or affinity services. Human resource managers need to understand what their unions want and what they are willing to give in return.

3. The 1970s and 1980s became a time of conflict, concession bargaining, and some notable bitter struggles, but the 1990s brought signs of new cooperative efforts. Managers must try to explore and develop these areas, which is not easy.

4. A variety of laws, including the Sherman-Clayton Act, Taft-Hartley Act, Wagner Act, and Landrum-Griffin Act, clearly spell out the legal rights and responsibilities of labor and management. In addition, a plethora of court decisions affect the general legal framework. Managers need the advice of legal experts when dealing with unions.

5. Management needs to be clear about its strategic goals and then align its labor policy with those goals. For example, if a company wants to serve a high-quality, high-price niche, it may be more flexible in negotiating wages but more stringent on flexible work assignments that will allow it to take advantage of highly skilled craftspeople without cumbersome job classifications.

6. The negotiating team must be very well prepared before it goes into the negotiating sessions. Preparations should include the following:
   a. A thorough review of past contracts.

     b. A listing of disagreements, disputes, and grievances since the last contract.

     c. An analysis of what the union will ask for and a careful assessment of the personalities of the negotiators on each side as well as the issues that are likely to arise.

     d. A list of objectives that the team wants to accomplish.

7. Once an agreement is worked out, the manager should ensure that supervisors understand the provisions of the contract with particular focus on how it is different from the last contract. The human resource department should ensure that the contract is distributed to all management personnel. It is also wise to hold workshops or briefing sessions to be sure that everyone understands the precise language.

Questions for Review

1. What, if anything, could the management and labor unions have done at Caterpillar to avoid the bitter struggle?

2. How will the changing demographics of the workforce affect union attempts at organizing?

3. In your opinion, should management resist the formation of a union? Why or why not? What are the advantages for the company? Are there any disadvantages to having a union?

4. Suppose you were attempting to organize a union in a large restaurant of 150 employees. How would you convince fellow employees they should vote for a union? Now reverse the role. How would you as a manager respond?

5. What are the most important roles that unions play today? Are they the same as they were 20 years ago? Why or why not?

6. What is meant by jointness efforts? Provide an example where a jointness effort is being tried.

7. Have unions outlived their usefulness? Make a case for and against this issue.

8. What is your forecast for union-management relations for the year 2005?

9. What are the most important reasons that some unions and managers now believe that a more collaborative relationship is in their best interest?

10. How does the relative power of the company and union affect the negotiating process?

11. What connection is there between a company's strategy and its approach to negotiating? How would the issues differ for a low-cost producer strategy versus a company that produces high-quality, high-priced luxury items focused on a special market niche?

12. What are some ways in which companies that have unions try to eliminate them? What are some methods that companies without unions use to remain union free? What are the legal and ethical issues involved in each case?

13. Regarding the collective bargaining process, what is the difference between mandatory, permissible, and prohibited issues? Give an example of each.

14. When negotiations break down, what are some tactics employed by unions to try to force a settlement? What tactics might a company use?

15. "The next 10 years are likely to be a period of increasing strife between labor and management based on the resurgence of militant union power." Do you agree or disagree with this statement? Explain your answer.

United Parcel Services (UPS)[71]

"It is imperative that we take a stand now, or we won't have a future." These are the words of Connie McArthur, a 19-year employee picketing a UPS distribution center in Seattle. The walkout at 12:01 AM EST on Monday, August 4, 1997, was the first nationwide strike in the 90-year history of UPS. The major issues that led to the strike were Teamsters union comments on part-time job opportunities, subcontracting, and the proposed employee pension plans. Along with increases in pensions and pay, the Teamsters demanded limits on subcontracting, better safety and health provisions, and more full-time jobs. The 16-day strike caused a plummet in daily deliveries from 12 million to 1 million. Some UPS customers even laid off workers because of the strike.

About UPS

In 1907, 19-year-old James E. Casey borrowed $100 from a friend and established the American Messenger Company in Seattle, Washington. Despite stiff competition, the company did well because of James' strict policies of customer courtesy, reliability, round-the-clock service, and low rates. In 1913 the company began focusing on package delivery for retail stores and merged with a competitor, Evert McCabe, to form Merchants Parcel Delivery. In 1929 the company opened United Air Express, offering package delivery via airplane to major West Coast cities. Due to the stock market crash of 1929, the air service was discontinued after only 8 months. The name United Parcel Service was adopted in the 1930s: "united" because shipments were consolidated; "service" because, as Charlie Soderstrom observed, "Service is all we have to offer." All UPS vehicles were painted brown because it was neat, dignified, and professional. With the fuel and rubber shortages during WWII, retail stores began to encourage customers to carry home their packages rather than have them delivered. UPS managers began looking for other opportunities and decided to expand their services by acquiring "common carrier" rights to deliver packages between all addresses. Over the next three decades, UPS fought to obtain authorization in all 48 contiguous states and in 1975 forged the "Golden Link" that made national parcel delivery service a reality.

Results of the Strike

The agreement reached on August 18, 1997, was seen as one of the most important victories, not just for the Teamsters' Union, but for all unions and workers. UPS members were allowed to vote on the contract by mail, and UPS management and the union agreed unanimously to approve the tentative agreement. The chart following shows what concessions were made by both the union and UPS:

Issue	Final UPS Offer	What Union Won
Full-time jobs	One thousand new full-time jobs over 5 years.	Ten thousand new full-time jobs over 5 years.
Subcontracting	Expand use of subcontractors to do feeder work.	No subcontracting of feeder work except during peak season, and then only if local union agrees.

Issue	Final UPS Offer	What Union Won
Package car work	Use part-time car drivers for any "time definite" deliveries.	No shift of package car work to part-timers.
Wages	Full-timers $1.50 for 5 years plus 2 bonuses.	Full-timers: $3.10 for 5 years Part-timers: Same as full-timers plus $1.00 more for part-timers hired after 1982.
	Part-timers in progression (3 of 4 part-timers): $0 plus 25 cents per year. Part-timers out of progression (1 of 4 part-timers): $2.50 over 5 years plus 2 bonuses. No increase in start rate for part-timers.	Part-time wage increases apply to all part-timers who have attained seniority as of August 1, 1997. 50-cent increase in start rate for part-timers.
Pensions	Force all UPSers into company-controlled plan.	Stay in Teamster plans with equal or better benefits than company offer for almost all workers.
Part-timers	No increase in guaranteed hours.	3.5-hour guarantee, except air operations.
Air drivers	Starting pay for new air drivers frozen at $10.00 per hour. Pay for exception drivers remains frozen.	Starting rate of $11.00 for part-timers and $13.00 for full-timers. Exception drivers paid part-time rate, which increases with general wage.
Over 70 pounds	UPS can increase weight limit above 150 pounds at any time without union agreement.	No right to increase weight limit above 150 pounds without union agreement. Right to Teamster help and lifting devices for over 70 pounds.
Health and welfare	Push all UPSers into managed care plans and HMOs. Eliminate family coverage copay for all newly hired workers.	Maintain current plans.
Right to honor union picket lines	Force UPS workers to scab on other union members.	Maintain our right to honor union picket lines.
Innocent until proven guilty	Expand the list of infractions called "cardinal sins" where innocent until proven guilty does not apply.	Maintain the current language of innocent until proven guilty except for "cardinal sins" as defined in the supplement.

Teamsters End Strike

Teamsters President Ron Carey announced a unanimous approval with UPS on Tuesday, August 21. The agreement called for the creation of 10,000 full-time jobs over the 5-year contract period. There were also pay increases in the base pay, driver average pay, and part-time hourly rates. Although UPS pushed to withdraw from the Teamsters' multi-employer pension plan and create a new retirement plan solely for the UPS workers, the final agreement was to keep the existing system. Despite company officials' beliefs that a strike would mean layoffs because of a loss of customers, no employees were laid off. In fact, UPS began hiring more employees after the strike.

Questions

1. What effect will the success of the Teamsters' Union in this case have on the membership of the unions and on the management-union relationship at other companies?

2. Will the signing of a 5-year rather than a 2- or 3-year contract mean a success for the Teamsters or management?

3. In your opinion, who "won" the strike?

4. Does this case show that union power may be increasing or decreasing? Support your answer.

Additional Readings

AFLCIO, *Work in Progress: This Week with America's Unions.* Available at **www.aflcio.org/publ/workin.htm**.

Arthur, Jeffrey, and James Dworking. "Current Topics in Industrial and Labor Relations Research and Practice." *Journal of Management* 17 (1991), pp. 515–551.

Ballott, Michael. *Labor-Management Relations in a Changing Environment.* New York: Wiley, 1992.

Barling, Julian, E. Kevin Kelloway, and Eric Brenermann. "Preemployment Predictors of Union Attitudes: The Role of Family Socialization and Work Belief." *Journal of Applied Psychology* 76 (1991), pp. 725–731.

Bernstein, Aaron. "Sweeney's Blitz." *Business Week*, February 17, 1997.

Bronfenbrenner, Kate, ed. *Organizing to Win: New Research on Union Strategies.* Ithaca, NY: ILR Press, 1998.

Carrell, Michael R., and Christina Heavrin. *Labor Relations and Collective Bargaining: Cases, Practices, and Law*, 6th ed. Upper Saddle River, NJ: Prentice Hall, 2001.

Chelius, James, and James Dworking, eds. *Reflections on the Transformation of Industrial Relations.* Metuchen, NJ: IMLR Press/Rutgers University, 1990.

Cimini, Michael. "Union Members in 1989." *News: United States Department of Labor.* Washington, DC: Bureau of Labor Statistics, February 7, 1990.

Clawson, Dan, and Mary Ann Clawson. "What has happened to the US labor movement? Union decline and renewal." *Annual Review of Sociology* 25 (1999), pp. 95–119.

Coleman, Charles J. *Managing Labor Relations in the Public Sector.* San Francisco: Jossey-Bass, 1990.

Estreicher, Samuel ed. *Employee Representation in the Emerging Workplace: Alternatives/ Supplements to Collective Bargaining: Proceedings of New York University 50th annual.* The Hague: Kluwer Law International, 2000.

Evans, Martin G., and Daniel A. Ondrack. "The Role of Job Outcomes and Values in Understanding the Union's Impact of Job Satisfaction: A Replication." *Human Relations*, May 1990.

Freeman, Richard B., and Joel Rogers. *What Workers Want.* Ithaca, NY: ILR Press, 1999.

Fulmer, William E., and Ann C. Casey. "Employment at Will: Options for Managers." *Academy of Management Executive* 4, no. 2 (1990), pp. 102–107.

Gini, Al. *My Job, My Self: Work and Creation of the Modern Individual.* New York: Routledge, 2000.

Goldberg, Beverly. *Age Works: What Corporate America Must Do to Survive the Graying of the Workforce.* New York: Free Press, 2000.

Grantham, Charles E. *The Future of Work: The Promise of the New Digital Work Society.* New York: McGraw-Hill, 2000.

Hathaway, Dale, A. *Allies Across the Border.* Cambridge, MA: South End Press, 2000.

Herrick, Neal Q. *Joint Management and Employee Participation: Labor and Management at the Crossroads.* San Francisco: Jossey-Bass, 1990.

Ichniowski, Casey, and Jeffrey Zax. "Today's Associations, Tomorrow's Unions." *Industrial and Labor Relations Review* 43 (1990), pp. 191–208.

Iverson, Torben, Jonas Pontusson, and David Soskice, eds. *Unions, Employers and Central Banks: Macroeconomic Coordination and Institutional Change in Social Market Economies*. New York, NY: Cambridge University Press, 1999.

Judy, Richard W., and Carol D'Amico. *Workforce 2020: Work and Workers in the 21st Century*. Indianapolis, IN: Hudson Institute, 1997.

Katz, Harry Charles, and Owen Darbishire. *Converging Divergences: Worldwide Changes in Employment Systems*. Ithaca, NY: ILR Press, 2000.

Krupat, Kitty, and Patrick McCreery, eds. *Out at Work: Building a Gay-Labor Alliance*. Minneapolis, MN: University of Minnesota Press, 2001.

Lareau, N. Peter. *Drafting the Union Contract*. Albany, NY: Matthew Bender, 1988.

Lawler, John J. *Unionization and Deunionization: Strategy, Tactics, and Outcomes*. Columbia, SC: University of South Carolina Press, 1990.

Lyndes, C. *Labor Unions*. Available at **www.hal-pc.org/~clyndes/political-unions.html**.

Martin, James E. *Two-Tier Compensation Structures: Their Impact on Unions, Employers, and Employees*. Kalamazoo, MI: Upjohn Institute, 1990.

Munro, Anne. *Women, Work, and Trade Unions*. New York, Mansell, 1999.

Palokangas, Tapio. *Labour Unions, Public Policy and Economic Growth*. New York: Cambridge University Press, 2000.

Rachleff, Peter. *Hard-Pressed in the Heartland: The Hormel Strike and the Future of the American Labor Movement*. Boston: South End Press, 1993.

Reshef, Yonatan, Mark Kizilos, and D. Gerald Jr. "Employee involvement programs: Should unions get involved?" *Journal of Labor Research* 20, no. 4 (1999), pp. 557–569.

Robertson, David Brian. *Capital, Labor, and State: the Battle for American Markets from the Civil War to the New Deal*. Lanham, MD: Rowman & Littlefield Publishers, 2000.

Sloane, Arthur A., and Fred Witney. *Labor Relations*, 10th ed. Upper Saddle River, NJ: Prentice Hall, 2001.

Strauss, George; Dan Gallagher; and Jack Fiorito, eds. *The State of the Unions*. Madison, WI: Industrial Relations Research Association, 1991.

Stodghill II, Ron. "The Mob on Wall Street: Why You Can't See It." *Business Week*, March 24, 1997.

Thompson, Leigh L. *The Mind and the Heart of the Negotiator*, 2nd ed. Upper Saddle River, NJ: Prentice Hall, 2001.

Weil, David. *Turning the Tide: Strategic Planning for Labor Unions*. New York: Lexington Books, 1994.

Zweig, Michael. *The Working Class Majority: America's Best Kept Secret*. Ithaca, NY: ILR Press, 2000.

Notes

[1] "UAW Blasts New Caterpillar Takeaways," *UAW Washington Report*, December 11, 1992, p. 2; Bill Casstevens, "UAW vs. Caterpillar—The Battle Continues," *The Wall Street Journal*, April 22, 1993, p. A15; Dennis Farley, "Workers at Caterpillar Hope against Hope Clinton Will Be True," *The Wall Street Journal*, July 26, 1993, p. A1; Kevin Kelly, "Cat Is Purring, but They're Hissing on the Floor," *Business Week*, May 16, 1994, p. 33; Robert L. Rose and Alex Kotlowitz, "Strife between UAW and Caterpillar Blights Promising Labor Idea," *The Wall Street Journal*, p. A1; Robert L. Rose, "Caterpillar, Aided by Economy's Gains, Posts Profit Surge, but Stock Falls 4.5%," *The Wall Street Journal*, April 21, 1994, p. A2; "UAW Rejects Caterpillar Bid for Negotiations," *The Wall Street Journal*, May 16, 1994, p. A9; "Labor Strife Threatens Caterpillar's Booming Business," *The Wall Street Journal*, June 10, 1994, p. B4; "Caterpillar Refuses to Let Strikers Resume Their Jobs," *The Wall Street Journal*, June 14, 1994, p. B11; "UAW Applauds NLRB Decision Upholding Posting of Pro-Union Materials at Caterpillar," August 15, 1997, available at **www.uaw.org/publications/releases/1997/815cat.html**; "Former Graduate Trainee Becomes Caterpillar CEO," *Financial Times*, January 13, 1999, p. 30; and "Caterpillar Expects Lower Profit," *The New York Times*, January 19, 2001, p. C12, available at **www.cat.com** and **www.uaw.org**.

[2] *Brief History of the American Labor Movement* (Washington, DC: U.S. Department of Labor Statistics, 1970), Bulletin 1000, p. 1.

[3]Arthur A. Sloane and Fred Whitney, *Labor Relations*, 4th ed. (Englewood Cliffs, NJ: Prentice-Hall, 1981), pp. 69–76.

[4]Aaron Bernstein, "Why America Needs Unions, but Not the Kind It Has Now," *Business Week*, May 23, 1994, pp. 70–82; and "Union affiliation of employed wage and salary workers by selected characteristics," Bureau of Labor Statistics, US Department of Labor, January 2001, available at **www.bls.gov/news.release/union2.t01.htm**.

[5]Ron Suskind, "Where Have All the Unions Gone?" *The Wall Street Journal*, July 28, 1992, p. A11; "Union membership of employed wage and salary workers, government and private industry, 1999 and 2000," Bureau of Labor Statistics, US Department of Labor, January 2001, available at **www.bls.gov/opub/ted/2001/jan/wk5/art04.txt**.

[6]"Fast Track Win Boosts Labor," *UAW: Washington Report* 37, no. 17 (November 21, 1997), available at **www.org/uawreleases/washington-report/3717/wr371701.html**.

[7]Bernstein, "Why America Needs Unions, but Not the Kind It Has Now," *Business Week*, May 23, 1994, pp. 70–82.

[8]Raju Narisetti, "Labor Letter," *The Wall Street Journal*, November 29, 1999, p. A1.

[9]*Economic Report of the President* (Washington, DC: U.S. Government Printing Office, 1994).

[10]E. McDonnell (executive producer), J. Judd (host), and A. Haeg (reporting). *Morning Edition*, June 29, 2000. Washington, D.C.: National Public Radio. Radio broadcast.

[11]Bernstein, "Why America Needs Unions, but Not the Kind It Has Now," *Business Week*, May 23, 1994, pp. 70–82.

[12]Larry Reynolds, "Labor's Leaders Changing to Meet the Times," *Management Review*, February 1988, pp. 57–58; and Peter Lazes and Jane Savage, "Embracing the Future: Union Strategies for the 21st Century," *The Journal for Quality and Participation*, Fall 2000, pp. 18–23.

[13]Peggy Connerton, "Union's Future Is Bright," *Personnel Administrator*, December 1989, pp. 99–100; Peter Lazes and Jane Savage, "Embracing the Future: Union Strategies for the 21st Century," *The Journal for Quality and Participation*, Fall 2000, pp. 18–23.

[14]Stephanie Overman, "Commission to Tackle Pittston Strike Issues," *HRNews*, February 1990, pp. A1, A4.

[15]Bernstein, "Why America Needs Unions, but Not the Kind It Has Now."

[16]Rebecca Blumenstein, "Auto Makers Attack High Health-Care Bills with a New Approach," *The Wall Street Journal*, December 9, 1996, pp. A1, A6.

[17]John Hoerr and Wendy Zellner, "A Japanese Import That's Not Selling," *Business Week*, February 26, 1990, pp. 86–87.

[18]Sloane and Whitney, *Labor Relations*, 4th ed. (Englewood Cliffs, NJ: Prentice-Hall, 1981), pp. 69–76.

[19]George Strauss, "Toward the Study of Human Resources Policy," in *Reflections on the Transformation of Industrial Relations*, James Chelius and James Dworkin, ed. (Metuchen, NJ: IMLR Press-Rutgers University, 1990), pp. 73–106.

[20]Dana Milbank, "National Steel Claims Strength in Its Labor-Management Alloy," *The Wall Street Journal*, April 30, 1992, p. B11.

[21]Don Nichols, "The Management Revolution and Loss of Union Clout" (an interview with Dr. Richard I. Lyles), *Management Review*, February 1988, pp. 25–26; and Constance DiCesare, "The Law at Work," *Monthly Labor Review* 119, no. 1, 2 (January 1996), pp. 79–80.

[22]Ben Fisher, "Union Busting or Empowerment?" *Across the Board*, April 1990, pp. 11–12.

[23]Steve Gunderson, "NLRB Muddies Regulatory Water," *The Wall Street Journal*, February 1, 1993, p. A10.

[24]Alexander B. Trowbridge, "Avoiding Labor-Management Conflict," *Management Review*, February 1988, pp. 14–21; and Peter Lazes and Jane Savage, "Embracing the Future: Union Strategies for the 21st Century," *The Journal for Quality and Participation*, Fall 2000, pp. 18–23.

[25]Jeremy Main, "The Labor Rebel Leading the Hormel Strike," *Fortune*, June 9, 1986, pp. 105–110.

[26]Rod Willis, "Can American Unions Transform Themselves?" *Management Review*, February 1988, pp. 14–21; and Silja J.A. Talvi, "Labor's New Front Lines," *The Christian Science Monitor*, January 29, 2001, p. 11.

[27]James Neff, *Mobbed Up: Jackie Presser's High-Wire Life in the Teamsters, the Mafia, and the FBI* (New York: Atlantic Monthly Press, 1989); and Silja J. A. Talvi, "Labor's New Front Lines."

[28]Mark Suzman, "America's labour unions strike back against tide of steady," *The Financial Times*, October 14, 1999, p. 4.

[29]Willis, "Can American Unions Transform Themselves?" *Management Review*, February 1988, pp. 14–21.

[30]Aaron Bernstein, "Tough Love for Labor" (an interview with Richard Bensinger), *Business Week*, October 16, 2000, pp. 118–120.

[31]John Naisbitt and Patricia Aburdeen, *Megatrends 2000-Ten New Directions for the 1990's* (New York: Morrow, 1990), p. 42.

[32]Douglas Braddock, "Occupational employment projections to 2008," *Monthly Labor Review*, November 1999, pp. 51–77; and Julie Hatch and Angela Clinton, "Job growth in the 1990s: a retrospect," *Monthly Labor Review*, December 2000, pp. 3–18.

[33]Robert Kuttner, "The Fed's Thermostat Is on the Fritz," *Business Week*, April 11, 1994, p. 18.

[34]John Hoerr et. al., "Beyond Unions," *Business Week*, July 8, 1985, p. 72; and "Ignore New Workplace Legislation at Your Peril, Warn Authors of Law Guide," *Managements Services* 44, no. 6 (June 2000), p. 3.

[35]Peter Drucker, "Reinventing Unions," *Across the Board*, September 1989, pp. 12–13.

[36]Audrey Freedman, "Unions' Future Is Bleak," *Personnel Administrator*, December 1989, p. 98.

[37]Ibid.

[38]Stephie Overman, "Nissan Sees Union's Loss as Management Style's Win," *Resource*, September 1989, p. 1.

[39]Joe Laws and Thomas Li-Ping Tang, "Japanese Transplants and Union Membership: The Case of Nissan Motor Manufacturing Corporation," *S.A.M. Advanced Management Journal* 64, no. 2 (Spring 1999), pp. 16–25.

[40]Thomas A. Kochan, Harry C. Katz, and Robert B. McKersie, *The Transformation of American Industrial Relations* (New York: Basic Books, 1986).

[41]Howard N. Fullerton, Jr., "Labor Force Participation: 75 Years of Change, 1950–98 and 1998–2025," *Monthly Labor Review*, December 1999, pp. 3–12.

[42]Willis, "Can American Unions Transform Themselves?"

[43]Edward E. Lawler III and Susan A. Mohrman, "Unions and the New Management," *Academy of Management Review* 13, no. 4 (1988), pp. 639–652; and "Trends in U.S. Labor Movement," *The Futurist* 30, no.1 (January/February 1996), p. 44.

[44]Alan I. Murray and Yonatan Reshef, "American Manufacturing Unions' Stasis: A Paradigmatic Perspective," *Academy of Management Review* 13, no. 4 (1988), pp. 639–652; and Hill Kemp and Bob Stump, "Getting Unions and Management Together," *The Journal for Quality and Participation* 22, no. 3 (May/June 1999), pp. 42–44.

[45]Adrienne Eaton and Paula Voos, "The Ability of Unions to Adapt to Innovative Workplace Arrangements," *AEA Papers and Proceedings* 79 (May 1989), pp. 172–176.

[46]Maureen Minehan, "Unions Target Nontraditional Industries," *HRMagazine* 42, no. 6 (June 1997), p. 272.

[47]Mary Beth Regan, "Shattering the AFL-CIO's Glass Ceiling," *Business Week*, Novermber 13, 1995, p. 46.

[48]Benjamin Aaron, Joyce M. Najita, and James L. Stern, eds, *Public Sector Bargaining*, 2nd ed. (Washington, DC: The Bureau of National Affairs, 1988).

[49]R. L. Rose, N. M. Christian, and A. Q. Nomani, "Union Merger Sounds Painless, But It Won't Be," *The Wall Street Journal*, July 28, 1995, p. B1; and Yochi Dreazen, "Labor Unions Turn to Mergers in Pursuit of Growth," *The New York Times*, September 1, 2000, p. A2, A6.

[50]Robert Frank, "UPS, Teamsters Reach Accord, Ending Strike," *The Wall Street Journal*, February 8, 1994, p. A2.

[51]Robert T. Thompson, "An Anti-Worker Labor Bill," *The Wall Street Journal*, August 31, 1990, p. A10.

[52]Leon Rubis, "Striker Order Argued in Congress, Court," *HRNews*, May 1995, p. 14; and "A Ruling on Striker Replacement," *The Washington Post*, May 15, 1996, p. A18.

[53]Robert Blake and Jane S. Mouton, "How to Achieve the Integration on the Human Side of the Merger," *Organizational Dynamics* 13, no. 3 (1985), pp. 41–56; and Charlene Marmer Solomon, "Corporate Pioneers Navigate Global Mergers," *Workforce* 3, no. 5 (September 1998), pp. 12–17.

[54]James Fraze, "After Model Merger Taking Two Years, USAir Growing Pilot Seniority Issue Unresolved," *Resource*, September 1989, p. 11.

[55]Frank Swoboda and Don Phillips, "Airlines' Deal May Hinge on Pilots' Seniority," *The Washington Post*, May 28, 2000, p. H01.

[56]Daily Congressional Record 3954 (April 23, 1947).

[57]Francis T. Coleman, "Once a Union Not Always a Union," *Personnel Journal*, March 1985, pp. 42–45; and Catherine Meeker, "Defining 'ministerial aid': Union Decertification Under the National Labor Relations Act," *The University of Chicago Law Review* 66, no. 3 (Summer 1999), pp. 999–1028.

[58]R. Wayne Mondy and Robert M. Noe III, *Human Resource Management*, 4th ed. (Boston: Allyn & Bacon, 1990), p. 650.

[59]Marc Singer, *Human Resource Management* (Boston: PWS-Kent, 1990), p. 414.

[60]Joseph B. White, "Worker's Revenge: Factory Towns Start to Fight Back Angrily When Firms Pull Out," *The Wall Street Journal*, March 8, 1988, p. A11.

[61]Ibid.

[62]Paul D. Straudohar, "New Plant Closing Law Aids Workers in Transition," *Personnel Journal*, January 1989, pp. 87–90; and "Plant Closings and Layoffs Follow Special Rules," *HRMagazine* 36, no. 7 (July 1991), p. 71.

[63]James F. Rand, "Preventive-Maintenance Techniques for Staying Union-Free," *Personnel Journal* 59 (June 1980), p. 497; Jonathan A. Segal, "The 'U' Word," *HRMagazine* 37, no. 8 (August 1992), pp. 89–90; and Mary Helen Yarborough, "Unions are Targeting Pro-Management States," *HR Focus* 71, no. 4 (April 1994), pp. 1–3.

[64]Singer, *Human Resource Management* (Boston: PWS-Kent, 1990), p. 437.

[65]Richard Johnson, "Interest Arbitration Examined," *Personnel Administrator*, January 1983, pp. 53–57; and Jeffery Sloan, "Let's Keep Control of Local Spending," *Los Angeles Times*, May 12, 1999, p. B7.

[66]William H. Holley and Kenneth M. Jennings, *The Labor Relations Process*, 3d ed. (Chicago: The Dryden Press, 1988), p. 246.

[67]Cynthia T. Gramm, "The Determinants of Strike Incidence and Severity: A Micro-Level Study," *Industrial and Labor Relations Review* 39 (April 1986), pp. 361–376; and "Work Stoppages Summary," Bureau of Labor Statistics, U.S. Department of Labor, February 24, 2000, available at **stats.bls.gov/news.release/wkstp.nr0.htm**.

[68]"Work Stoppages Summary," Bureau of Labor Statistics, February 24, 2000.

[69]Thompson, "An Anti-Worker, Labor Bill," *The Wall Street Journal*, August 31, 1990, p. A10.

[70]Andrew Kupfis, "Caterpillar's Union Fallout," *Fortune*, May 18, 1992, p. 16.

[71]Ken Hoover and Ilana Debare, "UPS, Teamsters Reach a Deal: Tentative Pact to End Strike Adds Full-Time Jobs, Lets Union Control Pension Fund," *San Francisco Chronicle*, August 19, 1997, p. A 1; **www.ups.com**; Louise Schiavone, "Teamsters Strike UPS," August 4, 1997, available at **www.cnn.com**; and "Members to Vote on New Contract," *Teamsters Update*, August 21, 1997, available at **www.teamster.org**.

V

Strategic Separation

**Chapter 17   Strategic Restructuring and the
              Virtual Organization**

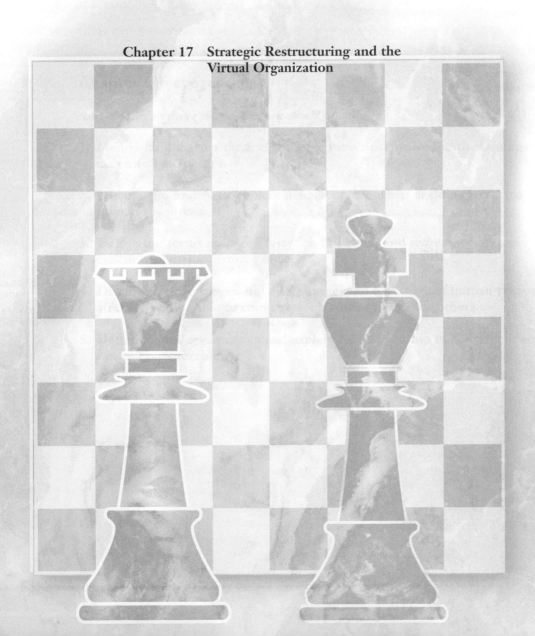

EXHIBIT 17.2	WORLDCOM'S STOCK PRICE

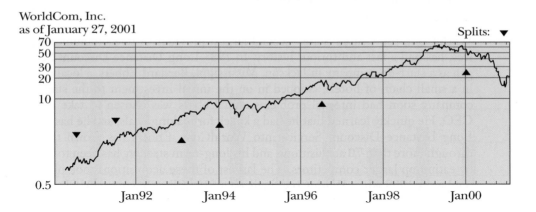

WorldCom, Inc.
as of January 27, 2001

Splits: ▼

Splits: 18-Jul-90 [3:2], 26-Jun-91 [3:2], 15-Jan-93 [3:2], 7-Jan-94 [2:1], 5-Jul-96 [2:1], 31-Dec-99 [3:2]

SOURCE: **www.yahoo.finance.com**

market for voice service is growing at a sluggish pace of 3 percent a year and will perhaps even decline as people increasingly use their wireless phones for cross-country calls and as the Bell telephone companies win permission to offer long-distance service. Because of this current shift in the market, WorldCom has recognized the need to refocus its business. In the early 1990s WorldCom began offering data services, and in 2000 it claims half of this market. WorldCom also began offering Internet service to corporate customers and in 2000 it was the largest competitor in this market. Although the prices are falling in this market as they are in the voice market, growth of the data and Internet services are expected to grow at more than ten times the rate of long-distance.

In response to the shifting market, WorldCom has taken a path that is exactly opposite of its previous growth scheme. Ebbers announced in October of 2000 that it again plans to do a major restructuring, only this time it will split into two different companies. One will offer the more conventional voice-based services, the other focused on data and Internet service. Ebbers hopes that the split will allow each new company to be small enough to react to the changes in each market while still maintaining the overhead cost advantage that comes with being a large competitor. Just as with a merger, the split will involve a major effort by the human resource department in the restructuring of both new companies.

The Present and Future

The telecommunications industry is very different from the stable, regulated, slow-growing business Ebbers entered nearly 20 years ago. Competition is fierce, prices are falling, technology is in constant flux, and the capital markets have ground to a halt. Like everyone else, WorldCom will have to figure out a way to drive growth in data revenues by selling complicated add-on services to corporate customers. It is now a world that favors new products over cost-cutting, and growth in sales as well as in the bottom line.[5] And for the time being, Bernie Ebbers remains as the top man in charge at WorldCom. His supporters aren't ready to give up on him yet. Unlike many of his competitors in the cutthroat communications business, Ebbers is an entrepreneur, someone who has shown he can move quickly to exploit new opportunities. If any telecom executive can reinvent himself for new market conditions, friends and colleagues say it is Ebbers.

For more on WorldCom and its history, see **www.worldcom.com**.

Strategic Choices

As in the case of WorldCom, the human resource unit plays a strategic role in periods of restructuring for several reasons. Human resources are used to increase efficiency, achieve a competitive position, and contribute to the company's survival. To achieve these goals, human resource managers must make strategic decisions that are frequently difficult to make. Some examples of these choices follow:

1. How should a newly merged company handle duplicate positions? Does the company need to retain all employees from both previous companies in a particular job description? Or will the company be more efficient by eliminating a portion of these jobs?

2. Merging companies bring together two corporate cultures. Should the larger company force the smaller company to completely change cultural values and organizational structure? If so, how long does the larger company phase this change in? And under what circumstances is an employee terminated for resisting this change? If a complete cultural overhaul is not forced, then how should the human resources department handle the restructuring?

3. The company must decide transition issues in the downsizing. Shall severance pay be issued? Shall outplacement services be provided? What about job and financial counseling?

4. Often managers must decide which employees will be laid off. If the company is not unionized and restricted by a contract, the decisions about whom to let go is management's responsibility. The criteria by which these decisions will be made must be developed.

5. Managers must decide on how to best restructure two firms if a split takes place. Which employees are best suited for each company? Will there be a need to cut jobs or create jobs after the split?

restructuring
Any major change in the way an organization operates.

cutbacks Attempts by an organization to react to temporary changes in the marketplace by reducing spending and controlling costs.

Restructuring Options

downsizing
The process by which a firm seeks to reduce its overall size and scope permanently, usually as the result of changes in either the organization's strategy or the marketplace.

Broadly defined, **restructuring** is any major change in the way an organization operates. Exhibit 17.1 shows the number of jobs lost through downsizing in recent years. Note that downsizing continued throughout the 1990s and into the 21st century, with 1993 being the peak year of the decade. The goal of restructuring is to reduce the number of employees serving the same function at the same level of efficiency.[6] Restructuring usually involves cutbacks, downsizing, and consolidation. **Cutbacks** are attempts by organizations to react to temporary changes in the marketplace by reducing spending and controlling costs. They are the most general type of restructuring. Typically more long term in its focus, **downsizing** is the process by which a firm seeks to reduce its overall size and scope permanently, usually the result of changes in

EXHIBIT 17.3	AN ORGANIZATION'S STRATEGIC RESTRUCTURING VARIABLES

Variable	Aspects
The Organization's Competitive Strategy	Overall Cost Leadership
Differentiation	
Focus	
Stuck in the Middle	
Management Philosophy Concerning	Attitudes about Employees
Employees and Technology	Attitudes about Skills/Training
Attitudes about Automation and Flexibility	
Business Cycle Effects	Prosperity
Recession	
Depression	
Recovery	
Type of Cost Restructuring of the Organization	Goals of Restructuring
	Cause of Restructuring

consolidations
Actions to cut functions or activities that may be redundant within an organization.

Chapter 11 bankruptcy A bankruptcy filing in which a firm seeks to reorganize its operations and continue operating.

the organization's strategy or in the marketplace. **Consolidations** are actions to cut functions or activities that may be redundant within an organization. Consolidations are frequently the result of mergers and acquisitions of firms, but they may also occur independently of those activities. Of course, cutbacks, downsizing, and consolidations are not mutually exclusive activities. One, two, or all three may occur simultaneously, depending on the scope of the restructuring.

In particularly difficult circumstances, the only restructuring choice for a firm may be bankruptcy. Under **Chapter 11 bankruptcy**, the firm may be able to reorganize as a smaller operation. Under a **Chapter 7 bankruptcy**, however, the firm ceases operations. Global Graphics Inc. bankruptcy in 2000 is an example of a Chapter 7 filing. Heilig-Meyers bankruptcy in 2000 is an example of a Chapter 11 filing.

Strategic Variables

Chapter 7 bankruptcy A bankruptcy filing in which a firm ceases to operate.

An organization's decision to restructure results from an examination of several different strategic variables. The strategic variables involved in the restructuring decision include (1) the organization's competitive strategy, (2) management's philosophy toward employees and technology, (3) business cycles, and (4) the goals and types of cost restructuring of the organization, or a combination of these. All of these variables affect the choices that the organization's management must make about the type of restructuring that it will undertake. Exhibit 17.3 briefly summarizes these variables, and each is explored following.

Competitive Strategy

Often, an organization will restructure as a result of a change in its **competitive strategy**. In *Competitive Strategy*, Michael Porter defines an organization's competitive strategy as a combination of the ends (goals) for which the firm is striving and the means (policies) by which it is seeking to get there.[7] Porter identifies three generic types of strategies that an organization may pursue: an overall cost leadership, a differentiation, or a focus strategy in relation to its competitors.[8]

Firms pursuing an **overall cost leadership strategy** seek to sell products that are less expensive in price than their competitors' products. This strategy involves vigorous pursuit of organizational efficiency. Managers emphasize efficient and large-scale assembly line and manufacturing techniques and strict control of operating and overhead costs. In addition, they reduce spending on perceived nonessential areas such as research and development (R&D), maintenance, and sales. Often when an organization adopts a cost leadership strategy, it seeks to reduce what it views as nonessential workers by cutting levels of bureaucracy, reducing redundant functions within the organization, and trimming staffing in nonessential departments. It also tries to reduce the number of workers on the assembly line by investing heavily in automation, robotics, and other related techniques. Southwest Airlines is an example of an organization that pursued this strategy in the 1990s.

Firms pursuing a **differentiation strategy** seek to create a product or service that is unique within the industry and thus gain a competitive advantage. Firms using this strategy try to build a brand loyalty in their customer's sensitivity to price and substitute product. Product design, quality, customer service, dealer networks, technology, features, or a combination of these factors serves to increase brand loyalty. A differentiation strategy does not allow firms to ignore costs, but many of its parts are costly. Organizations that adopt a differentiation strategy must build some form of strength. This strength may be in marketing, R&D, manufacturing skill, or other related capabilities. This strategy requires personnel who are highly skilled, creative, and talented. Critical areas include R&D labs, marketing departments, and product design engineering shops. Quality people in these areas are always in high demand. As a result, getting the necessary skills to be a strong competitor using the differentiation strategy is time consuming and expensive. This strategy is often costlier to adopt than other strategies because success is more difficult to measure. The basis of employee performance ratings is subjective, not quantitative, because output is difficult to measure. Mercedes-Benz, BMW, and other luxury car makers use this strategy.

Firms adopting a **focus strategy** seek to get back to the basics. Instead of trying to compete in many markets with a wide range of products, they concentrate on a narrow segment that matches their skills.[9] Firms cut nonessential functions and personnel not directly serving the organization's focus. Many focused firms are smaller than those using a low-cost or differentiation strategy. Management often organizes focused firms functionally to avoid waste and duplication. It puts its resources into doing one or two jobs well. Segmentation may occur by focusing on certain buyers, products, or geographic locations. A firm with a focus orientation may be the low-cost producer or may have high differentiation in the market segment it serves. Kentucky Fried Chicken is a good example of a firm that has successfully pursued a focus strategy: "We do chicken right."

A final strategy is essentially a lack of strategy. Porter calls this the **stuck in the middle strategy**. Firms stuck in the middle are unable to adopt successfully a generic strategy because of a lack of capital, market share, products, or managerial skill. They wander from one strategy to another and do poorly in each. This results in declining profits and market share. Decisive action may be the only solution to this problem if the firm wishes to remain a real competitor. This action almost always includes some form of

---

competitive strategy The combination of the ends (goals) for which a firm is striving and the means (policies) by which it seeks to achieve those goals.

overall cost leadership strategy A competitive strategy in which a firm seeks to sell products that are less expensive than its competitors' products.

Differentiation strategy A competitive strategy in which a firm seeks to create a product or service that is unique within the industry.

focus strategy A competitive strategy in which a firm seeks to concentrate on a narrow industry segment that matches its skills.

stuck in the middle strategy A situation in which a firm essentially lacks a competitive strategy.

EXHIBIT 17.4	COMMON ORGANIZATIONAL REQUIREMENTS OF PORTER'S THREE GENERIC STRATEGIES
Generic Strategy	**Common Organizational Requirements**
Overall Cost Leadership	Tight cost control Frequent, detailed control reports Structured organization and responsibilities Incentives based on meeting strict quantitative targets
Differentiation	Strong coordination among functions in R&D, product development, and marketing Subjective measurement and incentives instead of quantitative measures Amenities to attract highly skilled labor, scientists, or creative people
Focus	Combination of the above policies directed at the particular strategic target

SOURCE: Michael Porter, *Competitive Strategy*, (New York: Free Press, 1980) pp. 40–41.

restructuring. Exhibit 17.4 summarizes the common organizational requirements necessary for each of Porter's three generic strategies. Continental Airlines was an example of this strategy when, in the mid 1990s, it instituted a low-cost strategy called Continental Lite, only to abandon it after a number of months in Chapter 11 bankruptcy. Continental has since reorganized and became profitable in the late 1990s.

Management Philosophy Concerning Employees and Technology

The philosophy of the firm's managers concerning its employees and technology may also influence restructuring. Some firms, such as Japanese automobile producers, commit themselves to no-layoff policies, although during the early and mid 1990s this policy was modified somewhat during Japan's most severe recession since World War II. Honda in Marysville, Ohio, employs 12,000 workers and is the region's largest employer. It has not laid off one worker. Other organizations view personnel as easily replaced assets. Many organizations that require skilled people, such as those in the electronics industry, believe that it is cheaper to keep employees than to let them go during a restructuring and then have to rehire and train new people later.

Firms in some industries can easily replace employees because of the low level of skills needed to perform many of the jobs. This is particularly true of service industries, such as fast-food restaurants. Many firms in these industries have relatively low training costs for new employees. If not, they are willing to pay for the increased training costs due to high employee turnover because alternatives are less appealing. These alternatives may include automation or increased salaries for employees. Exhibit 17.5 highlights some of the jobs that are easy and not so easy to refill.

automation
Replacing people with machines and equipment.

Management philosophy toward **automation** may also affect a firm's restructuring decision. Some firms believe that high levels of automation are necessary to compete effectively in the market. As a result, employees in these organizations become more expendable during times of restructuring. Other firms place an emphasis on the flexibility of humans more than robots. In these cases capital investment may suffer during times of restructuring compared with employment levels. In any situation

EXHIBIT 17.5	EASY-TO-FILL AND HARD-TO-FILL JOBS

**Hard-to-fill Jobs:
Try to Avoid Laying Off Workers in These Areas**

Physical Therapists	Electrical Engineers
Veterinarians	Computer Scientists
Computer Systems Analysts	Dietitians
Physicians	Chemical Engineers
Pharmacists	Dentists
Biological Scientists	Lawyers
Vocational Counselors	Actuaries
Registered Nurses	

**Easy-to-fill jobs:
Layoffs in This Area Should Not Result in Problems**

Telephone Operators	Butchers/Meat Cutters
Rail Transport Workers	Telephone Installers
Machine Operators	Typists
Water Transport Workers	Statistical Clerks
Barbers	Data Processors
Photographers	Stenographers
Metalworkers	Firefighters
Plumbers	Postal Clerks

SOURCE: **www.bls.gov**

management's philosophy toward its employees and its technology plays a significant role in determining the form of the restructuring.

Business Cycles

Business cycle stages may also influence a firm's restructuring decision. Each stage of the business cycle prosperity, recession, depression, and recovery has a unique effect on an organization. Weak economic conditions often force restructuring decisions on firms. In other instances restructuring can arise from the opportunities to make changes in times of prosperity. Restructuring during these times is often less painful to carry out than during slowdowns.

prosperity and recovery A period of the business cycle characterized by strong economic times and increasing sales.

Characteristics of **prosperity and recovery** in economic terms are strong and increasing sales. Organizations have extra resources and capital as a result of the prosperous times, and restructuring often causes little disruption to the organization. Firms typically add extra employees to meet the strong demand from the market. Other firms may choose to restructure by putting a freeze on hiring or filling only critical positions, thus limiting the size of the organization. Still other firms may restructure by reassigning personnel from noncritical to critical positions. This enables

---

FOCUS ON HR

What Happens to Workers after Losing Jobs?

A recent study by the U.S. Department of Labor indicates that many workers have a hard time finding another job after losing their job through downsizing. What is particularly troublesome about this finding is that this occurred during a booming economy in the United States. Of 2.2 million full-time workers laid off in 1993 and 1994, only two thirds had full-time jobs again in early 1996. Half of this group were earning less than at their former jobs, and more than one third had pay cuts of 20 percent or more. Many older workers remained unemployed or just retired early. Those in their late 50s and early 60s who did find another job had pay cuts averaging 37 percent. However, 47 percent of full-timers who did find new jobs did as well or better in their new jobs salarywise, and about one in five actually experienced salary gains of 20 percent or more in the new jobs.

The Department of Labor concludes that downsizing appears to be a permanent fixture in our economy even in good times and that many people will continue to have difficulties finding a job comparable to the one they left.

SOURCE: Gene Koretz, "Downsizing's Painful Effects," *Business Week*, April 13, 1998, p. 23.

---

organizations to emphasize areas that are essential to their success. Many firms transfer employees out of corporate headquarters or support roles into sales and marketing positions.

recession A period of the business cycle characterized by economic slowdowns, rising unemployment, lack of market demand for goods and services, and excess productive capacity.

Restructuring often occurs during times of recession or depression. **Recessions** are periods of general economic slowdowns. Rising unemployment, lack of market demand for goods and services, and excess productive capacity characterize recessions. **Depressions** are severe forms of recessions. Unemployment may reach 25 percent of the total workforce, and firm bankruptcies increase significantly. Fortunately, business cycles do not always pass through all four stages. The last general depression in the United States occurred during the 1930s and ended with the start of World War II.

Not all segments of the economy are at the same stage of the business cycle. Thus the electronics industry may be in a period of prosperity while the steel industry is in a recession. Recessions and depressions often force firms to restructure to survive. Restructuring during these times is often more radical as a result. In times of prosperity firms consider the optimal number of employees they need to succeed. During recessions and depressions, they consider how many employees they can cut and still function. However, recessions and depressions allow organizations to make changes that they may not have been able to make during prosperous times, such as automating to cut costs or closing marginally profitable plants and offices.

depression A severe recession characterized by prolonged economic slowdowns, extremely high unemployment levels, severely declining market demand for goods and services, and high levels of excess productive capacity.

Many union contracts forbid layoffs or worker reassignments during strong economic periods but allow them during downturns. Resistance to restructuring may be high during periods of prosperity because it is difficult to justify cutbacks when the latest quarter just produced record profits. Resistance is often much lower if the organization's members are convinced that a restructuring is necessary to ensure the organization's continued existence. As a result, restructuring is often easier to accomplish during periods of recession or depression, and greater changes are possible than in stable economic times. However, once workers are laid off during poor economic times, they may not be rehired when the economy turns around. More and more companies are deciding to remain lean and make the job cuts permanent.[10]

Cost Restructure

The 1980s and 1990s saw great changes in U.S. business practices. Many organizations underwent radical changes in their operating methods. These changes were largely due to the increase in international competition and rapidly changing technology. Many U.S. firms discovered that their decades-old methods of operating were unsuitable to match the increase in foreign competition. Many foreign firms began to sell products that were both less expensive and higher in quality than those produced by their American counterparts. Peter Reid, in the book *Well Made in America*, described the reaction of a group of Harley-Davidson managers and employees who toured the Honda motorcycle plant in Marysville, Ohio, in 1982. He remembers that Honda's total overhead staff at Marysville (president, secretaries, personnel department, accounting, material planning, and so on) numbered 30 of 500 employees. Harley's managers were surprised that they could find no squadrons of engineers and planners stashed in the back room. Further, Harley manager's couldn't even conceive of how to do such a thing. This episode was a sobering lesson in the basic difference between Honda's costs and Harley's overhead staff.[11]

cost restructuring The process by which a firm seeks to change certain costs within the organization, usually with the goal of reducing costs to a lower level.

Harley-Davidson's reaction to this problem was typical of many U.S. firms facing similar situations in the 1980s and 1990s. It began a process of **cost restructuring**, a process in which a firm seeks to change certain costs within the organization, usually with the goal of reducing them. Cost restructuring is usually a common goal of any organization restructuring strategy. In Harley-Davidson's case one of its main cost restructuring goals was to reduce its overhead. A joint survey of 1837 firms, undertaken by the Society for Human Resource Management and the Commerce Clearing House, reported that the main goal of almost 50 percent of all restructuring efforts is labor cost reduction. The survey also found that more than two thirds of the firms that had restructured experienced a decrease in the size of their workforce. Exhibit 17.6 shows that cost control is the most common reason firms undertake a restructuring program.[12]

Other common cost restructuring goals include reducing production costs, inventory costs, and capital spending costs. Firms such as Oryx, a Texas oil and gas producer, have achieved significant cost restructuring by cutting or reducing bureaucratic red tape. This red tape may include rules, procedures, reviews, reports, and approval processes.[13] Kodak has restructured five times since 1982 to make it more efficient and allow it to post better earnings. Kodak also wanted the restructuring to put it on the growth track again. In 1991 it had a 5.7 percent drop in profit after adjusting for inflation. Even Kodak conceded that some of the restructuring attempts have not achieved their goals.[14] In January 1998 Kodak announced a cut of 10,000 jobs as part of restructuring, and in 2000 another 5000 jobs were cut. The struggling photo company announced weaker-than-expected quarterly profits for 1999.[15]

leveraged buyout (LBO) The takeover of a company with borrowed funds, using the acquired company's assets as collateral.

junk bonds High-yield, low-grade bonds often used as the basis for LBO financing plans.

Another major cause of cost restructuring that began in the 1980s is the widespread use of the **leveraged buyout (LBO)**. An LBO is the takeover of a company, usually using borrowed funds, either in the form of bank loans or low-rated junk bonds. Collateral for the buyout is usually the target company's own assets. The acquirer generally pledges to repay the loans out of the cash flow of the acquired company.[16] As LBO mania peaked in the middle to late 1980s, financing methods often became poorly thought out or unsound. **Junk bonds**, which are high-yielding low-grade bonds, formed the basis of many LBO financing plans. In short, junk-bond buyers were paid high rates of interest to offset the inherent risk.

| EXHIBIT 17.6 | REASONS COMPANIES RESTRUCTURE |

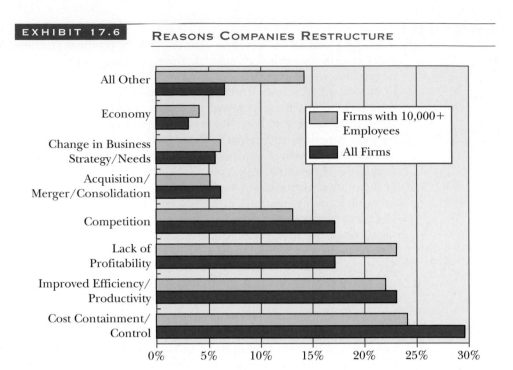

SOURCE: *People Trends*, September 1993, p. 2.

Many LBOs gave firms the unique opportunity to restructure their costs. This is true because LBOs often involve the arrival of a new management team not tied to old ways. As a result, the new management team may sell off operations that are not part of the organization's core business, thereby shifting the organization's emphasis from one business to another and achieving a cost restructuring in the process. Other LBOs are successful because they force firms to be aware of their cost structures. This may occur because the debt covenant has strict rules about the organizations cost structure. Management may also seek to control costs that would cause the organization to default on its debt payments. Payment defaults often force the firm into bankruptcy.

The main problem with less successful LBOs is the inability to meet the debt payments. Many organizations are unable to reduce costs enough to generate the extra cash necessary to make the debt payments. These payments are large because the interest rate on the debt is usually high. Other organizations run into problems when economic conditions change.

Finally, LBOs can lead to failures on the part of recently placed executives. With LBOs come new management teams who may not be familiar with current procedures and cultures. The entrance of new management can be advantageous to the firm from a cost-cutting perspective, but it can be detrimental to the manager's career. LBOs often do not provide sufficient time for managers to become familiar with key players and understand what is expected of them before they must make major decisions that can cause the LBO to succeed or fail.[17]

mergers When two firms join together as one firm.

More recently, the United States has experienced record growth in a different type of cost restructuring known as **mergers**. In 2000 the largest merger in U.S.

FOCUS ON HR

Honesty Is the Best Cost-Cutting Strategy

Against the better judgment of everyone he knew, Hugh Aaron, CEO of a small plastics firm, decided that the best way to make his workers understand why he had to make major cost-cutting changes was to let them see the books. He decided that his hourly workers should be made privy to the profit and loss statement. By showing them the facts and figures, they would surely agree with his plans.

So one day Aaron closed the plant for an hour and a half and with the use of a chalkboard, he explained the financial picture of the firm to all of his workers. As he began to explain the situation, he was asked many questions. Some, such as "What is gross profit?" made him realize that just explaining the situation would not be enough. He would first have to educate the workers about the business of being in business.

One of his managers volunteered to hold daily work sessions with the employees to explain business concepts to them. He was also given the task of explaining the profit and loss statement to the workers. At that meeting the workers began to accuse the management of having two sets of books: the ones it was sharing with the workers to show

how bad things were to garner wage cuts and the real set the accountants and lawyers used.

To combat these fears, the lawyers and accountants were present at the next meeting to reassure the workers that the figures they saw were the figures that the firm actually reported. Once the workers began to believe that the numbers were accurate, things started to change.

Some of the changes were small; others were not. For example, the workers noticed that there was a $4,000 entry on the books for renting and laundering uniforms. They suggested that the firm purchase an industrial washing machine to use at the end of the shift to save the laundering costs. This one change saved the firm $12,000 a year, approximately the same amount of money as one worker's yearly salary.

The only workers who did not seem to enjoy the new open information format were the managers. They seemed to thrive under the old traditional style of closed shops, which is exactly where Aaron asked them to go.

SOURCE: Adapted from Hugh Aaron, "In Troubled Times, Run an Open Company," *The Wall Street Journal*, December 10, 1990, p. A10.

history took place between media giants America Online (AOL) and Time Warner. The transaction was valued at $183 billion, making it the fourth highest stock market–valued company after the merger.

The Impact of Restructuring on Human Resources

Once an organization decides to restructure, its managers must make several broad choices to determine the type of human resource restructuring it will use. These choices are based on the answers to four basic questions:

1. Should the firm use a no-layoff strategy?
2. If the firm does not use a no-layoff strategy, should it use wage cuts?
3. If the firm uses layoffs, should they be temporary layoffs or permanent plant closings?
4. Should the organization cushion its terminations or use harsh terminations?

These issues represent the increasing severity of the impact of restructuring on employees. No-layoff strategies usually represent the least severe impact on employees as a whole in the organization. They are, however, often the most difficult for the firm to control and implement. Terminations, at the other end, are often the easiest form of restructuring for the organization to control and implement. Terminations

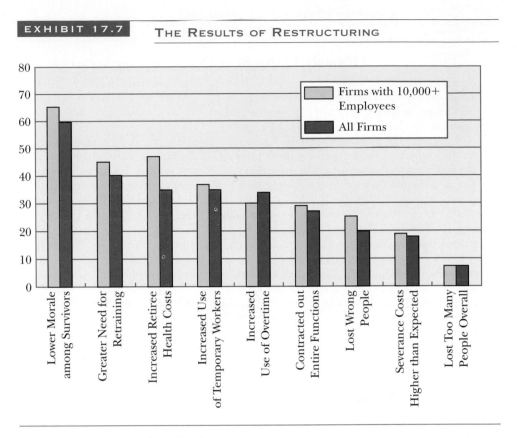

| EXHIBIT 17.7 | THE RESULTS OF RESTRUCTURING |

SOURCE: *People Trends*, September 1993, p. 3.

hurt because they usually have the greatest negative impact on the employees. The timeframe of each type of strategy also creates problems. No-layoff strategies usually take the longest to implement but often have the greatest long-term benefits to the organization if they are successful. Layoff and termination strategies, on the other hand, can take effect almost immediately after management has chosen them.

Layoffs may have unintended long-term side effects that are difficult to control, however. These side effects include losing valuable employees and long-term employee morale problems. Of course, a firm that is facing imminent bankruptcy may need the immediate benefits of massive layoffs to survive. For other firms the shock of large-scale layoffs may be the solution for revitalizing a lethargic and unresponsive organization.[18] Each strategy has its own unique characteristics and advantages and disadvantages. These issues will be discussed in the remainder of this chapter.

Exhibit 17.7 illustrates some of the negative effects companies have reported as a result of implementing restructuring programs. Exhibit 17.8 lists practices best suited in helping businesses restructuring goals.

No-Layoff Strategies

Many firms view their employees as their most valuable assets. They recognize that employees have unique skills gained over years of service to the organization. Other employees have skills that are rare in the marketplace, thus increasing their value to

EXHIBIT 17.8	EFFECTIVE PRACTICES USED TO ATTAIN RESTRUCTURING GOALS		

Practice	Percentage Terming It "Very Effective"	Percentage Who Used It
Creating restructuring project teams	64%	56%
Small-group meetings with employees	63	65
Involving employees on task forces	60	60
One-on-one counseling on early retirement	52	63
Briefings for managers and supervisors	51	74
Eliminating low-value work	51	58
Conducting team-building activities	45	61
Total-quality-management initiatives	41	68
Developing a restructuring communications strategy	41	63

SOURCE: Gilbert Fuchsberg, "Why Shakeups Work for Some, Not for Others," *The Wall Street Journal*, October 1, 1993, p. B1.

no-layoff restructuring An organizational strategy that seeks to reduce the size of a firm's workforce without having to lay off or terminate employees.

the firm. In other cases groups of employees have unique combinations of skills that make them valuable to the organization. The need to reduce the number of active employees on the payroll conflicts with their need of the employee's special skills. If the organization lays off employees, they may never return, or the unique combination of skills that made particular work teams valuable may be lost forever. On the other hand, if the organization does not reduce the size of its workforce, its operating costs may be too high. Many firms in this position choose to use a **no-layoff restructuring policy**.

reduction through attrition A no-layoff strategy in which a firm tries to stop the growth in the total number of its employees and reduce the total number without laying off employees.

No-layoff strategies are organization actions that seek to reduce the size of an organization's workforce without having to lay off or terminate anyone. No-layoff policies usually involve some combination of three alternatives: (1) reduce the workforce through attrition, (2) provide for worker reassignment and retraining, or (3) loan employees to other firms.

Workforce Reduction Through Attrition

Reduction through attrition is perhaps the most common method of no-layoff restructuring. Firms that use this method try to reduce the total number of people employed by the firm without laying off anyone. This is a popular method in government organizations. There are three basic types of attrition: hiring freezes in new and planned jobs, nonreplacement of current job vacancies, and nonreplacement of fired workers. The three methods are different from one another, but they share some similarities. Most firms use all three to some extent when carrying out a workforce attrition strategy.

hiring freeze A workforce attrition method in which a firm forgoes all new, planned hirings.

Perhaps the most common method that firms use for workforce attrition is the **hiring freeze**. Firms operating under hiring freezes forgo all new planned hirings. In many instances hiring freezes are organizationwide. In other instances firms selectively implement hiring freezes. In these situations firms stop hiring in most departments while continuing to hire in areas critical to the success of the organization. Both methods are used in practice; the remainder of this discussion concentrates on total, or organizationwide, hiring freezes.

Hiring freezes have several advantages and disadvantages. One advantage is that firms can immediately control and predict their wage and benefit expenses. Because no new employees are being hired, the firm can easily calculate how much it is spending and decide how to control these costs in the future. Another advantage lies in controlling costs related to recruitment and training of new employees. These costs include advertising funds, the time and money spent by managers interviewing potential employees, the internal costs related to new hires such as placement on payroll, the assignment of office supplies and equipment, and the funds allocated to train and orient new employees. Other costs saved include state and federal taxes paid on employees' wages and benefits. For example, if a firm chooses not to fill a $60,000-a-year position in the engineering department, the actual savings could be much higher:

Salary saved	$60,000
Benefits saved (such as insurance and vacation)	20,000
Taxes saved (Social Security, Workers' Compensation, etc.)	7000
Training costs saved (such as orientation, familiarization with rules and procedures, and job education)	4000
Office supplies and equipment (desk, chair, computer, supplies)	10,000
Hiring costs saved (such as entering in payroll, establishing employee file, and insurance policy paperwork)	2000
Recruitment costs saved (such as campus interviews, advertising, managers' interviewing time, and committee decision time)	10,000
Total savings	$113,000

This example shows that the actual savings from not hiring new employees are much higher than just an employee's salary. Savings may be higher or lower, depending on the nature of the job and the company, but either way the savings can be significant.

Such a strategy has several possible disadvantages, however. First, not hiring new employees may overburden current employees. This may result in decreased productivity and lower morale. Hiring freezes may have additional effects on employees who are seeking promotion within the organization because the freezes either explicitly or accidentally result in promotion freezes when current workers become more necessary in the positions that they now hold. As a result, many employees in line for promotions may become frustrated at a perceived lack of advancement potential. This, coupled with the additional workload that accompanies hiring freezes, may cause these employees to seek other employment opportunities.

In addition, firms that compete in technology-based industries may find themselves falling behind the competition as they fail to hire employees with new and valuable skills. For example, let's return to the example of the firm that did not hire the new engineer. If the firm needed a civil engineer, it probably would not experience too many competitive problems in the future because the supply of civil engineers is relatively good compared with the demand. If the position was for a computer engineer, however, the firm may soon experience severe problems because the average computer technology lasts for less than 3 years before it becomes obsolete; well-trained computer engineers are therefore relatively scarce. Firms that choose to use selective hiring freezes can often escape this problem, as mentioned earlier.

In summary, hiring freezes have two main advantages and disadvantages. They can help a firm immediately control costs and can save other related costs in hiring new employees. On the other hand, hiring freezes can have a negative impact on current employees and can result in the loss of competitive advantage from failing to gain new and valuable skills.

Another attrition method that firms use is *not to replace those people who naturally leave the organization*. Unlike hiring freezes, which try to stop growth by halting the creation of new jobs, this method seeks to reduce total employment by not filling current positions as they become vacant. People who quit, retire, die, or leave at the end of a contract are considered to have naturally left the organization. Organizations often offer some form of incentive to employees to accelerate this process. These incentives include cash bonuses to people who leave during a specified period, accelerated or early retirement benefits, and free outplacement services (discussed in more depth later in the chapter).[19] This method has several advantages. First, organizations can save a considerable amount of money in the recruitment, hiring, and training of new employees. This is the same type of advantage gained by organizations that use the no-new-hire strategy discussed earlier.

Another advantage of the attrition method is the ability to cut positions that have become unneeded or inefficient within the organization. A position that was important in the past may become obsolete as the organization changes. Positions created to fit certain needs during periods of success with little forethought or planning may have outlived their benefits. These positions may become redundant or unnecessary during periods of retrenchment.

When a firm decides to downsize, it may be difficult to cut positions because of several factors, such as the building of an empire by the individuals holding the positions. **Empire building** occurs when individuals entrench themselves in positions through a combination of politics, length of time in the job, and the ability to project a perceived value to the firm. Management may also be reluctant to fire or lay off an individual who is close to retirement. Finally, struggles by individual managers to protect the size of their departments may affect downsizing. These struggles often serve as a surrogate measure of the individual who is close to retirement.

A main disadvantage of using an attrition strategy is that the organization is unable to control exactly who leaves and who stays. It may seek to reduce its overhead positions, but it may also lose a significant number of people in marketing and R&D in the process. Another disadvantage is that this method may take a long time to carry out. Unlike other strategies, such as worker layoffs, which take only days or weeks, a nonreplacement strategy may take months or even years to reach its full potential. Because the organization is not forcing employees to leave, it must wait for individuals to decide to leave. The incentives mentioned earlier can help to speed the process, but even they do not guarantee that the firm will reach its goals in the time desired. Finally, the nonreplacement of workers who naturally leave can be problematic in the short term. Many of the incentives designed to encourage workers to leave (e.g., early retirement bonuses) require the organization to spend large sums of money up front. This is often contrary to the immediate goals of a restructuring.

Another major type of no-layoff restructuring is **worker reassignment and retraining**. Firms that use this strategy often do not want to reduce the size of their

empire building
Actions by individuals to entrench themselves in positions through a combination of politics, length of time on the job, and the ability to project a perceived value to the firm, thus making it more difficult for the firm to eliminate their jobs or lay them off.

worker reassignment and retraining
Moving workers out of one job and into another job that may be more important to the organization, often accompanied by the teaching of new and previously unrelated job skills.

workforce but instead want to move workers from one job and into another that may be more important to the organization. For example, a common reassignment involves transferring workers to sales and manufacturing jobs and out of support and overhead positions. This is typical because sales and manufacturing jobs often create real value for the organization because they both directly generate revenues. A larger sales force can generate more sales for the company, and a larger manufacturing force can produce more items and become more specialized. Because support and overhead positions such as clerical staff, maintenance workers, and corporate headquarters staff do not directly produce real value for the organization, they may be treated as a "necessary evil." In fact, some firms use **value chain analysis**, which attempts to determine the amount of added value produced by each position and unit in the organization. Those positions and units not producing sufficient added value are the first to go.

value chain analysis Determining the amount of value added to the organization by each job and unit.

In addition, worker productivity is more easily measured in sales and manufacturing jobs. Sales employees productivity measures are based on sales volume. The productivity of manufacturing employees is based on the number of units produced and the percentage of defective units produced. The productivity of support and overhead positions is not as easily measured as it is in sales and manufacturing. For example, how can the value of a raw materials price forecast prepared by a corporate analyst be determined? Is one good forecast equivalent to three average forecasts produced by another analyst? Could the money spent by the organization in preparing the forecast (employee salaries, purchasing or development of economic information, use of computer resources, and so on) be better used in other areas, such as purchasing a more efficient milling machine for the assembly line? How can one tell today if the forecast for the future is good or poor? How would the organization's performance be affected if the forecast was not produced? Clearly, it is difficult to determine how helpful these positions are to the organization. Many of these questions can be answered, but often only after a long time and at a great expense. Thus many firms are willing to move workers into sales and manufacturing because it is much easier to measure their contribution in terms of how well the organization is operating.

Organizations often use worker reassignments as a prelude to or with other types of restructuring. The transfer of workers into sales and manufacturing, in addition to directly affecting the firm's performance, enables the organization to begin the process of cutting workers. The productivity measures in sales and manufacturing jobs make it easier to determine which employees are worthwhile to the organization and which are not. Hence, it is easier to document and release poor performers in these areas. In addition, these transfers can either be voluntary programs or mandated by the organization. If the transfers are voluntary, the organization is often able to keep good employees who may have been getting stale in their previous positions. In these situations the transfers often result in improved employee morale and performance.

Voluntary transfers present problems to organizations seeking to lay off workers, however. Many poorer performing employees will choose to stay in their current jobs out of a fear of failing in a new job. Again, it may be difficult to lay off or replace these workers because productivity measures are difficult to determine in these positions. Employees who are valuable in these support and overhead positions may also transfer into manufacturing and sales. This can hurt the organization because they may be more valuable in their original positions. For example, a purchasing agent may have spent years learning the dynamics of the firm's industry and may have built strong relationships with many suppliers. The loss of these intangible benefits to the organization may be far greater than the immediate additional revenues generated by transferring the purchasing agent to sales. The chance also exists that a good performer in one position may transfer into a new position and become a poor performer because individual skills, interests, and abilities may not be transferable.

Mandatory transfers also have specific advantages and disadvantages. Unlike voluntary transfers, the results of mandatory transfers are more certain. Firms using mandatory transfers can target areas they consider to be less important and reduce them while emphasizing other areas with a virtual certainty of achieving their goals. Mandatory transfer programs often permit firms to target specific employees for transfer. This can produce a better match of job skills and can essentially force unwanted employees to leave the organization. This method is not without its problems, however. Mandatory transfers can hurt employee morale as the organization moves people into positions they do not want. They can also disrupt synergies that have developed in various work groups over the years.

Union contracts often prohibit organizations from implementing these policies, and they may meet fierce resistance from unions with contracts that do not prohibit such strategies. Unions have recently begun to accept contracts that allow firms to transfer employees to remain competitive. In recognizing this need in contracts, unions are, in turn, having more say in determining the nature of these transfers. Members of nonunion firms may also fight the transfers. Their fights may range from subtle resistance to open hostility or even to legal challenges. Finally, mandatory transfers may also result in valued employees leaving the organization.

worker retraining An upgrade or improvement of an employee's existing job skills.

Another complementary method to worker reassignment is organizational incentives to employees to undergo **worker retraining**, or career development. Although worker reassignment often involves some form of skills retraining, worker retraining refers to an upgrading or improvement of jobs skills, not the learning of new and unrelated ones. Organization incentives to retrain include paid sabbaticals, financing of education, a partial release from duties, and possible future promotions.

Such a policy has many advantages. First, the strategy can help to reduce employee anxiety caused by the restructuring. With the organization sponsoring or encouraging retraining, employees often feel more secure about their futures with the organization. If retraining programs are offered on a large scale, the resistance to the restructuring may decrease dramatically or at least help the employees accept what is happening.[20] Another advantage is that retraining programs during restructuring are often complementary to the new work systems and new directions that the organization seeks to achieve with the restructuring. Finally, the organization is often able to reduce the immediate direct and indirect labor costs that would result if the employee were working full-time during the restructuring.

worker loan-out program Lending of workers from one organization to another for a specified period, such as lending employees to government or charitable organizations.

Of course, some disadvantages do exist. Some employees who may benefit the most from retraining may be the employees who are most needed to help the organization successfully complete the restructuring. Furthermore, without a specific contract binding the employee to the company after the retraining period is over, the employee may take his or her additional skills to a new job. Despite these potential disadvantages, the case for further training during restructuring is strong. It is important that firms understand that career development training should still be used under these conditions, but designing it within such an environment may be challenging.

A final no-layoff restructuring strategy that has emerged within the past few years is the **worker loan-out program**. Although this strategy is somewhat rare, it might become more common in the 21st century. Worker loan-out programs involve one organization lending workers to another for a specified period, such as to government

---

EXHIBIT 17.9   SAVED BY THE BOSS

Brooks Beverage Management of Holland, Michigan, lent 20 workers to Haworth, Inc., and office furniture maker, rather than lay them off after an unexpectedly sharp seasonal decline. Brooks pays the employees' insurance benefits and compensates them for salary cuts so that when business picks up, the company can avoid the expense of recruiting and training new workers.

SOURCE: Rochelle Sharpe, "Labor Letter," *The Wall Street Journal*, September 13, 1994, p. A1.

or charitable organizations. For example, IBM and Polaroid support programs that allow their employees to work as teachers in public schools and universities for up to 2 years while still drawing a salary from their companies.[21] Motorola has begun training workers to pass on their knowledge to students through an advisement program, and Sears has assigned officials to work with schools to build stronger curriculums.[22] Exhibit 17.9 provides an example of an employer loaning employees to another noncompetitive firm.

Lockheed Martin's loan-out of employees to Boeing is another example of the loan strategy. Lockheed Martin's aircraft division derives most of its business from military orders. Cutbacks in U.S. military budgets resulted in a work slowdown for Lockheed Martin. In contrast, Boeing is the world's leading manufacturer of commercial aircraft. Some of its planes have order backlogs as long as 10 years. Rather than having to lay off, and possibly lose, highly skilled employees, Lockheed Martin agreed to lend 670 of its workers to Boeing, which, because of its recent success, needs more employees than it can recruit. Boeing agreed to use Lockheed Martin's workers and pay their salaries for the loan-out period.[23] Hewlett-Packard used an internal employee loan program, among other plans, to deal with more than 400 employees who were displaced when it made the strategic decision to exit the fabrication business. Employees were loaned to other divisions in which short-term hiring needs existed. Some of the loans were for as short a duration as 1 day; others lasted up to a year. H-P provided housing and transportation costs if the loan crossed regional boundaries.[24]

There are several advantages to both organizations involved in these situations. The organization loaning out its employees can keep them as its employees, often without having to incur the expenses of paying their salaries or to lay them off, during the loan-out period. Consequently, the organization can gain many of the advantages of a layoff and restructuring without incurring all of the related expenses, such as severance pay, outplacement services, and the recruitment and training costs of new employees in the future. These programs also enable the loaning company's employees to keep their skills up to date or to learn new skills without incurring the retraining expenses. Another advantage for the loaning organization is that its employees often return with new ideas and new outlooks as a result of their experiences. This may result in significant improvements in the organizations operations. These programs often generate large amounts of goodwill within the organization's home community, especially if the organization receiving the employees is a local government agency or charity. This goodwill can result in positive press and publicity and favorable attitudes toward the organization by the receiving organization.

These programs also can generate goodwill with the organization's employees, who may interpret the move in several different ways. Employees may perceive that the organization is willing to let them become involved in activities that are personally important without hurting their careers in the organization. In addition, employee loyalty to an organization that is not willing to let its employees join the unemployment line is likely to increase.

There are a number of advantages for the organization receiving the loaned-out employees. One advantage is the training expenses saved by borrowing workers who are already skilled. Another is the saving of recruiting costs. Because the length of the worker loan-out is usually fixed, the receiving firm saves money by having workers for only as long as they are needed. The receiving firm also avoids having to incur layoff and separation expenses. Receiving organizations can also gain the same type of benefit from the fresh outlook of the loaned-out employees. Finally, charities and government organizations obtain employees and skills that they would not be able to afford under normal circumstances.

Of course, this type of strategy has some disadvantages. If there is a sudden change in the circumstances of the loan-out (for example, the loaning company's business suddenly picks up), the workers cannot return until the end of the agreed loan-out period. Hence a firm may be unable to recover workers that it needs. There is also the chance that the loaning firm may permanently lose its employees, possibly even to competitors. Some loan-out agreements may specifically forbid a receiving firm from hiring loaned-out employees after the expiration of the loan-out period, but nothing prevents individuals from deciding not to return to their first organization. Finally, an organization may inadvertently give up some of its skills or secrets in loaning out its employees.

layoff A restructuring strategy in which an organization seeks to temporarily reduce the size of its workforce, usually through the release of employees from work for a specified time.

Layoff Strategies

indefinite layoff A layoff strategy in which the organization permanently releases an employee from the company after a fixed layoff period, such as 6 months or a year.

supplemental unemployment benefit (SUB) A layoff strategy in which employees receive a fixed percentage of their wages through a combination of state and federal unemployment benefits and organizational payments for periods of up to 1 year.

Layoffs are among the most common strategies used in restructuring (Exhibit 17.10). Layoffs usually involve some form of temporary reduction in the organization's workforce and are particularly common in cyclical industries. Under this strategy the organization releases employees from work for a specific time, but they remain employees of the organization and continue to receive benefits. Under an **indefinite layoff** the organization may release the employees from the company after a fixed period, such as 6 months or a year. An indefinite layoff strategy is typical in situations in which the workforce is highly skilled and the costs of recruiting and training new employees may be high. Thus the organization tries to keep its employees as long as possible without terminating them. Firms primarily use layoffs to reduce labor costs temporarily without losing valuable employees. Layoffs are commonly found in industries in which union contracts may prohibit the firing of employees because of changes in business conditions. Layoffs are common in automobile manufacturing, agriculture, steel making, and tourism.

Several layoff methods are available. One popular method within the automobile and steel industries is the use of **supplemental unemployment benefits (SUBs)**. They provide a fixed percentage (up to 95 percent in some instances) of a laid-off employee's wages through a combination of state and federal unemployment benefits and additional organization payments for periods up to 1 year. SUBs are common in these industries because they are cyclical or they involve periods of major plant shutdowns for renovations. For example, most U.S. automobile plants shut down for a period each summer to allow the company to change or gear up assembly lines for the new automobile model year that begins in October. Steel plants often close for routine maintenance or major upgrades in equipment.

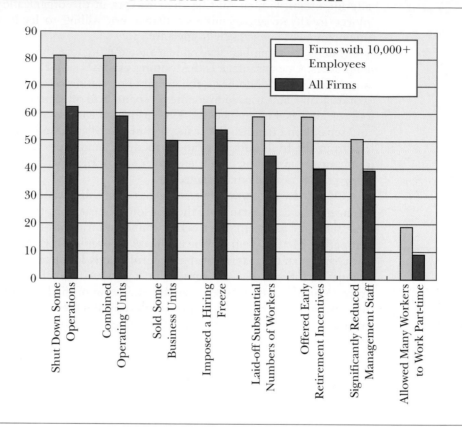

EXHIBIT 17.10   STRATEGIES USED TO DOWNSIZE

SOURCE: *People Trends*, September 1993, p. 2.

A major advantage of SUBs is that they allow firms to lay off their skilled employees for up to 1 year with little risk of losing them to other firms. Critics of SUBs, however, point out that the high level of benefits often discourages employees from seeking other jobs. This may hurt the laid-off workers more than it helped when the benefits expire at the end of the year and the firm chooses not to bring the employees back to work. Another disadvantage of SUBs is their high cost to the firm, but these costs must be weighed against the costs of hiring and training new employees.

reduced work-week A layoff strategy in which a firm lowers its payroll costs by reducing the number of hours worked every week by each employee.

Another common layoff strategy is the use of the **reduced workweek** for employees. The reduced workweek allows organizations to reduce their payroll costs while still holding employees and providing work for them. The size of the reduction varies from firm to firm, but most reduced workweeks are between 20 and 30 hours for full-time employees.[25] Like SUBs, the reduced workweek enables firms to keep their valuable employees, but it also enables employees to keep their skills up to date. Many firms also try to lessen the impact of the reduced workweek by scheduling special work that would not be done during normal company operations. Examples include repair and maintenance of plant and equipment to reorganizing plants and warehouses or taking special inventories. Some states even make up the difference in the workers pay if the firm keeps them on at least part time. The money spent by the state is less than the firms would spend for unemployment benefits, and the workers have the chance to go back full time if the company's business picks up.[26]

Reduced workweeks have several disadvantages. A main disadvantage involves predicting the number of hours that employees are needed each week. Reduced work-weeks may also require that many staff members continue to work full time to support those employees working reduced weeks because it is difficult to cut back support functions only partially. An example of this includes the need to keep a fully staffed payroll department, where the volume of work does not depend on the number of hours worked by line employees. Finally, reduced workweeks may prevent employees from seeking other jobs because they cannot predict when they will be available for work because of the unpredictable hours of the first job.

reduced shift A layoff strategy in which an organization cuts back on the total number of hours it operates, either by cutting back on the total number of employees per shift or eliminating one or more shifts entirely.

A third layoff strategy includes the use of **reduced shifts**, which involves cutting the total number of hours that the organization operates. Reduced shift layoffs can take one of two forms. One type cuts back on the total number of employees per shift. For example, a firm may usually operate three 8-hour shifts per day during normal conditions with 300 employees per shift. The first type of reduced shift strategy may be to reduce the total number of employees to 200 per shift. This approach affects all shifts equally. Another form of reduced shifts is to eliminate one or more shifts from the schedule entirely. In this example the firm may choose to cut the midnight-to-8:00 AM shift entirely while maintaining the other two shifts at full capacity.

Organizations may, of course, take a middle ground between these two extremes. They may decide to drop one shift and partially cut back on other shifts or use some other combination of cutbacks. Several factors usually determine the type of reduced shift approach used. The first factor is the nature of the work being done on each shift and the skills of the employees. If each shift performs essentially the same job, many organizations consider cutting entire shifts, especially the late-evening/early-morning shifts that have some form of salary differential. If a job takes several shifts to complete, with each shift performing a specialized function, the organization may consider laying off some employees on each shift but maintaining all shifts to some extent.

plant and office closings A layoff strategy in which an organization either temporarily or permanently shuts down independent work units as part of a restructuring.

Other factors may also affect the choice of reduced shift. A major factor in many decisions is the type of production process that the organization uses. If the organization's equipment is geared toward long continuous runs that would be expensive to interrupt (such as in the glass, steel, or paper-making industries), it may choose to reduce the number of employees per shift. This is typical of the paper-making industry in which it is expensive to start up and shut down machinery—the process of paper making is a round-the-clock effort.[27]

If the organization employs a batch production process, with each shift capable of producing a complete job, the decision may be to close down an entire shift instead of reducing all shifts. This is typical of clothing manufacturers. A similar situation exists in the automobile industry, where the production process is a machine-paced line flow. Because the production process is standardized over each shift and the cost of shutting down and starting up machinery is not prohibitively expensive, reduced shift layoffs are often an entire shift approach.

Plant and Office Closings

Another common layoff strategy is the use of **plant or office closings**. Unlike reduced shifts, which affect only a portion of the employees of the work unit, plant and office closings affect all employees of the unit. Plant and office closings are the temporary or permanent shutdown of independent work units as part of an organization's restructuring. Plants may be entire production facilities; for example, General Motors closed many car plants in 1990 and through 2000.[28] An example of an office closing is the closing of a district sales office by a national organization. Of course, other closings also qualify under this definition, even though they are not offices or plants. Burger King closed some of its older stores and Ames closed many of its retail stores as part of their bankruptcy reorganization.

Closings may occur for a variety of reasons. They may be part of a focus strategy discussed earlier in this chapter. The closings may be the result of a downsizing because of bankruptcy, as is the case with Ames. Or, as is the case with GM, they may result from the modernization or the conversion of facilities to meet a change in strategic orientation. Closings are often the only practical means of conversion or modernization because an attempt to undertake such an operation while still operating may be prohibitively expensive and time consuming.

Management must consider several human resource side effects of plant and office closings. First, closings affect all employees of the unit. Unlike other layoff strategies, closings affect everyone from the plants part-time personnel to its upper-level management. Thus a firm may inadvertently lose some of its best people if it does not plan the closing carefully. This means that the organization will lose its 30-year veterans as well as its recent hires. The advantage of this strategy, however, is that the firm may be able to keep its best employees by offering to move them to other parts of the organization. Of course, the organization may find itself in the position of having nowhere to send its skilled individuals, even though it does not want to lose them. Plant closings may be expensive because they often involve some form of lay-off pay, such as the supplemental unemployment benefits used by the automobile and steel industries mentioned earlier.

Plant closings can often have serious effects on morale in other parts of the organization. This is particularly true if the organization is undertaking a large restructuring and is not completely communicating its plans to its employees; that is, closings are not announced and explained in advance. In such situations employees begin to wonder if their plant or office will be the next one closed. In addition to damaging morale organizationwide, plant closings often affect worker productivity and may result in higher employee turnover in other parts of the organization as employees begin to seek what they perceive to be safer employment.

Worker Adjustment and Retraining Notification Act (WARN) A federal law that requires employers of 50 or more to give 60 days' written notice to employees of large-scale layoffs and plant closings.

Federal legislation, the federal **Worker Adjustment and Retraining Notification Act (WARN)**, mandates that organizations with at least 50 employees announce the decision to close plants or engage in massive layoffs at least 60 days in advance of the action. Critics argue that it is unnecessary because it will hurt productivity in the plant as employees seek new jobs and take time off to do so. They also argue that early announcements of plant closings hurt the competitiveness of U.S. firms because they are, in effect, forced prematurely to reveal valuable information about their strategies in a tough marketplace. Finally, critics of the legislation assert that because many decisions to close plants are made less than 60 days before an actual closing, the law puts management in a bind of having to make crucial decisions earlier than they would normally have been made. Supporters of the law argue that productivity losses are minimal. They also assert that management has an obligation to inform its employees of decisions affecting their future employment as soon as they are made. Finally, supporters argue that management should plan ahead in situations that have as broad an impact on employees as plant and office closings.

Criteria for Layoffs

employee seniority layoff criterion A layoff method in which employees are laid off according to the length of time each employee has worked with the firm.

A final issue in using a layoff strategy is how organizations determine whom to lay off and whom it gets to keep. In plant closings the issue is rather clear: Everyone is laid off. In other situations, such as reduced shifts, the task is not so easy. Two of the most common methods for determining layoffs are the use of employee seniority layoff criterion and the use of employee ability criterion. Firms that use **employee seniority layoff criterion** lay off workers according to the length of time that each employee has been with the firm. This is common in unionized firms. Most systems based on this method give greater protection to the employees with the most tenure or seniority, all other things being equal. If a firm has to lay off one of two welders, with each performing the same job, the welder who has been with the organization the longest will be kept.

employee ability layoff criterion A layoff method in which employees are laid off according to each employee's skill level and productivity.

Organizations that use an **employee ability layoff criterion** take a different approach. These firms lay off workers according to the skill level and productivity of each employee. Using the example of the two welders, the firm would keep the better of the two welders and lay off the other one. When the U.S. Air Force cut back its total troop levels by 25 percent as a result of budget cuts in the Department of Defense in the 1990s, it used a standard proficiency test as a measure of ability to determine which pilots and aircraft mechanics to retain and which ones to let go.

Advantages and Disadvantages of Seniority and Ability Based Layoffs

Each layoff approach has a number of advantages and disadvantages. Perhaps the greatest advantage of using a seniority-based layoff strategy is the objective manner in which it can be applied. Layoffs using this type of strategy are based on length of service to the organization, so workers know what their position is in a layoff program. It is also very hard to accuse management of playing favorites with employees using a seniority-based system because the layoff order is well known in advance. Any deviation from this system is likely to be noticed immediately by the workforce. The appearance of fairness and the ease of checking deviations from policy have made seniority-based layoff systems particularly popular in unionized organizations.

A main rationale behind a seniority-based layoff strategy is that employees who have been with the organization a long time have earned the right to be insulated from temporary changes in the firm's environment. Another belief behind a seniority-based layoff system is that it is easier for younger employees to find work and adapt their lives to layoffs than it is for older workers.

There are two disadvantages to a seniority-based system. The first is that it ignores worker talent and effort. Critics of the system argue that adherence to such rules is arbitrary and without merit. The long-standing ethic of rewarding good work often loses its value in organizations that adhere to seniority-based layoff systems. If workers know in advance that layoffs will be based on seniority, the incentive for them to operate at their peak levels is reduced. Instead, they may do only the minimal work necessary to ensure that they keep their jobs. In short, critics argue that this system shifts the focus from rewarding good work to job survival. If this is the case, the organization should experience higher labor costs, lower productivity, and lower work quality compared with its competitors that use other types of layoff strategies. Critics also argue that this system may keep the organization's payroll bloated because more experienced workers tend to earn higher wages. Hence, a seniority-based layoff system tends to cut back on the lower-paid employees while keeping the higher-paid ones. Of course, the counterargument is that the more experienced employee has a greater familiarity with the organization and how it operates. Ideally, this should make him or her more valuable to the organization because it has already sunk a great deal of money into training and developing the employee over the years. Either way, this can be a particularly problematic decision when the main goal is some form of cost restructuring.

Ability-based layoff systems seek to address some of the problems of seniority-based systems. Perhaps the greatest advantage of ability-based systems is that they keep the best workers during layoffs, often enabling the firm to maintain or increase productivity and quality levels during a restructuring. Firms using ability-based layoff systems should also realize a greater cost savings than firms using seniority-based layoffs. Further, ability-based systems appeal to the ethics of rewarding good work and should give workers incentives to seek to improve their performance. This approach may run into problems in reality, however. The most serious problem of such a system is defining ability. In many instances this is not a problem, especially when the work is standardized. For example, in the textile industry, in which productivity is based on the volume of material produced, determining the best workers is usually a straightforward process. The problem becomes more complex in other situations, however, especially in white-collar and skilled craft positions. As we discussed earlier, how does one place a quality figure on a raw materials price forecast prepared by a corporate analyst? The situation can even be complex in assembly-line situations, in which one worker's productivity depends on the output of another worker. Management must devise a system for determining how much one employee's work affects another. This is often a complicated and expensive process. Even when a fair system is in place, it is often difficult to communicate all of its aspects to employees in a clear and understandable manner.

In addition, ability-based systems encourage political behavior by workers. These systems sometimes generate the impression that it is the managers favorite workers, not the best workers, who are kept during layoffs. Many workers oppose such a system as a result of the difficulty in understanding the rules of the system and the perception of managerial favoritism. Consequently, ability-based systems are more likely to generate hostility with unions and possibly lead to lawsuits against the organization than are seniority-based systems.[29]

Termination Strategies

employee terminations Actions initiated by an organization to permanently separate employees from the organization.

Finally, organizations may choose to use **employee terminations** as part of a restructuring strategy. These are actions initiated by the organization to permanently separate employees from the organization, and they may come in many forms. Terminations may be the end result of an indefinite layoff or plant closing. They may also be the first action taken by a firm in a restructuring. Unlike firings, where employees are released from the organization for causes such as poor performance or high absenteeism, terminations are initiated with the purpose of reducing the size of the workforce. Massive terminations were a particularly popular method of downsizing in the early 1990s as companies have struggled to reduce costs and increase productivity. Exhibit 17.11 lists the companies who had major layoffs in the year 2000.

protection and compensation plans Organizational policies relating to the handling of employees during termination situations.

Termination Issues Organizations that pursue termination strategies must consider a number of issues. For example, all termination decisions must consider the organization's employee **protection and compensation plans**, which are its policies relating

EXHIBIT 17.11	MAJOR LAYOFFS IN 2000
AT&T	WorldCom
Polaroid	Priceline.com
Kodak	Aetna
AOL	Gillette
Lucent	Motorola
MarchFirst	Unisys
Whirlpool	Chrysler

to the handling of employees during termination situations. Many organizations have clearly defined plans for their employees. Others have no formal policies in place. Either way, the organization must deal with these issues. They typically include tenure, golden parachutes, severance pay, outplacement services, and career counseling.

tenure A measure of the time an employee has worked in an organization and the rights and benefits the person has accrued as a result.

Tenure relates to the length of time that an employee has worked in an organization and the rights that the person has accrued as a result. It is similar to seniority. In many instances employees with longer tenure, or length of service (seniority), have more rights and benefits than less-tenured or nontenured employees. These rights may include added benefits such as increased vacation time, sick leave, and insurance benefits, office and parking space privileges, stock options, and company cars. Many organizations also offer greater job protection to tenured employees. In universities and colleges, tenure for professors means guaranteed employment for life, as long as the professor continues to do his or her job. Even if the professor becomes incompetent or fails to do his or her job, tenure results in a long and formal termination process.

Consequently, organizations that use terminations as part of a restructuring must examine their tenure policies. Many of these tenure benefits are given as rewards for service, and many represent a long-term commitment by the organization to the employee. For example, an organization may guarantee stock options worth 20 percent of an executive's pay over 10 years as part of his or her promotion to upper management. Suppose, however, that the organization decides to close the executive's division and terminate all employees in the division (including the manager) 3 years after the manager has taken over the division. The organization must consider how to handle the stock options. The manager has been guaranteed the options based on performance, but a change in the organization's strategy variable beyond the manager's control eliminates the firm's need for the manager's services. This issue is complicated further by the fact that the manager is not being released for incompetence but as a change in organization strategy.

employment at will A doctrine stating that workers are employed at the will of the organization and the organization is free to end this employment at any time it chooses and for any reason it chooses.

In previous years U.S. law has given precedence to the **employment-at-will doctrine**. It states that workers are employed at the will of the organization and that the organization is free to end this employment at any time it chooses and for any reason it chooses. This doctrine also applies in reverse; employees are free to choose the organizations that they work for and can leave the organization at any time they choose and for any reason they wish. As we saw in Chapter 15, this concept has been challenged in recent years, and its validity is no longer guaranteed, especially when applied

Developing a Strong Outplacement Program

Traditionally, outplacement programs have been established by organizations to minimize the negative experiences associated with the loss of a job and to avoid the possibility of litigation by dismissed employees. However, companies are now realizing that it is important that employees who are joining or leaving the organization have a positive experience. Developing an effective and cost-efficient outplacement program is one way to ensure departing employees receive a positive experience.

Developing an effective outplacement program should be done as soon as possible. If brought in early, an outplacement company can help managers more effectively handle the termination interview. Often if the interview is inappropriately handled, employees do not understand why they have been terminated and spend a great deal of time pondering the reason. This takes away from the time they could be preparing for a new job.

Companies should introduce the employee to the outplacement program early in the week of termination so that they can begin immediately to prepare themselves for the job market. By focusing the terminated employee's attention on the outplacement process rather than on the termination, more positive outcomes occur. Further, by introducing the employee to the outplacement program immediately after termination, the outplacement company can be ready to offer crisis interventions if necessary.

A company should be prepared to pay for a good outplacement program. In general, the base cost for a full-service outplacement program is 15 percent of the outplaced worker's W-2 earnings for the previous year plus an administrative fee that averages about $1000. Some firms set a minimum fee of between $6000 and $7000 per program. Group programs can also be arranged. Costs for these services include a per diem charge of $1000 to $1500, plus an additional charge of $40 to $50 for each participant. Programs that are significantly lower than these ranges may not be of a high quality.

SOURCE: Adapted from Virginia Gibson, "The Ins and Outs of Outplacement," *Management Review*, October 1991, pp. 59–61.

---

to employees who may have built up tenure within an organization. Courts have been increasingly sensitive to instances that are deemed wrongful or abusive discharges on the part of the employer.[30] Wrongful or abusive discharge situations involve firing without cause, discrimination of almost any kind, failure to properly document the cause of the firing, or situations in which the procedure for firing is not standardized. Even if the organization is sure that it is in a situation in which the employment-at-will doctrine is valid, tenure-related issues often ensure that terminated employees may bring legal action against the organization to recover or be compensated for lost benefits and privileges.[31] The average jury verdict in wrongful discharge cases is more than $500,000. To avoid such litigation, companies are retraining poor performers, using overtime or temporary workers, offering generous severance, and adopting collaborate screening and performance review processes.[32]

golden parachutes Guarantees by organizations to employees (usually top managers) detailing the types of benefits they will receive in termination situations.

Golden Parachutes   Many organizations are responding to these problems by offering **golden parachutes** to their employees, especially top managers. Golden parachutes are guarantees by organizations to employees detailing the type of benefits they will receive in termination situations. Golden parachutes are offered as enticements to convince managers to take on the responsibility of joining a struggling firm for the purpose of turning it around. They are popular in organizations that are targets of mergers or hostile takeovers. As we mentioned earlier, many mergers end with the replacement of the old management team by a new one. In these situations the board of directors may vote to offer golden parachutes to key managers as a reward for their performance with the organization and because it makes it prohibitively expensive for a new management to replace the old management. Finally, golden parachutes are also popular because they represent a contractual agreement between the firm and the employee. Hence, if the employee is terminated, there is less chance of a legal challenge by the employee.

A main problem with golden parachutes is that they tend to be rather expensive to the organization. It is not uncommon to find golden parachutes containing provisions that range from one to two years' salary and other substantial cash payments. As a result, golden parachutes are mainly used for key managers. They are rarely offered to rank-and-file employees. Golden parachutes, if their existence is made known in the organization, may cause a great deal of hostility among members who are not protected in a similar manner. For example, in the bankruptcy of Drexel Burnham Lambert, top managers of the organization received $260 million in bonuses just weeks before the firm was forced into bankruptcy. When the organization filed for bankruptcy, all of its employees were terminated without any form of compensation, even though the organization owed them approximately $40 million in severance payments, which they never received. Many employees are upset that such bonus payments were made because the nature of their timing resembled that of a golden parachute to upper management. Even though the bonuses were, in reality, regularly scheduled payments to management, their perceived appearance as golden parachutes alienated many former organization members.[33]

Even with their negative connotations, golden parachutes can serve broader organization purposes. Eastman Kodak has added a unique twist to golden parachutes to protect itself from the threat of a hostile takeover. Kodak's plan, nicknamed "tin-parachutes," guarantees all 80,000 of its employees severance pay, health and life insurance benefits, and outplacement assistance if they lose their jobs in the wake of a takeover. Such a plan means that any organization that took over Kodak could also face another $12 billion in debt if it started releasing Kodak employees.[34] Of course, the main advantages of golden parachutes are that they can convince key individuals to join or remain in particularly risky situations for the organization, and they reduce the chances of legal action against the organization by terminated employees. Kodak's case illustrates that parachutes, whether made of gold or tin, can be highly effective weapons against unwanted takeover attempts.

Severance Pay A related and more common approach to terminations than golden parachutes is the use of **severance pay**. It is a payment to terminated workers based on their years of service to the organization and their salary. A typical severance pay might be four weeks of full pay for each year the employee has worked for the organization. For example, an employee who has worked for an organization for seven years and earned $400 per week would receive the following severance pay:

severance pay
A payment to terminated workers based on their years of service to the organization and on their salary.

(7 years × 4 weeks per year) = 28 weeks × $400 per week = $11,200

Severance pay may also include other payments such as accrued vacation and sick leave and possibly some medical coverage. How the pay is provided varies by organization. Some firms offer a lump-sum payment. Others offer the money over a specified period of time, like a weekly paycheck. Other firms use a combination of these tactics or let the employee decide how he or she wants the money.[35] Like golden parachutes, a clearly defined severance pay policy may reduce the chances of legal action

Disadvantages of Downsizing

It is a mystery to many observers, in light of the devastating impact on employee morale, why companies continue downsizing when there seems to be no benefits. A recent study done by three professors at the University of Colorado at Denver suggests that layoffs are not a route to increased profits. The professors found that firms that downsize are generally no more profitable than other companies in their industries and are less profitable than S&P 500 companies that are stable employers. Downsizers' return from stocks mostly lag behind those of stable employers as well.

A new Wharton School analysis shows that financial restructuring (LBOs, recapitalizations, etc.) had the highest payoff in subsequent years, followed by portfolio restructuring such as spin-offs and sell-offs. On average, organizational restructuring (downsizing) had little positive impact on earnings or stock market performance. In fact, more negative impacts are becoming apparent, such as low morale and mistrust of management. Also, job cutting can come back to haunt companies when managers sue for wrongful discharge. Well over half of executive and middle managers filing wrongful termination suits win settlements according to an article in *Across the Board*, a Conference Board magazine.

SOURCE: Gene Koretz, "The Downside of Downsizing," *Business Week*, April 28, 1997, p. 26; and Linda Micco, "Study Finds Downsizing Can Reduce Profitability," *Society for Human Resource Management*, January 1998, p. 15.

against the organization if widespread terminations occur. But where golden parachutes are designed as incentives and rewards to top management, severance pay is usually a hardship compensation to all employees. A main advantage of a severance package is that it immediately clears most of the organization's obligations to its former employees.

Severance packages are also used by organizations to help them improve employee relations. Many organizations use the existence of the severance programs as a recruiting tool for new employees. Firms that terminate employees with the possible intention of rehiring them at a later date face a much better chance of getting them back if there is some form of severance pay involved in the termination.

The main disadvantage of severance pay is that it requires the organization to spend large sums of money almost immediately. This may be particularly difficult for the organization, especially if the terminations are a result of a restructuring or bankruptcy. In mergers or consolidations, severance pay may be an ideal solution. Because both mergers and consolidations often involve the acquisition of one organization by another, severance pay is a convenient way to accelerate the transition process. The reason is that many restructuring costs are tax deductible, and the organization may write off the severance expense and realize a tax savings or reduction as a result.

The cost of firing a manager differs by country. In the United States it costs about $19,000 to fire a $50,000 manager. Only Ireland has a lower termination cost, $13,000. Italy and Spain spend more than $100,000 when terminating the same $50,000 manager, but Greece falls somewhere between at $67,000.[36]

Outplacement   Another issue that an organization must consider before it begins terminating employees is its outplacement policy. Outplacement programs are corporate programs whose purpose is to help terminated employees adjust to their terminations and to assist them in finding other jobs.[37] Most outplacement programs assist terminated employees in three areas: financial support, psychological support, and job search support. Financial support functions typically include wage/salary continuation, health insurance, unemployment compensation, and credit management. Psychological support functions usually include self-esteem counseling, stress management, spouse and family counseling, and counseling for retained employees. Job search support includes secretarial services, office space, telephones, self-assessment, job search skills, resume writing, interviewing, follow-up and evaluation, and other forms of career counseling.

Well-run outplacement programs can greatly ease the former employee's transition into a new job or career while maintaining the organization's image both internally and within its community. On the other hand, outplacement programs can quickly become expensive if they are not managed properly. Most organizations cannot afford to offer all of these services, and consequently they are placed in the position of having to decide the level of outplacement services to offer. Because an outplacement program can have such a large impact on the outcome of a termination strategy, its design should be tailored carefully to meet the most critical needs of the organization's overall termination strategy.

Types of Terminations An organization may pursue three basic types of termination strategies. The first is a **leave them naked termination** strategy. Firms that pursue this strategy essentially release employees from the organization without providing any protection or compensation benefits or outplacement services. Such a strategy has two main advantages. First, it involves relatively little up-front cash investment on the part of the organization because it provides no severance pay, outplacement, or counseling benefits. Second, the firm can decide exactly whom it wishes to release from the organization and whom it wishes to keep. These advantages can also be its main liabilities, however, because they often expose the organization to lawsuits by terminated employees with wrongful or abusive discharge claims. Other disadvantages include the likely adverse reactions from the remaining employees, the terminated employees, and the community at large. This is due to the fact that leave them naked strategies can easily be perceived as the action of a firm with only its own concerns in mind. Even with these disadvantages, many firms still choose to pursue this type of strategy, especially if immediate cash-flow problems are the main concern of the organization.

Two other common strategies are early retirement incentives and forced resignation before proceeding with terminations. **Early retirement termination** usually provides some form of inducements for employees to retire from the organization before they reach the normal retirement age. Typical inducements are called "5-5-4" packages. These packages add 5 years of service to the employees' record with the company and 5 years to the employees' age when calculating early retirement benefits. The "4" part of the package is typically the number of weeks of full pay that the employee will receive for each year he or she has worked for the organization. Other common packages include "3-3-2" or "2-2-1" plans.

Telecommunications giant AT&T is one of several firms that operates with a 5-5-4 early retirement plan as a part of its restructuring strategy. In late 1989 the firm expanded the scope of its program. Approximately 34,000 AT&T managers qualified for the program, and the company expected as many as one third of all eligible managers to take advantage of it in 1990. The total savings from the program reached $450 million in 1990.[38] AT&T also extended a similar program to at least some of its

leave them naked termination A termination strategy in which a firm releases employees from the organization without providing any protection or compensation benefits or outplacement services.

early retirement termination A termination strategy in which an organization provides some form of inducements for employees to retire from the organization before they reach normal retirement age.

173,500 nonmanagement workers. Once this second plan was adopted, AT&T's total savings reached $1 billion annually.[39] Added benefits are in the form of lower costs when firms select to implement an early retirement plan. As health-care costs soar, companies have responded by cutting the number of the most expensive employees to cover: older workers.[40,41]

forced resignation termination
A termination strategy in which employees are offered the option of either resigning or being terminated outright.

constructive discharge Making the work environment and the job so intolerable that the employee eventually quits.

Forced resignation terminations are more direct in nature. They are usually offered as alternatives to outright terminations. Each of these strategies has its own unique comparative restructuring advantages and disadvantages. The two types of strategies (early retirement and forced resignation) differ in cash outlays, legal issues, risks of losing valued employees, impacts on organization climate and culture, and impacts on the organization's public image. Exhibit 17.12 compares these two methods of downsizing.[42]

Finally, some organizations use a type of termination which is known as **constructive discharge**. This involves making the work environment so disagreeable for a person that the person eventually quits. For example, a person might have his/her hours changed, office moved, or disagreeable duties added to his/her job. His/her boss might shun the person or otherwise be unavaible for counsel. At some point, the person finds that the work environment has become so intolerable that he/she quits. There are legal issues here, of course, so the employer must be very careful if this policy is used. The may violate an express or implied employment contract or civil service or union provisions. It also cannot be taken just toward a particular class such as women, older workers, African Americans or other protected classes. It cannot be done in retaliation for an employee who files a discrimination or sexual harassment complaint. Finally, it may cause a significant morale problem among the employees who witness this action if they believe the employer is being unfair to the employee involved.

The organization must consider the impact of these types of terminations. It should determine the cash outlays involved in deciding whether to use an early retirement or a forced resignation termination strategy. It must make early retirement financially attractive enough to employees that they will accept it. Consequently, an organization that chooses to use an early retirement program should be prepared to spend large sums of money early on to induce employees to retire. In addition, the costs of the program may increase rapidly as the size of the program grows. In contrast, forced resignation programs require relatively little up-front cash investment on the part of the organization. Usually, forced resignations offer little to employees. At best, they offer a small severance package.

The organization must also consider the legal aspects of each program. Because early retirement programs are strictly voluntary on the part of the employees, there is relatively little chance of legal action against organizations using them. Forced resignations, on the other hand, incur a great risk of legal action, especially when issues such as tenure or age are involved or wrongful discharge can be proven.

The type of strategy that the organization undertakes also determines whether it loses valuable employees. Because voluntary retirements must generally be offered to all eligible employees, organizations run the risk of losing valuable employees as well as less valuable ones. In addition, valuable employees usually have skills that enable them to continue working with another organization. By taking early retirement from one organization and going to work for another, they are often able to increase their incomes dramatically as they receive funds from both organizations. As a result, the organization may wind up losing its most valuable employees to competitors during

EXHIBIT 17.12	COMPARISON OF TWO METHODS OF DOWNSIZING AND THEIR IMPACT ON CRITICAL ORGANIZATIONAL VARIABLES

	Method of Downsizing	
Variable	**Early Retirement**	**Forced Resignations**
Cash outlays	Relatively high	Relatively low
Possible litigation	Relatively low risk	Relatively high risk
Losing valued employees	Relatively high risk	Relatively low risk
Impact on organization climate and culture	Minimal	Relatively high likelihood of negative impact
Impact on public image	Relatively low risk of negative impact	Relatively high risk of negative impact

SOURCE: Frank E. Kuzmits and Lyle Sussman, "Early Retirement or Forced Resignation: Policy Issues for Downsizing Human Resources," *SAM Advanced Management Journal*, Winter 1988, p. 32.

voluntary retirement programs. Forced resignations generally do not suffer from these problems. Again, the organization essentially decides who is going to resign and who is going to be kept, and it is natural to assume that the organization is not going to ask its key members to resign.

Finally, the organization must consider the impact of each strategy on its culture, climate, and public image. Because forced resignations are involuntary in nature, they tend to have a large negative impact both internally and externally. The public is likely to interpret such actions as cold and uncaring on the part of the organization, especially if the program affects members with long tenure in the organization, which does not fully explain the rationale behind its actions. Internally, forced resignations are likely to foster hostility toward and resentment of upper management by employees. Even generous severance packages, which are usually rare in these situations, generally cannot overcome the resentment generated by making employees leave the organization. The level of resentment felt may differ by employee, but research has found that women executives cope better with forced resignations than do men. It appears that men take the firing personally. They view it as age discrimination or a conflict in personalities. Women, on the other hand, more readily accept the fact that the change is due to downsizing or economic conditions rather than a problem with them.[43] Early retirement terminations, on the other hand, do not suffer from such a stigma. Many organizations make employee retirement an occasion for celebration, and the community is likely to react positively to an organization that offers generous incentives to those employees who wish to retire early.[44]

Whatever method of termination is selected, human resource managers generally offer an exit interview so that terminated employees can have the opportunity to candidly discuss their work experience. Topics covered during this interview include the worker's impressions of the supervisor's performance, the adequacy of the training and development received, company policies, advancement opportunities, and overall job satisfaction. Managers can learn much about how employees feel during these interviews and should endeavor to hold one whenever an employee leaves.

HR CHALLENGES

Preparing Managers to Terminate Employees

Handling the termination process effectively can go a long way to ease tensions and reduce the chances of employee retaliation. The following suggestions may help managers to be better prepared for terminating employees:

1. Plan the termination for early in the week so that the employee does not get the weekend to mull it over.

2. Do not let the termination interview last longer than 15 minutes. Long meetings allow time for debate. Simply state your case and move on.

3. Meet in the worker's office so that he or she does not have to leave the meeting and explain it to workers on the way back to his or her office. Make sure that the location is private.

4. Do not plan the meeting on important dates such as birthdays or holidays or when the employee has just returned from a vacation.

5. Don't leave room for confusion. Tell the employee in the first sentence that he or she is terminated. Make it clear that the decision is final.

6. Clearly communicate all aspects of the severance package offered to the employee.

7. Be prepared for a terminated employee to be emotional and hostile.

8. Outline the remaining steps in the termination process, such as the last day and key return policies.

9. Provide the employee with the name of an individual at the outplacement service if one is being offered. If possible, personally introduce the employee to the counselor.

10. Discuss the transfer of the employee's responsibilities and work to other employees.

11. Wish the employee luck and express confidence in his or her ability to find a new job.

SOURCE: Adapted from Phyllis Macklin and Lester Minsuk, "10 Ways to Ease Dismissal Dread," *HRMagazine*, November 1991, pp. 104–105; and Susan Alexander, "Firms Get Plenty of Practice at Layoffs, but They Often Bungle the Firing Process," *The Wall Street Journal*, October 14, 1991, p. B1.

Organizations that consider a termination strategy as part of a restructuring plan must contend with many issues. Each strategy has its own advantages and shortcomings. In many instances termination strategies can help the organization achieve its restructuring more quickly than either layoff or no-layoff strategies. The risks and costs may be greater, however, depending on the type of strategy used. About the only absolute in determining the type of strategy to use is that management should carefully consider all alternatives and the likely impact of each. Often the best solution is not a single restructuring approach but a combination of methods. Rarely can one organization's experiences be applied directly to those of another organization.

Does Downsizing Work?

corporate anorexia The effect of too much downsizing that results in a very "thin" but very unhealthy organization.

Hamel and Prahalad argue that downsizing is a form of **corporate anorexia** in that it can make a company thinner but not necessarily healthier. [45] They argue that downsizing is merely an inefficient attempt to overcome bad management. In this view it results from a firm's failure to recognize its core competencies—the firm's key skills and resources—and to leverage them to the greatest extent possible. Downsizing is a meat cleaver way to cut costs and often results in throwing out the baby with the bath water. It takes great management insight to go beyond these quick fixes. [46]

To bolster their argument, Hamel and Prahalad provide data to show that downsized companies have not performed any better than other firms. Downsizing results in immediate labor savings as well as skill shortages and increased workloads for the employees left to do the work. Although employees are happy to have a job, they are also *unhappy* because of the increased workload and uncertainty surrounding their jobs.

HR CHALLENGES

Separation Agreements

When downsizing, or for other employment cutbacks, many firms ask employees to sign a release from employment in exchange for monetary payment and a promise not to sue. These are often called "separation agreements" or "termination agreements."

The Older Workers Benefit Protection Act of 1990, which amends the Age Discrimination in Employment Act, provides protection to employees who are asked to sign these agreements. These protections were upheld in a 1998 court ruling (*Oubre* vs. *Entergy Operations, Inc.*).

The key factors a separation agreement must meet are as follows:

1. It must be agreed to knowingly and voluntarily. There cannot be any compulsion on the part of the employer.

2. The individual must be advised in writing to consult with an attorney (not advisor or other language) before signing the agreement.

3. The individual must be given 21 days to consider the agreement or at least 45 days if the agreement is offered to a group or class of employees.

4. The individual must be allowed seven days after signing to revoke the agreement.

5. If the agreement is given to a class, unit, or group of employees, the agreement must state the class, group, or unit; any time limits; the job titles and ages of all individuals eligible for the program; and the ages and job titles of all individuals in the unit or class not eligible or selected for the program.

SOURCE: Linda Micco, "Keeping Severance Pay Doesn't Bar Age Bias Suit, Justices Rule," *HRNews*, March 1998, p. 11, 29; and U.S.C.Section 626(f) (f)(H). DKR. 24, p.2.

Studies done by Drake Beam Morin, Inc., found that more than half of the executives ended up making a higher salary when they found a new job.[47] However, executives spent about an average of 7.4 months to find the new job.[48]

Despite the Hamel and Prahalad study, it is still too early to assess adequately the effects of downsizing. More time is needed to determine whether corporate performance is better in downsized firms compared with similar firms.

The Virtual Organization, Contingent Workers, and Outsourcing

virtual organization Fungible modules built around information networks, flexible workforces, outsourcing, and webs of strategic partnerships.

To cope with the changes they are experiencing, organizations are experimenting with new forms of employment. One form is the emergence of the virtual organization, also known as the **virtual corporation**. The virtual corporation is composed of "fungible modules built around information networks, flexible workforces, outsourcing, and webs of strategic partnerships."[49] Unlike typical images of organizations where all workers show up for work at the plant at 9:00 AM and leave at 5:00 PM, the virtual organization is something very different. Employees may indeed begin work at 9:00, but the office might mean the old spare bedroom down the hall from the kid's room that has been converted into an office. Workers may never have to leave their homes thanks to computers, telephones, fax machines, videoconferencing, and modems, which enable them to be just as productive as they would be at corporate headquarters. Other workers may not start work until after 3:30 when the kids get home from school. In addition, some workers may work for the organization only on a temporary or part-time basis. Finally, the organization's payroll might be issued by another company specializing in payroll management. The following are six trends that are helping to create the virtual organization:

FOCUS ON HR

Telecommuting Takes Off

With today's technology, people no longer need to work in an office. Computers, hand held devices, cell phones, and fax machines make it possible for people to work just about anywhere. For example, Paolo Concini works in a bathing suit from his home in Bali, Indonesia, even though his company's offices and work are in China and Europe. This is known as "extreme telecommuting." This breed of telecommuters lives in countries and even continents far away from their company's work.

While this type of telecommuting is still relatively rare—people who do this tend to be owners of companies—all telecommuting is becoming more popular. In the U.S. in 2000 an estimated 24 million people regularly or occasionally telecommuted, according to the International Telework Association and Council. This is up 21 percent from 1999. In Europe an estimated 10 million people now telecommute. In 16 Asia-Pacific countries, at least 3.3 million workers telecommuted in 2000 at least one day a month, up 27 percent over 1999. As technology and communications tools continue to become more sophisticated and as firms seek greater flexibility, we are likely to see these figures increase.

SOURCE: Kevin Voigt, "For 'Extreme Telecommuters,' Remote Work Means Really Remote," *The Wall Street Journal*, January 31, 2001, p. B1.

1. The average company will become smaller, employing fewer people.
2. The traditional hierarchical organization will give way to a variety of organizational forms, the network of specialists foremost among these.
3. Technicians, ranging from computer repairers to radiation therapists, will replace manufacturing operatives as the worker elite.
4. The vertical division of labor will be replaced by a horizontal division.
5. The paradigm of doing business will shift from making a product to providing a service.
6. Work itself will be redefined, emphasizing constant learning and high-order thinking and deemphasizing set work hours.[50]

The basic tenant of the virtual organization is that traditional organizations, characterized by hierarchical management and rigid 9-to-5 work schedules, are being made obsolete by global competition, advances in information and communication technologies, changes in workers' skills and expectations, and the switch from manufacturing to services as the basis of capital creation.

The impact of global competition cannot be understated. The quality challenge provided by Asian and European manufacturers, the need to sell in international markets, and the need to conduct business with organizations that are literally oceans and continents away have forced U.S. businesses to adapt to global competition. Simple logistical problems such as cultural differences and how to communicate with employees in separate time zones and who may speak one of 100 different languages have forced companies to change if they wish to remain competitive. Some of these problems have been alleviated by computer and communications technologies. Instead of having to work an extra hour at the end of the day to telephone the United States to get permission from the headquarters to undertake a new project, a European employee can send the request via e-mail and have it waiting for his boss when she arrives for work at 8:00 AM in Los Angeles. When the European employee arrives at work the next day, he can quickly check his e-mail to see what the boss's answer is.

Domestically, computer and communication technologies can provide the same advantages they can internationally. With a computer, a fax machine, a telephone, and a modem at home, a book editor may have all the tools she needs to do her job and the company doesn't have to worry about costs associated with office assignments, parking spaces, and other work amenities for the employee. Computer networks can even allow for employees who may be spread across huge distances, such as continents and oceans, to work together on projects.

Further, many U.S. companies and workers have undergone a change in attitude about what they expect from a job. The Family-Leave Act, enacted in 1993, enables workers to take unpaid leave time for pregnancy or family illness. Many workers have taken advantage of this law to start families, attend to their own illnesses, or take care of ill or older family members. It does appear that the career orientation of the baby-boomer generation of the 1980s has changed to a greater desire to spend time with the family. Post–baby-boomers, often referred to as *Generation X*, have displayed a tendency to hold many jobs before settling down with a permanent full-time position. In addition, many of the fastest-growing jobs require highly specialized skills. Employees with these skills often have strong bargaining leverage with potential employers.

A final component of the virtual corporation is the switch from value creation through manufacturing to value creation through knowledge creation. Traditional businesses depended on the factory floor for the creation of wealth. A key component of the factory floor was immobility: Workers came to the factory, not the other way around. Today, many of the fast-growing industries, such as computer software, are based on the creation of knowledge. These service-based industries do not depend on the production of physical products for their wealth. Instead, they rely on the creation of knowledge by workers. A computer programmer can just as easily do her job at home as she can in the office if she has a computer. Ernst & Young's information technology consulting division is typical of this type of knowledge creation. It estimates that its consultants and auditors spend from 50 percent to 80 percent of their time in the field.[51]

For our discussion, two components of the virtual corporation have a direct impact on how firms strategically manage their human resources. The first component is the increased use of **contingent workers** by organizations. The second is the trend of firms to contract, or outsource, components of their operations to outside firms.

The number of contingent workers in the workforce has increased dramatically in recent years. In essence, a contingent worker is any person who works for an organization but not on a permanent or full-time basis. Temporary employees, part-time workers, contract laborers, and leased employees are examples. *The Wall Street Journal* estimates that temporary, contract, and part-time workers account for approximately 25 percent of the U.S. workforce.[52] Exhibit 17.13 reports the results of a poll of CEOs regarding their use of contingent workers.[53]

The use of contingent workers by corporations provides a number of advantages and disadvantages. The advantages include reduced payroll and benefit costs and increased flexibility in operations. The disadvantages include increased costs in training employees, failure to develop in-house skills, potential morale problems, difficulties in scheduling work, and lower levels of employee loyalty.

Perhaps the main reason that most companies are increasingly using contingency workers is to *save money*. Firms that shift a position from being full-time to contingent can save money in a number of areas, including benefit packages such as health insurance, vacation salaries, and sick days. And, depending on the type of contingency

contingent worker Any person who works for an organization, but not on a permanent or full-time basis.

When Is a Worker an Employee or an Independent Contractor?

The Internal Revenue Manual lists the following 20 factors that the IRS considers in determining the existence of an employer-employee relationship:

- Whether a worker is required to comply with other person's directions about how the work is to be performed, whether or not instructions are actually given.
- Whether a worker is trained by requiring an experienced worker to work with the worker or by using other methods to indicate that the employer wants the services performed in a particular manner.
- Whether the worker's services are integrated into the business operations.
- Whether services are rendered personally.
- Whether the person for whom services are performed hires, supervises, or pays assistants.
- Whether there is a continuing relationship between the parties.
- Whether set hours of work are established for the worker.
- Whether the worker must devote substantially full time to the person for whom services are performed.
- Whether work is performed on the premises of the person for whom services are performed.
- Whether a worker must perform tasks in an order prescribed by the person for whom services are performed.
- Whether the worker must submit oral or written reports.
- Whether the method of payment is regular or on a job-by-job basis.
- Whether the worker's business or travel expenses are paid by the person for whom services are performed.
- Whether tools and materials are furnished to the worker.
- Whether the worker invests in facilities used by him in performance of the service.
- Whether the worker takes a risk of profit or loss.
- Whether the worker works for more than one firm at a time.
- Whether the services are made generally available to the public.
- Whether the worker has a right to terminate the relationship without incurring liability.
- Whether the worker has a right to quit his or her job at anytime without incurring liability.

Generally, physicians, lawyers, dentists, veterinarians, contractors, subcontractors, public stenographers, auctioneers, and others who pursue an independent trade, business, or profession in which they offer their services to the public are not employees. Furthermore, if the relationship of employer and employee exists, the designation or description of the relationship by the parties as anything other than that of employer and employee is immaterial. Thus, if such relationship exists, it is of no consequence that the employee is designated as a partner, coadventurer, agent, or independent contractor.

SOURCE: Internal Revenue Manual Audit, Vol. III8463. These factors have been cited by the Senate as the factors generally considered under the common law in determining whether or not an employer-employee relationship exists. S. Rep. No. 494, 97th Cong. 2nd Sess. 359-60, reprinted in 1982 U. S. Code Cong. & Admin. News 781, 1092-93. The IRS described these factors in Rev. Rule 87-41, 1987-1 C. B. 296. Adopted from Tax Practice Series Analysis, Rev. 1/98, pp. 1–2.

EXHIBIT 17.13	CEOs' Use of Contingent Workers	
	Compared to 1988, My Company's Use of Contingent Workers Has	**Five Years from Now, My Company's Use of Them Will Have**
Increased	44%	44%
Decreased	13	9
Remained the same	43	44
Not sure	—	3

SOURCE: Joclyn Fierman, "The Contingency Workforce," *Fortune*, January 24, 1994, p. 31. Reprinted with permission.

worker the company uses, it may be able to shift most of the employee's tax burden to the employee or the outside contractor providing the employee. It is estimated that the average contingent worker costs an organization 20 percent to 40 percent less than the average full-time worker.

The other reason that companies use contingent workers is to increase their *flexibility* in responding to changing conditions. By using contingent workers, companies can easily increase or decrease the sizes of their staffs to meet increases or decreases in consumer demand. A typical use of contingent workers in this situation is the annual hiring of temporary workers by retail stores to meet the demands of the holiday buying rush. Further, companies can hire contingent workers to complete special one-time tasks or projects. Many people are familiar with agencies that provide temporary secretarial services, but they may not be aware of other organizations that exist to temporarily provide firms with highly skilled workers such as engineers, computer programmers, and even top managers. Prior to the advent of these specialized contingent workers, an organization was forced to hire the workers permanently, even if it needed them only for a single project. Once the organization has completed its project, it no longer has to worry about what to do with the contingent worker.

There can be several *disadvantages* associated with contingent workers, however. One disadvantage is that companies that indiscriminately use contingency workers may actually wind up *increasing their training costs*. This situation often arises when companies have unique or nonstandard methods of doing business. For example, most secretaries from temporary services are usually trained in the use of three of four specific word processors. If a company uses an uncommon one, it may find that it has to train its temporary workers how to use it before they can be productive. The chances are that the more unique or specialized the requirements are for a job, the higher the probability that the organization will have to invest in the training of the contingent worker.

Related to the first disadvantage is that companies could *potentially fail to adequately develop their own knowledge base*, or even worse, allow that knowledge to be copied by competitors if they rely too heavily on contingent workers. Like people, most organizations learn through trial and error. Over time, the organization builds a pool of experiences that it relies on to accomplish its goals efficiently. If the organization relies too heavily on contingent workers, especially those in key positions, it may fail to develop that knowledge necessary for competitive success. Because contingent workers often by design are not meant to be permanent or long-term workers with the organization, they frequently do not take part in organization rituals designed to pass along the organization's accumulated knowledge. Consequently, whatever skills or knowledge the contingent worker has may never be passed along to the organization. An even worse scenario for many organizations is that a contingent worker does learn valuable knowledge or skills from the organization and then goes to work for its competitor. Therefore organizations that use an unusually high number of contingent workers or use them in positions directly related to the organization's key skills may find themselves in the situation, in which the process of creating organizational knowledge is stunted. If this problem is not corrected in time, the organization may find that it has lost its key competitive skills or has become a "hollow corporation."

Another key problem associated with contingent workers is *low morale*. Many employees voluntarily choose to become contingent workers. Contingency status often provides workers with flexible schedules that enable them to work second jobs, spend more time with their families, provide additional family income for special occasions such as vacations, or pursue additional education. Many employees, however, become contingency workers because it is forced on them by their employers or because they are unable to find permanent full-time work. Permanent employees who are forced into contingency status by their employers often resent the loss of wages and benefits that are usually associated with contingent status. Further, they resent the organization's expectation of them to perform the same job at the same level as that of permanent employees but at the reduced rate. Organizations that make shifts to contingency work without clearly communicating their plan may incur morale problems from employees who are worried about their jobs. Another problem occurs when employees join a firm on a contingency status and seek to become permanent members. If the firm indicates that permanent status may be an option in the future, employees will gear their work and attitudes toward the achievement of permanent status. If the organization does not come through with what the employee perceives as a promise of a reward for good work, his or her morale and productivity are likely to suffer.

Another problem with contingent workers may occur with *scheduling work*. Because contingent workers often work part-time schedules or on fixed schedules, many organizations find it difficult to get all of their employees involved in a project together at the same time for important meetings. Further, organizations must take into account that the schedule of contingent workers may often affect the schedule of permanent workers, especially when both types of workers are involved in a task together. Failure to anticipate these needs may bring chaos to an organization's scheduling and result in severe productivity declines.

As noted, contingent workers seldom develop loyalty to the organization. Their temporary status allows them to develop a "here today, gone tomorrow" attitude. Although certainly all do not develop this attitude, the job situation they face is less stable than that of regular employees.

Outsourcing

Firms have three basic options in deciding how to achieve a specific task or goal. First, they can rely on full-time workers who are permanently assigned to performing the duties that the goal requires. Second, they can rely on contingent workers to fulfill the goal. Finally, they can strike a balance between the two and *contract out*, or *outsource*, their operations to another organization. Most organizations today use at least two, if not all three, options. An example of this is Digital Equipment's decision to outsource responsibility for sales and support for 7000 of its customers while still continuing to provide sales and support for its 1000 biggest customers.

Like the use of contingent workers, firms that outsource are frequently able to achieve cost savings by contracting small or inefficient operations to outside organizations. Outsourcing activities range from manufacturing machined parts to job recruitment function. Exhibit 17.15 shows human resource functions that are commonly outsourced by organizations. For example, among the most commonly outsourced activities are those related to payroll processing, especially in small organizations. Instead of maintaining a staff dedicated to processing the organization's payroll each week or taking the time away from persons with other duties, the organization can contract the work to firms that specialize in payroll processing. The firm immediately saves money by being able to free up employees for other tasks or by eliminating the department dedicated to payroll processing. Further, much outsourced work can be done less expensively by specialty organizations than it can be done in-house. By outsourcing small or inefficient activities, the organization is free to focus on those activities it does well.

FOCUS ON HR

Professional Employer Organizations (PEOs)

A Professional Employer Organization (PEO) is defined as an organization that provides an integrated and cost effective approach to the management and administration of the human resources and employer risk of its clients, by contractually assuming substantial employer rights, responsibilities, and risks, and through the establishment and maintenance of an employer relationship with the workers assigned to its clients. The role of PEOs in the day-to-day operations of small and medium-sized businesses across the country is growing. More and more business owners are turning to PEOs to help them efficiently handle the daunting load of administrative tasks that comes with running a company.

About 2000 PEOs across the country are responsible for managing approximately $18 billion in employee wages and benefits. The PEO industry is growing at a rate of 30 percent a year. PEOs operate in every state, and experts predict this growth rate can be sustained for 5 to 10 years in response to the increased need for their services. The PEO industry's target market is the estimated 53 percent of employees in the United States who work at companies with fewer than 500 people each.

PEOs help to level the playing field in the competition for employees, allowing small and medium-sized businesses to offer the same caliber of benefits as large companies. They handle a wide range of personal matters, including payroll, employment tax issues, government compliance, workers' compensation, employee benefits and unemployment insurance claims. PEOs become co-employers with their clients, reducing employment-related liabilities for the business owner.

Benefits of PEO Services

For the Business

- Controls costs.
- Saves time and paperwork hassles.
- Provides professional compliance (e.g., payroll, IRCA, EEOC).
- Reduces turnover and attracts better employees.

- Claims management (e.g., workers' compensation, unemployment insurance).
- Provides better benefits packages(s).
- Provides professional human resource services (e.g., employee handbooks, forms, policies and procedures).
- Reduces accounting costs.

For the Employee

- Comprehensive benefits previously unavailable.
- Better employer/employee communications.
- Payroll on time and accurate.
- Professional assistance with employment-related problems.
- Professional orientation and employee handbook.
- Statutory protection extended to more employees.
- Up-to-date information on labor regulations and workers' rights, worksite safety.
- Efficient and responsive claims processing.
- Portable benefits (employees can move from one PEO client to another without loss of eligibility for benefits).

For the Government

- Consolidates several small companies' employment tax filings into one.
- Creates more professional preparation and reporting.
- Accelerates collection of taxes.
- Extends medical benefits to more workers.
- Expands the communication of government requirements and changes to small businesses.
- Resolves many problems before they reach court.
- Allows government agencies to reach business through a single-employer entity.

SOURCE: **www.iapeo.org** (accessed February 26, 2001).

EXHIBIT 17.14	SOME CAUTIONS IN USING TEMPORARY WORKERS
Employee Development	Using temporary workers can decimate employers' reservoir of knowledge, skills, and abilities (KSAs) because training investment in temporary workers is not made.
Loyalty	Temporary employees show little commitment or loyalty to the organization and its vision and long-term goals.
Customer Service	Temporaries may be unlikely to build relationships with customers based on a commitment to the organization.
Corporate Culture	Temporary employees may not buy into or reinforce the corporate culture.
Safety	Temporary employees may not be fully trained and educated on unique employee safety requirements and hazards.
Discrimination	Because temporaries are usually paid lower wages and no benefits compared to regular employees, they may feel discriminated against and may not perform adequately.
Social Responsibility	Because temporaries work intermittently, employers who use them extensively may be relying on supplements by federal, state, and local unemployment and welfare benefits during gaps between work engagements.
Impact on Human Resource Professionals	Extensive use of temporaries may hurt the professional image of human resource professionals because they become primarily work schedulers, running people in and out of the organization rather than being builders of an organization's human resource assets.

SOURCE: Adapted from Earnest R. Archer, "Words of Caution on the Temporary Workforce," *HRMagazine*, September 1994, pp. 164–168.

Another advantage of outsourcing is that it gives the organization flexibility to change its mind. The organization is free to shop around to various organizations for the services or jobs it needs done, and it can specify the criteria it needs to have met whether those criteria are cost, quality, delivery time, quantity, and so on. Also, if at a later date the organization chooses to bring the activities in-house, it is free to do so.

Outsourcing shares many of the same disadvantages as using contingent workers. These include a loss of skills, which could lead to a possible hollowing of the corporation and possible morale problems associated with the inevitable downsizing of the organization that comes with the outsourcing. Like the problems associated with contingent workers, management must pay careful attention to the course of action it takes. Finally, the organization must make sure that it dedicates adequate resources to coordinating its activities with the activities of the organization(s) to which it has outsourced its work. Like the problems associated with scheduling contingent workers, failure to provide adequate coordination between the organization and its outsources may result in lost productivity, increased costs, lowered quality, and depressed morale.

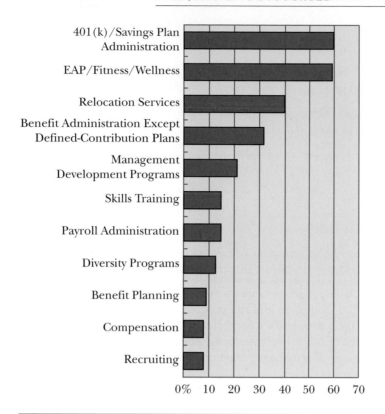

*Based on employers with outsourcing experiences or plans (N = 67).
SOURCE: *People Trends*, September 1993, p. 2.

FOCUS ON HR

Rapid Growth in Temporary Agencies

Temporary employment agencies grew rapidly during the decades of the 1980s and 1990s. About 10 percent of job growth during the 1990s was in temp agencies, twice as much as in the 1980s. Manpower, Inc., a temp agency, now boasts of being America's largest employer. In 2001 more than 3.3 million workers were in temp firm placements, primarily in light manufacturing and clerical jobs.

Why has temp employment grown so fast? Primarily because it gives employers flexibility. Employees come trained and work for only the period needed. Employers can dismiss an employee (send him or her back to the agency) for any reason—lack of work, poor performance, etc., without incurring legal hassles for wrongful termination. Furthermore, temp agencies serve as proving grounds for new employees. Employers can test employees by employing temps and then hiring them as regular employees if they work out. Some employers also can pay temps lower wages than their regular workers; however, by the time the fees for the agency are factored in, the total hourly wage paid can easily exceed the wage paid to regular employees.

What lies ahead? In good times, temp employees will remain in high demand. In bad times, they will be the first to be let go. That is the advantage of temporary employment—it allows employers to readily adapt their employment patterns to the business cycle.

SOURCE: David Wessel, "Capital: Temp Workers Have a Lasting Effect," *The Wall Street Journal*, February, 1, 2001, p. A1.

EXHIBIT 17.16	SOME SAMPLE OUTSOURCED PRODUCTS

Product	Manufacturer
Rayovac's battery recharger	Avex Electronics
Apple's PowerPC	Solectron
General Mills' Granola Bars	Coosa Baking
Snapple	Various local bottlers
Cytogen's Oncscint	Celltech

SOURCE: Thomas Martin, "You'll Never Guess Who Really Makes . . . ," *Fortune*, October 3, 1994, p. 125.

Management Guidelines

Based on the information presented in this chapter, several guidelines for managers who face an organizational restructuring can be offered.

1. Any organization restructuring involves a trade-off between the impact on the employees and the immediate benefits to the organization. It is the managers responsibility to balance the impact against the benefits.
2. Each type of restructuring strategy has its own time horizon for implementation. The manager must match the strategy to the time frame needed for the restructuring.
3. Each type of restructuring strategy has a different basic cost structure. The manager must consider the costs involved in each type of restructuring and the organization's ability to pay for it.
4. A critical determinant of a successful reorganization is the amount of managerial communication about the reasons for and goals of the restructuring. Poor communication between managers and employees may ruin the best planned restructuring.
5. There are several laws and doctrines concerning organization restructuring. Managers should make sure that they are in compliance with these laws and doctrines before they begin a restructuring.
6. All types of restructuring involve organizational trauma. To reduce trauma and ensure a successful restructuring, managers should attempt to plan the elements of a restructuring before they begin.
7. The strategic variables and choices facing an organization are often strong determinants of the type of restructuring that the organization undertakes. Managers should carefully examine these variables and choices before embarking on a restructuring.
8. The three types of restructuring strategies are not mutually exclusive. Managers should always consider using elements of all three types of restructuring strategies before making a final decision on the way to organize the restructuring.
9. Investigating the use of outsourcing, contingent workers, and the virtual organization may allow the organization to better cut costs and meet the variable changes in demand for the firm's goods and services.

Questions for Review

1. What is organization restructuring? What does it usually involve?
2. Identify and briefly discuss the three general types of restructuring. How are they alike? How do they differ?
3. What is the role of the human resource professional in a restructuring?
4. Briefly identify and discuss the strategic variables involved in a restructuring decision. Describe the elements of each variable.
5. What is an LBO? How is it usually related to a restructuring decision?
6. Identify the four broad strategic choices that an organization must make in deciding to restructure. Discuss the general impact on both the employees and the organization in each type of restructuring decision.
7. What are no-layoff strategies? Briefly compare and contrast the different types of no-layoff strategies.
8. What are layoff strategies? List the various types of layoff strategies and discuss the advantages and disadvantages of each.
9. What are termination strategies? How do they differ from other restructuring strategies?
10. What roles do tenure and protection and compensation plans have in a termination strategy?
11. What is the employment-at-will doctrine? How does it relate to termination strategies?
12. Briefly describe the role of golden parachutes in termination strategies.
13. How is severance pay used in a termination strategy? What are its main advantages and disadvantages?
14. Discuss an organization's outplacement policy in relation to termination strategies. What are the three elements of a typical outplacement policy?
15. Identify and discuss the three basic types of termination strategies that an organization may pursue. How are they alike? How do they differ?
16. What is the virtual organization? Why is it being considered by many organizations? How is it related to the contingent workforce and outsourcing?

CASE

The Aftermath of the Dot-Com Boom

With the growing emphasis of the Internet in recent years, many technologically savvy individuals saw an opportunity grow right before their eyes. The vast area of cyberspace was waiting to be discovered and cultivated, and it only took a few entrepreneurial minds to get the ball rolling. Multiple people flocked to the upstart dot-com companies for a chance to get in before the real growth started. These new hires included recent college graduates, as well as *Fortune* 500 executives who had defected from their stable but slow-growing jobs. Even though many of these individuals who were with the dot-coms from the beginning got rich really quickly, some were not so lucky—especially those who joined after the initial growth spurt. Currently, these dot-com companies are decreasing in number and will continue to do so throughout 2001 as more and more run out of capital and potential investors.

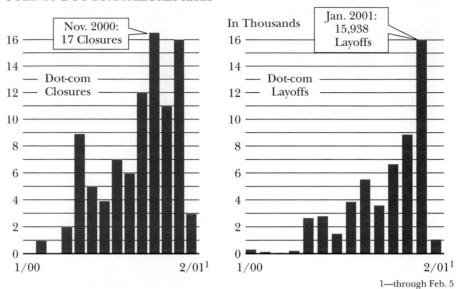

TOLL OF DOT-COM FAILURES RISES

SOURCE: *USA Today*, February 7, 2001, p. 2A.

The Layoffs

One by one, Internet companies ran into financial trouble—and, in many cases, mishandled the delicate task of layoffs. Axed staffers often walked away disillusioned by their treatment, complaining of scant or no severance pay and the absence of outplacement counseling.[54] Most of the companies did not offer their employees severance because more times than not, the remaining money was already claimed by creditors. Companies that did offer severance typically gave 2 weeks' worth. Of course, they were under no legal obligation to pay anything—and under most circumstances they had the right to terminate as many employees as they wanted. Some Internet companies are facing legal troubles regarding their massive terminations. The WARN act requires that companies with more than 100 employees give 60 days' notice when doing mass layoffs. Many dot-coms, however, would be exempt from the WARN act because they employ fewer than 100 people who have been working at the company at least 6 months. Many of the complaints could have been avoided had these dot-coms employed seasoned human resources managers or even written human resources policies. A lot of the companies started out with a great idea, but issues of disability, family leave, and severance went unheeded. Thus, as employees were pushed out the door, so did any positive feeling about their dot-com experience.

In the meantime, dot-commers are networking at pink-slip parties across the country. The buzz from these events: It would be nice to have a secure job, a healthy salary, and good benefits—in other words, making money the old-fashioned way.[55] Dot-commers go to commiserate and often come away with new job offers. Job churning makes the economy more efficient; it directs workers to the positions where they are most useful. But it comes at some psychic cost to employees and weakens the social fabric. Workers who shift from job to job do not have the security or form the same workplace bonds.[56] Despite this new climate of caution, plenty of companies are still hiring—even in the hard-hit high tech field. Microsoft is snapping up dot-com refugees, and Dell Computer says recruiting highly skilled engineers hasn't gotten easier.[57]

The Year 2000

At least 275 Internet companies ran out of funding and folded in 2000—about 75 percent of them B2C (business to customer) companies (see Exhibit 17.17). Along with that figure is one from a recent survey by job-placement firm Challenger, Gray & Christmas. They place the number of layoffs in 496 dot-com companies at 41,515 during the year 2000. The two halves of 2000 were like night and day for dot-commers. In the first 6 months all they heard about were job fairs, lavish recruiting parties and after-hours mixers where would-be entrepreneurs hoped to meet free-spending venture capitalists.[58] Now, pink-slip parties are the rage. According to an end-of-year study by Challenger, Gray & Christmas, between January and June of 2000, the Internet sector cut a total of 5097 jobs. From July through December, 36,177 reductions were made. Most of the job losses occurred at dot-com companies that specialize in services such as consulting and financial information. Internet retail firms saw the second-largest number of cuts. Even with a lot of dot-coms going belly up, the faster-growing communications companies are absorbing the good talent as it becomes available.

The Future

Among the remaining dot-com companies, some real restructuring is going to have to occur. These companies are going to be forced to use measurable marketing programs that are heavy on direct marketing and focus on the profitability of their customers. Experts say that fierce competition online—with rivals just a click away—means companies will have to personalize their sites and offerings if they hope to garner customer loyalty. Personalization is expected to be predominant on the web in 2001, as competition for customer loyalty continues to build. Right now, 70 percent of sites are not doing anything to personalize. Offers are going to have to become more appealing and relevant in order to hold a customer's attention. Three such companies currently in survival mode are Priceline.com, Bluefly.com, and Webvan.com. Exhibit 17.18 highlights their struggle to stay afloat.

After allowing many startups to succeed and then fail in the dot-com world, a new group of leaders is emerging. Call it the revenge of the real-world retailers. Recently, visits to "multi-channel" dot-coms (those with a catalog or store behind them) have shot up 67 percent. Sites like Walmart.com and Target.com are suddenly the fastest-growing destinations on the web. These multi-channels, of course, have the maddening advantage of starting out with trustworthy names—and bottomless parent-company purses. Traditional companies will turn their focus toward developing a much more strategic approach to integrating all of their online and offline channels in 2001. For 70 percent to 80 percent of the categories, the ultimate winners will be the brands established offline. The established stores offer the convenience of the Internet and the personal touch, brand name, and reach of a network of stores.

EXHIBIT 17.18   SURVIVAL MODE: THREE PIONEERS STRUGGLE TO STAY AFLOAT

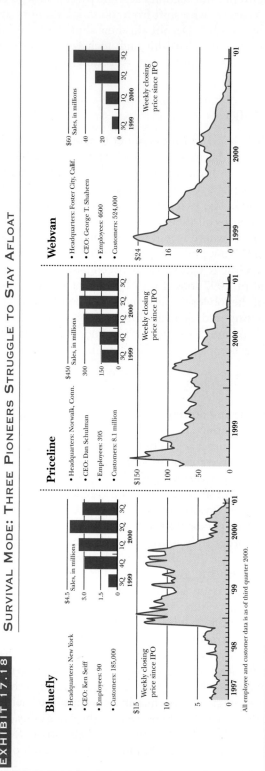

Bluefly

- Headquarters: New York
- CEO: Ken Seiff
- Employees: 90
- Customers: 185,000

Priceline

- Headquarters: Norwalk, Conn.
- CEO: Dan Schulman
- Employees: 395
- Customers: 8.1 million

Webvan

- Headquarters: Foster City, Calif.
- CEO: George T. Shaheen
- Employees: 4600
- Customers: 524,000

All employee and customer data is as of third quarter 2000.

SOURCE: *The Wall Street Journal*, January 25, 2001, p. B1.

Additional Readings

Baldwin, Michell C., and Dennis G. Pappas. *Surviving Corporate Downsizing with Dignity and Grace!* Birmingham, AL: Smart Publishing, 1999.

Bolman, Lee, and Terrence Deal. *Reframing Organizations.* San Francisco, CA: Jossey-Bass, 1991.

Boyette, Joseph, and Henry Conn. *Workplace 2000: The Revolution Reshaping American Business.* New York: Dutton, 1991.

Bramson, Robert, and Susan Bramson. *First Hired, Last Fired: How to Make Yourself Indispensable in an Age of Downsizing, Mergers, and Restructuring.* Lincolnwood, IL: Contemporary Books, 1999.

Bridges, William. *Managing Transitions.* Reading, MA: Addison-Wesley, 1991.

Cameron, Kim, Sarah Freeman, and Aneil Mishra. "Best Practices in White-collar Downsizing: Managing Contradictions." *Academy of Management Executive* 5 (1991), pp. 57–73.

Coulson, Robert. *Empowered at Forty: How to Negotiate the Best Time and Terms of Your Retirement.* New York: Harper-Business, 1992.

Downes, John, and Jordan Goodman. *Dictionary of Finance and Investment Terms.* 2nd ed. New York: Barron's, 1987.

Farrell, Christopher. "LBOs: The Stars, the Strugglers, the Flops." *Business Week*, January 15, 1990, pp. 58–62.

Fox, Isaac, and Alfred Marcus. "The Causes and Consequences of Leveraged Buyouts." *Academy of Management Journal* 17 (1992), pp. 62–65.

Gallie, Duncan, Michael White, Yuan Cheng, and Mark Tomlinson. *Restructuring the Employment Relationship.* New York: Clarendon Press, 1998.

Gaughan, Patrick A. *Mergers, Acquisitions, and Corporate Restructuring.* New York: Wiley 1999.

Geneen, Harold, and Brent Bowers. *Synergy and Other Lies: Downsizing, Bureaucracy, and Corporate Culture Debunked.* New York: Griffin Trade Paperback, 1999.

Hartley, Jean, Dan Jacobson, Bert Klandermans, and Tinka Van Vuuren. *Job Insecurity.* Newbury Park, CA: Sage, 1991.

Henkoff, Ronald. "Cost Cutting: How to Do It Right." *Fortune*, April 9, 1990, p. 41.

Hymowitz, Carol. "Kodak Passes Out Tin Parachutes to All Its Employees." *The Wall Street Journal*, January 12, 1990, p. B1.

Karr, Albert. "As the Army Shrinks, the Civilian Market Will Tighten for Job Seekers." *The Wall Street Journal*, June 19, 1990, p. A1.

Keller, John. "AT&T Weighs Early Retirement Plan that May Slash Non-Management Staff." *The Wall Street Journal*, March 15, 1990, p. A3.

Kissler, Gary. *Change Riders.* Reading, MA: Addison-Wesley, 1991.

Mainiero, Lisa, and Paul Upham. "Beating a Stacked Deck-Restructuring vs. Career Development." *Personnel Journal*, June 1987, p. 126.

Marchand, Marianne H., and Anne Sisson Runyan. *Gender and Global Restructuring: Sightings, Sites, and Resistances.* London: Routledge, 2000.

Messmer, Max. "Right-Sizing Reshapes Staffing Strategies." *HRMagazine*, October 1991, pp. 60–62.

Petras, Kathryn, and Ross Petras. *The Only Retirement Guide You'll Ever Need.* New York: Poseidon, 1992.

"Plant-Closing Law Affects Casino." *HRM News/Society for Human Resource Management*, February 1990, p. A11.

Reid, Peter. *Well Made in America: Lessons from Harley-Davidson on Being the Best.* New York: McGraw-Hill, 1990.

Shao, Maria. "Boeing: A Backlog Strains Its Assembly Line." *Business Week*, May 8, 1989, pp. 35–36.

Shoven, John B., and Joel Wladfogel. *Debt, Taxes, and Corporate Restructuring.* Washington, DC: Brookings Institute, 1990.

Siconolfi, Michael. "Drexel Owes Its Former Employees about $40 Million in Severance Fees." *The Wall Street Journal*, February 26, 1990, pp. A4,1.

Siehl, C., and D. Smith. "Avoiding the Loss of a Gain: Retraining Top Managers in an Acquisition." *Human Resource Management* 29 (1991), pp. 167–185.

Soukup, William, Miriam Rothman, and Dennis Brisco. "Outplacement Services: A Vital Component of Personnel Policy." *SAM Advanced Management Journal*, Autumn 1987, pp. 19–23.

Stewart, Paul, Phillip Garrahan, and Stuart Crowther. *Restructuring for Economic Flexibility.* Brookfield, VT: Avebury, 1990.

Sweet, Donald. *A Manager's Guide to Conducting Terminations.* Lexington, MA: Lexington Books, 1990.

Walsh, J., and J. Ellwood. "Mergers, Acquisitions, and the Pruning of Managerial Deadwood." *Strategic Management Journal* 12 (1991), pp. 210–217.

Weston, J. Fred, Kwang S. Chung, and Juan A. Siu. *Takeovers, Restructuring, & Corporate Governance.* Englewood Cliffs, NJ: Prentice Hall, 1998.

Notes

[1]Adam Geller, "Large-Scale Layoffs Make a Come Back," *Tallahassee Democrat*, December 19, 2000, pp. 1E, 2E.

[2]James Bandler, Daniel Golden, and John Hechinger, "Xerox Seeks to Survive on Tuna Sandwiches, Shared Cubicles, Layoffs," *The Wall Street Journal*, December 20, 2000, pp. B1, B8.

[3]Brian Dumaine, "The Bureaucracy Busters," *Fortune*, June 17, 1991, pp. 36–50.

[4]Ibid.; and Frank Kuzmits and Lyle Sussman, "Early Retirement or Forced Resignation: Policy Issues for Downsizing Human Resources," *SAM Advanced Management Journal*, Winter 1988, p. 28.

[5]Stephanie Mehta, "Can Bernie Bounce Back?" *Fortune*, January 22, 2001, pp. 84–90.

[6]John Wilke, "At Digital Equipment, Slowdown Reflects Industry's Big Changes," *The Wall Street Journal*, September 15, 1989, pp. A1; John R. Wilke, "Digital Plans at Least 20,000 More Job Cuts," *The Wall Street Journal*, May 6, 1994, p. A3; Joseph Weber, "Desperate Hours at DEC," *Business Week*, May 9, 1994, pp. 26–30; William M. Bulkeley, "Digital Equipment to Slash 14,000 Jobs in Core Computer Lines by Restructuring," *The Wall Street Journal*, July 19, 1994, p. B3; and Carrie Dolan, "Quantum Set to Pay about $400 Million for Digital Line," *The Wall Street Journal*, July 20, 1994, p. B6.

[7]Dean Tjosvold, "Foolproof Your Restructuring Plan," *HRMagazine*, November 1991, pp. 79–84.

[8]Michael Porter, *Competitive Strategy* (New York: Free Press, 1980), p. xvi.

[9]Ibid., pp. 34–46.

[10]Alan Meyer, "Adapting to Environmental Jolts," *Administrative Science Quarterly*, 1982, pp. 515–537.

[11]Albert Karr, "Staying Lean," *The Wall Street Journal*, July 16, 1991, p. A1.

[12]Peter C. Reid, *Well Made in America: Lessons from Harley-Davidson on Being the Best* (New York: McGraw-Hill, 1990), p. 14.

[13]*Human Resources Management Implications of Corporate Restructuring* (American Society for Personnel Administration–Commerce Clearing House, 1989), pp. 2–3.

[14]Ronald Henkoff, "Cost Cutting: How to Do It Right," *Fortune*, April 9, 1990, p. 41.

[15]**www.kodak.com**, (accessed November 5, 2000).

[16]John Downes and Jordan Goodman, *Dictionary of Finance and Investment Terms*, 2nd ed. (New York: Barron's, 1987), p. 209.

[17]William Starbuck and Bo Hedberg, "Saving an Organization from a Stagnating Environment," in H. Thorelli, ed., *Strategy 1 Structure 5 Performance* (Bloomington: Indiana University Press, 1977), pp. 249–258.

[18]Lisa Mainiero and Paul Upham, "Beating a Stacked Deck Restructuring vs. Career Development," *Personnel Journal*, June 1987, p. 126.

[19]Susan Kuhn, "How Business Helps Schools," *Fortune*, Education 1990 Issue, pp. 91–106.

[20]"Job-Based Learning: Some Firms Build Closer Ties between School and Work" *The Wall Street Journal*, September 10, 1991, p. A1.

[21]Maria Shao, "Boeing: A Backlog Strains Its Assembly Line," *Business Week*, May 8, 1989, p. 36.

[22]James Francis, John Mohr, and Kelly Anderson, "HR Balancing: Alternative Downsizing," *Personnel Journal*, January 1992, pp. 71–78.

[23]"The Axeman Cometh," *The Economist*, December 1990, pp. 15–16.

[24]Udayan Gupta, "Cutting Payrolls Without Axing Any Employees," *The Wall Street Journal*, March 26, 1991, pp. B1.

[25]For more information, see Roger W. Schmenner, *Production/Operations Management*, 3rd ed. (Chicago: SRA, 1987), pp. 5–23.

[26]Ibid., pp. 52–85.

[27]Joseph White, "GM's Plant Closings Help It Win Wall Street Applause," *The Wall Street Journal*, May 25, 1990, p. C1.

[28]Gregory L. White, "In Order to Grow, GM Finds that the Order of the Day is Cutbacks," *The Wall Street Journal*, December 18, 2000, pp. A1, A13.

[29]Gabriella Stren, Paul Carroll, and Michel McQueen, "In a Weak Economy, Some Top-Level Aides Are Bound to Topple," *The Wall Street Journal*, December 13, 1991, pp. A1.

[30]George Milkovich and John Boudreau, *Personnel/Human Resource Management: A Diagnostic Approach* (Plano, TX: Business Publications, 1988), pp. 465–467.

[31]Christopher Conte, "Litigation Losses," *The Wall Street Journal*, May 12, 1992, p. A1.

[32]Michael Siconolfi, "Drexel Owes Its Former Employees About $40 Million in Severance Fees," *The Wall Street Journal*, February 26, 1990, p. A4.

[33]Carol Hymowitz, "Kodak Passes Out Tin Parachutes to All Its Employees," *The Wall Street Journal*, January 12, 1990, pp. B1.

[34]"Severance: The Corporate Response," *The Right Research Report* (Fort Lauderdale: Right Associates).

[35]"Goodbyes Can Cost Plenty in Europe," *Fortune*, April 6, 1992, p. 16; and Christopher Conte, "Terminating Workers," *The Wall Street Journal*, May 12, 1992, p. A1.

[36]William Heery, "Outplacement through Specialization," *Personnel Administrator*, June 1989, p. 151.

[37]William Soukup, Miriam Rothman, and Dennis Brisco, "Outplacement Services: A Vital Component of Personnel Policy," *SAM Advanced Management Journal*, Autumn 1987, pp. 19–23.

[38]Laurie P. Cohen, "AT&T Expands Early-Retirement Plan—Earnings Climb 19 percent in Third Period," *The Wall Street Journal*, October 20, 1989, p. A4.

[39]John Keller, "AT&T Weighs Early Retirement Plan That May Slash Non-Management Staff," *The Wall Street Journal*, March 15, 1990, p. A3.

[40]Lenore Schiff, "Is Health Care a Job Killer?" *Fortune*, April 6, 1992, p. 30.

[41]The following discussion is based on Frank E. Kuzmits and Lyle Sussman, "Early Retirement or Forced Resignation: Policy Issues for Downsizing Human Resources," *SAM Advanced Management Journal*, Winter 1988, pp. 28–32.

[42]J. E. Rigdon, "Women Appear to Take Firings Less Personally," *The Wall Street Journal*, December 6, 1991, p. B1.

[43]Gregory Patterson, "More Employers Offer Early Retirement to Help Shrink Blue-Collar Work Force," *The Wall Street Journal*, August 30, 1991, p. B1.

[44]Robert Wolfe, "Most Employers Offer Exit Interviews," *HRNews*, June 1991, p. A2.

[45]Gary Hamel and C. K. Prahalad, *Competing for the Future* (Cambridge, MA: Harvard Business School Press, 1994).

[46]John Huey, "The New Post-Heroic Leadership," *Fortune*, February 21, 1994, p. 44.

[47]Walter Kiechel III, "How We Will Work in the Year 2000," *Fortune*, May 17, 1993,

[48]Alison L. Sprout, "Moving into the Virtual Office," *Business Week*, May 2, 1994, p. 103.

[49]Clare Ansberry, "Hired Out," *The Wall Street Journal*, March 11, 1993, p. A1.

[50]Jaclyn Fierman, "The Contingency Workforce," *Fortune*, January 24, 1994, pp. 30–31.

[51]Ansberry, "Hired Out."

[52]Fierman, "The Contingency Workforce," *Fortune*, January 24, 1994, p. 33.

[53]David Gold and Beth Unger, "Communication Boosts Morale after Downsizing," *HRNews*, February 1992, p. A7.

[54]Kemba Dunham, "Laid-Off Internet Workers Cite Shabby Treatment As They Are Shown Door," *The Wall Street Journal*, October 17, 2000, pp. B1 and B16.

[55]Melanie Warner, "Pity the poor dot-commer (a little bit)," *Fortune*, January 22, 2001, p. 40.

[56]Adam Cohen, "This Time It's Different," *Time*, January 8, 2001, pp. 18–21.

[57]Robert Berner, "Pink Slip Blues," *Business Week*, December 25, 2000, pp. 54–55.

[58]"Dot-com Job Cuts Rise in December," *The Wire—News from The AP*, December 27, 2000.

1

FedEx Corporation*

FedEx Express, formerly Federal Express, became a leader in the air transport industry in only a few years.[1] The company founded the small-package/document express market in 1973, and it constantly adds products and services while extending its service areas. Its main air freight forwarding competitors, most notably United Parcel Service (UPS), were content with the market positions they occupied before FedEx "changed the rules of the game" and took the market by storm.[2]

Industry

Firms involved in cargo movement include all-cargo air carriers, traditional freight forwarders, passenger airlines, ground transportation companies, and air couriers. Competitors directly involved in the small-package and document express market include FedEx Express, UPS, Airborne Express, DHL Worldwide Express, and the U.S. Postal Service.

Regulation for this industry falls under the Federal Aviation Act of 1958 and is enforced by the Federal Aviation Administration (FAA). The FAA's regulatory authority relates primarily to the safety aspects of air transportation, which includes aircraft standards and maintenance.

FedEx operations are also subject to regulation by the Federal Communications Act of 1934 because of the use of radio and communication equipment in ground and air units. In addition, the Department of Transportation exercises regulatory authority over the company.

Company Background

Frederick W. Smith, founder of FedEx Express earned his pilot's license before entering college. His experience as an aviator and his observation of material shipments out of airports while a student majoring in political science and economics at Yale University in the 1960s were the impetus for developing his firm in 1973.

*This case was prepared by Mark Dawkins and Erich Brockmann; it was revised by Cathie Anthony Mathe, Leslie Smith, Craig Mathe, Amanda Stephens, and Seanna Peters.

His initial conceptualization of FedEx Express was that of an air cargo firm that specialized in overnight package delivery on a door-to-door basis using its own planes.

The idea for FedEx Express was first laid out in an overdue economics paper. To cut cost and time, packages from all over the country would be flown to a central point, or hub, late at night when the traffic lanes were comparatively empty. At the hub the packages would be sorted, redistributed, and flown out again to their ultimate locations. Airports in sizable cities would be used, and trucks would carry the packages to their final destinations. The destinations served would include the airport locations and smaller communities in the vicinity. The goal was to deliver equipment and documents shipped from any location in the United States to any other location within the United States the next day.[3]

FedEx Express received its original name because of Smith's ambition to serve the Federal Reserve and to create a name with a broad geographic connotation. He wanted to assist the Federal Reserve in its float management efforts by selling them a delivery system that would cut down on float time (the period between receipt of a check and collection of funds). Unfortunately, Smith's contract bid was turned down by the Federal Reserve.

After college, Smith served two tours of duty in Vietnam. He decided to give his air express idea a try after returning home. A study showed that Memphis, Tennessee, was near the center of business shipping in the continental United States. Its airport offered long runways, a large abandoned ramp, and a pair of inexpensive hangars from World War II, and it was closed only an average of ten hours per year due to adverse weather conditions.[4] Thus Smith chose Memphis as a home base and started his firm with $4 million he had inherited.

Financing

Because $4 million was not enough for an entire fleet of planes, Smith went to New York and Chicago in search of additional funds. With his impressive knowledge of the air freight industry and his ability to impress investors, Smith raised $72 million in loans and equity investment within 1 year.

With fresh capital, FedEx Express expanded its focus from operating a charter service to its present business. It began transporting packages weighing less than 70 pounds from 13 airports in April 1973. Volume increased rapidly, resulting in extended service. FedEx Express appeared to be an overnight success. The success, however, did not last long as the Organization of Petroleum Exporting Countries' inflation of fuel prices increased expenses faster than revenues were growing. By mid 1974, the company was losing more than $1 million per month.[5]

Bankruptcy became a real possibility, forcing Smith to return to his disappointed investors for more money to keep the company growing until revenues could catch up with expenses. He raised $11 million in additional funds. Having lost $27 million during its first 2 years, FedEx Express posted profits of $3.6 million and revenues of $75 million in 1976.

Management/Personnel

Smith's charisma enabled him to motivate investors and employees to share his vision for FedEx Express. A man of great integrity, Smith attributed his drive to scars from his military service tours. He stated that he would not have the same perspective if not for his Vietnam experiences.[6]

Despite many challenges, Smith never relinquished his entrepreneurial vision. He courted investors for more money when the Arab oil embargo resulted in skyrocketing fuel costs. He went to Washington and lobbied for airline deregulation when the Civil Aeronautics Board (CAB) regulations made it impossible for FedEx Express to use the larger aircraft it needed. He jumped at the opportunity to deliver overnight letter service when the postal service relaxed its regulations against private delivery of extremely urgent mail.[7]

Smith's colleagues had the same entrepreneurial attitude towards FedEx Express. All were former pilots and entrepreneurs. Although most thought his idea very strange, the camaraderie and loyalty exhibited by employees of FedEx Express were strong from day one. This camaraderie and loyalty strengthened FedEx Express. By the late 1970s, however, FedEx Express had grown too large for the entrepreneurial approach to management used by Smith and his colleagues.

Company President Art Bass, one of the initial team members, decided to leave in 1979. He took five vice-presidents with him—all but one of whom had been with FedEx Express from the start. Bass and his colleagues felt that FedEx Express had matured and that they lacked the ability to adapt their entrepreneurial perspectives to managing this mature operation. In 1990 Smith replaced his former colleagues, including several key executives, with managers who were comfortable with the traditional corporate organization.[8]

Now, Smith is the chairman, president, and CEO of FedEx Corporation (formerly FDX Corporation), the parent company for the FedEx family of services worldwide. FedEx has been recognized for the strength of its management team, but the backbone of the company from the beginning has been its employees. The dedication of more than 200,000 employees worldwide to professional, faultless service has kept FedEx at the forefront of global transportation and logistics.[9,10] Currently, FedEx Express is led by David J. Bronczek, president and CEO, and employs approximately 96,000 permanent full-time and 53,000 permanent part-time employees, of which approximately 20 percent are employed in Memphis. Employees of FedEx Express international branches and subsidiaries represent approximately 13 percent of all employees. FedEx Ground's president and CEO is Daniel J. Sullivan, and the company has approximately 35,000 employees and contractors in North America.[11]

Each employee hired is viewed as a long-term investment. Part-time employees are scheduled to permit operations to expand or contract according to traffic levels, thereby avoiding the need to furlough full-time employees.[12] In addition, by employing part-time college students who come and go as they complete their education, FedEx has created a buffer between its operations and the entrance of unions to the hub.[13] This has allowed FedEx to keep its labor costs lower than any other company in the industry.[14]

However, they have not been totally successful. The flight-crew members decided to form a collective bargaining unit. Therefore, on August 26, 1993, the company began interim negotiations with the Air Line Pilots Association (ALPA), a powerful and active organization. Negotiations toward a comprehensive collective bargaining agreement began in May 1994. ALPA and FedEx Express reached an agreement in 1997, which resulted in FedEx pilots being paid well above any other pilots in the commercial or cargo business. Other concessions were made as well. For example, FedEx promised to use mostly American pilots on international routes.[15]

Since May 31, 1999, FedEx Express and the FedEx Pilots Association (FPA), the collective bargaining representative for the FedEx pilots, have been operating under a 5-year collective bargaining agreement which provides, in part, for a 17 percent pay increase over the term of the contract (3.4 percent average annual increase), enhanced retirement benefits, direct pilot input on scheduling issues, and limits on types of trips scheduled during certain times of the day.[16]

Strategy

According to the FedEx Corporation 2000 Annual Report, the company's mission is to produce superior financial returns for its shareowners as it serves its customers with the highest quality transportation, logistics, and e-commerce solutions.[17]

Recently, FedEx Corporation conducted extensive research to develop a new strategic plan, which was unveiled in January 2000. The new strategic plan is based on three principles: (1) to leverage a significant point of competitive differentiation where each company of the FedEx family operates independently but competes collectively; (2) to extend the strength of the powerful FedEx brand name to three subsidiaries and to the holding company, previously named FDX Corporation; and (3) to provide a single point of access to customers for sales, customer service, billing, and automation systems.[18]

FedEx expects its new strategic plan to generate substantial incremental revenues and profits beginning in fiscal year 2001 as the company focuses on several strategic growth opportunities: (1) to generate incremental volume in its core transportation business by cross-selling all FedEx services, (2) to attract new business from small- and medium-sized customers, (3) to create new revenue streams with the new FedEx Trade Networks subsidiary and the new FedEx Home Delivery service, (4) to capitalize on e-commerce, and (5) to provide meaningful supply chain solutions.[19]

The FedEx Corporation Family

FedEx Corporation is the premier global provider of transportation, logistics, e-commerce, and supply chain management services. All transportation and logistics needs are met by one organization: FedEx Corporation. FedEx Corporation is comprised of a powerful family of companies that operate independently but compete collectively. Independently each company is free to focus on the distinct needs of its market segment without compromising networks or service although, collectively, the entire FedEx organization works together to cross-sell services and provide customer solutions.[20]

FedEx Corporation is primarily composed of FedEx Express, the world's largest express transportation company, and FedEx Ground, a ground small-package carrier. FedEx has determined its reportable operating segments to be FedEx Express and FedEx Ground, both of which operate in single lines of business. Other companies included in the FedEx Corporation portfolio are the following:[21]

- FedEx Logistics, which offers complete supply chain solutions by combining worldwide transportation, information, and physical logistics services.
- FedEx Custom Critical (formerly known as Roberts Express), which is the world's leading surface-expedited carrier for time-critical shipments and those requiring special handling.

- FedEx Trade Networks, which provides customs brokerage and trade facilitation solutions, principally through its Tower Group International, Inc. subsidiary.
- Viking, which is a less-than-truckload freight carrier operating principally in the western United States.

Collectively, the FedEx Corporation companies leverage cross-company synergies to create end-to-end business solutions. Furthermore, the power of its advanced system of networks allows the FedEx Corporation companies to combine visibility and velocity in order to deliver a true competitive advantage. Through its physical networks, its companies deliver nearly 5 million shipments every business day.[22]

Operations

FedEx Express provides overnight express delivery service for high-priority packages and documents on a door-to-door basis. It delivers more than 3.3 million express shipments each business day worldwide. Services are available Monday through Saturday to 210 countries—the majority of the industrial world.[23] On March 6, 1998, FedEx launched Sunday delivery via FedEx Priority Overnight. Sunday delivery is to select zip codes in 50 major U.S. metropolitan areas from many U.S. origins.[24] These services are provided through FedEx Express' hub-and-spoke system, an intricate ground-air network.

FedEx Express has five headquarters: worldwide headquarters are located in Memphis, Tennessee; Asian headquarters, in Hong Kong; Canadian headquarters, in Toronto, Ontario; European headquarters, in Brussels, Belgium; and Latin American headquarters, in Miami, Florida.[25]

FedEx Express' central, primary sorting facility in Memphis (the SuperHub) has made its service operation unique in the field. A second national hub is located in Indianapolis. In addition, FedEx Express operates regional hubs in Newark, Oakland, and Fort Worth and major metropolitan sorting facilities in Los Angeles and Chicago. Facilities in Anchorage, Paris, and Subic Bay, the Philippines, serve as sorting facilities for express package and freight traffic moving to and from Asia, Europe, and North America. Additional major sorting and freight handling facilities are located at Narita Airport in Tokyo, Stansted Airport outside London, and Pearson Airport in Toronto. Facilities in Subic Bay and Paris are also designed to serve as regional hubs for their respective market areas.[26] This structure allows FedEx Express to provide service between many points worldwide within 24 to 48 hours.[27]

Hub operations are fine-tuned for maximum efficiency. Packages are collected in sorting facilities and offices during the day in hundreds of cities. Packages are then transported to the local airport and flown to the nearest hub. The planes are unloaded, and the packages are then sorted and loaded back onto the planes headed for their intended destinations. Couriers then transport the packages from sorting facilities at local airports to local offices, where they are routed to the receiver.

Contact with couriers is maintained through the use of digitally assisted dispatch units (DADs). Dispatch information can be left in couriers' vans, even when unoccupied.[28] FedEx Express also uses an advanced computer network for package tracking and billing. The satellite and telephone network, called COSMOS, can locate a package as it passes through numerous electronic gates during transit. Each parcel is barcoded for monitoring and recording each step of the journey.[29] In addition, the

COSMOS network provides proof of delivery information and an electronically re-produced air bill for the customer. For international shipments FedEx Express has de-veloped FedEx Expressclear, a worldwide electronic customs clearance system, which speeds up customs clearance by allowing customs agents in destination countries to review information about shipments before they arrive.[30]

FedEx Express has more than 46,000 drop-off locations and operates 663 aircraft and 49,000 delivery vehicles worldwide.[31] Other vehicles owned by the company in-clude ground support equipment, cargo loaders, transports, and aircraft tugs.

FedEx Ground handles more than 1.4 million packages daily. Like FedEx Ex-press, FedEx Ground uses a hub-and-spoke sorting and distribution system. Its 27 hubs are equipped with sophisticated package-sorting technology, with average pro-cessing speeds of 15,000 to 20,000 packages per hour. In January 1999 FedEx Ground announced its intention to boost its package processing capacity by 50 percent through a 3-year expansion program. Plans include the opening of three new state-of-the-art distribution hubs that will support New York, Chicago, and Los Angeles, as well as the relocation and expansion of more than 50 local terminals. FedEx Ground also expanded existing hubs in Toledo and Denver during 2000 and expects to com-plete expansion of its Sacramento hub in 2001. As of May 31, 2000, FedEx Ground operated 369 facilities in the United States and Canada.[32]

Using overhead laser scanners, hub conveyors electronically guide packages to their appropriate destination chute, where they are loaded for transport to their des-tination terminals for local delivery. FedEx Ground conducts its operations primarily with 9800 owner-operated vehicles and, in addition, owns more than 10,800 trailers. FedEx Ground is headquartered in Pittsburgh, Pennsylvania.[33]

FedEx Express and FedEx Ground maintain electronic connections with cus-tomers via FedEx Ship, FedEx interNetship, and FedEx Tracking.[34]

With the success of COSMOS, FedEx leveraged its information management to spin off a subsidiary called FedEx Logistics, specializing in managing inventory flows and worldwide distribution.[35] FedEx Logistics' comprehensive services include ware-housing, inventory control, order entry, packing, and delivery. With hub warehouses strategically located throughout the United States, Canada, Europe, and Asia, FedEx Express Distribution Centers enable non-store retailers or product suppliers to ex-pand their distribution capabilities without capital investment or long-term risk.[36] For instance, fashion retailer Laura Ashley signed a contract with FedEx to handle all aspects of the company's order-fulfillment and distribution operations. Not only does FedEx run all of Laura Ashley's warehouses—handling everything from inven-tory management to packing and shipping—but when mail-order customers call Laura Ashley's service numbers, they unknowingly speak to FedEx employees.[37]

Delivery Services

On a domestic level, FedEx Express offers three U.S. overnight delivery services: FedEx First Overnight, FedEx Priority Overnight, and FedEx Standard Overnight. Overnight document and package service extends to virtually the entire U.S. popula-tion. FedEx SameDay service is for urgent shipments up to 70 pounds to virtually any U.S. destination. Two U.S. deferred services are available for less urgent shipments: FedEx 2Day and FedEx Express Saver. U.S. overnight and second-day services are backed by money-back guarantees and are primarily used by customers for shipment of time-sensitive documents and goods.[38]

FedEx Express also offers express freight services to handle the needs of the time-definite freight market. FedEx Express offers customers the option of 1-, 2-, or 3-business-day service backed by two money-back guarantees. Shipments must be 151 pounds to 2200 pounds and must be forkliftable, stackable, banded, and shrink-wrapped.[39]

In addition, FedEx Express offers FedEx Dangerous Goods Service, FedEx Collect on Delivery (COD) Service, and Saturday Service. Moreover, the company offers FedEx Air Charter, in which FedEx provides the plane and crew and the client chooses the time and route.

FedEx Express offers various international package and document delivery services and international freight services to 210 countries. These services include: FedEx International Next Flight, FedEx International First, FedEx International Priority, FedEx International Economy, FedEx International Priority Direct Distribution, FedEx International Priority Plus, FedEx International MailService, FedEx International Priority Freight, FedEx International Economy Freight, FedEx International Express Freight, FedEx International Airport-to-Airport, and the FedEx Expressclear Electronic Customs Clearance, and FedEx International Broker Select service feature options.[40]

FedEx Express offers next business day 10:30 AM express cargo service from Asia to the United States. In fact, FedEx has a direct flight from Osaka, Japan to Memphis, Tennessee. International freight and express delivery markets, particularly outbound from Asia, are growing rapidly. FedEx Express offers the most competitive international freight service in the industry. In June 2000 FedEx Express announced the expansion of its international freight service to provide more delivery options to more countries. Detailed information about all of FedEx Express' delivery services can be found on the FedEx Web site at **www.fedex.com**.[41]

By focusing on business-to-business customers, maintaining a low cost structure, and efficiently using information technology, FedEx Ground has become the second-largest ground small-package carrier in the United States. FedEx Ground serves customers in the small-package market in North America, focusing primarily on the business-to-business delivery of packages weighing up to 150 pounds. FedEx Ground provides ground service to 100 percent of the U.S. population and overnight service to approximately 80 percent of the U.S. population. Through its subsidiary, FedEx Ground Package System, Ltd., service is provided to 100 percent of the Canadian population. In addition, FedEx Ground provides service to Mexico, Puerto Rico, Alaska, and Hawaii in cooperation with other transportation providers.[42]

In March 2000 FedEx Ground began providing FedEx Home Delivery to approximately 50 percent of the U.S. population. FedEx Home Delivery was created to respond to business-to-customer demand for a better ground delivery solution for the residential market. FedEx Home Delivery introduced new ideas to business-to-customer delivery to help retailers address mounting fulfillment challenges. In June 2000 FedEx Ground announced the accelerated expansion of the FedEx Home Delivery network. FedEx Home Delivery expects to increase its reach from 50 percent to 70 percent of the U.S. population by March 31, 2001, and to approximately 80 percent of the U.S. population by September 2001. Full coverage of the U.S. population is expected to be achieved by September 2002.[43]

FedEx Ground provides other specialized transportation services to meet specific customer requirements in the small-package market. FedEx Ground provides a money-back guarantee on all business-to-business ground deliveries within the continental United States.[44]

Marketing/Advertising

FedEx Express was an innovator. Having founded the small-package/document express market, FedEx Express hoped to dominate it. Smith stated that FedEx Express was selling time, thereby allowing people to be more effective in their day-to-day activities.[45] Smith went all out to get the message across. Initial emphasis was on building the public's trust by convincing customers that FedEx Express would do what it claimed to do: "Get it there overnight." Flying its own aircraft is indeed one of FedEx's competitive edges. With a tag line that says "We Live to Deliver," the company drives market share through its quality of service, which is based on speed, reliability, and information availability.[46]

In 1994 FedEx made a drastic change in its image. It decided to update its identity in an effort to set it apart from its competition. By adopting the ubiquitous "FedEx" in lieu of the previous "Federal Express," it established itself as responsive and global. The intent of the user-friendly logo was to increase the likelihood that the worldwide customer would think of FedEx first for express delivery. Furthermore, dropping the "Federal" eliminated the mistaken assumption of a government connection.

Now FedEx has adopted a new branding strategy, extending the FedEx brand name even further to three subsidiaries and to the holding company, previously named FDX Corporation. Changes have occurred quickly, including new logos and colors.

FedEx, a pioneer in customer self-service on the Web, is also taking great measures to stay up-to-date with the information age, mainly through the Internet. In fact, the FedEx Web site has been heralded as one of the best on the Web. One of its most well-known features is its Web package-tracking information capability. This feature was pioneered by FedEx and has become an industry norm.

In June 2000 FedEx launched its "single point of contact" hub for customers. The company redesigned its Web site so that U.S. customers could operate more efficiently with the site's easy, one-click access to FedEx Express and FedEx Ground package tracking, customer service, billing, and automation systems. The single point of contact hub enhances the customer experience although making it simpler to access FedEx services on the Internet.[47] The company also rolled out a service called Virtual Order that puts customers' catalogs on their Web sites for them and provides 24-hour technical support. These measures have allowed FedEx to become a major player in Internet commerce.[48]

More than 2.5 million customers are connected electronically through the FedEx information network and approximately two thirds of its U.S. domestic transactions are now handled online. Through the company's virtual networks, it handles more than 100 million electronic transactions a day while it continues to invest about $1.5 billion each year in information technology (IT) and IT people.[49]

Acquisitions

In 1987 FedEx purchased the assets of the Island Courier Companies and acquired Cansica, Inc. In 1989 the company acquired Tiger International for $895 million, a major strategic acquisition. In 1989 it also acquired East-West Couriers, Ltd., Yuill Courier Services, Ltd., and Bluejay Courier Services in Canada; Winchmore Developments, Ltd. and Home Delivery Services, Ltd. in the United Kingdom; Transport Group Alvarcht in Holland; Elbe-Klaus in Germany; Saimex in Italy; Rainer's in Australia; the Daisei Companies in Japan; and the Binghalib Express in the United Arab Emirates. In 1990 the company acquired Transports Transvendeens Chronoservice in France and Aeroenvios in Mexico.[50]

On January 27, 1998, FedEx Express became a wholly-owned subsidiary of FedEx Corp. in connection with the acquisition of Caliber System, Inc. On September 10, 1999, FedEx Logistics acquired the assets of GeoLogistics Air Services, Inc., an air freight forwarder servicing freight shipments between the United States and Puerto Rico. This business operates under the name Caribbean Transportation Services, Inc. Then on February 29, 2000, FedEx acquired the common stock of Tower Group International, a leader in the business of providing international customs clearance services. This business is operating as a subsidiary of FedEx Trade Networks. Finally, on March 31, 2000, FedEx acquired the common stock of World Tariff, Ltd., a premier source of customs duty and tax information around the globe. This business is also operating as a subsidiary of FedEx Trade Networks.[51]

Competition

The express package and freight markets are both highly competitive and sensitive to price and service. The ability to compete effectively depends on price, frequency and capacity of scheduled service, ability to track packages, extent of geographic coverage, and reliability. In 2000 FedEx Express' major competitors in the domestic market are UPS, Airborne Express, DHL Worldwide Express, passenger airlines offering express package services, regional express delivery entities, air freight forwarders, and the U.S. Postal Service. FedEx Express' principal competitors in the international market are DHL Worldwide Express, UPS, foreign postal authorities such as Deutsche Poste and TNT Post Group, passenger airlines, and all-cargo airlines.[52]

UPS provides transportation services primarily to deliver small packages. The company is the giant in package delivery and occupies a strong position in the transportation industry. Only the U.S. Postal Service can rival its package volume. Service is offered throughout the United States, Western Europe, and Canada. Service is also provided to many locations in the Soviet Union, Eastern Europe, Asia, the Middle East, Africa, and Central and South America.

The company entered the overnight package delivery market late in 1982 with its rates substantially lower than those charged by FedEx.[53] UPS enjoyed an established reputation of dependability, productivity, and efficiency until the union strike in the summer of 1997. Now the company operates a delivery fleet of 149,000 vehicles, utilizes more than 500 aircraft, and employs a workforce of 344,000 worldwide. Reported revenue for 1999 was $27.1 billion.[54]

The U.S. Postal Service competes in the overnight package delivery business with its Express Mail next-day service, which guarantees delivery to the addressee the following day by 3:00 PM. The addressee, at his or her option, can pick up the package as early as 10:00 AM on the delivery day. Customers can obtain full refunds for shipments that do not arrive on time. Postal Service statistics show that 95 percent of its shipments arrive on time.[55] Regularly scheduled package pickup is also available for a flat charge, regardless of the number of packages.

The U.S. Postal Service employs 797,795 people and has an annual operating revenue of $63 billion.[56] Its service areas include most major metropolitan areas in the United States, with international service to major cities in the United Kingdom, Australia, Brazil, Japan, Belgium, France, Hong Kong, and the Netherlands.[57] The U.S. Postal Service handles 46 percent of the world's mail volume.[58]

FedEx Ground's primary competitors are UPS and the U.S. Postal Service. Competition focuses largely on providing competitive pricing and dependable service.[59]

Financial

FedEx Express was not an immediate financial success. It took 4 years, $70 million in venture capital, and several perches on the edge of bankruptcy before the company reported its first profitable period in late 1975. The initial offering in 1974-1975 raised only $32 million, and new capital for 1975 was $10 million. The company constantly asked banks, other corporations, and venture capitalists for additional loans and equity participation arrangements. The company survived because a dozen or more equity groups participated in three rounds of critical financing. During this difficult period, Smith gave up virtually all of his equity in FedEx Express but earned true loyalty from his employees for his determination and steadfast belief in the company. Smith recaptured a substantial portion of his equity in later refinancing and currently owns 9 percent of the company.

Exhibit 1 contains selected financial information about FedEx Corporation and its operations. FedEx Corp. closed fiscal 2000 with solid financial results. Revenue

EXHIBIT 1	SELECTED CONSOLIDATED FINANCIAL DATA

Years Ended May 31, In Thousands, Except Per Share Amounts and Other Operating Data

	2000	1999	1998
OPERATING RESULTS			
Revenues	$18,265,945	$16,773,470	$15,872,810
Operating income[1]	1,221,074	1,163,086	1,010,660
Income from continuing operations before income taxes	1,137,740	1,061,064	899,518
Income from continuing operations	688,336	$ 631,333	498,155
Income (loss) from discontinued operations[2]	—	—	4,875
Net income[1]	$ 688,336	$ 631,333	$ 503,030
PER SHARE DATA			
Earnings (loss) per share:			
Basic:			
Continuing operations	$ 2.36	$ 2.13	$ 1.70
Discontinued operations[2]	—	—	.02
	$ 2.36	$ 2.13	$ 1.72
Assuming dilution:			
Continuing operations	$ 2.32	$ 2.10	$ 1.67
Discontinued operations[2]	—	—	.02
	$ 2.32	$ 2.10	$ 1.69
Average shares of common stock	291,727	295,983	293,401
Average common and common equivalent shares	296,326	300,643	298,408
Cash dividends[3]	—	—	—

[1]In connection with its restructuring, Viking recorded a pretax asset impairment charge of $225,000,000 ($175,000,000, net of tax) in 1997.
[2]Discontinued operations include the operations of Roadway Express, Inc., a wholly-owned subsidiary of Caliber, whose shares were distributed to Caliber stockholders on January 2, 1996, and Roadway Global Air, Inc., a wholly-owned subsidiary of Caliber, which exited the airfreight business in calendar 1995.
SOURCE: FedEx Corporation, *2000 Annual Report*, p. 34.

EXHIBIT 1   SELECTED CONSOLIDATED FINANCIAL DATA—CONT'D

Years Ended May 31, In Thousands, Except Per Share Amounts and Other Operating Data

	2000	1999	1998
FINANCIAL POSITION			
*Property and equipment, net	$ 7,083,527	$ 6,559,217	$ 5,935,050
Total assets	11,527,111	10,648,211	9,686,060
Long-term debt, less current portion	1,776,253	1,359,668	1,385,180
Common stockholders' investment	4,785,243	4,663,692	3,961,230
OTHER OPERATING DATA			
**FedEx Express			
Operating weekdays	257	256	254
Aircraft fleet	663	634	613
FedEx Ground:			
Operating weekdays	254	253	256
Average full-time			
equivalent employees	163,324	156,386	150,823

[3]Caliber declared dividends of $3,899,000, $28,184,000, and $54,706,000, for 1998, 1997, and 1996, respectively. Caliber declared additional dividends of $10,833,000 from January 1, 1997 to May 25, 1997 that are not included in the preceding amounts. FedEx has never paid cash dividends on its common stock.

*FedEx does not own any material real properties. FedEx leases two facilities in the Memphis area for its corporate headquarters and administrative offices.

**FedEx Express's principal owned or leased properties include its aircraft, vehicles, national, regional and metropolitan sorting facilities, administration buildings, FedEx World Service Centers, FedEx Drop Boxes and data processing and telecommunications equipment.

AIRCRAFT AND VEHICLES

FedEx Express's aircraft fleet at May 31, 2000 consisted of the following:

Description	Number[1]	Maximum Gross Structural Payload Pounds per Aircraft[2]
McDonnell Douglas MD11	30	195,000
McDonnell Douglas DC10-30	22	176,000
McDonnell Douglas DC10-10	69	139,000
Airbus A300-600	36	116,000
Airbus A310-200	41	82,000
Boeing B727-200	95	60,000
Boeing B727-100	66	45,000
Fokker F27-500	24	13,500
Fokker F27-600	8	12,500
Shorts 3-60	11	8,300
Cessna 208B	251	3,400
Cessna 208	10	3,000
Total	663	

SOURCE: FedEx Corporation, *2000 From 10-K.*
[1]Except as described in the following sentence, all of FedEx's aircraft are owned. The following aircraft are subject to operating leases: MD11 (29); DC10-30 (17); DC10-10 (4): A300 (36); A310 (16); B727-200 (13); B727-100 (5); and Shorts 3-60 (11).
[2]Maximum gross structural payload includes revenue payload and container.

rose 9 percent to $18.3 billion, and net income increased 9 percent to $688 million.[60] With continued strong growth in the company's international express business and modest growth in its domestic express and ground business, FedEx Corp. achieved record revenues.[61] Results for 2000 reflect strong international package volume growth, particularly in Asia and Europe, and improved revenue per package (yield), which lessened the effect of higher fuel prices. U.S. domestic package volume growth during 2000 was less than that experienced over the past 2 years. However, cost containment and productivity enhancement programs helped mitigate the impact of this decline in volume growth.[62] In addition, with the FedEx Express core global network in place, the company was able to reduce capital expenditures compared with 1999.[63]

In 2000 international operations accounted for 24 percent of the company's revenue, a $589 million year-over-year improvement. That follows the previous $222 million improvement in 1999. Express freight and express package now account for 91 percent of the $4.5 billion international revenue.

Regarding the domestic market, for fiscal 2000, FedEx Express' average revenue per package (yield) increased a little more than 1 percent for U.S overnight, where as the yield for U.S. deferred increased almost 4 percent for the same period. Average revenue per pound (yield) rose from $0.40 in 1999 to $0.47 in 2000, an increase of 18 percent. List price increases, fuel surcharges implemented in the second half of the year, an ongoing yield management program, and a slight increase in average weight per package all contributed to the increases in yields in fiscal 2000.[64]

For FedEx Ground, revenue per package rose about 4 percent. The increase in yield is due to a price increase, which was effective in February 1999, and a slight increase in the mix of higher-yielding packages.[65]

Human Resource Policies and Programs

FedEx management believes that the company's most important component is the human one: employees whose commitment and dedication to the company result in continuing prosperity.[66] The company is equally committed to its employees. In the past the company has been cited routinely for its no-layoff policy, minority recruitment efforts, and guaranteed fair treatment practice (GFTP). It has frequently been referred to as having a premier human resources program. It won the 1987 Strategic Human Resource Management Award for Excellence, had a manager selected as a Fellow of the National Academy of Human Resource (NAHR), won a Personnel Journal Optima Award, is treated as a benchmark by other companies (the truest measure of success, being recognized by its peers), and won the 1990 Malcolm Baldrige National Quality Award. In 1994 the Mid-South Minority Purchasing Council (MMPC) selected FedEx as the recipient of its prestigious Robert R. Church, Sr., Corporation of the Year Achievement Award for FedEx's continued support of minority business interests nationwide.[67]

Human resource practices at FedEx epitomize the popular views. The corporate philosophy is "People-Service-Profit." It has executive and upper management support. Its PRISM Human Resource Information System (HRIS) makes the best use of technology. The Survey-Feedback-Action (SFA) system and GFTP generate empowered employees. Also, the company makes good use of Total Quality Management (TQM) practices. Personnel and human resources staff ensure that FedEx maintains a highly motivated, productive, and satisfied workforce by providing leading-edge training, technology tracking capabilities, outstanding safety, renowned benefits, and dedicated personnel services.[68]

The emphasis on human resources begins at the top. The corporate philosophy of "People-Service-Profit" places people first by no accident. Smith reportedly spends 25 percent of his time on personnel issues—nearly five times that of the average CEO.[69] Smith implements his philosophy by having programs that answer three basic questions. First, "What is expected of me, and what do you want me to do?" This is answered by extensive orientation programs that pervade an employee's career. Second is "What's in it for me?" This is addressed by the promotion-from-within policy, the career progression policy, and incentives such as tuition reimbursement. Third is "Where do I go to resolve a problem?" This is answered in the open-door and guaranteed fair treatment practices. All encompassing is Smith's personal philosophy that training is one of the most important events at the company to meet the goal of 100-percent customer satisfaction.[70]

Likewise, independent organizations have recognized the support by senior management. Smith, while CEO of FedEx Express, was the 1997 recipient of the Strategic Leadership Forum's Peter F. Drucker Leadership Award. The Drucker Leadership Award is given to business leaders who have created strategic competitive advantages in their companies while serving humanitarian, medical, and personal needs around the world.[71] In addition, James A. Perkins, senior vice-president and chief personnel officer, was awarded the highest honor of the human resource profession. He was selected as a Fellow of the NAHR for the individual who has led the development of the human resource profession. Previous recognition occurred in 1987 with his receipt of the Strategic Human Resource Management Award for Excellence.[72] Other awards include Stephen Rutherford's receipt of the First Annual Human Resource Award of Excellence sponsored by the Olsten Staffing Services and the American Management Association in 1993. He is responsible for FedEx's Survey-Feedback-Action (SFA) program. FedEx also won the Second Annual Personnel Journal Optima Award in 1992. It was 1 of 10 companies recognized as having a human resource department that participates in corporate decision making, has human resource policies and strategies that are integrated so that a decision in one area considers the others, has human resource programs that are consistent with overall business goals, and is cost effective. In particular, FedEx was singled out from the other nine winners because of its commitment to training.[73]

All of these people, along with other senior managers, routinely participate in interactive discussions and question-and-answer programs.[74]

To help administer the human resource programs, FedEx uses its PRISM HRIS.[75] This is virtually a paperless system that affects all areas of the company. It maintains a job applicant database and processes new hires. When someone is hired, PRISM automatically creates an employee record and transfers it to the employee database after adding all applicable information. The employee database is updated by employees who are empowered and expected to maintain their own personal data. Typically, 25,000 such transactions occur daily. PRISM also supports job posting and bidding. Any interested employee can apply online for a position anywhere in the company's worldwide net. It provides the necessary data to hiring managers so that they can select those to interview. It then automatically updates the organizational chart when staff changes occur. Routinely, 1700 positions are posted and 7000 applications are processed each month. Job training and testing, one of the CEO's three most important events, is coordinated through PRISM. It controls all aspects of enrollment, training, and testing on 1200 personal computers and 25,000 online terminals. More than 4000 different courses are available with 5000 job-knowledge tests administered and scored monthly. The results are often available the next day.

The Managing-by-Objective (MBO) point system and reward program is tracked by PRISM. Here, employees can monitor their individual progress at any time. The system automatically forwards information to the payroll department so that bonus checks can be cut. PRISM has vastly improved FedEx's compliance with equal employment and affirmative action programs. It tracks employment data and provides a daily report comparing minority- or gender-based availability versus employment level by each group.

Another widely used tool is FedEx's Survey-Feedback-Action (SFA) program. This is the foundation for many of the human resource initiatives, as well as other initiatives (for example, safety). It is often used as a benchmark by other companies and has been cited as the key human resource system strength by the Baldrige Award examiners when FedEx won in 1990. The SFA complements the GFTP and other communication tools. It is an annual survey of employee attitude toward both specific departments and the company in general. Management never sees the individual responses, which are anonymous. The applicable area manager is required to meet and discuss employee concerns within 6 weeks after group results have been tallied—a process requiring about a month.[76] The manager must then develop and implement corrective action if his or her department was identified as having problems.[77] Another indicator of employee importance is the drive to minimize safety risks. Through feedback received by frontline employees via the SFA, safety improvement teams have replaced safety managers.[78]

The success of the SFA system is due, in no small part, to its automation via the FedEx PRISM system. In the United States the entire SFA questionnaire can be completed through the use of the company intranet that is accessible to employees through the Internet. The benefits of automation have made the SFA process more efficient, more user-friendly, and less time consuming. The success of the automation is due to the PRISM system's high level of accuracy and the simple fact that all FedEx employees have extensive training and experience with the PRISM system. FedEx's next step was to take the automation of the SFA system global. The first step in the globalization of the survey system was to implement it in the company's Canadian operations. The challenges of available technical infrastructure and sophistication in Canada, and simply the fact that computer systems are less widely used there than in the United States, made automation of the SFA system more difficult. Furthermore, the automation would not provide the type of savings achieved in the U.S. market because of the smaller size of the employee base in Canada. FedEx continued with the automation process in line with its commitment to its employee-first philosophy and implemented the automation of the SFA function with resounding success. Once Canadian employees believed in the system and were sure of its confidentiality, 99 percent of eligible employees participated in the automated SFA system. This has led to increased use of computer systems in the Canadian market. Expanded e-mail use has increased communication throughout the Canadian market and with FedEx U.S. Furthermore, the development of a bilingual survey system in Canada has created a model for the future expansion of automation of the SFA survey system in other global markets. The SFA automation is another example of FedEx's commitment to utilizing available technology to its benefit.[79,80]

Total Quality Management

The Baldrige Award confirms incorporation of many TQM principles in FedEx's human resource policies. Employee action teams permeate FedEx. They have improved safety results,[81] saved $3.5 million in a single year through reduced training time,[82] and eased implementation of the online system for SFA. Likewise, quality action teams are used to reach the goal of 100-percent customer satisfaction—4000 such teams are used at FedEx.[83] Everyone attends two programs: "Quality Advantage," which covers the basics of quality management, and "Quality Action Teams," where team development is learned. Through these programs, employees are empowered and learn that they can make a difference. Company policy allows every employee to do whatever is necessary to ensure customer satisfaction—a fairly broad statement. Employees are allowed to take appropriate risks and are not penalized for occasional errors.[84] Well-intentioned efforts are considered as important as successes. Furthermore, the SFA is an excellent example of continuous improvement.

Communications

Timely communication, another tool to empower employees, is used to keep everyone informed, to boost morale, and to make employees feel important. Three examples are FedEx Television (FXTV), the internal television network; the Open Door policy, an internal employee response program; and the GFTP, a practice similar to formal grievance procedures in union plants. FXTV reaches people in the United States, Canada, and overseas. The program "FedEx Overnight" is a daily broadcast of nightly progress. It allows daytime employees to get a recap of operations worldwide so that they can prevent errors and respond to customer problems either before or as they occur.[85] The network is also used as an interactive call-in program.[86] It allows key managers to respond immediately to questions and concerns. The Open Door policy is an extension of this program. It allows employees to find answers to situations they regard as disagreeable, controversial, or contrary to existing policy. No time limit is placed on the employee; however, management must respond to concerns within 14 days. To keep the program robust, the CEO receives a printout of every concern submitted and how and when it was answered.

The more formal GFTP is available automatically whenever an employee is disciplined and gives the employee the right to have any eligible issue go through a systematic review by progressively higher levels of management without fear of retribution.[87] Three basic steps are used. First, a management review is conducted. A written complaint is submitted within 7 days of the questionable occurrence. A response is required within 10 days of receipt of the complaint. If the employee is still dissatisfied, the complaint is forwarded within 7 days to the Officer Review, where a vice-president or senior vice-president can uphold, modify, or overturn any previous decision. If the employee is still dissatisfied, the complaint can go to the Executive Review, where an appeals board makes a final determination within 14 days. As with most of these processes, the time requirements can be relaxed if agreed on by both parties. FedEx's policy is to answer these complaints as soon as possible so that problems do not fester.[88]

Cross-functional communication has led to the benefits of improved customer service and cost savings. Such an example is exhibited in the unlikely pairing of marketing representatives and technology experts. This cross-functional team was designed in order to develop a database for customer complaints. The information technology experts created the framework for the database and then educated the marketing representatives on its use. The team created a database that more accurately defined the needs and expectations of customers, which ultimately allowed FedEx to become more in tune with them. Furthermore, the database was so effective that it provided the same number of responses from 30 percent of its customer base as the company's old system produced from surveys sent to 100 percent of its customers. FedEx was also able to cut postage costs by 70 percent.[89]

Training

Training is obviously important to any company that implements 1500 changes in any year.[90] FedEx has 650 full-time trainers in quality alone. The tie between human resource and corporate goals is best expressed by Larry W. McMahan, vice-president of human resources:

> Because we expect our employees to keep up with a lot of changes, we have to equip them with enough tools to give them a good running chance at satisfying customers. Therefore we can't support a customer-oriented objective without having a strong emphasis on training.[91]

For FedEx, training is a continuous process. Every 6 months, employees are required to pass a job knowledge test. In 1986 an interactive video training system was incorporated, allowing employees to work at their own pace, repeat necessary sections, and take advantage of slack periods to train themselves. Anyone failing a test is removed from customer-related duties until able to pass the test. Job training, however, is not the only program available. For instance, FedEx offers the Leadership Evaluation and Awareness Program (LEAP) that qualifies nonmanagement employees for management positions; the Management Applied Personnel Skills (MAPS) program, a 3-day in-depth program of background information and practical application of personnel and legal issues normally encountered in the workplace; and the Leadership Institute, a full week of required management training for all new managers covering quality management, leadership concepts, and company philosophy.

Retention

Good employee relations, following good recruiting, translate into good retention.[92] FedEx has the benefit of a turnover rate of about 4 percent.[92] It accomplishes this with 25 centers nationwide using a peer recruiter program. In this way recruits receive a more realistic idea of what is expected of them and what their potential positions entail. Retention is also aided by FedEx's excellent use and support of its part-time employees, who represent about 36 percent of the workforce. And although not required, they receive full medical coverage, a guaranteed workweek, and wage parity. Furthermore, they are given credit towards seniority for local full-time positions—a change adopted because of the SFA process. Previously, more senior full-time employees from outside the local area were cutting off local part-time employees' opportunities to advance.

Training is also a key asset in the drive to retain employees, and Fed Ex has spared no expense in the areas of money, people, and time. According to an article in *Business Week* earlier this year, turnover at FedEx is low, in part because the company invests 3 percent of total expenses in training. That is six times the level at most companies. The training is not just for managers, as is the case in many organizations. Virtually thousands of FedEx employees have completed a week-long leadership institute that educates employees on company culture and operations. The company's commitment to continuous learning allowed service representatives to ask for, and receive, the systems training they needed to be able to solve customer problems themselves.[94] These programs gradually develop FedEx employees that are both technically and informationally empowered. Ultimately, this investment by the company leads to enhanced employee satisfaction, improved job performance, superior customer service, and increased revenues.

Incentives and recognition, in addition to career advancement, provide another means of retaining employees. Nearly 85 percent of the employees at FedEx participate in some type of incentive program. Key executives can earn up to 40 percent of their salary in performance-based bonuses.[95] Awards programs reinforce desired behavior such as quality work and customer focus. Acknowledging effort is essential for a motivated and satisfied workforce. It stimulates new ideas and encourages better performance and team spirit.[96]

FedEx has a wide range of incentive and recognition programs. The Bravo Zulu (BZ) Voucher Program recognizes individual performance that surpasses normal job responsibilities. It is based on the U.S. Navy code flags "B-Z," which decode into "well done." Awards range from nonfinancial BZ letters of recognition to cash or noncash awards presented by management. The Suggestion Awards Program encourages employees to submit ideas to improve company performance. These are usually in the areas of lowering costs, increasing productivity, increasing revenues, or promoting safer working conditions. Awards range from $100 to $25,000 for ideas that are implemented. The Golden Falcon Award is for any full-time employee who has demonstrated service to the customer that goes above and beyond the call of duty. It is based on unsolicited internal, as well as external, letters citing outstanding performance. Winners are announced monthly through company publications and video programs, with winners receiving an award and shares of stock. The ultimate Five-Star Award is for individuals who materially helped the company enhance service, profitability, and teamwork. These awards demonstrate empowerment, senior management support, and company philosophies. Similarly, performance evaluations routinely include peer evaluations. Evaluations use internal and external customers and suppliers and cover such areas as quality of work and customer service dimensions.[97]

Benefits

FedEx companies provide a variety of excellent benefit plans and programs to employees:[98]

- Healthcare (Medical, Dental, and Vision)
- Life, Disability, and Accidental Death Insurance
- Retirement and Savings (401K and Pension)
- Quality of Life Programs
- Vacation and Paid Time Off
- Incentive Pay Programs
- Career Advancement
- Tuition Refund
- Training and Development
- Employee Activities
- Employee Discounts

Some benefit plans, programs, and privileges offered by individual FedEx companies vary.

Questions

1. At a time when technology is becoming the key distinction among transportation firms, FedEx recently announced plans to shrink its 4000-employee IT division by about 200 workers. The move has been considered jarring by some because FedEx traditionally has used layoffs only as a measure of last resort.[99] How could this action affect the company's organizational culture and employee relations, especially in lieu of its corporate philosophy? What steps should FedEx take in order to prevent or minimize possible negative effects?

2. In the past FedEx's human relations programs have kept the desire and need for union representation low. Research indicates that employees join unions because they are dissatisfied with their employer and believe the union can improve the situation. How should FedEx continue to improve its labor relations so employees are satisfied with management's treatment? Develop a strategy for FedEx in order to prevent further unionization.

3. The use of part-time labor continues to be a major strategy of the FedEx senior management team. Discuss the key challenges of employing such a large group of part-time workers and how FedEx should overcome them.

Notes

[1]*Standard & Poor's Industry Surveys*, December 6, 1984, p. A36.
[2]Geoffrey Colvin, "Federal Express Dives into Air Mail," *Fortune*, June 15, 1981, pp. 106–108.
[3]Henry Altman, "A Business Visionary Who Really Delivered," *Nation's Business*, November 1981, p. 50.
[4]Colvin, "Federal Express Dives," p. 107.
[5]Altman, "Business," p. 54.
[6]*Creativity with Bill Moyers: Fred Smith and the Federal Express*, PBS Video, 1981 .
[7]"The Memphis Connection," *Marketing and Media Decisions*, May 1982, p. 62.
[8]Federal Express, *1994 Annual Report*, pp. 20–21.
[9]**www.fedex.com/us** (accessed December 31, 2000)
[10]**interactive.wsj.com**, (accessed March 2, 1998).
[11]FedEx Corporation, *2000 Form 10-K.*
[12]Federal Express, *1982 Annual Report*, p. 14.
[13]Colvin, "Federal Express Dives," p. 107.
[14]Ibid., p. 108.
[15]G. Tomas M. Hult, Ph.D., Director and Assistant Professor, International Business, College of Business, Florida State University, March 1, 1998.
[16]FedEx Corporation, *2000 Form 10-K.*
[17]FedEx Corporation, *2000 Annual Report.*
[18]Ibid., p. 2.
[19]Ibid., pp. 3–5.
[20]Ibid., p. 2.
[21]FedEx Corporation, *2000 Annual Report.*
[22]**www.fedex.com/us**, (accessed December 31, 2000).
[23]**www.fedex.com**, (accessed December 31, 2000).
[24]**www.fedex.com/us/services**, accessed March 1, 1998, (accessed December 31, 2000).
[25]**www.fedex.com**, (accessed December 31, 2000).
[26]FedEx Corporation, *2000 Form 10-K.*
[27]**www.fedex.com/us/about**, (accessed February 26, 1998).

[28]Colvin, "Federal Express Dives," pp. 6–7.

[29]Ibid., p. 9.

[30]FedEx Corporation, *2000 Form 10-K.*

[31]Ibid.

[32]Ibid.

[33]Ibid.

[34]Ibid.

[35]**www.fedex.com/us/about**, (accessed March 1, 1998).

[36]**www.fedex.com/us/services**, (accessed February 26, 1998).

[37]**www.fedex.com/us/about**, (accessed March 1, 1998).

[38]FedEx Corporation, *2000 Form 10-K.*

[39]Ibid.

[40]Ibid.

[41]Ibid.

[42]Ibid.

[43]Ibid.

[44]Ibid.

[45]Sean Milmo, "British Air Couriers Welcome U.S. Entrant," *Business Marketing*, April 1984, p. 9.

[46]Eirmalasare Bani, "Only 1% of Cargo Transported by Air: FedEx," *Business Times*, September 19, 2000, p. 4.

[47]**www.fedex.com**, *FedEx Corp. Press Releases*, (accessed December 31, 2000).

[48]**www.fedex.com**, (accessed December 31, 2000).

[49]**www.fedex.com/us**, (accessed December 31, 2000).

[50]*Moody's Transportation Manual*, 1990, p. 1173.

[51]FedEx Corporation, *2000 Annual Report*, p. 22.

[52]FedEx Corporation, *2000 Form 10-K.*

[53]"Behind the UPS Mystique: Puritanism and Productivity," *Business Week*, June 6, 1983, p. 66.

[54]**www.ups.com**, (accessed December 31, 2000).

[55]U.S. Postal Service, *Express Mail Next Day Service*, Pamphlet Notice #43, July 1977, p. 2.

[56]**www.usps.com**, (accessed December 31, 2000).

[57]U.S. Postal Service, *Express Mail Next Day Service*, Pamphlet Notice #43, July 1977, p. 6.

[58]**www.usps.com**, (accessed December 31, 2000).

[59]FedEx Corporation, *2000 Form 10-K.*

[60]FedEx Corporation, *2000 Annual Report*, p. 2.

[61]Ibid., p. 6.

[62]Ibid., p. 7.

[63]Ibid., p. 6.

[64]Ibid., p. 9.

[65]Ibid., p. 11.

[66]Federal Express, *1994 Annual Report*, p. 24.

[67]"FedEx Receives Award," *FedEx World Update*, March/April 1995, p. 36.

[68]**www.fedex.com/us/careers**, (accessed December 31, 2000).

[69]D. Keith Denton, "Keeping Employees: The Federal Express Approach," *Advanced Management Journal*, Summer 1992, pp. 10–13.

[70]"1992 Optimas Awards," *Personnel Journal*, January 1992, pp. 51–61.

[71]John Geci, "Presenting the 1997 Peter F. Drucker Strategic Leadership Award," *Strategic Leadership Forum*, September 19, 1997, p. 30.

[72]"National Academy of Human Resources Installs 1992 Class," *HRMagazine*, January 1993, pp. 52–53.

[73]"1992 Optimas Awards."

[74]Stephen Stapleton, "Reducing Customer Irritation," *Across the Board*, November/December 1993, p. 48.

[75]Prashant Palvia, Sherry Sullivan, and Steven Zeltman, "PRISM Profile: An Employee-Oriented System," *HR Focus*, June 1993, p. 19.

[76]Bob Smith, "Award Honors Excellence in Human Resources," *HR Focus*, July 1993, p. 9.

[77]Denton, "Keeping Employees: The Federal Express Approach."

[78]Rosa Lindahl and Stacey Leary, "A Joint Effort Strengthens Safety Policies," *HR Focus*, October 1992, p. 13.

[79]Rosa V. Lindahl, "Automation Breaks the Language Barrier," *HR Magazine*, March 1996, p. 79.

[80]James Martin, "HR in the Cybercorp," *HR Focus*, April 1997, p. 3.

[81]Lindahl and Leary, "A Joint Effort Strengthens Safety Policies."

[82]"1992 Optimas Awards."

[83]Richard Blackburn and Benson Rosen, "Total Quality and Human Resources Management: Lessons Learned from Baldrige Award-Winning Companies," *Executive*, August 1993, pp. 49–66.

[84]Stapleton, "Reducing Customer Irritation."

[85]Ibid.

[86]Blackburn and Rosen, "Total Quality and Human Resources Management: Lessons Learned from Baldrige Award-Winning Companies."

[87]Denton, "Keeping Employees: The Federal Express Approach."

[88]Ibid.

[89]Robert Heibler, Thomas B. Kelley, and Charles Ketteman, *Best Practices* (New York: Simon and Schuster, 1998), p. 180–181.

[90]"1992 Optimas Awards."

[91]Ibid.

[92]Denton, "Keeping Employees: The Federal Express Approach."

[93]"FedEx's Commitment to Training," *Managing Training and Development*, September 2000, p. 8.

[94]Ibid.

[95]Blackburn and Rosen, "Total Quality and Human Resources Management: Lessons Learned from Baldrige Award-Winning Companies."

[96]Denton, "Keeping Employees: The Federal Express Approach."

[97]Blackburn and Rosen, "Total Quality and Human Resources Management: Lessons Learned from Baldrige Award-Winning Companies."

[98]**www.fedex.com**, (accessed December 31, 2000).

[99]Dave Hirschman, "FedEx to Trim Technology Division by 200 Workers," *Atlanta Journal and Constitution*, August 23, 2000.

Additional References Not Cited

interactive.wsj.com/inap-bin/bb?sym5FDX&page 54, accessed February 23, 1998.

www.fedex.com//, accessed March 1, 1998.

FedEx World Update, March/April 1995, p. 34.

2

Delta Air Lines, Inc.*

Delta has always understood the value of human resources within the organization. Whereas other airlines were established by war aces or financiers, Delta was founded by C. E. Woolman, an agricultural extension agent.[1] As a result, Delta has not been biased toward a military style of command leadership common to other airlines. Likewise, because Woolman was not a financier, Delta has not historically relied on financial strategies to create competitive advantage.[2] Delta has always differentiated itself from other airlines by its customer service. This was true when it was a regional airline, and it continued after it became one of the six largest domestic carriers through its 1986 merger with Western Airlines.

History[3,4]

Organizational History

Delta achieved customer service through the support of its personnel. As a regional carrier, Delta was noted for its Southern hospitality and charm. It introduced stewardesses to the industry in the 1940s. Delta retained a loyal workforce by paying competitive wages, treating personnel equitably as it grew, and adopting a "no-layoff policy." Unlike most airlines, Delta approached its early mergers with an eye toward accommodating its workers and pilots. This was true when it merged with Chicago Southern Airlines in 1953, when it acquired Northeastern Airlines in 1972, and when it merged with Western Airlines in 1986.[5] Delta faced personnel issues during each of these mergers and worked with the employees to allow the merging entities to retain both position and dignity in the organization. Whereas other merging airlines fell victim to sabotage, vandalism, slowdowns, and poor customer relations, each of Delta's mergers were followed by increased productivity and generally better customer relations.[6]

The key to Delta's success was its focus on human relations. For example, when it merged with Western, Delta promised job security and higher wages for existing Western employees. To generate excitement and support among the new employees,

---

*This case was prepared by Mark Dawkins and revised by Patricia Duffy, Daniel Griffin, Kris Inchcombe, and Patty Pinholster. This case was updated by Jon Alden, Cynthia Campbell, Eric Hamilton, Ed Nelson, Laura Wilson, and Cathie Mathe.

Delta adopted the slogan "The best get better." Delta promised to honor previously negotiated labor provisions, and rather than ignoring or provoking a conflict with an existing union, Delta recognized the Air Line Pilots Association (ALPA) as the union representing its pilots. Delta's management worked closely with the union to merge pilot seniority lists. Delta convinced nonunion personnel at Western to decertify three existing unions, using its reputation for fair dealing with its employees.

Delta's employees were historically some of the highest paid among the major carriers. In the past, Delta employees have earned approximately 21 percent more than the industry average,[7] which led to high productivity and good service.[8] The good service rendered by employees resulted in Delta having the fewest number of consumer complaints of any major carrier for over 20 years.[9]

Delta's commitment to its employees is evidenced in how it reacted to the recession of the early '80s. While other airlines were cutting wages or filing for bankruptcy to restructure their labor contracts, Delta kept its wages high for existing personnel and achieved cost reductions by requiring new hires to accept lower wages. This tactic, although protested by other airline groups, was accepted by Delta employees as the cost of staying competitive. Likewise, Delta had refused to layoff any employees during the oil embargo of 1976. From its inception through the 1980s, Delta was a paradigm of human relations within the airline industry. This was Delta's heritage and hoped-for legacy.

However, in the early 1990s, Delta fell victim to rising fuel prices, greater competition domestically and abroad, and a global recession. The first operating loss for the company in almost 40 years occurred in 1993 and was followed by another loss in 1994. This led its then CEO, Ronald Allen, to eschew his human relations philosophy and training (having been promoted from Delta's human relations division), to embark on a severe cost-cutting program. Leadership 7.5, as the strategic initiative was called, sought to reduce the airline's average cost per available seat per mile flown (CASM) to 7.5 cents. Delta's costs had reached a high of 9.59 cents per available seat mile (ASM) in March 1994. Leadership 7.5 compelled the reduction of Delta's workforce by 11,000 employees, the change of many employees from full time to part time (associate employees), and the outsourcing of a great deal of work formerly done by Delta employees. The efforts succeeded in reducing costs to 8.5 cents per ASM and returning the airline to profitability in 1995 but at a considerable price. (In fiscal 2000, the operating cost per available seat mile was 9.25 cents.)[10]

As noted, Leadership 7.5 was accepted by the management of Delta as a desperate effort for survival. Many airlines were failing, and without a dramatic change Delta would likely have joined them. But the covenant that it had previously had with its employees was broken. Delta's pilots and flight crews accepted pay cuts, and Delta's nonunion personnel received layoffs. Leadership 7.5 decimated employee morale at Delta, and this soon resulted in a drop in customer service (evidenced by a meteoric rise in customer complaints), efforts to unionize, and disaffection among personnel. The year 1995 may have shown positive net income, but Delta's human capital was breached and the damage could have been fatal.

By 1996 revenues had increased, and Delta was able to reverse the layoff trends and recall 472 furloughed pilots.[11,12] In January 1996, Delta added 665 customer-service jobs, which were filled largely by employees that had been relegated to part-time status.[13] Pay increases of 5 percent to nonunionized workers restored pay cuts taken in 1993.[14] Nonunion workers received pay increases of 2 percent to 5 percent again in 1997.[15]

Delta's vision is to become the *world's* best airline.[16] In order to accomplish this lofty goal, the company has developed five key strategic objectives that are at the center of its efforts: to become "number one" in customer service, to develop a truly global airline network, to build a superior team of employees, to continue its strong financial performance, and to find innovative ways to maximize the value of the company's core resources.[17]

Operational History

Delta Air Lines is one of the most successful air carriers in the United States. Delta Air Service began its climb to prominence when it received a U.S. government airmail contract in 1930. The company, then renamed Delta Air Corporation, received three more airmail contracts in 1941. During World War II, Delta devoted itself to the allied war effort by transporting troops and supplies. Delta returned to civilian service in 1945, entering an age of growth and competition never seen before in the airline industry.

Delta prospered as a major regional trunk carrier through the 1950s and 1960s. Delta continued its expansion into international operations by forming alliances with other carriers. It was slower than its competitors to form alliances that would provide hub access in key European and Asian cities.[18] However, at the end of the last decade, Delta participated in alliances with Austrian Airlines, Sabena, and Swissair (the Atlantic Excellence Alliance). In fiscal year 2000, another alliance was created—SkyTeam—partnering Delta with Aeromexico, Air France, and Korean Air. These alliances include codesharing, reciprocal frequent flyer programs, and coordinated cargo operations.[19] Further, Delta introduced the concept of codesharing, and it has formed codesharing partnerships with several airlines, including Aer Lingus, Aeromexico, Air Jamaica, Finnair, Korean Air, Malev, TAP Air Portugal, and Transbrasil. Finally, Delta has alliance agreements with All Nippon Airways and China Southern Antitrust Immunity partnerships receive permission to jointly set prices and schedules, and codesharing alliance partners book seats and issue tickets for each other's flights.

Delta's consistent growth is partially attributed to its successful transition of leadership. At Eastern, Pan Am, and TWA, the founding pioneers established almost dictatorial operations. Many were majority stockholders who refused to share their power or prepare a successor to operate the company after they resigned or died. As a result, those airline companies faced a difficult period of adjustment to new management after their chairmen left.

Woolman's departure at Delta was not surrounded by such difficulties. After suffering a heart attack, he had delegated some of his duties to other Delta board members. The board members gradually assumed more duties as Woolman's health deteriorated. When Woolman died at the age of 76, the airline was able to make a smooth transition to a more modern, corporate style of collective management.

Management

Delta Air Lines' board of directors signaled a change in management strategy when Allen announced that his ten-year contract would not be extended beyond July 31, 1997.[20] Allen's forced departure was attributed to an autocratic leadership style he adopted during Leadership 7.5 and the resulting decline of employee morale and customer service. Allen had completed cost-cutting restructuring that included the elimination of 11,000 employees. Although the restructuring resulted in a healthier balance sheet and a competitive position against domestic low-cost carriers, Allen's heavy-handed approach disenfranchised Delta employees. "By late 1996, 61 percent of Delta's employees felt they could not trust management and 57 percent said service had declined."[21]

The selection of Leo F. Mullin as CEO and president on August 15, 1997, indicated the extent of Delta's interest in a new leadership style. Mullin, a Harvard MBA and former banker, has been described as having an open management style and as being particularly adept at handling people. Within 24 hours of being selected CEO and president, the slim and bespectacled 54-year-old was roaming Hartsfield International Airport in Atlanta interviewing baggage handlers, ticket agents, pilots, and flight attendants before catching his flight home to Chicago. Mullin opined, "It's a cliché, but inclusion breeds commitment."[22] During his tenure, Mullin has traveled three weeks every month for employee and investor meetings. He has also decentralized management by delegating more day-to-day authority to managers. Mullin initiated several significant changes in Delta's organization and corporate culture.

Mullin's selection also represented a departure from several Delta traditions—the promotion of top executives from within the company and the top executive position holding the chairman of the board, CEO, and president positions. Delta had previously selected executive managers from within the company. Not only was Mullin an outsider, he had never been employed in the airline industry. In addition, Gerald Grinstein, the powerful board member credited with orchestrating Allen's departure, assumed the chairman of the board position. This was the first time Delta employed separate individuals for the chairman and CEO positions. Now, however, Mullin holds all three positions—CEO and president, as well as chairman.[23]

A trend of selecting senior airline executives from outside the industry has been developing over the past decade. As commercial air transport becomes more complex, competitive, and fast-paced, senior executives who understand and react to rapidly changing structural and market forces become essential for the survival of a company. However, the development of internal talent to fill senior executive positions has been inadequate in the majority of airline companies in the past. After deregulation in 1978, airline companies experienced dramatic restructuring, primarily to reduce costs. One of the cost reduction steps was the elimination of middle- and low-management positions where future talented individuals were previously identified and placed on a senior executive track. The restructuring also reduced the mobility across business units and, therefore, further inhibited the development of general managerial skills. Now Delta has a corporate succession planning system and mentoring process that provides the foundation for developing and retaining a leadership team. Through mentoring and coaching, the knowledge, skills, and experience of current leaders are transferred to emerging ones, allowing Delta to build a diverse pool of potential leaders.[24]

Shortly after his selection, Mullin outlined plans to overhaul Delta. Some of the more visible issues included upgrading interiors of all of its planes, remodeling outdated and rundown concourses and frequent flyer waiting rooms, modernizing reservation lines to decrease unanswered calls and hold times, and improving customer service.[25] Mullin also conceded Delta's information management system required immediate attention. In the past, the yield management programs of American Airlines and United Airlines provided a significant competitive advantage over Delta. This was a primary reason why a technology subsidiary called Delta Technology Inc. was created.[26] The mission of this subsidiary was to revamp Delta's existing information systems (IS) organization. Mullin hired a new chief information officer, who began by simplifying job descriptions and creating a team of 40 IS directors to serve on a leadership counsel. During the last three years, Delta has invested heavily in developing a cross-functional technology platform that communicates with every part of the organization. The center of the program is called Airport Renewal. During fiscal 2000, Delta implemented Airport Renewal in its top 54 airports. Airport Renewal provides the infrastructure for planned technology deployments and allows all operating units to be connected real time to key operational information.[27]

The first major management change under Mullin occurred when Thomas J. Roeck, Jr., Delta's chief financial officer, stepped down in November 1997. Roeck and Mullin mutually decided that their strategic visions differed. Roeck was credited with a central role during Allen's restructuring of Delta. In particular, Roeck was instrumental in reclaiming investment grade stature for Delta bonds on Wall Street. His replacement has been charged with further enhancing Delta's shareholders' value and the company's image to investors and analysts.[28] More resignations came in May of 1998, when Robert Coggin (a 42-year veteran with Delta) resigned as executive vice-president of marketing, and Robert Adams (a former Pan Am employee with 33 years' experience) retired as senior vice-president of personnel.[29] Delta sought replacements from outside the company.[30] In 1999, Delta was named "Best Managed Major Airline" by *Aviation Week & Space Technology* magazine.[31]

Human Resources

In 1997 Delta felt secure enough in the economy and its own financial recovery to begin efforts at healing the rift that had been created between it and its personnel. This was no small task. Delta employs approximately 81,000 people worldwide, including ASA and Comair. About 16 percent, or 12,960 employees, are represented by unions.[32] In the past, Delta has forced concessions from its pilots; it has been charged with hiring practice discrimination by its flight attendants;[33] and it has laid off almost 15 percent of its nonunion workforce. As a result, Delta believed it was necessary to change its management and its relations with its personnel. In July of 1997, after 34 years with the company, Allen resigned and was replaced by Mullin. Although an outsider and not a student of human relations, Mullin understood the task ahead and began a series of initiatives to rebuild employee trust, confidence, and loyalty.

The first task was to reestablish those advantages enjoyed by Delta workers that had inspired their loyalty and dedication in the years before Leadership 7.5. One of Delta's first steps was to give nonunion personnel a pay raise. Another was to offer virtually every employee who had been laid off a position back at Delta. Although this came too late for many who had found work elsewhere and was not an option for those who were unwilling or unable to relocate, it was a significant gesture by the company to the employees (and one taken advantage of by many). In addition to salary increases, Delta initiated a profit sharing program, under which virtually every employee benefits from the success of the company. Independent of the profit-sharing program, Delta has established a Family Care Savings Plan, a tax-qualified retirement plan in which Delta matches up to 15 percent of salary contributed to the plan on a 2:1 ratio. All of these measures have been helpful in rebuilding employee relations.

Delta recognizes and rewards high performance. In fact, it initiated an awards program called "Above and Beyond" (Appendix A). Every month this program awards employees nominated by their peers for extraordinary work performance. There are quarterly awards of more significant tangible value and an annual ceremony in which the top hundred employees are elected to the "Chairman's Club," where they are honored at a dinner and receive an award and shares of stock in the company. This concerted effort at recognition has served to reinvolve many employees in the goals of the company.

Taking advantage of its improved information technology (IT), Delta disseminates an electronic newsletter. The e-newsletter, "Newsline," is an intranet page that complements Delta's open door policy to allow employees access to information and a forum for asking questions and voicing grievances or concerns.

Delta has also established continuous improvement teams (CITs) throughout the organization (Appendix B). This effort allows panels of elected representatives to meet with division heads and supervisors to voice concerns and complaints, request changes, and provide feedback on current policies and initiatives. The CITs also have nonvoting representatives on Delta's Board Council. The council coordinates between divisions, CITs, and the actual board of directors. There are seven representatives on the Board Council, representing everyone from the flight crews to baggage handlers to senior management.

To find out even more about what its employees think, Delta completed a broad-reaching survey called Delta Survey 2000. It measured employee opinions in areas such as leadership trust, customer service, safety, job satisfaction, and rewards and recognition and was conducted by an independent surveying firm. In addition, Delta executives have held nearly 100 face-to-face meetings with frontline employees across the company. Employee opinions and concerns are a vital part of building a highly motivated team at Delta. As a result of listening to its workforce, new enhancements, such as a two-year leave of absence program and a part-time employment category with a full benefits package, have been added.[34] Delta also offers paid time-off benefits like vacations and holidays, flextime, and educational and adoption assistance.[35]

Delta is creating a learning environment to drive performance and to develop and retain talented employees. Training is offered worldwide via classroom, computer, and web-based programs. Further, Delta is establishing alliances with a global network of academic partners to form Delta University, which gives employees access to college credit and degree programs at those institutions. Delta is also partnering with the American Council on Education to approve in-house company training courses for college credit.[36] In addition, Delta offers tuition reimbursement for job-related courses, and it conducts in-house training in leadership and management skills, as well as for flight attendant positions. Delta trains reservation personnel and has created satellite reservation offices at several college campuses. These satellite offices allow college students to learn skills, earn a wage, and become familiar with the Delta culture in a convenient location offering flexible hours. The experience and training are an advantage if they continue with the company after graduation.

Delta has also created a personnel assistance office (Appendix C). This office administers substance recovery, critical incidents response, and workplace violence programs. Although it originally was formed to comply with the Drug Free Workplace regulation, the personnel assistance office is a human resource management function that can produce significant cost benefits to the company.

All of these initiatives have helped Delta improve the morale of its employees. As a result, there has been a dramatic drop in customer complaints, and Delta is continuing to regain the customer satisfaction, loyalty, and image that it lost from Leadership 7.5.

Human resource issues also affect Delta's aircraft and fleet size. For instance, in February 1999, Delta and ALPA began negotiations on pay rates and working conditions for 777 aircraft. In June 1999, the company announced that it would indefinitely defer the delivery of the eleven 777 aircraft on order and, on November 1, 1999, would remove from service the two 777 aircraft it operated because Delta and ALPA still had not reached an agreement.[37] Finally, an agreement was reached in 2000 on industry-leading pilot pay rates and work rules for new Boeing 767 and 777 aircraft. In the comprehensive negotiations now underway, Delta's leadership team has already indicated its willingness to provide top-level compensation. Delta's goal is to reach a timely, mutually rewarding outcome.[38]

Recent Disputes

In the spring of 2001 Delta narrowly avoided a strike of its pilots when it settled on a 4-year contract that made the Delta pilots the highest paid in the industry. A Boeing 777 captain with 12 years of seniority will get a base pay of $287,600 starting in May 2004, up from $232,000 in April 2001. Overall, raises ranged from 24 percent to 34 percent over the life of the contract, depending on the aircraft type. This pay rate is 1 percent above United's, which, until spring 2001, had the industry's highest paid pilots. Mr. Leo Mullin, Delta's CEO, said the company would have to find more ways to become even more efficient to pay for the higher salaries of pilots.

Delta's pilots were credited with a well-financed and impeccably organized campaign to secure higher wages, which included a refusal to work overtime during the later part of bargaining negotiations. This caused many flight delays and cancellations and upset many Delta passengers. Many Delta pilots are highly educated with law and MBA degrees. Many are ex-military officers with extensive leadership and control skills. Charles S. Giambusso, leader of the pilot's union, says "More than half the pilots at Delta could be the CEO or chairman of the board at Delta." The skill, knowledge, and organizing abilities of the pilots enabled them to obtain their desired goals in the collective bargaining agreement.

At the time of this writing, (spring, 2001) Comair, a Delta subsidiary serving mostly commuter routes, was in the midst of a 2 months-long strike resulting from an inability to reach an agreement with its pilots. As of April 30, Comair had laid off half of its non-pilot workforce as a result of the strike. Comair pilots have less seniority and much lower pay than Delta's and often fly prop planes and smaller jets instead of the large jets flown by Delta. The pilots struck for higher pay, pay for time spent waiting before and after flights, and a better pension system. Their negotiation tactics and bargaining power were not sufficient to avoid a strike as were those of the Delta pilots.[39]

Operations

Delta was the first airline to employ the "hub-and-spoke" system. Under this system, a number of flights are scheduled to land at a hub airport within a 30-minute time span. Passengers can then make connections for final destinations conveniently and quickly, thus avoiding long layovers. Delta has efficient and strategically located hubs in Atlanta, Dallas/Fort Worth, Salt Lake City, and Cincinnati. Smaller markets have been transferred to Delta Connection carriers, and certain less profitable transatlantic and transpacific flights were discontinued. Significant capacity has been shifted from its Dallas/Fort Worth hub to Cincinnati. The Dallas/Fort Worth operations have been refocused on east-west connecting traffic.[40] Recently, Delta has been building on its strong position at the Atlanta Worldport and strengthening its East Coast presence, including plans for a new consolidated airport terminal at Boston-Logan International Airport.[41] Delta has also increased its international position at New York-Kennedy airport. Delta currently offers nonstop service from the United States to the largest number of European destinations of any U.S. airline. Delta offers the most daily departures and carries the most passengers between the United States and Europe of any United States carrier.[42]

In fiscal year 2000, Delta's operating income was nearly $1.9 billion—virtually unchanged from the previous year. For the same period, net income decreased 6 percent to $1 billion, excluding nonrecurring items (the third consecutive year Delta has reached or exceeded the billion-dollar threshold). Delta achieved unit costs for fiscal 2000 of 9.25 cents per available seat mile. This represented a continued 6 percent unit cost advantage over the industry. Delta's low-cost leadership position, combined with strong revenue performance, generated an operating margin for 2000 of 11.8 percent.[43,44] Delta is proud of its financial performance and for exceeding industry averages.

Delta has shifted lower-yielding point-to-point markets from its hubs in order to gain higher-yielding business markets. This move attracts business travelers by increasing the frequency of flights to business destinations, adding nonstop service to West Coast destinations, and introducing hourly flights to Chicago and Reagan International Airport from Atlanta.[45] To retain its position against low-cost carriers serving the Southeast between Northeast and Midwest cities, Delta initiated Delta Express. This highly productive low-cost operation preserved Delta's market position in Florida, one of the largest revenue-producing segments of the system. Point-to-point low-fare flying is one of the fastest growing segments in the airline industry, and since the launch of Delta Express on October 1, 1996, it has established a leadership position in this market.[46]

Delta Express is in a dedicated terminal wing of the Orlando International Airport, enabling Delta Express to manage 168 daily flights. Delta Express provides point-to-point service between 17 Northeast and Midwest cities to five popular Florida cities—Orlando, Tampa, Fort Myers, West Palm Beach, and Fort Lauderdale. Delta Express consists of 37 Boeing 737-200s with all-economy cabins. (The 12 first-class seats were replaced with 24 economy seats for a total of 119 economy seats.) During fiscal 2000, plans were to increase to forty-one 737-200 aircraft.[47]

To deter new entrants, Delta Express offers services typically not associated with other low-cost carriers, such as advanced seat selection and mileage credit for each flight. In addition, Delta Express promotes its "safety, reliability, and dependability" in an attempt to obtain market share from the smaller commuter and discount lines.[48]

Delta's jetliner fleet is among the most modern fleets in domestic service. As of June 30, 1999, Delta owned 358 and leased 226 aircraft, with an average age of 12.3 years. To maintain a young and technologically advanced fleet, Delta has entered into long-term aircraft purchase agreements with the Boeing Company for 159 firm aircraft orders, with an additional 135 options and 418 rolling options through calendar year 2017. (Delta employs a 20-year acquisition plan on fleet development.) The majority of the new aircraft will be used to replace older existing aircraft, primarily the L-1011 and B-727 models (with an average current age of 21.3 years). Delta's long-term plan is to simplify its fleet by reducing aircraft family types from seven to three, while replacing older aircraft types with newer Boeing 767s and 737s over several years. The increased efficiencies of the more standardized fleet are expected to improve reliability and result in long-term cost savings in maintenance, parts, scheduling, and training.[49]

Once considered a competitive disadvantage, Delta's IT has been transformed from trailing edge to leading edge. Delta launched a companywide initiative that centralized information and reengineered technology and decision making around four application areas: customer, operations, revenue, and business support. Delta's goal is to continue to simplify the technological infrastructure, improve efficiency, and deliver state-of-the-art solutions for business needs. One of its new technology platforms is the

Customer Relationship Management (CRM) program, which began development in fiscal 2000. The platform will store information about customer preferences, such as preferred seating, special meals, personal contact information, and special handling requirements, as well as detailed information about travel patterns and experiences. Building on information obtained from the SkyMiles program, the CRM database serves as the centralized information source for all customer interactions. Eventually, all customer areas—from Marketing to Customer Service to Operations—will have access to this data, allowing Delta to tailor products, marketing programs, and services to individual needs and preferences. Ultimately, CRM will reduce transaction times and enhance customer service.[50]

Delta owns 40 percent of a computer reservation system (CRS) partnership called WORLDSPAN. This partnership is with Northwest Airlines and TWA, and offers CRS services to travel agents around the world. Based on the number of travel agents in the United States using a CRS, WORLDSPAN ranks third, behind SABRE and Galileo International, Inc., in market share among travel agents in the United States.[51] Further, Delta has consolidated its reservations offices in an effort to improve customer service. The result of the consolidation has utilized improved telecommunications technology in larger full-service offices while cutting operating costs significantly. In addition, Delta's ongoing initiatives include matching staffing levels to customer volumes. Reportedly, Delta has paid more than $300 million per year in CRS fees. Consequently, it has pioneered self-ticketing, which allows customers to book their own flights through Delta's Web site or at kiosks situated within an airport.[52] As an incentive for the customer, the Delta program offers additional frequent flyer miles for self-serve tickets. Self-ticketing lessens the demand for reservation services and, therefore, reduces some of the associated costs.

Industry Consolidation and Expansion

The airline industry has been a significant factor in the recent corporate globalization trend. Nations have historically required local airlines to be majority-owned and controlled by citizens of their countries to protect a vital aspect of their transportation infrastructure. Only individual carriers have been able to build worldwide route systems. Within the past several years, however, airline companies have been able to skirt local regulations preventing the international mergers that have benefited other industries through various forms of alliances. Delta was slow to react to the initial agreements arranged in Europe, and alliances with the larger airlines (like British Airways and Lufthansa) had been formed with American Airlines and United Airlines.[53]

A key issue facing the airline industry today is the possibility of consolidation and restructuring. The primary industry concern is that if any two current airlines combine, the resulting "mega" airline would have a significant destabilizing effect on the industry.[54] For example, in the late 1990s, Delta was outbid by Northwest Airlines in an effort by each to merge with Continental Airlines. A combined Delta-Continental Airline would have made Delta the largest carrier in the United States. Then, on May 24, 2000, United Airlines Corp. announced an $11.6 billion deal to buy US Airways Group Inc. Since then, AMR, parent of American Airlines Inc., the nation's second-largest carrier, has approached Northwest and number three Delta about a marriage. Delta has voiced interest in Northwest. So, the Big Six in the United States could be on the brink of becoming the Big Three, with 85 percent of the domestic market. The moves could also fuel mergers in Europe, where on June 6, 2000, British Airways declared its intention to pursue a merger with KLM.[55]

In recent years, Delta has experienced constant growth. In fiscal 2000 Delta carried approximately 117 million passengers to their destinations, more than any other airline in the world. Based on calendar 1999 data, Delta is the third-largest U.S. airline as measured by operating revenues and revenue passenger miles flown. As of September 1, 2000, Delta (including its wholly-owned subsidiaries, ASA, Inc. and Comair, Inc.) served 205 domestic cities in 45 states, the District of Columbia, Puerto Rico, and the U.S. Virgin Islands, as well as 44 cities in 28 countries. With its domestic and international codeshare partners, Delta's route network covers 221 domestic cities in 48 states and 118 cities in 47 countries.[56] Its customers have access to a global network of 5360 flights each day to 356 cities in 57 countries on Delta, Delta Express, Delta Shuttle, the Delta Connection carriers, and Delta's Worldwide Partners.[57]

Delta has been increasingly successful in recent years in infiltrating "new" markets. Delta's preferred method of expansion has been through so-called alliances, partnerships, and codesharing with other airlines. These arrangements between airlines allow seamless service to customers by synchronizing flight schedules, coordinating pricing, and offering joint marketing. Codesharing partners buy seats on flights of partner airlines and sell them through their own scheduling system.

Delta has long had a codesharing agreement with three European airlines—Austrian Airlines, Swissair, and Sabena (the Atlantic Excellence Alliance). This arrangement has allowed Delta to provide passengers nonstop flights between a large number of European cities. Unfortunately for Delta, other major U.S. carriers have formed alliances with larger European carriers (such as United Airlines with Lufthansa and Northwest Airlines with KLM) that gave them access to larger markets. In addition, Swissair has historically had a poor history of holding its alliances together and is struggling to keep its access to European hubs.[58] Nonetheless, Delta flies nonstop to more European cities than any U.S. airline, and in 2000 it added new or increased service to Dublin, London, Lyon, Venice, and Zurich.[59]

Codesharing agreements allow passengers on any approved flight to accrue frequent flyer miles that may be redeemed with any of the participating airlines. Codesharing has allowed Delta to enter other markets as well. For instance, it has entered the Jamaican market through an agreement with Air Jamaica. In addition, Delta is strengthening its presence in Asia through agreements with China Southern and Korean Air.[60]

Some airline alliances have been challenged in Europe recently. The European Union (EU) is conducting ongoing antitrust investigations of alliances between Lufthansa and UAL, SAS and UAL, Northwest and KLM, and US Airways and British Airways. The EU's antitrust concerns are most pointed over the US Airways alliance involving coveted slots at London's Heathrow airport. The modern paradigm of merger and consolidation has taken a strong hold in industries from banking to waste disposal, however, and the airline industry is not likely to evolve without it.[61]

Delta is also expanding by adding new flights to its schedule. For instance, it has received approval by the Department of Transportation (DOT) to offer daily nonstop flights from Atlanta to Tokyo and increased flights from Los Angeles to Tokyo. Delta has petitioned the DOT to allow several more nonstop flights to selected Japanese cities. Likewise, Delta has increased flights to Central and South America. The DOT has approved daily flights between Lima, Peru, and Atlanta. This follows the approval of Delta flights to Guatemala, Panama, Costa Rica, and Venezuela.[62] As Delta enters the third year of its Latin America expansion strategy, it has become a major competitor in the region, with service to 11 destinations in eight countries. In Fall 2000, it continued that growth as it added new flights to Bogota, Colombia; Leon, Los Cabos,

Monterrey, and Puebla, Mexico; and Santiago, Chile.[63] In addition, Delta has opened new larger, more modern ticket offices in Sao Paulo and Rio de Janeiro. Moreover, Delta has expanded its international system by adding Caribbean destinations from two new gateways, Cincinnati and New York-Kennedy.[64] Expansion opportunities generally arise from effective scheduling and the purchase of new planes.

Marketing

In July of 1997, Delta unveiled its slogan "On Top of the World."[65] The slogan reflected the success of the three years of cost-cutting measures in Leadership 7.5 and the reemergence of Delta as the largest passenger carrier on the globe. Delta's most recent ad campaign, however, eschews a single slogan or theme in favor of airport vignettes and fill-in-the-blank luggage tags that focus on simple passenger needs. Many spots close with personalized bag tags in which passengers have scribbled in their desires. The accompanying narration or copy conveys Delta's efforts to meet them. "We wanted to highlight the customer and the basic experiences that affect them," said Martin White, vice-president of consumer marketing at Delta, whose ad account is valued at about $100 million annually. He hopes the ads will communicate Delta's eagerness to respond to passengers' basic concerns.[66] Clearly, the new ad campaign illustrates the company's continued emphasis on customer service and complements its recently released 12 customer service commitments (Appendix D).

Delta utilizes cooperative marketing programs planned with Swissair, Aeromexico, and Singapore Airlines, which include codesharing, schedule coordination, possible joint services on certain routes, around-the-world fares, joint advertising and promotional activities, and frequent flyer programs.[67] In 2000 Delta served 27 million frequent flyers.[68]

Advertising and promotional programs support Delta's marketing efforts for business and leisure travel, military and government travel, and package tours. Delta also has a program called the Meeting Network, through which Delta makes the air travel arrangements for attendees of incentive programs, meetings, or conventions.[69] Delta's Fantastic Flyer program for children, a natural tie-in with the company's official airline relationships with Walt Disney World in Florida and Disneyland in California, continues to be successful.[70] Other continuing official airline relationships include the Professional Golf Association of America (PGA) and the PGA Tour.[71] Furthermore, Delta sponsored the 1996 Summer Olympic Games in Atlanta, Georgia, and it will sponsor the 2002 Winter Olympic Games in Salt Lake City, Utah.

Delta is proud of its community involvement. Its financial support to the community is provided by The Delta Air Lines Foundation, corporate contributions, and employee-giving through the United Way. During fiscal 2000, Delta contributed over $10 million to charitable organizations. Also, company employees contribute their time, energies, and skills by building homes, leading organizations, and participating in charity walks. In addition, Delta sponsors four organizations, known as "Signature Partners," that focus on Youth Wellness and Youth Leadership Development: American Red Cross, CARE, Children's Miracle Network, and the Juvenile Diabetes Foundation. Last year Delta donated over $1 million, and its employees volunteered more than 5000 hours to these organizations.[72]

In February 2000, Delta completed the redesign of its Web site to provide users with quicker and easier access to information. To leverage the strength of the Delta brand, Delta has recently changed its Web site URL address from **www.delta-air.com**

to **www.delta.com**. The new address makes it easier for customers to locate its site. Future enhancements to **www.delta.com** include an award calendar showing destinations available to SkyMiles members using mileage awards and the ability to redeem mileage credits online. On the Delta website, customers can already check up-to-date information on flight schedules, rates, sky miles, services offered, and advertising opportunities, as well as make flight reservations.[73]

By 1993 Delta's cargo marketing efforts resulted in its being the second largest passenger/cargo combination carrier in terms of U.S. domestic mail ton miles (a measure of cargo volume).[74] Its mission is to be "the worldwide air cargo carrier of choice, creating a competitive advantage for Delta and our customers by providing reliable service and time-definite products tailored to customer and market needs through a motivated, professional workforce."[75] In fiscal 2000, Delta changed the name of its cargo operation to Air Logistics to better represent the comprehensive service it provides to its customers. Its services range from sourcing, warehousing, and inventory management to distribution and supply to the end user.[76] Four of the specific services it provides to meet the needs of its customers are Delta DASH, small package service with 30-minute drop-off and recovery times; Delta Priority First Freight, express service for larger shipments that cannot be sent by DASH; Delta Priority Second Day, airport-to-airport service for general cargo; and Delta Priority Third Day, services all markets with deferred air freight. Today, Air Logistics offers over 4800 flights per day for shipment.[77] During fiscal year 2000, cargo revenues increased 4 percent from the previous year.[78] The airline's cargo operating unit contributed one third of Delta's net income during the past fiscal year.[79] Delta has led U.S. airlines in market share for both domestic and overseas military traffic.[80]

To continue efforts of improving its financial performance, Delta has reallocated aircraft on several domestic flight segments in the past. The aircraft have been redeployed to markets that provide greater revenue potential, including the Atlanta, Cincinnati, and Dallas/Fort Worth hubs. In addition, Delta has added more daily flights and new destinations from Atlanta. Delta continues to realign its routes to maximize assets. It has increased the flights to its major hubs in Atlanta, Cincinnati, and Salt Lake City.[81] Delta's Atlanta hub is the largest hub operation in the world. The Cincinnati hub has also expanded to include additional daily departures and new destinations. The Delta Connection partners have continued to expand in short-haul markets. This enables the affected markets to be accommodated more efficiently by smaller aircraft and, consequently, permits Delta to reallocate aircraft to long-haul routes with better revenue potential.

Delta's international capacity continues to grow. Recently, Delta's global reach received a significant boost the summer of 2000 when it joined Aeromexico, Air France, and Korean Air to launch SkyTeam.[82] According to Delta's most recent annual report, "With the launch of our global SkyTeam alliance this year, Delta and its partners now offer customers access to an unsurpassed network that covers the world's major travel markets."[83] Major expansions are already planned at SkyTeam's key hubs—Paris-Charles deGaulle, Seoul, and Atlanta Worldport—during the coming years. Integration of operations and services among SkyTeam partners is expected to bring significant value to the Delta network. For instance, Air France has added new transatlantic frequencies at Atlanta, Boston, and Philadelphia, and Delta has expanded codeshare services with Air France via Paris-Charles deGaulle. Delta's codeshare relationship with Aeromexico is now the most extensive partnership of any airline alliance in the industry.[84]

Delta continues to try to increase its international flight traffic and alliances. Delta's international efforts have included strengthening its presence at the New York–Kennedy Airport to build its North Atlantic travel operations.[85] To increase transoceanic service, Delta has even developed a Transoceanic Business Class of travel, which is intended to provide comfort and versatility for the busy traveler. Delta is strongest in the U.S. and Latin American markets but lacks any significant route system in Asia. Thus it is lobbying for landing rights in Beijing, making it the third U.S. passenger carrier to do so in China.[86]

Financial Condition

Delta was once known for having the most conservative balance sheet in the airline industry. Financial results for Delta Air Lines are presented in Exhibits 1 through 4. In the early 1990s, the company began to hit hard times. Delta reported its second loss since 1947, with the first occurring in 1983. The company suffered financial losses through 1994. A number of factors such as increased fuel prices because of the Middle East crisis; increased fare competition; massive expenses related to the company's expanded route system through purchase agreements with Pan Am; continued poor economic conditions, both domestic and international; and expansion costs were found as causes for this half-billion dollar loss.[87]

As a result of these losses, Delta began several cost-cutting steps such as the reduction of planned aircraft, facilities, and ground equipment expenditures through fiscal year 1995. Delta's directors even voluntarily cut their own compensation by 20 percent.[88] The company also consolidated reservation offices by closing eight of its 19 U.S. reservations facilities. These consolidations were completed between June 1993 and fall 1994.[89]

In summary, over the last five years, Delta's operating revenues have increased 28 percent while operating expenses have increased 22 percent.[90] During 2000, Delta delivered consistent financial and operational results with cost levels that remain below the industry average, according to Leo Mullin.[91] Its financial performance is attributed to a number of factors, such as effective fuel hedging, strong cash returns, a solid capital structure, improved asset utilization, and favorable economic conditions.[92]

For fiscal 2000, operating revenues were $15.9 billion, increasing 9 percent from $14.6 billion in fiscal 1999.[93] Passenger revenues accounted for 94 percent of Delta's consolidated operating revenues, and cargo revenues and other sources accounted for 6 percent for that period.[94] Passenger revenue grew 9 percent, reflecting a 6 percent increase in revenue passenger miles (RPMs) on 5 percent capacity growth and a 3 percent increase in passenger mile yield. The company's North American passenger mile yield rose 5 percent, largely because of the inclusion of ASA and Comair, and partially offset by increased low-fare competition and capacity increases by competitors. On the other hand, Delta's international passenger mile yield declined 4 percent primarily because of increased pricing pressures resulting from industry-wide capacity growth in the Atlantic market.[95]

Cargo revenues increased 4 percent to $579 million, reflecting a 7 percent increase in cargo ton miles and a 3 percent decrease in ton mile yield. The increase in cargo ton miles is primarily due to capacity increases and higher mail volume. The decrease in ton mile yield is due to pricing pressure resulting from industry-wide capacity growth in international markets. Other revenues increased 22 percent to $433 million, mainly as a result of higher revenues from codeshare activity and frequent flyer partnership programs.[96]

EXHIBIT 1   CONSOLIDATED SUMMARY OF OPERATIONS (IN MILLIONS, EXCEPT PER SHARE DATA)

For the Fiscal Years Ended June 30

	2000	1999	1998	1997	1996
Operating revenues	$15,888	$14,597	$14,057	$13,517	$12,418
Operating expenses	14,600	12,727	12,363	11,986	11,953
Operating income (loss)	1,288	1,870	1,694	1,531	465
Interest expense (net)	(305)	(153)	(148)	(174)	(243)
Miscellaneous income (net)	1,300	109	102	58	43
Income (loss) before income taxes	2,283	1,826	1,648	1,415	276
Income tax (provision) benefit	(914)	(725)	(647)	(561)	(120)
Net income (loss) before cumulative effect of change in accounting principle	1,369	1,101	1,001	854	156
Net income (loss) after cumulative effect of change in accounting principle	1,303	1,101	1,001	854	156
Preferred stock dividends	(12)	(11)	(11)	(9)	(82)
Net income (loss) attributable to common shareowners	$ 1,291	$ 1,090	$ 990	$ 845	$74
Earnings (loss) per share:					
Basic	$ 9.92	$ 7.63	$ 6.64	$ 5.70	$ 0.72
Diluted	$ 9.42	$ 7.20	$ 6.34	$ 5.52	$ 0.72
Dividends declared					
On common stock	$ 13	$ 14	$ 15	$15	$ 10
Per common share	$ 0.10	$ 0.10	$ 0.10	$ 0.10	$ 0.10

SOURCE: Delta Air Lines, Inc., *2000 Annual Report*, p. 54.

| EXHIBIT 2 | OTHER FINANCIAL AND STATISTICAL DATA (FINANCIAL DATA IN MILLIONS) |

For the Fiscal Years Ended June 30

	2000	1999	1998	1997	1996
Total assets	$ 20,566	$ 16,750	$ 14,603	$ 12,741	$ 12,226
Long-term debt and capital leases (excluding current maturities)	$ 4,525	$ 1,952	$ 1,782	$ 1,797	$ 2,175
Share owner's equity	$ 4,873	$ 4,448	$ 4,023	$ 3,007	$ 2,540
Shares of common stock outstanding at year end	122,639,566	138,553,719	150,450,394	147,391,974	135,556,212
Revenue passengers enplaned (thousands)	116,595	106,902	104,148	101,147	91,341
Available seat miles (millions)	151,913	144,003	140,149	136,821	130,751
Revenue passenger miles (millions)	110,347	104,575	101,136	97,758	88,673
Operating revenue per available seat mile	10.46¢	10.14¢	10.03¢	9.88¢	9.50¢
Passenger mile yield	13.48¢	13.09¢	13.03¢	12.98¢	13.19¢
Operating cost per available seat mile	9.61¢	8.84¢	8.82¢	8.76¢	9.14¢
Passenger load factor	72.6%	72.6%	72.2%	71.4%	67.8%
Break even passenger load factor	66.4%	62.7%	62.9%	62.8%	65.1%
Available ton miles (millions)	22,068	20,627	19,890	18,984	18,084
Revenue ton miles (millions)	12,504	12,115	11,859	11,308	10,235
Operating cost per available ton mile	66.16¢	61.70¢	62.16¢	63.14¢	66.10¢

SOURCE: Delta Air Lines, Inc., *2000 Annual Report*, p. 54.

EXHIBIT 3	OPERATING REVENUES BY GEOGRAPHIC REGION (IN MILLIONS)		
Region	**2000**	**1999**	**1998**
North America	$13,211	$11,956	$11,416
Atlantic	1,960	1,973	2,092
Pacific	302	326	304
Latin America	415	342	245
Total	15,888	14,597	14,057

SOURCE: Delta Air Lines, Inc., *2000 Annual Report*, p. 49.

EXHIBIT 4	DELTA AIR LINES, INC.

Consolidated Statements of Income (in Millions, Except Per Share Data)
for the years ended June 30, 2000, 1999, and 1998

	2000	1999	1998
Operating Revenues:			
Passenger	$14,876	$13,685	$13,180
Cargo	579	557	582
Other, net	433	355	295
Total operating revenues	$15,888	$14,597	$14,057
Operating Expenses:			
Salaries and related costs	$ 5,597	$ 4,993	$ 4,850
Aircraft fuel	1,646	1,360	1,507
Passenger commissions	722	867	980
Contracted services	893	772	694
Depreciation and amortization	1,146	961	860
Other selling expenses	644	641	600
Aircraft rent	694	590	552
Aircraft maintenance material and outside repairs	681	561	495
Passenger service	471	500	450
Landing fees and other rents	742	707	649
Asset writedowns and other special charges	555	—	—
Other	809	775	726
Total operating expenses	$14,600	$12,727	$12,363

SOURCE: Delta Air Lines, Inc., *2000 Annual Report*, p. 33.

Continued

EXHIBIT 4	DELTA AIR LINES, INC.—CONT'D			
		2000	**1999**	**1998**
Operating Income		1,288	1,870	1,694
Other Income (Expense):				
Interest income (expense), net		(197)	(101)	(69)
Gains from the sale of investments		1,202	26	—
Miscellaneous income (expense), net		(10)	31	23
Total other income (expense)		995	(44)	(46)
Income Before Income Taxes		2,283	1,826	1,648
Income Taxes Provided		(914)	(725)	(647)
Net Income Before Cumulative Effect of Accounting Change, Net of Tax		1,369	1,101	1,001
Cumualtive Effect of Accounting Change, Net of Tax		(66)	—	—
Net Income		1,303	1,101	1,001
Preferred Stock Dividends		(12)	(11)	(11)
Net Income Available to Common Shareowners		1,291	1,090	990

Operating expenses totaled $14.6 billion for fiscal 2000, increasing 15 percent from $12.7 billion in fiscal 1999. Operating capacity rose 5 percent to 152 billion available seat miles. Operating cost per available seat mile increased 9 percent to 9.61 cents. Salaries and related costs increased 12 percent during fiscal 2000. The number of full-time employees increased 9 percent, largely from the inclusion of ASA and Comair. The increase in salaries and related costs also reflects salary increases for most domestic employees of 2 percent on December 1, 1999, and 3 percent on April 1, 2000.[97] Delta's financial performance over the last three years has translated into total compensation packages that rank at or near the top among its competitive peers for all employee groups.[98]

Fuel prices are very important factors in total operating costs. Aircraft fuel expense increased 21 percent in fiscal 2000 compared with fiscal 1999, with the average fuel price per gallon rising 15 percent to 57.23 cents. Total gallons consumed increased 5 percent because of increased operations on a 5 percent rise in capacity. Delta's innovative fuel hedging program saved the company $442 million during fiscal 2000.[99]

Delta's Jet Fuel Consumption and Costs for Fiscal Years 1996 - 2000

	Gallons Consumed (Millions)	Cost (Millions)	Avg. Price Per Gallon	Percent of Operating Expenses
1996	2,500	$1,464	$58.53	13%
1997	2,599	$1,722	$66.23	14%
1998	2,664	$1,507	$56.54	12%
1999	2,730	$1,360	$49.83	11%
2000	2,876	$1,646	$57.23	12%

SOURCE: Delta Air Lines, Inc., *Online Form 10-K 2000*, p. 11.

Conclusion

The airline industry is highly competitive and is characterized by substantial price competition. In this environment, Delta must constantly evaluate possibilities of merger, alliance, and expansion. However, Delta's greatest challenge is to find a way to continue to differentiate itself through unparalleled customer service. Although the industry has changed dramatically since 1929, Delta's customer service philosophy has not. Superior customer service continues to be at the heart of the company and defines its focus for the next 70 years and beyond.

---

*This case was prepared by Mark Dawkins and revised by Patricia Duffy, Daniel Griffin, Kris Inchcombe, and Patty Pinholster. This case was updated by Jon Alden, Cynthia Campbell, Eric Hamilton, Cathie Mathe, Ed Nelson, and Laura Wilson.

A

Rewards & Recognition

Delta's corporate Rewards & Recognition program *Above & Beyond* was launched in October 1997. It is an initiative of the Integrated Customer Service (ICS) team, which selected 125 of Delta's best people to poll frontline coworkers. The selected personnel, called ambassadors, polled 7084 people. The input and comments from these frontline people helped formulate the development of ideas and solutions that would improve Delta's customer service. Their recommendations were to change some of the processes, integrate technology, and create a high-performing work environment that would recognize and reward employees for superior performance. The *Above & Beyond* program does this. In addition, it supports the company's reward-for-performance strategy. It provides Delta personnel at all levels an opportunity to recognize and be recognized for exceptional job performance and outstanding customer service.

The program objectives are to:

- Instill a sense of ownership in Delta and its customers.
- Motivate people to improve customer satisfaction levels.
- Build teamwork and camaraderie among Delta people.

Functions of the department include:

- Educating Delta people about the corporate goal of a 95 percent overall customer satisfaction ranking.
- Developing and coordinating policies and procedures for the monthly awards drawings.
- Soliciting low- and no-cost awards from Delta partners and vendors.
- Communicating and promoting the importance and power of recognizing employees.
- Researching and implementing guidelines regarding the tax ramifications associated with awards.
- Acting as a clearinghouse for departmental rewards and recognition programs.
- Establishing and monitoring the business unit committees charged with selecting Delta's "best-of-the-best" as Chairman's Club honorees.
- Creating and coordinating the annual Chairman's Club Recognition Banquet.

Critical Issues Facing Rewards & Recognition

- The Above & Beyond program needs to be more meaningful at a business unit and departmental level.
- An acceptable method to include Delta's Contractors in the program needs to be determined.
- Objective means must be found to measure the results of the program.
- Communications: Continue to address the challenge of communicating to a diverse workforce in order to effectively promote the program and raise visibility.

- The senior coordinator's role regarding monitoring of awards and programs for individual business units and/or departments should be clarified.
- Motivation: Continue to motivate employees to strive to reach our corporate goal of 95 percent overall customer satisfaction, when many perceive the goal as too high.
- Streamline the administration of the program via automation or outsourcing.

Major Accomplishments of Rewards & Recognition

- Focused attention on the 95 percent overall customer satisfaction goal, which significantly increased awareness and educated employees on the Customer Satisfaction Tracking Study.
- Created enthusiasm and interest among employees with various contests and team rally meetings.
- Introduced simple and effective tools that all Delta people can use to immediately recognize superior customer service and outstanding job performance (People-to-People Recognition Cards and Team Recognition Cards).
- Designed, planned, produced, and mailed quarterly Above & Beyond brochures and packets.
- Established The Chairman's Club, an annual tradition at Delta that rewards honorees based on performance rather than tenure.
- Partnered with consumer marketing to provide SkyMiles customers with recognition cards to give on-the-spot recognition to those Delta people who provide distinguished customer service. (Customer response has been very positive.)
- Garnered significant senior management support of the Above & Beyond program.
- Provided role preparation training to supervisors, demonstrating how the reward and recognition program can be used as an effective management tool.
- Raised visibility of the program by setting up booths at the Flight Attendant Forum Meeting, Leadership Conference, ACS Fair, and Volunteer Fair.
- Conducted focus groups with key people to identify strengths and weaknesses of program.
- Initiated a task force to determine award eligibility and taxation for management review and approval.

B

Continuous Improvement Teams

Continuous Improvement Team Support Group

The Continuous Improvement Team Support Group is responsible for establishing, training, supporting, and recognizing continuous improvement teams (CITs) at Delta Air Lines.

The CIT process is a problem-solving effort that allows employees to work as a team to identify, analyze, and solve problems that affect their work.

To form a CIT, a volunteer manager/supervisor is trained during a four-day concentrated leadership course in the continuous improvement team process (effective meetings, teamwork, presentation skills, problem solving, and practical application of presentation skills and problem-solving tools). This volunteer "sponsor" is responsible as the team "coach." The sponsor is a resource for the team in working closely with management and provides guidance in team meetings and presentations to management. The sponsor works with the team support group (TSG) and area management to solicit volunteers to participate by becoming CIT members. Management overviews are given by the TSG to enlighten supervisory personnel about the establishment and benefits of an area CIT.

The team members are responsible for attending team meetings; accepting team roles (team leader, scribe, timekeeper, etc.); and identifying, investigating, and solving problems in their work areas. The team makes presentations to applicable management in order to obtain approval for idea implementation.

The team support group is responsible for recognizing teams by developing and administering a corporate CIT recognition program. The TSG also arranges and implements high-visibility events to showcase productive CITs. One example is the annual CIT EXPO.

Critical Issues Facing Continuous Improvement Teams

- Managerial (top down) involvement, support, and encouragement of employee teamwork. Upper-level managers need to involve themselves by visiting team meetings and CIT-related functions. Management involvement builds trust and motivation within the ranks.
- Management needs to place more emphasis on investing time to allow teams/employees to be involved in identifying improvements, data gathering, problem solving, and implementation of ideas. Numerous opportunities are curtailed because of narrow supervisory emphasis on quotas and production designed to achieve high ratings on leadership performance appraisals.
- Employee involvement and CITs need to be driven from the top with accountability for team function and productivity throughout the ranks.

C

Delta's Personnel Assistance Programs Office

The Personnel Assistance Programs Office provides programs and resources designed to generate solutions to workplace productivity problems and remove barriers to optimal performance, such as:

Alcohol Recovery Program

Designed to assist employees with an alcohol or prescription medication addiction, Delta's alcohol recovery program provides quality treatment and support to maintain their sobriety. The recovery program includes two years of aftercare monitoring. Mandatory training is provided for management and employees volunteering as peer monitors.

Critical Incident Response Program (CIRP)

The CIRP provides trained peer support, as well as professional resources, as needed for personnel who may be at risk for emotional trauma after experiencing a work-related critical incident. (Any sudden event that is outside the range of normal human experience has the potential to overwhelm normal coping mechanisms and trigger traumatic consequences). CIRP goals are accomplished by providing emotional support and stress management services. The major objective is to assist "normal people having normal responses to abnormal events" and to return them to healthy functioning as quickly as possible.

Management Consultations

Management consultations help supervisors work more effectively with employees who have performance or productivity problems. Address health concerns that require immediate attention and facilitate timely access to assessment and referral services.

Mental Health Benefits

Mental health benefits ensure that employees and eligible family members have access to quality mental health services. Oversee contracts with managed-care vendors (Aetna, MCC) to provide effective service delivery. Provide information on illness prevention, coping skills, stress management, and maintenance of good mental health.

Workplace Violence

Delta's workplace violence program works with management team to help provide a safe environment for employees to work free of threats, fear, or intimidation.

Lunch & Learn

Seminars are offered on a variety of topics from stress management to sleep problems.

Personnel Assistance was created in the fall of 1989 with the primary role of enforcing the DOT/FAA mandated Drug-Free Workplace Act. That role included procedures for drug testing safety-sensitive employees and providing access to benefits for those seeking treatment. In January of 1993, all enforcement responsibilities were referred to other departments and Personnel Assistance focused strictly on the EAP-related functions. Employees can access individual counseling and treatment programs.

Delta's benefit plan covers counseling for a full range of issues from marital/family problems to DSM IV diagnoses. Personnel Assistance does not function as a gatekeeper for mental health benefits.

Personnel Assistance provides supervisory and management training and consultation on working with employees who have emotional or substance abuse problems that affect job performance. It contracts with a trainer to provide the initial training for members of the critical incident response team but provides all of the recurrent quarterly training itself.

D

Delta Customer Commitment

In response to the tremendous growth of air travel and the demanding need for excellence in customer service, Delta has joined other U.S. airlines and the Air Transport Association (ATA) in an effort to provide passengers with a clear understanding of our industry's commitment to meet essential performance objectives.

We have outlined our responsibilities below in 12 key points. We intend to ensure that your air travel experience will encompass, to the best of our abilities, the most comprehensive customer service possible.

Twelve Customer Service Commitments

Before You Fly:

1. We will offer, through our telephone reservation system, the lowest fare for which the customer is eligible for the date, flight, and class of service requested.
2. We will give you time to compare our fares with those of other airlines.
3. We will issue refunds for eligible tickets within seven business days for domestic credit card purchases and 20 business days for purchases made by cash or check.
4. We will inform you, upon your request by telephone, if the flight on which you are ticketed is overbooked. We also will provide information at airports about our policies and procedures for handling situations when all ticketed customers cannot be accommodated on a flight.
5. We will provide you with timely and complete information about policies and procedures that affect your travel.
6. We will ensure our domestic codeshare partners commit to providing comparable consumer plans and policies. Our partners are regional airlines that connect small- and medium-sized markets with Delta's network.

At the Airport:

7. We will provide you with information about our policies and procedures for accommodating disabled and special-needs customers and unaccompanied minors.
8. We will provide full and timely information on the status of delayed and canceled flights.
9. We will provide full and timely information regarding the status of a flight if there is an extreme delay after you have boarded or after the plane has landed, and we will provide for your essential needs while onboard.

After Landing:

10. We will strive to return your misplaced baggage within 24 hours, and we will attempt to contact owners of unclaimed baggage when a name and address or telephone number is available.

11. We support a U.S. Department of Transportation proposal to increase the per passenger domestic baggage liability limitation from $1250 to $2500.
12. We will respond to written customer complaints within 30 days, exceeding the 60-day response standard adopted by ATA member airlines.

Questions

1. Delta has made great strides, but there is room for improvement. How should Delta continue to regain the commitment of its employees in order to attain "#1" status? Discuss your strategic recommendations. How are your suggestions linked to improved customer satisfaction?
2. As Delta continues to expand globally, how should the company face the on-going challenge of finding the right balance between profits and employees? Discuss how management should be accountable for employees' needs and concerns.

Notes

[1] The company was originally founded as a crop-dusting service in 1924. This start resulted from a conversation between Collet Everman Woolman, an associate, and some Louisiana farmers concerned about the threat to their crops from boll weevils. Woolman, an agricultural scientist and pilot, knew that calcium arsenate would kill boll weevils. Woolman wanted to drop the chemical from an airplane and engineered a "hooper" for the chemical. After perfecting the system he began selling his services to farmers throughout the region, forming the world's first crop-dusting service. Woolman left the agricultural extension service in 1925 to take charge of the duster's entomological work. The crop-dusting operation was separated from its parent company in 1928 to form a new company named Delta Air Service. Woolman expanded his crop-dusting business into Mexico, South America, and throughout the South. The company also diversified by securing airmail contracts. Passenger service was inaugurated in 1929, with initial service to Jackson, Dallas, Atlanta, and Charleston.

[2] Swiercz and Spencer, "HRM and Sustainable Competitive Advantage: Lessons from Delta," *Human Resource Planning* 15, no. 2 (1992).

[3] The section's information, prior to the 1990s, is principally a reproduction of Delta's corporate history as compiled by the *International Directory of Company Histories* 1, 1988, pp. 99–100. Information for the 1990s comes from cited sources.

[4] "Delta Air Lines, Inc.," *Hoover's Handbook of American Business* 1, 1996, Companies A-L.

[5] Several mergers were consummated during these two decades. On May 1, 1953, Delta merged with Chicago and Southern Airlines. In June of 1967, Delta merged with Delaware Airlines and officially adopted the name of Delta Air Lines. Delta acquired Northeast Airlines on August 1, 1972. Delta also purchased Storer Leasing in July of 1976. In March 1988, Delta acquired 20 percent of the voting securities of SkyWest Incorporated. In 1991, Delta acquired Pan Am Corporation.

[6] I. Cohen, "Political Climate and Two Airline Strikes: Century Air in 1982 and Continental Airlines in 1985," *Industrial and Labor Relations Review* 42, no. 2 (1990), pp. 308–323.

[7] Seth Lubove, "Full Speed Ahead—but Cautiously," *Forbes*, October 29, 1990, pp. 36–38.

[8] Ibid.

[9] Ibid.

[10] Delta Air Lines, Inc., *2000 Annual Report*, p. 27.

[11] "Pilots' Union Accepts Pay Cut in Return for Options," *The New York Times*, February 22, 1996, pp. C4 (N), D4(L), col. 1.

[12] "Furloughed Delta Pilots Now All Rehired," *The New York Times*, June 8, 1996, pp. 30(N), 44(L), col. 4.

[13]"Delta Air Lines to Add 665 Customer-Service Jobs," *The New York Times*, January 31, 1996, pp. C4(N), D4(L), col. 1.

[14]"Delta Restoring Pay Cut to Nonunion Workers," *The New York Times*, January 31, 1996, pp. C4(N), D4(L), col. 1.

[15]"Delta to Give Raises to 50,000 Workers," *The New York Times*, April 19, 1997, pp. 20(N), 34(L), col. 1.

[16]Delta Air Lines, Inc., *2000 Annual Report*, p. 17.

[17]Ibid., p. 3.

[18]Terril Yue Jones, "Musical Chairs," *Forbes*, no. 1, January 12, 1998, p. 60.

[19]Delta Air Lines, Inc., *Online Form 10-K 2000*, p. 9.

[20]Martha Brannigan, "Delta Chief Is Mum about the Reasons Why He Will Retire," *The Wall Street Journal*, May 14, 1997, p. A4.

[21]David Greising, "A Break in the Clouds for Delta," *Business Week*, no. 3558, December 22, 1997, p. 93.

[22]Martha Brannigan and JoAnn S. Lublin, "Delta Airlines Changes Style with New Chief," *The Wall Street Journal*, August 18, 1997, p. B1.

[23]Delta Air Lines, Inc., *Online Form 10-K 2000*, p. 20.

[24]Delta Air Lines, Inc., *2000 Annual Report*, p. 17.

[25]Martha Brannigan, "Delta's New CEO Lays Out Big Agenda to Upgrade Airline's Customer Service," *The Wall Street Journal*, November 10, 1997, p. B3.

[26]Julia King, "Leadership Deal Lands Delta Hot CIO," *Computerworld*, 31, no. 51, December 22, 1997.

[27]Delta Air Lines, Inc., *2000 Annual Report*, p. 7.

[28]Martha Brannigan, "Delta's CEO Ousts Chief Financial Officer in Search of a Partner on Strategic Level," *The Wall Street Journal*, November 21, 1997, p. A4.

[29]Brannigan, "Two Delta Executives to Retire As New CEO Creates Own Team," *The Wall Street Journal*, April 14, 1998.

[30]"Delta Air Lines' Exec. V.P. Marketing to Retire," *Dow Jones Newswire*, April 13, 1998.

[31]"Delta Airlines Forms Advisory Board for Passengers with Special Needs; Strengthens Commitment to Customers with Disabilities," *PR Newswire*, April 24, 2000.

[32]Delta Air Lines, Inc., *Online Form 10-K 2000*, p. 12.

[33]Helen Lippman, "Courts Weigh in on Obesity," *Business and Health* 16, no. 2 (February 1998); *Rich v. Delta Airlines*, 921 F. Supp. 767 (D.C. N.D. Ga 1996).

[34]Delta Air Lines, Inc., *2000 Annual Report*, p. 16.

[35]Delta Air Lines, Inc., *1999 Annual Report*, p. 13.

[36]Delta Air Lines, Inc., *2000 Annual Report*, p. 17.

[37]Delta Air Lines, Inc., *1999 Annual Report*, p. 33.

[38]Delta Air Lines, Inc., *2000 Annual Report*, pp. 4–5.

[39]**www.delta.com**, (accessed May 4, 2001); Martha Brannigan, "How Delta Pilots Mobilized in the Battle Against Management," *The Wall Street Journal*, April 24, 2001, pp. A1, A12; and Rick Rooks and Martha Brannigan, "Delta's Tentative Pact with Pilots Will Be Costly, May Raise Salary Expectations," *The Wall Street Journal*, April 24, 2001, pp. A3, A12.

[40]Delta Air Lines, Inc., *1997 Annual Report*.

[41]Delta Air Lines, Inc., *2000 Annual Report*, p. 4.

[42]Delta Air Lines, Inc., *1997 Annual Report*.

[43]Delta Air Lines, Inc., *2000 Annual Report*, p. 1.

[44]Ibid, p. 5.

[45]Delta Air Lines, Inc., *1997 Annual Report*.

[46]Delta Air Lines, Inc., *1999 Annual Report*, p. 19.

[47]Ibid.

[48]"Delta Express: It's a Delta Jet," *Air Transport World* 34, no. 7, 1998 p. 35.

[49]Delta Air Lines, Inc., *1999 Annual Report*, p. 18.

[50]Delta Air Lines, Inc., *2000 Annual Report*, pp. 8–9.

[51]Delta Air Lines, Inc., *Online Form 10-K 2000*, p. 10.

[52]Clinton Wilder, "Online Incentive," *Information Week*, no. 61, February 3, 1997, p. 58.

[53]William H. Miller, "Growing Globally, at Last," *Industry Week* 246, no. 5 (March 3, 1997), pp. 64–71.

[54]Delta Air Lines, Inc., *2000 Annual Report*, p. 2.

[55]Wendy Zellner, Dan Carney, and Michael Arndt, "How Many Airlines Will Stay Aloft?" *Business Week*, June 19, 2000, p. 50.

[56]Delta Air Lines, Inc., *2000 Annual Report*, inside cover.

[57]"Delta Airlines Forms Advisory Board for Passengers with Special Needs; Strengthens Commitment to Customers with Disabilities," *PR Newswire*, April 24, 2000.

[58]Allison Bisbey, "Swissair's Delta Alliance at Risk from Franco-U.S. Treaty," *Dow Jones Newswire*, April 8, 1998.

[59]Delta Air Lines, Inc., *2000 Annual Report*, p. 4.

[60]Delta Air Lines, Inc., *1997 Annual Report*.

[61]Carey and McCartney, "Airline Alliances," *The Wall Street Journal*, April 6, 1998.

[62]*Delta press release*, **www.delta.com**.

[63]Delta Air Lines, Inc., *2000 Annual Report*, p. 10.

[64]Ibid.

[65]James Woolsey, "On Top of the World," *Air Transport World* 34, no. 7 (July 1997).

[66]Scott Thurston, "Delta Airlines' New Advertising Campaign Highlights Simple Pleasures," *The Atlanta Journal and Constitution*, March 8, 2000.

[67]Delta Air Lines, Inc., *1990 Annual Report*, p. 14.

[68]Delta Air Lines, Inc., *2000 Annual Report*, p. 19.

[69]**www.delta.com** (accessed March 2, 1998).

[70]Delta Air Lines, Inc., *1990 Annual Report*, p. 14.

[71]Ibid.

[72]Delta Air Lines, Inc., *2000 Annual Report*, p. 20.

[73]Ibid., p. 18.

[74]Delta Air Lines, Inc., *1990 Annual Report*, p. 14.

[75]**www.delta.com**.

[76]Delta Air Lines, Inc., *2000 Annual Report*, p. 9.

[77]**www.delta.com**.

[78]Delta Air Lines, Inc., *2000 Annual Report*, p. 27.

[79]"Delta Cargo Unit Gets New Senior Manager," *The Atlanta Journal and Constitution*, August 5, 2000, p. 2F.

[80]Delta Air Lines, Inc., *1990 Annual Report*, p. 14.

[81]Delta Air Lines, Inc., *1997 Annual Report*.

[82]Delta Air Lines, Inc., *2000 Annual Report*, p. 4.

[83]Ibid, p. 10.

[84]Ibid, p. 11.

[85]Delta Air Lines, Inc., *1997 Annual Report*.

[86]Betty Liu, "Delta Pilots Look Into Merger Possibility," *Financial Times* (London), June 6, 2000, p. 38.

[87]Delta Air Lines, Inc., *1993 Annual Report*.

[88]*Moody's Transportation Manual*, 1993.

[89]Ibid.

[90]Delta Air Lines, Inc., *2000 Annual Report*, pp. 54–55.

[91]Ibid., p. 2.

[92]Ibid., p. 5.

[93]Ibid., p. 27.

[94]Delta Air Lines, Inc., *Online Form 10-K 2000*, p. 5.

[95]Delta Air Lines, Inc., *2000 Annual Report*, p. 27.

[96]Ibid.

[97]Ibid.

[98]Ibid., pp. 16–17.

[99]Ibid., p. 27.

3

McDonald's Corporation*

Introduction

History

McDonald's is the world's largest restaurant chain. Its innovative marketing, superior products, impeccable operations, and devoted franchisees[1] have set the standard for the fast-food industry. The company philosophy of Q.S.C.&V. (quality food; fast, friendly service; restaurant cleanliness; and a menu that provides value) and its family-oriented image are the product of Ray Kroc. In addition, it is one of the world's most recognized brand names, along with Coca-Cola, Kodak, Gillette, Sony, and Walt Disney. Operations in 119 countries highlight the truly global nature of McDonald's in the new millennium.[2]

The first McDonald's was a drive-in restaurant started in San Bernardino, California, by two brothers, Dick and Mac McDonald, in 1948. Ray Kroc, the man who made McDonald's the household name it is today, became a franchising agent for the McDonald brothers in 1954 and opened his first McDonald's in Illinois in 1955. The McDonald brothers sold the company to Ray Kroc in 1961 for $2.7 million. In 1999 alone, McDonald's generated more than $13.2 billion in total revenues.[3] The company menu, which originally consisted only of hamburgers, cheeseburgers, french fries, sodas, milkshakes, milk, and coffee, has grown considerably since.

A more technical definition of McDonald's is an organization that develops, operates, franchises, and services a worldwide system of restaurants that prepare, assemble, package, and sell a limited menu of quickly prepared, moderately priced foods.[4] The McDonald's system is the largest and best-known food service organization in the world. The company franchises joint-venture partners, and restaurant managers operate nearly 27,000 restaurants in 119 countries, each offering a limited menu of high-quality food that can be part of a well-balanced meal plan. McDonald's has pioneered food quality specifications, equipment technology, marketing and training programs, and operational and supply systems, all of which are considered the standards of the industry throughout the world.[5] Q.S.C.&V.—Quality, Service, Cleanliness, and Value—are the standards upon which McDonald's was built and are the reasons McDonald's continues to operate so successfully today.[6]

*This case was prepared by Alexandra Orsin, Mike Martin, Ken Nielson, and Robert Graves; revised by Phillip Carlton, Stuart Henry, Cathie Mathe, Lucy Reams, Katrina Tew, and Jeff Younger.

EXHIBIT 1	CONSOLIDATED STATEMENT OF INCOME			
(In Millions, Except Per Share Data)	Years Ended December 31,	1999	1998	1997
Revenues				
Sales by Company-operated restaurants		$9,512.5	$8,894.9	$8,136.5
Revenues from franchised and affiliated restaurants		3,746.8	3,526.5	3,272.3
Total revenues		**13,259.3**	**12,421.4**	**11,408.8**
Operating costs and expenses				
Food and packaging		3,204.6	2,997.4	2,772.6
Payroll and employee benefits		2,418.3	2,220.3	2,025.1
Occupancy and other operating expenses		2,206.7	2,043.9	1,851.9
Total Company-operated restaurant expenses		**7,829.6**	**7,261.9**	**6,649.6**
Franchised restaurants-occupancy expenses		737.7	678.0	613.9
Selling, general and administrative expenses		1,477.6	1,458.5	1,450.5
Other operating (income) expenses		(124.1)	(60.2)	(113.5)
Made For You Costs		18.9	161.6	
Special charges			160.0	
Total operating costs and expenses		**9,939.7**	**9,659.5**	**8,600.5**
Operating income		**3,319.6**	**2,761.9**	**2,808.3**
Interest expense–net of capitalized interest of $14.3, $17.9 and $22.7		396.3	413.8	364.4
Nonoperating (income) expense		39.2	40.7	36.6
Income before provision for income taxes		**2,884.1**	**2,307.4**	**2,407.3**
Provision for income taxes		936.2	757.3	764.8
Net income		**$1,947.9**	**$1,550.1**	**$1,642.5**
Net income per common share		**$1.44**	**$1.14**	**$1.17**
Net income per common share–diluted		1.39	1.10	1.15
Dividends per common share		**$.20**	**$.18**	**$.16**
Weighted-average shares		1,355.3	1,365.3	1,378.7
Weighted-average shares–diluted		1,404.2	1,405.7	1,410.2

SOURCE: www.mcdonalds.com/corporate (accessed December 31, 2000).

EXHIBIT 2 CONSOLIDATED BALANCE SHEET		
(In Millions, Except Per Share Data)	December 31, 1999	1998
Assets		
Current assets		
Cash and equivalents	$419.5	$299.2
Accounts and notes receivable	708.1	609.4
Inventories, at cost, not in excess of market	82.7	77.3
Prepaid expenses and other current assets	362.0	323.5
Total current assets	1,572.3	1,309.4
Other assets		
Investments in and advances to affiliates	1,002.2	854.1
Intangible assets–net	1,261.8	973.1
Miscellaneous	822.4	606.2
Total other assets	3,086.4	2,433.4
Property and equipment		
Property and equipment, at cost	22,450.8	21,758.0
Accumulated depreciation and amortization	(6,126.3)	(5,716.4)
Net property and equipment	16,324.5	16,041.6
Total assets	$20,983.2	$19,784.4

SOURCE: www.mcdonalds.com/corporate

EXHIBIT 2 CONSOLIDATED BALANCE SHEET—CONT'D

(In Millions, Except Per Share Data)	December 31, 1999	1998
Liabilities and shareholders' equity		
Current liabilities		
Notes payable	$1,073.1	$686.8
Accounts payable	585.7	621.3
Income taxes	117.2	94.2
Other taxes	160.1	143.5
Accrued interest	131.4	132.3
Other accrued liabilities	660.0	651.0
Current maturities of long-term debt	546.8	168.0
Total current liabilities	**3,274.3**	**2,497.1**
Other liabilities		
Long-term debt	5,632.4	6,188.6
Other long-term liabilities and minority interests	538.4	492.6
Deferred income taxes	1,173.6	1,081.9
Common equity put options	725.4	59.5
Shareholders' equity		
Preferred stock, no par value; authorized–165.0 million shares; issued–none		
Common stock, $.01 par value; authorized–3.5 billion shares; issue	16.6	16.6
Additional paid-in capital	1,288.3	989.2
Unearned ESOP compensation	(133.3)	(148.7)
Retained earnings	15,562.8	13,879.6
Accumulated other comprehensive income	(886.8)	(522.5)
Common stock in treasury, at cost; 309.8 and 304.4 million shares	(6,208.5)	(4,749.5)
Total shareholders' equity	**9,639.1**	**9,464.7**
Total liabilities and shareholders' equity	**$20,983.2**	**$19,784.4**

EXHIBIT 3   SYSTEMWIDE SALES (IN MILLIONS)

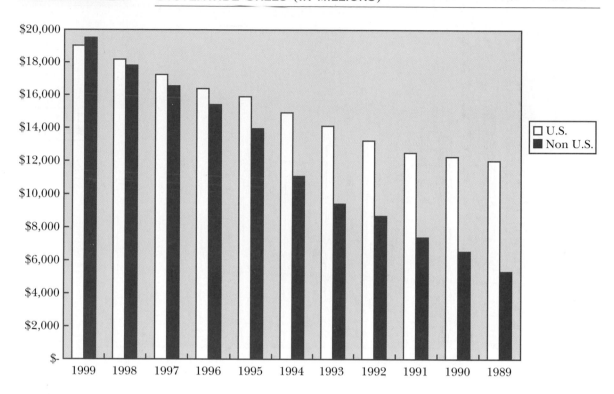

SOURCES: *McDonald's 1999 Online Annual Report*, p. 9; *McDonald's 1996 Annual Report*, p. 1.

Financial Information

Most aspects of McDonald's' consolidated statement of income (Exhibit 1) and consolidated balance sheet (Exhibit 2) reflect the company's growth. Total revenues in 1999 increased almost 7 percent and net income increased nearly 26 percent.

Sales increases in 1999 and 1998 were primarily due to restaurant expansion and positive comparable sales (Exhibit 3). In 1999, 1998, and 1997, more than 80 percent of systemwide sales were in the following eight markets: Australia, Brazil, Canada, France, Germany, Japan, the United Kingdom, and the United States. Systemwide sales in 1999 were affected less negatively by foreign currency translation than were revenues from the stronger Japanese yen and the company's affiliate structure in Japan.[7]

On a constant currency basis, total revenues increased at a higher rate than sales in 1999 and 1998 because of the higher unit growth rate of company-operated restaurants relative to systemwide restaurants. In both years this was primarily due to expansion in Europe and the consolidation of several affiliate markets because of an increase in ownership.[8]

Lackluster performance of the company's stock has done little to encourage dissatisfied Wall Street analysts. In falling to its lowest closing price since March 1998, the stock is down 34 percent for the year and has lost nearly half its value since reaching an all-time high of $49.56 November 1999.[9] Because McDonald's believes its

| EXHIBIT 4 | NUMBER OF SYSTEMWIDE RESTAURANTS |

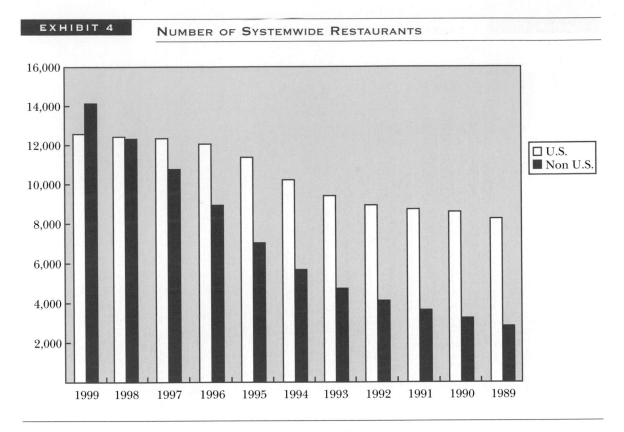

SOURCES: *McDonald's 1999 Online Annual Report*, p. 9; *McDonald's 1996 Annual Report*, p. 1.

stock is undervalued, it is using its substantial and growing free cash flow plus debt capacity to aggressively repurchase shares. In 1999 the company generated more than $1.1 billion in free cash flow, an increase of 29 percent over 1998. In April it increased its three-year share repurchase program by $1 billion, bringing it to $4.5 billion. The program is scheduled to be completed by the end of 2001.[10]

Historical Growth

The McDonald's strategy for growth focuses on three key elements: adding restaurants, maximizing sales and profits at existing restaurants, and improving international profitability. Adding restaurants can be achieved with people and capital resources. Maximizing sales and profits at existing restaurants can be accomplished through better operations, reinvestment, product development, effective marketing, and lower development costs. Improvement of international profitability can be realized as economies of scale are achieved in individual markets.[11]

In 1967, McDonald's moved into Canada and Puerto Rico, the first countries outside the United States to have a McDonald's franchise. McDonald's operated 12,629 restaurants in the United States in 1999, a growth of only 2 percent since 1997. In the same timeframe, restaurants in the international market increased nearly 32 percent to number 14,177 (Exhibit 4). This supports McDonald's' continued emphasis on traditional restaurants primarily in locations outside the United States.[12]

Franchise

The unprecedented growth of the McDonald's Corporation is largely due to its successful use of franchisee entrepreneurs to promote the McDonald's product. Approximately 80 percent of McDonald's' global restaurants are owned and operated by independent franchisees.[13] McDonald's is highly selective in choosing its franchisees and thoroughly trains them before they join the system. Before franchisees open their restaurant, they generally spend more than two years in training and work about 2000 uncompensated hours in a McDonald's restaurant.

A franchise arrangement in the United States is generally for a term of 20 years and requires a minimum of $175,000 of nonborrowed personal resources. McDonald's does not provide financing or loan guarantees. New franchisees enter the McDonald's system by acquiring a franchise for a new or existing restaurant. The purchase price of an existing restaurant is dependent upon a number of factors and is negotiated with the selling franchisee. For a new restaurant, typical preopening costs range from $432,800 to $715,150—60 percent of which may be financed from traditional sources. In a small number of cases, McDonald's sometimes grants a Business Facilities Lease (BFL) franchise to individuals who do not have sufficient capital, but who excel in all other criteria. Candidates for this program generally must have liquid assets of approximately $100,000.[14]

With limited exceptions, McDonald's does not supply food, paper, or equipment to any of its restaurants but approves suppliers from which franchised and company-operated restaurants can purchase these items. Franchisees are required to pay related occupancy costs, which include property taxes, insurance, maintenance, and a refundable, noninterest-bearing security deposit.[15]

Revenues from franchised restaurants are based on fees paid as a percent of sales, with specified minimum payments. Expenses associated with these restaurants are rent and depreciation, which are relatively fixed. Accordingly, the franchise margins are positively affected by increases in sales yet protected from rises in operating costs. Fees from franchises to McDonald's typically include rent and service fees. A monthly fee is based on the restaurant's sales performance (currently a service fee of 4 percent of monthly sales) plus the greater of (a) monthly base rent, or (b) percentage rent that is at least 8.5 percent of monthly sales.[16]

In the past, some domestic franchisee unrest has developed. In fact, some disgruntled franchisees have banded together in a loose organization called "The Consortium."[17] The primary source of dissension among franchisees is attributed to an aggressive growth strategy McDonald's decided to pursue in the early 1990s. The strategy involved adding more restaurants and taking on new franchise agreements, and it was successful in terms of domestic growth, but it angered existing franchisees as it cut into their margins.[18]

Product

McDonald's restaurants offer a substantially uniform menu consisting of hamburgers and cheeseburgers. The menu includes the Big Mac, Quarter Pounder with Cheese, the Big Xtra!, the Filet-O-Fish, several chicken sandwiches, french fries, Chicken McNuggets, salads, low-fat shakes, McFlurries, sundaes, cones, pies, cookies, and soft drinks, as well as other beverages. In addition, the restaurants sell a variety of products during limited promotional time periods. McDonald's restaurants operating in the United States and certain international markets are open during breakfast hours and offer a full or limited breakfast menu including the Egg McMuffin and the

Sausage McMuffin with Egg sandwiches; hotcakes and sausage; three varieties of biscuit sandwiches; bagel sandwiches; hashbrowns; and apple-bran muffins.[19] McDonald's restaurants in countries around the world offer many of these same products as well as other products and limited breakfast menus. The company tests new products on an ongoing basis.[20] Regardless, McDonald's has not had a successful new product introduction since the Chicken McNugget in 1983.

Competition

McDonald's restaurants compete with international, national, regional, and local retailers of food products. McDonald's competes on the basis of price, convenience, and service and by offering quality food products. McDonald's views its competition in the broadest perspectives: restaurants, quick-service eating establishments, pizza parlors, coffee shops, street vendors, convenience food stores, delicatessens, and supermarkets.

In the United States, the quick service restaurant business consists of about 465,000 restaurants that generate nearly $261 billion in annual sales. McDonald's accounts for about 2.7 percent of those restaurants and approximately 7.3 percent of those sales.[21] That leaves 92.7 percent, or nearly $242 billion, to competing restaurants. Competitors include, but are not limited to, Burger King, Wendy's, Hardees, Taco Bell, and KFC.[22]

Employees

Employees of eating and drinking establishments are paid considerably less than employees of any other nonagricultural industry. Most of the employees are students and other young people working for the first time. Wages in the fast-food industry in the United States are largely unaffected by collective bargaining or the threat of unionization.

The typical McDonald's restaurant does $1.6 million in sales a year. According to Alan Feldman, president of McDonald's USA, the chain's stores are better staffed, with the average crew size up to 44 from 40.[23] During 1999 the company's average number of employees worldwide, including company-operated restaurant employees, was approximately 314,000.[24] Currently, the minimum wage is $5.15 an hour, but bills to raise it to $6.15 are pending in Congress.[25] Nevertheless, McDonald's pays its employees what the market will bear, and it pays better than minimum wage.[26]

Executives, staff, and restaurant managers participate in profit-sharing contributions and shares released under the leveraged employee stock ownership program, based on their compensation.[27]

McDonald's' employee strategy hinges on its ability to infuse every store with its gung-ho culture and standardized procedures. Every job is broken down into the smallest of steps, and the whole process is automated. So rule bound is McDonald's that one sociologist claimed jobs in its restaurants are unfit for young people. "These are breeding grounds for robots working for yesterday's assembly lines, not tomorrow's high-tech posts," contends Professor Anitai Ezioni of George Washington University.[28]

Agency Costs

One relevant market parameter that can make agency costs high is the physical dispersion of operations. Franchising avoids the monitoring costs of specialization because the local manager is now an investor whose wealth is strongly dependent on the performance of her or his local unit, thus making franchising more common with physically dispersed operations, as in rural areas. Also, for a given level of output, monitoring costs will rise with an increasing labor/output ratio. The use of local managers who make heavy site-specific investments and post a large bond in the form of a franchise fee makes quality debasing less likely because a franchisee has much more to lose upon termination than a local employee-manager.[29]

Turnover

McDonald's finds a strong link between the quality of its labor force at the store level and the sales of a given restaurant. A key priority for the chain has been reducing restaurant-level employee turnover. According to Feldman, current turnover is about 130 to 135 percent, down from a peak of 170 percent about five years ago.[30] Periodically placemats used on trays are employment applications—every customer is a potential employee!

Overall Corporate Strategy

McDonald's is the largest food service organization in the world, with nearly 27,000 stores. Its goal has been to provide the highest quality products and friendly service in clean restaurants at good values (Q.S.C. & V.). Internationally, its strategies are to provide 100 percent customer satisfaction, increase market share, and optimize profitability by reducing costs.[31] Its vision is to be the world's best quick service restaurant experience. To achieve this vision, McDonald's is focused on three worldwide strategies: (1) To be the best employer for its people in each community around the world, (2) to deliver operational excellence to its customers in each of its restaurants, and (3) to achieve enduring profitable growth by expanding the brand and leveraging the strengths of the McDonald's system through innovation and technology.[32] In 2000, McDonald's added about 1,800 restaurants worldwide, with about 200 new restaurants in the United States.[33] To meet this goal, McDonald's' current strategies have focused on the following factors.

Customer Satisfaction

McDonald's was founded on the principle of uniformity. An operations manual of 600 pages ensured the consistency and quality of products served by McDonald's. Although this strategy worked well in the past, customers are now demanding more than consistency. In response to the changing market, McDonald's has taken a "do whatever it takes to make a customer happy"[34] strategy and has given its employees, managers, and stores the flexibility to carry out this new strategy.

Healthier Foods Customers are demanding that restaurants provide healthier foods. McDonald's has heard their cry, and it has changed the way foods are prepared: hamburgers are made with lean ground beef and enriched sandwich buns; french fries and hash browns are fried in 100 percent vegetable oil; milkshakes are made with 1 percent low-fat milk; and the amount of sodium used has been decreased. It has also added more nutritious foods to the menu: low-fat apple-bran muffins, fresh fruit and vegetables, and low-fat frozen yogurt. As one advertisement stated, "McDonald's is committed to making sure that when you've got an appetite for healthy food [McDonald's will] always have the choices to satisfy you."[35]

Food Quality and Nutrition The safety and quality of McDonald's food is maintained through a combination of stringent product standards, strict enforcement of operating procedures, and close working relationships with suppliers. Specifications for both raw and cooked product quality are established and enforced by the quality assurance labs in the United States, Europe, and Asia/Pacific. This quality assurance process involves ongoing testing and thorough on-site inspections of suppliers' facilities. Food preparation is also closely monitored, as well as cooking and equipment maintenance and procedures.[36]

Last year, the new Made For You food preparation system was installed in virtually all restaurants in the United States and Canada.[37] It is expected to improve food taste and quality by enabling McDonald's to deliver hot, fresh, made-to-order sandwiches.[38] Through advances in equipment and technology, the new system allows the restaurants to serve fresher, better-tasting food at the customary speed for which McDonald's is known. The system also supports future growth through product development because it can more easily accommodate an expanded menu.[39]

McDonald's has nutritional information on products available to customers so that they can make informed decisions about how McDonald's can be part of a healthy, well-balanced diet. Posters are displayed with complete nutritional and ingredient information in U.S. and international restaurants. In addition, this information is available for standard U.S. menu items, as well as new items, on the McDonald's Web site at **www.mcdonalds.com**.

McDonald's also takes it upon itself to educate healthcare professionals about the menu through advertising, convention exhibits, and patient education materials. Efforts like these have led to partnership programs with leading health associations, including the American Dietetic Association for the Food FUNdamentals Happy Meal, and "What's on Your Plate?"—a nutrition education program for children established through the Society for Nutrition Education.[40]

Larger Menus   In addition to healthy foods, customers want more choices. In response, McDonald's added a breakfast menu that includes eggs, sausage, biscuits, ham, danishes, and hot cakes. Other items, such as chicken sandwiches, Chicken McNuggets, and salads, have also been added. The latest menu items to be added include The Big Xtra!, Chicken McGrill, Crispy Chicken, McSalad Shakers, Breakfast Bagels, and Fruit 'n Yogurt Parfaits.

Restaurant Diversity   When Ray Kroc was CEO of McDonald's, each restaurant looked the same and served the same food. He wanted products to look and taste the same no matter where the customer was. In the 1990s, the customer wanted more than just fast food. McDonald's' management recognized these changes and allowed individual stores to experiment with their formats. The new store formats include self-service stores, drive-through only stores, cafes, and customized outlets. The utilization of these small, often limited-menu "satellite" restaurants has allowed profitable expansion into areas that would otherwise not have been feasible.[41] Generally, satellites are opened in Wal-Marts, Home Depots, service stations, and other nontraditional locations. At the end of 1999, satellite units numbered 3244.[42] The company recently stated that greater emphasis will be placed on the growth of traditional restaurants primarily in locations outside the United States.[43] Flexibility also exists in selecting menu items. Stores no longer have to carry a standard menu. Franchisees can experiment with new items and alter the menu to conform to regional and ethnic tastes.

Kids

According to projections, the U.S. population in the 5- to 13-year-old age group is expected to grow through the year 2002.[44] In response to the growing influence children have on family dining decisions, McDonald's has targeted them with nonfood-related products. For example, it has installed playlands at its stores and marketed

McDonald's clothes and toys. In the past decade the company even started a venture called Leaps & Bounds, a chain of play centers that allowed parents and children to play together, but it was ultimately sold to Discovery Zone. In addition, after witnessing rival Burger King lure kids with product tie-ins from blockbuster movies such as *The Lion King* and *Toy Story*, McDonald's entered into a ten-year joint-marketing alliance with Disney. The agreement has also resulted in the building of Ronald's Fun House at Walt Disney World in Florida and the operating of restaurants at Disney theme parks (Disney employees already sell McDonald's french fries at Walt Disney World).[45] McDonald's admits that kids are key to its business and hopes that these strategies will make children think of McDonald's when it is time to eat.

Untapped Markets

According to Jack Greenberg, McDonald's Chairman and Chief Executive Officer, even though McDonald's now serves 43 million people a day, the numbers are not big enough. In the vernacular of McDonald's, there are 18 billion "meal opportunities" a day worldwide. Greenberg states that if McDonald's could obtain just 1 percent of that, the company could triple its sales. In order to achieve that kind of growth, the company is extending beyond its core hamburger business, as well as focusing on international expansion.

Diversification   Having hit a ceiling in the hamburger-saturated United States, the maker of Big Macs has no choice but to diversify.[46] Recently, McDonald's began a series of acquisitions. Now the company operates several restaurant concepts: Aroma Café, a small chain of coffeehouses serving prepared sandwiches and pastries in the United Kingdom; Chipotle Mexican Grill, a fresh-mex grill located in the United States serving gourmet burritos and tacos; and Donatos Pizza, a restaurant business located in the United States that sells pizza, subs, and salads.[47] In May 2000, the company also welcomed Boston Market, a U.S. chain specializing in fresh, convenient meals, featuring homestyle entrees, fresh vegetables, sandwiches, salads, and side dishes, to the "McFamily."

McDonald's' nonhamburger brands still represent just a fraction of the company's business, accounting for $91 million of its $38.5 billion in systemwide sales last year.[48] The McDonald's brand offers enormous long-term opportunity, and the company believes it can leverage its competencies to add value to these concepts and potentially grow them into major brands.[49] There is little doubt that McDonald's will use its considerable operations expertise to impose the same standards of consistency it maintains with its hamburger restaurants.[50] Clearly, McDonald's is hoping that these smaller chains jump-start its domestic revenues, boost dinner sales, and offer franchisees new growth options.

International   Systemwide, 1790 McDonald's restaurants were added in 1999, with more than 90 percent of them outside the United States.[51] In 2000 the company added about 1800 restaurants, with only about 200 of those in the United States.

In 1999 international systemwide sales posted a 9 percent gain, following an 8 percent increase in 1998. In addition, last year the international segment comprised 51 percent of systemwide sales and 55 percent of operating income. International growth is expected to continue because McDonald's, which currently operates in 119 countries, added about 650 stores in Asia/Pacific, 550 in Europe, and 350 in Latin America in the year 2000 alone and plans to add more during 2001.

EXHIBIT 5   CONTROVERSY SIZZLES IN BRAZIL

On June 30, 2000, McDonald's Corporation reached a milestone as it proudly opened its 500th restaurant in Brazil. Because of the company's recent astounding growth in the Latin American country, Brazil has become McDonald's eighth-largest market while McDonald's has become Brazil's third-largest corporate employer with 34,800 employees. This is all part of McDonald's carefully planned expansion strategy to double the number of its Brazilian restaurants by 2003.

McDonald's brisk growth in Brazil is not met without controversy, however. Its aggressive tactics have created both disgruntled franchisees and unhappy employees in Brazil. The sources of contention for a group of franchisees are the chain's fast rate of growth—which was meant to preempt competitors—and the high rental fees the chain charges for their restaurants. Consequently, these franchisees have taken McDonald's to court. Apparently, at the very core of their lawsuit are the rental fees, which average 17 percent of sales in Brazil but only 8.5 percent of sales in the United States.

Meanwhile, some employees have been so dissatisfied with their short work hours that many cooks and counter clerks have filed complaints, prompting an investigation by the Sao Paulo Labor Ministry into McDonald's labor practices. These employees actually want to work longer and more regular hours, but this interferes with the company's global practice of tailoring work shifts around its peak business hours. Therefore, for efficiency, McDonald's employs some staff for as little as eight hours a week.

The outcomes of these challenges are uncertain, especially in lieu of Latin American law, which is often considered antiquated and vague. McDonald's does not apologize for its strong growth strategy, and it insists that it will not change its work-shift scheduling system. McDonald's has been in Brazil for 21 years, enduring the high inflation of the Brazilian economy and watching other fast-food businesses come and go; it is accustomed to hanging tough.

McDonald's Restaurants
In Selected Cities

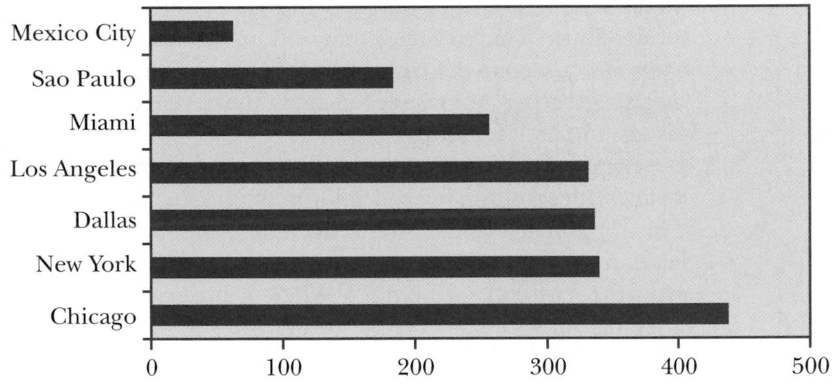

SOURCE: Miriam Jordan, "McDonald's Strikes Sparks With Fast Growth in Brazil," *The Wall Street Journal*, October 4, 2000, p. A23.

Social Responsibility

McDonald's' annual report states that "being a good corporate citizen means treating people with fairness and integrity, and sharing success with the communities in which we do business."[52] Because of this, McDonald's' overall corporate strategy includes many charitable programs.

Healthy Growing Up—A program designed to encourage students from kindergarten through third grade to adopt lifelong habits of good nutrition, exercise, and positive self-esteem, approved by the President's Council on Physical Fitness & Sports.[53]

Book Some Time Together—McDonald's partnered with the American Library Association to encourage families to read together through their local libraries.[54]

Cartoon All-Stars to the Rescue—McDonald's sponsored this animated, anti-substance abuse television special, which was broadcast on every major network in North America.[55]

Education   Supporting and providing education is one way McDonald's helps society. McDonald's is committed to making the work in the restaurant part of the learning process by teaching self-confidence, self-esteem, responsibility, people skills, and time and money management. McDonald's Education Department also works with educators, schools, and its franchises and employees to coordinate the company's diverse educational initiatives. McDonald's has developed a comprehensive variety of educational curriculum and programs for students at all levels. The topics range from environmental awareness, nutrition, and fitness to stay-in-school and drug prevention programs. Some of the programs that educators and students participate in include Black History Makers of Tomorrow, the Ray A. Kroc Youth Achievement Award, and the McDonald's Education Award.

McDonald's' commitment to the responsible student employee consists of balancing part-time work with school by over-complying with minor labor laws, recognizing scholastic achievement, and assisting employees in pursuing their education through book/tuition reimbursement programs and local scholarships.[56] In addition to sponsoring events that encourage and recognize achievement, it has created five programs designed to further education. Two of the programs, "When I Grow Up" and "Stay in School" focus on the importance of education, whereas the "It's Our Business" program teaches economic principles to students in grades 7 through 10 and the "Hispanic American Commitment to Education Resources" program provides college scholarships. McDonald's Crew College Education program also provides financial aid grants through an agreement with the United Negro College Fund to promote higher education.[57]

Equal Opportunity   Equal opportunity is also an ideal supported by McDonald's. McJobs, McMasters, and affirmative action programs are aimed at ensuring full and equal participation by all members in society.[58]

Equal opportunity is a major issue in today's business world. McDonald's has made it a point to attract and retain a diversified workforce.[59] McDonald's has been listed as one of *The Top Companies for Minorities to Work*.[60] McDonald's has also received awards for fostering leadership development of women.[61] In the United States, minorities and women currently represent more than 34 percent of franchisees and 70 percent of the applicants in training to become franchisees.[62] Furthermore, in 1999, McDonald's purchased about $3 billion worth of goods and services from women and minority suppliers.[63]

Children's Charities   McDonald's is "dedicated to helping children achieve their fullest potential."[64] The Ronald McDonald Charities provide grants to programs that support education, drug awareness, health care, medical research, and rehabilitation.

To help families of seriously ill children, the Ronald McDonald House program provides a place for families to stay while their children are hospitalized. The Ronald McDonald House program serves some 4000 family members every night.[65] At year-end 1999, there were more than 200 houses in 19 countries.[66]

Environment   Environmental issues have taken a prominent place in today's society, and McDonald's is doing what it can to make the world a better place to live. Ten years ago, McDonald's began a groundbreaking alliance with the Environmental Defense Fund (EDF) to reduce, reuse, and recycle. Since then, it has eliminated 150,000 tons of packaging, purchased more than $3 billion of recycled products, and recycled more than 1 million tons of corrugated cardboard in the United States.[67] Furthermore, McDonald's joined the Paper Task Force to develop recommendations for increasing the use of environmentally preferable paperboard products. It is also working with local communities and teachers in schools by providing educational materials to promote sound environmental practices and values.[68] McDonald's has even established the McDonald's All-Star Green Teens award, which recognizes and rewards high-school students who have demonstrated exceptional environmental leadership.[69] McDonald's' environmental concerns also extend to the conservation of natural resources, protection of the tropical rain forests, preservation of clean air, humane treatment of animals, and the pioneering of a smoke-free atmosphere.[70]

Human Resource Strategy

Managing Diversity/Labor Shortage

The economic expansion of the last decade has resulted in the lowest U.S. unemployment rate (4 percent in June 2000) in more than a generation. The labor market has become tighter at a time when the growth in the labor pool has slowed considerably. Well known is the foodservice industry's growing need for workers. One prediction is that by the year 2006, the restaurant industry is projected to need an additional 2 million individuals to round out its ranks.[71] In fact, franchise owners are already going to extraordinary new lengths to find workers.[72] Another prediction is that the majority of the new entrants to the workforce will be minorities, elderly, and women. The buzz word for recruiting, training, and retaining this new rainbow coalition of human resources is "managing diversity." In recognition of the changing demographics and the shrinking labor force, McDonald's has created programs to deal with employee diversity.

In addition to billions of hamburgers every year, McDonald's is serving up employment opportunities to two growing segments of the workforce: the disabled and the elderly. The McDonald's corporate identification is strategically named in these employment programs, which are known as McJobs and McMasters.

At sites across the country, more than 9000 mentally and physically disabled people between the ages of 16 and 60 have graduated from the McJobs program and have begun work at McDonald's restaurants.[73] Specially selected and trained managers serve as job coaches and work closely with local vocational rehabilitation agencies to monitor each candidate's progress. Job coaches work one-on-one with four or five candidates at a time. Each receives standard McDonald's training—classroom instruction, demonstration, and supervised practice at various job stations.[74]

McMasters is a nationwide program that identifies, recruits, trains, and retains workers who are 55 years of age and older. It also features job coaches, who function in much the same manner as the coaches in McJobs, as well as a referral program that alerts older workers to the opportunities at McDonald's. Workers hired through McDonald's' referral program are immediately teamed up with a "partner"—an experienced worker who helps the team member through the initial training. McDonald's is looking specifically to increase the share of older workers in its company-owned restaurants. Right now, about 7 percent, or three workers per restaurant, are 60 or older.[75]

The corporation offers its managers solid diversity training, including a workshop designed to help managers deal with older workers, minorities, and the mentally and physically handicapped. "We believe that management must understand what diversity is, and how it works to the company's and the individual's advantage," said Monica Boyles, past director of McDonald's Changing Workforce program. She adds the following:

> Not only do we want a representative workforce, but we want to clearly empower cultural differences so that we have full advantage of what everybody brings; we want to ensure that people at all levels of McDonald's are free to be themselves and to bring their energy and creativity into the work environment.[76]

In addition, McDonald's offers career-development programs designed for various minority groups and training for managers that identifies diversity from a value-added perspective. As a result of their programs, more than half of the top managers at restaurants owned by McDonald's are women and minorities.[77]

Training

Today, more than 65,000 managers in McDonald's restaurants have graduated with a degree in hamburgerology from Hamburger University, Oak Brook, Illinois.[78] Hamburger U. is now located in a 130,000-square-foot state-of-the-art facility on the McDonald's Home Office Campus. All of the company's managers and franchise holders must attend. In fact, H.U. teaches about 7000 students a year.[79] Formal classroom sessions are provided in which participants learn management skills, market evaluation, financial budgets, and the reinforcement of Ray Kroc's philosophy of Q.S.C. & V. A two-week curriculum covers four major areas: equipment, operations, human relations skills, and interpersonal/communication skills.[80]

Training for employees begins with in-store videotapes and one-on-one instruction "even before the crew member cooks their first french fry."[81] "The book" at McDonald's—the company's policies and procedures manual—spells out the precise details at each station in the restaurant. "Cooks must turn, never flip, hamburgers one, never two, at a time." Or, "If they haven't been purchased, Big Macs must be discarded ten minutes after being cooked and french fries in seven."

The company aims to build its reputation as a premier training organization by creating an environment that encourages career-long training. It is rolling out a new crew and restaurant management curriculum worldwide and redoubling the emphasis on coaching and training.[82] Training programs are always being refined and updated to provide the crew with the tools needed to handle the challenges of operating a McDonald's restaurant.[83] McDonald's has also added a class to its career-development program designed to build leadership and communication skills. Training competencies extend to McDonald's Quality Management (MQM) programs, whereby quality tools such as long-range planning, process reengineering, benchmarking, and continuous improvement are taught.[84]

Careers: The Golden Opportunity Under the Arches

McDonald's is not only the biggest fast-food restaurant chain in America; it is also the nation's largest youth employer. "Its impact on the U.S. workforce greatly exceeds its current employment, because it trains so many high school students for their first jobs."[85] In fact, about one eighth of the current American workforce has worked at McDonald's.[86]

Every new employee begins as a trainee on the easiest of jobs—cooking french fries. Once that station is perfected, an employee moves to the next designated station, and so on. McDonald's functions as a de facto job-training program by teaching youth discipline and the basics of how to work.[87] For workers who show initiative, McDonald's offers opportunities for quick advancement. An employee can work his or her way up to "crew chief" where he or she can manage an entire operation and its crew.

The youth will continue to work as crew chief—given that the annual turn-over rate is more than 100 percent—until promotion to a manager. McDonald's has a long tradition of promoting from within on the basis of skill and hustle, not academic credentials.[88] More than half of its corporate executives never graduated from college. This fits right into the philosophy of Ray Kroc on what education should be:

> Career education, that's what this country needs. Many young people emerge from college unprepared to hold down a steady job or to cook or do housework and it makes them depressed. No wonder! They should train for a career, learn how to support themselves and how to enjoy work first. Then if they have a thirst for advanced learning, they can go to night school.[89]

The possibilities for advancing to corporate headquarters are also attainable. More than half of McDonald's' top corporate management started out as crew members. However, the organizational chart is flat for being one of the nation's biggest employers. As Kroc stated, "I believe that *less is more* in the case of corporate management; for its size, McDonald's is the most unstructured corporation I know and I don't think you could find a happier, more secure, harder working group of executives anywhere."[90]

Lately, however, some 500 positions at the home office proved to be not that secure after all. At the end of 1999, McDonald's completed a large productivity initiative which reorganized its home office. The productivity plan was designed to improve staff alignment, focus, and productivity, as well as reduce ongoing selling, general, and administrative expenses. As a result, the company reduced home office staffing and restructured the organization to decentralize many core functions.[91] The franchisees were unhappy with the previous structure and pressured the home office to make these changes. Now McDonald's is hoping to capitalize on a more decentralized, entrepreneurial style.

McDonald's' corporate management does have its critics. Many companies, including IBM and AT&T, have brought in outside managerial talent to cope with the changing marketplace, whereas McDonald's continues to look inward to its "McFamily" for leadership. The McDonald's board is also a tribute to company loyalty, because only about one third of the members are independent, meaning they do not work for McDonald's, do outside business with the company, nor have a McDonald's executive on their own board. The insular nature of McDonald's' board is unusual for such a large company, especially when viewed in light of the evolution of corporate-governance standards during the past decade. Most companies of McDonald's' size have a majority of board of directors who are independent. In fact, nearly every company that produces a strong brand identity will have the majority of its directors as independent.[92]

Benefits

One of the increasing concerns of McDonald's is matching and effectively communicating corporate benefits to all segments of its increasingly diverse workforce. The main emphasis is good communication about the benefits plan itself.

McDonald's, which self-insures its benefits programs, provides health insurance to its full-time employees in the United States. These include the employees of company-owned restaurants, regional offices, and the corporate headquarters.

Benefit Communication Planning Teams are established to reflect the employment demographics: an exceptionally young workforce with the average age being in the low 30s, few employees above the age of 65, large employment of minorities, and a domination of women in management. The teams are also designed to include a variety of people from various corporate departments to ensure a diverse representation. These teams simplify and streamline materials to improve communication with the diverse workforce.

The accomplishments of the Benefit Communication Planning Team include:

- Plastic insurance cards with a magnetic strip to automatically bill for prescriptions.
- Coworker communication programs, which allow a group of trained employees to explain the program to other workers.

The McDonald's benefit plan also emphasizes the concept of simplicity. Mike Quinlan, McDonald's' previous chairman and CEO, simplified health plan enrollment by including a chart in the benefits package that outlines which of the medical plans would be most cost effective for an individual or a family based on anticipated future medical costs. The plans differ only in deductible and coinsurance requirements, and McDonald's pays 80 percent of the premium.

Simplicity has also affected written benefit materials. McDonald's provides Spanish-speaking language materials; Spanish-speaking representatives to answer questions about the plan; and interactive communication, including telephone enrollment, slide shows, and videos.

Profit Sharing   The company's program for U.S. employees includes profit sharing, 401(k), McDonald's Employee Stock Ownership Plan (McDESOP), and leveraged employee stock ownership (ESOP) features.[93] McDESOP allows participants to make contributions that are partly matched from shares released under ESOP. Certain foreign subsidiaries also offer profit sharing, stock purchase, or other similar benefit plans.

Preferred Provider Organization (PPO)[94]   PPO applies to all full-time staff and store management selecting McDonald's medical coverage. PPO is a network of hospitals across the United States that provides quality care and a discount to McDonald's employees who use these facilities for either inpatient or outpatient services.

Educational Assistance Program[95]   McDonald's supports the educational objectives of its employees and offers a job-related education assistance program (EAP). Eligible employees (store management and its assistants with at least six months of service) will be reimbursed for 75 percent of their course fees to a maximum of $400 per course (two courses per semester). Home office approval is required.

Sabbaticals[96]   McDonald's believes that sabbaticals are the best way to replenish its employees' energy. After ten years of service, workers are eligible for a sabbatical leave program acknowledging "the need to nurture individuals within a corporate culture dedicated, in part, to mass-producing an identical, high-quality product and service."[97]

Child Care[98]   McDonald's makes available to all employees, through Kinder Care and La Petite Academy, a tuition discount for child care.

Accomplishments

Domination of the Industry

McDonald's corporation operates, licenses, and services the world's largest chain of fast-food restaurants and competes with virtually all restaurants (as well as with food stores on certain items). McDonald's corporation has broadened its menu over the years to compete, to some extent, in virtually all areas. Although McDonald's' market share within the quick serve restaurant business in the United States is about 7.3 percent, it remains king of the fast-food burger segment with 43.1 percent of the market.[99] Hence, it appears that the company has room to grow from its current base, although it may need to do so in the nonburger fast-food market.[100]

Growth

In recent years, domestic growth has slowed as a result of market saturation. Transactions and sales have been described as sluggish. Same-store sales in the United States have grown only about 1 percent annually in recent years. However, Greenberg commented recently that in the first six months of 2000, McDonald's' global food service business delivered good results: systemwide sales increased 7 percent and revenues increased 10 percent. On a global basis the increases in sales and revenues were due to expansion and positive comparable sales. Foreign currency translation had a negative effect on the growth rates for both systemwide sales and revenues for the six months. For the same time period, U.S. sales increased 3 percent because of restaurant expansion and positive comparable sales.[101]

For the company as a whole, McDonald's said sales at its restaurants worldwide rose 4.5 percent in August 2000 to $3.6 billion, led by sales in the United States and Canada, as well as sales at such nonhamburger chains as Boston Market, Donatos Pizza, and Chipotle Mexican Grill. For the same time period, U.S. sales rose as much as 2 percent. In the year 2000, sales at all U.S. McDonald's rose just 3 percent and were unchanged in Europe from 1999.[102]

International Sector

Since the first international restaurant opened in Canada in 1967, McDonald's restaurants have expanded throughout the globe. Between 1994 and 1999, the number of McDonald's international restaurants has more than doubled. By December 31, 1999, there were 14,177 units in foreign countries, mostly in Japan, Canada, Germany, the United Kingdom, France, Australia, and Brazil.[103]

Because it presents the most growth potential, the international market is being emphasized to address the sluggish sales problem. McDonald's opened 1831 restaurants outside the United States during 1999, and about the same number in the year 2000. Record first-day sales are common for restaurants located outside the United States. Around 30,000 customers visited McDonald's in Moscow on its first day of operation, and even more waited to try their first taste of McDonald's when it opened in Shenzhen, China.[104] In 1999, international operations accounted for 62 percent of

McDonald's systemwide revenues, 55 percent of operating income, and 58 percent of income before provision for income taxes. In fact, sales for 1999 surpassed those of the much larger U.S. restaurant system.

With operations in 119 countries, McDonald's has considerable profit growth potential in the international sector. Its biggest market outside the United States is Japan, which now has more than 3000 outlets. Germany and Britain follow with more than 1000 apiece. Already, McDonald's' market share outside the United States is as big as all of its competitors combined. Recently, however, McDonald's acknowledged that a strong dollar compared with local currencies, especially Europe's common currency, the Euro, as well as rising fuel costs, would cut into profits more than previously expected. In addition, on the basis of stores open at least one year, analysts estimated that August sales at McDonald's overseas fell 1 percent. McDonald's said European sales fell 4.1 percent while its operations in Asia-Pacific and Latin America gained.[105]

The impact of currency fluctuations and unfavorable currency translations—concerns for any global enterprise—will continue to be growing concerns as McDonald's increases its dependence on the income from international operations. In addition, analysts are worried about political instability in some countries.

Questions

1. Discuss the inherent conflicts that exist between McDonald's' company philosophy and its reformed organizational structure.
2. As McDonald's continues to expand internationally, discuss the many human resource issues that may arise and how the company may manage differences in culture.

Notes

[1]Shelly Branch, "What's Eating McDonald's," *Fortune*, October 13, 1997, p. 84.
[2]David Leonhardt, "McDonald's, Can It Regain Its Golden Touch?" *Business Week*, March 9, 1997, p. 71.
[3]**www.mcdonalds.com/corporate** (accessed December 31, 2000).
[4]"The McDonald's Franchise," Brochure, June 10, 1994.
[5]Ibid.
[6]"McDonald's Franchising," The McDonald's Corporation 65-1555/McD 19373 2/94, p. 2.
[7]*McDonald's 1999 Online Annual Report*, p. 9.
[8]Ibid., p. 10.
[9]Dave Carpenter, "McDonald's Shares Fall on Currency Worries," *The Associated Press State and Local Wire*, September 15, 2000.
[10]**www.mcdonalds.com/corporate**.
[11]*McDonald's 1990 Annual Report*.
[12]*McDonald's 1999 Online Annual Report*, p. 13.
[13]**www.mcdonalds.com/corporate**.
[14]**www.mcdonalds.com/countries**.
[15]*McDonald's 1993 Annual Report*, p. 46.
[16]**www.mcdonalds.com**.
[17]Leonhardt, "McDonald's, Can It Regain Its Golden Touch?" p. 76.
[18]Ibid., p. 74.
[19]*McDonald's On-line Form 10-K*, 2000, p. 4.
[20]*McDonald's Form 10-K*. 1993, p. 2.

[21]*McDonald's On-line Form 10-K*, 2000, p. 6.

[22]*McDonald's Form 10-K*, 1996, p. 5.

[23]Amy Zuber, "McDonald's Is Sweet on Reinvention," *Nation's Restaurant News*, July 17, 2000, p. 1.

[24]*McDonald's Online Form 10-K*, 2000, p. 6.

[25]Noshua Watson, "Scarce Labor: Then and Now," *Fortune*, May 15, 2000, p. 496+.

[26]Bob Lewis, "IS Survival Guide: Even Those in IS Who Hate McDonald's Can Learn Some Good Lessons From It," *Info World*, September 20, 1999, p. 84.

[27]*McDonald's Online Form 10-K*, 2000, p. 61.

[28]Kathleen Deveney, "McWorld?" *Business Week*, October 13, 1986, pp. 78–86.

[29]Seth W. Norton, "Empirical Look at Franchising as an Organization Form," *The Journal of Business* 61 (April 1988), pp. 197–218.

[30]Zuber, "McDonald's Is Sweet on Reinvention," p. 1.

[31]**www.mcdonalds.com/corporate**.

[32]Ibid.

[33]Ibid.

[34]Lois Therrien, "McRisky," *Business Week*, October 19, 1991, p. 117.

[35]"McDonald's at the Crossroads," *Time*, September 9, 1991, pp. 38–39.

[36]*McDonald's 1993 Annual Report*, pp. 8–9.

[37]*McDonald's 1999 Online Annual Report*, p. 12.

[38]**www.mcdonalds.com/corporate**.

[39]*McDonald's 1999 Online Annual Report*, p. 12.

[40]*McDonald's 1993 Annual Report*, pp. 8–9.

[41]*McDonald's 1999 Online Annual Report*, p. 10.

[42]*McDonald's On-line Form 10-K*, 2000, p. 28.

[43]*McDonald's 1999 Online Annual Report*, p. 13.

[44]**www.census.gov** (accessed December 31, 2000).

[45]Richard Gibson and Bruce Orwall, "New Mission for Mickey Mouse, Mickey D," *The Wall Street Journal Interactive Edition*, January 23, 1998.

[46]Deborah L. Cohen, "McDonald's is Going to Market: Must Use Locations to Spur Growth," *Crain's Chicago Business*, December 6, 1999, p. 4.

[47]*McDonald's Online Form 10-K*, 2000, p. 3.

[48]Alby F. Gallun, "McDonald's Faces a Tricky Menu of Options; Non-burger Biz Could Burn Franchisees," *Crain's Chicago Business*, July 31, 2000, p. 3.

[49]**www.mcdonalds.com/corporate**.

[50]Cohen, "McDonald's is Going to Market: Must Use Locations to Spur Growth," p. 4.

[51]*McDonald's 1999 Online Annual Report*, p. 1.

[52]*McDonald's 1990 Annual Report*.

[53]"Welcome to McDonald's," Brochure, 1998, p. 43.

[54]*McDonald's Student Packet 1993*, MCD1-1274, pp. 9–10.

[55]Ibid.

[56]"McDonald's Commitment to Education," Pamphlet, MCD1-1332.

[57]Ibid.

[58]These programs are discussed in further detail in the "Human Resources" section of the case.

[59]*McDonald's 1993 Annual Report*, p. 13.

[60]Ibid.

[61]Ibid.

[62]**www.mcdonalds.com/corporate**.

[63]*McDonald's 1999 Online Annual Report*, p. 6.

[64]*McDonald's 1990 Annual Report*, p. 18.

[65]"Welcome to McDonald's," Brochure, 1998, p. 41.

[66]*McDonald's 1999 Online Annual Report*, p. 6.

[67]Ibid.

[68]"McDonald's Commitment to the Environment," Pamphlet, 1994, McDonald's Corporation, MCD-4/94.

[69]*McDonald's Student Packet*, 1994, McDonald's Corporation, MCD 1-1274.

[70]*McDonald's 1993 Annual Report*, p. 13.

[71]"From Beginning to End, Foodservice Industry Offers Students a Career Path, Not Just a Job," *Nation's Restaurant News*, March 15, 1999, p. 35.

[72]Dan Morse, "Labor Shortage Has Franchisees Hustling for Workers," *The Wall Street Journal*, August 22, 2000, p. B2.

[73]*McDonald's Student Packet*, 1994, McDonald's Corporation, MCD 19169-4/94.

[74]Jennifer J. Laabs, "The Golden Arches Provide Golden Opportunities," *Personnel Journal*, July 1991, pp. 52–57.

[75]Fred Brock, "Seniority; The Labor Shortage: Color it Gray," *The New York Times*, February 6, 2000, p. 14.

[76]Telephone interview with Monica Boyles, past director of McDonald's Changing World Force Program.

[77]Laabs, "The Golden Arches Provide Golden Opportunities," pp. 52–57.

[78]**www.mcdonalds.com/corporate**.

[79]"The Burger King," *The Economist*, October 23, 1999.

[80]*McDonald's 1993 Annual Report*, p. 9.

[81]*McDonald's 1990 Annual Report*.

[82]*McDonald's Annual Shareholders Meeting*, May 18, 2000.

[83]Ray Kroc, *Grinding It Out: The Making of McDonald's* (Chicago: Contemporary Books, 1977).

[84]*McDonald's 1993 Annual Report*, p. 9.

[85]John F. Love, *McDonald's: Behind the Arches* (Toronto: Bantam Books, 1986).

[86]"Welcome to McDonald's," Brochure, 1998, p. 23.

[87]Marcus Mabry, "Inside the Golden Arches," *Newsweek*, December 18, 1989, pp. 46–47.

[88]Ibid.

[89]Kroc, *Grinding It Out: The Making of McDonald's*.

[90]Ibid.

[91]*McDonald's 1999 Online Annual Report*, p. 12.

[92]Leonhardt, "McDonald's, Can It Regain Its Golden Touch?" p. 72.

[93]Deborah Shalowitz-Cowans, "Expanding the Menu: Broadened Efforts Help McDonald's Explain Benefits," *Business Insurance*, May 9, 1994, p. 3.

[94]Ibid.

[95]Ibid.

[96]Ibid.

[97]Ibid.

[98]Ibid.

[99]Elaine Walker, "Miami-Based Burger King to Face Challenges, Benefits as a Public Company," *The Miami Herald*, June 24, 2000.

[100]*McDonald's Form 10-K*, 1996.

[101]"McDonald's Reports Global Results," *PR Newswire*, July 25, 2000.

[102]Judith Schoolman, "Overseas Woes Eating Away at Gains in McDonald's U.S. Sales," *Daily News*, September 15, 2000, p. 47.

[103]*McDonald's Online Form 10-K*, 2000, p. 28.

[104]Gibson, "McDonald's Quarterly Earnings Fall Short of Analysts' Forecasts," January 23, 1998.

[105]Schoolman, "Overseas Woes Eating Away at Gains in McDonald's U.S. Sales," p. 47.

4

The Walt Disney Company*

Introduction

Overview of the Company

The Walt Disney Company has become one of the most recognized organizations in the world. The company is spirited by the success of its theme parks, resort hotels, consumer goods, and movies. Even those who have not visited one of Disney's many theme parks or resorts, nor seen a Disney movie, have certainly seen or heard about the likes of one of the most notable characters of all time: Mickey Mouse. He has been a key to Disney's success. From the creation of Mickey Mouse to the exciting play of the National Hockey League's Anaheim Mighty Ducks, Disney has grown through diversification in the entertainment and leisure markets. Disney currently operates many different businesses while continuing its strong alliances with licensees, manufacturers, and retail outlets. This diverse and successful company was spawned from the success of a mouse and the talents of Walter E. Disney.

The last ten years comprised a spectacular decade for Disney. Unfortunately, in financial terms it ended on a down note. Revenues have been flat and profits are down. Although revenue has doubled since 1995, profits have been cut in half, down from 11.4 percent to only 5.6 percent. For fiscal year 1999, revenues increased only 2 percent to $23.4 billion while operating income declined 21 percent to $3.2 billion.[1] In creative terms, however, the decade ended strongly, with the company's entertainment product continuing to attract wide audiences around the world. Michael D. Eisner, Disney's chairman and CEO, says of Disney, "I feel the same way about Disney as I like to feel about my family—solid, on the right track, with strong fundamentals and an enthusiasm for the future."[2]

Company History

Because Walt Disney's personality, dreams, and attitudes still influence the company, a look at both his and his company's history offers insights into the Disney of today. His successes and battles with distributors, strikers, merchandisers, and even friends left an indelible mark on the man and the realization of his dream.

---

*This case was prepared by Alexandria Orsin, Mike Martin, Ken Nelson, and Robert Graves. It was revised by Heather Brymer, Nicolas Catel, Remy DeVlieghere, Marisa Feldman, Pamela Hemmen, Matt Lee, Cathie Mathe, and Lori Unger.

The Beginning Walter Elias Disney was born in 1901 in Chicago, but his family moved to a farm near Marcilene, Missouri, in 1906. It was this place that proved to be the inspiration for things to come and also the place where 4-year-old Walter first learned to draw. The story goes that Walt and his sister, Ruth, discovered a barrel of tar on the farm and proceeded to draw on the newly whitewashed fence with sticks dipped in the black liquid. Because his father, Elias, was rather a strict disciplinarian, Walt and Ruth were appropriately punished. Despite this, Walt's Aunt Margaret encouraged him by bringing paper and crayons from Kansas City, where she lived.[3]

Walt was an avid reader, but in grammar school his first love remained drawing. His unusual style sometimes got him in trouble though. Once, when he was asked to draw a pot of flowers, he added faces to the blooms and arms instead of leaves. He attended children's art classes at the Kansas City Art Institute and persuaded his father to pay for a correspondence course in art. As Walt grew older, he spent his time in school at McKinley High, washing bottles at his father's jelly factory, and drawing.[4]

Walt was eager to play his part in the war effort and, in 1918, enlisted in the American Ambulance Corps. He convinced his mother to sign his passport application, which showed Walt to be of age, and he was sent to France. He kept up with his drawing, and when he returned to the United States, he applied for jobs as a cartoonist at several papers. He failed to find an opening but soon signed on at the Pesmin-Rubin Commercial Art Studio for the sum of $50 per week.[5]

Walt's Early Efforts

Walt did not realize that he was taken on to meet a seasonal increase in work, and he was laid off after the Christmas rush. He and a friend, Ub Iwerks, created a company called Iwerks-Disney Commercial Artists, which quickly failed. This trend continued with a slightly less disastrous experience at a company called Laugh-O-Grams, which Walt and other investors formed in 1920. Following his brother Roy's advice to "get out of there," Walt traveled to Hollywood in 1923, after the firm went bankrupt.[6]

Hollywood met all of Walt's expectations, and he set up shop in a small office and got some stationery printed that boldly said "Walt Disney—Cartoonist." He contacted a distributor to whom he had sent information in New York while with Laugh-O-Grams and explained an idea for a cartoon/live-action series called "Alice Comedies." He prevailed upon the creditors of Laugh-O-Grams to allow him to release the only existing cartoon to the distributor. With a few changes, a deal was struck, and Walt found a site on Hollywood Boulevard for live-action filming. He rented a shop adjacent to the premises and emblazoned the words "Disney Bros. Studio," with his brother, Roy, as partner.[7]

Temporary Success

Roy had more of a talent for managing the money than for animation, and Walt had quite a talent for spending what little money they had. This was characteristic of the quest for quality that obsessed Walt, and the early days were a preamble of what was to come. Walt and Roy begged for loans from anyone they could, and the company was in a perilous situation in 1924. Walt had no choice but to continue on with the relationship.[8]

About this time, Universal Pictures was looking for a new cartoon series featuring a rabbit, and it was suggested that Walt be given the project, with the Alice series' company as the distributor. Walt gladly accepted and created "Oswald, the lucky rabbit." The series was a critical and financial success, and all seemed to be going well for the studios. Frequent checks were now being delivered by Walt's distributors.[9]

During this time Walt married Lillian Bounds, who was employed as an ink-and-paint worker at the studios. She and Walt took a trip to New York to negotiate a deal with his distributor for the next series of Oswald cartoons. Walt had intended to ask the distributor for an increase in the fee per picture, but instead they offered Walt a reduced price. Walt angrily refused and was informed that if he chose to refuse the offer, the distributor would take his whole firm away from him. (The distributor had signed up all of his animators.) A quick phone call to Roy revealed that what the distributor said was true, and Walt started to look frantically for an alternative distributor. However, Walt's distributor informed him that even if he did find another distributor, Universal held all of the rights to the character he had created. Walt and Lillian took the train back to Hollywood, and Walt vowed never to lose control over his interests again.[10]

The Mouse

"DON'T WORRY EVERYTHING OK GIVE DETAILS WHEN I ARRIVE." This was the cable that Walt sent Roy before leaving New York for home, and it is an example of the incredible optimism that truly characterized Walt Disney. The truth, however, was that things were not okay, but Walt viewed the situation as an opportunity to create a character that could be even more successful than Oswald, the not-so-lucky rabbit.

No one really knows how the idea of the character Mickey Mouse came about. To the delight of Walt Disney, so much of the tale is shrouded in myth that we may never know exactly what happened. What we do know is that out of the turmoil of that visit to New York came a character that would become perhaps the best-known icon of our time and the key to the success of Disney Studios. As Walt would later remark to his employees, "I hope we never lose sight of one fact . . . that this was all started by a mouse. . . ."[11]

When he arrived back in Hollywood, Walt had to break the news about the loss to Roy and the only other loyal animator, Ub Iwerks. He was able to temper it with news about the new cartoon series he had envisioned. The mouse, originally to be named Mortimer, would be called Mickey (at the insistence of Lillian). The defecting animators would not be leaving for another 3 months, so Walt and Ub had to labor in secret and very quickly to boot. The cartoon, called *Plane Crazy*, was churned out in only 2 weeks, with Ub averaging an amazing 700 drawings per day—one per minute! The plot revolved around a rickety plane built by Mickey and his barnyard friends after Mickey reads about Charles Lindbergh. Mickey then sets off with his girlfriend, Minnie, with the two characters symbolizing youth, optimism, and adventure.[12]

The cartoon was received warmly, but no distributor could be found. It seemed that the mouse was likable enough, but he did not have a unique hook to set him apart from the other cartoon characters. After *The Jazz Singer*, the first movie with synchronized sound, was released, Walt decided that this would be what made Mickey different—sound. He authorized Roy to hock everything, including his car. With the company teetering on the edge of bankruptcy, Walt made the first cartoon to incorporate sound—*Steamboat Willie*.[13]

The film was held over 2 weeks at the Roxy Theater and was no less than a triumph. The next three Mickey Mouse cartoons had sound added, and "the mouse" was soon so popular that more animators had to be added to the staff. More films came, including the *Silly Symphony* series, and soon Mickey and Minnie were as popular as any flesh-and-blood movie actor. In 1929 Walt was approached by a man offering him $300 to put the image of Mickey and Minnie on children's notebooks. As usual, the money was needed, and Walt agreed. Within a year, hundreds of manufacturers were producing officially licensed products, and the fortunes of the company seemed safe at last.[14]

The Company Takes Off

Mickey's place among the public was secure, and the offshoots of the cartoons were bringing in substantial revenues. Consumer products, such as the Mickey Mouse watch, sold like hotcakes, and the Mickey Mouse Clubs that cinema owners across the country put together boasted a million members. In 1930 one of the most well-regarded promoters in the country, Herman Kamen, offered to manage the licensing of Disney characters, and the brothers jumped at the opportunity.[15]

The cartoons were the core business of the studios, after all, and they were turned out one after another. In addition to the *Silly Symphonies* and Mickey Mouse cartoons, the studios put out *The Ugly Duckling, Three Blind Mouseketeers*, and *The Three Little Pigs*. In the 1930s Mickey got such sidekicks as Clara Cluck, Pluto, Goofy, and the irrepressible Donald Duck. These characters were successful, but Walt had a more ambitious project in mind—a full-length animated film.

Snow White—A New Era

No one else had dared to make a full-length animated feature previously. The task was daunting, and the amount of drawings alone would be enormous. But Walt was positive that it could be done and that it would be successful. He began preparation for this full-length cartoon as a general would prepare for battle. By the time it was over, the *Snow White* team would include 85 animators, story and gag writers, inkers, painters, and several departments of technicians. Not only did *Snow White* have to be produced, but the regular quota of short films had to be continued also. Both tasks were accomplished, but the financial and personal pressures were great. Production took 5 years.[16]

What had been called "Disney's folly" was an absolute success, both nationally and internationally, with its release on February 4, 1938. The studio's place in history had been assured, and the genius of Disney and his artists was without question. Adding to the success of the film were the revenues from various consumer products, including seeds, shampoos, and even diapers.[17]

"The Golden Years"

As the company grew, it was clear to Walt that the current studio was not adequate to meet the needs of an ambitious schedule, so a suitable site was located in Burbank and construction began. During this time Walt also felt it necessary to reorganize the company. In 1938 a huge document detailing organizational structure and job descriptions was drawn up—a far cry from the ad hoc type of arrangement that had been operating for years.

Disney Goes Public

Germany invaded Poland on September 1, 1939. As the war consumed more and more of Europe, the 45 percent in revenues that Disney enjoyed from that part of the world quickly dried up. As income diminished, costs escalated (particularly on the production of *Fantasia*). Disney had more than 1000 people working for him, and despite *Pinocchio's* critical success, the film did not do well at the box office. The new studios were just being completed and payment was due. Roy Disney confronted his brother in the spring of 1940 with the news—the company was $4.5 million in debt.[18]

Walt's first response was to laugh because he remembered a time in the not-so-distant past when the studio could not borrow even a thousand dollars—much less a million. But the situation was serious, so the Disney brothers opted for an issue of stock on the public market. In April of 1940, the company offered 155,000 shares of 6 percent cumulative convertible preferred stock at $25 par value and 600,000 shares of common stock at $5 per share. The offering raised $3.5 million in much-needed capital.[19]

An ominous threat was brewing, however, and it would prove more trying to Walt than merely funding the company.

The Strike

It seemed that ever since the move from the old studios, the atmosphere of camaraderie and creativity had been waning. The artists felt cut off from the creative process and, worst of all, from Walt himself. Rumors about the staff and management, ranging from the cost of the number of waitresses in the cafeteria to a fictitious "inner ring" of Walt's employees who enjoyed privileges that others did not, began to circulate. The legalistic job descriptions and organizational charts did nothing to help, and it was not long before there was unrest in the Disney organization.

The disharmony was evident, and when the price of Disney stock began to fall, many employees chose to cash in. Walt demonstrated his strong belief in the company by buying the shares of anyone who wanted to sell. The stage was set for some type of union organization, and the Disney animators became the prime target for activists.

Disney had always operated a closed shop with various other trades, but the animators were not organized. Two separate unions canvassed the animators: the independent Federation of Screen Cartoonists and the Screen Cartoonists Guild, led by Herbert Sorrell and affiliated with the Brotherhood of Painters, Paperhangers, and Decorators of America. Many animators, being a bit naive, joined both unions, whereas some joined neither. Sorrell tried to get Walt Disney to join his union, claiming that a majority of his animators already had. Walt told Sorrell that he wanted the matter put to a ballot organized by the National Labor Relations Board, but Sorrell refused.[20]

Walt tried to calm the rumors and increase communication with his staff by issuing a recorded speech addressing the concerns of the animators. He stressed that he had never been interested in a personal gain or profit and said that instead of complaining, the employees of the company should count their blessings. Despite this plea, the tensions came to a head when Goofy's chief animator, Art Babbit, was dismissed. He had long been a supporter of the Guild, and Herb Sorrell maintained that the dismissal was in reprisal for union activities. The long-threatened strike was called in May of 1941. Walt said, "To me, the entire situation is a catastrophe."[21]

The strike was settled in October of 1941, with Sorrell claiming victory for the unions. Walt said that the strike was settled in the simplest way—"the negotiators gave Sorrell everything he wanted."[22] The animosities and confrontations were not easily forgotten, and within 2 years, many of the strikers, including Art Babbit, had left the company. A noticeable change came over Walt, and wary of further trouble, he insisted that every employee—down to the gardeners—join the proper union. He became more cautious and remote in his relationships.

The Years 1940-1966

A New Outlook on Costs

The financial problems that had always plagued the company did not vanish, however, and Walt announced a new policy regarding costs. Staff was urged to adopt "a constructive attitude toward every dollar that went into developing, producing, and selling the scheduled pictures."[23] From now on, there would be a production schedule to which workers would adhere; movies would come in within budgets; stories would be prepared more thoroughly to eliminate costly changes; and all departments would be policed in order to prevent unnecessary expenses. Selling and exploiting the pictures to the fullest also would be of utmost importance.

Under the new rules, the studio continued to produce hits. *Cinderella* was released in 1950, followed by *Alice in Wonderland* in 1951. *Peter Pan* arrived in 1953, along with the Disney signature fairy, Tinkerbell. Also, in the 1950s Disney turned to films with live characters, such as *Treasure Island* (1950), *20,000 Leagues Under the Sea* (1954), and the musical fantasy, *Mary Poppins* (1964). In addition, Disney turned to the filmed entertainment area for nature films, whose fine photography was marred for some critics by the sentimentality of approach. Disney also produced many films for television audiences: the "Davy Crockett" series and the "Mickey Mouse Club" helped revive the old cartoon figures for several new generations of children. The Disney Channel today offers "Disneyfied" entertainment to subscribing cable television viewers. However, in the early 1950s the greatest production of all was just beginning to brew in the mind of its creator.

Disneyland

The original concept for Disneyland came to Walt's mind in early 1939, but the details were not thought out until 1951. Walt formed WED Enterprises so that stockholders would not object to the new venture, and he attempted to persuade investors to fund the project. This proved difficult, so Walt backed his idea with his own money. A site was selected in 1953—160 acres in Anaheim, California, just 25 miles from Los Angeles. As Walt put it:

> There's nothing like it in the whole world—I know, because I've looked. That's why it can be great; because it will be unique. A new concept in entertainment, and I think—I *know*—it can be a success.[24]

Disneyland opened on July 17, 1955. That morning traffic was jammed for more than 7 miles on the roads leading to the park, and by midday more than 30,000 people had passed through the turnstiles. The staff had been hired from agencies, and they treated the guests with the same belligerence they used for dealing with crowds at racetracks and ballparks. Several rides broke down, and others were dangerously overcrowded. The food and drinks ran out; water fountains were inadequate; and the park became littered with trash. The day was a disaster, and Walt later referred to it as "Black Sunday."

To make the necessary changes, Walt built an apartment over the Main Street Fire Station and spent 24 hours a day at the park for 2 weeks. An army of young men was employed to clean up the litter; standards for staff courtesy and efficiency were established; and ways of speeding up the waiting times for rides were found. It was a headache, but this experience afforded an opportunity not found in the movies—a chance for continual improvement. Disneyland, as it turned out, was a turning point in the fortunes of the company. After 16 months, net profits were the highest in the company's history.[25]

For the World's Fair in 1964, Walt approached a number of corporations and asked to design their attractions. It was a decision that would have far-reaching consequences. The Ford Motor Company bought Walt's design for a car ride through history from caveman to spaceman, and Pepsi helped develop the idea that would eventually become the boat ride known as "It's a Small World." The president of the World's Fair commissioned what would become one of the fair's major attractions—a three-dimensional, talking and moving Abraham Lincoln. Audiences experienced the sensation of being in the crowd listening to a Lincoln speech. The Disney-designed exhibits drew more than 46 million visitors.

During this time Walt also began to acquire land for "Disneyland East," another theme park to be located in Orlando, Florida. The idea of a prototype community, later to be known as EPCOT, was also taking shape, and Walt began sharing his dream with the world—after the land was purchased, however. The cost of the two projects was estimated at $500 million.[26]

Unbeknownst to anyone but his closest aides, Walt Disney was very ill. He was admitted to the hospital on November 2, 1966, and x-ray films showed a spot on his left lung. It was found to be cancerous and was removed, and Walt seemed to be recovering. He went back to work but soon fell ill again. After 2 more weeks in the hospital, he rallied somewhat, and on December 14 he even spoke with Roy about details of the Disneyland project. The next morning, Walt Disney died of acute circulatory collapse. As Richard Zanuck said, "No eulogy will be read or monument built to equal the memorial Walt Disney has left in the hearts and minds and imaginations of the world's peoples."[27]

Life After Walt

The years after Walt Disney's death were marked by feuds between "Roy men," the financial types, and "Walt men," the creative types. Nearly everything, including filmmaking, was undertaken only after a discussion over what Walt would have done. This philosophy worked for a while but eventually led to the deterioration of the company's film segment. This was marked by Disney's refusal to produce *Raiders of the Lost Ark* and *E.T.* simply because of the creator's desire to have a share of the profits. The dismal decisions led to a devaluation of Disney's stock and a takeover effort in 1984 by Roy Disney, Jr., among others.[28]

Sid Bass and Stanley Gold were the "white knights" that helped stave off the raiders. On the inside, they insisted upon a shakeup in management. This resulted in the hiring of Michael Eisner, Frank Wells, and Jeffry Katzenberg. These individuals engineered a remarkable turnaround in the film division, as well as other divisions within the company, and consequently, Disney showed record earnings and growth over the next few years. In 1995 after Frank Wells' death, Disney hired as its president Michael Ovitz, Hollywood's premier power broker from Creative Artists Agency. His contacts with celebrities have helped Disney in movies and films.[29]

Corporate Strategy

Because of the expansion that took place during the past decade, Disney enters the new decade as a substantially different company. It now has seven theme parks (with four more in the works), 27 hotels with 36,888 rooms, two cruise ships, 728 Disney Stores, one broadcast network, ten television stations, nine international Disney

Channels, 42 radio stations, an Internet portal, five major Internet Web sites, interests in nine U.S. cable networks. In the past decade Disney has enhanced its library with animated films, live-action films, animated television episodes, and live-action television episodes.[30]

This enormous expansion reflected a two-fold corporate strategy: (1) to build the greatest entertainment asset base in the world and (2) to simultaneously create the greatest entertainment product in the world. Now Disney enters the first decade of the 21st century with a strategy that is four-pronged, focusing on revitalizing underperforming areas (developing new strategies for Consumer Products and Home Video); achieving greater profitability from existing assets; exploring capital-efficient initiatives to drive long-term growth; and continuing development of creative, innovative, and engaging products.[31]

In addition, the company introduced a new financial reporting structure in 1999. Instead of the three operating segments it previously reported—Theme Parks and Resorts, Broadcasting, and Creative Content—Disney now reports along five lines of businesses. Theme Parks and Resorts is reported as before. Broadcasting is now referred to as Media Networks, with a further breakdown separating cable networks from broadcast-related businesses. Creative Content is now reported in three parts: Studio Entertainment, Consumer Products, and Internet and Direct Marketing.[32]

Consumer Products

Disney sells a vast array of merchandise, including books, toys, apparel, computer software, magazines, artwork, and collectibles, outside of the settings of its theme parks.[33] The company licenses the name "Walt Disney," as well as the company's characters, visual and literacy properties, and songs and music to various consumer manufacturers, retailers, show promoters, and publishers throughout the world. The company also engages in direct retail distribution principally through the general public in the United States and Europe. In addition, the company produces audio products for all markets, as well as film, video, and computer software products for the educational marketplace.[34] The main components of Consumer Products are licensing, The Disney Stores, Walt Disney Art Classics, Disney Interactive, and Walt Disney Children's Books.

Even though each event within the Disney Company (such as the opening of the Animal Kingdom in Florida, the arrival of each new film, the celebration of the 70th anniversary of Mickey and Minnie, and the 75th anniversary of the company) is a pretext to create new merchandising products and to develop sales, Consumer Products has taken a downturn recently. In 1999 revenue for Consumer Products fell 5 percent and operating income declined 24 percent.[35] In fact, this is a primary reason for Disney's disappointing financial results last year. The challenge in Consumer Products has two major facets—licensing and The Disney Stores. One major step the company has just taken to improve both of these areas is the appointment of Andrew Mooney as President of Disney Consumer Products.[36]

During recent years Disney's licensing business has been a victim of its own success. It built market share by signing as many licensees as possible, reaching a peak of more than 4000. This became far too many relationships to productively manage, especially when the market shifted. Thus Disney is cutting the number of licensees in half. By having broader relationships with fewer licensees, the company believes it will be able to more effectively build new merchandise campaigns to strengthen such established characters as Mickey Mouse and Winnie the Pooh.[37]

EXHIBIT 1 | SELECTED FINANCIAL DATA

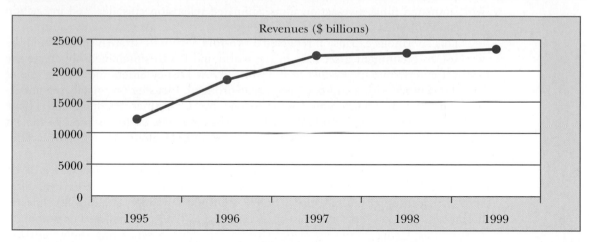

Revenues ($ billions)

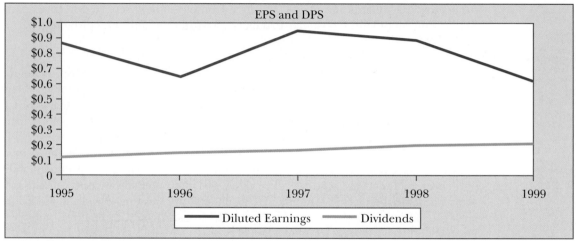

EPS and DPS

— Diluted Earnings — Dividends

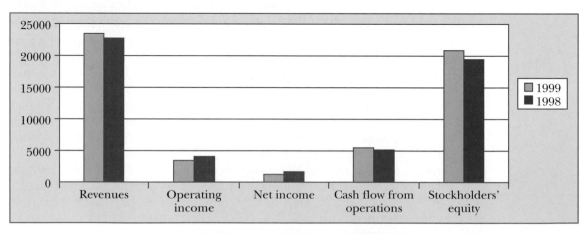

SOURCE: The Walt Disney Company, *1999 Online Annual Report*, p. 70.

Furthermore, Disney has several joint ventures or alliances with companies in related businesses. For example, it has a contract with Nestle that allows Nestle to produce food products using Disney characters. Also, the Disney name can be found on Mattel products since the two companies joined forces in the toy industry. From this alliance comes "Mattel-sponsored attractions at Disney theme parks, the development of park-related toys, and the expansion of Disney's lucrative toy-licensing pacts with Mattel." In addition, Toys 'R' Us is rolling out front-of-the-store Disney-themed spaces, and Disney is developing merchandise exclusives featuring its characters for Target and Macy's. These ventures and others will help Disney make a strong stand in the consumer products market.[38]

Consumer Products is also inspired by Disney's increasing prominence in sports. In May of 1996, Disney purchased a 25-percent interest in the Anaheim Angels, a major league baseball team, and it has owned the National Hockey League franchise of the Mighty Ducks of Anaheim since 1992. Disney's expansion into the ownership and marketing of professional sports has continued with the opening of one of the most modern sports complexes in the world, Disney's Wide World of Sports Complex in Florida. Consumer Products is also enlivened by ABC with a lineup of products capitalizing on the strength of ESPN, ABC Sports, and Monday Night Football.[39]

In 1987 the people who brought us everything from Mickey Mouse to *Pretty Woman* decided to open their first retail store outside their theme parks. The first store was opened in the Glendale Galleria, near the Disney headquarters in Anaheim, California. By 1991 The Disney Store had become one of the most sought-after chains in the shopping center industry.[40] Although The Disney Stores hit a milestone of 700 total stores last March, overall sales were down in 1999. To help return The Disney Store to strong growth, a new merchandise strategy with an emphasis on young boys and girls, pre-teens, and adults has been implemented. It is being backed with direct consumer advertising and an all-new store design that will see existing Disney Store locations thoroughly renovated. The new store design will include computer kiosks that will make it possible for consumers to purchase items not available in a particular store through The Disney Store Online.[41] Accordingly, Disney is also reducing the number of items of merchandise in each store by more than half to focus on key, showcase products. In addition, new merchandise lines are being developed, and the new management team of the stores is working to better define shopping "events" like Halloween, back-to-school, Christmas, and Valentine's Day.[42]

Globalization

On April 2, 1992, The Walt Disney Company expanded to Marne la Vallee, France, in an effort to further diversify within the theme park segment. Two years after its grand opening, Euro Disney, the holding company of which Disney holds a 35 percent stake, was showing heavy losses cumulating to more than $7 billion. The losses were due to the combined effect of higher costs and lower visitor spending than predicted. How could an organization like Disney have been so wrong in Europe? Some consultants have brought forward the "Icarus Paradox" hypothesis. Could it be that some of Disney's historical strengths were preventing senior management from understanding the project's weakness?[43]

Finally, after many years of surprising losses, Euro Disney has now turned around. After its debt was restructured, admission prices lowered, the surrounding areas developed, and the park renamed Disneyland Paris, it is on its way towards

EXHIBIT 2	FINANCIAL HIGHLIGHTS

(In millions, except per share data)	1999	1998	1997	1996	1995
Statements of income					
Revenues	$23,402	$22,976	$22,473	$18,739	$12,151
Operating income	3,444	4,015	4,447	3,033	2,466
Net income	1,300	1,850	1,966	1,214	1,380
Per share					
Earnings					
Diluted	$0.62	$0.89	$0.95	$0.65	$0.87
Basic	0.63	0.91	0.97	0.66	0.88
Dividends	0.21	0.20	0.17	0.14	0.12
Balance sheets					
Total assets	$43,679	$41,378	$38,497	$37,341	$14,995
Borrowings	11,693	11,685	11,068	12,342	2,984
Stockholders' equity	20,975	19,388	17,285	16,086	6,651
Statements of cash flows					
Cash provided by operations	$5,588	$5,115	$5,099	$3,707	$3,510
Investing activities	(5,310)	(5,665)	(3,936)	(12,546)	(2,288)
Financing activities	9	360	(1,124)	8,040	(332)

SOURCE: The Walt Disney Company, *1999 Online Annual Report*, p. 11, and 12, 70.

success and profitability. Construction has even begun on a second Paris theme park, Disney Studios, which is set to open in the spring of 2002.

The early performance of Euro Disney contrasts greatly with the early success of Tokyo Disneyland, which recently celebrated its 15th anniversary and set attendance records last year. Tokyo Disneyland was Disney's first associated theme park outside of the United States, and it has been a huge success. The park gets more than 15 million visitors each year, which by some industry estimates makes it the most visited amusement park in the world, exceeding other Disney theme parks. Although Tokyo Disneyland earns huge profits, The Walt Disney Company does not get a direct share of them because it refused to buy an interest in the park when it was developed, believing it too risky. However, Disney does have control over the artistic side of Tokyo Disneyland, and it receives a royalty on the admission fees.[44] Attendance grew by more than 10 percent during the first several years, but then the situation of the amusement industry in Japan dipped, following the collapse of the bubble economy. With the current Japanese economy, the owner of Tokyo Disneyland is searching for ways to cut costs and gain economies of scale while building a second park, Tokyo DisneySea.[45] The new park is scheduled to open in 2001 and will include 23 attractions, live entertainment, restaurants, and shops centered around seven "ports of call." Two Disney-branded hotels are available. The Disney Ambassador opened in 2000, and Disney's Mira Costa opened in 2001 as part of Tokyo DisneySea.[46]

As if the new theme parks at its existing international locations are not enough, Disney has announced plans to build Disneyland Hong Kong, scheduled to open in 2005. The government will construct a sea wall in Hong Kong's Penny Bay and reclaim approximately 200 acres of usable land through dredging. In addition, another section of the bay could be used, should Disney decide a second park is feasible.[47]

In 1999 Disney created Walt Disney International in order to better manage its existing international assets. Disney's growth overseas has been strong, but it has not duplicated the level of success it has achieved in North America. The United States contains only 5 percent of the world's population, but it accounts for 80 percent of the company's revenues. With Walt Disney International coordinating its lines of business overseas, the company is hoping to strengthen its international performance.[48]

Disney films have been successful in the global marketplace for quite some time. *Dead Poets Society* is one example in which 25 percent more business occurred in foreign countries than in the United States. There are still some additional markets, such as China, to be penetrated. In 1997 Disney faced some difficult issues with the Chinese authorities after the release of the movie *Seven Years in Tibet* because of the cultural differences between the two countries. The production in 1998 of *Mulan*, a historical Chinese character, can be interpreted as a desire to open the doors to the markets in Asia. In 2000 *Toy Story 2*, *Dinosaur*, *Gone in 60 Seconds*, and *Mission to Mars* were strong entries in the international market.[49]

Theme Parks and Resorts

Included in the company's Theme Parks and Resorts are the following: Walt Disney World in Florida; Disneyland Park, the Disneyland Hotel, and the Disneyland Pacific Hotel in California; Disney Regional Entertainment; the Disney Vacation Club; the Mighty Ducks of Anaheim; and the Anaheim Angels. The company's Imagineering unit designs and develops new theme park concepts and attractions, as well as resort properties.[50] Theme Parks and Resorts represented more than 40 percent of Disney's operating income in 1999. For the same period, the segment's revenues increased 10 percent and operating income grew by about 12 percent. Revenues were driven by growth at the Walt Disney World Resort, reflecting increased guest spending and record attendance, as well as increases from Disney Cruise Line, Anaheim Sports, Inc., and increased guest spending at Disneyland. The increase in operating income resulted primarily from revenue growth at the Walt Disney World Resort and a full period of operations at Disney Cruise Line.[51]

Disney California Disneyland opened on July 17, 1955, in Anaheim, California, with 18 major attractions. This year it celebrates its 45th anniversary with more than

60 attractions throughout the park. Some of the recently added attractions include "Indiana Jones Adventures," which allows guests to go on an Indiana Jones adventure through the Temple of the Forbidden Eye, and "The Spirit of Pocahontas" stage show. In addition, last summer, the Adventureland site of the Swiss Family Robinson Treehouse was transformed into Tarzan's Treehouse, a climb-through attraction featuring characters and stories from the animated movie.[52]

One of Disneyland's largest renovation projects, Tomorrowland, reopened in spring 1998, and it is an updated look into the future, inspired by Jules Verne. Disney embarked on a total renovation of Tomorrowland in order to bring the park into its long anticipated "voyage into imagination and beyond." The renovation included an exciting new-generation 3-D experience, a high-speed journey throughout the land in rocket cars of the future, an interactive pavilion of technology and imagination, and a landmark orbiter attraction at Tomorrowland's entrance. Also, the redesigned Autopia ride is now presented by Chevron and has updated cars, landscaping, and marquees along the motorway. Classic attractions, such as Space Mountain and Star Tours, have remained the same and are expected to benefit from the surrounding updated designs and new attractions.[53]

In 2001 Disney opened the newest West Coast resort that redefines the California vacation experience. Disney's California Adventure follows the Disney tradition of fun and magic, and it includes the Disney studio district where guests can explore the process of television production; the California wilderness that showcases the beauty of natural California; lakefront leisure that includes shoreline shops and dining reminiscent of coastal communities like Monterey and Carmel; and the Boardwalk, which houses classical amusement rides. As a part of the new resort, Disney opened The Grand Californian, which is a 750-room hotel that is the first hotel ever completely situated inside a Disney theme park. Outside the park, as a part of the Anaheim Resort District, is Downtown Disney, a 300,000-square-foot retail, dining, and entertainment complex with venues including House of Blues, Rainforest Café, and ESPN Zone.[54]

Disneyland offers many specialized services to make the Disney experience a complete one. For example, Disney offers the fairy tale wedding at Disneyland Park, the Disneyland Hotel, and the Disneyland Pacific Hotel. Disney provides all the needed services, such as catering and entertainment, to make a truly memorable wedding celebration. Disney also offers the "practically perfect tea," which allows friends and family to enjoy a traditional intimate tea with a Disney twist.[55]

Disney Florida October 1, 1971, marked the opening of the Magic Kingdom Park in Orlando, Florida. From the modest start of 23 attractions in six themed areas, Walt Disney World Florida has grown into a city. The Walt Disney World Resort currently encompasses the Magic Kingdom, EPCOT, Disney-MGM Studios, Disney's Animal Kingdom, 13 resort hotels and a complex of villas and suites, a sports complex, conference centers, campgrounds, golf courses, water parks, and other recreational facilities. In addition, the resort operates Disney Cruise Line from Port Canaveral, Florida.[56] This continuous expansion was made possible with Disney's initial purchase of 43 square miles of land in Central Florida. Just a few years ago, Walt Disney World celebrated its 25th anniversary by turning Cinderella's Castle into a 20-story-tall anniversary cake. Now the Magic Kingdom comprises 34 attractions, 8 exhibits, 32 food locations, and 48 merchandise locations. Recent additions include Mickey's Toontown and Minnie's Country House.[57]

Disney's Experimental Prototype Community of Tomorrow (EPCOT) opened on October 1, 1982, 11 years after the Magic Kingdom. EPCOT includes two main areas: the World Showcase and Future World. In the World Showcase, visitors may learn the history, feel the culture, and taste the cuisine of 11 different countries from around the world.[58] In addition, The Millennium Celebration, centered at EPCOT, features nightly parades and exhibits celebrating cultures from around the world. The Millennium Celebration kicked off in October 1999 and ran for 15 months.[59] Future World allows visitors to view and test technological innovations of the future. The Disney Imagineers have not only been giving certain attractions a much-needed face-lift—or updated image—but they have been designing new, exciting attractions also. Such attractions include Test Track, where guests can "test drive" one of the most advanced ride vehicles ever developed by Walt Disney's Imagineers.

The third major theme park, Disney-MGM Studios, opened in 1989. This theme park is a tribute to the world of Hollywood magic. Here visitors play a starring role in both the scenes and behind the stage. Disney-MGM Studios captures the history, the glamour, the glitz, and a lot of action, special effects, and stunts from the movie and television industries.[60] The park is filled with rides, actual working soundstages and production buildings, and plenty of entertainment.

Pleasure Island can be characterized as a party town. During the day it is a popular place to eat and shop, whereas the nighttime brings streets filled with visitors enjoying comedy, country, rock, live entertainment, and a large New Year's Eve party every night of the year. The BET SoundStage Club, the newest addition to Pleasure Island, opened in spring 1998 and features jazz, rhythm and blues, soul, and hip-hop. Pleasure Island has expanded to include the Downtown Disney Marketplace and the West Side. During the summer of 1998, Downtown Disney opened DisneyQuest, where guests can take an interactive journey through four distinctive entertainment environments. The attraction boasts five stories of virtual games.[61] In addition, gymnasts and dancers have been performing the Cirque du Soleil show, La Nouba, in a new 1600-seat theater in Downtown Disney.

Typhoon Lagoon is a water park set in a tropical village. The park contains many water slides, a giant wave pool, and a large children's water area. The success of this park prompted Disney to open a second water theme park. A legend states that a freak winter storm dropped tons of snow over this section of Florida. Disney quickly used the snow mountains to build Blizzard Beach and Disney's Winter Summerland, the only two parks built in Florida around a winter theme.[62]

The town of Celebration, Florida, located near Walt Disney World, is Disney's visionary community. Celebration offers its residents leading-edge health, education, and technology systems while providing a comfortable sense of community. The large demand for homes in Celebration led officials to use a lottery system to grant homes to first bidders. Residents began moving in on July 4, 1996.[63] Currently, Celebration is home to more than 2500 residents, and the growth of the town is expected to reach 20,000 residents.[64]

Animal Kingdom is Disney's newest theme park, which opened in April of 1998 at the Walt Disney World Resort. This is not just a zoo, but an adventure through many different lands and eras. The park is home to more than a thousand live animals, Audio-Animatronics creations, and classic characters. Sitting on 500 acres, this park tells the story of all animals—real, imaginary, and extinct. The goal of the park is to educate guests about endangered species and global conservation while providing a natural setting for wildlife. In 1999 the Animal Kingdom opened a new area called Asia, a land rich with rainforests and wildlife of southern Asia.[65] This new land includes a white-water rafting journey, as well as a jungle trek that traverses dense rainforests and ancient ruins where tigers appear to be roaming free.[66]

Disney is constantly searching for new ways to exploit the Disney brand and image. The newest business Disney has entered is the cruise line industry with its Disney Cruise Line, which includes two 85,000-ton superships, *Disney Magic* and *Disney Wonder*. The maiden voyage of the *Disney Magic* embarked in the summer of 1998.[67] The cruise line offers a 7-day package that includes a 3- or 4-night stay at the Walt Disney World Resort and then a 3- or 4-night cruise to the Bahamas. The ships have been designed especially for Disney, enabling the company to offer extraordinary entertainment for guests of all ages. On-board amenities include four restaurants, an ESPN sky box, a teen-only coffee house with live music, an entire deck devoted to children only, a variety of nighttime activities and clubs, a Buena Vista Theater, and several adults-only areas including an Italian restaurant and a secluded beach section on Disney's own Castaway Island.

The company also manages and markets vacation ownership interests in the Disney Vacation Club. The club includes several resort facilities, including the Disney Old Key West Resort and Disney's Boardwalk Resort at the Walt Disney World Resort; a resort in Vero Beach, Florida; and a resort on Hilton Head Island, South Carolina. An expansion at Disney's Old Key West opened in 2000, and an expansion adjacent to Disney's Wilderness Lodge is scheduled for opening in late 2001.[68]

The Walt Disney World Resort has come a long way since its modest beginning. Throughout the past few decades, Disney has continued to entertain and enlighten people—young and old—from all over the world.

Studio Entertainment

In 1999 revenues for Studio Entertainment decreased 4 percent, driven by declines in domestic home video. For the same period, operating income decreased 85 percent, reflecting declines in worldwide home video and network television production and distribution.[69]

Last year, The Walt Disney Studios released 15 live-action films. This was the culmination of a long-term strategy to reduce production costs from the level of 3 years earlier, when about twice as many films were released. In addition, the studios reorganized all of its businesses, which resulted in an overall live-action film investment reduction of $400 million compared with 1998. The year 1999 was strong at the box office for the film group with live-action and animated hits from all of its labels, but Miramax and Buena Vista performed exceptionally well.[70]

Disney movies have always been known as major players in the field of family entertainment. The Walt Disney Studios has produced such recent blockbusters as *The Sixth Sense*, *A Bug's Life*, *Tarzan*, and *The Waterboy*.[71] These complement long-standing hits such as *Bambi*, *Snow White*, and *Dumbo*. These movies, along with others from Disney's Touchstone/Hollywood Pictures, Buena Vista, and Miramax, have led to Disney's continued success in film entertainment.[72]

Disney Studios has produced some of the biggest blockbusters of all time with record-breaking profits. Its list of such hits includes *The Little Mermaid* (1991), *Beauty and the Beast* (1992), *Aladdin* (1993), *The Lion King* (1994), *Toy Story* (1995), *Pocahontas* (1996), *Hercules* (1997), *Mulan* (1998), and *A Bug's Life* (1999). Disney has continued its one-hit-per-year approach with the release of the spine-tingling *The Sixth Sense* in the fall of 1999 and *Remember the Titans* in 2000.

EXHIBIT 3   REVENUES AND OPERATING INCOME BY SEGMENT

"Business Segments"	1999	1998	1997
Revenues			
Media Networks	$7,512	$7,142	$6,522
Studio Entertainment			
Third Parties	6,472	6,755	6,840
Intersegment	76	94	141
	6,548	6,849	6,981
Theme Parks and Resorts	6,106	5,532	5,014
Consumer Products			
Third Parties	3,106	3,287	3,923
Intersegment	(76)	(94)	(141)
	3,030	3,193	3,782
Internet and Direct Marketing	206	260	174
Total Consolidated Revenues	$23,402	$22,976	$22,473
Operating Income			
Media Networks	$1,611	$1,746	$1,699
Studio Entertainment	116	769	1,079
Theme Parks and Resorts	1,446	1,288	1,136
Consumer Products	607	801	893
Internet and Direct Marketing	(93)	(94)	(56)
Amortization of Intangible Assets	(456)	(431)	(439)
	3,231	4,079	4,312
Restructuring Charges	(132)	(64)	—
Gain on Sale of Starwave	345	—	—
Gain on Sale of KCAL	—	—	135
Total Consolidated Operating Income	$3,444	$4,015	$4,447
Capital Expenditures			
Media Networks	$159	$245	$152
Studio Entertainment	51	117	171
Theme Parks and Resorts	1,758	1,693	1,266
Consumer Products	106	77	109
Internet and Direct Marketing	17	27	21
Corporate	43	155	203
Total Consolidated Capital Expenditures	$2,134	$2,314	$1,922
Depreciation Expense			
Media Networks	$131	$122	$104
Studio Entertainment	64	115	86
Theme Parks and Resorts	498	443	408
Consumer Products	124	85	95
Internet and Direct Marketing	8	10	6
Corporate	26	34	39
Total Consolidated Depreciation Expense	$851	$809	$738

	1999	1998	1997
Amortization Expense			
Media Networks	$423	$421	$405
Studio Entertainment	1	1	—
Theme Parks and Resorts	21	1	—
Consumer Products	6	1	27
Internet and Direct Marketing	5	7	7
Total Consolidated Amortization Expense	$456	$431	$439
Identifiable Assets			
Media Networks	$19,326	$18,749	$18,415
Studio Entertainment	7,865	8,089	6,864
Theme Parks and Resorts	10,272	9,214	8,051
Consumer Products	1,964	1,975	2,065
Internet and Direct Marketing	214	336	168
Corporate*	4,038	3,015	2,934
Total Consolidated Assets	$43,679	$41,378	$38,497
Supplemental Revenue Data			
Media Networks Advertising	$5,486	$5,287	$4,937
Theme Parks and Resorts Merchandise, Food and Beverage	1,878	1,780	1,754
Admissions	1,860	1,739	1,603

"Geographic Segments"	1999	1998	1997
Revenues			
United States	$18,657	$18,106	$17,868
U.S. Exports	1,147	1,036	874
Europe	2,059	2,215	2,073
Asia Pacific	974	996	987
Latin America, Canada and Other	565	623	671
Total Consolidated Revenues	$23,402	$22,976	$22,473
Operating Income			
United States	$3,142	$3,468	$3,712
Europe	229	369	499
Asia Pacific	228	217	335
Latin America, Canada and Other	115	173	62
Total Consolidated Operating Income	$3,444	$4,015	$4,447
Identifiable Assets			
United States	$41,938	$39,462	$36,706
Europe**	1,238	1,468	1,275
Asia Pacific	319	270	341
Latin America, Canada and Other	184	178	175
	$43,679	$41,378	$38,497

*Primarily investments accounted for under the equity method, deferred tax assets, other investments, fixed and other assets
**Primarily current assets and investment in Euro Disney
SOURCE: The Walt Disney Company, *1999 Online Annual Report*, p. 65.

Home videos have allowed The Walt Disney Studios to benefit from the return of its rereleased classics, such as *Dumbo, Snow White*, and *Bambi*. Recently, however, home video sales have dipped, contributing to the company's disappointing 1999 financial results. Throughout the past decade, Disney's approach to home video was to release all of its major library titles for relatively brief designated periods of availability. That strategy worked well during the rapid-growth phase of the video business, but now Disney believes that consumers are better served by making most titles available on a year-round basis. Accordingly, in January 2000, Disney began sequencing into the video market all but ten of the titles that were previously held in limited availability. The other ten classic animated films will be released each fall on a ten-year cycle, starting with *Snow White* in the fall of 2001. Disney's strategy is to build a company-wide marketing event around each release, thereby maximizing the value of these ten films and reinforcing their special appeal among consumers.[73]

Walt Disney Network Television continues to experience success. *Boy Meets World* started its seventh season as a part of ABC's "TGIF" lineup in fall 1999, and it ranked number one in its time-slot among all youth demographics in 1999. In addition, the more recognized title of *The Wonderful World of Disney* ended the 1998-1999 season number one among teens and kids in its time period. New Disney television movies on *The Wonderful World of Disney* in the 1999-2000 season include *Annie* and *Geppetto*, as well as the network television premieres of *Jungle 2 Jungle, A Bug's Life*, and *Mulan*.[74]

Walt Disney Feature Animation, under the leadership of chairman Roy Disney and president Thomas Schumacher, released three animated films—*A Bug's Life, Tarzan*, and *Toy Story 2*—from November 1998 to Thanksgiving 1999. *Fantasia 2000, Dinosaur*, and *Kingdom in the Sun* greeted the new millenium.[75]

Media Networks

Media Networks consists of Broadcast Networks, Cable Networks, and Publishing. In 1999 revenues for Media Networks increased 5 percent, driven by increases at the Cable Networks. On the other hand, operating income decreased 8 percent, reflecting higher Broadcasting and Cable Network costs and expenses and lower Broadcasting revenues.[76]

Broadcasting became a major part of Disney with the acquisition of Capital Cities/ABC, Inc., on February 9, 1996. The ABC Television Network reaches 99.9 percent of all U.S. television households.[77] ABC has captured the attention of audiences and critics with its lineup of new shows and returning favorites. Successful shows during the 1999-2000 season included *Once and Again, The Practice, Dharma & Greg*, and *The Drew Carey Show*. ABC also delivered the season's biggest hit show, *Who Wants to Be a Millionaire*, which has become ABC's most-watched new series in 6 years, drawing an average of 24.2 million viewers each episode.[78]

In addition, ABC News continues to be the leader in television news with *Good Morning America, World News Tonight with Peter Jennings*, and *Nightline*. ABC Sports continues its *Monday Night Football*, the highest-rated regularly scheduled sports program on network TV. In 2000 the sports network also carried the women's World Cup Soccer final, a prime-time golf match between Woods and Duval, and Super Bowl XXXIV in January. Furthermore, ABC, in affiliation with MTV, recently released a new show called *Making the Band*.[79]

Disney also owns ten (ABC-owned) television stations that reach 24 percent of the nation's households. The station group posted excellent ratings last year, with six of the ten stations ranked number one in household delivery during the total broadcast day in their markets. By the end of 1999, the seven largest of these stations were broadcasting selected network programs in high definition (HDTV).[80]

In addition to the wholly owned Disney Channel, Toon Disney, and SoapNet, ABC owns 80 percent of ESPN and 50 percent of Lifetime Television and holds significant minority positions in E! Entertainment Television, A&E Television Network, and The History Channel.[81]

In 1999 ESPN celebrated its 20th anniversary. Today, ESPN, one of the most recognized brands in the world, provides a broad multimedia platform in sports, syndication, radio, Internet, print, retail, and location-based dining and entertainment ventures. ESPN reaches an estimated 77 million homes. ESPN's NFL telecasts, Sunday Night Football, drew increased viewership and remained the most-watched series on cable last year. Other programming includes the NHL's Stanley Cup playoffs, Major League Baseball playoffs, and women's World Cup Soccer. Recently, ESPN and ABC Sports broke new ground in the marketplace by merging their sales staffs to offer advertisers and marketers depth and flexibility in creating innovative packages across their different sports properties and media. Furthermore, ESPN International is one of the world's largest distributors of sports programming, with ESPN-branded sportscasting reaching more than 150 countries in 21 languages.[82] ESPN also has several other brand extensions, including ESPN Radio, the largest radio sports network in the United States, distributed through ABC Radio to more than 620 stations; ESPN The Magazine published by Disney Publishing, included in the Consumer Products segment; and ESPN Zones, sports-themed dining and entertainment facilities managed by Disney Regional Entertainment, included in the Theme Parks and Resorts segment.[83]

The Disney Channel, which features programming for kids and families, added 17 million homes to its audience last year and now reaches a total of 59 million homes in the United States. As one of the fastest growing cable networks, the Disney Channel consistently ranks among the top five basic cable outlets in prime-time ratings.[84]

The launch of a Disney Channel in Germany, strong performance in distribution activities, and new local and international productions contributed to the growth of Walt Disney Television International during 1999. Overall Disney Channel subscriptions were up by more than 20 percent. New Disney Channels are scheduled to launch in the next 2 years in Latin America, Scandinavia, and several countries in Asia through the region's Disney Channel Asia Network. In addition, new equity investments have positioned Walt Disney Television International to capitalize on growth opportunities that exist in Central Europe.[85]

Internet and Direct Marketing

Disney's Internet business develops, publishes, and distributes content for online services intended to appeal to a broad consumer interest in sports, news, family, and entertainment. The company's Internet Web sites include **www.Disney.com**, **www.Family.com**, **www.ESPN.com**, **www.ABCNEWS.com**, **www.ABCSports.com**, and **www.ABC. com**. Internet commerce activities include **www.DisneyStore.com**, which markets Disney-themed merchandise online; Disney Travel Online, which offers travel packages to the Walt Disney World Resort and other Disney destinations; and **www. ESPNStore.com**, which offers ESPN-themed and other sports-related merchandise.[86]

Last year Disney launched the GO Network. GO offers Web users many services, including e-mail, a search engine, chat rooms, auctions, stock updates, maps, and weather. The GO Network also brings together all of Disney's Web sites into one user-friendly interactive hub.[87] In addition, **www.GO.com** includes Direct Marketing activities, which manage merchandise sales through The Disney Catalog. Disney views its Direct Marketing business as a strategic asset that provides an infrastructure for its e-commerce services on the Internet. The company's goal is to build a more powerful, market-leading Internet business. The establishment of **www.GO.com** should help position Disney to seize opportunities as the Internet continues to evolve.[88]

Human Resources

Walt Disney once said, "You can dream, create, design, and build the most wonderful place in the world, but it requires people to make that dream a reality." Essentially, this is the Disney approach to human resources management. Disney has never let the importance of its employees go overlooked. Disney's Human Resources department consists of ten separate entities, including such areas as Employee Relations, Benefits Administration, The Disney University, Employee Development, Employee Activities and Services, and Employee Communications.[89] The success of the entire Disney empire is built on the excellent customer service that Disney provides to its guests. Disney calls this customer service "Disney courtesy." The company employs approximately 120,000 people.[90] So, what is the key for getting the Disney cast members to live, eat, breathe, and sleep Disney courtesy? The answer is the Disney orientation process, which is a part of Disney's well-organized, structured approach to human relations. It is during orientation that cast members learn the art of bringing value to guests. Each of Disney's cast members works for a company whose products hold special meaning for millions of people throughout the world. Disney delivers magical and memorable entertainment experiences that create a sense of joy in their guests.

Disney's Culture

Disney is "rich in heritage, traditions, quality standards, and values that it believes are critical factors to its success."[91] This foundation and environment creates the Disney culture that is the cornerstone of the company. Its cast members share the values of honesty, integrity, respect, courage, openness, diversity, and balance. These values are demonstrated through such traits and behaviors like making guests happy, caring about fellow cast members, working as a team, delivering quality, fostering creativity, paying attention to every detail, and having an emotional commitment to Disney.[92]

As diversity in the workplace continues to become a focus for nearly every company, Disney works to make this vision a reality. "By providing the cast members with the opportunity to express their own creative thoughts and direction, Disney has fostered a greater 'buy-in' to the company vision."[91] One way this has come to the attention of the cast members and the public is via GayDays at Walt Disney World. It may have been Orlando's biggest annual tourist event ever with 100,000 visitors during the tenth annual GayDays celebration, May 30-June 5, 2000. Although no theme park officially endorses the event, special days are designated at all major theme parks, and gays and lesbians usually visit them in droves.[93]

In recognition of exceptional young people who have had a positive impact on their communities, Disney and McDonald's teamed up to form the Millennium Dreamers program. This new and exciting program searches for young people who have made a significant difference in their lives and the lives of the people around them, and it honors them with an official recognition ceremony at the Walt Disney World Resort. Celebrities have been added to provide additional excitement at the ceremony for the 2000 young people during the 3-day celebration.[94]

VoluntEARism

Individualism is also passed on to the community through the cast members and employees of Walt Disney with their long-standing reputation for community service. Every year, Disney VoluntEARS provide meals to the elderly, raise funds for breast and ovarian cancer research, and mentor children and young people. Disney volunteers contribute more than a quarter of a million hours annually in community service. Between 1998 and 2000, Disney employees pledged 1 million Magical Hours of volunteerism.[95]

This volunteerism began at the Disneyland Resort in 1983. The VoluntEARS from Disneyland worked on such projects as turning inner-city vacant lots into playgrounds and raising money for the Children's Hospital of Orange County.[96] Today's VoluntEARS are working on projects like the Probation Department's Gang Alternative Programs. One VoluntEAR from the Disney Channel has mentored a young person for several years who has now graduated from high school and is mentoring another youth.[97]

Orientation

Disney's orientation process is ongoing for all Disney cast members, beginning with the recruitment stage. It continuously reinforces the values, philosophies, and guest service standards on which Disney has prided itself for so many years. Exhibit 4 shows Disney's comprehensive approach to employee relations. It is reinforced with activities, management style, and language. Employees at Disney are called "cast members." They do not work at a job; instead, they are "cast in a role for the show." Disney uses this terminology to immerse its employees in an environment that constantly reinforces the image Disney wants to project to the public. Also, cast members work either onstage or backstage, and they wear costumes rather than uniforms. Because they can interact with guests at any time, all Disney employees—whether onstage cast members or backstage cast members—are required to learn and use Disney courtesy at all times. (See Exhibit 5.)

Recruitment

Disney has a clean-cut image and conservative approach that helps potential employees self-select; thus Disney usually attracts the type of applicants it wants. The Disney "casting" department (human resources) is responsible for hiring qualified applicants who will be cast for a role in Disney's show. This department hires for general employment and college, international, and professional staffing. Hiring for general employment can come from both internal and external sources. Approximately 85 percent of Disney's middle- and executive-level management is hired from within; therefore the majority of new general employment applicants come from internal sources.

All new-to-Disney applicants go through the same recruitment process. First, there is an 8- to 10-minute preliminary interview that involves a great number of applicants. The main emphasis of this initial interview is to give a realistic view of employment at Disney, to eliminate those who are not interested or are not qualified, and to reschedule a full interview for those applicants who are still interested in becoming a Disney cast member. Would-be cast members need to understand that a job at Disney is not all glamour and that it takes a lot of hard work. For example, Disney theme parks, resorts, and hotels are open 365 days a year, and cast members work early mornings, days, evenings, weekends, and holidays. In addition, all cast members

| EXHIBIT 4 | EMPLOYEE RELATIONS PHILOSOPHY |

We believe in
1. Being air and impartial in our relations with all employees without regard to race, religion, color, national origin, age, sex, marital status, and handicaps.
2. Providing an opportunity for all employees to reach their personal goals while accomplishing the goals of the organization.
3. Providing a safe and meaningful working environment that contributes to a feeling of worth and individual dignity for each member of our "family."
4. Providing opportunities for growth and development on the job through comprehensive training programs.
5. Providing competitive pay and benefits that recognize employee loyalty, dedication, and individual contribution.
6. Promoting from within our organization when and where feasible.
7. An informal, friendly management style, encouraging open lines of communications at all levels.
8. Teamwork—each of us working together toward common, understood goals.

| EXHIBIT 5 | THE DISNEY PRODUCT GUEST SERVICE |

In providing the Disney brand of GUEST SERVICE, our cast members are . . .
I.   COURTEOUS
  • Tone of voice
  • Smile
  • Considerate
  • Hospitable
II. IMAGE-CONSCIOUS
  • Appearance
  • Demeanor
  • Attitude
  • Eye Contact
III. HIGH PERFORMERS
  • Knowledgeable
  • Accurate
  • Thorough
  • Helpful
  • Creative

must adhere to strict grooming standards. All would-be employees are shown a film that details the discipline, grooming, and dress codes to which Disney expects all cast members to adhere at all times. People with extreme styles will know at this point of the interview process if they will be able to adapt in order to be a part of Disney's show. The next step, the full interview, is conducted with three prospective candidates for 45 minutes. These peer interviews allow the interviewer to get a closer look at the applicant by observing how each interacts with the others. One Disney manager stated, "This is a good indication of how they'll work with fellow cast members and guests. We're looking for human relations and communications skills. We can train them in the technical skills."[98]

Disney University

Disney University is the corporate structure that teaches Disney courtesy, translates company policy, and trains employees.[99] In other words, it is the framework that keeps all of those things together. The concept of the Disney University started in Disneyland in 1955, along with Walt Disney's vision of an amusement park unlike any other. Walt dreamed of a safe and friendly family park to which people would return. Thus he decided that Disneyland (the only theme park at that time) needed a training facility to introduce new employees to the business of entertainment as he imagined it. What started as a 1-hour program called "You Create Happiness" grew as Disneyland grew. In the 1960s the Disney University was officially established.

Today, because each Disney facility has unique challenges and varying employee needs, each Disney facility has its own Disney University. Each university is responsible for training and development, employee activities, employee communications, researching and analyzing the organization's people needs, proposing plans to meet those needs, and continually researching the effectiveness of the orientation and training programs.

Traditions I and II at Disney University

All new cast members at any Disney facility begin their Disney careers with a 2-day orientation seminar called "Traditions" that is conducted at the Disney University (see Exhibit 6). The role of the Disney University and the Traditions seminar is to provide cast members with a sound understanding of Disney's corporate tradition and values, skills essential to job performance, and accredited continuing professional growth and development (see Exhibit 7). The Traditions 2-day seminar is carefully scripted and conducted in a comfortable, specially designed training room. During the first day of orientation, Traditions I, cast members learn the history, traditions, and milestones of the worldwide Disney team; Walt Disney's philosophy and the standards of guest service; and where they fit into the corporate structure (their role in the show). They also receive a tour of the Disney property where they will work and are introduced to the intangible product of happiness and their role in creating it. The second day of orientation, Traditions II, is devoted to the Disney policies and practices cast members must know in order to perform their jobs; an overview of what social, recreational, and personal services the company provides cast members; and a 4-hour orientation of their specific work area, which includes meeting with their supervisors, learning what costumes they will wear, and reviewing general policies and procedures.

When the 2-day Traditions orientation is completed, cast members begin a series of learning experiences at onsite practice sessions and classes at the university. This training may run for 8 to 16 hours before cast members are allowed to go to their specific work area after closing to practice.

The next step, paired training, allows exceptional cast members to act as role models. The benefits of paired training include the new cast member rehearsing with a respected member of the troupes; the veteran cast member is recognized by management, as well as by peers, and held in esteem. These new cast members are required to have between 16 to 48 hours of paired training and are not allowed to interact solo with guests until they have completed paired training and have answered questions on the training checklist.

Adapting the Disney Approach to Improve Your Organization

Disney also is known for offering programs to train employees of other firms and to provide the equivalent level of service. Insight can be gained to assist a company in the

EXHIBIT 6	ORIENTATION AND DEVELOPMENT PROCESS

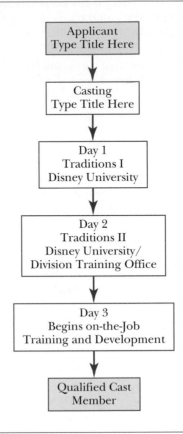

EXHIBIT 7	WHY EXTENSIVE ORIENTATION?

- To establish the corporate culture and overall company knowledge
- To strengthen the self-image of cast members
- To communicate employee benefits, activities, and services
- To communicate the why and wherefore of company policies and procedures
- To transmit to cast members the people skills and attitudes prerequisite to the job skills needed to perform their roles in the show
- To create a team spirit among new members of the Disney cast

selection, training, communication, and care that comprises a company's culture. The motivation and coaching of employees, as well as listening and responding to their needs, are strategies that remain a focus of this program. Techniques include communicating with front-line employees, implementing training programs, communicating a vision, and developing low-cost employee activity programs that contribute to job satisfaction and productivity. Methods consist of strengthening workforce morale and productivity, recruiting and hiring full-time and part-time personnel, and adapting the Disney approach to improve organizations in certain industry areas.

| EXHIBIT 8 | UNIONS TARGET DISNEY WORLD |

In the Spring of 2001, Disney World's unions pressed demands for improved wages and other employment issues as a three year collective bargaining contract approached its expiration date. The Services Trades Council Union consists of six union locals representing almost 25,000 of 55,000 employees. The unions are as follows:

Hotel Employees & Restaurant Employees Union, Local 737, **representing housekeepers, hotel restaurant workers, cooks, chef assistants, chef prep workers and bakers.**

Hotel Employees & Restaurant Employees Union, Local 362, **representing custodians, animal caretakers, vacation planners, ticket takers and laundresses.**

International Brotherhood of Teamsters, Local 385, **representing bus drivers and costumed workers.**

Transportation Communications International Union, Local 1908, **representing boat operators, valets, bellhops, and hotel front desk workers.**

United Food and Commercial Workers, Local 1625, **representing food and beverage handlers.**

International Alliance of Theatrical Stage Employees, Local 631, **representing stagehands and theater workers.**

In the spring of 2001, Disney World announced 1400 job cuts and a hiring freeze as a result of a slowdown in economic activity. Even though the freeze lasted only a few days and did not affect union employees, the unions believe this action signals a much tougher negotiation stance on the part of management, although the company denies this.

One of the major demands the union is making is an increase in the starting minimum wage by $2.33 per hour to $8.68 per hour with a 9.25 percent wage increase over the contract's three-year life. They are also asking that the hourly workers at the top of the pay scale receive nothing less than a 6 percent increase.

Mike Stapleton, President of the Teamsters Local, states that, "This is a very difficult company to work for in terms of regimentation. As part of their uniform, they have to smile, even on days when the last thing they want to do is smile."

Jerry Montgomery, Disney World's V.P. of employee relations, said, "We look forward to a fair exchange of ideas and views."

SOURCE: Mike Schneider, "Unions Take Aim at Disney," *Tallahassee Democrat*, April 15, 2001, p. 5B.

The Disney seminar experience is as unique as the program content. Prices for open-enrollment program packages range from $2795 to $3295, and the fee for each $3\frac{1}{2}$ day program includes:

- Accommodations at the Disney Institute.
- Visits to "onstage" and behind-the-scenes locations to see how textbook theory becomes operational reality.
- Meetings with Disney leaders for insight into management "best practices."
- A list of program participants for future networking.
- Continental breakfast and lunch daily.
- Preprogram and classroom materials.
- A comprehensive reference manual of course content.
- An opening-night work session with a dinner buffet and beverages.

- Complimentary access to the Disney Institute Sports and Fitness Center.
- Theme park admission and unlimited use of the Walt Disney World Resort Transportation System.[100]

The University Professional Development Program is designed for leaders who want to stimulate their staff. Human resource representatives discover valuable people-management strategies for industries such as healthcare, financial services, utilities, telecommunications, trade associations, independent consulting, education, retail merchandising, tourism and resorts, food service, government, manufacturing, transportation, museums, insurance, wholesale, and retail. Regardless of the size or focus of the company, Disney will provide effective ideas and solutions that pertain to all human resource issues.[101]

Development: An Ongoing Process

Training does not stop when cast members learn their roles. Hourly, cast members are offered career development, goal setting, and interviewing technique classes. Clerical staff are offered courtesy and clerical stress management classes. Disney's leaders (hourly workers who have been given a leadership role for their job classification) and trainers receive special development, including performance appraisals and instruction in how to train and lead development, which strengthen their human resource skills. Salaried cast members can attend classes such as counseling and listening, understanding people as individuals, Disney's courtesy, stress and time management, and an array of specific skill-related programs.

Because Disney promotes 85 percent of its middle- and executive-level management from within, Disney has developed the Disney Intern Program. Cast members with management potential from different divisions of the company go through 6 months of on-the-job training. Halfway through the program, these students are given an assignment to develop an idea or modify an existing process at Disney. Small groups work together to develop a presentation for top management. The program ends with an exam and graduation. Unfortunately, completion of the internship is no guarantee of a job, but cast members know this going into the program. Rather than promote and then train them for the job, Disney trains them in advance. Most college students are offered a starting salary of $5.60 an hour with some increase in pay for certain positions. Overtime is often required and results in time-and-a-half pay. Interns work anywhere from 4 to 8 hours a day, 5 days a week with some overtime and weekend work required, and are only paid a stipend.[101] Division managers project how many salaried people they think that they will need, and the company tries to make sure that there will be enough interns to meet those needs.

Benefits

Disney continues to offer its cast members competitive wage rates, premium benefits, and outstanding growth opportunities. Today, the company offers cast members multiple health plans, including a free HMO. Financial options include an employee stock purchase plan, defined benefit retirement program, salaried 401(k) program, credit union, and insurance discounts.[103] Besides the traditional benefits packages, Disney also offers discounts at other local and national companies and free park admissions.

For instance, before the opening of Animal Kingdom to guests, cast members were given exclusive access to the park during "cast preview days."

Conclusion

The Walt Disney Company has become one of the world's most recognized corporate entities. In pursuing its goals, Disney continues to focus on the key factors that have driven strong results since its inception: the ongoing development of the company's powerful brand and character franchises, and an emphasis on creative excellence and high quality in all Disney products.[104] Much of the company's growth and success is due to its expansion into many diverse businesses. Now The Walt Disney Company is a vast multinational corporation, which stands at the forefront of the entertainment industry. Disney is known nearly all over the world for its intangible product of happiness, but it must continue to overcome certain challenges to ensure its position as the world's preeminent entertainment company.

Questions

1. From the beginning of his tenure, Michael Eisner has played a significant role in Disney's management. Discuss the steps Disney should take to ensure success in the future.
2. Disney now has five lines of businesses. How successful do you think Disney will be in the future with its endeavors to integrate entertainment inside and outside the home? Will its theme parks, restaurants, and movies complement its plans to expand into the markets of the Internet and broadcasting? Explain.
3. How should Disney maintain its corporate culture as it continues to expand into global markets?
4. With the current labor market and competitive conditions dictating wage rates, should Disney and other large companies in the tourist industry be required to pay higher wages?

Notes

[1]The Walt Disney Company, *1999 Online Annual Report*, p. 2.
[2]**www.disney.com**, (accessed September 1, 2000).
[3]Richard Hollis and Brian Sibley, *The Disney Studio Story* (London: Octopus Books Ltd., 1988).
[4]Ibid.
[5]Adrian Bailey, *Walt Disney's World of Fantasy* (Secaucus, NJ: Chartwell Books, 1982).
[6]Hollis and Sibley, *The Disney Studio Story*.
[7]Ibid.
[8]Ibid.
[9]Ibid.
[10]Ibid.
[11]Bailey, *Walt Disney's World of Fantasy*.
[12]Hollis and Sibley, *The Disney Studio Story*.
[13]Ibid.
[14]Ibid.

[15]Ibid.

[16]Bailey, *Walt Disney's World of Fantasy.*

[17]Hollis and Sibley, *The Disney Studio Story.*

[18]Ibid.

[19]Ibid.

[20]Ibid.

[21]Ibid.

[22]Ibid.

[23]Ibid.

[24]Ibid.

[25]Ibid.

[26]Ibid.

[27]Ibid.

[28]Roy Grover, *The Disney Touch* (Homewood, IL: Business One Irwin, 1991).

[29]Ronald Grover and Michael O'Neal, "Disney: Room for Two Lion Kings," *Business Week*, August 28, 1995, pp. 28–29.

[30]The Walt Disney Company, *1999 Online Annual Report*, p. 2.

[31]Ibid.

[32]Ibid, p. 10.

[33]Ibid, p. 39.

[34]Ibid, p. 58. 30.

[35]Ibid, pp. 48–49.

[36]Ibid, p. 3.

[37]Ibid, pp. 3–4.

[38]Ibid, p. 4.

[39]Scott Kauffman, "Eisner Surprises Braves with a Visit," **www.lexis-nexis.com/universe**, (accessed September 1, 2000).

[40]"Mice, Magic, and Malls," *Shopping Centers Today*, May 1991, pp. 27–43.

[41]The Walt Disney Company, *1999 Online Annual Report*, p. 39.

[42]Ibid, p. 4.

[43]Frank Kane, "Disneyland Paris Needs Boost from Uncle Walt," *Sunday Times*, August 31, 1997, **www.lexi-nexis.com/universe**.

[44]Yomiri Shimbum, "Theme Parks Introduce Japanese to Fun," *The Daily Yomiuri*, June 2, 1995, p. 17, **www.lexis-nexis.com/universe.docm**, (accessed September 1, 2000).

[45]Ibid.

[46]The Walt Disney Company, *1999 Online Annual Report*, p. 19.

[47]Ibid.

[48]Ibid, p. 6.

[49]Ibid, p. 29.

[50]Ibid, p. 58.

[51]Ibid, p. 48.

[52]Ibid, p. 15.

[53]Ibid.

[54]Ibid.

[55]**www.disney.com**, (accessed September 1, 2000).

[56]The Walt Disney Company, *1999 Online Annual Report*, p. 58.

[57]Disney History Packet.

[58]**www.funandsun.com/1tocf/Disney/dis2.html**, (accessed September 1, 2000).

[59]The Walt Disney Company, *1999 Online Annual Report*, p. 16.

[60]Alan Bryman, *Disney and His Worlds* (Routledge: New York, 1995), p. 74.

[61]David Molyneaux, "Disney in Florida Is Still Growing," *The Plain Dealer*, February 15, 1998, Travel Section, p. 1.

[62]**www.disney.com**, (accessed September 1, 2000).

[63]Disney History Packet.

[64]The Walt Disney Company, *1999 Online Form 10-K.*

[65]*1999 Factbook.*

[66]The Walt Disney Company, *1999 Online Annual Report*, p. 15.

[67]Nancy Keates and Bruce Orwall, "Disney Ship's Maiden Voyage Delayed Again," *The Wall Street Journal*, February 19, 1998, p. B5.

[68]The Walt Disney Company, *1999 Online Form 10-K*.

[69]The Walt Disney Company, *1999 Online Annual Report*, p. 47.

[70]Ibid, p. 25.

[71]Ibid, p. 47.

[72]**www.disney.com**, (accessed September 1, 2000).

[73]The Walt Disney Company, *1999 Online Annual Report*, p. 3.

[74]Ibid, p. 26.

[75]Ibid, p. 27.

[76]Ibid, p. 46.

[77]**www.disney.com**, (accessed September 1, 2000).

[78]The Walt Disney Company, *1999 Online Annual Report*, p. 33.

[79]**www.disney.com**, (accessed September 1, 2000).

[80]The Walt Disney Company, *1999 Online Annual Report*, p. 34.

[81]Ibid, p. 36.

[82]Ibid.

[83]The Walt Disney Company, *1999 Online Form 10-K*.

[84]The Walt Disney Company, *1999 Online Annual Report*, p. 36.

[85]Ibid, p. 35.

[86]Ibid, p. 58.

[87]Ibid, p. 42.

[88]Ibid, p. 43.

[89]**guest.btinternet.com/~alan.price/hrm/Disney.htm**, (accessed September 1, 2000).

[90]The Walt Disney Company, *1999 Online Form 10-K*.

[91]**www.disney.com/factbook98**, (accessed September 1, 2000).

[92]Judson Green, "Performance Excellence," *Walt Disney Attraction*, April 1994, p. 4.

[93]"Gays and Lesbians Flock to World's #1 Tourist Destination For 10th Annual GayDays Celebration," *PR Newswire*, May 17, 2000.

[94]"Making the Vision a Reality," **www.gay.com**, (accessed September 1, 2000).

[95]**www.mcdonalds.com/corporate**, (accessed September 1, 2000).

[96]"Disney Volunteerism: Thousands of Helping Hands," **http://www.disney.com**.

[97]Ibid.

[98]Charlene Marmer Soloman, "How Does Disney Do It?" *Personal Journal*, December 1989, pp. 50–57.

[99]Ibid.

[100]**www.disney.go.com/DisneyWorld/DisneyInstitute/ProfessionalPrograms**, (accessed September 1, 2000).

[101]Dee Anne Neri, "Thought, Talk, and Speculation," *CBN Report*, March 9, 1998, p. 4.

[102]"The Working Experience," *Walt Disney World College Program*, p. 2.

[103]*1997 Annual Report*, **www.disney.com**, (accessed September 1, 2000).

[104]The Walt Disney Company, *1999 Online Annual Report*, p. 10.

5

Wal-Mart Stores, Inc.*

When J.C. Penney let Samuel Moore Walton slip away from its management trainee program in 1942, the company had no warning of the resounding impact that resignation would have on its industry in the coming decades. After 3 years in the Army, Sam Walton opened the first Walton's Ben Franklin store in Newport, Arkansas, in September 1945.

In 1950, Sam Walton, after losing the lease on his Newport store, relocated to Bentonville, Arkansas. During the 1950s, Mr. Sam (as he would be known to his associates) increased the number of Walton-owned Ben Franklin stores to nine. In 1962 Mr. Sam and his brother, Bud, opened the first Wal-Mart Discount City in Rogers, Arkansas. Growth was anything but exponential during that period; the second Wal-Mart store did not open for 2 more years. David Glass, former president and CEO and now chairman of the executive committee of the board of directors, attended that grand opening in Harrison:

> It was the worst retail store I had ever seen. Sam had brought a couple of trucks of watermelons and stacked them on the sidewalk. He also had donkey rides out in the parking lot. It was 115 degrees, and the watermelons began to pop, and the donkeys began to do what donkeys do, and it got all mixed together and ran all over the parking lot. And when you went inside the store, the mess continued. He was a nice fellow, but I wrote him off. It was just terrible.[1]

From that dubious beginning, Wal-Mart Corporation has surprised Wall Street, as well as its competitors, by becoming America's largest retailer by 1990.[2] Late in 1969, the company was incorporated; 12 months later, its stock was publicly traded over the counter. In another 2 years, the stock was approved and listed on the New York Stock Exchange. Sales for 1970 were $44 million and by 1979 had reached more than $1 billion.[3] For fiscal 2000, sales exceeded $165 billion with net income more than $5 billion. (See Appendix A for Wal-Mart's current financial position). The company's sales growth of 20 percent in fiscal 2000, when compared with fiscal 1999, is

---

*This case was prepared by Steve R. Avera, Elizabeth D. Ellis, Don W. Reinhard, Andrew M. Thomas, and Tammy Wilkerson. It was revised by Cheri Beacht, Mike Johnson, Brad Mabry, Catherine Mathe, Keishia Roberts, and Sandi Smith.

the result of the company's expansion program, including international acquisition, and a domestic comparative store sales increase of 8 percent. [4]

A unique feature of Wal-Mart's retailing is that it is virtually recession proof. In times of economic downturn, consumers flock to discount retailers. During the recession of 1974-75, sales expanded 42 percent; in the 1981-82 recession, sales grew 44 percent; and in the recession of the 1990s, sales grew 30 percent. As such, Wal-Mart is not affected by economic downturns like many other retailers.[5]

Wal-Mart has obtained a distinct competitive advantage by targeting small, rural communities, which leads to lower operating costs. This advantage results from lower rents, moderate wages, and the absence of unionization. In addition, real estate is significantly cheaper, and smaller communities have a more loyal and productive workforce.

Although the store location strategy was innovative, several other factors have played a strong role in vaulting Wal-Mart to the top of the retail mountain. For instance, Mr. Sam's management practices were even more trend setting than his store location strategy. A strong advocate of participatory management practices, Wal-Mart has been a prototype in employee relations. For example, employees are not referred to as employees; instead, they are called "associates," a term coined by Mr. Sam at the very first Wal-Mart store. Other factors that have contributed to Wal-Mart's success include rigorous cost control, an excellent distribution network, and a technological advantage.

Wal-Mart proudly moved up in *Fortune's* list of the top ten "America's Most Admired Companies" in 2000, rising to fifth on the list. In ranking the top ten, *Fortune* surveyed more than 10,000 executives, directors, and securities analysts, who were asked to choose the companies they admired most, regardless of industry.[6]

Efficient Operations

Wal-Mart is proud of its efficient operations, which have been a decisive factor in its ascension to become America's top discount store. With its stated goal to be the low-cost leader,[7] Wal-Mart has built a network of stores and offices that serves two important functions: it avoids the cost of building separate administrative offices, and it creates a close feeling between store management and customers while promoting a better working bond among coworkers. This design allows managers to interact with the customers during business hours. It also has the added feature of allowing managers close contact with associates.

The low-overhead style of management Wal-Mart has developed has allowed the company to keep its operating expenses under control. Since 1990 sales have risen from more than $25 billion to $165 billion in 2000.[8] During this same period, the company has continued to expand its number of store locations. According to the Wal-Mart 2000 Annual Report, it has grown to 2373 discount stores, 512 SAM'S Clubs, and 1104 Supercenters worldwide.[9] Even with this considerable growth taking place, Wal-Mart has managed to keep its operating, selling, general, and administrative expenses, expressed as a percentage of sales, relatively low at about 16 percent in recent years.[10]

Support systems such as excellent distribution, a state-of-the-art communications network, and certainly the associates have given management the ability to manage this large-scale growth while controlling operating costs. Wal-Mart is careful to provide each associate with the technological tools needed in order to work smarter. In early 1997 the company was recognized by *Computerworld* and *Smithsonian Magazine* as one of the top five innovators in information technology. The award recognized the Retail Link system, which provides sales data—by item, by store, by day—to vendor-partners. This helps suppliers save time and expense in planning their production and distribution, which translates to lower merchandise costs.

Another measure of efficiency that Wal-Mart is particularly proud of is inventory shrinkage. Shrinkage occurs as a result of shoplifting, inventory shortages, and employee theft. Although the discount retail industry's average shrinkage per store is 2 percent, Wal-Mart employees pride themselves on a per-store shrinkage of around 1 percent.[11] With this low shrinkage rate comes clear rewards: stores that achieve target shrinkage rates earn bonuses of several hundred dollars each.

Clearly, operating efficiencies have played a critical role in the success of Wal-Mart. These operating efficiencies have allowed Wal-Mart to offer services that customers notice, such as keeping extra checkout lines open and posting a "greeter" at the entrance to each Wal-Mart store. This results in what Stephen F. Mandel, Jr., an analyst with Tiger Management Corporation, calls the "productivity loop," in which Wal-Mart's ability to offer lower prices and better service will inevitably attract more shoppers. This prompts more sales, making the company more efficient and able to lower prices even further.

Distribution Network

Wal-Mart's distribution system is another key component of its efficiency strategy. Its distribution centers strategically blanket Wal-Mart's market areas. Most stores are located within 1 day's drive of a distribution center. Deliveries are made daily to each Wal-Mart store. The company recognizes that communication is the backbone to an efficient distribution system. Based on this reasoning, Wal-Mart budgets $500 million annually to its communication and information systems staff of 1200 professionals.[12]

Between 70 and 80 percent of all purchasing is done centrally, taking advantage of Wal-Mart's state-of-the-art satellite network. (See the discussion of computer technology that follows.) Similarly, during fiscal 2000, approximately 83 percent of the purchases made by Wal-Mart discount stores and Supercenters were shipped from Wal-Mart's distribution centers. The remaining 17 percent was shipped directly to the stores from suppliers.[13]

All but one of the distribution centers are automated, utilizing a complex conveyor system that involves up to eleven *miles* of belts. Laser scanners route the goods (up to 190,000 cases per day), which are also strategically tied to the satellite network core in Bentonville. In addition, Wal-Mart built a state-of-the-art 600,000-square-foot distribution center featuring technological and logistical advancements. The distribution center replaced the one located in Bentonville.[14]

In an effort to further cut costs and improve grocery distribution center efficiency, Wal-Mart has added a voice-based, order-filling system. Inventory and order personnel simply strap on a headset connected to a portable unit worn on a waist belt and orally make stock requests. The associate's voice automatically directs the request to the location in the warehouse where the product is stored. Subsequently, the quantity ordered is verified and filled. This technology has effectively eliminated paper lists and product labeling—costs formerly associated with the traditional process. Today, Wal-Mart has distribution centers in 62 locations around the world.[15]

Computer Technology

Wal-Mart boasts the world's largest private, fully integrated satellite network.[16] This satellite network connects the Wal-Mart management information system (MIS) to every Wal-Mart store and distribution center in 45 states, as well as to its foreign operations in Mexico, Canada, Brazil, China, and other South Pacific rim countries. By using audio, video, and data signals via more than 1400 earth stations, it maintains constant communication between the organization's communications center and all of its operations and suppliers. As a result, every store is connected in real time to the corporate information center in Bentonville so that each and every transaction is made online. The network not only monitors inventory and orders replacement stock, but it also electronically approves credit transactions. Authorization is sent back to the remote store from the network in less than 6 seconds.

The operational goal of this network is to provide better customer service and improve business efficiency. For instance, if a credit authorization transaction can be completed in 25 percent less time, one checker can handle four customers in the time it took to handle three using the manual system. Hence, a checker can process more customers in the same amount of time. Customers spend less time in the checkout line and leave with positive feelings toward the store.

Other business efficiencies that result from the network include the monitoring of inventory and movement, the ability to track trends by item, and the assurance of a smooth product flow from suppliers to distribution centers to retail stores to consumers. Products that are in demand flow into the stores at the desired rate. This rapid response time has allowed Wal-Mart to maintain an enviable in-stock rate, a high asset utilization rate, and industry leadership in holding both waste and costs down while keeping productivity and profits high.[17]

In the event that a particular store location does experience a stock-out, associates are equipped to scan an item and electronically check on its availability in other area stores. Associates are even given "magic wands," hand-held computers linked by a radio-frequency network to in-store terminals that serve as a high-tech conduit to an internal information system that gives every associate access to Wal-Mart merchandise inventory. The wands help keep up-to-the-minute track of the inventory on hand, deliveries, and backup merchandise in stock at Wal-Mart distribution centers.[18]

Online Wal-Mart Retailing

On July 30, 1996, Wal-Mart and SAM'S Club went live with the introduction of online shopping. The online sites offer shoppers the "high technology of cyberspace shopping with the familiar, friendly settings of Wal-Mart and SAM'S Club."[19] Similar to the real-life experience at any Wal-Mart store, shoppers are immediately greeted at the door and assisted throughout the shopping journey. Shoppers are even given virtual shopping carts in which to place their selections.[20]

Wal-Mart Online (**www.wal-mart.com**), relaunched on January 1, 2000, offers the well-known products found in traditional stores plus additional products offered only to online users. "Virtual shelves" are always well stocked with the latest software, videos, music, home products, office furniture, toys, tools, and collectibles. Similarly, SAM'S Club Online (**www.samsclub.com**) offers the familiar products found in SAM'S Clubs, and the club's members still enjoy discounted prices.

Recently, Wal-Mart formed a new partnership with the Internet venture-capital firm Accel Partners. The new venture, Wal-Mart.com Inc., will be based in Palo Alto, California, and its financial results will be consolidated into Wal-Mart's financials because Wal-Mart Stores, Inc. is the majority shareholder. Furthermore, the separate company will have its own management team and board of directors.[21]

In February of 1998, Florists' Transworld Delivery, Inc., (FTD) announced that it had partnered with Wal-Mart to launch an online flower shop in conjunction with Wal-Mart's Web site. The partnership allows FTD to sell holiday and everyday arrangements, flowers, gourmet food items, and other gift-giving solutions. FTD provides merchandising support and fulfills floral orders through its international affiliated network of more than 54,000 FTD florists.[22]

An investment in technology has helped to assure online consumers of the safety and convenience of electronic retailing. Regarding their safety, credit card transactions utilize the Secure Sockets Layer (SSL) system. The security system applies high-tech encryption technology to ensure that credit card numbers are kept away from undesirable fraud artists. Purchases are made conveniently with the help of support representatives who are available 24 hours a day, 7 days a week at 1-800-WMON-LINE. Finally, purchases are shipped via UPS within 48 hours of receipt of the order.[23]

Support American Made

The Buy American program has evolved in the past few years but still provides opportunities for many domestic suppliers to succeed in the face of daunting foreign competition.

Originally, Wal-Mart targeted American manufacturers that simply could not compete with the cheaper and equal—if not better quality—foreign goods. Sam Walton was making an effort to help out the small merchants and manufacturers because he remembered that Wal-Mart used to be a small company as well.

The Buy American program has evolved into the Support American Made program. Support American Made not only provides business for smaller American manufacturers, but it also has an emphasis on better production and marketing of the products. Support American Made specifically assists the many small manufacturers whose production or distribution capabilities for providing products to nationwide retailers are limited. Furthermore, Wal-Mart focuses on assisting these companies in finding more efficient and profitable ways of doing business.

The Support American Made program will help any manufacturer of American-made products with a sales history of 6 months or more. These businesses can easily learn about and apply for membership in the program through Wal-Mart's website. Support American Made is a free service from Wal-Mart that is coordinated by Southwest Missouri State University in Springfield and conducted at Wal-Mart's Home Office in Bentonville, Arkansas. Wal-Mart has become a global company, taking the philosophy of helping local communities into every area it enters. Even in the global economy, Wal-Mart promotes local jobs.

The program can also connect smaller manufacturers with a network of Support American Made partners that have experience in assisting companies with increasing their effectiveness in competitive markets. In addition, financial advice, management guidance, and technical assistance are available from these partners.

Wal-Mart promotes the production of goods by American manufacturers, which helps the economics of the local areas. The real problem often associated with these programs is that they do not help consumers by promoting the best and most inexpensive products available. Wal-Mart distributes products made by local manufacturers when the products that are made overseas are potentially cheaper for the American people. Does this really put the interests of the worker in the foreground?

Here is an example story that was published on Wal-Mart's Web site:

BLACK & DECKER
> Flavor Scenter Food Steamers—Asheboro, North Carolina
>
> Of the 16,000 good people who live in Asheboro, more than 1500 work at Black & Decker making Snake Lights, toaster ovens, coffee makers, Dustbusters, and Flavor Scenter Food Steamers. The Flavor Scenter adds the taste of your favorite herbs and spices as you steam rice, vegetables, or other foods. It's a quick, easy way to make healthful, flavorful meals.
>
> Traditionally, a team at Black & Decker headquarters in Shelton, Connecticut, is responsible for product development. However, for the Flavor Scenter Food Steamer, Black & Decker turned to its Asheboro plant.
>
> The Asheboro employees built a diverse team, representing every critical part of the process, including design, engineering, manufacturing, and quality control. Working in partnership with Wal-Mart, they designed the product and developed the manufacturing. In the process, they not only created a great new product that brings flavor to your table; they brought 76 new jobs to their home town.[24]

Unlike some corporations whose financial growth does not translate into more jobs, Wal-Mart's phenomenal growth has been an engine for making jobs. Now Wal-Mart employs more than 885,000 associates in the United States and more than 225,000 internationally for a total of more than 1,140,000 worldwide.[25] The company is currently the largest private-sector employer in the United States.[26]

The Wal-Mart Effect

During the 1980s and early 1990s, Wal-Mart was presented with multiple predatory pricing lawsuits, and these were settled out of court. Then, in 1993 an Arkansas state court ruled that Wal-Mart was guilty of practicing these anti-small business pricing practices. However, that case was later reversed by the Supreme Court of Arkansas on January 9, 1995, as given in state court document no. 94-235.

Wal-Mart has worked very hard over the years to create an image that it is the working person's store. The stores are staffed with local, "everyday" people who relate well with the types of people to which Wal-Mart is marketing. But for some people, the image of this wholesome American store is tainted by the predatory pricing lawsuits.[27]

Since the court's ruling, Wal-Mart has expanded into numerous towns and cities in the United States. There are also expansion efforts into Mexico and Canada, and the pressures to compete with this giant discount retailer are causing companies in these countries to worry about their future.

Wal-Mart is working to correct the predatory pricing image by pushing the "All-American small town provider" image even more. Although the company is the leading retail employer in small towns, it also promotes local economic growth by donating about $3 million in Economic Development Grants each year. In addition, the company has formed alliances with the National Association of Towns and Townships to bolster its image.

Wal-Mart's image on the streets of America is still mixed even after these efforts to correct the damage done by their alleged illegal actions in the past. *The Wall Street Journal* compares Wal-Mart's choice-reducing practices to the recent Microsoft antitrust investigations and calls the years past "Wal-Mart tyranny."[28]

Wal-Mart is also affecting the Canadian marketplace by moving into the food retailing business by opening mini-supermarket test centers. "The prices (in those stores) have been incredibly aggressive," says an executive of Loblaw, a Canadian food retailer.[29]

Wal-Mart Operating Segments

Wal-Mart, as a whole, has a company trade territory serving more than 100 million customers weekly in 50 states, Puerto Rico, Canada, China, Mexico, Brazil, Germany, the United Kingdom, Argentina, and South Korea.[30] Wal-Mart is principally engaged in the operation of mass merchandising stores, which serve its customers primarily through the operation of three segments. The company identifies segments based on management responsibility within the U.S. and geographically for all international units. The Wal-Mart Stores segment includes the company's discount stores and Supercenters in the United States. The SAM'S Club segment includes the warehouse membership clubs in the United States. The international segment includes all operations in countries outside of the United States.[31]

Wal-Mart Stores

The Wal-Mart Discount City, the original format for Wal-Mart stores, is still emphasizing the lowest prices for a variety of brand name merchandise. These products are purchased mostly from local providers and are of comparable quality and price to overseas competitors. The theme of "everyday low prices" is prominent throughout Wal-Mart's advertising campaigns. These Wal-Marts are the prominent format in the company, and it currently operates 1801 of these discount stores in the United States.[32]

Currently, there are 721 Wal-Mart Supercenters in the United States,[33] and these stores offer a wide variety of goods from retail merchandise to food products in a one-stop shopping format. These stores are being placed throughout the United States, and the concept is being experimented with in Canada and Mexico where Wal-Mart currently has contracts with other vendors.

Sales for the company's Wal-Mart Stores segment increased by 14 percent in fiscal 2000 compared with fiscal 1999. The fiscal 2000 growth is the result of comparative store sales increases and the company's expansion program. Segment expansion during fiscal 2000 included the opening of 29 Wal-Mart stores and 157 Supercenters (including the conversion of 96 existing Wal-Mart stores into Supercenters). Operating income for the segment for fiscal 2000 increased by 19 percent when compared with fiscal 1999. The increase in operating income for 2000 was driven by margin improvements resulting from improvements in markdowns and shrinkage.[34]

SAM'S Clubs

SAM'S Clubs, formerly Sam's Wholesale Club until the name was revised when prices were discovered to be a bit higher than true wholesale prices, caters to small businesses by selling bulk items at very low prices. These stores are simply warehouses that handle an assortment of items stacked to the ceiling on pallets. There is no atmosphere or decoration added to the stores, which lowers overhead and helps SAM'S offer the lowest possible prices. SAM'S Clubs sell items that turn over quickly, but it limits the types of items offered to curb the cannibalization of other Wal-Mart ventures' profits. Currently, there are 463 clubs operating in the United States.[35]

Sales for the company's SAM'S Club segment increased by 8.4 percent in fiscal 2000 compared with fiscal 1999. SAM'S Club sales continued to decrease as a percentage of total company sales, decreasing from 17.5 percent in fiscal 1998 to 15.0 percent in fiscal 2000. This decrease as a percentage of total company sales is primarily the result of the increased growth rate in the international segment. The expansion of the SAM'S Club segment during fiscal 2000 and 1999 consisted of the opening of 12 and 8 clubs, respectively, and the company has plans for continued new club openings in fiscal 2001. In addition, the company intends to continue its program of remodeling its existing SAM'S Clubs. Operating income for the segment in fiscal 2000 increased by 16.8 percent.[36]

Also, during fiscal 2000, SAM'S Clubs launched an Elite Membership program that offers additional benefits such as long distance service, roadside assistance, Internet access, home improvement, Telebank, business insurance, financial planning, auto brokering, pharmacy discounts, and entertainment savings guides to Elite Members.[37]

International

International sales accounted for approximately 13.8 percent of the total company sales in fiscal 2000 compared with 8.9 percent in fiscal 1999. The largest portion of the increase in international sales is the result of the acquisition of the ASDA Group PLC, a British supermarket chain, which consisted of 229 stores, during the third quarter of fiscal 2000.[38] Wal-Mart's largest acquisition to date gave the company a major presence in the United Kingdom.[39]

Expansion in the international segment for fiscal 2000 consisted of the opening or acquisition of 288 units.[40] Total international sales increased more than 85 percent to $22.7 billion in fiscal 2000. Operating profit was $817 million, an increase of almost 49 percent compared with the previous fiscal year.[41] In less than 10 years, the international division has grown to more than 1000 stores and should exceed $30 billion in sales for fiscal 2001.[42]

Wal-Mart's foreign operations are composed of wholly owned operations in Argentina, Canada, Germany, Korea, Puerto Rico, and the United Kingdom; joint ventures in China; and majority-owned subsidiaries in Brazil and Mexico. At the end of fiscal 2000, Wal-Mart operated 1004 international units, including 572 discount stores, 383 Supercenters, and 49 SAM'S Clubs.[43] (See Appendix A.)

Expansion

Domestically, the company plans to open approximately 40 new Wal-Mart stores and approximately 165 new Supercenters in fiscal 2000. Relocations or expansions of existing discount stores will account for 107 of the Supercenters, and approximately 58 will be new locations.[44]

Because of the continued positive customer feedback on the Neighborhood Market concept, which is being tested in seven locations, the company plans to add five to ten new locations.[45] Wal-Mart believes that this complements its existing Supercenter strategy and offers extra convenience. The smaller format of the Neighborhood Markets gives the company the flexibility to serve markets where it may not have a Supercenter because of demographic or real estate constraints.[46]

Also planned for fiscal 2001 are 19 new SAM'S Clubs, including eight relocations. In addition, the company will remodel approximately 140 of the existing SAM'S Clubs and expand two units. In order to serve these and future developments, the company will begin shipping from eleven new distribution centers in the next fiscal year.[47]

Internationally, plans are to develop or relocate 90 to 100 retail units. These units are planned in Argentina, Brazil, Canada, China, Germany, Korea, Mexico, Puerto Rico, and the United Kingdom.[48]

Total planned growth represents approximately 34.9 million square feet of net additional retail space.[49] Over the next 5 years, 60 to 70 percent of Wal-Mart's growth in sales and earnings is expected to come from the domestic markets with its Wal-Mart stores and Supercenters, and another 10 to 15 percent from SAM'S Club and McLane. The remaining 20 percent of the growth will come from its planned growth in international markets.[50]

Human Resources

Corporate Culture and Philosophy

Our philosophy is that management's role is simply to get the right people in the right places to do a job and then encourage them to use their own inventiveness to accomplish the task at hand.[51]
-Sam Walton

We have no superstars at Wal-Mart; we have average people operating in an environment that encourages everyone to perform way above average.[52]
-David Glass

Most of us wear a button that says, "Our People Make the Difference." That is not a slogan at Wal-Mart; it is a way of life. Our people really do make a difference.[53]
-David Glass

In the late 1960s when Sam and his brother, Bud, owned about 20 Wal-Marts, a union tried to organize two stores in Missouri, and Sam hired labor lawyer John Tate, now an executive vice-president of Wal-Mart, to help. Tate told Walton, "You can approach this one of two ways. Hold people down, and pay me or some other lawyer to make it work. Or devote time and attention to proving to people that you care." Sam chose the latter and subsequently held his first management seminar, entitled "We care."

Sam insisted upon calling all employees "associates" because it implies a partnership. Department managers see figures that many companies never show general managers. Profit goals are set for each store, and if exceeded, hourly associates share a part of the additional profit. This "partnership" goes past monetary participation to open-door policies and an atmosphere that says, "Hey, if you've got a problem, talk to somebody. Don't talk about it in the lounge or the parking lot; come to management." This is ingrained in Wal-Mart's culture.

Wal-Mart's culture is its most fearsome weapon. The company gospel is "Be an agent for consumers, find out what they want, and sell it to them for the lowest possible price."[54] One source described Wal-Mart as follows:

The key to Wal-Mart's success is the quality of their management, its style, and its recognition of the importance of the individual player in the overall team effort. Other companies are striving to achieve the same cultural level, but no other retail company is close. Wal-Mart people work harder than most, probably because they have more fun. They are constantly being challenged by one another and forced to laugh at themselves. They take pride in working for perhaps the finest company in the world and their individual contributions are recognized.[55]

It is Wal-Mart's family-like environment that emphasizes teamwork and encourages employees' ideas and participation. The work atmosphere is a down-home "concern for the individual." Individual contributions to the team effort are welcomed and rewarded. Participatory management from top to bottom is stressed, and listening is an important part of a manager's job. According to Mr. Sam, "99 percent of the best ideas we ever had came from our employees."[56] His explanation was simplistic but to the point: "If people believe in themselves, it's truly amazing what they can accomplish."[57]

Sam Walton "managed by walking around" and expected the same from his managers. Lee Scott, president and CEO, along with other top executives, spends several days a week visiting the stores. To heighten associates' sense of mission, they are given plenty of responsibility. Managers for each of the 40 departments within a typical Wal-Mart are expected to run their operations as if they were running their own businesses.[58] According to one manager, 90 percent of his day is spent walking around stores communicating with associates—he praises them for well-done jobs, discusses how improvements could be made, and listens to comments and solicits suggestions. This management style also encourages the steady stream of ideas that Wal-Mart receives from its associates.

Low threshold of change (LTC) is a highly valued concept at Wal-Mart. The planning process begins with store management asking each associate what he or she could do individually to improve or how store operations could improve. Associates are encouraged to challenge and change any policies perceived to detract from operations.

Wal-Mart's corporate culture is defined by ten basic principles:[59]

1. The customer is always right.
2. We are a merchandise-driven company.
3. Our people make the difference.
4. We communicate with our associates.
5. We maintain a strong work ethic.
6. Associates are partners.
7. Our leaders are also servants.
8. Associates are empowered.
9. We have integrity in all we do.
10. We control our expenses.

In 1999 *Discount Store News* honored Wal-Mart Stores, Inc. as "Retailer of the Century." According to Tony Lisanti, editor and associate publisher of *DSN*, "The reason we chose Wal-Mart as Retailer of the Century is that Wal-Mart cares about the individual, whether he or she is an associate or a customer." *DSN* believes that the secret that has allowed Wal-Mart to outpace every other retailer in history is the spirit that pervades the company's culture.[60]

Store Meetings

Every morning before stores open and every evening after stores close, associates and managers meet for ten minutes to discuss overall operations, expectations, how things went, and so on. Every Friday morning, each store has a general store meeting during which associates at every level can ask questions and expect to get straightforward answers from management. These meetings communicate to associates information on new company initiatives and policy change announcements. Video training films are also shown from time to time. As a part of these meetings, corporate management, via satellite, emphasizes the company's five most important priorities for the upcoming week, which gives employees goals and keeps them focused.[61]

Each week department and store figures are posted on the back wall of each store so associates can see how they rank. If the figures are better than average, associates are praised. Associates in departments that regularly out-perform averages can expect annual bonuses and raises. Performances lower than average are discussed so solutions can be found.[62]

Saturday Morning Meetings at Headquarters

Since 1961, on every Saturday at 7:30 AM in Bentonville, Arkansas, Wal-Mart conducts a very informal and relaxed meeting; employees dress casually—some in hunting or tennis clothes for after-meeting fun. Those attending include top officers, merchandising staff, regional managers who oversee store districts, and the Bentonville headquarters staff. They meet to discuss Wal-Mart issues, such as the week's sales; payroll percentages; special promotional items; unusual problems; and reports on transportation, loss prevention, and information systems.[63]

People Division

Instead of a personnel department, Wal-Mart has a people division. According to Von Johnston, director of the people division, "We deal with people; people are our job. One of our board members suggested that we change our name to reflect our job and we did."[64]

This division is divided into five functions: store operations, warehouse personnel, training and development, general office personnel staff, and the Walton Life Fitness Center staff. A primary focus of the people division is the recruitment of new associates.

"The Wal-Mart Way"

"The Wal-Mart Way" summarizes the company's unconventional approach to business and the determination of its associates. This commitment to "total quality" is essential to the company's future success; it proliferates the very best qualities of the company while incorporating the new ideas of company employees.[65] "Quality the Wal-Mart Way" is an ongoing focus, with the emphasis on doing everything right the first time because that is the most efficient way. Key elements are productivity, teamwork, the "elimination of dumb things," innovation that calls for "breaking the frame," and an effort to continuously improve. This mind set has also been adopted by SAM'S Clubs, which has adopted HEATKTE—"high expectations are the key to everything"—as its strategic rally cry.[66]

Wal-Mart's senior management is able to keep on top of all that is happening because management believes in delegating authority, sharing decisions, and trusting the people charged with specific responsibilities. "The esprit de corps and the desire of the individuals to excel are so engendered as to assure that the best possible job is performed in practically every sector of Wal-Mart."[67] Wal-Mart's people are focused, responsive, willing to change, and willing to execute their jobs in a superior fashion. The company has grown tremendously without losing sight of the basic principles that made it great in the first place. Wal-Mart's corporate culture is very much ingrained in all of its associates.

Helping the Community

Welfare-to-Work

Wal-Mart is a strong supporter of the Welfare Reform of 1996, which strives to move people from welfare to work. Among the hourly associates Wal-Mart has hired since the beginning of 1997, almost 12 percent were receiving public assistance at the time they were hired.[68]

The company hired about 70,000 associates in the year 2000, and plans to continue hiring to both replace turnover and meet store growth.[69] Wal-Mart is in a unique position to continue to support the Welfare-to-Work program. Wal-Mart also encourages other companies to participate in the program. Its Web site provides information on how to get involved.

Education

Wal-Mart provides a supportive atmosphere for personal and career development of its associates. The company reimburses associates and their spouses for expenses incurred in obtaining a GED if they want to finish their education. In 1999 Wal-Mart awarded approximately 3000 scholarships, totaling more than $8.4 million, to deserving high school seniors.[70]

Youths with Disabilities

In Toronto, Ottawa, and Vancouver, a Skills Training Partnership for Youths with Disabilities has been funded by Human Resources Development Canada under the Opportunities Fund for Persons with Disabilities and coordinated by the Canadian Council on Rehabilitation and Work.[71] The youths with disabilities are guaranteed entry-level positions at Wal-Mart.[72]

On July 5, 2000, eleven young people with disabilities celebrated their graduation into permanent retail customer service jobs. Goodwill Toronto facilitated the recruitment, screening, classroom training, and follow-up. The students spent twelve weeks of in-class preemployment training at Goodwill, focusing on customer service, Wal-Mart's corporate culture, and lifelong learning. Following the classroom training, they spent another twelve weeks of paid on-the-job training in Toronto area Wal-Mart stores. Every successful graduate moved from placement into a job as a Wal-Mart Sales Associate. This recent initiative follows three earlier joint training projects that resulted in the successful placement of 45 youths with disabilities into full-time jobs at Wal-Mart stores in Toronto, Mississauga, and Calgary. To date 85 percent of the original graduates are still with Wal-Mart.[73]

Making a Difference in Hometowns and America

Sam Walton believed that each Wal-Mart store should reflect the values of its customers and support the vision they hold for their community.[74] Wal-Mart associates lead community outreach programs in the areas in which they spent their childhood.

In local communities Wal-Mart provides varying forms of assistance. Wal-Mart underwrites college scholarships for high-school seniors, educates the public about recycling, and provides fund-raisers that benefit schools, churches, Boy and Girl Scouts, and police and fire charities.

One of Wal-Mart's favorite causes each year is the Children's Miracle Network (CMN), which raises money for 170 children's hospitals across the United States. In June of 1999, Wal-Mart donated $29 million to CMN, the largest single contribution ever made to the cause. Wal-Mart is the largest corporate sponsor of CMN and has raised more than $160 million for the network during its 12 years of sponsorship.[75]

Furthermore, Wal-Mart is a devoted sponsor of the Missing Children's Network, a cooperative project with the non-profit National Center for Missing and Exploited Children. In fiscal 2000, Wal-Mart raised and contributed $163.8 million to charitable causes.[76]

On a broader scope, Wal-Mart contributes more than $3 million in grants annually to support communities across America.[77] In addition, the company has developed the Competitive Edge Scholarship Program for technical degree-seeking students; created an Environmental Demonstration Store that tests environment-friendly products; and sponsored the American Hometown Leadership Award, which rewards outstanding government leaders of small communities.[78] For these reasons and more, Wal-Mart was voted "Most Admired General Merchandiser of 1997" in the March 1998 issue of *Fortune* magazine.[79]

The Dating Game

Because Wal-Mart's corporate culture encourages high interaction between associates, it is bound to create personal bonds among them. Most of the time the relationships that occur do not affect employment status, except in the case of Laural Allen and Samuel Johnson. They were dismissed from their jobs because they dated while working at a Wal-Mart in Johnstown, New York.

At issue in the case is a section in the 1989 company handbook entitled "Fraternization." In it, the company cautions its sales associates to maintain "sound business relationships" with their coworkers. Wal-Mart strongly believes and supports the "family unit," and the handbook states, "A dating relationship between a married associate, other than his or her own spouse, is not consistent with this belief and is prohibited."

The relationship between Ms. Allen and Mr. Johnson began when her husband, David, a 27-year-old machinist, moved out of their house in December. Ms. Allen said she met Mr. Johnson a few weeks before her husband had left, and they became friends, getting to know each other at informal gatherings with other coworkers over a frame of bowling or a meal. At no time, she said, did the two show any affection in the store. The relationship came to the attention of the Wal-Mart managers when the lawyer for Ms. Allen's estranged husband served her with custody papers at the store. Distraught, she said that she shared the papers, which included a reference to Mr. Johnson, with a supervisor. After management confirmed the relationship with the two, they were both promptly dismissed.

The New York state legislature passed a law in July 1993 that makes it unlawful for a business to terminate employment based on "an individual's legal recreational activities outside of work hours and off of the employer's premises." The couple sued Wal-Mart for $2 million for wrongful discharge. New York Attorney General Robert

Abrams said, "What's problematic about it is the fact that the employer is terminating the employee not on the basis of job performance, but on what they're doing in their private lives outside the workplace. When they were dismissed, there was no allegation of this relationship interfering with their job performance."

On January 5, 1995, the Supreme Court of New York, Appellate Division, ruled on the Wal-Mart fraternization policy. The court stated that the "defendant employer did not violate Labor Law 201d in discharging two of its employees for violating its fraternization policy, which prohibits a dating relationship between a married employee and another employee other than his or her own spouse, since a dating relationship does not fall within the definition of statutorily protected off-hours recreational activity."[80]

Staffing

In-store employees at Wal-Mart consist of two categories: manager (salaried) and associates (hourly). Every retail outlet is managed by a store manager and one or more assistants. Managers are hired in one of three ways: (1) people from other retail companies with outstanding merchandising skills are recruited, (2) college graduates are hired, and (3) hourly associates move up through the ranks.

Approximately 60 percent of all managers began in hourly positions, 30 percent are recent college graduates, and 10 percent are from other retailers. Wal-Mart hires more than 1500 people into management per year just to maintain staffing levels in its stores and corporate headquarters.[81] In addition to store operations, Wal-Mart associates may also develop careers in fields such as merchandising, finance, international business, real estate, loss prevention, and information systems. The Walton Institute of Retailing for Management Associates helps identify and prepare associates to assume greater responsibility and leadership.[82]

Training and Development

Wal-Mart considers people development its number one priority. Developing people allows the company to push decision making down to lower levels. Extensive training is provided to managers at the corporate level; managers, in turn, are expected to train hourly associates.

Management Training and Succession

In order to ensure well-trained future store managers, Wal-Mart is committed to an ongoing training program for store managers, assistant managers, and department managers. All managers complete a structured management training program that consists of on-the-job training and book work.[83] Areas studied include management topics such as internal/external theft; scheduling; store staffing; retail math; merchandise replenishment; and the Wal-Mart "keys to supervision" series, which deals with interpersonal skills and personnel responsibilities. After completing the training program, trainees are given responsibility of an area in a store. The length of time they are in this position varies according to how the trainee progresses. Subsequent to this training, the trainee is promoted to assistant manager.

As an assistant manager, training continues with the 1-week Retail Management Training Seminar.[84] According to Suzanne Allford, former vice-president of the people division:

We believe our store and club managers are our best teachers and instructors; corporately, it's our job to provide them with the very best tools and facilities; our belief that this can only be done using practical hands-on methods led us to move our retail management seminars from our home office out to ten of our distribution centers, near to the store and clubs, to expose our management team to the heart of our distribution network.

In 1985 Wal-Mart created the Walton Institute of Retailing, which was opened in affiliation with the University of Arkansas. Currently, every Wal-Mart corporate and store manager is expected to participate in the institute's special programs to strengthen and develop the company's managerial capabilities.[85]

Wal-Mart believes that good people need new challenges. Therefore, with respect to senior management, Wal-Mart offers cross-training to enable them to master new areas.

Wal-Mart faces the challenge of having to attract, retain, and develop a constant stream of new leaders at all management levels in order to maintain its rate of growth. Accordingly, the company recently adopted a formal process of managing succession it calls People Asset Review, or PAR. The executive vice-president of Wal-Mart's people division, Cole Peterson, along with senior management and division presidents, reviews areas in the organization where development is needed, tracks promotable individuals, and develops specific succession plans. Then the company comes up with avenues of growth, determining who the successors are and how close they are to assuming that role. The purpose of the biannual PAR review is to ensure that the company has management depth and strong succession in place. The process focuses on people already working for Wal-Mart.[86]

Associate Training

"If you are not looking at those people who are at the bottom of the line and looking to train and develop them, you're going to continue having employment problems," according to Von Johnston.[87]

Upon being hired, all new associates must complete a "new hire" checklist and a 3-day orientation,[88] and they are immediately placed in positions for on-the-job training (OJT). No formal training is provided from Wal-Mart headquarters for hourly associates. OJT (sometimes supplemented by computer-based learning modules[89]) is Wal-Mart's philosophy regarding associate training. Store managers and department managers train and supervise employees. The use of video films is a popular training technique, shown from time to time in the Friday morning meetings.[90] Topics of the videos vary from new cash register functionality to security policies.[91] Wal-Mart also uses satellite television broadcasts and retail management seminars to disseminate information from headquarters.[92,93]

Associates have every opportunity for advancement. The Management Trainee Program is designed to give associates an opportunity to learn and apply basic skills necessary to advance to the assistant manager position. The program is a structured 20-week period with each week including a specific focus or emphasis area. The objectives of the program are to build a strong knowledge and experience base in the following areas: personnel functions and administration, operations, merchandising, and supervisory skills.[94] The trainee program is implemented via extensive on-the-job training and computer-based learning (CBL). A CBL program provides training on approximately 200 task areas and tests the associate at the end of each learning module.[95] CBL programs also are used to train newly hired associates.[96]

Performance Evaluations and Reward Systems

Performance Evaluations

Wal-Mart calls the process of performance appraisals "evaluations."[97] All managers and associates are evaluated annually.

Associates are hired at higher than minimum wage and can expect a raise within the first year. New associates receive two evaluations during their first year—the first at 90 days and the second on their anniversary date.[98] The four performance "levels" are below standard, standard, above standard, and outstanding. Assuming performance is above standard, the employee receives raises at the 90-day evaluation and at the annual evaluation.[99] Employees who are performing at outstanding levels may receive merit raises any time during the year. After successfully completing the first year, associates receive annual evaluations. Exceptions to this include promotions or ratings other than "marginal progress."[100] All employees must be in their current position for at least 6 months before they can be promoted to the next level (such as associate to assistant manager, or assistant manager to manager).[101]

Reward Systems

As previously indicated, management positions are salaried. Store managers receive additional compensation based on their store's profits. Assistant store managers receive additional compensation based on the company's profitability. All other personnel are compensated on an hourly basis with the opportunity of receiving additional incentive bonuses based on the company's productivity and profitability.[102]

Relatively speaking, Wal-Mart's people are highly motivated, well trained, and very productive. Ideas for productivity and efficiency are quickly disseminated. For example, each week an average of 1200 stores submit approximately 5000 suggestions. The best of these ideas are adopted, leading to substantial sales gains, cost reductions, and improved productivity. Successful ideas receive companywide recognition, such as in Saturday morning meetings at headquarters or even the personal praise of the chairperson. This reward system motivates employees to think of ways to improve operations, like how to decrease shoplifting or improve merchandising.

Shrinkage bonuses were implemented in 1980 to control losses from theft and damage. If a store holds shrinkage below the corporate goal, every associate in that store receives a bonus.[103] In a single quarter, Wal-Mart has paid several million dollars in bonuses to stores for improving their shrinkage problem.[104]

A very successful incentive program is its Volume Producing Item contests, whereby departments within a store have special promotions and pricing on items they want to feature. The contest is initially among departments within a store; ultimately, though, contest results are compared at both the store-to-store and region-to-region levels. This program helps boost sales and sell slow-moving items. It also encourages employees to be innovative.

Benefits

Benefits Package

Wal-Mart's benefits program is extensive and very competitive in the industry.[105] The highlights of the benefits package include:[106]

- Profit sharing.
- Comprehensive healthcare plan and dental insurance for employee and his/her dependents.
- Group life insurance and optional term life insurance plans.
- Business travel accident policy.
- Salary continuance.
- Long-term disability insurance.
- Paid vacations.
- Purchase discounts.
- Generous stock purchase plan.
- Store manager's bonus program.

Profit Sharing and Stock Options Plans

Wal-Mart believes that each of its associates is a partner in the company and encourages stock ownership. In fact, in an effort to maintain the feeling of company ownership and to keep employees informed, the company's stock price is announced storewide at the end of each business day.[107] Eighty percent of Wal-Mart's full-time associates own stock.[108]

The company maintains a profit-sharing plan under which most full-time and many part-time employees become participants. Every associate is eligible to participate in the plan after the first 90 days of employment and become fully vested after 7 years of employment.[109] During fiscal 2000, participants could contribute up to 10 percent of their earnings. Effective fiscal 2001, the allowable participant contributions were increased to 15 percent. Annual company contributions, based on the profitability of the company, are made at the sole discretion of the company and were $429 million, $388 million, and $321 million in 2000, 1999, and 1998, respectively.[110] For fiscal years ending January 31, 1991, through January 31, 2000, the contributions were made as shown in the table, "Annual Contributions to Profit Sharing.[111,112,113]

Wal-Mart's stock purchase plan (also called associate stock ownership plan) allows eligible associates a means of voluntarily purchasing shares of common stock at market prices through regular payroll deductions of no more than $75 per biweekly pay period, or $1800 per year. Wal-Mart contributes a 15-percent match to each participant's purchase on up to $1800 of annual stock purchases.[114] Most associates participate in incentive programs, which provide the opportunity to receive additional compensation based upon the company's productivity or profitability.[115]

ANNUAL CONTRIBUTIONS TO PROFIT SHARING			
1991	$ 98,327,000	1996	$204,000,000
1992	$129,635,000	1997	$247,000,000
1993	$166,035,000	1998	$321,000,000
1994	$166,000,000	1999	$388,000,000
1995	$175,000,000	2000	$429,000,000

Executive Compensation and Director Compensation Plan

Wal-Mart uses the Compensation and Nominating Committee and the Stock Option Committee (both of which are two of the five committees of Wal-Mart's Board of Directors) to help determine executive compensation parameters. The Stock Option Committee administers Wal-Mart's Stock Options and Restricted Stock Plans, except with respect to executive officers. The Compensation and Nominating Committee administers Wal-Mart's Stock Options and Restricted Stock Plans, sets the interest rate applicable to the Deferred Compensation Plan, and reviews the salary and benefits structure for executive officers. This committee also makes recommendations to the board regarding nominees for directors. According to the Wal-Mart 2000 Annual Report, the Compensation and Nominating Committee consists of John Cooper, Jr., Stanley Gault (chairman), Betsy Sanders, and Jose Villarreal; the Stock Option Committee consists of David Glass, Lee Scott, Don Soderquist, and Rob Walton (chairman).[116]

Wal-Mart's executive compensation program is designed to (1) provide fair compensation to executives based on their performance and contributions to Wal-Mart; (2) provide incentives to attract and retain key executives; and (3) instill a long-term commitment to Wal-Mart and develop pride and a sense of company ownership.[117] The executive officers' compensation package has three main parts: (1) base salary, which is reviewed annually; (2) equity compensation consisting of stock options and, for certain executives, restricted stock; and (3) incentive payments under the company's Management Incentive Plan (which may be earned annually depending on Wal-Mart's achievement of performance goals). Wal-Mart has a Deferred Compensation Plan under which executives may defer compensation, with interest accruing on amounts deferred. Incentive payments on the amounts deferred are accrued annually starting ten years after the initial deferral. Executives also participate in the Profit Sharing Plan, which is a defined contribution retirement plan with its assets primarily invested in Wal-Mart stock.[118]

During the calendar year ended December 31, 1999, outside directors were paid $50,000. At least one half of the retainer is paid in Wal-Mart stock or stock units. Chairpersons of board committees receive an additional retainer of $3000. Outside directors are paid $1500 per day, not to exceed 30 days per year, for Board-related work outside the scope of their regular director duties. Directors are not paid for meeting attendance but are reimbursed for expenses incurred in attending the meetings. In June of 1999, outside directors also received a stock option grant of 2174 shares each to more closely link their compensation to the interests of shareholders. The grant vests 1 year from the date of grant and has a term of 10 years.[119]

Questions

1. Wal-Mart's international segment is continuing to be a growing piece of the business. What challenges do you think this division will face in the future? How do you expect the Wal-Mart culture to transcend international boundaries?
2. Discuss some of Wal-Mart's recruitment challenges.

A

EXHIBIT 1

CONSOLIDATED STATEMENTS OF INCOME
(IN MILLIONS EXCEPT PER SHARE DATA)

Fiscal Years Ended January 31	2000	1999	1998
Revenues:			
Net sales	$165,013	$137,634	$117,958
Other income-net	$ 1,796	$ 1,574	$ 1,341
Cost and Expenses:			
Cost of sales	$ 129,664	$108,725	$93,438
Operating, selling, general, & administrative	$ 27,040	$22,363	$19,358
Interest Costs:			
Debt	$ 756	$ 529	$ 555
Capital leases	$ 266	$ 268	$ 229
	$157,726	$131,885	$113,580
Income before Income Taxes	$ 9,083	$ 7,323	$ 5,719
Provision for Income Taxes:			
Current	$ 3,476	$ 3,380	$ 2,095
Deferred	$ (138)	$ (640)	$ 20
	$ 3,338	$ 2,740	$ 2,115
Net Income	$ 5,377	$ 4,430	$ 3,526
Net Income per Share	$ 1.20	$ 0.99	$ 0.78

SOURCE: Wal-Mart, *2000 Online Annual Report*, **www.walmartstores.com/newsstand**, (accessed September 9, 2000).

EXHIBIT 2

ANNUAL EARNINGS PER SHARE

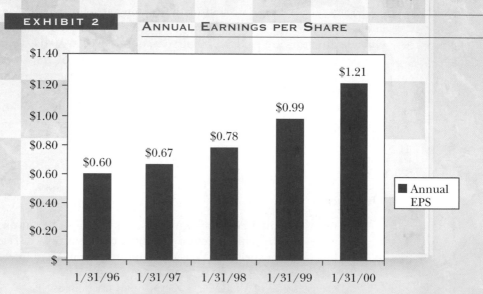

SOURCE: Wal-Mart, *2000 Online Annual Report*, **www.walmartstores.com/newsstand**, (accessed September 9, 2000).

ANNUAL NET SALES IN MILLIONS

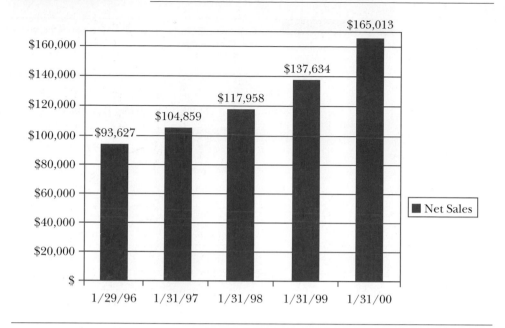

SOURCE: Wal-Mart, *2000 Online Annual Report*, **www.walmartstores.com/newsstand**, (accessed September 9, 2000).

WAL-MART STORES, INC. ANNUAL NET INCOME IN MILLIONS

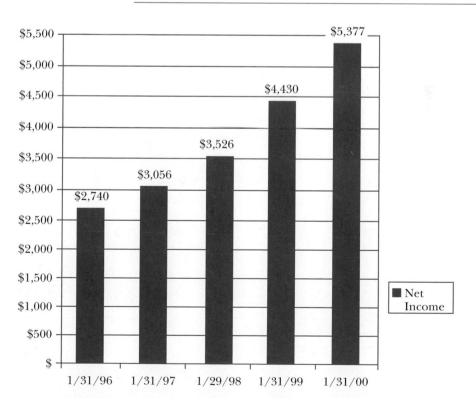

SOURCE: Wal-Mart, *2000 Online Annual Report*, **www.walmartstores.com/newsstand**, (accessed September 9, 2000).

EXHIBIT 5

FISCAL 2000 END-OF-YEAR STORE COUNT BY COUNTRY

Country	Discount Stores	Supercenters	SAM'S Clubs
U.S. Total	**1801**	**721**	**463**
Argentina	0	10	3
Brazil	0	9	5
Canada	166	0	0
China	0	5	1
Germany	0	95	0
Korea	0	5	0
Mexico	397*	27	34
Puerto Rico	9	0	6
United Kingdom	0	232	0
INT'L Total	**572**	**383**	**49**
Worldwide Grand Total	**2373**	**1104**	**512**

*Includes 36 Aurreras, 68 Bodegas, 51 Suburbias, 38 Superamas, and 204 Vips.

SOURCE: Wal-Mart, *2000 Online Annual Report*, p. 6.

Notes

[1] John Huey, "America's Most Successful Merchant," *Fortune*, September 23, 1991, pp. 46–59.
[2] *Facts About Wal-Mart Stores, Inc.* (Wal-Mart Stores, Inc., 1991).
[3] Subrata N. Chakravarty, "A Tale of Two Companies," *Forbes*, May 27, 1991, pp. 86–96.
[4] Wal-Mart, *2000 Online Annual Report*, **www.walmartstores.com/newsstand**, (accessed September 9, 2000).
[5] Wal-Mart, *1993 Annual Report*.
[6] Wal-Mart, *2000 Online Annual Report*, p. 13.
[7] Wal-Mart, *1991 Annual Report*.
[8] Wal-Mart, *2000 Online Annual Report*.
[9] Ibid, p. 6.
[10] Ibid.
[11] Huey, "America's Most Successful Merchant."
[12] Wal-Mart, *1997 Annual Report*.
[13] Wal-Mart, *2000 Online Form 10-K*, p. 6.
[14] Dale Ingram, "Wal-Mart to Relocate Distribution Center in Bentonville," Wal-Mart Stores, Inc., **www.wal-mart.com/newsroom/prdc.html**, (accessed September 9, 2000).
[15] **www.walmartstores.com/newsstand**.
[16] Jamal Munshi, *MIS:Cases in Action* (New York: McGraw-Hill, 1990).
[17] Ibid.
[18] Bryan Stanley, Wal-Mart Stores, Inc., Corporate Offices, Public Relations, telephone interview, February 24, 1998.
[19] "Wal-Mart and Sam's Club Journey into Cyberspace," Wal-Mart Stores, Inc., **www.wal-mart.com/newsroom/wmonline.html**, (accessed September 9, 2000).
[20] "Wal-Mart and Sam's Club Journey into Cyberspace," Wal-Mart Stores, Inc., Corporate Offices, Public Relations, press release comments, July 1996.
[21] Wal-Mart, *2000 Online Annual Report*, p. 7.
[22] "FTD Teams with Wal-Mart to Offer Online Store," Wal-Mart press release, February 1998
[23] "Wal-Mart and Sam's Club Journey into Cyberspace," Wal-Mart press release, July 1996.
[24] **www.wal-mart.com/community/mrh/decker2.html**, (accessed September 9, 2000).
[25] **www.walmartstores.com/newsstand**.
[26] Wal-Mart, *1997 Annual Report*, p. 11.
[27] Hurt, "The Irrational Antitrust Case against Wal-Mart."
[28] Rich Karlgaard, "Bust These Trusts," *The Wall Street Journal* Interactive Edition, Edit Page Features, February 18, 1998.
[29] Loblaw, "Shrs Up 2: Analyst Has 'Sell' Rating on Stock," *Dow Jones Newswires*, February 17, 1998.
[30] **www.walmartstores.com/newsstand**.
[31] Wal-Mart, *2000 Online Form 10-K*, p. 4.
[32] Wal-Mart, *2000 Online Annual Report*, p. 6.
[33] Ibid.
[34] Ibid.
[35] Ibid, p. 6.
[36] Ibid.
[37] Wal-Mart, *2000 Online Form 10-K*, p. 7.
[38] Wal-Mart, *2000 Online Annual Report*.
[39] Ibid, p. 2.
[40] Ibid.
[41] **www.walmartstores.com/newsstand**.
[42] Wal-Mart, *2000 Online Annual Report*, p. 2.
[43] Ibid, p. 6.
[44] Ibid.
[45] Ibid.
[46] Ibid, p. 3.
[47] Ibid.
[48] Ibid.
[49] Ibid.
[50] Ibid, p. 2.

[51]Ken A. King, "Wal-Mart Stores, Inc.," *Strategic Management* (Homewood, IL: Richard D. Irwin, 1985).

[52]"Quality of Management," *Fortune*, January 29, 1990.

[53]King, "Wal-Mart Stores, Inc."

[54]Bill Saporito, "Is Wal-Mart Unstoppable?" *Fortune*, May 6, 1991, pp. 50–59.

[55]Wal-Mart Stores, Inc., The First Boston Corp., *Equity Research Report*, Number RT2697, December 3, 1990.

[56]Saporito, "Is Wal-Mart Unstoppable?"

[57]John Huey, "Wal-Mart: Will It Take Over the World?" *Fortune*, January 30, 1989, pp. 52–61.

[58]"Quality of Management."

[59]"Wal-Mart Culture: The Payback," February 24, 1998.

[60]Wal-Mart, *2000 Online Annual Report*, p. 12.

[61]Joan Bergman, "Saga of Sam Walton," *Stores*, January 1988, pp. 129–142.

[62]King, "Wal-Mart Stores, Inc."

[63]Ibid.

[64]Allan Halcrow, "Voices of HR Experience—Part II," *Personnel Journal* 68, no. 5 (May 1989), pp. 38–53.

[65]Wal-Mart, *1997 Annual Report*.

[66]Ibid.

[67]Wal-Mart Stores, Inc., The First Boston Corp., *Equity Research Report*.

[68]"Welfare to Work," Community Involvement, **www.wal-mart.com/community/welfare-work.shtml**, (accessed September 9, 2000).

[69]"Wal-Mart Taps Personic to Take Corporate Recruiting to New Heights," *Business Wire*, February 28, 2000.

[70]**www.walmartstores.com/newsstand**.

[71]"Wal-Mart Program Guarantees Jobs for Youth with Disabilities," *Canada NewsWire*, July 5, 2000.

[72]"Employment Program Guarantees Jobs for Youth with Disabilities at Wal-Mart Canada, *Wal-Mart Student Packet* (Wal-Mart Stores Inc., February 1998)."

[73]"Wal-Mart Program Guarantees Jobs for Youth with Disabilities," *Canada NewsWire*, July 5, 2000.

[74]"The Story of Wal-Mart," *Wal-Mart Student Packet* (Wal-Mart Stores Inc., February 1998).

[75]Wal-Mart, *2000 Online Annual Report*, p. 17.

[76]Ibid, p. 16.

[77]**www.walmartstores.com/newsstand**.

[78]"The Story of Wal-Mart," *Wal-Mart Student Packet*, February 1998.

[79]"America's Most Admired Companies," *Fortune*, March 2, 1998, p. F–3.

[80]*Respondent-Appellant* v. *Wal-Mart Stores, Inc.* Supreme Court of New York, Appellate Division, Third Department, **web.lexis-nexis.com/universe/document**.

[81]"Land of Opportunity," **www.wal-mart.com/newsroom/opportunity.html**.

[82]Ibid.

[83]Sandy Brummett, telephone interview with public relations assistant of Wal-Mart Stores, Inc., Bentonville, Arkansas, November 19, 1991.

[84]Ibid.

[85]Ibid.

[86]Mike Troy, "Finding Successors to the Dynasty Starts by Winning the Turnover War," *DSN Retailing Today*, June 5, 2000, p. 145.

[87]Halcrow, "Voices of HR Experience—Part II."

[88]Theresa McKenzie, personal interview with personnel assistant of Wal-Mart store, Tallahassee, Florida, Store #1408, February 27, 1998.

[89]Ibid.

[90]George Wilkins, telephone interview with assistant manager of Wal-Mart Store, Capital Circle Southeast, Tallahassee, Florida, November 18, 1991.

[91]McKenzie, personal interview.

[92]"The Story of Wal-Mart."

[93]McKenzie, personal interview.

[94]"Wal-Mart Pamphlet" (distributed to potential new hires via Florida State University Career Center).

[95]"The Story of Wal-Mart."

[96]McKenzie, personal interview.

[97]Halcrow, "Voices of HR Experience–Part II."

[98]McKenzie, personal interview.

[99]Ibid.

[100]Wilkins, personal interview.

[101]McKenzie, personal interview.

[102]Wal-Mart, *1991 Form 10-K.*

[103]Wilkins, personal interview.

[104]M. A. Gilliam, *Company Report,* The First Boston Corp., Wal-Mart Stores, Inc., July 8, 1991.

[105]"Wal-Mart Pamphlet."

[106]Gilliam, *Company Report.*

[107]McKenzie, personal interview.

[108]Wal-Mart, *1991 Form 10-K.*

[109]Wal-Mart, *1997 Annual Report, Form 10-K,* submitted to Securities and Exchange Commission, included in *Wal-Mart Student Packet,* February 1998.

[110]Wal-Mart, *2000 Online Annual Report.*

[111]Wal-Mart, *1997 Annual Report,* Form 10-K submitted to Securities and Exchange Commission included in *Wal-Mart Student Packet,* February 1998.

[112]Wal-Mart, *1991 Form 10-K.*

[113]Wal-Mart, *2000 Online Annual Report.*

[114]Wal-Mart, *1991 Form 10-K.*

[115]Wal-Mart, *2000 Form 10-K,* p. 10.

[116]**www.walmartstores.com/newsstand**.

[117]Wal-Mart, *1997 Annual Report, Notice of Annual Meeting of Shareholders.*

[118]Ibid.

[119]**www.walmartstores.com/newsstand**.

6

Microsoft*

When new employees join Microsoft, they are invited to "be part of something that starts with listening, that believes in learning, that thrives on risk, that embraces change, that doesn't follow, that creates a product that changes everything, including the world."[1] This self-portrait as a dynamic, cutting-edge environment is the image that Microsoft uses to attract highly skilled technical professionals. The publicly promoted Microsoft culture stresses the importance of technology, autonomy, and workplace diversity. A closer look at the management of Microsoft and its approach to employee recruiting, hiring, retention, and relations will help in understanding how it leverages its 39,904 worldwide employees (as of June 30, 2000)[2] to continue posting impressive growth.

History of Microsoft

Visionary Youth

The students at Lakeside School in Seattle, Washington, were given an incredible opportunity in 1968. The Mothers' Club paid to put a teletype machine in the school for the students to use to communicate via telephone line with a PDP-10 minicomputer owned by General Electric. At this time, computer technology was in its infancy with most adults never having seen a computer, never mind getting to experiment with one. Two young Lakeside students, eighth-grader Bill Gates and sophomore Paul Allen quickly discovered a common passion in programming. The boys studied all the manuals they could find and spent every spare moment at the terminal. This shared boyhood interest in computers would eventually lead to the founding of Microsoft.

The arrangement with General Electric required the school to pay for the computer time used by the students. The thirst for knowledge among the Lakeside students quickly exceeded the budgets of the Mothers' Club and the parents. Gates, Allen, and a few other students were offered computer time in exchange for testing software and documenting bugs on the PDP-10 for a young company, Computer Center Corporation. Opportunities to improve their expertise would continue to come to both Gates and Allen. In December 1970 Information Sciences offered Gates

---

*This case was prepared by Roger J. Boutin, Monique Emmanuel, Vicki Lockamy, Sue Lewkowitz, and Eva Somaan.

and Allen $10,000 worth of computer hours in exchange for writing a payroll program in COBOL. They were also called on to write a rather complex class scheduling program for Lakeside High. Later, Bill couldn't resist modifying this program so that his own schedule would have him, whenever possible, as the only boy in a class of cute girls.[3]

In 1971 Gates and Allen purchased one of Intel's early microprocessor chips and had an electronics technician build them a programmable machine. For this machine they created software that would analyze the traffic data gathered by punch cards in gray boxes on Seattle streets. During Bill's senior year in high school and while Allen was attending Washington State University as a computer science major, their company, Traf-O-Data would earn $20,000 from selling traffic data analysis to other governmental agencies. Competition brought their business to an end when the federal government offered this same service at no charge.[4] Their first real jobs in 1973 for TRW came as a result of their early expertise with the PDP-10s. Allen left Washington State University and went to work for TRW full-time. Incredibly, all of this occurred before Gates had even graduated from high school. Upon graduation from Lakeside, Gates enrolled at Harvard. A year later, Allen followed him east as a programmer for Honeywell.

The Beginning of Microsoft

In 1975, during Gates' sophomore year at Harvard, he and Allen set out to adapt BASIC, a computer language they had learned at Lakeside, for the MITS Altair, considered by many as the world's first microcomputer.[5] (Although Apple is most widely known for the introduction of the microcomputer, controversy exists because many others consider the MITS as the first microcomputer.) Within weeks they had finished it and set out to persuade MITS to sell it. Allen soon accepted a position with MITS as Director of Software Development in Albuquerque, New Mexico. Later that year, Gates followed Allen to form an informal partnership, Micro-Soft (the hyphen in the name would soon be dropped), for their negotiations with MITS.[6] Although a formal partnership was not formed until 1977, their goal was to develop languages for the Altair and for future microcomputers. From the beginning, there was a natural division of labor between the two, with Allen concentrating on the new technology and products while Gates handled more of the negotiations and business deals.[7] This separation of duties was evidence that even in the early stages of Microsoft, albeit informal, Gates and Allen were already learning how to leverage the human resource element to achieve the best results.

Their first contract with MITS set the stage for future software contracts by specifying that Gates and Allen would retain ownership of the actual software although licensing its use by MITS. In 1976 Microsoft hired its first four employees, all programmers, who mainly worked from home. Bill Gates checked every line of code they wrote. At the end of 1976, Allen left MITS and Gates dropped out of Harvard to concentrate on their business. Within a year, Microsoft moved into its first real office with a staff of six, and Microsoft licensed the use of its BASIC software to GE, NCR, and other national corporations. Microsoft followed a policy of charging a very low price for its software, much lower than the in-house production cost of microcomputer manufacturers.[8]

In 1977 the company started shipping programs in a second computer language, FORTRAN. The growth of Microsoft at this time was closely tied to changes occurring in the microcomputer industry. The MITS Altair was unreliable and had very limited ability. Steve Wozniak, an employee of Hewlett-Packard, had been trying in vain to persuade his company to build a microcomputer.[9] Wozniak and a friend, Steve Jobs, ended up building a computer in Wozniak's garage. This was the birth of Apple. In 1977 they introduced APPLE II at the first West Coast Computer Faire. The APPLE II weighed less than 15 pounds and was priced at a consumer friendly $1350. The configuration of the APPLE II allowed for future enhancements of the computer's graphics, printing, and communications by the consumer. In the fall of 1977, Microsoft granted a license for Apple to use its BASIC. Other microcomputers also appeared in the marketplace in 1977, including the TRS-80 by Tandy and the PET by Commodore.[10] Like the Apple, the PET Commodore and the TRS-80 both used Microsoft's BASIC.

The Early Years

By 1978, because MITS was no longer the only manufacturer of personal computers, the decision was made to move Microsoft, which by now had grown to yearly sales of $1.3 million and had more than a dozen employees, to Bellevue, Washington.[11] A strategic partnership was formed with ASC II Corporation in Japan to market Microsoft products in Japan to original equipment manufacturers (OEMs), dealers, and end users. Gates and Allen were negotiating with so many potential clients that they never really figured out how many employees they needed to cover their growing number of commitments. When they started selling to the Japanese companies, Gates and Allen had really promised more than they could deliver because they lacked the needed human resources to complete the work on time.[12] Fortunately for them, their competitors were not able to take advantage of this situation. Had Microsoft's competitors been poised to act, this HR blunder could have destroyed this upstart company by allowing competitors who had the needed manpower to deliver the product and capture much of the market from Microsoft. In 1979 Microsoft enjoyed sales of $2.4 million, and the number of employees more than doubled. Microsoft had a BASIC compiler for virtually every microcomputer on the market. More importantly, its reputation and expertise allowed it to be involved in the development of hardware by computer manufacturers. Gates and Allen early on believed that eventually there would be a computer on every desk and in every home.[13]

In 1980 Microsoft's first professional business manager was hired to serve as the first assistant to the president. Steve Ballmer, a Harvard buddy of Gates, came to them from Procter & Gamble and removed some of the administrative burdens that Gates had assumed. Other administrative changes were made to systematize the operations as the yearly sales reached $8 million and the employees numbered 40. For the first time, Microsoft expanded beyond the business of developing languages to sell its first hardware product, the MS Soft Card. However, IBM's signing a contract with Microsoft would prove to be the factor that would shape the destiny of this still relatively small company. IBM was looking for an operating system for the personal computer it was developing. Paul Allen had been in negotiations with a nearby computer company, Seattle Computer, to purchase its operating system, Q-DOS. Gates and Ballmer offered to license Q-DOS to IBM, even though they did not yet own the software.[14] Fortunately, for Microsoft, they were able to close the deal with Seattle Computer before Microsoft had to present the system to IBM. The IBM personal computer with Microsoft's Disk Operating System (MS-DOS) debuted the following year. During the next 16 months, Microsoft licensed the use of its DOS operating system to 50 hardware manufacturers with Microsoft modifying MS-DOS for each machine.[15] Microsoft enjoyed phenomenal growth as the sales reached $16 million. In July 1981 the partnership of Gates and Allen was reorganized as a private corporation. Microsoft's 128 employees could now buy shares of stock for about $1 a share. This incentive helped to compensate for Microsoft's lower salaries and it made it easier to attract good people.

Expanding Products and Sales

Although Microsoft was making a name for itself as a supplier of operating systems, it began to explore business applications with a spreadsheet format in 1980 and 2 years later introduced Multiplan to the market. Another business application was addressed in 1983 with the debut of Microsoft Word and the mouse, which allowed users to point and click to operate the computer. Development was started on software that came to be known as Microsoft Windows. The goal was to create an easy-to-use graphical interface that would allow users to run multiple applications at once. Internationally, Microsoft continued its expansion of its global sales territory going into Europe and England. The purchase of Wiser Laboratories of Australia gave Microsoft direct distribution in this area. One sad note for the company in 1982 was the departure of cofounder Paul Allen from Microsoft after his recovery from Hodgkin's Disease. Allen decided to "get a life" and do other things besides Microsoft.[16] He did, however, remain as a director of Microsoft.

By 1983 programmers made up more than 100 of the nearly 450 company employees. Gates and Ballmer would look for highly intelligent candidates with a background in science, math, or computers and who had drive and initiative.[17] The option to purchase stock played an important role in helping Microsoft to recruit the very best. In August 1983 Gates recruited John Shirley from Tandy to be Microsoft's president. The company was growing so rapidly that Steve Ballmer was having trouble handling accounting, recruitment, and other functions. Even though revenues had grown to nearly $50 million per year, Microsoft was still using a small Tandy microcomputer and inadequate software to handle its accounting functions. Shirley ordered a central computer to manage accounting and inventory records.[18] He believed in using delegation to develop excellent managers, which Microsoft needed if it was to grow successfully. Shirley would stay with Microsoft until his retirement in 1990, leading the company through a period of incredible growth.

Over the next few years, the increasing growth of personal computers created an expanding marketplace for the Microsoft products. Microsoft continued its practice of adapting software for personal computer manufacturers. In 1984 Apple introduced the Macintosh with BASIC and Multiplan. Computer manufacturers received their first application kits for Windows, and the company continued to update the languages in its product line. Organizational changes were made in the company with the separation of the systems group, headed by Steve Ballmer, and the applications group, led by former Apple marketing director Ida Cole. These changes allowed Gates to devote himself to future products. Communications between all of Microsoft's subsidiaries improved because all were now linked by e-mail. By its tenth anniversary the corporation had started construction on its new headquarters in Redmond, Washington, as well as construction of its first foreign production facility in Ireland. Sales in fiscal 1985 reached $140 million, and the number of employees was 910.[19]

The Second Decade and Beyond

The initial public offering (IPO), with the release of 2.5 million shares at $21 per share, highlighted the start of the second decade of Microsoft. This IPO made Gates the world's youngest billionaire at age 30. Corporate growth did not slow down, and acquisitions were made to complement the existing product line, including acquisition of Forethought, Inc., the maker of PowerPoint. By 1988 Microsoft became the top software vendor when it surpassed Lotus Development Corporation. This rapid growth, coupled with the absorption of new companies into Microsoft, forced the firm to address its human resource needs and company structure. As a result, the corporation again reorganized, this time into five business units: graphics, analysis, data access, office, and entry. To handle the growing number of requests for product support, a product support services facility was established, which at that time handled 1 million calls a month. International sales continued to grow as distributors were added. By 1989 international sales accounted for more than half of the annual sales. By Microsoft's 15th anniversary, the corporation, now with 5635 employees, had become the first software company to exceed the $1 billion sales mark. The acceptance of Windows 3.0 had been exceptional, with 100,000 copies sold in 2 weeks. Within the next year, 4 million copies of Windows 3.0 were shipped to 24 countries in 12 languages, and computer manufacturers included Windows as part of the standard computer package. This year also marked the start of investigations by the Department of Justice into possible antitrust violations by Microsoft. Meanwhile, research and development continued to find new products that fit the corporation's mission—that is, "software for the personal computer that enriches people in the workplace, at school, at home."[20]

In 1992 Microsoft's revenues reached $2.7 billion although the number of employees doubled in only a 2-year period. To handle the growing problems of running a company this large, an "Office of the President" was organized with three executive vice-presidents dividing the responsibilities of president. By now Word for Windows was available in 22 languages. The number of licensed users of Windows reached more than 25 million in the next year.[21] Internationally, sales continued to grow, and a Japanese version of Microsoft Windows 3.1 was introduced. During 1994 more than 5000 employees were handling just international operations, and a Latin office opened in Florida to put operations close to South American customers. By the company's 20th anniversary, revenues approached the $6 billion mark and employees numbered nearly 18,000. Microsoft headed into the Internet with the introduction of Internet Explorer, and the company launched the Microsoft Network (MSN) online service. On August 24, 1995, Microsoft launched Windows 95 with a huge marketing extravaganza. Customers obtained more than 1 million copies during the first 4 days of availability in North America.[22]

In 2000, as Microsoft marks its 25th anniversary, it is the world's largest software company with nearly 40,000 employees, $23 billion in revenue, and a wide range of powerful software and Internet products, including the most popular PC operating system, productivity software, and Internet network. With the release of Windows 2000, the continuing strength of Microsoft Office, its expanding enterprise server family, and the surging popularity of MSN, Microsoft has strong core businesses. At the same time the company is making significant strategic investments for the future in key growth areas, including wireless technologies, digital devices, games, TV, small business, and the new Microsoft.NET platform. Over the next year, Microsoft plans to invest more than $4 billion in research and development to advance its core businesses, build on its strategic investments, and deliver its important software initiative—Microsoft.NET.[23]

"Permatemps"

The rapid employee growth that was necessary to support Microsoft's growing operations over the years has not been without its problems. In addition to hiring regular employees to staff its growth, Microsoft also hired "independent contractors." Independent contractors are people who work for a company but not as regular employees. For example, they have few job rights and are not awarded employee benefits like insurance, 401(k) plans, and stock options. In the early 1990s the IRS accused Microsoft of avoiding payroll taxes on several of its independent contractors. The IRS argued that these independent contractors performed the same work as normal employees at Microsoft and thus should have been subject to the same payroll taxes. As shown in Chapter 17 in the HR Challenges box "When Is a Worker an Employee or an Independent Contractor?" there are 20 factors that the IRS considers in determining the existence of an employer-employee relationship. Some of the determining factors include whether there is a continuing relationship between the parties, whether the person must submit an oral or written report, whether tools and materials are furnished for the worker, whether there is a right to discharge the worker, and whether the worker's services are integrated into the business operations. The IRS made this determination, even though these "employees" signed contracts that identified them as independent contractors and explicitly stated that they were forfeiting their rights to employee benefits. In return for this concession, these individuals were paid higher wages than Microsoft employees doing similar work. After Microsoft made amends with the IRS (in the form of huge back tax payments), some of the reclassified employees were offered regular employment with the company, whereas others were offered continued work if they became employees of a temporary agency. Eight of the former independent contractors refused to become employees of the temporary agency and sued the company and its various pension plans *(Vizcaino* v. *Microsoft Corporation)* claiming rights to *all* benefits provided to regular employees. They did so using the IRS determination that the workers, previously classified as independent contractors, were indeed employees of Microsoft. The district court granted summary judgment in favor of Microsoft. The plaintiffs appealed the judgment relating to 401(k) and the employee stock purchase plan (ESPP) only. On July 24, 1997, the decision was reversed, stating that the workers were regular employees who were improperly excluded from participating in the benefit plans. Based on the fact that these individuals were now classified as employees, any other issues regarding the rights of the workers to participate in the ESPP was to be decided by the plan administrator upon remand. Microsoft appealed this decision, however, but in early 1998, the U.S. Supreme Court refused to hear the case.[24] Experts believe that the outcome of the case could have a rippling effect on corporate-sponsored employee stock purchase plans (ESPP) because nonemployee workers, such as consultants, can be potentially classified as employees.

After losing a series of legal battles, Microsoft recently settled a class action filed by temporary workers 8 years ago. The company agreed to hand over $97 million to settle claims that it treated thousands of temps as full-time employees in every regard but compensation. So-called permatemps worked for years at Microsoft but did not participate in the company's ESPP in which workers can buy Microsoft stock at a discount. The law firm representing the temps has asked the court to award it $27 million in fees. If approved, the remaining $70 million would be split among an estimated 8000 to 12,000 eligible temporary workers. That comes to an average of $7000 per temp, much less than they would have received if they had been allowed to invest in the employee stock plan.[25]

This ruling, and its far-reaching implications, will have a serious effect not only on Microsoft, but on corporate America. Many companies have turned to long-term temporaries as a way to reduce personnel costs or to fill the void in a tight labor market.[26] Because firms do not pay federal or state employment taxes or benefits for these employees (benefits are typically about 35 percent of salary), substantial savings are realized. The ESPP, which will be discussed in greater detail later, is also an expensive part of the employee benefits package for Microsoft. Rulings like these may force the company to scale back its plan for all employees because of the additional costs generated by the need to offer the plan to more employees. In 2000, however, the company made changes in its policy, requiring the agencies it does business with to provide benefits. Microsoft now also requires permatemps to take a 100-day absence after a full year of employment.[27]

Microsoft Products and Marketing

Microsoft has always held notoriously high standards for its technical workers, but it has also pursued talented marketers. From a marketing standpoint, Microsoft operates much like a large packaged goods company. It has separated its varied products into separate divisions, with a manager in charge of each division, much like a product manager in the packaged goods industry. Microsoft has also established extensive and far-reaching channels of distribution, which are crucial to successful packaged goods companies. Given these similarities, it is no wonder that the only two members of Microsoft's Executive Committee that are from outside the technical industry (Steve Ballmer, president and CEO, and Robert Herbold, executive vice president and COO) are both from the packaged goods giant Procter & Gamble.

In order to compete in the plethora of related segments in the software industry, Microsoft follows a pioneer strategy that dominates evolving mass markets. The company's basic strategy emphasizes the following:

- It enters evolving mass markets early or stimulates new markets with special products that set industry standards.
- It incrementally improves new products and periodically makes old products obsolete.
- It pushes volume sales and exclusive contracts to ensure that company products become and remain industry standards.
- It takes advantage of being the standards provider with new products and product linkages.
- It integrates, extends, and simplifies products to reach new mass markets.[28]

The company's organizational structure and fundamental approach to business reflect the needs of its customers. As such, Microsoft has three major segments: Windows Platforms; Productivity Applications and Developer; and Consumer and Other. Windows Platforms includes the Windows Division, which is primarily responsible for developing and marketing Windows NT Workstation, Windows 2000 Professional, Windows 98, Windows 95, Windows NT Server, and Windows 2000 Server. Productivity Applications and Developer includes the Business Productivity Division, which is responsible for developing and marketing desktop applications, server applications, and developer tools. Consumer and Other products and services include primarily learning, entertainment, and PC input device products; WebTV and PC online access; and portal and vertical properties.[29]

Product Research and Development

Mindful that innovation is the key to success in his industry, Microsoft Chairman and Chief Software Architect Bill Gates has put together a team of experts to create the next great research lab. Some of the researchers on staff, under the direction of chief researcher Dr. Nathan Myhrvold, include Rick Rashid, mastermind of a state-of-the-art operating system called *Mach*, and Dan Ling, a former IBM researcher with several patents to his credit. Also on board are Karen Jensen, Stephen Richardson, and George Heidorn, natural-language researchers from IBM. These three scientists invented MindNet, a program that allows a computer to teach itself how words in a sentence are connected to one another.[30]

Rapid technological changes affect the software industry and increase competitive pressures. Microsoft puts emphasis on responding to market pressures quickly and effectively without sacrificing product quality. Research and product development are two areas in which Microsoft dedicates its valuable resources in order to keep ahead of the market as technology advances and consumers' usage patterns change. During 1998, 1999, and 2000, the company spent $2.6 billion (17.0 percent of revenues), $3.0 billion (15.0 percent of revenues), and $3.8 billion (16.4 percent of revenues), respectively, on product research and development.[31] Microsoft products are "interpreted" in order to accommodate foreign countries' needs in terms of local languages and conventions, user messages, documentation, and monetary references.

Microsoft research is committed to basic and applied research in computer science. The company develops new technologies that revolutionize the ways people and computers interact. Its research team consists of outstanding professionals from a wide spectrum of disciplines. They originate from leading academic institutions to industrial research labs and actively serve on conference program committees, editorial boards, and advisory panels. The company's R&D team, which consists of about 250 scientists, also participates in the worldwide research community and collaborates with numerous universities.[32,33]

Microsoft's scientists research a wide array of technologies, including programming productivity tools; applications of artificial intelligence to operating systems and user interfaces; computer-based decision making; speech processing and understanding; supercomputer design; video-on-demand server technology; the mixing of video, audio, and text for pocket information systems (for example, "wallet PC"); multimedia products; and interactive TV. The research division is responsible for the online service, Windows and NT operating systems, and new user interfaces that provide assistance to nonsophisticated users. The involvement of Bill Gates with the research group's strategy reflects the company's philosophy that successful research is tied directly to the heart of the company's operations.[34] The heavy emphasis on R&D clearly demonstrates Microsoft's dependence on "knowledge capital." Recruiting, hiring, managing, and retaining the employees who provide this knowledge are crucial to the success of the firm.

Microsoft develops many of its software products internally. Internal development grants the company the freedom of choosing the types of modifications and enhancements that the organization considers the most critical, as well as the ability to implement its own schedule. A number of proprietary developmental tools and methodologies have been created by the Microsoft people, which enable the company to create new products and enhance its existing products. These tools and methodologies make the Microsoft products portable across various operating systems, microprocessors, and computers. Microsoft not only develops its products, but it also purchases technology, licenses intellectual property rights, and oversees third-party development.

Manufacturing

Microsoft began outsourcing most of its production when the company sold its domestic manufacturing and distribution operation in July 1996. Because of the avalanche of Microsoft family products, outsourcing was deemed a more cost-effective and efficient way of producing products. Third-party vendors now handle much of Microsoft production. Microsoft has established a multitude of alternate custom manufacturers of various components if outsourcing becomes unavailable from current suppliers. The company has in place a quality control system on purchased parts, finished disks, CD-ROMs, and other products to ensure that they meet the required specifications.[35] The company owns and operates manufacturing facilities outside of the United States in Puerto Rico and Ireland. These two locations were chosen for their distinct strategic and financial benefits.

Puerto Rico (which is a Commonwealth of the United States) offers tax incentives, as well as special location-dictated incentives in the form of cash grants to companies that establish manufacturing facilities in areas of high unemployment. The cash grants are given to companies that (1) provide its services to clients outside of Puerto Rico, (2) perform 80 percent of the work in Puerto Rico, and (3) utilize local resources to perform 80 percent of the invoiced value of a given project.[36]

Puerto Rico offers the advantage of a bilingual population and a unique mixture of Latin American heritage and North American culture. Its integration with the U.S. constitutional system and geographical proximity to the Caribbean and South and Central America makes it a strategic distribution location.[37] The Puerto Rico facility manufactures the CD-ROMs, assembles other purchased parts, and packages final products.

Ireland is a land of opportunity in terms of state-of-the-art communications, low employment costs, competitive suppliers, and sophisticated transportation logistics that make it an ideal place for Microsoft's operations. Profits derived from manufacturing and qualifying services are only subject to a 10 percent tax rate, which will be in effect until at least December of 2010. These profits can be repatriated freely and are not subject to taxation upon their return to the United States. For companies engaged in R&D, patent royalty income on products developed in Ireland is tax-free. This combination of affordable labor and advantageous tax laws makes Ireland a strategically sensible location for manufacturing.[38] The Irish manufacturing facility reproduces disks, assembles purchased parts, and packages final products.

The traditional avenues of purchasing and installing software are gradually becoming a thing of the past. More and more, companies offer their software over the Internet, providing consumers with a better, more convenient, and expedient service. Selling software over the Internet enables consumers to choose, download, purchase, and install new software right from their home PC. This type of purchase makes the costly manufacturing and packaging of software on CDs unnecessary. Microsoft currently offers software over the Internet, and some of it is free of charge. The long-term implications of such a trend may have a devastating effect on the wholesalers and retailers of this type of merchandise. As this trend continues, the need for manufacturing facilities, and the employees who operate them, will continue to diminish. Microsoft is well known for its vision of the future, and it is anticipated that as the trend continues, the company will take steps to focus on ways to distribute its products to consumers in the most convenient and cost-effective way possible.

Marketing and Distribution

The influence of the two former Procter & Gamble employees on the Microsoft Executive Committee seems to have had an effect on the marketing strategy of the firm. Despite the high-tech nature of the company, its marketing and distribution systems are similar to large packaged goods companies. The products that service each customer type are much like the varied brands within a packaged goods giant like P&G. Microsoft focuses its sales and marketing efforts on various customer types, such as original equipment manufacturers (OEMs), end-users, organizations, Internet content providers (ICPs), applications developers, infrastructure owners, and enterprises. Microsoft has three major geographic sales and marketing organizations: the United States and Canadian, European (United Kingdom), and international.

- *The OEM customer unit sales force* works with original equipment manufacturers to preinstall Microsoft software on their PCs.
- *The end-user unit* targets the segment of population that makes individual decisions for PCs at work and at home. It includes developing and administering reseller relationships, sales terms and conditions, marketing programs, support policies, seminars, marketing promotions, and sales training for resellers. The main products for the end-users customer unit are desktop applications, operating systems, and interactive media products.
- *The organization customer unit* aims at small to medium-sized companies. This unit works with Solution Providers, distributors, and value-added resellers to serve this market segment. It also provides technical training to Solution Providers and channel resellers and develops support policies along with seminars and sales training for its channel partners.
- *The Internet customer unit* focuses on introducing products and technologies to the public infrastructure owners (telephone and cable companies), and ICPs, who build and operate public networks and provide content for the Web.
- *The application developer unit* focuses on corporate developers and independent software vendors (ISVs) who create their business applications with a development platform in line with Microsoft Windows and BackOffice design.
- *The enterprise customer unit* targets sales and marketing to large organizations. It works directly with these organizations through large account resellers to create and support their mission critical decisions and business computing needs the best way possible.[39]

Distribution channels

Large Accounts   The Microsoft network of large account resellers together with the Microsoft Select Program focuses the marketing efforts towards large multinational organizations. They offer flexible software acquisition, licensing, and maintenance options customized to fit each company's needs. The target markets are technology specialists, large enterprises, and end-users.[40]

Distributors and Resellers   Microsoft markets its finished products mainly through independent distributors like CHS Electronics, Computer 2000, Tech Data, Merisell, SoftBank, and Ingram Micro. The company also markets its finished goods through resellers like Software Spectrum and Stream International. A network of sales representatives solicits orders from distributors and resellers and provides product training and support.[41] Microsoft's customers range from end-users and application developers to ISPs and OEMs. End-users obtain Microsoft products through these distributors, resellers, and OEMs, who bundle the software with their hardware.

Solution Providers' Channels   Solution Providers are part of Microsoft's comprehensive program of building relationships with independent organizations that provide network and system integration, custom development, and technical support for businesses. Microsoft provides sales and product information, development services, early access to its products, as well as customer support tools (e.g., education and business development support). Microsoft's Consulting Services Division works with Solution Providers to create enterprise-wide computing solutions. The Solution Provider Program covers under its umbrella Internet service and hosting organizations, value-added resellers (VARs), system integrators, consultants, custom application developers, and technical support/training organizations.[42,43]

Original Equipment Manufacturers as a Channel of Distribution   Microsoft has licensed its operating systems to original equipment manufacturers and has granted them the right to distribute desktop applications and interactive media programs with their computers but under Microsoft trademarks. OEMs also distribute hardware components, such as the Microsoft mouse and keyboard, with the computers to their customers. The company has OEM agreements covering one or more of its products with virtually all of the major OEMs, including, Acer, Actebis, Compaq, Dell, eMachines, Fujitsu, Fujitsu Siemens Computers, Gateway, Hewlett Packard, IBM, Micron, NEC, Samsung, Sony, and Toshiba.[44]

International Channels of Distribution   Microsoft has a network of marketing and support subsidiaries in more than 70 countries. Much of what has been achieved in the United States has been replicated in Japan and Europe. Microsoft's strategy to compete in these markets has been through the formation of alliances and use of a variety of pricing tactics and long-term agreements whereby companies bundle Microsoft software with the local hardware. The company's international operations including OEMs and finished goods are subject to each country's laws and regulations, import restrictions, and foreign exchange rate volatility.[45]

Advertising Channels   Microsoft works with large advertising and direct marketing firms, and it maintains its advertising campaign with a focus on building Microsoft brand loyalty. The company targets a broad consumer base through television, radio, and business publications. It also utilizes direct marketing, worldwide packaging, and marketing materials to reach its end-users. Some of the company's OEMs and resellers advertise Microsoft products and then get reimbursed for their advertising expenditures. Sales and marketing expenses amounted to $4.1 billion for fiscal year 2000, which represented 18.0 percent of revenue, compared with 16.4 percent for fiscal year 1999. The total expense as a percentage of revenue increased because of higher relative marketing costs associated with new product releases and online marketing.[46]

Microsoft Partners, Mergers, and Acquisitions

Over the past several years, Microsoft has used partnering and acquisitions as an effective way to gain control of new technologies, as well as talented employees.

Although Microsoft still develops many of its own technologies, the past few years have seen several acquisitions expand Microsoft's service and product menu.

The most recent acquisitions have been companies that develop Internet-based products and services. "Understanding usage patterns on your Web site is the best way to see what your customers are interested in so you can deliver the most targeted content" were the words of Bill Gates when his company acquired Interse.[47] Microsoft not only acquires the technologies when it purchases companies, but it also acquires the valuable human capital that these firms possess. "More world-class talent means Microsoft can move even faster on its goal to deliver the world's best solutions for developers of Java and other object-oriented languages," said John Ludwig, vice-president of the Internet Client and Collaboration Division at Microsoft, of the acquisition of Cooper & Peters.[48] It is clear that Microsoft is strategically targeting companies to purchase, not only for their products, but also for their human capital.

Microsoft Human Resources

Microsoft has been widely recognized as one of America's most successful companies. Its success is not limited to its phenomenal financial growth. *Fortune* magazine ranked Microsoft as the eighth best company to work for in the United States[49] and the second most admired company in America (behind GE). In another publication, *Forbes* magazine (in its online version, *Forbes ASAP*) named Microsoft to its annual list of the 100 Most Dynamic Companies in America. *Forbes ASAP* ranked Microsoft fifth overall and gave the company the highest mark possible for its "Human Capital." *Forbes ASAP* lists human capital as one of the six deciding factors for its rankings, noting that, "This factor's importance reflects the truism that real value is created by intellectual capital, not bricks and mortar."[50] *Forbes ASAP* commented that much of Microsoft's success was attributable to "brilliant management, [and] a devoted cult of engineers. . . ."[51] This string of impressive accomplishments begs the question: How does Microsoft do it? As is the case with many successful entrepreneurial companies, the dynamic leadership at the top has strongly influenced Microsoft's culture. A closer look reveals an amazing, but sometimes contradictory, company culture.

Executive Management

Although Microsoft touts diversity as one of its strengths in reaching customers in more than 50 countries, the executive management is markedly uniform. All top nine executive managers, including founder and Chairman Bill Gates, are white males. In addition, seven out of the nine senior staff come from other technological companies although the other two come from Proctor & Gamble. The oldest member of the committee is 58-year-old Robert Herbold. The remaining members are all in their 40s.[52,53]

Leveraging Employee Growth

From modest beginnings in 1975, Microsoft has expanded its employee base rapidly during its 25-year existence. Both revenues and profits have increased by no less than 16 percent from 1988 though 2000.[54] Growth in staffing has followed, but not at the expense of efficiency. Microsoft has continued to post impressive financial results by leveraging its human resources. Microsoft has not only grown its employee ranks (see Exhibits 1 and 2) but also its revenues and profits. The growth in revenues and profits has been at a faster rate than the increase in head count. In 1989 Microsoft generated $804 million in revenues and $171 million in net income from its 4037 employees. This came to $199,158 in revenues and $42,358 in profits *per employee*. In

EXHIBIT.1	EMPLOYEE GROWTH: 1975–2000	

Year	Employees	% Change
1975	3	—
1976	7	133%
1977	9	29%
1978	13	44%
1979	28	115%
1980	40	43%
1981	128	220%
1982	220	72%
1983	476	116%
1984	608	28%
1985	910	50%
1986	1,153	27%
1987	1,816	58%
1988	4,037	122%
1989	2,793	−31%
1990	5,635	102%
1991	8,226	46%
1992	11,542	40%
1993	14,430	25%
1994	15,257	6%
1995	17,801	17%
1996	20,561	16%
1997	22,276	8%
1998	27,055	21%
1999	31,575	17%
2000	39,904	26%

SOURCE: Cusumano and Selby, *Microsoft Secrets*, p. 3; and Microsoft Corporation, **www.microsoft.com/corpinfo/fastfact.htm**, (accessed January 31, 1998); **www.microsoft.com/presspass/fastfacts.asp**, (accessed January 23, 2001).

2000 Microsoft generated $22.96 billion in revenues and $9.42 billion in net income from 39,904 employees.[55] This breaks down to $575,281 in revenues and $236,092 in profits *per employee*. (See Exhibit 3 and Exhibits 3A-3C for a complete listing.) This drastic and continual increase in productivity is of course due in part to the continued market penetration of Microsoft. However, the human resource element cannot be ignored. How has Microsoft continually been successful in securing more and more productivity out of each employee?

EXHIBIT 2 **MICROSOFT EMPLOYEE GROWTH**

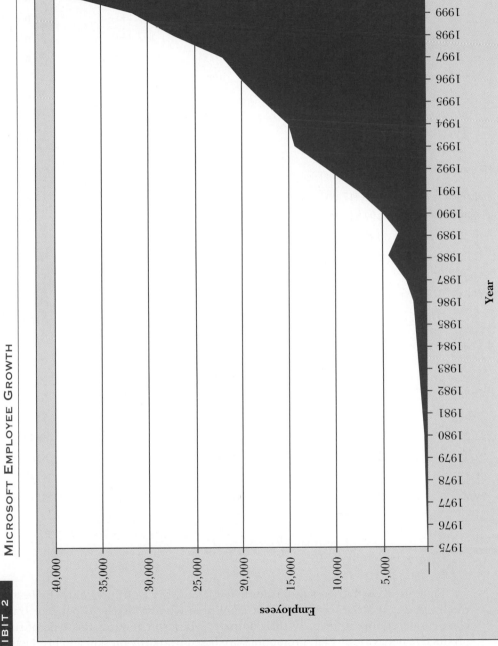

SOURCES: Cusumano and Selby, *Microsoft Secrets*, p. 3; and Microsoft Corporation, **www.microsoft.com/corpinfo/fastfact.htm**, (accessed January 31, 1998), **www.microsoft.com/presspass/fastfacts.asp**, (accessed January 23, 2001).

| EXHIBIT 3 | EMPLOYEE AND PROFIT GROWTH |

Fiscal Year*	Worldwide Head Count	Net Revenue	Net Income	Revenue Per Employee	Income Per Employee
1975	3	16,000	n/a	$5,333	n/a
1976	7	22,000	n/a	$3,143	n/a
1977	9	382,000	n/a	$42,444	n/a
1978	13	1,356,000	n/a	$104,308	n/a
1979	28	2,390,000	n/a	$85,357	n/a
1980	38	8,000,000	n/a	$210,526	n/a
1981	130	16,000,000	n/a	$123,077	n/a
1982	220	24,486,000	n/a	$111,300	n/a
1983	476	50,065,000	n/a	$105,179	n/a
1984	778	97,479,000	n/a	$125,294	n/a
1985	1,001	140,417,000	n/a	$140,277	n/a
1986	1,442	197,514,000	n/a	$136,972	n/a
1987	2,258	345,890,000	78,100,000	$153,184	$ 34,588
1988	2,793	590,827,000	124,000,000	$211,538	$ 44,397
1989	4,037	803,530,000	171,000,000	$199,041	$ 42,358
1990	5,635	1,183,000,000	279,000,000	$209,938	$ 49,512
1991	8,226	1,843,000,000	463,000,000	$224,046	$ 56,285
1992	11,542	2,759,000,000	708,000,000	$239,040	$ 61,341
1993	14,430	3,753,000,000	953,000,000	$260,083	$ 66,043
1994	15,017	4,649,000,000	1,146,000,000	$309,582	$ 76,314
1995	17,801	5,937,000,000	1,450,000,000	$333,521	$ 81,456
1996	20,561	8,671,000,000	2,195,000,000	$421,721	$106,756
1997	22,276	11,360,000,000	3,450,000,000	$509,966	$154,875
1998	27,055	15,262,000,000	4,490,000,000	$564,110	$165,958
1999	31,575	19,747,000,000	7,785,000,000	$625,400	$246,556
2000	39,904	22,956,000,000	9,421,000,000	$575,281	$236,092

*Fiscal year ends June 30.
SOURCE: Cusumano & Selby, *Microsoft Secrets*, p. 3; and Microsoft Corporation, **www.microsoft.com**, (accessed January 23, 2001).

First, as we will discuss in further detail later, Microsoft hires only the best and the brightest. It strives to hire driven employees who are likely to put in extra uncompensated hours to increase their output.[56] Microsoft rewards this type of superproductive behavior. In fact, promotions are based primarily on skill and productivity. For example, team leaders in the development area are expected to perform two roles. They are expected to supervise their team although continuing their programming. Employees are promoted to these positions because they are capable of doing a full

EXHIBIT 3A

NET INCOME: 1990–2000

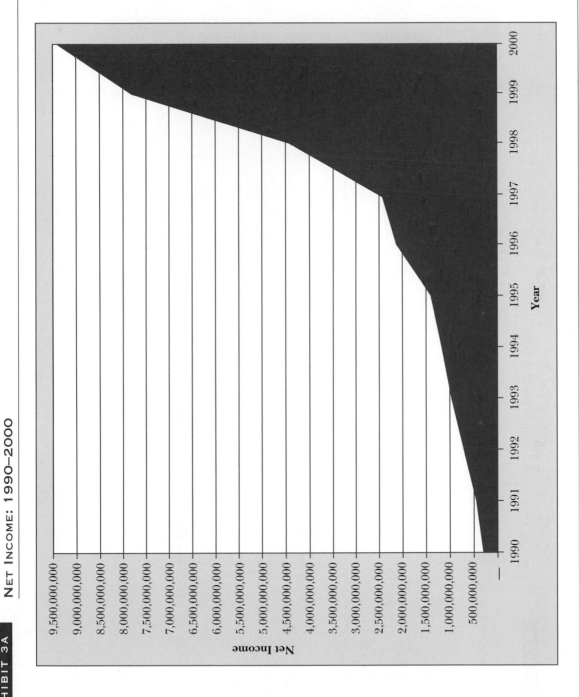

SOURCE: Cusumano and Selby, *Microsoft Secrets*, p. 3; and Microsoft Corporation, **www.microsoft.com**, (accessed January 23, 2001).

EXHIBIT 3B   REVENUE PER EMPLOYEE: 1975–2000

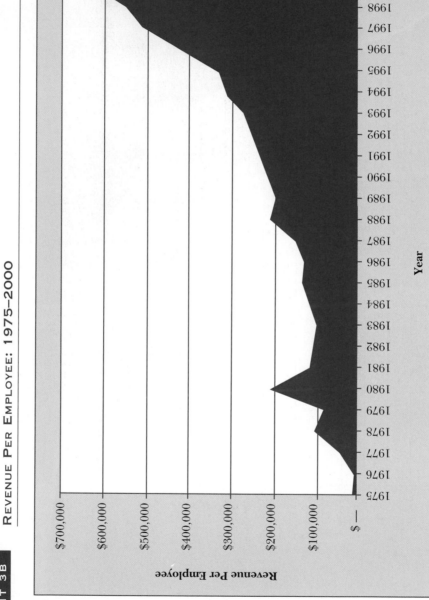

SOURCE: Cusumano and Selby, *Microsoft Secrets*, p. 3; and Microsoft Corporation, **www.microsoft.com**, (accessed January 23, 2001).

EXHIBIT 3C   NET INCOME PER EMPLOYEE: 1990–2000

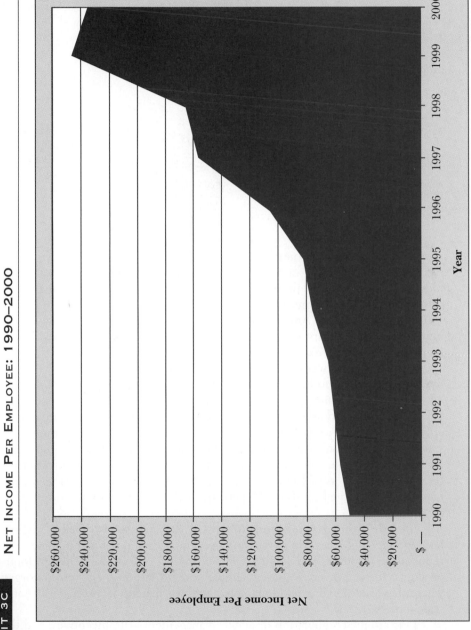

SOURCE: Cusumano and Selby, *Microsoft Secrets*, p. 3; and Microsoft Corporation, **www.microsoft.com**, (accessed January 23, 2001).

EXHIBIT 4	STOCK OPTION LEADERS*

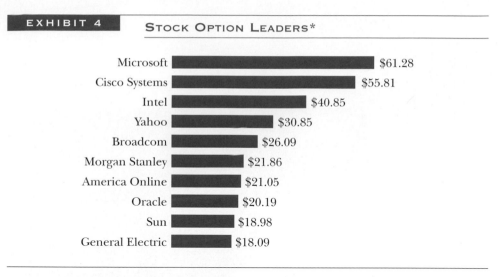

Microsoft	$61.28
Cisco Systems	$55.81
Intel	$40.85
Yahoo	$30.85
Broadcom	$26.09
Morgan Stanley	$21.86
America Online	$21.05
Oracle	$20.19
Sun	$18.98
General Electric	$18.09

SOURCE: "UBS Warburg," *The Wall Street Journal*, August 8, 2000, p. B6.
*Ranked by market value of stock options as of June 30, 2000 in billions.

week's worth of programming in 3 days, then spend the other two with managerial duties.[57] This dual role not only makes Microsoft more productive, but it sends a clear message to workers that productivity is not only valued, but also the key to promotions. The talent and management skills of Microsoft employees do not go unnoticed. In *Fortune's* rankings of America's 100 most admired companies, Microsoft was ranked number one in the software industry. Its talent was ranked number one, and its quality of management ranked number five.[58]

Microsoft employees are clearly given incentives to achieve high levels of productivity. Microsoft follows Bill Gates' philosophy of reasonably low base salaries for *all* employees but high incentive compensation—like bonuses and stock options.[59] Employee stock options are a vital tool for technology companies, which use them to attract and retain key employees. Microsoft has long been a leader in the practice. The stock option portion of compensation has reached nearly unbelievable heights. Recently, UBS Warburg released a study that put the market value of Microsoft's options, outstanding as of June 30, 2000, at $61.3 billion, ahead of other publicly held companies and equal to about 15 percent of the company's shares outstanding (see Exhibit 4).[60]

Growth through acquisitions (discussed earlier) has also enabled Microsoft to leverage its employees. By purchasing previously developed technologies, Microsoft reduces the resources it would have to put toward researching and developing these products. Instead, it takes these technologies and inserts them into its organization where they can be refined and marketed with the benefit of Microsoft's economies of scale in these areas.

This unique combination of talent, management skill, incentives, and the ability to grow both internally and through acquisitions has enabled Microsoft to leverage its human resources to continue to achieve a higher return on each employee. The strain on employees may be great, but the results are difficult to dispute (see Exhibit 3).

EXHIBIT 5	AGE AND GENDER (DOMESTIC ONLY)*	
Male	19,999	73.4%
Female	7,234	26.5%
Under 20	17	<0.1%
20–29	7,805	28.6%
30–39	13,716	50.3%
40+	5,711	21.0%
Total	27,249	

SOURCE: Microsoft Corporation: **www.microsoft.com/presspass/fastfacts.asp.**
*As of June 30, 2000.

EXHIBIT 6	FUNCTIONAL BREAKDOWN (WORLDWIDE)*	
Division	**Employees**	**Percentage of Workforce**
R&D	16,501	41.4%
Sales & Support	18,533	46.4%
Operations	4,870	12.2%
Worldwide Total	39,904	100%

SOURCE: Microsoft Corporation, **www.microsoft.com/presspass/fastfacts.asp.**
*As of June 30, 2000.

Current Employee Demographics

The technical expertise of the Executive Committee members is reflected throughout the Microsoft workforce. Even those employees classified as sales and service are expected to be knowledgeable in technical aspects. None of Microsoft's 39,904 employees worldwide are covered by a collective bargaining agreement.[61] This lack of union representation may explain some of the extraordinary workload that employees assume. Domestically, males make up more than 73 percent of the Microsoft workforce. As of June 2000, employees between ages 30 and 39 constituted more than 50 percent of employees, with the average age being 34.2 years old. R&D employees comprise 41.4 percent of the workforce, whereas sales and support constitutes 46.4 percent, and operations the remaining 12.2 percent.[62] (See Exhibits 5 and 6 for complete listings.)

Recruiting and Hiring

Although the number of employees has increased dramatically year after year, Microsoft has not simply thrown warm bodies into positions. The hiring process is renowned for its grueling selectivity. In the early days, Bill Gates and Paul Allen (the founders) and Charles Simonyi (chief architect of Microsoft Research) would interview most new potential employees. Today, technical managers still perform all interviews after the initial screening process. Bill Gates is known to look for four important qualities in all new hires: ambition, IQ, technical expertise, and business judgment, with IQ being the most important. In order to secure employees who possess these essential qualities, Microsoft employs a rigorous screening and interviewing process.[63]

The typical recruiting and hiring process for Microsoft follows the general flow and guidelines presented here. To initiate the process, recruiters visit 40 to 50 well-regarded universities each year. Although most of the recruiting is done at these "elite" schools, Microsoft also looks closely at students in colleges and universities close to Microsoft's Redmond, Washington site, especially for customer support engineers and testers. The role of human resource professionals is to orchestrate this process, with interviews performed by experienced employees from technical and product groups. It is important to note here that recruiters do not hire employees; they *manage the process*.[64] In other words, the managers who staff the units where the employees will *work* actually do the hiring.

The aim of the interview process is to determine how smart recruits are in the abstract, not necessarily how much they know about the specific areas to which they have applied. Microsoft has been known to ask prospective employees to estimate the volume of water flowing down the Mississippi River or the number of gas stations in the United States. The answer is unimportant, but the approach to analyzing the problem is critical.[65] Microsoft emphasizes substance more than form with its prospective employees. Microsoft warns interviewees not to be surprised if their interviewer is dressed in jeans and a T-shirt, and employment candidates are told to wear "whatever makes you comfortable" to an interview.[66]

Of the thousands of university students that are screened by Microsoft, only 10 percent to 15 percent will receive additional interviews. From that group, only 10 percent to 15 percent are typically hired. That means that only 2 percent to 3 percent of all recruits expressing an interest in Microsoft are eventually hired.[67]

IT Labor Shortage

To address the growing IT labor shortage, Microsoft and some of its leading technology partners started a multimillion-dollar initiative, Microsoft Skills 2000. The goal of the Skills 2000 is to bring new individuals into the industry and promote continued development among current IT professionals.[68] Included in this initiative are Web pages that enable interested parties to take an information technology aptitude skills test; obtain information regarding Microsoft product-related training and certification options; and technical training options with instructor-led, online, and self-paced formats. These Web sites also provide information regarding universities, colleges, and schools that participate in the Microsoft Authorized Academic Training Program and information about the Microsoft Skills 2000 IT Career Loan Program, which allows students and current professionals to obtain low-cost financing for their IT training. Information regarding jobs in IT are also provided through Microsoft Skills 2000 Career Expos. This series of job fairs brings together training experts, as well as employers waiting to hire qualified candidates.

On February 2, 1998, Microsoft and its business partners held the first National Groundhog Job Shadow Day to provide 5000 students nationwide with the opportunity to spend the day following IT professionals, including network managers, interactive digital media specialists, software developers, system administrators, and technical writers. The goal of the program was to highlight the tremendous job opportunities available in IT. According to James B. Hayes, president and CEO of Junior Achievement, "Microsoft's involvement in this initiative underscores the business community's commitment to emphasize marketable skills to young people in a very real and tangible way."[69] There is no doubt that other IT companies will need to get involved in similar initiatives to address the problems arising from the growing IT workforce shortage.

The lack of skilled computer labor has forced Microsoft to alter some of its recruiting practices. Although the Internet job site and college recruiting are still used to obtain potential employee candidates, Microsoft increasingly depends on employee referrals to obtain skilled labor. Microsoft is very aggressive when it comes to recruiting from a competitor's labor force if the potential employee has the needed skills. Microsoft is still very careful about recruiting from its partners and solution providers and will not approach them directly. If, however, the applicant approaches Microsoft regarding possible future employment, that person is fair game. According to Mickey Howard, Microsoft's regional director for the Southeastern United States, Microsoft does not offer perks or salary as an incentive but rather its current and future dominant position in the software industry. Some competitors would argue this point with Howard. It is clear that the tight labor market and increasing demand for skilled workers will force Microsoft to compete with other firms not only for market share but also for human capital.

Culture

Once hired, employees blend into and help shape the corporate culture. The Microsoft culture has been described as one that successfully provides a structure in which incremental, as well as "cutting edge," approaches are used to develop both small- and large-scale products. This means that Microsoft encourages iterative development of projects although enabling employees the freedom to "reinvent the wheel" in order to make large leaps in technological advances. This unique atmosphere is in large part driven by the programmers, who are zealously anti-bureaucratic.[70] This is just one way that Microsoft molds its culture to fit its workers in order to create an environment that is conducive to the productivity of employees. This atmosphere allows Microsoft to operate like a small company, by giving employees the freedom to take risks that could lead to advances, without the cumbersome burden of red tape hindering the process. The highly intelligent and technologically competent employees are talented problem solvers and decision makers. Employing skilled workers, as Microsoft has done, enables a firm to extend this type of autonomy to its employees.

Microsoft describes its employees as "part brainiacs, part free-spirited individuals, and 100 percent passionate about technology."[71] With more than 40 percent of its workforce involved in R&D, it is clear that the pursuit of technological innovations and breakthroughs is a core value at Microsoft. Evidence of the autonomy just mentioned is the fact that employees in technology groups have the freedom to move in a number of directions. Microsoft describes the ability of employees to work on several emerging projects simultaneously as "work[ing] for dozens of start-ups under one roof."[72]

However, the work environment at Microsoft does have its drawbacks. Microsoft pays relatively low salaries and often does not pay for overtime. In 1982, under pressure to pay overtime, Gates settled on a plan that offered year-end bonuses and the stock option plan.[73] (The current compensation plan will be covered in detail later.) Although total compensation becomes generous once stock options are computed, burnout and turnover still remain significant problems. The flexible, technology-driven culture described earlier also promotes demanding work schedules. Dave

Moore, the director of development at Microsoft, describes a typical day at work: "The Microsoft way: Wake up, go to work, do some work. 'Oh, I'm hungry.' Go down and eat some breakfast. Do some work. 'Oh, I'm hungry.' Eat some lunch. Work until you drop. Drive home. Sleep."[74] To survive and be considered valuable at Microsoft, working 14-hour days and most weekends is the norm. It is not uncommon for workers to stay at the office and work 3 or 4 days straight on a project. In addition, employees rarely take vacations, and when they do, they are typically very short ones. This high-pressure environment coupled with the fact that Microsoft ". . . tend[s] to select people who would burn themselves out anyway . . ."[75] leads to significant turnover for professional employees.

Microsoft estimates that 10 percent of new hires leave within the first year and that another 10 percent leave each subsequent year up through the fifth year.[76] A simple numerical example using this estimate is quite revealing. Suppose Microsoft hired 100 fresh new college recruits. After the first year, ten employees (10 percent) would be gone, leaving 90 employees remaining. At the end of the second year, nine employees would have left (again 10 percent), leaving 81 employees. Carrying this example out through year five, Microsoft would lose eight employees in year three, seven in year four, and at least six in year five. This means that of the 100 new hires in year one, only 59 would remain after 5 years. However, once employees have survived the first 5 grueling years, they tend to remain. After 5 years with Microsoft, most employees usually just take a leave of absence rather than leave the company altogether.

How does this demanding environment affect the attitudes of Microsoft employees? Cusumano and Selby, in their book *Microsoft Secrets*, surveyed employees on a number of issues. A selected list of replies about Microsoft includes:

- 25 percent *strongly agree* that "pace . . .[is] too frenetic."
- 39 percent *strongly agree* that "there are a lot of politics involved in getting promotions and recognition."
- 43 percent *strongly agree* that "[there is a] conflict . . . between quality of performance and quantity of work."
- 32 percent *strongly agree* that "I feel pressured to work many more hours/days than I am comfortable with."
- 44 percent *strongly disagree* that "new employees receive adequate training."
- 41 percent *strongly disagree* that "salary is equitable." (Only 30 percent *strongly agree* with this statement.)
- 26 percent *strongly disagree* that "[there is a] high degree of cooperation among business units." (Only 29 percent *strongly agree* with this statement.)[77]

As the survey indicates, many employees have strong feelings regarding Microsoft's shortcomings. Although most employees are pleased with the company overall, these answers indicate selected areas where employees are unhappy.

Diversity

Although not reflected in its executive ranks, Microsoft attempts to reflect its diverse customer base in its employees. Several "support groups" have been initiated and chartered by individual employees. These groups have been formed for a variety of reasons, including networking, social activities, continuing education, career development, and community outreach. All of these groups are members of the Microsoft Diversity Advisory Council (DAC). The DAC is an internal council that attempts to

EXHIBIT 7	DIVERSITY EMPLOYEE GROUPS

African American	Indian
Attention deficit disorder (ADD)	Korean
Chinese	Native American
Deaf/hard of hearing	Single parents
Filipino	Women
Gay, lesbian, bisexual, and transgender	Working parents
	Hispanic

SOURCE: Microsoft Corporation, **www.microsoft.com/corpinfo/fastfacts.asp**, (accessed January 31, 1998).

ensure that Microsoft remains an attractive place to work for a wide variety of skilled candidates.[78] Exhibit 7 indicates the wide variety of organizations formed by Microsoft employees. Microsoft offers two interactive diversity-training programs: Diversity Awareness and the Business of Diversity Programs.

The Diversity Awareness program serves as an introduction to diversity. It attempts to educate employees on their "ability to influence stereotypes, identify elements that make each participant a diverse person, and sharing communication strategies that help participants in a diverse environment."[79]

Employees are then encouraged to attend the Business of Diversity program, which functions as a sequel to the awareness program. This program looks directly at diversity in the workplace, providing real-life situations, problems, and solutions for employees to learn from. Both of these programs are geared to attract and keep talented employees who come from a wide array of backgrounds (see Exhibit 7).[80]

Benefits

The benefits plan at Microsoft is appropriately free from bureaucracy. All employee choices and changes are done directly via an online interface from employees' desktop PCs (except for salary increases, of course).

Compensation   As mentioned earlier, salary alone at Microsoft is somewhat low. All employees, including executives like Gates himself, receive salaries that are fair, but on the low end of industry averages. Although still competitive in the industry, it is the other benefits that make the complete compensation package more attractive.

Healthcare   Microsoft pays the full premium cost of medical, dental, and vision coverage for all eligible employees. This premium includes coverage for employees' spouse, same sex domestic partner, and eligible children. The programs are customizable using the online interface. Additional supplemental insurance is also available, including life insurance, short- and long-term disability insurance, and a group legal plan.

Financial Plans   Microsoft offers a myriad of financial options for its employees. After 6 months of employment, workers are eligible for the Savings Plus 401(k) Plan, which allows them to defer up to 15 percent of pretax salary, with Microsoft matching 50 cents of every dollar on all contributions up to 6 percent. The firm also offers diversified investment options and short-term loan provisions. The ESPP enables all full-time employees to purchase stock (through payroll deduction) at 85 percent of the closing fair-market value. Each employee is allowed to invest 2 percent to 10 percent of his or her after-tax salary in stock options.[81,82] Employees can exercise 25 percent of the options after working 18 months, and 12.5 percent every 6 months from that time forward, at any time within ten years.[83] Most Microsoft employees take advantage of the stock options. Other options include pretax deductions to cover healthcare and dependent costs.

Microsoft Extras   Claiming to offer "more perks than Seattle has coffee houses,"[84] Microsoft makes numerous other benefits available to its employees. These include a health club membership for employees in the Puget Sound area, up to $5000 for adoption assistance, paid maternity and paternity leave, and a matching charitable gifts program (up to $12,000). It also offers tuition assistance for qualified work-related university courses, encourages ergonomic consultations for health work environments, provides discounts on all Microsoft products, and offers Counseling Assistance Referral and Education Services (CARES) to assist employees in personal crisis situations.

On the Job with Microsoft

Career Path   Career paths at Microsoft generally run within a functional specialty. A typical progression is from new hire to being a mentor, team leader, then to a manager of a functional area for an entire product unit. Beyond this are special positions that involve responsibilities that extend over other functional areas.[85] As previously mentioned, managers at the upper levels of Microsoft must not only be extremely intelligent and skilled but also ultra-productive.

Training and Development   Speaking to the U.S. Congress on February 25, 1998, Mike Murray, Microsoft's head of human resources, testified that "the lifeblood of our industry is not capital equipment, but human capital." Murray and other top HR managers from technical companies relayed to Congress the critical shortage of highly skilled technical workers.[86] Despite the recognition of this situation, Microsoft still operates much like it did in its early entrepreneurial days. The company does not devote much of its resource to training programs, formal rules and procedures, or product documentation. Rather, it depends heavily on learning by doing. Less-experienced employees learn from more-experienced employees and through trial and error. The firm relies heavily on these knowledgeable employees to guide and teach the new ones.[87] Apparently, because it hires people based on their intellect and ability to learn, Microsoft seems to consider that this type of "training" is adequate. Although this method can help to make these highly skilled workers feel empowered to take control of their own learning, it does have some drawbacks. Highly skilled employees must spend considerable time answering questions from new employees. This takes away from the skilled employee's productive time. The extensive use of trial-and-error learning can also lead to costly mistakes in the fast-paced software industry.

"Ladder Levels"   In order to allow for the consistent appraisal and promotion of employees across functional areas, Microsoft developed "ladder levels" for employees in each specialty in 1983 and 1984. It began as a way to normalize salaries and attract new developers to Microsoft, and it was soon expanded to all functional areas. The ladder begins at a level 9 and progresses up to a level 15. Each level is "achieved" based on experience with the company, performance, and raw skill. A formal review by senior management is required for the promotion from one level to the next, and salary increases are directly tied to an increase in levels. Most college graduates begin at a level 9 or 10 with Microsoft. Moving up to higher "ladder levels" varies for each employee and even slightly from one function group to another. Across all function groups the progression, *on average*, from level to level is as follows:

- *Level 9 or 10:* New employees (mostly recent graduates) are hired at this level based on their knowledge and experience. Most employees spend from 6 to 18 months at this level.
- *Level 11:* Employees at this level are able to function on their own with minimal supervision. Employees normally stay at a level 11 for 2 or 3 years, although many stay at this level for several years.
- *Level 12:* From this point forward, there are no "typical" time progressions. It is all merit based. Employees who have shown that they can handle every aspect of a project advance to level 12. These employees have "significant impact on the project."[88]
- *Level 13:* Employees that begin to make an impact across business units have the opportunity to move to level 13. This requires extensive questioning from the division director regarding employee skills and contributions.
- *Level 14:* These employees have demonstrated the ability to contribute across an entire division. This requires an exhaustive review, which includes the employee's manager describing the contributions of the employee to the division head. People are promoted to this level only with the approval of Bill Gates. People considered to be part of the company "brain trust" are level 14 or 15.
- *Level 15:* There are very few level 15 employees. Promotion to this level also requires Gates' approval. All of these individuals are considered part of the strategic "brain trust" of Microsoft.[89]

Dave Moore, director of development, estimated that the breakdown for developers (which is fairly indicative of the entire company) was as follows:

Level 9-11:	50%-60%
Level 12:	20%
Level 13:	15%
Level 14-15:	5%-8%

Microsoft Competition

Microsoft's current dominance in the software industry, and its expansion into other markets, gives the impression that no one can compete with Microsoft. Despite this possible perception, Microsoft has many markets in which it competes to obtain the top market position.

Software

The Internet has drastically changed how people use computers (see Exhibit 8), and that in turn has changed what they expect of desktop applications. What Internet-savvy users need today are applications fully integrated with the Internet. The

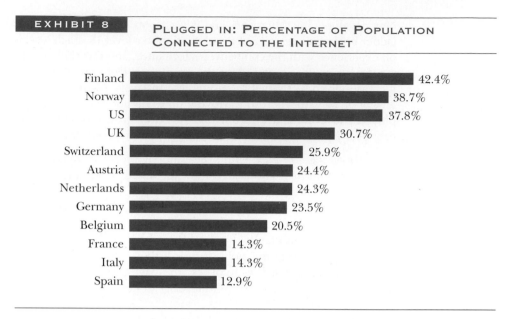

| EXHIBIT 8 | PLUGGED IN: PERCENTAGE OF POPULATION CONNECTED TO THE INTERNET |

Country	Percentage
Finland	42.4%
Norway	38.7%
US	37.8%
UK	30.7%
Switzerland	25.9%
Austria	24.4%
Netherlands	24.3%
Germany	23.5%
Belgium	20.5%
France	14.3%
Italy	14.3%
Spain	12.9%

SOURCE: Donaldson, Lufkin, and Jenrette, *The Wall Street Journal*, October 16, 2000, p. B13.

company continues to face movements from PC-based applications to server-based applications or Web-based application hosting services, from proprietary software to open source software, and from PCs to Internet-based devices. A number of Microsoft's most significant competitors, including IBM, Sun Microsystems, Oracle, and AOL, are collaborating with one another on various initiatives directed at competing with Microsoft. These initiatives relate in part to efforts to move software from individual PCs to centrally managed servers. Other competitive collaborative efforts also include the development of new platform technologies that are intended to replicate much of the value of Microsoft Windows operating systems. New computing from factors including non-PC information devices are gaining popularity and competing with PCs running Microsoft's software products. The company also faces relentless competition from software pirates who unlawfully copy and distribute Microsoft's copyrighted software products, depriving the company of large amounts of revenue on an annual basis.[90]

Windows software runs on 90 percent of PCs. Microsoft's strategic power in the computer software industry presents significant challenges for its competitors. Microsoft has and is using its success with Windows to expand its reach beyond the desktop to other areas of business where software is needed. This has led software competitors to complain very loudly to the Federal Trade Commission and the Justice Department about Microsoft's domination of the software market and for the Justice Department to closely scrutinize Microsoft for anticompetitive behavior. Its biggest rivals—Netscape, Sun Microsystems, Oracle, and IBM—have united to form a front against their common foe. Their rhetoric is increasingly vitriolic. "Microsoft is feared and loathed, and that drives companies together against them," says George Paolini, director of corporate marketing for Sun's JavaSoft Division.[91] James H. Clark, chairman of Netscape Communications Corp. said, "Microsoft, I think, is fundamentally an evil company."[92] Samuel Goodhope, a special assistant in the Texas Attorney

General's Office and its point man in its antitrust investigation into Microsoft Corporation, thinks the software maker is a lot like the Star Trek characters, the Borg. These characters—part flesh, part machine—prowl the universe conquering and assimilating other races and incorporating them into their own.[93]

This kind of Microsoft bashing has been going on for years, partly because it is the leader everyone wants to beat, and also because of its aggressiveness with competitors, distributors, and even business partners.[94] Thus far the flexibility of the Microsoft culture and the productivity of its employees have enabled it to respond rapidly and effectively to these continual threats.

Antitrust Case   In July 1994 Microsoft and the United States Department of Justice (DOJ) signed a consent decree that stated that Microsoft might not require computer manufacturers (OEMs) who license Windows also to license any other software product. However, the consent decree did not prohibit Microsoft from developing integrated products. In July 1995 Microsoft launched Windows 95 with integrated Internet Explorer features. The DOJ found Microsoft in contempt of the consent decree, claiming that Internet Explorer was a separate product. Linking the two products violated the consent decree.[95] On January 22, 1998, the software giant accepted the DOJ's terms to avoid a contempt of court violation. Some say that Microsoft's efforts to sandbag compliance have committed a public relations blunder, provoking both the presiding judge and the antitrust regulators.

Microsoft has many supporters such as Compaq Computer, the world's biggest personal computer maker. Compaq continues to package Microsoft's browser. The primary reason is that Windows operating systems have become the computer industry standard.[96] A survey published in *Fortune* found that Americans love Microsoft. The survey showed that 73 percent of Americans think Microsoft is one of the country's greatest businesses, and 78 percent agree that Microsoft produces high-quality products.[97] The negative publicity surrounding the company's dispute with the DOJ over its marketing practices for its Internet software has not severely affected the company's popularity with American people.[98] However, a more recent survey conducted by Merrill Lynch found that the computer giant's standing among technology opinion leaders has suffered. In the survey of 50 corporate chief information officers, 59 percent said they believe Microsoft abuses its power. Sixty-two percent of those surveyed disagree with the U.S. DOJ antitrust actions against Microsoft. They believe Microsoft should be able to integrate its browser and operating system.[99]

In December 1997 the government began sending civil subpoenas to companies doing business with Microsoft, including software makers, providers of Internet content and entertainment, and online service providers. On March 3, 1998, Microsoft's then-CEO Bill Gates, along with CEOs from two of the rivals, Sun Microsystem's Scott McNealy and Netscape's Jim Barksdale, testified before a Senate Judiciary Committee investigating alleged antitrust violations by Microsoft. The hearing was an opportunity for rivals of Microsoft to argue that it was indeed a monopoly that needed to be regulated. Barksdale posed this question to a packed house in the hearing room: "I would like a show of hands. How many of you use Intel-based PCs in this audience? [Nearly the entire room raised their hands.] Of that group who use PCs, how many of you use a PC *without* Microsoft's operating system? [Every hand dropped.] Gentlemen, that's a monopoly. That's a lock. That's 100 percent."[100] McNealy also argued that Microsoft is a monopoly when he stated: "Well, it has the opportunity to leverage a monopoly. The only thing I'd rather own than Windows is English or Chinese or Spanish, because then I could charge you $249 to speak English and I could charge you an upgrade fee when I add new letters like 'N' and 'T.'"[101]

When Bill Gates was given his opportunity to defend Microsoft, he pointed out the dominance of IBM in the 1970s. "People said that any start-up who tried to take on this company was doomed to failure . . . people who feared IBM were wrong . . . innovation depends on freedom to move constantly from one frontier to the next."[102] Gates argued that because of the fast-paced changes in the technology industry, a current advantage in the market could be lost very quickly.

Although these testimonies made for some interesting sound bites on the evening news, the real issue being explored at these hearings was whether Microsoft was engaging in anticompetitive activities. When asked repeatedly by Senator Orin Hatch of Utah whether Microsoft restricts its Internet partners from dealing with Microsoft rivals, Gates conceded that it did. He noted that the most prominent Web sites featured in its Internet software (Internet Explorer) are barred from promoting Netscape. Gates said "On those pages, you don't promote [rival] browsers."[103] This statement by Gates was surprising in the sense that news of Microsoft's revising existing browser deals had reached the popular press *before* his testimony. On March 1, 1998, Microsoft announced that it had revised deals with 30 Internet providers in Europe and 12 in the United States that would allow them to promote rival browsers. Microsoft had made formal notification to the European Commission 2 days earlier, on February 27.[104] Microsoft spokesman Mark Murray told the *Washington Post*, "This change makes sense from a business perspective, and if it helps to alleviate any potential government concerns, then it's a change we're happy to make."[105] The fact that Gates did not point this out to the hearing committee is somewhat confusing.

The effects of this antitrust issue have not been lost on the human resource element of Microsoft. Because the Justice Department filed the suit, Microsoft has funneled most of its communications through an internal team of about 20 people reporting to Public Relations Manager Mitch Mathews. This extensive strategy formulation has also involved lawyers, executive VPs Steve Ballmer and Bob Herbold, and Bill Gates himself.[106] Microsoft's legal issues have not only diverted strategic resources to deal with their effects, but the negative publicity has shaken some employees.

Other Competition   Microsoft's long-held vision of a computer on every desk and in every home continues to be at the core of everything the company does. Microsoft believes that software is the tool that empowers people both at work and at home. Since Microsoft was founded in 1975, its charter has been to deliver on its vision of the power of personal computing. Now its vision has expanded to include every business in which software matters: the corporate-enterprise market, computerized home appliances, and Internet commerce.

Although Microsoft dominates the desktop, other information technologies are dominated by different companies. In the mainframe systems and software technology, IBM is Microsoft's most formidable competitor. After stumbling in the early '90s, IBM has made a remarkable comeback by using PC technology to sell mainframe computers costing less than one tenth what customers paid in the late 1980s.[107] It has a large entrenched customer base of legacy mainframe customers dating from the 1970s. These customers still run IBM mainframe software. IBM's strategy to retain its market share included the purchase of Lotus Notes and the integration of the dominant GroupWise software with its mainframe systems. It has also integrated Java technology in its offerings to customers, allowing them access to Internet technology while retaining their mainframe systems.

Operating Systems   Microsoft's operating system products face substantial competition from a wide variety of companies. Competitors such as IBM, Apple Computer, Sun Microsystems, and others are vertically integrated in both software development and hardware manufacturing and have developed operating systems that they preinstall on computers of their own manufacture. Many of these operating system software products are also licensed to third-party OEMs for preinstallation on their computers. Microsoft's operating system products compete with UNIX-based operating systems from a wide range of companies, including IBM, AT&T, Hewlett-Packard, Sun Microsystems, The Santa Cruz Operation, and others. Variants of UNIX run on a wide variety of computer platforms and have gained increasing acceptance as desktop operating systems. With an increased attention toward open-source software, the Linux operating system has gained increasing acceptance. Several computer manufacturers preinstall Linux on PC Servers, and many leading software developers have written applications that run on Linux. Microsoft Windows operating systems are also threatened by alternative platforms, such as those based on Internet-browsing software and Java technology promoted by AOL and Sun Microsystems.[108]

Consumer Platforms   A wide variety of companies develop operating systems for information appliances, including Palm, Apple, Motorola, 3Com, Psion Software, Sun Microsystems, Microworkz, Be, Inc., WindRiver, Symbian and others. The company's WebTV offerings and other multimedia consumer products face competitors such as AOL, Oracle, Liberate Technologies, NetChannel, and others. An enormous range of companies, including media conglomerates, telephone companies, cable companies, retailers, hardware manufacturers, and software developers, are competing to make interactive services widely available to the home.[109]

Desktop Applications   The company's competitors include many software application vendors, such as IBM (Lotus), Oracle, Apple (Filemaker, Inc.), Sun Microsystems, Corel, Qualcomm, and local application developers in Europe and Asia. IBM and Corel have large installed bases with their spreadsheet and word-processor products, respectively, and both have aggressive pricing strategies. Also, IBM and Apple preinstall certain application software products on various models of their PCs, competing directly with Microsoft's desktop application software. In addition, Web-based application hosting services provide an alternative to PC-based applications such as Microsoft Office.[110]

Business Solutions   The company competes in the business of providing enterprise-wide computing solutions with several competitors that enjoy a larger share of sales and larger installed bases. Many companies offer operating system software for mainframes and midrange computers, including IBM, Hewlett-Packard, and Sun Microsystems. Because legacy business systems are typically support intensive, these competitors also offer substantial support services. Software developers that provide competing server applications for PC-based distributed client/server environments include Oracle, IBM, Computer Associates, Sybase, and Informix. There are also several software vendors who offer connectivity servers. As mentioned previously, there are numerous companies and organizations offering Internet and intranet server software that compete against the company's business systems. In addition, IBM has a large installed base of Lotus Notes and cc:Mail, both of which compete with the company's collaboration and e-mail products.[111]

Internet   Microsoft's competition with rival Netscape is probably the best example of its technology market strategy in recent memory. Even though Microsoft bundled the first version of Internet Explorer with Windows, Netscape's Navigator's technical superiority allowed it to dominate the lion's share of the market, overshadowing such early entrants as Quarterdeck and Spyglass. With the launch of its Internet Explorer version 3.0, Microsoft had matched many of Netscape's browser features. Netscape Communication pioneered the Internet business model of giving software away to build up market share and then selling related products.[112] However, while Microsoft copied Netscape's plan of giving its browser away for free by bundling it into Windows 95, Netscape began to charge for its browser. After Microsoft had already gained ground in the battle for Web browser market share, Netscape announced plans to market its browser software for free in an attempt to hold onto its market share.[113] Microsoft has also put pressure on Netscape in the Web server market, supplying its Internet software with other server products for free. Netscape sells its browser and server as stand-alone products.

Online Services

Microsoft's online services network, MSN, faces formidable competition from AOL (including its CompuServe unit), Yahoo, and a vast array of Web sites and portals that offer content of all types and e-mail, instant messaging, calendaring, chat, and search and shopping services, among other things. In addition, the ease of entry into Internet services has allowed numerous Web-based service companies to build significant businesses in areas such as e-mail, electronic commerce, Web search engines, directories, and information of numerous types. Competitors include AOL, Yahoo, Excite, Lycos, Infoseek, AltaVista, and many others. The company's MSNBC joint ventures face formidable competition from other 24-hour cable and Internet news organizations such as CNN, CNN Headline News, and Fox News Network. MSNBC also competes with traditional news media such as newspapers, magazines, and broadcast TV.[114]

E-commerce   Microsoft competes with many companies in the e-commerce business and its major components, including business-to-consumer, business-to-business, procurement, and supply chain integration. In the development and marketing of Internet and intranet solutions, major commerce software competitors provide many different ranges of products and solutions that compete with Microsoft, including IBM, Oracle, AOL, Sun Microsystems, Broadvision, and many others.[115]

Future Competition

Microsoft's Windows software runs on 90 percent of PCs, and the company dominates the home computing market.[116] Considering the amount of software Microsoft bundles, this does not leave a lot of market share for new companies to exploit. Most venture capitalists now view this market as mature with little room for growth; there just is not a lot of market share left. Personal productivity software must now be able to tap into today's distributed computing environment in the areas known as Group-Ware or online applications to interest consumers. New ventures into this market are either absorbed or eliminated by Microsoft.

The dilemma that most software entrepreneurs face today is what strategic direction to pursue. Start-up companies that go head-to-head against Microsoft risk annihilation; however, companies that cooperate with Microsoft as partners also risk

EXHIBIT 9	MICROSOFT'S FINANCIAL PERFORMANCE

Financial Highlights (In Millions, Except EPS)

Year Ended June 30	1996	1997	1998	1999	2000
Revenue	9,050	11,936	15,262	19,747	22,956
Net income	2,195	3,454	4,490	7,785	9,421
Diluted EPS	0.43	0.66	0.84	1.42	1.70
Cash and short-term investments	6,940	8,966	13,927	17,236	23,798
Total assets	10,093	14,387	22,357	38,625	52,150
Stockholders' equity	6,908	10,777	16,627	28,438	41,368

SOURCE: **www.microsoft.com**, (accessed January 23, 2001).

annihilation through assimilation. Microsoft executives advise venture capitalists against sinking money into start-up companies that challenge its control of the desktop platform.[117] Start-up companies today now target niches that they can build up so that Microsoft will pay to take over the company rather than simply bypassing it and freezing it out of the marketplace.

Financial Highlights

The company's revenue growth rate was 28 percent in fiscal 1998, 29 percent in fiscal 1999, and 16 percent in fiscal 2000 (Exhibit 9). Revenue growth in fiscal 2000 was driven by strong licensing of the Microsoft suite of products including Microsoft Windows NT Workstation, Windows 2000 Professional, Windows NT Server, Windows 2000 Server, Microsoft Office 2000, and SQL Server 7.0. Windows 2000, released during fiscal 2000, is the newest version of the Windows NT operating system. Consumer revenue, including Internet access, the online properties, entertainment software, and hardware peripherals also grew strongly. Partially offsetting those items was slower growth from Windows operating systems sold through the OEM channel because of slow demand for business PCs throughout a significant portion of fiscal 2000. Revenue growth in fiscal 1998 and 1999 reflected the continued adoption of Windows operating systems and Microsoft Office. Software organizational license increases in 1998, 1999, and 2000 have been a significant factor in the company's revenue growth. The average selling price per license has decreased, primarily because of general shifts in the sales mix from retail packaged products to licensing programs, from new products to product upgrades, and from stand-alone desktop applications to integrated product suites. Average revenue per license from OEM licenses and organizational license programs is lower than average revenue per license from retail versions. Likewise, product upgrades have lower prices than new products.[118]

The Future for Microsoft

One of Microsoft's many challenges going forward is fending off attacks on its corporate policies and culture. On January 3, 2001, a suit was filed in federal court claiming that Microsoft's flat hierarchical structure discriminates against minorities.[119] This flat reporting structure, being one of the cornerstones of Microsoft's corporate culture, allows junior employees to interact freely with their superiors in hopes of increasing productivity and knowledge transfer, as well as simply tearing down walls between employees. The suit alleges that this structure creates a hostile work environment where junior white male employees are permitted to publicly challenge and defy their minority superiors and bypass them in the chain of command. The suit also alleges that Microsoft's employee review system, in which managers are asked to grade their employees, has allowed white employees to be promoted faster and more often than their minority counterparts. This review style is intended to promote a corporate culture in which promotions, pay increases, and bonus stock options are given to employees who are the most skilled and not base the reward structure around seniority and length of service. The suit alleges that this grading system is subjective in nature and allows managers to discriminate against employees based on their race, age, or sex. In answering this suit, Microsoft must decide if it is willing to change corporate policy to correct these alleged discriminatory management practices and must weigh their impact on Microsoft's corporate culture.

In an industry in which competitors can change overnight, one can only speculate what the future will hold for Microsoft. Financially, Microsoft's revenues and profits continue to grow at a phenomenal rate. However, there is no doubt that Microsoft has some challenges ahead. As a growing company, Microsoft continues to face problems with human resources. To be a highly successful company, Microsoft must constantly find ways to attract the best and the brightest, especially in light of the growing information technology workforce shortage. The Microsoft Skills 2000 program, which aims to bring new individuals into the industry and encourages those in it to keep their skills current, will hopefully have positive results for the company and the industry. However, Microsoft needs to address the reasons for the high employee turnover and must find ways to reduce the number of employees who leave. Microsoft's future also depends on the strengths and talents of the individuals who may eventually step into Bill Gates' and CEO Steve Ballmer's shoes. Adequate planning for succession will be critical for the company to survive should the driving force of Bill Gates no longer be there to lead Microsoft into the future.

Questions

1. Microsoft has recognized the shortage of skilled workers by initiating the Skills 2000 program. However, it still has no structured training program for its new employees. How will this affect them in the future? Should they change this policy?

2. The "learn as you go" work method can be vulnerable to costly mistakes that set a company back on a deadline or project. Why is Microsoft even more vulnerable to this threat because of their industry? Stock options are an expensive part of Microsoft's labor costs. If these were eliminated, what impact would it have on its ability to hire "the best and the brightest"? Should it alter its current ESPP plan?

3. How should Microsoft react to the federal lawsuit alleging that ingrained Microsoft corporate practices, such as the performance grading system and flat hierarchical structure, discriminate against minorities?

4. Microsoft is in many ways dominated by the persona of Bill Gates. What effect would his absence (untimely illness or death, etc.) have on the company?

Notes

[1]**www.microsoft.com**, (accessed June 31, 2000).

[2]**www.microsoft.com/presspass**, (accessed June 31, 2000).

[3]Daniel Ichbiah and Susan Knepper, *The Making of Microsoft* (Rocklin, CA: Prima Publishing, 1991), p. 10.

[4]James Wallace and Jim Erickson, *Hard Drive: Bill Gates and the Making of the Microsoft Empire* (New York: Wiley, 1992), p. 59.

[5]Schlender, Brenton, "Bill Gates & Paul Allen Talk," *Fortune*, October 2, 1995, p. 71.

[6]Ichbiah and Knepper, *The Making of Microsoft*, p. 26.

[7]Schlender, "Bill Gates & Paul Allen Talk," p. 71.

[8]Ibid., p. 72.

[9]Ichbiah and Knepper, *The Making of Microsoft*, p. 47.

[10]Ibid.

[11]Schlender, "Bill Gates & Paul Allen Talk," p. 72.

[12]Ibid.

[13]"Corporate Information," **www.microsoft.com**, (accessed January 21, 1998).

[14]Schlender, "Bill Gates & Paul Allen Talk," p. 76.

[15]"Microsoft Past and Present," **www.microsoft.com**, (accessed January 29, 1998).

[16]Schlender, "Bill Gates & Paul Allen Talk," p. 78.

[17]Wallace and Erickson, *Hard Drive: Bill Gates and the Making of the Microsoft Empire* , p. 259.

[18]Ichbiah and Knepper, *The Making of Microsoft*, p. 124.

[19]Ibid.

[20]"Corporate Information."

[21]"Microsoft Past and Present."

[22]Ibid.

[23]Microsoft, *2000 Annual Report*, p. 3.

[24]*Vizcaino* v. *Microsoft Corp.*, 120 F. 3d 1006, 97-2 USTC p. 50,572,21 Employee Benefits Cas. 1273, 97 Cal. Daily Op. Serv.5847, 97 Daily Journal D.A.R. 9429, Pens.Plan Guide P 23935S (9th Cir., Washington, DC, July 24, 1997) (No. 94-35770).

[25]"At Microsoft, A Consolation Prize," *Business Week*, December 25, 2000, p. 60.

[26]Lawrence Lore and Karyn-Siobhan Robinson, "Microsoft 'Permatemp' Settlement Seen As Warning To Employers," *HRNews*, February 2001, p. 8.

[27]Ibid.

[28]Michael Cusumano and Richard W.Selby, *Microsoft Secrets*, New York: Simon and Shorter, 1998, pp. 127–128.

[29]Microsoft, *2000 Annual Report*, p. 25.

[30]Randall E. Stross, "Mr. Gates Builds His Brain Trust," *Fortune*, December 8, 1997, pp. 84–87.

[31]Microsoft, *2000 Annual Report*, p. 11.

[32]**www.research.microsoft.com**, (accessed February 22, 1998).

[33]Microsoft Corporation, *SEC Form 10K*, September 29, 1997.

[34]Cusumano and Selby, *Microsoft Secrets*, pp. 55–58.

[35]Microsoft Corporation, *SEC Form 10K*, September 29, 1997.

[36]**www.pr-eda.com/partner.html**, (accessed February 23, 1998).

[37]**www.businessnetpr.com/tradenet0197b.htm**, (accessed February 22, 1998).

[38]**www.ida.ie/consusec.htm**, (accessed February 22, 1998).

[39]Microsoft Corporation, *SEC Form 10K*, September 29, 1997.

[40]Ibid.

[41]Ibid.

[42]Ibid.

[43]Cusumano and Selby, *Microsoft Secrets*.

[44]Microsoft Corporation, *SEC Form 10K*, 2000, pp. 10–11.

[45]Cusumano and Selby, *Microsoft Secrets*.

[46]Microsoft, *2000 Annual Report*, p. 15.

[47]"Press Release," **www.microsoft.com**, (accessed February 22, 1998).

[48]"Press Release," **www.microsoft.com**, (accessed February 22, 1998).

[49]Ronald B. Lieber, "You Inc.: 100 Best Companies to Work for in America," *Fortune*, January 12, 1998.

[50]"The ASAP Dynamic 100," *Forbes ASAP*, February 23, 1998, **www.forbes.com**.

[51]Max Anguilera-Hellweg, "A Round of Applause," *Forbes ASAP*, February 23, 1998, **www.forbes.com**.

[52]Microsoft Corporation, **www.microsoft.com**, (accessed January 31, 1998).

[53]Microsoft Corporation, *SEC Form 10K*, September 29, 1997.

[54]Microsoft Corporation, **www.microsoft.com**.

[55]Ibid.

[56]Cusumano and Selby, *Microsoft Secrets*, p. 94.

[57]Ibid., p. 120.

[58]Thomas A. Stewart, "America's Most Admired Companies," *Fortune*, March 2, 1998, pp. 70–82.

[59]Cusumano and Selby, *Microsoft Secrets*, p. 116.

[60]Don Clark and Rebecca Buckman, "Microsoft To Resume Buybacks To Provide For Employee Options, Prevent Dilution," *The Wall Street Journal*, August 8, 2000, p. B6.

[61]Cusumano and Selby, *Microsoft Secrets*, p. 90.

[62]Microsoft Corporation, **www.microsoft.com**.

[63]Cusumano and Selby, *Microsoft Secrets*, p. 92.

[64]Ibid., p. 91.

[65]Ibid., p. 92.

[66]Microsoft Corporation, **www.microsoft.com**.

[67]Cusumano and Selby, *Microsoft Secrets*, p. 92.

[68]"Microsoft Skills 2000," March 2, 1998, **www.microsoft.com**.

[69]Microsoft and Its Business Partners to Mentor 5,000 Students during National Groundhog Job Shadow Day '98," March 2, 1998, **www.microsoft.com**.

[70]Cusumano and Selby, *Microsoft Secrets*, p. 15.

[71]Microsoft Corporation, **www.microsoft.com**.

[72]Microsoft Corporation, **www.microsoft.com**.

[73]Cusumano and Selby, *Microsoft Secrets*, p. 93.

[74]Ibid.

[75]Ibid.

[76]Ibid., pp. 93–95.

[77]Ibid., pp. 465–467.

[78]Microsoft Corporation, **www.microsoft.com**.

[79]Ibid.

[80]Ibid.

[81]*Microsoft Benefits*, Microsoft Corporation, Recruiting Brochure, 0695 Part No. 098-60768.

[82]Cusumano and Selby, *Microsoft Secrets*, p. 93.

[83]Ibid.

[84]Microsoft Corporation, **www.microsoft.com**.

[85]Cusumano and Selby, *Microsoft Secrets*, p. 116.

[86]Patricia Wilson, "Tech Firms Seek Foreign Employees to Fill Void," *Reuters Service*, February 26, 1998.

[87]Cusumano and Selby, *Microsoft Secrets*, p. 104.

[88]Ibid., p. 119.

[89]Ibid., pp. 116–119.

[90]Microsoft Corporation, *SEC Form 10K*, 2000.

[91]Steve Hamm, "The Long Shadow of Bill Gates," *BusinessWeek*, August 25, 1997, p. 85.

[92]Ibid.

[93]Steve Hamm et al., "Microsoft's Future," p. 58.

[94]Gartner Group, Inc., "Microsoft's Road Ahead—What It Means for Your Business," *Business Technology Journal*, (February 28, 1998).

[95]Microsoft, "Timeline of Events," **www.microsoft.com**.

[96]David Bank and John Wilke, "Microsoft and Justice End a Skirmish, yet War Could Escalate," *The Wall Street Journal*, January 23, 1998, p. A1.

[97]David Kirkpatrick, "America Loves Microsoft," *Fortune*, February 2, 1998, pp. 80–86.

[98]David Bank, "Microsoft Beats 2nd Period Net Outlook," *The Wall Street Journal*, January 22, 1998, p. A3.

[99]Bank and Wilke, "Microsoft and Justice End a Skirmish," p. A1.

[100]"In Their Own Words: Three High-Tech CEOs Testify," *The Wall Street Journal*, March 4, 1998, p. B1.

[101]Ibid.

[102]Ibid.

[103]John R. Wilke and David Bank, "Microsoft's Chief Concedes Hardball Tactics," *The Wall Street Journal*, March 4, 1998, p. B1.

[104]"Microsoft Allows Promotion of Rival Browsers," **www.yahoo.com/headlines/980302/tech/stories/browser_1html**, (accessed March 2, 1998).

[105]"Microsoft Reveals Browser Deal," *The Associated Press*, AP-NY-03-01-98 2351EST (March 2, 1998).

[106]Don Clark, "A Master Programmer Updates His Code," *The Wall Street Journal*, March 4, 1998, p. B1.

[107]Hamm et al., "Microsoft's Future," p. 61.

[108]Microsoft Corporation, *SEC Form 10K*, 2000.

[109]Ibid.

[110]Ibid.

[111]Ibid.

[112]Heather Green, "Has Netscape Hit the 'Innovation Ceiling?'" *BusinessWeek*, January 19, 1998, p. 69.

[113]Peter B. Dushkin, "Wrestling with Redmond," *Internet Business Report*, (February 28, 1998).

[114]Microsoft Corporation, *SEC Form 10K*, 2000.

[115]Ibid.

[116]Hamm et al., "Microsoft's Future," p. 61.

[117]Hamm, "The Long Shadow of Bill Gates," p. 85.

[118]**www.microsoft.com**.

[119]Yochi J. Dreazen and Jess Bravin, "Bias Suit Against Microsoft Aims At 'Flat' Workplace Hierarchies," *The Wall Street Journal*, January 4, 2001, p. A10.

7

Intel

Introduction

Overview of the Company

In 1968 Gordon Moore and Bob Noyce decided to leave Fairchild Semiconductor and create a competing company: Intel.[1] Once they had the financing for their new company, Moore and Noyce needed two additional pieces to complete their management puzzle. The company needed an operations manager and a marketing manager. Choosing these two individuals has had more impact on Intel than any other choice made during Intel's infancy. Bob Graham was selected as marketing manager, and Andy Grove became the operations manager. Grove came on board several months before Graham, while Graham took care of prior commitments. This is of importance because Graham had virtually no impact on Intel's early hiring decisions. As the story unfolds, Andy Grove has gone on to become the CEO of Intel and the driving force behind the unique corporate culture of Intel. On the other hand, Graham eventually left Intel after several years once it became clear that Intel was developing into Grove's company.

By 1971 Intel had invented the first computer on a chip, known as the microprocessor, and in 1980 IBM chose Intel's 8086 chip as the central component of the original IBM PC.[2] Since then Intel has gone on to obtain a 90 percent share of the world's PC microprocessor market[3] and to have annual profits of $12.1 billion in 2000 and an average annual return to investors of 35.4 percent during the past 10 years.[4] Intel has also grown from its original production facility in the old Union Carbide Plant in Mountain View, California, with more than 100 employees, to an international corporation with major locations spanning the globe (Exhibit 1) and more than 70,000 employees worldwide.

Intel's mission is to be the preeminent building block supplier to the worldwide Internet economy. The company supplies the computing industry with the chips, boards, systems, and software that are the ingredients of computer architecture and used to create advanced computing systems.

Intel's current emphasis is on the newest PC market that focuses on "sub-$1000" PCs, with sales in U.S. retail units reaching an estimated 25 percent in 2000. A mid-1998 release of the Celeron Microprocessor was aimed at what Intel labels the Basic PC Market. However, they are not abandoning their strength of being able to introduce the next generation of microprocessor while their competitors try to duplicate the current Intel chips. Intel released a 1.5-gegahertz Pentium 4 in November 2000, thus continuing their string of new chip releases.

EXHIBIT 1	INTEL'S LOCATIONS

North America

United States, Argentina, Brazil, Canada, Chile, Colombia, Costa Rica, Mexico

Asia

Australia, Hong Kong, China, India, Indonesia, Japan, Korea, Malaysia, New Zealand, Pakistan, Philippines, Singapore, Taiwan, Thailand, Vietnam

Europe and Other

Belgium, Czech Republic, Denmark, Finland, France, Germany, Greece, Holland, Hungary, Ireland, Israel, Italy, Lithuania, Poland, Russia, South Africa, Spain, Sweden, Turkey, Ukraine, United Arab Emirates, United Kingdom

Human Resources

Corporate Culture

Andy Grove, *Time* magazine 1997 man of the year and Intel CEO, is the driving force behind the corporate culture of Intel. His demanding, confrontational style has created an environment that is both criticized for putting too much stress on employees and praised for bringing out the best in employees. The atypical culture at Intel is about encouraging employees to challenge ideas and solutions and to take risks. Trusting employees and expecting them to make million-dollar decisions is central to the company's culture. This creates a focus on recruiting individuals with intense personalities who are not only able to give open and honest feedback but are also willing to take the same kind of scrutiny. Because of this intense, highly productive environment, Intel is not known for its "show." Plush executive offices are not the norm; more typical are doorless cubicles in a campus-like facility where expertise is more important than rank and hierarchy.

Intel focuses on a set of values and views that employees are expected to demonstrate in their projects and teams (Exhibit 2).

All newly hired employees complete an orientation course focusing on performance that meets the company values. And training continues beyond orientation; Intel estimates that it spends more than $200 million in training annually. More importantly, the company expects the responsibility of each individual's employability in the dynamic environment to fall on the employee: each employee is responsible for all aspects of their work. Intel focuses on giving employees the tools and training and then expecting them to excel using those tools and training.

This direct and challenging environment is at the core of Intel's corporate culture. One competitive advantage that Intel enjoys is its ability to stay ahead of the pack, and its culture is the reason that it has been able to remain one, or sometimes two, steps ahead. Intel recently was ranked 42nd in *Fortune* magazine's top 100 best companies to work for in America (January 8, 2001), showing that its culture is having a positive effect on its employees, which reflects positively on the company. Intel also finished eighth overall in *Fortune's* 2000 annual survey of most admired companies (February 22, 2000), including a top-five ranking in quality of management (Exhibit 3).

EXHIBIT 2	INTEL'S VALUES

Results Orientation

- Set challenging and competitive goals.
- Focus on output.
- Assume responsibility.
- Constructively confront and solve problems.
- Execute flawlessly.

Risk Taking

- Foster innovation and creative thinking.
- Embrace change and challenge the status quo.
- Listen to all ideas and viewpoints.
- Learn from our successes and mistakes.
- Encourage and reward informed risk taking.

Great Place to Work

- Be open and direct.
- Promote a challenging work environment that develops our workforce.
- Work as a team with respect and trust for each other.
- Recognize and reward accomplishments.
- Manage performance fairly and firmly.
- Be an asset to our communities worldwide.

Customer Orientation

- Listen and respond to our customers, suppliers, and stakeholders.
- Clearly communicate mutual intentions and expectations.
- Make it easy to work with us.
- Be the vendor of choice.

Quality

- Achieve the highest standards of excellence.
- Do the right things right.
- Continuously learn, develop, and improve.
- Take pride in our work.

Discipline

- Conduct business with uncompromising integrity and professionalism.
- Ensure a safe, clean, and injury free workplace.
- Make and meet commitments.
- Properly plan, fund, and staff projects.
- Pay attention to detail.

Intel drives home the point that it is a different kind of company, much along the lines of the dot-com companies, but with a history and stability. Exhibit 4 shows material from the corporate Web page as to what Intel is and is not.

Organization

In November 1997 Intel reorganized its internal functions to better meet the demands of customers and better prepare for future changes in the computer industry. Under the new structure the former desktop products group split into the Consumer

Survey Results

Category	Rank	Score
Quality of Management	5	8.78
Quality of Products/Services	13	8.40
Innovativeness	23	7.80
Long-Term Investment Value	33	7.73
Financial Soundness	2	9.43
Employee Talent	12	7.98
Social Responsibility	48	7.11
Use of Corporate Assets	10	8.10
Overall Company Results	10	8.16
Overall Industry Results	1	8.16

SOURCE: **www.fortune.com,** (accessed December 20, 2000).

EXHIBIT 4   WHAT INTEL IS AND WHAT INTEL ISN'T

Here's a quick look at what you'll find when you come to work at Intel—and some of what you won't find.

Intel is...

Teams—many different people working together toward common goals.

Open communication—people are always willing to help or answer questions, every idea counts, and being straightforward is valued.

Comprehensive compensation and benefits—this is a productive environment with a focus on rewarding performance and developing your career.

Acronyms—Intel probably gets the prize for the greatest number of abbreviated words used inside the company. If you don't know what they mean, we have an acronym dictionary to help you.

State-of-the-art technological communications—in addition to having the latest features in our e-mail and Internet systems, we routinely use teleconferencing and videoconferencing with remote data-sharing.

EXHIBIT 4	WHAT INTEL IS AND WHAT INTEL ISN'T—CONT'D

Food—on-site cafeterias and espresso bars make it easy to grab a snack or lunch with a colleague.

Fitness centers—we help you stay fit and healthy on-site.

Community volunteers—we are a company full of people who like to get involved. Check out Intel's community involvement.

Cool logo merchandise—everything from baby clothes to jewelry to chocolate bars. Visit the Shop Intel store right now.

Intel isn't...

One personality—our employees, customers and stakeholders have diverse backgrounds. With facilities around the world, we believe our diversity enriches our corporate culture.

Hierarchical management—our environment is informal and egalitarian. The best idea wins, whether it's from an intern or a senior manager.

Suits—neckties get in the way of thinking. Success at Intel is based on your performance, not appearance.

Closed offices—nobody gets an office with a door. Don't believe us? Here's Chairman Andy Grove's cubicle.

Priority parking—yes, that's your car in the first slot. And President Craig Barrett's way out there in the corner (unless he got to work first.)

A lot of time for computer solitaire—we're noted for our technological advancements and lively pace. That keeps us challenged and excited.

Slow-paced—from hallway meetings to online teleconferences, everyone makes the best use of every minute.

EXHIBIT 4   WHAT INTEL IS AND WHAT INTEL ISN'T—CONT'D

What you think it is—you have the
opportunity to create your own career
path, which means Intel is something
different to everyone.

Intel's Workforce Diversity

Intel is clear about its diverse worldwide workforce as this page from it's Web site explains:

Our workforce spans over 40 nations and includes more than
70,000 employees worldwide, which represents a rich assortment
of countries and cultures. We believe that the wide-ranging
experiences and perspectives of our varied population is exciting
and necessary for our success. We want to continue to expand as
a global company and to do this, we need the broad range of ideas
and experiences of our employees, community and suppliers.

To support our commitment to diversity, we have three key areas in
which we focus our efforts.

Our Workforce
Education
Our Suppliers

Workforce

We recognize that to be a leading technology company, we need to have
great talent from around the world in our company. To do this, we focus on both
recruiting and retaining the best. Following are some of the ways we do this.

Employee Groups (U.S.)

Volunteers have formed a number of U.S. employee groups
that are supported by the company to provide networking,
integration, development and outreach through their activities.
Following is a list of our active groups.

African-Americans
Asians
Christians
Employees from India
Gay, lesbian, bi-sexual, or transgender
Latinos
Native Americans
Muslims
Women

College Recruiting

About 38 percent of our worldwide hires (42 percent in the U.S.) were
made through our college recruiting program in 1999. We
partner with key schools and universities to develop and
attract top graduates into our intern programs and to hire
graduates straight out of school.

EXHIBIT 4	WHAT INTEL IS AND WHAT INTEL ISN'T—CONT'D

In the U.S., we have developed recruiting programs which help us attract and hire women and people from underrepresented demographic groups into technical positions.

Company Culture and Values

Our culture is based on teamwork, open communication and an idea that all employees are equal. All employees, from our CEO to interns, work in similar cubicles, park in the same parking lots and eat in the same cafeterias.
Our culture has what's called an "open door philosophy." It means that all employees can approach any level of manager if they feel that an issue needs to be raised. We want employees to be able to voice concerns quickly and effectively to seek resolution.

Training and Mentoring

We want to ensure that each and every one of our employees is given the opportunity for a challenging and rewarding career.

Newly hired employees complete an orientation to learn about our culture and values. Managers take a series of courses to develop their people management skills.

Courses such as "Managing in a Diverse Work Environment"; "Working with Differences, Practicing Respect and Trust"; and "Harassment Avoidance" are available to all employees worldwide.

Mentoring is a key element in our corporate growth and development programs. A number of business groups have mentoring processes to foster opportunities for a personal learning relationship.

Education

Our goal is to inspire students to explore new ideas, develop breakthrough technologies and bring a fresh perspective to the challenges facing our world. Each year, we spend more than $100 million to improve math, science, engineering and technology education in our communities throughout the world.

Intel Teaches to the Future

Our goal is to train more than 400,000 classroom teachers in 20 countries around the world on the use of technology and computers in the classroom. The teachers will then be able to encourage students to explore technology.

| EXHIBIT 4 | WHAT INTEL IS AND WHAT INTEL ISN'T—CONT'D |

Intel Computer Clubhouse Network

By 2005, we will establish 100 community-based technology centers in neighborhoods around the world to provide more than 50,000 underserved youth with access to technology and tutoring.

In addition, we provide grants to schools, and for more information, check out our Intel Innovation in Education site.

Suppliers

Our recently established supplier diversity program promotes the growth of businesses owned by women and members of other underrepresented demographic groups. The program aims to build a competitive supplier network that will foster diversity in our providers.

Products Group (CPG) and the Business Platform Group (BPG). The CPG targets the consumer desktop PCs, but the BPG focuses on the all-business computers. The former Internet and communications group also split, forming the Small Business and Networking Group (SBNG) and the Intel Architecture Labs (IAL). The SBNG includes networking products and business communications, and the IAL will continue to develop emerging platforms and applications technologies. The Computing Enhancement Group (CEG) continues to work on peripheral silicon solutions associated with PCs, with additional responsibilities for chip sets and graphic controllers. Finally, a new division, Digital Imaging and Video Division (DIVD), is associated with digital imaging and the emergence of digital cameras.

According to CEO Craig Barrett, this new organization was developed to help deal with segmentation of the growing personal computer industry.

Careers at Intel

Intel is a technical computer company that specializes in microprocessor design and production. They are looking toward the future with an emphasis on integrating and developing products into all facets of computers. However, Intel's successes cannot only be attributed to its technical skills, but also to its management and marketing skills. Careers at Intel fall under the following categories:

Technical Careers

- Integrated circuit engineering
- Integrated circuit manufacturing
- Hardware engineering
- Hardware manufacturing
- Software engineering
- Information technology

Business Careers:

- Marketing
- Finance and accounting

- Planning and logistics
- Material and corporate services
- Human resources
- Management
- Legal

The range of work covered in these jobs is seen by comparing the major functions for several of the careers. Hardware engineers work on the design, development, and support of new system products and PC boards. Members of the information technology group spend time on a range of areas covering topics such as telecommunications protocols and technology, and database design and management. Marketing focuses on the less technical, but just as important, functions of market development, pricing and demand, competitive analysis, and advertising, to name a few.

Intel has been very aggressive in hiring new college graduates into its ranks. Intel begins with a very attractive internship program with about 1400 slots offered per year. Pay for interns ranges from $2000 per month for college freshmen to $5000 per month for experienced graduate students. Other benefits include relocation and moving expenses as well as a shared rental car. This may seem like a large investment in an intern, but Intel expects to hire 70 percent of its yearly college quota from former interns.

Intel continues to attract college graduates with its entry-level rotation program for engineers. Recent graduates are rotated through several technical areas such as manufacturing, design, and marketing for a period of 4 months in each. Once completed, the employee and Intel select the best-suited field for the engineer. The natural progression takes 2 to 3 years to make senior engineer and another 2 to 3 years to make manager. Intel has recently come under fire for its dependence on new college graduates. This policy has allowed Intel to keep down the average age of its workforce and the average salaries paid to employees by hiring young, entry-level professionals.

Pay and Benefits

Intel's rewards and recognition program is directly tied to performance and results. The total compensation is made up of base pay, benefits, and results-driven bonuses. In 2000 the employee cash bonus totaled about an additional 10 percent of annual salary for every participating individual. One specific benefit that is not monetary in nature is the 8-week sabbatical with pay that every employee is entitled to after 7 years of full-time employment.

Intel pay is typically around the industry average; however, most Intel employees will confirm that the base pay is not the proper measure of compensation for work at Intel. Typical salaries at Intel are as follows:

- Microprocessor group engineer, 1 year entry level: $42,000 to $60,000.
- Software manager, 1 year: $60,000 to $95,000 plus bonus (typically a month to a month and a half salary per year).
- Senior analyst, finance or marketing, without MBA: $45,000 to $60,000.
- Senior analyst, finance or marketing, with MBA: $70,000 to $90,000 plus bonus (typically a month to a month and a half of salary per year).

Stock Purchase and Stock Options, and Other Incentives

The biggest perk offered by the company is the stock purchase plan. Intel allows employees to purchase stock at a price 15 percent lower than the market value. Employees can invest up to 10 percent of their pay in this purchase plan, and historically this has been very profitable. By the end of fiscal 2000, an employee who purchased 100 shares for $2350 in 1970 would have more than 17,000 shares worth well more than $2 million. Employees may receive stock options based on past performance levels and anticipated future contributions. All employees are eligible for stock option consideration. An employee who receives a stock option has the right to purchase a certain amount of Intel stock at a set price during a specified time in the future.

The Employee Cash Bonus Plan (ECBP) ties employee rewards directly to the company's financial performance. Twice a year, employees receive a cash bonus based on corporate pretax profits. In addition to the ECBP, the Employee Bonus is a variable pay program for all noncommissioned, regular Intel employees worldwide. Once a year a payout is determined based on the employee's bonus target, the financial performance of the corporation, and the performance of the employee's business group against preset goals.

Other Benefits

Intel Home PC Program

The Intel Home PC Program offers a computer and Internet access and services to all Intel employees (tax allowance provided). This program helps employees and their families participate fully in the Internet revolution and take advantage of the educational and e-Commerce opportunities offered on the Internet. All employees receive baseline PC configurations using high-performance processors (currently a Pentium III processor) and unlimited Internet access. In addition, the package will include: printer, Intel PC Camera Pack, keyboard, mouse, monitor, graphics adapter, software and technical support.

Vacation, Personal Absence, Sick Time

Salaried employees receive about 3 weeks per year of vacation and personal time. After 10 years of service, salaried employees receive 4 weeks' leave. Nonexempt employees accrue up to 80 hours per year of vacation time, plus up to 80 hours per year of personal absence/sick time.

Holidays

Intel exempt employees in the United States have ten paid holidays each year, one of which is an employee-specified "floater" holiday. Non-exempt employees receive 80 hours of paid holiday time, 8 hours of which are employee-specified "floater" holiday hours.

Sabbatical Leave

Intel provides an 8-week sabbatical, with full salary, after each 7 years of full-time service. When combined with your annual 3 or 4 weeks of vacation, a sabbatical leave can provide up to 12 weeks of paid time off.

Employee Assistance Program

Intel contracts with an independent employee assistance service to support employees experiencing personal problems or crises. Employees and eligible dependents may receive a confidential, professional assessment for mental health, chemical dependency, family or general living problems. Trained counselors, who are not employed by Intel, can also refer callers to local resources for assistance.

LifeWorks Resource and Referral Services
This program provides access to referral services designed to assist employees and their families with everyday concerns such as child care, tutoring, elder care, adoption referral, and parenting.

Dependent Care Assistance

Employees may pay for eligible dependent care expenses on a before-tax basis so that employee and spouse can work, look for work, or attend school full-time. Certain dependent definitions and IRS regulations may also apply.

Recreation

Intel's major U.S. campuses have on-site facilities that offer recreational opportunities such as basketball, volleyball, jogging, aerobics, and other activities. Specific recreational offerings vary from site to site.

Evaluation

February is a tense time at Intel because "rank and rating" is done during that month. The evaluation process is disliked by most employees because it involves direct ranking of employees against each other. In what is already a competitive environment with results being primary, competing for supervisors' attention can reach an all-time high. Ranking employees against each other is very difficult by definition when Intel employees are already among the best and brightest in the industry.

Former and Current Employees of Intel ("Face")

Evaluation time may not be the only thing Intel employees dislike about their company. "Face Intel" is a separate organization driven by both former and current employees whose goal it is to "influence positive human resources policies and practices and create true long-term employee opportunities at Intel." The group regularly maintains a Web site that contains information about the group and many testimonials from ex-Intel employees (**www.faceintel.com**).

The general attitude of the group is that Intel is discriminatory in many of its personnel policies. Face Intel attacks Intel, citing the constant age of its workforce, dependence on new collegiate hires, and increasing amount of contract workers. The Web site also takes some stabs at Intel with examples of ethnicity and race discrimination. Suggestions are offered for students and even the media to further publicize the organization's findings.

Lawsuits involving Intel and its workers are also documented at the Web site. Decisions involving labor lawsuits, as well as defamation, libel, and slander, are listed. Further, a survival guide is offered to potential applicants to avoid legal conflicts.

Intellectual Property Rights

Intel is known as an extremely aggressive protector of its intellectual property. The company spends about $2.5 billion a year on research and development, and it files about 650 patents a year as one method of protecting its investment in intellectual property. Intel also is particularly known for zealous enforcement of nondisclosure agreements. Peter Detkin, Intel's director of litigation, states that the knowledge within the heads of Intel's employees is worth more than $2 billion a year. He continues by noting that not only is current knowledge important to protect, but even technology used in some of Intel's older chips such as the 386 must be closely guarded. "If some former employee would want to write his memoirs about working on the 386, we'd want to see it before publication. Some of that technology is still used in the Pentium." Intel itself is an example of former employees putting their employer out of business when, in 1968, three former members of the now defunct Fairchild Semiconductor left to form their own start-up.[5]

Employers like Intel use nondisclosure agreements to prevent employees from taking their knowledge to other companies. Very often these nondisclosure agreements are introduced right after employees have been hired. This creates a dilemma for them as to whether they should sign the agreement and lose their rights or refuse to sign it and risk losing their job. Criminal laws are increasingly being enforced in trade secret cases. Also, trade secret laws have been broadened to cover not only scientific and technical information but also such items as marketing plans and rolodex files. One recent example of an Intel employee stealing secrets involves Bill Gaede. In March 1996 Gaede was sentenced to 33 months in a California jail after pleading guilty to charges that he stole secrets from Intel. The secrets were worth an estimated $10 million to $20 million. Gaede obtained Pentium and 486 manufacturing specifications after he downloaded them from an Intel database into his home computer. He then copied the information by videotaping the data as it scrolled by on the screen. After moving back to his native Argentina, Gaede reportedly mailed the tapes to Advanced Micro Devices (AMD). However, AMD notified Intel when it received the tapes in January 1995, and Intel promptly notified federal authorities. Gaede was caught by federal agents as he was in the process of trying to sell the information to government agents from Cuba, China, and Iran.[6]

One example of Intel's commitment to protect its intellectual property is the highly publicized case involving George Hwang and a former Intel employee named Alfred Chan. Hwang was the president of USLI Systems Inc., and Chan was an engineer then working for USLI. After a USLI employee notified Intel that Chan had taken documents from Intel, Hwang returned the documents to Intel and asked Intel to inspect USLI to determine if any proprietary information had been used. Intel responded by turning this information over to the Santa Clara police. The result was criminal charges being filed against Hwang and Chan by a prosecutor who had once consulted for Intel as a result of an investigation by a police investigator who had also consulted for Intel. In addition, Intel filed a civil suit against USLI.

After several years of court battles, a jury acquitted both Hwang and Chan of any criminal acts after finding that the documents were not private property but, instead, public documents. Also, the civil case was settled out of court. However, during that time Chan was forced to leave USLI and found it very difficult to find another job because of his reputation. As a result of the bad publicity generated by the litigation, Hwang and USLI found it difficult to recruit senior engineers, lost a $25 million deal between it and AMD, and lost an estimated $40 million to $50 million in profits. Also, USLI spent close to $3 million in legal expenses, which was equal to the amount spent on the entire company. Although these events took place during the late 1980s, this incident still reflects Intel's attitude regarding protecting its intellectual property.[7]

Environmental Health and Safety

Intel employees continued to improve their world-class health and safety performance by again dramatically reducing workplace injuries and illnesses in 1999. Over the past 4 years, the company has reduced the Occupational Safety and Health Administration (OSHA) recordable injury rate an average of 40 percent each year and the lost-day case rate an average of 38 percent each year. The Center for Office Ergonomics, an external organization of computer users and manufacturers, recognized Intel with its annual Outstanding Office Ergonomics Award for promoting the successful implementation of a sound office ergonomics program that is measurable and sustainable. An ergonomics steering team and a comprehensive program has delivered ergonomics to at least 90 percent of all employees and all new hires. The Design for Environment efforts have reduced air emissions as well as water and energy use per manufacturing unit in each of the last five product generations. Intel's Northwest Region received the U.S. Environmental Protection Agency's Evergreen Award for environmental excellence, and the Costa Rica site received the Preventico Global Award for exhibiting the highest OSHA standards. The inaugural Environmental Excellence Award went to a team implementing a program for reusing shipping trays that reduced waste generation and saved Intel more than $50 million.

Products

The first microprocessor produced by Intel was the 4004. The 4004 was introduced in 1971, and it contained 2300 transistors. The 8088 ran at 8 megahertz but could be boosted to 10 megahertz. In comparison, today's Pentium 4 processor can run at 1.5 gigahertz.

Microprocessors serve as the brains inside personal computers, but they also deliver intelligence to many other devices as well. For example, they provide telephones with speed-dial and redial options, they automatically turn down home thermostats at night, and they make cars safer and more energy efficient.

In 1971 the 4004 powered the Busicom calculator and provided a means for embedding intelligence in inanimate objects, as well as in the personal computer. In 1972 the 8008 was twice as powerful as the 4004. According to *Radio Electronics* magazine, Don Lancaster, a dedicated computer hobbyist, used the 8008 to create a predecessor to the first personal computer, a device *Radio Electronics* dubbed a "TV typewriter." It was used as a dumb terminal. In 1974 the 8080 became the brains of the first personal computer, the Altair, allegedly named for a destination of the *Starship Enterprise* from the *Star Trek* television show. Computer hobbyists could purchase a kit for the Altair for $395. Within months it sold tens of thousands and created the first PC back orders in history. In 1978 a pivotal sale to IBM's new personal computer division made the 8088 the brains of IBM's new hit product, the IBM PC. The 8088's success propelled Intel into the ranks of the *Fortune* 500, and *Fortune* magazine named the company one of the "Business Triumphs of the Seventies." In 1982 the 286, also known as the 80286, was the first Intel processor that could run all the software written for its predecessor. This software compatibility remains a hallmark of Intel's family of microprocessors. Within 6 years of its release, there were an estimated 15 million 286-based personal computers installed around the world. In 1985 the Intel 386 microprocessor featured 275,000 transistors, which was more than 100 times as many transistors as the original 4004. It was also a 32-bit chip and was "multi-tasking," meaning it could run multiple programs at the same time. In 1989 the 486 generation microprocessor allowed a user to go from command-level computing to point-and-click computing. "I could have a color computer for the first time and do desktop publishing at a significant speed," recalls technology historian David K. Alison of the Smithsonian's National Museum of American History. The Intel 486 processor was the first microprocessor to offer a built-in math coprocessor that sped up computing because the coprocessor was able to perform complex math functions for the central processor.

More recently, the Pentium processor has allowed computers to more easily incorporate "real world" data, such as speech, sound, handwriting, and photographic images. The Pentium brand, mentioned in the comics and on television talk shows, became a household word soon after its introduction. In 1995 the Pentium Pro processor was designed to fuel 32-bit server and workstation-level applications, enabling fast computer-aided design, mechanical engineering, and scientific computation. Each Pentium Pro processor is packaged together with a second speed-enhancing cache memory chip. The powerful Pentium Pro processor boasts 5.5 million transistors. In 1997 the 7.5 million-transistor Pentium II processor incorporated Intel MMX technology, which is designed specifically to process video, audio, and graphics data efficiently. At 333 MHz, the Pentium II processor delivered a 75 percent to 150 percent performance boost, compared to the 233 MHz Pentium processor, with MMX technology and approximately 50 percent more performance on multimedia benchmarks. With this chip, PC users can capture, edit, and share digital photos with friends and family via the Internet; edit and add text, music, or between-scene transitions to home movies; and, with a video phone, send video over standard phone lines and the Internet. Intel has incorporated its MMX technology into the entire family of Pentium processors. On the Intel Media Benchmark, which measures multimedia performance, a Pentium processor with MMX technology runs more than 60 percent faster than it does on the original Pentium processor at the same clock speed. The improvement will be determined by the type of application and the degree to which it has been designed for Intel MMX technology.[8] Currently, Intel offers microprocessors optimized for each segment of the computing market: Pentium III Xeon processor for mid-range to high-end servers and workstations; Pentium III processor for entry-level servers and workstations and performance desktop PCs; Intel Celeron processor for value PC systems; Mobile Pentium II and Pentium III processors for performance in mobile PC systems Chipsets, which perform essential logic functions surrounding the CPU in computers and support and extend the graphics, video, and other capabilities of many Intel processor-based systems. Motherboards combine Intel microprocessors and chipsets to form the basic subsystem of a PC or server.

Intel also offers wireless communications and computing products. These products are component-level hardware and software focusing on digital cellular communications and other applications needing both low-power processing and reprogrammable, retained memory capability (flash memory). These products are used in mobile phones, handheld devices, two-way pagers, and many other products.

Networking and communications products are another product category. System-level products consist of hardware, software and support services for e-business data centers, and building blocks for communications access solutions. These products include e-commerce infrastructure appliances; hubs, switches, and routers for Ethernet networks; and computer telephony components. Component-level products include communications silicon components and embedded control chips designed to perform specific functions in networking and communications applications, such as telecommunications, hubs, routers, and wide-area networking. Embedded control chips are also used in laser printers, imaging, storage media, automotive systems, and other applications.

Finally, Intel offers solutions and services. These products and services include e-commerce data center services as well as connected peripherals and security access software.

Intel's major customers include: (1) original equipment manufacturers (OEMs) of computer systems, telecommunications and data communications equipment, and peripherals PC users—including individuals, large and small businesses, and Internet service providers—who buy Intel's PC enhancements; (2) business communications products and networking products through reseller, retail, and OEM channels; and (3) other manufacturers, including makers of a wide range of industrial and communications equipment.

Intel Corp. continues to seek ways to strengthen its competitive advantages. One way it does this is by developing cooperative alliances with several other companies in its industry. For example:

1. In September 1997 Intel announced an alliance with Compaq Computer Corp. for joint development of networking products.
2. In 1999 Intel started producing the Merced chip that it developed with Hewlett-Packard. This chip embodies a large shift in microprocessor design.

Competition

Competition to Intel comes from other producers of chips used to build PCs. Companies such as Cyrix and Advanced Micro Devices, Inc. are developing chips that are almost as powerful as Intel's and offering low costs to computer companies. Compaq and Hewlett-Packard, among others, are using these chips in the development of low-cost PCs. In early 2001 these full-featured corporate PCs were sold for around $1000.

Strategies Intel Is Following

Strong demand for the sub-$1000 PCs has made this segment the fastest growing of the PC market. Nearly one of every two PCs sold costs less than $1000. Only 75 percent of these use Intel's chips, compared to 90 percent for the rest of the market. In an effort to increase its share of this important market segment, Intel introduced the Celeron, a processor designed for basic PCs. Basic PCs meet the core needs and affordability requirements common to many new PC users. Intel's Celeron processor is based on the same Intel P6 microarchitecture on which the Pentium II processor is based and offers a cost-effective solution for PC manufacturers who design basic PC systems. At the Intel Developer Forum, Andrew Grove outlined Intel's strategy of developing products for a broad range of market segments, saying that the company is aggressively moving its architecture into the entry level.

Intel's single freight strategy is another way the company has improved its competitive position. This global freight strategy, which emerged from a carrier reduction program launched in 1993, puts 90 percent of the semiconductor maker's freight dollars, about $400 million a year, in the hands of just four transportation providers. The plan has increased Intel's negotiating leverage and improved delivery and service to its customers. The new system has changed the way the computer chip maker handles its distribution.

Financial Success

Intel Corporation's revenues were $33.7 billion for the fiscal year ended December 27, 2000. This represented a 15 percent increase over 1999. Its net earnings were $12.1 billion, up 49 percent from the $8.1 billion reported for 1999. Powered by strong microprocessor sales, both revenues and earnings set a new record. For 2000 earnings excluding acquisition-related costs were $1.73 per share, an increase of 48 percent from $1.17 in 1999.

A set of financial report summaries, including income statements, balance sheets, and cash flow statements for the last 5 years is included in Appendix A.

Conclusion

The title of Andrew Grove's book says it all: *Only the Paranoid Survive*. With 90 percent market share, most companies would be more than happy to rest on their laurels. Intel refuses to rest. Aggressively pursuing the next generation of microprocessor and using its intellectual capital have given Intel an overwhelming competitive advantage that it has used to the fullest. The risk-taking corporate culture at Intel has paid great dividends, and the company continues to rely on this culture to continue its dominance of the microprocessor industry.

Questions

1. Critique Intel's forced ranking evaluation process.
2. Evaluate the benefit program of Intel.
3. What are the dangers of delegating so much authority to employees? Does this undermine the role of supervisors as coaches and counselors?
4. What human resource strategies do you recommend for Intel for the next 2 or 3 years, and why?
5. How well does Intel's human resource strategies match up with overall corporate strategy?

A

Financial summary
Ten years ended December 25, 1999

intel.

(In millions—except employees)	Employees at year-end (in thousands)	Net investment in property, plant & equipment	Long-term debt & put warrants	Total assets	Stock-holders' equity	Additions to property, plant & equipment [A]	Weighted average diluted shares outstanding
1999	70.2	$ 11,715	$ 1,085	$ 43,849	$ 32,535	$ 3,403	3,470
1998	64.5	$ 11,609	$ 903	$ 31,471	$ 23,377	$ 4,032	3,517
1997	63.7	$ 10,666	$ 2,489	$ 28,880	$ 19,295	$ 4,501	3,590
1996	48.5	$ 8,487	$ 1,003	$ 23,735	$ 16,872	$ 3,024	3,551
1995	41.6	$ 7,471	$ 1,125	$ 17,504	$ 12,140	$ 3,550	3,536
1994	32.6	$ 5,367	$ 1,136	$ 13,816	$ 9,267	$ 2,441	3,496
1993	29.5	$ 3,996	$ 1,114	$ 11,344	$ 7,500	$ 1,933	3,528
1992	25.8	$ 2,816	$ 622	$ 8,089	$ 5,445	$ 1,228	3,436
1991	24.6	$ 2,163	$ 503	$ 6,292	$ 4,418	$ 948	3,344
1990	23.9	$ 1,658	$ 345	$ 5,376	$ 3,592	$ 680	3,247

(In millions—except per share amounts)	Net revenues	Cost of sales [B]	Research & development [C]	Amortization of goodwill & other acquisition-related intangibles	Operating income	Net income	Basic earnings per share	Diluted earnings per share	Dividends declared per share
1999	$ 29,389	$ 11,836	$ 3,111	$ 411	$ 9,767	$ 7,314	$ 2.20	$ 2.11	$ .110
1998	$ 26,273	$ 12,088	$ 2,509	$ 56	$ 8,379	$ 6,068	$ 1.82	$ 1.73	$ .050
1997	$ 25,070	$ 9,945	$ 2,347	$ -	$ 9,887	$ 6,945	$ 2.12	$ 1.93	$ .058
1996	$ 20,847	$ 9,164	$ 1,808	$ -	$ 7,553	$ 5,157	$ 1.57	$ 1.45	$ .048
1995	$ 16,202	$ 7,811	$ 1,296	$ -	$ 5,252	$ 3,566	$ 1.08	$ 1.01	$ .038
1994	$ 11,521	$ 5,576	$ 1,111	$ -	$ 3,387	$ 2,288	$ .69	$ .65	$ .029
1993	$ 8,782	$ 3,252	$ 970	$ -	$ 3,392	$ 2,295	$ .69	$ .65	$ .025
1992	$ 5,844	$ 2,557	$ 780	$ -	$ 1,490	$ 1,067	$ .32	$ .31	$ .013
1991	$ 4,779	$ 2,316	$ 618	$ -	$ 1,080	$ 819	$ .25	$ .24	$ -
1990	$ 3,921	$ 1,930	$ 517	$ -	$ 858	$ 650	$ .21	$ .20	$ -

Share and per share amounts shown have been adjusted for stock splits through 1999.

[A] Additions to property, plant and equipment in 1998 include $475 million for capital assets acquired from Digital Equipment Corporation.

[B] Cost of sales for 1998 reflects the reclassification of amortization of goodwill and other acquisition-related intangibles to a separate line item.

[C] Research and development excludes in-process research and development of $392 million and $165 million for 1999 and 1998, respectively.

Consolidated statements of income

Three years ended December 25, 1999

(In millions—except per share amounts)

	1999	1998	1997
Net revenues	$ 29,389	$ 26,273	$ 25,070
Cost of sales	11,836	12,088	9,945
Research and development	3,111	2,509	2,347
Marketing, general and administrative	3,872	3,076	2,891
Amortization of goodwill and other acquisition-related intangibles	411	56	-
Purchased in-process research and development	392	165	-
Operating costs and expenses	19,622	17,894	15,183
Operating income	**9,767**	**8,379**	**9,887**
Interest expense	(36)	(34)	(27)
Interest income and other, net	1,497	792	799
Income before taxes	**11,228**	**9,137**	**10,659**
Provision for taxes	3,914	3,069	3,714
Net income	**$ 7,314**	**$ 6,068**	**$ 6,945**
Basic earnings per common share	**$ 2.20**	**$ 1.82**	**$ 2.12**
Diluted earnings per common share	**$ 2.11**	**$ 1.73**	**$ 1.93**
Weighted average common shares outstanding	3,324	3,336	3,271
Weighted average common shares outstanding, assuming dilution	3,470	3,517	3,590

See accompanying notes.

Note: Share and per share amounts shown have been adjusted for stock splits through 1999.
Certain prior year amounts have been reclassified to conform to the 1999 presentation.

Consolidated balance sheets

December 25, 1999 and December 26, 1998

intel.

(In millions—except per share amounts)

	1999	1998
Assets		
Current assets:		
Cash and cash equivalents	$ 3,695	$ 2,038
Short-term investments	7,705	5,272
Trading assets	388	316
Accounts receivable, net of allowance for doubtful accounts of $67 ($62 in 1998)	3,700	3,527
Inventories	1,478	1,582
Deferred tax assets	673	618
Other current assets	180	122
Total current assets	**17,819**	**13,475**
Property, plant and equipment:		
Land and buildings	7,246	6,297
Machinery and equipment	14,851	13,149
Construction in progress	1,460	1,622
	23,557	21,068
Less accumulated depreciation	11,842	9,459
Property, plant and equipment, net	**11,715**	**11,609**
Marketable strategic equity securities	**7,121**	**1,757**
Other long-term investments	**790**	**3,608**
Goodwill and other acquisition-related intangibles	**4,934**	**111**
Other assets	**1,470**	**911**
Total assets	**$ 43,849**	**$ 31,471**
Liabilities and stockholders' equity		
Current liabilities:		
Short-term debt	$ 230	$ 159
Accounts payable	1,370	1,244
Accrued compensation and benefits	1,454	1,285
Deferred income on shipments to distributors	609	606
Accrued advertising	582	458
Other accrued liabilities	1,159	1,094
Income taxes payable	1,695	958
Total current liabilities	**7,099**	**5,804**
Long-term debt	**955**	**702**
Deferred tax liabilities	**3,130**	**1,387**
Put warrants	**130**	**201**
Commitments and contingencies		
Stockholders' equity:		
Preferred stock, $.001 par value, 50 shares authorized; none issued	-	-
Common stock, $.001 par value, 4,500 shares authorized; 3,334 issued and outstanding (3,315 in 1998) and capital in excess of par value	7,316	4,822
Retained earnings	21,428	17,952
Accumulated other comprehensive income	3,791	603
Total stockholders' equity	**32,535**	**23,377**
Total liabilities and stockholders' equity	**$ 43,849**	**$ 31,471**

See accompanying notes.

Note: Share and per share amounts shown have been adjusted for stock splits through 1999.
Certain prior year amounts have been reclassified to conform to the 1999 presentation.

Consolidated statements of cash flows

Three years ended December 25, 1999

intel.

(In millions)	1999	1998	1997
Cash and cash equivalents, beginning of year	$ 2,038	$ 4,102	$ 4,165
Cash flows provided by (used for) operating activities:			
Net income	7,314	6,068	6,945
Adjustments to reconcile net income to net cash provided by (used for) operating activities:			
Depreciation	3,186	2,807	2,192
Amortization of goodwill and other acquisition-related intangibles	411	56	-
Purchased in-process research and development	392	165	-
Gains on sales of marketable strategic equity securities	(883)	(185)	(106)
Net loss on retirements of property, plant and equipment	193	282	130
Deferred taxes	(219)	77	6
Changes in assets and liabilities:			
Accounts receivable	153	(38)	285
Inventories	169	167	(404)
Accounts payable	79	(180)	438
Accrued compensation and benefits	127	17	140
Income taxes payable	726	(211)	179
Tax benefit from employee stock plans	506	415	224
Other assets and liabilities	(819)	(249)	(21)
Total adjustments	4,021	3,123	3,063
Net cash provided by operating activities	**11,335**	**9,191**	**10,008**
Cash flows provided by (used for) investing activities:			
Additions to property, plant and equipment	(3,403)	(3,557)	(4,501)
Acquisitions, net of cash acquired	(2,979)	(906)	-
Purchases of available-for-sale investments	(7,055)	(10,925)	(9,224)
Sales of available-for-sale investments	831	201	153
Maturities and other changes in available-for-sale investments	7,156	8,681	6,713
Net cash used for investing activities	**(5,450)**	**(6,506)**	**(6,859)**
Cash flows provided by (used for) financing activities:			
Increase (decrease) in short-term debt, net	69	(83)	(177)
Additions to long-term debt	118	169	172
Retirement of long-term debt	-	-	(300)
Proceeds from sales of shares through employee stock plans and other	543	507	317
Proceeds from exercise of 1998 step-up warrants	-	1,620	40
Proceeds from sales of put warrants	20	40	288
Repurchase and retirement of common stock	(4,612)	(6,785)	(3,372)
Payment of dividends to stockholders	(366)	(217)	(180)
Net cash used for financing activities	**(4,228)**	**(4,749)**	**(3,212)**
Net increase (decrease) in cash and cash equivalents	**1,657**	**(2,064)**	**(63)**
Cash and cash equivalents, end of year	**$ 3,695**	**$ 2,038**	**$ 4,102**
Supplemental disclosures of cash flow information:			
Cash paid during the year for:			
Interest	$ 40	$ 40	$ 37
Income taxes	$ 2,899	$ 2,784	$ 3,305

See accompanying notes.

Note: Certain prior year amounts have been reclassified to conform to the 1999 presentation.

Consolidated statements of stockholders' equity
Three years ended December 25, 1999

intel.

(In millions–except per share amounts)	Common stock and capital in excess of par value Number of shares	Amount	Retained earnings	Accumulated other com- prehensive income	Total
Balance at December 28, 1996	**3,283**	**$ 2,897**	**$ 13,853**	**$ 122**	**$ 16,872**
Components of comprehensive income:					
Net income	-	-	6,945	-	6,945
Change in unrealized gain on available-for-sale investments, net of tax	-	-	-	(64)	(64)
Total comprehensive income					6,881
Proceeds from sales of shares through employee stock plans, tax benefit of $224 and other	61	581	(1)	-	580
Proceeds from sales of put warrants	-	288	-	-	288
Reclassification of put warrant obligation, net	-	(144)	(1,622)	-	(1,766)
Repurchase and retirement of common stock	(88)	(311)	(3,061)	-	(3,372)
Cash dividends declared ($.058 per share)	-	-	(188)	-	(188)
Balance at December 27, 1997	**3,256**	**3,311**	**15,926**	**58**	**19,295**
Components of comprehensive income:					
Net income	-	-	6,068	-	6,068
Change in unrealized gain on available-for-sale investments, net of tax	-	-	-	545	545
Total comprehensive income					6,613
Proceeds from sales of shares through employee stock plans, tax benefit of $415 and other	66	922	-	-	922
Proceeds from exercise of 1998 step-up warrants	155	1,620	-	-	1,620
Proceeds from sales of put warrants	-	40	-	-	40
Reclassification of put warrant obligation, net	-	53	588	-	641
Repurchase and retirement of common stock	(162)	(1,124)	(4,462)	-	(5,586)
Cash dividends declared ($.050 per share)	-	-	(168)	-	(168)
Balance at December 26, 1998	**3,315**	**4,822**	**17,952**	**603**	**23,377**
Components of comprehensive income:					
Net income	-	-	7,314	-	7,314
Change in unrealized gain on available-for-sale investments, net of tax	-	-	-	3,188	3,188
Total comprehensive income					10,502
Proceeds from sales of shares through employee stock plans, tax benefit of $506 and other	56	1,049	-	-	1,049
Proceeds from sales of put warrants	-	20	-	-	20
Reclassification of put warrant obligation, net	-	7	64	-	71
Repurchase and retirement of common stock	(71)	(1,076)	(3,536)	-	(4,612)
Issuance of common stock in connection with Level One Communications acquisition	34	1,963	-	-	1,963
Stock options assumed in connection with acquisitions	-	531	-	-	531
Cash dividends declared ($0.110 per share)	-	-	(366)	-	(366)
Balance at December 25, 1999	**3,334**	**$ 7,316**	**$ 21,428**	**$ 3,791**	**$ 32,535**

See accompanying notes.

Note: Share and per share amounts shown have been adjusted for stock splits through 1999.

Intel facts and figures
10-year graph plot points

intel.

	1990	1991	1992	1993	1994	1995	1996	1997	1998	1999
1 Net revenues *Dollars in billions*	3.9	4.8	5.8	8.8	11.5	16.2	20.8	25.1	26.3	29.4
2 Diluted earnings per share *Dollars, adjusted for stock splits*	0.20	0.24	0.31	0.65	0.65	1.01	1.45	1.93	1.73	2.11
3 Stock price trading ranges by fiscal year *Dollars, adjusted for stock splits*										
High	3.20	3.66	5.63	9.16	9.03	19.11	34.38	50.25	62.50	89.31
Low	1.82	2.38	2.94	5.41	7.06	7.95	12.50	32.59	32.97	50.50
Close	2.37	2.97	5.63	7.77	7.99	14.19	33.84	35.44	62.50	83.13
4 Research and development *Dollars in millions, excluding purchased in-process research and development*	517	618	780	970	1,111	1,296	1,808	2,347	2,509	3,111
5 Return on average stockholders' equity *Percent*	21.2	20.4	21.6	35.5	27.3	33.3	35.6	38.4	28.4	26.2
6 Book value per share at year-end *Dollars, adjusted for stock splits*	1.12	1.35	1.63	2.24	2.80	3.69	5.14	5.93	7.05	9.76
7 Geographic breakdown of 1999 revenues *Percent*										
North America										43%
Europe										27%
Asia-Pacific										23%
Japan										7%
Total										100%
8 Capital additions to property, plant and equipment *Dollars in millions*										
Land, buildings & improvements	170	352	457	604	819	1,471	1,043	1,165	895	785
Machinery & equipment	510	596	771	1,329	1,622	2,079	1,981	3,336	3,137	2,618
Total	680	948	1,228	1,933	2,441	3,550	3,024	4,501	4,032	3,403

Additions in 1998 include capital assets acquired from Digital Equipment Corporation

Note: Past performance does not guarantee future results.
Share and per share amounts shown have been adjusted for stock splits through 1999.

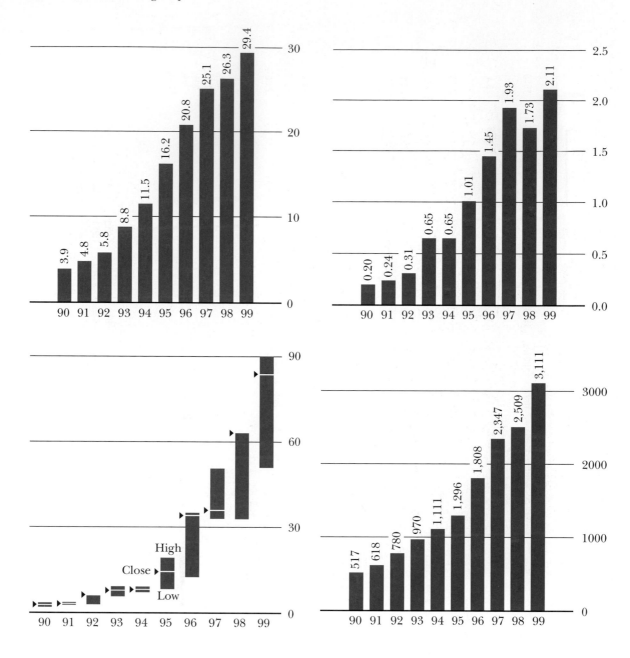

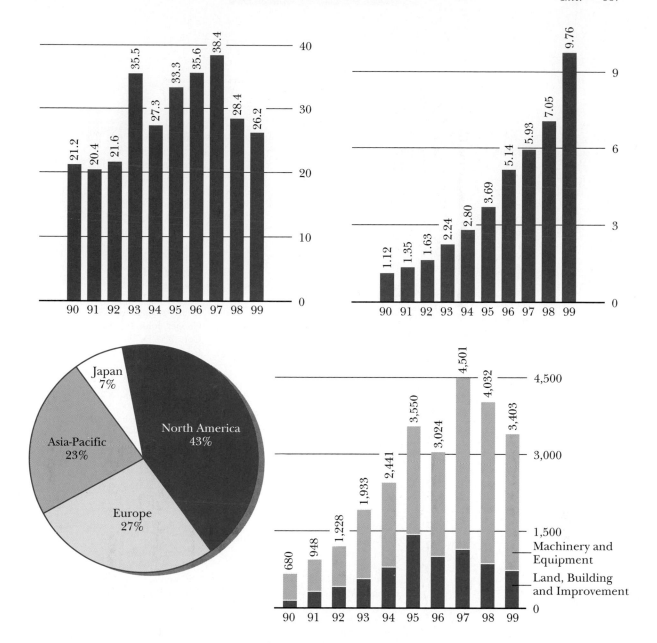

Notes

1. Tim Jackson, *Inside Intel*, (New York: Dutton, 1997), p. 31.
2. Ibid.
3. Brian Fuller, "Cleared, USLI's Hwang Picks Up Pieces," *Electronic Engineering Times*, June 1993.
4. **www.intel.com**. Unless indicated otherwise, most of the data presented in this case was found on the Intel Web site, accessed between September 2000, and January 2001.
5. Jackson, *Inside Intel*.
6. "Ex-Intel Employee Pleads Guilty," *Electronic News*, March 25, 1996, p. 2.
7. Fuller, "Cleared, USLI's Hwang Picks Up Pieces."
8. Ibid.

Social responsibility at McDonald's, 745–748

Social Security, 474–475, 476
  funding for, 474
  future of, 475

Social Security Act of 1935, 473, 474

Social security cards, 140

Societal environment, 70–77

Societal forces, 47–48, 284

Sociocultural and demographic forces, 76–77

Sociotechnical model, 287, 289

Soroka v. Dayton, 260

Soviet Union, 88

Special assignments, 330

Specialization, 11, 98

Specification of work rules, disagreements, and grievances, 589

Speech impairments, 177

SPHR. *See* Senior Professional in Human Resources

Split-half method in realibility estimation, 255

Spouses, 35

Stability, 259

Staff development meetings, 329

Staff involvement levels, 31–32

Staff positions, 20

Staff-line conflicts, 20, 54–56

Stakeholders, 558, 559
  analysis of, 45–46
  in the human resource subunit, 46
  in the organization, 45

Standard hour plan, 410

Standard methods and procedures (SMPs), 437

Standards for safety and health, 512–513

State programs for safety and health, 533–534

Stay bonuses, 412

Steel industry, 21, 30

Stereotyping, 378–379

Stock options, 23, 416–417

Stock ownership plans, 415–416

Stock purchase investment, 417, 494

Straight piece-work plan, 410

Strategic approach, 3–38
  and corporate strategies, 24–26
  corporate strategy integration, 16–17
  decision-making focus, 15–16
  definition, 9–10
  environment-organization link, 21–22

and functional approach, 17–20, 24–26

including all personnel, 16

labor market, 15

long-range focus, 15

management guidelines, 33–34

and managers, 20

organizational chart, 17, 18

outside environment, 12, 13, 15

process in, 26–28

see also Strategic decisions

Strategic decisions, 15–16, 28–33
  capital versus labor, 28–29
  human resource unit role, 31
  impact on people, 29–30
  line authority in, 32
  political influences, 30–31
  staff involvement levels, 31–32
  strategy, globalization, and technology, 33
  see also Strategic approach

Strategic Human Resource Management Award for Excellence, 699, 700

"Strategic Human Resource Management" (Lengnick-Hall and Lengnick-Hall), 51, 52

Strategy, 9–10, 33

Strategy and Structure (Chandler), 9

Stress response, 524

Stress in the workplace, 523–528
  causes of, 524–527
  consequences and expenses of, 527–528
  reduction techniques, 528
  stress indicators checklist, 527

Striker Replacement legislation, 607

Strikes, 621

Strong Vocational Inventory Blank (SVIB), 260

Structural capital, 132

Structural hiearchy, 314

Structured interviews, 262–264

Stuck in the middle strategy, 643

Subcontracting, 128

SUBs. *See* Supplemental unemployment benefits

Substance abuse programs, 489, 529–530

Substance abuse rehabilitation, 316

Suggestion boxes, 451

Sunbelt states, 48, 77, 120, 595, 601

Superconductivity, 75

Superpowers, 87

Supervisors and work teams, 291

Supplemental unemployment benefits (SUBs), 476, 657–658

Survey-Feedback Action (SFA) program, 701

Survival training exercises, 333

Sustainable competitive advantage, 21

Sutton v. United Airlines, 178

SVBI. *See* Strong Vocational Inventory Blank

Sweatshops, 96

Swing generation, 446

Synergy, 16–17

Systematic error, 253

Systems, 134

Taft-Hartley Act of 1947, 609, 614, 618, 622

Takeovers, 76

Talent search techniques, 315

Talladega, Alabama, 189

Tardy/absent employee, 564

Tariff barrier problems, 91–92

Task Design (Griffin), 301

Task environment, 70–71, 77–82

Task in hierarchy of work activities, 206

Task identity, 295, 297

Task needs assessment, 328

Task significance, 295, 297

Tax benefits, 91

Team support groups, 728

Team-building experiences, 333

Teams 360 Degree Feedback, 357

Teams, 591

Technical positions, 84

Technical schools, 120

Technological forces, 72, 75

Technology, 33
  and dislocations, 29
  and human resource strategy, 22
  and job design, 285, 286–287
  and privacy rights, 554
  in recruitment, 235–236
  see also Human resource planning and information systems

Telecommunications, 177

Telecommuting, 233, 299–300, 497, 672

Telephone, 141

Telerecruiting, 236

Temp-to-lease programs, 248

Temp-to-perm programs, 248

Temporary agencies, 679

Temporary workers, 98, 247, 248, 678

Tenure, 663

Terminal diseases, 490

Terminations, 316, 662–670
  on-line companies, 25
  wrongful discharge, 319, 321

Test-retest method in realibility estimation, 255

25   HR Challenges   Bill Leonard, "HR Not a Priority at Dot-Coms," *HR Magazine* (October 2000), p. 27. Reprinted with the permission of *HR Magazine* published by the Society for Human Resource Management, Alexandria, VA.

89   Exhibit 3.13   Graph from **www.fortune.com**. Copyright © 2000 Time, Inc. Reprinted by permission of *Fortune*, all rights reserved.

99   Focus on HR   Chikako Mogi, "Japan's Diligent Work Force is Woefully Inefficient," *Tallahassee Democrat* (December 20, 2000), p. 7E. Reprinted with permission of The Associated Press.

479   Exhibit 13.5   Timothy L. O'Brien, "Many Firms Abandon Defined-Benefit Plans," *The Wall Street Journal* (February 12, 1993), p. B1. Copyright © 1993 Dow Jones & Co., Inc. Reproduced with permission of Dow Jones & Co., Inc. via Copyright Clearance Center.

481   Exhibit 13.6   Roger Thompson, "The Positive Side of Negative Elections," *HR Magazine* (November 1997), p. 115. Reprinted with the permission of *HR Magazine* published by the Society for Human Resource Management, Alexandria, VA.

485   Exhibit 13.7   Judith Harkham Semans, "Taking Off from the Hi-Tech Grind," *HR Magazine* (September 1997), p. 128. Reprinted with the permission of *HR Magazine* published by the Society for Human Resource Management, Alexandria, VA.

514   HR Challenges   A. Gerlin, "A Matter of Degree: How a Jury Decided That a Coffee Spill is Worth $2.9 Million," *The Wall Street Journal* (September 1, 1994), p. A1. Copyright © 1994 Dow Jones & Co., Inc. Reproduced with permission of Dow Jones & Co., Inc. via Copyright Clearance Center.

597   Focus on HR   Nick Wingfield, "Amazon's Layoffs Include Agreement Linking Benefits to Speech Curbs," *The Wall Street Journal* (February 1, 2001), p. B1. Copyright © 2001 Dow Jones & Co., Inc. Reproduced with permission of Dow Jones & Co., Inc. via Copyright Clearance Center.

646   Focus on HR   Gene Koretz, "Downsizing's Painful Effects," *Business Week* (April 13, 1998), p. 23. Reprinted with special permission of *Business Week*. Copyright © 1998 by The McGraw-Hill Companies, Inc.

651   Exhibit 17.8   Gilbert Fuchsberg, "Why Shakeups Work for Some, Not for Others," *The Wall Street Journal* (October 1, 1993), p. B1. Reproduced with permission of Dow Jones & Co., Inc. Copyright © 1993 Dow Jones & Co., Inc. via Copyright Clearance Center.

679   Exhibit 17.15   Bill Leonard, "Human Resource Services Most Frequently Outsourced," *HR Magazine* (July 1994), p. 53. Reprinted with the permission of *HR Magazine* published by the Society for Human Resource Management, Alexandria, VA.

682   Exhibit 17.17   "Toll of dot-com failures rises," *USA Today* (February 7, 2001), p. 2A. Reprinted with permission of *USA Today*. Copyright © 2001 *USA Today*.

684   Exhibit 17.18   *The Wall Street Journal* (January 25, 2001), p. B1. Reproduced with permission of Dow Jones & Co., Inc. Copyright © 2001 Dow Jones & Co., Inc. via Copyright Clearance Center.

671   HR Challenges   Linda Micco, "Keeping Severance Pay Doesn't Bar Age Bias Suit, Justices Rule," *HR News* (March 1998), pp. 11, 29. Reprinted with the permission of *HR News* published by the Society for Human Resource Management, Alexandria, VA.

672   Focus on HR   Kevin Voigt, "For 'Extreme Telecommuters,' Remote Work Means Really Remote," *The Wall Street Journal* (January 31, 2001), p. B1. Reproduced with permission of Dow Jones & Co., Inc. Copyright © 2001 Dow Jones & Co., Inc. via Copyright Clearance Center.

679   Focus on HR   David Wessel, "Capital: Temp Workers have a Lasting Effect," *The Wall Street Journal* (February 1, 2001), p. A1. Reproduced with permission of Dow Jones & Co., Inc. Copyright © 2001 Dow Jones & Co., Inc. via Copyright Clearance Center.